INTERNATIONAL FINANCIAL STATEMENT ANALYSIS

CFA Institute is the premier association for investment professionals around the world, with over 95,000 members in 134 countries. Since 1963 the organization has developed and administered the renowned Chartered Financial Analyst® Program. With a rich history of leading the investment profession, CFA Institute has set the highest standards in ethics, education, and professional excellence within the global investment community, and is the foremost authority on investment profession conduct and practice.

Each book in the CFA Institute Investment Series is geared toward industry practitioners, along with graduate-level finance students, and covers the most important topics in the industry. The authors of these cutting-edge books are themselves industry professionals and academics and bring their wealth of knowledge and expertise to this series.

INTERNATIONAL FINANCIAL STATEMENT ANALYSIS

Thomas R. Robinson, CFA

Hennie van Greuning, CFA

Elaine Henry, CFA

Michael A. Broihahn, CFA

WILEY

John Wiley & Sons, Inc.

Library of Congress Cataloging-in-Publication Data:

International financial statement analysis / Thomas R. Robinson . . . [et al.].

     p.   cm.—(CFA Institute investment series)

   Includes index.

   ISBN 978-0-470-28766-8 (cloth)

    1. Financial statements.   2. International business enterprises—Accounting.   I. Robinson, Thomas R.

HF5681.B2I5788   2008

657'.3—dc22

                                 2008014644

Printed in the United States of America

10 9 8 7 6 5 4

CONTENTS

CHAPTER 3
Financial Reporting Standards   79

CHAPTER 8
International Standards Convergence   323

CHAPTER 12
Income Taxes 469

CHAPTER 15
Intercorporate Investments 605

FOREWORD

Investors now routinely scour the globe looking for diversification and investment opportunities. At the same time they seek new and profitable opportunities, the economies in which they invest directly benefit from greater access to capital for development and growth, and from a lower and more competitive cost of capital. Because of the benefits to cross-border investors and economies alike, the increasing globalisation of securities markets and capital is likely to be a defining hallmark of the twenty-first century.

Although globalisation has been gradually increasing for many years, the final building blocks—the infrastructure necessary to ensure both free and unfettered movements of capital across borders and the investor protections required to support the flows—are just now being put in place. They include cross-border stock exchanges, financial institutions with global reach that can facilitate the efficient movement of capital from investors to companies, and the gradual development of cooperative arrangements among global regulators essential for the monitoring, oversight, and enforcement of consistent regulations and standards for investment.

However, among the most critical and urgent of these changes is the development of a common financial reporting standard, really a common language applicable and understandable across the globe, and the importance of a single, high-quality standard cannot be overstated. The effective functioning of capital markets and the economic benefits that they could bring depend largely on the investors who participate in those markets. It is investors who must interpret financial information, who evaluate the potential risks and rewards of investments, and who ultimately make investment decisions.

In the absence of such a standard, the barriers to free movement of capital to those who most need it and can most efficiently use it can be formidable. Investors, both large institutions and individuals, are required to invest large sums of resources to try to compensate, if they can do so at all. Their efforts must include not only understanding the language in which the financial reports are prepared but also gaining expert knowledge in the local GAAP standards and their idiosyncrasies, as well as attempts to try to transform the various reporting systems into a consistent and comparable format for the comparison of various investment opportunities with the limited patchwork of information available. The attractiveness of a single, high-quality standard is immediately apparent.

Although accounting standards are written with these global investors in mind, historically they have varied widely across borders because of the existence of differing accounting and enforcement regimes. Our goal at the International Accounting Standards Board (IASB) is to develop accounting principles that will span borders and require a company, whether in New York, London, Tokyo, Mumbai, or Shanghai, to report a transaction in the same way. In this way, we aim to enable investors and other decision makers to make informed judgements and to allocate capital efficiently, wherever they are based.

The establishment of a single set of high-quality accounting standards used throughout the world's capital markets would greatly assist in the analysis and comparison of financial information. For investors, the good news is that within just seven years of the IASB's establishment, International Financial Reporting Standards (IFRSs) are now permitted or required by over 100 countries around the world, with the remaining major economies following a path toward convergence and adoption. The adoption of IFRSs, combined with rigorous audits and effective enforcement regimes, should serve as the basis of a sound financial reporting infrastructure for increasingly integrated capital markets.

However, despite this excellent progress, much work remains to be done before the dream of globally integrated financial markets with a single financial reporting system becomes reality. First, financial statement preparers worldwide must have the tools they need to understand and be able to apply IFRSs correctly and uniformly, regardless of the jurisdiction or the regulatory regime. Second, auditors in all countries and of all companies that choose to apply IFRSs must have the tools to gain the technical competence they need to perform audits of financial statements prepared according to the standards and to be able to demonstrate that knowledge through formal coursework in university curricula as well as rigorous examinations. Third, investors must have the necessary tools to gain the expert knowledge of IFRSs required to understand, analyze, and interpret financial statements prepared according to IFRSs.

Unfortunately, the rapid developments in financial markets, regulation, and standard setting at the global level have not been accompanied by ground-level development of the learning tools essential to support the market infrastructure. Specifically, until now, the textbooks and other in-depth instructional materials suitable for use in the global environment have not been developed. Development necessarily takes a long time and requires substantial investment of resources. Thus, we welcome the resolve and commitment of CFA Institute to do its part to enhance and support the globalization of financial markets by developing this text for the use of one of the core financial reporting constituencies worldwide, investors.

Importantly, this text bridges the current changes under way in financial reporting by presenting the information investors need in both IFRSs, the emerging global standard, and U.S. GAAP, the system still currently in use in the world's largest financial market. As more countries adopt IFRSs, the remaining national systems in place will gradually disappear. Thus, this text will provide the information most investors will require to analyze financial reports of companies regardless of the country of the reporting company or the reporting regime in use in that country. The U.S. standard setter, the Financial Accounting Standards Board (FASB), and the IASB have formally committed to work toward convergence in all major respects of their respective standard systems within the next several years. Thus, in a relatively short time, the last remaining significant differences in the systems will be removed. CFA Institute is committed to following the progress in standards development and convergence with regularly scheduled updates in this text so that it will remain current and an invaluable resource for the global investment profession.

The IASB's emphasis on serving the needs of capital providers is why IFRSs have been developed with significant input from the global investment community and why we at the IASB greatly appreciate the support and encouragement offered by CFA Institute. It is also why I am delighted to have been asked to introduce this first financial analysis text in the CFA Institute Investment Series.

CFA Institute rightly sets the bar very high to become a CFA charterholder, and this publication has an important role to play in assisting current and aspiring investment professionals to achieve the highest standards of ethics, integrity, education, and professional excellence.

SIR DAVID TWEEDIE, Chairman
International Accounting Standards Board

PREFACE

International Financial Statement Analysis is a practically oriented introduction to financial statement analysis. Each chapter covers one major area of financial statement analysis and is written by highly credentialed experts. By taking a global perspective on accounting standards, with a focus on International Financial Reporting Standards (IFRS), and by selecting a broad range of companies for illustration, the book well equips the reader for practice in today's global marketplace.

The book adopts a structured presentation style, clearly explaining and illustrating each major concept, tool, or technique as it is introduced. Technical terms are defined in their first major occurrence, and terminology is used consistently across the chapters. No prior accounting background is assumed of the reader. In more detail, chapter coverage is as follows:

Chapter 1, Financial Statement Analysis: An Introduction, provides an integrative perspective on financial statement analysis and a foundation for the entire book. After motivating the uses of financial statement analysis, the chapter discusses the key financial statements and other information sources relevant to financial analysis. The chapter concludes by presenting a framework for conducting any financial statement analysis.

Chapter 2, Financial Reporting Mechanics, explains how accounting systems record a company's transactions with suppliers, customers, employees, capital suppliers, and taxing authorities and how those transactions are eventually summarized in financial statements. Understanding financial reporting mechanics enables an analyst to understand the interrelationships of financial accounts and statements and, therefore, to better assess a company's financial performance.

Chapter 3, Financial Reporting Standards, introduces the accounting standard-setting and regulatory contexts within which companies prepare their financial statements. The chapter explains the conceptual framework behind the preparation of financial statements, focusing on IFRS. Understanding that framework will help the reader evaluate the securities valuation implications of any financial statement element or transaction.

Chapter 4, Understanding the Income Statement, explains the income statement, which summarizes an entity's revenue and expenses over a stated time period. The chapter explains revenue and expense recognition principles, the interpretation of income statement elements, and the calculation of earnings per share. The chapter illustrates a range of tools for analyzing and interpreting the income statement.

Chapter 5, Understanding the Balance Sheet, explains the balance sheet, which presents the financial position of a company at a point in time. The information in this chapter should help the reader to better assess a company's ability to meet debt obligations, generate future cash flows, and make distributions to owners. The chapter explains the balance sheet's components, alternative formats, and the measurement bases of assets and liabilities. Tools relevant for analyzing and interpreting the balance sheet are illustrated.

Chapter 6, Understanding the Cash Flow Statement, explains the cash flow statement, which summarizes cash receipts and disbursements over a stated time period. After presenting the components and alternative formats of the cash flow statement in detail, the chapter offers clear discussions of the linkages of the cash flow statement with the income statement and balance sheet and of the steps in cash flow statement preparation. The chapter also introduces cash flow statement analysis and interpretation. This chapter completes the overview of the most important financial statements.

Chapter 7, Financial Analysis Techniques, builds on the prior chapters to present a comprehensive overview of the techniques used by analysts to evaluate the performance and financial condition of a company. The chapter illustrates the use of ratio analysis, common-size financial statements, decomposition (DuPont) analysis, and analyst adjustments to reported financials. The use of financial statement analysis by both equity analysts and credit analysts is illustrated.

Chapter 8, International Standards Convergence, provides an overview of a very important development in accounting: the planned convergence of IFRS and U.S. generally accepted accounting principles (U.S. GAAP). The chapter also illustrates some typical analyst adjustments used to facilitate valid comparisons of financials prepared according to IFRS with financials prepared according to U.S. GAAP.

Chapter 9, Financial Statement Analysis: Applications, consolidates and extends skills and knowledge from earlier chapters by illustrating four major applications of financial statement analysis: evaluating past financial performance, projecting future financial performance, assessing credit risk, and screening for potential equity investments. An overview of analyst adjustments to reported financials often used in such applications concludes the chapter.

Chapter 10, Inventories, begins a series of chapters that take a more detailed look at important accounting topics than was possible in the chapters covering the major financial statements. For merchandising and manufacturing companies, inventory is an important asset, and inventory cost flow is a major determinant of net income. This chapter presents the major issues associated with accounting for and analyzing inventories.

Chapter 11, Long-Lived Assets, presents such important topics related to long-lived (noncurrent) assets as accounting for tangible and intangible assets; depreciation of tangible assets; amortization of intangible assets with finite useful lives; accounting for asset retirement obligations; accounting for the disposal of long-lived operating assets; impairment of long-lived assets; and asset revaluation.

Chapter 12, Income Taxes, explains the issues that arise because of potential differences between the accounting used for reporting income taxes and the accounting used for preparing a company's financial statements.

Chapter 13, Long-Term Liabilities and Leases, discusses accounting for debt, debt with equity features, leases, and off-balance-sheet liabilities.

Chapter 14, Employee Compensation: Postretirement and Share-Based, explains such issues as accounting for defined-benefit pensions and executive stock options. These means of compensation are complex, but need to be understood by analysts because they can have substantial effects on a company's actual financial position and performance.

Chapter 15, Intercorporate Investments, provides an overview of the accounting-related issues arising from the investments companies make in other companies. The chapter covers the classification of intercorporate investments and for each type explains the accounting issues relevant to the analyst.

Chapter 16, Multinational Operations, presents two major topics: the accounting for foreign currency-denominated transactions that arise in international trade and the translation of foreign currency financial statements of overseas subsidiaries into the parent company's currency for the purpose of preparing consolidated financial statements.

Chapter 17, Evaluating Financial Reporting Quality, deals with evaluating the accuracy with which a company's reported financials reflect its operating performance and their usefulness for forecasting future cash flows. Besides illustrating a generally applicable framework for evaluating financial reporting quality, the chapter introduces concepts and techniques being used in leading investment management firms to interpret reported financial results.

ACKNOWLEDGMENTS

We would like to thank the many individuals who played a role in producing this book.

Robert R. Johnson, CFA, Managing Director of the Education Division at CFA Institute, originally saw the need for specialized curriculum materials and initiated their development. We appreciate his support. Dennis W. McLeavey, CFA, initiated the project and John D. Stowe, CFA, oversaw its final development during their respective terms as Head of Curriculum Development. Jerald E. Pinto, CFA, had primary responsibility for the delivery of the first nine chapters and the chapter on financial reporting quality, while Christopher B. Wiese, CFA, oversaw organization, writing, and editing of the other chapters.

Individual manuscript reviews were provided by Evan Ashcraft, CFA; Donna Bernachi, CFA; Sean D. Carr; Harold Evensky; Philip Fanara, CFA; Jane Farris, CFA; Jacques Gagne, CFA; Mui Cheng Heng, CFA; David Jessop; Lisa Joublanc, CFA; Swee Sum Lam, CFA; Asjeet Lamba, CFA; Barbara MacLeod, CFA; Rebecca McEnally, CFA; Lewis Randolph, CFA; Raymond D. Rath, CFA; Sanjiv Sabherwal; Zouheir Tamim El Jarkass; William A. Trent, CFA; Lavone Whitmer, CFA; and Geoffrey Whittington. End-of-chapter problems and solutions were written by William A. Trent, CFA. We thank all of them for their excellent and detailed work.

Nicole Robbins of CFA Institute and Sophia Battaglia provided copyediting that substantially contributed to the book's readability. Wanda Lauziere of CFA Institute expertly served as project manager for the book's production.

INTRODUCTION

CFA Institute is pleased to provide you with this Investment Series covering major areas in the field of investments. These texts are thoroughly grounded in the highly regarded CFA Program Candidate Body of Knowledge that serves as the anchor for the three levels of the CFA Program. Currently, nearly 200,000 aspiring investment professionals are devoting hundreds of hours each to master this material, as well as other elements of the Candidate Body of Knowledge, to obtain the coveted CFA charter. We provide these materials for the same reason we have been chartering investment professionals for over 40 years: to lead the investment profession globally by setting the highest standards of ethics, education, and professional excellence.

HISTORY

This book series draws on the rich history and origins of CFA Institute. In the 1940s, a handful of societies for investment professionals developed around common interests in the evolving investment industry. At that time, the idea of purchasing common stock as an investment—as opposed to pure speculation—was still a relatively new concept for the general public. Just 10 years before, the U.S. Securities and Exchange Commission had been formed to help referee a playing field marked by robber barons and stock market panics.

In January 1945, a fundamental analysis–driven professor and practitioner from Columbia University and Graham-Newman Corporation wrote an article in the precursor of today's CFA Institute *Financial Analysts Journal*, making the case that people who research and manage portfolios should have some sort of credential to demonstrate competence and ethical behavior. This person was none other than Benjamin Graham, the father of security analysis and future mentor to well-known modern investor Warren Buffett.

Creating such a credential took 16 years. By 1963, 284 brave souls—all over the age of 45—took an exam and successfully launched the CFA credential. What many do not fully understand is that this effort was driven by a desire to create professional standards for practitioners dedicated to serving individual investors. In so doing, a fairer and more productive capital market would result.

Most professions—including medicine, law, and accounting—have certain hallmark characteristics that help to attract serious individuals and motivate them to devote energy to their life's work. First, there must be a body of knowledge. Second, there need to be entry requirements, such as those required to achieve the CFA credential. Third, there must be a commitment to continuing education. Finally, a profession must serve a purpose beyond one's individual interests. By properly conducting one's affairs and putting client interests first, the investment professional encourages general participation in the incredibly productive global capital markets. This encourages the investing public to part with their hard-earned savings for redeployment in the fair and productive pursuit of appropriate returns.

As C. Stewart Sheppard, founding executive director of the Institute of Chartered Financial Analysts, said:

> *Society demands more from a profession and its members than it does from a professional craftsman in trade, arts, or business. In return for status, prestige, and autonomy, a profession extends a public warranty that it has established and maintains conditions of entry, standards of fair practice, disciplinary procedures, and continuing education for its particular constituency. Much is expected from members of a profession, but over time, more is given.*

"The Standards for Educational and Psychological Testing," put forth by the American Psychological Association, the American Educational Research Association, and the National Council on Measurement in Education, state that the validity of professional credentialing examinations should be demonstrated primarily by verifying that the content of the examination accurately represents professional practice. In addition, a practice analysis study, which confirms the knowledge and skills required for the competent professional, should be the basis for establishing content validity.

For more than 40 years, hundreds upon hundreds of practitioners and academics have served on CFA Institute curriculum committees, sifting through and winnowing out all the many investment concepts and ideas to create a body of investment knowledge and the CFA curriculum. One of the hallmarks of curriculum development at CFA Institute is its extensive use of practitioners in all phases of the process. CFA Institute has followed a formal practice analysis process since 1995. Most recently, the effort involves special practice analysis forums held at 20 locations around the world. Results of the forums were put forth to 70,000 CFA charterholders for verification and confirmation. In 2007, CFA Institute moved to implement a continuous practice analysis by making use of a collaborative web-based site and "wiki" technology. This will open the process to thousands more charterholders and significantly reduce the lag effect of concepts and techniques moving from practice to the Candidate Body of Knowledge.

What this means for the reader is that the concepts highlighted in these texts were selected by practitioners who fully understand the skills and knowledge necessary for success. We are pleased to put this extensive effort to work for the benefit of the readers of the Investment Series.

BENEFITS

This series will prove useful to those contemplating entry into the extremely competitive field of investment management, as well as those seeking a means of keeping one's knowledge fresh and up to date. Regardless of its use, this series was designed to be both user friendly and highly relevant. Each chapter within the series includes extensive references for those who would like to dig deeper into a given concept. The workbooks provide a summary of each chapter's key points to help organize your thoughts, as well as sample questions and answers to test yourself on your progress.

I believe that the general public seriously underestimates the disciplined processes needed for the best investment firms and individuals to prosper. This material will help you better understand the investment field. For those new to the industry, the essential concepts that any investment professional needs to master are presented in a time-tested fashion. These texts lay the basic groundwork for many of the processes that successful firms use on a day-to-day basis. Without this base level of understanding and an appreciation for how the capital markets work, it becomes challenging to find competitive success. Furthermore, the concepts herein provide a true sense of the kind of work that is to be found managing portfolios, doing research, or pursuing related endeavors.

The investment profession, despite its relatively lucrative compensation, is not for everyone. It takes a special kind of individual fundamentally to understand and absorb the teachings from this body of work and then apply it in practice. In fact, most individuals who enter the field do not survive in the long run. The aspiring professional should think long and hard about whether this is the right field. There is no better way to make such a critical decision than by reading and evaluating the classic works of the profession.

The more experienced professional understands that the nature of the capital markets requires a commitment to continuous learning. Markets evolve as quickly as smart minds can find new ways to create exposure, attract capital, or manage risk. A number of the concepts in these texts did not exist a decade or two ago when many were starting out in the business. Hedge funds, derivatives, alternative investment concepts, and behavioral finance are just a few examples of the new applications and concepts that have altered the capital markets in recent years.

As markets invent and reinvent themselves, a best-in-class foundation investment series is of great value. Investment professionals must continuously hone their skills and knowledge if they are to compete with the young talent that constantly emerges. In fact, as we talk to major employers about their training needs, we are often told that one of the biggest challenges they face is how to help the experienced professional keep up with the recent graduates. This series can be part of that answer.

CONVENTIONAL WISDOM

It doesn't take long for the astute investment professional to realize two common characteristics of markets. First, prices are set by conventional wisdom, as a function of the many variables in the market. Truth in markets is, at its essence, what the market believes it is and how it assesses pricing credits or debits based on those beliefs. Second, inasmuch as conventional wisdom is a product of the evolution of general theory and learning, by definition conventional wisdom is often wrong or at the least subject to material change.

When I first entered this industry in the mid-1970s, conventional wisdom held that the concepts examined in these texts were a bit too academic for use in the competitive marketplace. What were considered to be the best investment firms of the time were led by men who had an eclectic style, an intuitive sense of markets, and a great track record. In the rough-and-tumble world of the practitioner, some of these concepts were considered to be of no use. Could conventional wisdom have been more wrong?

During the years of my tenure in the profession, the practitioner investment management firms that evolved successfully were full of determined, intelligent, intellectually curious investment professionals who endeavored to apply these concepts in a serious and disciplined manner. Today, the best firms are run by those who carefully form investment hypotheses and test them rigorously in the marketplace, whether it be in a quant strategy, comparative shopping for stocks within an industry, or hedge fund strategies. Their goal is to create investment processes that can be replicated with some statistical reliability. I believe those who embraced the so-called academic side of the learning equation have been much more successful as real-world investment managers.

THE TEXTS

One of the most prominent texts over the years in the investment management industry has been Maginn and Tuttle's *Managing Investment Portfolios: A Dynamic Process*. The third edition updates key concepts from the 1990 second edition. Some of the more experienced members of our community own the prior two editions and will add the third edition to their library. Not only does this seminal work take the concepts from the other readings and put them in a portfolio context, but it also updates the concepts of alternative investments, performance presentation standards, portfolio execution and, very importantly, managing individual investor portfolios. Focusing attention away from institutional portfolios, and toward the individual investor, makes this edition an important and timely work.

Quantitative Investment Analysis focuses on some key tools that are needed for today's professional investor. In addition to classic time value of money, discounted cash flow applications, and probability material, there are two aspects that can be of value over traditional thinking.

The first involves the chapters dealing with correlation and regression that ultimately figure into the formation of hypotheses for purposes of testing. This gets to a critical skill that many professionals are challenged by: the ability to distinguish useful information from the overwhelming quantity of available data. For most investment researchers and managers, their analysis is not solely the result of newly created data and tests that they perform. Rather, they synthesize and analyze primary research done by others. Without a rigorous manner by which to understand quality research, you cannot understand good research, nor do you have a basis on which to evaluate less rigorous research. What is often put forth in the applied world as good quantitative research frequently lacks rigor and validity.

Second, the last chapter of *Quantitative Investment Analysis* on portfolio concepts takes the reader beyond the traditional capital asset pricing model (CAPM) type of tools and into the more practical world of multifactor models and arbitrage pricing theory. This chapter also helps address the concerns of those who thought the text had a CAPM bias.

Equity Asset Valuation is a particularly cogent and important resource for anyone involved in estimating the value of securities and understanding security pricing. A well-informed professional knows that the common forms of equity valuation—dividend discount modeling, free cash flow modeling, price/earnings models, and residual income models—can all be reconciled to one another under certain assumptions. With a deep understanding of the underlying assumptions, the professional investor can better understand what other investors assume when calculating their valuation estimates. In my prior life as the head of an equity investment team, this knowledge gave us an edge over other investors.

Fixed Income Analysis has been at the forefront of new concepts in recent years, and this particular text offers some of the most recent material for the seasoned professional who is not a fixed-income specialist. The application of option and derivative technology to the once staid province of fixed income has helped contribute to an explosion of thought in this area. Not only are professionals challenged to stay up to speed with credit derivatives, swaptions, collateralized mortgage securities, mortgage-backed securities, and other vehicles, but this explosion of thought also puts a strain on the world's central banks to provide sufficient oversight. Armed with a thorough grasp of the new exposures, the professional investor is much better able to anticipate and understand the challenges our central bankers and markets face.

Corporate Finance: A Practical Approach is a solid foundation for those looking to achieve lasting business growth. In today's competitive business environment, companies must find innovative ways to enable rapid and sustainable growth. This text equips readers with the foundational knowledge and tools for making smart business decisions and formulating strategies to maximize company value. It covers everything from managing relationships between stakeholders to evaluating mergers and acquisitions bids as well as the companies behind them.

Through extensive use of real-world examples, readers will gain critical perspective into interpreting corporate financial data, evaluating projects, and allocating funds in ways that increase corporate value. Readers will gain insights into the tools and strategies employed in modern corporate financial management.

International Financial Statement Analysis is designed to address the ever-increasing need for investment professionals and students to think about financial statement analysis from a global perspective. The text is a practically oriented introduction to financial statement analysis that is distinguished by its combination of a true international orientation, a structured presentation style, and abundant illustrations and tools covering concepts as they are introduced in the text. The authors cover this discipline comprehensively and with an eye to ensuring the reader's success at all levels in the complex world of financial statement analysis.

I hope you find this new series helpful in your efforts to grow your investment knowledge, whether you are a relatively new entrant or an experienced veteran ethically bound to keep up-to-date in the ever-changing market environment. CFA Institute, as a long-term committed participant of the investment profession and a not-for-profit association, is pleased to give you this opportunity.

JEFF DIERMEIER, CFA
President and Chief Executive Officer
CFA Institute
October 2008

CHAPTER 1

FINANCIAL STATEMENT ANALYSIS: AN INTRODUCTION

Thomas R. Robinson, CFA

CFA Institute
Charlottesville, Virginia

Hennie van Greuning, CFA

World Bank
Washington, DC

Elaine Henry, CFA

University of Miami
Miami, Florida

Michael A. Broihahn, CFA

Barry University
Miami, Florida

LEARNING OUTCOMES

After completing this chapter, you will be able to do the following:

- Discuss the roles of financial reporting and financial statement analysis.
- Discuss the roles of the key financial statements (income statement, balance sheet, cash flow statement, and statement of changes in owners' equity) in evaluating a company's performance and financial position.

1

- Discuss the importance of financial statement notes and supplementary information (including disclosures of accounting methods, estimates, and assumptions) and management's discussion and analysis.
- Discuss the objective of audits of financial statements, the types of audit reports, and the importance of effective internal controls.
- Identify and explain information sources besides annual financial statements and supplementary information that analysts use in financial statement analysis.
- Describe the steps in the financial statement analysis framework.

1. INTRODUCTION

Analysts are employed in a number of functional areas. Commonly, analysts evaluate an investment in some type of security that has characteristics of equity (representing an ownership position) or debt (representing a lending position). In arriving at investment decisions or recommendations, analysts need to evaluate the performance, financial position, and value of the company issuing the securities. Company financial reports, which include financial statements and other data, provide the information necessary to evaluate the company and its securities. Consequently, the analyst must have a firm understanding of the information provided in each company's financial reports, including the financial notes and other forms of supplementary information.

This chapter is organized as follows: Section 2 discusses the scope of financial statement analysis. Section 3 describes the sources of information used in financial statement analysis, including the primary financial statements (income statement, balance sheet, and cash flow statement). Section 4 provides a framework for guiding the financial statement analysis process, and section 5 summarizes the key points of the chapter. Practice problems in the CFA Institute multiple-choice format conclude the chapter.

2. SCOPE OF FINANCIAL STATEMENT ANALYSIS

The role of financial reporting by companies is to provide information about their performance, financial position, and changes in financial position that is useful to a wide range of users in making economic decisions.[1] The role of financial statement analysis is to take financial reports prepared by companies, combined with other information, to evaluate the past, current, and prospective performance and financial position of a company for the purpose of making investment, credit, and other economic decisions.

In evaluating financial reports, analysts typically have an economic decision in mind. Examples include the following:

- Evaluating an equity investment for inclusion in a portfolio.
- Evaluating a merger or acquisition candidate.
- Evaluating a subsidiary or operating division of a parent company.

---

[1]See paragraph 12 of the *Framework for the Preparation and Presentation of Financial Statements,* originally published by the International Accounting Standards Committee in 1989 and then adopted by the International Accounting Standards Board in 2001.

- Deciding whether to make a venture capital or other private equity investment.
- Determining the creditworthiness of a company that has made a loan request.
- Extending credit to a customer.
- Examining compliance with debt covenants or other contractual arrangements.
- Assigning a debt rating to a company or bond issue.
- Valuing a security for making an investment recommendation to others.
- Forecasting future net income and cash flow.

There are certain themes in financial analysis. In general, analysts seek to examine the performance and financial position of companies as well as forecast future performance and financial position. Analysts are also concerned about factors that affect risks to the company's future performance and financial position. An examination of performance can include an assessment of a company's profitability (the ability to earn a profit from delivering goods and services) and its cash flow–generating ability (the ability to produce cash receipts in excess of cash disbursements). Profit and cash flow are not equivalent. Profit represents the excess of the prices at which goods or services are sold over all the costs of providing those goods and services (regardless of when cash is received or paid). Example 1-1 illustrates the distinction between profit and cash flow.

Profit vs. Cash Flow

EXAMPLE 1-1   Profit versus Cash Flow

Sennett Designs (SD) sells imported furniture on a retail basis. SD began operations during December 2006 and sold furniture for cash of €250,000. The furniture that was sold by SD was delivered by the supplier during December, but the supplier has granted SD credit terms, according to which payment is not due until January 2007. SD is obligated to pay €220,000 in January for the furniture it sold during December.

1. How much is SD's profit for December 2006 if no other transactions occurred?
2. How much is SD's cash flow for December 2006?

Solution to 1. SD's profit for December 2006 is the excess of the sales price (€250,000) over the cost of the goods that were sold (€220,000), or €30,000.

Solution to 2. The December 2006 cash flow is €250,000.

Although profitability is important, so is the ability to generate positive cash flow. Cash flow is important because, ultimately, cash is needed to pay employees, suppliers, and others to continue as a going concern. A company that generates positive cash flow from operations has more flexibility in funding needed investments and taking advantage of attractive business opportunities than an otherwise comparable company without positive cash flow. Additionally, cash flow is the source of returns to providers of capital. Therefore, the expected magnitude of future cash flows is important in valuing corporate securities and in determining the company's ability to meet its obligations. The ability to meet short-term obligations is generally referred to as **liquidity**, and the ability to meet long-term obligations is generally referred to as **solvency**. However, as shown in Example 1-1, cash flow in a given period is not a complete measure of performance in that period; for example, a company may be obligated to make future cash payments as a result of a transaction generating positive cash flow in the current period.

As noted earlier, profits reflect the ability of a company to deliver goods and services at prices in excess of the costs of delivering the goods and services. Profits also provide useful information about future (and past) cash flows. If the transaction of Example 1-1 were repeated year after year, the long-term average annual cash flow of SD would be €30,000, its annual profit. Many analysts not only evaluate past profitability but also forecast future profitability.

Exhibit 1-1 shows how news media coverage of corporate earnings announcements places corporate results in the context of analysts' expectations. Furthermore, analysts frequently use earnings in valuation, for example, when they value shares of a company on the basis of the price-to-earnings ratio (P/E) in relation to peer companies' P/Es or when they use a present value model of valuation that is based on forecasted future earnings.

Analysts are also interested in the current financial position of a company. The financial position can be measured by comparing the resources controlled by the company in relation to the claims against those resources. An example of a resource is cash. In Example 1-1, if no other transactions occur, the company should have cash on 31 December 2006 of €250,000.

EXHIBIT 1-1   An Earnings Release and Analyst Reaction

Panel A. Excerpt from Apple Earnings Release

Apple Reports Third-Quarter Results
Posts Second-Highest Quarterly Revenue and Earnings in Company's History

CUPERTINO, California—July 19, 2006—Apple® today announced financial results for its fiscal 2006 third quarter ended July 1, 2006. The Company posted revenue of $4.37 billion and a net quarterly profit of $472 million, or $0.54 per diluted share. These results compare to revenue of $3.52 billion and a net profit of $320 million, or $0.37 per diluted share, in the year-ago quarter. Gross margin was 30.3 percent, up from 29.7 percent in the year-ago quarter. International sales accounted for 39 percent of the quarter's revenue.

Apple shipped 1,327,000 Macintosh® computers and 8,111,000 iPods during the quarter, representing 12 percent growth in Macs and 32 percent growth in iPods over the year-ago quarter. . . .

Panel B. Excerpt from CNET News.com Report

"Mac Sales Up 12 Percent as Apple Profits Soar" by Tom Krazit

Apple Computer's third-quarter revenue fell a little short of expectations, but profitability was far higher than expected and Mac sales increased at a healthy clip.

. . . Net income was $472 million, or 54 cents per share, an improvement of 48 percent compared with last year's results of $320 million in net income and 37 cents per share. Analysts surveyed by Thomson First Call had been expecting Apple to report $4.4 billion in revenue and earn 44 cents per share.

. . . The outlook for the next period will probably disappoint some investors. The company predicted fourth-quarter revenue would be about $4.5 billion to $4.6 billion, less than the $4.9 billion analysts had been expecting. Apple executives will hold a conference call later Wednesday to discuss results.

Sources: www.apple.com/pr/library/2006/jul/19results.html, http://news.com/Mac+sales+up+12+ percent+as+Apple+profits+soar/2100-1047_3-6096116.html.

EXHIBIT 1-2   Grupo Imsa Press Release Dated 18 January 2005

Standard & Poor's and Fitch Upgrade Grupo Imsa's Credit Rating

---

MONTERREY, Mexico: Grupo Imsa (NYSE: IMY) (BMV: IMSA) announces that Standard & Poor's has recently upgraded the Company's local currency corporate credit rating from BBB– to BBB and its national scale rating from mxAA to mxAA+. Fitch Mexico also increased Grupo Imsa's domestic rating from AA(mex) to AA+(mex). These rating upgrades reflect the positive results of Grupo Imsa's main businesses and the strengthening of its financial position, combined with the Company's geographic diversification, market leadership, state-of-the-art technology and high operational efficiency.

Mr. Marcelo Canales, Grupo Imsa's CFO, explained: "Grupo Imsa follows a policy of maintaining a solid financial position that ensures the Company's continuity for the benefit of our employees, shareholders and creditors. We take our financial commitments very seriously, as can be seen from the fact that during our 70 years of existence we have always complied with our financial obligations. The change in rating also reflects the strength of our business model and its capacity to generate cash." Mr. Canales added: "These upgrades in credit rating should translate into a better valuation of our debt to reflect Grupo Imsa's new financial reality."

Grupo Imsa, a holding company, dates back to 1936 and is today one of Mexico's leading diversified industrial companies, operating in three core businesses: steel processed products; steel and plastic construction products; and aluminum and other related products. With manufacturing and distribution facilities in Mexico, the United States, Europe and throughout Central and South America, Grupo Imsa currently exports to all five continents. Grupo Imsa's shares trade on the Mexican Stock Exchange (IMSA) and, in the United States, on the NYSE (IMY).

This document contains forward-looking statements relating to Grupo Imsa's future performance or its current expectations or beliefs, including statements regarding the intent, belief or current expectations of the Company and its management. Investors are cautioned that any such forward-looking statements are not guarantees of future performance and involve a number of risks and uncertainties pertaining to the industries in which the Company participates. Grupo Imsa does not intend, and does not assume any obligation, to update these forward-looking statements.

Source: Business Wire, 18 January 2005.

This cash can be used by the company to pay the obligation to the supplier (a claim against the company) and may also be used to make distributions to the owner (who also has a claim against the company for any profits that have been earned). Financial position is particularly important in credit analysis, as depicted in Exhibit 1-2.

In conducting a financial analysis of a company, the analyst will regularly refer to the company's financial statements, financial notes and supplementary schedules, and a variety of other information sources. The next section introduces the major financial statements and most commonly used information sources.

3. MAJOR FINANCIAL STATEMENTS AND OTHER INFORMATION SOURCES

In order to perform an equity or credit analysis of a company, an analyst must collect a great deal of information. The nature of the information will vary based on the individual task but will typically include information about the economy, industry, and company as well as information about comparable peer companies. Much of this information will come from outside the company, such as economic statistics, industry reports, trade publications, and databases containing information on competitors. The company itself provides some of the core information for analysis in its financial reports, press releases, and conference calls and webcasts.

Companies prepare financial reports to report to investors and creditors on financial performance and financial strength at regular intervals (annually, semiannually, and/ or quarterly). Financial reports include financial statements and supplemental information necessary to assess the performance and financial position of the company. Financial statements are the end results of an accounting record-keeping process that records the economic activities of a company. They summarize this information for use by investors, creditors, analysts, and others interested in a company's performance and financial position. In order to provide some assurances as to the information provided in the financial statements and related notes, the financial statements are audited by independent accountants, who express an opinion on whether the financial statements fairly portray the company's performance and financial position.

3.1. Financial Statements and Supplementary Information

The key financial statements that are the focus of analysis are the income statement, balance sheet, statement of cash flows, and statement of changes in owners' equity. The income statement and statement of cash flows portray different aspects of a company's performance over a period of time. The balance sheet portrays the company's financial position at a given point in time. The statement of changes in owners' equity provides additional information regarding the changes in a company's financial position. In addition to the financial statements, a company provides other information in its financial reports that is useful to the financial analyst. As part of his or her analysis, the financial analyst should read and assess this additional information, which includes:

- Notes to the financial statements (also known as footnotes) and supplementary schedules.
- Management's discussion and analysis (MD&A).
- The external auditor's report(s).

The following sections illustrate the major financial statements.

3.1.1. Income Statement

The income statement presents information on the financial results of a company's business activities over a period of time. The income statement communicates how much revenue the company generated during a period and what costs it incurred in connection with generating that revenue. Net income (revenue minus all costs) on the income statement is often referred to as the "bottom line" because of its proximity to the bottom of the income statement.[2] Income statements are reported on a consolidated basis, meaning that they include the revenues and expenses of affiliated companies under the control of the parent (reporting) company. The income statement is sometimes referred to as a **statement of operations** or **profit and loss** (P&L) **statement**. The basic equation underlying the income statement is Revenue − Expenses = Net income.

In Exhibit 1-3, the income statement is presented with the most recent year in the first column and the earliest year in the last column. Although this is a common presentation,

---

[2]Net income is also referred to as net earnings or net profit. In the event that costs exceed revenues, it is referred to as net loss.

EXHIBIT 1-3   Wal-Mart Consolidated Statements of Income (in millions except per share data)

Fiscal years ended 31 January	2005	2004	2003
Revenues			
Net sales	$285,222	$256,329	$229,616
Other income, net	2,767	2,352	1,961
	287,989	258,681	231,577
Costs and Expenses			
Cost of sales	219,793	198,747	178,299
Operating, selling, general, and administrative expenses	51,105	44,909	39,983
Operating Income	17,091	15,025	13,295
Interest			
Debt	934	729	799
Capital lease	253	267	260
Interest income	(201)	(164)	(132)
Interest, net	986	832	927
Income from continuing operations before income taxes and minority interest	16,105	14,193	12,368
Provision for Income Taxes			
Current	5,326	4,941	3,883
Deferred	263	177	474
Total	5,589	5,118	4,357
Income from continuing operations before minority interest	10,516	9,075	8,011
Minority interest	(249)	(214)	(193)
Income from continuing operations	10,267	8,861	7,818
Income from discontinued operations, net of tax	—	193	137
Net Income	$ 10,267	$ 9,054	$ 7,955
Basic Net Income per Common Share			
Income from continuing operations	$ 2.41	$ 2.03	$ 1.77
Income from discontinued operations	—	0.05	0.03
Basic net income per common share	$ 2.41	$ 2.08	$ 1.80
Diluted Net Income per Common Share			
Income from continuing operations	$ 2.41	$ 2.03	$ 1.76
Income from discontinued operations	—	0.04	0.03
Diluted net income per common share	$ 2.41	$ 2.07	$ 1.79
Weighted Average Number of Common Shares			
Basic	4,259	4,363	4,430
Diluted	4,266	4,373	4,446
Dividends per Common Share	$ 0.52	$ 0.36	$ 0.30

analysts should be careful when reading an income statement because in other cases, the years may be listed from most distant to most recent.

Exhibit 1-3 shows that Wal-Mart's total revenue for the fiscal year ended 31 January 2005 was (in millions) $287,989. Wal-Mart then subtracted its operating costs and expenses to arrive at an operating income (profit) of $17,091. Operating income reflects a company's profits from its usual business activities, before deducting interest expense or taxes. Operating income is thus often referred to as EBIT, or earnings before interest and taxes. Operating income reflects the company's underlying performance independent of the use of financial leverage. Wal-Mart's total interest cost (net of the interest income that was earned from investments) for 2005 was $986; its earnings before taxes was, therefore, $16,105. Total income tax expense for 2005 was $5,589, and the minority interest expense (income earned by the minority share-holders from Wal-Mart subsidiary companies) was $249. After deducting these final expenses, Wal-Mart's net income for fiscal 2005 was $10,267.

Companies present their basic and diluted earnings per share on the face of the income statement. Earnings per share represents the net income divided by the number of shares of stock outstanding during the period. Basic earnings per share uses the weighted average number of common shares that were actually outstanding during the period, whereas diluted earnings per share uses **diluted shares**—the number of shares that would be outstanding if potentially dilutive claims on common shares (e.g., stock options) were exercised by their holders. Wal-Mart's basic earning per share for 2005 was $2.41 ($10,267 net income ÷ 4,259 basic shares outstanding). Likewise, Wal-Mart's diluted earnings per share for 2005 was also $2.41 ($10,267 net income ÷ 4,266 diluted shares).

An analyst examining the income statement might note that Wal-Mart was profitable in each year and that revenue, operating income, net income, and earnings per share—all measures of profitability—increased over the three-year period. The analyst might formulate questions related to profitability, such as the following:

- Is the growth in revenue related to an increase in units sold, an increase in prices, or some combination?
- After adjusting for growth in the number of stores, is the company still more profitable over time?
- How does the company compare with other companies in the industry?

Answering such questions requires the analyst to gather, analyze, and interpret facts from a number of sources, including the income statement. The chapter on understanding the income statement will explain the income statement in greater detail. The next section illustrates the balance sheet, the second major financial statement.

3.1.2. Balance Sheet

The **balance sheet** (also known as the **statement of financial position** or **statement of financial condition**) presents a company's current financial position by disclosing resources the company controls (assets) and what it owes (liabilities) at a specific point in time. **Owners' equity** represents the excess of assets over liabilities. This amount is attributable to the owners or shareholders of the business; it is the residual interest in the assets of an entity after deducting its liabilities. The three parts of the balance sheet are formulated in an accounting relationship known as the accounting equation: Assets = Liabilities + Owners' equity (that is, the total amount for assets must *balance* to the combined total amounts for liabilities and owners' equity). Alternatively, the three parts of the balance sheet of the accounting relationship may be formulated as Assets − Liabilities = Owners' equity. Depending on the form of the organization, owners' equity also goes by several alternative titles, such as "partners' capital" or "shareholders' equity."

Exhibit 1-4 presents Wal-Mart's consolidated balance sheets for the fiscal years ended 31 January 2004 and 2005.

EXHIBIT 1-4   Wal-Mart Consolidated Balance Sheets (in millions except per-share data)

Fiscal Years Ended 31 January	2005	2004
Assets		
Current assets:		
Cash and cash equivalents	$ 5,488	$ 5,199
Receivables	1,715	1,254
Inventories	29,447	26,612
Prepaid expenses and other	1,841	1,356
Total current assets	38,491	34,421
Property and equipment, at cost:		
Land	14,472	12,699
Buildings and improvements	46,582	40,192
Fixtures and equipment	21,461	17,934
Transportation equipment	1,530	1,269
Property and equipment, at cost	84,045	72,094
Less accumulated depreciation	18,637	15,684
Property and equipment, net	65,408	56,410
Property under capital lease:		
Property under capital lease	4,997	4,286
Less accumulated amortization	1,838	1,673
Property under capital lease, net	3,159	2,613
Goodwill	10,803	9,882
Other assets and deferred charges	2,362	2,079
Total assets	$120,223	$105,405
Liabilities and shareholders' equity		
Current liabilities:		
Commercial paper	$ 3,812	$ 3,267
Accounts payable	21,671	19,425
Accrued liabilities	12,155	10,671
Accrued income taxes	1,281	1,377
Long-term debt due within one year	3,759	2,904
Obligations under capital leases due within one year	210	196
Total current liabilities	42,888	37,840
	(Continued)	

EXHIBIT 1-4 *Continued*

Fiscal Years Ended 31 January	2005	2004
Long-term debt:	$20,087	$17,102
Long-term obligations under capital leases	3,582	2,997
Deferred income taxes and other	2,947	2,359
Minority interest	1,323	1,484
Shareholders' equity:		
Preferred stock ($0.10 par value; 100 shares authorized, none issued)	—	—
Common stock ($0.10 par value; 11,000 shares authorized, 4,234 and 4,311 issued and outstanding in 2005 and 2004, respectively)	423	431
Capital in excess of par value	2,425	2,135
Other accumulated comprehensive income	2,694	851
Retained earnings	43,854	40,206
Total shareholders' equity	49,396	43,623
Total Liabilities and Shareholders' Equity	**$120,223**	**$105,405**

On 31 January 2005, Wal-Mart's total resources or assets were $120,223 (in millions). Shareholders' equity (in millions) was $49,396. Although Wal-Mart does not give a total amount for all the balance sheet liabilities, it may be determined from the accounting relationship as Total assets − Total shareholders' equity or $120,223 − $49,396 = $70,827.[3] Using the balance sheet and applying financial statement analysis, the analyst will be able to answer such questions as:

- Has the company's liquidity (ability to meet short-term obligations) improved?
- Is the company solvent (does it have sufficient resources to cover its obligations)?
- What is the company's financial position relative to the industry?

The chapter on understanding the balance sheet will cover the analysis of the balance sheet in more depth. The next section illustrates the cash flow statement.

3.1.3. Cash Flow Statement

Although the income statement and balance sheet provide a measure of a company's success in terms of performance and financial position, cash flow is also vital to a company's long-term success. Disclosing the sources and uses of cash helps creditors, investors, and other statement users evaluate the company's liquidity, solvency, and financial flexibility. **Financial flexibility** is the ability to react and adapt to financial adversities and opportunities. The cash flow statement classifies all company cash flows into operating, investing,

---

[3]Note that this computation includes an amount labeled "minority interest in liabilities." Minority interest represents ownership in a subsidiary company by others (not the parent company). Accounting rule makers are currently considering reclassifying this amount as part of owners' equity.

and financing activity cash flows. **Operating activities** involve transactions that enter into the determination of net income and are primarily activities that comprise the day-to-day business functions of a company. **Investing activities** are those activities associated with the acquisition and disposal of long-term assets, such as equipment. **Financing activities** are those activities related to obtaining or repaying capital to be used in the business.

Exhibit 1-5 presents Wal-Mart's consolidated statement of cash flows for the fiscal years ended 31 January 2003, 2004, and 2005.

EXHIBIT 1-5   Wal-Mart Consolidated Statements of Cash Flows (in millions)

Fiscal Years Ended 31 January	2005	2004	2003
Cash Flows from Operating Activities			
Income from continuing operations	$ 10,267	$ 8,861	$ 7,818
Adjustments to reconcile net income to net cash provided by operating activities:			
Depreciation and amortization	4,405	3,852	3,364
Deferred income taxes	263	177	474
Other operating activities	378	173	685
Changes in certain assets and liabilities, net of effects of acquisitions:			
Decrease (increase) in accounts receivable	(304)	373	(159)
Increase in inventories	(2,635)	(1,973)	(2,219)
Increase in accounts payable	1,694	2,587	1,748
Increase in accrued liabilities	976	1,896	1,212
Net cash provided by operating activities of continuing operations	15,044	15,946	12,923
Net cash provided by operating activities of discontinued operations	—	50	82
Net cash provided by operating activities	15,044	15,996	13,005
Cash Flows from Investing Activities			
Payments for property and equipment	(12,893)	(10,308)	(9,245)
Investment in international operations	(315)	(38)	(749)
Proceeds from the disposal of fixed assets	953	481	311
Proceeds from the sale of McLane	—	1,500	—
Other investing activities	(96)	78	(73)
Net cash used in investing activities of continuing operations	(12,351)	(8,287)	(9,756)
Net cash used in investing activities discontinued operations	—	(25)	(83)
Net cash used in investing activities	(12,351)	(8,312)	(9,839)
Cash Flows from Financing Activities			
Increase in commercial paper	544	688	1,836
Proceeds from issuance of long-term debt	5,832	4,099	2,044

(Continued)

EXHIBIT 1-5 *Continued*

Fiscal Years Ended 31 January	2005	2004	2003
Purchase of company stock	(4,549)	(5,046)	(3,383)
Dividends paid	(2,214)	(1,569)	(1,328)
Payment of long-term debt	(2,131)	(3,541)	(1,261)
Payment of capital lease obligations	(204)	(305)	(216)
Other financing activities	113	111	(62)
Net cash used in financing activities	(2,609)	(5,563)	(2,370)
Effect of exchange rate changes on cash	205	320	(199)
Net increase in cash and cash equivalents	289	2,441	597
Cash and cash equivalents at beginning of year	5,199	2,758	2,161
Cash and cash equivalents at end of year	$ 5,488	$ 5,199	$ 2,758
Supplemental Disclosure of Cash Flow Information			
Income tax paid	$ 5,593	$ 4,358	$ 4,539
Interest paid	1,163	1,024	1,085
Capital lease obligations incurred	377	252	381

In the cash flows from operating activities section of Wal-Mart's cash flow statement, the company reconciles its net income to net cash provided by operating activities. This emphasizes the different perspectives of the income statement and cash flow statement. Income is reported when earned, not necessarily when cash is received. The cash flow statement presents another aspect of performance: the ability of a company to generate cash flow from running its business. Ideally, the analyst would like to see that the primary source of cash flow is from operating activities (as opposed to investing or financing activities). Note that Wal-Mart had a large amount of operating cash flow, which increased from 2003 to 2004 but decreased slightly in 2005. Although operating cash flow was high, an analyst might question why net income increased but operating cash flow decreased in 2005.

The summation of the net cash flows from operating, investing, and financing activities and the effect of exchange rates on cash equals the net change in cash during the fiscal year. For Wal-Mart, the summation of these four cash flow activities in 2005 was $289, which thus increased the company's cash from $5,199 on 31 January 2004 (beginning cash balance) to $5,488 on 31 January 2005 (ending cash balance). Note that these beginning and ending cash balances agree with the cash reported on Wal-Mart's balance sheets in Exhibit 1-4.

The cash flow statement will be treated in more depth in the chapter on understanding the cash flow statement.

3.1.4. Statement of Changes in Owners' Equity

The income statement, balance sheet, and cash flow statements represent the primary financial statements used to assess a company's performance and financial position. A fourth financial statement is also available, variously called a "statement of changes in owners' equity," "statement of shareholders' equity," or "statement of retained earnings." This statement primarily serves to report changes in the owners' investment in the business over time and assists the analyst in understanding the changes in financial position reflected on the balance sheet.

3.1.5. Financial Notes and Supplementary Schedules

Financial notes and supplementary schedules are an integral part of the financial statements. By way of example, the financial notes and supplemental schedules provide explanatory information about the following:

- Business acquisitions and disposals
- Commitments and contingencies
- Legal proceedings
- Stock option and other employee benefit plans
- Related-party transactions
- Significant customers
- Subsequent events
- Business and geographic segments
- Quarterly financial data

Additionally, the footnotes contain information about the methods and assumptions used to prepare the financial statements. Comparability of financial statements is a critical requirement for objective financial analysis. Financial statement comparability occurs when information is measured and reported in a similar manner over time and for different companies. Comparability allows the analyst to identify and analyze the real economic substance differences and similarities between companies. The International Accounting Standards Board based in London sets forth standards under which international financial statements should be prepared. These are referred to as International Financial Reporting Standards (IFRS). Similarly, the Financial Accounting Standards Board (FASB) in the United States sets forth standards (called statements of financial accounting standards) that constitute the key part of the body of principles known as generally accepted accounting principles (U.S. GAAP). These two organizations are working to make their standards similar, but there are key differences. When comparing a U.S. company with a European company, an analyst must understand differences in these standards, which can relate, for example, to the period in which to report revenue.

Even within each of these sets of standards there can be choices for management to make that can reduce comparability between companies. Both IFRS and U.S. GAAP allow the use of alternative accounting methods to measure company financial performance and financial condition where there are differences in economic environments between companies. Additionally, some principles require the use of estimates and assumptions in measuring performance and financial condition. This flexibility is necessary because, ideally, a company will select those methods, estimates, and assumptions within the principles that fairly reflect the unique economic environment of the company's business and industry. Although this flexibility in accounting principles ostensibly meets the divergent needs of many businesses, it creates a problem for the analyst because comparability is lost when flexibility occurs. For example, if a company acquires a piece of equipment to use in its operations, accounting standards require that the cost of the asset be reported as an expense in a systematic manner over the life of the equipment (estimating the process of the equipment's wearing out). This allocation of the cost is known as **depreciation**. The standards permit a great deal of flexibility, however, in determining the manner in which each year's expense is determined. Two companies may acquire similar equipment but use different methods and assumptions to record the expense over time. Comparing the companies' performance directly is then impaired by this difference.

A company's accounting policies (methods, estimates, and assumptions) are generally presented in the notes to the financial statements. A note containing a summary of significant accounting policies reveals, for example, how the company recognizes its revenues and depreciates its capital assets. Analysts must be aware of the methods, estimates, and assumptions used by a company to determine if they are similar to those of other companies that are being used as benchmarks. If they are not similar, the analyst who understands accounting techniques can make adjustments to make the financial statements more comparable.

3.1.6. Management's Discussion and Analysis

Publicly held companies are often required to include in their financial reports a section called Management's Discussion and Analysis (MD&A). In it, management must highlight any favorable or unfavorable trends and identify significant events and uncertainties that affect the company's liquidity, capital resources, and results of operations. The MD&A must also provide information about the effects of inflation, changing prices, or other material events and uncertainties that may cause the future operating results and financial condition to materially depart from the current reported financial information. Companies should also provide disclosure in the MD&A that discusses the critical accounting policies that require management to make subjective judgments and that have a significant impact on reported financial results. The MD&A section of a company's report provides a good starting place for understanding what is going on in the financial statements. Nevertheless, it is only one input for the analyst in seeking an objective and independent perspective on a company's performance and prospects.

3.1.7. Auditor's Reports

Financial statements presented in company annual financial reports are often required to be audited (examined) by an independent accounting firm that then expresses an opinion on the financial statements. Audits may be required by contractual arrangement, law, or regulation. Just as there are standards for preparing financial statements, there are standards for auditing and for expressing the resulting auditor's opinion. International standards for auditing have been developed by the International Auditing and Assurance Standards Board of the International Federation of Accountants. These standards have been adopted by many countries. Other countries, such as the United States, have developed their own standards. With the enactment of the Sarbanes–Oxley Act in the United States, auditing standards are being promulgated by the Public Company Accounting Oversight Board (PCAOB). Under International Standard on Auditing 200:

> *The objective of an audit of financial statements is to enable the auditor to express an opinion whether the financial statements are prepared, in all material respects, in accordance with an applicable financial reporting framework.*[4]

Publicly traded companies may also have requirements set by regulators or stock exchanges, such as appointing an independent audit committee of the board of directors to oversee the audit process. The audit process provides a basis for the independent auditor to express an audit opinion on the fairness of the financial statements that were audited. Because audits are designed and conducted by using audit sampling techniques, independent auditors cannot express an opinion that provides absolute assurance about the accuracy or precision of the financial statements. Instead, the independent audit report provides

---

[4]International Federation of Accountants, *Handbook of International Auditing, Assurance, and Ethics Pronouncements*, 2006 edition, p. 230, available at www.ifac.org.

reasonable assurance that the financial statements are *fairly presented*, meaning that there is a high degree of probability that the audited financial statements are free from *material* error, fraud, or illegal acts that have a direct effect on the financial statements.

The standard independent audit report for a publicly traded company normally has several paragraphs under both the international and U.S. auditing standards. The first or "introductory" paragraph describes the financial statements that were audited and the responsibilities of both management and the independent auditor. The second or "scope" paragraph describes the nature of the audit process and provides the basis for the auditor's expression about reasonable assurance on the fairness of the financial statements. The third or "opinion" paragraph expresses the auditor's opinion on the fairness of the audited financial statements. An *unqualified* audit opinion states that the financial statements give a "true and fair view" (international) or are "fairly presented" (international and U.S.) in accordance with applicable accounting standards. This is often referred to as a "clean" opinion and is the one that analysts would like to see in a financial report. There are several other types of opinions. A *qualified* audit opinion is one in which there is some limitation or exception to accounting standards. Exceptions are described in the audit report with additional explanatory paragraphs so that the analyst can determine the importance of the exception. An *adverse* audit opinion occurs when the financial statements materially depart from accounting standards and are not fairly presented. An adverse opinion makes analysis of the financial statements easy: Don't bother, because the company's financial statements cannot be relied upon. Finally, a *disclaimer of opinion* occurs when, for some reason, the auditors are unable to issue an opinion. Exhibit 1-6 presents the independent auditor's report for Wal-Mart. Note that Wal-Mart received a "clean" or unqualified audit opinion from Ernst & Young LLP for the company's fiscal year ended 31 January 2005.

In the United States, under the Sarbanes-Oxley Act, the auditors must also express an opinion on the company's internal control systems. This information may be provided in a separate opinion or incorporated as a fourth paragraph in the opinion related to the financial statements. The internal control system is the company's internal system that is designed, among other things, to ensure that the company's process for generating financial reports is sound.

Although management has always been responsible for maintaining effective internal control, the Sarbanes-Oxley Act greatly increases management's responsibility for demonstrating that the company's internal controls are effective. Publicly traded companies in the United States are now required by securities regulators to:

- Accept responsibility for the effectiveness of internal control.
- Evaluate the effectiveness of internal control using suitable control criteria.
- Support the evaluation with sufficient competent evidence.
- Provide a report on internal control.

The Sarbanes-Oxley Act specifically requires management's report on internal control to:

- State that it is management's responsibility to establish and maintain adequate internal control.
- Identify management's framework for evaluating internal control.
- Include management's assessment of the effectiveness of the company's internal control over financial reporting as of the end of the most recent year, including a statement as to whether internal control over financial reporting is effective.
- Include a statement that the company's auditors have issued an attestation report on management's assessment.
- Certify that the company's financial statements are fairly presented.

EXHIBIT 1-6   Wal-Mart's Independent Audit Report

Report of Independent Registered Accounting Firm

WAL-MART
The Board of Directors and Shareholders,
Wal-Mart Stores, Inc.

We have audited the accompanying consolidated balance sheets of Wal-Mart Stores, Inc. as of January 31, 2005 and 2004, and the related consolidated statements of income, shareholders' equity and cash flows for each of the three years in the period ended January 31, 2005. These financial statements are the responsibility of the company's management. Our responsibility is to express an opinion on these financial statements based on our audits.

We conducted our audits in accordance with the standards of the Public Company Accounting Oversight Board (United States). Those standards require that we plan and perform the audit to obtain reasonable assurance about whether the financial statements are free of material misstatement. An audit includes examining on a test basis, evidence supporting the amounts and disclosures in the financial statements. An audit also includes assessing the accounting principles used and significant estimates made by management, as well as evaluating the overall financial statement presentation. We believe that our audits provide a reasonable basis for our opinion.

In our opinion, the financial statements referred to above present fairly, in all material respects, the consolidated financial position of Wal-Mart Stores, Inc. at January 31, 2005 and 2004, and the consolidated results of its operations and its cash flows for each of the three years in the period ended January 31, 2005, in conformity with U.S. generally accepted accounting principles.

We also have audited, in accordance with the standards of the Public Accounting Oversight Board (United States), the effectiveness of Wal-Mart Stores, Inc.'s internal control over financial reporting as of January 31, 2005, based on criteria established in *Internal Control – Integrated Framework* issued by the Committee of Sponsoring Organizations of the Treadway Committee and our report dated March 25, 2005 expressed an unqualified opinion thereon.

Ernst & Young LLP
Rogers, Arkansas
March 25, 2005

Source: 2005 Wal-Mart Stores, Inc. annual report.

Exhibit 1-7 presents Wal-Mart management's report on internal control to its company's shareholders. Note that Wal-Mart has fully complied with each of the reporting criterion that were discussed in the preceding paragraph.

Although these reports provide some assurances to analysts, they are not infallible. The analyst must always use a degree of healthy skepticism when analyzing financial statements.

3.2. Other Sources of Information

The information described in the previous section is generally provided to shareholders on an annual basis. Interim reports are also provided by the company either semiannually or quarterly. Interim reports generally present the four key financial statements and footnotes but are not audited. These interim reports provide updated information on a company's performance and financial position since the last annual period. Companies also prepare proxy statements for distribution to shareholders on matters that are to be put to a vote at the company's annual (or special) meeting of shareholders. The proxy statement typically provides useful information regarding management and director compensation and company stock performance and discloses any potential conflicts of interest that may exist between management,

EXHIBIT 1-7   Wal-Mart's Report to Shareholders on Corporate Governance and Internal Control

Management's Report to Our Shareholders

WAL-MART

Management of Wal-Mart Stores, Inc. ("Wal-Mart") is responsible for the preparation, integrity and objectivity of Wal-Mart's consolidated financial statements and other financial information contained in this Annual Report to Shareholders. Those consolidated financial statements were prepared in conformity with accounting principles generally accepted in the United States. In preparing those consolidated financial statements, Management was required to make certain estimates and judgments, which are based upon currently available information and Management's view of current conditions and circumstances.

The Audit Committee of the Board of Directors, which consists solely of independent directors, oversees our process of reporting financial information and the audit of our consolidated financial statements. The Audit Committee stays informed of the financial condition of Wal-Mart and regularly reviews Management's financial policies and procedures, the independence of our independent auditors, our internal control and the objectivity of our financial reporting. Both the independent financial auditors and the internal auditors have free access to the Audit Committee and meet with the Audit Committee periodically, both with and without Management present.

We have retained Ernst & Young LLP, an independent registered public accounting firm, to audit our consolidated financial statements found in this annual report. We have made available to Ernst & Young LLP all of our financial records and related data in connection with their audit of our consolidated financial statements.

We have filed with the Securities and Exchange Commission the required certifications related to our consolidated financial statements as of and for the year ended January 31, 2005. These certifications are attached as exhibits to our Annual Report on Form 10-K for the year ended January 31, 2005. Additionally, we have also provided to the New York Stock Exchange the required annual certification of our Chief Executive Officer regarding our compliance with the New York Stock Exchange's corporate governance listing standards.

Report on Internal Control over Financial Reporting

Management has responsibility for establishing and maintaining adequate internal control over financial reporting. Internal control over financial reporting is a process designed to provide reasonable assurance regarding the reliability of financial reporting and the preparation of financial statements for external reporting purposes in accordance with accounting principles generally accepted in the United States. Because of its inherent limitations, internal control over financial reporting may not prevent or detect misstatements. Management has assessed the effectiveness of the company's internal control over financial reporting as of January 31, 2005. In making its assessment, Management has utilized the criteria set forth by the Committee of Sponsoring Organizations ("COSO") of the Treadway Commission in *Internal Control–Integrated Framework*. Management concluded that based on its assessment, Wal-Mart's internal control over financial reporting was effective as of January 31, 2005. Management's assessment of the effectiveness of the company's internal control over financial reporting as of January 31, 2005 has been audited by Ernst & Young LLP, an independent registered public accounting firm, as stated in their report which appears in this Annual Report to Shareholders.

Evaluation of Disclosure Controls and Procedures

We maintain disclosure controls and procedures designed to provide reasonable assurance that information, which is required to be timely disclosed, is accumulated and communicated to Management in a timely fashion. Management has assessed the effectiveness of these disclosure controls and procedures as of January 31, 2005 and determined that they were effective as of that date to provide reasonable assurance that information required to be disclosed by us in the reports we file or submit under the Securities Exchange Act of 1934, as amended, is accumulated and communicated to Management, as appropriate, to allow timely decisions regarding required disclosure and are effective to provide reasonable assurance that such information is recorded, processed, summarized and reported within the time periods specified by the SEC's rules and forms.

(Continued)

EXHIBIT 1-7   *Continued*

Report on Ethical Standards

Our company was founded on the belief that open communications and the highest standard of ethics are necessary to be successful. Our long-standing "Open Door" communication policy helps Management be aware of and address issues in a timely and effective manner. Through the open door policy all associates are encouraged to inform Management at the appropriate level when they are concerned about any matter pertaining to Wal-Mart.

Wal-Mart has adopted a Statement of Ethics to guide our associates in the continued observance of high ethical standards such as honesty, integrity and compliance with the law in the conduct of Wal-Mart's business. Familiarity and compliance with the Statement of Ethics is required of all associates who are part of Management. The company also maintains a separate Code of Ethics for our senior financial officers. Wal-Mart also has in place a Related-Party Transaction Policy. This policy applies to all of Wal-Mart's Officers and Directors and requires material related-party transactions to be reviewed by the Audit Committee. The Officers and Directors are required to report material related-party transactions to Wal-Mart. We maintain an ethics office which oversees and administers an ethics hotline. The ethics hotline provides a channel for associates to make confidential and anonymous complaints regarding potential violations of our statement of ethics, including violations related to financial or accounting matters.

H. Lee Scott
President and Chief Executive Officer
Thomas M. Schoewe
Executive Vice President and Chief Financial Officer

Source: 2005 Wal-Mart Stores, Inc. annual report.

the board, and shareholders. Companies also provide relevant current information on their web sites and in press releases and as part of conference calls. When performing financial statement analysis, analysts should review all these company sources of information as well as information from external sources regarding the economy, the industry, the company, and peer (comparable) companies. Information on the economy, industry, and peer companies is useful in putting the company's financial performance and position in perspective and in assessing the company's future. The next section presents a framework for using all this information in financial statement analysis.

4. FINANCIAL STATEMENT ANALYSIS FRAMEWORK

Analysts work in a variety of positions. Some are equity analysts whose main objective is to evaluate potential equity (share) investments to determine whether a prospective investment is attractive and what an appropriate purchase price might be. Others are credit analysts who evaluate the creditworthiness of a company to decide whether (and with what terms) a loan should be made or what credit rating should be assigned. Analysts may also be involved in a variety of other tasks, such as evaluating the performance of a subsidiary company, evaluating a private equity investment, or finding stocks that are overvalued for purposes of taking a short position. This section presents a generic framework for financial statement analysis that can be used in these various tasks. The framework is summarized in Exhibit 1-8.[5]

---

[5]Components of this framework have been adapted from van Greuning and Bratanovic (2003, p. 300) and from Benninga and Sarig (1997, pp. 134–156).

EXHIBIT 1-8   Financial Statement Analysis Framework   *Process*

Phase	Sources of Information	Output
1. Articulate the purpose and context of the analysis.	The nature of the analyst's function, such as evaluating an equity or debt investment or issuing a credit rating. Communication with client or supervisor on needs and concerns. Institutional guidelines related to developing specific work product.	Statement of the purpose or objective of analysis. A list (written or unwritten) of specific questions to be answered by the analysis. Nature and content of report to be provided. Timetable and budgeted resources for completion.
2. Collect data.	Financial statements, other financial data, questionnaires, and industry/economic data. Discussions with management, suppliers, customers, and competitors. Company site visits (e.g., to production facilities or retail stores).	Organized financial statements. Financial data tables. Completed questionnaires, if applicable.
3. Process data.	Data from the previous phase.	Adjusted financial statements. Common-size statements. Ratios and graphs. Forecasts.
4. Analyze/interpret the processed data.	Input data as well as processed data.	Analytical results.
5. Develop and communicate conclusions and recommendations (e.g., with an analysis report).	Analytical results and previous reports. Institutional guidelines for published reports.	Analytical report answering questions posed in Phase 1. Recommendation regarding the purpose of the analysis, such as whether to make an investment or grant credit.
6. Follow up.	Information gathered by periodically repeating above steps as necessary to determine whether changes to holdings or recommendations are necessary.	Updated reports and recommendations.

The following sections discuss the individual phases of financial statement analysis.

4.1.   Articulate the Purpose and Context of Analysis

Prior to undertaking any analysis, it is essential to understand the purpose of the analysis. An understanding of the purpose is particularly important in financial statement analysis because of the numerous available techniques and the substantial amount of data.

Some analytical tasks are well defined, in which case articulating the purpose of the analysis requires little decision making by the analyst. For example, a periodic credit review of an investment-grade debt portfolio or an equity analyst's report on a particular company may be guided by institutional norms such that the purpose of the analysis is given. Furthermore, the format, procedures, and/or sources of information may also be given.

For other analytical tasks, articulating the purpose of the analysis requires the analyst to make decisions. The purpose of an analysis guides further decisions about the approach, the tools, the data sources, the format in which to report results of the analysis, and the relative importance of different aspects of the analysis.

When facing a substantial amount of data, a less experienced analyst may be tempted to just start crunching numbers and creating output. It is generally advisable to resist the temptation and thus avoid the black hole of pointless number crunching. Consider the questions: If you could wave a magic wand and have all the numbers crunched, what conclusion would you be able to draw? What question would you be able to answer? What decision would your answer support?

The analyst should also define the context at this stage. Who is the intended audience? What is the end product—for example, a final report explaining conclusions and recommendations? What is the time frame (i.e., when is the report due)? What resources and resource constraints are relevant to completion of the analysis? Again, the context may be predefined (i.e., standard and guided by institutional norms).

Having clarified the purpose and context of the financial statement analysis, the analyst should next compile the specific questions to be answered by the analysis. For example, if the purpose of the financial statement analysis (or, more likely, the particular stage of a larger analysis) is to compare the historical performance of three companies operating in a particular industry, specific questions would include: What has been the relative growth rate of the companies and what has been the relative profitability of the companies?

4.2. Collect Data

Next, the analyst obtains the data required to answer the specific questions. A key part of this step is obtaining an understanding of the company's business, financial performance, and financial position (including trends over time and in comparison with peer companies). For historical analyses, financial statement data alone are adequate in some cases. For example, to screen a large number of alternative companies for those with a minimum level of profitability, financial statement data alone would be adequate. But to address more in-depth questions, such as why and how one company performed better or worse than its competitors, additional information would be required. As another example, to compare the historical performance of two companies in a particular industry, the historical financial statements would be sufficient to determine which had faster-growing sales or earnings and which was more profitable; however, a broader comparison with overall industry growth and profitability would obviously require industry data.

Furthermore, information on the economy and industry is necessary to understand the environment in which the company operates. Analysts often take a top-down approach whereby they (1) gain an understanding of the macroeconomic environment, such as prospects for growth in the economy and inflation, (2) analyze the prospects of the industry in which the subject company operates based on the expected macroeconomic environment, and (3) determine the prospects for the company in the expected industry and macroeconomic environments. For example, an analyst may need to forecast future growth in earnings for a company. To project future growth, past company data provide one basis for statistical forecasting; however, an understanding of economic and industry conditions can improve the analyst's ability to forecast a company's earnings based on forecasts of overall economic and industry activity.

4.3. Process Data

After obtaining the requisite financial statement and other information, the analyst processes this data using appropriate analytical tools. For example, processing the data may involve computing ratios or growth rates; preparing common-size financial statements; creating charts; performing statistical analyses, such as regressions or Monte Carlo simulations; performing equity valuation; performing sensitivity analyses; or using any other analytical tools or combination of tools that are available and appropriate to the task. A comprehensive financial analysis at this stage would include the following:

- Reading and evaluating financial statements for each company subject to analysis. This includes reading the footnotes and understanding what accounting standards have been used (e.g., IFRS or U.S. GAAP), what accounting choices have been made (e.g., when to report revenue on the income statement), and what operating decisions have been made that affect reported financial statements (e.g., leasing versus purchasing equipment).
- Making any needed adjustments to the financial statements to facilitate comparison, when the unadjusted statements of the subject companies reflect differences in accounting standards, accounting choices, or operating decisions. Note that commonly used databases do not make such analyst adjustments.
- Preparing or collecting common-size financial statement data (which scale data to directly reflect percentages [e.g., of sales] or changes [e.g., from the prior year]) and financial ratios (which are measures of various aspects of corporate performance based on financial statement elements). On the basis of common-size financial statements and financial ratios, analysts can evaluate a company's relative profitability, liquidity, leverage, efficiency, and valuation in relation to past results and/or peers' results.

4.4. Analyze/Interpret the Processed Data

Once the data have been processed, the next step—critical to any analysis—is to interpret the output. The answer to a specific financial analysis question is seldom the numerical answer alone; the answer to the analytical question relies on the interpretation of the output and the use of this interpreted output to support a conclusion or recommendation. The answers to the specific analytical questions may themselves achieve the underlying purpose of the analysis, but usually, a conclusion or recommendation is required. For example, an equity analysis may require a buy, hold, or sell decision or a conclusion about the value of a share of stock. In support of the decision, the analysis would cite such information as target value, relative performance, expected future performance given a company's strategic position, quality of management, and whatever other information was important in reaching the decision.

4.5. Develop and Communicate Conclusions/Recommendations

Communicating the conclusion or recommendation in an appropriate format is the next step in an analysis. The appropriate format will vary by analytical task, by institution, and/or by audience. For example, an equity analyst report would typically include the following components:[6]

- Summary and investment conclusion
- Business summary
- Risks
- Valuation
- Historical and pro forma tables

The contents of reports many also be specified by regulatory agencies or professional standards. For example, the CFA Institute *Standards of Practice Handbook* (SOPH) dictates standards that must be followed in communicating recommendations. The SOPH provides, in part:

> *Standard V(B) states the responsibility of members and candidates to include in their communications those key factors that are instrumental to the investment recommendation presented. A critical part of this requirement is to distinguish clearly between opinions and facts. In preparing a research report, the member or candidate must present the basic characteristics of the security being analyzed, which will allow the reader to evaluate the report and incorporate information the reader deems relevant to his or her investment decision making process.[7]*

The SOPH requires that limitations to the analysis and any risks inherent to the investment be disclosed. Furthermore, the SOPH requires that any report include elements important to the analysis and conclusions so that readers can evaluate the conclusions themselves.

4.6. Follow Up

The process does not end with the report. If an equity investment is made or a credit rating assigned, periodic review is required to determine if the original conclusions and recommendations are still valid. In the case of a rejected investment, follow-up may not be necessary but may be appropriate to determine if the analysis process should be refined (e.g., if a rejected investment turns out to be successful in the market). Follow-up may involve repeating all the above steps in the process on a periodic basis.

5. SUMMARY

This chapter has presented an overview of financial statement analysis. Among the major points covered are the following:

- The primary purpose of financial reports is to provide information and data about a company's financial position and performance, including profitability and cash flows. The information presented in financial reports—including the financial statements, financial notes, and management's discussion and analysis—allows the financial analyst to assess a company's financial position and performance and trends in that performance.

---

[6]Stowe, Robinson, Pinto, and McLeavey (2002, p. 27).
[7]*Standards of Practice Handbook* (2006, p. 105).

- Key financial statements that are a primary focus of analysis include the income statement, balance sheet, cash flow statement, and statement of owners' equity.
- The income statement presents information on the financial results of a company's business activities over a period of time. The income statement communicates how much revenue the company generated during a period and what costs it incurred in connection with generating that revenue. The basic equation underlying the income statement is Revenue − Expense = Net income.
- The balance sheet discloses what a company owns (assets) and what it owes (liabilities) at a specific point in time. Owners' equity represents the portion belonging to the owners or shareholders of the business; it is the residual interest in the assets of an entity after deducting its liabilities. The three parts of the balance sheet are formulated in the accounting relationship of Assets = Liabilities + Owners' equity.
- Although the income statement and balance sheet provide a measure of a company's success, cash and cash flow are also vital to a company's long-term success. Disclosing the sources and uses of cash in the cash flow statement helps creditors, investors, and other statement users evaluate the company's liquidity, solvency, and financial flexibility.
- The statement of changes in owners' equity reflects information about the increases or decreases to a company's owners' equity.
- In addition to the financial statements, a company provides other sources of financial information that are useful to the financial analyst. As part of his or her analysis, the financial analyst should read and assess the information presented in the company's financial note disclosures and supplementary schedules as well as the information contained in the MD&A. Analysts must also evaluate footnote disclosures regarding the use of alternative accounting methods, estimates, and assumptions.
- A publicly traded company must have an independent audit performed on its year-end financial statements. The auditor's opinion provides some assurance about whether the financial statements fairly reflect a company's performance and financial position. In addition, for U.S. publicly traded companies, management must demonstrate that the company's internal controls are effective.
- The financial statement analysis framework provides steps that can be followed in any financial statement analysis project, including the following:
  - Articulate the purpose and context of the analysis.
  - Collect input data.
  - Process data.
  - Analyze/interpret the processed data.
  - Develop and communicate conclusions and recommendations.
  - Follow up.

PRACTICE PROBLEMS

1. Providing information about the performance and financial position of companies so that users can make economic decisions *best* describes the role of
   A. auditing.
   B. financial reporting.
   C. financial statement analysis.

2. A company's current financial position would *best* be evaluated using the
   A. balance sheet.
   B. income statement.
   C. cash flow statement.

3. A company's profitability for a period would *best* be evaluated using the
   A. balance sheet.
   B. income statement.
   C. cash flow statement.

4. Accounting methods, estimates, and assumptions used in preparing financial statements are found
   A. in footnotes.
   B. in the auditor's report.
   C. in the proxy statement.

5. Information about management and director compensation would *best* be found
   A. in footnotes.
   B. in the auditor's report.
   C. in the proxy statement.

6. Information about material events and uncertainties would *best* be found in
   A. footnotes.
   B. the proxy statement.
   C. management's discussion and analysis.

7. What type of audit opinion is preferred when analyzing financial statements?
   A. Qualified.
   B. Adverse.
   C. Unqualified.

8. Ratios are an input into which step in the financial analysis framework?
   A. Process data.
   B. Collect input data.
   C. Analyze/interpret the processed data.

CHAPTER 2

FINANCIAL REPORTING MECHANICS

Thomas R. Robinson, CFA

CFA Institute
Charlottesville, Virginia

Hennie van Greuning, CFA

World Bank
Washington, DC

Elaine Henry, CFA

University of Miami
Miami, Florida

Michael A. Broihahn, CFA

Barry University
Miami, Florida

LEARNING OUTCOMES

After completing this chapter, you will be able to do the following:

- Identify the groups (operating, investing, and financing activities) into which business activities are categorized for financial reporting purposes and classify any business activity in the appropriate group. ✓
- Explain the relationship of financial statement elements and accounts, and classify accounts into the financial statement elements. ✓

- Explain the accounting equation in its basic and expanded forms. ✓
- Explain the process of recording business transactions using an accounting system based on the accounting equations. ° *Debit* ° *Credit*
- Explain the need for accruals and other adjustments in preparing financial statements. ✓
- Prepare financial statements given account balances and/or other elements in the relevant accounting equation, and explain the relationships among the income statement, balance sheet, statement of cash flows, and statement of owners' equity. ✓
- Describe the flow of information in an accounting system.
- Explain the use of the results of the accounting process in security analysis.

1. INTRODUCTION

The financial statements of a company are end products of a process for recording transactions of the company related to operations, financing, and investment. The structures of financial statements themselves reflect the system of recording and organizing transactions. To be an informed user of financial statements, the analyst must be knowledgeable about the principles of this system. This chapter will supply that essential knowledge, taking the perspective of the user rather than the preparer. Learning the process from this perspective will enable an analyst to grasp the critical concepts without being overwhelmed by the detailed technical skills required by the accountants who prepare financial statements that are a major component of financial reports.

This chapter is organized as follows: Section 2 describes the three groups into which business activities are classified for financial reporting purposes. Any transaction affects one or more of these groups. Section 3 describes how the elements of financial statements relate to accounts, the basic content unit of classifying transactions. The section is also an introduction to the linkages among the financial statements. Section 4 provides a step-by-step illustration of the accounting process. Section 5 explains the consequences of timing differences between the elements of a transaction. Section 6 provides an overview of how information flows through a business's accounting system. Section 7 introduces the use of financial reporting in security analysis, and Section 8 presents a summary of key points. Practice problems in the CFA Institute multiple-choice format conclude the chapter.

2. THE CLASSIFICATION OF BUSINESS ACTIVITIES

Accountants give similar accounting treatment to similar types of business transactions. Therefore, a first step in understanding financial reporting mechanics is to understand how business activities are classified for financial reporting purposes.

Business activities may be classified into three groups for financial reporting purposes: operating, investing, and financing activities.

- **Operating activities** are those activities that are part of the day-to-day business functioning of an entity. Examples include the sale of meals by a restaurant, the sale of services by a consulting firm, the manufacture and sale of ovens by an oven-manufacturing company, and taking deposits and making loans by a bank.
- **Investing activities** are those activities associated with acquisition and disposal of long-term assets. Examples include the purchase of equipment or sale of surplus equipment

EXHIBIT 2-1   Typical Business Activities and Financial Statement Elements Affected

Assets (A), Liabilities (L), Owners' Equity (E), Revenue (R), and Expenses (X) *A, L, O e, R, X*	
Operating activities	Sales of goods and services to customers: (R)
	Costs of providing the goods and services: (X)
	Income tax expense: (X)
	Holding short-term assets or incurring short-term liabilities directly related to operating activities: (A), (L)
Investing activities	Purchase or sale of assets, such as property, plant, and equipment: (A)
	Purchase or sale of other entities' equity and debt securities: (A)
Financing activities	Issuance or repurchase of the company's own preferred or common stock: (E)
	Issuance or repayment of debt: (L)
	Payment of distributions (i.e., dividends to preferred or common stockholders): (E)

(such as an oven) by a restaurant (contrast this to the sale of an oven by an oven manufacturer, which would be an operating activity), and the purchase or sale of an office building, a retail store, or a factory.

- **Financing activities** are those activities related to obtaining or repaying capital. The two primary sources for such funds are owners (shareholders) or creditors. Examples include issuing common shares, taking out a bank loan, and issuing bonds.

Understanding the nature of activities helps the analyst understand where the company is doing well and where it is not doing so well. Ideally, an analyst would prefer that most of a company's profits (and cash flow) come from its operating activities. Exhibit 2-1 provides examples of typical business activities and how these activities relate to the elements of financial statements described in the following section.

Not all transactions fit neatly in this framework for purposes of financial statement presentation. For example, interest received by a bank on one of its loans would be considered *OCF* part of operating activities because a bank is in the business of lending money. In contrast, interest received on a bond investment by a restaurant may be more appropriately classified as an investing activity because the restaurant is not in the business of lending money.

The next section discusses how transactions resulting from these business activities are reflected in a company's financial records.

3. ACCOUNTS AND FINANCIAL STATEMENTS

Business activities resulting in transactions are reflected in the broad groupings of financial statement elements: assets, liabilities, owners' equity, revenue, and expenses.[1] In general terms, these elements can be defined as follows: **assets** are the economic resources of a

---

[1]International Financial Reporting Standards use the term *income* to include revenue and gains. Gains are similar to revenue; however, they arise from secondary or peripheral activities rather than from a

company; **liabilities** are the creditors' claims on the resources of a company; **owners' equity** is the residual claim on those resources; **revenues** are inflows of economic resources to the company; and **expenses** are outflows of economic resources or increases in liabilities.[2]

Accounts provide individual records of increases and decreases in a *specific* asset, liability, component of owners' equity, revenue, or expense. The financial statements are constructed using these elements.

3.1. Financial Statement Elements and Accounts

Within the financial statement elements, accounts are subclassifications. **Accounts** are individual records of increases and decreases in a specific asset, liability, component of owners' equity, revenue, or expense. For financial statements, amounts recorded in every individual account are summarized and grouped appropriately within a financial statement element. Exhibit 2-2 provides a listing of common accounts. These accounts will be described throughout this chapter or in following chapters. Unlike the financial statement elements, there is no standard set of accounts applicable to all companies. Although almost every company has certain accounts, such as cash, each company specifies the accounts in its accounting system based on its particular needs and circumstances. For example, a company in the restaurant business may not be involved in trading securities and, therefore, may not need an account to record such an activity. Furthermore, each company names its accounts based on its business. A company in the restaurant business might have an asset account for each of its ovens, with the accounts named "Oven-1" and "Oven-2." In its financial statements, these accounts would likely be grouped within long-term assets as a single line item called *property, plant, and equipment.*

A company's challenge is to establish accounts and account groupings that provide meaningful summarization of voluminous data but retain enough detail to facilitate decision making and preparation of the financial statements. The actual accounts used in a company's accounting system will be set forth in a **chart of accounts**. Generally, the chart of accounts is far more detailed than the information presented in financial statements.

Certain accounts are used to offset other accounts. For example, a common asset account is accounts receivable, also known as *trade accounts receivable* or *trade receivables*. A company uses this account to record the amounts it is owed by its customers. In other words, sales made on credit are reflected in accounts receivable. In connection with its receivables, a company often expects some amount of uncollectible accounts and, therefore, records an estimate

---

company's primary business activities. For example, for a restaurant, the sale of surplus restaurant equipment for more than its cost is referred to as a gain rather than revenue. Similarly, a loss is like an expense but arises from secondary activities. Gains and losses may be considered part of operations on the income statement (for example, a loss due to a decline in value of inventory) or may be part of nonoperating activities (for example, the sale of nontrading investments). Under U.S. GAAP, financial statement elements are defined to include assets, liabilities, owners' equity, revenue, expenses, gains, and losses. To illustrate business transactions in this reading, we will use the simple classification of revenues and expenses. All gains and revenue will be aggregated in revenue, and all losses and expenses will be aggregated in expenses.

[2]The authoritative accounting standards provide significantly more detailed definitions of the accounting elements. Also note that *owners' equity* is a generic term, and more specific titles are often used such as *shareholders' equity, stockholders' equity,* or *partners' capital.* The broader terms *equity* and *capital* are also used on occasion.

EXHIBIT 2-2   Common Accounts

Assets	Cash and cash equivalents
	Accounts receivable, trade receivables
	Prepaid expenses
	Inventory
	Property, plant, and equipment
	Investment property
	Intangible assets (patents, trademarks, licenses, copyright, goodwill)
	Financial assets, trading securities, investment securities
	Investments accounted for by the equity method
	Current and deferred tax assets
	(for banks, Loans [receivable])
Liabilities	Accounts payable, trade payables
	Provisions or accrued liabilities
	Financial liabilities
	Current and deferred tax liabilities
	Reserves
	Minority interest
	Unearned revenue
	Debt payable
	Bonds (payable)
	(for banks, Deposits)
Owners' equity	Capital, such as common stock par value
	Additional paid-in capital
	Retained earnings
	Other comprehensive income
Revenue	Revenue, sales
	Gains
	Investment income (e.g., interest and dividends)
Expense	Cost of goods sold
	Selling, general, and administrative expenses (SG&A; e.g., rent, utilities, salaries, advertising)
	Depreciation and amortization
	Interest expense
	Tax expense
	Losses

of the amount that may not be collected. The estimated uncollectible amount is recorded in an account called **allowance for bad debts**. Because the effect of the allowance for bad debts account is to reduce the balance of the company's accounts receivable, it is known as a contra asset account. Any account that is offset or deducted from another account is called a **contra account**. Common contra asset accounts include allowance for bad debts (an offset to accounts receivable for the amount of accounts receivable that are estimated to be uncollectible), **accumulated depreciation** (an offset to property, plant, and equipment reflecting the amount of the cost of property, plant, and equipment that has been allocated to current and previous accounting periods), and **sales returns and allowances** (an offset to revenue reflecting any cash refunds, credits on account, and discounts from sales prices given to customers who purchased defective or unsatisfactory items).

For presentation purposes, assets are sometimes categorized as "current" or "noncurrent." For example, Tesco (a large European retailer) presents the following major asset accounts in its 2006 financial reports:

Noncurrent assets

- Intangible assets including goodwill
- Property, plant, and equipment
- Investment property
- Investments in joint ventures and associates
- Current assets
- Inventories
- Trade and other receivables
- Cash and cash equivalents

Noncurrent assets are assets that are expected to benefit the company over an extended period of time (usually more than one year). For Tesco, these include the following: intangible assets, such as goodwill;[3] property, plant, and equipment used in operations (e.g., land and buildings); other property held for investment, and investments in the securities of other companies.

Current assets are those that are expected to be consumed or converted into cash in the near future, typically one year or less. **Inventories** are the unsold units of product on hand (sometimes referred to as inventory stock). **Trade receivables** (also referred to as **commercial receivables**, or simply **accounts receivable**) are amounts customers owe the company for products that have been sold as well as amounts that may be due from suppliers (such as for returns of merchandise). **Other receivables** represent amounts owed to the company from parties other than customers. **Cash** refers to cash on hand (e.g., petty cash and cash not yet deposited to the bank) and in the bank. **Cash equivalents** are very liquid short-term investments, usually maturing in 90 days or less. The presentation of assets as current or noncurrent will vary from industry to industry and from country to country. Some industries present current assets first, whereas others list noncurrent assets first. This is discussed further in later chapters.

3.2. Accounting Equations

The five financial statement elements noted previously serve as the inputs for equations that underlie the financial statements. This section describes the equations for three of the financial statements: balance sheet, income statement, and statement of retained earnings. A statement of retained earnings can be viewed as a component of the statement of stockholders' equity, which shows *all* changes to owners' equity, both changes resulting from retained

---

[3]**Goodwill** is an intangible asset that represents the excess of the purchase price of an acquired company over the value of the net assets acquired.

earnings and changes resulting from share issuance or repurchase. The fourth basic financial statement, the statement of cash flows, will be discussed in a later section.

The **balance sheet** presents a company's financial position at a *particular point in time*. It provides a listing of a company's assets and the claims on those assets (liabilities and equity claims). The equation that underlies the balance sheet is also known as the basic accounting equation. A company's financial position is reflected using the following equation:

$$\text{Assets} = \text{Liabilities} + \text{Owners' equity} \qquad (2\text{-}1a)$$

Presented in this form, it is clear that claims on assets are from two sources: liabilities or owners' equity. Owners' equity is the **residual claim** of the owners (i.e., the owners' remaining claim on the company's assets after the liabilities are deducted). The concept of the owners' residual claim is well illustrated by the slightly rearranged balance sheet equation, roughly equivalent to the structure commonly seen in the balance sheets of U.K. companies:

$$\text{Assets} - \text{Liabilities} = \text{Owners' equity} \qquad (2\text{-}1b)$$

Other terms are used to denote owners' equity, including shareholders' equity, stockholders' equity, net assets, equity, net worth, net book value, and partners' capital. The exact titles depend upon the type of entity, but the equation remains the same. Owners' equity at a given date can be further classified by its origin: capital contributed by owners, and earnings retained in the business up to that date:[4]

$$\text{Owners' equity} = \text{Contributed capital} + \text{Retained earnings} \qquad (2\text{-}2)$$

The **income statement** presents the performance of a business for a *specific period of time*. The equation reflected in the income statement is the following:

$$\text{Revenue} - \text{Expenses} = \text{Net income (loss)} \qquad (2\text{-}3)$$

Note that **net income (loss)** is the difference between two of the elements: revenue and expenses. When a company's revenue exceeds its expenses, it reports net income; when a company's revenues are less than its expenses, it reports a net loss. Other terms are used synonymously with revenue, including *sales* and *turnover* (in the United Kingdom). Other terms used synonymously with net income include *net profit* and *net earnings*.

Also, as noted earlier, revenue and expenses generally relate to providing goods or services in a company's primary business activities. In contrast, gains (losses) relate to increases (decreases) in resources that are not part of a company's primary business activities. Distinguishing a company's primary business activities from other business activities is important in financial analysis; however, for purposes of the accounting equation, gains are included in revenue and losses are included in expenses.

The balance sheet and income statement are two of the primary financial statements. Although these are the common terms for these statements, some variations in the names occur. A balance sheet can be referred to as a *statement of financial position* or some similar

---

[4]This formula reflects the fundamental origins of owners' equity and reflects the basic principles of accounting. The presentation is somewhat simplified. In practice, the owners' equity section of a company's balance sheet may include other items, such as treasury stock (which arises when a company repurchases and holds its own stock) or other comprehensive income. **Comprehensive income** includes all income of the company. Some items of comprehensive income are not reported on the income statement. These items as a group are called **other comprehensive income**; such items arise, for example, when there are changes in the value of assets or liabilities that are not reflected in the income statement.

EXHIBIT 2-3   Simplified Balance Sheet and Income Statement

ABC Company, Inc. Balance Sheet As of 31 December 20X1		ABC Company, Inc. Income Statement For the Year Ended 31 December 20X1	
Assets	2,000	Revenue	250
Liabilities	500		
Owners' equity	1,500	Expense	50
	2,000	Net income	200

term that indicates it contains balances at a point in time. Income statements can be titled *statement of operations, statement of income, statement of profit and loss,* or some other similar term showing that it reflects the company's operating activity for a period of time. A simplified balance sheet and income statement are shown in Exhibit 2-3.

The balance sheet represents a company's financial position at a point in time, and the income statement represents a company's activity over a period of time. The two statements are linked together through the retained earnings component of owners' equity. Beginning retained earnings is the balance in this account at the beginning of the accounting period, and ending retained earnings is the balance at the end of the period. A company's ending retained earnings is composed of the beginning balance (if any), plus net income, less any distributions to owners (dividends). Accordingly, the equation underlying retained earnings is:

$$\text{Ending retained earnings} = \text{Beginning retained earnings} + \text{Net income} - \text{Dividends} \tag{2-4a}$$

Or, substituting Equation 2-3 for Net income, equivalently:

$$\text{Ending retained earnings} = \text{Beginning retained earnings} + \text{Revenues} - \text{Expenses} - \text{Dividends} \tag{2-4b}$$

As its name suggests, retained earnings represent the earnings (i.e., net income) that are retained by the company—in other words, the amount not distributed as dividends to owners. Retained earnings is a component of owners' equity and links the "as of" balance sheet equation with the "activity" equation of the income statement. To provide a combined representation of the balance sheet and income statement, we can substitute Equation 2-2 into Equation 2-1a. This becomes the expanded accounting equation:

$$\text{Assets} = \text{Liabilities} + \text{Contributed capital} + \text{Ending retained earnings} \tag{2-5a}$$

Or equivalently, substituting Equation 2-4b into Equation 2-5a, we can write:

$$\text{Assets} = \text{Liabilities} + \text{Contributed capital} + \text{Beginning retained earnings} + \text{Revenue} - \text{Expenses} - \text{Dividends} \tag{2-5b}$$

The last five items, beginning with contributed capital, are components of owners' equity.

The **statement of retained earnings** shows the linkage between the balance sheet and income statement. Exhibit 2-4 shows a simplified example of financial statements for a company that began the year with retained earnings of $250 and recognized $200 of net income

EXHIBIT 2-4   Simplified Balance Sheet, Income Statement, and Statement of Retained Earnings

Point in Time: **Beginning of Period** **Balance Sheet**	**Change over Time:** **Income Statement and** **Changes in Retained Earnings**	**Point in Time:** **End-of-Period** **Balance Sheet**

ABC Company, Inc. **(Beginning) Balance Sheet** **As of 31 December 20X0**		**ABC Company, Inc.** **Income Statement** **Year Ended 31 December 20X1**		**ABC Company, Inc.** **(Ending) Balance Sheet** **As of 31 December 20X1**	
Assets	2,000	Revenue	250	Assets	2,200
		Expense	50		
Liabilities	500	Net income	200	Liabilities	500
Contributed equity	1,250			Contributed equity	1,250
Retained earnings	**250**			**Retained earnings**	**450**
Owners' equity	1,500			Owners' equity	1,700
	2,000				2,200

ABC Company, Inc. **Statement of Retained Earnings** **Year Ended 31 December 20X1**	
Beginning retained earnings	250
Plus net income	200
Minus dividends	0
Ending retained earnings	450

during the period. The example assumes the company paid no dividends and, therefore, had ending retained earnings of $450.

The basic accounting equation reflected in the balance sheet (Assets = Liabilities + Owners' equity) implies that every recorded transaction affects at least two accounts in order to keep the equation in balance, hence the term **double-entry accounting** that is sometimes used to describe the accounting process. For example, the use of cash to purchase equipment affects two accounts (both asset accounts): cash decreases and equipment increases. As another example, the use of cash to pay off a liability also affects two accounts (one asset account and one liability account): cash decreases and the liability decreases. With each transaction, the accounting equation remains in balance, which is a fundamental accounting concept. Example 2-1 presents a partial balance sheet for an actual company and an application of the accounting equation. Examples 2-2 and 2-3 provide further practice for applying the accounting equations.

EXAMPLE 2-1   Using Accounting Equations (1)

Canon is a manufacturer of copy machines and other electronic equipment. Abbreviated balance sheets as of 31 December 2004 and 2005 are presented below.

Canon and Subsidiaries: Consolidated Balance Sheets (¥millions)

	31 DEC 2005	31 DEC 2004
Assets		
Total assets	¥4,043,553	¥3,587,021
Liabilities and stockholders' equity		
Total liabilities	1,238,535	1,190,331
Total stockholders' equity	?	2,396,690
Total liabilities and stockholders' equity	¥4,043,553	¥3,587,021

Using Equation 2-1a, address the following:

1. Determine the amount of stockholders' equity as of 31 December 2005.
2. A. Calculate and contrast the absolute change in total assets in 2005 with the absolute change in total stockholders' equity in 2005.
   B. Based on your answer to 2A, state and justify the relative importance of growth in stockholders' equity and growth in liabilities in financing the growth of assets over the two years.

Solution to 1. Total stockholders' equity is equal to assets minus liabilities; in other words, it is the residual claim to the company's assets after deducting liabilities. For 2005, the amount of Canon's total stockholders' equity was thus ¥4,043,553 million − ¥1,238,535 million = ¥2,805,018 million.

Solutions to 2:
   A. Total assets increased by ¥4,043,553 million − ¥3,587,021 million = ¥456,532 million. Total stockholders' equity increased by ¥2,805,018 million − ¥2,396,690 million = ¥408,328 million. Thus, in 2005, total assets grew by more than total stockholders' equity (¥456,532 million is larger than ¥408,328 million).
   B. Using the relationship Assets = Liabilities + Owners' equity, the solution to 2A implies that total liabilities increased by the difference between the increase in total assets and the increase in total stockholders' equity, that is, by ¥456,532 million − ¥408,328 million = ¥48,204 million. (If liabilities had not increased by ¥48,204 million, the accounting equation would not be in balance.) Contrasting the growth in total stockholders' equity (¥408,328 million) with the growth in total liabilities (¥48,204 million), we see that the growth in stockholders' equity was relatively much more important than the growth in liabilities in financing total asset growth in 2005.

EXAMPLE 2-2   Using Accounting Equations (2)

An analyst has collected the following information regarding a company in advance of its year-end earnings announcement (amounts in millions):

Estimated net income	$ 150
Beginning retained earnings	$ 2,000
Estimated distributions to owners	$ 50

The analyst's estimate of ending retained earnings (in millions) should be closest to

A. $2,000.
B. $2,100.
C. $2,150.
D. $2,200.

Solution. B is correct. Beginning retained earnings is increased by net income and reduced by distributions to owners: $2,000 + $150 − $50 = $2,100.

EXAMPLE 2-3   Using Accounting Equations (3)

An analyst has compiled the following information regarding RDZ, Inc.

Liabilities at year-end	€1,000
Contributed capital at year-end	€1,000
Beginning retained earnings	€ 500
Revenue during the year	€4,000
Expenses during the year	€3,800

There have been no distributions to owners. The analyst's estimate of total assets at year-end should be closest to

A. €2,000.
B. €2,300.
C. €2,500.
D. €2,700.

Solution. D is correct. Ending retained earnings is first determined by adding revenue minus expenses to beginning retained earnings to obtain €700. Total assets would be equal to the sum of liabilities, contributed capital, and ending retained earnings: €1,000 + €1,000 + €700 = €2,700.

Having described the components and linkages of financial statements in abstract terms, we now examine more concretely how business activities are recorded. The next section illustrates the accounting process with a simple step-by-step example.

4. THE ACCOUNTING PROCESS

The accounting process involves recording business transactions such that periodic financial statements can be prepared. This section illustrates how business transactions are recorded in a simplified accounting system.

4.1. An Illustration

Key concepts of the accounting process can be more easily explained using a simple illustration. We look at an illustration in which three friends decide to start a business, Investment Advisers, Ltd. (IAL). They plan to issue a monthly newsletter of securities trading advice and to sell investment books. Although they do not plan to manage any clients' funds, they will manage a trading portfolio of the owners' funds to demonstrate the success of the recommended strategies from the newsletter. Because this illustration is meant to present accounting concepts, any regulatory implications will not be addressed. Additionally, for this illustration, we will assume that the entity will not be subject to income taxes; any income or loss will be passed through to the owners and be subject to tax on their personal income tax returns.

As the business commences, various business activities occur. Exhibit 2-5 provides a listing of the business activities that have taken place in the early stages of operations. Note that these activities encompass the types of operating, investing, and financing business activities discussed above.

4.2. The Accounting Records

If the owners want to evaluate the business at the end of January 2006, Exhibit 2-5 does not provide a sufficiently meaningful report of what transpired or where the company currently stands. It is clear that a system is needed to track this information and to address three objectives:

- Identify those activities requiring further action (e.g., collection of outstanding receivable balances).
- Assess the profitability of the operations over the month.
- Evaluate the current financial position of the company (such as cash on hand).

An accounting system will translate the company's business activities into usable financial records. The basic system for recording transactions in this illustration is a spreadsheet with each of the different types of accounts represented by a column. The accounting equation provides a basis for setting up this system. Recall the accounting Equation 2-5b:

$$\text{Assets} = \text{Liabilities} + \text{Contributed capital} + \text{Beginning retained earnings} + \text{Revenue} - \text{Expenses} - \text{Dividends}$$

$A = L + CC + beg\ RE + Rev - Ex - Dividends$

EXHIBIT 2-5   Business Activities for Investment Advisers, Ltd.

#	Date	Business Activity
1	31 December 2005	File documents with regulatory authorities to establish a separate legal entity. Initially capitalize the company through deposit of $150,000 from the three owners.
2	2 January 2006	Set up a $100,000 investment account and purchase a portfolio of equities and fixed-income securities.
3	2 January 3006	Pay $3,000 to landlord for office/warehouse. $2,000 represents a refundable deposit, and $1,000 represents the first month's rent.
4	3 January 2006	Purchase office equipment for $6,000. The equipment has an estimated life of two years with no salvage value.[5]
5	3 January 2006	Receive $1,200 cash for a one-year subscription to the monthly newsletter.
6	10 January 2006	Purchase and receive 500 books at a cost of $20 per book for a total of $10,000. Invoice terms are that payment from IAL is due in 30 days. No cash changes hands. These books are intended for resale.
7	10 January 2006	Spend $600 on newspaper and trade magazine advertising for the month.
8	15 January 2006	Borrow $12,000 from a bank for working capital. Interest is payable annually at 10 percent. The principal is due in two years.
9	15 January 2006	Ship first order to a customer consisting of five books at $25 per book. Invoice terms are that payment is due in 30 days. No cash changes hands.
10	15 January 2006	Sell for cash 10 books at $25 per book at an investment conference.
11	30 January 2006	Hire a part-time clerk. The clerk is hired through an agency that also handles all payroll taxes. The company is to pay $15 per hour to the agency. The clerk works six hours prior to 31 January, but no cash will be paid until February.
12	31 January 2006	Mail out the first month's newsletter to customer. This subscription had been sold on 3 January. See item 5.
13	31 January 2006	Review of the investment portfolio shows that $100 of interest income was earned and the market value of the portfolio has increased by $2,000. The balance in the investment account is now $102,100. The securities are classified as "trading" securities.

---

[5]**Salvage value** is the amount the company estimates that it can sell the asset for at the end of its useful life.

The specific accounts to be used for IAL's system include the following:

Asset Accounts

Cash
Investments
Prepaid rent (cash paid for rent in advance of recognizing the expense)
Rent deposit (cash deposited with the landlord, but returnable to the company)
Office equipment
Inventory
Accounts receivable

Liability Accounts

Unearned fees (fees that have not been earned yet, even though cash has been received)
Accounts payable (amounts owed to suppliers)
Bank debt

Equity Accounts

Contributed capital
Retained earnings
Income
Revenue
Expenses
Dividends

Exhibit 2-6 presents the spreadsheet representing IAL's accounting system for the first 10 transactions. Each event is entered on a new row of the spreadsheet as it occurs. To record events in the spreadsheet, the financial impact of each needs to be assessed and the activity expressed as an accounting transaction. In assessing the financial impact of each event and converting these events into accounting transactions, the following steps are taken:

1. Identify which accounts are affected, by what amount, and whether the accounts are increased or decreased.
2. Determine the element type for each account identified in Step 1 (e.g., cash is an asset) and where it fits in the basic accounting equation. Rely on the economic characteristics of the account and the basic definitions of the elements to make this determination.
3. Using the information from Steps 1 and 2, enter the amounts in the appropriate column of the spreadsheet.
4. Verify that the accounting equation is still in balance.

At any point in time, basic financial statements can be prepared based on the subtotals in each column.

The discussion that follows identifies the accounts affected and the related element (Steps 1 and 2) for the first 10 events listed in Exhibit 2-5. The accounting treatment shows the account affected in bold and the related element in brackets. The recording of these entries into a basic accounting system (Steps 3 and 4) is depicted on the spreadsheet in Exhibit 2-6.

EXHIBIT 2-6   Accounting System for Investment Advisers, Ltd.

#	Assets =			Liabilities +		Owners' Equity				
	Cash	Other Assets	Account	Amount	Account	Contributed Capital	Beginning Retained Earnings	Revenue	Expense	Dividends
Beg. Balance	0	0		0		0	0	0	0	0
1 Capitalize	150,000					150,000				
2 Investments	(100,000)	100,000	Investments							
3 Pay landlord	(3,000)	1,000 2,000	Prepaid rent Rent deposit							
4 Buy equipment	(6,000)	6,000	Office equipment							
5 Sell subscription	1,200			1,200	Unearned fees					
6 Buy books		10,000	Inventory	10,000	Accounts payable					
7 Advertise	(600)								(600)	
8 Borrow	12,000			12,000	Bank debt					
9 Sell books on account		125 (100)	Accounts receivable Inventory					125	(100)	
10 Cash sale	250	(200)	Inventory					250	(200)	
Subtotal	**53,850**	**118,825**		**23,200**		**150,000**		**375**	**(900)**	

39

Because this is a new business, the accounting equation begins at zero on both sides. There is a zero beginning balance in all accounts.

31 December 2005

	Business Activity	Accounting Treatment
1	File documents with regulatory authorities to establish a separate legal entity. Initially capitalize the company through deposit of $150,000 from the three owners.	**Cash [A]** is increased by $150,000, and **contributed capital [E]**[6] is increased by $150,000.

Accounting Elements: Assets (A), Liabilites (L), Equity (E), Revenue (R), and Expenses (X).

This transaction affects two elements: assets and equity. Exhibit 2-6 demonstrates this effect on the accounting equation. The company's balance sheet at this point in time would be presented by subtotaling the columns in Exhibit 2-6:

Investment Advisers, Ltd.
Balance Sheet

31 December 2005

Assets	
Cash	$150,000
Total assets	$150,000
Liabilities and owners' equity	
Contributed capital	$150,000
Total liabilities and owners' equity	$150,000

The company has assets (resources) of $150,000, and the owners' claim on the resources equals $150,000 (their contributed capital) as there are no liabilities at this point.

For this illustration, we present an unclassified balance sheet. An **unclassified balance sheet** is one that does not show subtotals for current assets and current liabilities. Assets are simply listed in order of liquidity (how quickly they are expected to be converted into cash). Similarly, liabilities are listed in the order in which they are expected to be satisfied (or paid off).

2 January 2006

	Business Activity	Accounting Treatment
2	Set up a $100,000 investment account and purchase a portfolio of equities and fixed-income securities.	**Investments [A]** were increased by $100,000, and **cash [A]** was decreased by $100,000.

Accounting Elements: Assets (A), Liabilites (L), Equity (E), Revenue (R), and Expenses (X).

This transaction affects two accounts, but only one element (assets) and one side of the accounting equation, as depicted in Exhibit 2-6. Cash is reduced when the securities are purchased. Another type of asset, investments, increases. We examine the other transaction from 2 January before taking another look at the company's balance sheet.

---

[6]The account title will vary depending upon the type of entity (incorporated or not) and jurisdiction. Alternative account titles are common shares, common stock, members' capital, partners' capital, etc.

2 January 2006

	Business Activity	Accounting Treatment
3	Pay $3,000 to landlord for office/warehouse. $2,000 represents a refundable deposit, and $1,000 represents the first month's rent.	**Cash [A]** was decreased by $3,000, **deposits [A]** were increased by $2,000, and **prepaid rent [A]** was increased by $1,000.

Accounting Elements: Assets (A), Liabilites (L), Equity (E), Revenue (R), and Expenses (X).

Once again, this transaction affects only asset accounts. Note that the first month's rent is initially recorded as an asset, prepaid rent. As time passes, the company will incur rent expense, so a portion of this prepaid asset will be transferred to expenses and thus will appear on the income statement as an expense.[7] This will require a later adjustment in our accounting system. Note that the transactions so far have had no impact on the income statement. At this point in time, the company's balance sheet would be:

Investment Advisers, Ltd.
Balance Sheet
As of 2 January 2006

Assets	
Cash	$ 47,000
Investments	100,000
Prepaid rent	1,000
Deposits	2,000
Total assets	$150,000
Liabilities and owners' equity	
Contributed capital	$150,000
Total liabilities and owners' equity	$150,000

Note that the items in the balance sheet have changed, but it remains in balance; the amount of total assets equals total liabilities plus owners' equity. The company still has $150,000 in resources, but the assets now comprise cash, investments, prepaid rent, and deposits. Each asset is listed separately because they are different in terms of their ability to be used by the company. Note also that the owners' equity claim on these assets remains $150,000 because the company still has no liabilities.

3 January 2006

	Business Activity	Accounting Treatment
4	Purchase office equipment for $6,000 in cash. The equipment has an estimated life of two years with no salvage value.	**Cash [A]** was decreased by $6,000, and **office equipment [A]** was increased by $6,000.

Accounting Elements: Assets (A), Liabilites (L), Equity (E), Revenue (R), and Expenses (X).

---

[7]An argument can be made for treating this $1,000 as an immediate expense. We adopt the approach of recording a prepaid asset in order to illustrate accrual accounting. A situation in which a company prepays rent (or insurance or any similar expense) for a time span covering multiple accounting periods more clearly requires the use of accrual accounting.

The company has once again exchanged one asset for another. Cash has decreased while office equipment has increased. Office equipment is a resource that will provide benefits over multiple future periods and, therefore, its cost must also be spread over multiple future periods. This will require adjustments to our accounting records as time passes. **Depreciation** is the term for the process of spreading this cost over multiple periods.

3 January 2006

Business Activity	Accounting Treatment
5 Receive $1,200 cash for a one-year subscription to the monthly newsletter.	**Cash [A]** was increased by $1,200, and **unearned fees [L]** was increased by $1,200.

Accounting Elements: Assets (A), Liabilites (L), Equity (E), Revenue (R), and Expenses (X).

In this transaction, the company has received cash related to the sale of subscriptions. However, the company has not yet actually earned the subscription fees because it has an obligation to deliver newsletters in the future. So, this amount is recorded as a liability called **unearned fees** (or **unearned revenue**). In the future, as the company delivers the newsletters and thus fulfills its obligation, this amount will be transferred to revenue. If the company fails to deliver the newsletters, the fees will need to be returned to the customer. As of 3 January 2006, the company's balance sheet would appear as

Investment Advisers, Ltd.
Balance Sheet
As of 3 January 2006

Assets	
Cash	$ 42,200
Investments	100,000
Prepaid rent	1,000
Deposits	2,000
Office equipment	6,000
Total assets	$151,200
Liabilities and owners' equity	
Liabilities	
Unearned fees	$ 1,200
Equity	
Contributed capital	150,000
Total liabilities and owners' equity	$151,200

The company now has $151,200 of resources, against which there is a claim by the subscription customer of $1,200 and a residual claim by the owners of $150,000. Again, the balance sheet remains in balance, with total assets equal to total liabilities plus equity.

10 January 2006

Business Activity	Accounting Treatment
6 Purchase and receive 500 books at a cost of $20 per book for a total of $10,000. Invoice terms are that payment from IAL is due in 30 days. No cash changes hands. These books are intended for resale.	**Inventory [A]** is increased by $10,000, and **accounts payable [L]** is increased by $10,000.

Accounting Elements: Assets (A), Liabilites (L), Equity (E), Revenue (R), and Expenses (X).

The company has obtained an asset, inventory, which can be sold to customers at a later date. Rather than paying cash to the supplier currently, the company has incurred an obligation to do so in 30 days. This represents a liability to the supplier that is termed accounts payable.

10 January 2006

	Business Activity	Accounting Treatment
7	Spend $600 on newspaper and trade magazine advertising for the month.	**Cash [A]** was decreased by $600, and **advertising expense [X]** was increased by $600.

Accounting Elements: Assets (A), Liabilites (L), Equity (E), Revenue (R), and Expenses (X).

Unlike the previous expenditures, advertising is an expense, not an asset. Its benefits relate to the current period. Expenditures such as advertising are recorded as an expense when they are incurred. Contrast this expenditure with that for equipment, which is expected to be useful over multiple periods and thus is initially recorded as an asset, and then reflected as an expense over time. Also, contrast this treatment with that for rent expense, which was paid in advance and can be clearly allocated over time, and thus is initially recorded as a prepaid asset and then reflected as an expense over time. The advertising expenditure in this example relates to the current period. If the company had paid in advance for several years worth of advertising, then a portion would be capitalized (i.e., recorded as an asset), similar to the treatment of equipment or prepaid rent and expensed in future periods. We can now prepare a partial income statement for the company reflecting this expense:

Investment Advisers, Ltd.
Income Statement
For the Period 1 January through 10 January 2006

Total revenue		$ 0
Expenses		
Advertising	$ 600	
Total expense		600
Net income (loss)		$ (600)

Because the company has incurred a $600 expense but has not recorded any revenue (the subscription revenue has not been earned yet), an income statement for Transactions 1 through 7 would show net income of minus $600 (i.e., a net loss). To prepare a balance sheet for the company, we need to update the retained earnings account. Beginning retained earnings was $0 (zero). Adding the net loss of $600 (made up of $0 revenue minus $600 expense) and deducting any dividend ($0 in this illustration) gives ending retained earnings of minus $600. The ending retained earnings covering Transactions 1–7 is included in the interim balance sheet:

Investment Advisers, Ltd.
Balance Sheet
As of 10 January 2006

Assets	
Cash	$ 41,600
Investments	100,000
Inventory	10,000
Prepaid rent	1,000
Deposits	2,000
Office equipment	6,000
Total assets	$160,600
Liabilities and owners' equity	
Liabilities	
Accounts payable	$ 10,000
Unearned fees	1,200
Total liabilities	11,200
Equity	
Contributed capital	150,000
Retained earnings	(600)
Total equity	149,400
Total liabilities and owners' equity	$160,600

As with all balance sheets, the amount of total assets equals total liabilities plus owners' equity—both are $160,600. The owners' claim on the business has been reduced to $149,400. This is due to the negative retained earnings (sometimes referred to as a retained "deficit"). As noted, the company has a net loss after the first seven transactions, a result of incurring $600 of advertising expenses but not yet producing any revenue.

15 January 2006

	Business Activity	Accounting Treatment
8	Borrow $12,000 from a bank for working capital. Interest is payable annually at 10 percent. The principal is due in two years.	**Cash [A]** is increased by $12,000, and **bank debt [L]** is increased by $12,000.

Accounting Elements: Assets (A), Liabilites (L), Equity (E), Revenue (R), and Expenses (X).

Cash is increased, and a corresponding liability is recorded to reflect the amount owed to the bank. Initially, no entry is made for interest that is expected to be paid on the loan. In the future, interest will be recorded as time passes and interest accrues (accumulates) on the loan.

15 January 2006

	Business Activity	Accounting Treatment
9	Ship first order to a customer consisting of five books at $25 per book. Invoice terms are that payment is due in 30 days. No cash changes hands.	**Accounts receivable [A]** increased by $125, and **revenue [R]** increased by $125. Additionally, **inventory [A]** decreased by $100, and **cost of goods sold [X]** increased by $100.

Accounting Elements: Assets (A), Liabilites (L), Equity (E), Revenue (R), and Expenses (X).

The company has now made a sale. Sale transaction records have two parts. One part represents the $125 revenue to be received from the customer, and the other part represents the $100 cost of the goods that have been sold. Although payment has not yet been received from the customer in payment for the goods, the company has delivered the goods (five books) and so revenue is recorded. A corresponding asset, accounts receivable, is recorded to reflect amounts due from the customer. Simultaneously, the company reduces its inventory balance by the cost of the five books sold and also records this amount as an expense termed **cost of goods sold**.

		15 January 2006
	Business Activity	**Accounting Treatment**
10	Sell for cash 10 books at $25 per book at an investment conference.	**Cash [A]** is increased by $250, and **revenue [R]** is increased by $250. Additionally, **inventory [A]** is decreased by $200, and **cost of goods sold [X]** is increased by $200.

Accounting Elements: Assets (A), Liabilites (L), Equity (E), Revenue (R), and Expenses (X).

Similar to the previous sale transaction, both the $250 sales proceeds and the $200 cost of the goods sold must be recorded. In contrast with the previous sale, however, the sales proceeds are received in cash. Subtotals from Exhibit 2-6 can once again be used to prepare a preliminary income statement and balance sheet to evaluate the business to date:

Investment Advisers, Ltd.
Income Statement
For the Period 1 January through 15 January 2006

Total revenue		$ 375
Expenses		
Cost of goods sold	$300	
Advertising	600	
Total expenses		900
Net income (loss)		$(525)

Investment Advisers, Ltd.
Balance Sheet
As of 15 January 2006

Assets	
Cash	$ 53,850
Accounts receivable	125
Investments	100,000
Inventory	9,700
Prepaid rent	1,000
Deposits	2,000
Office equipment	6,000
Total assets	$172,675

(Continued)

Investment Advisers, Ltd.
Balance Sheet
As of 15 January 2006 (*Continued*)

Liabilities and owners' equity	
Liabilities	
Accounts payable	$ 10,000
Unearned fees	1,200
Bank debt	12,000
Total liabilities	23,200
Equity	
Contributed capital	150,000
Retained earnings	(525)
Total equity	149,475
Total liabilities and owners' equity	$172,675

An income statement covering Transactions 1–10 would reflect revenue to date of $375 for the sale of books minus the $300 cost of those books and minus the $600 advertising expense. The net loss is $525, which is shown in the income statement as $(525) using the accounting convention that indicates a negative number using parentheses. This net loss is also reflected on the balance sheet in retained earnings. The amount in retained earnings at this point equals the net loss of $525 because retained earnings had $0 beginning balance and no dividends have been distributed. The balance sheet reflects total assets of $172,675 and claims on the assets of $23,200 in liabilities and $149,475 owners' equity. Within assets, the inventory balance represents the cost of the 485 remaining books (a total of 15 have been sold) at $20 each.

Transactions 1–10 occurred throughout the month and involved cash, accounts receivable, or accounts payable; accordingly, these transactions clearly required an entry into the accounting system. The other transactions, items 11–13, have also occurred and need to be reflected in the financial statements, but these transactions may not be so obvious. In order to prepare complete financial statements at the end of a reporting period, an entity needs to review its operations to determine whether any accruals or other adjustments are required. A more complete discussion of accruals and adjustments is set forth in the next section, but generally speaking, such entries serve to allocate revenue and expense items into the correct accounting period. In practice, companies may also make adjustments to correct erroneous entries or to update inventory balances to reflect a physical count.

In this illustration, adjustments are needed for a number of transactions in order to allocate amounts across accounting periods. The accounting treatment for these transactions is shown in Exhibit 2-7. Transactions are numbered sequentially, and an "a" is added to a transaction number to denote an adjustment relating to a previous transaction. Exhibit 2-8 presents the completed spreadsheet reflecting these additional entries in the accounting system.

A final income statement and balance sheet can now be prepared reflecting all transactions and adjustments as shown on page 49.

EXHIBIT 2-7   Investment Advisers, Ltd. Accruals and Other Adjusting Entries on
31 January 2006

Items 11–13 are repeated from Exhibit 2-5. Items 3a, 4a, and 8a reflect adjustments relating to items 3, 4, and 8 from Exhibit 2-5.

	Business Activity	**Accounting Treatment**
11	Hire a part-time clerk. The clerk is hired through an agency that also handles all payroll taxes. The company is to pay $15 per hour to the agency. The clerk works six hours prior to 31 January, but no cash will be paid until February.	The company owes $90 for wages at month end. Under accrual accounting, expenses are recorded when incurred, not when paid. **Accrued wages [L]** is increased by $90, and **payroll expense [X]** is increased by $90. The accrued wage liability will be eliminated when the wages are paid.
12	Mail out the first month's newsletter to customer. This subscription had been sold on 3 January.	One month (or 1/12) of the $1,200 subscription has been satisfied, so $100 can be recognized as revenue. **Unearned fees [L]** is decreased by $100, and **fee revenue [R]** is increased by $100.
13	Review of the investment portfolio shows that $100 of interest income was earned and the market value of the portfolio has increased by $2,000. The balance in the investment account is now $102,100. The securities are classified as "trading" securities.	**Interest income [R]** is increased by $100, and the **investments** account **[A]** is increased by $100. The $2,000 increase in the value of the portfolio represents unrealized gains that are part of income for traded securities. The **investments** account **[A]** is increased by $2,000, and **unrealized gains [R]** is increased by $2,000.
3a	In item 3, $3,000 was paid to the landlord for office/warehouse, including a $2,000 refundable deposit and $1,000 for the first month's rent. Now, the first month has ended, so this rent has become a cost of doing business.	To reflect the full amount of the first month's rent as a cost of doing business, **prepaid rent [A]** is decreased by $1,000, and **rent expense [X]** is increased by $1,000.
4a	In item 4, office equipment was purchased for $6,000 in cash. The equipment has an estimated life of two years with no salvage value. Now, one month (or 1/24) of the useful life of the equipment has ended, so a portion of the equipment cost has become a cost of doing business.	A portion (1/24) of the total $6,000 cost of the office equipment is allocated to the current period's cost of doing business. **Depreciation expense [X]** is increased by $250, and **accumulated depreciation [A]** (a contra asset account) is increased by $250. Accumulated depreciation is a contra asset account to office equipment.
8a	The company borrowed $12,000 from a bank on 15 January, with interest payable annually at 10 percent and the principal due in two years. Now, one-half of one month has passed since the borrowing.	One-half of one month of interest expense has become a cost of doing business. $12,000 × 10% = $1,200 of annual interest, equivalent to $100 per month or $50 for one-half month. **Interest expense [X]** is increased by $50, and **interest payable [L]** is increased by $50.

Accounting Elements: Assets (A), Liabilites (L), Equity (E), Revenue (R), and Expenses (X).

EXHIBIT 2-8 Accounting System for Investment Advisers, Ltd.

#	Cash	Other Assets	Account	Amount	Account	Contributed Capital	Beginning Retained Earnings	Revenue	Expense (enter as negative)	Dividends (enter as negative)
Beg. Bal	0	0		0		0	0	0	0	0
1 Capitalize	150,000					150,000				
2 Investments	(100,000)	100,000	Investments							
3 Pay landlord	(3,000)	1,000 / 2,000	Prepaid rent / Rent deposit							
4 Buy equipment	(6,000)	6,000	Office equipment							
5 Sell subscript.	1,200			1,200	Unearned fees					
6 Buy books		10,000	Inventory	10,000	Accounts payable					
7 Advertise	(600)								(600)	
8 Borrow	12,000			12,000	Bank debt					
9 Sell books on account		(100) / 125	Inventory / Accounts receivable					125		
10 Cash sale	250	(200)	Inventory					250	(200)	
11 Accrue wages				90	Accrued wages				(90)	
12 Earn subscription fees				(100)	Unearned fees			100		
13 Investment income		100 / 2,000	Investments / Investments					100 / 2,000		
3A Rent expense		(1,000)	Prepaid rent						(1,000)	
4A Depreciate equipment		(250)	Accumulated depreciation (equipment)						(250)	
8A Accrue interest				50	Interest payable				(50)	
Subtotal	53,850	119,675		23,240		150,000		2,575	(2,290)	

48

Investment Advisers, Ltd.
Income Statement
For the Period 1 January through 31 January 2006

Revenues	
Fee revenue	$ 100
Book sales	375
Investment income	2,100
Total revenues	$2,575
Expenses	
Cost of goods sold	$ 300
Advertising	600
Wage	90
Rent	1,000
Depreciation	250
Interest	50
Total expenses	2,290
Net income (loss)	$ 285

Investment Advisers, Ltd.
Balance Sheet
As of 31 January 2006

Assets	
Cash	$ 53,850
Accounts receivable	125
Investments	102,100
Inventory	9,700
Prepaid rent	0
Office equipment, net	5,750
Deposits	2,000
Total assets	$173,525
Liabilities and owners' equity	
Liabilities	
Accounts payable	$ 10,000
Accrued wages	90
Interest payable	50
Unearned fees	1,100
Bank debt	12,000
Total liabilities	23,240
Equity	
Contributed capital	150,000
Retained earnings	285
Total equity	150,285
Total liabilities and owners' equity	$173,525

From the income statement, we can determine that the business was profitable for the month. The business earned $285 after expenses. The balance sheet presents the financial position. The company has assets of $173,525, and claims against those assets included liabilities of $23,240 and an owners' claim of $150,285. The owners' claim reflects their initial investment plus reinvested earnings. These statements are explored further in the next section.

4.3. Financial Statements

The spreadsheet in Exhibit 2-8 is an organized presentation of the company's transactions and can help in preparing the income statement and balance sheet presented above. Exhibit 2-9 presents all financial statements and demonstrates their relationships. Note that the data for the income statement come from the revenue and expense columns of the spreadsheet (which include gains and losses). The net income of $285 (revenue of $2,575 minus expenses of $2,290) was retained in the business rather than distributed to the owners as dividends. The net income, therefore, becomes part of ending retained earnings on the balance sheet. The detail of retained earnings is shown in the statement of owners' equity.

The balance sheet presents the financial position of the company using the assets, liabilities, and equity accounts from the accounting system spreadsheet. The statement of cash flows summarizes the data from the cash column of the accounting system spreadsheet to enable the owners and others to assess the sources and uses of cash. These sources and uses of cash are categorized according to group of business activity: operating, investing, or financing. The format of the statement of cash flows presented here is known as the **direct format**, which refers to the operating cash section appearing simply as operating cash receipts less operating cash disbursements. An alternative format for the operating cash section, which begins with net income and shows adjustments to derive operating cash flow, is known as the **indirect format**. The alternative formats and detailed rules are discussed in the statement of cash flows chapter.

Financial statements use the financial data reported in the accounting system and present this data in a more meaningful manner. Each statement reports on critical areas. Specifically, a review of the financial statements for the IAL illustration provides the following information:

- **Balance sheet.** This statement provides information about a company's financial position at a point in time. It shows an entity's assets, liabilities, and owners' equity at a particular date. Two years are usually presented so that comparisons can be made. Less significant accounts can be grouped into a single line item. One observation from the IAL illustration is that although total assets have increased significantly (about 16 percent), equity has increased less than 0.2 percent—most of the increase in total assets is due to the increase in liabilities.
- **Income statement.** This statement provides information about a company's profitability over a period of time. It shows the amount of revenue, expense, and resulting net income or loss for a company during a period of time. Again, less significant accounts can be grouped into a single line item—in this illustration, expenses other than cost of goods sold are grouped into a single line item. The statement shows that IAL has three sources of revenue and made a small profit in its first month of operations. Significantly, most of the revenue came from investments rather than subscriptions or book sales.
- **Statement of cash flows.** This statement provides information about a company's cash flows over a period of time. It shows a company's cash inflows (receipts) and outflows

EXHIBIT 2-9   Investment Advisors, Ltd. Financial Statements

<table>
<tr><th colspan="3" align="center">Investment Advisers, Ltd.
Balance Sheet
As of</th></tr>
<tr><td></td><td align="center">12/31/2005</td><td align="center">1/31/2006</td></tr>
<tr><td>Assets</td><td></td><td></td></tr>
<tr><td>Cash</td><td align="right">150,000</td><td align="right">53,850</td></tr>
<tr><td>Accounts receivable</td><td align="right">0</td><td align="right">125</td></tr>
<tr><td>Investments</td><td align="right">0</td><td align="right">102,100</td></tr>
<tr><td>Inventory</td><td></td><td align="right">9,700</td></tr>
<tr><td>Office equipment, net</td><td></td><td align="right">5,750</td></tr>
<tr><td>Deposits</td><td></td><td align="right">2,000</td></tr>
<tr><td>Total assets</td><td align="right">150,000</td><td align="right">173,525</td></tr>
<tr><td>Liabilities</td><td></td><td></td></tr>
<tr><td>Accounts payable</td><td align="right">0</td><td align="right">10,000</td></tr>
<tr><td>Accrued expenses</td><td></td><td align="right">140</td></tr>
<tr><td>Unearned fees</td><td></td><td align="right">1,100</td></tr>
<tr><td>Bank debt</td><td></td><td align="right">12,000</td></tr>
<tr><td>Total liabilities</td><td></td><td align="right">23,240</td></tr>
<tr><td>Owners' equity</td><td></td><td></td></tr>
<tr><td>Contributed capital</td><td align="right">150,000</td><td align="right">150,000</td></tr>
<tr><td>Retained earnings</td><td align="right">0</td><td align="right">285</td></tr>
<tr><td>Total equity</td><td align="right">150,000</td><td align="right">150,285</td></tr>
<tr><td>Total liabilities and equity</td><td align="right">150,000</td><td align="right">173,525</td></tr>
</table>

<table>
<tr><th colspan="2" align="center">Investment Advisers, Ltd.
Income Statement
For the Month Ended 1/31/2006</th></tr>
<tr><td>Fee revenue</td><td align="right">100</td></tr>
<tr><td>Book sales revenue</td><td align="right">375</td></tr>
<tr><td>Investment income</td><td align="right">2,100</td></tr>
<tr><td>Total revenue</td><td align="right">2,575</td></tr>
<tr><td>Cost of goods sold</td><td align="right">300</td></tr>
<tr><td>Other expense</td><td align="right">1,990</td></tr>
<tr><td>Total expense</td><td align="right">2,290</td></tr>
<tr><td>Net income (loss)</td><td align="right">285</td></tr>
</table>

<table>
<tr><th colspan="2" align="center">Investment Advisers, Ltd.
Statement of Cash Flows
For the Month Ended 1/31/2006</th></tr>
<tr><td>Cash received from customers</td><td align="right">1,450</td></tr>
<tr><td>Cash paid to landlord</td><td align="right">(3,000)</td></tr>
<tr><td>Cash paid for advertising</td><td align="right">(600)</td></tr>
<tr><td>Investments in trading securities</td><td align="right">(100,000)</td></tr>
<tr><td>Operating cash flows</td><td align="right">(102,150)</td></tr>
<tr><td>Capital expenditures</td><td align="right">(6,000)</td></tr>
<tr><td>Investing cash flows</td><td align="right">(6,000)</td></tr>
<tr><td>Borrowing</td><td align="right">12,000</td></tr>
<tr><td>Financing cash flows</td><td align="right">12,000</td></tr>
<tr><td>Net decrease in cash</td><td align="right">(96,150)</td></tr>
<tr><td>Cash at 12/31/05</td><td align="right">150,000</td></tr>
<tr><td>Cash at 1/31/06</td><td align="right">53,850</td></tr>
</table>

<table>
<tr><th colspan="4" align="center">Investment Advisers, Ltd.
Statement of Owners' Equity
31 January 2006</th></tr>
<tr><td></td><td align="center">Contributed Capital</td><td align="center">Retained Earnings</td><td align="center">Total</td></tr>
<tr><td>Balance at 12/31/05</td><td align="right">150,000</td><td align="right">0</td><td align="right">150,000</td></tr>
<tr><td>Issuance of stock</td><td></td><td></td><td></td></tr>
<tr><td>Net income (loss)</td><td></td><td align="right">285</td><td align="right">285</td></tr>
<tr><td>Distributions</td><td></td><td></td><td></td></tr>
<tr><td>Balance at 1/31/06</td><td align="right">150,000</td><td align="right">285</td><td align="right">150,285</td></tr>
</table>

(payments) during the period. These flows are categorized according to the three groups of business activities: operating, financing, and investing. In the illustration, IAL reported a large negative cash flow from operations ($102,150), primarily because its trading activities involved the purchase of a portfolio of securities but no sales were made from the portfolio. (Note that the purchase of investments for IAL appears in its operating section because the company is in the business of trading securities. In contrast, for a nontrading company, investment activity would be shown as investing cash flows rather than operating cash flows.) IAL's negative operating and investing cash flows were funded by $12,000 bank borrowing and a $96,150 reduction in the cash balance.

- **Statement of owners' equity**. This statement provides information about the composition and changes in owners' equity during a period of time. In this illustration, the only change in equity resulted from the net income of $285. A **statement of retained earnings** (not shown) would report the changes in a company's retained earnings during a period of time.

These statements again illustrate the interrelationships among financial statements. On the balance sheet, we see beginning and ending amounts for assets, liabilities, and owners' equity. Owners' equity increased from $150,000 to $150,285. The statement of owners' equity presents a breakdown of this $285 change. The arrow from the statement of owners' equity to the owners' equity section of the balance sheet explains that section of the balance sheet. In the IAL illustration, the entire $285 change resulted from an increase in retained earnings. In turn, the increase in retained earnings resulted from $285 net income. The income statement presents a breakdown of the revenues and expenses resulting in this $285. The arrow from the income statement to the net income figure in the owners' equity section explains how reported net income came about.

Also on the balance sheet, we see that cash decreased from $150,000 at the beginning of the month to $53,850 at the end of the month. The statement of cash flows provides information on the increases and decreases in cash by group of business activity. The arrow from the cash flow statement to the ending cash figure shows that the cash flow statement explains in detail the ending cash amount.

In summary, the balance sheet provides information at a point in time (financial position), whereas the other statements provide useful information regarding the activity during a period of time (profitability, cash flow, and changes in owners' equity).

5. ACCRUALS AND VALUATION ADJUSTMENTS

In a simple business model such as the investment company discussed in the illustration above, many transactions are handled in cash and settled in a relatively short time frame. Furthermore, assets and liabilities have a fixed and determinable value. Translating business transactions into the accounting system is fairly easy. Difficulty usually arises when a cash receipt or disbursement occurs in a different period than the related revenue or expense, or when the reportable values of assets vary. This section will address the accounting treatment for these situations—namely, accruals and valuation adjustments.

5.1. Accruals

Accrual accounting requires that revenue be recorded when earned and that expenses be recorded when incurred, irrespective of when the related cash movements occur. The purpose of accrual entries is to report revenue and expense in the proper accounting period. Because accrual entries occur due to timing differences between cash movements and accounting recognition of revenue or expense, it follows that there are only a few possibilities. First, cash movement and accounting recognition can occur at the same time, in which case there is no need for accruals. Second, cash movement may occur before or after accounting recognition, in which case accruals are required.

EXHIBIT 2-10   Accruals

	Cash Movement Prior to Accounting Recognition	Cash Movement in the Same Period as Accounting Recognition	Cash Movement after Accounting Recognition
Revenue	**Unearned (Deferred) Revenue** Originating entry—record cash receipt and establish a liability (such as unearned revenue) Adjusting entry—reduce the liability while recording revenue	Settled transaction—no accrual entry needed	**Unbilled (Accrued) Revenue** Originating entry—record revenue and establish an asset (such as unbilled revenue) Adjusting entry—when billing occurs, reduce unbilled revenue and increase accounts receivable. When cash is collected, eliminate the receivable.
Expense	**Prepaid Expense** Originating entry—record cash payment and establish an asset (such as prepaid expense) Adjusting entry—reduce the asset while recording expense		**Accrued Expenses** Originating entry—establish a liability (such as accrued expenses) and record an expense Adjusting entry—reduce the liability as cash is paid

The possible situations requiring accrual entries are summarized into four types of accrual entries shown in Exhibit 2-10 and discussed below. Each type of accrual involves an originating entry and at least one adjusting entry at a later date or dates.

Unearned (or **deferred**) **revenue** arises when a company receives cash prior to earning the revenue. In the IAL illustration, in Transaction 5, the company received $1,200 for a 12-month subscription to a monthly newsletter. At the time the cash was received, the company had an obligation to deliver 12 newsletters and thus had not yet earned the revenue. Each month, as a newsletter is delivered, this obligation will decrease by 1/12th (i.e., $100). And at the same time, $100 of revenue will be earned. The accounting treatment involves an originating entry (the initial recording of the cash received and the corresponding liability to deliver newsletters) and, subsequently, 12 future adjusting entries, the first one of which was illustrated as Transaction 12. Each adjusting entry reduces the liability and records revenue.

In practice, a large amount of unearned revenue may cause some concern about a company's ability to deliver on this future commitment. Conversely, a positive aspect is that increases in unearned revenue are an indicator of future revenues. For example, a large liability on the balance sheet of an airline relates to cash received for future airline travel. Revenue will be recognized as the travel occurs, so an increase in this liability is an indicator of future increases in revenue.

Unbilled (or **accrued**) **revenue** arises when a company earns revenue prior to receiving cash but has not yet recognized the revenue at the end of an accounting period. In such cases, the accounting treatment involves an originating entry to record the revenue earned through the end of the accounting period and a related receivable reflecting amounts due from customers. When the company receives payment (or if goods are returned), an adjusting entry eliminates the receivable.

Accrued revenue specifically relates to end-of-period accruals; however, the concept is similar to any sale involving deferred receipt of cash. In the IAL illustration, in Transaction 9, the company sold books on account, so the revenue was recognized prior to cash receipt. The accounting treatment involved an entry to record the revenue and the associated receivable. In the future, when the company receives payment, an adjusting entry (not shown) would eliminate the receivable. In practice, it is important to understand the quality of a company's receivables (i.e., the likelihood of collection).

Prepaid expense arises when a company makes a cash payment prior to recognizing an expense. In the illustration, in Transaction 3, the company prepaid one month's rent. The accounting treatment involves an originating entry to record the payment of cash and the prepaid asset reflecting future benefits, and a subsequent adjusting entry to record the expense and eliminate the prepaid asset. (See the boxes showing the accounting treatment of Transaction 3, which refers to the originating entry, and Transaction 3a, which refers to the adjusting entry.) In other words, prepaid expenses are assets that will be subsequently expensed. In practice, particularly in a valuation, one consideration is that prepaid assets typically have future value only as future operations transpire, unless they are refundable.

Accrued expenses arise when a company incurs expenses that have not yet been paid as of the end of an accounting period. Accrued expenses result in liabilities that usually require future cash payments. In the IAL illustration, the company had incurred wage expenses at month end, but the payment would not be made until after the end of the month (Transaction 11). To reflect the company's position at the end of the month, the accounting treatment involved an originating entry to record wage expense and the corresponding liability for wages payable, and a future adjusting entry to eliminate the liability when cash is paid (not shown because wages will be paid only in February). Similarly, the IAL illustration included interest accrual on the company's bank borrowing. (See the boxes showing the accounting treatment of Transaction 8, where Transaction 8 refers to the originating entry, and Transaction 8a, which refers to the adjusting entry.)

As with accrued revenues, accrued expenses specifically relate to end-of-period accruals. Accounts payable are similar to accrued expenses in that they involve a transaction that occurs now but the cash payment is made later. Accounts payable is also a liability but often relates to the receipt of inventory (or perhaps services) as opposed to recording an immediate expense. Accounts payable should be listed separately from other accrued expenses on the balance sheet because of their different nature.

Overall, in practice, complex businesses require additional accruals that are theoretically similar to the four categories of accruals discussed above but which require considerably more judgment. For example, there may be significant lags between a transaction and cash settlement. In such cases, accruals can span many accounting periods (even 10–20 years!), and it is not always clear when revenue has been earned or an expense has been incurred. Considerable judgment is required to determine how to allocate/distribute amounts across periods. An example of such a complex accrual would be the estimated annual revenue for a contractor on a long-term construction project, such as building a nuclear power plant. In general, however, accruals fall under the four general types and follow essentially the same pattern of originating and adjusting entries as the basic accruals described.

5.2. Valuation Adjustments

In contrast to accrual entries that allocate revenue and expenses into the appropriate accounting periods, valuation adjustments are made to a company's assets or liabilities—only where required by accounting standards—so that the accounting records reflect the current market value rather than the historical cost. In this discussion, we focus on valuation adjustments to assets. For example, in the IAL illustration, Transaction 13 adjusted the value of the company's investment portfolio to its current market value. The income statement reflects the $2,100 increase (including interest), and the ending balance sheets report the investment portfolio at its current market value of $102,100. In contrast, the equipment in the IAL illustration was not reported at its current market value and no valuation adjustment was required.

As this illustration demonstrates, accounting regulations do not require all types of assets to be reported at their current market value. Some assets (e.g., trading securities) are shown on the balance sheet at their current market value, and changes in that market value are reported in the income statement. Some assets are shown at their historical cost (e.g., specific classes of investment securities being held to maturity). Other assets (e.g., a particular class of investment securities) are shown on the balance sheet at their current market value, but changes in market value bypass the income statement and are recorded directly into shareholders' equity under a component referred to as *other comprehensive income*. This topic will be discussed in more detail in later chapters.

In summary, where valuation adjustment entries are required for assets, the basic pattern is the following for increases in assets: An asset is increased with the other side of the equation being a gain on the income statement or an increase to other comprehensive income. Conversely for decreases: An asset is decreased with the other side of the equation being a loss on the income statement or a decrease to other comprehensive income.

6. ACCOUNTING SYSTEMS

The accounting system set forth for the IAL illustration involved a very simple business, a single month of activity, and a small number of transactions. In practice, most businesses are more complicated and have many more transactions. Accordingly, actual accounting systems, although using essentially the same logic as discussed in the illustration, are both more efficient than a spreadsheet and more complex.

6.1. Flow of Information in an Accounting System

Accounting texts typically discuss accounting systems in detail because accountants need to understand each step in the process. While analysts do not need to know the same details, they should be familiar with the flow of information through a financial reporting system. This flow and the key related documents are described in Exhibit 2-11.

6.2. Debits and Credits

Reviewing the example of IAL, it is clear that the accounting treatment of every transaction involved at least two accounts and the transaction either increased or decreased the value of any affected account. Traditionally, accounting systems have used the terms **debit** and **credit** to describe changes in an account resulting from the accounting processing of a transaction. The correct usage of "debit" and "credit" in an accounting context differs from how these terms are used in everyday language.[8] The accounting definitions of debit and credit ensure

---

[8]In accounting, debits record increases of asset and expense accounts or decreases in liability and owners' equity accounts. Credits record increases in liability, owners' equity, and revenue accounts or decreases in asset accounts. Appendix 2A provides more details.

EXHIBIT 2-11   Accounting System Flow and Related Documents

Journal entries and adjusting entries	A journal is a document or computer file in which business transactions are recorded in the order in which they occur (chronological order). The general journal is the collection of all business transactions in an accounting system sorted by date. All accounting systems have a general journal to record all transactions. Some accounting systems also include special journals. For example, there may be one journal for recording sales transactions and another for recording inventory purchases.
	Journal entries—recorded in journals—are dated, and show the accounts affected and the amounts. If necessary, the entry will include an explanation of the transaction and documented authorization to record the entry. As the initial step in converting business transactions into financial information, the journal entry is useful for obtaining detailed information regarding a particular transaction.
	Adjusting journal entries, a subset of journal entries, are typically made at the end of an accounting period to record items such as accruals that are not yet reflected in the accounting system.

General ledger and T-accounts	A ledger is a document or computer file that shows all business transactions by account. Note that the general ledger, the core of every accounting system, contains all of the same entries as that posted to the general journal—the only difference is that the data are sorted by date in a journal and by account in the ledger. The general ledger is useful for reviewing all of the activity related to a single account. T-accounts, explained in Appendix 2A, are representations of ledger accounts and are frequently used to describe or analyze accounting transactions.

Trial balance and adjusted trial balance	A trial balance is a document that lists account balances at a particular point in time. Trial balances are typically prepared at the end of an accounting period as a first step in producing financial statements. A key difference between a trial balance and a ledger is that the trial balance shows only total ending balances. An initial trial balance assists in the identification of any adjusting entries that may be required. Once these adjusting entries are made, an adjusted trial balance can be prepared.

Financial statements	The financial statements, a final product of the accounting system, are prepared based on the account totals from an adjusted trial balance.

that, in processing a transaction, the sum of the debits equals the sum of the credits, which is consistent with the accounting equation (i.e., Equation 2-7) always remaining in balance.

Although mastering the usage of the terms *debit* and *credit* is essential for an accountant, an analyst can still understand financial reporting mechanics without speaking in terms of debits and credits. In general, this text avoids the use of debit/credit presentation; however, for reference, Appendix 2A presents the IAL illustration in a debit and credit system.

The following section broadly describes some considerations for using financial statements in security analysis.

7. USING FINANCIAL STATEMENTS IN SECURITY ANALYSIS

Financial statements serve as a foundation for credit and equity analysis, including security valuation. Analysts may need to make adjustments to reflect items not reported in the statements (certain assets/liabilities and future earnings). Analysts may also need to assess the reasonableness of management judgment (e.g., in accruals and valuations). Because analysts typically will not have access to the accounting system or individual entries, they will need to infer what transactions were recorded by examining the financial statements.

7.1. The Use of Judgment in Accounts and Entries

Quite apart from deliberate misrepresentations, even efforts to faithfully represent the economic performance and position of a company require judgments and estimates. Financial reporting systems need to accommodate complex business models by recording accruals and changes in valuations of balance sheet accounts. Accruals and valuation entries require considerable judgment and thus create many of the limitations of the accounting model. Judgments could prove wrong or, worse, be used for deliberate earnings manipulation. An important first step in analyzing financial statements is identifying the types of accruals and valuation entries in an entity's financial statements. Most of these items will be noted in the critical accounting policies/estimates section of management's discussion and analysis (MD&A) and in the significant accounting policies footnote, both found in the annual report. Analysts should use this disclosure to identify the key accruals and valuations for a company. The analyst needs to be aware, as Example 2-4 shows, that the manipulation of earnings and assets can take place within the context of satisfying the mechanical rules governing the recording of transactions.

EXAMPLE 2-4   The Manipulation of Accounting Earnings

As discussed in this chapter, the accounting equation can be expressed as Assets = Liabilities + Contributed capital + Ending retained earnings (Equation 2-5a). Although the equation must remain in balance with each transaction, management can improperly record a transaction to achieve a desired result. For example, when a company spends cash and records an expense, assets are reduced on the left side of the equation and expenses are recorded, which lowers retained earnings on the right side. The balance is maintained. If, however, a company spent cash but did not want to record an expense in order to achieve higher net income, the company could manipulate the system by reducing cash and increasing another asset. The equation would remain in balance and the right-hand side of the equation would not be affected at all. This was one of the techniques used by managers at WorldCom to manipulate financial reports, as summarized in a U.S. Securities and Exchange Commission complaint against the company (emphasis added):

> *In general, WorldCom manipulated its financial results in two ways. First, WorldCom reduced its operating expenses by improperly releasing certain reserves held against operating expenses. Second,* **WorldCom improperly reduced its operating expenses by recharacterizing certain expenses as capital assets**. *Neither practice was in conformity with generally accepted accounting principles (GAAP). Neither practice was disclosed to WorldCom's investors, despite the fact that both practices constituted changes from WorldCom's previous accounting practices. Both practices falsely reduced WorldCom's expenses and, accordingly, had the effect of artificially inflating the income WorldCom reported to the public in its financial statements from 1999 through the first quarter of 2002.*[9]

In 2005, the former CEO of WorldCom was sentenced to 25 years in prison for his role in the fraud.[10] The analyst should be aware of the possibility of manipulation of earnings and be on the lookout for large increases in existing assets, new unusual assets, and unexplained changes in financial ratios.

7.2. Misrepresentations

It is rare in this age of computers that the mechanics of an accounting system do not work. Most computer accounting systems will not allow a company to make one-sided entries. It is important to note, however, that just because the mechanics work does not necessarily mean that the judgments underlying the financial statements are correct. An unscrupulous accountant could structure entries to achieve a desired result. For example, if a manager wanted to record fictitious revenue, a fictitious asset (a receivable) could be created to keep the accounting equation in balance. If the manager paid for something but did not want to record an expense, the transaction could be recorded in a prepaid asset account. If cash is received but the manager does not want to record revenue, a liability could be created. Understanding that there has to be another side to every entry is key in detecting inappropriate accounting because—usually in the course of "fixing" one account—there will be another account with a balance that does not make sense. In the case of recording fictitious revenue, there is likely to be a growing receivable whose collectibility is in doubt. Ratio analysis, which is discussed further in later chapters, can assist in detecting suspect amounts in these accounts. Furthermore, the accounting equation can be used to detect likely accounts where aggressive or even fraudulent accounting may have occurred.

---

[9]SEC vs. WorldCom, 5 November 2002: www.sec.gov/litigation/complaints/comp17829.htm.
[10]"Ebbers Is Sentenced to 25 Years For $11 Billion WorldCom Fraud," *Wall Street Journal*, 14 July 2005, A1.

8. SUMMARY

The accounting process is a key component of financial reporting. The mechanics of this process convert business transactions into records necessary to create periodic reports on a company. An understanding of these mechanics is useful in evaluating financial statements for credit and equity analysis purposes and in forecasting future financial statements. Key concepts are as follows:

- Business activities can be classified into three groups: operating activities, investing activities, and financing activities.
- Companies classify transactions into common accounts that are components of the five financial statement elements: assets, liabilities, equity, revenue, and expense.
- The core of the accounting process is the basic accounting equation: Assets = Liabilities + Owners' equity.
- The expanded accounting equation is Assets = Liabilities + Contributed capital + Beginning retained earnings + Revenue − Expenses − Dividends.
- Business transactions are recorded in an accounting system that is based on the basic and expanded accounting equations.
- The accounting system tracks and summarizes data used to create financial statements: the balance sheet, income statement, statement of cash flows, and statement of owners' equity. The statement of retained earnings is a component of the statement of owners' equity.
- Accruals are a necessary part of the accounting process and are designed to allocate activity to the proper period for financial reporting purposes.
- The results of the accounting process are financial reports that are used by managers, investors, creditors, analysts, and others in making business decisions.
- An analyst uses the financial statements to make judgments on the financial health of a company.
- Company management can manipulate financial statements, and a perceptive analyst can use his or her understanding of financial statements to detect misrepresentations.

PRACTICE PROBLEMS

1. Which of the following items would most likely be classified as an operating activity?
   A. Issuance of debt
   B. Acquisition of a competitor
   C. Sale of automobiles by an automobile dealer

2. Which of the following items would most likely be classified as a financing activity?
   A. Issuance of debt
   B. Payment of income taxes
   C. Investments in the stock of a supplier

3. Which of the following elements represents an economic resource?
   A. Asset
   B. Liability
   C. Owners' equity

4. Which of the following elements represents a residual claim?
   A. Asset
   B. Liability
   C. Owners' equity

5. An analyst has projected that a company will have assets of €2,000 at year-end and lia-
   bilities of €1,200. The analyst's projection of total owners' equity should be closest to
   A. €800.
   B. €2,000.
   C. €3,200.

6. An analyst has collected the following information regarding a company in advance of
   its year-end earnings announcement (in millions):

Estimated net income	$200
Beginning retained earnings	$1,400
Estimated distributions to owners	$100

   The analyst's estimate of ending retained earnings (in millions) should be closest to
   A. $1,300.
   B. $1,500.
   C. $1,700.

7. An analyst has compiled the following information regarding Rubsam, Inc.

Liabilities at year-end	€1,000
Contributed capital at year-end	€ 500
Beginning retained earnings	€ 600
Revenue during the year	€5,000
Expenses during the year	€4,300

   There have been no distributions to owners. The analyst's most likely estimate of total
   assets at year-end should be closest to
   A. €2,100.
   B. €2,300.
   C. €2,800.

8. A group of individuals formed a new company with an investment of $500,000. The
   most likely effect of this transaction on the company's accounting equation at the time
   of the formation is an increase in cash and
   A. an increase in revenue.
   B. an increase in liabilities.
   C. an increase in contributed capital.

9. HVG, LLC paid $12,000 of cash to a real estate company upon signing a lease on 31
   December 2005. The payment represents a $4,000 security deposit and $4,000 of rent
   for each of January 2006 and February 2006. Assuming that the correct accounting is
   to reflect both January and February rent as prepaid, the most likely effect on HVG's
   accounting equation in December 2005 is

A. no net change in assets.

B. a decrease in assets of $8,000.

C. a decrease in assets of $12,000.

10. TRR Enterprises sold products to customers on 30 June 2006 for a total price of €10,000. The terms of the sale are that payment is due in 30 days. The cost of the products was €8,000. The most likely net change in TRR's total assets on 30 June 2006 related to this transaction is
    A. €0.
    B. €2,000.
    C. €10,000.

11. On 30 April 2006, Pinto Products received a cash payment of $30,000 as a deposit on production of a custom machine to be delivered in August 2006. This transaction would most likely result in which of the following on 30 April 2006?
    A. No effect on liabilities
    B. A decrease in assets of $30,000
    C. An increase in liabilities of $30,000

12. Squires & Johnson, Ltd., recorded €250,000 of depreciation expense in December 2005. The most likely effect on the company's accounting equation is
    A. no effect on assets.
    B. a decrease in assets of €250,000.
    C. an increase in liabilities of €250,000.

13. An analyst who is interested in assessing a company's financial position is most likely to focus on which financial statement?
    A. Balance sheet
    B. Income statement
    C. Statement of cash flows

14. The statement of cash flows presents the flows into which three groups of business activities?
    A. Operating, nonoperating, and financing
    B. Operating, investing, and financing
    C. Operating, nonoperating, and investing

15. Which of the following statements about cash received prior to the recognition of revenue in the financial statements is *most* accurate? The cash is recorded as
    A. deferred revenue, an asset.
    B. accrued revenue, a liability.
    C. deferred revenue, a liability.

16. When, at the end of an accounting period, a revenue has been recognized in the financial statements but no billing has occurred and no cash has been received, the accrual is to
    A. unbilled (accrued) revenue, an asset.
    B. deferred revenue, an asset.
    C. unbilled (accrued) revenue, a liability.

17. When, at the end of an accounting period, cash has been paid with respect to an expense incurred but not yet recognized in the financial statements, the business should then record
   A. an accrued expense, an asset.
   B. a prepaid expense, an asset.
   C. an accrued expense, a liability.

18. When, at the end of an accounting period, cash has not been paid with respect to an expense that has been incurred but not recognized yet in the financial statements, the business should then record
   A. an accrued expense, an asset.
   B. a prepaid expense, an asset.
   C. an accrued expense, a liability.

19. The collection of all business transactions sorted by account in an accounting system is referred to as
   A. a trial balance.
   B. a general ledger.
   C. a general journal.

20. If a company reported fictitious revenue, it could try to cover up its fraud by
   A. decreasing assets.
   B. increasing liabilities.
   C. creating a fictitious asset.

APPENDIX 2A: A DEBIT/CREDIT ACCOUNTING SYSTEM

The main section of this chapter presented a basic accounting system represented as a spreadsheet. An alternative system that underlies most manual and electronic accounting systems uses debits and credits. Both a spreadsheet and a debit/credit system are based on the basic accounting equation:

$$Assets = Liabilities + Owners' equity$$

Early generations of accountants desired a system for recording transactions that maintained the balance of the accounting equation and avoided the use of negative numbers (which could lead to errors in recording). The system can be illustrated with T-accounts for every account involved in recording transactions. The T-account is so named for its shape:

T-Account

Debit	Credit

The left-hand side of the T-account is called a *debit,* and the right-hand side is termed a *credit.* The names should not be construed as denoting value. A debit is not better than a credit and vice versa. Debit simply means the left side of the T-account, and credit simply means the right side. Traditionally, debit is abbreviated as "DR," whereas credit is abbreviated "CR." The T-account is also related to the balance sheet and accounting equation as follows:

Balance Sheet

| Assets | Liabilities |
| | Owners' Equity |

Assets are referred to as the left side of the balance sheet (and accounting equation) and hence are on the left side of the T-account. Assets are, therefore, recorded with a debit balance. In other words, to record an increase in an asset, an entry is made to the left-hand side of a T-account. A decrease to an asset is recorded on the right side of a T-account. Liabilities and owners' equity are referred to as the right side of the balance sheet (and accounting equation). Increases to liabilities and owners' equity are recorded on the right side of a T-account; decreases to liabilities and owners' equity are recorded on the left side.

At any point in time, the balance in an account is determined by summing all the amounts on the left side of the account, summing all the amounts on the right side of the account, and calculating the difference. If the sum of amounts on the left side of the account is greater than the sum of amounts on the right side of the account, the account has a debit balance equal to the difference. If the sum of amounts on the right side of the account is greater than the sum of amounts on the left side of the account, the account has a credit balance.

A T-account is created for each asset account, liability account, and owners' equity account. The collection of these T-accounts at the beginning of the year for a fictitious company, Investment Advisers, Ltd. (IAL), is presented in Exhibit 2A-1. Each balance sheet T-account is termed a *permanent* or *real* account because the balance in the account carries over from year-to-year.

T-accounts are also set up for each income statement account. These T-accounts are referred to as *temporary* or *nominal* accounts because they are transferred at the end of each fiscal year by transferring any net income or loss to the balance sheet account, retained earnings. Income statement T-accounts for IAL are presented in Exhibit 2A-2.

The collection of all business transactions sorted by account, real and temporary, for a company comprise the general ledger. The general ledger is the core of every accounting system, where all transactions are ultimately entered. To illustrate the use of T-accounts, we will use the transactions for IAL summarized in Exhibit 2A-3. We will first enter each transaction into the general ledger T-accounts, then use the information to prepare financial statements.

Because this is a new business, the company's general ledger T-accounts initially have a zero balance.

EXHIBIT 2A-1   Balance Sheet T-Accounts for Investment Advisers, Ltd.

Cash	Accounts Receivable	Inventory

Investments	Office Equipment	Accumulated Depreciation

Deposits	Prepaid Rent	Accounts Payable

Accrued Wages	Unearned Fees	Bank Debt

Accrued Interest	Contributed Capital	Retained Earnings

EXHIBIT 2A-2   Income Statement T-Accounts for Investment Advisers, Ltd.

Fee Revenue	Book Sales Revenue	Investment Income

Cost of Goods Sold	Advertising Expense	Rent Expense

Depreciation Expense	Wage Expense	Interest Expense

EXHIBIT 2A-3   Business Transactions for Investment Advisers, Ltd.

#	Date	Business Activity
1	31 December 2005	File documents with regulatory authorities to establish a separate legal entity. Initially capitalize the company through deposit of $150,000 from the three owners.
2	2 January 2006	Set up a $100,000 investment account and purchase a portfolio of equities and fixed-income securities.
3	2 January 2006	Pay $3,000 to landlord for office/warehouse. $2,000 represents a refundable deposit, and $1,000 represents the first month's rent.
4	3 January 2006	Purchase office equipment for $6,000. The equipment has an estimated life of two years with no salvage value.
5	3 January 2006	Receive $1,200 cash for a one-year subscription to the monthly newsletter.
6	10 January 2006	Purchase and receive 500 books at a cost of $20 per book for a total of $10,000. Invoice terms are that payment from IAL is due in 30 days. No cash changes hands. These books are intended for resale.
7	10 January 2006	Spend $600 on newspaper and trade magazine advertising for the month.
8	15 January 2006	Borrow $12,000 from a bank for working capital. Interest is payable annually at 10 percent. The principal is due in two years.
9	15 January 2006	Ship first order to a customer consisting of five books at $25 per book. Invoice terms are that payment is due in 30 days. No cash changes hands.
10	15 January 2006	Sell for cash 10 books at $25 per book at an investment conference.
11	30 January 2006	Hire a part-time clerk. The clerk is hired through an agency that also handles all payroll taxes. The company is to pay $15 per hour to the agency. The clerk works six hours prior to 31 January, but no cash will be paid until February.
12	31 January 2006	Mail out the first month's newsletter to customer. This subscription had been sold on 3 January. See item 5.
13	31 January 2006	Review of the investment portfolio shows that $100 of interest income was earned and the market value of the portfolio has increased by $2,000. The balance in the investment account is now $102,100. Securities are classified as "trading" securities.

31 December 2005

	Business Activity	Accounting Treatment
1	File documents with regulatory authorities to establish a separate legal entity. Initially capitalize the company through deposit of $150,000 from the three owners.	**Cash [A]** is increased by $150,000, and **contributed capital [E]**[11] is increased by $150,000.

Accounting Elements: Assets (A), Liabilites (L), Equity (E), Revenue (R), and Expenses (X).

---

[11]The account title will vary depending upon the type of entity (incorporated or not) and jurisdiction. Alternative account titles are common shares, common stock, members' capital, partners' capital, etc.

This transaction affects two accounts: cash and contributed capital. (Cash is an asset, and contributed capital is part of equity.) The transaction is entered into the T-accounts as shown below. The number in parentheses references the transaction number.

Cash		Contributed Capital	
150,000 (1)			150,000 (1)

Cash is an asset account, and assets are on the left-hand side of the balance sheet (and basic accounting equation); therefore, cash is increased by recording the $150,000 on the debit (left) side of the T-account. Contributed capital is an equity account, and equity accounts are on the right-hand side of the balance sheet; therefore, contributed capital is increased by recording $150,000 on the credit (right) side of the T-account. Note that the sum of the debits for this transaction equals the sum of the credits:

DR = $150,000
CR = $150,000
DR = CR

Each transaction must always maintain this equality. This ensures that the accounting system (and accounting equation) is kept in balance. At this point in time, the company has assets (resources) of $150,000, and the owners' claim on the resources equals $150,000 (their contributed capital) because there are no liabilities at this point.

Transactions are recorded in a journal, which is then "posted to" (recorded in) the general ledger. When a transaction is recorded in a journal, it takes the form:

Date	Account	DR	CR
13 Dec 2005	Cash	150,000	
	Contributed Capital		150,000

This kind of entry is referred to as a *journal entry*, and it is a summary of the information that will be posted in the general ledger T-accounts.

2 January 2006	
Business Activity	**Accounting Treatment**
2 Set up a $100,000 investment account and purchase a portfolio of equities and fixed-income securities.	**Investments [A]** were increased by $100,000, and **cash [A]** was decreased by $100,000.

Accounting Elements: Assets (A), Liabilites (L), Equity (E), Revenue (R), and Expenses (X).

This transaction affects two accounts but only one side of the accounting equation. Cash is reduced when the investments are purchased. Another type of asset, investments, increases. The T-account entries are shown below:

Cash		**Investments**	
150,000 (1)	100,000 (2)	100,000 (2)	

The cash account started with a $150,000 debit balance from the previous transaction. Assets are reduced by credit entries, so the reduction in cash is recorded by entering the $100,000 on the credit (right) side of the cash T-account. The investment account is also an asset, and the increase in investments is recorded by entering $100,000 on the debit side of the investments T-account. Transaction 2 balances because Transaction 2 debits equal Transaction 2 credits.

Going forward, we will use the traditional accounting terms of *debit (debiting, debited)* to indicate the action of entering a number in the debit side of an account, and *credit (crediting, credited)* to indicate the action of entering an amount on the credit side of an account.

2 January 2006

	Business Activity	**Accounting Treatment**
3	Pay $3,000 to landlord for office/warehouse. $2,000 represents a refundable deposit, and $1,000 represents the first month's rent.	**Cash [A]** was decreased by $3,000, **deposits [A]** were increased by $2,000, and **prepaid rent [A]** was increased by $1,000.

Accounting Elements: Assets (A), Liabilites (L), Equity (E), Revenue (R), and Expenses (X).

Cash is reduced once again by crediting the account by $3,000. On the other side of the transaction, two asset accounts increase. Deposits are increased by debiting the account for $2,000, while prepaid rent is increased by debiting that account for $1,000:

Cash		**Deposits**		**Prepaid Rent**	
150,000 (1)	100,000 (2)	2,000 (3)		1,000 (3)	
	3,000 (3)				

The sum of the debits for Transaction 3 equals the sum of the credits (i.e., $3,000).

3 January 2006

	Business Activity	**Accounting Treatment**
4	Purchase office equipment for $6,000 in cash. The equipment has an estimated life of two years with no salvage value.	**Cash [A]** was decreased by $6,000, and **office equipment [A]** was increased by $6,000.

Accounting Elements: Assets (A), Liabilites (L), Equity (E), Revenue (R), and Expenses (X).

Cash is credited for $6,000, while office equipment is debited for $6,000. Both are asset accounts, so these entries reflect a reduction in cash and an increase in office equipment.

Cash		Office Equipment	
150,000 (1)	100,000 (2)	6,000 (4)	
	3,000 (3)		
	6,000 (4)		

3 January 2006

	Business Activity	Accounting Treatment
5	Receive $1,200 cash for a one-year subscription to the monthly newsletter.	**Cash [A]** was increased by $1,200, and **unearned fees [L]** was increased by $1,200.

Accounting Elements: Assets (A), Liabilites (L), Equity (E), Revenue (R), and Expenses (X).

In this transaction, the company has received cash related to the sale of subscriptions. However, the company has not yet actually earned the subscription fees because it has an obligation to deliver newsletters in the future. So, this amount is recorded as a liability called *unearned fees* (or *unearned revenue*). In the future, as the company delivers the newsletters and thus fulfills its obligation, this amount will be transferred to revenue. If they fail to deliver the newsletters, the fees will need to be returned to the customer. To record the transaction, cash is debited (increased), while a liability account, unearned fees, is credited. Liabilities are on the right-hand side of the balance sheet and are, therefore, increased by crediting the T-account.

Cash		Unearned Fees	
150,000 (1)	100,000 (2)		1,200 (5)
1,200 (5)	3,000 (3)		
	6,000 (4)		

The sum of Transaction 5 debits and credits each equal $1,200.

10 January 2006

	Business Activity	Accounting Treatment
6	Purchase and receive 500 books at a cost of $20 per book for a total of $10,000. Invoice terms are that payment from IAL is due in 30 days. No cash changes hands. These books are intended for resale.	**Inventory [A]** is increased by $10,000, and **accounts payable [L]** is increased by $10,000.

Accounting Elements: Assets (A), Liabilites (L), Equity (E), Revenue (R), and Expenses (X).

The company has obtained an asset, inventory, which can be sold to customers at a later date. Rather than paying cash to the supplier currently, the company has an obligation to do so in 30 days. This represents a liability (accounts payable) to the supplier. Inventory is debited for $10,000, while the liability, accounts payable, is credited for $10,000. Note that there is no impact on the cash account.

Inventory		Accounts Payable	
10,000 (6)			10,000 (6)

10 January 2006

	Business Activity	Accounting Treatment
7	Spend $600 on newspaper and trade magazine advertising for the month	**Cash [A]** was decreased by $600, and **advertising expense [X]** was increased by $600.

Accounting Elements: Assets (A), Liabilites (L), Equity (E), Revenue (R), and Expenses (X).

Unlike the previous expenditures, advertising is not an asset. Its future economic benefits are unclear, unlike equipment, which is expected to be useful over multiple periods. Expenditures such as advertising are recorded as an expense when they are incurred. To record the advertising expense, cash is credited for $600, and advertising expense is debited for $600. Expenses reduce net income, and thus reduce retained earnings. Decreases in retained earnings, as with any equity account, are recorded as debits. The entries with respect to retained earnings will be presented later in this section after the income statement.

Cash		Advertising Expense	
150,000 (1)	100,000 (2)	600 (7)	
1,200 (5)	3,000 (3)		
	6,000 (4)		
	600 (7)		

15 January 2006

	Business Activity	Accounting Treatment
8	Borrow $12,000 from a bank for working capital. Interest is payable annually at 10 percent. The principal is due in two years.	**Cash [A]** is increased by $12,000, and **Bank debt [L]** is increased by $12,000.

Accounting Elements: Assets (A), Liabilites (L), Equity (E), Revenue (R), and Expenses (X).

Cash is debited, and a corresponding liability is credited. Initially, no entry is made for interest that is expected to be paid on the loan. Interest will be recorded in the future as time passes and interest accrues (accumulates) on the loan.

Cash		Bank Debt	
150,000 (1)	100,000 (2)		12,000 (8)
1,200 (5)	3,000 (3)		
12,000 (8)	6,000 (4)		
	600 (7)		

The debits and credits of Transaction 8 each total $12,000.

15 January 2006

	Business Activity	Accounting Treatment
9	Ship first order to a customer consisting of five books at $25 per book. Invoice terms are that payment is due in 30 days. No cash changes hands.	**Accounts receivable [A]** increased by $125, and **book sales revenue [R]** increased by $125. Additionally, **inventory [A]** decreased by $100, and **cost of goods sold [X]** increased by $100.

Accounting Elements: Assets (A), Liabilites (L), Equity (E), Revenue (R), and Expenses (X).

The company has now made a sale. Sale transaction records have two parts. One part records the $125 revenue to be received from the customer, and the other part records the $100 cost of the goods that have been sold. For the first part, accounts receivable is debited (increased) for $125, and a revenue account is credited for $125.

Accounts Receivable		Book Sales Revenue	
125 (9)			125 (9)

For the second part, inventory is credited (reduced) for $100, and an expense, cost of goods sold, is debited (increased) to reflect the cost of inventory sold.

Inventory		Cost of Goods Sold	
10,000 (6)	100 (9)	100 (9)	

Note that the sum of debits and the sum of credits for Transaction 9 both equal $225. The $225 is not meaningful by itself. What is important is that the debits and credits balance.

15 January 2006

	Business Activity	Accounting Treatment
10	Sell for cash 10 books at $25 per book at an investment conference.	**Cash [A]** is increased by $250, and **book sales revenue [R]** is increased by $250. Additionally, **inventory [A]** is decreased by $200, and **cost of goods sold [X]** is increased by $200.

Accounting Elements: Assets (A), Liabilites (L), Equity (E), Revenue (R), and Expenses (X).

Similar to the previous transaction, both the sales proceeds and cost of the goods sold must be recorded. In this case, however, the sales proceeds are received in cash. To record the sale proceeds, the entries include a debit to cash for $250 and a corresponding credit to book sales revenue for $250. To record cost of goods sold, the entries include a debit to cost of goods sold and a credit to inventory.

Cash		Book Sales Revenue	
150,000 (1)	100,000 (2)		125 (9)
1,200 (5)	3,000 (3)		250 (10)
12,000 (8)	6,000 (4)		
250 (10)	600 (7)		

Inventory		Cost of Goods Sold	
10,000 (6)	100 (9)	100 (9)	
	200 (10)	200 (10)	

Transaction 10's debits and credits are equal, maintaining the accounting system's balance.

30 January 2006

11	Hire a part-time clerk. The clerk is hired through an agency that also handles all payroll taxes. The company is to pay $15 per hour to the agency. The clerk works six hours prior to 31 January, but no cash will be paid until February.	The company owes $90 for wages at month-end. Under accrual accounting, expenses are recorded when incurred, not when paid. **Accrued wages [L]** is increased by $90, and **wage expense [X]** is increased by $90. The accrued wage liability will be eliminated when the wages are paid.

Accounting Elements: Assets (A), Liabilites (L), Equity (E), Revenue (R), and Expenses (X).

Accrued wages is a liability that is increased by crediting that account, whereas payroll is an expense account that is increased with a debit.

Accrued Wages		Wage Expense	
	90 (11)	90 (11)	

31 January 2006

12	Mail out the first month's newsletter to customer. This subscription had been sold on 3 January.	One month (or 1/12) of the $1,200 subscription has been satisfied, and thus $100 can be recognized as revenue. **Unearned fees [L]** is decreased by $100, and **fee revenue [R]** is increased by $100.

Accounting Elements: Assets (A), Liabilites (L), Equity (E), Revenue (R), and Expenses (X).

To record the recognition of one month of the subscription fee, the account fee revenue is credited (increased) by $100, and the related liability is debited (decreased) by $100.

Fee Revenue		Unearned Fees	
	100 (12)	100 (12)	1,200 (5)

31 January 2006

13	Review of the investment portfolio shows that $100 of interest income was earned and the market value of the portfolio has increased by $2,000. The balance in the investment account is now $102,100. The securities are classified as "trading" securities.	**Investment income [R]** is increased by $100, and the **investments** account **[A]** is increased by $100. The $2,000 increase in the value of the portfolio represents unrealized gains that are part of income for traded securities. The **investments** account **[A]** is increased by $2,000, and **investment income [R]** is increased by $2,000.

Accounting Elements: Assets (A), Liabilites (L), Equity (E), Revenue (R), and Expenses (X).

The investments account is an asset account that is debited (increased) for $2,100, and investment income is a revenue account that is credited (increased) by $2,100.

Investments		Investment Income	
100,000 (2)			2,100 (13)
2,100 (13)			

These entries complete the recording of the first 13 transactions. In this illustration, there are three adjustments. An adjustment must be made related to Transaction 3 to account for the fact that a month has passed and rent expense has been incurred. We refer to this as Transaction 3a. Adjustments must also be made for an estimate of the depreciation of the office equipment (Transaction 4a) and for interest that has accrued on the loan (Transaction 8a).

3a	In item 3, $3,000 was paid to the landlord for office/warehouse, including a $2,000 refundable deposit and $1,000 for the first month's rent. Now, the first month has ended, so this rent has become a cost of doing business.	To reflect the full amount of the first month's rent as a cost of doing business, **prepaid rent [A]** is decreased by $1,000, and **rent expense [X]** is increased by $1,000.

Accounting Elements: Assets (A), Liabilites (L), Equity (E), Revenue (R), and Expenses (X).

Prepaid rent (an asset) is credited for $1,000 to reduce the balance, and rent expense is debited for the same amount to record the fact that the expense has now been incurred. After this entry, the balance of the prepaid rent asset account is $0.

Prepaid Rent		**Rent Expense**	
1,000 (3)	1,000 (3a)	1,000 (3a)	

4a	In item 4, office equipment was purchased for $6,000 in cash. The equipment has an estimated life of two years with no salvage value.	A portion (1/24) of the total $6,000 cost of the office equipment is allocated to the current period's cost of doing business.
	Now, one month (or 1/24) of the useful life of the equipment has ended so a portion of the equipment cost has become a cost of doing business.	**Depreciation expense [X]** is increased by $250, and **accumulated depreciation** is increased by $250.
		Accumulated depreciation is a contra asset account to office equipment

Accounting Elements: Assets (A), Liabilites (L), Equity (E), Revenue (R), and Expenses (X).

Because some time has passed, accounting principles require that the estimated depreciation of the equipment be recorded. In this case, one could directly credit office equipment for $250; however, a preferred method is to credit an account called *accumulated depreciation*, which is associated with the office equipment account. This accumulated depreciation account "holds" the cumulative amount of the depreciation related to the office equipment. When financial reports are prepared, a user is able to see both the original cost of the equipment as well as the accumulated depreciation. The user, therefore, has insight into the age of the asset, and perhaps how much time remains before it is likely to be replaced. Accumulated depreciation is termed a *contra* asset account and is credited for $250, while depreciation expense is debited (increased) for $250.

Accumulated Depreciation		**Depreciation Expense**	
	250 (4a)	250 (4a)	

8a	The company borrowed $12,000 from a bank on 15 January, with interest payable annually at 10 percent and the principal due in two years.	One-half of one month of interest expense has become a cost of doing business. $12,000 times 10% equals $1,200 of annual interest, equivalent to $100 per month and $50 for one-half month.
	Now, one-half of one month has passed since the borrowing.	**Interest expense [X]** is increased by $50, and **accrued interest [L]** is increased by $50.

Accrued interest is a liability that is credited (increased) for $50, and interest expense is debited (increased) for $50. Accrued interest is also sometimes referred to as *interest payable*.

Accrued Interest		**Interest Expense**	
	50 (8a)	50 (8a)	

Exhibit 2A-4 summarizes the general ledger T-accounts for IAL at this point in time. For accounts with multiple entries, a line is drawn and the debit and credit columns are summed and netted to determine the current balance in the account. The balance is entered below the line. These individual account totals are then summarized in a trial balance as depicted in Exhibit 2A-5. A trial balance is a summary of the account balances at a point in time. An accountant can prepare a trial balance at any time to ensure that the system is in balance and to review current amounts in the accounts. Note that the debit and credit columns each

EXHIBIT 2A-4   General Ledger T-Accounts for Investment Advisers, Ltd.

Cash		Accounts Receivable		Inventory	
150,000 (1)	100,000 (2)	125 (9)		10,000 (6)	100 (9)
1,200 (5)	3,000 (3)				200 (10)
12,000 (8)	6,000 (4)			9,700	
250 (10)	600 (7)				
53,850					

Investments		Office Equipment		Accumulated Depreciation	
100,000 (2)		6,000 (4)			250 (4a)
2,100 (13)					
102,100					

Deposits		Prepaid Rent		Accounts Payable	
2,000 (3)		1,000 (3)	1,000 (3a)		10,000 (6)
		0			

Accrued Wages		Unearned Fees		Bank Debt	
	90 (11)	100 (12)	1,200 (5)		12,000 (8)
			1,100		

Accrued Interest		Contributed Capital		Retained Earnings	
	50 (8a)		150,000 (1)		

Fee Revenue		Book Sales Revenue		Investment Income	
	100 (12)		125 (9)		2,100 (13)
			250 (10)		
			375		

Cost of Goods Sold	Advertising Expense	Rent Expense
100 (9)	600 (7)	1,000 (3a)
200 (10)		
300		

Depreciation Expense	Wage Expense	Interest Expense
250 (4a)	90 (11)	50 (8a)

EXHIBIT 2A-5   Investment Advisers, Ltd. Trial Balance

	DR	CR
Cash	53,850	
Accounts receivable	125	
Inventory	9,700	
Investments	102,100	
Office equipment	6,000	
Accumulated depreciation		250
Deposits	2,000	
Prepaid rent	0	
Accounts payable		10,000
Accrued wages		90
Unearned fees		1,100
Bank debt		12,000
Accrued interest		50
Contributed capital		150,000
Retained earnings		
Fee revenue		100
Book sales revenue		375
Investment income		2,100
Cost of goods sold	300	
Advertising expense	600	
Rent expense	1,000	
Depreciation expense	250	
Wage expense	90	
Interest expense	50	
Total	**176,065**	**176,065**

total $176,065, confirming that the system is in balance. Any difference in the column totals would indicate an error had been made. The trial balance totals have no particular significance and are not used in preparing financial statements. These totals are simply the sum of debits and credits in the accounting system at that point in time.

After ensuring that the balances in the trial balance are correct (if there are errors, they are corrected and an adjusted trial balance is prepared), we prepare the financial statements. The trial balance provides the information necessary to prepare the balance sheet and the income statement. The detail in the general ledger must be reviewed to prepare the statement of cash flows and statement of owners' equity. After the income statement is prepared, the temporary accounts are closed out (i.e., taken to a zero balance) by transferring each of their balances to retained earnings. This typically occurs at year-end and is termed the *closing process*. Exhibits 2A-6 and 2A-7 show the post-closing general ledger and trial balance, respectively.

EXHIBIT 2A-6 Post-Closing General Ledger T-Accounts for Investment Advisers, Ltd.

Cash			Accounts Receivable		Inventory	
150,000 (1)	100,000 (2)		125 (9)		10,000 (6)	100 (9)
1,200 (5)	3,000 (3)					200 (10)
12,000 (8)	6,000 (4)				9,700	
250 (10)	600 (7)					
53,850						

Investments		Office Equipment		Accumulated Depreciation	
100,000 (2)		6,000 (4)			250 (4a)
2,100 (13)					
102,100					

Deposits		Prepaid Rent		Accounts Payable	
2,000 (3)		1,000 (3)	1,000 (3a)		10,000 (6)
		0			

Accrued Wages		Unearned Fees		Bank Debt	
	90 (11)	100 (12)	1,200 (5)		12,000 (8)
			1,100		

Accrued Interest		Contributed Capital		Retained Earnings	
	50 (8a)		150,000 (1)		285

Fee Revenue	Book Sales Revenue	Investment Income
0	0	0

Cost of Goods Sold	Advertising Expense	Rent Expense
0	0	0

Depreciation Expense	Wage Expense	Interest Expense
0	0	0

EXHIBIT 2A-7   Investment Advisers, Ltd. Postclosing Trial Balance

	DR	CR
Cash	53,850	
Accounts receivable	125	
Inventory	9,700	
Investments	102,100	
Office equipment	6,000	
Accumulated depreciation		250
Deposits	2,000	
Prepaid rent	0	
Accounts payable		10,000
Accrued wages		90
Unearned fees		1,100
Bank debt		12,000
Accrued interest		50
Contributed capital		150,000
Retained earnings		285
Fee revenue		0
Book sales revenue		0
Investment income		0
Cost of goods sold	0	

(Continued)

EXHIBIT 2A-7 *Continued*

	DR	CR
Advertising expense	0	
Rent expense	0	
Depreciation expense	0	
Wage expense	0	
Interest expense	0	
Total	**173,775**	**173,775**

Financial statements are identical whether using a spreadsheet approach or a debit/credit approach. Accordingly, the financial statements for IAL that would be prepared using the trial balances are identical to those presented in the main body of the chapter as Exhibit 2-9.

CHAPTER 3

FINANCIAL REPORTING STANDARDS

Thomas R. Robinson, CFA

CFA Institute
Charlottesville, Virginia

Hennie van Greuning, CFA

World Bank
Washington, DC

Elaine Henry, CFA

University of Miami
Miami, Florida

Michael A. Broihahn, CFA

Barry University
Miami, Florida

LEARNING OUTCOMES

After completing this chapter, you will be able to do the following:

- Explain the objective of financial statements and the importance of reporting standards in security analysis and valuation.
- Explain the role of financial reporting standard-setting bodies (including the International Accounting Standards Board and the U.S. Financial Accounting Standards Board) and

regulatory authorities such as the International Organization of Securities Commissions, the U.K. Financial Services Authority, and the U.S. Securities and Exchange Commission in establishing and enforcing reporting standards.

- Discuss the status of global convergence of accounting standards and the ongoing barriers to developing one universally accepted set of financial reporting standards.
- Describe the International Financial Reporting Standards (IFRS) framework, including the objective of financial statements, their qualitative characteristics, required reporting elements, and the constraints and assumptions in preparing financial statements.
- Explain the general requirements for financial statements.
- Compare and contrast the key concepts of financial reporting standards under IFRS and alternative reporting systems, and discuss the implications for financial analysis of differing financial reporting systems.
- Identify the characteristics of a coherent financial reporting framework and barriers to creating such a framework.
- Discuss the importance of monitoring developments in financial reporting standards and evaluate company disclosures of significant accounting policies.

1. INTRODUCTION

Financial reporting standards determine the types and amounts of information that must be provided to investors and creditors so that they may make informed decisions. This chapter focuses on the broad framework within which these standards are created. An understanding of the underlying framework of financial reporting standards, which is broader than knowledge of specific accounting rules, will allow an analyst to assess the valuation implications of *any* financial statement element or transaction—including newly developed transactions that are not specifically addressed by the standards.

Section 2 of this chapter discusses the objective of financial statements and the importance of financial standards in security analysis and valuation. Section 3 describes the financial reporting standard-setting bodies and regulatory authorities that establish financial reporting standards. Section 4 examines the trend toward convergence of global financial reporting standards. The International Financial Reporting Standards (IFRS) framework is presented in section 5, and section 6 compares IFRS with alternative reporting systems.[1] Section 7 discusses the characteristics of an effective financial reporting framework. Section 8 discusses the importance of monitoring developments in financial reporting standards. Section 9 summarizes the key points of the chapter, and practice problems in the CFA Institute multiple-choice format conclude the chapter.

2. THE OBJECTIVE OF FINANCIAL REPORTING

Financial reporting begins with a simple enough premise. The International Accounting Standards Board (IASB), which is the international accounting standard-setting body, expresses it as follows in its *Framework for the Preparation and Presentation of Financial Statements*:

---

[1]The body of standards issued by the IASB is referred to as International Financial Reporting Standards, which include previously issued International Accounting Standards (IAS). *Financial reporting* is a broad term including reporting on accounting, financial statements, and other information found in company financial reports.

> *The objective of financial statements is to provide information about the financial position, performance, and changes in financial position of an entity; this information should be useful to a wide range of users for the purpose of making economic decisions.*[2]

Until recently, financial reporting standards were developed mostly independently by each country's standard-setting body. This has created a wide range of standards, some of which are quite comprehensive and complex, and others more general. Recent accounting scandals have raised awareness of the need for more uniform global financial reporting standards and provided the impetus for stronger coordination among the major standard-setting bodies. Such coordination is also a natural outgrowth of the increased globalization of capital markets.

Developing financial reporting standards is complicated because the underlying economic reality is complicated. The financial transactions and organizations that financial statements purport to represent are complicated. There is often uncertainty about transactions, resulting in the need for accruals and estimates. These accruals and estimates necessitate judgment. Judgment varies from one preparer to the next. Accordingly, standards are needed to achieve some type of consistency in these judgments. Even with such standards there will be no one right answer. Nevertheless, financial reporting standards try to limit the range of acceptable answers to ensure some measure of consistency in financial statements.

EXAMPLE 3-1   Estimates in Financial Reporting

In order to make comparisons across companies (cross-sectional analysis) and over time for a single company (time-series analysis), it is important that accounting methods are comparable and consistently applied. However, accounting standards must be flexible enough to recognize that there are differences in the underlying economics between businesses.

Suppose two companies buy the same model of machinery to be used in their respective businesses. The machine is expected to last for several years. Financial reporting standards should require that both companies account for this equipment by initially recording the cost of the machinery as an asset. Without such a standard, the companies could report the purchase of the equipment differently. For example, one company might record the purchase as an asset and the other might record the purchase as an expense. An accounting standard ensures that both companies would be required to record the transaction in a similar manner.

Accounting standards typically would require the cost of the machine to be apportioned over the estimated useful life of an asset as an expense called depreciation. Because the two companies may be operating the machinery differently, financial reporting standards must retain some flexibility. One company might operate the machinery only a few days per week, whereas the other company operates the equipment continuously throughout the week. Given the difference in usage, it would not be appropriate for the two companies to report an identical amount of depreciation expense each period. Financial reporting standards must allow for some discretion such that management can match their financial reporting choices to the underlying economics of their business while ensuring that similar transactions are recorded in a similar manner between companies.

---

[2]*Framework for the Preparation and Presentation of Financial Statements*, International Accounting Standards Committee, 1989, adopted by IASB 2001, paragraph 12.

The IASB and the U.S. Financial Accounting Standards Board (FASB) have developed similar financial reporting frameworks, both of which specify the overall objective and qualities of information to be provided. Financial reports are intended to provide information to many users, including investors, creditors, employees, customers, and others. As a result of this multipurpose nature, financial reports are *not* designed with only asset valuation in mind. However, financial reports provide important inputs into the process of valuing a company or the securities a company issues. Understanding the financial reporting framework—including how and when judgments and estimates can affect the numbers reported—enables an analyst to evaluate the information reported and to use the information appropriately when assessing a company's financial performance. Clearly, such an understanding is also important in assessing the financial impact of business decisions and in making comparisons across entities.

3. FINANCIAL REPORTING STANDARD-SETTING BODIES AND REGULATORY AUTHORITIES

A distinction needs to be made between standard-setting bodies and regulatory authorities. Standard-setting bodies, such as the IASB and FASB, are typically private-sector organizations consisting of experienced accountants, auditors, users of financial statements, and academics. Regulatory authorities, such as the Securities and Exchange Commission (SEC) in the United States and the Financial Services Authority (FSA) in the United Kingdom, are governmental entities that have the legal authority to enforce financial reporting requirements and exert other controls over entities that participate in the capital markets within their jurisdiction.

In other words, *generally*, standard-setting bodies make the rules and regulatory authorities enforce the rules. Note, however, that regulators often retain the legal authority to establish financial reporting standards in their jurisdiction and can overrule the private sector standard-setting bodies.

EXAMPLE 3-2   Industry-Specific Regulation

In certain cases, there exist multiple regulatory bodies that affect a company's financial reporting requirements. For example, in almost all jurisdictions around the world, banking-specific regulatory bodies establish requirements related to risk-based capital measurement, minimum capital adequacy, provisions for doubtful loans, and minimum monetary reserves. An awareness of such regulations provides an analyst with the context to understand a bank's business, including the objectives and scope of allowed activities.

In the United States, the Office of the Comptroller of the Currency charters and regulates all national banks. In the United Kingdom, the FSA regulates the financial services industry. In some countries, a single entity serves both as the central bank and as the regulatory body for the country's financial institutions.

This section provides a brief overview of the most important international standard-setting body, the IASB, followed by a description of the International Organization of

Securities Commissions (IOSCO), capital markets regulation in the European Union (EU), and an overview of the U.S. SEC.

3.1.   International Accounting Standards Board

The IASB is the standard-setting body responsible for developing international financial reporting and accounting standards. The four goals of the IASB are:

(a) to develop, in the public interest, a single set of high quality, understandable and enforceable global accounting standards that require high quality, transparent and comparable information in financial statements and other financial reporting to help participants in the world's capital markets and other users make economic decisions;

(b) to promote the use and rigorous application of those standards;

(c) in fulfilling the objectives associated with (a) and (b), to take account of, as appropriate, the special needs of small and medium-sized entities and emerging economies; and

(d) to bring about convergence of national accounting standards and International Accounting Standards and International Financial Reporting Standards to high quality solutions.[3]

The predecessor of the IASB, the International Accounting Standards Committee (IASC), was founded in June 1973 as a result of an agreement by accountancy bodies in Australia, Canada, France, Germany, Japan, Mexico, the Netherlands, the United Kingdom and Ireland, and the United States. By 1998, the IASC had expanded membership to 140 accountancy bodies in 101 countries. In 2001, the IASC was reconstituted into the IASB. The IASB has 14 full-time board members who deliberate new financial reporting standards.[4]

The IASB is overseen by the International Accounting Standards Committee Foundation, which has 19 trustees who appoint the members of the IASB, establish the budget, and monitor the IASB's progress. The IASB is advised by the Standards Advisory Council, which is composed of about 50 members representing organizations and individuals with an interest in international financial reporting.

3.2.   International Organization of Securities Commissions

IOSCO, formed in 1983 as the successor organization of an inter-American regional association (created in 1974), has 181 members that regulate more than 90 percent of the world's financial capital markets.

---

[3]International Accounting Standards Committee Foundation Constitution, IASCF, July 2005, part A, paragraph 2.

[4]Although the name of the IASB incorporates "Accounting Standards" and early standards were titled International Accounting Standards (IAS), the term *International Financial Reporting Standards* is being used for new standards. The use of the words *financial reporting* recognizes the importance of disclosures outside of the core financial statements, such as management discussion of the business, risks, and future plans.

In 1998, IOSCO adopted a comprehensive set of *Objectives and Principles of Securities Regulation*, which is recognized as international benchmarks for all markets. IOSCO sets out three core objectives of securities regulation:

1. Protecting investors.
2. Ensuring that markets are fair, efficient, and transparent.
3. Reducing systematic risk.

Standards related to financial reporting, including accounting and auditing standards, are key components in achieving these objectives. IOSCO's *Objectives and Principles of Securities Regulation* states:

> *Full disclosure of information material to investors' decisions is the most important means for ensuring investor protection. Investors are, thereby, better able to assess the potential risks and rewards of their investments and, thus, to protect their own interests. As key components of disclosure requirements, accounting and auditing standards should be in place and they should be of a high and internationally acceptable quality.*[5]

Historically, regulation and related financial reporting standards were developed within individual countries and were often based on the cultural, economic, and political norms of each country. As financial markets have become more global, it has become desirable to establish comparable financial reporting standards internationally. Ultimately, laws and regulations are established by individual jurisdictions, so this also requires cooperation among regulators. In order to ensure adherence to international financial standards, it is important to have uniform regulation across national boundaries. IOSCO aims to assist in attaining this goal of uniform regulation.

3.3. Capital Markets Regulation in Europe

Each individual member state of the EU regulates capital markets in its jurisdiction. There are, however, certain regulations that have been adopted at the EU level. These include standards and directives related to enforcement of IFRS, a proposed directive to adopt International Standards on Auditing, and proposed directives concerning the board of directors' responsibility for a company's financial statements. The EU, under its Accounting Regulation, will likely serve a role similar to the SEC in the United States as it must endorse each international standard for use in Europe.

In 2001, the European Commission established two committees related to securities regulation: the European Securities Committee (ESC) and the Committee of European Securities Regulators (CESR). The ESC consists of high-level representatives of member states and advises the European Commission on securities policy issues. The CESR is an independent advisory body composed of representatives of regulatory authorities of the member states.

As noted earlier, regulation still rests with the individual member states and, therefore, requirements for registering shares and filing periodic financial reports vary from country to country. Over time, this process is expected to become more uniform in the EU.

---

[5]*Objectives and Principles of Securities Regulation,* IOSCO, May 2003, section 4.2.1.

3.4.   Capital Markets Regulation in the United States

Any company issuing securities within the United States, or otherwise involved in U.S. capital markets, is subject to the rules and regulations of the U.S. SEC. The SEC, one of the oldest and most developed regulatory authorities, originated as a result of reform efforts made after the great stock market crash of 1929, sometimes referred to as simply the "Great Crash."

3.4.1.   Significant Securities-Related Legislation

There are numerous SEC rules and regulations affecting reporting companies, broker/dealers, and other market participants. From a financial reporting and analysis perspective, the most significant of these acts are the Securities Acts of 1933 and 1934 and the Sarbanes–Oxley Act of 2002.

- *Securities Act of 1933 (The 1933 Act).* This act specifies the financial and other significant information that investors must receive when securities are sold, prohibits misrepresentations, and requires initial registration of all public issuances of securities.
- *Securities Exchange Act of 1934 (The 1934 Act).* This act created the SEC, gave the SEC authority over all aspects of the securities industry, and empowered the SEC to require periodic reporting by companies with publicly traded securities.
- *Sarbanes-Oxley Act of 2002.* The Sarbanes-Oxley Act of 2002 created the Public Company Accounting Oversight Board (PCAOB) to oversee auditors. The SEC is responsible for carrying out the requirements of the act and overseeing the PCAOB. The act addresses auditor independence; for example, it prohibits auditors from providing certain nonaudit services to the companies they audit. The act strengthens corporate responsibility for financial reports; for example, it requires the chief executive officer and the chief financial officer to certify that the company's financial reports fairly present the company's condition. Furthermore, section 404 of the Sarbanes-Oxley Act requires management to report on the effectiveness of the company's internal control over financial reporting and to obtain a report from its external auditor attesting to management's assertion about the effectiveness of the company's internal control.

Internal Controls

3.4.2.   SEC Filings: Key Sources of Information for Analysts

Companies satisfy compliance with these acts principally through the completion and submission (i.e., filing) of standardized forms issued by the SEC. There are more than 50 different types of SEC forms that are used to satisfy reporting requirements; the discussion herein will be limited to those forms most relevant for financial analysts.

In 1993, the SEC began to mandate electronic filings of the required forms through its Electronic Data Gathering, Analysis, and Retrieval (EDGAR) system. As of 2005, most SEC filings are required to be made electronically. EDGAR has made corporate and financial information more readily available to investors and the financial community. Most of the SEC filings that an analyst would be interested in can be retrieved from the Internet from one of many web sites, including the SEC's own web site. Some filings are required upon the initial offering of securities, whereas others are required on a periodic basis thereafter. The following are some of the more common information sources used by analysts.

- *Securities offerings registration statement.* The 1933 Act requires companies offering securities to file a registration statement. New issuers as well as previously registered companies that are issuing new securities are required to file these statements. Required information and the precise form vary depending upon the size and nature of the offering. Typically, required information includes: (1) disclosures about the securities being offered for sale,

(2) the relationship of these new securities to the issuer's other capital securities, (3) the information typically provided in the annual filings, (4) recent audited financial statements, and (5) risk factors involved in the business.

EXAMPLE 3-3   Initial Registration Statement

In 2004, Google filed a Form S-1 registration statement with the U.S. SEC to register its initial public offering of securities (Class A common stock). In addition to copious amounts of financial and business information, the registration statement provided a 20-page discussion of risks related to Google's business and industry. This type of qualitative information is helpful, if not essential, in making an assessment of a company's credit or investment risk.

- *Forms 10-K, 20-F, and 40-F.* These are forms that companies are required to file *annually*. Form 10-K is for U.S. registrants, Form 40-F is for certain Canadian registrants, and Form 20-F is for all other non-U.S. registrants. These forms require a comprehensive overview, including information concerning a company's business, financial disclosures, legal proceedings, and information related to management. The financial disclosures include a historical summary of financial data (usually 10 years), management's discussion and analysis (MD&A) of the company's financial condition and results of operations, and audited financial statements.
- *Annual report.* In addition to the SEC's annual filings (e.g., Form 10-K), most companies prepare an annual report to shareholders. This is not a requirement of the SEC. The annual report is usually viewed as one of the most significant opportunities for a company to present itself to shareholders and other external parties; accordingly, it is often a highly polished marketing document with photographs, an opening letter from the chief executive officer, financial data, market segment information, research and development activities, and future corporate goals. In contrast, the Form 10-K is a more legal type of document with minimal marketing emphasis. Although the perspectives vary, there is considerable overlap between a company's annual report and its Form 10-K. Some companies elect to prepare just the Form 10-K or a document that integrates both the 10-K and annual report.
- *Proxy statement/Form DEF-14A.* The SEC requires that shareholders of a company receive a proxy statement prior to a shareholder meeting. A proxy is an authorization from the shareholder giving another party the right to cast its vote. Shareholder meetings are held at least once a year, but any special meetings also require a proxy statement. Proxies, especially annual meeting proxies, contain information that is often useful to financial analysts. Such information typically includes proposals that require a shareholder vote, details of security ownership by management and principal owners, biographical information on directors, and disclosure of executive compensation. Proxy statement information is filed with the SEC as Form DEF-14A.
- *Forms 10-Q and 6-K.* These are forms that companies are required to submit for interim periods (quarterly for U.S. companies on Form 10-Q, semiannually for many non-U.S. companies on Form 6-K). The filing requires certain financial information, including unaudited financial statements and a MD&A for the interim period covered by the report. Additionally, if certain types of nonrecurring events—such as the adoption of a significant accounting policy,

commencement of significant litigation, or a material limitation on the rights of any holders of any class of registered securities—take place during the period covered by the report, these events must be included in the Form 10-Q report. Companies may provide the 10-Q report to shareholders or may prepare a separate, abbreviated, quarterly report to shareholders.

- *Other filings.* There are other SEC filings that a company or its officers make—either periodically, or, if significant events or transactions have occurred, in between the periodic reports noted above. By their nature, these forms sometimes contain the most interesting and timely information and may have significant valuation implications.
- *Form 8-K.* In addition to filing annual and interim reports, SEC registrants must report material corporate events on a more current basis. Form 8-K (6-K for non-U.S. registrants) is the "current report" companies must file with the SEC to announce such major events as acquisitions or disposals of corporate assets, changes in securities and trading markets, matters related to accountants and financial statements, corporate governance and management changes, and Regulation FD disclosures.[6]
- *Form 144.* This form must be filed with the SEC as notice of the proposed sale of restricted securities or securities held by an affiliate of the issuer in reliance on Rule 144. Rule 144 permits limited sales of restricted securities without registration.
- *Forms 3, 4, and 5.* These forms are required to report beneficial ownership of securities. These filings are required for any director or officer of a registered company as well as beneficial owners of greater than 10 percent of a class of registered equity securities. Form 3 is the initial statement, Form 4 reports changes, and Form 5 is the annual report. These forms, along with Form 144, can be used to examine purchases and sales of securities by officers, directors, and other affiliates of the company.
- *Form 11-K.* This is the annual report of employee stock purchase, savings, and similar plans. It might be of interest to analysts for companies with significant employee benefit plans because it contains more information than that disclosed in the company's financial statements.

4. CONVERGENCE OF GLOBAL FINANCIAL REPORTING STANDARDS

Recent activities have moved the goal of one set of universally accepted financial reporting standards out of the theoretical sphere into the realm of reality.

In 2002, the IASB and FASB each acknowledged their commitment to the development of high-quality, compatible accounting standards that could be used for both domestic and cross-border financial reporting (in an agreement referred to as the "Norwalk Agreement"). Both the IASB and FASB pledged to use their best efforts to (1) make their existing financial reporting standards fully compatible as soon as practicable, and (2) to coordinate their future work programs to ensure that, once achieved, compatibility is maintained. The Norwalk Agreement was certainly an important milestone, and both bodies are working toward convergence through an ongoing short-term convergence project, a convergence research project, and joint projects such as revenue recognition and business combinations.

---

[6]Regulation FD provides that when an issuer discloses material nonpublic information to certain individuals or entities—generally, securities market professionals such as stock analysts or holders of the issuer's securities who may trade on the basis of the information—the issuer must make public disclosure of that information. In this way, the rule aims to promote full and fair disclosure.

In 2004, the IASB and FASB agreed that, in principle, any significant accounting standard would be developed cooperatively. It is likely to take considerable time to work out differences on existing IFRS and U.S. generally accepted accounting principles (GAAP) because of other pressing priorities and honest differences in principles. Development of one universally accepted financial reporting framework is a major undertaking and is expected to take a number of years. Exhibit 3-1 provides a summary of the worldwide adoption status of IFRS.

EXHIBIT 3-1   International Adoption Status of IFRS as of December 2006

Europe	The EU requires companies listed in EU countries to adopt IFRS for the 2005 financial statements.
	The IASB decides in late 2006 that it will not require the application of new IFRS or major amendments to existing standards before 1 January 2009.
	Switzerland requires that multinational main board companies must choose either U.S. GAAP or IFRS.
United States	The SEC accepts IFRS for non-U.S. registrants but currently requires a reconciliation to U.S. GAAP. It has indicated that it will revisit this requirement after the filing of 2005 financial statements.
	The FASB is engaged in numerous projects with the IASB to achieve convergence of U.S. GAAP to IFRS. Full convergence, however, is not expected to be completed in the foreseeable future.
Canada	In 2006, Canada's Accounting Standards Board decided to converge Canadian GAAP with IFRS.
Central and South America	Guatemala, Costa Rica, Ecuador, Nicaragua, Panama, Peru, and Honduras require IFRS for all domestic listed companies.
	Venezuela required adoption of IFRS beginning in 2006 for listed companies and 2007 for others.
	El Salvador permits IFRS for domestic listed companies.
Caribbean	Bahamas, Barbados, Jamaica, Trinidad and Tobago, Dominican Republic, and Haiti require IFRS for all domestic listed companies.
Asia Pacific Countries	Bangladesh requires the use of IFRS, and Australia and New Zealand have adopted IFRS "equivalent" standards for the 2005 and 2007, respectively, financial statements.
	Japan has launched a joint project with the IASB to reduce differences between Japanese accounting standards and IFRS.
	China requires IFRS for some domestic listed companies.
	Hong Kong and Philippines have adopted national standards that are equivalent to IFRS except for some effective dates and transition.
	Singapore has adopted many IFRS.
	Myanmar and Sri Lanka permit the use of IFRS for domestic listed companies.
Africa and the Middle East	South Africa, Tanzania, Kenya, Egypt, and Malawi require IFRS for all domestic listed companies.
Russian Federation and former Soviet Union	The Russian Federation requires IFRS for banks and has proposed phasing in requiring all domestic listed companies to use IFRS beginning in 2006.

Sources: Based on data from www.iasb.org and www.iasplus.com.

In some ways, the move toward one global set of financial reporting standards has made the barriers to full convergence more apparent. Standard-setting bodies and regulators can have differing views. In addition, they may be influenced by strong industry lobbying groups and others that will be subject to these reporting standards. For example, the FASB faced strong opposition when it first attempted to adopt standards requiring companies to expense employee stock compensation plans.[7] The IASB has experienced similar political pressures. The issue of political pressure is compounded when international standards are involved, simply because there are many more interested parties and many more divergent views and objectives. The integrity of the financial reporting framework depends on the standard setter's ability to balance various points of view.

5.   THE INTERNATIONAL FINANCIAL REPORTING STANDARDS FRAMEWORK

The IFRS *Framework for the Preparation and Presentation of Financial Statements* (referred to here as the "Framework") sets forth the concepts that underlie the preparation and presentation of financial statements for external uses. The Framework is designed to assist the IASB in developing standards and to instruct preparers of financial statements on the principles of financial statement construction. Importantly, the Framework is also designed to assist users of financial statements—including financial analysts—in interpreting the information contained therein.

The Framework is diagrammed in Exhibit 3-2. The top part shows how the objective of financial statements determines the characteristics that the reporting elements (relating to performance and financial position) should embody. In practice, decisions in financial statement preparation must satisfy a number of constraints, such as cost–benefit trade-offs. Finally, underlying financial statement preparation, and, therefore, placed at the bottom of the exhibit, are certain important assumptions.

In the following, we discuss the Framework starting at the center: the objective of financial statements.

5.1.   Objective of Financial Statements

At the center of the Framework is the objective: fair presentation of the company's financial position, its financial performance, and its cash flows. All other aspects of the Framework flow from that central objective.

Fair presentation to whom? And for what purpose? The introduction to the Framework states that the objective of financial statements is to provide information about the financial position, performance, and changes in financial position of an entity; this information should be useful to a wide range of users for the purpose of making economic decisions.[8]

The range of users includes investors, employees, lenders, suppliers, other creditors, customers, government agencies, the public, and analysts. The purpose of all this information

---

[7]The second attempt was successful and FASB Statement 123R now requires the expensing of stock options.

[8]*Framework for the Preparation and Presentation of Financial Statements,* IASC, 1989, adopted by IASB 2001, paragraph 12.

EXHIBIT 3-2   IFRS Framework for the Preparation and Presentation of Financial Statements

*Reliability = Faithful representation, substance over form, neutrality, prudence, completeness

is to be useful in making economic decisions. The types of economic decisions differ by users, so the specific information needed differs as well. However, although these users may have unique information needs, there are some information needs that are common across all users. One common need is for information about the company's financial position: its resources and its financial obligations. Information about a company's financial performance explains how and why the company's financial position changed in the past and can be useful in evaluating potential changes in the future. The third common information need reflected in the Framework diagram is the need for information about a company's cash. How did the company obtain cash? By selling its products and services, borrowing, other? How did the company use cash? Paying expenses, investing in new equipment, paying dividends, other?

5.2. Qualitative Characteristics of Financial Statements

Flowing from the central objective of providing a *fair presentation* of information that is *useful* to decision makers, the Framework elaborates on what constitutes usefulness. The Framework identifies four principal qualitative characteristics that make financial information useful: understandability, relevance, reliability, and comparability.[9]

1. *Understandability.* Understandability of information is defined in terms of who should be able to understand it. The Framework specifies that the information should be readily understandable by users who have a basic knowledge of business, economic activities, and accounting, and who have a willingness to study the information with reasonable diligence.
2. *Relevance.* Relevance of information is defined in terms of whether the information influences economic decisions of users, helping them to evaluate past, present, and future events, or to confirm or correct their past evaluations. Relevant information is typically timely, rather than dated. Relevant information is detailed enough to help users assess the risks and opportunities of a company (e.g., information on business segments or geographical segments). In choosing the level of detail to present, a criterion of materiality is applied. **Materiality** means that omission or misstatement of the information could make a difference to users' decisions.
3. *Reliability.* Reliable information is free from material error and bias. It is information that a user can depend upon to represent a company's financial situation faithfully and completely (within the bounds of materiality and cost). Reliable information also reflects economic reality, not just the legal form of a transaction or event. The following factors contribute to reliability:
   - *Faithful representation.* Information must represent faithfully the transactions and other events it either purports to represent or could reasonably be expected to represent.
   - *Substance over form.* It is necessary that transactions and other events be accounted for and represented in accordance with their substance and economic reality and not merely their legal form.
   - *Neutrality.* Information contained in the financial statements must be neutral—that is, free from bias.
   - *Prudence.* Prudence is the inclusion of a degree of caution in making the estimates required under conditions of uncertainty. It does not, however, allow the deliberate misstatement of elements in the financial statements in an attempt to be conservative by providing for hidden reserves or excessive provisions.
   - *Completeness.* Financial statements must be complete within the bounds of materiality and cost.
4. *Comparability.* Information should be presented in a consistent manner over time and in a consistent manner between entities to enable users to make significant comparisons.

Financial information exhibiting these principal qualitative characteristics normally results in fair presentation (sometimes termed a *true and fair view*).

CRRU

[9]Ibid., paragraphs 24–42.

5.3.   Constraints on Financial Statements

Although it would be ideal for financial statements to exhibit all of these qualitative characteristics and thus to achieve maximal usefulness, there are several constraints in achieving this goal.[10]

One constraint is the necessity for trade-offs across the desirable characteristics. For example, to be relevant, information must be timely; however, it may take considerable time to ensure the information is error-free (i.e., reliable). The aim is a balance between relevance and reliability.

Another constraint on useful financial information is the cost of providing this information. Optimally, benefits derived from information should exceed the cost of providing it. Again, the aim is a balance between costs and benefits.

A further constraint involves what financial statements omit. Financial statements, by necessity, omit information that is nonquantifiable. For example, the creativity, innovation, and competence of a company's work force are not directly captured in the financial statements. Similarly, customer loyalty, a positive corporate culture, environmental respectfulness, and many other nonquantifiable aspects about a company are not directly reflected in the financial statements. Of course, to the extent that these nonquantifiable items result in superior financial performance, a company's financial reports will reflect the results.

EXAMPLE 3-4   Balancing Qualitative Characteristics of Useful Information

A trade-off between qualitative characteristics often occurs. For example, when a company records sales revenue, it is required to simultaneously estimate and record an expense for potential bad debts (uncollectible accounts). This is considered to provide relevant information about the net profits for the accounting period. However, because bad debts may not be known with certainty until a later period, there is a sacrifice of reliability. The bad debt expense is simply an estimate. It is apparent that it is not always possible to simultaneously fulfill all qualitative characteristics.

5.4.   The Elements of Financial Statements

Financial statements portray the financial effects of transactions and other events by grouping them into broad classes (elements) according to their economic characteristics.

Three elements of financial statements are directly related to the measurement of the financial position: assets, liabilities, and equity.[11]

- *Assets.* Resources controlled by the enterprise as a result of past events and from which future economic benefits are expected to flow to the enterprise. Assets are what a company owns (e.g., inventory and equipment).

---

[10]Ibid., paragraphs 43–45.
[11]Ibid., paragraph 49.

- *Liabilities.* Present obligations of an enterprise arising from past events, the settlement of which is expected to result in an outflow of resources embodying economic benefits. Liabilities are what a company owes (e.g., bank borrowings).
- *Equity* (commonly known as *shareholders' equity*). Assets less liabilities. Equity is the residual interest in the assets after subtracting the liabilities.

The elements of financial statements directly related to the measurement of performance are income and expenses.[12]

- *Income.* Increases in economic benefits in the form of inflows or enhancements of assets, or decreases of liabilities that result in an increase in equity (other than increases resulting from contributions by owners). Income includes both revenues and gains. Revenues represent income from the ordinary activities of the enterprise (e.g., the sale of products). Gains may result from ordinary activities or other activities (the sale of surplus equipment).
- *Expenses.* Decreases in economic benefits in the form of outflows or depletions of assets, or increases in liabilities that result in decreases in equity (other than decreases because of distributions to owners). Expenses include losses, as well as those items normally thought of as expenses, such as the cost of goods sold or wages.

5.4.1. Underlying Assumptions in Financial Statements

At the base of the Framework, two important assumptions underlying financial statements are shown: accrual basis and going concern. These assumptions determine how financial statement elements are recognized and measured.[13]

Accrual basis refers to the underlying assumption that financial statements aim to reflect transactions when they actually occur, not necessarily when cash movements occur. For example, accrual accounting specifies that a company reports revenues *when they are earned*, regardless of whether the company received cash before delivering the product, after delivering the product, or at the time of delivery.

Going concern refers to the assumption that the company will continue in business for the foreseeable future. To illustrate, consider the value of a company's inventory if it is assumed that the inventory can be sold over a normal period of time versus the value of that same inventory if it is assumed that the inventory must all be sold in a day (or a week). Companies with the intent to liquidate or materially curtail operations would require different information for a fair presentation.

EXAMPLE 3-5   Going Concern

In reporting the financial position of a company that is assumed to be a going concern, it may be appropriate to list assets at some measure of a current value based upon normal market conditions. However, if a company is expected to cease operations and be liquidated, it may be more appropriate to list such assets at an appropriate liquidation value, namely, a value that would be obtained in a forced sale.

---

[12]Ibid., paragraph 70.
[13]Ibid., paragraphs 22 and 23.

5.4.2. Recognition of Financial Statement Elements

Recognition is the process of incorporating in the balance sheet or income statement an item that meets the definition of an element and satisfies the criteria for recognition. A financial statement element (assets, liabilities, equity, income, and expenses) should be recognized in the financial statements if[14]

- It is *probable* that any future economic benefit associated with the item will flow to or from the enterprise; and
- The item has a cost or value that can be *measured with reliability.*

5.4.3. Measurement of Financial Statement Elements

Measurement is the process of determining the monetary amounts at which the elements of the financial statements are to be recognized and carried in the balance sheet and income statement. The following alternative bases of measurement are used to different degrees and in varying combinations to measure assets and liabilities:

- *Historical cost.* Historical cost is simply the amount of cash or cash equivalents paid to purchase an asset, including any costs of acquisition and/or preparation. If the asset was not bought for cash, historical cost is the fair value of whatever was given in order to buy the asset. When referring to liabilities, the historical cost basis of measurement means the amount of proceeds received in exchange for the obligation.
- *Current cost.* In reference to assets, current cost is the amount of cash or cash equivalents that would have to be paid to buy the same or an equivalent asset today. In reference to liabilities, the current cost basis of measurement means the undiscounted amount of cash or cash equivalents that would be required to settle the obligation today.
- *Realizable (settlement) value.* In reference to assets, realizable value is the amount of cash or cash equivalents that could currently be obtained by selling the asset in an orderly disposal. For liabilities, the equivalent to realizable value is called *settlement value*—that is, settlement value is the undiscounted amount of cash or cash equivalents expected to be paid to satisfy the liabilities in the normal course of business.
- *Present value.* For assets, present value is the present discounted value of the future net cash inflows that the asset is expected to generate in the normal course of business. For liabilities, present value is the present discounted value of the future net cash outflows that are expected to be required to settle the liabilities in the normal course of business.
- *Fair value.* Fair value is the amount at which an asset could be exchanged, or a liability settled, between knowledgeable, willing parties in an arm's-length transaction, which may involve either market measures or present value measures.

5.5. General Requirements for Financial Statements

The Framework provides a basis for establishing standards and the elements of financial statements, but it does not address the contents of the financial statements. Having discussed the Framework, we now need to address the general requirements for financial statements.

The required financial statements, the fundamental principles underlying their presentation, and the principles of presentation are provided by International Accounting Standard (IAS) No. 1, *Presentation of Financial Statements.* These general requirements are illustrated in Exhibit 3-3 and described in the subsections below.

---

[14]Ibid., paragraph 83.

EXHIBIT 3-3   IASB General Requirements for Financial Statements

> **Required Financial Statements**
>
> - Balance sheet
> - Income statement
> - Statement of changes in equity
> - Cash flow statement
> - Accounting policies and notes

Fundamental Principles

- Fair presentation
- Going concern
- Accrual basis
- Consistency
- Materiality

Presentation Requirements

- Aggregation where appropriate
- No offsetting
- Classified balance sheet
- Minimum information on face
- Minimum note disclosures
- Comparative information

In the following, we discuss required financial statements, the fundamental principles underlying the preparation of financial statements, and the principles of presentation in greater detail.

5.5.1. Required Financial Statements

Under IAS No. 1, a complete set of financial statements includes:[15]

- A balance sheet.
- An income statement.
- A statement of changes in equity showing either
  - all changes in equity, or
  - changes in equity other than those arising from transactions with equity holders acting in their capacity as equity holders.[16]
- A cash flow statement.
- Notes comprising a summary of significant accounting policies and other explanatory notes.

Entities are encouraged to furnish other related financial and nonfinancial information in addition to the financial statements. Financial statements need to present fairly the financial position, financial performance, and cash flows of an entity.

---

[15]IAS No. 1, *Presentation of Financial Statements,* paragraph 8.

[16]Examples of transactions with equityholders acting in their capacity as equityholders include sale of equity securities to investors, distributions of earnings to investors, and repurchases of equity securities from investors.

5.5.2. Fundamental Principles Underlying the Preparation of Financial Statements

A company that applies the IFRS states explicitly in the notes to its financial statements that it is in compliance with the standards. Except in extremely rare circumstances, such a statement is only made when a company is in compliance with *all* requirements of IFRS.

IAS No. 1 specifies a number of fundamental principles underlying the preparation of financial statements. These principles clearly reflect the Framework.

- *Fair presentation.* The application of IFRS is presumed to result in financial statements that achieve a fair presentation. The IAS describes fair presentation as follows:

  Fair presentation requires faithful representation of the effects of transactions, events and conditions in accordance with the definitions and recognition criteria for assets, liabilities, income and expenses set out in the Framework.[17]

- *Going concern.* Financial statements are prepared on a going concern basis unless management either intends to liquidate the entity or to cease trading, or has no realistic alternative but to do so. If not presented on a going concern basis, the fact and rationale should be disclosed.
- *Accrual basis.* Financial statements (except for cash flow information) are to be prepared using the accrual basis of accounting.
- *Consistency.* The presentation and classification of items in the financial statements are usually retained from one period to the next. Comparative information of prior periods is disclosed for all amounts reported in the financial statements, unless an IFRS requires or permits otherwise.
- *Materiality.* Omissions or misstatements of items are material if they could, individually or collectively, influence the economic decisions of users taken on the basis of the financial statements. Any material item shall be presented separately.

5.5.3. Presentation Requirements

IAS No. 1 also specifies a number of principles that guide the presentation of financial statements. These principles include the following:

- *Aggregation.* Each material class of similar items is presented separately. Dissimilar items are presented separately unless they are immaterial.
- *No offsetting.* Assets and liabilities, and income and expenses, are not offset unless required or permitted by an IFRS.
- *Classified balance sheet.* The balance sheet should distinguish between current and noncurrent assets, and between current and noncurrent liabilities unless a presentation based on liquidity provides more relevant and reliable information (e.g., in the case of a bank or similar financial institution).
- *Minimum information on the face of the financial statements.* IAS No. 1 specifies the minimum line item disclosures on the face of, or in the notes to, the balance sheet, the income statement, and the statement of changes in equity. For example, companies are specifically required to disclose the amount of their plant, property, and equipment as a line item on the face of the balance sheet. The specific requirements are listed in Exhibit 3-4.

---

[17]IAS No. 1, *Presentation of Financial Statements,* paragraph 13.

EXHIBIT 3-4   IAS No. 1: Minimum Required Line Items in Financial Statements

On the face of the balance sheet	Plant, property, and equipment
	Investment property
	Intangible assets
	Financial assets (not listed in other line items)
	Investments accounted for using the equity method
	Biological assets
	Inventories
	Trade and other receivables
	Cash and cash equivalents
	Trade and other payables
	Provisions
	Financial liabilities (not listed in other line items)
	Liabilities and assets for current tax
	Deferred tax liabilities and deferred tax assets
	Minority interest, presented within equity
	Issued capital and reserves attributable to equity holders of the parent
On the face of the income statement	Revenue
	Finance costs
	Share of the profit or loss of associates and joint ventures accounted for using the equity method
	Pretax gain or loss recognized on the disposal of assets or settlement of liabilities attributable to discontinuing operations
	Tax expense
	Profit or loss
	Profit or loss attributable to minority interest
	Profit or loss attributable to equity holders of the parent
On the face of the statement of changes in equity	Profit or loss for the period
	Each item of income and expense for the period that, as required by other Standards or by Interpretations, is recognized directly in equity, and the total of these items
	Total income and expense for the period, showing separately the total amounts attributable to equity holders of the parent and to minority interest
	For each component of equity, the effects of changes in accounting policies and corrections of errors recognized in accordance with IAS No. 8

- *Minimum information in the notes* (or on face of financial statements). IAS No. 1 specifies disclosures about information to be presented in the financial statements. This information must be provided in a systematic manner and cross-referenced from the face of the financial statements to the notes. The required information is summarized in Exhibit 3-5.

EXHIBIT 3-5   Summary of IFRS Required Disclosures in the Notes to the Financial Statements

Disclosure of accounting policies	Measurement bases used in preparing financial statements
	Each accounting policy used even if not covered by the IFRS
	Judgments made in applying accounting policies that have the most significant effect on the amounts recognized in the financial statements
Estimation uncertainty	Key assumptions about the future and other key sources of estimation uncertainty that have a significant risk of causing material adjustment to the carrying amount of assets and liabilities within the next year
Other disclosures	Description of the entity, including its domicile, legal form country of incorporation, and registered office or business address
	Nature of operations or principal activities, or both
	Name of parent and ultimate parent

- *Comparative information.* For all amounts reported in a financial statement, comparative information should be provided for the previous period unless another standard requires or permits otherwise. Such comparative information allows users to better understand reported amounts.

6. COMPARISON OF IFRS WITH ALTERNATIVE REPORTING SYSTEMS

The recent adoption of IFRS as the required financial reporting standard by the EU and other countries has advanced the goal of global convergence. Nevertheless, there are still significant differences in financial reporting in the global capital markets. Arguably, the most critical are the differences that exist between IFRS and U.S. GAAP. After the EU adoption of IFRS in 2005, these two reporting standards account for a significant number of the world's listed companies.

This section will discuss the differences between IFRS and U.S. GAAP that affect the framework and general financial reporting requirements. The chapters on individual financial statements will review in more detail the differences in these financial reporting standards as they apply to specific financial statements. The chapter on the convergence of international standards also makes relevant points.

6.1. U.S. GAAP

The FASB or its predecessor organizations have been issuing financial reporting standards in the United States since the 1930s. Currently, the FASB is the primary body setting these standards. There are, however, several other organizations that have issued guidance in the past. These include the American Institute of Certified Public Accountants' (AICPA) Accounting Standards Executive Committee (AcSEC), the Emerging Issues Task Force (EITF), and the FASB staff. Since the introduction of the Sarbanes–Oxley Act, changes have been made that essentially limit these other bodies from providing any new guidance unless it is directly under the direction of the FASB. The EITF has come under the more formal oversight of the FASB, and the AICPA's AcSEC will no longer issue new standards applicable to public companies.

6.1.1. U.S. GAAP Authoritative Guidance

Together, the standards and interpretations issued by these bodies comprise U.S. GAAP. A "GAAP hierarchy" was established to provide guidance as to the order of authority of the various sources of accounting pronouncements. In other words, the GAAP hierarchy defines the sources of accounting principles and a framework for selecting the right principle. This hierarchy is especially important for new transactions and those policies where there is no explicit authoritative guidance. The GAAP hierarchy was originally established in the auditing area rather than the accounting area, but it is currently being reexamined by the FASB. The FASB is also working on a project to bring all authoritative guidance from these various sources into one set of authoritative literature called the "Codification."

The top level of the hierarchy includes standards issued by the FASB. If an answer is not found at that level, preparers and auditors consider other sources of GAAP. The literature referred to in the GAAP hierarchy that comprises U.S. GAAP is extensive. The FASB has stated that there are more than 2,000 pronouncements comprising U.S. GAAP. The FASB alone has issued 7 concept statements, 153 standards, 47 interpretations, and numerous technical bulletins. Recently, the FASB began issuing FASB staff positions, which provide still another source of U.S. GAAP.

As these standards have been developed over many years and by various bodies, they are more a patchwork than a cohesive framework. Although U.S. GAAP does have an explicit conceptual framework that was developed in the late 1970s/early 1980s, not all of the standards adhere completely to the framework. Some standards were developed prior to the framework and certain of the more recent standards are rule based as preparers and auditors request detailed rules and clear-cut do's and don'ts in an effort to reduce the need for judgment.

6.1.2. Role of the SEC in U.S. GAAP

U.S. GAAP, as established by the standard-setting bodies noted above, is officially recognized as authoritative by the SEC (Financial Reporting Release No. 1, section 101, and reaffirmed in the April 2003 Policy Statement). However, the SEC retains the authority to establish standards. Although it has rarely overruled the FASB, the SEC does issue staff accounting bulletins (SABs). SABs reflect the SEC's views regarding accounting-related disclosure practices and can be found on the SEC web site.

6.1.3. Convergence of the U.S. GAAP and IASB Framework

A joint IASB–FASB project was begun in October 2004 to develop a common conceptual framework. The project, which currently has a five-year timetable, is divided into seven phases. The initial focus is on achieving the convergence of the frameworks and improving particular aspects of the framework dealing with objectives, qualitative characteristics, elements recognition, and measurement. A December 2004 discussion paper presented the broad differences between the two frameworks. These differences are summarized in Exhibit 3-6. Additionally, under U.S. GAAP, there is not a single standard like IAS No. 1 that specifies the presentation of financial statements; instead, standards for presentation of financial statements are dispersed in many different FASB pronouncements and SEC regulations.

6.2. Implications of Other Reporting Systems

As more countries adopt IFRS, the need to examine other financial reporting systems will be minimized. Additionally, the IASB and FASB are considering frameworks from other jurisdictions in developing their joint framework. Nevertheless, analysts are likely

EXHIBIT 3-6   Summary of Differences between IFRS and U.S. GAAP Frameworks

	U.S. GAAP (FASB) Framework
Purpose of the framework	The FASB framework is similar to the IASB framework in its purpose to assist in developing and revising standards, but it resides at a lower level in the hierarchy—a very important difference. Under IFRS, management is expressly required to consider the framework if there is no standard or interpretation for that issue. The FASB framework does not have a similar provision.
Objectives of financial statements	There is general agreement on the objectives of financial statements: Both frameworks have a broad focus to provide relevant information to a wide range of users. The principle difference is that the U.S. GAAP framework provides separate objectives for business entities versus nonbusiness entities rather than one objective as in the IASB framework.
Underlying assumptions	Although the U.S. GAAP framework recognizes the importance of the accrual and going concern assumptions, these are not given as much prominence as in the IASB framework. In particular, the going concern assumption is not well developed in the FASB framework.
Qualitative characteristics	The U.S. GAAP framework identifies the same qualitative characteristics but also establishes a hierarchy of those characteristics. Relevance and reliability are considered primary qualities, whereas comparability is deemed to be a secondary quality under the FASB framework. The fourth qualitative characteristic, understandability, is treated as a user-specific quality in the U.S. GAAP framework and is seen as a link between the characteristics of individual users and decision-specific qualities of information. The FASB framework indicates that it cannot base its decisions on the specific circumstances of individual users.
Constraints	There is similar discussion of the constraints in both frameworks.
Financial statement elements (definition, recognition, and measurement)	*Performance elements.* The FASB framework includes three elements relating to financial performance in addition to revenue and expenses: gains, losses, and comprehensive income. Comprehensive income is a more encompassing concept than net income, as it includes all changes in equity during a period except those resulting from investments by and distributions to owners.
	Financial position elements. The FASB framework defines an asset as "a future economic benefit" rather than the "resource" from which future economic benefits are expected to flow to the entity as in the IASB framework. It also includes the term *probable* to define the assets and liabilities elements. As discussed below, the term *probable* is part of the IASB framework recognition criteria. Additionally, the frameworks have different meanings of probable.
	Recognition of elements. The FASB framework does not discuss the term *probable* in its recognition criteria, whereas the IASB framework requires that it is probable that any future economic benefit flow to/from the entity. The FASB framework also has a separate recognition criterion of relevance.
	Measurement of elements. Measurement attributes (historical cost, current cost, settlement value, current market value, and present value) are broadly consistent, and both frameworks lack fully developed measurement concepts. Furthermore, the FASB framework prohibits revaluations except for certain categories of financial instruments, which have to be carried at fair value.

to encounter financial statements that are prepared on a basis other than IFRS. Although the number and relevance of different local GAAP reporting systems are likely to decline, industry-specific financial reports—such as those required for banking or insurance companies—will continue to exist.

6.3. Reconciliation of Financials Prepared According to Different Standards

When analyzing financial statements created under different frameworks, reconciliation schedules and disclosures regarding the significant differences between the reporting bases are usually available. For example, the SEC currently requires reconciliation for foreign private issuers that do not prepare financial statements in accordance with U.S. GAAP. The EU is currently considering requiring reconciliations for companies trading on European markets that do not prepare financial statements using IFRS. Such reconciliations can reveal additional information related to the more judgmental components of the financial statements and can have important implications for security valuation.

A first look at the disclosure related to any such differences can sometimes be daunting, particularly if the reconciliation is lengthy. For example, Syngenta's 2005 U.S. SEC Form 20-F filing discusses these differences in Note 33, "Significant Differences between IFRS and United States Generally Accepted Accounting Principles." This note is longer than 15 pages!

Given the length of reconciliation disclosure, a systematic method to quickly digest the information can be helpful. A good starting point is the chart that provides the numerical reconciliation of net income and shareholders' equity (see Exhibit 3-7). These reconciliations can

EXHIBIT 3-7   Reconciliation of GAAP Income—Syngenta (US$ millions)

	2005	2004	2003 (adjusted)
Net income (loss) reported under IFRS attributable to Syngenta AG shareholders	622	460	248
U.S. GAAP adjustments:			
Purchase accounting: Zaneca agrochemicals business	(7)	62	43
Purchase accounting: other acquisitions	(80)	(62)	(67)
Restructuring charges	(9)	47	32
Pension provisions (including post-retirement benefits)	(15)	43	2
Deferred taxes on stock-based compensation	3	(3)	2
Deferred taxes on unrealized profit in inventory	(33)	(61)	36
Impairment losses	(7)	(1)	
Other items	28	(17)	(4)
Valuation allowance against deferred tax assets	26	(34)	—
Tax on undistributed earnings of subsidiaries	1	(27)	—
Deferred tax effect of U.S. GAAP adjustments	27	(55)	(42)
Net income/(loss) reported under U.S. GAAP	556	352	250

Source: 2005 U.S. SEC Form 20-F.

be reviewed to identify the significant items; large amounts should be examined in more detail. The Syngenta disclosure indicates that the company's 2005 net income based on U.S. GAAP was $556 million, compared with the $622 million of net income reported under IFRS. The reconciliation indicates that most significant differences relate to accounting for acquisitions (purchase accounting adjustments include a $7 million decrease and an $80 million decrease), accounting for pension provisions ($15 million), and accounting for various tax-related items. In some instances, further analysis would be undertaken to determine the implications of each significant difference based on disclosures in the indicated notes.

7. EFFECTIVE FINANCIAL REPORTING

A discussion of the characteristics of an effective framework and the barriers to the creation of such a framework offer additional perspective on the financial reporting frameworks reviewed above.

7.1. Characteristics of an Effective Financial Reporting Framework

Any effective financial reporting system needs to be a coherent one (i.e., a framework in which all the pieces fit together according to an underlying logic). Such frameworks have several characteristics: _TCC_

- _Transparency._ A framework should enhance the transparency of a company's financial statements. Transparency means that users should be able to see the underlying economics of the business reflected clearly in the company's financial statements. Full disclosure and fair presentation create transparency.
- _Comprehensiveness._ To be comprehensive, a framework should encompass the full spectrum of transactions that have financial consequences. This spectrum includes not only transactions currently occurring but also new types of transactions as they are developed. So, an effective financial reporting framework is based on principles that are universal enough to provide guidance for recording both existing and newly developed transactions.
- _Consistency._ An effective framework should ensure reasonable consistency across companies and time periods. In other words, similar transactions should be measured and presented in a similar manner regardless of industry, company size, geography, or other characteristics. Balanced against this need for consistency, however, is the need for sufficient flexibility to allow companies sufficient discretion to report results in accordance with underlying economic activity.

7.2. Barriers to a Single Coherent Framework

Although effective frameworks all share the characteristics of transparency, comprehensiveness, and consistency, there are some conflicts that create inherent limitations in any financial reporting standards framework. Specifically, it is difficult to completely satisfy all these characteristics concurrently, so any framework represents an attempt to balance the relative importance of these characteristics. Three areas of conflict include valuation, standard-setting approach, and measurement.

- _Valuation._ As discussed, various bases for measuring the value of assets and liabilities exist, such as historical cost, current cost, realizable value, and present value. Historical cost valuation, under which an asset's value is its initial cost, requires minimal judgment. In contrast, other valuation approaches require considerable judgment. Over time, both the IASB and FASB have recognized that it may be more appropriate to measure certain elements of financial statements using some fair value method in spite of the judgment required.[18] Fair value is the amount at which an asset could be exchanged, or a liability settled, between knowledgeable willing parties in an arm's-length transaction; clearly, in many cases, determining fair value requires considerable judgment. Fair value may be more relevant, whereas historical cost may be more reliable.

- *Standard-setting approach.* Financial reporting standards can be established based on (1) principles, (2) rules, or (3) a combination of principles and rules (sometimes referred to as "objectives oriented"). A principles-based approach provides a broad financial reporting framework with little specific guidance on how to report a particular element or transaction. Such principles-based approaches require the preparers of financial reports and auditors to exercise considerable judgment in financial reporting. In contrast, a rules-based approach establishes specific rules for each element or transaction. Rules-based approaches are characterized by a list of yes-or-no rules, specific numerical tests for classifying certain transactions (known as *bright-line tests*), exceptions, and alternative treatments. The third alternative, an objectives-oriented approach, combines the other two approaches by including both a framework of principles and appropriate levels of implementation guidance.

   IFRS has been referred to as a "principles-based approach." The FASB, which has been criticized for having a rules-based approach in the past, has explicitly stated that it is moving to adopt a more objectives-oriented approach to standard setting. There is a joint project underway to develop a common conceptual framework, and this is likely to be more objectives oriented.

- *Measurement.* The balance sheet presents elements at a point in time, whereas the income statement reflects changes during a period of time. Because these statements are related, standards regarding one of the statements have an effect on the other statement. Financial reporting standards can be established taking an "asset/liability" approach, which gives preference to proper valuation of the balance sheet, or a "revenue/expense" approach that focuses more on the income statement. This conflict can result in one statement being reported in a theoretically sound manner, but the other statement reflecting less relevant information. In recent years, standard setters have predominantly used an asset/liability approach.

EXAMPLE 3-6   Conflicts between Measurement Approaches

Prime Retailers (PR), a U.S.-based distributor of men's shirts, has a policy of marking its merchandise up by $5 per unit. At the beginning of 2005, PR had 10,000 units of inventory on hand, which cost $15 per unit. During 2006, PR purchased 100,000 units of inventory at a cost of $22 per unit. Also during 2006, PR sold

---

[18]The FASB is currently developing a Fair Value Measurement standard that will be also be reviewed by the IASB. This standard is expected to be effective for fiscal years beginning after 15 November 2007 in the United States.

100,000 units of inventory at $27 per unit. How shall PR reflect the cost of the inventory sold: $15 or $22?

In order to match current costs with current revenues, PR (which does not operate in an IFRS jurisdiction) may decide that it is appropriate to use a method of inventory costing that assumes that the most recently purchased inventory is sold first. So, the assumption is that the 100,000 units of sales had a cost of $22. A partial income statement for PR would be:

Sales	$2,700,000
Cost of sales	2,200,000
Gross profit	$500,000

The gross profit reflected in this manner reflects the current cost of goods matched with the current level of revenues.

But PR still has 10,000 units of inventory on hand. The assumption must be that the 10,000 remaining units had a cost of $15 per unit. Therefore, the value of the inventory reflected on the balance sheet would be $150,000.

Although the income statement reflects current costs, the remaining inventory on the balance sheet does not reflect current information. The inventory is reflected at the older cost of $15 per unit. An analyst would likely find this older cost less relevant than the current cost of that inventory.

8. MONITORING DEVELOPMENTS IN FINANCIAL REPORTING STANDARDS

In studying financial reporting and financial statement analysis in general, the analyst needs to be aware that reporting standards are evolving rapidly. Analysts need to monitor ongoing developments in financial reporting and assess their implications for security analysis and valuation. The need to monitor developments in financial reporting standards does not mean that analysts should be accountants. An accountant monitors these developments from a preparer's perspective; an analyst needs to monitor from a user's perspective. More specifically, analysts need to know how these developments will affect financial reports.

Analysts can remain aware of developments in financial reporting standards by monitoring three areas: new products or transactions, actions of standard setters and other groups representing users of financials statements (such as CFA Institute), and company disclosures regarding critical accounting policies and estimates.

8.1. New Products or Types of Transactions

New products and new types of transactions can have unusual or unique elements to them such that no explicit guidance in the financial reporting standards exists. New products or transactions typically arise from economic events, such as new businesses (e.g., the Internet), or from a newly developed financial instrument or financial structure. Financial instruments, exchange-traded or not, are typically designed to enhance a company's business or to mitigate inherent risks. However, at times, financial instruments or structured transactions have been developed primarily for purposes of financial report "window dressing."

Although companies might discuss new products and transactions in their financial reports, the analyst can also monitor business journals and the capital markets to identify such items. Additionally, when one company in an industry develops a new product or transaction, other companies in the industry often do the same. Once new products, financial instruments, or structured transactions are identified, it is helpful to gain an understanding of the business purpose. If necessary, an analyst can obtain further information from a company's management, which should be able to describe the economic purpose, the financial statement reporting, significant estimates, judgments applied in determining the reporting, and future cash flow implications for these items. The financial reporting framework presented here is useful in evaluating the potential effect on financial statements even though a standard may not have been issued as to how to report a particular transaction.

8.2. Evolving Standards and the Role of CFA Institute

Although the actions of standard setters and regulators are unlikely to be helpful in identifying new products and transactions given the lag between new product development and regulatory action, monitoring the actions of these authorities is, nonetheless, important for another reason: Changes in regulations can affect companies' financial reports and, thus, valuations. This is particularly true if the financial reporting standards change to require more explicit identification of matters affecting asset/liability valuation or financial performance. For example, a recent regulatory change requires companies to report the value of employee stock options as an expense in the income statement. Prior to the required expensing, an analyst could assess the impact of stock options on a company's performance and the dilutive effect to shareholders by reviewing information disclosed in the notes to the financial statements. To the extent that some market participants do not examine financial statement details and thus ignore this expense when valuing a company's securities, more explicit identification could affect the value of the company's securities.

The IASB and FASB have numerous major projects under way that will most likely result in new standards. It is important to keep up to date on these evolving standards. The IASB (www.iasb.org) and FASB (www.fasb.org) provide a great deal of information on their web sites regarding new standards and proposals for future changes in standards. In addition, the IASB and FASB seek input from the financial analyst community—those who regularly use financial statements in making investment and credit decisions. When a new standard is proposed, an exposure draft is made available and users of financial statements can draft comment letters and position papers for submission to the IASB and FASB in order to evaluate the proposal.

CFA Institute is active through its CFA Centre for Financial Market Integrity in advocating improvements to financial reporting. Volunteer members of CFA Institute serve on several liaison committees that meet regularly to make recommendations to the IASB and FASB on proposed standards and to draft comment letters and position papers. You can view the CFA Centre's positions on financial reporting issues at www.cfainstitute.org/cfacentre/.

In October 2005, the CFA Centre issued a position paper titled *A Comprehensive Business Reporting Model: Financial Reporting for Investors*, which provides a suggested model for significantly improving financial reporting. The position paper states:

> *Corporate financial statements and their related disclosures are critical to sound investment decision making. The well being of the world's financial markets, and of the millions of investors who entrust their financial present and future to those markets, depends*

directly on the quality of the information financial statements and disclosures provide. Consequently, the quality of the information drives global financial markets. The quality, in turn, depends directly on the quality of the principles and standards by which managers recognize and measure the economic activities and events affecting their companies' operations. To succeed, a partnership is needed among standard setters, common shareowners, and other investors to bring full transparency and the highest integrity to the standards and the processes by which those standards are developed. CFA Institute and the CFA Centre for Financial Market Integrity are committed to join in a partnership to improve financial market integrity in the 21st century.[19]

Among other principles, the proposed model stresses the importance of information regarding the current fair value of assets and liabilities, of neutrality in financial reporting, and of providing detailed information on cash flows to investors through the choice of the so-called direct format for the cash flow statement.[20]

In summary, analysts can improve their investment decision making by keeping current on financial reporting standards, and various web-based sources provide the means to do so. In addition, analysts can contribute to improving financial reporting by sharing their users' perspective with standard-setting bodies, which typically invite comments concerning proposed changes.

8.3. Company Disclosures

A good source for obtaining information regarding the effect of financial reporting standards on a company's financial statements is typically the company itself. This information is provided in the footnotes to the financial statements and accompanying discussion.

8.3.1. Disclosures Relating to Critical and Significant Accounting Policies

As noted earlier, financial reporting standards need to restrict alternatives but retain flexibility in allowing enterprises to match their accounting methods with underlying economics. As a result, companies choose among alternative accounting policies (e.g., depreciation methods) and use estimates (e.g., depreciable lives of assets). Under both IFRS and U.S. GAAP, companies are required to disclose their accounting policies and estimates in the footnotes to the financial statements. Public companies must discuss their accounting policies and estimates in management's discussion and analysis (MD&A). This disclosure indicates the policies that management deems most important. Although many of the policies are discussed in both the MD&A and the footnotes to the financial statement, there is typically a distinction between the two discussions. The MD&A disclosure relates to those policies that require significant judgments and estimates, whereas the footnote discusses all accounting policies, irrespective of whether judgment was required. Each disclosure has value.

In analyzing financial reporting disclosures, the following questions should be addressed:

- What policies have been discussed?
- Do these policies appear to cover all of the significant balances on the financial statements?
- Which policies are identified as requiring significant estimates?
- Have there been any changes in these disclosures from one year to the next?

---

[19]*A Comprehensive Business Reporting Model: Financial Reporting for Investors*, CFA Institute Centre for Financial Market Integrity, 24 October 2005, p. 3.

[20]See the chapter on understanding the cash flow statement for further information on the direct format.

Example 3-7 summarizes the accounting policies discussed in Disney's 2004 annual report MD&A and Note 2, "Summary of Significant Accounting Policy."

Two items usually requiring significant judgment include revenue recognition and timing of reporting the related expenses. As a result, the types of judgments and estimates in revenue recognition and expense reporting are usually discussed in both the MD&A and in the footnotes.

EXAMPLE 3-7   List of Significant Accounting Policy Disclosures: Disney MD&A Notes

- Film and television revenue and costs
- Revenue recognition
- Pension and post-retirement benefit plan actuarial assumptions
- Goodwill, intangible assets, long-lived assets, and investments
- Contingencies and litigation
- Income tax audit
- Principles of consolidation
- Accounting changes
- Use of estimates
- Advertising expenses
- Cash and cash equivalents
- Investments
- Translation policy
- Inventories
- Film and television costs
- Capitalized software costs
- Parks, resorts, and other property
- Goodwill and other intangible assets
- Risk management contracts
- Earnings per share
- Stock options
- Reclassifications

8.3.2. Disclosures Regarding the Impact of Recently Issued Accounting Standards

Internationally, public companies face disclosure requirements related to recently issued accounting standards. In the United States, the SEC (in its SABs) also requires public companies to provide information regarding the likely future impact of recently issued accounting standards. Under IFRS, IAS No. 8 similarly requires discussion about pending implementations of new standards and the known or estimable information relevant to assessing the impact of the new standards. These disclosures can alert an analyst to significant changes in reported financial statement amounts that could affect security valuation.

Although each discussion will be different, the conclusions that a company can reach about a new standard include:

- The standard does not apply.
- The standard will have no material impact.
- Management is still evaluating the impact.
- The impact of adoption is discussed.

Exhibit 3-8 provides some of the disclosures provided by Syngenta in its 2004 Form 20-F relating to recently issued accounting standards. In the exhibit, "IFRIC" refers to the International Financial Reporting Interpretations Committee—formerly known as the Standing Interpretations Committee or SIC—which is responsible for interpreting IAS and IFRS.

Clearly, disclosures indicating the expected impact provide the most meaningful information. In addition, disclosures indicating that the standard does not apply or will not have a material effect are also helpful. However, disclosures indicating that management is still evaluating the impact of a new standard create some uncertainty about whether the change might materially affect the company.

EXHIBIT 3-8   Impact of Recently Issued Accounting Standards: Syngenta (emphasis added)

Standard does not apply	IFRIC amendment to SIC-12, "Special Purpose Entities," was published in October 2004 and requires employee share trusts and similar entities established under share participation plans to be consolidated with effect from 1 January 2005. *Syngenta operates its employee share participation plans without using entities of this type, and the amendment will have no effect on the consolidated financial statements.*
No material impact	Amendment to IAS No. 39, "Transition and Initial Recognition of Financial Assets and Financial Liabilities," was issued in December 2004. It will be effective from Syngenta as from 1 January 2005. The amendment changes the transitional requirements on adoption of IAS No. 39 (revised December 2003). *Syngenta does not expect the amendment to have a material effect on its consolidated financial statements.*
Evaluating the impact	IFRIC 4, "Determining Whether an Arrangement Contains a Lease," was issued in December 2004 and requires contracts for the supply of goods or services that depend upon the use of a specific asset to be treated in certain circumstances as containing a lease of that asset in addition to a supply contract. IFRIC 4 will be mandatory for Syngenta with effect from 1 January 2006. *During 2005, Syngenta will assess the impact on its consolidated financial statements from adopting IFRIC 4.*
Impact described	As stated in Note 2 above, Syngenta will apply IFRS 3, "Business Combinations," and the related revisions to IAS No. 36 and IAS No. 38, to all previous business combinations with effect from 1 January 2005. *Goodwill amortization expense will no longer be recorded. Goodwill amortization expense on these acquisitions in 2004 was US$56 million. The related tax credit was US$2 million because in most cases the amortization is not tax deductible. Syngenta will test goodwill for impairment annually.*

9. SUMMARY

An awareness of the reporting framework underlying financial reports can assist in security valuation and other financial analysis. The framework describes the objectives of financial reporting, desirable characteristics for financial reports, the elements of financial reports, and the underlying assumptions and constraints of financial reporting. An understanding of the framework, broader than knowledge of a particular set of rules, offers an analyst a basis from which to infer the proper financial reporting, and thus security valuation implications, of *any* financial statement element or transaction.

We have discussed how financial reporting systems are developed, the conceptual objectives of financial reporting standards, the parties involved in standard-setting processes, and how financial reporting standards are converging into one global set of standards. A summary of the key points for each section is noted below:

- *The objective of financial reporting:*
  - The objective of financial statements is to provide information about the financial position, performance, and changes in financial position of an entity; this information should be useful to a wide range of users for the purpose of making economic decisions.[21]
  - Financial reporting requires policy choices and estimates. These choices and estimates require judgment, which can vary from one preparer to the next. Accordingly, standards are needed to attempt to ensure some type of consistency in these judgments.
- *Financial reporting standard-setting bodies and regulatory authorities.* Private sector standard-setting bodies and regulatory authorities play significant but different roles in the standard-setting process. In general, standard-setting bodies make the rules, and regulatory authorities enforce the rules. However, regulators typically retain legal authority to establish financial reporting standards in their jurisdiction.
- *Convergence of global financial reporting standards.* The IASB and FASB, along with other standard setters, are working to achieve convergence of financial reporting standards. Listed companies in many countries are adopting IFRS. Barriers to full convergence still exist.
- *The IFRS Framework.* The IFRS Framework sets forth the concepts that underlie the preparation and presentation of financial statements for external users, provides further guidance on the elements from which financial statements are constructed, and discusses concepts of capital and capital maintenance.
  - The objective of fair presentation of useful information is the center of the Framework. The qualitative characteristics of useful information include understandability, relevance, reliability, and comparability.
  - The IFRS Framework identifies the following elements of financial statements: assets, liabilities, equity, income, expense, and capital maintenance adjustments.
  - The Framework is constructed based on the underlying assumptions of accrual basis and going concern but acknowledges three inherent constraints: timeliness, benefit versus cost, and balance between qualitative characteristics.
- *IFRS financial statements.* IAS No. 1 prescribes that a complete set of financial statements includes a balance sheet, an income statement, a statement of changes in equity, a cash flow statement, and notes. The notes include a summary of significant accounting policies and other explanatory information.

---

[21] *Framework for the Preparation and Presentation of Financial Statements,* IASC, 1989, adopted by IASB 2001, paragraph 12.

- ○ Financial statements need to adhere to the fundamental principles of fair presentation, going concern, accrual basis, consistency, and materiality.
  - ○ Financial statements must also satisfy the presentation requirements of appropriate aggregation, no offsetting, and a classified balance sheet. Statements must provide the required minimum information on the face of the financial statements and note disclosures.
- *Comparison with alternative reporting systems.* A significant number of the world's listed companies report under either IFRS or U.S. GAAP. Although these standards are moving toward convergence, there are still significant differences in the framework and individual standards. Frequently, companies provide reconciliations and disclosures regarding the significant differences between reporting bases. These reconciliations can be reviewed to identify significant items that could affect security valuation.
- *Characteristics of a coherent financial reporting framework.* Effective frameworks share three characteristics: transparency, comprehensiveness, and consistency. Effective standards can, however, have conflicting approaches on valuation, the bases for standard setting (principle or rules based), and resolution of conflicts between balance sheet and income statement focus.
- *Monitoring developments.* Analysts can remain aware of ongoing developments in financial reporting by monitoring three areas: new products or transactions, standard setters' and regulators' actions, and company disclosures regarding critical accounting policies and estimates.

PRACTICE PROBLEMS

1. Which of the following is not an objective of financial statements as expressed by the International Accounting Standards Board?
   A. To provide information about the performance of an entity
   B. To provide information about the financial position of an entity
   C. To provide information about the users of an entity's financial statements

2. International accounting standards are currently developed by which entity?
   A. Financial Services Authority
   B. International Accounting Standards Board
   C. International Accounting Standards Committee

3. U.S. Financial Accounting Standards are currently developed by which entity?
   A. U.S. Congress
   B. Financial Services Authority
   C. Financial Accounting Standards Board

4. The SEC requires which of the following be issued to shareholders before a shareholder meeting?
   A. Form 10-K
   B. Statement of cash flow
   C. Proxy statement

5. According to the *Framework for the Preparation and Presentation of Financial Statements*, which of the following is a qualitative characteristic of information in financial statements?
   A. Accuracy
   B. Timeliness
   C. Comparability

6. Which of the following is *not* a constraint on the financial statements according to the IFRS Framework?
   A. Timeliness
   B. Understandability
   C. Benefit versus cost

7. The assumption that an entity will continue to operate for the foreseeable future is called
   A. accrual basis.
   B. comparability.
   C. going concern.

8. The assumption that the effects of transactions and other events are recognized when they occur, not necessarily when cash movements occur, is called
   A. accrual basis.
   B. going concern.
   C. relevance.

9. Neutrality of information in the financial statements most closely contributes to which qualitative characteristic?
   A. Relevance
   B. Reliability
   C. Comparability

10. Does fair presentation entail full disclosure and transparency?

	Full Disclosure	Transparency
A.	No	Yes
B.	Yes	No
C.	Yes	Yes

11. Valuing assets at the amount of cash or equivalents paid, or the fair value of the consideration given to acquire them at the time of acquisition, most closely describes which measurement of financial statement elements?
    A. Current cost
    B. Realizable cost
    C. Historical cost

12. The valuation technique under which assets are recorded at the amount that would be received in an orderly disposal is
    A. current cost.
    B. present value.
    C. realizable value.

13. Which of the following is not a required financial statement according to IAS No. 1?
    A. Income statement
    B. Statement of changes in equity
    C. Statement of changes in income

14. Which of the following elements of financial statements is most closely related to measurement of performance?
    A. Assets
    B. Expenses
    C. Liabilities

15. Which of the following elements of financial statements is most closely related to measurement of financial position?
    A. Equity
    B. Income
    C. Expenses

16. Which of the following is not a characteristic of a coherent financial reporting framework?
    A. Timeliness
    B. Consistency
    C. Transparency

17. In the past, the Financial Accounting Standards Board has been criticized as having
    A. a rules-based approach to standards.
    B. a principles-based approach to standards.
    C. an objectives-oriented approach to standards.

18. Which of the following types of discussions regarding new accounting standards in management's discussion would provide the most meaningful information to an analyst?
    A. The standard does not apply.
    B. The impact of adoption is discussed.
    C. The standard will have no material impact.

CHAPTER 4

UNDERSTANDING THE INCOME STATEMENT

Thomas R. Robinson, CFA

CFA Institute
Charlottesville, Virginia

Hennie van Greuning, CFA

World Bank
Washington, DC

Elaine Henry, CFA

University of Miami
Miami, Florida

Michael A. Broihahn, CFA

Barry University
Miami, Florida

LEARNING OUTCOMES

After completing this chapter, you will be able to do the following:

- Describe the components of the income statement and the alternative presentation formats of that statement.
- Discuss the general principles of revenue recognition and accrual accounting, specific revenue recognition applications (including accounting for long-term contracts, installment sales, barter transactions, gross and net reporting of revenue), and the implications of revenue recognition principles for financial analysis.

- Discuss the general principles of expense recognition, such as the matching principle, specific expense recognition applications (including depreciation of long-term assets and inventory methods), and the implications of expense recognition principles for financial analysis.
- Distinguish between the operating and nonoperating components of the income statement.
- Discuss the financial reporting treatment and analysis of nonrecurring items, including discontinued operations, extraordinary items, unusual or infrequent items, and changes in accounting standards.
- Describe the components of earnings per share and calculate a company's earnings per share (both basic and diluted earnings per share) for both a simple and complex capital structure.
- Evaluate a company's financial performance using common-size income statements and financial ratios based on the income statement.
- State the accounting classification for items that are excluded from the income statement but affect owners' equity, and list the major types of items receiving that treatment.
- Describe and calculate comprehensive income.

1. INTRODUCTION

The income statement presents information on the financial results of a company's business activities over a period of time. The income statement communicates how much revenue the company generated during a period and what costs it incurred in connection with generating that revenue. The basic equation underlying the income statement is: Revenue − Expense = Net income. The income statement is also called the *statement of operations* or *statement of earnings* or, sometimes, in business jargon, it is called the *P&L* (for profit and loss).

Investment analysts intensely scrutinize companies' income statements. Equity analysts are interested in them because equity markets often reward relatively high- or low-earnings growth companies with above-average or below-average valuations, respectively. Fixed-income analysts examine the components of income statements, past and projected, for information on companies' abilities to make promised payments on their debt over the course of the business cycle. Corporate financial announcements frequently emphasize income statements more than the other financial statements.

This chapter is organized as follows: Section 2 describes the components of the income statement and its format. Section 3 describes basic principles and selected applications related to the recognition of revenue, and section 4 describes basic principles and selected applications related to the recognition of expenses. Section 5 covers nonrecurring items and nonoperating items. Section 6 explains the calculation of earnings per share. Section 7 introduces income statement analysis. Section 8 explains comprehensive income and its reporting. Section 9 summarizes the chapter. Practice problems in the CFA Institute multiple-choice format complete the chapter.

2. COMPONENTS AND FORMAT OF THE INCOME STATEMENT

On the top line of the income statement, companies typically report revenue. **Revenue** refers to amounts charged for the delivery of goods or services in the ordinary activities of a business. The term **net revenue** means that the revenue number is shown after adjustments

EXHIBIT 4-1   Groupe Danone: Consolidated Statements of Income (€ millions)

	Year ended 31 December		
	2002	**2003**	**2004**
Net sales	€13,555	€13,131	€13,700
Cost of goods sold	(6,442)	(5,983)	(6,369)
Selling expenses	(4,170)	(4,176)	(4,294)
General and administrative expenses	(964)	(977)	(997)
Research and development expenses	(133)	(130)	(131)
Other (expense) income	(256)	(261)	(204)
Operating income	1,590	1,604	1,705
Nonrecurring items	458	(60)	(105)
Interest expense, net	(110)	(70)	(73)
Income before provision for income taxes and minority interests	1,938	1,474	1,527
Provision for income taxes	(490)	(488)	(457)
Income before minority interests	1,448	986	1,070
Minority interests	(182)	(184)	(189)
Share in net income of affiliates	17	37	(564)
Net income	€1,283	€839	€317

(e.g., for estimated returns or for amounts unlikely to be collected). *Revenue* is often used synonymously with *sales*.[1] Exhibits 4-1 and 4-2 show the income statements for Groupe Danone, a French food manufacturer, and Kraft Foods, a U.S. food manufacturer. For the year ended 31 December 2004, Danone reports €13.7 billion of net sales, whereas Kraft reports $32.2 billion of net revenues.[2]

Note that Groupe Danone lists the years in increasing order from left to right with the most recent year in the last column, whereas Kraft lists the years in decreasing order, with the most recent year listed in the first column. These alternative formats are common. There are also differences in presentations of items, such as expenses. Groupe Danone shows expenses such as cost of goods sold in parentheses to explicitly show that these are subtracted from revenue. Kraft, however, does not place cost of sales in parentheses. Rather, it is implicitly understood that this is an expense and is subtracted in arriving at subtotals and totals. The analyst should always verify the order of years and presentation of negative items before analysis is begun because there is flexibility in how companies may present the income statement.

---

[1]**Sales** is sometimes understood to refer to the sale of goods, whereas *revenue* can include the sale of goods or services; however, the terms are often used interchangeably. In some countries, **turnover** is used in place of *revenue*.

[2]Following net income, the income statement will also present **earnings per share**, the amount of earnings per common share of the company. Earnings per share will be discussed in detail later in this reading, and the per-share display has been omitted from these exhibits to focus on the core income statement.

EXHIBIT 4-2   Kraft Foods and Subsidiaries: Consolidated Statements of Earnings ($ millions except per-share data)

| | Year Ended 31 December | | |
	2004	2003	2002
Net revenues	$32,168	$30,498	$29,248
Cost of sales	20,281	18,531	17,463
Gross profit	11,887	11,967	11,785
Marketing, administration, and research costs	6,658	6,136	5,644
Integration costs and a loss on sale of a food factory		(13)	111
Asset impairment and exit costs	603	6	142
Losses (gains) on sales of businesses	3	(31)	(80)
Amortization of intangibles	11	9	7
Operating income	4,612	5,860	5,961
Interest and other debt expense, net	666	665	847
Earnings from continuing operations before income taxes and minority interest	3,946	5,195	5,114
Provision for income taxes	1,274	1,812	1,813
Earnings from continuing operations before minority interest	2,672	3,383	3,301
Minority interest in earnings from continuing operations, net	3	4	4
Earnings from continuing operations	2,669	3,379	3,297
(Loss) earnings from discontinued operations, net of income taxes	(4)	97	97
Net earnings	$2,665	$3,476	$3,394

At the bottom of the income statement, companies report net income (or, essentially synonymously, net earnings or profit). For 2004, Danone reports €317 million of net income and Kraft reports $2,665 million of net earnings. Net income is often referred to as the *bottom line*. The basis for this expression is that net income is the final—or bottom—line in an income statement. Because net income is often viewed as the single most relevant number to describe a company's performance over a period of time, the term *bottom line* sometimes is used in general business jargon to mean any final or most relevant result.

Net income also includes **gains** and **losses,** which are asset inflows and outflows, respectively, not directly related to the ordinary activities of the business. For example, if a company sells products, these are reported as revenue and the costs are listed separately. However, if a company sells surplus land that is not needed, the cost of the land is subtracted from the sales price and the net result is reported as a gain or a loss.

In addition to presenting the net income, income statements also present subtotals that are significant to users of financial statements. Some of the subtotals are specified by International Financial Reporting Standards (IFRS), particularly nonrecurring items, but

Analysts focus on core earnings.

other subtotals are not specified.[3] International Accounting Standard (IAS) No. 1, *Presentation of Financial Statements*, requires that certain items, such as revenue, finance costs, and tax expense, be separately stated on the face of the income statement. IAS No. 1 also requires that headings and subtotals should also "be presented on the face of the income statement when such presentation is relevant to an understanding of the entity's financial performance."[4] IAS No. 1 states that expenses may be grouped together either by their nature or function. For example, grouping together expenses such as depreciation on manufacturing equipment and depreciation on administrative facilities into a single line item called *depreciation* represents a **grouping by nature** of the expense. An example of **grouping by function** would be grouping together expenses into a category such as cost of goods sold, which would include some salaries (e.g., salespeople's), material costs, depreciation, and other direct sales-related expenses.

One subtotal often shown in an income statement is **gross profit** (or, synonymously, **gross margin**). When an income statement shows a gross profit subtotal, it is said to use a multi-step format rather than a **single-step format**. The Kraft Foods income statement is an example of the multi-step format, whereas the Danone income statement is a single step. For manufacturing and merchandising companies, for whom gross profit is most relevant, gross profit is calculated as revenue minus the cost of the goods that were sold.[5] For service companies, gross profit is calculated as revenue minus the cost of services that were provided. In summary, gross profit is the amount of revenue available after subtracting the costs of delivering goods or services such as material and labor. Other expenses related to running the business are subtracted after gross profit.

Another important subtotal shown on the income statement is **operating profit** (or, synonymously, *operating income*). Operating profit further deducts operating expenses such as selling, general, administrative, and research and development expenses. Operating profit reflects a company's profits on its usual business activities before deducting taxes. For financial firms, interest expense would be included in operating expenses and subtracted in arriving at operating profit. For nonfinancial companies, interest expense would not be included in operating expenses and would be subtracted after operating profit because it relates to nonoperating activities for such companies. For some companies composed of a number of separate business segments, operating profit can be useful in evaluating the performance of the individual businesses, reflecting the reality that interest and tax expenses are more relevant at the level of the overall company rather than an individual segment level. For example, in its Investor Relations information, DaimlerChrysler notes, "Especially on the pre-tax level, Operating Profit is the principal earnings indicator for the Segments, Divisions and Business Units."[6] The specific calculations of gross margin and operating profit may vary by company, and a reader of financial statements can consult the notes to the statements to identify significant variations across companies.

Note that both Groupe Danone and Kraft Foods include a line item on their income statements referring to minority interest. Danone and Kraft both consolidate subsidiaries

---

[3]The body of standards issued by the International Accounting Standards Board is now referred to as International Financial Reporting Standards, which include previously issued International Accounting Standards. *Financial reporting* is a broad term including reporting on accounting, financial statements, and other information found in company financial reports.

[4]IAS No. 1, *Presentation of Financial Statements*, paragraph 83.

[5]Later chapters will provide additional information about alternative methods to calculate cost of goods sold.

[6]DaimlerChrysler/Investor Relations/Basic Information/Controlling systems at www.daimlerchrysler.com.

EXHIBIT 4-3   Charles River Associates Incorporated: Consolidated Statements of Income
($ thousands except per-share data)

	Year Ended		
	27 Nov. 2004 (52 weeks)	29 Nov. 2003 (52 weeks)	30 Nov. 2002 (53 weeks)
Revenues	$216,735	$163,458	$130,690
Cost of services	127,716	100,168	80,659
Gross profit	89,019	63,290	50,031
Selling, general, and administrative expenses	57,286	43,055	36,600
Income from operations	31,733	20,235	13,431
Interest income	904	429	486
Interest expense	(1,751)	(38)	(120)
Other expense	(260)	(306)	(29)
Income before provision for income taxes and minority interest	30,626	20,320	13,768
Provision for income taxes	(13,947)	(8,737)	(5,879)
Income before minority interest	16,679	11,583	7,889
Minority interest	(335)	(154)	547
Net income	$16,344	$11,429	$8,436

over which they have control. Consolidation means that they include all of the revenues and expenses of those subsidiaries even if they own less than 100 percent. Minority interest represents the portion of income that belongs to minority shareholders of these consolidated subsidiaries, as opposed to the parent company.

Exhibit 4-3 shows the income statement for CRA International (then known as Charles River Associates), a company providing management consulting services. These examples illustrate basic points about the income statement, including variations across the statements—some of which depend on the industry, whereas others reflect differences in accounting policies and practices of a particular company. In addition, some differences within an industry are primarily differences in terminology, whereas others are more fundamental accounting differences. Footnotes to the financial statements are helpful in identifying such differences.

Having introduced the components and format of an income statement, the next objective is to understand the actual reported numbers in it. To accurately interpret reported numbers, the analyst needs to be familiar with the principles of revenue and expense recognition—that is, how revenue and expenses are measured and attributed to a given accounting reporting period. Revenue and expense recognition are our next topics.

3. REVENUE RECOGNITION

Revenue is the top line in an income statement, so we begin the discussion with revenue recognition. A first task is to explain some relevant accounting terminology.

The terms *revenue, sales, gains, losses,* and *net income* (*profit, net earnings*) have been previously briefly defined. The IFRS *Framework for the Preparation and Presentation of Financial Statements* (referred to here as the Framework) provides further relevant details. The Framework provides that profit is a frequently used measure of performance that is composed of income and expenses.[7] It defines **income** as follows:

> *Income is increases in economic benefits during the accounting period in the form of inflows or enhancements of assets or decreases of liabilities that result in increases in equity, other than those relating to contributions from equity participants.*[8]

International Financial Reporting Standards use the term *income* to include revenue and gains. Gains are similar to revenue; however, they arise from secondary or peripheral activities rather than from a company's primary business activities. For example, for a restaurant, the sale of surplus restaurant equipment for more than its cost is referred to as a gain rather than as revenue. Similarly, a loss is like an expense but arises from secondary activities. Gains and losses may be considered part of operating activities (e.g., a loss due to a decline in the value of inventory) or may be considered part of nonoperating activities (e.g., the sale of nontrading investments).

In a simple hypothetical scenario, revenue recognition would not be an issue. For instance, a company sells goods to a buyer for cash with no returns allowed: When should the company recognize revenue? In this instance, it is clear that revenue should be recognized when the exchange of goods for cash takes place. In practice, however, determining when revenue should be recognized can be somewhat more complex for a number of reasons discussed in the following sections.

3.1. General Principles

An important concept concerning revenue recognition is that it can occur independently of cash movements. For example, assume a company sells goods to a buyer on credit and so does not actually receive cash until some later time. A fundamental principle of accrual accounting is that revenue is recognized when it is earned, so the company's financial records reflect the sale when it is made and a related accounts receivable is created. Later, when cash changes hands, the company's financial records simply reflect that cash has been received to settle an account receivable. Similarly, there are situations when a company receives cash upfront and actually delivers the product or service later, perhaps over a period of time. In this case, the company would record **unearned revenue,** which is then recognized as being earned over time. (One example would be a subscription payment received up front for a publication that is to be delivered periodically over time, the accounting for which was illustrated earlier.)

The basic revenue recognition principles promulgated by accounting regulators deal with the definition of "earned." The International Accounting Standards Board (IASB) provides that revenue for the sale of goods is to be recognized (reported on the income statement) when the following conditions are satisfied:[9]

- The entity has transferred to the buyer the significant risks and rewards of ownership of the goods.

---

[7]IASB, *International Framework for the Preparation and Presentation of Financial Statements,* paragraph 69.
[8]Ibid., paragraph 70.
[9]IASB, IAS No. 18, *Revenue,* paragraph 14.

- The entity retains neither continuing managerial involvement to the degree usually associated with ownership nor effective control over the goods sold.
- The amount of revenue can be measured reliably.
- It is probable that the economic benefits associated with the transaction will flow to the entity.
- The costs incurred or to be incurred in respect of the transaction can be measured reliably.

The IASB notes that the transfer of the risks and rewards of ownership normally occurs when goods are delivered to the buyer or when legal title to goods transfers. However, as noted by the above remaining conditions, transfer of goods will not always result in the recognition of revenue. For example, if goods are delivered to a retail store to be sold on consignment and title is not transferred, the revenue would not yet be recognized.[10]

The Financial Accounting Standards Board (FASB)[11] specifies that revenue should be recognized when it is "realized or realizable and earned." The U.S. Securities and Exchange Commission (SEC),[12] motivated in part because of the frequency with which overstating revenue occurs in connection with fraud and/or misstatements, provides guidance on how to apply the accounting principles. This guidance names four criteria to determine when revenue is realized or realizable and earned:

1. There is evidence of an arrangement between buyer and seller. For instance, this would disallow the practice of recognizing revenue in a period by delivering the product just before the end of an accounting period and then completing a sales contract *after* the period end.
2. The product has been delivered, or the service has been rendered. For instance, this would preclude revenue recognition when the product has been shipped but the *risks and rewards of ownership have not actually passed* to the buyer.
3. The price is determined, or determinable. For instance, this would preclude a company from recognizing revenue that is based on some *contingency*.
4. The seller is reasonably sure of collecting money. For instance, this would preclude a company from recognizing revenue when the customer is *unlikely to pay*.

The IASB standards separately deal with the recognition of revenue for services:[13]

- When the outcome of a transaction involving the rendering of services can be estimated reliably, revenue associated with the transaction shall be recognized by reference to the stage of completion of the transaction at the balance sheet date.
- The outcome of a transaction can be estimated reliably when all the following conditions are satisfied:
  ○ The amount of revenue can be measured reliably.
  ○ It is probable that the economic benefits associated with the transaction will flow to the entity.

---

[10]IAS No. 18 describes a *consignment sale* as one in which the recipient undertakes to sell the goods for the shipper. Revenue is recognized when the recipient sells the goods to a third party. IAS No. 18, Appendix, paragraph 2.

[11]See Statement of Financial Accounting Concepts No. 5, paragraph 83(b).

[12]See SEC Staff Accounting Bulletin 101.

[13]IASB, IAS No. 18, paragraph 20.

EXHIBIT 4-4   Partial Revenue Recognition Footnote for DaimlerChrysler

Revenue for sales of vehicles, service parts, and other related products is recognized when persuasive evidence of an arrangement exists, delivery has occurred or services have been rendered, the price of the transaction is fixed and determinable, and collectability is reasonably assured.

Revenues are recognized net of discounts, cash sales incentives, customer bonuses and rebates granted. Noncash sales incentives that do not reduce the transaction price to the customer are classified within cost of sales. Shipping and handling costs are recorded as cost of sales in the period incurred.

DaimlerChrysler uses price discounts to adjust market pricing in response to a number of market and product factors, including: pricing actions and incentives offered by competitors, economic conditions, the amount of excess industry production capacity, the intensity of market competition, and consumer demand for the product. The Group may offer a variety of sales incentive programs at any point in time, including: cash offers to dealers and consumers, lease subsidies which reduce the consumer's monthly lease payment, or reduced financing rate programs offered to consumers.

The Group records as a reduction to revenue at the time of sale to the dealer the estimated impact of sales incentives programs offered to dealers and consumers. This estimated impact represents the incentive programs offered to dealers and consumers as well as the expected modifications to these programs in order for the dealers to sell their inventory.

- ○ The stage of completion of the transaction at the balance sheet date can be measured reliably.
- ○ The costs incurred for the transaction and the costs to complete the transaction can be measured reliably.

Companies must disclose their revenue recognition policies in the footnotes to their financial statements. Analysts should review these policies carefully to understand how and when a company recognizes revenue, which may differ depending upon the types of product sold and services rendered. Exhibit 4-4 presents a portion of the revenue recognition footnote for DaimlerChrysler from its 2005 annual report prepared under IFRS.

The topic of revenue recognition remains important, and new challenges have evolved, particularly in areas of e-commerce and services such as software development. Standard setters continue to evaluate current revenue recognition standards and issue new guidance periodically to deal with new types of transactions. Additionally, there are occasional special cases for revenue recognition, as discussed in the next section.

3.2. Revenue Recognition in Special Cases

The general principles discussed above are helpful for dealing with most revenue recognition issues. There are some areas where revenue recognition is more difficult to determine. For example, in limited circumstances, revenue may be recognized before or after goods are delivered or services are rendered, as summarized in Exhibit 4-5.

The following sections discuss revenue recognition in the case of long-term contracts, installment sales, and barter.

3.2.1. Long-Term Contracts

A **long-term contract** is one that spans a number of accounting periods. Such contracts raise issues in determining when the earnings process has been completed. How should a company

EXHIBIT 4-5   Revenue Recognition in Special Cases

Before **Goods Are Delivered or** **Services Rendered**	**At the Time** **Goods Are Delivered or** **Services Rendered**	**After Goods Are Delivered or** **Services Rendered**
For example, with long-term contracts where the outcome can be reliably measured, the percentage-of-completion method is used.	Recognize revenues using normal revenue recognition criteria (IAS, FAS, SEC).	For example, with real estate sales where there is doubt about the buyer's ability to complete payments, the installment method and cost recovery method are appropriate.

apportion the revenue earned under a long-term contract to each accounting period? If, for example, the contract is a service contract or a licensing arrangement, the company may recognize the revenue ratably over the period of time of the contract rather than at the end of the contract term. As stated in IAS No. 18 regarding the rendering of services:

> The recognition of revenue by reference to the stage of completion of a transaction is often referred to as the percentage-of-completion method. Under this method, revenue is recognized in the accounting periods in which the services are rendered. The recognition of revenue on this basis provides useful information on the extent of service activity and performance during a period. IAS 11 Construction Contracts also requires the recognition of revenue on this basis. The requirements of that Standard are generally applicable to the recognition of revenue and the associated expenses for a transaction involving the rendering of services.[14]

As noted in IAS No. 18, construction contracts are another example of contracts that may span a number of accounting periods. IAS No. 11 provides that when the outcome of a construction contract can be measured reliably, revenue and expenses should be recognized in reference to the stage of completion. U.S. generally accepted accounting principles (U.S. GAAP) have a similar requirement. In both cases, the percentage-of-completion method of accounting is used. Under the **percentage-of-completion** method, in each accounting period, the company estimates what percentage of the contract is complete and then reports that percentage of the total contract revenue in its income statement. Contract costs for the period are expensed against the revenue. Therefore, net income or profit is reported each year as work is performed.

Under IAS No. 11, if the outcome of the contract cannot be measured reliably, then revenue is only reported to the extent of contract costs incurred (if it is probable the costs will be recovered). Costs are expensed in the period incurred. Under this method, no profit would be reported until completion of the contract. Under U.S. GAAP, a different method is used when the outcome cannot be measured reliably, termed the *completed contract method*. Under the **completed contract** method, the company does not report any revenue until the contract is finished. Under U.S. GAAP, the completed contract method is also appropriate when the contract is not a long-term contract. Note, however, that when a contract is started and completed in the same period, there is no difference between the percentage-of-completion and completed contract methods.

---

[14]IAS No. 18, paragraph 21.

Examples 4-1, 4-2, and 4-3 provide illustrations of these revenue recognition methods. As shown, the percentage-of-completion method results in revenue recognition sooner than the completed contract method and thus may be considered a less conservative approach. In addition, the percentage-of-completion method relies on management estimates and is thus not as objective as the completed contract method. However, an advantage of the percentage-of-completion method is that it results in better matching of revenue recognition with the accounting period in which it was earned. Because of better matching with the periods in which work is performed, the percentage-of-completion method is the preferred method of revenue recognition for long-term contracts and is required when the outcome can be measured reliably under both IFRS and U.S. GAAP. Under both IFRS and U.S. GAAP, if a loss is expected on the contract, the loss is reported immediately, not upon completion of the contract, regardless of the method used (e.g., percentage-of-completion or completed contract).

EXAMPLE 4-1   Revenue Recognition for Long-Term Contracts: Recognizing Revenue Ratably

New Era Network Associates has a five-year license to provide networking support services to a customer. The total amount of the license fee to be received by New Era is $1 million. New Era recognizes license revenue ratably regardless of the time at which cash is received. How much revenue will New Era recognize for this license?

Solution. For this license, New Era Network Associates will recognize $200,000 each year for five years (calculated as $1 million divided by 5).

EXAMPLE 4-2   Revenue Recognition for Long-Term Contracts: Percentage-of-Completion Method

Stelle Technology has a contract to build a network for a customer for a total sales price of $10 million. The network will take an estimated three years to build, and total building costs are estimated to be $6 million. Stelle recognizes long-term contract revenue using the percentage-of-completion method and estimates percentage complete based on expenditure incurred as a percentage of total estimated expenditures.

1. At the end of Year 1, the company has spent $3 million. Total costs to complete are estimated to be another $3 million. How much revenue will Stelle recognize in Year 1?
2. At the end of Year 2, the company has spent $5.4 million. Total costs to complete are estimated to be another $0.6 million. How much revenue will Stelle recognize in Year 2?
3. At the end of Year 3, the contract is complete. The company spent a total of $6 million. How much revenue will Stelle recognize in Year 3?

Solution to 1. Stelle has spent 50 percent of the total project costs ($3 million divided by $6 million), so in Year 1, the company will recognize 50 percent of the total contract revenue (i.e., $5 million).

Solution to 2. Because Stelle has spent 90 percent of the total project costs ($5.4 million divided by $6 million), by the end of Year 2, it will need to have recognized 90 percent of the total contract revenue (i.e., $9 million). Stelle has already recognized $5 million of revenue in Year 1, so in Year 2, the company will recognize $4 million revenue ($9 million minus $5 million).

Solution to 3. Because Stelle has spent 100 percent of the total project costs, by the end of Year 3, it will need to have recognized 100 percent of the total contract revenue (i.e., $10 million). Stelle had already recognized $9 million of revenue by the end of Year 2, so in Year 3, the company will recognize $1 million revenue ($10 million minus $9 million).

	Year 1	Year 2	Year 3	Total
Revenue	$5 million	$4 million	$1 million	$10 million

EXAMPLE 4-3   Revenue Recognition for Long-Term Contracts: Completed Contract Method

Kolenda Technology Group has a contract to build a network for a customer for a total sales price of $10 million. This network will take an estimated three years to build, but considerable uncertainty surrounds total building costs because new technologies are involved. Kolenda recognizes contract revenue using the completed contract method.

1. At the end of Year 1, Kolenda has spent $3 million. How much revenue will the company recognize in Year 1?
2. At the end of Year 2, Kolenda has spent $5.4 million. How much revenue will the company recognize in Year 2?
3. At the end of Year 3, the contract is complete. Kolenda spent a total of $6 million. How much revenue will the company recognize in Year 3?

Solution to 1. No revenue will be recognized until the contract is complete. In Year 1, Kolenda will recognize $0.

Solution to 2. No revenue will be recognized until the contract is complete. In Year 2, Kolenda will recognize $0.

Solution to 3. Because the contract is complete, Kolenda will recognize the total contract revenue (i.e., $10 million).

	Year 1	Year 2	Year 3	Total
Revenue	$0 million	$0 million	$10 million	$10 million

3.2.2. Installment Sales

As noted above, revenue is normally reported when goods are delivered or services are rendered, independent of the period in which cash payments for those goods or services are received. This principle applies even to **installment sales**—sales in which proceeds are to be paid in installments over an extended period. Under limited circumstances, recognition of revenue or profit may be required to be deferred for some installment sales.

An example of such deferral arises for certain sales of real estate on an installment basis. Revenue recognition for sales of real estate[15] varies depending on specific aspects of the sale transaction. Under normal conditions, sales of real estate are reported at the time of sale using the normal revenue recognition conditions. International standards note that in the case of real estate sales, the time at which legal title transfers may differ from the time at which the buyer acquires a vested interest. Continuing involvement in the real estate by the seller may also indicate that risks and rewards of ownership of the property have not been transferred. There may also be significant doubt of the ability of the buyer to complete payment for a real estate sales contract. IAS No. 18 provides that in the case of real estate where the down payment and payments received do not provide sufficient evidence of the commitment of the buyer, revenue should be reported only to the extent cash is received. This is a conservative treatment because the reporting of revenue is deferred. Similar provisions exist under U.S. GAAP except that under U.S. GAAP the full revenue is shown in the year of sale but some of the profit is deferred.

Two methods may be appropriate in these limited circumstances and relate to the amount of profit to be recognized each year from the transaction: the **installment method** and the **cost recovery method**. Under the installment method, the portion of the total profit of the sale that is recognized in each period is determined by the percentage of the total sales price for which the seller has received cash. Exhibit 4-6 presents an example of a disclosure of an installment sale of real estate under U.S. GAAP where a portion of the profit was recognized and the remainder was deferred.

EXHIBIT 4-6   Installment Sale Disclosure for First Bancshares

---

On June 22, 2004, an agreement was entered into to sell the property and equipment of South Central Missouri Title Company, Inc for $252,000. In addition, South Central entered into a covenant not to compete agreement with the purchaser. Expense related to the sale totaled $61,512. As of the date of the sale, the assets sold had a net book value of $100,166. The majority of the sales price was in the form of a promissory note to South Central with a five year maturity. The transaction closed on July 16, 2004. As a result of this sale, the subsidiary will no longer offer sales of title insurance or real estate closing services. The company accounted for this sale on the installment method because the initial investment by the buyer was not substantial enough to warrant full recognition of the gain. However, the recovery of the cost of the property is reasonably assured if the buyer defaults. The following schedule summarizes certain information for the transaction:

Revenue	$252,000
Cost of Sale	161,678
Deferred gain	90,322
Deferred gain recognized during FY 2005	8,026
Deferred gain at June 30, 2005	$82,296

Source: First Bancshares Form 10K, filed 11/1/2005.

---

[15]IAS No. 18, Appendix, paragraph 9, and FASB Statement No. 66, *Accounting for Sales of Real Estate.*

The cost recovery method of revenue recognition is an appropriate alternative for many of the same situations as the installment method. Under the cost recovery method, the seller does not report any profit until the cash amounts paid by the buyer—including principal and interest on any financing from the seller—are greater than all the seller's costs of the property. Example 4-4 below provides an example of the differences between the installment method and the cost recovery method.

Installment sales and cost recovery treatment of revenue recognition are rare for financial reporting purposes, especially for assets other than real estate. IAS No. 18 provides that installment sales other than real estate generally require revenue to be recognized at the time of sale; however, it further provides that the guidance found in IAS No. 18 must be considered in light of local laws regarding the sale of goods in a particular country.

EXAMPLE 4-4   The Installment and Cost Recovery Methods of Revenue Recognition

Assume the total sales price and cost of a property are $2,000,000 and $1,100,000, respectively, so that the total profit to be recognized is $900,000. The amount of cash received by the seller as a down payment is $300,000, with the remainder of the sales price to be received over a 10-year period. It has been determined that there is significant doubt about the ability and commitment of the buyer to complete all payments. How much profit will be recognized attributable to the down payment if:

1. The installment method is used?
2. The cost recovery method is used?

Solution to 1. The installment method apportions the cash receipt between cost recovered and profit using the ratio of profit to sales value; here, this ratio equals $900,000 ÷ $2,000,000 = 0.45 or 45 percent. Therefore, the seller will recognize the following profit attributable to the down payment: 45 percent of $300,000 = $135,000.

Solution to 2. Under the cost recovery method of revenue recognition, the company would not recognize any profit attributable to the down payment because the cash amounts paid by the buyer still do not exceed the cost of $1,100,000.

3.2.3. Barter

Revenue recognition issues related to barter transactions became particularly important as e-commerce developed. As an example, if Company A exchanges advertising space for computer equipment from Company B but no cash changes hands, can Company A and B both report revenue? Such an exchange is referred to as a *barter transaction.*

An even more challenging revenue recognition issue evolved from barter transactions—round-trip transactions. As an example, if Company A sells advertising services (or energy contracts, or commodities) to Company B and almost simultaneously buys an almost identical product from Company B, can Company A report revenue at the fair value of the product sold? Because the company's revenue would be approximately equal to its expense, the net effect of the transaction would have no impact on net income or cash flow. However, the amount of revenue reported would be higher, and the amount of revenue can be important to a company's valuation. In the earlier stages of e-commerce, for example, some equity valuations were based on sales (because many early Internet companies reported no net income).

Under IFRS, revenue from barter transactions must be measured based on the fair value of revenue from similar nonbarter transactions with unrelated parties (parties other than the barter partner).[16] Similarly, the FASB states that revenue can be recognized at fair value only if a company has historically received cash payments for such services and can thus use this historical experience as a basis for determining fair value.[17]

3.2.4. Gross versus Net Reporting

Another revenue recognition issue that became particularly important with the emergence of e-commerce is the issue of gross versus net reporting. Merchandising companies typically sell products that they purchased from a supplier. In accounting for their sales, the company records the amount of the sale proceeds as sales revenue and their cost of the products as the cost of goods sold. As Internet-based merchandising companies developed, many sold products that they had never held in inventory; they simply arranged for the supplier to ship the products directly to the end customer. In effect, many such companies were agents of the supplier company, and the net difference between their sales proceeds and their costs was equivalent to a sales commission. What amount should these companies record as their revenues—the gross amount of sales proceeds received from their customers, or the net difference between sales proceeds and their cost?

U.S. GAAP indicates that the approach should be based on the specific situation and provides guidance for determining when revenue should be reported gross versus net.[18] To report gross revenues, the following criteria are relevant: The company is the primary obligor under the contract, bears inventory risk and credit risk, can choose its supplier, and has reasonable latitude to establish price. If these criteria are not met, the company should report revenues net. Example 4-5 provides an illustration.

EXAMPLE 4-5   Gross versus Net Reporting of Revenues

Flyalot has agreements with several major airlines to obtain airline tickets at reduced rates. The company pays only for tickets it sells to customers. In the most recent period, Flyalot sold airline tickets to customers over the internet for a total of $1.1 million. The cost of these tickets to Flyalot was $1 million. The company's direct selling costs were $2,000. Once the customers receive their ticket, the airline is responsible for providing all services associated with the customers' flight.

1. Demonstrate the reporting of revenues under
   A. gross reporting.
   B. net reporting.

---

[16]IASB, SIC Interpretation 31, *Revenue—Barter Transactions Involving Advertising Services,* paragraph 5.
[17]See Emerging Issues Task Force EITF 99-17, "Accounting for Advertising Barter Transactions."
[18]See Emerging Issues Task Force EITF 99-19, "Reporting Revenue Gross as a Principal versus Net as an Agent."

2. Determine and justify the appropriate method for reporting revenues.

Solution to 1. The table below shows how reporting would appear on a gross and a net basis.

	A. Gross Reporting	B. Net Reporting
Revenues	$1,100,000	$100,000
Cost of sales	1,002,000	2,000
Gross margin	$ 98,000	$ 98,000

Solution to 2. Flyalot should report revenue on a net basis. Flyalot pays only for tickets it sells to customers and thus did not bear inventory risk. In addition, the airline—not Flyalot—is the primary obligor under the contract. Revenues should be reported as $100,000.

3.3. Implications for Financial Analysis

As we have seen, companies use a variety of revenue recognition methods. Furthermore, a single company may use different revenue recognition policies for different businesses. Companies disclose their revenue recognition policies in the footnotes to their financial statement, often in the first note.

The following aspects of a company's revenue recognition policy are particularly relevant to financial analysis: whether a policy results in recognition of revenue sooner rather than later (sooner is less conservative), and to what extent a policy requires the company to make estimates. In order to analyze a company's financial statements, and particularly to compare one company's financial statements with those of another company, it is helpful to understand any differences in their revenue recognition policies. Although it may not be possible to calculate the monetary effect of differences between particular companies' revenue recognition policies and estimates, it is generally possible to characterize the relative conservatism of a company's policies and to qualitatively assess how differences in policies might affect financial ratios.

EXAMPLE 4-6   Revenue Recognition Policy for Motorola

As disclosed in the footnotes to the financial statements shown below (emphasis added), Motorola (NYSE: MOT) uses different revenue recognition policies depending on the type of revenue-producing activity, including product sales, long-term contracts, contracts involving unproven technology, revenue for services, and revenue for licensing agreements.

Revenue Recognition: *The Company recognizes revenue for* **product sales** *when title transfers, the risks and rewards of ownership have been transferred to the customer, the fee is fixed and determinable, and collection of the related receivable is probable, which is generally at the time of shipment. Accruals are established, with the related reduction to revenue, for allowances for discounts and price protection, product returns and incentive programs for distributors and end customers related to these sales based on actual historical exposure at the time the related revenues are recognized. For* **long-term contracts,** *the Company uses the percentage-of-completion method to recognize revenues and costs based on the percentage of costs incurred to date compared to the total estimated contract costs. For* **contracts involving new unproven technologies,** *revenues and profits are deferred until technological feasibility is established, customer acceptance is obtained and other contract-specific terms have been completed. Provisions for losses are recognized during the period in which the loss first becomes apparent.* **Revenue for services** *is recognized ratably over the contract term or as services are being performed.* **Revenue related to licensing agreements** *is recognized over the licensing period or at the time the Company has fulfilled its obligations and the fee to be received is fixed and determinable.*

Source: Motorola 10-K financial statement footnotes for the year ended 31 December 2004, as filed with the SEC; emphasis added.

EXAMPLE 4-7   Revenue Recognition of i2 Technologies

On 9 June 2004, the SEC announced it had settled a securities fraud case against i2 Technologies (NASDAQ: ITWO) involving the misstatement of approximately $1 billion in revenues. The SEC announcement explains that the company recognized revenue up front on its software licenses, which was inappropriate because some of the software lacked complete functionality either for general use or for use by a particular customer.

Source: SEC Accounting and Auditing Enforcement Release No. 2034.

With familiarity of the basic principles of revenue recognition in hand, the next section begins a discussion of expense recognition.

4. EXPENSE RECOGNITION

Expenses are deducted against revenue to arrive at a company's net profit or loss. Under the IASB Framework, **expenses** are "decreases in economic benefits during the accounting period in the form of outflows or depletions of assets or incurrences of liabilities that result in decreases in equity, other than those relating to distributions to equity participants."[19]

---

[19]IASB, *Framework for the Preparation and Presentation of Financial Statements,* paragraph 70.

The IASB Framework also states:

The definition of expenses encompasses losses as well as those expenses that arise in the course of the ordinary activities of the enterprise. Expenses that arise in the course of the ordinary activities of the enterprise include, for example, cost of sales, wages and depreciation. They usually take the form of an outflow or depletion of assets such as cash and cash equivalents, inventory, property, plant and equipment.

Losses represent other items that meet the definition of expenses and may, or may not, arise in the course of the ordinary activities of the enterprise. Losses represent decreases in economic benefits and as such they are no different in nature from other expenses. Hence, they are not regarded as a separate element in this Framework.

Losses include, for example, those resulting from disasters such as fire and flood.[20]

Similar to the issues with revenue recognition, in a simple hypothetical scenario, expense recognition would not be an issue. For instance, assume a company purchased inventory for cash and sold the entire inventory in the same period. When the company paid for the inventory, absent indications to the contrary, it is clear that the inventory cost has been incurred and should be recognized as an expense (cost of goods sold) in the financial records. Assume also that the company paid all operating and administrative expenses in cash within each accounting period. In such a simple hypothetical scenario, no issues of expense recognition would arise. In practice, however, as with revenue recognition, determining when expenses should be recognized can be somewhat more complex.

4.1. General Principles

In general, a company recognizes expenses in the period that it consumes (i.e., uses up) the economic benefits associated with the expenditure, or loses some previously recognized economic benefit.[21]

A general principle of expense recognition is the **matching principle,** also known as the "matching of costs with revenues."[22] Under the matching principle, a company directly matches some expenses (e.g., cost of goods sold) with associated revenues. Unlike the simple scenario in which a company purchases inventory and sells all of the inventory within the same accounting period, in practice, it is more likely that some of the current period's sales are made from inventory purchased in a previous period. It is also more likely that some of the inventory purchased in the current period will remain unsold at the end of the current period and so will be sold in the following period. The matching principle requires that the company match the cost of goods sold with the revenues of the period.

Period costs, expenditures that less directly match the timing of revenues, are reflected in the period when a company makes the expenditure or incurs the liability to pay. Administrative expenses are an example of period costs. Other expenditures that also less directly match the timing of revenues relate more directly to future expected benefits; in this

---

[20]Ibid., paragraphs 78–80.
[21]Ibid., paragraph 94.
[22]Ibid., paragraph 95.

case, the expenditures are allocated systematically with the passage of time. An example is depreciation expense (discussed below).

Examples 4-8 and 4-9 demonstrate the matching principle applied to inventory and cost of goods sold.

EXAMPLE 4-8   The Matching of Inventory Costs with Revenues

Kahn Distribution Limited (KDL) purchases inventory items for resale. During 2006, Kahn had the following transactions:

Inventory Purchases	
First quarter	2,000 units at $40 per unit
Second quarter	1,500 units at $41 per unit
Third quarter	2,200 units at $43 per unit
Fourth quarter	1,900 units at $45 per unit
Total	7,600 units at a total cost of $321,600

Inventory sales during the year were 5,600 units at $50 per unit. KDL determines that there were 2,000 remaining units of inventory and specifically identifies that 1,900 were those purchased in the fourth quarter and 100 were purchased in the third quarter. What are the revenue and expense associated with these transactions during 2006?

Solution. The revenue for 2006 would be $280,000 (5,600 units × $50 per unit). Initially, the total cost of the goods purchased would be recorded as inventory (an asset) in the amount of $321,600. During 2006, the cost of the 5,600 units sold would be expensed (matched against the revenue) while the cost of the 2,000 remaining unsold units would remain in inventory as follows:

Cost of Goods Sold		
From the first quarter	2,000 units at $40 per unit =	$ 80,000
From the second quarter	1,500 units at $41 per unit =	$61,500
From the third quarter	2,100 units at $43 per unit =	$90,300
Total cost of goods sold		$231,800
Cost of Goods Remaining in Inventory		
From the third quarter	100 units at $43 per unit =	$4,300
From the fourth quarter	1,900 units at $45 per unit =	$85,500
Total remaining (or ending) inventory cost		$89,800

To confirm that total costs are accounted for: $231,800 + $89,800 = $321,600

The cost of the goods sold would be expensed against the revenue of $280,000 as follows:

Revenue	$280,000
Cost of goods sold	231,800
Gross profit	$ 48,200

The remaining inventory amount of $89,800 will be matched against revenue in a future year when the inventory items are sold.

EXAMPLE 4-9   Alternative Inventory Costing Methods

In Example 4-8, KDL was able to specifically identify which inventory items were sold and which remained in inventory to be carried over to later periods. That method is called the **specific identification method.** It is not always possible to specifically identify which items were sold, so the accounting standards permit the assignment of inventory costs to costs of goods sold and to ending inventory using cost flow assumptions. Under both IFRS and U.S. GAAP, companies may use either of two methods to assign costs: the first in, first out (FIFO) method, or the weighted average cost method. Under the **FIFO method,** it is simply assumed that the earliest items purchased were sold first. Ending inventory would, therefore, include only the latest purchases. It turns out that those items specifically identified as sold in Example 4-8 were also the first items purchased, so in this example, under FIFO, the cost of goods sold would also be $231,800, calculated as above. The **weighted average cost method** simply averages the total available costs over the total available units.

For KDL, the weighted average cost would be

$$\$ 321,600/7,600 \text{ units} = \$42.3158 \text{ per unit}$$

Cost of goods sold using the weighted average cost method would be

$$5,600 \text{ units at } \$42.3158 = \$236,968$$

Ending inventory using the weighted average cost method would be

$$2,000 \text{ units at } \$42.3158 = \$ 84,632$$

Another method is available under U.S. GAAP but is not permitted under IFRS. This method is the last in, first out (LIFO) method. Under the **LIFO method,** it is assumed that the most recent items purchased were sold first. Although this may seem contrary to common sense, it is logical in certain circumstances. For example, lumber in a lumberyard may be stacked up with the oldest lumber on the bottom. As lumber is sold, it is sold from the top of the stack, so the last lumber in is the first lumber out. Theoretically, a company should choose this method under U.S. GAAP if the physical inventory flows in this manner.[23] Under the LIFO method, in the KDL example, it would be assumed that the 2,000 units remaining in ending inventory would have come from the first quarter's purchases:[24]

Ending inventory 2,000 units at $40 per unit = $80,000

The remaining costs would be allocated to cost of goods sold under LIFO:

Total costs of $321,600 less $80,000 remaining in ending inventory = $241,600

Alternatively, the cost of the last 5,600 units purchased is allocated to cost of goods sold under LIFO:

1,900 units at $45 per unit + 2,200 units at $43 per unit
+ 1,500 units at $41 per unit = $241,600

Exhibit 4-7 summarizes and compares inventory costing methods.

CFA Mandatory

EXHIBIT 4-7   Summary Table on Inventory Costing Methods

Method	Description	Cost of Goods Sold When Prices Are Rising, Relative to Other Two Methods	Ending Inventory When Prices Are Rising, Relative to Other Two Methods
FIFO (first in, first out)	Assumes that earliest items purchased were sold first	Lowest	Highest
LIFO (last in, first out)	Assumes most recent items purchased were sold first	Highest[a]	Lowest[a]
Weighted average cost	Averages total costs over total units available	Middle	Middle

[a]Assumes no LIFO layer liquidation. **LIFO layer liquidation** occurs when the volume of sales rises above the volume of recent purchases so that some sales are made from existing, relatively low-priced inventory rather than from more recent purchases.

---

[23]Practically, the reason some companies choose to use LIFO in the United States is to reduce taxes. When prices and inventory quantities are rising, LIFO will normally result in lower income and hence lower taxes. U.S. tax regulations require that if LIFO is used on a company's tax return, it must also be used on the company's GAAP financial statements.

[24]If data on the precise timing of quarterly sales were available, the answer would differ because the cost of goods sold would be determined during the quarter rather than at the end of the quarter.

4.2. Issues in Expense Recognition

The following sections cover applications of the principles of expense recognition to certain common situations.

4.2.1. Doubtful Accounts

When a company sells its products or services on credit, it is likely that some customers will ultimately default on their obligations (i.e., fail to pay). At the time of the sale, it is not known which customer will default. (If it were known that a particular customer would ultimately default, presumably a company would not sell on credit to that customer.) One possible approach to recognizing credit losses on customer receivables would be for the company to wait until such time as a customer defaulted and only then recognize the loss (**direct write-off method**). Such an approach would usually not be consistent with generally accepted accounting principles.

Under the matching principle, at the time revenue is recognized on a sale, a company is required to record an estimate of how much of the revenue will ultimately be uncollectible. Companies make such estimates based on previous experience with uncollectible accounts. Such estimates may be expressed as a proportion of the overall amount of sales, the overall amount of receivables, or the amount of receivables overdue by a specific amount of time. The company records its estimate of uncollectible amounts as an expense on the income statement, not as a direct reduction of revenues.

4.2.2. Warranties

At times, companies offer warranties on the products they sell. If the product proves deficient in some respect that is covered under the terms of the warranty, the company will incur an expense to repair or replace the product. At the time of sale, the company does not know the amount of future expenses it will incur in connection with its warranties. One possible approach would be for a company to wait until actual expenses are incurred under the warranty and to reflect the expense at that time. However, this would not result in a matching of the expense with the associated revenue.

Under the matching principle, a company is required to estimate the amount of future expenses resulting from its warranties, to recognize an estimated warranty expense in the period of the sale, and to update the expense as indicated by experience over the life of the warranty.

4.2.3. Depreciation and Amortization

Companies commonly incur costs to obtain long-lived assets. **Long-lived assets** are assets expected to provide economic benefits over a future period of time greater than one year. Examples are land (property), plant, equipment, and **intangible assets** (assets lacking physical substance) such as trademarks. The costs of most long-lived assets are allocated over the period of time during which they provide economic benefits. The two main types of long-lived assets whose costs are *not* allocated over time are land and those intangible assets with indefinite useful lives.

Depreciation is the process of systematically allocating costs of long-lived assets over the period during which the assets are expected to provide economic benefits. Depreciation is the term commonly applied to this process for physical long-lived assets such as plant and equipment (land is not depreciated), and **amortization** is the term commonly applied to this process for intangible long-lived assets with a finite useful life.[25] Examples of intangible long-lived assets with a finite useful life include an acquired mailing list, an acquired patent with a set expiration date, and an acquired copyright with a set legal life. The term amortization is also commonly applied to the systematic allocation of a premium or discount relative to the face value of a fixed-income security over the life of the security.

IAS No. 16, *Property, Plant, and Equipment*, requires that the depreciable amount (cost less residual value) be allocated on a systematic basis over the remaining useful life of the asset. The method used to compute depreciation must reflect the pattern over which the economic benefits of the asset are expected to be consumed. IAS No. 16 does not prescribe a particular method for computing depreciation but notes that several methods are commonly used, such as the straight-line method, diminishing balance method (accelerated depreciation), and the units of production method (depreciation varies depending upon production or usage).

The **straight-line method** allocates evenly the cost of long-lived assets less estimated residual value over the estimated useful life of an asset. (The term *straight line* derives from the fact that the annual depreciation expense, if represented as a line graph over time, would be a straight line. In addition, a plot of the cost of the asset minus the cumulative amount of annual depreciation expense, if represented as a line graph over time, would be a straight line with a negative downward slope.) Calculating depreciation and amortization requires two significant estimates: the estimated useful life of an asset and the estimated residual value (also known as *salvage value*) of an asset. Under IAS No. 16, the residual value is the amount that the company expects to receive upon sale of the asset at the end of its useful life. Example 4-10 assumes that an item of equipment is depreciated using the straight-line method and illustrates how the annual depreciation expense varies under different estimates of the useful life and estimated residual value of an asset. As shown, annual depreciation expense is sensitive to both the estimated useful life and to the estimated residual value.

EXAMPLE 4-10   Sensitivity of Annual Depreciation Expense to Varying Estimates of Useful Life and Residual Value

Using the straight-line method of depreciation, annual depreciation expense is calculated as

$$\frac{\text{Cost} - \text{Residual value}}{\text{Estimated useful life}}$$

Assume the cost of an asset is \$10,000. If, for example, the residual value of the asset is estimated to be \$0 and its useful life is estimated to be 5 years, the annual depreciation expense under the straight-line method would be (\$10,000 − \$0)/5 years = \$2,000.

---

[25]Under SFAS No. 142, intangible assets with indefinite life are not amortized. Instead, they are tested at least annually for impairment (i.e., if the current value of an intangible asset is materially lower than its value in the company's books, the value of the asset is considered to be impaired and its value must be decreased).

In contrast, holding the estimated useful life of the asset constant at 5 years but increasing the estimated residual value of the asset to $4,000 would result in annual depreciation expense of only $1,200 [calculated as ($10,000 − $4,000)/5 years]. Alternatively, holding the estimated residual value at $0 but increasing the estimated useful life of the asset to 10 years would result in annual depreciation expense of only $1,000 [calculated as ($10,000 − $0)/10 years]. Exhibit 4-8 shows annual depreciation expense for various combinations of estimated useful life and residual value.

EXHIBIT 4-8   Annual Depreciation Expense (in dollars)

Estimated Useful Life (years)	Estimated Residual Value					
	0	1,000	2,000	3,000	4,000	5,000
2	5,000	4,500	4,000	3,500	3,000	2,500
4	2,500	2,250	2,000	1,750	1,500	1,250
5	2,000	1,800	1,600	1,400	1,200	1,000
8	1,250	1,125	1,000	875	750	625
10	1,000	900	800	700	600	500

Generally, alternatives to the straight-line method of depreciation are called **accelerated methods of depreciation** because they accelerate (i.e., speed up) the timing of depreciation. Accelerated depreciation methods allocate a greater proportion of the cost to the early years of an asset's useful life. These methods are appropriate if the plant or equipment is expected to be used up faster in the early years (e.g., an automobile). A commonly used accelerated method is the **diminishing balance method,** as mentioned in IAS No. 16 (also known as the **declining balance method**). The diminishing balance method is demonstrated in Example 4-11.

EXAMPLE 4-11   An Illustration of Diminishing Balance Depreciation

Assume the cost of computer equipment was $11,000, the estimated residual value is $1,000, and the estimated useful life is five years. Under the diminishing or declining balance method, the first step is to determine the straight-line rate, the rate at which the asset would be depreciated under the straight-line method. This rate is measured as 100 percent divided by the useful life or 20 percent for a five-year useful life. Under the straight-line method, 1/5 or 20 percent of the depreciable cost of the asset (here, $11,000 − $1,000 = $10,000) would be expensed each year for five years: The depreciation expense would be $2,000 per year.

The next step is to determine an acceleration factor that approximates the pattern of the asset's wear. Common acceleration factors are 150 percent and 200 percent. The latter is known as **double-declining balance depreciation** because it depreciates the asset at double the straight-line rate. Using the 200 percent acceleration factor, the diminishing balance rate would be 40 percent (20 percent × 2.0). This rate is then applied to the remaining undepreciated balance of the asset each period (known as the **net book value**).

At the beginning of the first year, the net book value is $11,000. Depreciation expense for the first full year of use of the asset would be 40 percent of $11,000, or $4,400. Under this method, the residual value, if any, is generally not used in the computation of the depreciation each period (the 40 percent is applied to $11,000 rather than to $11,000 minus residual value). However, the company will stop taking depreciation when the salvage value is reached.

At the beginning of Year 2, the net book value is measured as

Asset cost	$11,000
Less: Accumulated depreciation	(4,400)
Net book value	$ 6,600

For the second full year, depreciation expense would be $6,600 × 40 percent, or $2,640. At the end of the second year (i.e., beginning of the third year), a total of $7,040 ($4,400 + $2,640) of depreciation would have been recorded. So, the remaining net book value at the beginning of the third year would be

Asset cost	$11,000
Less: Accumulated depreciation	(7,040)
Net book value	$ 3,960

For the third full year, depreciation would be $3,960 × 40 percent, or $1,584. At the end of the third year, a total of $8,624 ($4,400 + $2,640 + $1,584) of depreciation would have been recorded. So, the remaining net book value at the beginning of the fourth year would be

Asset cost	$11,000
Less: Accumulated depreciation	(8,624)
Net book value	$ 2,376

For the fourth full year, depreciation would be $2,376 × 40 percent, or $950. At the end of the fourth year, a total of $9,574 ($4,400 + $2,640 + $1,584 + $950) of depreciation would have been recorded. So, the remaining net book value at the beginning of the fifth year would be

Asset cost	$11,000
Less: Accumulated depreciation	(9,574)
Net book value	$ 1,426

For the fifth year, if deprecation were determined as in previous years, it would amount to $570 ($1,426 × 40 percent). However, this would result in a remaining net book value of the asset below its estimated residual value of $1,000. So, instead, only $426 would be depreciated, leaving a $1,000 net book value at the end of the fifth year.

Asset cost	$11,000
Less: Accumulated depreciation	(10,000)
Net book value	$ 1,000

Companies often use a zero or small residual value, which creates problems for diminishing balance depreciation because the asset never fully depreciates. In order to fully depreciate the asset over the initially estimated useful life when a zero or small residual value is assumed, companies often adopt a depreciation policy that combines the diminishing balance and straight-line methods. An example would be a deprecation policy of using double-declining balance depreciation and switching to the straight-line method halfway through the useful life.

Under accelerated depreciation methods, there is a higher depreciation expense in early years relative to the straight-line method. This results in higher expenses and lower net income in the early depreciation years. In later years, there is a reversal with accelerated depreciation expense lower than straight-line depreciation. Accelerated deprecation is sometimes referred to as a conservative accounting choice because it results in lower net income in the early years of asset use.

For those intangible assets that must be amortized (those with an identifiable useful life), the process is the same as for depreciation; only the name of the expense is different. IAS No. 38, *Intangible Assets*, states that if a pattern cannot be determined over the useful life, then the straight-line method should be used. In most cases under international accounting standards and U.S. GAAP, amortizable intangible assets are amortized using the straight-line method with no residual value. **Goodwill**[26] and intangible assets with indefinite life are not amortized. Instead, they are tested at least annually for impairment (i.e., if the current value of an intangible asset or goodwill is materially lower than its value in the company's books, the value of the asset is considered to be impaired and its value in the company's books must be decreased).

In summary, to calculate depreciation and amortization, a company must choose a method, estimate the asset's useful life, and estimate residual value. Clearly, different choices have a differing effect on depreciation or amortization expense and, therefore, on reported net income.

---

[26]Goodwill is recorded in acquisitions and is the amount by which the price to purchase an entity exceeds the amount of net identifiable assets acquired (the total amount of identifiable assets acquired less liabilities assumed).

4.3.   Implications for Financial Analysis

A company's estimates for doubtful accounts and/or for warranty expenses can affect its reported net income. Similarly, a company's choice of depreciation or amortization method, estimates of assets' useful lives, and estimates of assets' residual values can affect reported net income. These are only a few of the choices and estimates that affect a company's reported net income.

As with revenue recognition policies, a company's choice of expense recognition can be characterized by its relative conservatism. A policy that results in recognition of expenses later rather than sooner is considered less conservative. In addition, many items of expense require the company to make estimates that can significantly affect net income. Analysis of a company's financial statements, and particularly comparison of one company's financial statements with those of another, requires an understanding of differences in these estimates and their potential impact.

If, for example, a company shows a significant year-to-year change in its estimates of uncollectible accounts as a percentage of sales, warranty expenses as percentage of sales, or estimated useful lives of assets, the analyst should seek to understand the underlying reasons. Do the changes reflect a change in business operations (e.g., lower estimated warranty expenses reflecting recent experience of fewer warranty claims because of improved product quality)? Or are the changes seemingly unrelated to changes in business operations and thus possibly a signal that a company is manipulating estimates in order to achieve a particular effect on its reported net income?

As another example, if two companies in the same industry have dramatically different estimates for uncollectible accounts as a percentage of their sales, warranty expenses as a percentage of sales, or estimated useful lives as a percentage of assets, it is important to understand the underlying reasons. Are the differences consistent with differences in the two companies' business operations (e.g., lower uncollectible accounts for one company reflecting a different, more creditworthy customer base or possibly stricter credit policies)? Another difference consistent with differences in business operations would be a difference in estimated useful lives of assets if one of the companies employs newer equipment. Or, alternatively, are the differences seemingly inconsistent with differences in the two companies' business operations, possibly signaling that a company is manipulating estimates?

Information about a company's accounting policies and significant estimates are described in the footnotes to the financial statements and in the management discussion and analysis section of a company's annual report.

When possible, the monetary effect of differences in expense recognition policies and estimates can facilitate more meaningful comparisons with a single company's historical performance or across a number of companies. An analyst can use the monetary effect to adjust the reported expenses so that they are on a comparable basis.

Even when the monetary effects of differences in policies and estimates cannot be calculated, it is generally possible to characterize the relative conservatism of the policies and estimates and, therefore, to qualitatively assess how such differences might affect reported expenses and thus financial ratios.

5.   NONRECURRING ITEMS AND NONOPERATING ITEMS

From a company's income statements, we can see its earnings from last year and in the previous year. Looking forward, the question is: What will the company earn next year and in the years after?

To assess a company's future earnings, it is helpful to separate those prior years' items of income and expense that are likely to continue in the future from those items that are less likely to continue.[27] Some items from prior years are clearly not expected to continue in the future periods and are separately disclosed on a company's income statement. Two such items are (1) discontinued operations, and (2) extraordinary items (the latter category is no longer permitted under IFRS). These two items, if applicable, must be reported separately from continuing operations.[28]

For other items on a company's income statement, such as unusual items, accounting changes, and nonoperating income, the likelihood of their continuing in the future is somewhat less clear and requires the analyst to make some judgments.

5.1. Discontinued Operations

When a company disposes of or establishes a plan to dispose of one of its component operations and will have no further involvement in the operation, the income statement reports separately the effect of this disposal as a "discontinued" operation under both IFRS and U.S. GAAP. Financial standards provide various criteria for reporting the effect separately, which are generally that the discontinued component must be separable both physically and operationally.[29]

Because the discontinued operation will no longer provide earnings (or cash flow) to the company, an analyst can eliminate discontinued operations in formulating expectations about a company's future financial performance.

In Exhibit 4-2, Kraft reported a loss from discontinued operations of $4 million in 2004 and earnings of $97 million in both 2003 and 2002. In Footnote 5 of its financial statements, Kraft explains that it sold substantially all of its sugar confectionary business (including brands such as Life Savers and Altoids). The $4 million loss and $97 million earnings refer to the amount of loss (earnings) of the sugar confectionary business in each of those years.

5.2. Extraordinary Items — *Unusual & Infrequent*

IAS No. 1 prohibits classification of any income or expense items as being "extraordinary."[30] Under U.S. GAAP, an extraordinary item is one that is both unusual in nature and infrequent in occurrence. Extraordinary items are presented separately on the income statement and allow a reader of the statements to see that these items are not part of a company's operating activities and are not expected to occur on an ongoing basis. Extraordinary items are shown net of tax and appear on the income statement below discontinued operations. An example of an extraordinary item is provided in Example 4-12.

---

[27]In business writing, items expected to continue in the future are often described as "persistent" or "permanent," whereas those not expected to continue are described as "transitory."

[28]These requirements apply to material amounts.

[29]IFRS No. 5, *Non-Current Assets Held for Sale and Discontinued Operations*, paragraphs 31–33.

[30]IAS No. 1, *Presentation of Financial Statements*, paragraph 85, effective 2005. In prior years, classification of items as extraordinary was permitted.

EXAMPLE 4-12   Extraordinary Gain: Purchase of a Business for Less than the Fair Value of the Identifiable Net Assets

Vicon Industries in its annual report made the following disclosure:

> *On October 1, 2004, the Company entered into an agreement to purchase all of the operating assets of Videotronic Infosystems GmbH ("Videotronic"), a Germany based video system supplier which was operating under insolvency protection, for 700,000 Eurodollars [sic] (approximately $868,000). . . . During the year ended September 30, 2005, the Company recognized a $211,000 extraordinary gain on the recovery of Videotronic net assets in excess of their allocated purchase price. Such gain includes adjustments to assigned values of accounts receivable, inventories, trade payables and severance liabilities.*

Source: Vicon Industries 10-K Report for fiscal year ended 30 September 2005, filed 29 December 2005: Note 15.

Companies apply judgment to determine whether an item is extraordinary based on guidance from accounting standards (Accounting Practices Board Opinion No. 30). Judgment on whether an item is unusual in nature requires consideration of the company's environment, including its industry and geography. Determining whether an item is infrequent in occurrence is based on expectations of whether it will occur again in the near future. Standard setters offer specific guidance in some cases. For example, following Hurricanes Katrina and Rita in 2005, the American Institute of Certified Public Accountants issued Technical Practice Aid 5400.05, which states (the material in square brackets has been added): "A natural disaster [such as a hurricane, tornado, fire, or earthquake] of a type that is reasonably expected to re-occur would not meet both conditions [for classification as an extraordinary item]."

Given the requirements for classification of an item as extraordinary—unusual and infrequent—an analyst can generally eliminate extraordinary items from expectations about a company's future financial performance unless there is some indication that such an extraordinary item may reoccur.

5.3.   Unusual or Infrequent Items

Items that do not meet the definition of extraordinary are shown as part of a company's continuing operations. Items that are unusual or infrequent—but not both—cannot be shown as extraordinary. For example, restructuring charges, such as costs to close plants and employee termination costs, are considered part of a company's ordinary activities. As another example, gains and losses arising when a company sells an asset or part of a business for more or less than its carrying value are also disclosed separately on the income statement but are not considered extraordinary because such sales are considered ordinary business activities.[31]

Highlighting the unusual or infrequent nature of these items assists an analyst in judging the likelihood that such items will reoccur.

In Exhibit 4-2, Kraft's income statement showed several such infrequent but not unusual items, all of which are included as part of operating income. The company reported a $111 million loss in 2002 from "integration costs and a loss on sale of a food factory," followed by a $13 million reduction of these costs in 2003. In Note 14 of its financial statements, the company explains that these costs arose from consolidating production lines in North America. Also, the company reported $142 million, $6 million, and $603 million in 2002, 2003, and 2004, respectively, for "asset impairment and exit costs" and explains in the footnotes that the large costs in 2004 are related to its restructuring program and reflect asset disposals, severance, and other implementation aspects.

Finally, Kraft reported an $80 million gain on the sale of businesses in 2002 and a $31 million gain in 2003, followed by a $3 million loss on the sale of businesses in 2004. In Note 14 of its financial statements, Kraft explains that the $80 million gain in 2002 arose from the sale of its Latin American bakery ingredient business and several small food businesses; the $31 million gain in 2003 arose from the sale of a European rice business and an Italian fresh cheese business; and the $3 million loss in 2004 arose from the sale of a Brazilian snack nuts business and Norwegian candy business trademarks. An analyst would seek to understand how these disposals fit with the company's strategy and what effect, if material, these disposals would have on the company's future operations.

Generally, in forecasting future operations, an analyst would assess whether the items reported are likely to reoccur and also possible implications for future earnings. It is generally not advisable simply to ignore all unusual items.

5.4. Changes in Accounting Standards

At times, standard setters issue new pronouncements that require companies to change accounting principles. In other cases, changes in accounting principles (e.g., from one acceptable inventory costing method to another) are made for other reasons, such as providing a better reflection of the company's performance. Changes in accounting principles are reported through retrospective application,[32] unless it is impractical to do so. *Retrospective application* means that the financial statements for all fiscal years shown in a company's financial report are presented as if the newly adopted accounting principle had been used throughout the entire period. Footnotes to the financial statements describe the change and explain the justification for the change.

Because changes in accounting principles are retrospectively applied, the financial statements that appear within a financial report are comparable. So, if a company's annual report for 2006 includes its financial statements for fiscal years 2004, 2005, and 2006, all of these statements will be comparable.

---

[31]In its financial statement footnotes, Groupe Danone provides a reconciliation between operating income under French GAAP, which excludes certain exceptional items (such as gains and losses on disposals), and U.S. GAAP.

[32]IAS No. 8, *Accounting Policies, Changes in Accounting Estimates and Errors,* and FASB Financial Accounting Statement No. 154, *Accounting Changes and Error Corrections.*

In years prior to 2005, under both IFRS and U.S. GAAP, the cumulative effect of changes in accounting policies was typically shown at the bottom of the income statement in the year of change instead of using retrospective application. It is possible that future accounting standards may occasionally require a company to report the change differently than retrospective application. Footnote disclosures are required to explain how the transition from the old standard to the new one was handled. During the period when companies make the transition from the old standard to the new, an analyst would examine disclosures to ensure comparability across companies.

In contrast to changes in accounting policies (such as whether to expense the cost of employee stock options), companies sometimes make *changes in accounting estimates* (such as the useful life of a depreciable asset). Changes in accounting estimates are handled prospectively, with the change affecting the financial statements for the period of change and future periods.[33] No adjustments are made to prior statements, and the adjustment is not shown on the face of the income statement. Significant changes should be disclosed in the footnotes.

Another possible adjustment is a *correction of an error for a prior period* (e.g., in financial statements issued for an earlier year). This cannot be handled by simply adjusting the current period income statement. Correction of an error for a prior period is handled by restating the financial statements (including the balance sheet, statement of owners' equity, and cash flow statement) for the prior periods presented in the current financial statements.[34] Footnote disclosures are required regarding the error. These disclosures should be examined carefully because they may reveal weaknesses in the company's accounting systems and financial controls.

5.5. Nonoperating Items: Investing and Financing Activities

Nonoperating items are reported separately from operating income. For example, if a nonfinancial service company invests in equity or debt securities issued by another company, any interest, dividends, or profits from sales of these securities will be shown as nonoperating income. In general, for nonfinancial services companies,[35] nonoperating income that is disclosed separately on the income statement (or in the notes) includes amounts earned through investing activities.

Among nonoperating items on the income statement (or accompanying notes), nonfinancial service companies also disclose the interest expense on their debt securities, including amortization of any discount or premium. The amount of interest expense is related to the amount of a company's borrowings and is generally described in the financial footnotes. For financial service companies, interest income and expense are likely components of operating activities.

In practice, investing and financing activities may be disclosed on a net basis, with the components disclosed separately in the footnotes. In its income statement for 2004, Kraft, for example, disclosed net interest and other debt expense of $666 million. The financial statement footnotes (not shown) further disclose that Kraft's total interest expense was $679 million and interest income was $13 million, thus the net $666 million. Groupe Danone's footnotes provide similar disclosures.

---

[33]Ibid.

[34]Ibid.

[35]Examples of financial services firms are insurance companies, banks, brokers, dealers, and investment companies.

For purposes of assessing a company's future performance, the amount of financing expense will depend on the company's financing policy (target capital structure) and borrowing costs. The amount of investing income will depend on the purpose and success of investing activities. For a nonfinancial company, a significant amount of financial income would typically warrant further exploration. What are the reasons underlying the company's investments in the securities of other companies? Is the company simply investing excess cash in short-term securities to generate income higher than cash deposits, or is the company purchasing securities issued by other companies for strategic reasons, such as access to raw material supply or research?

6. EARNINGS PER SHARE

One metric of particular importance to an equity investor is earnings per share (EPS). EPS is an input into ratios such as the price/earnings ratio. Additionally, each shareholder in a company owns a different number of shares. A presentation of EPS, therefore, enables each shareholder to compute his or her share of the company's earnings. Under IFRS, IAS No. 33, *Earnings per Share*, requires the presentation of EPS on the face of the income statement for net profit or loss (net income) and profit or loss (income) from continuing operations. Similar presentation is required under U.S. GAAP by Financial Accounting Statement No. 128, *Earnings per Share*. This section outlines the calculations for EPS and explains how the calculation differs for a simple versus complex capital structure.

6.1. Simple versus Complex Capital Structure

A company's capital is composed of its equity and debt. Some types of equity have preference over others, and some debt (and other instruments) may be converted into equity. Under IFRS, the type of equity for which EPS is presented are ordinary shares. **Ordinary shares** are those equity shares that are subordinate to all other types of equity. This is the basic ownership of the company—the equity holders who are paid last in a liquidation of the company and who benefit the most when the company does well. Under U.S. GAAP, this equity is referred to as **common stock** or **common shares**, reflecting U.S. language usage. The terms *ordinary shares, common stock,* and *common shares* are used equivalently in the remaining discussion.

When a company has any securities that are potentially convertible into common stock, it is said to have a complex capital structure. Specific examples of securities that are potentially convertible into common stock include convertible bonds, convertible preferred stock, employee stock options, and warrants.[36] If a company's capital structure does not include securities that are potentially convertible into common stock, it is said to have a simple capital structure.

The distinction between simple versus complex capital structure is relevant to the calculation of EPS because any securities that are potentially convertible into common stock

---

[36]A warrant is a call option typically attached to securities issued by a company, such as bonds. A warrant gives the holder the right to acquire the company's stock from the company at a specified price within a specified time period. IFRS and U.S. GAAP standards regarding earnings per share apply equally to call options, warrants, and equivalent instruments.

could, as a result of conversion, potentially dilute (i.e., decrease) EPS. Information about such a potential dilution is valuable to a company's current and potential shareholders; therefore, accounting standards require companies to disclose what their EPS would be if all dilutive securities were converted into common stock. The EPS that would result if all dilutive securities were converted is called **diluted EPS**. In contrast, **basic EPS** is calculated using the actual earnings available to common stock and the weighted average number of shares outstanding.

Companies are required to report both their basic EPS and their diluted EPS. In Exhibit 4-2, Kraft reported basic EPS of $1.56 and diluted EPS of $1.55 for 2004, lower than EPS (from continuing operations) of $1.95 for 2003. In Exhibit 4-1, Danone reported basic EPS of 1.26 and diluted EPS of 1.25 for 2004, much lower than 2003. An analyst would try to determine the causes underlying the changes in EPS, a topic we will address following an explanation of the calculations of both basic and diluted EPS.

6.2. Basic EPS

Basic EPS is the amount of income available to common shareholders divided by the weighted average number of common shares outstanding over a period. The amount of income available to common shareholders is the amount of net income remaining after preferred dividends (if any) have been paid. Thus, the formula to calculate basic EPS is:

$$\text{Basic EPS} = \frac{\text{Net income} - \text{Preferred dividends}}{\text{Weighted average number of shares outstanding}} \qquad (4\text{-}1)$$

The weighted average number of shares outstanding is a time weighting of common shares outstanding, and the methodology applies to calculating diluted EPS. As an example, assume a company began the year with 2,000,000 shares outstanding and repurchased 100,000 shares on 1 July. The weighted average number of shares outstanding would be the sum of 2,000,000 shares × 1/2 year + 1,900,000 shares × 1/2 year, or 1,950,000 shares. So, the company would use 1,950,000 shares in calculating its basic EPS.

If the number of shares of common stock increases as a result of a stock dividend, stock bonus, or a stock split (all three represent the receipt of additional shares by existing shareholders), the EPS calculation reflects the change retroactively to the beginning of the period.

Examples of a basic EPS computation are presented in Examples 4-13, 4-14, and 4-15.

EXAMPLE 4-13　A Basic EPS Calculation (1)

For the year ended 31 December 2006, Shopalot Company had net income of $1,950,000. The company had an average of 1,500,000 shares of common stock outstanding, no preferred stock, and no convertible securities. What was Shopalot's basic EPS?

Solution. Shopalot's basic EPS was $1.30, calculated as $1,950,000 divided by 1,500,000 shares.

EXAMPLE 4-14   A Basic EPS Calculation (2)

For the year ended 31 December 2006, Angler Products had net income of $2,500,000. The company declared and paid $200,000 of dividends on preferred stock. The company also had the following common stock share information:

Shares outstanding on 1 January 2006	1,000,000
Shares issued on 1 April 2006	200,000
Shares repurchased (treasury shares) on 1 October 2006	(100,000)
Shares outstanding on 31 December 2006	1,100,000

1. What is the company's weighted average number of shares outstanding?
2. What is the company's basic EPS?

Solution to 1. The weighted average number of shares outstanding is determined by the length of time each quantity of shares was outstanding:

1,000,000 × (3 months/12 months)	=	250,000
1,200,000 × (6 months/12 months)	=	600,000
1,100,000 × (3 months/12 months)	=	275,000
Weighted average number of shares outstanding		1,125,000

Solution to 2. Basic EPS is (Net income − Preferred dividends)/Weighted average number of shares = ($2,500,000 − $200,000)/1,125,000 = $2.04

EXAMPLE 4-15   A Basic EPS Calculation (3)

Assume the same facts as in Example 4-14 except that on 1 December 2006, the company institutes a two-for-one stock split. Each shareholder receives two shares in exchange for each current share that he or she owns. What is the company's basic EPS?

Solution. For EPS calculation purposes, a stock split is treated as if it occurred at the beginning of the period. The weighted average number of shares would, therefore, be 2,250,000, and the basic EPS would be $1.02.

6.3. Diluted EPS

If a company has a simple capital structure (i.e., one with no potentially dilutive securities), then its basic EPS is equal to its diluted EPS. If, however, a company has dilutive securities, its diluted EPS is lower than its basic EPS. The sections below describe the effects of three types of potentially dilutive securities: convertible preferred, convertible debt, and employee stock options.

6.3.1. Diluted EPS When a Company Has Convertible Preferred Stock Outstanding

When a company has convertible preferred stock outstanding, diluted EPS is calculated using the **if-converted method** (i.e., what EPS would have been *if* the convertible preferred securities had been converted at the beginning of the period). What would have been the effect if the securities had been converted? If the convertible preferred securities had converted, these securities would no longer be outstanding; instead, additional common stock would be outstanding. Therefore, if such a conversion had taken place, the company would not have paid preferred dividends and would have had more shares of common stock.

The diluted EPS using the if-converted method for convertible preferred stock is equal to the amount of net income divided by the weighted average number of shares outstanding plus the new shares of common stock that would be issued upon conversion of the preferred. Thus, the formula to calculate diluted EPS using the if-converted method for preferred stock is:

$$\text{Diluted EPS} = (\text{Net income})/(\text{Weighted average number} \\ \text{of shares outstanding} + \text{New common shares} \\ \text{that would have been issued at conversion}) \qquad (4\text{-}2)$$

A diluted EPS calculation using the if-converted method for preferred stock is provided in Example 4-16 on page 148.

6.3.2. Diluted EPS When a Company Has Convertible Debt Outstanding

When a company has convertible debt outstanding, the diluted EPS calculation is similar to the calculation for convertible preferred: Diluted EPS is calculated using the if-converted method (i.e., what EPS would have been *if* the convertible debt had been converted at the beginning of the period). If the convertible debt had been converted, the debt securities would no longer be outstanding; instead, additional common stock would be outstanding. Therefore, if such a conversion had taken place, the company would not have paid interest on the convertible debt and would have had more shares of common stock.

To calculate diluted EPS using the if-converted method for convertible debt, the amount of net income available to common shareholders must be increased by the amount of after-tax interest related to the convertible debt. In addition, the weighted average number of shares in the denominator increases by the number of new shares of common stock that would be issued upon conversion of the convertible debt. Thus, the formula to calculate diluted EPS using the if-converted method for convertible debt is:

$$\text{Diluted EPS} = (\text{Net income} + \text{After-tax interest on convertible debt} \\ - \text{Preferred dividends})/(\text{Weighted average number of} \\ \text{shares outstanding} + \text{New common shares that could} \\ \text{have been issued at conversion}) \qquad (4\text{-}3)$$

A diluted EPS calculation using the if-converted method for convertible debt is provided in Example 4-17.

EXAMPLE 4-16   A Diluted EPS Calculation Using the If-Converted Method for Preferred Stock

For the year ended 31 December 2006, Bright-Warm Utility Company had net income of $1,750,000. The company had an average of 500,000 shares of common stock outstanding, 20,000 shares of convertible preferred, and no other potentially dilutive securities. Each share of preferred pays a dividend of $10 per share, and each is convertible into five shares of the company's common stock. Calculate the company's basic and diluted EPS.

Solution. If the 20,000 shares of convertible preferred had each converted into 5 shares of the company's common stock, the company would have had an additional 100,000 shares of common stock (5 shares of common for each of the 20,000 shares of preferred). If the conversion had taken place, the company would not have paid preferred dividends of $200,000 ($10 per share for each of the 20,000 shares of preferred). As shown in Exhibit 4-9, the company's basic EPS was $3.10 and its diluted EPS was $2.92.

EXHIBIT 4-9   Calculation of Diluted EPS for Bright-Warm Utility Company

Using the If-Converted Method: Case of Preferred Stock		
	Basic EPS	**Diluted EPS Using If-Converted Method**
Net income	$1,750,000	$1,750,000
Preferred dividend	−200,000	0
Numerator	$1,550,000	$1,750,000
Weighted average number of shares outstanding	500,000	500,000
If converted	0	100,000
Denominator	500,000	600,000
EPS	**$3.10**	**$2.92**

EXAMPLE 4-17   A Diluted EPS Calculation Using the If-Converted Method for Convertible Debt

Oppnox Company reported net income of $750,000 for the year ended 31 December 2005. The company had an average of 690,000 shares of common stock outstanding. In addition, the company has only one potentially dilutive security: $50,000 of 6 percent convertible bonds, convertible into a total of 10,000 shares. Assuming a tax rate of 30 percent, calculate Oppnox's basic and diluted EPS.

Solution. If the convertible debt had been converted, the debt securities would no longer be outstanding; instead, an additional 10,000 shares of common stock would be outstanding. Also, if such a conversion had taken place, the company would not have paid interest on the convertible debt of $3,000, equivalent to $3,000(1 − 0.30) = $2,100 on an after-tax basis. To calculate diluted EPS using the if-converted method for convertible debt, the amount of net income available to common shareholders is increased by $2,100. Also, the weighted average number of shares in the denominator increases by 10,000 shares.

EXHIBIT 4-10   Calculation of Diluted EPS for Oppnox Company

Using the If-Converted Method: Case of a Convertible Bond

	Basic EPS	**Diluted EPS Using If-Converted Method**
Net income	$750,000	$750,000
After-tax cost of interest		2,100
Numerator	$750,000	$752,100
Weighted average number of shares outstanding	690,000	690,000
If converted	0	10,000
Denominator	690,000	700,000
EPS	**$1.09**	**$1.07**

6.3.3. Diluted EPS When a Company Has Stock Options, Warrants, or Their Equivalents Outstanding

Under U.S. GAAP, when a company has stock options, warrants, or their equivalents[37] outstanding, the diluted EPS is calculated using the **treasury stock method** (i.e., what EPS would have been *if* the options had been exercised and the company had used the proceeds to repurchase common stock). If the options had been exercised, the company would have received cash for the amount of the option exercise price. The options would no longer be outstanding; instead, additional common stock would be outstanding. Under the treasury stock method, a further calculation is made to adjust the number of shares outstanding by the number of shares that could have been purchased with the cash received upon exercise of the options.

To calculate diluted EPS using the treasury stock method for options, the weighted average number of shares in the denominator increases by the number of new shares of common stock that would be issued upon exercise of the options minus the number of shares that could have been purchased with the cash received upon exercise of the options. No change is

---

[37]Hereafter, options, warrants, and their equivalents will be referred to simply as *options* because the accounting treatment is interchangeable for these instruments under IFRS and U.S. GAAP.

made to the numerator. Thus, the formula to calculate diluted EPS using the treasury stock method for options is

$$\text{Diluted EPS} = \text{(Net income} - \text{Preferred dividends)/(Weighted average}$$
$$\text{number of shares outstanding} + \text{New shares that could have}$$
$$\text{been issued at option exercise} - \text{Shares that could have been}$$
$$\text{purchased with cash received upon exercise)} \qquad (4\text{-}4)$$

A diluted EPS calculation using the treasury stock method for options is provided in Example 4-18.

EXAMPLE 4-18   A Diluted EPS Calculation Using the Treasury Stock Method for Options

Hihotech Company reported net income of $2.3 million for the year ended 30 June 2005 and had an average of 800,000 common shares outstanding. The company has outstanding 30,000 options with an exercise price of $35 and no other potentially dilutive securities. Over the year, the company's market price has averaged $55 per share. Calculate the company's basic and diluted EPS.

Solution. Using the treasury stock method, we first calculate that the company would have received $1,050,000 ($35 for each of the 30,000 options exercised) if all the options had been exercised. The options would no longer be outstanding; instead, 30,000 new shares of common stock would be outstanding. Under the treasury stock method, we reduce the number of new shares by the number of shares that could have been purchased with the cash received upon exercise of the options. At an average market price of $55 per share, the $1,050,000 proceeds from option exercise could have purchased 19,091 shares of treasury stock. Therefore, the net new shares issued would have been 10,909 (calculated as 30,000 minus 19,091). No change is made to the numerator. As shown in Exhibit 4-11, the company's basic EPS was $2.88 and the diluted EPS was $2.84.

EXHIBIT 4-11   Calculation of Diluted EPS for Hihotech Company

Using the Treasury Stock Method: Case of Stock Options		
	Basic EPS	**Diluted EPS Using Treasury Stock Method**
Net income	$2,300,000	$2,300,000
Numerator	$2,300,000	$2,300,000
Weighted average number of shares outstanding	800,000	800,000
If converted	0	10,909
Denominator	800,000	810,909
EPS	**$2.88**	**$2.84**

Under IFRS, IAS No. 33 requires a similar computation but does not refer to it as the "treasury stock method." The company is required to consider that any assumed proceeds are received from the issuance of new shares at the average market price for the period. These new "inferred" shares would be disregarded in the computation of diluted EPS, but the excess of the new shares issued under options contracts over the new "inferred" shares would be added into the weighted average number of shares outstanding. The results are similar to the treasury stock method, as shown in Example 4-19.

EXAMPLE 4-19   Diluted EPS for Options under IFRS

Assuming the same facts as in Example 4-18, calculate the weighted average number of shares outstanding for diluted EPS under IFRS.

Solution. If the options had been converted, the company would have received $1,050,000. If this amount had been received from the issuance of new shares at the average market price of $55 per share, the company would have sold 19,091 shares. The excess of the shares issued under options (30,000) over the shares the company could have sold at market prices (19,091) is 10,909. This amount is added to the weighted average number of shares outstanding of 800,000 to get diluted shares of 810,909. Note that this is the same result as that obtained under U.S. GAAP; it is just derived in a different manner.

6.3.4. Other Issues with Diluted EPS

It is possible that some potentially convertible securities could be **antidilutive** (i.e., their inclusion in the computation would result in an EPS higher than the company's basic EPS). Under accounting standards, antidilutive securities are not included in the calculation of diluted EPS. In general, diluted EPS reflects maximum potential dilution. Example 4-20 provides an illustration of an antidilutive security.

EXAMPLE 4-20   An Antidilutive Security

For the year ended 31 December 2006, Dim-Cool Utility Company had net income of $1,750,000. The company had an average of 500,000 shares of common stock outstanding, 20,000 shares of convertible preferred, and no other potentially dilutive securities. Each share of preferred pays a dividend of $10 per share, and each is convertible into three shares of the company's common stock. What was the company's basic and diluted EPS?

Solution. If the 20,000 shares of convertible preferred had each converted into 3 shares of the company's common stock, the company would have had an additional 60,000 shares of common stock (3 shares of common for each of the 20,000 shares of preferred). If the conversion had taken place, the company would not have paid preferred dividends of $200,000 ($10 per share for each of the 20,000 shares of preferred). The effect of using the if-converted method would be EPS of $3.13, as shown in Exhibit 4-12. Because this is greater than the company's basic EPS of $3.10, the securities are said to be antidilutive and the effect of their conversion would not be included in diluted EPS. Diluted EPS would be the same as basic EPS (i.e., $3.10).

EXHIBIT 4-12   Calculation for an Antidilutive Security

	Basic EPS	Diluted EPS Using If-Converted Method	
Net income	$1,750,000	$1,750,000	
Preferred dividend	−200,000	0	
Numerator	$1,550,000	$1,750,000	
Weighted average number of shares outstanding	500,000	500,000	
If converted	0	60,000	
Denominator	500,000	560,000	
EPS	**$3.10**	$3.13	←Exceeds basic EPS; security is antidilutive and, therefore, not included.

7. ANALYSIS OF THE INCOME STATEMENT

In this section, we apply two analytical tools to analyze the income statement: common-size analysis and income statement ratios. In analyzing the income statement, the objective is to assess a company's performance over a period of time—compared with its own historical performance or to the performance of another company.

7.1. Common-Size Analysis of the Income Statement

Common-size analysis of the income statement can be performed by stating each line item on the income statement as a percentage of revenue.[38] Common-size statements facilitate comparison across time periods (time-series analysis) and across companies of different sizes (cross-sectional analysis).

---

[38]This format can be distinguished as *vertical common-size analysis*. As the reading on financial statement analysis discusses, there is another type of common-size analysis, known as *horizontal common-size analysis,* that states items in relation to a selected base year value. Unless otherwise indicated, text references to *common-size analysis* refer to vertical analysis.

EXHIBIT 4-13   Income Statements for Company A, B, and C

Panel A: Income Statements for Company A, Company B, and Company C

($)	A	B	C
Sales	$10,000,000	$10,000,000	$2,000,000
Cost of sales	3,000,000	7,500,000	600,000
Gross profit	7,000,000	2,500,000	1,400,000
Selling, general, and administrative expenses	1,000,000	1,000,000	200,000
Research and development	2,000,000	–	400,000
Advertising	2,000,000	–	400,000
Operating profit	2,000,000	1,500,000	400,000

Panel B: Common-Size Income Statements for Companies A, B, and C

(%)	A	B	C
Sales	100%	100%	100%
Cost of sales	30	75	30
Gross profit	70	25	70
Selling, general, and administrative expenses	10	10	10
Research and development	20	0	20
Advertising	20	0	20
Operating profit	20	15	20

Note: Each line item is expressed as a percentage of the company's sales.

To illustrate, Panel A of Exhibit 4-13 presents an income statement for three hypothetical companies. Company A and Company B, each with $10 million in sales, are larger (as measured by sales) than Company C, which has only $2 million in sales. In addition, Companies A and B both have higher operating profit: $2 million and $1.5 million, respectively, compared with Company C's operating profit of only $400,000.

How can an analyst meaningfully compare the performance of these companies? By preparing a common-size income statement, as illustrated in Panel B, an analyst can readily see that the percentages of Company C's expenses and profit relative to its sales are exactly the same as for Company A. Furthermore, although Company C's operating profit is lower than Company B's in absolute dollars, it is higher in percentage terms (20 percent for Company C compared with only 15 percent for Company B). For each $100 of sales, Company C generates $5 more operating profit than Company B. In other words, Company C is more profitable than Company B based on this measure.

The common-size income statement also highlights differences in companies' strategies. Comparing the two larger companies, Company A reports significantly higher gross profit as a percentage of sales than does Company B (70 percent compared with 25 percent). Given that both companies operate in the same industry, why can Company A generate so much higher gross profit? One possible explanation is found by comparing the operating expenses of the two companies. Company A spends significantly more on research and development and on advertising than Company B. Expenditures on research and development likely result in products with superior technology. Expenditures on advertising likely result in greater brand awareness. So, based on these differences, it is likely that Company A is selling technologically superior products with a better brand image. Company B may be selling its products more cheaply (with a lower gross profit as a percentage of sales) but saving money by not investing in research and development or advertising. In practice, differences across companies are more subtle, but the concept is similar. An analyst, noting significant differences, would seek to understand the underlying reasons for the differences and their implications for the future performance of the companies.

For most expenses, comparison to the amount of sales is appropriate. However, in the case of taxes, it is more meaningful to compare the amount of taxes with the amount of pretax income. Using financial footnote disclosure, an analyst can then examine the causes for differences in effective tax rates. To project the companies' future net income, an analyst would project the companies' pretax income and apply an estimated effective tax rate determined in part by the historical tax rates.

Vertical common-size analysis of the income statement is particularly useful in cross-sectional analysis—comparing companies with each other for a particular time period or comparing a company with industry or sector data. The analyst could select individual peer companies for comparison, use industry data from published sources, or compile data from databases based on a selection of peer companies or broader industry data. For example, Exhibit 4-14 presents common-size income statement data compiled for the components of the Standard & Poor's 500 classified into the 10 S&P/MSCI Global Industrial Classification System (GICS) sectors using 2005 data. Note that when compiling aggregate data such as this, some level of aggregation is necessary and less detail may be available than from peer company financial statements. The performance of an individual company can be compared with industry or peer company data to evaluate its relative performance.

7.2. Income Statement Ratios

One aspect of financial performance is profitability. One indicator of profitability is **net profit margin**, also known as **profit margin** and **return on sales**, which is calculated as net income divided by revenue (or sales).[39]

$$\text{Net profit margin} = \frac{\text{Net income}}{\text{Revenue}}$$

Net profit margin measures the amount of income that a company was able to generate for each dollar of revenue. A higher level of net profit margin indicates higher profitability and is thus more desirable. Net profit margin can also be found directly on the common-size income statements.

For Kraft Foods, net profit margin for 2004 was 8.3 percent (calculated as earnings from continuing operations of $2,669 million, divided by net revenues of $32,168 million).

---

[39]In the definition of margin ratios of this type, *sales* is often used interchangeably with *revenue*. *Return on sales* has also been used to refer to a class of profitability ratios having revenue in the denominator.

EXHIBIT 4-14   Common-Size Income Statement Statistics for the S&P 500

Classified by S&P/MSCI GICS
Sector
Data for 2005

	Energy	Materials	Industrials	Consumer Discretionary	Consumer Staples	Health Care	Financials	Information Technology	Telecom. Services	Utilities
Panel A: Median Data										
No. observations	29	30	49	85	36	52	87	73	9	31
Operating margin	17.24	11.85	11.94	11.15	12.53	16.73	34.62	12.59	22.85	13.52
Pretax margin	19.17	10.95	10.55	10.17	10.76	14.03	23.28	13.60	18.18	9.27
Taxes	5.63	2.87	2.94	3.59	3.26	4.69	6.51	4.06	4.27	3.12
Profit margin	13.97	7.68	7.28	6.87	6.74	9.35	16.09	11.60	10.91	6.93
Cost of goods sold	66.52	68.35	69.02	63.29	56.24	45.29	42.29	47.17	41.76	76.79
Selling, general, and administrative expenses	3.82	10.20	15.88	22.46	25.07	31.77	28.98	31.81	22.40	4.91
Panel B: Mean Data										
No. observations	29	30	49	85	36	52	87	73	9	31
Operating margin	23.13	14.12	13.16	12.69	14.51	17.84	35.45	15.13	20.66	14.60
Pretax margin	23.96	12.58	11.09	10.38	12.03	15.83	23.42	15.25	15.19	8.00
Taxes	7.72	3.38	3.33	3.94	3.81	4.94	6.65	4.98	5.14	2.48
Profit margin	16.02	8.58	7.69	6.32	8.15	10.80	16.37	10.26	9.52	5.68
Cost of goods sold	62.36	67.87	68.92	62.41	56.62	49.20	51.47	46.65	40.61	76.51
Selling, general, and administrative expenses	5.44	13.05	17.45	22.82	25.88	30.48	27.68	33.06	22.81	4.91
Average tax rate computed on mean	32.22	26.89	30.04	37.98	31.65	31.21	28.40	32.66	33.82	30.99

Source: Based on data from Compustat.

155

To judge this ratio, some comparison is needed. Kraft's profitability can be compared with that of another company or with its own previous performance. Compared with previous years, Kraft's profitability has declined. In 2003, net profit margin was 11.1 percent, and in 2002, it was 11.3 percent.

Another measure of profitability is the gross profit margin. Gross profit is calculated as revenue minus cost of goods sold, and the **gross profit margin** is calculated as the gross profit divided by revenue.

$$\text{Gross profit margin} = \frac{\text{Gross profit}}{\text{Revenue}}$$

The gross profit margin measures the amount of gross profit that a company generated for each dollar of revenue. A higher level of gross profit margin indicates higher profitability and thus is generally more desirable, although differences in gross profit margins across companies reflect differences in companies' strategies. For example, consider a company pursuing a strategy of selling a differentiated product (e.g., a product differentiated based on brand name, quality, superior technology, or patent protection). The company would likely be able to sell the differentiated product at a higher price than a similar, but undifferentiated, product and, therefore, would likely show a higher gross profit margin than a company selling an undifferentiated product. Although a company selling a differentiated product would likely show a higher gross profit margin, this may take time. In the initial stage of the strategy, the company would likely incur costs to create a differentiated product, such as advertising or research and development, which would not be reflected in the gross margin calculation.

Kraft's gross profit (shown in Exhibit 4-2) was $11,785 in 2002 and $11,887 in 2004. In other words, in absolute terms, Kraft's gross profit increased. However, expressing gross profit as a percentage of net revenues,[40] it is apparent that Kraft's gross profit margin declined, as Exhibit 4-15 illustrates. From over 40 percent in 2002, Kraft's profit margin declined to 36.95 percent in 2004.

The net profit margin and gross profit margin are just two of the many subtotals that can be generated from common-size income statements. Other margins used by analysts include the **operating margin** (operating income divided by revenue) and **pretax margin** (earnings before taxes divided by revenue).

EXHIBIT 4-15   Kraft's Gross Profit Margin

	2004		2003		2002	
	$ millions	%	$ millions	%	$ millions	%
Net revenues	32,168	100.00	30,498	100 00	29,248	100.00
Cost of sales	20,281	63.05	18,531	60.76	17,463	59.71
Gross profit	11,887	**36.95**	11,967	**39.24**	11,785	**40.29**

[40]Some items disclosed separately in Kraft's actual income statement have been summarized as "other operating costs (income)" for this display.

8. COMPREHENSIVE INCOME

The general expression for net income is revenue minus expenses. There are, however, certain items of revenue and expense that, by accounting convention, are excluded from the net income calculation. To understand how reported shareholders' equity of one period links with reported shareholders' equity of the next period, we must understand these excluded items, known as **other comprehensive income**.

Comprehensive income is defined as "the change in equity [net assets] of a business enterprise during a period from transactions and other events and circumstances from non-owner sources. It includes all changes in equity during a period except those resulting from investments by owners and distributions to owners."[41] So, comprehensive income includes *both* net income and other revenue and expense items that are excluded from the net income calculation (other comprehensive income). Assume, for example, a company's beginning shareholders' equity is €110 million, its net income for the year is €10 million, its cash dividends for the year are €2 million, and there was no issuance or repurchase of common stock. If the company's actual ending shareholders' equity is €123 million, then €5 million [€123 − (€110 + €10 − €2)] has bypassed the net income calculation by being classified as other comprehensive income. (If the company had no other comprehensive income, its ending shareholders' equity would have been €118 million [€110 + €10 − €2].)

In U.S. financial statements, according to U.S. GAAP, four types of items are treated as other comprehensive income.

- *Foreign currency translation adjustments.* In consolidating the financial statements of foreign subsidiaries, the effects of translating the subsidiaries' balance sheet assets and liabilities at current exchange rates are included as other comprehensive income.
- *Unrealized gains or losses on derivatives contracts accounted for as hedges.* Changes in the fair value of derivatives are recorded each period, but these changes in value for certain derivatives (those considered hedges) are treated as other comprehensive income and thus bypass the income statement.
- *Unrealized holding gains and losses on a certain category of investment securities, namely, available-for-sale securities.*
- *Changes in the funded status of a company's defined benefit postretirement plans.*
   pension plans

The third type of item is perhaps the simplest to illustrate. Holding gains on securities arise when a company owns securities over an accounting period, during which time the securities' value increases. Similarly, holding losses on securities arise when a company owns securities over a period during which time the securities' value decreases. If the company has not sold the securities (i.e., realized the gain or loss), its holding gain or loss is said to be unrealized. The question is: Should the company reflect these unrealized holding gains and losses in its income statement?

According to accounting standards, the answer depends on how the company has categorized the securities. Categorization depends on what the company intends to do with the securities. If the company intends to actively trade the securities, the answer is yes; the company should categorize the securities as **trading securities** and reflect unrealized holding gains and losses in its income statement. However, if the company does not intend to

---

[41]See SFAS No. 130, Concepts Statement 6, paragraph 70.

actively trade the securities, the securities may be categorized as **available-for-sale securities**. For available-for-sale securities, the company does not reflect unrealized holding gains and losses in its income statement. Instead, unrealized holding gains and losses on available-for-sale securities bypass the income statement and go directly to shareholders' equity.

Even though unrealized holding gains and losses on available-for-sale securities are excluded from a company's net income, they are *included* in a company's comprehensive income.

The fourth item, concerning defined benefit postretirement plans, has changed. Until recently, so-called minimum pension liability adjustments were treated as other comprehensive income; however, a new standard (SFAS No. 158, effective for public companies as of the end of fiscal years after 15 December 2006) will eliminate the need for minimum pension liability adjustments. The need for those adjustments resulted from pension accounting that often created a divergence between a pension plan's funded status and the amount reported on the balance sheet. Under the new standard, companies are required to recognize the overfunded or underfunded status of a defined benefit postretirement plan as an asset or a liability on its balance sheet.[42]

SFAS No. 130 allows companies to report comprehensive income at the bottom of the income statement, on a separate statement of comprehensive income, or as a column in the statement of shareholders' equity; however, presentation alternatives are currently being reviewed by both U.S. and non-U.S. standard setters.

Particularly in comparing financial statements of two companies, it is relevant to examine significant differences in comprehensive income.

EXAMPLE 4-21   Other Comprehensive Income

Assume a company's beginning shareholders' equity is €200 million, its net income for the year is €20 million, its cash dividends for the year are €3 million, and there was no issuance or repurchase of common stock. The company's actual ending shareholders' equity is €227 million.

1. What amount has bypassed the net income calculation by being classified as other comprehensive income?
   A. €0
   B. €7 million
   C. €10 million
   D. €30 million

2. Which of the following statements best describes other comprehensive income?
   A. Income earned from diverse geographic and segment activities.
   B. Income earned from activities that are not part of the company's ordinary business activities.

---

[42]A defined benefit plan is said to be *overfunded* if the amount of assets in a trust fund for that plan exceeds that plan's obligations. If the amount of assets in a trust fund for that plan is less than the plan's obligations, it is *underfunded*.

C. Income related to the sale of goods and delivery of services.

D. Income that increases stockholders' equity but is not reflected as part of net income.

Solution to 1. C is correct. If the company's actual ending shareholders' equity is €227 million, then €10 million [€227 − (€200 + €20 − €3)] has bypassed the net income calculation by being classified as other comprehensive income.

Solution to 2. D is correct. Answers A and B are not correct because they do not specify whether such income is reported as part of net income and shown in the income statement. Answer C is not correct because such activities would typically be reported as part of net income on the income statement.

EXAMPLE 4-22   Other Comprehensive Income in Analysis

An analyst is looking at two comparable companies. Company A has a lower price/earnings (P/E) ratio than Company B, and the conclusion that has been suggested is that Company A is undervalued. As part of examining this conclusion, the analyst decides to explore the question: What would the company's P/E look like if total comprehensive income per share—rather than net income per share—were used as the relevant metric?

	Company A	Company B
Price	$35	$30
EPS	$ 1.60	$ 0.90
P/E ratio	21.9x	33.3x
Other comprehensive income (loss) $ million	($16.272)	$ (1.757)
Shares (millions)	22.6	25.1

Solution. As shown by the following table, part of the explanation for Company A's lower P/E ratio may be that its significant losses—accounted for as other comprehensive income (OCI)—are not included in the P/E ratio.

	Company A	Company B
Price	$35	$ 30
EPS	$ 1.60	$0.90
OCI (loss) $ million	($16.272)	$ (1.757)
Shares (millions)	22.6	25.1
OCI (loss) per share	$ (0.72)	$ (0.07)
Comprehensive EPS = EPS + OCI per share	$ 0.88	$ 0.83
Price/Comprehensive EPS ratio	39.8x	36.1x

9. SUMMARY

This chapter has presented the elements of income statement analysis. The income statement presents information on the financial results of a company's business activities over a period of time; it communicates how much revenue the company generated during a period and what costs it incurred in connection with generating that revenue. A company's net income and its components (e.g., gross margin, operating earnings, and pretax earnings) are critical inputs into both the equity and credit analysis processes. Equity analysts are interested in earnings because equity markets often reward relatively high- or low-earnings growth companies with above-average or below-average valuations, respectively. Fixed-income analysts examine the components of income statements, past and projected, for information on companies' abilities to make promised payments on their debt over the course of the business cycle. Corporate financial announcements frequently emphasize income statements more than the other financial statements. Key points to this chapter include the following:

- The income statement presents revenue, expenses, and net income.
- The components of the income statement include: revenue; cost of sales; sales, general, and administrative expenses; other operating expenses; nonoperating income and expenses; gains and losses; nonrecurring items; net income; and EPS.
- An income statement that presents a subtotal for gross profit (revenue minus cost of goods sold) is said to be presented in a multi-step format. One that does not present this subtotal is said to be presented in a single-step format.
- Revenue is recognized in the period it is earned, which may or may not be in the same period as the related cash collection. Recognition of revenue when earned is a fundamental principal of accrual accounting.
- In limited circumstances, specific revenue recognition methods may be applicable, including percentage of completion, completed contract, installment sales, and cost recovery.
- An analyst should identify differences in companies' revenue recognition methods and adjust reported revenue where possible to facilitate comparability. Where the available information does not permit adjustment, an analyst can characterize the revenue recognition as more or less conservative and thus qualitatively assess how differences in policies might affect financial ratios and judgments about profitability.
- The general principles of expense recognition include the matching principle. Expenses are matched either to revenue or to the time period in which the expenditure occurs (period costs) or to the time period of expected benefits of the expenditures (e.g. depreciation).
- In expense recognition, choice of method (i.e., depreciation method and inventory cost method), as well as estimates (i.e., uncollectible accounts, warranty expenses, assets' useful life, and salvage value) affect a company's reported income. An analyst should identify differences in companies' expense recognition methods and adjust reported financial statements where possible to facilitate comparability. Where the available information does not permit adjustment, an analyst can characterize the policies and estimates as more or less conservative and thus qualitatively assess how differences in policies might affect financial ratios and judgments about companies' performance.
- To assess a company's future earnings, it is helpful to separate those prior years' items of income and expense that are likely to continue in the future from those items that are less likely to continue.
- Some items from prior years clearly are not expected to continue in future periods and are separately disclosed on a company's income statement. Two such items are (1) discontinued

operations and (2) extraordinary items. Both of these items are required to be reported separately from continuing operations.

• For other items on a company's income statement, such as unusual items and accounting changes, the likelihood of their continuing in the future is somewhat less clear and requires the analyst to make some judgments.

• Nonoperating items are reported separately from operating items. For example, if a non-financial service company invests in equity or debt securities issued by another company, any interest, dividends, or profits from sales of these securities will be shown as nonoperating income.

• Basic EPS is the amount of income available to common shareholders divided by the weighted average number of common shares outstanding over a period. The amount of income available to common shareholders is the amount of net income remaining after preferred dividends (if any) have been paid.

• If a company has a simple capital structure (i.e., one with no potentially dilutive securities), then its basic EPS is equal to its diluted EPS. If, however, a company has dilutive securities, its diluted EPS is lower than its basic EPS.

• Diluted EPS is calculated using the if-converted method for convertible securities and the treasury stock method for options.

• Common-size analysis of the income statement involves stating each line item on the income statement as a percentage of sales. Common-size statements facilitate comparison across time periods and across companies of different sizes.

• Two income-statement-based indicators of profitability are net profit margin and gross profit margin.

• Comprehensive income includes *both* net income and other revenue and expense items that are excluded from the net income calculation.

PRACTICE PROBLEMS

1. Expenses on the income statement may be grouped by
   A. nature, but not by function.
   B. function, but not by nature.
   C. either function or nature.

2. An example of an expense classification by function is
   A. tax expense.
   B. interest expense.
   C. cost of goods sold.

3. Denali Limited, a manufacturing company, had the following income statement information:

Revenue	$4,000,000
Cost of goods sold	$3,000,000
Other operating expenses	$500,000
Interest expense	$100,000
Tax expense	$120,000

Denali's gross profit is equal to
A. $280,000.
B. $500,000.
C. $1,000,000.

4. Under IFRS, income includes increases in economic benefits from
   A. increases in owners' equity related to owners' contributions.
   B. increases in liabilities not related to owners' contributions.
   C. enhancements of assets not related to owners' contributions.

5. Fairplay had the following information related to the sale of its products during 2006, which was its first year of business:

Revenue	$1,000,000
Returns of goods sold	$100,000
Cash collected	$800,000
Cost of goods sold	$700,000

Under the accrual basis of accounting, how much net revenue would be reported on Fairplay's 2006 income statement?
A. $200,000
B. $800,000
C. $900,000

6. If the outcome of a long-term contract can be measured reliably, the preferred accounting method under both IFRS and U.S. GAAP is
   A. the installment method.
   B. the completed contract method.
   C. the percentage-of-completion method.

7. At the beginning of 2006, Florida Road Construction entered into a contract to build a road for the government. Construction will take four years. The following information as of 31 December 2006 is available for the contract:

Total revenue according to contract	$10,000,000
Total expected cost	$8,000,000
Cost incurred during 2006	$1,200,000

Under the completed contract method, how much revenue will be reported in 2006?
A. None
B. $300,000
C. $1,500,000

8. During 2006, Argo Company sold 10 acres of prime commercial zoned land to a builder for $5,000,000. The builder gave Argo a $1,000,000 down payment and will pay the remaining balance of $4,000,000 to Argo in 2007. Argo purchased the land in 1999 for $2,000,000. Using the installment method, how much profit will Argo report for 2006?

A. None
B. $600,000
C. $1,000,000

9. Using the same information as in Question 8, how much profit will Argo report for 2006 by using the cost recovery method?
   A. None
   B. $1,000,000
   C. $3,000,000

10. Under IFRS, revenue from barter transactions should be measured based on the fair value of revenue from
    A. similar barter transactions with related parties.
    B. similar barter transactions with unrelated parties.
    C. similar nonbarter transactions with unrelated parties.

11. Apex Consignment sells items over the Internet for individuals on a consignment basis. Apex receives the items from the owner, lists them for sale on the Internet, and receives a 25 percent commission for any items sold. Apex collects the full amount from the buyer and pays the net amount after commission to the owner. Unsold items are returned to the owner after 90 days. During 2006, Apex had the following information:

    • Total sales price of items sold during 2006 on consignment was €2,000,000.
    • Total commissions retained by Apex during 2006 for these items was €500,000.

    How much revenue should Apex report on its 2006 income statement?
    A. €500,000
    B. €2,000,000
    C. €1,500,000

12. During 2007, Accent Toys Plc., which began business in October of that year, purchased 10,000 units of its most popular toy at a cost of £10 per unit in October. In anticipation of heavy December sales, Accent purchased 5,000 additional units in November at a cost of £11 per unit. During 2007, Accent sold 12,000 units at a price of £15 per unit. Under the first in, first out (FIFO) method, what is Accent's cost of goods sold for 2007?
    A. £105,000
    B. £120,000
    C. £122,000

13. Using the same information as in Question 12, what would Accent's cost of goods sold be under the weighted average cost method?
    A. £120,000
    B. £122,000
    C. £124,000

14. Which inventory method is least likely to be used under IFRS?
    A. First in, first out (FIFO)
    B. Last in, first out (LIFO)
    C. Weighted average

15. At the beginning of 2007, Glass Manufacturing purchased a new machine for its assembly line at a cost of $600,000. The machine has an estimated useful life of 10 years and estimated residual value of $50,000. Under the straight-line method, how much depreciation would Glass take in 2008 for financial reporting purposes?
    A. None
    B. $55,000
    C. $60,000

16. Using the same information as in Question 15, how much depreciation would Glass take in 2007 for financial reporting purposes under the double-declining balance method?
    A. $60,000
    B. $110,000
    C. $120,000

17. Which combination of depreciation methods and useful lives is most conservative in the year a depreciable asset is acquired?
    A. Straight-line depreciation with a long useful life.
    B. Straight-line depreciation with a short useful life.
    C. Declining balance depreciation with a short useful life.

18. Under IFRS, a loss from the destruction of property in a fire would most likely be classified as
    A. continuing operations.
    B. an extraordinary item.
    C. discontinued operations.

19. For 2007, Flamingo Products had net income of $1,000,000. On 1 January 2007, there were 1,000,000 shares outstanding. On 1 July 2007, the company issued 100,000 new shares for $20 per share. The company paid $200,000 in dividends to common shareholders. What is Flamingo's basic earnings per share for 2007?
    A. $0.73
    B. $0.91
    C. $0.95

20. Cell Services (CSI) had 1,000,000 average shares outstanding during all of 2007. During 2007, CSI also had 10,000 options outstanding with exercise prices of $10 each. The average stock price of CSI during 2007 was $15. For purposes of computing diluted earnings per share, how many shares would be used in the denominator?
    A. 1,000,000
    B. 1,003,333
    C. 1,010,000

CHAPTER 5

UNDERSTANDING THE BALANCE SHEET

Thomas R. Robinson, CFA

CFA Institute
Charlottesville, Virginia

Hennie van Greuning, CFA

World Bank
Washington, DC

Elaine Henry, CFA

University of Miami
Miami, Florida

Michael A. Broihahn, CFA

Barry University
Miami, Florida

LEARNING OUTCOMES

After completing this chapter, you will be able to do the following:

- Define and interpret the asset and liability categories on the balance sheet, and discuss the uses of a balance sheet.
- Describe the various formats of balance sheet presentation.
- Compare and contrast current and noncurrent assets and liabilities.

- Explain the measurement bases (e.g., historical cost and fair value) of assets and liabilities, including current assets, current liabilities, tangible assets, and intangible assets.
- List and explain the appropriate classifications and related accounting treatments for financial instruments.
- List and explain the components of shareholders' equity.
- Interpret balance sheets, common-size balance sheets, the statement of changes in equity, and commonly used balance sheet ratios.

1. INTRODUCTION

The starting place for analyzing a company's financial position is typically the balance sheet. Creditors, investors, and analysts recognize the value of the balance sheet and also its limitations. The balance sheet provides such users with information on a company's resources (assets) and its sources of capital (its equity and liabilities/debt). It normally also provides information about the future earnings capacity of a company's assets as well as an indication of cash flows that may come from receivables and inventories.

However, the balance sheet does have limitations, especially relating to how assets and liabilities are measured. Liabilities and, sometimes, assets may not be recognized in a timely manner. Furthermore, the use of historical costs rather than fair values to measure some items on the balance sheet means that the financial analyst may need to make adjustments to determine the real (economic) net worth of the company. By understanding how a balance sheet is constructed and how it may be analyzed, the reader should be able to make appropriate use of it.

This chapter is organized as follows: In section 2, we describe and illustrate the format, structure, and components of the balance sheet. Section 3 discusses the measurement bases for assets and liabilities. Section 4 describes the components of equity and illustrates the statement of changes in shareholders' equity. Section 5 introduces balance sheet analysis. Section 6 summarizes the chapter, and practice problems in the CFA Institute multiple-choice format conclude the chapter.

2. COMPONENTS AND FORMAT OF THE BALANCE SHEET

The **balance sheet** discloses what an entity owns and what it owes at a specific point in time; thus, it is also referred to as the **statement of financial position.**[1]

The financial position of an entity is described in terms of its assets, liabilities, and equity:

- **Assets (A)** are resources controlled by the company as a result of past events and from which future economic benefits are expected to flow to the entity.
- **Liabilities (L)** represent obligations of a company arising from past events, the settlement of which is expected to result in an outflow of economic benefits from the entity.
- **Equity (E)** Commonly known as **shareholders' equity** or **owners' equity**, equity is determined by subtracting the liabilities from the assets of a company, giving rise to the accounting equation: $A = L + E$ or $A - L = E$. Equity can be viewed as a residual or balancing amount, taking assets and liabilities into account.

---

[1]The balance sheet is also known as the **statement of financial condition**.

EXHIBIT 5-1   Listing of Assets, Liabilities, and Owners' Equity Funds

Element	20X7	20X6	Financial Statement Element	Equation
Inventory	€20,000	€16,000	Asset	
Property, plant, and equipment	53,000	27,000	Asset	+ A
Subtotal	**73,000**	**43,000**		
Trade creditors	(14,000)	(7,000)	Liability	
Bond repayable in 5 years' time	(37,000)	(16,000)	Liability	– L
Owners' equity	**€22,000**	**€20,000**	**Equity** (balancing amount)	= E

Assets and liabilities arise as a result of business transactions (e.g., the purchase of a building or issuing a bond.) The accounting equation is useful in assessing the impact of transactions on the balance sheet. For example, if a company borrows money in exchange for a note payable, assets and liabilities increase by the same amount. Assets and liabilities also arise from the accrual process. As noted in earlier chapters, the income statement reflects revenue and expenses reported on an accrual basis regardless of the period in which cash is received and paid. Differences between accrued revenue and expenses and cash flows will result in assets and liabilities. Specifically:

- Revenue reported on the income statement before cash is received; this results in accrued revenue or accounts receivable, which is an asset. This is ultimately reflected on the balance sheet as an increase in accounts receivable and an increase in retained earnings.
- Cash received before revenue is to be reported on the income statement; this results in a deferred revenue or unearned revenue, which is a liability. For example, if a company pays in advance for delivery of custom equipment, the balance sheet reflects an increase in cash and an increase in liabilities.
- Expense reported on the income statement before cash is paid; this results in an accrued expense, which is a liability. This is reflected on the balance sheet as an increase in liabilities and a decrease in retained earnings.
- Cash paid before an expense is to be reported on the income statement; this results in a deferred expense, also known as a *prepaid expense,* which is an asset. On the balance sheet, cash is reduced and prepaid assets are increased.

Exhibit 5-1 illustrates what an unformatted balance sheet might look like, providing examples of a selection of assets and liabilities. The account *trade creditors* (also known as *accounts payable*) arises when goods are purchased on credit and received into inventory before their purchase price is paid in cash. Because an expense is recognized before cash is paid, it is an example of the type of accrual described in the third bullet point.

2.1. Structure and Components of the Balance Sheet

As noted above, the balance sheet presents the financial position of a company. The financial position shows the relative amounts of assets, liabilities, and equity held by the enterprise at a particular point in time.

2.1.1. Assets

Assets are generated either through purchase (investing activities), or generated through business activities (operating activities), or financing activities, such as issuance of debt.

Through the analysis of the liabilities and equity of an entity, the analyst is able to determine *how* assets are acquired or funded. Funding for the purchase may come from shareholders (financing activities) or from creditors (either through direct financing activities, or indirectly through the surplus generated through operating activities that may be funded by current liabilities/trade finance).

The chapter on financial reporting standards defined **assets** as "resources controlled by the enterprise as a result of past events and from which future economic benefits are expected to flow to the enterprise." This formal definition of an asset tells us that its essence lies in its capability to generate future benefits, which, therefore, alerts the reader of the financial statements about the future earnings capability of the entity's assets. A simpler definition of an asset is that it is a store of wealth (such as cash, marketable securities, and property).

Turning back to the official definition of assets, we note that financial statement elements (such as assets) should be recognized in the financial statements only if:

- It is probable that any future economic benefit associated with the item will flow to the entity.
- The item has a cost or value that can be *measured* with reliability (this aspect will be discussed more fully in section 3 of this chapter).

Values that are typically included in assets will include amounts that have been spent but which have not been recorded as an expense on the income statement (as in the case of inventories) because of the matching principle, or amounts that have been reported as earned on an income statement but have not been received (as in the case of accounts receivable).

Exhibit 5-1 included inventories as well as property, plant, and equipment as examples of assets. Exhibit 5-2 provides a more complete list of assets that may be found on the face of the balance sheet.

EXHIBIT 5-2   Typical Assets Disclosed on the Balance Sheet

Cash and cash equivalents

Inventories

Trade and other receivables

Prepaid expenses

Financial assets

Deferred tax assets

Property, plant, and equipment

Investment property

Intangible assets

Investments accounted for using the equity method

Natural resource assets

Assets held for sale

2.1.2. Liabilities

Liabilities (and equity capital) represent the ways in which the funds were raised to acquire the assets. **Liabilities** are technically defined as probable future sacrifices of economic benefits arising from present obligations of an entity to transfer assets or provide services to other entities in the future as a result of past transactions or events. Alternatively, a liability can be described as:

- Amounts received but which have not been reported as revenues or income on an income statement and/or will have to be repaid (e.g., notes payable).
- Amounts that have been reported as expenses on an income statement but have not been paid (e.g., accounts payable, accruals, and taxes payable).

Exhibit 5-1 included trade creditors as well as a long-term bond payable as examples of liabilities. Exhibit 5-3 provides a more complete list of liabilities that may be found on the face of the balance sheet.

EXHIBIT 5-3   Typical Liabilities
Disclosed on the Balance Sheet

Bank borrowings/notes payable
Trade and other payables
Provisions
Unearned revenues
Financial liabilities
Accrued liabilities
Deferred tax liabilities

2.1.3. Equity

Equity represents the portion belonging to the owners or shareholders of a business. **Equity** is the residual interest in the assets of an entity after deducting its liabilities, also referred to as **net asset value**:

$$\text{Equity} = \text{Assets} - \text{Liabilities}$$

Equity is increased by contributions by the owners or by profits (including gains) made during the year and is decreased by losses or withdrawals in the form of dividends.

Almost every aspect of a company is either directly or indirectly influenced by the availability and/or the cost of equity capital. The adequacy of equity capital is one of the key factors to be considered when the safety and soundness of a particular company is assessed. An adequate equity base serves as a safety net for a variety of risks to which any entity is exposed in the course of its business. Equity capital provides a cushion to absorb possible losses and thus provides a basis for maintaining creditor confidence in a company. Equity capital also is the ultimate determinant of a company's borrowing capacity. In practice, a company's balance sheet cannot be expanded beyond a level determined by its equity capital without increasing the risk of financial distress to an unacceptable level; the availability of equity capital consequently determines the maximum level of assets.

The cost and amount of capital affect a company's competitive position. Because shareholders expect a return on their equity, the obligation to earn such a return impacts the

EXHIBIT 5-4   Typical Equity Information Disclosed on the Balance Sheet

Minority interest, presented within equity

Issued capital and paid-in capital attributable to equity holders of the parent

Earnings retained in the company

Parent shareholders' equity

Information that is usually disclosed for each class of equity on the face of the balance sheet or in notes to the financial statements includes:

Number of shares authorized

Number of shares issued and fully paid

Number of shares issued and not fully paid

Par (or stated) value per share, or a statement that it has no par (stated) value

Reconciliation of shares at beginning and end of reporting period

Rights, preferences, and restrictions attached to that class

Shares in the entity held by entity, subsidiaries, or associates

Shares reserved for issue under options and sales contracts

---

pricing of company products. There is also another important aspect to the level of capital, namely, the perspective of the market. The issuance of debt requires public confidence in a company, which, in turn, can best be established and maintained by an equity capital buffer. If a company faces a shortage of equity capital or if the cost of capital is high, a company stands to lose business to its competitors.

The key purposes of equity capital are to provide stability and to absorb losses, thereby providing a measure of protection to creditors in the event of liquidation. As such, the capital of a company should have three important characteristics:

- It should be permanent.
- It should not impose mandatory fixed charges against earnings (in the case of banks).
- It should allow for legal subordination to the rights of creditors.

Exhibit 5-4 provides a list of equity information that is disclosed on the balance sheet.

The total amount of equity capital is of fundamental importance. Also important is the nature of the company ownership—the identity of those owners who can directly influence the company's strategic direction and risk management policies. This is particularly critical for financial institutions, such as banks. For example, a bank's ownership structure must ensure the integrity of its capital and owners must be able to supply more capital if and when needed.

2.2. Format of the Balance Sheet

As the balance sheet provides information about the financial position of the company, it should distinguish between major categories and classifications of assets and liabilities.

Detail and formats of balance sheets vary from company to company. The basic information contained in balance sheets is the same though, regardless of the format. When using the **report format**, assets, liabilities, and equity are listed in a single column. The **account format** follows the pattern of the traditional general ledger accounts, with assets at the left and liabilities and equity at the right of a central dividing line. The report format is most commonly preferred and used by financial statement preparers.

If a company were to have many assets and liabilities, the balance sheet might become quite difficult to read. Grouping together the various classes of assets and liabilities, therefore, results in a balance sheet format described as a **classified balance sheet**.

Classification, in this case, is the term used to describe the grouping of accounts into subcategories—it helps readers to gain a quick perspective of the company's financial position. Classification assists in drawing attention to specific amounts and also to groups of accounts.

Classifications most often distinguish between current and noncurrent assets/liabilities, or by financial and nonfinancial categories—all in order to provide information related to the liquidity of such assets or liabilities (albeit indirectly in many cases).

2.2.1. Current and Noncurrent Distinction

The balance sheet should distinguish between current and noncurrent assets and between current and noncurrent liabilities unless a presentation based on liquidity provides more relevant and reliable information (e.g., in the case of a bank or similar financial institution).

From Exhibit 5-5, it should be clear that in essence, the current/noncurrent distinction is also an attempt at incorporating liquidity expectations into the structure of the balance sheet. Assets expected to be liquidated or used up within one year or one operating cycle of the business, whichever is greater, are classified as current assets. A company's operating cycle is the amount of time that elapses between spending cash for inventory and supplies and collecting the cash from its sales to customers. Assets not expected to be liquidated or used up within one year or one operating cycle of the business, whichever is greater, are classified as noncurrent (long-term) assets.

The excess of current assets over current liabilities is called **working capital**. The level of working capital tells analysts about the ability of an entity to meet liabilities as they fall due. Yet, working capital should not be too large because funds could be tied up that could be used more productively elsewhere.

Some **current assets** are allocated to expenses immediately (e.g., inventory) when sales or cash transactions take place, whereas noncurrent assets are allocated over the useful lives of such assets. Current assets are maintained for operating purposes and represent cash or items

EXHIBIT 5-5   Balance Sheet: Current versus Noncurrent Distinction

Apex Corporation	20X7	20X6
Assets		
Current assets	€ 20,000	€ 16,000
Noncurrent assets	53,000	27,000
Total assets	**€73,000**	**€43,000**
Liabilities and equity		
Current liabilities	14,000	7,000
Noncurrent liabilities	37,000	16,000
Total liabilities	**51,000**	**23,000**
Equity	**22,000**	**20,000**
Total liabilities and equity	**€73,000**	**€43,000**

expected to be converted into cash or used up (e.g., prepaid expenses) in the current period. Current assets, therefore, tell us more about the operating activities and the operating capability of the entity.

Noncurrent assets represent the infrastructure from which the entity operates and are not consumed or disposed in the current period. Such assets represent potentially less liquid investments made from a strategic or longer-term perspective (e.g., to secure trading advantages, supply lines, or other synergies, such as equity securities held, investments in associates, or investments in subsidiaries).

A **current liability** is a liability that satisfies any of the following criteria:

Could be one year, could be something else.

- It is expected to be settled in the entity's normal operating cycle.
- It is held primarily for the purpose of being traded.
- It is due to be settled within one year after the balance sheet date.
- The entity does not have an unconditional right to defer settlement of the liability for at least one year after the balance sheet date.

Financial liabilities are classified as current if they are due to be settled within one year after the balance sheet date, even if the original term was for a period longer than one year. All other liabilities are classified as **noncurrent**.

International Accounting Standard (IAS) No. 1 specifies that some current liabilities, such as trade payables and some accruals for employee and other operating costs, are part of the working capital used in the entity's normal operating cycle. Such operating items are classified as current liabilities even if they will be settled more than one year after the balance sheet date. When the entity's normal operating cycle is not clearly identifiable, its duration is assumed to be one year.

Noncurrent liabilities include financial liabilities that provide financing on a long-term basis, and they are, therefore, not part of the working capital used in the entity's normal operating cycle; neither are they due for settlement within one year after the balance sheet date.

2.2.2. Liquidity-Based Presentation

Paragraph 51 of IAS No. 1 requires the use of the current/noncurrent format of presentation for the balance sheet, except when a presentation based on liquidity provides information that is reliable and is more relevant. When that exception applies, all assets and liabilities shall be presented broadly in order of liquidity.

Entities such as banks are clearly candidates for such a liquidity-based presentation in their balance sheets. Exhibit 5-6 shows how the asset side of a bank's balance sheet could be ordered using a liquidity-based presentation.

2.2.3. IFRS and U.S. GAAP Balance Sheet Illustrations

This section illustrates actual corporate balance sheets prepared under International Financial Reporting Standards (IFRS) and generally accepted accounting principles (GAAP) via examples from Roche Group and Sony Corporation, respectively.

Roche is a leading international health care company based in Switzerland and prepares its financial statements in accordance with IFRS. Exhibit 5-7 presents the comparative balance sheets from the company's annual report for the fiscal years ended 31 December 2005 and 2004.

Roche prepares its balance sheets using the report format. The balance sheet also gives noncurrent assets before current assets and long-term liabilities before current liabilities,

EXHIBIT 5-6   Bank Balance Sheet: Asset Side Order. Using a Liquidity-Based Presentation

Assets

1. Cash and balances with the central bank

2. Trading securities

3. Securities held for stable liquidity portfolio purposes

4. Placements with and loans to banks and credit institutions (net of specific provisions)

5. Loans and advances to other customers

6. Investments—long-term interests in other entities

7. Property, plant, and equipment

8. Other assets (prepayments, etc.)

Total Assets

EXHIBIT 5-7   Roche Group—Consolidated Balance Sheets (CHF millions)

	31 December	
	2005	**2004**
Noncurrent assets		
Property, plant, and equipment	15,097	12,408
Goodwill	6,132	5,532
Intangible assets	6,256	6,340
Investments in associated companies	58	55
Financial long-term assets	2,190	1,227
Other long-term assets	660	484
Deferred income tax assets	1,724	1,144
Post-employment benefit assets	1,622	1,577
Total noncurrent assets	**33,739**	**28,767**
Current assets		
Inventories	5,041	4,614
Accounts receivables	7,698	7,014
Current income tax assets	299	159
Other current assets	1,703	2,007
Receivable from Bayer Group collected on 1 January 2005	—	2,886
Marketable securities	16,657	10,394
Cash and cash equivalents	4,228	2,605
Total current assets	**35,626**	**29,679**
Total assets	**69,365**	**58,446**
Noncurrent liabilities		
Long-term debt	(9,322)	(7,077)
Deferred income tax liabilities	(3,518)	(3,564)
		(*Continued*)

EXHIBIT 5-7   (*Continued*)

| | 31 December | |
	2005	2004
Post-employment benefits liabilities	(2,937)	(2,744)
Provisions	(1,547)	(683)
Other noncurrent liabilities	(806)	(961)
Total noncurrent liabilities	**(18,130)**	**(15,029)**
Current Liabilities		
Short-term debt	(348)	(2,013)
Current income tax liabilities	(811)	(947)
Provisions	(833)	(1,223)
Accounts payable	(2,373)	(1,844)
Accrued and other current liabilities	(5,127)	(4,107)
Total current liabilities	**(9,492)**	**(10,134)**
Total liabilities	**(27,622)**	**(25,163)**
Total net assets	**41,743**	**33,283**
Equity		
Capital and reserves attributable to Roche shareholders	34,922	27,998
Equity attributable to minority interests	6,821	5,285
Total equity	**41,743**	**33,283**

following common practice under IFRS. Note also that Roche shows the minority interest for its consolidated subsidiary companies in the shareholders' equity section as required under IFRS. **Minority interest** represents the portion of consolidated subsidiaries owned by others. For example, if a company owns 85 percent of a subsidiary, 100 percent of the subsidiary's assets and liabilities are included in the consolidated balance sheet. Minority interest represents the 15 percent of the net assets of the subsidiary not owned by the parent company.

Sony Corporation and its consolidated subsidiaries are engaged in the development, design, manufacture, and sale of various kinds of electronic equipment, instruments, and devices for consumer and industrial markets. Sony is also engaged in the development, production, and distribution of recorded music and image-based software. Sony Corporation has prepared a set of consolidated financial statements in accordance with U.S. GAAP. Exhibit 5-8 presents the comparative balance sheets from the company's U.S. GAAP annual report for the fiscal years ended 31 March 2005 and 2004.

Sony prepares its balance sheets using the report format. Under U.S. GAAP, current assets are presented before long-term assets, and current liabilities are presented before long-term liabilities. The current/long-term presentation rule is applicable for all manufacturing, merchandising, and service companies, although there are some regulated industry exceptions (e.g., utility companies) where the presentation is reversed (similar to the common

EXHIBIT 5-8   Sony Corporation: Consolidated Balance Sheets (¥ millions)

	31 March	
	2005	**2004**
Assets		
Current Assets		
Cash and cash equivalents	779,103	849,211
Time deposits	1,492	4,662
Marketable securities	460,202	274,748
Notes and accounts receivable, trade	1,113,071	1,123,863
Allowance for doubtful accounts and sales returns	(87,709)	(112,674)
Inventories	631,349	666,507
Deferred income taxes	141,154	125,532
Prepaid expenses and other current assets	517,509	431,506
Total current assets	3,556,171	3,363,355
Film costs	278,961	256,740
Investments and Advances		
Affiliated companies	252,905	86,253
Securities investments and other	2,492,784	2,426,697
	2,745,689	2,512,950
Property, Plant, and Equipment		
Land	182,900	189,785
Buildings	925,796	930,983
Machinery and equipment	2,192,038	2,053,085
Construction in progress	92,611	98,480
Less—Accumulated depreciation	(2,020,946)	(1,907,289)
	1,372,399	1,365,044
Other Assets		
Intangibles, net	187,024	248,010
Goodwill	283,923	277,870
Deferred insurance acquisition costs	374,805	349,194
Deferred income taxes	240,396	203,203
Other	459,732	514,296
	1,545,880	1,592,573
Total assets	9,499,100	9,090,662
Liabilities and Stockholders' Equity		
Current Liabilities		
Short-term borrowings	63,396	91,260
Current portion of long-term debt	166,870	383,757

(*Continued*)

EXHIBIT 5-8   *(Continued)*

	31 March	
	2005	**2004**
Notes and accounts payable, trade	806,044	778,773
Accounts payable, other and accrued expenses	746,466	812,175
Accrued income and other taxes	55,651	57,913
Deposits from customers in the banking business	546,718	378,851
Other	424,223	479,486
Total current liabilities	2,809,368	2,982,215
Long-Term Liabilities		
Long-term debt	678,992	777,649
Accrued pension and severance costs	352,402	368,382
Deferred income taxes	72,227	96,193
Future insurance policy benefits and other	2,464,295	2,178,626
Other	227,631	286,737
	3,795,547	3,707,587
Minority Interest in Consolidated Subsidiaries	23,847	22,858
Stockholders' Equity		
Subsidiary tracking stock, no par value		
Authorized 100,000,000 shares, outstanding 3,072,000 shares	3,917	3,917
Common stock, no par value		
2004—Authorized 3,500,000,000 shares, outstanding 926,418,280 shares		476,350
2005—Authorized 3,500,000,000 shares, outstanding 997,211,213 shares	617,792	
Additional paid-in capital	1,134,222	992,817
Retained earnings	1,506,082	1,367,060
Accumulated other comprehensive income		
Unrealized gains on securities	62,669	69,950
Unrealized losses on derivative investments	(2,490)	(600)
Minimum pension liability adjustments	(90,030)	(89,261)
Foreign currency translation adjustments	(355,824)	(430,048)
	(385,675)	(449,959)
Treasury stock, at cost		
Subsidiary tracking stock (2004—0 shares, 2005-32 shares)	(0)	(0)
Common stock (2004—2,468,258 shares, 2005-1,118,984 shares)	(6,000)	(12,183)
	2,870,338	2,378,002
Total liabilities and stockholders' equity	9,499,100	9,090,662

IFRS practice of presenting long-term assets before current assets and long-term liabilities before current liabilities). Note also that Sony shows the minority interest for its consolidated subsidiary companies in an "in-between" or "mezzanine" section between the liabilities and shareholders' equity sections. This mezzanine presentation for minority interest is common under U.S. GAAP; however, minority interest may also be shown under either liabilities or shareholders' equity. By contrast, under IFRS, a minority interest is presented in the shareholders' equity section. The Financial Accounting Standards Board (FASB) is considering a change to U.S. GAAP to conform their standards to IFRS.

3. MEASUREMENT BASES OF ASSETS AND LIABILITIES

In portraying an asset or liability on the balance sheet, the question arises as to how it should be measured. For example, an asset may have been acquired many years ago at a cost of $1 million but may have a current value of $5 million. Should this asset be listed at its historic cost or its current value? On the one hand, historical cost provides a reliable and objectively determined measurement base—there would be no dispute regarding what the asset cost. On the other hand, users of financial statements (e.g., creditors) may prefer to know what the asset could be sold for currently if the company needed to raise cash. Some assets and liabilities can be more objectively valued in the marketplace than others (e.g., when an established market exists in which the asset or liability trades regularly, such as an investment in another publicly traded company). As a result, the balance sheet under current standards is a mixed model: Some assets and liabilities are reported based on historical cost, sometimes with adjustments, whereas other assets and liabilities are measured based upon a current value intended to represent the asset's fair value. Fair value and historical value can be defined as follows:

- *Fair value.* Fair value is the amount at which an asset could be exchanged, or a liability settled, between knowledgeable willing parties in an arm's-length transaction. When the asset or liability trades regularly, its fair value is usually readily determinable from its market price (sometimes referred to as **fair market value**).
- *Historical cost.* The historical cost of an asset or liability is its cost or fair value at acquisition, including any costs of acquisition and/or preparation.

In limited circumstances other measurement bases are sometimes used, such as **current cost** (the cost to replace an asset) or **present value** (the present discounted value of future cash flows). The key question for analysts is how the reported measures of assets and liabilities on the balance sheet relate to economic reality and to each other. To answer this question, the analyst needs to understand the accounting policies applied in preparing the balance sheet and the measurement bases used. Analysts may need to make adjustments to balance sheet measures of assets and liabilities in assessing the investment potential or creditworthiness of a company. For example, land is generally reported at historical cost on the balance sheet because this measure is objective and any measure of current value (other than an actual sale) would be very subjective. Through diligent research, an analyst may find companies that own valuable land that is not adequately reflected on the balance sheet.[2]

---

[2]See, for example, "Beyond the Balance-Sheet: Land-Ho," *Forbes*, 4 September 2006, pp. 84–85, which examines a handful of stocks with valuable land holdings not reflected on the balance sheet.

For all of these reasons, the balance sheet value of total assets should not be accepted as an accurate measure of the total value of a company. The value of a company is a function of many factors, including future cash flows expected to be generated by the company and current market conditions. The balance sheet provides important information about the value of some assets and information about future cash flows but does not represent the value of the company as a whole.

Once individual assets and liabilities are measured, additional decisions may be necessary as to how these measures are reflected on the balance sheet. Accounting standards generally prohibit the offsetting of assets and liabilities other than in limited circumstances. For example, if a building is purchased for $10 million subject to a mortgage of $8 million, the building is reported as an asset for $10 million while the mortgage is shown separately as a liability ($8 million). It is important that these assets and liabilities be reported separately. Offsetting in the balance sheet, except when offsetting reflects the substance of the transaction or other event, detracts from the ability of users to understand the transactions, events, and conditions that have occurred and to assess the entity's future cash flows. However, disclosing or measuring assets net of valuation allowances (e.g., obsolescence allowances on inventories and doubtful accounts allowances on receivables) is not considered to be offsetting. Offsetting is also permitted in limited circumstances where there are restrictions on the availability of assets (such as with pension plans).

According to IFRS, fair presentation requires the faithful representation on the balance sheet of the effects of transactions, other events, and conditions in accordance with the definitions and recognition criteria for assets, liabilities, income, and expenses set out in the IFRS Framework, as presented in the chapter on financial reporting standards. The application of IFRS is presumed to result in fair presentation.

The financial statements should disclose the following information related to the measures used for assets and liabilities shown on the balance sheet:

- Accounting policies, including the cost formulas used.
- Total carrying amount of inventories and amount per category.
- Amount of inventories carried at fair value less costs to sell.
- Amount of any write-downs and reversals of any write-down.
- Circumstances or events that led to the reversal of a write-down.
- Inventories pledged as security for liabilities.
- Amount of inventories recognized as an expense.

The notes to financial statements and management's discussion and analysis are integral parts of the U.S. GAAP and IFRS financial reporting processes. They provide important required detailed disclosures, as well as other information provided voluntarily by management. This information can be invaluable when determining whether the measurement of assets is comparable to other entities being analyzed. The notes include information on such topics as the following:

- Specific accounting policies that were used in compiling the financial statements.
- Terms of debt agreements.
- Lease information.
- Off-balance-sheet financing.
- Breakdowns of operations by important segments.
- Contingent assets and liabilities.
- Detailed pension plan disclosure.

The notes would also provide information in respect of:

Disclosure of accounting policies	Measurement bases used in preparing financial statements.
	Each accounting policy used.
	Judgments made in applying accounting policies that have the most significant effect on the amounts recognized in the financial statements.
Estimation uncertainty	Key assumptions about the future and other key sources of estimation uncertainty that have a significant risk of causing material adjustment to the carrying amount of assets and liabilities within the next year.
Other disclosures	Description of the entity, including its domicile, legal form, country of incorporation, and registered office or business address.
	Nature of operations or principal activities, or both.
	Name of parent and ultimate parent.

EXAMPLE 5-1   Analysis of Off-Balance-Sheet Disclosures

Hewitt Associates (NYSE: HEW) posted the following table on page 43 of its SEC Form 10-K for the fiscal year ending 30 September 2005. The table was included in the Management Discussion and Analysis.

Contractual Obligations (in millions)

	Payments Due in Fiscal Year				
	Total	**2006**	**2007–08**	**2009–10**	**Thereafter**
Operating leases (1)	737	89	149	123	376
Capital leases:					
Principal	80	4	9	11	56
Interest	41	6	11	9	15
Total leases:	121	10	20	20	71
Debt:					
Principal	259	36	50	30	143
Interest	50	12	18	13	7
Total debt	309	48	68	43	150
Purchase commitments	73	34	37	2	—
Other long-term liabilities	72	8	16	9	39
Total contractual obligations	$1,312	$189	$290	$197	$636

On pages 56–57 of the 10-K, Hewitt posted the following balance sheet (abbreviated below). Of the obligations listed above, only the capital leases and other long-term liabilities are included explicitly on the balance sheet.

Hewitt Associates, Inc.: Consolidated Balance Sheets (Dollars in thousands except share and per-share amounts)

	30 September	
	2005	**2004**
Assets		
Current assets:		
Cash and cash equivalents	$163,928	$129,481
Short-term investments	53,693	183,205
Client receivables and unbilled work in process	595,691	522,882
Refundable income taxes	23,100	—
Prepaid expenses and other current assets	60,662	50,546
Funds held for clients	97,907	14,693
Deferred income taxes, net	5,902	246
Total current assets	1,000,883	901,053
Noncurrent assets:		
Deferred contract costs	253,505	162,602
Property and equipment, net	302,875	236,099
Capitalized software, net	110,997	85,350
Other intangible assets, net	261,999	107,322
Goodwill	694,370	285,743
Other assets, net	32,711	29,805
Total noncurrent assets	1,656,457	906,921
Total assets	2,657,340	1,807,974
Liabilities		
Current liabilities:		
Accounts payable	57,412	20,909
Accrued expenses	156,575	83,226
Funds held for clients	97,907	14,693
Advanced billings to clients	156,257	106,934
Accrued compensation and benefits	141,350	181,812
Short-term debt and current portion of long-term debt	35,915	13,445
Current portion of capital lease obligations	3,989	5,373
Employee deferred compensation and accrued profit sharing	30,136	49,450
Total current liabilities	679,541	475,842

Long-term liabilities:		
Deferred contract revenues	140,474	118,025
Debt, less current portion	222,692	121,253
Capital lease obligations, less current portion	76,477	79,982
Other long-term liabilities	127,376	83,063
Deferred income taxes, net	99,423	70,456
Total long-term liabilities	666,442	472,779
Total liabilities	1,345,983	948,621
Commitments and contingencies (Notes 12 and 17)		
Stockholders' Equity		
Total stockholders' equity	1,311,357	859,353
Total liabilities and stockholders' equity	$2,657,340	$1,807,974

Operating leases represent assets used by the company but for which accounting standards do not currently require the assets or related obligations be reported on the company's balance sheet. Analysts, however, frequently prefer to adjust the balance sheet to determine how it would look if the assets had been purchased and financed. Credit analysts, such as Standard & Poor's, also make this adjustment to better reflect the creditworthiness of the company. Ideally, the analyst would like to know the implied interest rate in the lease agreements and use this to determine the present value of the asset and related liability, because each lease payment effectively has an interest and a principal component. For this initial example, we will use a shortcut method. Assuming operating leases can be segregated into principal and interest components at approximately the same rate as the capital leases, they represent a liability worth nearly $500 million that is not recorded on the balance sheet. The analyst would adjust the balance sheet by adding that amount to fixed assets and liabilities to examine the current economic position. This information would not have been uncovered based solely upon a review of the balance sheet. Important disclosures about assets and liabilities can be found in the footnotes to the financial statements and in management's discussion of the financial statements.

3.1. Current Assets

Current assets are assets expected to be realized or intended for sale or consumption in the entity's normal operating cycle. Typical current assets that appear on the face of the balance sheet include:

- Assets held primarily for trading.
- Assets expected to be realized within 12 months after the balance sheet date.
- Cash or cash equivalents, unless restricted in use for at least 12 months.
- Marketable securities—debt or equity securities that are owned by a business, traded in a public market, and whose value can be determined from price information in a public

market. Examples of marketable securities include treasury bills, notes, bonds, and equity securities, such as common stocks and mutual fund shares.

- Trade receivables—amounts owed to a business by its customers for products and services already delivered are included as trade receivables. Allowance has to be made for bad debt expenses, reducing the gross receivables amount.
- Inventories—physical products on hand such as goods that will eventually be sold to an entity's customers, either in their current form (finished goods) or as inputs into a process to manufacture a final product (raw materials and work-in-process).
- Other current assets—short-term items not easily classifiable into the above categories (e.g., prepaid expenses).

Exhibit 5-9 illustrates how the current asset amounts of €20,000 (20X7) and €16,000 (20X6) have been expanded from the one amount shown in Exhibit 5-5. In the sections below, some of the issues surrounding the measurement principles for inventories and prepaid expenses are discussed.

EXHIBIT 5-9   Apex Current Assets

	20X7	20X6
Current Assets	**€20,000**	**€16,000**
Cash and cash equivalents	3,000	2,000
Marketable securities	3,000	4,000
Trade receivables	5,000	3,000
Inventories	7,000	6,000
Other current assets—prepaid expenses	2,000	1,000

3.1.1. Inventories

Inventories should be measured at the lower of cost or net realizable value. The cost of inventories comprises all costs of purchase, costs of conversion, and other costs incurred in bringing the inventories to their present location and condition. The following amounts should be excluded in the determination of inventory costs:

- Abnormal amounts of wasted materials, labor, and overhead.
- Storage costs, unless they are necessary prior to a further production process.
- Administrative overheads.
- Selling costs.

The net realizable value (NRV) is the estimated selling price less the estimated costs of completion and costs necessary to make the sale.

Accounting standards allow different valuation methods. For example, IAS No. 2 allows only the first in, first out (FIFO), weighted average cost (WAC), and specific identification methods. Some accounting standard setters (such as U.S. GAAP) also allow LIFO (last in, first out) as an additional inventory valuation method, whereas LIFO is not allowed under IFRS.

The following techniques can be used to measure the cost of inventories if the resulting valuation amount approximates cost:

- **Standard cost,** which should take into account the normal levels of materials, labor, and actual capacity. The standard cost should be reviewed regularly in order to ensure that it approximates actual costs.   *Mongerial Accounting*
- The **retail method** in which the sales value is reduced by the gross margin to calculate cost. An average gross margin percentage should be used for each homogeneous group of items. In addition, the impact of marked-down prices should be taken into consideration.

EXAMPLE 5-2   Analysis of Inventory

Cisco Systems is the world's leading provider of networking equipment. In its third quarter 2001 Form 10-Q filed with the U.S. Securities and Exchange Commission (SEC) on 1 June 2001, the company made the following disclosure:

> *We recorded a provision for inventory, including purchase commitments, totaling $2.36 billion in the third quarter of fiscal 2001, of which $2.25 billion related to an additional excess inventory charge. Inventory purchases and commitments are based upon future sales forecasts. To mitigate the component supply constraints that have existed in the past, we built inventory levels for certain components with long lead times and entered into certain longer-term commitments for certain components. Due to the sudden and significant decrease in demand for our products, inventory levels exceeded our requirements based on current 12-month sales forecasts. This additional excess inventory charge was calculated based on the inventory levels in excess of 12-month demand for each specific product. We do not currently anticipate that the excess inventory subject to this provision will be used at a later date based on our current 12-month demand forecast.*

Even after the inventory charge, Cisco held approximately $2 billion of inventory on the balance sheet, suggesting that the write-off amounted to half its inventory. In addition to the obvious concerns raised as to management's poor performance anticipating how much they would need, many analysts were concerned about how the write-off would affect Cisco's future reported earnings. When this inventory is sold in a future period, a "gain" could be reported based on a lower cost basis for the inventory. In this case, management indicated that the intent was to scrap the inventory. When the company subsequently released its annual earnings, the press release stated:[3]

> *Net sales for fiscal 2001 were $22.29 billion, compared with $18.93 billion for fiscal 2000, an increase of 18%. Pro forma net income, which excludes the effects of acquisition charges, payroll tax on stock option exercises, restructuring costs and*

---

[3]Cisco Press Release dated 7 August 2001 from www.cisco.com.

other special charges, excess inventory charge (benefit), and net gains realized on minority investments, was $3.09 billion or $0.41 per share for fiscal 2001, compared with pro forma net income of $3.91 billion or $0.53 per share for fiscal 2000, decreases of 21% and 23%, respectively.

Actual net loss for fiscal 2001 was $1.01 billion or $0.14 per share, compared with actual net income of $2.67 billion or $0.36 per share for fiscal 2000.

Note that the company focused on "pro forma earnings" initially, which excluded the impact of many items, including the inventory write-off. The company only gave a brief mention of actual (U.S. GAAP) results.

3.1.2. Prepaid Expenses

Prepaid expenses are normal operating expenses that have been paid in advance. The advance payment creates an asset out of a transaction that would normally have resulted in an expense. Examples might include prepaid rent or prepaid insurance. Prepaid expenses will be expensed in future periods as they are used up. Generally, expenses are reported in the period in which they are incurred as opposed to when they are paid. If a company pays its insurance premium for the next calendar year on 31 December, the expense is not incurred at that date; the expense is incurred as time passes (in this example, 1/12 in each following month).

3.2. Current Liabilities

Current liabilities are those liabilities that are expected to be settled in the entity's normal operating cycle, held primarily for trading and due to be settled within 12 months after the balance sheet date.

Exhibit 5-10 illustrates how the current liabilities amounts of €14,000 (20X7) and €7,000 (20X6) have been expanded from the one amount shown in Exhibit 5-5. In the sections below, some of the issues surrounding the measurement principles for payables, accrued liabilities, and unearned revenue are discussed.

EXHIBIT 5-10   Apex Current Liabilities

	20X7	20X6
Current Liabilities	€14,000	€7,000
Trade and other payables	5,000	2,000
Notes payable	3,000	1,000
Current portion of noncurrent borrowings	2,000	1,000
Current tax payable	2,000	2,000
Accrued liabilities	1,000	500
Unearned revenue	1,000	500

Noncurrent interest-bearing liabilities to be settled within 12 months after the balance sheet date can be classified as noncurrent liabilities if:

* The original term of the liability is greater than 12 months,
* It is the intention to refinance or reschedule the obligation, or
* The agreement to refinance or reschedule the obligation is completed on or before the balance sheet date.

3.2.1. Trade and Other Payables (Accounts Payable)

Accounts payable are amounts that a business owes its vendors for goods and services that were purchased from them but which have not yet been paid.

3.2.2. Notes Payable

Notes payable are amounts owed by a business to creditors as a result of borrowings that are evidenced by a (short-term) loan agreement. Examples of notes payable include bank loans and other current borrowings other than those arising from trade credit. Notes payable may also appear in the long-term liability section of the balance sheet if they are due after one year or the operating cycle, whichever is longer.

3.2.3. Current Portion of Noncurrent Borrowings

By convention, liabilities expected to be repaid or liquidated within one year or one operating cycle of the business, whichever is greater, are classified as current liabilities. Other liabilities are classified as noncurrent. For example, Exhibit 5-10 shows that €2,000 of Apex's noncurrent borrowings will come due within a year; therefore, the €2,000 constitutes a current liability.

3.2.4. Current Tax Payable

Current taxes payable are tax expenses that have been determined and recorded on a company's income statement but which have not yet been paid.

3.2.5. Accrued Liabilities

Accrued liabilities (also known as **accrued expenses**) are expenses that have been reported on a company's income statement but which have not yet been paid because there is no legal obligation to pay them as of the balance sheet date. Common examples of accrued liabilities are accrued interest payable and accrued wages payable.

3.2.6. Unearned Revenue

Unearned revenue (also known as **deferred revenue**) is the collection of money in advance of delivery of the goods and services associated with the revenue. Examples include rental income received in advance, advance fees for servicing office equipment, and advance payments for magazine subscriptions received from customers.

EXAMPLE 5-3   Analysis of Unearned Revenue

Germany's SAP AG is one of the world's leading providers of business software solutions and one of the world's three largest independent software companies based on market capitalization. At year-end 2005, SAP reported the following assets and liabilities on its balance sheet (in € thousands):[4]

	2005	2004
Assets		
Goodwill	626,546	456,707
Other intangible assets	139,697	68,186
Property, plant, and equipment	1,094,965	999,083
Financial assets	534,155	100,382
Fixed assets	2,395,363	1,624,358
Inventories	19,376	11,692
Accounts receivable, net	2,251,027	1,929,100
Other assets	635,554	537,645
Accounts receivable and other assets	2,886,581	2,466,745
Marketable securities	209,565	10,164
Liquid assets	3,213,572	3,196,542
Nonfixed assets	6,329,094	5,685,143
Deferred taxes	250,698	205,601
Prepaid expenses and deferred charges	87,587	70,370
Total assets	9,062,742	7,585,472
thereof total current assets	6,241,125	4,849,537
Shareholders' Equity and Liabilities		
Subscribed capital[(1)]	316,458	316,004
Treasury stock	(775,318)	(569,166)
Additional paid-in capital	372,767	322,660
Retained earnings	5,986,186	4,830,156
Accumulated other comprehensive loss	(117,855)	(305,401)
Shareholders' equity	5,782,238	4,594,253

---

[4]In its annual report, SAP AG chose to provide the subtotal of current assets and current liabilities at the bottom of the respective portions of the balance sheet rather than within the balance sheet to distinguish how much of its nonfixed assets are current. According to Footnote 1 of SAP AG's 2005 annual report: "Non-fixed assets are comprised of Inventories, Accounts receivable, Other assets, Marketable securities, and Liquid assets including amounts to be realized in excess of one year."

Minority interests	7,615	21,971
Pension liabilities and similar obligations	183,619	139,690
Other reserves and accrued liabilities	1,839,140	1,768,723
Reserves and accrued liabilities	2,022,759	1,908,413
Bonds	6,927	7,277
Other liabilities	838,778	728,838
Other liabilities	845,705	736,115
Deferred income	404,425	324,720
Total shareholders' equity and liabilities	9,062,742	7,585,472
thereof current liabilities	2,781,685	2,591,872

The final line shows that deferred income rose nearly 25 percent to end 2005 with a value of $404.4 million. SAP describes the line as follows:

> *Deferred income consists mainly of prepayments for maintenance and deferred software license revenues. Such amounts will be recognized as software, maintenance, or service revenue, depending upon the reasons for the deferral when the basic criteria in SOP 97-2 have been met (see Note 3).*

Although investors prefer to see many liabilities minimized, deferred revenue represents money the company has already been paid for services that will be delivered in the future. Because it will then be recognized as revenue, many investors monitor the deferred income line (when significant) as an indicator of future revenue growth.

3.3. Tangible Assets

Tangible assets are long-term assets with physical substance that are used in company operations. These noncurrent assets are carried at their historical cost less any accumulated depreciation or accumulated depletion. Historical cost generally consists of vendor invoice cost, freight cost, and any other additional costs incurred to make the asset operable. Examples of tangible assets include land, buildings, equipment, machinery, furniture, and natural resources owned by the company, such as copper mines, oil and gas properties, and timberlands. If any of these assets are not used in company operations, they must be classified as investment assets.

3.4. Intangible Assets

Intangible assets are amounts paid by a company to acquire certain rights that are not represented by the possession of physical assets. A distinction can be made between identifiable intangibles and unidentifiable intangibles. An **identifiable intangible** can be acquired singly and is typically linked to specific rights or privileges having finite benefit periods. Examples include patents and trademarks. An **unidentifiable intangible** cannot be acquired singly and typically possesses an indefinite benefit period. An example is accounting goodwill, discussed further in section 3.4.2.

A company should assess whether the useful life of an intangible asset is finite or infinite and, if finite, the length of its life, or number of production or similar units constituting its useful life. Amortization and impairment principles apply as follows:

- An intangible asset with a finite useful life is amortized on a systematic basis over the best estimate of its useful life.
- An intangible asset with an infinite useful life should be tested for impairment annually but not amortized.

The balance sheet and notes should disclose the gross carrying amount (book value) less accumulated amortization for each class of asset at the beginning and the end of the period.

Companies may also have intangible assets that are not recorded on their balance sheets. These intangible assets might include management skill, valuable trademarks and name recognition, a good reputation, proprietary products, and so forth. Such assets are valuable and would fetch their worth if a company were to be sold.

Financial analysts have traditionally viewed the values assigned to intangible assets, particularly unidentifiable intangibles, with caution. Consequently, in assessing financial statements, they often exclude the book value assigned to intangibles, particularly unidentifiable intangibles, reducing net equity by an equal amount and increasing pretax income by any amortization expense or impairment associated with the intangibles. An arbitrary assignment of zero value to intangibles is not advisable. The analyst should examine each listed intangible and assess whether an adjustment should be made.

3.4.1. Specifically Identifiable Intangibles

Under IFRS, specifically identifiable intangible assets are nonfinancial assets without physical substance but which can be identified. Such assets are recognized on the balance sheet if it is probable that future economic benefits will flow to the company and the cost of the asset can be measured reliably. Examples of identifiable intangible assets include patents, trademarks, copyrights, franchises, and other rights. Identifiable intangible assets may have been created or purchased by a company. Determining the cost of internally created intangible assets can be difficult and subjective. For these reasons, internally created identifiable intangibles are less likely to be reported on the balance sheet under IFRS or U.S. GAAP. IAS No. 38 applies to all intangible assets that are not specifically dealt with in other international accounting standards. This standard determines that the intangible assets reported on a balance sheet are only those intangibles that have been *purchased* or *created* (in strictly limited instances).

IAS No. 38 provides that for internally created intangible assets, the company must identify the research phase and the development phase. The research phase includes activities that seek new knowledge or products. The development phase occurs after the research phase and includes design or testing of prototypes and models. IAS No. 38 prohibits the capitalization of costs as intangible assets during the research phase. Instead, these costs must be expensed on the income statement. Costs incurred in the development stage can be capitalized as intangible assets if certain criteria are met, including technological feasibility, the ability to use or sell the resulting asset, and the ability to complete the project.

All other expenses related to the following categories are **expensed**. They include:

- Internally *generated* brands, mastheads, publishing titles, customer lists, etc.
- Start-up costs.
- Training costs.

- Administrative and other general overhead costs.
- Advertising and promotion.
- Relocation and reorganization expenses.
- Redundancy and other termination costs.

U.S. GAAP prohibits the capitalization as an asset of almost all research and development costs. All such costs usually must be expensed. Generally, under U.S. GAAP, acquired intangible assets are reported as separately identifiable intangibles (as opposed to goodwill) if they arise from contractual rights (such as a licensing agreement), other legal rights (such as patents), or have the ability to be separated and sold (such as a customer list).

EXAMPLE 5-4   Measuring Intangible Assets

Alpha Inc., a motor vehicle manufacturer, has a research division that worked on the following projects during the year:

Project 1: Research aimed at finding a steering mechanism that does not operate like a conventional steering wheel but reacts to the impulses from a driver's fingers.

Project 2: The design of a prototype welding apparatus that is controlled electronically rather than mechanically, which has been determined to be technologically feasible.

The following is a summary of the expenses of the particular department:

	General	Project 1	Project 2
	€'000	€'000	€'000
Material and Services	128	935	620
Labor			
Direct labor	—	620	320
Administrative personnel	720	—	—
Overhead			
Direct	—	340	410
Indirect	270	110	60

Five percent of administrative personnel costs can be attributed to each of Projects 1 and 2. Explain the capitalization of Alpha's development costs for Projects 1 and 2 under IFRS.

Solution. Under IFRS, the capitalization of development costs for Projects 1 and 2 would be as follows:

	€'000
Project 1: Classified as research so all costs are recognized as expenses.	NIL
Project 2: (620 + 320 + 410 + 60)	1,410

Note that Project 2 is in the development stage and costs related to the project should be capitalized under IFRS. However, under IAS No. 38, administrative personnel costs should be expensed.

3.4.2. Goodwill

In a purchase acquisition, the excess of the cost of acquisition over the acquirer's interest in the fair value of the identifiable assets and liabilities acquired is described as goodwill and is recognized as an asset.

The subject of recognizing goodwill in financial statements has found both proponents and opponents among professionals. The proponents of goodwill recognition assert that goodwill is the "present value of excess returns that a company is able to earn." This group claims that determining the present value of these excess returns is analogous to determining the present value of future cash flows associated with other assets and projects. Opponents of goodwill recognition claim that the prices paid for acquisitions often turn out to be based on unrealistic expectations, thereby leading to future write-offs of goodwill.

Analysts should distinguish between accounting goodwill and economic goodwill. Economic goodwill is based on the economic performance of the entity, whereas accounting goodwill is based on accounting standards and only reported for past acquisitions. Economic goodwill is what should concern analysts and investors, and it is often not reflected on the balance sheet. This economic goodwill should be reflected in the stock price. Many analysts believe that goodwill should not be listed on the balance sheet, as it cannot be sold separately from the entity. These analysts believe that only assets that can be separately identified and sold be reflected on the balance sheet. Other financial statement users may desire to analyze goodwill and any subsequent impairment charges to assess management's performance on prior acquisitions.

Under IFRS and U.S. GAAP, goodwill should be capitalized and tested for impairment annually. Goodwill is not amortized. Impairment of goodwill is a noncash expense. If goodwill is deemed to be impaired, it is charged against income in the current period. This charge reduces current earnings. Assets are also reduced, so some performance measures, such as return on assets (net income divided by average total assets), may actually increase in future periods.

Under IFRS No. 3, the purchase method of accounting can be summarized by the following steps:

- The cost of acquisition is determined.
- The fair value of the acquiree's assets is determined.
- The fair value of the acquiree's liabilities and contingent liabilities is determined.
- Calculate the goodwill arising from the purchase as follows:
  - The book value of the acquirer's assets and liabilities should be combined with the fair value adjustments of the acquiree's assets, liabilities, and contingent liabilities.
  - Any goodwill should be recognized as an asset in the combined entity's balance sheet.

Despite the clear guidance incorporated in IFRS No. 3, many analysts believe that the determination of fair values involve considerable management discretion. Values for intangible assets, such as computer software, might not be easily validated when analyzing purchase acquisitions.

Management judgment can be particularly apparent in the allocation of the excess purchase price (after all other allocations to assets and liabilities). If, for example, the remaining excess purchase price is allocated to goodwill, there will be no impact on the company's net income because goodwill is not amortized (but is tested for impairment). If the excess were to be allocated to fixed assets, depreciation would rise, thus reducing net income and producing incorrect financial statements. (**Depreciation** is the allocation of the costs of a long-term [tangible] asset over its useful life.)

Goodwill can significantly affect the comparability of financial statements between companies using different accounting methods. As such, an analyst should remove any distortion that the recognition, amortization, and impairment of goodwill might create by adjusting the company's financial statements. Adjustments should be made by:

- Computing financial ratios using balance sheet data that exclude goodwill.
- Reviewing operating trends using data that exclude the amortization of goodwill or impairment to goodwill charges.
- Evaluating future business acquisitions by taking into account the purchase price paid relative to the net assets and earnings prospects of the acquired company.

IFRS No. 3 requires disclosure of the factors that contributed to goodwill and a description of each intangible asset that was not recognized separately from goodwill.

EXAMPLE 5-5   Goodwill Impairment

Vodafone Group, PLC, is a leading international provider of mobile communications services. It entered many of its international markets by acquiring local carriers. On 27 February 2006, Vodafone issued a press release that included the following information:

> *Reflecting the increasingly competitive environment in the industry, Vodafone has incorporated into its latest ten year plan a lower view of growth prospects for a number of key operating companies, particularly in the medium to long term, than those it has used previously.*

> *The result of these factors is that Vodafone expects to report:*

> *1. An impairment of the Group's goodwill in the range of GBP 23 billion to GBP 28 billion in respect of reductions in the aggregate goodwill for Vodafone Germany, Vodafone Italy and, potentially, Vodafone Japan. It is expected that most of the total will be attributable to Vodafone Germany.*

> *2. No impairment for any other subsidiary, joint venture or investment in associated undertakings.*

> *3. No impairment in respect of finite lived assets.*

A summary of the Group's goodwill in respect of subsidiary undertakings and joint ventures as of 30 September 2005 is set out below:

	GBP Billion
Germany	35.5
Italy	19.7
Japan	9.0

Spain	10.3
United Kingdom	0.7
Other subsidiaries and joint ventures	6.3
	81.5

How significant is this goodwill impairment and, with reference to acquisition prices, what might it indicate?

Solution. Given that the goodwill impairment was approximately equal to one-third the total value of goodwill recorded, it would appear to be significant. According to the press release, the impairment has arisen due to a competitive environment and lower expected growth rates. The operations involved appear now to be worth less than the price that was paid for their acquisition.

3.5. Financial Instruments: Financial Assets and Financial Liabilities

International accounting standards define a financial instrument as a contract that gives rise to a financial asset of one entity, and a financial liability or equity instrument of another entity. Financial instruments, both assets and liabilities, come in a variety of forms. Financial assets include investments in stocks and bonds and similar instruments. Financial liabilities include bonds, notes payable, and similar instruments. Some financial instruments may be classified as either an asset or a liability depending upon the contractual terms and current market conditions. One example of such a complex financial instrument is a derivative. A **derivative** is a financial instrument for which the value is derived based on some underlying factor (interest rate, exchange rate, commodity price, security price, or credit rating) and for which little or no initial investment is required. Derivatives may be used to hedge business transactions or for speculation.

Mark-to-market (fair value adjustments to financial assets and liabilities) is the process whereby the value of most trading assets (e.g., those held for trading and that are available for sale) and trading liabilities are adjusted to reflect current fair value. Such adjustments are often made on a daily basis, and cumulative balances are reversed on the subsequent day, prior to recalculating a fresh cumulative mark-to-market adjustment.

All financial assets and financial liabilities (including derivatives) should be recognized when the entity becomes a party to the contractual provisions of an instrument. For the purchase or sale of financial assets where market convention determines a fixed period between trade and settlement dates, the trade or settlement date can be used for recognition. Interest is not normally accrued between trade and settlement dates, but mark-to-market adjustments are made regardless of whether the entity uses trade date or settlement date accounting. Although IAS No. 39 allows the use of either date, trade date accounting is preferred by most treasury accountants.

Exhibit 5-11 provides a summary of how various financial assets and liabilities are classified and measured.

From Exhibit 5-11, marketable securities such as stocks and bonds may be classified as trading, available for sale, and held to maturity. To illustrate the different accounting

EXHIBIT 5-11   Measurement of Financial Assets and Liabilities

Measured at Fair Value	Measured at Cost or Amortized Cost
Financial Assets	**Financial Assets**
Financial assets held for trading (e.g., stocks and bonds)	Unlisted instruments (investments where the fair value is not reliably measurable)
Available-for-sale financial assets (e.g., stocks and bonds)	Held-to-maturity investments (bonds intended to be held to maturity)
Derivatives whether stand-alone or imbedded in nonderivative instruments	Loans and receivables
Nonderivative instruments (including financial assets) with fair value exposures *hedged* by derivatives	
Financial Liabilities	**Financial Liabilities**
Derivatives	All other liabilities (such as bonds payable or notes payable)
Financial liabilities held for trading	
Nonderivative instruments (including financial liabilities) with fair value exposures *hedged* by derivatives	

treatments of the gains and losses on marketable securities, consider an entity that invests €100 million in a 5 percent coupon fixed-income security portfolio. After six months, the company receives the first coupon payment of €2,500,000. Additionally, interest rates have declined and the value of the fixed-income securities has increased by €2 million. Exhibit 5-12 illustrates how this situation will be portrayed in the balance sheet assets and equity, as well as the income statement of the entity concerned, under each of the following three accounting policies for marketable securities: assets held for trading purposes, assets available for sale, and held-to-maturity assets.

In the case of marketable securities classified as either trading or available for sale, the investments are listed under assets at fair market value. For exposition purposes, Exhibit 5-12 shows the unrealized gain on a separate line. Practically, the investments would be listed at their fair value of €102 million on one line within assets. In the case of trading securities, the unrealized gain is included on the income statement and thus reflected in retained earnings. In the case of available-for-sale securities, the unrealized gain is not included on the income statement; rather, it is deferred as part of other comprehensive income within owners' equity. As noted in the chapter on the income statement, other comprehensive income includes gains and losses that have not yet been reported on the income statement due to particular accounting standards. In the case of held-to-maturity securities, the unrealized gain is not reflected on either the balance sheet or income statement.

In the case of liabilities such as bonds issued by a company, these are normally reported at amortized cost on the balance sheet, as noted in Exhibit 5-12. For example, if a company issues bonds with a total par value of $10 million at a price of $9,750,000 (issued at a discount), the bonds are reported as a liability of $9,750,000 (cost). As time passes, the discount of $250,000 is amortized such that the bond will be listed as a liability of $10 million at maturity. Similarly, any bond premium would be amortized for bonds issued at a premium.

EXHIBIT 5-12   Accounting for Gains and Losses on Marketable Securities

BALANCE SHEET As of 30 June 200X	Trading Portfolio	Available-for- Sale Portfolio	Held to Maturity
Assets			
Deposits	2,500,000	2,500,000	2,500,000
Cost of securities	100,000,000	100,000,000	100,000,000
Unrealized gains (losses) on securities	2,000,000	2,000,000	—
	104,500,000	104,500,000	102,500,000
Liabilities			
Equity			
Paid-in capital	100,000,000	100,000,000	100,000,000
Retained earnings	4,500,000	2,500,000	2,500,000
Other comprehensive income (losses)	—	2,000,000	—
	104,500,000	104,500,000	102,500,000

INCOME STATEMENT For period 1 January–30 June 200X			
Interest income	2,500,000	2,500,000	2,500,000
Unrealized gains (losses)	2,000,000	—	—
	4,500,000	2,500,000	2,500,000

4. EQUITY

Equity is the residual claim on a company's assets after subtracting liabilities. It represents the claim of the owner against the company. Equity includes funds directly invested in the company by the owners, as well as earnings that have been reinvested over time. Equity can also include items of gain or loss that are not yet recognized on the company's income statement.

4.1. Components of Equity

IFRS and U.S. GAAP both define equity (or net assets) as the residual interest in the assets of an entity that remain after deducting its liabilities. There are five potential components that comprise the owners' equity section of the balance sheet:

1. *Capital contributed by owners*. Capital ownership in a corporation is evidenced through the issuance of common stock, although preferred stock (a hybrid security with some characteristics of debt) may be issued by some companies in addition to common stock. Preferred shares have rights that take precedence over the rights of common shareholders—rights that generally pertain to receipt of dividends (not always cumulative if omitted by the board of directors) and receipt of assets if the company is liquidated. Common and preferred shares

may have a par value (or stated value) or may be issued as no par shares (depending on governmental requirements at the time of incorporation). Where par or stated value requirements exist, it must be disclosed in the stockholders' equity section of the balance sheet. In addition, the number of shares authorized, issued, and outstanding must be disclosed for each class of stock issued by the company. The number of authorized shares is the number of shares that may be sold by the company under its articles of incorporation. The number of issued shares is those shares that have been sold to investors while the number of outstanding shares consists of the issued shares less those shares repurchased (treasury stock) by the company.

2. *Minority interest (or noncontrolling interest).* The equity interests of minority shareholders in the subsidiary companies that have been consolidated by the parent (controlling) company but that are not wholly owned by the parent company.

3. *Retained earnings (or retained deficit).* Amounts that have been recognized as cumulatively earned in the company's income statements but which have not been paid to the owners of the company through dividends.

4. *Treasury stock (or own shares repurchased).* The repurchase of company shares may occur when management considers the shares undervalued or when it wants to limit the effects of dilution from various employee stock compensation plans. Treasury stock is a reduction of shareholders' equity and a reduction of total shares outstanding. Treasury shares are nonvoting and do not receive dividends if declared by the company.

5. *Accumulated comprehensive income (or other reserves).* Amounts that may either increase or decrease total shareholders' equity but are not derived from the income statement or through any company transactions in its own equity shares.

In June 1997, the FASB released Statement of Financial Accounting Standard (SFAS) No. 130, *Reporting of Comprehensive Income.* This statement established certain standards for reporting and presenting comprehensive income in the general-purpose financial statements. SFAS No. 130 was issued in response to users' concerns that certain changes in assets and liabilities were bypassing the income statement and appearing in the statement of changes in stockholders' equity. The purpose of SFAS No. 130 was to report all items that met the definition of *comprehensive income* in a prominent financial statement for the same period in which they were recognized. In accordance with the definition provided by Statement of Financial Accounting Concepts No. 6, **comprehensive income** was to include all changes in owners' equity that resulted from transactions of the business entity with nonowners. Comprehensive income can be defined as:

$$\text{Comprehensive income} = \text{Net income} + \text{Other comprehensive income}$$

According to SFAS No. 130, **other comprehensive income** (OCI) is part of total comprehensive income but generally excluded from net income. Prior to SFAS No. 130, these three items—foreign currency translation adjustments, minimum pension liability adjustments, and unrealized gains or losses on available-for-sale investments—were disclosed as separate components of stockholders' equity on the balance sheet. Under SFAS No. 130, they are to be reported as OCI. Furthermore, they must be reported separately, as the FASB decided that information about each component is more important than information about the aggregate. Later, under SFAS No. 133, net unrealized losses on derivatives were also included in the definition of OCI. The intent of SFAS No. 130 was that "if used with related disclosures and other information in financial statements, the information provided by reporting comprehensive income would assist investors, creditors, and other financial statement users in assessing an enterprise's economic activities and its timing and magnitude of future cash flows."

EXHIBIT 5-13   Apex Stockholders' Equity

	20X7	20X6
Equity	**€22,000**	**€20,000**
Share capital	10,000	10,000
Preferred shares	2,000	2,000
Share premium (paid-in capital)	—	—
Other reserves (unrealized gains and losses)	1,000	—
Retained earnings	9,000	8,000
Own shares repurchased (treasury shares)	—	—

Although the FASB required that "an enterprise shall display total comprehensive income and its components in a financial statement that is displayed with the same prominence as other financial statements that constitute a full set of financial statements," it did not specify which format was required, except that net income should be shown as a component of comprehensive income in that financial statement. According to SFAS No. 130, three alternative formats are allowed for presenting OCI and total comprehensive income:

1. Below the line for net income in a traditional income statement (as a combined statement of net income and comprehensive income).
2. In a separate statement of comprehensive income that begins with the amount of net income for the year.
3. In a statement of changes in stockholders' equity.

Under IFRS, the component changes are also reported in the statement of equity; however, it is not presently required that a comprehensive income amount be reported.

Exhibit 5-13 illustrates how the equity amounts of €22,000 (20X7) and €20,000 (20X6) have been expanded from the one amount shown in Exhibit 5-5.

4.2. Statement of Changes in Shareholders' Equity

The **statement of changes in shareholders' equity** reflects information about the increases or decreases to a company's net assets or wealth. With respect to comprehensive income, the following items, if present, must be disclosed:

- Unrealized gains or losses on available-for-sale investments.
- Gains or losses from derivatives that qualify as net investment hedges or cash flow hedges.
- Minimum pension liability adjustments from underfunded defined-benefit plans.
- Foreign currency translation adjustments on foreign subsidiary companies.

Other information in the changes in equity statement or in notes includes the following:

- Capital transactions with owners and distributions to owners.
- Reconciliation of the balance of accumulated profit or loss (retained earnings) at the beginning and end of the year.

- Reconciliation of the carrying amount of each class of equity capital, share premium (paid-in capital), and accumulated comprehensive income (reserve) at the beginning and end of the period.

Exhibit 5-14 presents Sony Corporation's Consolidated Statement of Changes in Stockholders' Equity for the fiscal years ended 31 March 2004 and 2005. In this statement, Sony complies with the reconciliation and disclosure requirements that were discussed above.

EXHIBIT 5-14 Sony Corporation and Consolidated Subsidiaries: Consolidated Statement of Changes in Stockholders' Equity (¥ millions)

	Subsidiary Tracking Stock	Common Stock	Additional Paid-In Capital	Retained Earnings	Accumulated Other Comprehensive Income	Treasury stock, at Cost	Total
Balance on 31 March 2003	3,917	472,361	984,196	1,301,740	(471,978)	(9,341)	2,280,895
Conversion of convertible bonds		3,989	3,988				7,977
Stock issued under exchange offering			5,409				5,409
Comprehensive income:							
Net income				88,511			88,511
Other comprehensive income, net of tax							
Unrealized gains on securities:							
Unrealized holding gains or losses arising during period					57,971		57,971
Less:							
Reclassification adjustment for gains or losses included in net income					(5,679)		(5,679)
Unrealized losses on derivative instruments:							
Unrealized holding gains or losses arising during period					7,537		7,537
Less:							
Reclassification adjustment for gains or losses included in net income					(3,344)		(3,344)

(Continued)

EXHIBIT 5-14   (*Continued*)

	Subsidiary Tracking Stock	Common Stock	Additional Paid-In Capital	Retained Earnings	Accumulated Other Comprehensive Income	Treasury stock, at Cost	Total
Minimum pension liability adjustment					93,415		93,415
Foreign currency translation adjustments:							
Translation adjustments arising during period					(129,113)		(129,113)
Less:							
Reclassification adjustment for losses included in net income					1,232		1,232
Total comprehensive income							110,530
Stock issue costs, net of tax				(53)			(53)
Dividends declared				(23,138)			(23,138)
Purchase of treasury stock						(8,523)	(8,523)
Reissuance of treasury stock			(776)			5,681	4,905
Balance on 31 March 2004	**3,917**	**476,350**	**992,817**	**1,367,060**	**(449,959)**	**(12,183)**	**2,378,022**
Balance on 31 March 2004	3,917	476,350	992,817	1,367,060	(449,959)	(12,183)	2,378,022
Exercise of stock acquisition rights		52	53				105
Conversion of convertible bonds		141,390	141,354				282,744
Stock-based compensation			340				340
Comprehensive income:							
Net income				163,838			163,838
Other comprehensive income, net of tax							

	Subsidiary Tracking Stock	Common Stock	Additional Paid-In Capital	Retained Earnings	Accumulated Other Comprehensive Income	Treasury stock, at Cost	Total
Unrealized gains on securities:							
Unrealized holding gains or losses arising during period					5,643		5,643
Less:							
Reclassification adjustment for gains or losses included in net income					(12,924)		(12,924)
Unrealized losses on derivative instruments:							
Unrealized holding gains or losses arising during period					(209)		(209)
Less:							
Reclassification adjustment for gains or losses included in net income					(1,681)		(1,681)
Minimum pension liability adjustment					(769)		(769)
Foreign currency translation adjustments:							
Translation adjustments arising during period					74,224		74,224
Total comprehensive income							228,122
Stock issue costs, net of tax				(541)			(541)
Dividends declared				(24,030)			(24,030)
Purchase of treasury stock						(416)	(416)
Reissuance of treasury stock			(342)	(245)		6,599	6,012
Balance on 31 March 2005	3,917	617,792	1,134,222	1,506,082	(385,675)	(6,000)	2,870,338

5. USES AND ANALYSIS OF THE BALANCE SHEET

The classified sections of Apex Corporation's balance sheets have been discussed and illustrated throughout this chapter. Exhibit 5-15 now presents the complete detailed balance sheets for Apex, which we will use as the basis for a discussion of how to analyze a balance sheet.

EXHIBIT 5-15   Apex Detailed Balance Sheets

Balance Sheet (000)	20X7	20X6
Assets		
Current Assets	**€20,000**	**€16,000**
Cash and cash equivalents	3,000	2,000
Marketable securities: 3 types	3,000	4,000
Trade receivables	5,000	3,000
Inventories	7,000	6,000
Other current assets	2,000	1,000
Noncurrent Assets	**53,000**	**27,000**
Property, plant, and equipment	35,000	20,000
Goodwill	5,000	1,000
Other intangible assets	3,000	1,000
Noncurrent investments (subsidiaries, associates, joint ventures)	10,000	5,000
Total Assets	**€73,000**	**€43,000**
Liabilities and Equity		
Current Liabilities	**14,000**	**7,000**
Trade and other payables	5,000	2,000
Current borrowings	3,000	1,000
Current portion of noncurrent borrowings	2,000	1,000
Current tax payable	2,000	2,000
Accrued liabilities	1,000	500
Unearned revenue	1,000	500
Noncurrent Liabilities	**37,000**	**16,000**
Noncurrent borrowings	30,000	10,000
Deferred tax	6,000	5,000
Noncurrent provisions	1,000	1,000
Total Liabilities	**51,000**	**23,000**
Equity	**22,000**	**20,000**
Share capital	10,000	10,000
Preference shares	2,000	2,000
Share premium (paid-in capital)	—	—
Other reserves (unrealized gains and losses)	1,000	—
Retained earnings	9,000	8,000
Own shares repurchased (treasury shares)	—	—
Total Liabilities and Shareholders' Equity	**€73,000**	**€43,000**

If a company is growing or shrinking, comparing balance sheet amounts from year to year may not clearly show trends. Additionally, comparing companies is difficult unless adjustments are made for size. Two techniques used to analyze balance sheets adjusted for differences or changes are common-size analysis and ratio analysis.

5.1. Common-Size Analysis of the Balance Sheet

The first technique, common-size analysis, involves stating all balance sheet items as a percentage of total assets.[5] Common-size statements are useful in comparing a company's current balance sheet with prior-year balance sheets or to other companies in the same industry. Horizontal common-size analysis provides a format to accomplish the former but not the latter. Exhibit 5-16 illustrates vertical common-size balance sheets for Apex Corporation. Horizontal common-size analysis is demonstrated in a later chapter.

EXHIBIT 5-16   Apex Common-Size Balance Sheets

Balance Sheet (Percent of Total Assets)	20X7	20X6
Assets		
Current Assets	**27.4**	**37.2**
Cash and cash equivalents	4.1	4.7
Marketable securities: 3 types	4.1	9.3
Trade receivables	6.8	7.0
Inventories	9.6	14.0
Other current assets	2.7	2.3
Noncurrent Assets	**72.6**	**62.8**
Property, plant, and equipment	47.9	46.5
Goodwill	6.8	2.3
Other intangible assets	4.1	2.3
Noncurrent investments (subsidiaries, associates, joint ventures)	13.7	11.6
Total Assets	**100.0**	**100.0**
Liabilities and Equity		
Current Liabilities	**19.2**	**16.3**
Trade and other payables	6.8	4.7
Current borrowings	4.1	2.3
Current portion of noncurrent borrowings	2.7	2.3
Current tax payable	2.7	4.7
		(Continued)

[5]This format can be distinguished as *vertical common-size analysis.* As the chapter on financial statement analysis will discuss, another type of common-size analysis, known as *horizontal common-size analysis,* states quantities in terms of a selected base-year value. Unless otherwise indicated, text references to *common-size analysis* refer to vertical analysis.

EXHIBIT 5-16   (*Continued*)

Balance Sheet (Percent of Total Assets)	20X7	20X6
Accrued liabilities	1.4	1.2
Unearned revenue	1.4	1.2
Noncurrent Liabilities	**50.7**	**37.2**
Noncurrent borrowings	41.1	23.3
Deferred tax	8.2	11.6
Noncurrent provisions	1.4	2.3
Total Liabilities	**69.9**	**53.5**
Shareholders' Equity	**30.1**	**46.5**
Share capital	13.7	23.3
Preference shares	2.7	4.7
Share premium (paid-in capital)	—	—
Other reserves (unrealized gains and losses)	1.4	—
Retained earnings	12.3	18.6
Own shares repurchased (treasury shares)	—	—
Total Liabilities and Shareholders' Equity	**100.0**	**100.0**

The common-size analysis for Apex clearly shows that for 20X7, the company is less liquid and is more leveraged than it was in 20X6. Regarding liquidity, current assets have decreased and current liabilities have increased when compared with the prior year. With respect to leverage, both noncurrent and total liabilities have increased when compared with the prior year.

EXAMPLE 5-6   Common-Size Analysis

Applying common-size analysis to the Roche Group balance sheets presented in Exhibit 5-7, which one of the following line items increased in 2005 relative to 2004?

A. Goodwill
B. Inventories
C. Long-term debt
D. Accounts receivables

Solution. C is correct. Long-term debt increased as a percentage of total assets from 12.1 percent of total assets in 2004 (CHF7,077 ÷ CHF58,446) to 13.4 percent in 2005 (CHF9,322 ÷ CHF69,365).

Although goodwill, inventories, and accounts receivables all increased in absolute Swiss franc amounts during 2005, they declined as a percentage of total assets when compared with the previous year.

Vertical common-size analysis of the balance sheet is particularly useful in cross-sectional analysis—comparing companies to each other for a particular time period or comparing a company with industry or sector data. The analyst could select individual peer companies for comparison, use industry data from published sources, or compile data from databases. Some common sources of published data are:

- *Annual Statement Studies*, published by the Risk Management Association (RMA). This volume provides abbreviated common-size (and ratio) data by industry. The source of data includes both public and nonpublic company data collected by financial institutions and may reflect non-GAAP, unaudited data.
- *Almanac of Business and Industrial Financial Ratios*, by Leo Troy. This is an annually revised publication, currently published by CCH.

When analyzing a company, many analysts prefer to select the peer companies for comparison or to compile their own industry statistics. For example, Exhibit 5-17 presents common-size balance sheet data compiled for the 10 sectors of Standard & Poor's 500 using 2005 data. The sector classification follows the S&P/MSCI Global Industrial Classification System (GICS). The exhibit presents mean and median common-size balance sheet data for those companies in the S&P 500 for which 2005 data was available in the Compustat database.[6]

Some interesting general observations can be made from these data:

- Energy and utility companies have the largest amounts of property, plant, and equipment. Utilities also have the highest level of long-term debt and use some preferred stock.
- Financial companies have the greatest percentage of liabilities.
- Telecommunications services and utility companies have the lowest level of receivables.
- Inventory levels are highest for consumer discretionary and consumer staples companies.
- Information technology companies use the least amount of leverage as evidenced by the entries for long-term debt and total liabilities.

Example 5-7 shows an analyst using cross-sectional common-size balance sheet data.

---

[6]An entry of zero for an item (e.g., current assets) was excluded from the data, except in the case of preferred stock. Note that most financial institutions did not provide current asset or current liability data, so these are reported as not available in the database.

EXHIBIT 5-17   Common-Size Balance Sheet Statistics for the S&P 500: Grouped by S&P/MSCI GICS Sector (in percent except No. of Observations; data for 2005)

Panel A. Median Data

	Energy	Materials	Industrials	Consumer Discretionary	Consumer Staples	Health Care	Financials	Information Technology	Telecom. Services	Utilities
No. observations	29	30	49	85	36	52	87	73	9	31
Cash	7.55	6.07	4.89	7.60	4.50	18.50	5.32	28.35	2.05	1.61
Receivables	11.16	13.56	16.50	9.60	9.92	11.91	28.95	10.64	4.71	5.49
Inventories	3.98	10.21	10.38	15.43	14.67	7.49	1.37	5.52	0.95	2.13
Other current	1.64	2.51	3.59	3.33	2.75	3.85	0.98	4.00	1.49	4.59
Current assets	27.29	35.65	36.58	43.92	33.18	41.61	NA	56.05	10.06	16.89
PP&E	54.70	37.21	15.79	20.99	27.53	13.70	1.06	9.80	42.57	55.04
Accts payable	7.50	7.01	6.91	6.99	8.54	4.54	34.73	4.14	2.49	3.89
Current liabilities	17.94	20.18	24.48	27.13	29.55	23.87	NA	22.90	13.70	17.13
LT debt	14.77	19.86	17.43	17.81	21.39	11.43	11.98	8.01	23.13	29.35
Total liabilities	50.72	63.82	62.29	56.73	65.36	47.87	89.81	37.10	58.39	75.28
Preferred stock	0.00	0.00	0.00	0.00	0.00	0.00	0.00	0.00	0.00	0.28
Common equity	49.28	36.18	37.71	43.27	34.64	52.13	10.19	62.90	41.61	22.89
Total equity	49.28	36.18	37.71	43.27	34.64	52.13	10.19	62.90	41.61	24.72

Panel B. Mean Data

	Energy	Materials	Industrials	Consumer Discretionary	Consumer Staples	Health Care	Financials	Information Technology	Telecom. Services	Utilities
No. observations	29	30	49	85	36	52	87	73	9	31
Cash	7.56	9.16	7.91	10.19	7.45	19.55	10.49	33.43	3.32	2.85
Receivables	11.83	14.30	17.92	12.46	9.92	12.96	34.02	12.78	5.16	6.78
Inventories	5.32	10.82	10.21	19.36	15.54	9.23	6.88	6.51	0.94	2.62
Other current	2.98	2.73	4.07	3.74	3.09	4.08	1.09	4.60	2.49	6.44
Current assets	27.14	36.82	36.41	40.18	36.35	44.62	NA	56.71	11.59	18.60
PP&E	54.84	35.70	24.83	25.38	30.77	16.76	1.92	13.05	48.53	57.48
Accts payable	9.07	8.80	7.12	10.46	9.82	8.75	35.09	7.03	2.76	4.53
Current liabilities	19.00	21.02	25.48	27.71	28.66	25.50	NA	23.99	13.56	18.92
LT debt	17.84	20.18	18.78	19.05	23.51	14.83	18.16	10.60	31.00	31.94
Total liabilities	53.16	61.72	61.10	57.64	64.67	48.88	80.50	40.05	65.74	76.83
Preferred stock	0.50	0.76	0.14	0.11	0.01	0.18	0.93	0.06	0.04	0.60
Common equity	46.33	37.52	38.76	42.25	35.32	50.94	18.60	59.89	34.22	22.57
Total equity	46.84	38.28	38.90	42.36	35.33	51.12	19.50	59.95	34.26	23.17

LT = long term, PP&E = property, plant, and equipment.
Source: Based on data from Compustat.

EXAMPLE 5-7   Cross-Sectional Common-Size Analysis

Jason Lu is examining four companies in the computer industry to evaluate their relative financial position as reflected on their balance sheet. He has compiled the following vertical common-size data for Dell, Hewlett-Packard Co., Gateway, and Apple Computer.

Cross-Sectional Analysis, Consolidated Balance Sheets (in percent of total assets)

Company	DELL	HPQ	GTW	AAPL
Fiscal year	3 Feb 2006	31 Oct 2005	31 Dec 2005	30 Sep 2005
Assets				
Current assets:				
Cash and cash equivalents	30.47	17.99	21.99	30.22
Short-term investments	8.72	0.02	8.50	41.30
Accounts receivable, net	17.69	16.11	17.97	7.75
Financing receivables, net	5.90	NA	NA	NA
Inventories	2.49	8.89	11.42	1.43
Other current assets	11.34	13.03	22.06	8.48
Total current assets	76.62	56.05	81.94	89.17
Property, plant, and equipment, net	8.68	8.34	4.33	7.07
Investments	11.64	9.70	0.00	0.00
Long-term financing receivables, net	1.41	NA	NA	NA
Other assets	1.65	25.91	13.73	3.76
Total Assets	100.00	100.00	100.00	100.00
Liabilities and Stockholders' Equity				
Current liabilities:				
Accounts payable	42.58	13.22	39.66	15.40
Short-term debt	0.00	2.37	2.60	0.00
Accrued and other	26.34	25.10	23.60	14.76
Total current liabilities	68.92	40.69	65.86	30.16
Long-term debt	2.18	4.39	15.62	0.00
Other liabilities	11.03	6.84	2.98	5.20
Commitments and contingent liabilities	0.00	0.00	0.00	0.00
Total liabilities	82.13	51.92	84.46	35.36
Stockholders' equity				
Total stockholders' equity	17.87	48.08	15.54	64.64

Source: Based on data from Bloomberg.

HPQ = Hewlett-Packard Co., GTW = Gateway, APPL = Apple Computer, NA = not available.

From this data, Lu learns the following:

- All four companies have a high level of cash, consistent with the information technology sector. Dell and Apple have a much higher than normal balance in cash and investments combined. This may reflect their business models, which have generated large operating cash flows in recent years.
- Apple has the lowest level of accounts receivable. Further research is necessary to learn if this is related to Apple's cash sales through retail stores or if the company has been selling/factoring receivables to a greater degree than the other companies.
- Dell and Apple both have an extraordinarily low level of inventory. Both utilize a just-in-time inventory system and rely on suppliers to hold inventory until needed. Additional scrutiny of the footnotes accompanying their annual reports reveals that Dell includes some "in-transit" inventory in other current assets and that Apple regularly makes purchase commitments that are not currently recorded as inventory and uses contract manufacturers to assemble and test some finished products. Dell has a smaller relative amount of purchase commitments. Hewlett-Packard has similar purchase commitments to Apple, and all of the companies make some use of contract manufacturers, but no mention is made of them about the extent that inventory may be "understated" through such use. Overall, it appears that the inventory levels may be understated somewhat for Dell and Apple but that, all things considered, they have been more efficient at managing inventory than Hewlett-Packard or Gateway.
- All four companies have a level of property, plant, and equipment below that of the sector, with Gateway having the lowest level.
- Hewlett-Packard has a large amount of "other assets." Further analysis reveals that this represents purchased intangibles, particularly goodwill from acquisitions.
- Dell and Gateway have a large amount of accounts payable. Due to Dell's high level of cash and investments, this is likely not a problem for Dell; however, it could indicate that Gateway could have difficulty in paying suppliers. An analysis of Gateway's cash flows would be warranted.
- Consistent with the industry, Dell, Hewlett-Packard, and Apple have very low levels of long-term debt. Gateway has a high level relative to the industry, which warrants further examination to assess the company's financial risk.

5.2. Balance Sheet Ratios

The second technique permitting comparison across time (time-series analysis) and across companies (cross-sectional analysis) is ratio analysis. In ratio analysis, the analyst may examine the level and trend of a ratio in relation to past values of the ratio for the company, thereby providing information on changes in the financial position of a company over time. The analyst may also compare a ratio against the values of the ratio for comparable companies, thereby providing information on the financial position of a company in relation to that of its peer group. So-called **balance sheet ratios** are those involving balance sheet items only. Balance sheet ratios fall under the heading of **liquidity ratios** (measuring the company's ability to meet its short-term obligations) or **solvency ratios** (measuring the company's ability to meet long-term and other obligations). The use of these ratios along with other balance sheet ratios and ratios combining balance sheet data

EXHIBIT 5-18   Balance Sheet Ratios

Liquidity Ratios	Calculation	Measurement
Current	Current assets ÷ Current liabilities	Ability to meet current liabilities
Quick (acid test)	(Cash + Marketable securities + Receivables) ÷ Current liabilities	Ability to meet current liabilities
Cash	(Cash + Marketable securities) ÷ Current liabilities	Ability to meet current liabilities
Solvency Ratios		
Long-term debt to equity	Total long-term debt ÷ Total equity	Financial risk and financial leverage
Debt to equity	Total debt ÷ Total equity	Financial risk and financial leverage
Total debt	Total debt ÷ Total assets	Financial risk and financial leverage
Financial leverage	Total assets ÷ Total equity	Financial risk and financial leverage

with other financial statement data are discussed in a later chapter. Exhibit 5-18 summarizes the calculation and interpretation of selected balance sheet ratios.

Some have questioned the usefulness of financial statement analysis in a world where capital markets are said to be efficient. After all, they say, an efficient market is forward looking, whereas the analysis of financial statements is a look at the past. However, the value of financial analysis is that it enables the analyst to gain insights that can assist in making forward-looking projections required by an efficient market. Financial ratios serve the following purposes:

- They provide insights into the microeconomic relationships within a company that help analysts project earnings and free cash flow (which is necessary to determine entity value and creditworthiness).
- They provide insights into a company's financial flexibility, which is its ability to obtain the cash required to meet financial obligations or to make asset acquisitions, even if unexpected circumstances should develop. Financial flexibility requires a company to possess financial strength (a level and trend of financial ratios that meet or exceed industry norms), lines of credit, or assets that can be easily used as a means of obtaining cash, either by their outright sale or by using them as collateral.
- They provide a means of evaluating management's ability. Key performance ratios can serve as quantitative measures for ranking management's ability relative to a peer group.

EXAMPLE 5-8   Ratio Analysis

For the following ratio questions, refer to the balance sheet information for Roche Group presented in Exhibit 5-7.

1. The current ratio for Roche Group at 31 December 2005 is closest to
   A. 1.29.
   B. 1.86.
   C. 1.97.
   D. 3.75.

2. Using the balance sheet information presented in Exhibit 5-7 for Roche Group, which one of the following ratios increased in 2005 relative to 2004?
   A. Current ratio
   B. Total debt ratio
   C. Debt-to-equity ratio
   D. Financial leverage ratio

Solution to 1. D is correct. The current ratio (current assets ÷ current liabilities) is 3.75 (CHF35,626 ÷ CHF9,492).

Solution to 2. A is correct. The current ratio (current assets ÷ current liabilities) increased from 2.93 (CHF29,679 ÷ CHF10,134) in 2004 to 3.75 (CHF35,626 ÷ CHF9,492) in 2005. The total debt ratio declined from 43.1 percent in 2004 to 39.8 percent in 2005; the debt-to-equity ratio declined from 75.6 percent in 2004 to 66.2 percent in 2005; and the financial leverage ratio declined from 1.756 in 2004 to 1.662 in 2005.

Financial ratio analysis is limited by:

- *The use of alternative accounting methods.* Accounting methods play an important role in the interpretation of financial ratios. It should be remembered that ratios are usually based on data taken from financial statements. Such data are generated via accounting procedures that might not be comparable among companies because companies have latitude in the choice of accounting methods. This lack of consistency across companies makes comparability difficult to analyze and limits the usefulness of ratio analysis. Some accounting alternatives currently found include the following:
  ○ FIFO or LIFO inventory valuation methods.
  ○ Cost or equity methods of accounting for unconsolidated associates.
  ○ Straight-line or accelerated consumption pattern methods of depreciation.
  ○ Capitalized or operating lease treatment.
- *The homogeneity of a company's operating activities.* Many companies are diversified with divisions operating in different industries. This makes it difficult to find comparable industry ratios to use for comparison purposes. It is better to examine industry-specific ratios by lines of business.
- *The need to determine whether the results of the ratio analysis are mutually consistent.* One set of ratios might show a problem, and another set might indicate that this problem is short term in nature.
- *The need to use judgment.* The analyst must use judgment when performing ratio analysis. A key issue is whether a ratio for a company is within a reasonable range for an industry, with this range being determined by the analyst. Although financial ratios are used to help assess the growth potential and risk of a business, they cannot be used alone to directly value a company or determine its creditworthiness. The entire operation of the business must be examined, and the external economic and industry setting in which it is operating must be considered when interpreting financial ratios.

6. SUMMARY

The starting place for analyzing a company is typically the balance sheet. It provides users such as creditors or investors with information regarding the sources of finance available for projects and infrastructure. At the same time, it normally provides information about the future earnings capacity of a company's assets as well as an indication of cash flows implicit in the receivables and inventories.

The balance sheet has many limitations, especially relating to the measurement of assets and liabilities. The lack of timely recognition of liabilities and, sometimes, assets, coupled with historical costs as opposed to fair value accounting for all items on the balance sheet, implies that the financial analyst must make numerous adjustments to determine the economic net worth of the company.

The balance sheet discloses what an entity owns (assets) and what it owes (liabilities) at a specific point in time, which is why it is also referred to as the statement of financial position. Equity represents the portion belonging to the owners or shareholders of a business. Equity is the residual interest in the assets of an entity after deducting its liabilities. The value of equity is increased by any generation of new assets by the business itself or by profits made during the year and is decreased by losses or withdrawals in the form of dividends.

The analyst must understand the structure and format of the balance sheet in order to evaluate the liquidity, solvency, and overall financial position of a company. Key points are:

- The "report format" of the balance sheet lists assets, liabilities, and equity in a single column. The "account format" follows the pattern of the traditional general ledger accounts, with assets at the left and liabilities and equity at the right of a central dividing line.
- The balance sheet should distinguish between current and noncurrent assets and between current and noncurrent liabilities unless a presentation based on liquidity provides more relevant and reliable information.
- Assets expected to be liquidated or used up within one year or one operating cycle of the business, whichever is greater, are classified as current assets. Assets not expected to be liquidated or used up within one year or one operating cycle of the business, whichever is greater, are classified as noncurrent assets.
- Liabilities expected to be settled or paid within one year or one operating cycle of the business, whichever is greater, are classified as current liabilities. Liabilities not expected to be settled or paid within one year or one operating cycle of the business, whichever is greater, are classified as noncurrent liabilities.
- Asset and liability values reported on a balance sheet may be measured on the basis of fair value or historical cost. Historical cost values may be quite different from economic values. Balance sheets must be evaluated critically in light of accounting policies applied in order to answer the question of how the values relate to economic reality and to each other.
- The notes to financial statements are an integral part of the U.S. GAAP and IFRS financial reporting processes. They provide important required detailed disclosures, as well as other information provided voluntarily by management. This information can be invaluable when determining whether the measurement of assets is comparable to other entities being analyzed.
- Tangible assets are long-term assets with physical substance that are used in company operations.
- Intangible assets are amounts paid by a company to acquire certain rights that are not represented by the possession of physical assets. A company should assess whether the useful life of an intangible asset is finite or infinite and, if finite, the length of its life.

- Under IFRS and U.S. GAAP, goodwill should be capitalized and tested for impairment annually. Goodwill is not amortized.
- Financial instruments are contracts that give rise to both a financial asset of one entity and a financial liability of another entity. Financial instruments come in a variety of instruments, including derivatives, hedges, and marketable securities.
- There are five potential components that comprise the owners' equity section of the balance: contributed capital, minority interest, retained earnings, treasury stock, and accumulated comprehensive income.
- The statement of changes in equity reflects information about the increases or decreases to a company's net assets or wealth.
- Ratio analysis is used by analysts and managers to assess company performance and status. Another valuable analytical technique is common-size (relative) analysis, which is achieved through the conversion of all balance sheet items to a percentage of total assets.

PRACTICE PROBLEMS

1. Resources controlled by a company as a result of past events are
   A. equity.
   B. assets.
   C. liabilities.

2. Equity equals
   A. Assets − Liabilities.
   B. Liabilities − Assets.
   C. Assets + Liabilities.

3. Distinguishing between current and noncurrent items on the balance sheet and presenting a subtotal for current assets and liabilities is referred to as
   A. the report format.
   B. the account format.
   C. a classified balance sheet.

4. All of the following are current assets *except*
   A. cash.
   B. goodwill.
   C. inventories.

5. Debt due within one year is considered
   A. current.
   B. preferred.
   C. long term.

6. Money received from customers for products to be delivered in the future is recorded as
   A. revenue and an asset.
   B. an asset and a liability.
   C. revenue and a liability.

7. The carrying value of inventories reflects
   A. their original cost.
   B. their current value.
   C. the lower of original cost or net realizable value.

8. When a company pays its rent in advance, its balance sheet will reflect a reduction in
   A. assets and liabilities.
   B. liabilities and shareholders' equity.
   C. one category of assets and an increase in another.

9. Accrued liabilities are
   A. balanced against an asset.
   B. expenses that have been paid.
   C. expenses that have been reported on the income statement.

10. The initial measurement of goodwill is
    A. not subject to management discretion.
    B. based on an acquisition's purchase price.
    C. based on the acquired company's book value.

11. Defining total asset turnover as revenue divided by average total assets, all else equal, impairment write-downs of long-lived assets owned by a company will most likely result in an increase for that company in
    A. the debt-to-equity ratio but not the total asset turnover.
    B. the total asset turnover but not the debt-to-equity ratio.
    C. both the debt-to-equity ratio and the total asset turnover.

12. For financial assets classified as trading securities, how are unrealized gains and losses reflected in shareholders' equity?
    A. They are not recognized.
    B. As an adjustment to paid-in capital.
    C. They flow through income into retained earnings.

13. For financial assets classified as available for sale, how are unrealized gains and losses reflected in shareholders' equity?
    A. They are not recognized.
    B. They flow through retained earnings.
    C. As a separate line item (other comprehensive income).

14. For financial assets classified as held to maturity, how are unrealized gains and losses reflected in shareholders' equity?
    A. They are not recognized.
    B. They flow through retained earnings.
    C. As a separate line item (valuation gains/losses).

15. Under IFRS, the minority interest in consolidated subsidiaries is presented on the balance sheet
    A. as a long-term liability.
    B. separately, but as a part of shareholders' equity.
    C. as a mezzanine item between liabilities and shareholders' equity.

16. Retained earnings are a component of
    A. liabilities.
    B. minority interest.
    C. owners' equity.

17. When a company buys shares of its own stock to be held in treasury, it records a reduction in
    A. both assets and liabilities.
    B. both assets and shareholders' equity.
    C. assets and an increase in shareholders' equity.

18. A common-size analysis of the balance sheet is most likely to signal investors that the company
    A. has increased sales.
    B. is using assets efficiently.
    C. is becoming more leveraged.

19. An investor concerned whether a company can meet its near-term obligations is most likely to calculate the
    A. current ratio.
    B. debt-to-equity ratio.
    C. return on total capital.

20. The most stringent test of a company's liquidity is its
    A. cash ratio.
    B. quick ratio.
    C. current ratio.

21. An investor worried that a company may go bankrupt would *most likely* examine its
    A. current ratio.
    B. return on equity.
    C. debt-to-equity ratio.

22. Using the information presented in Exhibit 5-8 in the chapter, the quick ratio for Sony Corp. on 31 March 2005 is *closest* to
    A. 0.44.
    B. 0.81.
    C. 0.84.

23. Applying common-size analysis to the Sony Corp. balance sheets presented in Exhibit 5-8, which one of the following line items increased in 2005 relative to 2004?
    A. Goodwill
    B. Securities investments and other
    C. Deferred insurance acquisition costs

24. Using the information presented in Exhibit 5-8, the financial leverage ratio for Sony Corp. on 31 March 2005 is *closest* to
    A. 2.30.
    B. 2.81.
    C. 3.31.

CHAPTER 6

UNDERSTANDING THE CASH FLOW STATEMENT

Thomas R. Robinson, CFA

CFA Institute
Charlottesville, Virginia

Hennie van Greuning, CFA

World Bank
Washington, DC

Elaine Henry, CFA

University of Miami
Miami, Florida

Michael A. Broihahn, CFA

Barry University
Miami, Florida

LEARNING OUTCOMES

After completing this chapter, you will be able to do the following:

- Compare and contrast cash flows from operating, investing, and financing activities and classify cash flow items as relating to one of those three categories given a description of the items.
- Describe how noncash investing and financing activities are reported.

- Compare and contrast the key differences in cash flow statements prepared under international financial reporting standards (IFRS) and U.S. generally accepted accounting principles (U.S. GAAP).
- Explain the difference between the direct and indirect method of presenting cash from operating activities and the arguments in favor of each method.
- Describe how the cash flow statement is linked to the income statement and the balance sheet.
- Explain the steps in the preparation of direct and indirect cash flow statements, including how cash flows can be computed using income statement and balance sheet data.
- Analyze and interpret a cash flow statement using both total currency amounts and common-size cash flow statements.
- Explain and compute free cash flow to the firm, free cash flow to equity, and other cash flow ratios.

1. INTRODUCTION

The cash flow statement provides information about a company's *cash receipts* and *cash payments* during an accounting period, showing how these cash flows link the ending cash balance to the beginning balance shown on the company's balance sheet. The cash-based information provided by the cash flow statement contrasts with the accrual-based information from the income statement. For example, the income statement reflects revenues when earned rather than when cash is collected; in contrast, the cash flow statement reflects cash receipts when collected as opposed to when the revenue was earned. A reconciliation between reported income and cash flows from operating activities provides useful information about when, whether, and how a company is able to generate cash from its operating activities. Although income is an important measure of the results of a company's activities, cash flow is also essential. As an extreme illustration, a hypothetical company that makes all sales on account, without regard to whether it will ever collect its accounts receivable, would report healthy sales on its income statement and might well report significant income; however, with zero cash inflow, the company would not survive. The cash flow statement also provides a reconciliation of the beginning and ending cash on the balance sheet.

In addition to information about cash generated (or, alternatively, cash used) in operating activities, the cash flow statement provides information about cash provided (or used) in a company's investing and financing activities. This information allows the analyst to answer such questions as:

- Does the company generate enough cash from its operations to pay for its new investments, or is the company relying on new debt issuance to finance them?
- Does the company pay its dividends to common stockholders using cash generated from operations, from selling assets, or from issuing debt?

Answers to these questions are important because, in theory, generating cash from operations can continue indefinitely, but generating cash from selling assets, for example, is possible only as long as there are assets to sell. Similarly, generating cash from debt financing is possible only as long as lenders are willing to lend, and the lending decision depends on expectations that the company will ultimately have adequate cash to repay its obligations. In summary, information about the sources and uses of cash helps creditors, investors, and other statement users evaluate the company's liquidity, solvency, and financial flexibility.

This chapter explains how cash flow activities are reflected in a company's cash flow statement. The chapter is organized as follows: Section 2 describes the components and format of the cash flow statement, including the classification of cash flows under international financial reporting standards (IFRS) and U.S. generally accepted accounting principles (GAAP) and the direct and indirect formats for presenting the cash flow statement. Section 3 discusses the linkages of the cash flow statement with the income statement and balance sheet and the steps in the preparation of the cash flow statement. Section 4 demonstrates the analysis of cash flow statements, including the conversion of an indirect cash flow statement to the direct method and how to use common-size cash flow analysis, free cash flow measures, and cash flow ratios used in security analysis. Section 5 summarizes the chapter. Finally, practice problems in CFA Institute multiple-choice format are provided.

2. COMPONENTS AND FORMAT OF THE CASH FLOW STATEMENT

The analyst needs to be able to extract and interpret information on cash flows from financial statements prepared according to any allowable format. The basic components and allowable formats of the cash flow statement are well established.

- The cash flow statement has subsections relating specific items to the operating, investing, and financing activities of the company.
- Two presentation formats are available: the direct and the indirect.

The following discussion presents these topics in greater detail.

2.1. Classification of Cash Flows and Noncash Activities

All companies engage in operating, investing, and financing activities. These activities are the classifications used in the cash flow statement under both IFRS and U.S. GAAP. Under IFRS, International Accounting Standard No. 7, (IAS No. 7), *Cash Flow Statements*, provides that cash flows are categorized as follows:[1]

- **Operating activities** include the company's day-to-day activities that create revenues, such as selling inventory and providing services. Cash inflows result from cash sales and from collection of accounts receivable. Examples include cash receipts from the provision of services and royalties, commissions, and other revenue. To generate revenue, companies undertake activities such as manufacturing inventory, purchasing inventory from suppliers, and paying employees. Cash outflows result from cash payments for inventory, salaries, taxes, and other operating-related expenses and from paying accounts payable. Additionally, operating activities include cash receipts and payments related to securities held for dealing or trading purposes (as opposed to being held for investment, as discussed below).
- **Investing activities** include purchasing and selling investments. Investments include property, plant, and equipment; intangible assets; other long-term assets; and both long-term and short-term investments in the equity and debt (bonds and loans) issued by other companies.

---

[1]IAS No. 7 became effective on 1 January 1994.

For this purpose, investments in equity and debt securities exclude: (a) any securities considered cash equivalents (very short-term, highly liquid securities) and (b) **dealing** or **trading securities,** the purchase and sale of which are considered operating activities even for companies where this is not a primary business activity. Cash inflows in the investing category include cash receipts from the sale of nontrading securities; property, plant, and equipment; intangibles; or other long-term assets. Cash outflows include cash payments for the purchase of these assets.

- **Financing activities** include obtaining or repaying capital, such as equity and long-term debt. The two primary sources of capital are shareholders and creditors. Cash inflows in this category include cash receipts from issuing stock (common or preferred) or bonds and cash receipts from borrowing. Cash outflows include cash payments to repurchase stock (e.g., treasury stock), to pay dividends, and to repay bonds and other borrowings. Note that indirect borrowing using accounts payable is not considered a financing activity—such borrowing would be classified as an operating activity.

EXAMPLE 6-1   Net Cash Flow from Investing Activities

A company recorded the following in Year 1:

Proceeds from issuance of long-term debt	$300,000
Purchase of equipment	$200,000
Loss on sale of equipment	$70,000
Proceeds from sale of equipment	$120,000
Equity in earnings of affiliate	$10,000

On the Year 1 statement of cash flows, the company would report net cash flow from investing activities *closest* to

A. −$150,000.
B. −$80,000.
C. $200,000.
D. $300,000.

Solution. The only two items that would affect the investing section are the purchase of equipment and the proceeds from sale of equipment. The loss on sale of equipment and the equity in earnings of affiliate affect net income but are not investing cash flows. The issuance of debt is a financing cash flow. B is correct: ($200,000) + $120,000 = ($80,000).

Under IFRS, there is some flexibility in reporting some items of cash flow, particularly interest and dividends. IAS No. 7 notes that while for a financial institution interest paid and received would normally be classified as operating activities, for other entities, alternative classifications may be appropriate. For this reason, under IFRS, interest received may be classified either as an operating activity or as an investing activity. Under IFRS, interest paid may be classified as either an operating activity or as a financing activity. Furthermore, under IFRS, dividends received may be classified as either an operating activity or an investing activity. On the other hand, dividends paid may be classified as either an operating activity or a financing activity. Companies must use a consistent classification from year to year and disclose where the amounts are reported.

Under U.S. GAAP, this discretion is not permitted: Interest received and paid is reported as operating activities for all companies.[2] Under U.S. GAAP, dividends received are always reported as operating activities and dividends paid are always reported as financing activities.

EXAMPLE 6-2   Operating versus Financing Cash Flows

On 31 December 2006, a company issued a $30,000, 90-day note at 8 percent to pay for inventory purchased that day and issued $110,000 long-term debt at 11 percent annually to pay for new equipment purchased that day. Which of the following *most* accurately reflects the combined effect of both transactions on the company's cash flows for the year ended 31 December 2006 under U.S. GAAP? Cash flow from

A. operations increases $30,000.
B. financing increases $110,000.
C. operations decreases $30,000.
D. financing decreases $110,000.

Solution. C is correct because the increase in inventories would decrease cash flow from operations. The issuance of both short-term and long-term debt is part of financing activities. Equipment purchased is an investing activity. Note that because no interest was paid or received in this example, the answer would be the same under IFRS.

Companies may also engage in noncash investing and financing transactions. A noncash transaction is any transaction that does not involve an inflow or outflow of cash. For example, if a company exchanges one nonmonetary asset for another nonmonetary asset, no cash is involved. Similarly, no cash is involved when a company issues common stock either for dividends or in connection with conversion of a convertible bond or convertible preferred stock. Because no cash is involved in noncash transactions (by definition), these transactions are not incorporated in the cash flow statement. However, any significant noncash transaction is required to be disclosed, either in a separate note or a supplementary schedule to the cash flow statement.

2.2.   A Summary of Differences between IFRS and U.S. GAAP

As highlighted in the previous section, there are some differences in cash flow statements prepared under IFRS and U.S. GAAP that the analyst should be aware of when comparing the cash flow statements of companies using U.S. GAAP or IFRS. The key differences are

---

[2]See Financial Accounting Standard No. 95, *Statement of Cash Flows*. This was originally issued in 1987 and modified somewhat in recent years.

EXHIBIT 6-1   Cash Flow Statements: Differences between IFRS and U.S. GAAP

Topic	IFRS	U.S. GAAP
Classification of Cash Flows:		
Interest received	Operating or investing	Operating
Interest paid	Operating or financing	Operating
Dividends received	Operating or investing	Operating
Dividends paid	Operating or financing	Financing
Bank overdrafts	Considered part of cash equivalents	Not considered part of cash and cash equivalents and classified as financing
Taxes paid	Generally operating, but a portion can be allocated to investing or financing if it can be specifically identified with these categories	Operating
Format of statement	Direct or indirect; direct is encouraged	Direct or indirect; direct is encouraged. If direct is used, a reconciliation of net income and operating cash flow must also be provided
Disclosures	Tax cash flows must be separately disclosed in the cash flow statement	Interest and taxes paid must be disclosed in footnotes if not presented on the statement of cash flows

Sources: IAS No. 7, FAS No. 95, and "Similarities and Differences: A Comparison of IFRS and U.S. GAAP," PricewaterhouseCoopers, October 2004, available at www.pwc.com.

summarized in Exhibit 6-1. In short, the IASB allows more flexibility in the reporting of items such as interest paid or received and dividends paid or received, and in how income tax expense is classified.

U.S. GAAP classifies interest and dividends received from investments as operating activities, whereas IFRS allows companies to classify those items as either operating or investing cash flows. Likewise, U.S. GAAP classifies interest expense as an operating activity, even though the principal amount of the debt issued is classified as a financing activity. IFRS allows companies to classify interest expense as either an operating activity or a financing activity. U.S. GAAP classifies dividends paid to stockholders as a financing activity, whereas IFRS allows companies to classify dividends paid as either an operating activity or a financing activity.

U.S. GAAP classifies all income tax expenses as an operating activity. IFRS also classifies income tax expense as an operating activity, unless the tax expense can be specifically identified with an investing or financing activity (e.g., the tax effect of the sale of a discontinued operation could be classified under investing activities).

Under either of the two sets of standards, companies currently have a choice of formats for presenting cash flow statements, as discussed in the next section.

2.3. Direct and Indirect Cash Flow Formats for Reporting Operating Cash Flow

There are two acceptable formats for reporting **cash flow from operations** (also known as **cash flow from operating activities** or **operating cash flow**), defined as the net amount of cash provided from operating activities: the direct and the indirect methods. The *amount* of operating cash flow is identical under both methods; only the *presentation format* of the operating cash flow section differs. The presentation format of the cash flows from investing and financing is exactly the same, regardless of which method is used to present operating cash flows.

The **direct method** shows the specific cash inflows and outflows that result in reported cash flow from operating activities. It shows each cash inflow and outflow related to a company's cash receipts and disbursements, adjusting income statement items to remove the effect of accruals. In other words, the direct method eliminates any impact of accruals and shows only cash receipts and cash payments. The primary argument in favor of the direct method is that it provides information on the specific sources of operating cash receipts and payments in contrast to the indirect method, which shows only the net result of these receipts and payments. Just as information on the specific sources of revenues and expenses is more useful than knowing only the net result—net income—the analyst gets additional information from a direct-format cash flow statement. The additional information is useful in understanding historical performance and in predicting future operating cash flows.

The **indirect method** shows how cash flow from operations can be obtained from reported net income as the result of a series of adjustments. The indirect format begins with net income. To reconcile net income with operating cash flow, adjustments are made for noncash items, for nonoperating items, and for the net changes in operating accruals. The main argument for the indirect approach is that it shows the reasons for differences between net income and operating cash flows. (It may be noted, however, that the differences between net income and operating cash flows are equally visible on an indirect-format cash flow statement and in the supplementary reconciliation required if the company uses the direct method.) Another argument for the indirect method is that it mirrors a forecasting approach that begins by forecasting future income and then derives cash flows by adjusting for changes in balance sheet accounts that occur due to the timing differences between accrual and cash accounting.

Under IFRS, IAS No. 7 encourages the use of the direct method but permits either. Similarly, under U.S. GAAP, the Financial Accounting Standards Board (FASB) in Financial Accounting Standard No. 95 encourages the use of the direct method but allows companies to use the indirect method. Under FAS No. 95, if the direct method is presented, footnote disclosure must also be provided of the indirect method. If the indirect method is chosen, no direct-format disclosures are required. As a result, few U.S. companies present the direct format for operating cash flows.

Many users of financial statements prefer the direct format, particularly analysts and commercial lenders, because of the importance of information about operating receipts and payments to assessing a company's financing needs and capacity to repay existing obligations. In 1987, at the time the FASB was adopting FAS No. 95, some companies argued that it is less costly to adjust net income to operating cash flow, as in the indirect format, than it is to report gross operating cash receipts and payments, as in the direct format. With subsequent progress in accounting systems and technology, it is not clear that this argument remains valid. CFA Institute has advocated that standard setters require the use of the direct format for the main presentation of the cash flow statement, with indirect cash flows as supplementary disclosure.[3]

2.3.1. An Indirect-Format Cash Flow Statement Prepared under IFRS

Exhibit 6-2 presents cash flow statements prepared under IFRS from Roche Group's annual report for the fiscal years ended 31 December 2005 and 2004, which show the use of the indirect method. Roche is a leading international health care company based in Switzerland.[4]

EXHIBIT 6-2   Roche Group: Consolidated Cash Flow Statements (CHF millions)

Fiscal Years Ended 31 December	2005	2004
Cash Flows from Operating Activities		
Net income	6,730	7,063
Add back nonoperating (income) expense:		
Income from associated companies	(1)	43
Financial income	(678)	(369)
Financing costs *Analyst will remove or adjust*	382	602
~~Exceptional income from bond conversion and redemption~~	—	(872)
Income taxes	2,224	1,865
Discontinued businesses	12	(2,337)
Operating profit	8,669	5,995
Depreciation of property, plant, and equipment	1,302	1,242
Amortization of goodwill	—	572
Amortization of intangible assets	1,011	1,000
Impairment of long-term assets	66	39
Changes in group organization	—	199
Major legal cases	356	—
Expenses for defined-benefit postemployment plans	313	532
Expenses for equity-settled equity compensation plans	364	169
Other adjustments	445	(335)
Cash generated from continuing operations	12,526	9,413
Operating cash flows generated from discontinued businesses	(5)	335
Cash generated from operations	12,521	9,748
(Increase) decrease in working capital	488	227

---

[3] *A Comprehensive Business Reporting Model: Financial Reporting for Investors*, CFA Institute Centre for Financial Market Integrity, October 2005, p. 27.

[4] The cash flow statement presented here includes a reconciliation of net income to cash generated from operations, which Roche Group reported in the footnotes to the financial statement rather than on the statement itself.

Fiscal Years Ended 31 December	2005	2004
Vitamin case payments	(82)	(66)
Major legal cases	(98)	(65)
Payments made for defined-benefit postemployment plans	(303)	(653)
Utilization of restructuring provisions	(119)	(163)
Utilization of other provisions	(310)	(128)
Other operating cash flows	(125)	(75)
Income taxes paid	(1,997)	(1,490)
Total Cash Flows from Operating Activities	9,975	7,335
Cash Flows from Investing Activities		
Purchase of property, plant, and equipment	(3,319)	(2,344)
Purchase of intangible assets	(349)	(191)
Disposal of property, plant, and equipment	353	196
Disposal of intangible assets	2	12
Disposal of products	56	431
Acquisitions of subsidiaries and associated companies	(233)	(1,822)
Divestments of discontinued businesses and associated companies	2,913	696
Interest and dividends received	383	255
Sales of marketable securities	9,859	4,965
Purchases of marketable securities	(15,190)	(4,281)
Other investing cash flows	(161)	64
Total Cash Flows from Investing Activities	(5,686)	(2,019)
Cash Flows from Financing Activities		
Proceeds from issue of long-term debt instruments	2,565	—
Repayment of long-term debt instruments	(1,178)	(3,039)
Increase (decrease) in other long-term debt	(1,083)	(1,156)
Transactions in own equity instruments	779	237
Increase (decrease) in short-term borrowings	(422)	(939)
Interest and dividends paid	(1,983)	(1,971)
Exercises of equity-settled equity compensation plans	1,090	643
Genentech and Chugai share repurchases	(2,511)	(1,699)
Other financing cash flows	(38)	61
Total Cash Flows from Financing Activities	(2,781)	(7,863)
Net effect of currency translation on cash and cash equivalents	115	(124)
Increase (Decrease) in Cash and Cash Equivalents	1,623	(2,671)
Cash and cash equivalents at 1 January	2,605	5,276
Cash and Cash Equivalents on 31 December	4,228	2,605

In the cash flows from operating activities section of Roche's cash flow statement, the company reconciles its net income to net cash provided by operating activities. Under IFRS, payments for interest and taxes are disclosed in the body of the cash flow statement. Note that Roche discloses the income taxes paid (CHF 1,997 million in 2005) as a separate item in the cash flows from operating activities section. Separate disclosure of this is not useful if an analyst is trying to assess the impact on cash flow of changes in tax rates (income tax expense provided on the income statement does not reflect the flow of cash due to prepaid and deferred items). Roche reports its interest paid in the cash flows from financing activities section, showing a total of CHF 1,983 million in interest and dividends paid in 2005. As noted earlier under U.S. GAAP, interest paid—or the reconciliation adjustment for the net change in interest payable—must be reported in the operating section of the cash flow statement. Furthermore, U.S. GAAP does not require that interest and taxes paid be disclosed as separate line items on the cash flow statement; however, it does require that these amounts be provided in a supplemental note.

Roche reports its dividends and interest received (CHF 383 million in 2005) in the cash flows from investing activities section. Under U.S. GAAP, investment income received (or the reconciliation adjustment for the net change in investment income receivable) must be reported in the operating section of the cash flow statement.

2.3.2. A Direct-Format Cash Flow Statement Prepared under IFRS

Exhibit 6-3 presents a direct-method format cash flow statement prepared under IFRS for Telefónica Group, a diversified telecommunications company based in Madrid.[5] Note that in this format of the cash flow statement, the cash received from customers, as well as other operating items, is clearly shown. The analyst can then contrast the change in revenues from the income statement with the change in cash received from customers. An increase in revenues coupled with a decrease in cash received from customers could signal collection problems. However, in the case of Telefónica Group, cash received from customers has increased.

2.3.3. Illustrations of Cash Flow Statements Prepared under U.S. GAAP

Previously, we presented a cash flow statement prepared under IFRS. In this section, we illustrate cash flow statements prepared under U.S. GAAP. This section presents the cash flow statements of two companies, Tech Data Corporation and Wal-Mart. Tech Data reports its operating activities using the direct method, whereas Wal-Mart reports its operating activities using the more common indirect method.

Tech Data Corporation is a leading distributor of information technology products. Exhibit 6-4 on page 226 presents comparative cash flow statements from the company's annual report for the fiscal years ended 31 January 2005 and 2004.[6]

Tech Data Corporation prepares its cash flow statements under the direct method. In the cash flows from operating activities section of Tech Data's cash flow statements, the company identifies the amount of cash it received from customers, $19.7 billion for 2005, and the amount of cash that it paid to suppliers and employees, $19.6 billion for 2005. Net cash provided by operating activities of $106.9 million was adequate to cover the company's investing activities, primarily purchases of property and equipment ($25.9 million) and software

---

[5]Excludes supplemental cash flow reconciliation provided at the bottom of the original cash flow statement by the company.

[6]Under U.S. GAAP, companies present three years of the cash flow statement. For purposes of presentation and comparison with the IFRS statements presented above, only two years are presented here.

IFRS   Direct method

EXHIBIT 6-3   Telefónica Group: Consolidated Cash Flow Statements for Years Ended 31 December (€ millions)

Cash can be e drag

	2005	2004
Cash Flows from Operating Activities		
Cash received from customers	44,353.14	36,367.10
Cash paid to suppliers and employees	(30,531.54)	(24,674.10)
Dividends received	70.58	71.24
Net interest and other financial expenses paid	(1,520.00)	(1,307.11)
Taxes paid	(1,233.04)	(326.00)
Net Cash from Operating Activities This is different	11,139.14	10,131.13
Cash Flows from Investing Activities		
Proceeds on disposals of property, plant, and equipment and intangible assets	113.20	241.27
Payments on investments in property, plant, and equipment and intangible assets	(4,423.22)	(3,488.15)
Proceeds on disposals of companies, net of cash, and cash equivalents disposed	501.59	531.98
Payments on investments in companies, net of cash, and cash equivalents acquired	(6,571.40)	(4,201.57)
Proceeds on financial investments not included under cash equivalents	147.61	31.64
Payments made on financial investments not included under cash equivalents	(17.65)	(76.35)
Interest received on short-term investments not included under cash equivalents	625.18	1,139.51
Capital grants received	32.67	13.51
Net Cash Used in Investing Activities	(9,592.02)	(5,808.16)
Cash Flows from Financing Activities		
Dividends paid	(2,768.60)	(2,865.81)
Proceeds from issue of stock	(2,054.12)	(1,938.56)
Proceeds on issue of debentures and bonds	875.15	572.99
Proceeds on loans, credits, and promissory notes	16,533.96	10,135.11
Cancellation of debentures and bonds	(3,696.52)	(1,790.57)
Repayments of loans, credits, and promissory notes	(9,324.54)	(8,049.77)
Net Cash from Financing Activities Capital	(434.67)	(3,936.61)
Effect of foreign exchange rate changes on collections and payments	165.73	74.18
Effect of changes in consolidation methods and other nonmonetary effects	9.62	(36.76)
Net Increase (Decrease) in Cash and Cash Equivalents during the Year	1,287.80	423.78
Cash and cash equivalents at beginning of year	914.35	490.57
Cash and Cash Equivalents at End of Year	2,202.15	914.35

Cash Flow Transactional Analysis.

U.S. GAAP

EXHIBIT 6-4   Tech Data Corporation and Subsidiaries: Consolidated Cash Flow Statements, Years Ended 31 January ($ thousands)

	2005	2004
Cash Flows from Operating Activities:		
Cash received from customers	$19,745,283	$17,390,674
Cash paid to suppliers and employees	(19,571,824)	(17,027,162)
Interest paid	(18,837)	(17,045)
Income taxes paid	(47,677)	(43,233)
Net Cash Provided by Operating Activities	106,945	303,234
Cash Flows from Investing Activities		
Acquisition of businesses, net of cash acquired	—	(203,010)
Proceeds from sale of property and equipment	5,130	4,484
Expenditures for property and equipment	(25,876)	(31,278)
Software development costs	(17,899)	(21,714)
Net Cash Used in Investing Activities	(38,645)	(251,518)
Cash Flows from Financing Activities		
Proceeds from the issuance of common stock	32,733	28,823
Net repayments on revolving credit loans	(11,319)	(138,039)
Principal payments on long-term debt	(9,214)	(1,492)
Net Cash Provided by (Used in) Financing Activities	12,200	(110,708)
Effect of exchange rate changes on cash	5,755	10,602
Net Increase (Decrease) in Cash and Cash Equivalents	86,255	(48,390)
Cash and cash equivalents at beginning of year	108,801	157,191
Cash and Cash Equivalents at End of Year	$195,056	$108,801
Reconciliation of net income to net cash provided by operating activities:		
Net income	$162,460	$104,147
Adjustments to reconcile net income to net cash provided by operating activities:		
Depreciation and amortization	55,472	55,084
Provision for losses on accounts receivable	13,268	29,214
Deferred income taxes	(3,616)	7,369
Changes in operating assets and liabilities, net of acquisitions:		
Accounts receivable	(44,305)	(15,699)
Inventories	(119,999)	(140,203)
Prepaid and other assets	(32,193)	14,713
Accounts payable	55,849	300,350
Accrued expenses and other liabilities	20,000	(51,741)
Total adjustments	(55,515)	199,087
Net cash provided by operating activities	$106,945	$303,234

development ($17.9 million). In 2005, the company issued $32.7 million of common stock, providing net cash from financing activities of $12.2 million after its debt repayments. Overall, the company's cash increased by $86.3 million, from $108.8 million at the beginning of the year to $195.1 million at the end of the year.

Whenever the direct method is used, FAS No. 95 mandates a disclosure note and schedule that reconciles net income with the net cash flow from operating activities. Tech Data shows this reconciliation at the bottom of its consolidated statements of cash flows. The disclosure note and reconciliation schedule are exactly the information that would have been presented in the body of the cash flow statement if the company had elected instead to use the indirect method.

Wal-Mart is a global retailer that conducts business under the names of Wal-Mart and Sam's Club. Exhibit 6-5 presents the comparative cash flow statements from the company's annual report for the fiscal years ended 31 January 2005 and 2004.[7]

Wal-Mart prepares its cash flow statements under the indirect method. In the cash flows from operating activities section of Wal-Mart's cash flow statement, the company reconciles its net income of $10.3 billion to net cash provided by operating activities of $15 billion. Whenever the indirect method is used, U.S. GAAP mandates a supplemental note that discloses how much cash was paid for interest and income taxes. Wal-Mart discloses the amount of cash paid for income tax ($5.6 billion), interest ($1.2 billion), and capital lease obligations (i.e., the interest expense component of the capital lease payments) at the bottom of its cash flow statements.

EXHIBIT 6-5   Wal-Mart Cash Flow Statements, Fiscal Years Ended 31 January ($ millions)

	2005	2004
Cash Flows from Operating Activities		
Income from continuing operations	$10,267	$ 8,861
Adjustments to reconcile net income to net cash provided by operating activities:		
Depreciation and amortization	4,405	3,852
Deferred income taxes	263	177
Other operating activities	378	173
Changes in certain assets and liabilities, net of effects of acquisitions:		
Decrease (increase) in accounts receivable	(304)	373
Increase in inventories	(2,635)	(1,973)
Increase in accounts payable	1,694	2,587
Increase in accrued liabilities	976	1,896
Net cash provided by operating activities of continuing operations	15,044	15,946
Net cash provided by operating activities of discontinued operations	—	50
Net Cash Provided by Operating Activities	15,044	15,996
		(Continued)

---

[7]Under U.S. GAAP, companies present three years of the cash flow statement. For purposes of presentation and comparison with the IFRS statements presented above, only two years are presented here.

EXHIBIT 6-5   (*Continued*)

	2005	2004
Cash Flows from Investing Activities		
Payments for property and equipment	(12,893)	(10,308)
Investment in international operations	(315)	(38)
Proceeds from the disposal of fixed assets	953	481
Proceeds from the sale of McLane	—	1,500
Other investing activities	(96)	78
Net cash used in investing activities of continuing operations	(12,351)	(8,287)
Net cash used in investing activities discontinued operations	—	(25)
Net Cash Used in Investing Activities	(12,351)	(8,312)
Cash Flows from Financing Activities		
Increase in commercial paper	544	688
Proceeds from issuance of long-term debt	5,832	4,099
Purchase of company stock	(4,549)	(5,046)
Dividends paid	(2,214)	(1,569)
Payment of long-term debt	(2,131)	(3,541)
Payment of capital lease obligations	(204)	(305)
Other financing activities	113	111
Net Cash Used in Financing Activities	(2,609)	(5,563)
Effect of exchange rate changes on cash	205	320
Net Increase in Cash and Cash Equivalents	289	2,441
Cash and cash equivalents at beginning of year	5,199	2,758
Cash and Cash Equivalents at End of Year	$5,488	$5,199
Income tax paid	$5,593	$4,358
Interest paid	1,163	1,024
Capital lease obligations incurred	377	252

3. THE CASH FLOW STATEMENT: LINKAGES AND PREPARATION

The indirect format of the cash flow statement demonstrates that changes in balance sheet accounts are an important factor in determining cash flows. The next section addresses the linkages between the cash flow statement and other financial statements.

3.1. Linkages of the Cash Flow Statement with the Income Statement and Balance Sheet

Recall the accounting equation that summarizes the balance sheet:

$$\text{Assets} = \text{Liabilities} + \text{Owners' equity}$$

Cash is an asset. The statement of cash flows ultimately shows the change in cash during an accounting period. The beginning and ending balances of cash are shown on the company's balance sheets for the previous and current years, and the bottom of the cash flow statement reconciles beginning cash with ending cash. For example, the Roche Group's cash flow statement for 2005, presented in Exhibit 6-2, shows that operating, investing, and financing activities during the year imply a CHF 1,623 increase in cash and cash equivalents, which is the amount by which end-of-year cash and cash equivalents (CHF 4,228) exceeds beginning-of-year cash and cash equivalents (CHF 2,605). The relationship, stated in general terms, is as shown below.

Beginning Balance Sheet on 31 December 20X6	**Statement of Cash Flows for Year Ended 31 December 20X7**		**Ending Balance Sheet on 31 December 20X7**
Beginning cash	Plus: Cash receipts (from operating, investing, and financing activities)	Less: Cash payments (for operating, investing, and financing activities)	Ending cash

In the case of cash held in foreign currencies, there would also be an impact from changes in exchange rates. The body of the cash flow statement shows why the change in cash occurred; in other words, it shows the company's operating, investing, and financing activities (as well as the impact of foreign currency translation). The beginning and ending balance sheet values of cash and cash equivalents are linked through the cash flow statement. The linkage is similar to the one that relates net income and dividends as shown in the income statement to the beginning and ending values of retained earnings in the owners' equity section of the balance sheet, as shown below.

Beginning Balance Sheet on 31 December 20X6	**Statement of Owners' Equity for Year Ended 31 December 20X7**		**Ending Balance Sheet on 31 December 20X7**
Beginning retained earnings	Plus: Net income or minus net loss from the income statement for year ended 31 December 20X7	Minus: Dividends	Ending retained earnings

A company's operating activities are reported on an accrual basis in the income statement, and any differences between the accrual basis and the cash basis of accounting for an operating transaction result in an increase or decrease in some (usually) short-term asset or liability on the balance sheet. For example, if revenue reported using accrual accounting is higher than the cash actually collected, the result will be an increase in accounts receivable. If expenses reported using accrual accounting are lower than cash actually paid, the result will be a decrease in accounts payable.

A company's investing activities typically relate to the long-term asset section of the balance sheet, and its financing activities typically relate to the equity and long-term debt sections of the balance sheet. Each item on the balance sheet is also related to the income statement and/or cash flow statement through the change in the beginning and ending balance. Consider, for example, accounts receivable:

Beginning Balance Sheet on 31 December 20X6	Income Statement for Year Ended 31 December 20X7	Statement of Cash Flows for Year Ended 31 December 20X7	Ending Balance Sheet on 31 December 20X7
Beginning accounts receivable	Plus: Revenues	Minus: Cash collected from customers	Ending accounts receivable

Knowing any three of these four items makes it easy to compute the fourth. For example, if you know beginning accounts receivable, revenues, and cash collected from customers, you can easily compute ending accounts receivable. Understanding these interrelationships between the balance sheet, income statement, and cash flow statement is useful in not only understanding the company's financial health but also in detecting accounting irregularities. The next section demonstrates the preparation of cash flow information based on income statement and balance sheet information.

3.2. Steps in Preparing the Cash Flow Statement

The preparation of the cash flow statement uses data from both the income statement and the comparative balance sheets.

As noted earlier, companies often only disclose indirect operating cash flow information, whereas analysts prefer direct-format information. Understanding how cash flow information is put together will enable you to take an indirect statement apart and reconfigure it in a more useful manner. The following demonstration of how a cash flow statement is prepared uses the income statement and the comparative balance sheets for Acme Corporation (a fictitious retail company) shown in Exhibits 6-6 and 6-7.

EXHIBIT 6-6   Acme Corporation Income Statement, Year Ended 31 December 2006 ($ thousands)

Revenue		$23,598
Cost of goods sold		11,456
Gross profit		12,142
Salary and wage expense	4,123	
Depreciation expense	1,052	
Other operating expenses	3,577	
Total operating expenses		8,752
Operating profit		3,390
Other revenues (expenses):		
Gain on sale of equipment	205	
Interest expense	(246)	(41)
Income before tax		3,349
Income tax expense		1,139
Net income		$ 2,210

EXHIBIT 6-7   Acme Corporation Comparative Balance Sheets, 31 December 2006 and 2005 ($ thousands)

	2006	2005	Net Change
Cash	$1,011	$1,163	$(152)
Accounts receivable	1,012	957	55
Inventory	3,984	3,277	707
Prepaid expenses	155	178	(23)
Total current assets	6,162	5,575	587
Land	510	510	—
Buildings	3,680	3,680	—
Equipment*	8,798	8,555	243
Less: accumulated depreciation	(3,443)	(2,891)	(552)
Total long-term assets	9,545	9,854	(309)
Total assets	$15,707	$15,429	278
Accounts payable	$3,588	$3,325	263
Salary and wage payable	85	75	10
Interest payable	62	74	(12)
Income tax payable	55	50	5
Other accrued liabilities	1,126	1,104	22
Total current liabilities	4,916	4,628	288
Long-term debt	3,075	3,575	(500)
Common stock	3,750	4,350	(600)
Retained earnings	3,966	2,876	1,090
Total liabilities and equity	$15,707	$15,429	278

*During 2006, Acme purchased new equipment for a total cost of $1,300. No items impacted retained earnings other than net income and dividends.

The first step in preparing the cash flow statement is to determine the total cash flows from operating activities. The direct method of presenting cash from operating activities will be illustrated first, followed by the indirect method. Cash flows from investing activities and from financing activities are identical under either method.

3.2.1. Operating Activities: Direct Method

We first determine how much cash Acme received from its customers, followed by how much cash was paid to suppliers and to employees as well as how much cash was paid for other operating expenses, interest, and income taxes.

3.2.1.1. Cash Received from Customers   The income statement for Acme reported revenue of $23,598 (in thousands) for the year ended 31 December 2006. To determine the cash receipts from its customers, it is necessary to adjust this revenue amount by the net change in accounts receivable for the year. If accounts receivable increase during the year, revenue on an accrual basis is higher than cash receipts from customers, and vice versa. For Acme Corporation, accounts receivable increased by $55, so cash received from customers was $23,543, as follows:

Revenue	$23,598
Less: Increase in accounts receivable	(55)
Cash received from customers	**$23,543**

Cash received from customers affects the accounts receivable account as follows:

Beginning accounts receivable	$957
Plus revenue	23,598
Minus cash collected from customers	**(23,543)**
Ending accounts receivable	$1,012

The accounts receivable account information can also be presented as follows:

Beginning accounts receivable	$957
Plus revenue	23,598
Minus ending accounts receivable	(1,012)
Cash collected from customers	**$23,543**

EXAMPLE 6-3 | Computing Cash Received from Customers

Blue Bayou, an advertising company, reported revenues of $50 million, total expenses of $35 million, and net income of $15 million in the most recent year. If accounts receivable decreased by $12 million, how much cash did the company receive from customers?

A. $62 million
B. $50 million
C. $38 million
D. $15 million

Solution. A is correct. Revenues of $50 million plus the decrease in accounts receivable of $12 million equals $62 million cash received from customers. The decrease in accounts receivable means that the company received more in cash than the amount of revenue it reported.

"Cash received from customers" is sometimes referred to as *cash collections from customers* or *cash collections.*

3.2.1.2. ██████ **d to Suppliers** For Acme, the cash paid to suppliers was $11,900, determi██ ███ ws:

Cost of goods sold	$11,456
Plus: Increase in inventory	707
Equals purchases from suppliers	$12,163
Less: Increase in accounts payable	(263)
Cash paid to suppliers	**$11,900**

These are all various methods to backout the cash flow.

There are two pieces to this calculation: the amount of inventory purchased and the amount paid for it. To determine purchases from suppliers, cost of goods sold is adjusted for the change in inventory. If inventory increased during the year, then purchases during the year exceeded cost of goods sold, and vice versa. Acme reported cost of goods sold of $11,456 for the year ended 31 December 2006. For Acme Corporation, inventory increased by $707, so purchases from suppliers was $12,163. Purchases from suppliers affects the inventory account, as shown below:

Beginning inventory	$3,277	*B*
Plus purchases	12,163	*P*
Minus cost of goods sold	(11,456)	*COOS*
Ending inventory	$3,984	*E*

Acme purchased $12,163 of inventory from suppliers this year, but is this the amount of cash that Acme paid to its suppliers during the year? Not necessarily. Acme may not have yet paid for all of these purchases and may yet owe for some of the purchases made this year. In other words, Acme may have paid less cash to its suppliers than the amount of this year's purchases, in which case Acme's liability (accounts payable) will have increased by the difference. Alternatively, Acme may have paid even more to its suppliers than the amount of this year's purchases, in which case Acme's accounts payable will have decreased.

Therefore, once purchases have been determined, cash paid to suppliers can be calculated by adjusting purchases for the change in accounts payable. If the company made all purchases for cash, then accounts payable would not change and cash outflows would equal purchases. If accounts payable increased during the year, then purchases on an accrual basis are higher than they are on a cash basis, and vice versa. In this example, Acme made more purchases than it paid in cash, so the balance in accounts payable has increased. For Acme, the cash paid to suppliers was $11,900, determined as follows:

Purchases from suppliers	$12,163
Less: Increase in accounts payable	(263)
Cash paid to suppliers	**$11,900**

The amount of cash paid to suppliers is reflected in the accounts payable account, as shown below:

Beginning accounts payable	$3,325
Plus purchases	12,163
Minus cash paid to suppliers	**(11,900)**
Ending accounts payable	$3,588

EXAMPLE 6-4   Computing Cash Paid to Suppliers

Orange Beverages Plc., a manufacturer of tropical drinks, reported cost of goods sold for the year of $100 million. Total assets increased by $55 million, but inventory declined by $6 million. Total liabilities increased by $45 million, but accounts payable decreased by $2 million. How much cash did the company pay to its suppliers during the year?

A. $110 million
B. $108 million
C. $104 million
D. $96 million

Solution. D is correct. Cost of goods sold of $100 million less the decrease in inventory of $6 million equals purchases from suppliers of $94 million. The decrease in accounts payable of $2 million means that the company paid $96 million in cash ($94 million plus $2 million).

3.2.1.3. Cash Paid to Employees   To determine the cash paid to employees, it is necessary to adjust salary and wage expense by the net change in salary and wage payable for the year. If salary and wage payable increased during the year, then salary and wage expense on an accrual basis is higher than the amount of cash paid for this expense, and vice versa. For Acme, salary and wage payable increased by $10, so cash paid for salary and wages was $4,113, as follows:

Salary and wage expense	$4,123
Less: Increase in salary and wage payable	(10)
Cash paid to employees	**$4,113**

The amount of cash paid to employees is reflected in the salary and wage payable account, as shown below:

Beginning salary and wages payable	$75
Plus salary and wage expense	4,123
Minus cash paid to employees	**(4,113)**
Ending salary and wages payable	$85

3.2.1.4. Cash Paid for Other Operating Expenses   To determine the cash paid for other operating expenses, it is necessary to adjust the other operating expenses amount on the income statement by the net changes in prepaid expenses and accrued expense liabilities for the year. If prepaid expenses increased during the year, other operating expenses on a cash basis were higher than on an accrual basis, and vice versa. Likewise, if accrued expense liabilities increased during the year, other operating expenses on a cash basis were lower than on an accrual basis, and vice versa. For Acme Corporation, the amount of cash paid for operating expenses in 2006 was $3,532, as follows:

Other operating expenses	$3,577
Less: Decrease in prepaid expenses	(23)
Less: Increase in other accrued liabilities	(22)
Cash paid for other operating expenses	**$3,532**

EXAMPLE 6-5   Computing Cash Paid for Other Operating Expenses

Black Ice, a sportswear manufacturer, reported other operating expenses of $30 million. Prepaid insurance expense increased by $4 million, and accrued utilities payable decreased by $7 million. Insurance and utilities are the only two components of other operating expenses. How much cash did the company pay in other operating expenses?

A. $41 million
B. $33 million
C. $27 million
D. $19 million

Solution. A is correct. Other operating expenses of $30 million plus the increase in prepaid insurance expense of $4 million plus the decrease in accrued utilities payable of $7 million equals $41 million.

3.2.1.5. Cash Paid for Interest   The company is either subject to U.S. GAAP, which requires that interest expense be included in operating cash flows, or it is subject to IFRS, which gives companies the option to treat interest expense in this manner. To determine the cash paid for interest, it is necessary to adjust interest expense by the net change in interest payable for the year. If interest payable increases during the year, then interest expense on an accrual basis is higher than the amount of cash paid for interest, and vice versa. For Acme Corporation, interest payable decreased by $12 and cash paid for interest was $258, as follows:

Interest expense	$246
Plus: Decrease in interest payable	12
Cash paid for interest	**$258**

Alternatively, cash paid for interest may also be determined by an analysis of the interest payable account, as shown below:

Beginning interest payable	$74
Plus interest expense	246
Minus cash paid for interest	**(258)**
Ending interest payable	$62

3.2.1.6. Cash Paid for Income Taxes   To determine the cash paid for income taxes, it is necessary to adjust the income tax expense amount on the income statement by the net changes in taxes receivable, taxes payable, and deferred income taxes for the year. If taxes receivable or deferred tax assets increase during the year, income taxes on a cash basis will be higher than on an accrual basis, and vice versa. Likewise, if taxes payable or deferred tax liabilities increase during the year, income tax expense on a cash basis will be lower than on an accrual basis, and vice versa. For Acme Corporation, the amount of cash paid for income taxes in 2006 was $1,134, as follows:

Income tax expense	$1,139
Less: Increase in income tax payable	(5)
Cash paid for income taxes	**$1,134**

3.2.2. Investing Activities: Direct Method

The second and third steps in preparing the cash flow statement are to determine the total cash flows from investing activities and from financing activities. The presentation of this information is identical, regardless of whether the direct or indirect method is used for operating cash flows. Investing cash flows are always presented using the direct method.

Purchases and sales of equipment were the only investing activities undertaken by Acme in 2006, as evidenced by the fact that the amounts reported for land and buildings were unchanged during the year. An informational note in Exhibit 6-7 tells us that Acme *purchased* new equipment in 2006 for a total cost of $1,300. However, the amount of equipment shown on Acme's balance sheet increased by only $243 (ending balance of $8,798 minus beginning balance of $8,555); therefore, Acme must have also *sold* some equipment during the year. To determine the cash inflow from the sale of equipment, we analyze the equipment and accumulated depreciation accounts as well as the gain on the sale of equipment from Exhibits 6-6 and 6-7.

The historical cost of the equipment sold was $1,057. This amount is determined as follows:

Beginning balance equipment (from balance sheet)	$8,555
Plus equipment purchased (from informational note)	1,300
Minus ending balance equipment (from balance sheet)	(8,798)
Equals historical cost of equipment sold	$1,057

The accumulated depreciation on the equipment sold was $500, determined as follows:

Beginning balance accumulated depreciation (from balance sheet)	$2,891
Plus depreciation expense (from income statement)	1,052
Minus ending balance accumulated depreciation (from balance sheet)	(3,443)
Equals accumulated depreciation on equipment sold	$500

The historical cost information, accumulated depreciation information, and information from the income statement about the gain on the sale of equipment can be used to determine the cash received from the sale.

Historical cost of equipment sold (calculated above)	$1,057
Less accumulated depreciation on equipment sold (calculated above)	(500)
Equals: Book value of equipment sold	557
Plus: Gain on sale of equipment (from the income statement)	205
Equals: Cash received from sale of equipment	**$762**

EXAMPLE 6-6   Computing Cash Received from the Sale of Equipment

Copper, Inc., a brewery and restaurant chain, reported a gain on the sale of equipment of $12 million. In addition, the company's income statement shows depreciation expense of $8 million and the cash flow statement shows capital expenditure of $15 million, all of which was for the purchase of new equipment.

Balance sheet item	12/31/2005	12/31/2006	Change
Equipment	$100 million	$109 million	$9 million
Accumulated depreciation—equipment	$30 million	$36 million	$6 million

Using the above information from the comparative balance sheets, how much cash did the company receive from the equipment sale?

A. $16 million
B. $9 million
C. $6 million
D. $3 million

Solution. A is correct. Selling price (cash inflow) minus book value equals gain or loss on sale; therefore, gain or loss on sale plus book value equals selling price (cash inflow). The amount of gain is given, $12 million. To calculate the book value of the equipment sold, find the historical cost of the equipment and the accumulated depreciation on the equipment.

Beginning balance of equipment of $100 million plus equipment purchased of $15 million minus ending balance of equipment of $109 million equals historical cost of equipment sold, or $6 million.

Beginning accumulated depreciation on equipment of $30 million plus depreciation expense for the year of $8 million minus ending balance of accumulated depreciation of $36 million equals accumulated depreciation on the equipment sold, or $2 million.

Therefore, the book value of the equipment sold was $6 million minus $2 million, or $4 million.

Because the gain on the sale of equipment was $12 million, the amount of cash received must have been $16 million.

3.2.3. Financing Activities: Direct Method
As with investing activities, financing activities are always presented using the direct method.

3.2.3.1. Long-Term Debt and Common Stock   The change in long-term debt, based on the beginning and ending balance sheets in Exhibit 6-7, was a decrease of $500. Absent other information, this indicates that Acme retired $500 of long-term debt. Retiring long-term debt is a cash outflow relating to financing activities.

Similarly, the change in common stock during 2006 was a decrease of $600. Absent other information, this indicates that Acme repurchased $600 of its common stock. Repurchase of common stock is also a cash outflow related to financing activity.

3.2.3.2. Dividends   Recall the following relationship:

Beginning retained earnings + Net income − Dividends = Ending retained earnings

Based on this relationship, the amount of cash dividends paid in 2006 can be determined from an analysis of retained earnings, as follows:

Beginning balance of retained earnings (from the balance sheet)	$2,876
Plus net income (from the income statement)	2,210
Minus ending balance of retained earnings (from the balance sheet)	(3,966)
Equals dividends paid	**$1,120**

3.2.4. Overall Statement of Cash Flows: Direct Method

Exhibit 6-8 summarizes the information about Acme's operating, investing, and financing cash flows in the statement of cash flows. At the bottom of the statement, the total net change in cash is shown to be a decrease of $152 (from $1,163 to $1,011). This can also be seen on the comparative balance sheet in Exhibit 6-7. The cash provided by operating activities of $2,606 was adequate to cover the net cash used in investing activities of $538; however, the company's debt repayments, cash payments for dividends, and repurchase of common stock (i.e., its financing activities) of $2,220 resulted in an overall decrease of $152.

EXHIBIT 6-8   Acme Corporation Cash Flow Statement (Direct Method) for Year Ended 31 December 2006 ($ thousands)

Cash Flow from Operating Activities	
Cash received from customers	$23,543
Cash paid to suppliers	(11,900)
Cash paid to employees	(4,113)
Cash paid for other operating expenses	(3,532)
Cash paid for interest	(258)
Cash paid for income tax	(1,134)
Net cash provided by operating activities	2,606
Cash Flow from Investing Activities	
Cash received from sale of equipment	762
Cash paid for purchase of equipment	(1,300)
Net cash used for investing activities	(538)
Cash Flow from Financing Activities	
Cash paid to retire long-term debt	(500)
Cash paid to retire common stock	(600)
Cash paid for dividends	(1,120)
Net cash used for financing activities	(2,220)
Net decrease in cash	(152)
Cash balance, 31 December 2005	1,163
Cash balance, 31 December 2006	$1,011

3.2.5. Overall Statement of Cash Flows: Indirect Method

Using the alternative approach to reporting cash from operating activities, the indirect method, we will present the same amount of cash provided by operating activities. Under this approach, we reconcile Acme's net income of $2,210 to its operating cash flow of $2,606.

To perform this reconciliation, net income is adjusted for the following: (a) any nonoperating activities; (b) any noncash expenses; and (c) changes in operating working capital items.

The only nonoperating activity in Acme's income statement, the sale of equipment, resulted in a gain of $205. This amount is removed from the operating cash flow section; the cash effects of the sale are shown in the investing section.

Acme's only noncash expense was depreciation expense of $1,052. Under the indirect method, depreciation expense must be added back to net income because it was a noncash deduction in the calculation of net income.

Changes in working capital accounts include increases and decreases in the current operating asset and liability accounts. The changes in these accounts arise from applying accrual accounting; that is, recognizing revenues when they are earned and expenses when they are incurred instead of when the cash is received or paid. To make the working capital adjustments under the indirect method, any increase in a current operating asset account is subtracted from net income while a net decrease is added to net income. As described above, the increase in accounts receivable, for example, resulted from Acme recording income statement revenue higher than the amount of cash received from customers; therefore, to reconcile back to operating cash flow, that increase in accounts receivable must be deducted from net income. For current operating liabilities, a net increase is added to net income while a net decrease is subtracted from net income. As described above, the increase in wages payable, for example, resulted from Acme recording income statement expenses higher than the amount of cash paid to employees.

Exhibit 6-9 presents a tabulation of the most common types of adjustments that are made to net income when using the indirect method to determine net cash flow from operating activities.

EXHIBIT 6-9 Adjustments to Net Income Using the Indirect Method

Additions	**Noncash Items**
	Depreciation expense of tangible assets
	Amortization expense of intangible assets
	Depletion expense of natural resources
	Amortization of bond discount
	Nonoperating Losses
	Loss on sale or write down of assets
	Loss on retirement of debt
	Loss on investments accounted for under the equity method
	Increase in Deferred Income Tax Liability
	Changes in Working Capital Resulting from Accruing Higher Expenses than Cash Payments, or Lower Revenues than Cash Receipts
	Increase in current operating liabilities (e.g., accounts payable and accrued expense liabilities)
	Decrease in current operating assets (e.g., accounts receivable, inventory, and prepaid expenses)

(Continued)

EXHIBIT 6-9   (*Continued*)

Subtractions	**Noncash Items (e.g., Amortization of Bond Premium)**
	Nonoperating Items
	Gain on sale of assets
	Gain on retirement of debt
	Income on investments accounted for under the equity method
	Decrease in Deferred Income Tax Liability
	Changes in Working Capital Resulting from Accruing Lower Expenses than Cash Payments, or Higher Revenues than Cash Receipts
	Decrease in current operating liabilities (e.g., accounts payable and accrued expense liabilities)
	Increase in current operating assets (e.g., accounts receivable, inventory, and prepaid expenses)

Accordingly, for Acme Corporation, the $55 increase in accounts receivable and the $707 increase in inventory are subtracted from net income while the $23 decrease in prepaid expenses is added to net income. For Acme's current liabilities, the increases in accounts payable, salary and wage payable, income tax payable, and other accrued liabilities ($263, $10, $5, and $22, respectively) are added to net income while the $12 decrease in interest payable is subtracted from net income. Exhibit 6-10 presents the cash flow statement for Acme Corporation under the indirect method by using the information that we have determined from our analysis of the income statement and the comparative balance sheets. Note that the investing and financing sections are identical to the statement of cash flows prepared using the direct method.

EXHIBIT 6-10   Acme Corporation Cash Flow Statement (Indirect Method) Year Ended 31 December 2006 ($ thousands)

Cash Flow from Operating Activities	
Net income	$2,210
Depreciation expense	1,052
Gain on sale of equipment	(205)
Increase in accounts receivable	(55)
Increase in inventory	(707)
Decrease in prepaid expenses	23
Increase in accounts payable	263
Increase in salary and wage payable	10
Decrease in interest payable	(12)
Increase in income tax payable	5
Increase in other accrued liabilities	22
Net cash provided by operating activities	2,606

Cash Flow from Investing Activities

Cash received from sale of equipment	762
Cash paid for purchase of equipment	(1,300)
Net cash used for investing activities	(538)

Cash Flow from Financing Activities

Cash paid to retire long-term debt	(500)
Cash paid to retire common stock	(600)
Cash paid for dividends	(1,120)
Net cash used for financing activities	(2,220)
Net decrease in cash	(152)
Cash balance, 31 December 2005	1,163
Cash balance, 31 December 2006	$1,011

EXAMPLE 6-7   Adjusting Net Income to Compute Operating Cash Flow

Based on the following information for Pinkerly Inc., what are the total adjustments that the company would make to net income in order to derive operating cash flow?

	Year Ended	
Income Statement Item	**12/31/2006**	
Net income	**$ 30 million**	
Depreciation	**$7 million**	
Balance sheet item	12/31/2005	12/31/2006	Change
Accounts receivable	$15 million	$30 million	$15 million
Inventory	$16 million	$13 million	($3 million)
Accounts payable	$10 million	$20 million	$10 million

A. Add $5 million.
B. Add $29 million.
C. Subtract $ 5 million.
D. Subtract $29 million.

Solution. A is correct. To derive operating cash flow, the company would make the following adjustments to net income: add depreciation (a noncash expense) of $7 million; add the decrease in inventory of $3 million; add the increase in accounts payable of $10 million; and subtract the increase in accounts receivable of $15 million. Total additions would be $20 million, and total subtractions would be $15 million for net additions of $5 million.

3.3. Conversion of Cash Flows from the Indirect to the Direct Method

An analyst may desire to review direct-format operating cash flow to review trends in cash receipts and payments (such as cash received from customers or cash paid to suppliers). If a direct-format statement is not available, cash flows from operating activities reported under the indirect method can be converted to the direct method. Accuracy of conversion depends on adjustments using data available in published financial reports. The method described here is sufficiently accurate for most analytical purposes.

The three-step conversion process is demonstrated for Acme Corporation in Exhibit 6-11. Referring again to Exhibits 6-6 and 6-7 for Acme Corporation's income statement and balance sheet information, begin by disaggregating net income of $2,210 into total revenues and total expenses (Step 1). Next, remove any nonoperating and noncash items (Step 2). For Acme, we

EXHIBIT 6-11   Conversion from the Indirect to the Direct Method

Step 1	Total revenues	$23,803
Aggregate all revenue and all expenses	Total expenses	21,593
	Net income	$ 2,210

Step 2	Total revenue less noncash item revenues:
Remove all noncash items from aggregated revenues and expenses and break out remaining items into relevant cash flow items	($23,803 − $205) = $23,598
	Revenue $23,598
	Total expenses less noncash item expenses:
	($21,593 − $1,052) = $20,541
	Cost of goods sold $11,456
	Salary and wage expenses 4,123
	Other operating expenses 3,577
	Interest expense 246
	Income tax expense 1,139
	Total $20,541

Step 3	[a]Cash received from customers	$23,543
Convert accrual amounts to cash flow amounts by adjusting for working capital changes	[b]Cash paid to suppliers	11,900
	[c]Cash paid to employees	4,113
	[d]Cash paid for other operating expenses	3,532
	[e]Cash paid for interest	258
	[f]Cash paid for income tax	1,134

Calculations for Step 3

[a]Revenue of $23,598 less increase in accounts receivable of $55.

[b]Cost of goods sold of $11,456 plus increase in inventory of $707 less increase in accounts payable of $263.

[c]Salary and wage expense of $4,123 less increase in salary and wage payable of $10.

[d]Other operating expenses of $3,577 less decrease in prepaid expenses of $23 less increase in other accrued liabilities of $22.

[e]Interest expense of $246 plus decrease in interest payable of $12.

[f]Income tax expense of $1,139 less increase in income tax payable of $5.

therefore remove the nonoperating gain on the sale of equipment of $205 and the noncash depreciation expense of $1,052. Then, convert accrual amounts of revenues and expenses to cash flow amounts of receipts and payments by adjusting for changes in working capital accounts (Step 3). The results of these adjustments are the items of information for the direct format of operating cash flows. These line items are shown as the results of Step 3.

[handwritten: source of capital   A/P increases or decreases]

4. CASH FLOW STATEMENT ANALYSIS

The analysis of a company's cash flows can provide useful information for understanding a company's business and earnings and for predicting its future cash flows. This section describes tools and techniques for analyzing the statement of cash flows, including the analysis of major sources and uses of cash, cash flow, common-size analysis, conversion of the cash flow statement from the indirect method to the direct method, and computation of free cash flow and cash flow ratios.

4.1. Evaluation of the Sources and Uses of Cash

Evaluation of the cash flow statement should involve an overall assessment of the sources and uses of cash between the three main categories as well as an assessment of the main drivers of cash flow within each category, as follows:

1. Evaluate where the major sources and uses of cash flow are between operating, investing, and financing activities.
2. Evaluate the primary determinants of operating cash flow.
3. Evaluate the primary determinants of investing cash flow.
4. Evaluate the primary determinants of financing cash flow.

[handwritten: R 100   R 110]

   Step 1: The major sources of cash for a company can vary with its stage of growth. For a mature company, it is desirable to have the primary source of cash be operating activities. Over the long term, a company must generate cash from its operating activities. If operating cash flow were consistently negative, a company would need to borrow money or issue stock (financing activities) to fund the shortfall. Eventually, these providers of capital need to be repaid from operations or they will no longer be willing to provide capital. Cash generated from operating activities can either be used in investing or financing activities. If the company has good opportunities to grow the business or other investment opportunities, it is desirable to use the cash in investing activities. If the company does not have profitable investment opportunities, the cash should be returned to capital providers, a financing activity. For a new or growth stage company, operating cash flow may be negative for some period of time as it invests in inventory and receivables (extending credit to new customers) in order to grow the business. This cannot sustain itself over the long term, so eventually the cash must start to come primarily from operating activities so that capital can be returned to the providers of capital. Finally, it is desirable that operating cash flows are sufficient to cover capital expenditures (in other words, the company has free cash flow as discussed further below). In summary, major points to consider at this step are:

• What are the major sources and uses of cash flow?
• Is operating cash flow positive and sufficient to cover capital expenditures?

Step 2: Turning to the operating section, the analysts should examine the most significant determinants of operating cash flow. Some companies need to raise cash for use in operations (to hold receivables, inventory, etc.), while occasionally a company's business model generates cash flow (e.g., when cash is received from customers before it needs to be paid out to suppliers). Under the indirect method, the increases and decreases in receivables, inventory, payables, and so on can be examined to determine whether the company is using or generating cash in operations and why. It is also useful to compare operating cash flow with net income. For a mature company, because net income includes noncash expenses (depreciation and amortization), it is desirable that operating cash flow exceeds net income. The relationship between net income and operating cash flow is also an indicator of earnings quality. If a company has large net income but poor operating cash flow, it may be a sign of poor earnings quality. The company may be making aggressive accounting choices to increase net income but not be generating cash for its business. You should also examine the variability of both earnings and cash flow and consider the impact of this variability on the company's risk as well as the ability to forecast future cash flows for valuation purposes. In summary:

• What are the major determinants of operating cash flow?
• Is operating cash flow higher or lower than net income? Why?
• How consistent are operating cash flows?

Step 3: Within the investing section, you should evaluate each line item. Each line item represents either a source or use of cash. This enables you to understand where the cash is being spent (or received). This section will tell you how much cash is being invested for the future in property, plant, and equipment; how much is used to acquire entire companies; and how much is put aside in liquid investments, such as stocks and bonds. It will also tell you how much cash is being raised by selling these types of assets. If the company is making major capital investments, you should consider where the cash is coming from to cover these investments (e.g., is the cash coming from excess operating cash flow or from the financing activities described in Step 4?).

Step 4: Within the financing section, you should examine each line item to understand whether the company is raising capital or repaying capital and what the nature of its capital sources are. If the company is borrowing each year, you should consider when repayment may be required. This section will also present dividend payments and repurchases of stock that are alternative means of returning capital to owners.

Example 6-8 provides an example of a cash flow statement evaluation.

EXAMPLE 6-8   Analysis of the Cash Flow Statement

Derek Yee, CFA, is preparing to forecast cash flow for Groupe Danone as an input into his valuation model. He has asked you to evaluate the historical cash flow statement of Groupe Danone, which is presented in Exhibit 6-12. Groupe Danone prepares its financial statements in conformity with International Financial Reporting Standards as adopted by the European Union.

EXHIBIT 6-12   Groupe Danone: Consolidated Financial Statements, Consolidated Statements of Cash Flows, Years Ended 31 December (€ millions)

	2004	2005
Net income	449	1,464
Minority interests in net income of consolidated subsidiaries	189	207
Net income from discontinued operations	(47)	(504)
Net income (loss) of affiliates	550	(44)
Depreciation and amortization	481	478
Dividends received from affiliates	45	45
Other flows	(93)	70
Cash Flows Provided by Operations	1,574	1,716
(Increase) decrease in inventories	(70)	(17)
(Increase) decrease in trade accounts receivable	(27)	(87)
Increase (decrease) in trade accounts payable	143	123
Changes in other working capital items	74	112
Net change in current working capital	120	131
Cash Flows Provided by Operating Activities	1,694	1,847
Capital expenditures	(520)	(607)
Purchase of businesses and other investments net of cash and cash equivalent acquired	(98)	(636)
Proceeds from the sale of businesses and other investments net of cash and cash equivalent disposed of	650	1,659
(Increase) decrease in long-term loans and other long-term assets	130	(134)
Changes in cash and cash equivalents of discontinued operations	52	30
Cash Flows Provided by Investing Activities	214	312
Increase in capital and additional paid-in capital	38	61
Purchases of treasury stock (net of disposals)	(213)	(558)
Dividends	(456)	(489)
Increase (decrease) in noncurrent financial liabilities	(290)	(715)
Increase (decrease) in current financial liabilities	(536)	(191)
(Increase) decrease in marketable securities	(415)	(210)
Cash flows used in financing activities	(1,872)	(2,102)
Effect of exchange rate changes on cash and cash equivalents	(21)	53
Increase (Decrease) in Cash and Cash Equivalents	15	110
Cash and cash equivalents at beginning of period	451	466
Cash and Cash Equivalents at End of Period	466	576
Supplemental Disclosures:		
Cash paid during the year:		
Interest	152	172
Income tax	439	424

Yee would like answers to the following questions:

- What are the major sources of cash for Groupe Danone?
- What are the major uses of cash for Groupe Danone?
- What is the relationship between net income and cash flow from operating activities?
- Is cash flow from operating activities sufficient to cover capital expenditures?
- Other than capital expenditures, is cash being used or generated in investing activities?
- What types of financing cash flows does Groupe Danone have?

Solution. The major categories of cash flows can be summarized as follows (€ millions):

	2004	2005
Cash flows from operating activities	1,694	1,847
Cash flows from investing activities	214	312
Cash flows from financing activities	(1,872)	(2,102)
Exchange rate effects on cash	(21)	53
Increase in cash	15	110

The primary source of cash for Groupe Danone is operating activities. The secondary source of cash is investing activities. Most of this cash flow is being spent in financing activities. The fact that the primary source of cash is from operations is a good sign. Additionally, operating cash flow exceeds net income in both years—a good sign. Operating cash flows is much higher than capital expenditures, indicating that the company can easily fund capital expenditures from operations. The company has generated investing cash flows by selling business and investments in the two years presented. In the financing category, Groupe Danone is spending cash by repurchasing its own stock, paying dividends, and paying down debt. This could be an indicator that the company lacks investment opportunities and is, therefore, returning cash to the providers of capital.

4.2. Common-Size Analysis of the Statement of Cash Flows

In common-size analysis of a company's income statement, each income and expense line item is expressed as a percentage of net revenues (net sales). For the common-size balance sheet, each asset, liability, and equity line item is expressed as a percentage of total assets. For the common-size cash flow statement, there are two alternative approaches. The first approach is to express each line item of cash inflow (outflow) as a percentage of total inflows (outflows) of cash, and the second approach is to express each line item as a percentage of net revenue.

Exhibit 6-13 demonstrates the total cash inflows/total outflows method for Acme Corporation. Under this approach, each of the cash inflows is expressed as a percentage of the total cash inflows, whereas each of the cash outflows is expressed as a percentage of the total

EXHIBIT 6-13 Acme Corporation: Common-Size Cash Flow Statement, Year Ended 31 December 2006

Panel A. Direct Format for Operating Cash Flow

Inflows		Percentage of Total Inflows
Receipts from customers	$23,543	96.86%
Sale of equipment	762	3.14
Total	$24,305	100.00%

Outflows		Percentage of Total Outflows
Payments to suppliers	$11,900	48.66%
Payments to employees	4,113	16.82
Payments for other operating expenses	3,532	14.44
Payments for interest	258	1.05
Payments for income tax	1,134	4.64
Purchase of equipment	1,300	5.32
Retirement of long-term debt	500	2.04
Retirement of common stock	600	2.45
Dividend payments	1,120	4.58
Total	$24,457	100.00%

Panel B. Indirect Format for Operating Cash Flow

Inflows		Percentage of Total Inflows
Operations	$2,606	77.38%
Sale of equipment	762	22.62
Total	$3,368	100.00%

Outflows		Percentage of Total Outflows
Purchase of equipment	1,300	36.93%
Retirement of long-term debt	500	14.20
Retirement of common stock	600	17.05
Dividend payments	1,120	31.82
Total	$3,520	100.00%

Operating Income / Cash Flow

cash outflows. In Panel A, Acme's common-size statement is based on a cash flow statement using the direct method of presenting operating cash flows. Operating cash inflows and outflows are separately presented on the cash flow statement and, therefore, the common-size cash flow statement shows each of these operating inflows (outflows) as a percentage of total inflows (outflows). In Panel B, Acme's common-size statement is based on a cash flow statement using the indirect method of presenting operating cash flows. When a cash flow statement has been presented using the indirect method, operating cash inflows and outflows are not separately presented; therefore, the common-size cash flow statement shows only the net operating cash flows as a percentage of total inflows or outflows, depending on whether the net amount

EXHIBIT 6-14   Acme Corporation: Common-Size Cash Flow Statement: Indirect Format, Year Ended 31 December 2006

Cash Flow from Operating Activities		Percentage of Net Revenue
Net income	$2,210	9.37
Depreciation expense	1,052	4.46
Gain on sale of equipment	(205)	(0.87)
Increase in accounts receivable	(55)	(0.23)
Increase in inventory	(707)	(3.00)
Decrease in prepaid expenses	23	0.10
Increase in accounts payable	263	1.11
Increase in salary and wage payable	10	0.04
Decrease in interest payable	(12)	(0.05)
Increase in income tax payable	5	0.02
Increase in other accrued liabilities	22	0.09
Net Cash Provided by Operating Activities	2,606	11.04
Cash Flow from Investing Activities		
Cash received from sale of equipment	762	3.23
Cash paid for purchase of equipment	(1,300)	(5.51)
Net Cash Used for Investing Activities	(538)	(2.28)
Cash Flow from Financing Activities		
Cash paid to retire long-term debt	(500)	(2.12)
Cash paid to retire common stock	(600)	(2.54)
Cash paid for dividends	(1,120)	(4.75)
Net Cash Used for Financing Activities	(2,220)	(9.41)
Net Decrease in Cash	$(152)	(0.64)

was an in- or out- cash flow. Because Acme's net operating cash flow is positive, it is shown as a percentage of total inflows.

Exhibit 6-14 demonstrates the net revenue common-size cash flow statement for Acme Corporation. Under the net revenue approach, each line item in the cash flow statement is shown as a percentage of net revenue. The common-size statement in this exhibit has been developed based on Acme's cash flow statement using the indirect method for operating cash flows. Each line item of the reconciliation between net income and net operating cash flows is expressed as a percentage of net revenue. The common-size format makes it easier to see trends in cash flow rather than just looking at the total amount. This method is also useful to the analyst in forecasting future cash flows because individual items in the common-size statement (e.g., depreciation, fixed capital expenditures, debt borrowing, and repayment) are expressed as a percentage of net revenue. Thus, once the analyst has forecast revenue, the common-size statement provides a basis for forecasting cash flows.

EXAMPLE 6-9   Analysis of a Common-Size Cash Flow Statement

Andrew Potter is examining an abbreviated common-size cash flow statement based on net revenues for Dell, which is reproduced below:

Period Ending:	3 Feb 2006	28 Jan 2005	30 Jan 2004	31 Jan 2003	1 Feb 2002
Net income	**6.39%**	**6.18%**	**6.38%**	**5.99%**	**4.00%**
Cash flows—operating activities					
Depreciation	0.70	0.68	0.63	0.60	0.77
Net income adjustments	0.93	−0.56	−0.92	−0.61	4.57
Changes in operating activities					
Accounts receivable	−1.84	0.00	−1.96	0.54	0.71
Inventory	−0.21	0.00	−0.13	−0.06	0.36
Other operating activities	−0.54	4.49	−0.34	−0.50	−0.20
Liabilities	3.22	0.00	5.19	4.04	1.98
Net Cash Flow—Operating	**8.66%**	**10.79%**	**8.86%**	**9.99%**	**12.18%**
Cash flows—investing activities					
Capital expenditures	−1.30	−1.07	−0.79	−0.86	−0.97
Investments	8.24	−3.64	−4.88	−3.04	−6.28
Other investing activities	0.00	0.00	−1.12	0.00	0.00
Net Cash Flows—Investing	**6.94%**	**−4.71%**	**−6.79%**	**−3.90%**	**−7.25%**
Cash flows—financing activities					
Sale and purchase of stock	−11.14	−6.36	−3.34	−5.72	−8.68
Other financing activities	0.00	0.00	0.00	0.00	0.01
Net Cash Flows—Financing	**−11.14%**	**−6.36%**	**−3.34%**	**−5.72%**	**−8.67%**
Effect of exchange rate	−0.35	1.15	1.48	1.30	−0.33
Net Cash Flow	**4.10%**	**0.87%**	**0.21%**	**1.67%**	**−4.07%**

Based on the information in the above exhibit, address the following:

1. Characterize the importance of
   A. depreciation.
   B. capital expenditures.
2. Contrast Dell's operating cash flow as a percentage of revenue with Dell's net profit margin (on a cash basis).
3. Identify Dell's major use of its positive operating cash flow.

Solution to 1.
    A. Dell has very little depreciation expense (less than 1 percent), which is added back to determine operating cash flow.
    B. Dell's level of capital expenditures is relatively small, less than 1 percent of revenues in most years, but this increased in the most recent year. This is consistent with Dell's low amount of depreciation.

Solution to 2. Dell's operating cash flow as a percentage of revenue is consistently much higher than net profit margin. Dell's business model appears to generate cash flow instead of requiring working capital, as many companies do. Dell collects cash flow customers, on average, sooner than cash is paid out to suppliers.

Solution to 3. Most of Dell's operating cash flow has been used to repurchase large amounts of its own stock (financing activities).

4.3. Free Cash Flow to the Firm and Free Cash Flow to Equity

In the initial evaluation of the cash flow statement above, it was mentioned that it is desirable that operating cash flows are sufficient to cover capital expenditures. The excess of operating cash flow over capital expenditures is known generically as **free cash flow**. For purposes of valuing a company or its equity securities, an analyst may want to determine a more precise free cash flow measure, such as free cash flow to the firm (FCFF) or free cash flow to equity (FCFE).

    FCFF is the cash flow available to the company's suppliers of debt and equity capital after all operating expenses (including income taxes) have been paid and necessary investments in working capital and fixed capital have been made. FCFF can be computed starting with net income as[8]

$$FCFF = NI + NCC + Int(1 - Tax\ rate) - FCInv - WCInv$$

where

        NI = Net income
    NCC = Noncash charges (such as depreciation and amortization)
      Int = Interest expense
   FCInv = Capital expenditures (fixed capital, such as equipment)
  WCInv = Working capital expenditures

    The reason for adding back interest is that FCFF is the cash flow available to the suppliers of debt capital as well as equity capital. Conveniently, FCFF can also be computed from cash flow from operating activities as

$$FCFF = CFO + Int(1 - Tax\ rate) - FCInv$$

CFO represents cash flow from operating activities under U.S. GAAP or under IFRS where the company has chosen to place interest expense in operating activities. Under IFRS, if

---

[8]See Stowe, Robinson, Pinto, and McLeavey (2002) for a detailed discussion of free cash flow computations.

This is in the spreadsheet.

the company has placed interest and dividends received in investing activities, these should be added back to CFO to determine FCFF. Additionally, if dividends paid were subtracted in the operating section, these should be added back in to compute FCFF.

The computation of FCFF for Acme Corporation (based on the data from Exhibits 6-6, 6-7, and 6-8) is as follows:

CFO	$2,606
Plus: Interest paid times (1 − income tax rate)	
{$258 [1 − ($1,139 ÷ $3,349)]}	170
Less: Net investments in fixed capital	
($1,300 − $762)	(538)
FCFF	$2,238

FCFE is the cash flow available to the company's common stockholders after all operating expenses and borrowing costs (principal and interest) have been paid and necessary investments in working capital and fixed capital have been made. FCFE can be computed as

$$FCFE = CFO - FCInv + Net\ borrowing - Net\ debt\ repayment$$

The computation of FCFE for Acme Corporation (based on the data from Exhibits 6-6, 6-7, and 6-8) is as follows:

CFO	$2,606
Less: Net investments in fixed capital [$1,300 − $762]	(538)
Less: Debt repayment	(500)
FCFE	$1,568

Positive FCFE means that the company has an excess of operating cash flow over amounts needed for investments for the future and repayment of debt. This cash would be available for distribution to owners.

4.4. Cash Flow Ratios

The statement of cash flows provides information that can be analyzed over time to obtain a better understanding of the past performance of a company and its future prospects. This information can also be effectively used to compare the performance and prospects of different companies in an industry and of different industries. There are several ratios based on cash flow from operating activities that are useful in this analysis. These ratios generally fall into cash flow performance (profitability) ratios and cash flow coverage (solvency) ratios. Exhibit 6-15 on page 252 summarizes the calculation and interpretation of some of these ratios.

EXAMPLE 6-10   A Cash Flow Analysis of Comparables

Andrew Potter is comparing the cash-flow-generating ability of Dell with that of several other computer manufacturers: Hewlett Packard, Gateway, and Apple. He collects the following information:

Operating Cash Flow

Revenue	2005	2004	2003
DELL	8.66%	10.79%	8.86%
HPQ	9.26%	6.37%	8.29%
GTW	−0.65%	−11.89%	2.15%
AAPL	18.20%	11.28%	4.66%

Average Total Assets	2005	2004	2003
DELL	20.89%	24.97%	21.10%
HPQ	10.46%	6.75%	8.33%
GTW	−1.35%	−22.84%	3.22%
AAPL	25.87%	12.57%	4.41%

AAPL = Apple, GTW = Gateway, HPQ = Hewlett Packard.

What is Potter likely to conclude about the relative cash-flow-generating ability of these companies?

Solution. Dell has consistently generated operating cash flow relative to both revenue and assets. Hewlett Packard also has a good level of operating cash flow relative to revenue, but its operating cash flow is not as strong as Dell relative to assets. This is likely due to Dell's lean business model and lack of a need for large amounts of property, plant, and equipment. Gateway has poor operating cash flow on both measures. Apple has dramatically improved its operating cash flow over the three years and in 2005 had the strongest operating cash flow of the group.

EXHIBIT 6-15   Cash Flow Ratios

Performance Ratios	Calculation	What It Measures
Cash flow to revenue	CFO ÷ Net revenue	Cash generated per dollar of revenue
Cash return on assets	CFO ÷ Average total assets	Cash generated from all resources
Cash return on equity	CFO ÷ Average shareholders' equity	Cash generated from owner resources
Cash to income	CFO ÷ Operating income	Cash generating ability of operations
Cash flow per share	(CFO − Preferred dividends) ÷ number of common shares outstanding	Operating cash flow on a per-share basis

Coverage Ratios	Calculation	What It Measures
Debt coverage	CFO ÷ Total debt	Financial risk and financial leverage
Interest coverage	(CFO + Interest paid + Taxes paid) ÷ Interest paid	Ability to meet interest obligations

estment	CFO ÷ Cash paid for long-term assets	Ability to acquire assets with operating cash flows
payment	CFO ÷ Cash paid for long-term debt repayment	Ability to pay debts with operating cash flows
lend payment	CFO ÷ Dividends paid	Ability to pay dividends with operating cash flows
Investing and financing	CFO ÷ Cash outflows for investing and financing activities	Ability to acquire assets, pay debts, and make distributions to owners

5. SUMMARY

The cash flow statement provides important information about a company's cash receipts and cash payments during an accounting period as well as information about a company's operating, investing, and financing activities. Although the income statement provides a measure of a company's success, cash and cash flow are also vital to a company's long-term success. Information on the sources and uses of cash helps creditors, investors, and other statement users evaluate the company's liquidity, solvency, and financial flexibility. Key concepts are as follows:

- Cash flow activities are classified into three categories: operating activities, investing activities, and financing activities. Significant noncash transaction activities (if present) are reported by using a supplemental disclosure note to the cash flow statement.
- The cash flow statement under IFRS is similar to U.S. GAAP; however, IFRS permits greater discretion in classifying some cash flow items as operating, investing, or financing activities.
- Companies can use either the direct or the indirect method for reporting their operating cash flow:
  - The direct method discloses operating cash inflows by source (e.g., cash received from customers, cash received from investment income) and operating cash outflows by use (e.g., cash paid to suppliers, cash paid for interest) in the operating activities section of the cash flow statement.
  - The indirect method reconciles net income to net cash flow from operating activities by adjusting net income for all noncash items and the net changes in the operating working capital accounts.
- The cash flow statement is linked to a company's income statement and comparative balance sheets and is constructed from the data on those statements.
- Although the indirect method is most commonly used by companies, the analyst can generally convert it to the direct format by following a simple three-step process.
- The analyst can use common-size statement analysis for the cash flow statement. Two prescribed approaches are the total cash inflows/total cash outflows method and the percentage of net revenues method.
- The cash flow statement can be used to determine FCFF and FCFE.
- The cash flow statement may also be used in financial ratios measuring a company's profitability, performance, and financial strength.

PRACTICE PROBLEMS

1. The three major classifications of activities in a cash flow statement are
   A. inflows, outflows, and balances.
   B. beginning balance, ending balance, and change.
   C. operating, investing, and financing.

2. The sale of a building for cash would be classified as what type of activity on the cash flow statement?
   A. Operating
   B. Investing
   C. Financing

3. Which of the following is an example of a financing activity on the cash flow statement under U.S. GAAP?
   A. Payment of dividends
   B. Receipt of dividends
   C. Payment of interest

4. A conversion of a face value $1 million convertible bond for $1 million of common stock would most likely be
   A. reported as a $1 million financing cash outflow and inflow.
   B. reported as supplementary information to the cash flow statement.
   C. reported as a $1 million financing cash outflow and a $1 million investing cash inflow.

5. Interest expense may be classified as an operating cash flow
   A. under U.S. GAAP, but may be classified as either operating or investing cash flows under IFRS.
   B. under IFRS, but may be classified as either operating or investing cash flows under U.S. GAAP.
   C. under U.S. GAAP, but may be classified as either operating or financing cash flows under IFRS.

6. Tax cash flows
   A. must be separately disclosed in the cash flow statement under IFRS only.
   B. must be separately disclosed in the cash flow statement under U.S. GAAP only.
   C. are not separately disclosed in the cash flow statement under IFRS or U.S. GAAP.

7. Which of the following components of the cash flow statement may be prepared under the indirect method under both IFRS and U.S. GAAP?
   A. Operating
   B. Investing
   C. Financing

8. Which of the following is most likely to appear in the operating section of a cash flow statement under the indirect method under U.S. GAAP?
   A. Net income
   B. Cash paid for interest
   C. Cash paid to suppliers

9. Red Road Company, a consulting company, reported total revenues of $100 million, total expenses of $80 million, and net income of $20 million in the most recent year. If accounts receivable increased by $10 million, how much cash did the company receive from customers?
   A. $110 million
   B. $90 million
   C. $30 million

10. Green Glory Corp., a garden supply wholesaler, reported cost of goods sold for the year of $80 million. Total assets increased by $55 million, including an increase of $5 million in inventory. Total liabilities increased by $45 million, including an increase of $2 million in accounts payable. How much cash did the company pay to its suppliers during the year?
    A. $90 million
    B. $83 million
    C. $77 million

11. Purple Fleur S.A., a retailer of floral products, reported cost of goods sold for the year of $75 million. Total assets increased by $55 million, but inventory declined by $6 million. Total liabilities increased by $45 million, and accounts payable increased by $2 million. How much cash did the company pay to its suppliers during the year?
    A. $85 million
    B. $79 million
    C. $67 million

12. White Flag, a women's clothing manufacturer, reported wage expense of $20 million. The beginning balance of wages payable was $3 million, and the ending balance of wages payable was $1 million. How much cash did the company pay in wages?
    A. $24 million
    B. $23 million
    C. $22 million

13. An analyst gathered the following information from a company's 2004 financial statements ($ millions):

Year Ended 31 December	2003	2004
Net sales	245.8	254.6
Cost of goods sold	168.3	175.9
Accounts receivable	73.2	68.3
Inventory	39.0	47.8
Accounts payable	20.3	22.9

Based only on the information above, the company's 2004 statement of cash flows prepared using the direct method would include amounts ($ millions) for cash received from customers and cash paid to suppliers, respectively, that are *closest* to:

	Cash Received from Customers	Cash Paid to Suppliers
A.	249.7	182.1
B.	259.5	169.7
C.	259.5	182.1

14. Golden Cumulus Corp., a commodities trading company, reported interest expense of $19 million and taxes of $6 million. Interest payable increased by $3 million, and taxes payable decreased by $4 million. How much cash did the company pay for interest and taxes?
    A. $22 million for interest and $2 million for taxes
    B. $16 million for interest and $2 million for taxes
    C. $16 million for interest and $10 million for taxes

15. An analyst gathered the following information from a company's 2005 financial statements ($ millions):

Balances as of Year Ended 31 December	2004	2005
Retained earnings	120	145
Accounts receivable	38	43
Inventory	45	48
Accounts payable	36	29

The company declared and paid cash dividends of $10 million in 2005 and recorded depreciation expense in the amount of $25 million for 2005. The company's 2005 cash flow from operations ($ millions) was *closest* to
    A. 25.
    B. 35.
    C. 45.

16. Silverago Incorporated, an international metals company, reported a loss on the sale of equipment of $2 million. In addition, the company's income statement shows depreciation expense of $8 million and the cash flow statement shows capital expenditure of $10 million, all of which was for the purchase of new equipment. Using the following information from the comparative balance sheets, how much cash did the company receive from the equipment sale?

Balance Sheet Item	12/31/2005	12/31/2006	Change
Equipment	$100 million	$105 million	$5 million
Accumulated depreciation—equipment	$40 million	$46 million	$6 million

    A. $6 million
    B. $5 million
    C. $1 million

17. Jaderong Plinkett Stores reported net income of $25 million, which equals the company's comprehensive income. The company has no outstanding debt. Using the following information from the comparative balance sheets ($ millions), what should the company report in the financing section of the statement of cash flows?

Balance Sheet Item	12/31/2005	12/31/2006	Change
Common stock	$100	$102	$2
Additional paid-in capital common stock	$100	$140	$40
Retained earnings	$100	$115	$15
Total stockholders' equity	$300	$357	$57

A. Issuance of common stock $42 million; dividends paid of $10 million
B. Issuance of common stock $38 million; dividends paid of $10 million
C. Issuance of common stock $42 million; dividends paid of $40 million

18. Based on the following information for Pinkerly Inc., what are the total net adjustments that the company would make to net income in order to derive operating cash flow?

		Year Ended	
Income Statement Item		**12/31/2006**	
Net income		$20 million	
Depreciation		$2 million	
Balance Sheet Item	**12/31/2005**	**12/31/2006**	**Change**
Accounts receivable	$25 million	$22 million	($3 million)
Inventory	$10 million	$14 million	$4 million
Accounts payable	$8 million	$13 million	$5 million

A. Add $6 million
B. Add $8 million
C. Subtract $6 million

19. The first step in evaluating the cash flow statement should be to examine
   A. individual investing cash flow items.
   B. individual financing cash flow items.
   C. the major sources and uses of cash.

20. Which of the following would be valid conclusions from an analysis of the cash flow statement for Telefónica Group presented in Exhibit 6-3?
   A. The company does not pay dividends.
   B. The primary use of cash is financing activities.
   C. The primary source of cash is operating activities.

21. Which is an appropriate method of preparing a common-size cash flow statement?
   A. Begin with net income and show the items that reconcile net income and operating cash flows.
   B. Show each line item on the cash flow statement as a percentage of net revenue.
   C. Show each line item on the cash flow statement as a percentage of total cash outflows.

22. Which of the following is an appropriate method of computing free cash flow to the firm?
   A. Add operating cash flows plus capital expenditures and deduct after-tax interest payments.
   B. Add operating cash flows plus after-tax interest payments and deduct capital expenditures.
   C. Deduct both after-tax interest payments and capital expenditures from operating cash flows.

23. An analyst has calculated a ratio using as the numerator the sum of operating cash flow, interest, and taxes, and as the denominator the amount of interest. What is this ratio, what does it measure, and what does it indicate?

   A. This ratio is an interest coverage ratio, measuring a company's ability to meet its interest obligations and indicating a company's solvency.

   B. This ratio is an effective tax ratio, measuring the amount of a company's operating cash flow used for taxes, and indicating a company's efficiency in tax management.

   C. This ratio is an operating profitability ratio, measuring the operating cash flow generated accounting for taxes and interest, and indicating a company's liquidity.

CHAPTER 7

FINANCIAL ANALYSIS TECHNIQUES

Thomas R. Robinson, CFA

CFA Institute
Charlottesville, Virginia

Hennie van Greuning, CFA

World Bank
Washington, DC

Elaine Henry, CFA

University of Miami
Miami, Florida

Michael A. Broihahn, CFA

Barry University
Miami, Florida

LEARNING OUTCOMES

After completing this chapter, you will be able to do the following:

- Identify the analytical phases, sources of information, and output of financial analysis.
- Differentiate between computation and analysis of ratios, and explain key questions that should be addressed in ratio analysis.

- Demonstrate and explain the use of ratio analysis, common-size financial statements, and graphs in company analysis and the value, purposes, and limitations of ratio analysis.
- Explain the common classifications of ratios and compute, analyze, and interpret activity, liquidity, solvency, profitability, and valuation ratios.
- Explain how ratios are related and how to evaluate a company using a combination of different ratios.
- Demonstrate the application of DuPont analysis (the decomposition of return on equity).
- Describe how ratios are useful in equity analysis.
- Describe how ratios are useful in credit analysis.
- Discuss segment reporting requirements and compute, analyze, and interpret segment ratios.
- Describe how the results of common-size and ratio analysis can be used to model/forecast earnings.

1. INTRODUCTION

Financial analysis applies analytical tools to financial data to assess a company's performance and trends in that performance. In essence, an analyst converts data into financial metrics that assist in decision making. Analysts seek to answer such questions as: How successfully has the company performed, relative to its own past performance and relative to its competitors? How is the company likely to perform in the future? Based on expectations about future performance, what is the value of this company or the securities it issues?

A primary source of data is a company's financial reports, including the financial statements, footnotes, and management's discussion and analysis. This text focuses on data presented in financial reports prepared under International Financial Reporting Standards (IFRS) and U.S. generally accepted accounting principles (U.S. GAAP). However, even financial reports prepared under these standards do not contain all the information needed to perform effective financial analysis. Although financial statements do contain data about the *past* performance of a company (its income and cash flows) as well as its *current* financial condition (assets, liabilities, and owners' equity), such statements may not provide some important nonfinancial information nor do they forecast *future* results. The financial analyst must be capable of utilizing financial statements in conjunction with other information in order to reach valid conclusions and make projections. Accordingly, an analyst will most likely need to supplement the information found in a company's financial reports with industry and economic data.

The purpose of this chapter is to describe various techniques used to analyze a company's financial statements. Financial analysis of a company may be performed for a variety of reasons, such as valuing equity securities, assessing credit risk, conducting due diligence related to an acquisition, or assessing a subsidiary's performance. This text will describe the techniques common to any financial analysis and then discuss more specific aspects for the two most common categories: equity analysis and credit analysis.

Equity analysis incorporates an owner's perspective, either for valuation or performance evaluation. Credit analysis incorporates a creditor's (such as a banker or bondholder) perspective. In either case, there is a need to gather and analyze information to make a decision (ownership or credit); the focus of analysis varies due to the differing interests of owners and creditors. Both equity and credit analysis assess the entity's ability to generate and grow earnings and cash flow, as well as any associated risks. Equity analysis usually places a greater emphasis on growth, whereas credit analysis usually places a greater emphasis on risks. The difference in emphasis reflects the different fundamentals of these types of investments: The value of a company's equity generally increases as the company's earnings and cash flow increase, whereas the value of a company's debt has an upper limit.[1]

The balance of this chapter is organized as follows: Section 2 recaps the framework for financial statements and the place of financial analysis techniques within it. Section 3 provides a description of analytical tools and techniques. Section 4 explains how to compute, analyze, and interpret common financial ratios. Sections 4 through 8 explain the use of ratios and other analytical data in equity analysis, debt analysis, segment analysis, and forecasting, respectively. Section 9 summarizes the key points of the chapter. Practice problems in the CFA Institute multiple-choice format conclude the chapter.

2. THE FINANCIAL ANALYSIS PROCESS

In financial analysis, as in any business task, a clear understanding of the end goal and the steps required to get there is essential. In addition, the analyst needs to know the typical questions to address when interpreting financial data and how to communicate the analysis and conclusions.

2.1. The Objectives of the Financial Analysis Process

Due to the variety of reasons for performing financial analysis, the numerous available techniques, and the often substantial amount of data, it is important that the analytical approach be tailored to the specific situation. Prior to embarking on any financial analysis, the analyst should clarify purpose and context, and clearly understand the following:

- What is the purpose of the analysis? What questions will this analysis answer?
- What level of detail will be needed to accomplish this purpose?
- What data are available for the analysis?
- What are the factors or relationships that will influence the analysis?
- What are the analytical limitations, and will these limitations potentially impair the analysis?

Having clarified the purpose and context of the analysis, the analyst can select the techniques (e.g., ratios) that will best assist in making a decision. Although there is no single approach to structuring the analysis process, a general framework is set forth in Exhibit 7-1.[2] The steps in this process were discussed in more detail in an earlier chapter. The primary focus of this chapter is on Phases 3 and 4, processing and analyzing data.

2.2. Distinguishing between Computations and Analysis

An effective analysis encompasses both computations and interpretations. A well-reasoned analysis differs from a mere compilation of various pieces of information, computations,

---

[1]The upper limit is equal to the undiscounted sum of the principal and remaining interest payments (i.e., the present value of these contractual payments at a zero percent discount rate).

[2]Components of this framework have been adapted from van Greuning and Bratanovic (2003, p. 300) and Benninga and Sarig (1997, pp. 134–156).

EXHIBIT 7-1   A Financial Statement Analysis Framework

Phase	Sources of Information	Output
1. Articulate the purpose and context of the analysis	The nature of the analyst's function, such as evaluating an equity or debt investment or issuing a credit rating.	Statement of the purpose or objective of analysis.
	Communication with client or superior on needs and concerns.	A list (written or unwritten) of specific questions to be answered by the analysis.
	Institutional guidelines related to developing specific work product.	Nature and content of report to be provided.
		Timetable and budgeted resources for completion.
2. Collect input data	Financial statements, other financial data, questionnaires, and industry/economic data.	Organized financial statements.
		Financial data tables.
	Discussions with management, suppliers, customers, and competitors.	Completed questionnaires, if applicable.
	Company site visits (e.g., to production facilities or retail stores).	
3. Process data	Data from the previous phase.	Adjusted financial statements.
		Common-size statements.
		Ratios and graphs.
		Forecasts.
4. Analyze/interpret the processed data	Input data as well as processed data.	Analytical results.
5. Develop and communicate conclusions and recommendations (e.g., with an analysis report)	Analytical results and previous reports.	Analytical report answering questions posed in Phase 1.
	Institutional guidelines for published reports.	Recommendation regarding the purpose of the analysis, such as whether to make an investment or grant credit.
6. Follow up	Information gathered by periodically repeating above steps as necessary to determine whether changes to holdings or recommendations are necessary.	Updated reports and recommendations.

tables, and graphs by integrating the data collected into a cohesive whole. Analysis of past performance, for example, should address not only what happened but also why it happened and whether it advanced the company's strategy. Some of the key questions to address include:

- What aspects of performance are critical for this company to successfully compete in this industry?
- How well did the company's performance meet these critical aspects? (This is established through computation and comparison with appropriate benchmarks, such as the company's own historical performance or competitors' performance.)

- What were the key causes of this performance, and how does this performance reflect the company's strategy? (This is established through analysis.)

If the analysis is forward looking, additional questions include:

- What is the likely impact of an event or trend? (Established through interpretation of analysis.)
- What is the likely response of management to this trend? (Established through evaluation of quality of management and corporate governance.)
- What is the likely impact of trends in the company, industry, and economy on future cash flows? (Established through assessment of corporate strategy and through forecasts.)
- What are the recommendations of the analyst? (Established through interpretation and forecasting of results of analysis.)
- What risks should be highlighted? (Established by an evaluation of major uncertainties in the forecast.)

Example 7-1 demonstrates how a company's financial data can be analyzed in the context of its business strategy and changes in that strategy. An analyst must be able to understand the "why" behind the numbers and ratios, not just what the numbers and ratios are.

EXAMPLE 7-1   Change in Strategy Reflected in Financial Performance

Motorola (NYSE: MOT) and Nokia (NYSE: NOK) engage in the design, manufacture, and sale of mobility products worldwide. Selected financial data for 2003 through 2005 for these two competitors are given below.

Selected Financial Data for Motorola ($ millions)

Years ended 31 December	2005	2004	2003
Net sales	36,843	31,323	23,155
Operating earnings	4,696	3,132	1,273

Selected Financial Data for Nokia Corporation (€ millions)

Years ended 31 December	2005	2004	2003
Net sales	34,191	29,371	29,533
Operating profit	4,639	4,326	4,960

Source: Motorola 10-K and Nokia 20-F, both filed 2 March 2006.

Although the raw numbers for Motorola and Nokia are not directly comparable because Motorola reports in U.S. dollars and Nokia in euros, the relative changes can be compared. Motorola reported a 35 percent increase in net sales from 2003 to 2004 and a further increase in 2005 of approximately 18 percent. Also, the company's operating earnings more than doubled from 2003 to 2004 and grew another 50 percent in 2005. Over the 2003 to 2004 time period, industry leader Nokia reported a decrease in both sales and operating profits, although sales growth was about 16 percent in 2005.

What caused Motorola's dramatic growth in sales and operating profits? One of the most important factors was the introduction of new products, such as the stylish RAZR cell phone in 2004. Motorola's 2005 10-K indicates that more than 23 million RAZRs had been sold since the product was launched. The handset segment represents 54 percent of the company's 2004 sales and nearly 58 percent of 2005 sales, so the impact on sales and profitability of the successful product introduction was significant. The introduction of branded, differentiated products not only increased demand but also increased the potential for higher pricing. The introduction of the new products was one result of the company's strategic shift to develop a consumer marketing orientation as a complement to its historically strong technological position.

Analysts often need to communicate the findings of their analysis in a written report. Their reports should, therefore, communicate how conclusions were reached and why recommendations were made. For example, a report might present the following:[3]

- The purpose of the report, unless it is readily apparent.
- Relevant aspects of the business context:
  - Economic environment (country, macro economy, sector).
  - Financial and other infrastructure (accounting, auditing, rating agencies).
  - Legal and regulatory environment (and any other material limitations on the company being analyzed).
- Evaluation of corporate governance.
- Assessment of financial and operational data.
- Conclusions and recommendations (including risks and limitations to the analysis).

An effective storyline and well-supported conclusions and recommendations are normally enhanced by using 3 to 10 years of data, as well as analytic techniques appropriate to the purpose of the report.

3. ANALYSIS TOOLS AND TECHNIQUES

The tools and techniques presented in this section facilitate evaluations of company data. Evaluations require comparisons. It is difficult to say that a company's financial performance was "good" without clarifying the basis for comparison.

In assessing a company's ability to generate and grow earnings and cash flow, and the risks related to those earnings and cash flows, the analyst draws comparisons to other companies (cross-sectional analysis) and over time (trend or time-series analysis).

For example, an analyst may wish to compare the profitability in 2004 of Dell and Gateway. These companies differ significantly in size, so comparing net income in raw dollars

---

[3]The nature and content of reports will vary depending on the purpose of the analysis and the ultimate recipient of the report. For an example of the contents of an equity research report, see Stowe, Robinson, Pinto, and McLeavey (2002, pp. 22–28).

is not useful. Instead, ratios (which express one number in relation to another) and common-size financial statements can remove size as a factor and enable a more relevant comparison.

The analyst may also want to examine Dell's performance relative to its own historic performance. Again, the raw dollar amounts of sales or net income may not highlight significant changes. However, using ratios (see Example 7-2), horizontal financial statements, and graphs can make such changes more apparent.

The following paragraphs describe the tools and techniques of ratio analysis in more detail.

EXAMPLE 7-2   Ratio Analysis

Dell computer reported the following data for three recent fiscal years:

Fiscal Year Ended (FYE)	Net Income (millions of US$)
1/31/2003	$2,122
1/30/2004	$2,645
1/28/2005	$3,043

Overall net income has grown steadily over the three-year period. Net income for FYE 2005 is 43 percent higher than net income in 2003, which is a good sign. However, has profitability also steadily increased? We can obtain some insight by looking at the **net profit margin** (net income divided by revenue) for each year.

Fiscal Year Ended	Net Profit Margin
1/31/2003	5.99%
1/30/2004	6.38%
1/28/2005	6.18%

The net profit margin indicates that profitability improved from FY2003 to FY2004 but deteriorated slightly from FY2004 to FY2005. Further analysis is needed to determine the cause of the profitability decline and assess whether this decline is likely to persist in future years.

3.1. Ratios

There are many relationships between financial accounts and between expected relationships from one point in time to another. Ratios are a useful way of expressing these relationships. Ratios express one quantity in relation to another (usually as a quotient).

Notable academic research has examined the importance of ratios in predicting stock returns (Ou and Penman, 1989b; Abarbanell and Bushee, 1998) or credit failure (Altman, 1968; Ohlson, 1980; Hopwood et al., 1994). This research has found that financial statement ratios are effective in selecting investments and in predicting financial distress. Practitioners routinely use ratios to communicate the value of companies and securities.

Several aspects of ratio analysis are important to understand. First, the computed ratio is not "the answer." The ratio is an *indicator* of some aspect of a company's performance, telling what happened but not why it happened. For example, an analyst might want to answer the question: Which of two companies was more profitable? The net profit margin, which expresses profit relative to revenue, can provide insight into this question. Net profit margin is calculated by dividing net income by revenue:[4]

$$\frac{\text{Net income}}{\text{Revenue}}$$

Assume Company A has €100,000 of net income and €2 million of revenue, and thus a net profit margin of 5 percent. Company B has €200,000 of net income and €6 million of revenue, and thus a net profit margin of 3.33 percent. Expressing net income as a percentage of revenue clarifies the relationship: For each €100 of revenue, Company A earns €5 in net income, while Company B earns only €3.33 for each €100 of revenue. So, we can now answer the question of which company was more profitable in percentage terms: Company A was more profitable, as indicated by its higher net profit margin of 5 percent. We also note that Company A was more profitable despite the fact that Company B reported higher absolute amounts of net income and revenue. However, this ratio by itself does not tell us *why* Company A has a higher profit margin. Further analysis is required to determine the reason (perhaps higher relative sales prices or better cost control).

Company size sometimes confers economies of scale, so the absolute amounts of net income and revenue are useful in financial analysis. However, ratios reduce the effect of size, which enhances comparisons between companies and over time.

A second important aspect of ratio analysis is that differences in accounting policies (across companies and across time) can distort ratios, and a meaningful comparison may, therefore, involve adjustments to the financial data. Third, not all ratios are necessarily relevant to a particular analysis. The ability to select a relevant ratio or ratios to answer the research question is an analytical skill. Finally, as with financial analysis in general, ratio analysis does not stop with computation; interpretation of the result is essential. In practice, differences in ratios across time and across companies can be subtle, and interpretation is situation specific.

3.1.1. The Universe of Ratios

There are no authoritative bodies specifying exact formulas for computing ratios or providing a standard, comprehensive list of ratios. Formulas and even names of ratios often differ from analyst to analyst or from database to database. The number of different ratios that can be created is practically limitless. There are, however, widely accepted ratios that have been found to be useful. Section 4 of this chapter will focus primarily on these broad classes and commonly accepted definitions of key ratios. However, the analyst should be aware that different ratios may be used in practice and that certain industries have unique ratios tailored to the characteristics of that industry. When faced with an unfamiliar ratio, the analyst can

---

[4]The term *sales* is often used interchangeably with the term *revenues*. Other times it is used to refer to revenues derived from sales of products versus services. Furthermore, the income statement usually reflects "revenues" or "sales" after returns and allowances (e.g., returns of products or discounts offered after a sale to induce the customer to not return a product). Additionally, in some countries, including the United Kingdom, the term *turnover* is used in the sense of *revenue*.

examine the underlying formula to gain insight into what the ratio is measuring. For example, consider the following ratio formula:

$$\frac{\text{Operating income}}{\text{Average total assets}}$$

Never having seen this ratio, an analyst might question whether a result of 12 percent is better than 8 percent. The answer can be found in the ratio itself. The numerator is operating income and the denominator is average total assets, so the ratio can be interpreted as the amount of operating income generated per unit of assets. For every €100 of average total assets, generating €12 of operating income is better than generating €8 of operating income. Furthermore, it is apparent that this particular ratio is an indicator of profitability (and, to a lesser extent, efficiency in use of assets in generating operating profits). When facing a ratio for the first time, the analyst should evaluate the numerator and denominator to assess what the ratio is attempting to measure and how it should be interpreted. This is demonstrated in Example 7-3.

EXAMPLE 7-3   Interpreting a Financial Ratio

An insurance company reports that its "combined ratio" is determined by dividing losses and expenses incurred by net premiums earned. It reports the following combined ratios:

	2005	2004	2003	2002	2001
Combined ratio	90.1%	104.0%	98.5%	104.1%	101.1%

Explain what this ratio is measuring and compare and contrast the results reported for each of the years shown in the chart. What other information might an analyst want to review before concluding on this information?

Solution. The combined ratio is a profitability measure. The ratio is explaining how much the costs (losses and expenses) were for every dollar of revenue (net premiums earned). The underlying formula indicates that a lower ratio is better. The 2005 ratio of 90.1 percent means that for every dollar of net premiums earned, the costs were $.901, yielding a gross profit of $.099. Ratios greater than 100 percent indicate an overall loss. A review of the data indicates that there does not seem to be a consistent trend in this ratio. Profits were achieved in 2005 and 2003. The results for 2004 and 2002 show the most significant losses at 104 percent.

The analyst would want to discuss this data further with management and understand the characteristics of the underlying business. He or she would want to understand why the results are so volatile. The analyst would also want to determine what ratio should be used as a benchmark.

The operating income/average total assets ratio shown above is one of many versions of the **return on assets** (ROA) ratio. Note that there are other ways of specifying this formula based on how assets are defined. Some financial ratio databases compute ROA using the ending value of assets rather than average assets. In limited cases, one may also see beginning assets in the denominator. Which one is right? It depends upon what you are trying to measure and the underlying company trends. If the company has a stable level of assets, the answer will not differ greatly under the three measures of assets (beginning, average, and ending). If, however, the assets are growing (or shrinking), the results will differ. When assets are growing, operating income divided by ending assets may not make sense because some of the income would have been generated before some assets were purchased, and this would understate the company's performance. Similarly, if beginning assets are used, some of the operating income later in the year may have been generated only because of the addition of assets; therefore, the ratio would overstate the company's performance. Because operating income occurs throughout the period, it generally makes sense to use some average measure of assets. A good general rule is that when an income statement or cash flow statement number is in the numerator of a ratio and a balance sheet number is in the denominator, then an average should be used for the denominator. It is generally not necessary to use averages when only balance sheet numbers are used in both the numerator and denominator because both are determined as of the same date. However, as we shall see later, there are occasions when even balance sheet data may be averages, e.g., in analyzing the components of **return on equity** (ROE), which is defined as net income divided by average shareholders' equity.

If an average is used, there is also judgment required as to what average should be used. For simplicity, most ratio databases use a simple average of the beginning and end-of-year balance sheet amounts. If the company's business is seasonal so that levels of assets vary by interim period (semiannual or quarterly), then it may be beneficial to take an average over all interim periods, if available (if the analyst is working within a company and has access to monthly data, this can also be used).

3.1.2. Value, Purposes, and Limitations of Ratio Analysis

The value of ratio analysis is that it enables the equity or credit analyst to evaluate past performance, assess the current financial position of the company, and gain insights useful for projecting future results. As noted previously, the ratio itself is not the answer but an indicator of some aspect of a company's performance. Financial ratios provide insights into:

- Microeconomic relationships within a company that help analysts project earnings and free cash flow.
- A company's financial flexibility, or ability to obtain the cash required to grow and meet its obligations, even if unexpected circumstances develop.
- Management's ability.

There are also limitations to ratio analysis:

- *The homogeneity of a company's operating activities.* Companies may have divisions operating in many different industries. This can make it difficult to find comparable industry ratios to use for comparison purposes.
- *The need to determine whether the results of the ratio analysis are consistent.* One set of ratios may indicate a problem, whereas another set may prove that the potential problem is only short term in nature.
- *The need to use judgment.* A key issue is whether a ratio for a company is within a reasonable range. Although financial ratios are used to help assess the growth potential and risk of a company, they cannot be used alone to directly value a company or its securities, or to determine its creditworthiness. The entire operation of the company must be examined,

and the external economic and industry setting in which it is operating must be considered when interpreting financial ratios.

- *The use of alternative accounting methods.* Companies frequently have latitude when choosing certain accounting methods. Ratios taken from financial statements that employ different accounting choices may not be comparable unless adjustments are made. Some important accounting considerations include the following:
  - FIFO (first in, first out), LIFO (last in, first out), or average cost inventory valuation methods (IFRS no longer allow LIFO).
  - Cost or equity methods of accounting for unconsolidated affiliates.
  - Straight-line or accelerated methods of depreciation.
  - Capital or operating lease treatment.

The expanding use of IFRS and the planned convergence between U.S. GAAP and IFRS seeks to make the financial statements of different companies comparable and so overcome some of these difficulties. Nonetheless, there will remain accounting choices that the analyst must consider.

3.1.3. Sources of Ratios

Ratios may be computed using data directly from companies' financial statements or from a database such as Reuters, Bloomberg, Baseline, FactSet, or Thomson Financial. These databases are popular because they provide easy access to many years of historical data so that trends over time can be examined. They also allow for ratio calculations based on periods other than the company's fiscal year, such as for the trailing 12 months (TTM) or most recent quarter (MRQ).

Analysts should be aware that the underlying formulas may differ by vendor. The formula used should be obtained from the vendor, and the analyst should determine whether any adjustments are necessary. Furthermore, database providers often exercise judgment when classifying items. For example, operating income may not appear directly on a company's income statement, and the vendor may use judgment to classify income statement items as "operating" or "nonoperating." Variation in such judgments would affect any computation involving operating income. It is, therefore, a good practice to use the same source for data when comparing different companies or when evaluating the historical record of a single given company. Analysts should verify the consistency of formulas and data classifications of the data source. Analysts should also be mindful of the judgments made by a vendor in data classifications and refer back to the source financial statements until they are comfortable that the classifications are appropriate.

Systems are under development that collect financial data from regulatory filings and can automatically compute ratios. The eXtensible Business Reporting Language (XBRL) is a mechanism that attaches "smart tags" to financial information (e.g., total assets), so that software can automatically collect the data and perform desired computations. The organization developing XBRL (www.xbrl.org) is a worldwide nonprofit consortium of organizations, including the International Accounting Standards Board.

Analysts can compare a subject company to similar (peer) companies in these databases or use aggregate industry data. For nonpublic companies, aggregate industry data can be obtained from such sources as *Annual Statement Studies* by the Risk Management Association or Dun & Bradstreet. These publications provide industry data with companies sorted into quartiles. Twenty-five percent of companies' ratios fall within the lowest quartile, 25 percent have ratios between the lower quartile and median value, and so on. Analysts can then determine a company's relative standing in the industry.

3.2. Common-Size Analysis

Common-size analysis involves expressing financial data, including entire financial statements, in relation to a single financial statement item, or base. Items used most frequently as the bases are total assets or revenue. In essence, common-size analysis creates a ratio between every financial statement item and the base item.

Common-size analysis was demonstrated in chapters for the income statement, balance sheet, and cash flow statement. In this section, we present common-size analysis of financial statements in greater detail and include further discussion of their interpretation.

3.2.1. Common-Size Analysis of the Balance Sheet

A vertical[5] common-size balance sheet, prepared by dividing each item on the balance sheet by the same period's total assets and expressing the results as percentages, highlights the composition of the balance sheet. What is the mix of assets being used? How is the company financing itself? How does one company's balance sheet composition compare with that of peer companies, and what is behind any differences?

A horizontal common-size balance sheet, prepared by computing the increase or decrease in percentage terms of each balance sheet item from the prior year, highlights items that have changed unexpectedly or have unexpectedly remained unchanged.

For example, Exhibit 7-2 presents a vertical common-size (partial) balance sheet for a hypothetical company in two different time periods. In this example, receivables have increased from 35 percent to 57 percent of total assets. What are possible reasons for such an increase? The increase might indicate that the company is making more of its sales on a credit basis rather than a cash basis, perhaps in response to some action taken by a competitor. Alternatively, the increase in receivables as a percentage of assets may have occurred because of a change in another current asset category, for example, a decrease in the level of inventory; the analyst would then need to investigate why that asset category had changed. Another possible reason for the increase in receivables as a percentage of assets is that the company has lowered its credit standards, relaxed its collection procedures, or adopted more aggressive revenue recognition policies. The analyst can turn to other comparisons and ratios (e.g., comparing the rate of growth in accounts receivable with the rate of growth in sales to help determine which explanation is most likely).

EXHIBIT 7-2   Vertical Common-Size (Partial) Balance Sheet for a Hypothetical Company

	Period 1 % of Total Assets	Period 2 % of Total Assets
Cash	25	15
Receivables	35	57
Inventory	35	20
Fixed assets, net of depreciation	5	8
Total assets	100	100

---

[5]The term **vertical analysis** is used to denote a common-size analysis using only one reporting period or one base financial statement, whereas **horizontal analysis** can refer either to an analysis comparing a specific financial statement with prior or future time periods or to a cross-sectional analysis of one company with another.

3.2.2. Common-Size Analysis of the Income Statement

A vertical common-size income statement divides each income statement item by revenue, or sometimes by total assets (especially in the case of financial institutions). If there are multiple revenue sources, a decomposition of revenue in percentage terms is useful. For example, Exhibit 7-3 presents a hypothetical company's vertical common-size income statement in two different time periods. Revenue is separated into the company's four services, each shown as a percentage of total revenue. In this example, revenues from Service A have become a far greater percentage of the company's total revenue (45 percent in Period 2). What are possible reasons for and implications of this change in business mix? Did the company make a strategic decision to sell more of Service A, perhaps because it is more profitable? Apparently not, because the company's earnings before interest, taxes, depreciation, and amortization (EBITDA) declined from 53 percent of sales to 45 percent, so other possible explanations should be examined. In addition, we note from the composition of operating expenses that the main reason for this decline in profitability is that salaries and employee benefits have increased from 15 percent to 25 percent of total revenue. Are more highly compensated employees required for Service A? Were higher training costs incurred in order to increase Service A revenues? If the analyst wants to predict future performance, the causes of these changes must be understood.

In addition, Exhibit 7-3 shows that the company's income tax as a percentage of sales has declined dramatically (from 15 percent to 8 percent). Furthermore, as a percentage of earnings before tax (EBT) (usually the more relevant comparison), taxes have decreased from 36 percent to 23 percent. Is Service A provided in a jurisdiction with lower tax rates? If not, what is the explanation?

EXHIBIT 7-3   Vertical Common-Size Income Statement for Hypothetical Company

	Period 1 **% of Total Revenue**	**Period 2** **% of Total Revenue**
Revenue source: Service A	30	45
Revenue source: Service B	23	20
Revenue source: Service C	30	30
Revenue source: Service D	17	5
Total revenue	**100**	**100**
Operating expenses (excluding depreciation)		
Salaries and employee benefits	15	25
Administrative expenses	22	20
Rent expense	10	10
EBITDA	**53**	**45**
Depreciation and amortization	4	4
EBIT	**49**	**41**
Interest paid	7	7
EBT	**42**	**34**
Income tax provision	15	8
Net income	**27**	**26**

EBIT = earnings before interest and tax.

The observations based on Exhibit 7-3 summarize the issues that can be raised through analysis of the vertical common-size income statement.

3.2.3. Cross-Sectional Analysis

As noted previously, ratios and common-size statements derive part of their meaning through comparison to some benchmark. **Cross-sectional analysis** (sometimes called *relative analysis*) compares a specific metric for one company with the same metric for another company or group of companies, allowing comparisons even though the companies might be of significantly different sizes and/or operate in different currencies.

Exhibit 7-4 presents a vertical common-size (partial) balance sheet for two hypothetical companies at the same point in time. Company 1 is clearly more liquid (liquidity is a function of how quickly assets can be converted into cash) than Company 2, which has only 12 percent of assets available as cash, compared with the highly liquid Company 1, where cash is 38 percent of assets. Given that cash is generally a relatively low-yielding asset and thus not a particularly efficient use of the balance sheet, why does Company 1 hold such a large percentage of total assets in cash? Perhaps the company is preparing for an acquisition, or maintains a large cash position as insulation from a particularly volatile operating environment. Another issue highlighted by the comparison in this example is the relatively high percentage of receivables in Company 2's assets, which (as discussed in section 3.2.1) may indicate a greater proportion of credit sales, overall changes in asset composition, lower credit or collection standards, or aggressive accounting policies.

3.2.4. Trend Analysis[6]

When looking at financial statements and ratios, trends in the data, whether they are improving or deteriorating, are as important as the current absolute or relative levels. Trend analysis provides important information regarding historical performance and growth and, given a sufficiently long history of accurate seasonal information, can be of great assistance as a planning and forecasting tool for management and analysts.

Exhibit 7-5A presents a partial balance sheet for a hypothetical company over five periods. The last two columns of the table show the changes for Period 5 compared with Period 4, expressed both in absolute currency (in this case, dollars) and in percentages. A small percentage

EXHIBIT 7-4   Vertical Common-Size (Partial) Balance Sheet for Two Hypothetical Companies

Assets	Company 1 % of Total Assets	Company 2 % of Total Assets
Cash	38	12
Receivables	33	55
Inventory	27	24
Fixed assets net of depreciation	1	2
Investments	1	7
Total Assets	**100**	**100**

---

[6]In financial statement analysis, the term *trend analysis* usually refers to comparisons across time periods of 3 to 10 years not involving statistical tools. This differs from the use of the term in the quantitative methods portion of the CFA curriculum, where *trend analysis* refers to statistical methods of measuring patterns in time-series data.

EXHIBIT 7-5A   Partial Balance Sheet for a Hypothetical Company over Five Periods

Assets ($ millions)	Period					Change 4 to 5 ($ million)	Change 4 to 5 (%)
	1	2	3	4	5		
Cash	39	29	27	19	16	−3	−15.8%
Investments	1	7	7	6	4	−2	−33.3%
Receivables	44	41	37	67	79	12	17.9%
Inventory	15	25	36	25	27	2	8%
Fixed assets net of depreciation	1	2	6	9	8	−1	−11.1%
Total assets	100	105	112	126	133	8	5.6%

change could hide a significant currency change and vice versa, prompting the analyst to investigate the reasons despite one of the changes being relatively small. In this example, the largest percentage change was in investments, which decreased by 33.3 percent.[7] However, an examination of the absolute currency amount of changes shows that investments changed by only $2 million, and the more significant change was the $12 million increase in receivables.

Another way to present data covering a period of time is to show each item in relation to the same item in a base year (i.e., a horizontal common-size balance sheet). Exhibit 7-5B presents the same partial balance sheet as in Exhibit 7-5A but with each item indexed relative to the same item in Period 1. For example, in Period 2, the company had $29 million cash, which is 75 percent of the amount of cash it had in Period 1, or expressed as an index relative to Period 1, 75 ($29/$39 = 0.75 × 100 = 75). Presenting data this way highlights significant changes. In this example, we see easily that the company has less than half the amount of cash in Period 1, four times the amount of investments, and eight times the amount of property, plant, and equipment.

An analysis of horizontal common-size balance sheets highlights structural changes that have occurred in a business. Past trends are obviously not necessarily an accurate predictor of the future, especially when the economic or competitive environment changes. An examination of past trends is more valuable when the macroeconomic and competitive environments are relatively stable and when the analyst is reviewing a stable or mature business. However, even in less stable contexts, historical analysis can serve as a basis for developing expectations. Understanding past trends is helpful in assessing whether these trends are likely to continue or if the trend is likely to change direction.

One measure of success is for a company to grow at a rate greater than the rate of the overall market in which it operates. Companies that grow slowly may find themselves unable to attract equity capital. Conversely, companies that grow too quickly may find that their administrative and management information systems cannot keep up with the rate of expansion.

3.2.5. Relationships among Financial Statements

Trend data generated by a horizontal common-size analysis can be compared across financial statements. For example, the growth rate of assets for the hypothetical company in

---

[7]Percentage change is calculated as: (Ending value − Beginning value)/Beginning value, or equivalently, (Ending value/Beginning value) − 1.

EXHIBIT 7-5B   Horizontal Common-Size (Partial) Balance Sheet for a Hypothetical Company over Five Periods, with Each Item Expressed Relative to the Same Item in Period One

	Period				
Assets	1	2	3	4	5
Cash	1.00	0.75	0.69	0.48	0.41
Investments	1.00	7.35	6.74	6.29	4.00
Receivables	1.00	0.93	0.84	1.52	1.79
Inventory	1.00	1.68	2.40	1.68	1.78
Fixed assets net of depreciation	1.00	2.10	5.62	8.81	8.00
Total assets	1.00	1.05	1.12	1.26	1.33

Exhibit 7-5 can be compared with the company's growth in revenue over the same period of time. If revenue is growing more quickly than assets, the company may be increasing its efficiency (i.e., generating more revenue for every dollar invested in assets).

As another example, consider the following year-over-year percentage changes for a hypothetical company:

Revenue	+20%
Net income	+25%
Operating cash flow	−10%
Total assets	+30%

Net income is growing faster than revenue, which indicates increasing profitability. However, the analyst would need to determine whether the faster growth in net income resulted from continuing operations or from nonoperating, nonrecurring items. In addition, the 10 percent decline in operating cash flow despite increasing revenue and net income clearly warrants further investigation because it could indicate a problem with earnings quality (perhaps aggressive reporting of revenue). Finally, the fact that assets have grown faster than revenue indicates the company's efficiency may be declining. The analyst should examine the composition of the increase in assets and the reasons for the changes. Example 7-4 provides a recent example of a company where comparisons of trend data from different financial statements can indicate aggressive accounting policies.

EXAMPLE 7-4   Use of Comparative Growth Information[8]

Sunbeam, a U.S. company, brought in new management to turn the company around during July 1996. For the following year, 1997, the following common-size trends were apparent:

Revenue	+ 19%
Inventory	+ 58%
Receivables	+ 38%

---

[8]Adapted from Robinson and Munter (2004, pp. 2–15).

It is generally more desirable to observe inventory and receivables growing at a slower (or similar) rate to revenue growth. Receivables' growing faster than revenue can indicate operational issues, such as lower credit standards or aggressive accounting policies for revenue recognition. Similarly, inventory growing faster than revenue can indicate an operational problem with obsolescence or aggressive accounting policies, such as an improper overstatement of inventory to increase profits.

In this case, the explanation lay in aggressive accounting policies. Sunbeam was later charged by the U.S. Securities and Exchange Commission (SEC) with improperly accelerating the recognition of revenue and engaging in other practices, such as billing customers for inventory prior to shipment.

3.3.   The Use of Graphs as an Analytical Tool

Graphs facilitate comparison of performance and financial structure over time, highlighting changes in significant aspects of business operations. In addition, graphs provide the analyst (and management) with a visual overview of risk trends in a business. Graphs may also be used effectively to communicate the analyst's conclusions regarding financial condition and risk management aspects.

Exhibit 7-6 presents the information from Exhibit 7-5A in a stacked column format. The graph makes the significant decline in cash and growth in receivables (both in absolute terms and as a percentage of assets) readily apparent.

Choosing the appropriate graph to communicate the most significant conclusions of a financial analysis is a skill. In general, pie graphs are most useful to communicate the composition of a total value (e.g., assets over a limited amount of time, say one or two periods). Line graphs are useful when the focus is on the change in amount for a limited number of

EXHIBIT 7-6   Stacked Column Graph of Asset Composition of Hypothetical Company over Five Periods

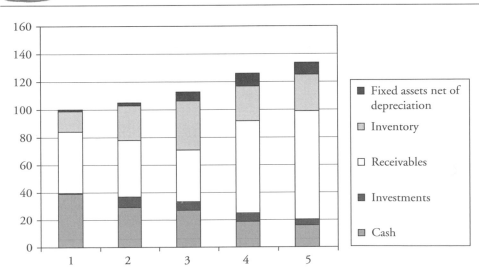

EXHIBIT 7-7   Line Graph of Growth of Assets of Hypothetical Company over Five Periods

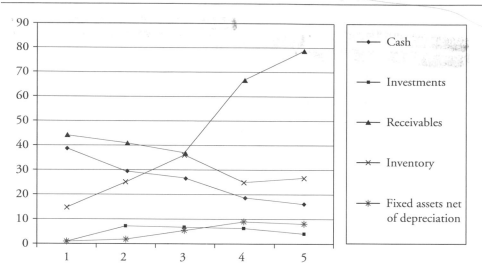

items over a relatively longer time period. When the composition and amounts, as well as their change over time, are all important, a stacked column graph can be useful.

When comparing Period 5 with Period 4, the growth in receivables appears to be within normal bounds, but when comparing Period 5 with earlier periods, the dramatic growth becomes apparent. In the same manner, a simple line graph will also illustrate the growth trends in key financial variables. Exhibit 7-7 presents the information from Exhibit 7-5 as a line graph, illustrating the growth of assets of a hypothetical company over five periods. The steady decline in cash, volatile movements of inventory, and dramatic growth of receivables is clearly illustrated.

3.4. Regression Analysis

When analyzing the trend in a specific line item or ratio, frequently it is possible simply to visually evaluate the changes. For more complex situations, regression analysis can help identify relationships (or correlation) between variables. For example, a regression analysis could relate a company's sales to gross domestic product (GDP) over time, providing insight into whether the company is cyclical. In addition, the statistical relationship between sales and GDP could be used as a basis for forecasting sales.

Other examples of such relationships are the relation between a company's sales and inventory over time, or the relation between hotel occupancy and a company's hotel revenues. In addition to providing a basis for forecasting, regression analysis facilitates identification of items or ratios that are not behaving as expected, given historical statistical relationships.

4. COMMON RATIOS USED IN FINANCIAL ANALYSIS

In the previous section, we focused on ratios resulting from common-size analysis. In this section, we expand the discussion to include other commonly used financial ratios and the broad classes into which they are categorized. There is some overlap with common-size financial

EXHIBIT 7-8   Categories of Financial Ratios

Category	Description
Activity	**Activity ratios** measure how efficiently a company performs day-to-day tasks, such as the collection of receivables and management of inventory.
Liquidity	**Liquidity ratios** measure the company's ability to meet its short-term obligations.
Solvency	**Solvency ratios** measure a company's ability to meet long-term obligations. Subsets of these ratios are also known as "leverage" and "long-term debt" ratios.
Profitability	**Profitability ratios** measure the company's ability to generate profitable sales from its resources (assets).
Valuation	**Valuation ratios** measure the quantity of an asset or flow (e.g., earnings) associated with ownership of a specified claim (e.g., a share or ownership of the enterprise).

statement ratios. For example, a common indicator of profitability is the net profit margin, which is calculated as net income divided by sales. This ratio appears on a common-size vertical income statement. Other ratios involve information from multiple financial statements or even data from outside the financial statements.

Due to the large number of ratios, it is helpful to think about ratios in terms of broad categories based on what aspects of performance a ratio is intended to detect. Financial analysts and data vendors use a variety of categories to classify ratios. The category names and the ratios included in each category can differ. Common ratio categories include activity, liquidity, solvency, and profitability. These categories are summarized in Exhibit 7-8. Each category measures a different aspect of analysis, but all are useful in evaluating a company's overall ability to generate cash flows from operating its business and the associated risks.

These categories are not mutually exclusive; some ratios are useful in measuring multiple aspects of the business. For example, an activity ratio measuring how quickly a company collects accounts receivable is also useful in assessing the company's liquidity because collection of revenues increases cash. Some profitability ratios also reflect the operating efficiency of the business. In summary, analysts appropriately use certain ratios to evaluate multiple aspects of the business. Analysts also need to be aware of variations in industry practice in the calculation of financial ratios. In the text that follows, alternative views on ratio calculations are often provided.

4.1.   Interpretation and Context

Financial ratios can only be interpreted in the context of other information, including benchmarks. In general, the financial ratios of a company are compared with those of its major competitors (cross-sectional and trend analysis) and to the company's prior periods (trend analysis). The goal is to understand the underlying causes of divergence between a company's ratios and those of the industry. Even ratios that remain consistent require understanding because consistency can sometimes indicate accounting policies selected to smooth earnings. An analyst should evaluate financial ratios based on the following:

1. *Company goals and strategy.* Actual ratios can be compared with company objectives to determine whether objectives are being attained and whether the results are consistent with the company's strategy.
2. *Industry norms (cross-sectional analysis).* A company can be compared with others in its industry by relating its financial ratios to industry norms or to a subset of the companies in an industry. When industry norms are used to make judgments, care must be taken because:
   - Many ratios are industry specific, and not all ratios are important to all industries.
   - Companies may have several different lines of business. This will cause aggregate financial ratios to be distorted. It is better to examine industry-specific ratios by lines of business.
   - Differences in accounting methods used by companies can distort financial ratios.
   - Differences in corporate strategies can affect certain financial ratios.
3. *Economic conditions.* For cyclical companies, financial ratios tend to improve when the economy is strong and weaken during recessions. Therefore, financial ratios should be examined in light of the current phase of the business cycle.

The following sections discuss activity, liquidity, solvency, and profitability ratios in turn. Selected valuation ratios are presented later in the section on equity analysis.

4.2. Activity Ratios

Activity ratios are also known as **asset utilization ratios** or **operating efficiency ratios**. This category is intended to measure how well a company manages various activities, particularly how efficiently it manages its various assets. Activity ratios are analyzed as indicators of ongoing operational performance—how effectively assets are used by a company. These ratios reflect the efficient management of both working capital and longer-term assets. As noted, efficiency has a direct impact on liquidity (the ability of a company to meet its short-term obligations), so some activity ratios are also useful in assessing liquidity.

4.2.1. Calculation of Activity Ratios

Exhibit 7-9 presents the most commonly used activity ratios. The exhibit shows the numerator and denominator of each ratio.

Activity ratios measure how efficiently the company utilizes assets. They generally combine information from the income statement in the numerator with balance sheet items in the denominator. Because the income statement measures what happened *during* a period whereas the balance sheet shows the condition only at the end of the period, average balance sheet data are normally used for consistency. For example, to measure inventory management efficiency, cost of goods sold (from the income statement) is divided by average inventory (from the balance sheet). Most databases, such as Bloomberg and Baseline, use this averaging convention when income statement and balance sheet data are combined. These databases typically average only two points: the beginning of the year and the end of the year. The examples that follow based on annual financial statements illustrate that practice. However, some analysts prefer to average more observations if they are available, especially if the business is seasonal. If a semiannual report is prepared, an average can be taken over three data

EXHIBIT 7-9   Definitions of Commonly Used Activity Ratios

Activity Ratios	Numerator	Denominator
Inventory turnover	Cost of goods sold	Average inventory
Days of inventory on hand (DOH)	Number of days in period	Inventory turnover
Receivables turnover	Revenue	Average receivables
Days of sales outstanding (DSO)	Number of days in period	Receivables turnover
Payables turnover	Purchases	Average trade payables
Number of days of payables	Number of days in period	Payables turnover
Working capital turnover	Revenue	Average working capital
Fixed asset turnover	Revenue	Average net fixed assets
Total asset turnover	Revenue	Average total assets

points (beginning, middle, and end of year). If quarterly data are available, a five-point average can be computed (beginning of year and end of each quarterly period) or a four-point average using the end of each quarterly period. Note that if the company's year ends at a low or high point for inventory for the year, there can still be bias in using three or five data points, because the beginning and end of year occur at the same time of the year and are effectively double counted.

Because cost of goods sold measures the cost of inventory that has been sold, this ratio measures how many times per year the entire inventory was theoretically turned over, or sold. (We say that the entire inventory was "theoretically" sold because in practice companies do not generally sell out their entire inventory.) If, for example, a company's cost of goods sold for a recent year was €120,000 and its average inventory was €10,000, the inventory turnover ratio would be 12. The company theoretically turns over (i.e., sells) its entire inventory 12 times per year (i.e., once a month). (Again, we say "theoretically" because in practice the company likely carries some inventory from one month into another.) Turnover can then be converted to days of inventory on hand (DOH) by dividing inventory turnover into the number of days in the accounting period. In this example, the result is a DOH of 30.42 (365/12), meaning that, on average, the company's inventory was on hand for about 30 days, or, equivalently, the company kept on hand about 30 days' worth of inventory, on average, during the period.

Activity ratios can be computed for any annual or interim period, but care must be taken in the interpretation and comparison across periods. For example, if the same company had cost of goods sold for the first quarter (90 days) of the following year of €35,000 and average inventory of €11,000, the inventory turnover would be 3.18 times. However, this turnover rate is 3.18 times per quarter, which is not directly comparable to the 12 times per year in the preceding year. In this case, we can annualize the quarterly inventory turnover rate by multiplying the quarterly turnover by 4 (12 months/3 months; or by 4.06, using 365 days/90 days) for comparison to the annual turnover rate. So, the quarterly inventory turnover is equivalent to a 12.72 annual inventory turnover (or 12.91 if we annualize the ratio using a 90-day quarter and a 365-day year). To compute the DOH using quarterly data, we can use the quarterly turnover rate and the number of days in the quarter for the numerator—or, we can use the annualized turnover rate and 365 days; either results in DOH of around 28.3, with slight differences due to rounding (90/3.18 = 28.30 and 365/12.91 = 28.27). Another time-related computational detail is that for companies using a 52/53-week annual period and for leap years, the actual days in the year should be used rather than 365.

In some cases, an analyst may want to know how many days of inventory are on hand at the end of the year rather than the average for the year. In this case, it would be appropriate to use the year-end inventory balance in the computation rather than the average. If the company is growing rapidly or if costs are increasing rapidly, analysts should consider using cost of goods sold just for the fourth quarter in this computation because the cost of goods sold of earlier quarters may not be relevant. Example 7-5 further demonstrates computation of activity ratios using Hong Kong Exchange–listed Lenovo Group Limited.

EXAMPLE 7-5   Computation of Activity Ratios

Ya-Wen Yang would like to evaluate how efficient Lenovo Group Limited is at collecting its trade accounts receivable on average during the fiscal year ended 31 March 2005. Yang has gathered the following information from Lenovo's annual and interim reports:

HK$ in Thousands	
Trade receivables as of 31 March 2004	1,230,944
Trade receivables as of 31 March 2005	851,337
Revenue for year ended 31 March 2005	22,554,678

What is Lenovo's receivables turnover and number of days of sales outstanding (DSO) for the fiscal year ended 31 March 2005?

Solution:

Receivables turnover = **Revenue/Average receivables**
                         = 22,554,678/[(1,230,944 + 851,337)/2]
                         = 22,554,678/1,041,140.50
                         = 21.6634 times
DSO   = **Number of days in period/Receivables turnover**
                         = 365/21.6634
                         = 16.85 days

On average, it took Lenovo 16.85 days to collect receivables during the fiscal year ended 31 March 2005.

4.2.2   Interpretation of Activity Ratios

In this section, we discuss the activity ratios that were defined in Exhibit 7-9.

Inventory turnover and DOH. Inventory turnover lies at the heart of operations for many entities. It indicates the resources (money) tied up in inventory (i.e., the carrying costs) and can, therefore, be used to indicate inventory management effectiveness. The higher the inventory turnover ratio, the shorter the period that inventory is held and so the lower DOH. In general, inventory turnover (and DOH) should be benchmarked against industry norms.

A high inventory turnover ratio relative to industry norms might indicate highly effective inventory management. Alternatively, a high inventory turnover ratio (and commensurately low DOH) could possibly indicate the company does not carry adequate inventory, so shortages could potentially hurt revenue. To assess which explanation is more likely, the analyst can compare the company's revenue growth with that of the industry. Slower growth combined with higher inventory turnover could indicate inadequate inventory levels. Revenue growth at or above the industry's growth supports the interpretation that the higher turnover reflects greater inventory management efficiency.

A low inventory turnover ratio (and commensurately high DOH) relative to the rest of the industry could be an indicator of slow-moving inventory, perhaps due to technological obsolescence or a change in fashion. Again, comparing the company's sales growth with the industry can offer insight.

Receivables turnover and DSO. The number of DSO represents the elapsed time between a sale and cash collection, reflecting how fast the company collects cash from customers it offers credit. Although limiting the numerator to sales made on credit would be more appropriate, credit sales information is not always available to analysts; therefore, revenue as reported in the income statement is generally used as an approximation.

A relatively high receivables turnover ratio (and commensurately low DSO) might indicate highly efficient credit and collection. Alternatively, a high receivables turnover ratio could indicate that the company's credit or collection policies are too stringent, suggesting the possibility of sales being lost to competitors offering more lenient terms. A relatively low receivables turnover ratio would typically raise questions about the efficiency of the company's credit and collections procedures. As with inventory management, comparison of the company's sales growth relative to the industry can help the analyst assess whether sales are being lost due to stringent credit policies. In addition, comparing the company's estimates of uncollectible accounts receivable and actual credit losses with past experience and with peer companies can help assess whether low turnover reflects credit management issues. Companies often provide details of receivables aging (how much receivables have been outstanding by age). This can be used along with DSO to understand trends in collection, as demonstrated in Example 7-6.

EXAMPLE 7-6   Evaluation of an Activity Ratio

Ya-Wen Yang has computed the average DSO for fiscal years ended 31 March 2004 and 2005:

	2005	2004
Days of sales outstanding	16.85	14.05

Yang would like to better understand why, on average, it took almost 17 days to collect receivables in 2005 versus 14 days in 2004. He collects accounts receivable aging information from Lenovo's annual reports and computes the percentage of accounts receivable by days outstanding. This information is presented below:

	31 March 2005		31 March 2004		31 March 2003	
	HK$000	Percent	HK$000	Percent	HK$000	Percent
0–30 days	588,389	69.11%	944,212	76.71%	490,851	88.68%
31–60 days	56,966	6.69%	84,481	6.86%	27,213	4.92%
61–90 days	40,702	4.78%	20,862	1.69%	10,680	1.93%
Over 90 days	165,280	19.41%	181,389	14.74%	24,772	4.48%
Total	851,337	100.00%	1,230,944	100.00%	553,516	100.00%

From these data, it appears that over the past three years there has been a trend of fewer receivables due within 30 days and more due for periods of longer than 90 days. Lenovo's footnotes disclose that general trade customers are provided with 30-day credit terms but that systems integration customers (consulting jobs) are given 180 days. Furthermore, the footnotes reveal that consulting revenues increased dramatically over the 2003 to 2004 period. In the third quarter of fiscal year ending 31 March 2005, Lenovo spun off its systems integration business to another company, retaining a small percentage interest. Yang concludes that the higher DSO in fiscal year ending 31 March 2005 appears to be due to the higher revenue in systems integration, which has longer credit terms. Yang may further surmise that DSO should drop in the next fiscal year since this business has been spun off.

Payables turnover and the number of days of payables. The number of days of payables reflects the average number of days the company takes to pay its suppliers, and the payables turnover ratio measures how many times per year the company theoretically pays off all its creditors. For purposes of calculating these ratios, an implicit assumption is that the company makes all its purchases using credit. If the amount of purchases is not directly available, it can be computed as cost of goods sold plus ending inventory less beginning inventory. Alternatively, cost of goods sold is sometimes used as an approximation of purchases.

A payables turnover ratio that is high (low days payable) relative to the industry could indicate that the company is not making full use of available credit facilities; alternatively, it could result from a company taking advantage of early payment discounts. An excessively low turnover ratio (high days payable) could indicate trouble making payments on time, or alternatively, exploitation of lenient supplier terms. This is another example where it is useful to look simultaneously at other ratios. If liquidity ratios indicate that the company has sufficient cash and other short-term assets to pay obligations and yet the days payable ratio is relatively high, the analyst would favor the lenient supplier credit and collection policies as an explanation.

Working capital turnover. **Working capital** is defined as current (expected to be consumed or converted into cash within one year) assets minus current liabilities. Working capital turnover indicates how efficiently the company generates revenue with its working capital. For example, a working capital turnover ratio of 4.0 indicates that the company generates €4 of revenue for every €1 of working capital. A high working capital turnover ratio indicates greater efficiency (i.e., the company is generating a high level of revenues relative to working capital). For some companies, working capital can be near zero or negative, rendering this ratio incapable of being interpreted. The following two ratios are more useful in those circumstances.

Fixed asset turnover. This ratio measures how efficiently the company generates revenues from its investments in fixed assets. Generally, a higher fixed-asset turnover ratio indicates more efficient use of fixed assets in generating revenue. A low ratio can indicate inefficiency, a capital-intensive business environment, or a new business not yet operating at full capacity—in which case the analyst will not be able to link the ratio directly to efficiency. In addition, asset turnover can be affected by factors other than a company's efficiency. The fixed-asset turnover ratio would be lower for a company whose assets are newer (and, therefore, less depreciated and so reflected in the financial statements at a higher carrying value) than the ratio for a company with older assets (that are thus more depreciated and so reflected at a lower carrying value). The fixed-asset ratio can be erratic because, although revenue may have a steady growth rate, increases in fixed assets may not follow a smooth pattern; so, every year-to-year change in the ratio does not necessarily indicate important changes in the company's efficiency.

Total asset turnover. The total asset turnover ratio measures the company's overall ability to generate revenues with a given level of assets. A ratio of 1.20 would indicate that the company is generating €1.20 of revenues for every €1 of average assets. A higher ratio indicates greater efficiency. Because this ratio includes both fixed and current assets, inefficient working capital management can distort overall interpretations. It is, therefore, helpful to analyze working capital and fixed-asset turnover ratios separately.

A low asset turnover ratio can be an indicator of inefficiency or of relative capital intensity of the business. The ratio also reflects strategic decisions by management: for example, the decision whether to use a more labor-intensive (and less capital-intensive) approach to its business or a more capital-intensive (and less labor-intensive) approach.

When interpreting activity ratios, the analysts should examine not only the individual ratios but also the collection of relevant ratios to determine the overall efficiency of a company. Example 7-7 demonstrates the evaluation of activity ratios, both narrow (e.g., number of days inventory) and broad (total asset turnover) for a Taiwanese semiconductor manufacturer.

EXAMPLE 7-7   Evaluation of Activity Ratios

United Microelectronics Corp. (UMC) is a semiconductor foundry company based in Taiwan. As part of an analysis of management's operating efficiency, an analyst collects the following activity ratios from Bloomberg:

Ratio	2004	2003	2002	2001
DOH	35.68	40.70	40.47	48.51
DSO	45.07	58.28	51.27	76.98
Total asset turnover	0.35	0.28	0.23	0.22

These ratios indicate that the company has improved on all three measures of activity over the four-year period. The company has fewer DOH, is collecting receivables faster, and is generating a higher level of revenues relative to total assets. The overall trend is good, but thus far, the analyst has only determined *what* happened. A more important question is *why* the ratios improved, because understanding good changes as well as bad ones facilitates judgments about the company's future performance. To answer this question, the analyst examines company financial reports as well as external information about the industry and economy. In examining the annual report, the analyst notes that in the fourth quarter of 2004, the company experienced an "inventory correction" and that the company recorded an allowance for the decline in market value and obsolescence of inventory of TWD 1,786,493, or about 15 percent of year-end inventory value (compared with about a 5.9 percent allowance in the prior year). This reduction in the value of inventory accounts for a large portion of the decline in DOH from 40.7 in 2003 to 35.68 in 2004. Management claims that this inventory obsolescence is a short-term issue; analysts can watch DOH in future interim periods to confirm this assertion. In any event, all else being equal, the analyst would likely expect DOH to return to a level closer to 40 days going forward.

More positive interpretations can be drawn from the total asset turnover. The analyst finds that the company's revenues increased more than 35 percent while total assets only increased by about 6 percent. Based on external information about the industry and economy, the analyst attributes the increased revenues largely to the recovery of the semiconductor industry in 2004. However, management was able to achieve this growth in revenues with a comparatively modest increase in assets, leading to an improvement in total asset turnover. Note further that part of the reason for the modest increase in assets is lower DOH and DSO.

4.3. Liquidity Ratios

Liquidity analysis, which focuses on cash flows, measures a company's ability to meet its short-term obligations. Liquidity measures how quickly assets are converted into cash. Liquidity ratios also measure the ability to pay off short-term obligations. In day-to-day operations, liquidity management is typically achieved through efficient use of assets. In the medium term, liquidity in the nonfinancial sector is also addressed by managing the structure of liabilities. (See discussion on financial sector below.)

The level of liquidity needed differs from one industry to another. A particular company's liquidity position may also vary according to the anticipated need for funds at any given time. Judging whether a company has adequate liquidity requires analysis of its historical funding requirements, current liquidity position, anticipated future funding needs, and options for reducing funding needs or attracting additional funds (including actual and potential sources of such funding).

Larger companies are usually better able to control the level and composition of their liabilities than smaller companies. Therefore, they may have more potential funding sources, including public capital and money markets. Greater discretionary access to capital markets also reduces the size of the liquidity buffer needed relative to companies without such access.

Contingent liabilities, such as letters of credit or financial guarantees, can also be relevant when assessing liquidity. The importance of contingent liabilities varies for the nonbanking and banking sector. In the nonbanking sector, contingent liabilities (usually disclosed in the footnotes to the company's financial statements) represent potential cash outflows, and when appropriate, should be included in an assessment of a company's liquidity. In the banking sector, contingent liabilities represent potentially significant cash outflows that are not dependent on the bank's financial condition. Although outflows in normal market circumstances typically may be low, a general macroeconomic or market crisis can trigger a substantial increase in cash outflows related to contingent liabilities because of the increase in defaults and business bankruptcies that often accompany such events. In addition, such crises are usually characterized by diminished levels of overall liquidity, which can further exacerbate funding shortfalls. Therefore, for the banking sector, the effect of contingent liabilities on liquidity warrants particular attention.

4.3.1. Calculation of Liquidity Ratios

Common liquidity ratios are presented in Exhibit 7-10. These liquidity ratios reflect a company's position at a point in time and, therefore, typically use data from the ending balance sheet rather than averages. The current, quick, and cash ratios reflect three measures of a company's ability to pay current liabilities. Each uses a progressively stricter definition of liquid assets.

The defensive interval ratio measures how long a company can pay its daily cash expenditures using only its existing liquid assets, without additional cash flow coming in. This ratio is similar to the "burn rate" often computed for start-up internet companies in the late 1990s or for biotechnology companies. The numerator of this ratio includes the same liquid assets used in the quick ratio, and the denominator is an estimate of daily cash expenditures. To obtain daily cash expenditures, the total of cash expenditures for the period is divided by the number of days in the period. Total cash expenditures for a period can be approximated by summing all expenses on the income statement—such as cost of goods sold; selling, general, and administrative expenses; and research and development expenses—and then subtracting any noncash expenses, such as depreciation and amortization. (Typically, taxes are not included.)

EXHIBIT 7-10   Definitions of Commonly Used Liquidity Ratios

Liquidity Ratios	Numerator	Denominator
Current ratio	Current assets	Current liabilities
Quick ratio	Cash + short-term marketable investments + receivables	Current liabilities
Cash ratio	Cash + short-term marketable investments	Current liabilities
Defensive interval ratio	Cash + short-term marketable investments + receivables	Daily cash expenditures
Additional Liquidity Measure		
Cash conversion cycle (net operating cycle)	DOH + DSO – number of days of payables	

The **cash conversion cycle**, a financial metric not in ratio form, measures the length of time required for a company to go from cash (invested in its operations) to cash received (as a result of its operations). During this period of time, the company needs to finance its investment in operations through other sources (i.e., through debt or equity).

4.3.2. Interpretation of Liquidity Ratios

In this section, we discuss the interpretation of the five basic liquidity ratios presented in Exhibit 7-10.

Current ratio. This ratio expresses current assets (assets expected to be consumed or converted into cash within one year) in relation to current liabilities (liabilities falling due within one year). A higher ratio indicates a higher level of liquidity (i.e., a greater ability to meet short-term obligations). A current ratio of 1.0 would indicate that the book value of its current assets exactly equals the book value of its current liabilities.

A lower ratio indicates less liquidity, implying a greater reliance on operating cash flow and outside financing to meet short-term obligations. Liquidity affects the company's capacity to take on debt. The current ratio implicitly assumes that inventories and accounts receivable are indeed liquid (which is presumably not the case when related turnover ratios are low).

Quick ratio. The quick ratio is more conservative than the current ratio because it includes only the more liquid current assets (sometimes referred to as "quick assets") in relation to current liabilities. Like the current ratio, a higher quick ratio indicates greater liquidity.

The quick ratio reflects the fact that certain current assets—such as prepaid expenses, some taxes, and employee-related prepayments—represent costs of the current period that have been paid in advance and cannot usually be converted back into cash. This ratio also reflects the fact that inventory might not be easily and quickly converted into cash, and furthermore, that a company would probably not be able to sell all of its inventory for an amount equal to its carrying value, especially if it were required to sell the inventory quickly. In situations where inventories are illiquid (as indicated, for example, by low inventory turnover ratios), the quick ratio may be a better indicator of liquidity than the current ratio.

Cash ratio. The cash ratio normally represents a reliable measure of an individual entity's liquidity in a crisis situation. Only highly marketable short-term investments and cash are included. In a general market crisis, the fair value of marketable securities could decrease significantly as a result of market factors, in which case even this ratio might not provide reliable information.

Defensive interval ratio. This ratio measures how long the company can continue to pay its expenses from its existing liquid assets without receiving any additional cash inflow. A defensive interval ratio of 50 would indicate that the company can continue to pay its operating expenses for 50 days before running out of quick assets, assuming no additional cash inflows. A higher defensive interval ratio indicates greater liquidity. If a company's defensive interval ratio is very low relative to peer companies or to the company's own history, the analyst would want to ascertain whether there is sufficient cash inflow expected to mitigate the low defensive interval ratio.

Cash conversion cycle (net operating cycle). This metric indicates the amount of time that elapses from the point when a company invests in working capital until the point at which the company collects cash. In the typical course of events, a merchandising company acquires inventory on credit, incurring accounts payable. The company then sells that inventory on credit, increasing accounts receivable. Afterwards, it pays out cash to settle its accounts payable, and it collects cash in settlement of its accounts receivable. The time between the outlay of cash and the collection of cash is called the *cash conversion cycle*. A shorter cash conversion cycle indicates greater liquidity. The short cash conversion cycle implies that the company needs to finance its inventory and accounts receivable for only a short period of time. A longer cash conversion cycle indicates lower liquidity; it implies that the company must finance its inventory and accounts receivable for a longer period of time, possibly indicating a need for a higher level of capital to fund current assets. Example 7-8 demonstrates the advantages of a short cash conversion cycle as well as how a company's business strategies are reflected in financial ratios.

EXAMPLE 7-8   Evaluation of Liquidity Ratios

An analyst is evaluating the liquidity of Dell and finds that Dell provides a computation of the number of days of receivables, inventory, and accounts payable, as well as the overall cash conversion cycle, as follows:

Fiscal Year Ended	28 Jan 2005	30 Jan 2004	31 Jan 2003
DSO	32	31	28
DOH	4	3	3
Less: Number of days of payables	73	70	68
Equals: Cash conversion cycle	(37)	(36)	(37)

The minimal DOH indicates that Dell maintains lean inventories, which is attributable to key aspects of the company's business model—namely, the company does not build a computer until it is ordered. Furthermore, Dell has a sophisticated just-in-time manufacturing system. In isolation, the increase in number of days payable (from 68 days in 2003 to 73 days in 2005) might suggest an inability to pay suppliers; however, in Dell's case, the balance sheet indicates that the company has almost $10 billion of cash and short-term investments, which would be more than enough to pay suppliers sooner if Dell chose to do so. Instead, Dell takes advantage of the favorable credit terms granted by its suppliers. The overall effect is a negative cash cycle, a somewhat unusual result. Instead of requiring additional capital to fund working capital as is the case for most companies, Dell has excess cash to invest for about 37 days (reflected on the balance sheet as short-term investments) on which it is earning, rather than paying, interest.

For comparison, the analyst computes the cash conversion cycle for three of Dell's competitors:

Fiscal Year	2004	2003	2002
HP Compaq	27	37	61
Gateway	(7)	(9)	(3)
Apple	(40)	(41)	(40)

The analyst notes that of the group, only HP Compaq has to raise capital for working capital purposes. Dell is outperforming HP Compaq and Gateway on this metric, its negative cash conversion cycle of minus 37 days indicating stronger liquidity than either of those two competitors. Apple, however, is slightly more liquid than Dell, evidenced by its slightly more negative cash conversion cycle, and Apple also has a similarly stable negative cash conversion cycle.

4.4. Solvency Ratios

Solvency refers to a company's ability to fulfill its long-term debt obligations. Assessment of a company's ability to pay its long-term obligations (i.e., to make interest and principal payments) generally includes an in-depth analysis of the components of its financial structure. Solvency ratios provide information regarding the relative amount of debt in the company's capital structure and the adequacy of earnings and cash flow to cover interest expenses and other fixed charges (such as lease or rental payments) as they come due.

Analysts seek to understand a company's use of debt for several main reasons. One reason is that the amount of debt in a company's capital structure is important for assessing the company's risk and return characteristics, specifically its financial leverage. Leverage is a magnifying effect that results from the use of **fixed costs**—costs that stay the same within some range of activity—and can take two forms: **operating leverage** and **financial leverage**. Operating leverage results from the use of fixed costs in conducting the company's business. Operating leverage magnifies the effect of changes in sales on operating income. Profitable companies may use operating leverage because when revenues increase, with operating leverage, their operating income increases at a faster rate. The explanation is that, although **variable costs** will rise proportionally with revenue, fixed costs will not. When financing a firm (i.e., raising capital for it), the use of debt constitutes financial leverage because interest payments are essentially fixed financing costs. As a result of interest payments, a given percent change in EBIT results in a larger percent change in earnings before taxes (EBT). Thus, financial leverage tends to magnify the effect of changes in EBIT on returns flowing to equity holders. Assuming that a company can earn more on the funds than it pays in interest, the inclusion of some level of debt in a company's capital structure may lower a company's overall cost of capital and increase returns to equity holders. However, a higher level of debt in a company's capital structure increases the risk of default and results in higher borrowing costs for the company to compensate lenders for assuming greater credit risk. Starting with Modigliani and Miller (1958, 1963), a substantial amount of research has focused on a company's optimal capital structure and the subject remains an important one in corporate finance. In analyzing financial statements, an analyst aims to understand levels and trends in a company's use of financial leverage in relation to past practices and the practices of peer companies. Analysts also need to be aware of the relationship between operating leverage and financial leverage. The greater a company's use of operating leverage, the greater the risk of the operating income stream available to cover debt payments; operating leverage can thus limit a company's capacity to use financial leverage.

A company's relative solvency is fundamental to valuation of its debt securities and its creditworthiness. Finally, understanding a company's use of debt can provide analysts with insight into the company's future business prospects because management's decisions about financing often signal their beliefs about a company's future.

4.4.1. Calculation of Solvency Ratios

Solvency ratios are primarily of two types. Debt ratios, the first type, focus on the balance sheet and measure the amount of debt capital relative to equity capital. Coverage ratios, the second type, focus on the income statement and measure the ability of a company to cover its debt payments. All of these ratios are useful in assessing a company's solvency and, therefore, in evaluating the quality of a company's bonds and other debt obligations.

Exhibit 7-11 describes commonly used solvency ratios. The first three of the debt ratios presented use total debt in the numerator. The definition of total debt used in these

EXHIBIT 7-11   Definitions of Commonly Used Solvency Ratios

Solvency Ratios	Numerator	Denominator
Debt ratios		
Debt-to-assets ratio[a]	Total debt[b]	Total assets
Debt-to-capital ratio	Total debt[b]	Total debt[b] + Total shareholders' equity
Debt-to-equity ratio	Total debt[b]	Total shareholders' equity
Financial leverage ratio	Average total assets	Average total equity
Coverage ratios		
Interest coverage	EBIT	Interest payments
Fixed charge coverage	EBIT + lease payments	Interest payments + lease payments

[a]*Total debt ratio* is another name sometimes used for this ratio.
[b]In this chapter, we take total debt in this context to be the sum of interest-bearing short-term and long-term debt.

ratios varies among informed analysts and financial data vendors, with some using the total of interest-bearing short-term and long-term debt, excluding liabilities such as accrued expenses and accounts payable. (For calculations in this chapter, we use this definition.) Other analysts use definitions that are more inclusive (e.g., all liabilities) or restrictive (e.g., long-term debt only, in which case the ratio is sometimes qualified as "long-term," as in "long-term debt-to-equity ratio"). If using different definitions of total debt materially changes conclusions about a company's solvency, the reasons for the discrepancies warrant further investigation.

4.4.2.   Interpretation of Solvency Ratios

In this section, we discuss the interpretation of the basic solvency ratios presented in Exhibit 7-11.

Debt-to-assets ratio. This ratio measures the percentage of total assets financed with debt. For example, a debt-to-assets ratio of 0.40 or 40 percent indicates that 40 percent of the company's assets are financed with debt. Generally, higher debt means higher financial risk and thus weaker solvency.

Debt-to-capital ratio. The debt-to-capital ratio measures the percentage of a company's capital (debt plus equity) represented by debt. As with the previous ratio, a higher ratio generally means higher financial risk and thus indicates weaker solvency.

Debt-to-equity ratio. The debt-to-equity ratio measures the amount of debt capital relative to equity capital. Interpretation is similar to the preceding two ratios (i.e., a higher ratio indicates weaker solvency). A ratio of 1.0 would indicate equal amounts of debt and equity, which is equivalent to a debt-to-capital ratio of 50 percent. Alternative definitions of this ratio use the market value of stockholders' equity rather than its book value (or use the market values of both stockholders' equity and debt).

Financial leverage ratio. This ratio (often called simply the *leverage ratio*) measures the amount of total assets supported for each one money unit of equity. For example, a value of 3 for this ratio means that each €1 of equity supports €3 of total assets. The higher the financial leverage ratio, the more leveraged the company is in the sense of using debt and other liabilities to finance assets. This ratio is often defined in terms of average total assets and average total equity and plays an important role in the DuPont decomposition of return on equity that will be presented in section 4.6.2.

Interest coverage. This ratio measures the number of times a company's EBIT could cover its interest payments. A higher interest coverage ratio indicates stronger solvency, offering greater assurance that the company can service its debt (i.e., bank debt, bonds, notes) from operating earnings.

Fixed charge coverage. This ratio relates fixed charges, or obligations, to the cash flow generated by the company. It measures the number of times a company's earnings (before interest, taxes, and lease payments) can cover the company's interest and lease payments.[9] Similar to the interest coverage ratio, a higher fixed charge coverage ratio implies stronger solvency, offering greater assurance that the company can service its debt (i.e., bank debt, bonds, notes, and leases) from normal earnings. The ratio is sometimes used as an indication of the quality of the preferred dividend, with a higher ratio indicating a more secure preferred dividend.

Example 7-9 demonstrates the use of solvency ratios in evaluating the creditworthiness of a company.

EXAMPLE 7-9   Evaluation of Solvency Ratios

A credit analyst is evaluating the solvency of Alcatel (now known as Alcatel-Lucent) as of the beginning of 2005. The following data are gathered from the company's 2005 annual report (in € millions):

	2004	2003
Total equity	4,389	4,038
Accrued pension	1,144	1,010
Other reserves	2,278	3,049
Total financial debt	4,359	5,293
Other liabilities	6,867	7,742
Total assets	19,037	21,132

The analyst concludes that, as used by Alcatel in its 2005 annual report, "total financial debt" consists of noncurrent debt and the interest-bearing, borrowed portion of current liabilities.

1. A. Calculate the company's financial leverage ratio for 2004.
   B. Interpret the financial leverage ratio calculated in Part A.
2. A. What are the company's debt-to-assets, debt-to-capital, and debt-to-equity ratios for the two years?
   B. Is there any discernable trend over the two years?

---

[9]For computing this ratio, an assumption sometimes made is that one-third of the lease payment amount represents interest on the lease obligation and that the rest is a repayment of principal on the obligation. For this variant of the fixed charge coverage ratio, the numerator is EBIT plus one-third of lease payments and the denominator is interest payments plus one-third of lease payments.

Solutions to 1:

A. Average total assets was $(19,037 + 21,132)/2 = 20,084.50$ and average total equity was $(4,389 + 4,038)/2 = 4,213.5$. Thus, financial leverage was $20,084.50/4,213.5 = 4.77$.

B. For 2004, every €1 in total equity supported €4.77 in total assets, on average.

Solutions to 2:

A. Debt-to-assets for 2003 $= 5,293/21,132 = 25.05\%$
Debt-to-assets for 2004 $= 4,359/19,037 = 22.90\%$
Debt-to-capital for 2003 $= 5,293/(5,293 + 4,038) = 56.72\%$
Debt-to-capital for 2004 $= 4,359/(4,359 + 4,389) = 49.83\%$
Debt-to-equity for 2003 $= 5,293/4,038 = 1.31$
Debt-to-equity for 2004 $= 4,359/4,389 = 0.99$

B. On all three metrics, the company's level of debt has declined. This decrease in debt as part of the company's capital structure indicates that the company's solvency has improved. From a creditor's perspective, higher solvency (lower debt) indicates lower risk of default on obligations.

4.5. Profitability Ratios

The ability to generate profit on capital invested is a key determinant of a company's overall value and the value of the securities it issues. Consequently, many equity analysts would consider profitability to be a key focus of their analytical efforts.

Profitability reflects a company's competitive position in the market, and by extension, the quality of its management. The income statement reveals the sources of earnings and the components of revenue and expenses. Earnings can be distributed to shareholders or reinvested in the company. Reinvested earnings enhance solvency and provide a cushion against short-term problems.

4.5.1. Calculation of Profitability Ratios

Profitability ratios measure the return earned by the company during a period. Exhibit 7-12 provides the definitions of a selection of commonly used profitability ratios. Return-on-sales profitability ratios express various subtotals on the income statement (e.g., gross profit, operating profit, net profit) as a percentage of revenue. Essentially, these ratios constitute part of a common-size income statement discussed earlier. Return on investment profitability ratios measure income relative to assets, equity, or total capital employed by the company. For operating ROA, returns are measured as operating income (i.e., prior to deducting interest on debt capital). For ROA and ROE, returns are measured as net income (i.e., after deducting interest paid on debt capital). For return on common equity, returns are measured as net income minus preferred dividends (because preferred dividends are a return to preferred equity).

EXHIBIT 7-12   Definitions of Commonly Used Profitability Ratios

Profitability Ratios	Numerator	Denominator
Return on Sales[10]		
Gross profit margin	Gross profit	Revenue
Operating profit margin	Operating income[11]	Revenue
Pretax margin	EBT (earnings before tax but after interest)	Revenue
Net profit margin	Net income	Revenue
Return on Investment		
Operating ROA	Operating income	Average total assets
ROA	Net income	Average total assets
Return on total capital	EBIT	Short- and long-term debt and equity
ROE	Net income	Average total equity
Return on common equity	Net income—Preferred dividends	Average common equity

4.5.2. Interpretation of Profitability Ratios

In the following, we discuss the interpretation of the profitability ratios presented in Exhibit 7-12. For each of the profitability ratios, a higher ratio indicates greater profitability.

Gross profit margin. Gross profit margin indicates the percentage of revenue available to cover operating and other expenditures. Higher gross profit margin indicates some combination of higher product pricing and lower product costs. The ability to charge a higher price is constrained by competition, so gross profits are affected by (and usually inversely related to) competition. If a product has a competitive advantage (e.g., superior branding, better quality, or exclusive technology), the company is better able to charge more for it. On the cost side, higher gross profit margin can also indicate that a company has a competitive advantage in product costs.

Operating profit margin. Operating profit is calculated as gross margin minus operating costs. So, an operating margin increasing faster than the gross margin can indicate improvements in controlling operating costs, such as administrative overheads. In contrast, a declining operating profit margin could be an indicator of deteriorating control over operating costs.

Pretax margin. Pretax income (also called *earnings before tax*) is calculated as operating profit minus interest, so this ratio reflects the effects on profitability of leverage and other

---

[10]*Sales* is being used as a synonym for *revenue*.

[11]Some analysts use EBIT as a shortcut representation of operating income. Note that EBIT, strictly speaking, includes nonoperating items such as dividends received and gains and losses on investment securities. Of utmost importance is that the analyst compute ratios consistently whether comparing different companies or analyzing one company over time.

(nonoperating) income and expenses. If a company's pretax margin is rising primarily as a result of increasing nonoperating income, the analyst should evaluate whether this increase reflects a deliberate change in a company's business focus and, therefore, the likelihood that the increase will continue.

Net profit margin. Net profit, or net income, is calculated as revenue minus all expenses. Net income includes both recurring and nonrecurring components. Generally, the net profit margin adjusted for nonrecurring items offers a better view of a company's potential future profitability.

ROA. ROA measures the return earned by a company on its assets. The higher the ratio, the more income is generated by a given level of assets. Most databases compute this ratio as:

$$\frac{\text{Net income}}{\text{Average total assets}}$$

The problem with this computation is net income is the return to equity holders, whereas assets are financed by both equity holders and creditors. Interest expense (the return to creditors) has already been subtracted in the numerator. Some analysts, therefore, prefer to add back interest expense in the numerator. In such cases, interest must be adjusted for income taxes because net income is determined after taxes. With this adjustment, the ratio would be computed as:

$$\frac{\text{Net income} + \text{Interest expense }(1 - \text{Tax rate})}{\text{Average total assets}}$$

Alternatively, some analysts elect to compute ROA on a pre-interest and pretax basis as:

$$\frac{\text{Operating income of EBIT}}{\text{Average total assets}}$$

As noted, returns are measured prior to deducting interest on debt capital (i.e., as operating income or EBIT). This measure reflects the return on all assets invested in the company, whether financed with liabilities, debt, or equity. Whichever form of ROA is chosen, the analyst must use it consistently in comparisons to other companies or time periods.

Return on total capital. Return on total capital measures the profits a company earns on all of the capital that it employs (short-term debt, long-term debt, and equity). As with ROA, returns are measured prior to deducting interest on debt capital (i.e., as operating income or EBIT).

ROE. ROE measures the return earned by a company on its equity capital, including minority equity, preferred equity, and common equity. As noted, return is measured as net income (i.e., interest on debt capital is not included in the return on equity capital). A variation of ROE is return on common equity, which measures the return earned by a company only on its common equity.

Both ROA and ROE are important measures of profitability and will be explored in more detail below. As with other ratios, profitability ratios should be evaluated individually and as a group to gain an understanding of what is driving profitability (operating versus nonoperating activities). Example 7-10 demonstrates the evaluation of profitability ratios and the use of management's discussion that accompanies financial statements to explain the trend in ratios.

EXAMPLE 7-10   Evaluation of Profitability Ratios.

An analyst is evaluating the profitability of DaimlerChrysler (NYSE: DCX) over a recent three-year period and collects the following profitability ratios:

	2004	2003	2002
Gross profit margin	19.35%	19.49%	18.99%
Operating profit margin	3.19%	2.83%	3.35%
Pretax margin	2.49%	0.44%	4.06%
Net profit margin	1.74%	0.33%	3.15%

DCX's 2003 annual report indicates that revenue declined in 2003. Furthermore, management's discussion of results in that report notes the following:

> General administrative expenses of €5.4 billion remained virtually flat on the prior-year level. General administrative expenses as a percentage of revenues were 3.9 percent in 2003 and 3.6 percent in 2002, reflecting the limited variability of these expenses. Slightly higher personnel expenses, primarily caused by higher net periodic pension and postretirement benefit costs, resulted in a moderate increase of general administrative expenses.

1. Contrast gross profit margins and operating profit margins over 2002 to 2004.
2. Explain the decline in operating profit margin in 2003.
3. Explain why the pretax margin might decrease to a greater extent than the operating profit margin in 2003.
4. Compare and contrast net profit margins and pretax margins over 2002 to 2004.

Solution to 1. Gross margin improved from 2002 to 2003 as a result of some combination of price increases and/or cost control. However, gross margin declined slightly in 2004. Operating profit margin, on the other hand, declined from 2002 to 2003, and then improved in 2004.

Solution to 2. The decline in operating profit from 3.35 percent in 2002 to 2.83 percent in 2003 appears to be the result of DCX's operating leverage, discussed in management's discussion. Revenue declined in 2003 but, according to management, general administrative expenses were virtually flat compared with 2002. These expenses thus increased as a proportion of revenue in 2003, lowering the operating profit margin. This is an example of the effects of fixed cost on profitability. In general, as revenues rise, to the extent that costs remain fixed, operating margins should increase. However, if revenue declines, the opposite occurs.

Solution to 3. Pretax margin was down substantially in 2003, indicating that the company may have had some nonoperating losses or high interest expense in that year. A review of the company's financial statement footnotes confirms that the cause was nonoperating losses: Specifically, the company had a significant impairment loss on investments in 2003.

Solution to 4. Net profit margin followed the same pattern as pretax margin, declining substantially in 2003, then improving in 2004 but not reaching 2002 levels. In the absence of major variation in the applicable tax rates, this would be the expected as net income is EBT (1 − tax rate).

4.6. Integrated Financial Ratio Analysis

In prior sections, the text presented separately activity, liquidity, solvency, and profitability ratios. In the following, we illustrate the importance of examining a portfolio of ratios, not a single ratio or category of ratios in isolation, to ascertain the overall position and performance of a company. Experience shows that the information from one ratio category can be helpful in answering questions raised by another category and that the most accurate overall picture comes from integrating information from all sources. Section 4.6.1 provides some introductory examples of such analysis, and section 4.6.2 shows how return on equity can be analyzed into components related to profit margin, asset utilization (activity), and financial leverage.

4.6.1. The Overall Ratio Picture: Examples

This section presents two simple illustrations to introduce the use of a portfolio of ratios to address an analytical task. Example 7-11 shows how the analysis of a pair of activity ratios resolves an issue concerning a company's liquidity. Example 7-12 shows that examining the overall ratios of multiple companies can assist an analyst in drawing conclusions about their relative performances.

EXAMPLE 7-11   A Portfolio of Ratios

An analyst is evaluating the liquidity of a Canadian manufacturing company and obtains the following liquidity ratios:

	2005	2004	2003
Current ratio	2.1	1.9	1.6
Quick ratio	0.8	0.9	1.0

The ratios present a contradictory picture of the company's liquidity. Based on the increase in its current ratio from 1.6 to 2.1, the company appears to have strong and improving liquidity; however, based on the decline of the quick ratio from 1.0 to 0.8, its liquidity appears to be deteriorating. Because both ratios have exactly the same denominator, current liabilities, the difference must be the result of changes in some asset that is included in the current ratio but not in the quick ratio (e.g., inventories). The analyst collects the following activity ratios:

DOH	55	45	30
DSO	24	28	30

The company's DOH has deteriorated from 30 days to 55 days, meaning that the company is holding increasingly greater amounts of inventory relative to sales. The decrease in DSO implies that the company is collecting receivables faster. If the proceeds from these collections were held as cash, there would be no effect on either the current ratio or the quick ratio. However, if the proceeds from the collections were used to purchase inventory, there would be no effect on the current ratio and a decline in the quick ratio (i.e., the pattern shown in this example). Collectively, the ratios suggest that liquidity is declining and that the company may have an inventory problem that needs to be addressed.

EXAMPLE 7-12   A Comparison of Two Companies (1).

An analyst collects the following information for two companies:

	2005	2004	2003	2002
Anson Industries				
Inventory turnover	76.69	89.09	147.82	187.64
DOH	4.76	4.10	2.47	1.95
Receivables turnover	10.75	9.33	11.14	7.56
DSO	33.95	39.13	32.77	48.29
Accounts payable turnover	4.62	4.36	4.84	4.22
Days payable	78.97	83.77	75.49	86.56
Cash from operations/Total liabilities	31.41%	11.15%	4.04%	8.81%
ROE	5.92%	1.66%	1.62%	−0.62%
ROA	3.70%	1.05%	1.05%	−0.39%
Net profit margin (Net income/Revenue)	3.33%	1.11%	1.13%	−0.47%
Total asset turnover (Revenue/Average assets)	1.11	0.95	0.93	0.84
Leverage (Average assets/Average equity)	1.60	1.58	1.54	1.60
Clarence Corporation				
Inventory turnover	9.19	9.08	7.52	14.84
DOH	39.73	40.20	48.51	24.59
Receivables turnover	8.35	7.01	6.09	5.16
DSO	43.73	52.03	59.92	70.79
Accounts payable turnover	6.47	6.61	7.66	6.52
Days payable	56.44	55.22	47.64	56.00
Cash from operations/Total liabilities	13.19%	16.39%	15.80%	11.79%
ROE	9.28%	6.82%	−3.63%	−6.75%
ROA	4.64%	3.48%	−1.76%	3.23%
Net profit margin (Net income/Revenue)	4.38%	3.48%	−1.60%	−2.34%
Total asset turnover (Revenue/Average assets)	1.06	1.00	1.10	1.38
Leverage (Average assets/Average equity)	2.00	1.96	2.06	2.09

Which of the following choices best describes reasonable conclusions an analyst might make about the companies' efficiency?

A. Over the past four years, Anson has shown greater improvement in efficiency than Clarence, as indicated by its total asset turnover ratio increasing from 0.84 to 1.11.

B. In 2004, Anson's DOH of only 4.76 indicated that it was less efficient at inventory management than Clarence, which had DOH of 39.73.

C. In 2004, Clarence's receivables turnover of 8.35 times indicated that it was more efficient at receivables management than Anson, which had receivables turnover of 10.75.

D. Over the past four years, Clarence has shown greater improvement in efficiency than Anson, as indicated by its net profit margin of 4.38 percent.

Solution. A is correct. Over the past four years, Anson has shown greater improvement in efficiency than Clarence, as indicated by its total asset turnover ratio increasing from 0.84 to 1.11. Over the same period of time, Clarence's total asset turnover ratio has declined from 1.38 to 1.06. Choice B is incorrect because it misinterprets DOH. Choice C is incorrect because it misinterprets receivables turnover. Choice D is incorrect because net profit margin is not an indicator of efficiency.

4.6.2. DuPont Analysis: The Decomposition of ROE

As noted earlier, ROE measures the return a company generates on its equity capital. To understand what drives a company's ROE, a useful technique is to decompose ROE into its component parts. (Decomposition of ROE is sometimes referred to as **DuPont analysis** because it was developed originally at that company.) Decomposing ROE involves expressing the basic ratio (i.e., net income divided by average shareholders' equity) as the product of component ratios. Because each of these component ratios is an indicator of a distinct aspect of a company's performance that affects ROE, the decomposition allows us to evaluate how these different aspects of performance affected the company's profitability as measured by ROE.[12]

Decomposing ROE is useful in determining the reasons for changes in ROE over time for a given company and for differences in ROE for different companies in a given time period. The information gained can also be used by management to determine which areas they should focus on to improve ROE. This decomposition will also show why a company's overall profitability, measured by ROE, is a function of its efficiency, operating profitability, taxes, and use of financial leverage. DuPont analysis shows the relationship between the various categories of ratios discussed in this chapter and how they all influence the return to the investment of the owners.

Analysts have developed several different methods of decomposing ROE. The decomposition presented here is one of the most commonly used and the one found in popular research databases, such as Bloomberg. Return on equity is calculated as:

$$\text{ROE} = \frac{\text{Net income}}{\text{Average shareholders' equity}}$$

---

[12]For purposes of analyzing ROE, this method usually uses average balance sheet factors; however, the math will work out if beginning or ending balances are used throughout. For certain purposes, these alternative methods may be appropriate. See Stowe et al. (2002, pp. 85–88).

The decomposition of ROE makes use of simple algebra and illustrates the relationship between ROE and ROA. Expressing ROE as a product of only two of its components, we can write:

$$ROE = \frac{\text{Net income}}{\text{Average shareholders' equity}} = \frac{\text{Net income}}{\text{Average total assets}} \times \frac{\text{Average total assets}}{\text{Average shareholders' equity}}$$

$$(7\text{-}1a)$$

which can be interpreted as:

$$ROE = ROA \times \text{Leverage}$$

In other words, ROE is a function of a company's ROA and its use of financial leverage ("leverage" for short, in this discussion). A company can improve its ROE by improving ROA or making more effective use of leverage. Consistent with the definition given earlier, leverage is measured as average total assets divided by average shareholders' equity. If a company had no leverage (no liabilities), its leverage ratio would equal 1.0 and ROE would exactly equal ROA. As a company takes on liabilities, its leverage increases. As long as a company is able to borrow at a rate lower than the marginal rate it can earn investing the borrowed money in its business, the company is making an effective use of leverage and ROE would increase as leverage increases. If a company's borrowing cost exceeds the marginal rate it can earn on investing, ROE would decline as leverage increased because the effect of borrowing would be to depress ROA.

Using the data from Example 7-12 for Anson Industries, an analyst can examine the trend in ROE and determine whether the increase from an ROE of -0.625 percent in 2002 to 5.925 percent in 2005 is a function of ROA or the use of leverage:

	ROE =	ROA ×	Leverage
2005	5.92%	3.70%	1.60
2004	1.66%	1.05%	1.58
2003	1.62%	1.05%	1.54
2002	−0.62%	−0.39%	1.60

Over the four-year period, the company's leverage factor was relatively stable. The primary reason for the increase in ROE is the increase in profitability measured by ROA.

Just as ROE can be decomposed, the individual components such as ROA can be decomposed. Further decomposing ROA, we can express ROE as a product of three component ratios:

$$\frac{\text{Net income}}{\text{Averages shareholders' equity}} = \frac{\text{Net income}}{\text{Revenue}} \times \frac{\text{Revenue}}{\text{Average total assets}}$$
$$\times \frac{\text{Average total assets}}{\text{Average shareholders' equity}} \qquad (7\text{-}1b)$$

which can be interpreted as:

$$ROE = \text{Net profit margin} \times \text{Asset turnover} \times \text{Leverage}$$

The first term on the right-hand side of this equation is the net profit margin, an indicator of profitability: how much income a company derives per one money unit (e.g., euro or dollar) of sales. The second term on the right is the asset turnover ratio, an indicator of efficiency: how much revenue a company generates per one money unit of assets. Note that ROA is decomposed into these two components: net profit margin and asset turnover. A company's ROA is a function of profitability (net profit margin) and efficiency (asset turnover). The third term on the right-hand side of Equation 7-1b is a measure of financial leverage, an indicator of solvency: the total amount of a company's assets relative to its equity capital. This decomposition illustrates that a company's ROE is a function of its net profit margin, its efficiency, and its leverage. Again, using the data from Example 7-12 for Anson Industries, the analyst can evaluate in more detail the reasons behind the trend in ROE:[13]

	ROE =	Net Profit Margin ×	Asset Turnover ×	Leverage
2005	5.92%	3.33%	1.11	1.60
2004	1.66%	1.11%	0.95	1.58
2003	1.62%	1.13%	0.93	1.54
2002	−0.62%	−0.47%	0.84	1.60

This further decomposition confirms that increases in profitability (measured here as net profit margin) are indeed an important contributor to the increase in ROE over the four-year period. However, Anson's asset turnover has also increased steadily. The increase in ROE is, therefore, a function of improving profitability and improving efficiency. As noted above, ROE decomposition can also be used to compare the ROEs of peer companies, as demonstrated in Example 7-13.

EXAMPLE 7-13   A Comparison of Two Companies (2)

Referring to the data for Anson Industries and Clarence Corporation in Example 7-12, which of the following choices best describes reasonable conclusions an analyst might make about the companies' ROE?

A. Anson's inventory turnover of 76.69 indicates it is more profitable than Clarence.
B. The main drivers of Clarence's superior ROE in 2004 are its greater use of debt financing and higher net profit margin.
C. The main driver of Clarence's superior ROE in 2004 is its more efficient use of assets.
D. Anson's days payable of 78.97 indicates it is more profitable than Clarence.

Solution. B is correct. The main driver of Clarence's superior ROE (9.29 percent compared with only 5.94 percent for Anson) in 2004 is its greater use of debt financing (leverage of 2.00 compared with Anson's leverage of 1.60) and higher net profit margin (4.38 percent compared with only 3.33 percent for Anson). A and D are incorrect because neither inventory turnover nor days payable is an indicator of profitability. C is incorrect because Clarence has less-efficient use of assets than Anson, indicated by turnover of 1.06 for Clarence compared with Anson's turnover of 1.11.

---

[13]Please note that ratios are expressed in terms of two decimal places and are rounded. Therefore, ROE may not be the exact product of the three ratios.

To separate the effects of taxes and interest, we can further decompose the net profit margin and write:

$$\frac{\text{Net income}}{\text{Average shareholder' equity}} = \frac{\text{Net income}}{\text{EBT}} \times \frac{\text{EBT}}{\text{EBIT}} \times \frac{\text{EBIT}}{\text{Revenue}} \times \frac{\text{Revenue}}{\text{Average total assets}}$$
$$\times \frac{\text{Average total assets}}{\text{Average shareholders' equity}} \qquad (7\text{-}1c)$$

which can be interpreted as:

ROE = Tax burden × Interest burden × EBIT margin × Asset turnover × Leverage

This five-way decomposition is the one found in financial databases such as Bloomberg. The first term on the right-hand side of this equation measures the effect of taxes on ROE. Essentially, it reflects one minus the average tax rate, or how much of a company's pretax profits it gets to keep. This can be expressed in decimal or percentage form. So, a 30 percent tax rate would yield a factor of 0.70 or 70 percent. A higher value for the tax burden implies that the company can keep a higher percentage of its pretax profits, indicating a lower tax rate. A decrease in the tax burden ratio implies the opposite (i.e., a higher tax rate leaving the company with less of its pretax profits).

The second term on the right-hand side captures the effect of interest on ROE. Higher borrowing costs reduce ROE. Some analysts prefer to use operating income instead of EBIT for this factor and the following one (consistency is required!). In such a case, the second factor would measure both the effect of interest expense and nonoperating income.

The third term on the right-hand side captures the effect of operating margin (if operating income is used in the numerator) or EBIT margin (if EBIT is used) on ROE. In either case, this factor primarily measures the effect of operating profitability on ROE.

The fourth term on the right-hand side is again the asset turnover ratio, an indicator of the overall efficiency of the company (i.e., how much revenue it generates per unit of assets). The fifth term on the right-hand side is the financial leverage ratio described above—the total amount of a company's assets relative to its equity capital.

This decomposition expresses a company's ROE as a function of its tax rate, interest burden, operating profitability, efficiency, and leverage. An analyst can use this framework to determine what factors are driving a company's ROE. The decomposition of ROE can also be useful in forecasting ROE based upon expected efficiency, profitability, financing activities, and tax rates. The relationship of the individual factors, such as ROA to the overall ROE, can also be expressed in the form of an ROE tree to study the contribution of each of the five factors, as shown in Exhibit 7-13 for Anson Industries.[14]

Exhibit 7-13 shows that Anson's ROE of 5.92 percent in 2005 can be decomposed into ROA of 3.7 percent and leverage of 1.60. ROA can further be decomposed into a net profit margin of 3.33 percent and total asset turnover of 1.11. Net profit margin can be decomposed into a tax burden of 0.70 (an average tax rate of 30 percent), an interest burden of 0.90, and an EBIT margin of 5.29 percent. Overall ROE is decomposed into five components.

Example 7-14 demonstrates how the five-component decomposition can be used to determine reasons behind the trend in a company's ROE.

---

[14]Note that a breakdown of net profit margin was not provided in Example 7-12, but is added here.

EXHIBIT 7-13   DuPont Analysis of Anson Industries' ROE: 2005

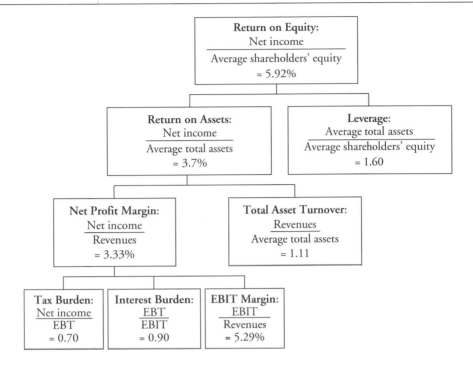

EXAMPLE 7-14   Five-Way Decomposition of ROE

An analyst examining BP PLC (BP) wishes to understand the factors driving the trend in ROE over a recent three-year period. The analyst obtains the following data from Bloomberg and ascertains that Bloomberg has included nonoperating income in the interest burden factor:

	2004	2003	2002
ROE	20.62%	14.42%	10.17%
Tax burden	64.88%	62.52%	60.67%
Interest burden	130.54%	112.60%	130.50%
EBIT margin	6.51%	6.40%	4.84%
Asset turnover	1.55	1.38	1.19
Leverage	2.42	2.32	2.24

What might the analyst conclude?

Solution. Because the tax burden reflects the relation of after-tax profits to pretax profits, the increase from 60.67 percent to 64.88 percent indicates that taxes declined as a percentage of pretax profits. This decline in average tax rates could be due to lower tax rates from new legislation or revenue in a lower tax jurisdiction. An interest burden factor greater than 100 percent means that nonoperating income exceeded interest expense in all three years. Operating margin (EBIT margin) improved, particularly from 2002 to 2003, indicating the company's operations were more profitable. The company's efficiency (asset turnover) increased each year as did its leverage. Overall, the trend in ROE (doubling in three years) did not result from a single aspect of the company's performance, but instead was a function of lower average tax rates, increasing operating profits, greater efficiency, and increased use of leverage. Additional research on the causes of the various changes is required in order to develop expectations about the company's future performance.

The most detailed decomposition of ROE that we have presented is a five-way decomposition. Nevertheless, an analyst could further decompose individual components of a five-way analysis. For example, EBIT margin (EBIT/Revenue) could be further decomposed into a nonoperating component (EBIT/Operating income) and an operating component (Operating income/Revenues). The analyst can also examine which other factors contributed to these five components. For example, an improvement in efficiency (total asset turnover) may have resulted from better management of inventory (DOH) or better collection of receivables (DSO).

5. EQUITY ANALYSIS

One application of financial analysis is to select securities as part of the equity portfolio management process. Analysts are interested in valuing a security to assess its merits for inclusion or retention in a portfolio. The valuation process has several steps, including:[15]

1. Understanding the business and the existing financial profile.
2. Forecasting company performance.
3. Selecting the appropriate valuation model.
4. Converting forecasts to a valuation.
5. Making the investment decision.

Financial analysis assists in providing the core information to complete the first two steps of this valuation process: understanding the business and forecasting performance.

Fundamental equity analysis involves evaluating a company's performance and valuing its equity in order to assess its relative attractiveness as an investment. Analysts use a variety of methods to value a company's equity, including valuation ratios (e.g., the price-to-earnings or P/E ratio), discounted cash flow approaches, and residual income approaches (ROE compared with the cost of capital), among others. The following section addresses the first of these approaches—the use of valuation ratios.

---

[15]Stowe et al. (2002, p. 6).

5.1. Valuation Ratios

Valuation ratios have long been used in investment decision making. A well-known example is the P/E ratio—probably the most widely used indicator in discussing the value of equity securities—which relates share price to the earnings per share (EPS). Additionally, some analysts use other market multiples, such as price to book value (P/B) and price to cash flow (P/CF). The following sections explore valuation ratios and other quantities related to valuing equities.

5.1.1. Calculation of Valuation Ratios and Related Quantities

Exhibit 7-14 describes the calculation of some common valuation ratios and related quantities.

The P/E ratio expresses the relationship between the price per share and the amount of earnings attributable to a single share. In other words, the P/E ratio tells us how much an investor in common stock pays per dollar of current earnings.

EXHIBIT 7-14   Definitions of Selected Valuation Ratios and Related Quantities

	Numerator	**Denominator**
Valuation ratios		
P/E	Price per share	Earnings per share
P/CF	Price per share	Cash flow per share
P/S	Price per share	Sales per share
P/B	Price per share	Book value per share
Per-Share Quantities		
Basic EPS	Net income minus preferred dividends	Weighted average number of ordinary shares outstanding
Diluted EPS	Adjusted income available for ordinary shares, reflecting conversion of dilutive securities	Weighted average number of ordinary and potential ordinary shares outstanding
Cash flow per share	Cash flow from operations	Average number of shares outstanding
EBITDA per share	EBITDA	Average number of shares outstanding
Dividends per share	Common dividends declared	Weighted average number of ordinary shares outstanding
Dividend-Related Quantities		
Dividend payout ratio	Common share dividends	Net income attributable to common shares
Retention rate (*b*)	Net income attributable to common shares − Common share dividends	Net income attributable to common shares
Sustainable growth rate	$b \times$ ROE	

Because P/E ratios are calculated using net income, the ratios can be sensitive to non-recurring earnings or one-off earnings events. In addition, because net income is generally considered to be more susceptible to manipulation than are cash flows, analysts may use **price to cash flow** as an alternative measure—particularly in situations where earnings quality may be an issue. EBITDA per share, because it is calculated using income before interest, taxes, and depreciation, can be used to eliminate the effect of different levels of fixed asset investment across companies. It facilitates comparison between companies in the same sector but at different stages of infrastructure maturity. **Price to sales** is calculated in a similar manner and is sometimes used as a comparative price metric when a company does not have positive net income.

Another price-based ratio that facilitates useful comparisons of companies' stock prices is **price to book value**, or P/B, which is the ratio of price to book value per share. This ratio is often interpreted as an indicator of market judgment about the relationship between a company's required rate of return and its actual rate of return. Assuming that book values reflect the fair values of the assets, a price to book ratio of one can be interpreted as an indicator that the company's future returns are expected to be exactly equal to the returns required by the market. A ratio greater than one would indicate that the future profitability of the company is expected to exceed the required rate of return, and values of this ratio less than one indicate that the company is not expected to earn excess returns.[16]

5.1.2. Interpretation of Earnings per Share

Exhibit 7-14 presented a number of per-share quantities that can be used in valuation ratios. In the following, we discuss the interpretation of one such critical quantity, EPS.

EPS is simply the amount of earnings attributable to each share of common stock. In isolation, EPS does not provide adequate information for comparison of one company with another. For example, assume that two companies have only common stock outstanding and no dilutive securities outstanding. In addition, assume the two companies have identical net income of $10 million, identical book equity of $100 million and, therefore, identical profitability (10 percent, using ending equity in this case for simplicity). Furthermore, assume that Company A has 100 million weighted average common shares outstanding, whereas Company B has 10 million weighted average common shares outstanding. So, Company A will report EPS of $0.10 per share, and Company B will report EPS of $1 per share. The difference in EPS does not reflect a difference in profitability—the companies have identical profits and profitability. The difference reflects only a different number of common shares outstanding.

Analysts should understand in detail the types of EPS information that companies report:

Basic EPS provides information regarding the earnings attributable to each share of common stock. International Accounting Standards (IAS) No. 33 contains the international principles for the determination and presentation of EPS. This standard applies to entities whose shares are publicly traded or in the process of being issued in public securities markets, and other entities that choose to disclose EPS. U.S. Financial Accounting Standards Board Statement No. 128 contains the standards for computing and presenting EPS.

To calculate basic EPS, the weighted average number of shares outstanding during the period is first calculated. The weighted average number of shares consists of the number of

---

[16]For more detail on valuation ratios as used in equity analysis, see Stowe et al. (2002).

ordinary shares outstanding at the beginning of the period, adjusted by those bought back or issued during the period, multiplied by a time-weighting factor.

Accounting standards generally require the disclosure of basic as well as diluted EPS (**diluted EPS** includes the effect of all the company's securities whose conversion or exercise would result in a reduction of basic EPS; dilutive securities include convertible debt, convertible preferred, warrants, and options). Basic EPS and diluted EPS must be shown with equal prominence on the face of the income statement for each class of ordinary share. Disclosure includes the amounts used as the numerators in calculating basic and diluted EPS, and a reconciliation of those amounts to the company's profit or loss for the period. Because both basic and diluted EPS are presented in a company's financial statements, an analyst does not need to calculate these measures for reported financial statements. Understanding the calculations is, however, helpful for situations requiring an analyst to calculate expected future EPS.

To calculate diluted EPS, earnings are adjusted for the after-tax effects assuming conversion, and the following adjustments are made to the weighted number of shares:

- The weighted average number of shares for basic EPS, *plus* those that would be issued on conversion of all dilutive potential ordinary shares. Potential ordinary shares are treated as dilutive when their conversion would decrease net profit per share from continuing ordinary operations.
- These shares are deemed to have been converted into ordinary shares at the beginning of the period or, if later, at the date of the issue of the shares.
- Options, warrants (and their equivalents), convertible instruments, contingently issuable shares, contracts that can be settled in ordinary shares or cash, purchased options, and written put options should be considered.

5.1.3. Dividend-Related Quantities

In the following, we discuss the interpretation of the dividend-related quantities presented in Exhibit 7-14. These quantities play a role in some present value models for valuing equities.

Dividend payout ratio. The dividend payout ratio measures the percentage of earnings that the company pays out as dividends to shareholders. The amount of dividends per share tends to be relatively fixed because any reduction in dividends has been shown to result in a disproportionately large reduction in share price. Because dividend amounts are relatively fixed, the dividend payout ratio tends to fluctuate with earnings. Therefore, conclusions about a company's dividend payout policies should be based on examination of payout over a number of periods. Optimal dividend policy, similar to optimal capital structure, has been examined in academic research and continues to be a topic of significant interest in corporate finance.

Retention rate. The retention rate is the complement of the payout ratio (i.e., 1 − payout ratio). Whereas the payout ratio measures the percentage of earnings that a company pays out as dividends, the retention rate is the percentage of earnings that a company retains. It is simply one minus the payout ratio. (Note that both the dividend payout ratio and retention rate are both percentages of earnings. The difference in terminology—*ratio* versus *rate* versus *percentage*—reflects common usage rather than any substantive differences.)

Sustainable growth rate. A company's sustainable growth rate is viewed as a function of its profitability (measured as ROE) and its ability to finance itself from internally generated funds (measured as the retention rate). A higher ROE and a higher retention rate result in a higher sustainable growth rate. This calculation can be used to estimate a company's growth rate, a factor commonly used in equity valuation.

5.2. Industry-Specific Ratios

As stated earlier in this chapter, a universally accepted definition and classification of ratios does not exist. The purpose of ratios is to serve as indicators of important aspects of a company's performance and value. Aspects of performance that are considered important in one industry may be irrelevant in another, and industry-specific ratios reflect these differences. For example, companies in the retail industry may report same-store sales changes because, in the retail industry, it is important to distinguish between growth that results from opening new stores and growth that results from generating more sales at existing stores. Industry-specific metrics can be especially important to the value of equity in early stage industries, where companies are not yet profitable.

In addition, regulated industries—especially in the financial sector—often are required to comply with specific regulatory ratios. For example, the banking sector's liquidity and cash reserve ratios provide an indication of banking liquidity and reflect monetary and political requirements. Banking capital adequacy requirements, although not perfect, do relate banks' solvency requirements directly to their specific levels of risk exposure.

Exhibit 7-15 presents some industry-specific and task-specific ratios.[17]

5.3. Research on Ratios in Equity Analysis

Some ratios should be expected to be particularly useful in equity analysis. The end product of equity analysis is often a valuation and investment recommendation. Theoretical valuation models are useful in selecting ratios that would be useful in this process. For example, a company's P/B is theoretically linked to ROE, growth, and the required return. ROE is also a primary determinate of residual income in a residual income valuation model. In both cases, higher ROE relative to the required return denotes a higher valuation. Similarly, profit margin is related to justified price-to-sales (P/S) ratios. Another common valuation method involves forecasts of future cash flows that are discounted back to the present. Trends in ratios can be useful in forecasting future earnings and cash flows (e.g., trends operating profit margin and collection of customer receivables). Future growth expectations are a key component of all of these valuation models. Trends may be useful in assessing growth prospects (when used in conjunction with overall economic and industry trends). The variability in ratios and common-size data can be useful in assessing risk, an important component of the required rate of return in valuation models. A great deal of academic research has focused on the use of these fundamental ratios in evaluating equity investments.

A classic study, Ou and Penman (1989a,b), found that ratios and common-size metrics generated from accounting data were useful in forecasting earnings and stock returns. Ou and Penman examined a variety of 68 such metrics and found that these variables could be reduced to a more parsimonious list and combined in a statistical model that was particularly useful for selecting investments. These variables included:

- Percentage change in current ratio.
- Percentage change in quick ratio.
- Percentage change in inventory turnover.

---

[17]These are provided for illustrative purposes only. There are many other industry-specific ratios that are outside the scope of this text. Resources such as Standard and Poor's Industry Surveys present useful ratios for each industry.

EXHIBIT 7-15   Definitions of Some Common Industry and Task-Specific Ratios

Ratios	Numerator	Denominator
Business Risk Ratios		
Coefficient of variation of operating income	Standard deviation of operating income	Average operating income
Coefficient of variation of net income	Standard deviation of net income	Average net income
Coefficient of variation of revenues	Standard deviation of revenue	Average revenue
Financial Sector Ratios		
Capital adequacy—banks	Various components of capital	Risk-weighted assets, market risk exposure, and level of operational risk assumed
Monetary reserve requirement	Reserves held at central bank	Specified deposit liabilities
Liquid asset requirement	Approved "readily marketable" securities	Specified deposit liabilities
Net interest margin	Net interest income	Total interest-earning assets
Retail Ratios		
Same (or comparable) store sales	Average revenue growth year over year for stores open in both periods	Not applicable
Sales per square foot (meter)	Revenue	Total retail space in feet or meters
Service Companies		
Revenue per employee	Revenue	Total number of employees
Net Income per employee	Net income	Total number of employees
Hotel		
Average daily rate	Room revenue	Number of rooms sold
Occupancy rate	Number of rooms sold	Number of rooms available

- Inventory/total assets (a common-size measure) and the percentage change in this metric.
- Percentage change in inventory.
- Percentage change in sales.
- Percentage change in depreciation.
- Change in dividend per share.
- Percentage change in depreciation to plant assets ratio.
- ROE.
- Change in ROE.
- Percentage change in capital expenditures to total assets ratio (contemporaneously and lagged).
- Debt-to-equity ratio and the percentage change in this ratio.
- Percentage change in total asset turnover.

- ROA.
- Gross margin.
- Pretax margin.
- Sales to total cash.
- Percentage change in total assets.
- Cash flow to debt.
- Working capital to total assets.
- Operating ROA.
- Repayment of long-term debt to total long-term debt.
- Cash dividend to cash flows.

Subsequent studies have also demonstrated the use of ratios in evaluation of equity investments and valuation. Lev and Thiagarajan (1993) examined fundamental financial variables used by analysts to assess whether they are useful in security valuation. They found that fundamental variables add about 70 percent to the explanatory power of earnings alone in predicting excess returns (stock returns in excess of those expected). The fundamental variables they found useful included percentage changes in inventory and receivables relative to sales, gross margin, sales per employee, and the change in bad debts relative to the change in accounts receivable, among others. Abarbanell and Bushee (1997) found some of the same variables useful in predicting future accounting earnings. Abarbanell and Bushee (1998) devised an investment strategy using these same variables and found that they can generate excess returns under this strategy.

Piotroski (2000) used financial ratios to supplement a value investing strategy and found that he can generate significant excess returns. Variables used by Piotroski include ROA, cash flow ROA, change in ROA, change in leverage, change in liquidity, change in gross margin, and change in inventory turnover.

This research shows that in addition to being useful in evaluating the past performance of a company, ratios can be useful in predicting future earnings and equity returns.

6. CREDIT ANALYSIS

Credit risk is the risk of loss caused by a counterparty's or debtor's failure to make a promised payment. For example, credit risk with respect to a bond is the risk that the obligor (the issuer of the bond) is not able to pay interest and principal according to the terms of the bond indenture (contract). **Credit analysis** is the evaluation of credit risk.

Approaches to credit analysis vary and, as with all financial analysis, depend on the purpose of the analysis and the context in which it is done. Credit analysis for specific types of debt (e.g., acquisition financing and other highly leveraged financing) often involves projections of period-by-period cash flows similar to projections made by equity analysts. Whereas the equity analyst may discount projected cash flows to determine the value of the company's equity, a credit analyst would use the projected cash flows to assess the likelihood of a company complying with its financial covenants in each period and paying interest and principal as due.[18] The analysis would also include expectations about asset sales and refinancing options open to the company.

---

[18]Financial covenants are clauses in bond indentures relating to the financial condition of the bond issuer.

Credit analysis may relate to the borrower's credit risk in a particular transaction or to its overall creditworthiness. In assessing overall creditworthiness, one general approach is credit scoring, a statistical analysis of the determinants of credit default.

Another general approach to credit analysis is the credit rating process that is used, for example, by credit rating agencies to assess and communicate the probability of default by an issuer on its debt obligations (e.g., commercial paper, notes, and bonds). A credit rating can be either long term or short term and is an indication of the rating agency's opinion of the creditworthiness of a debt issuer with respect to a specific debt security or other obligation. Where a company has no debt outstanding, a rating agency can also provide an issuer credit rating that expresses an opinion of the issuer's overall capacity and willingness to meet its financial obligations. The following sections review research on the use of ratios in credit analysis and the ratios commonly used in credit analysis.

6.1. The Credit Rating Process

The rating process involves both the analysis of a company's financial reports as well as a broad assessment of a company's operations. The credit rating process includes many of the following procedures:[19]

- Meeting with management, typically including the chief financial officer, to discuss, for example, industry outlook, overview of major business segments, financial policies and goals, distinctive accounting practices, capital spending plans, and financial contingency plans.
- Tours of major facilities, time permitting.
- Meeting of a ratings committee where the analyst's recommendations are voted on, after considering factors that include:
  - Business risk, including the evaluation of:
    - Operating environment.
    - Industry characteristics (e.g., cyclicality and capital intensity).
    - Success factors and areas of vulnerability.
    - Company's competitive position, including size and diversification.
  - Financial risk, including:
    - The evaluation of capital structure, interest coverage, and profitability using ratio analysis.
    - The examination of debt covenants.
  - Evaluation of management.
- Monitoring of publicly distributed ratings—including reconsideration of ratings due to changing conditions.

In assigning credit ratings, rating agencies emphasize the importance of the relationship between a company's business risk profile and its financial risk. "The company's business risk profile determines the level of financial risk appropriate for any rating category."[20]

When analyzing financial ratios, rating agencies normally investigate deviations of ratios from the median ratios of the universe of companies for which such ratios have been calculated and also use the median ratings as an indicator for the ratings grade given to

---

[19]Based on Standard & Poor's Corporate Ratings Criteria (2006).
[20]Standard & Poor's Corporate Ratings Criteria (2006), p. 23.

EXHIBIT 7-16   Selected Credit Ratios Used by Standard & Poor's

Credit Ratio	Numerator[a]	Denominator[b]
EBIT interest coverage	EBIT	Gross interest (prior to deductions for capitalized interest or interest income)
EBITDA interest coverage	EBITDA	Gross interest (prior to deductions for capitalized interest or interest income)
Funds from operations to total debt	FFO (net income adjusted for noncash items)	Total debt
Free operating cash flow to total debt	CFO (adjusted) less capital expenditures	Total debt
Total debt to EBITDA	Total debt	EBITDA
Return on capital	EBIT	Capital = Average equity (common and preferred stock) and short-term portions of debt, noncurrent deferred taxes, minority interest
Total debt to total debt plus equity	Total debt	Total debt plus equity

FFO, funds from operations; CFO, cash flow from operations.

[a]Emphasis is on earnings from *continuing* operations.

[b]Note that both the numerator and denominator definitions are adjusted from ratio to ratio and may not correspond to the definitions used in this chapter.

Source: Based on data from Standard & Poor's Corporate Ratings Criteria (2006), p. 43.

a specific debt issuer. This so-called universe of rated companies changes constantly, and any calculations are obviously affected by economic factors as well as by mergers and acquisitions. International ratings include the influence of country and economic risk factors. Exhibit 7-16 presents key financial ratios used by Standard & Poor's in evaluating industrial companies. Note that before calculating ratios, rating agencies make certain adjustments to reported financials such as adjusting debt to include off-balance sheet debt in a company's total debt.

6.2. Research on Ratios in Credit Analysis

A great deal of academic and practitioner research has focused on determining which ratios are useful in assessing the credit risk of a company, including the risk of bankruptcy.

One of the earliest studies examined individual ratios to assess their ability to predict failure of a company up to five years in advance. Beaver (1967) found that six ratios could correctly predict company failure one year in advance 90 percent of the time and five years in advance at least 65 percent of the time. The ratios found effective by Beaver were cash flow-to-total debt, ROA, total debt-to-total assets, working capital-to-total assets, the current ratio, and the no-credit interval ratio (the length of time a company could go without borrowing). Altman (1968) and Altman, Haldeman, and Narayanan (1977) found that financial ratios could be combined in an effective model for predicting bankruptcy. Altman's initial work involved creation of a Z-score that was able to correctly predict financial distress. The Z-score was computed as

$$Z = 1.2 \times \text{(Current assets} - \text{Current liabilities)/Total assets}$$
$$+ \ 1.4 \times \text{(Retained earnings/Total assets)}$$
$$+ \ 3.3 \times \text{(EBIT/Total assets)}$$
$$+ \ 0.6 \times \text{(Market value of stock/Book value of liabilities)}$$
$$+ \ 1.0 \times \text{(Sales/Total assets)}$$

In his initial study, a Z-score of lower than 1.81 predicted failure and the model was able to accurately classify 95 percent of companies studied into a failure group and a nonfailure group. The original model was designed for manufacturing companies. Subsequent refinements to the models allow for other company types and time periods. Generally, the variables found to be useful in prediction include profitability ratios, coverage ratios, liquidity ratios, capitalization ratios, and earnings variability (Altman 2000).

Similar research has been performed on the ability of ratios to predict bond ratings and bond yields. For example, Ederington, Yawitz, and Roberts (1987) found that a small number of variables (total assets, interest coverage, leverage, variability of coverage, and subordination status) were effective in explaining bond yields. Similarly, Ederington (1986) found that nine variables in combination could correctly classify more than 70 percent of bond ratings. These variables included ROA, long-term debt to assets, interest coverage, cash flow to debt, variability of coverage and cash flow, total assets, and subordination status. These studies have shown that ratios are effective in evaluating credit risk, bond yields, and bond ratings.

7. BUSINESS AND GEOGRAPHIC SEGMENTS

Analysts often need to evaluate the performance underlying business segments (subsidiary companies, operating units, or simply operations in different geographic areas) to understand in detail the company as a whole. Unfortunately, companies are not required to provide full financial statements for segments for which all of the traditional ratios can be computed. Publicly traded companies are required to provide limited segment information under both IFRS and U.S. GAAP.

7.1. IAS 14 Requirements

Under IAS 14 (Segment Reporting), disclosures are required for reportable segments. U.S. GAAP requirements are similar to IFRS but less detailed. One noticeable omission under U.S. GAAP is the disclosure of segment liabilities.

A reportable segment is defined as a business or geographical segment where both of the following apply:

- The majority (greater than 50 percent) of its revenue is earned externally.
- Its income from sales, segment result, or assets is greater than or equal to 10 percent of the appropriate total amount of all segments.

A business segment is a distinguishable component of a company that is engaged in providing an individual product or service or a group of related products or services and that is subject to risks and returns that are different from those of other business segments. A geographical segment is a distinguishable component of a company that is engaged in providing products or services within a particular economic environment.

Different business and geographical segments should be identified. A company's business and geographical segments for external reporting purposes should be those organizational units for which information is reported to the board of directors and to the chief executive officer. If a company's internal organizational and management structure and its system of internal financial reporting to the board of directors and the chief executive officer are not based on individual products, services, groups of related products or services, nor on geography, the directors and management of the company should choose either business segments or geographical segments as the company's primary segment reporting format, based on their assessment of which type of segment reflects the primary source of the company's risks and returns. Under this standard, most entities would identify their business and geographical segments as the organizational units for which information is reported to the nonexecutive board of directors and senior management.

If the total revenue from external customers for all reportable segments combined is less than 75 percent of the total company revenue, additional reportable segments should be identified until the 75 percent level is reached. Small segments might be combined as one if they share a substantial number of factors that define a business or geographical segment, or they might be combined with a similar significant reportable segment. If they are not separately reported or combined, they are included as an unallocated reconciling item.

The company must identify a primary segment reporting format (either business or geographical) with the other segment used for the secondary reporting format. The dominant source and nature of risks and returns govern whether a company's primary segment reporting format will be its business segments or its geographical segments. The company's internal organization and management structure, and its system of internal financial reporting to the board of directors and the chief executive officer, are normally the basis for identifying the predominant source and nature of risks and differing rates of return facing the company.

For each primary segment, the following should be disclosed:

- Segment revenue, distinguishing between revenue to external customers and revenue from other segments.
- Segment result (segment revenue minus segment expenses).
- Carrying amount of segment assets.
- Segment liabilities.
- Cost of property, plant, and equipment, and intangible assets acquired.
- Depreciation and amortization expense.
- Other noncash expenses.
- Share of the net profit or loss of an investment accounted for under the equity method.
- Reconciliation between the information of reportable segments and the consolidated financial statements in terms of segment revenue, result, assets, and liabilities.

For each secondary segment, the following should be disclosed:

- Revenue from external customers.
- Carrying amount of segment assets.
- Cost of property, plant, and equipment, and intangible assets acquired.

Other required disclosures are as follows:

- Revenue of any segment whereby the external revenue of the segment is greater than or equal to 10 percent of company revenue but that is not a reportable segment (because a majority of its revenue is from internal transfers).

- Basis of pricing intersegment transfers.
- Changes in segment accounting policies.
- Types of products and services in each business segment.
- Composition of each geographical segment.

7.2. Segment Ratios

Based on the limited segment information that companies are required to present, a variety of useful ratios can be computed, as shown in Exhibit 7-17.

The segment margin measures the operating profitability of the segment relative to revenues, whereas the segment ROA measures the operating profitability relative to assets. Segment turnover measures the overall efficiency of the segment: how much revenue is generated per unit of assets. The segment debt ratio examines the level of liabilities (hence solvency) of the segment. Example 7-15 demonstrates the evaluation of segment ratios.

EXHIBIT 7-17   Definitions of Segment Ratios

Segment Ratios	Numerator	Denominator
Segment margin	Segment profit (loss)	Segment revenue
Segment turnover	Segment revenue	Segment assets
Segment ROA	Segment profit (loss)	Segment assets
Segment debt ratio	Segment liabilities	Segment assets

EXAMPLE 7-15   The Evaluation of Segment Ratios

The following information relates to the business segments of Nokia for 2004 in millions of euros. Evaluate the performance of the segments using the segment margin, segment ROA, and segment turnover.

	Revenue	Operating Profit	Segment Assets
Mobile Phones	18,429	3,768	3,758
Multimedia	3,636	179	787
Enterprise Solutions	806	−199	210
Networks	6,367	878	3,055
	Segment Margin	Segment ROA	Segment Turnover
Mobile Phones	20.45%	100.27%	4.90
Multimedia	4.92%	22.74%	4.62
Enterprise Solutions	−24.69%	−94.76%	3.84
Networks	13.79%	28.74%	2.08

Solution. Mobile Phones is the best performing segment with the highest segment margin, segment ROA, and efficiency. Networks is the second highest in terms of profitability but lowest in efficiency (the ability to generate revenue from assets). Enterprise Solutions is not profitable; however, it is the smallest segment and may still be in the development stage.

8. MODEL BUILDING AND FORECASTING

Analysts often need to forecast future financial performance. For example, EPS forecasts of analysts are widely followed by Wall Street. Analysts use data about the economy, industry, and company in arriving at a company's forecast. The results of an analyst's financial analysis, including common-size and ratio analysis, are integral to this process, along with the judgment of the analysts.

Based on forecasts of growth and expected relationships among the financial statement data, the analyst can build a model (sometimes referred to as an *earnings model*) to forecast future performance. In addition to budgets, pro forma financial statements are widely used in financial forecasting within companies, especially for use by senior executives and boards of directors. Last but not least, these budgets and forecasts are also used in presentations to credit analysts and others in obtaining external financing.

For example, based on a revenue forecast, an analyst may budget expenses based on expected common-size data. Forecasts of balance sheet and cash flow statements can be derived from expected ratio data, such as DSO. Forecasts are not limited to a single point estimate but should involve a range of possibilities. This can involve several techniques:

- *Sensitivity analysis.* Also known as *what if* analysis, sensitivity analysis shows the range of possible outcomes as specific assumptions are changed; this could, in turn, influence financing needs or investment in fixed assets.
- *Scenario analysis.* This type of analysis shows the changes in key financial quantities that result from given (economic) events, such as the loss of customers, the loss of a supply source, or a catastrophic event. If the list of events is mutually exclusive and exhaustive and the events can be assigned probabilities, the analyst can evaluate not only the range of outcomes but also standard statistical measures such as the mean and median value for various quantities of interest.
- *Simulation.* This is computer-generated sensitivity or scenario analysis based on probability models for the factors that drive outcomes. Each event or possible outcome is assigned a probability. Multiple scenarios are then run using the probability factors assigned to the possible values of a variable.

9. SUMMARY

Financial analysis techniques, including common-size and ratio analysis, are useful in summarizing financial reporting data and evaluating the performance and financial position of a company. The results of financial analysis techniques provide important inputs into security valuation. Key facets of financial analysis include the following:

- Common-size financial statements and financial ratios remove the effect of size, allowing comparisons of a company with peer companies (cross-sectional analysis) and comparison of a company's results over time (trend or time-series analysis).
- Activity ratios measure the efficiency of a company's operations, such as collection of receivables or management of inventory. Major activity ratios include inventory turnover, days of inventory on hand, receivables turnover, days of sales outstanding, payables turnover, number of days of payables, working capital turnover, fixed asset turnover, and total asset turnover.
- Liquidity ratios measure the ability of a company to meet short-term obligations. Major liquidity ratios include the current ratio, quick ratio, cash ratio, and defensive interval ratio.
- Solvency ratios measure the ability of a company to meet long-term obligations. Major solvency ratios include debt ratios (including the debt-to-assets ratio, debt-to-capital ratio, debt-to-equity ratio, and financial leverage ratio) and coverage ratios (including interest coverage and fixed charge coverage).
- Profitability ratios measure the ability of a company to generate profits from revenue and assets. Major profitability ratios include return on sales ratios (including gross profit margin, operating profit margin, pretax margin, and net profit margin) and return on investment ratios (including operating ROA, ROA, ROE, and return on common equity).
- Ratios can also be combined and evaluated as a group to better understand how they fit together and how efficiency and leverage are tied to profitability.
- ROE can be analyzed as the product of the net profit margin, asset turnover, and financial leverage.
- Ratio analysis is useful in the selection and valuation of debt and equity securities and is a part of the credit rating process.
- Ratios can also be computed for business segments to evaluate how units within a business are doing.
- The results of financial analysis provide valuable inputs into forecasts of future earnings and cash flow.

PRACTICE PROBLEMS

1. Comparison of a company's financial results to other peer companies for the same time period is called
   A. horizontal analysis.
   B. time-series analysis.
   C. cross-sectional analysis.

2. In order to assess a company's ability to fulfill its long-term obligations, an analyst would *most likely* examine
   A. activity ratios.
   B. liquidity ratios.
   C. solvency ratios.

3. Which ratio would a company *most likely* use to measure its ability to meet short-term obligations?
   A. Current ratio
   B. Payables turnover
   C. Gross profit margin

4. Which of the following ratios would be *most useful* in determining a company's ability to cover its debt payments?
   A. ROA
   B. Total asset turnover
   C. Fixed charge coverage

5. John Chan is interested in assessing both the efficiency and liquidity of Spherion PLC. Chan has collected the following data for Spherion:

	2005	2004	2003
Days of inventory on hand	32	34	40
Days of sales outstanding	28	25	23
Number of days of payables	40	35	35

   Based on this data, what is Chan *least likely* to conclude?
   A. Inventory management has contributed to improved liquidity.
   B. Management of payables has contributed to improved liquidity.
   C. Management of receivables has contributed to improved liquidity.

6. Marcus Lee is examining the solvency of Apex Manufacturing and has collected the following data (in millions of euros):

	2005	2004	2003
Total debt	€2,000	€1,900	€1,750
Total equity	€4,000	€4,500	€5,000

   Which of the following would be the *most appropriate* conclusion for Lee?
   A. The company is becoming increasingly less solvent, as evidenced by the increase in its debt-to-equity ratio from 0.35 to 0.50 from 2003 to 2005.
   B. The company is becoming less liquid, as evidenced by the increase in its debt-to-equity ratio from 0.35 to 0.50 from 2003 to 2005.
   C. The company is becoming increasingly more liquid, as evidenced by the increase in its debt-to-equity ratio from 0.35 to 0.50 from 2003 to 2005.

7. With regard to the data in Problem 6, what would be a reasonable explanation of these financial results?
   A. The decline in the company's equity results from a decline in the market value of this company's common shares.
   B. The increase of €250 in the company's debt from 2003 to 2005 indicates that lenders are viewing the company as increasingly creditworthy.
   C. The decline in the company's equity indicates that the company may be incurring losses on its operations, paying dividends greater than income, and/or repurchasing shares.

8. Linda Roper observes a decrease in a company's inventory turnover. Which of the following would explain this trend?
   A. The company installed a new inventory management system, allowing more efficient inventory management.

  B. Due to problems with obsolescent inventory last year, the company wrote off a large amount of its inventory at the beginning of the period.
  C. The company installed a new inventory management system but experienced some operational difficulties resulting in duplicate orders being placed with suppliers.

9. Which of the following would best explain an increase in receivables turnover?
  A. The company adopted new credit policies last year and began offering credit to customers with weak credit histories.
  B. Due to problems with an error in its old credit scoring system, the company had accumulated a substantial amount of uncollectible accounts and wrote off a large amount of its receivables.
  C. To match the terms offered by its closest competitor, the company adopted new payment terms now requiring net payment within 30 days rather than 15 days, which had been its previous requirement.

10. Brown Corporation had an average days' sales outstanding of 19 days in 2005. Brown wants to decrease its collection period in 2006 to match the industry average of 15 days. Credit sales in 2005 were $300 million, and Brown expects credit sales to increase to $390 million in 2006. To achieve Brown's goal of decreasing the collection period, the change in the average accounts receivable balance from 2005 to 2006 that must occur is *closest* to
  A. −$1.22 million.
  B. −$0.42 million.
  C. $0.42 million.

11. An analyst gathered the following data for a company:

	2003	2004	2005
ROE	19.8%	20.0%	22.0%
Return on total assets	8.1%	8.0%	7.9%
Total asset turnover	2.0	2.0	2.1

Based only on the information above, the *most* appropriate conclusion is that, over the period 2003 to 2005, the company's
  A. net profit margin and financial leverage have decreased.
  B. net profit margin and financial leverage have increased.
  C. net profit margin has decreased but its financial leverage has increased.

12. A decomposition of ROE for Integra SA is as follows:

	2005	2004
ROE	18.90%	18.90%
Tax burden	0.70	0.75
Interest burden	0.90	0.90
EBIT margin	10.00%	10.00%
Asset turnover	1.50	1.40
Leverage	2.00	2.00

Which of the following choices *best* describes reasonable conclusions an analyst might make based on this ROE decomposition?
A. Profitability and the liquidity position both improved in 2005.
B. The higher average tax rate in 2005 offset the improvement in profitability, leaving ROE unchanged.
C. The higher average tax rate in 2005 offset the improvement in efficiency, leaving ROE unchanged.

13. A decomposition of ROE for Company A and Company B is as follows:

	Company A		Company B	
	2005	2004	2005	2004
ROE	26.46%	18.90%	26.33%	18.90%
Tax burden	0.7	0.75	0.75	0.75
Interest burden	0.9	0.9	0.9	0.9
EBIT margin	7.00%	10.00%	13.00%	10.00%
Asset turnover	1.5	1.4	1.5	1.4
Leverage	4	2	2	2

Which of the following choices *best* describes reasonable conclusions an analyst might make based on this ROE decomposition?
A. Company A's ROE is higher than Company B's in 2005, but the difference between the two companies' ROE is very small and was mainly the result of Company A's increase in its financial leverage.
B. Company A's ROE is higher than Company B's in 2005, apparently reflecting a strategic shift by Company A to a product mix with higher profit margins.
C. Company A's ROE is higher than Company B's in 2005, which suggests that Company A may have purchased new, more efficient equipment.

14. Rent-A-Center reported the following information related to total debt and shareholders' equity in its 2003 annual report.

($ thousands)	As of 31 December				
	2003	2002	2001	2000	1999
Total debt	698,000	521,330	702,506	741,051	847,160
Stockholders' equity	794,830	842,400	405,378	309,371	206,690

What would an analyst's most appropriate conclusion be based on this data?
A. The company's solvency improved from 1999 to 2002.
B. The company's solvency improved from 2002 to 2003.
C. The data suggest the company increased debt in 2002.

15. Frank Collins observes the following data for two companies:

	Company A	Company B
Revenue	$4,500	$6,000
Net income	$50	$1,000
Current assets	$40,000	$60,000
Total assets	$100,000	$700,000
Current liabilities	$10,000	$50,000
Total debt	$60,000	$150,000
Shareholders' equity	$30,000	$500,000

Which of the following choices best describes reasonable conclusions that Collins might make about the two companies' ability to pay their current and long-term obligations?

A. Company A's current ratio of 4.0x indicates it is more liquid than Company B, whose current ratio is only 1.2x, but Company B is more solvent, as indicated by its lower debt-to-equity ratio.

B. Company A's current ratio of 25 percent indicates it is less liquid than Company B, whose current ratio is 83 percent, and Company A is also less solvent, as indicated by a debt-to-equity ratio of 200 percent compared with Company B's debt-to-equity ratio of only 30 percent.

C. Company A's current ratio of 4.0x indicates it is more liquid than Company B, whose current ratio is only 1.2x, and Company A is also more solvent, as indicated by a debt-to-equity ratio of 200 percent compared with Company B's debt-to-equity ratio of only 30 percent.

Use the following information to answer Problems 16 through 19.

The data below appear in the five-year summary of a major international company. A business combination with another major manufacturer took place in 2003. The term *turnover* in this financial data is a synonym for revenue.

	2000	2001	2002	2003	2004
Financial statements	GBP m	GBP m	GBP m	GBP m	GBP m
Income statements					
Turnover (i.e., revenue)	4,390	3,624	3,717	8,167	11,366
Profit before interest and taxation (EBIT)	844	700	704	933	1,579
Net interest payable	−80	−54	−98	−163	−188
Taxation	−186	−195	−208	−349	−579
Minorities	−94	−99	−105	−125	−167
Profit for the year	484	352	293	296	645

(Continued)

(*Continued*)

	2000	2001	2002	2003	2004
Balance sheets					
Fixed assets	3,510	3,667	4,758	10,431	11,483
Current asset investments, cash at bank and in hand	316	218	290	561	682
Other current assets	558	514	643	1,258	1,634
Total assets	4,384	4,399	5,691	12,250	13,799
Interest bearing debt (long term)	−602	−1,053	−1,535	−3,523	−3,707
Other creditors and provisions (current)	−1,223	−1,054	−1,102	−2,377	−3,108
Total liabilities	−1,825	−2,107	−2,637	−5,900	−6,815
Net assets	2,559	2,292	3,054	6,350	6,984
Shareholders' funds	2,161	2,006	2,309	5,572	6,165
Equity minority interests	398	286	745	778	819
Capital employed	2,559	2,292	3,054	6,350	6,984
Cash flow					
Working capital movements	−53	5	71	85	107
Net cash inflow from operating activities	864	859	975	1,568	2,292

16. The company's total assets at year-end 1999 were GBP 3,500 million. Which of the following choices *best* describes reasonable conclusions an analyst might make about the company's efficiency?
    A. Comparing 2004 with 2000, the company's efficiency improved, as indicated by a total asset turnover ratio of 0.86 compared with 0.64.
    B. Comparing 2004 with 2000, the company's efficiency deteriorated, as indicated by its current ratio.
    C. Comparing 2004 with 2000, the company's efficiency deteriorated due to asset growth faster than turnover (i.e., revenue) growth.

17. Which of the following choices *best* describes reasonable conclusions an analyst might make about the company's solvency?
    A. Comparing 2004 with 2000, the company's solvency improved, as indicated by an increase in its debt-to-assets ratio from 0.14 to 0.27.
    B. Comparing 2004 with 2000, the company's solvency deteriorated, as indicated by a decrease in interest coverage from 10.6 to 8.4.
    C. Comparing 2004 with 2000, the company's solvency improved, as indicated by the growth in its profits to GBP 645 million.

18. Which of the following choices *best* describes reasonable conclusions an analyst might make about the company's liquidity?
    A. Comparing 2004 with 2000, the company's liquidity improved, as indicated by an increase in its debt-to-assets ratio from 0.14 to 0.27.

    B. Comparing 2004 with 2000, the company's liquidity deteriorated, as indicated by a decrease in interest coverage from 10.6 to 8.4.

    C. Comparing 2004 with 2000, the company's liquidity improved, as indicated by an increase in its current ratio from 0.71 to 0.75.

19. Which of the following choices *best* describes reasonable conclusions an analyst might make about the company's profitability?

    A. Comparing 2004 with 2000, the company's profitability improved, as indicated by an increase in its debt-to-assets ratio from 0.14 to 0.27.

    B. Comparing 2004 with 2000, the company's profitability deteriorated, as indicated by a decrease in its net profit margin from 11.0 percent to 5.7 percent.

    C. Comparing 2004 with 2000, the company's profitability improved, as indicated by the growth in its shareholders' equity to GBP 6,165 million.

20. In general, a creditor would consider a decrease in which of the following ratios to be positive news?

    A. Interest coverage (times interest earned)

    B. Debt to total assets

    C. Return on assets

21. Assuming no changes in other variables, which of the following would decrease ROA?

    A. A decrease in the effective tax rate

    B. A decrease in interest expense

    C. An increase in average assets

22. What does the P/E ratio measure?

    A. The "multiple" that the stock market places on a company's EPS.

    B. The relationship between dividends and market prices.

    C. The earnings for one common share of stock.

CHAPTER 8

INTERNATIONAL STANDARDS CONVERGENCE

Thomas R. Robinson, CFA

CFA Institute
Charlottesville, Virginia

Hennie van Greuning, CFA

World Bank
Washington, DC

Elaine Henry, CFA

University of Miami
Miami, Florida

Michael A. Broihahn, CFA

Barry University
Miami, Florida

LEARNING OUTCOMES

After completing this chapter, you will be able to do the following:

- State and explain key aspects of the International Financial Reporting Standards (IFRS) framework as they pertain to the objectives and qualitative characteristics of financial statements.

- Identify and explain the major international accounting standards for each asset and liability category on the balance sheet, and the key differences from U.S. generally accepted accounting principles (GAAP).
- Identify and explain the major international accounting standards for major revenue and expense categories on the income statement, and the key differences from U.S. GAAP.
- Identify and explain the major differences between international and U.S. GAAP accounting standards concerning the treatment of interest and dividends on the cash flow statement.
- Interpret the effect of differences between international and U.S. GAAP accounting standards on the balance sheet, income statement, and the statement of changes in equity for some commonly used financial ratios.

1. INTRODUCTION

The International Accounting Standards Board (IASB) is the standard-setting body of the International Accounting Standards Committee (IASC) Foundation. The objectives of the IASC Foundation are to develop a single set of global financial reporting standards and to promote the use of those standards. In accomplishing these objectives, the IASC Foundation explicitly aims to bring about convergence between national standards and international standards.

Around the world, many national accounting standard setters have adopted, or are in the process of adopting, the standards issued by the IASB: International Financial Reporting Standards, or IFRS.[1]

Over the past few years, convergence between IFRS and U.S. generally accepted accounting principles (U.S. GAAP), which are issued by the Financial Accounting Standards Board (FASB), has increased significantly. The two accounting standards boards now issue joint exposure drafts for a number of standards. In February 2006, the FASB and IASB published a memorandum of understanding outlining a "road map for convergence" over the next several years.

The IFRS *Framework for the Preparation and Presentation of Financial Statements* (referred to here as the "Framework") was introduced earlier. In this chapter, we review certain key aspects of the Framework. Section 2 provides an overview of the Framework. Sections 3, 4, and 5 provide additional descriptions of the IFRS relevant to each of the financial statements, noting some of the differences currently remaining between IFRS and U.S. GAAP. Section 6 summarizes the standard setters' agenda for convergence. Section 7 describes the effect on selected financial ratios of current differences between U.S. and international standards. Section 8 provides a summary of key concepts, and practice problems in the CFA multiple-choice format conclude the chapter.

A note of caution: The stated objective of the IASB/FASB convergence project is to eliminate differences between IFRS and U.S. GAAP. The convergence project implies that frequent changes to accounting standards are bound to continue for a number of years. Because a detailed comparison of current differences between IFRS and U.S. GAAP would

---

[1]International accounting standards also include standards with a numbering system identified as "IAS" (International Accounting Standards), which were issued by the board of the IASC prior to the formation of the IASB in 2001 and the handover of standard-setting functions from the IASC's board to the IASB.

be of limited practical value, this chapter aims to present basic principles and issues. Analysts should be aware of resources available to find the timeliest information on IFRS, including the web site of the IASB (www.iasb.org) and the website of the FASB (www.fasb.org).

2. THE IFRS FRAMEWORK

The IFRS Framework, which is currently being re-examined as part of the international convergence project, was originally published in 1989 and was designed to assist the IASB in developing standards as well as to assist users of financial statements in interpreting the information contained therein. The Framework sets forth the concepts that underlie the preparation and presentation of financial statements and provides guidance on the definition, recognition, and measurement of the elements from which financial statements are constructed. In addition, the Framework discusses the concepts of capital and capital maintenance.

2.1.   Key Aspects of the IFRS Framework

The objectives of financial statements, as stated in the Framework, are "to provide information about the financial position, performance, and changes in financial position of an entity; this information should be useful to a wide range of users for the purpose of making economic decisions."[2] The definition, therefore, covers the balance sheet (including the statement of changes in equity), income statement, and cash flow statement.

To achieve the objective of providing useful information, financial statements should have certain characteristics. Recent IASB updates emphasize the following qualitative characteristics related to the usefulness of information in financial statements:

- Relevance
- Predictive value
- Faithful representation (an emphasis on economic substance over form, reliability, and completeness)
- Neutrality (absence of bias)
- Verifiability

Financial statements provide information on the financial position and performance of an entity by grouping the effects of transactions and other events into the following five broad classes or elements:

Balance Sheet Elements (Financial Position)

- *Assets:* Resources controlled by an entity as a result of past events and from which future economic benefits are expected to flow to the entity.
- *Liabilities:* Present obligations of an entity arising from past events, the settlement of which is expected to result in an outflow of resources from the entity.
- *Equity:* Assets less liabilities (for companies, shareholders' equity), which is the residual interest in the assets of the entity.

---

[2] *Framework for the Preparation and Presentation of Financial Statements,* IASC, 1989, adopted by IASB 2001, paragraph 12.

Income Statement Elements (Performance)

- *Income:* Increases in economic benefits that result in an increase in equity, other than increases resulting from contributions by owners. The increases in economic benefits may be in the form of inflows of assets, enhancements to assets, or decreases in liabilities. Income includes both revenues and gains. Revenues are income from the ordinary activities of the entity (e.g., the sale of products). Gains result from activities other than ordinary activities (e.g., the sale of equipment no longer needed).
- *Expenses:* Decreases in economic benefits that result in decreases in equity, other than decreases because of distributions to owners. The decreases in economic benefits may be in the form of outflows of assets, depletions of assets, or increases in liabilities. (Expenses include losses as well as those items normally thought of as expenses, such as the cost of goods sold or wages.)

Changes in these five basic elements are portrayed in the statement of cash flow and the statement of changes in equity.

2.2. Challenges in Financial Statement Preparation: Timing and Amounts

Two key challenges for preparers of financial statements are determining when to recognize financial events and how to measure the financial effect of these events.

Recognition is the process of incorporating into the financial statement an item that meets the definition of a financial statement element (i.e., assets, liabilities, equity, income, and expenses) and satisfies the criteria for recognition. The IFRS criteria for recognition of an item are that it should be recognized in the financial statements if:

- It is *probable* that any future economic benefit associated with the item will flow to or from the entity.
- The item has a cost or value that can be *measured with reliability*.

Measurement is the process of determining the monetary effect of financial events and thus the amounts that are to be recognized and presented in the financial statements.

In meeting the challenges of recognition and measurement, financial statement preparers employ judgment about appropriate methods—many of which are constrained by IFRS requirements to use specific methods—and the estimation of relevant parameters. Such judgments and estimates can vary across companies and across time; therefore, analysts should develop awareness of the potential effect of these variations on financial statements.

3. THE BALANCE SHEET

A number of standards, including the Framework described above, apply to the majority of the components of the balance sheet. These include standards describing requirements for companies adopting international financial standards for the first time,[3] requirements for presenting

---

[3]IFRS No. 1.

financial statements under international financial standards,[4] and accounting for changes in accounting principles and estimates.[5]

Other standards apply more directly to specific components of the balance sheet. The sections below describe the key aspects of the standards relevant to each component of the balance sheet.

3.1. Marketable Securities

The international standards of accounting for marketable securities, contained in IAS No. 39, require that companies recognize securities initially at fair market value; for investments in marketable securities, this is typically the cost to acquire securities.

The fair market value of securities changes over time, and the central issue in accounting for securities is: Should securities continue to be presented at cost or adjusted as changes occur in their fair market value? Under the accounting standards, the answer depends on how the security is categorized.

Securities with fixed maturities and payments (e.g., bonds) that the company intends to hold until maturity (and has the ability to do so) can be categorized as held to maturity. **Held-to-maturity** securities are presented at their original cost, updated for any amortization of discount or premium. A debt security purchased for an amount greater than its principal value is said to have been purchased at a premium; if purchased for an amount less than its principal value it is said to have been purchased at a discount. Any premium or discount is amortized (i.e., reduced) over the remaining life of the security so that at maturity, the value of the security in the accounting records equals the principal value.

Securities that do not have fixed maturities (e.g., equity) and bonds that a company does not intend to hold until maturity are presented at their fair market value, and the reported value continues to be adjusted as changes occur in the fair market value. Such changes in a security's fair market value during an accounting period, assuming the security is not sold, give rise to unrealized gains or losses. An unrealized gain results from an increase in a security's value over the accounting period, and an unrealized loss results from a decrease in a security's value. If the security is sold, the gain or loss is said to be realized. When securities are sold, a company realizes a gain (loss) if the sale price is greater than (less than) the value of the security in the company's books.

The accounting for unrealized holding gains or losses differs for **held-for-trading securities** (trading securities) versus **available-for-sale securities**. Trading securities are simply those securities that the company intends to trade, and available-for-sale securities are those that do not fall into any other category. The category *trading securities* also includes derivatives.

Unrealized holding gains or losses on trading securities are recorded in the income statement. Unrealized holding gains or losses on available-for-sale securities are recorded in equity (as part of other comprehensive income) until the securities are sold. So, both trading and available-for-sale securities are valued at market value, but only the unrealized holding gains or losses on trading securities flow directly through the income statement. As a result, the performance of trading securities portfolios is more transparently reflected in the financial statements.

Exhibit 8-1 summarizes the different categories of marketable securities and their accounting treatment.

---

[4]IAS No. 1.
[5]IAS No. 8.

AVS securities

Marked to Market by

analysts mostly

EXHIBIT 8-1   Categories of Marketable Securities and Accounting Treatment

Category	How Measured	Unrealized and Realized Gains and Losses	Income (Interest and Dividends) Reported
Held to maturity	Amortized cost	Unrealized: not reported	In income statement
		Realized: reported in income statement	
Trading	Fair value	Unrealized: reported in income statement	In income statement
		Realized: reported in income statement	
Available for sale	Fair value	Unrealized: reported in equity	In income statement
		Realized: reported in income statement	

EXAMPLE 8-1   Accounting for Marketable Securities

Assume a company has the following portfolio of marketable securities:

Category	Value at Fiscal Year-End 2005	Value at Fiscal Year-End 2006
Held to maturity	$10,000,000	$10,000,000
Held for trading	$5,000,000	$5,500,000
Available for sale	$8,000,000	$7,000,000

1. What amount of unrealized holding gains or losses would the company report in total?
2. How much unrealized holding gains or losses would the company report in its income statement?

Solution to 1. The total amount of unrealized holding gains or losses that the company would report is determined by comparing the end-of-period value of held-for-trading and available-for-sale securities with their values as reported at the end of the previous period. In this example, the company would report a total of $500,000 as unrealized holding *losses*, calculated as the value of the held-for-trading and available-for-sale securities at the end of the period ($12,500,000) minus their value at the beginning of the period ($13,000,000).

Solution to 2. The company would report an unrealized holding *gain* of $500,000 in its income statement. The change in the market value of the available-for-sale securities (the unrealized loss of $1,000,000) would not be reported in the income statement. Instead, it would be shown as part of comprehensive income.

An analyst should obtain an understanding of management's rationale for categorizing securities as "trading securities" or as "available for sale." The performance of trading securities portfolios is more transparently reflected in the financial statements because the income statement shows both income (interest and dividends) and changes in value, whether realized or unrealized. In contrast, with available-for-sale securities, there is an asymmetrical treatment of income and changes in value. This asymmetrical treatment can cause an unsophisticated user of financial statements to misinterpret the performance of a company's marketable securities portfolio. It is possible, for example, that unrealized losses could accumulate in equity without affecting the income statement.

An additional standard relevant to marketable securities is the requirement that risk exposures arising from financial instruments be disclosed; requirements include specified minimum qualitative and quantitative disclosures about credit risk, liquidity risk, and market risk.[6] Qualitative disclosures require a description of management's objectives, policies, and processes for managing those risks. Quantitative disclosures refer to the provision of information regarding the *extent* to which an entity is exposed to risk. Together, these disclosures provide an overview of the entity's use of financial instruments and the resulting risk exposures.

3.2. Inventories

The chapter on balance sheets describes various methods by which companies determine the cost of goods in inventory. Unlike U.S. GAAP, International Accounting Standards[7] require that the choice of the accounting method used to value inventories should be based upon the order in which products are sold, relative to when they are put into inventory. Therefore, whenever possible, the cost of a unit of inventory should be assigned by specific identification of the unit's costs. In many cases, however, it is necessary to use a formula to calculate inventory costs.

International standards permit the use of two alternative formulas for assigning the cost of inventory: (1) weighted average cost, in which the cost per unit of inventory is determined as a weighted average of the cost of all units of inventory; and (2) first in, first out (FIFO), in which it is assumed that the costs associated with the first units purchased (first in) are considered to be the cost of the first units sold (first out).

Unlike U.S. GAAP, international standards do not allow the use of the LIFO (last in, first out) method to calculate the cost of inventory because the method is not considered a faithful model of inventory flows. The IASB has noted that the use of LIFO is often tax driven because this method results in lower taxable income during periods of rising prices; however, they concluded that tax considerations do not provide a conceptual basis for selecting an appropriate treatment.

Like U.S. GAAP, international standards require inventory to be reported at the lower of cost or net realizable value. However, IFRS permits the reversal of inventory write-downs, but no such provision exists in U.S. GAAP.

3.3. Property, Plant, and Equipment

The international standards of accounting for property, plant, and equipment, contained in IAS No. 16, require companies to recognize these assets initially at cost.

---

[6]IFRS No. 7.
[7]IAS No. 2.

Like U.S. GAAP, international standards allow property, plant, and equipment to be reported in the financial statements at cost less accumulated depreciation. *Depreciation* is the systematic allocation of the cost of the asset over its useful life, and *accumulated depreciation* is the cumulative amount of depreciation expense recorded in relation to the asset.

Unlike U.S. GAAP, International Accounting Standards allow another alternative: reporting property, plant, and equipment at a revalued amount. When property, plant, and equipment are revalued, they are reported in the financial statements at fair value as of the revaluation date, less accumulated depreciation subsequent to the revaluation. Any revaluation increase is reported as part of equity, unless it is reversing a previous revaluation decrease. (The reason for this is that the previous decrease was reported as a reduction in the company's net income.) Any revaluation decrease is reported in profit and loss unless it is reversing a previous revaluation increase.

3.4. Long-Term Investments

The overall IFRS Framework for accounting for a company's investments in the securities of another company is based on the extent of control that the investing company has on the investee company. In the discussion of marketable securities above, it was assumed that the equity investment gave the investing company no control over the investee. As discussed, in such cases, the investments are designated as "trading" or "available for sale" and reflected at fair value.

If, however, an equity investment *did* give the investing company some control over the investee, the accounting standards require a different treatment. The specific treatment depends on the amount of control. If an investor owns 20 percent or more of the voting power of an investee, such an ownership stake would provide significant influence, where significant influence is defined as "power to participate in financial and operating policy decisions of the investee but is not control or joint control over those policies."[8] When an investor has significant influence, international standards require that the investment be reported using the equity method of accounting. The equity method of accounting means that the investor reports its pro rata share of the investee's profits as an increase in the amount of investment.

If an investor owns more than 50 percent of the voting power of the investee, such an ownership stake would provide significant control and the investee's financial statements would be consolidated with those of the investor. Consolidation roughly means that the investee's assets, liabilities, and income are combined into those of the investor. *Note*: The IFRS standard on business combinations is an active agenda item of the convergence project and is, therefore, subject to change during coming years.

When an investor shares the ownership of an investee, as in a joint venture, control is shared and the investor would account for the investment using either the proportionate consolidation method or the equity method. Proportionate consolidation roughly means that the investor's financial statements include its proportionate share of the investee's assets, liabilities, and income.

Exhibit 8-2 summarizes the different levels of control associated with each level of ownership and the accounting treatment used in each situation.

---

[8]IAS No. 28.

EXHIBIT 8-2   Accounting Treatment for Different Levels of an Investor's Percentage Ownership in an Investee and Related Extent of Control

Extent of Control	Percent Ownership	Accounting Treatment	IFRS Reference
Significant influence	20–50%	Equity accounting	IAS No. 28
Control	More than 50%	Business combinations/consolidation	IAS No. 27/IFRS No. 3/SIC 12
Joint control	Shared	Joint ventures/proportionate consolidation or equity accounting	IAS No. 31/SIC 13

SIC = Standing Interpretations Committee.

Like U.S. GAAP, international standards use extent of control as a factor determining whether an investee should be consolidated. U.S. GAAP differs from IFRS in that it allows a dual model: one model based on extent of voting control, and one model based on an alternative assessment of economic control. The model based on economic control depends first on the economic substance of the investee and second on the investor's economic interests in the investee (liability for the investee's losses and opportunity to benefit from the investee's gains).

Unlike U.S. GAAP, international standards permit that interests in joint ventures may be accounted for using the proportionate consolidation method or the equity method,[9] whereas U.S. GAAP requires the equity method of accounting.

3.5. Goodwill

IFRS defines **goodwill** as the amount an acquirer pays to buy another company, minus the fair value of the net identifiable assets acquired. Goodwill is intended to represent future economic benefits arising from assets that are not capable of being individually identified and separately recognized. Goodwill is considered an **intangible asset** (i.e., an asset without physical substance). Whereas some intangible assets—so-called identifiable intangible assets, such as patents and trademarks—can be bought and sold individually, goodwill cannot. Goodwill is an **unidentifiable intangible**.

Under IFRS No. 3, goodwill is capitalized as an asset and tested for impairment annually. **Impairment** means diminishment in value. Impairment of goodwill is a noncash expense; however, the impairment of goodwill does affect reported net income. When impairment of goodwill is charged against income in the current period, current reported income decreases. This charge against income also leads to reduced net assets and reduced shareholders' equity, but potentially improved return on assets, asset turnover ratios, return on equity, and equity turnover ratios because equity, the denominator in these ratios, is smaller. Even if the market reacts indifferently to an impairment write-off, an analyst should understand the implications of a goodwill write-off and, more generally, evaluate whether reported goodwill has been impaired. Example 8-2 presents a partial goodwill impairment footnote for Prudential PLC.

---

[9]IAS No. 31.

EXAMPLE 8-2   Goodwill Impairment Testing

Susan Lee is examining the financial statements of Prudential PLC and notes that the income statement shows a goodwill impairment charge of £120 million. Lee finds the following footnote to Prudential's financial statements.

Prudential PLC
2005 Annual Report Footnote H1
Impairment testing

Goodwill does not generate cash flows independently of other groups of assets and thus is assigned to cash generating units (CGUs) for the purposes of impairment testing. These CGUs are based upon how management monitors the business and represent the lowest level to which goodwill can be allocated on a reasonable basis. An allocation of the Group's goodwill to CGUs is shown below:

	2005 (£ millions)	2004 (£ millions)
M&G	1,153	1,153
Japan life company	—	120
Venture investment subsidiaries of the PAC with-profits fund	607	784
Other	188	188
	1,948	2,245

'Other' represents goodwill amounts allocated across cash generating units in Asia and US operations. These goodwill amounts are not individually material. There are no other intangible assets with indefinite useful lives other than goodwill.

Assessment of whether goodwill may be impaired
With the exception of M&G and venture investment subsidiaries of the PAC with-profits fund the goodwill in the balance sheet relates to acquired life businesses. The Company routinely compares the aggregate of net asset value and acquired goodwill on an IFRS basis of acquired life business with the value of the business as determined using the EEV methodology, as described in section D1. Any excess of IFRS over EEV carrying value is then compared with EEV basis value of current and projected future new business to determine whether there is any indication that the goodwill in the IFRS balance sheet may be impaired.

Goodwill is tested for impairment by comparing the CGUs carrying amount, excluding any goodwill, with its recoverable amount.

M&G
The recoverable amount for the M&G CGU has been determined by calculating its value in use. This has been calculated by aggregating the present value of future

cash flows expected to be derived from the component businesses of M&G (based upon management projections) and its current surplus capital.

The discounted cash flow valuation has been based on a three-year plan prepared by M&G, and approved by the directors of Prudential plc, and cash flow projections for later years.

As a cross check to the discounted cash flow analysis, a review was undertaken of publicly available information for companies engaged in businesses comparable to the component businesses, including reported market prices for such companies' shares. In addition, a review was undertaken of publicly available terms of transactions involving companies comparable to the component businesses. In particular, comparison has been made of the valuation multiples implied by the discounted cash flow analysis to current trading multiples of companies comparable to the component businesses, as well as to multiples achieved in precedent transactions.

The value in use is particularly sensitive to a number of key assumptions, as follows:

(i)   The assumed growth rate on forecast cash flows beyond the terminal year of the budget. A growth rate of 2.5 per cent has been used to extrapolate beyond the plan period.

(ii)   The risk discount rate. Differing discount rates have been applied in accordance with the nature of the individual component businesses. For retail and institutional business a risk discount rate of 12 per cent has been applied. This represents the average implied discount rate for comparable UK listed asset managers calculated by reference to risk-free rates, equity risk premiums of 5 per cent and an average 'beta' factor for relative market risk of comparable UK listed asset managers. A similarly granular approach has been applied for the other component businesses of M&G.

(iii)   That asset management contracts continue on similar terms.

Management believes that any reasonable change in the key assumptions would not cause the carrying amount of M&G to exceed its recoverable amount.

Japanese life company

As noted above, the entire goodwill relating to the Japanese life operation of £120 million has been deemed to be impaired following impairment testing carried out in 2005. This testing was based on a recoverable amount for the Japanese company that was determined by calculating its value in use based on net present value cash flow projections. Such projections reflected existing business over the expected duration of the contracts and expected new business. A risk discount rate of 5 per cent was applied to the projected cash flows. On the basis of the results of this exercise it was determined that all goodwill held in relation to the Japanese business should be written off in 2005.

PAC with-profits fund venture investment subsidiaries

The recoverable amount for the ventures entities controlled by the Group through PPM Capital has been determined on a portfolio CGU basis by aggregating fair values calculated for each entity less costs to sell these entities.

The fair value of each entity is calculated by PPM Capital in accordance with the International Private Equity and Venture Capital Valuation Guidelines which set out industry best practice for determining the fair value of private equity investments. The guidelines require that an enterprise value is calculated for each investment, typically using an appropriate multiple applied to the Company's maintainable earnings. All amounts relating to financial instruments ranking higher in a liquidation than those controlled by PPM Capital are then deducted from the enterprise value and a marketability discount applied to the result to give a fair value attributable to the instruments controlled by PPM Capital. The marketability discount ranges from 10 per cent to 30 per cent, depending on PPM Capital's level of control over a realization process.

Management believes that any reasonable change in the key assumptions would not give rise to an impairment charge.

1. What operating unit resulted in a goodwill impairment charge, and how was the charge computed?
2. For the operating unit identified in Part 1, would an analyst anticipate subsequent goodwill impairments?

Solution to 1. The entire impairment charge for 2005 was related to the Japanese life company operating unit. The loss was determined by projecting future cash flows for this unit and discounting them at a rate of 5 percent.

Solution to 2. Because the impairment charge for 2005 represented all of the goodwill of the Japanese life company operating unit, subsequent goodwill impairments for this operating unit should not occur.

Because goodwill can significantly influence the comparability of financial statements between companies using different accounting methods, analysts sometimes make certain goodwill-related adjustments to a company's financial statements. The objective of such adjustments is to remove any distortion that goodwill and its recognition, amortization, and impairment might create. Adjustments include the following:

- Subtracting goodwill from assets and use of this adjusted data to compute financial ratios.
- Excluding goodwill impairment charges from income and use of this adjusted data when reviewing operating trends.
- Evaluating future business acquisitions by taking into account the purchase price paid relative to the net assets and earnings prospects of the acquired company.

If the amount an acquirer pays to buy another company is less than the fair value of the net identifiable assets acquired, it is not recognized as negative goodwill. Instead, a gain is recognized. However, before any gain is recognized, the acquirer should reassess the cost of acquisition and the fair values attributed to the acquiree's identifiable assets, liabilities, and contingent liabilities.

As noted, goodwill arises in connection with acquisitions. Several other aspects of international accounting for acquisitions may be noted. Under the purchase method of accounting,[10] the acquisition price must be allocated to all of the acquired company's identifiable tangible and intangible assets, liabilities, and contingent liabilities. The assets and liabilities of the acquired entity are combined into the financial statements of the acquiring company at their fair values on the acquisition date. Because the acquirer's assets and liabilities, measured at their historical costs, are combined with the acquired company's assets and liabilities, measured at their fair market value on the acquisition date, the acquirer's pre- and post-merger balance sheets are often not easily compared.

Furthermore, under the purchase method, the income statement and the cash flow statements include the operating performance of the acquiree from the date of the acquisition forward. Operating results prior to the acquisition are not restated and remain the same as historically reported by the acquirer. Consequently, although the financial statements of the acquirer will reflect the reality of the acquisition, they will not be comparable before and after the acquisition.

3.6.   Intangible Assets Other than Goodwill

IAS No. 38 includes standards for reporting certain intangible assets other than goodwill. These intangible assets are referred to as identifiable intangible assets. **Identifiable intangible assets arise either from contractual or other legal rights**, or must be capable of being separated from the company and sold, transferred, licensed, rented, or exchanged.

The standards for reporting identifiable intangible assets, contained in IAS No. 38, provide that an intangible asset is recognized—at cost—if it is probable that the future economic benefits attributable to the asset will flow to the company and if the cost of the asset can be measured reliably. Only those intangibles that have been purchased or manufactured (in limited instances) may be recognized as assets. Internally produced items, such as customer lists, are not recognized as assets.

Given that it meets the criteria for recognition, an intangible asset with a finite useful life is amortized on a systematic basis over the best estimate of its useful life. In other words, the cost of the identifiable intangible asset is allocated systematically over the asset's useful life. If the identifiable intangible asset does not have a finite useful life, it is not amortized. Instead, the asset is tested at least annually for impairment as with goodwill. Testing for impairment involves evaluating whether the current value of an asset is materially lower than its carrying value.

Like U.S. GAAP, international standards allow identifiable intangibles to be reported in the financial statements at cost less amortization and less any impairment charges.

Unlike U.S. GAAP, international accounting standards allow another alternative: reporting identifiable intangible assets at a revalued amount. When identifiable intangible assets are revalued, they are reported in the financial statements at fair value as of the revaluation date, less accumulated amortization subsequent to the revaluation. Any revaluation increase is reported as part of equity, unless it is reversing a previous revaluation decrease. Any revaluation decrease is reported in profit and loss unless it is reversing a previous revaluation increase. U.S. GAAP prohibits revaluations.

Companies also have intangible assets that accounting rules do not include as items that can be recorded in financial statements; these intangible assets include management skill,

---

[10]IFRS No. 3.

a positive corporate culture, trademarks, name recognition, a good reputation, proprietary products, and so forth. However, the costs related to these intangible assets—such as training, advertising, and research—must be expensed. An analyst must be aware of the potential value of such unrecorded assets.

3.7. Provisions (Nonfinancial Liabilities)

Nonfinancial liabilities include **provisions**, which are liabilities of uncertain timing or amount, such as warranty obligations, and contingent liabilities, which are liabilities contingent on the occurrence of some event. The standards for reporting nonfinancial liabilities, contained in IAS No. 37, provide that a company should recognize nonfinancial liabilities when it has a present obligation as a result of a past event and the company can reliably estimate the cost to settle the obligation.

The amount recognized as a nonfinancial liability should be the best estimate, as of the balance sheet date, of the cost that will be required to settle the obligation.

4. THE INCOME STATEMENT

A number of standards, including the Framework (described above), apply to the majority of the components of the income statement. These include standards describing requirements for companies adopting international financial standards for the first time, requirements for presenting financial statements under international financial standards, and accounting for changes in accounting principles and estimates.[11]

Other standards apply more directly to specific components of the income statement. The sections below describe the key aspects of the standards relevant to each component in the same order as the components described in the chapter discussing the income statement.

4.1. Revenue Recognition: General

The IASB Framework defines income as including both revenue and gains. In IAS No. 18, revenue is defined as the gross inflow of economic benefits during the period, arising in the ordinary course of activities, or resulting in increases in equity other than contributions by equity participants.

IAS No. 18 addresses how revenue is to be measured, namely, at the fair value of consideration received. The standard also addresses the timing of revenue recognition.

Some criteria for recognizing revenue are common to both the sale of goods and the provision of services: It must be possible to reliably measure the amount of revenue and costs of the transaction, and it must be probable that economic benefits of the transaction will flow to the seller. In addition, to recognize revenue from the sale of goods, it is necessary that the risks and rewards of ownership pass to the buyer and that the seller not have continued control over the goods sold. To recognize revenue from the provision of services, it is necessary that the stage of completion of the service can be measured reliably.

U.S. GAAP defines revenue in terms of actual or expected cash flows, and, for revenue recognition, U.S. GAAP focuses extensively on realization and earned status. U.S. GAAP also

---

[11]IFRS No. 1, IAS No. 1, and IAS No. 8, respectively.

provides more extensive guidance than IFRS regarding industry-specific issues. Despite such differences, the key principles are similar in U.S. GAAP and IFRS.

4.2.   Revenue Recognition for Construction Contracts

IAS No. 11 deals with the recognition of construction contract revenue and costs—in particular, the allocation of contract revenue and costs to the accounting periods in which construction work is performed. The standard applies to the accounting for construction contracts in the financial statements of contractors.

A construction contract is a contract specifically negotiated for the construction of an asset or a combination of assets that are closely interrelated or interdependent in terms of their design, technology, and function, or their ultimate purpose or use. Construction contracts include those for the construction or restoration of assets and the restoration of the environment.

When the outcome of a construction contract can be estimated reliably, revenue and costs (and, therefore, profit) should be recognized based on the stage of completion (percentage of completion method). When the outcome of a contract *cannot* be reliably estimated, revenue should be recognized to the extent that it is probable to recover contract costs. This requirement differs from U.S. GAAP, which requires that the completed contract method be used in such cases.

4.3.   Cost of Sales

Two international accounting standards, IAS No. 2 (accounting for the cost of inventories) and IAS No. 18 (revenue recognition), have an effect on cost of sales. As noted, under international standards, LIFO is not an acceptable method for the valuation of inventory. Consequently, financial statements prepared according to U.S. GAAP may differ significantly from those prepared under IFRS.

U.S. GAAP does, however, require that companies using LIFO disclose the information required to enable a user of financial statements to adjust the inventory and cost of sales figures to a basis comparable with financial statements prepared using IFRS.

4.4.   Administrative Expenses (Including Employee Benefits)

Administrative (or operating) expenses typically include overheads related to employee costs. The IASB Framework defines expenses to include losses because expenses are decreases in economic benefits that result in a decrease in equity. The inclusion of losses as expenses contrasts with U.S. GAAP, which differentiates expenses from losses by restricting the term *expenses* to refer to those outflows (of cash or the equivalent) that relate to the entity's ongoing primary business operations.

One type of administrative expense with specific international accounting principles is the expense related to employee benefits, such as salaries, bonuses, postemployment benefits, and termination benefits. Recognition and measurement principles, as well as the disclosure requirements, are provided in IAS No. 19. IFRS No. 2 deals with equity compensation benefits, such as share options.

4.5.   Depreciation Expenses

As discussed above, depreciation is the process of recognizing the costs of fixed assets over time by systematically decreasing the assets' value and reporting a commensurate expense on the income statement. The term *depletion* is used for this process when the asset is a natural resource, and the term *amortization* is used for this process when the asset is an intangible asset. The cost of acquiring land is not depreciated.

International standards require companies to review the depreciation method applied to an asset at least at each financial year-end. If there has been a significant change in the expected pattern of consumption of the future economic benefits embodied in the asset, companies must change the depreciation method to reflect the changed pattern. Similar to U.S. GAAP, such a change is accounted for as a change in accounting estimate[12] and thus reflected on future financial statements.

Various depreciation methods exist, including the straight-line method, which allocates evenly the cost of a long-lived asset over its estimated useful life, and accelerated methods, which allocate a greater proportion of the asset's cost in the earlier years of its useful life, thus accelerating the timing of the depreciation expense. In choosing the appropriate depreciation method, IFRS requires:

- The depreciable amount is allocated on a *systematic* basis over the useful life.
- The method used must reflect the pattern of expected *consumption*.

Whether the straight-line depreciation method or an accelerated method is used, the method complies with IFRS *only* if it reflects the pattern of the expected consumption of the assets.

4.6. Finance Costs

In general, borrowing costs—defined as interest and other costs incurred by an entity in connection with the borrowing of funds—are expensed in the period incurred.

IFRS offers an alternative to expensing borrowing costs immediately. When borrowing costs are incurred in connection with the acquisition, construction, or production of an asset that takes a long time to be ready for its intended use, such borrowing costs can be added to the total cost of the asset.[13] In other words, rather than expensing these costs immediately, a company has the alternative to capitalize these borrowing costs and depreciate them over time. This topic is an item on the list of IASB's short-term convergence projects as of December 2006.

U.S. GAAP requires the capitalization of interest costs for assets that take a substantial time to complete.

4.7. Income Tax Expense

IAS No. 12 prescribes the accounting treatment for income taxes and specifically addresses issues relating to the carrying amount of assets as well as transactions and other events of the current period, which are recognized in the entity's financial statements.

As with U.S. GAAP, international standards provide for the accounting treatment when differences exist between accounting methods allowed by the relevant taxing authority and accounting methods allowed for financial statement reporting (i.e., IFRS). Where differences exist between methods allowable by taxing authorities and by IFRS, differences will exist between taxable profit and financial statement pretax profit (also referred to as *accounting*

---

[12]IAS No. 8.
[13]IAS No. 23.

profit). Such differences give rise to differences in the value of a company's assets and liabilities recorded in its financial statements (balance sheet) and the tax bases of those assets and liabilities. In turn, these differences can result in future taxes payable or receivable, so-called deferred tax liabilities and deferred tax assets.

The primary differences between U.S. GAAP and IFRS are attributable to differences in exceptions to the application of the principles (i.e., differences in the scope of coverage of the principles).

4.8.   Nonrecurring Items

Nonrecurring items generally include discontinued operations, accounting changes, and unusual or infrequent items. As noted, analysts typically find it useful to break reported earnings down into recurring and nonrecurring components. Recurring earnings are viewed as permanent or sustainable, whereas nonrecurring earnings are considered to be somewhat random and unsustainable. Therefore, analysts often exclude the effects of nonrecurring items when performing a short-term analysis of an entity (e.g., estimating next year's earnings). However, even so-called nonrecurring events, such as sales of a part of a business, tend to recur from time to time, so analysts may include some average (per year) amount of nonrecurring items for longer-term analyses.

IFRS and U.S. GAAP differ in their treatment of these issues, although as with other areas, convergence is occurring.[14]

For discontinued operations, IFRS changed to align with U.S. GAAP. IFRS No. 5 generally converges with SFAS No. 144. The new international guidance, like the U.S. standards, requires that discontinued operations be reported when a company disposes of one of its business components (or when the component is being held for sale) and will no longer have management involvement.

For accounting changes, U.S. GAAP changed to align with IFRS. SFAS No. 154, issued in June 2005, generally converges with IAS No. 8. Changes in accounting principles are accounted for retrospectively, and changes in accounting estimates are accounted for prospectively.

For extraordinary items, convergence has not yet been achieved. U.S. GAAP continues to allow extraordinary items (i.e., items that are both unusual in nature and infrequent in occurrence) to be reported separately from net income.

Unlike U.S. GAAP, IFRS do not distinguish between items that are and are not likely to recur. Furthermore, IFRS do not permit any items to be classified as *extraordinary items*. However, IFRS do require the disclosure of all material information that is relevant to understanding a company's performance. The analyst generally can use this information, together with information from outside sources, to estimate amounts of recurring and nonrecurring items.

5.   THE CASH FLOW STATEMENT

Both international standards and U.S. GAAP require that a statement of cash flows be included among a company's full set of financial statements (FASB Statement No. 95, *Statement of Cash Flows,* and IAS No. 7, *Cash Flow Statements*) showing the changes in cash and cash equivalents over an accounting period.

---

[14]This topic is discussed in D. Herrmann and I. P. N. Hauge, "Convergence: In Search of the Best," *Journal of Accountancy* online edition, January 2006: www.aicpa.org/PUBS/JOFA/jan2006/herrmann.htm.

EXHIBIT 8-3   Statement of Cash Flows: Classification of Interest and Dividends under
International and U.S. Standards

Category	Classification in IFRS vs. U.S. GAAP

Cash flows from OPERATING activities

Cash from principal revenue-producing activities of the entity (i.e., cash receipts from customers less cash payments to suppliers and employees).

Interest received	IFRS alternatives: operating or investing section
	U.S. GAAP: mandated operating section
Dividends received	IFRS alternatives: operating or investing section
	U.S. GAAP: mandated operating section
Interest paid	IFRS alternatives: operating or financing section
	U.S. GAAP: mandated operating section
Dividends paid (IFRS only)	IFRS alternatives: operating or financing section

Cash flows from INVESTING activities

Purchases of long-term assets and other investments not included in cash equivalents; proceeds on sale.

Interest received (IFRS only)	IFRS alternatives: operating or investing section
Dividends received (IFRS only)	IFRS alternatives: operating or investing section

Cash flows from FINANCING activities

Cash from issuance or repayment of equity capital and/or long-term debt.

Dividends paid	IFRS alternatives: operating or financing section
	U.S. GAAP: mandated financing section
Interest paid	IFRS alternatives: operating or financing section

Both sets of standards require that the cash flow statement include sections covering operating, investing, and financing activities of the company. The differences between international and U.S. standards arise in the classification of certain cash flows.

International standards allow companies to report cash inflows from interest and dividends as either operating or investing activities and cash outflows for interest and dividends as either operating or financing activities (see Exhibit 8-3). In contrast, U.S. standards require the following: Interest and dividends received are classified as inflows from operating activities; interest paid is classified as an outflow for operating activities; and dividends paid are classified as financing activities.

6. STANDARD SETTERS' AGENDA FOR CONVERGENCE

As noted in the introduction to this chapter, in February 2006, the FASB and IASB published a memorandum of understanding outlining a "road map for convergence" over the next several years. This section summarizes the standard setters' agenda for convergence over the period 2006 to 2008.

By 2008, the IASB and FASB aim to conclude whether any major differences should be eliminated in the following topics for short-term convergence, and if so, to complete the work to do so: fair value option (allow companies to report financial assets and liabilities at fair value on a contract-by-contract basis, converging to IFRS); borrowing costs (eliminate alternative to expense immediately when in connection with longer-term projects, converging to U.S. GAAP); research and development; impairment; segment reporting; subsequent events; and income taxes.

Topics that are already on an active agenda for IASB and/or FASB include business combinations, consolidations, fair value measurement guidance, liabilities and equity distinctions, performance reporting, postretirement benefits (including pensions), and revenue recognition. Joint IASB and FASB goals for 2008 have been established for each of these topics.

7. EFFECT OF DIFFERENCES BETWEEN ACCOUNTING STANDARDS

As we note throughout this chapter, differences between international and U.S. accounting standards are decreasing as convergence between the two sets of standards occurs. Differences that do exist have an effect on commonly used financial ratios. We discuss several major differences here.

If comparing a U.S. company that uses LIFO accounting with an international company for whom this method is not allowable, an analyst will make adjustments. Specifically, using financial statement note disclosures, the analyst will adjust the U.S. company's profits (gross, operating, and net), ending inventory, and total assets. These adjustments will affect certain profitability, solvency, liquidity, and activity ratios. For comparison purposes, inventory is adjusted from LIFO to FIFO by adding the LIFO reserve to the LIFO inventory value on the balance sheet. Under U.S. GAAP, a company must disclose the LIFO reserve amount in the financial statement notes if the LIFO method is followed. In addition, cost of goods sold is adjusted from LIFO to FIFO by subtracting the net increase in the LIFO reserve that occurred during the fiscal year. Example 8-3 illustrates a LIFO to FIFO conversion.

EXAMPLE 8-3   LIFO Effects on Financial Statements and Ratios

Buccaneer Corporation prepares its financial statements (Exhibits 8-4 and 8-5) in accordance with U.S. GAAP and uses the LIFO inventory method. During the year, Buccaneer's LIFO reserve increased from $40 million to $64 million. The income tax rate is 30 percent.

EXHIBIT 8-4   Income Statement and Balance Sheet under LIFO and FIFO Inventory Accounting ($ millions)

Account	LIFO Method	LIFO to FIFO Adjustment	FIFO Method
Sales	1,800.0	—	1,800.0
Cost of sales	1,060.0	(24.0)	1,036.0
Gross profit	740.0	24.0	764.0
Operating expenses	534.0	—	534.0
Income before taxes	206.0	24.0	230.0

Account	LIFO Method	LIFO to FIFO Adjustment	FIFO Method
Income taxes	61.8	(7.2)	69.0
Net income	144.2	(16.8)	161.0
Cash	80.0	—	80.0
Inventory	356.0	64.0	420.0
Other current assets	344.0	—	344.0
Fixed assets, net	1,120.0	—	1,120.0
Total assets	1,900.0	64.0	1,964.0
Current liabilities	200.0	—	200.0
Noncurrent liabilities	424.0	19.2	443.2
Common stock	840.0	—	840.0
Retained earnings	436.0	44.8	480.8
Total liabilities and equity	1,900.0	64.0	1,964.0

The net increase in Buccaneer's LIFO reserve during the fiscal year was $24 million ($64 million − $40 million). To adjust from LIFO to FIFO, the net increase in the LIFO reserve must be subtracted from the LIFO reported cost of sales. (A net decrease in the LIFO reserve during the year would be added to LIFO reported cost of sales in a LIFO to FIFO conversion.) Accordingly, because reported gross profits are $24 million higher after the FIFO conversion, income tax expense will increase by $7.2 million ($24 million × 30% income tax rate), resulting in an increase to net income of $16.8 million. For the balance sheet conversion, the year-end LIFO reserve of $64 million is added to the LIFO reported inventory, resulting in an increase of $64 million to both inventory and total assets under FIFO. In addition, the deferred income tax liabilities will increase by $19.2 million ($64 million × 30% income tax rate), and retained earnings will increase by $44.8 million ($64 million × 70% after-tax retention).

Comparative selected profitability, solvency, liquidity, and activity ratios for Buccaneer Corporation under the two inventory methods are given in Exhibit 8-5.

EXHIBIT 8-5   Financial Ratios under LIFO and FIFO Inventory Accounting

Ratio	Formula	LIFO Method	FIFO Method
Net profit margin	Net income ÷ Net sales	8.01%	8.94%
Financial leverage	Total assets ÷ Total equity	1.489	1.487
Current ratio	Current assets ÷ Current liabilities	3.90	4.22
Inventory turnover	Cost of sales ÷ Ending inventory	2.98 turns	2.47 turns

If comparing an IFRS company with a U.S. company that reports extraordinary items separately from net income but reports certain unusual items as part of operating income, an analyst will examine the financial statement notes to identify similar items that have received different reporting treatment.

If comparing an IFRS company, which has written up the value of its intangible or tangible long-term assets, with a U.S. company, an analyst will eliminate the effect of the write-ups in calculating asset-based ratios. Example 8-4 illustrates a revaluation adjustment conversion.

EXAMPLE 8-4   Analyst Adjustments to Revaluations in IFRS/U.S. GAAP Comparisons

Aramis Ltd. prepares its financial statements in accordance with IFRS. During the current year, Aramis revalued its fixed assets upward by a total of €75 million to better reflect its present fair market value.

The analyst must reverse the revaluation adjustments that Aramis has made if Aramis is to be compared with a company that complies with U.S. GAAP. For Aramis, the analyst will reduce both fixed assets and other equity by the upward revaluation of €75 million. Exhibit 8-6 shows these adjustments.

EXHIBIT 8-6   Analyst Adjustments to Revaluation (€ millions)

Account	Unadjusted	Reversal of Revaluation	Post-Adjustment
Sales	1,700.0	—	1,700.0
Cost of sales	1,040.0	—	1,040.0
Gross profit	660.0	—	660.0
Operating expenses	475.0	—	475.0
Income before taxes	185.0	—	185.0
Income taxes	74.0	—	74.0
Net income	111.0	—	111.0
Fixed assets, net	1,150.0	(75.0)	1,075.0
Inventory	310.0	—	310.0
Other current assets	120.0	—	120.0
Cash	20.0	—	20.0
Total assets	1,600.0	(75.0)	1,525.0
Noncurrent liabilities	370.0	—	370.0
Current liabilities	225.0	—	225.0
Contributed capital	550.0	—	550.0
Earned and other equity	455.0	(75.0)	380.0
Total liabilities and equity	1,600.0	(75.0)	1,525.0

Selected comparative performance ratios for Aramis under the two approaches are given in Exhibit 8-7.

EXHIBIT 8-7   Financial Ratios Pre- and Post-Adjustment

Ratio	Formula	Unadjusted	Post-adjustment
Return on assets	Net income ÷ Total assets	6.94%	7.28%
Return on equity	Net income ÷ Total equity	11.04%	11.94%
Asset turnover	Net sales ÷ Total assets	1.063 turns	1.115 turns
Equity turnover	Net sales ÷ Total equity	1.692 turns	1.828 turns
Financial leverage	Total assets ÷ Total equity	1.592	1.640

8. SUMMARY

The IASB is the standard-setting body of the IASC Foundation. The objectives of the IASC Foundation are to develop a single set of global financial reporting standards and to promote the use of those standards. In accomplishing these objectives, the IASC Foundation explicitly aims to bring about convergence between national standards and international standards. Many national accounting standard setters have adopted, or are in the process of adopting, the IFRS.

This chapter discussed both the IFRS Framework and the IFRS standards for reporting accounting items on the balance sheet, income statement, and cash flow statement. Key points include the following:

- The objectives of financial statements, as stated in the Framework, are "to provide information about the financial position, performance, and changes in financial position of an entity; this information should be useful to a wide range of users for the purpose of making economic decisions."
- To achieve the objective of providing useful information, financial statements should have the following qualitative characteristics: relevance, predictive value, faithful representation, neutrality, and verifiability.
- Financial statements provide information on the financial position and performance of an entity by grouping the effects of transactions and other events into the following five broad elements: assets, liabilities, equity, income, and expenses.
- Both IFRS and U.S. GAAP require companies to present basic financial statements: balance sheet, income statement, statement of cash flows, and statement of changes in equity.
- One major difference between IFRS and U.S. GAAP affecting all three statements involves inventories: U.S. GAAP allows the LIFO method for inventory costing, whereas IFRS does not.
- Another major balance sheet difference between IFRS and U.S. GAAP is that IFRS allows companies to revalue property, plant, and equipment as well as intangible assets.
- Accounting for investments is another area of difference: IFRS uses a voting control model to determine need for consolidation, whereas U.S. GAAP uses a dual model based on voting control and economic control.

- An important difference between IFRS and U.S. GAAP is the treatment of some nonrecurring items. IFRS does not permit any items to be classified as extraordinary items.
- International standards allow companies to report cash inflows from interest and dividends as relating to either operating or investing activities, and cash outflows for interest and dividends as relating to either operating or financing activities.
- Convergence between IFRS and U.S. GAAP has increased significantly over the past few years and is continuing.
- Analysts should know how to make financial statement adjustments to better compare IFRS reporting companies with those companies reporting under U.S. GAAP.

PRACTICE PROBLEMS

1. According to the IFRS Framework, which of the following is a qualitative characteristic related to the usefulness of information in financial statements?
   A. Neutrality
   B. Timeliness
   C. Accrual basis

2. Under the IFRS Framework, changes in the elements of financial statements are *most likely* portrayed in the
   A. balance sheet.
   B. income statement.
   C. cash flow statement.

3. Under IASB standards, which of the following categories of marketable securities is *most likely* to incur an asymmetrical treatment of income and changes in value?
   A. Held for trading
   B. Held to maturity
   C. Available for sale

4. According to IASB standards, which of the following inventory methods is *most preferred*?
   A. Specific identification
   B. Weighted average cost
   C. First in, first out (FIFO)

5. According to IASB standards, which of the following inventory methods is not acceptable?
   A. Weighted average cost
   B. First in, first out (FIFO)
   C. Last in, first out (LIFO)

6. Under IASB standards, inventory write-downs are
   A. not allowed.
   B. allowed but not reversible.
   C. allowed and subject to reversal.

7. According to IASB standards, property, plant, and equipment revaluations are
   A. not allowed.
   B. allowed for decreases only.
   C. allowed for both increases and decreases.

8. Under IASB standards, a joint venture interest is accounted for by using
   A. consolidation.
   B. the equity method or consolidation.
   C. the equity method or proportionate consolidation.

9. Under IASB standards, goodwill
   A. may be written off when acquired.
   B. is subject to an annual impairment test.
   C. is amortized over its expected useful life.

10. Under IASB standards, negative goodwill
    A. must be recorded as a gain.
    B. is prorated to the noncurrent assets.
    C. is accounted for as an extraordinary item.

11. Under IASB standards, an identifiable intangible asset with an indefinite life
    A. may be written off when acquired.
    B. is amortized over a 20-year period.
    C. is accounted for in the same manner as goodwill.

12. Under IASB standards, identifiable intangible assets are
    A. only revalued downward, with the decrease reported to profit and loss.
    B. revalued upward and reported to equity when reversing a previous revaluation decrease.
    C. revalued upward and reported to profit and loss when reversing a previous revaluation decrease.

13. Under IASB standards, when the outcome of a construction contract cannot be estimated reliably, revenue and costs should be
    A. recognized by using the completed contract method.
    B. recognized by using the percentage of completion contract method.
    C. recognized to the extent that it is probable to recover contract costs.

14. Under IASB standards, fixed asset depreciation methods must be
    A. rational and systematic.
    B. rational and reviewed at least annually.
    C. systematic and reflect the pattern of expected consumption.

15. Under IASB standards, cash inflows for the receipt of interest and dividends are
    A. operating cash flows.
    B. either operating or investing cash flows.
    C. either investing or financing cash flows.

16. Under IASB standards, cash outflows for the payment of interest are
    A. operating cash flows.
    B. either investing or financing cash flows.
    C. either operating or financing cash flows.

17. Under IASB standards, cash outflows for the payment of dividends are
    A. financing cash flows.
    B. either operating or investing cash flows.
    C. either operating or financing cash flows.

18. When comparing a U.S. company that uses LIFO accounting with an IFRS company that uses FIFO accounting, an analyst will
    A. make no adjustment if the adjustment data are unavailable.
    B. adjust either company to achieve comparability with the other.
    C. adjust the U.S. company to achieve comparability with the IFRS company.

19. When comparing a U.S. company with an IFRS company that has written up the value of its intangible assets, an analyst will eliminate the effect of the write-ups in calculating the
    A. gross margin.
    B. earnings per share.
    C. financial leverage multiplier.

CHAPTER 9

FINANCIAL STATEMENT ANALYSIS: APPLICATIONS

Thomas R. Robinson, CFA

CFA Institute
Charlottesville, Virginia

Hennie van Greuning, CFA

World Bank
Washington, DC

Elaine Henry, CFA

University of Miami
Miami, Florida

Michael A. Broihahn, CFA

Barry University
Miami, Florida

LEARNING OUTCOMES

After completing this chapter, you will be able to do the following:

- Evaluate a company's past financial performance and explain how a company's strategy is reflected in past financial performance.
- Prepare a basic projection of a company's future net income and cash flow.

- Describe the role of financial statement analysis in assessing the cred f a potential debt investment.
- Discuss the use of financial statement analysis in screening tial equity investments.
- Determine and justify appropriate analyst adjustments to a compan l statements to facilitate comparison with another company.

1. INTRODUCTION

This chapter presents several important applications of financial statement analysis. Among the issues we will address are the following:

- What are the key questions to address in evaluating a company's past financial performance?
- How can an analyst approach forecasting a company's future net income and cash flow?
- How can financial statement analysis be used to evaluate the credit quality of a potential fixed-income investment?
- How can financial statement analysis be used to screen for potential equity investments?
- How can differences in accounting methods affect financial ratio comparisons between companies, and what are some adjustments analysts make to reported financials in the interests of comparability?

Prior to undertaking any analysis, an analyst should explore the purpose and context of the analysis because purpose and context guide further decisions about the approach, the tools, the data sources, and the format in which to report results of the analysis, and also suggest which aspects of the analysis are most important. The analyst should then be able to formulate the key questions that the analysis must address. The questions will suggest the data the analyst needs to collect to objectively address the questions. The analyst then processes and analyzes the data to answer these questions. Conclusions and decisions based on the analysis are communicated in a format appropriate to the context, and follow-up is undertaken as required. Although this chapter will not formally present applications as a series of steps, the process just described is generally applicable.

Section 2 describes the use of financial statement analysis to evaluate a company's past financial performance, and section 3 describes basic approaches to projecting a company's future financial performance. Section 4 presents the use of financial statement analysis in assessing the credit quality of a potential debt investment. Section 5 concludes the survey of applications by describing the use of financial statement analysis in screening for potential equity investments. Analysts often encounter situations in which they must make adjustments to a company's reported financial results to increase their accuracy or comparability with the financials of other companies. Section 6 illustrates several typical types of analyst adjustments. Section 7 summarizes the chapter, and practice problems in the CFA Institute multiple-choice format conclude the chapter.

2. APPLICATION: EVALUATING PAST FINANCIAL PERFORMANCE

Analysts often analyze a company's past financial performance to determine the comparability of companies for a market-based valuation,[1] to provide a basis for a forward-looking analysis of the company, or to obtain information for evaluating the company's management.

An evaluation of a company's past performance addresses not only *what* happened (i.e., how the company performed) but also *why* it happened—the causes behind the performance and how the performance reflects the company's strategy. Evaluative judgments assess whether the performance is better or worse, compared with a relevant benchmark such as the company's own historical performance, a competitor's performance, or market expectations. Some of the key analytical questions include:

- How have corporate measures of profitability, efficiency, liquidity, and solvency changed over the period being analyzed? Why?
- How do the level and trend in a company's profitability, efficiency, liquidity, and solvency compare with the corresponding results of other companies in the same industry? What explains any differences?
- What aspects of performance are critical for a company to successfully compete in its industry, and how did the company perform relative to those critical performance aspects?
- What are the company's business model and strategy, and how did they influence the company's performance as reflected, for example, in its sales growth, efficiency, and profitability?

Data available to answer these questions include the company's (and its competitors') financial statements, materials from the company's investor relations department, corporate press releases, and nonfinancial statement regulatory filings, such as proxies. Useful data also include industry information (e.g., from industry surveys, trade publications, and government sources), consumer information (e.g., from consumer satisfaction surveys), and information that is gathered by the analyst firsthand (e.g., through on-site visits). Processing the data will typically involve creating common-size financial statements, calculating financial ratios, and reviewing or calculating industry-specific metrics. Example 9-1 illustrates the effects of strategy on performance and the use of basic economic reasoning in interpreting results.

EXAMPLE 9-1   A Change in Strategy Reflected in a Change in Financial Performance

In analyzing the historical performance of Motorola (NYSE: MOT) as of the beginning of 2006, an analyst might refer to the information presented in Exhibit 9-1. Panel A presents selected data for Motorola from 2003 to 2005. Panel B presents an excerpt from

---

[1]Stowe, Robinson, Pinto, and McLeavey (2002) describe market-based valuation as using price multiples ratios of a stock's market price to some measure of value per share (e.g., price-to-earnings ratios). Although the valuation method may be used independently of an analysis of a company's past financial performance, such an analysis may explain reasons for differences in companies' price multiples.

the segment footnote, giving data for Motorola's mobile device business segment (the segment that manufactures and sells cellular phones). Panel C presents excerpts from the Management Discussion and Analysis (MD&A) describing the results of the segment.

Looking back to 1996, Motorola was the market leader with its StarTAC cellular phone, but since 1998, Nokia had become the largest player in the global mobile phone market. "The mood inside Motorola was grim in early 2003. Nokia, whose 'candy bar' phone designs were all the rage, had snatched Motorola's No. 1 worldwide market share" (*Fortune*, 12 June 2006, p. 126).

Following the arrival of new CEO Edward Zander at the end of 2003, Motorola radically revamped its strategy for new products: "Design leads, and engineering follows" (*Business Week*, 8 August 2005, p. 68). Motorola's strategy thereafter evolved to include a strong consumer marketing orientation to complement its historically strong technological position. The company launched 60 new products in 2004, an important one of which was the RAZR cellular phone with an ultra-thin profile that served to differentiate it from competitors' offerings. The successful introduction of new products in 2004 enabled the company to gain market share and increase profitability.

The changes at Motorola extended beyond the product strategy. An article in *Barron's* noted that in addition to the shift in product strategy, "Motorola has undergone a financial overhaul. . . . The company has reduced the percentage of working capital to sales to less than 12 percent from about 22 percent, a sign of increased efficiency" (*Barron's*, 25 July 2005, p. 23).

EXHIBIT 9-1   Selected Data for Motorola (Years Ended 31 December)

($ millions)	2005	2004	2003
Panel A. Data for Motorola			
Net sales	$36,843	$31,323	$23,155
Gross margin	11,777	10,354	7,503
Operating earnings	4,696	3,132	1,273
Total assets	35,649	30,922	26,809
Panel B. Data for Motorola's Mobile Device Segment from Segment Footnote			
Net sales	21,455	17,108	11,238
Operating earnings	2,198	1,728	511
Assets	7,548	5,442	3,900

Panel C. Excerpt from MD&A

2004   "Our wireless handset business had a very strong year in 2004, reflected by a 53% increase in net sales, a 257% increase in operating earnings and increased market share. The increase in net sales was driven by an increase in unit shipments, which increased 39% in 2004 compared to 2003, and improved ASP [average selling price], which increased 15% in 2004 compared to 2003. . . . This increase in net sales, accompanied by process improvements in the supply chain and benefits from ongoing cost reduction activities resulted in increased gross margin, which drove the increase in overall operating earnings for the business. . . ."

2005   "Net sales increased by $4.3 billion, or 25%, to $21.5 billion and operating earnings increased by 27% to $2.2 billion. We shipped 146 million handsets in 2005,
up 40% from 2004. . . . The increase in unit shipments was attributed to an
increase in the size of the total market and a gain in the segment's market share.
The gain in market share reflected strong demand for GSM handsets and consumers' desire for the segment's compelling products that combine innovative style
leading technology. The segment had increased net sales in all regions of the world
as a result of an improved product portfolio, strong market growth in emerging
markets, and high replacement sales in more mature markets. Average selling price
(ASP) decreased approximately 10% compared to 2004, driven primarily by a
higher percentage of lower-tier, lower-priced handsets in the overall sales mix."

Source: Motorola's 2005 10-K filed 2 March 2006 and 2004 10-K filed 4 March 2005.

Using the information provided, address the following:

1. Typically, products that are differentiated either through recognizable brand
   names, proprietary technology, or both can be sold at a higher price than com-
   modity products.
   A. In general, would the selling prices of differentiated products be more directly
      reflected in a company's operating profit margin or gross profit margin?
   B. Does Motorola's segment footnote (Panel B) reflect a successful differentiation
      strategy in its mobile devices business?
   C. Based on the excerpts from Motorola's MD&A (Panel C), compare and con-
      trast the drivers of the growth in sales in Motorola's mobile device business in
      2005 with the drivers in 2004.
2. The *Barron's* article refers to working capital as a percentage of sales, an indicator
   of efficiency.
   A. In general, what other ratios indicate a company's efficiency?
   B. Does the financial data for Motorola shown in this example reflect increased
      efficiency?

Solutions to 1:
   A. Sales of differentiated products at premium prices would generally be reflected
      more directly in the gross profit margin, increasing it, all else equal. The effect
      of premium pricing generally would also be reflected in a higher operating
      margin. However, expenditures on advertising and/or research in support of
      differentiating features mean that the effect on operating profit margins is
      often weaker than the effect on gross profit margins.
   B. Although Motorola's segment footnote does not include information on
      gross margins by segment, it does include sufficient information for calcu-
      lating operating profit margins, which should also be positively correlated
      with premium pricing. Dividing operating earnings by net sales, we find that
      operating margins in the mobile devices business increased from 4.5 percent
      ($511/11,238) in 2003 to 10.1 percent ($1,728/17,108) in 2004 and 10.2 per-
      cent ($2,198/21,455) in 2005. The data indicate successful results from the dif-
      ferentiation strategy in 2004, but no further meaningful improvement in 2005.

C. In both years, the MD&A attributes sales growth to an increase in Motorola's share of the handset market. The 2005 MD&A explicitly mentions growth of the total wireless handset market as another factor in sales growth for that year. The 2004 results benefited from both a 39 percent increase in units sales (compared with 2003) and a 15 percent increase in ASP. The sources of growth shifted somewhat from 2004 to 2005. Lower-tier, lower-price handsets became a larger part of Motorola's product mix in 2005, and ASP declined by 10 percent. Because sales grew by 25.4 percent [= (21,455 − 17,108)/17,108] in 2005, it is clear, however, that the growth in handset unit sales more than overcame the decline in ASP.

Solutions to 2:

A. Other ratios that indicate a company's efficiency include asset turnover, fixed-asset turnover, working capital turnover, receivables turnover, and inventory turnover. In addition, efficiency is indicated by days of inventory on hand, days of sales outstanding, and days of payables.

B. Yes, they do indicate increased efficiency. The data given permit the calculation of one efficiency ratio, total asset turnover. Motorola's total asset turnover improved from 0.864 (23,155/26,809) for 2003 to 1.013 (31,323/30,922) for 2004 to 1.033 (36,843/35,649) for 2005.

In calculating financial statement ratios, an analyst needs to be aware of the potential impact of companies reporting under different accounting standards, such as U.S. generally accepted accounting principles (U.S. GAAP) and International Financial Reporting Standards (IFRS). Furthermore, even within a given set of accounting standards, companies still have discretion to choose among acceptable methods and also must make certain estimates even when applying the same method. Therefore, it may be useful to make selected adjustments to a company's financial statement data in order to facilitate comparisons with other companies or with the industry overall. Examples of such analyst adjustments will be discussed in section 6. Example 9-2 illustrates how differences in accounting standards can affect financial ratio comparisons.

EXAMPLE 9-2   The Effect of U.S. GAAP versus IFRS on ROE Comparisons

Despite convergence between U.S. GAAP and IFRS, differences remain. Non-U.S. companies that use IFRS (or any other acceptable body of accounting standards) and file with the U.S. Securities and Exchange Commission (because their shares or depositary receipts based on their shares trade in the United States) are required to reconcile their net income and shareholders' equity accounts to U.S. GAAP. In comparing the historical performance of Motorola and Nokia, you have prepared Exhibit 9-2 to evaluate whether the difference in accounting standards affects the comparison of the two companies' return on equity (ROE). Panel A presents selected data for Motorola for 2004 and 2005, and Panel B presents data for Nokia under IFRS and under U.S. GAAP.

EXHIBIT 9-2   Data for Motorola and Nokia for an ROE Calculation (Years Ended 31 December)

	2005	2004
Panel A: Selected Data for Motorola		
U.S. GAAP	($ millions)	($ millions)
Net income	4,599	2,191
Shareholders' equity	16,676	13,331
Panel B: Selected Data for Nokia Corporation		
IFRS	(€ millions)	(€ millions)
Net income	3,616	3,192
Shareholders' equity	12,155	14,231
U.S. GAAP		
Net income	3,582	3,343
Shareholders' equity	12,558	14,576

Source: Motorola's 10-K and Nokia's 20-F, both filed 2 March 2006.

Does the difference in accounting standards affect the ROE comparison?

Solution. Motorola's return on average shareholders' equity for 2005 at 30.7 percent [net income of $4,599 divided by average shareholders' equity, calculated as ($16,676 + $13,331)/2] was higher than Nokia's, whether calculated under IFRS or U.S. GAAP. The difference in accounting standards does *not* affect the conclusion, though it does affect the magnitude of the difference in profitability. Under IFRS, Nokia's ROE was 27.4 percent [net income of €3,616 divided by average shareholders' equity, calculated as (€12,155 + €14,231)/2]. Under U.S. GAAP, Nokia's ROE was slightly lower at 26.4 percent [net income of €3,582 divided by average shareholders' equity, calculated as (€12,558 + €14,576)/2]. Results of the calculations are summarized in the following table:

Panel A: Motorola	
U.S. GAAP	
Return on average shareholders' equity	30.7%
Panel B: Nokia Corporation	
IFRS	
Return on average shareholders' equity	27.4%
U.S. GAAP	
Return on average shareholders' equity	26.4%

In Example 9-2, Nokia's ROE for 2005 under IFRS and U.S. GAAP differed only slightly. In some cases, the effect of applying IFRS and U.S. GAAP on ROE and other profitability ratios can be substantial. For example, the Swiss drug company Novartis, which has undertaken historically numerous business combinations, shows a return on average shareholders' equity of 19.0 percent in 2005 under IFRS compared with 13.7 percent under U.S. GAAP; the differences are largely due to differences in accounting for business combinations.[2] Research indicates that for most non-U.S. companies filing with the U.S. Securities and Exchange Commission (SEC), differences between U.S. GAAP and home-country GAAP net income average around 1 to 2 percent of market value of equity, but with large variation.[3]

Comparison of the levels and trends in the company's performance provide information for statements about *how* the company performed. The company's management presents its view about causes underlying its performance in the MD&A section of its annual report and during periodic conference calls. To gain additional understanding on the causes underlying a company's performance, an analyst can review industry information or seek additional sources of information.

The results of an analysis of past performance provide a basis for reaching conclusions and making recommendations. For example, an analysis undertaken as the basis for a forward-looking study might result in conclusions about whether a company's future performance is likely to reflect continuation of recent historical trends or not. As another example, an analysis to support a market-based valuation of a company might focus on whether the company's better (worse) profitability and growth outlook compared with the peer group median justify its relatively high (low) valuation, as judged by market multiples such as price-to-earnings ratio (P/E), market-to-book ratio (MV/BV), and total invested capital to earnings before interest, taxes, depreciation, and amortization (TIC/EBITDA).[4] As another example, an analysis undertaken as a component of an evaluation of the company's management might result in conclusions about whether the company has grown as fast as another company, or as the industry overall, and whether the company has maintained profitability while growing.

3. APPLICATION: PROJECTING FUTURE FINANCIAL PERFORMANCE

In some cases, evaluating a company's past performance provides a basis for forward-looking analyses. An evaluation of a company's environment and history may persuade the analyst that historical data constitute a valid basis for such analyses and that the analyst's projections may be based on the continuance of past trends, perhaps with some adjustments. Alternatively, in the case of a major acquisition or divestiture, a start-up company, or a company operating in a volatile industry, past performance may be less relevant to future performance.

Projections of future financial performance are used in determining the value of a company or of its equity component. Projections of future financial performance are also used in

---

[2]Henry and Yang (2006).

[3]Pownall and Schipper (1999). *Home country GAAP* can refer to IFRS in addition to non-IFRS GAAP other than U.S. GAAP.

[4]**Total invested capital** is the sum of market value of common equity, book value of preferred equity, and face value of debt.

credit analysis—particularly in project finance or acquisition finance—to determine whether a company's cash flows will be adequate to pay the interest and principal on its debt and to evaluate whether a company will likely be in compliance with its financial covenants.

Sources of data for analysts' projections include some or all of the following: the company's projections; the company's previous financial statements; industry structure and outlook; and macroeconomic forecasts.

Projections of a company's near-term performance may be used as an input to market-based valuation (valuation based on price multiples). Such projections may involve projecting next year's sales and using the common-size income statement to project major expense items or particular margins on sales (e.g., gross profit margin or operating profit margin). More complex projections of a company's future performance involve developing a more detailed analysis of components across multiple periods—for example, projections of sales and gross margin by product line, projection of operating expenses based on historical patterns, and projection of interest expense based on requisite debt funding, interest rates, and applicable taxes. Furthermore, a projection should include sensitivity analyses related to the major assumptions.

3.1.   Projecting Performance: An Input to Market-Based Valuation

One application of financial statement analysis involves projecting a company's near-term performance as an input to market-based valuation. For example, one might project a company's sales and profit margin to estimate earnings per share (EPS) and then apply a projected P/E to establish a target price for a company's stock.

Analysts often take a top-down approach to projecting a company's sales.[5] First, industry sales are projected based on their historical relation with some macroeconomic indicator or indicators such as real gross domestic product. In researching the automobile industry, for example, the analyst may find that the industry's annual domestic unit automobile sales (numbers of cars sold in domestic markets) bears a relation to annual changes in real GDP. Regression analysis is often used in establishing the parameters of such relations. Other factors in projecting sales may include consumer income or tastes, technological developments, and the availability of substitute products or services. After industry sales are projected, a company's market share is projected. Company-level market share projections may be based on historical market share and a forward-looking assessment of the company's competitive position. The company's sales are then estimated as its projected market share multiplied by projected total industry sales.

After developing a sales forecast for a company, an analyst can choose among various methods for forecasting income and cash flow. One decision is the level of detail in forecasts. For example, separate forecasts may be made for individual expense items or for more aggregated expense items, such as total operating expenses. Rather than stating a forecast in terms of expenses, the forecast might be stated in terms of a forecasted profit margin (gross, operating, or net). The net profit margin, in contrast to the gross or operating profit margins, is affected by financial leverage and tax rates, which are subject to managerial and legal/regulatory revisions; therefore, historical data may sometimes be more relevant for projecting gross or operating margins. Whatever the margin used, the forecasted amount of profit for a given period is the product of the forecasted amount of sales and the forecast of the selected profit margin.

---

[5]The discussion in this paragraph is indebted to Benninga and Sarig (1997).

Easier to Predict by Geographic Segment or Business Segment

As Example 9-3 illustrates, for relatively mature companies operating in nonvolatile product markets, historical information on operating profit margins can provide a useful starting point for forecasting future operating profits (at least over short forecasting horizons). For a new or relatively volatile business, or one with significant fixed costs (which can magnify the volatility of operating margins), historical operating profit margins are typically less reliable for projecting future margins.

EXAMPLE 9-3   Using Historical Operating Profit Margins to Forecast Operating Profit

---

One approach to projecting operating profit is to determine a company's average operating profit margin over the previous three years and apply that margin to a forecast of the company's sales. Consider the following three companies:

- *Johnson & Johnson (JNJ)*. This U.S. health care conglomerate founded in 1887 had 2005 sales of around $50.5 billion from its three main businesses: pharmaceuticals, medical devices and diagnostics, and consumer products.
- *BHP Billiton (BHP)*. This company, with group headquarters in Australia and secondary headquarters in London, is the world's largest natural resources company, reporting revenue of approximately US$32 billion for the fiscal year ended June 2006. The company mines, processes, and markets coal, copper, nickel, iron, bauxite, and silver and also has substantial petroleum operations.
- *TomTom*. This Dutch company, which went public on the Amsterdam Stock Exchange in 2005, provides personal navigation products and services in Europe, North America, and Australia. The company's revenues for 2005 were €720 million, an increase of 275 percent from 2004 and more than 18 times greater than revenues in 2003.

Address the following problems:

1. For each of the three companies given, state and justify whether the suggested forecasting method would be a reasonable starting point for projecting future operating profit.
2. Assume the suggested approach was applied to each of the three companies based on the realized level of sales provided. Consider the following additional information:
   - *JNJ:* For the three years prior to 2005, JNJ's average operating profit margin was approximately 26.6 percent. The company's actual operating profit for 2005 was $13.4 billion.
   - *BHP:* For the three years prior to the year ending June 2006, BHP's average operating profit margin was approximately 22.5 percent, based on data from Thompson Financial. The company's actual operating profit for the year ended June 2006, excluding profits from a jointly controlled entity, was $9.7 billion.
   - *TomTom:* Over the three years prior to 2005, TomTom's average operating profit margin was approximately 23.5 percent. The company's actual operating profit for 2005 was €195 million.

Using the additional information given, state and justify whether actual results supported the usefulness of the stable operating margin assumption.

Solution to 1:

JNJ: Because JNJ is an established company with diversified operations across relatively stable businesses, the suggested approach to projecting the company's operating profit might provide a reasonable starting point.

BHP: Because commodity prices tend to be volatile and the mining industry is relatively capital intensive, the suggested approach to projecting BHP's operating profit would probably not have provided a useful starting point.

TomTom: A new company such as TomTom has little operating history on which to judge stability of margins. Two aspects about the company suggest that the broad approach to projecting operating profit would not be a useful starting point for Tom-Tom. First, the company operates in an area of rapid technological change; and, second, the company appears to be in a period of rapid growth.

Solution to 2:

JNJ: JNJ's actual operating profit margin for 2005 was 26.5 percent ($13.4 billion divided by sales of $50.5 billion), which is very close to the company's three-year average operating profit margin of approximately 26.6 percent. If the average operating profit margin had been applied to perfectly forecasted 2005 sales to obtain forecasted operating profit, the forecasting error would have been minimal.

BHP: BHP's actual operating profit margin for the year ended June 2006 was 30.3 percent ($9.7 billion divided by sales of $32 billion). If the company's average profit margin of 22.5 percent had been applied to perfectly forecasted sales, the forecasted operating profit would have been approximately $7.2 billion, 26 percent less than actual operating profit.

TomTom: TomTom's actual operating profit margin for 2005 was 27.1 percent (€195 million divided by sales of €720 million). If the average profit margin of 23.5 percent had been applied to perfectly forecasted sales, the forecasted operating profit would have been approximately €169 million, or 13 percent below TomTom's actual operating profit.

Although prior years' profit margins can provide a useful starting point in projections for companies with relatively stable business, the underlying data should, nonetheless, be examined to identify items that are not likely to reoccur. Such nonrecurring (i.e., transitory) items should be removed from computations of any profit amount or profit margin that will be used in projections. Example 9-4 illustrates this principle.

EXAMPLE 9-4   Issues in Forecasting

In reviewing Motorola's 2005 performance, an analyst notes the following items. What is the relevance of each item in forecasting the item given in italics?

1. Of Motorola's $4,696 million of operating earnings, $458 million was from other income, primarily payment received from a former customer that had defaulted several years ago on obligations to Motorola. *Operating earnings.*
2. Motorola's income included $1.9 billion from gains on sales of investments. Investments at the end of 2005 were $1.6 billion compared with $3.2 billion at the end of 2004. *Net income.*
3. Motorola's effective tax rate for 2005 was 29.5 percent compared with 32.6 percent for each of the previous two years. A main reason for the lower effective tax rate was a one-time tax incentive for U.S. multinational companies to repatriate accumulated earnings from their foreign subsidiaries. *Net income.*
4. Motorola had losses from discontinued operations of $21 million and $659 million for the years 2005 and 2004, respectively. *Net income.*

Solution to 1. This item related to a specific former customer and is not an ongoing source of operating earnings. Therefore, it is not relevant in forecasting operating earnings.

Solution to 2. Gains on sales of investments are not a core part of Motorola's business, and the sale in 2005 halved the amount of Motorola's investments. Thus, this item should not be viewed as an ongoing source of earnings, and it is, therefore, not relevant to forecasting net income.

Solution to 3. The lower tax rate does not appear to reflect an ongoing change and, therefore, a projection would probably consider the previous years' higher rate as more representative and more useful in forecasting net income.

Solution to 4. Results of discontinued items should not be included either when assessing past performance or when forecasting future net income.

In general, when earnings projections are used as a basis for market-based valuations, an analyst will make appropriate allowance for transitory components of past earnings.

3.2. Projecting Multiple-Period Performance

Projections of future financial performance over multiple periods are needed in valuation models that estimate the value of a company or its equity by discounting future cash flows. The value of a company or its equity developed in this way can then be compared with the market price as a basis for investment decisions.

Projections of future performance are also used for credit analysis, in which case conclusions include an assessment of a borrower's ability to repay interest and principal of debt obligations. Investment recommendations depend on the needs and objectives of the client and on an evaluation of the risk of the investment relative to its expected return—both of which are a function of the terms of the debt obligation itself as well as financial market conditions. Terms of the debt obligation include amount, interest rate, maturity, financial covenants, and collateral.

Example 9-5 presents an elementary illustration of net income and cash flow forecasting to illustrate a format for analysis and some basic principles. In Example 9-5, assumptions are shown first and the period-by-period abbreviated financial statement that results from the assumption is shown below.

Depending on the use of the forecast, an analyst may choose to compute further, specific cash flow metrics. For example, free cash flow to equity, used in discounted cash flow approaches to equity valuation, can be found as net income adjusted for noncash items, minus investment in net working capital and in net fixed assets, plus net borrowing.[6]

EXAMPLE 9-5   Basic Example of Financial Forecasting

Assume a company is formed with $100 of equity capital, all of which is immediately invested in working capital. Assumptions are as follows:

Dividends	Nondividend Paying
First-year sales	$100
Sales growth	10% per annum
Cost of goods sold/sales	20%
Operating expense/sales	70%
Interest income rate	5%
Tax rate	30%
Working capital as percent of sales	90%

Based on the above information, forecast the company's net income and cash flow for five years.

Solution. Exhibit 9-3 below shows the net income forecasts in Line 7 and cash flow forecasts ("change in cash") in Line 18.

EXHIBIT 9-3   Basic Financial Forecasting

	Time					
	0	**1**	**2**	**3**	**4**	**5**
(1) Sales		100.0	110.0	121.0	133.1	146.4
(2) Cost of goods sold		(20.0)	(22.0)	(24.2)	(26.6)	(29.3)
(3) Operating expenses		(70.0)	(77.0)	(84.7)	(93.2)	(102.5)
(4) Interest income		0.0	0.9	0.8	0.8	0.7
(5) Income before tax		10.0	11.9	12.9	14.1	15.3
(6) Taxes		(3.0)	(3.6)	(3.9)	(4.2)	(4.6)
(7) Net income		7.0	8.3	9.0	9.9	10.7
(8) Cash/Borrowing	0.0	17.0	16.3	15.4	14.4	13.1
(9) Working capital (noncash)	100.0	90.0	99.0	108.9	119.8	131.8

(Continued)

---

[6]See Stowe et al. (2002) for further information.

EXHIBIT 9-3   (*Continued*)

	0	1	2	3	4	5
(10) Total assets	100.0	107.0	115.3	124.3	134.2	144.9
(11) Liabilities	0.0	0.0	0.0	0.0	0.0	0.0
(12) Equity	100.0	107.0	115.3	124.3	134.2	144.9
(13) Total liabilities + Equity	100.0	107.0	115.3	124.3	134.2	144.9
(14) Net income		7.0	8.3	9.0	9.9	10.7
(15) Plus noncash items		0.0	0.0	0.0	0.0	0.0
(16) Less: investment in working capital		−10.0	9.0	9.9	10.9	12.0
(17) Less: investment in fixed capital		0.0	0.0	0.0	0.0	0.0
(18) Change in cash		17.0	−0.7	−0.9	−1.0	−1.3
(19) Beginning cash		0.0	17.0	16.3	15.4	14.4
(20) Ending cash		17.0	16.3	15.4	14.4	13.1

To explain the exhibit, at time zero, the company is formed with $100 of equity capital (Line 12). All of the company's capital is assumed to be immediately invested in working capital (Line 9). In future periods, because it is assumed that no dividends are paid, equity increases each year by the amount of net income. Future periods' working capital is assumed to be 90 percent of annual sales.

Sales are assumed to be $100 in the first period and to grow at a constant rate of 10 percent per annum (Line 1). The cost of goods sold is assumed constant at 20 percent of sales (Line 2), so the gross profit margin is 80 percent. Operating expenses are assumed to be 70 percent of sales each year (Line 3). Interest income (Line 4) is calculated as 5 percent of the beginning cash/borrowing balance (Line 8) and is an income item when there is a cash balance, as it is in this example. (If available cash is inadequate to cover required cash outflows, the shortfall is presumed to be covered by borrowing. This borrowing would be shown as a negative balance on Line 8 and an associated interest expense on Line 4. Alternatively, a forecast can be presented with separate lines for cash and borrowing.) Taxes of 30 percent are deducted to obtain net income (Line 7).

To calculate each period's cash flow, we begin with net income (Line 7 = Line 14), add back any noncash items such as depreciation (Line 15), deduct investment in working capital (Line 16), and deduct investment in fixed capital (Line 17).[7] In this simple example, we are assuming that the company does not invest in any fixed capital (long-term assets) but, rather, rents furnished office space. Therefore, there is no depreciation, and thus noncash items are zero. Each period's change in cash (Line 18) is added to the beginning cash balance (Line 19) to obtain the ending cash balance (Line 20 = Line 8).

---

[7]Working capital represents funds that must be invested in the daily operations of a business such as to carry inventory and accounts receivable. The term *investment* in this context means *the addition to* or *increase*. The *investment in fixed capital* is also referred to as *capital expenditure* or *capex*. See Stowe et al. (2002), Chapter 3, for further information.

Example 9-5 is simplified to demonstrate some principles of forecasting. In practice, each aspect of a forecast presents substantial challenges. Sales forecasts may be very detailed, with separate forecasts for each year of each product line and/or each geographical or business segment. Sales forecasts may be based on past results (for relatively stable businesses), management forecasts, industry studies, and/or macroeconomic forecasts. Similarly, gross margins may be detailed and may be based on past results or forecast relationships. Expenses other than cost of goods sold may be broken down into more detailed line items, each of which may be forecasted based on its relationship with sales (if variable) or on its historical levels. Working capital requirements may be estimated as a proportion of the amount of sales (as in the example) or the change in sales, or as a compilation of specific forecasts for inventory, receivables, and payables. Most forecasts will involve some investment in fixed assets, in which case depreciation amounts affect taxable income and net income but not cash flow. Example 9-5 makes the simplifying assumption that interest is paid on the beginning-of-year cash balance.

Example 9-5 developed a series of point estimates for future net income and cash flow. In practice, forecasting generally includes an analysis of the risk in forecasts—in this case, an assessment of the impact on income and cash flow if the realized values of variables differ significantly from the assumptions used in the base case or if actual sales are much different from forecasts. Quantifying the risk in forecasts requires an analysis of the economics of the company's businesses and expense structures, and the potential impact of events affecting the company, the industry, and the economy in general. That investigation done, the analyst can assess risk using scenario analysis or Monte Carlo simulation. Scenario analysis involves specifying assumptions that differ from those included as the base case assumptions. In the above example, the projections of net income and cash flow could be recast using a more pessimistic scenario, with assumptions changed to reflect slower sales growth and higher costs. A Monte Carlo simulation involves specifying probability distributions of values for variables and random sampling from those distributions. In the above analysis, the projections would be repeatedly recast using randomly selected values for the drivers of net income and cash flow, thus permitting the analyst to evaluate the range of results possible and the probability of simulating the possible actual outcomes.

An understanding of financial statements and ratios can enable an analyst to make more detailed projections of income statement, balance sheet, and cash flow statement items. For example, an analyst may collect information on normal inventory and receivables turnover ratios and use this information to forecast accounts receivable, inventory, and cash flows based on sales projections rather than use a composite working capital investment assumption, as in the above example.

As the analyst makes detailed forecasts, he or she must ensure that they are mutually consistent. For instance, in Example 9-6, the analyst's forecast concerning days of sales outstanding (which is an estimate of the average time to collect payment from sales made on credit) should flow from a model of the company that yields a forecast of the change in the average accounts receivable balance given as the solution to the problem. Otherwise, predicted days of sales outstanding and accounts receivable would not be mutually consistent.

EXAMPLE 9-6   Consistency of Forecasts[8]

Brown Corporation had an average days-of-sales-outstanding (DSO) period of 19 days in 2005. An analyst thinks that Brown's DSO will decline to match the industry

---

[8]Adapted from a past CFA Institute examination question.

average of 15 days in 2006. Total sales (all on credit) in 2005 were $300 million, and Brown expects total sales (all on credit) to increase to $320 million in 2006. To achieve the lower DSO, the change in the average accounts receivable balance from 2005 to 2006 that must occur is *closest* to

    A. −$3.51 million.
    B. −$2.46 million.
    C. $2.46 million.
    D. $3.51 million.

Solution. B is correct. The first step is to calculate accounts receivable turnover from the DSO collection period. Receivable turnover equals 365/19 (DSO) = 19.2 for 2005, and 365/15 = 24.3 in 2006. Next, we use the fact that the average accounts receivable balance equals sales/receivable turnover to conclude that for 2005, average accounts receivable was $300,000,000/19.2 = $15,625,000, and for 2006, it must equal $320,000,000/24.3 = $13,168,724. The difference is a reduction in receivables of $2,456,276.

The next section illustrates the application of financial statement analysis to credit risk analysis.

4. APPLICATION: ASSESSING CREDIT RISK

Credit risk is the risk of loss caused by a counterparty's or debtor's failure to make a promised payment. For example, credit risk with respect to a bond is the risk that the obligor (the issuer of the bond) is not able to pay interest and principal according to the terms of the bond indenture (contract). **Credit analysis** is the evaluation of credit risk. Credit analysis may relate to the credit risk of an obligor in a particular transaction or to an obligor's overall creditworthiness.

In assessing an obligor's overall creditworthiness, one general approach is credit scoring, a statistical analysis of the determinants of credit default. As noted above, credit analysis for specific types of debt (e.g., acquisition financing and other highly leveraged financing) typically involves projections of period-by-period cash flows.

Whatever the techniques adopted, the analytical focus of credit analysis is on debt-paying ability. Unlike payments to equity investors, payments to debt investors are limited by the agreed contractual interest. If a company experiences financial success, its debt becomes less risky, but its success does not increase the amount of payments to its debtholders. In contrast, if a company experiences financial distress, it may be unable to pay interest and principal on its debt obligations. Thus, credit analysis has a special concern with the sensitivity of debt-paying ability to adverse events and economic conditions—cases in which the creditor's promised returns may be most at risk. Because those returns are generally paid in cash, credit analysis usually focuses on cash flow rather than accrual-income returns. Typically, credit analysts use return measures related to operating cash flow because it represents cash generated internally, which is available to pay creditors.

These themes are reflected in Example 9-7, which illustrates the application of four groups of quantitative factors in credit analysis to an industry group: scale and diversification, tolerance for leverage, operational stability, and margin stability. Scale and diversification relate to a company's sensitivity to adverse events and economic conditions as well as to other factors—such as market leadership, purchasing power with suppliers, and access to capital markets—that can affect debt-paying ability. Financial policies or tolerance for leverage relates to the obligor's ability to service its indebtedness (i.e., make the promised payments on debt). In the example, various solvency ratios are used to measure tolerance for leverage. One set of tolerance-for-leverage measures is based on retained cash flow (RCF). RCF is defined by Moody's as operating cash flow before working capital changes less dividends. A ratio of RCF/total debt of 0.5, for example, indicates that the company may be able to pay off debt in approximately $1/0.5 = 2$ years from cash flow retained in the business (at current levels of RCF and debt), assuming no capital expenditures; a ratio adjusting for capital expenditures is also used. Other factors include interest coverage ratios based on EBITDA, which is also chosen by Moody's in specifying factors for operational efficiency and margin stability. *Operational efficiency* as defined by Moody's relates to cost structure: Companies with lower costs are better positioned to deal with financial stress. *Margin stability* relates to the past volatility of profit margins: Higher stability should be associated with lower credit risk.

EXAMPLE 9-7   Moody's Evaluation of Quantifiable Rating Factors[9]

Moody's Investors Service indicates that when assigning credit ratings for the global paper and forest products industry, they look at a number of factors, including quantitative measures of four broad factors. These factors are weighted and aggregated in determining the overall credit rating assigned. The four broad factors, the subfactors, and weightings are as follows:

Broad Factor	Subfactors	Subfactor Weighting (%)	Broad Factor Weighting (%)
Scale and diversification	Average annual revenues	6.00	15
	Segment diversification	4.50	
	Geographic diversification	4.50	
Financial policies (tolerance for leverage)	Retained cash flow (RCF)/Total debt	11.00	55
	(RCF – Capital expenditures)/Total debt	11.00	
	Total debt/EBITDA	11.00	
	(EBITDA – Capital expenditures)/Interest	11.00	
	EBITDA/Interest	11.00	

---

[9]Moody's Investors Service (2006, pp. 8–19).

Broad Factor	Subfactors	Subfactor Weighting (%)	Broad Factor Weighting (%)
Operational efficiency	Vertical integration	5.25	15
	EBITDA margin	5.25	
	EBITDA/Average assets	4.50	
Margin stability	Average percentage change in EBITDA margin	15.00	15
Total		100.00	100

1. What are some reasons why Moody's may have selected these four broad factors as being important in assigning a credit rating?
2. Why might financial policies be weighted so heavily?

Solution to 1.

Scale and Diversification:
• Large scale can result in purchasing power over suppliers, leading to cost savings.
• Product and geographic diversification should lower risk.

Financial Policies:
• Strong financial policies should be associated with the ability of cash flow to service debt.

Operational Efficiency:
• Companies with high operational efficiency should have lower costs and higher margins than less efficient companies and so be able to withstand a downturn easier.

Margin Stability:
• Lower volatility in margins would imply lower risk relative to economic conditions.

Solution to 2. The level of debt relative to earnings and cash flow is a critical factor in assessing creditworthiness. The higher the current level of debt, the higher the risk of default.

A point to note regarding Example 9-7 is that the rating factors and the metrics used to represent each can vary by industry group. For example, for heavy manufacturing (manufacturing of the capital assets used in manufacturing and production processes), Moody's distinguishes order trends and quality as distinctive credit factors affecting future revenues, factory load, and profitability patterns.

Analyses of a company's historical and projected financial statements are an integral part of the credit evaluation process. As noted by Moody's, the rating process makes:

> . . . *extensive use of historic financial statements. Historic results help with understanding the pattern of a company's results and how the company compares to others. They also provide perspective, helping to ensure that estimated future results are grounded in reality.*[10]

---

[10]Ibid., p. 6.

As noted in the above example, Moody' computes a variety of ratios in assessing credit-worthiness. A comparison of a company's ratios to its peers is informative in evaluating relative creditworthiness, as demonstrated in Example 9-8.

EXAMPLE 9-8   Peer Comparison of Ratios

A credit analyst is assessing the tolerance for leverage for two paper companies based on the following subfactors identified by Moody's:[11]

	International Paper	Louisiana-Pacific
RCF/Debt	8.2 %	59.1%
(RCF—Capital expenditures)/Debt	0.2%	39.8%
Debt/EBITDA	5.6x	1.0x
(EBITDA—Capital expenditures)/Interest	1.7x	8.1x
EBITDA/Interest	3.1x	10.0x

Based solely on the data given, which company is more likely to be assigned a higher credit rating?

Solution. The ratio comparisons are all in favor of Louisiana-Pacific. Louisiana-Pacific has a much higher level of retained cash flow relative to debt whether capital expenditures are netted from RCF or not. Louisiana-Pacific has a lower level of debt relative to EBITDA and a higher level of EBITDA relative to interest expense. Louisiana-Pacific is likely to be assigned a higher credit rating.

Before calculating ratios such as those presented in Example 9-8, rating agencies make certain adjustments to reported financial statements, such as adjusting debt to include off-balance-sheet debt in a company's total debt.[12] A later section will describe some common adjustments. Financial statement analysis, especially financial ratio analysis, can also be an important tool used in selecting equity investments, as discussed in the next section.

5. APPLICATION: SCREENING FOR POTENTIAL EQUITY INVESTMENTS

Ratios using financial statement data and market data are used to screen for potential equity investments. **Screening** is the application of a set of criteria to reduce a set of potential investments to a smaller set having certain desired characteristics. Criteria involving financial ratios generally involve comparing one or more ratios with some prespecified cutoff values.

---

[11]Ibid., p. 12; the values reported are based on average historical data.
[12]Ibid., p. 6.

A security selection approach incorporating financial ratios may be used whether the investor uses top-down analysis or bottom-up analysis. **Top-down analysis** involves identifying attractive geographic segments and/or industry segments and then the most attractive investments within those segments. **Bottom-up analysis** involves selection from all companies within a specified investment universe. Regardless of the direction, screening for potential equity investments aims to identify companies that meet specific criteria. An analysis of this type may be used as the basis for directly forming a portfolio, or it may be undertaken as a preliminary part of a more thorough analysis of potential investment targets.

Fundamental to this type of analysis are decisions about which metrics to use as screens, how many metrics to include, what values of those metrics to use as cutoff points, and what weighting to give each metric. Metrics can include not only financial ratios but also characteristics such as market capitalization or membership as a component security in a specified index. Exhibit 9-4 is an example of a hypothetical simple stock screen based on the following criteria: a valuation ratio (price-to-sales) less than a specified value; a solvency ratio measuring financial leverage (total assets/equity) not exceeding a specified value; dividend payments; and positive one-year-ahead forecast EPS. The exhibit shows the results of applying the screen to a set of 4,203 U.S. securities that comprise a hypothetical equity manager's investment universe.

Several points about the screen in Exhibit 9-4 are observed in many screens seen in practice:

- Some criteria serve as checks on the interpretation of other criteria. In this hypothetical example, the first criterion selects stocks that are relatively cheaply valued. However, the stocks might be cheap for a good reason, such as poor profitability or excessive financial leverage. So, the criteria requiring forecast EPS and dividends to be positive serve as checks on profitability, and the criterion limiting financial leverage serves as a check on financial risk. Of course, financial ratios or other statistics cannot generally control for exposure to certain types of risk (e.g., related to regulatory developments or technological innovation).
- If all the criteria were completely independent of each other, the set of stocks meeting all four criteria would be 329, equal to 4,203 times 7.8 percent—the product of the fraction of stocks satisfying the four criteria individually (i.e., $0.371 \times 0.505 \times 0.594 \times 0.703 = 0.078$, or 7.8 percent). As the screen illustrates, criteria are often not independent, and the result is more securities passing the screen. In this example, 473 (or 11.3 percent) of the securities passed all four screens. As an example of the lack of independence, dividend-paying status is probably positively correlated with the ability to generate positive earnings

EXHIBIT 9-4   Example of a Stock Screen

Criterion	Stocks Meeting Criterion	
	Number	**Percent of Total**
Price per share/Sales per share < 1.5	1,560	37.1%
Total assets/Equity ≤ 2.0	2,123	50.5%
Dividends > 0	2,497	59.4%
Consensus forecast EPS > 0	2,956	70.3%
Meeting all four criteria simultaneously	473	11.3%

Source for data: http://finance.yahoo.com.

and the value of the fourth criterion. If stocks that pass one test tend to also pass the other, fewer would be eliminated after the application of the second test.

- The results of screens can sometimes be relatively concentrated in a subset of the sectors represented in the benchmark. The financial leverage criterion in Exhibit 9-4 would exclude all banking stocks, for example. What constitutes a high or low value of a measure of a financial characteristic can be sensitive to the industry in which a company operates.

Growth v. Value

Screens can be used by both **growth investors** (focused on investing in high-earnings-growth companies), **value investors** (focused on paying a relatively low share price in relation to earnings or assets per share), and **market-oriented investors** (an intermediate grouping for investors whose investment disciplines cannot be clearly categorized as value or growth). The criteria of growth screens would typically feature criteria related to earnings growth and/or momentum. Value screens, as a rule, feature criteria setting upper limits for the value of one or more valuation ratios. Market-oriented screens would not strongly emphasize valuation or growth criteria. The use of screens involving financial ratios may be most common among value investors.

There have been many studies researching the most effective items of accounting information for screening equity investments. Some research suggests that certain items of accounting information can help explain (and potentially predict) market returns (e.g., Chan et al., 1991; Lev and Thiagarajan, 1993; Lakonishok et al., 1994; Davis, 1994; Arbanell and Bushee, 1998). Representative of such investigations is Piotroski (2000), whose screen uses nine accounting-based fundamentals that aim to identify financially strong and profitable companies among those with high book value/market value ratios. For example, the profitability measures relate to whether the company reported positive net income, positive cash flow, and an increase in return on assets (ROA).

An analyst may want to evaluate how a portfolio based on a particular screen would have performed historically, using a process known as *backtesting*. **Backtesting** applies the portfolio selection rules to historical data and calculates what returns would have been earned if a particular strategy had been used. The relevance of backtesting to investment success in practice can, however, be limited. Haugen and Baker (1996) describe some of these limitations:

- *Survivorship bias.* If the database used in backtesting eliminates companies that cease to exist because of a merger or bankruptcy, then the remaining companies collectively will appear to have performed better.
- *Look-ahead bias.* If a database includes financial data updated for restatements (where companies have restated previously issued financial statements to correct errors or reflect changes in accounting principles),[13] then there is a mismatch between what investors would have actually known at the time of the investment decision and the information used in backtesting.
- *Data-snooping bias.* If researchers build models based on previous researchers' findings, then using the same data base to test the model is not actually a test. Under this scenario, the same rules may or may not produce similar results in the future. One academic study argues that the apparent ability of value strategies to generate excess returns is largely explainable as the result of collective data snooping (Conrad, Cooper, and Kaul, 2003).

---

[13]In the United States, restatements of previously issued financial statements have increased in recent years. The U.S. Government Accounting Office (2002) reports 919 restatements by 834 public companies in the period from January 1997 to June 2002. The number of restatements increased from 613 in 2004 to 1,195 in 2005 (*Wall Street Journal*, 2006.)

EXAMPLE 9-9   Ratio-Based Screening for Potential Equity Investments

Below are two alternative strategies under consideration by an investment firm:

Strategy A invests in stocks that are components of a global equity index, have a ROE above the median ROE of all stocks in the index, and a P/E ratio less than the median P/E.

Strategy B invests in stocks that are components of a broad-based U.S. equity index, have price to operating cash flow in the lowest quartile of companies in the index, and have shown increases in sales for at least the past three years.

Both strategies were developed with the use of backtesting.

1. How would you characterize the two strategies?
2. What concerns might you have about using such strategies?

Solution to 1. Strategy A appears to aim for global diversification and combines a requirement for profitability with a traditional measure of value (low P/E). Strategy B focuses on both large and small companies in a single market and apparently aims to identify companies that are growing and yet managing to generate positive cash flow from operations.

Solution to 2. The use of *any* approach to investment decisions depends on the objectives and risk profile of the investor. With that crucial consideration in mind, ratio-based benchmarks can offer an efficient way to screen for potential equity investments. However, in doing so, many types of questions arise.

First, unintentional selections can be made if criteria are not specified carefully. For example, Strategy A might unintentionally select a loss-making company with negative shareholders' equity because negative net income divided by negative shareholders' equity would arithmetically result in a positive ROE. Strategy B might unintentionally select a company with negative operating cash flow because price to operating cash flow would be negative and thus very low in the ranking. In both cases, the analyst can add additional screening criteria to avoid unintentional selection (e.g., criteria requiring positive shareholders' equity and operating cash flow).

Second, the inputs to ratio analysis are derived from financial statements, and companies may differ in the financial standards applied (e.g., IFRS versus U.S. GAAP); the specific accounting method chosen within those allowed under any body of reporting standards; and/or the estimates made in applying an accounting method.

Third, backtesting may not provide a reliable indication of future performance because of survivorship bias, look-ahead bias, or data snooping; furthermore, as suggested by finance theory and by common sense, the past is not necessarily indicative of the future. Fourth, implementation decisions can crucially affect returns. For example, decisions about frequency and timing of portfolio selection and reevaluation affect transaction costs and taxes paid out of the portfolio.

6. ANALYST ADJUSTMENTS TO REPORTED FINANCIALS

When comparing companies that use different accounting methods or estimate key accounting inputs in different ways, analysts frequently adjust a company's financials. In this section, we first provide a framework for considering potential analyst adjustments to facilitate such comparisons and then provide examples of such adjustments. In practice, required adjustments vary widely. The examples presented here are not intended to be comprehensive, but rather to illustrate the use of adjustments to facilitate comparison.

6.1. A Framework for Analyst Adjustments

In this discussion of potential analyst adjustments to a company's financial statements, we employ a balance sheet–focused framework. Of course, because the financial statements are interrelated, adjustments to items reported on one statement must also be reflected in adjustments to items on another statement. For example, an analyst adjustment to the balance sheet item inventory affects the income statement item cost of goods sold; and the owners' equity amount is affected by analyst adjustments relating to expense or revenue recognition.

Regardless of the particular order in which an analyst considers the items that may require adjustment for comparability, the following considerations are appropriate:

- *Importance.* Is an adjustment to this item likely to affect my conclusions? In other words, does it matter? For example, in an industry where companies require minimal inventory, does it matter that two companies use different inventory accounting methods?
- *Body of standards.* Is there a difference in the body of standards being used (U.S. GAAP versus IFRS)? If so, in which areas is the difference likely to affect a comparison?
- *Methods.* Is there a difference in methods?
- *Estimates.* Is there a difference in important estimates?

The following sections illustrate analyst adjustments—first those relating to the asset side of the balance sheet and then those relating to the liability side.

6.2. Analyst Adjustments Related to Investments

Accounting for investments in the debt and equity securities of other companies (other than investments accounted for under the equity method and investments in consolidated subsidiaries) depends on management's intention (i.e., to actively trade the securities, make them available for sale, or, in the case of debt securities, to hold them to maturity). When securities are classified as "trading" securities, unrealized gains and losses are reported in the income statement. When securities are classified as "available-for-sale" securities, unrealized gains and losses are not reported in the income statement and instead are recognized in equity. If two otherwise comparable companies have significant differences in the classification of investments, analyst adjustments may be useful to facilitate comparison.

Also, IFRS requires that those unrealized gains and losses on available-for-sale debt securities that arise due to exchange rate movements be recognized in the income statement, whereas U.S. GAAP does not. To facilitate comparison across companies, increases (decreases) in the value of available-for-sale debt securities arising from exchange rate movements can be deducted from (added to) the amount of income reported by the IFRS-reporting company.

EXAMPLE 9-10   Adjustment for a Company Using LIFO Method of Accounting for Inventories

An analyst is comparing the financial performance of SL Industries (AMEX: SLI), a U.S. company operating in the electric lighting and wiring industry, with a company that reports using IFRS. The IFRS company uses the FIFO method of inventory accounting, and you therefore must convert SLI's results to a comparable basis.

EXHIBIT 9-5   Data for SL Industries

	31 December	
	2005	2004
Total current assets	$44,194,000	$37,990,000
Total current liabilities	18,387,000	18,494,000

NOTE 6. INVENTORIES
Inventories consist of the following ($ in thousands):

Raw materials	$ 9,774	$ 9,669
Work in process	4,699	5,000
Finished goods	1,926	3,633
	16,399	18,302
Less: Allowances	(1,829)	(2,463)
	$14,570	$15,839

Source: 10-K for SL Industries, Inc. for the year ended 31 December 2005; filed with the SEC 24 March 2006.

The above includes certain inventories that are valued using the LIFO method, which aggregated $4,746,000 and $3,832,000 as of December 31, 2005, and December 31, 2004, respectively. The excess of FIFO cost over LIFO cost as of December 31, 2005, and December 31, 2004, was approximately $502,000 and $565,000, respectively.

1. Based on the information in Exhibit 9-5, calculate SLI's current ratio under FIFO and LIFO for 2004 and 2005.
2. Interpret the results of adjusting the current ratio to be consistent with inventory on a FIFO basis.

Solution to 1. The calculations of SLI's current ratio (current assets divided by current liabilities) are given below.

	2005	2004
I. Current Ratio (Unadjusted)		
Total current assets	$44,194,000	$37,990,000
Total current liabilities	18,387,000	18,494,000
Current ratio (unadjusted)	2.40	2.05

	2005	2004
II. Current Ratio (adjusted)		
Adjust the inventory to FIFO, add	502,000	565,000
Total current assets (adjusted)	$44,696,000	$38,555,000
Total current liabilities	18,387,000	18,494,000
Current ratio (adjusted)	2.43	2.08

To adjust the LIFO inventory to FIFO, the excess amounts of FIFO cost over LIFO cost are added to LIFO inventory, increasing current assets by an equal amount. The effect of adjusting inventory on the current ratio is to increase it from 2.05 to 2.08 in 2004 and from 2.40 to 2.43 in 2005.

Solution to 2. SLI appears to be somewhat more liquid based on the adjusted current ratio. However, the year-over-year improvement in the current ratio on an adjusted basis at 16.8 percent (2.43/2.08 − 1) was slightly less favorable than the improvement of 17.1 percent (2.40/2.05 − 1) on an unadjusted basis.

6.3.   Analyst Adjustments Related to Inventory

With inventory, adjustments may be required for different accounting methods. As described in previous chapters, a company's decision about the inventory method will affect the value of inventory shown on the balance sheet as well as the value of inventory that is sold (cost of goods sold). If one company, not reporting under IFRS,[14] uses LIFO (last in, first out) and another uses FIFO (first in, first out), comparison of the two companies may be difficult. However, companies that use the LIFO method must also disclose the value of their inventory under the FIFO method. To place inventory values for a company using LIFO reporting on a FIFO basis, the analyst would add the ending balance of the LIFO reserve to the ending value of inventory under LIFO accounting; to adjust cost of goods sold to a FIFO basis, the analyst would subtract the change in the LIFO reserve from the reported cost of goods sold under LIFO accounting. Example 9-10 illustrates the use of a disclosure of the value of inventory under the FIFO method to make a valid current ratio comparison between companies reporting on a LIFO and FIFO basis.

In summary, the information disclosed by companies using LIFO allows an analyst to calculate the value of the company's inventory as if it were using the FIFO method. In the example above, the portion of inventory valued using the LIFO method was a relatively small portion of total inventory, and the LIFO reserve (excess of FIFO cost over LIFO) was also relatively small. However, if the LIFO method is used for a substantial part of a company's inventory and the LIFO reserve is large relative to reported inventory, the adjustment to a FIFO basis can be important for comparison of the LIFO-reporting company with another company that uses the FIFO method of inventory valuation. Example 9-11 illustrates a case in which such an adjustment would have a major impact on an analyst's conclusions.

---

[14]IAS No. 2 does not permit the use of LIFO.

EXAMPLE 9-11   Analyst Adjustment to Inventory Value for Comparability in a Current Ratio Comparison

Company A reports under IFRS and uses the FIFO method of inventory accounting for its entire inventory. Company B reports under U.S. GAAP and uses the LIFO method. Exhibit 9-6 gives data pertaining to current assets, LIFO reserves, and current liabilities of these companies.

EXHIBIT 9-6   Data for Companies Accounting for Inventory on Different Bases

	Company A (FIFO)	Company B (LIFO)
Current assets (includes inventory)	$300,000	$80,000
LIFO reserve	NA	$20,000
Current liabilities	$150,000	$45,000

Based on the data given in Exhibit 9-6, compare the liquidity of the two companies as measured by the current ratio.

Solution. Company A's current ratio is 2.0. Based on unadjusted balance sheet data, Company B's current ratio is 1.78. Company A's higher current ratio indicates that Company A appears to be more liquid than Company B; however, the use of unadjusted data for Company B is not appropriate for making comparisons with Company A.

After adjusting Company B's inventory to a comparable basis (i.e., to a FIFO basis), the conclusion changes. The table below summarizes the results when Company B's inventory is left on a LIFO basis and when it is placed on a FIFO basis for comparability with Company A.

	Company A (FIFO)	Company B	
		Unadjusted (LIFO Basis)	Adjusted (FIFO Basis)
Current assets (includes inventory)	$ 300,000	$ 80,000	$ 100,000
Current liabilities	$ 150,000	$ 45,000	$ 45,000
Current ratio	2.00	1.78	2.22

When both companies' inventories are stated on a FIFO basis, Company B appears to be more liquid, as indicated by its current ratio of 2.22 versus Company A's ratio of 2.00.

The adjustment to place Company B's inventory on a FIFO basis was significant because Company B was assumed to use LIFO for its entire inventory and its inventory reserve was $20,000/$80,000 = 0.25, or 25 percent of its reported inventory.

As mentioned earlier, an analyst can also adjust the cost of goods sold for a company using LIFO to a FIFO basis by subtracting the change in the amount of the LIFO reserve from cost of goods sold. Such an adjustment would be appropriate for making profitability comparisons with a company reporting on a FIFO basis and would be important to make when the impact of the adjustment would be material.

6.4. Analyst Adjustments Related to Property, Plant, and Equipment

Management generally has considerable discretion in the determination of depreciation expense. Depreciation expense affects reported net income and reported net fixed asset values. Analysts often consider management's choices related to depreciation as one qualitative factor in evaluating the quality of a company's financial reporting and, in some cases, they may adjust reported depreciation expense for a specific analytic purpose.

The amount of depreciation expense depends on both the accounting method and the estimates used in the calculations. Companies can depreciate fixed assets (other than land) using the straight-line method, an accelerated method, or a usage method. The straight-line method reports an equal amount of depreciation expense each period, computed as the depreciable cost divided by the estimated useful life of the asset (when acquired, an asset's depreciable cost is calculated as its total cost minus its estimated salvage value). Accelerated methods depreciate the asset more quickly, apportioning a greater amount of the depreciable cost to depreciation expense in the earlier periods. Usage-based methods depreciate an asset in proportion to its usage. Apart from selecting a depreciation method, companies must estimate an asset's salvage value and useful life to compute depreciation.

Disclosures required for depreciation often do not facilitate specific adjustments, so comparisons across companies concerning their decisions in depreciating assets are often qualitative and general. The accounts that are associated with depreciation include the balance sheet accounts for gross property, plant, and equipment (gross PP&E); accumulated depreciation; the income statement account for depreciation expense; and the statement of cash flows disclosure of capital expenditure (capex) and asset disposals. The relationships between these items can reveal various pieces of information:

- Accumulated depreciation divided by gross PP&E, from the balance sheet, suggests how much of its useful life the company's overall asset base has passed.
- Accumulated depreciation divided by depreciation expense suggests how many years' worth of depreciation expense has already been recognized (i.e., the average age of the asset base).
- Net PP&E (net of accumulated depreciation) divided by depreciation expense is an approximate indicator of how many years of useful life remain for the company's overall asset base.
- Gross PP&E divided by depreciation expense can suggest the average life of the assets at installation.
- Capex divided by the sum of gross PP&E plus capex can suggest what percentage of the asset base is being renewed through new capital investment.
- Capex in relation to asset disposal provides information on growth of the asset base.

These relationships can be evaluated across companies in an industry to suggest differences in strategies for asset utilization or areas for further investigation.

EXAMPLE 9-12   Differences in Depreciation

An analyst is evaluating the financial statements for two companies in the same industry. The companies have similar strategies with respect to the use of equipment in manufacturing their products. The following information is provided (amounts in millions):

	Company A	Company B
Net PP&E	$1,200	$750
Depreciation expense	$120	$50

1. Based on the information given, estimate the average remaining useful lives of the asset bases of Company A and Company B.
2. Suppose that, based on a physical inspection of the companies' plants and other industry information, the analyst believes that the actual remaining useful lives of Company A's and Company B's assets is roughly equal at 10 years. Based only on the facts given, what might the analyst conclude concerning Company B's reported net income?

Solution to 1. The estimated average remaining useful life of Company A's asset base, calculated as net PP&E divided by depreciation expense, is $1,200/$120 = 10 years. For Company B, the average remaining useful life of the asset base appears to be far longer at 15 years ($750/$50).

Solution to 2. If Company B's depreciation expense were calculated using 10 years, it would be $75 million (i.e., $25 million higher than reported) and higher depreciation expense would decrease net income. The analyst might conclude that Company B's reported net income reflects relatively aggressive accounting estimates compared with Company A's reported net income.

6.5.   Analyst Adjustments Related to Goodwill

Goodwill is an example of an intangible asset (i.e., one without physical substance). Goodwill arises when one company purchases another for a price that exceeds the fair value of the assets acquired. Goodwill is recorded as an asset. For example, assume ParentCo purchases TargetCo for a purchase price of $400 million, the fair value of TargetCo's identifiable assets is $300 million, and the excess of the purchase price is attributed to TargetCo's valuable brands and well-trained workforce. ParentCo will record total assets of $400 million, consisting of $300 million in identifiable assets and $100 million of goodwill. The goodwill is tested annually for impairment, and if its value has declined, ParentCo will reduce the amount of the asset and report a write-off due to impairment.

One of the conceptual difficulties with goodwill arises in comparative financial statement analysis. Consider, for example, two hypothetical U.S. companies, one of which has grown by making an acquisition and the other one of which has grown internally. Assume that the economic value of the two companies is identical: Each has an identically valuable branded product, well-trained workforce, and proprietary technology. The company that has grown by acquisition will incur a related expenditure and will report assets on its balance sheet equal to the amount of the expenditure (assuming no write-offs). The company that has grown internally will have done so by incurring expenditures for advertising, staff training, and research, all of which are expensed as incurred under U.S. GAAP and are thus not directly reflected on the company's balance sheet. Ratios based on asset values and/or income, including profitability ratios such as return on assets and MV/BV, will generally differ for the two companies because of differences in the accounting values of assets and income related to goodwill, although by assumption the economic value of the companies is identical.

EXAMPLE 9-13   Ratio Comparisons for Goodwill

Miano Marseglia is an analyst who is evaluating the relative valuation of two footwear manufacturing companies: Phoenix Footwear Group (AMEX: PXG) and Rocky Brands (NASDAQ: RCKY). As one part of an overall analysis, Marseglia would like to see how the two companies compare with each other and with the industry based on price/book (P/B) ratios.[15] Because both companies are nondiversified, are small, and have high risk relative to larger, more diversified companies in the industry, Marseglia expects them to sell at a lower P/B ratio than the industry average of 3.68. Marseglia collects the following data on the two companies.

	PXG	**RCKY**
Market capitalization at 11 October 2006 (market price per share times the number of shares outstanding)	$37.22 million	$67.57 million
Total shareholders' equity as of the most recent quarter (MRQ)	$54.99 million	$100.35 million
Goodwill	$33.67 million	$24.87 million
Other intangible assets	$33.22 million	$38.09 million

Marseglia computes the P/B ratios as follows:

PXG $37.22/$54.99 $= 0.68$
RCKY $67.57/$100.35 = 0.67$

The companies have similar P/B ratios (i.e., they are approximately equally valued relative to MRQ shareholders' equity). As expected, each company also appears to be selling at a significant discount to the industry average P/B multiple of 3.68. Marseglia is concerned, however, because he notes that both companies have significant intangible assets, particularly goodwill. He wonders what the relative value would be if the

---

[15]Price/book, or P/B, is the price per share divided by stockholders' equity per share. It is also referred to as a market/book, or MV/BV, ratio because it can also be calculated as total market value of the stock (market capitalization) divided by total stockholders' equity.

P/B ratio were computed after adjusting book value first to remove goodwill and then to remove all intangible assets. Book value reduced by all intangible assets is known as *tangible book value*. The average price/tangible book value for the industry is 4.19.

1. Compute the P/B ratio adjusted for goodwill and the price/tangible book value ratio for each company.
2. Which company appears to be a better value based *solely* on this data? (Note that the P/B ratio is only one part of a broader analysis. Much more evidence on the valuation and the comparability of the companies would be required to reach a conclusion about whether one company is a better value.)

Solution to 1.

	PXG	RCKY
Total stockholders' equity	$54.99 million	$100.35 million
Less: Goodwill	$33.67 million	$24.87 million
Book value, adjusted	$21.32 million	$75.48 million

Adjusted P/B ratio $37.22/$21.32 = 1.75 $67.57/$75.48 = 0.90

	PXG	RCKY
Total stockholders' equity	$54.99 million	$100.35 million
Less: Goodwill	$33.67 million	$24.87 million
Less: Other intangible assets	$33.22 million	$38.09 million
Tangible book value	$(11.90) million	$37.39 million

Price/tangible book value ratio NM (not meaningful) $67.57/$37.39 = 1.81

Solution to 2. Based on an adjustment for goodwill accumulated in acquisitions, RCKY appears to be selling for a lower price relative to book value than PXG (0.90 versus 1.75). Both companies are selling at a significant discount to the industry, even after adjusting for goodwill.

Based on price/tangible book value, RCKY is also selling for a lower multiple than the industry (1.81 versus 4.19). PXG has a negative tangible book value, and its price/tangible book value ratio is not meaningful with a negative denominator. Based on this interpretation and based *solely* on this information, PXG appears relatively expensive compared with RCKY.

6.6. Analyst Adjustments Related to Off-Balance-Sheet Financing

A number of business activities give rise to obligations which, although they are economically liabilities of a company, are not required to be reported on a company's balance sheet. Including such off-balance-sheet obligations in a company's liabilities can affect ratios and conclusions based on such ratios. In this section, we describe adjustments to financial statements related to one type of off-balance-sheet obligation, the operating lease.

The rights of a lessee (the party that is leasing some asset) may be very similar to the rights of an owner, but if the terms of the lease can be structured so it can be accounted for as an operating lease, the lease is treated like a rental contract, and neither the leased asset nor the associated liability is reported on the balance sheet.[16] The lessee simply records the periodic lease payment as a rental expense in its income statement. In contrast, when a company actually owns an asset, the asset is shown on the balance sheet along with any corresponding liability, such as financing for the asset. Similarly, if a lease is accounted for as a capital lease—essentially equivalent to ownership—the leased asset and associated liability appear on the lessee's balance sheet. The issue of concern to analysts arises when a lease conveys to the lessee most of the benefits and risks of ownership but the lease is accounted for as an operating lease—the case of off-balance-sheet financing. International accounting standard setters have stated that the entities should not avoid balance sheet recording of leases through artificial leasing structures, seeking to avoid the substance of the transaction.

A 2005 report by the U.S. SEC on off-balance-sheet financing estimates that more than 63 percent of companies in the United States report having an operating lease. The SEC estimate of total future lease payments under operating leases was $1.2 trillion.

Because companies are required to disclose in their financial statements the amount and timing of lease payments, an analyst can use this information to answer the question: How would a company's financial position look if operating lease obligations were included in its total liabilities?

Exhibit 9-7 presents selected items from the balance sheet of AMR Corporation (the parent of American Airlines) and the text of the footnote from the financial statements about the company's leases. We can use the information in this exhibit to illustrate analyst adjustments:

To evaluate the company's solvency position, we can calculate the debt-to-assets ratio, defined in the chapter on financial analysis techniques as the ratio of total debt to total assets. Excluding obligations under capital leases (amounting to $1,088 in 2005) from the definition of total debt, we would calculate the ratio for 2005 as 46.1 percent (total long-term debt/total assets = $13,607/$29,495). Properly including obligations under capital leases in the definition of total debt, we would calculate the ratio as 49.8 percent ($14,695/$29,495).

The company's footnote on leases discloses a total of $12.2 billion of future payments for operating leases on an undiscounted basis. The footnote also indicates that, of this amount, only $1.4 billion is shown on the balance sheet. To determine the impact of including operating lease obligations in the total liabilities, we will calculate the present value of the future operating lease payments. Calculating the present value of the future operating lease payments requires a discount rate. We can estimate an appropriate discount rate from the information about the present value of the capital lease payments. The discount rate is the internal rate of return implied by the stream of lease payments and their present value.

For AMR, the present value of the capital lease payments is $1,088 million. Using the stream of payments shown in the footnote and assuming that all of the $794 million

---

[16]A lessee classifies a lease as an operating lease if certain guidelines concerning the term of the lease, the present value of the lease payments, and the ownership of the asset at the end of the lease term are satisfied. Under U.S. GAAP, FAS No. 13 specifies the criteria for classification.

EXHIBIT 9-7   Lease Arrangements of AMR Corporation (NYSE: AMR), Selected Items from Balance Sheet ($ millions)

	31 December	
	2005	**2004**
Total Assets	**$29,495**	**$28,773**
Current maturities of long-term debt	$1,077	$659
Long-term debt, less current maturities	12,530	12,436
Total long-term debt	13,607	13,095
Current obligations under capital leases	162	147
Obligations under capital leases, less current obligations	926	1,088
Total long-term debt and capital leases	$14,695	$14,330

From Footnote 5. Leases

AMR's subsidiaries lease various types of equipment and property, primarily aircraft and airport facilities. The future minimum lease payments required under capital leases, together with the present value of such payments, and future minimum lease payments required under operating leases that have initial or remaining non-cancelable lease terms in excess of one year as of December 31, 2005, were (in millions):

Year Ending December 31,	Capital Leases	Operating Leases
2006	$263	$1,065
2007	196	1,039
2008	236	973
2009	175	872
2010	140	815
2011 and thereafter	794	7,453
	$1,804	$12,217[a]
Less amount representing interest	716	
Present value of net minimum lease payments	$1,088	

[a]As of December 31, 2005, included in Accrued liabilities and Other liabilities and deferred credits on the accompanying consolidated balance sheet is approximately $1.4 billion relating to rent expense being recorded in advance of future operating lease payments.

Source: AMR Corporation's Form 10-K for period ending 31 December 2005, filed 24 February 2006.

payments are made in the year 2011 would give an internal rate of return of 13.7 percent. However, based on the schedule of payments shown, a better assumption is that the $794 million payments do not all occur in a single year. One approach to estimating the timing of these payments is to assume that the payments in 2011 and subsequent years equal the average annual payments in years 2006 to 2010 of $202 = ($263 + $196 + $236 + $175 + $140)/5. Using this approach, there are four annual payments in 2011 and thereafter and the internal rate of return of the capital lease is 12.1 percent. Given that lease payments have been generally declining over 2006 to 2010, another approach resulting in lower lease payments after 2010 would be to assume that the $794 million is paid equally over some longer time span, such as 10 years. Using this assumption, the internal rate of return of the capital lease payments is 10.0 percent.[17]

EXHIBIT 9-8   Present Value of Operating Lease Payments Using Discount Rate Derived from Present Value of Capital Lease Payments ($ millions)

	Capital Lease			**Operating Lease**	
	Payments (as given)	Payments incl. Estimated Annual Payments for 2011 and Thereafter	Payments incl. Estimated Annual Payments for 2011 and Thereafter	Payments (as given)	Payments incl. Estimated Annual Payments for 2011 and Thereafter
Present value, *given*	−$1,088	−$1,088	−$1,088		
Year 2006	$263	$263	$263	$1,065	$1,065
2007	$196	$196	$196	$1,039	$1,039
2008	$236	$236	$236	$973	$973
2009	$175	$175	$175	$872	$872
2010	$140	$140	$140	$815	$815
2011 and thereafter	$794	$202	$79	$7,453	$953
		$202	$79		$953
		$202	$79		$953
		$188	$79		$953
			$79		$953
			$79		$953
			$79		$953
			$79		$782
			$79		
			$79		
Internal rate of return	13.7%	12.1%	10.0%		

(Continued)

---

[17]If the term structure of the capital and operating leases can be assumed to be similar, an alternative, shortcut, way to estimate the present value of future operating lease payments that do not appear on the balance sheet is to assume that the relationship between the discounted and undiscounted operating lease payments is approximately the same as the relationship between the discounted and undiscounted capital lease payments. The discounted capital lease payments of $926 million as reported on the balance sheet are 56.4 percent of the undiscounted noncurrent capital lease payments of $1,642 million ($1,804 million total minus $162 million current payments). Applying the same relationship to operating lease payments, 56.4 percent of the undiscounted noncurrent operating lease payments of $10,817 million ($12,217 million total minus $1,400 million current) equals $6.1 billion, yielding $7.5 billion as the present value of operating lease payments including the current obligation of $1.4 billion.

EXHIBIT 9-8   (*Continued*)

Present value of operating lease payments using a 13.7% discount rate:	$5,671
Present value of operating lease payments using a 12.1% discount rate:	$6,106
Present value of operating lease payments using a 10.0% discount rate:	$6,767

Having estimated an appropriate discount rate, we can calculate the present value of the future operating lease payments. Exhibit 9-8 presents the results of these calculations and illustrates the sensitivity of the analysis to assumptions about the timing of cash flows. We developed discount rate estimates of 12.1 percent and 10 percent. Using a discount rate of 12.1 percent, the present value of future operating lease payments would be roughly $6.1 billion, and using a discount rate of 10.0 percent, the present value would be around $6.8 billion. Because $1.4 billion of the amounts related to operating leases already appear on the balance sheet (as disclosed in the company's lease footnote), the value of the future operating lease payments that do not appear on the balance sheet are estimated to be in the range of $6,106 million − $1,400 million = $4,706 million, or about $4.7 billion, to $6,767 million − $1,400 million = $5,367 million, or about $5.4 billion. The lower the assumed discount rate, the higher the present value of the lease payments.

We now add the present value of the off-balance-sheet future operating lease payments to the company's total assets and total debt. Making this adjustment increases the debt-to-assets ratio to an amount between ($14,695 + $4,706)/($29,495 + $4,706) = 56.7 percent and ($14,695 + $5,367)/($29,495 + $5,367) = 57.5 percent. If a point estimate of the debt-to-assets ratio were needed, in this case, the analyst might select the 57.5 percent estimate based on the lower discount rate because that discount rate is more consistent with yields on investment-grade bonds as of the date of the example.

EXAMPLE 9-14   Analyst Adjustment to Debt for Operating Lease Payments

An analyst is evaluating the capital structure of two (hypothetical) companies, Koller Semiconductor and MacRae Manufacturing, as of the beginning of 2006. Koller Semiconductor makes somewhat less use of operating leases than MacRae Manufacturing. The analyst has the following additional information:

	Koller Semiconductor	MacRae Manufacturing
Total debt	$1,200	$2,400
Total equity	$2,000	$4,000
Average interest rate on debt	10%	8%

Before and After

payments on operating leases		
	10	90
	18	105
2008	22	115
2009	25	128
2010 and thereafter	75	384

Based on the information given, discuss how adjusting for operating leases affects the companies' solvency based on their debt to debt-plus-equity ratios, assuming no adjustment to equity. (Assume payments after 2009 occur at the same rate as for 2009. For example, for Koller Semiconductor, the payments for 2010 through 2012 are assumed to be $25 each year.)

Solution. Before making the adjustment, the companies' debt to debt-plus-equity ratios are identical, both at 37.5 percent. To make the adjustment for operating leases, the first step is to calculate the present value of the operating lease payments. Assuming that payments after 2009 occur at the same rate as for 2009, Koller's payment would be $25 in 2010, 2011, and 2012. The present value of $25 discounted for five years at 10 percent is $15.52. MacRae's payment is assumed to be $128 in each of 2010, 2011, and 2012. The present value of $128 discounted for five years at 8 percent is $87.11. Calculations for the following two years are made in the same manner, resulting in the present values shown in the following table:

	Koller Semiconductor	MacRae Manufacturing
2006	$9.09	$83.33
2007	$14.88	$90.02
2008	$16.53	$91.29
2009	$17.08	$94.08
2010	$15.52	$87.11
2011	$14.11	$80.66
2012	$12.83	$74.69
Total present value (PV)	$100.04	$601.18

After adding the present value of capitalized lease obligations to total debt, MacRae Manufacturing's debt to debt-plus-equity ratio is significantly higher, at 42.9 percent, as shown in the following table. The higher ratio reflects the impact of lease obligations on MacRae's solvency:

	Koller Semiconductor		MacRae Manufacturing	
	Before Capitalizing	**After Capitalizing**	**Before Capitalizing**	**After Capitalizing**
Total debt	$1,200	$1,300	$2,400	$3,001
Total equity	$2,000	$2,000	$4,000	$4,000
Debt/(Debt + Equity)	37.5%	39.4%	37.5%	42.9%

EXAMPLE 9-15   Stylized Example of Effect on Coverage Ratio for Operating Lease Adjustment

The analyst is also evaluating the interest coverage ratio of the companies in the previous example, Koller Semiconductor and MacRae Manufacturing.

	Koller Semiconductor	MacRae Manufacturing
EBIT before adjustment	$850	$1,350
Interest expense before adjustment	$120	$192

The prior-year (2005) rent expense was $11 for Koller Semiconductor and $90 for MacRae Manufacturing.

Using the information in Example 9-14 and the additional information given above, discuss how adjustment for operating leases affects the companies' solvency as measured by their coverage ratios.

Solution. Interest coverage is calculated as EBIT divided by interest. For the adjustments, rent expense is the average of two years' rent. For Koller Semiconductor, rent expense is calculated as ($11 + $10)/2. The cost of interest on lease obligations is estimated as the interest rate multiplied by the present value of the lease payments. For Koller Semiconductor, this interest expense is calculated as 10% × $100.04, and for MacRae Manufacturing, it is calculated as 8% × $601.18. Depreciation is estimated on a straight-line basis by dividing the PV of lease payments by the number of years of lease payments (seven years). After the adjustment, both companies show a decline in interest coverage ratio, reflecting the increased obligation associated with the operating lease obligations. There is also a larger apparent difference in the coverage between the two companies.

	Koller Semiconductor	MacRae Manufacturing
Interest coverage before adjustment	**7.1**	**7.0**
EBIT before adjustment	**850**	**1,350**
Rent expense; an add-back to EBIT	10.5	90.0
Depreciation; a deduction from EBIT	(14.3)	(85.9)
EBIT after adjustment	846.2	1354.1
Interest expense before adjustment	120	192
Assumed cost of interest on lease obligation (to add to interest)	10.0	48.1
Interest expense after adjustment	130.0	240.1
Interest coverage after adjustment	**6.5**	**5.6**

The adjustment for operating leases essentially treats the transaction as if the asset had been purchased rather than leased. The present value of the capitalized lease obligations is the amount owed and the amount at which the asset is valued. Further adjustments reflect the reduction of rent expenses (if the asset is owned, rent would not be paid), the related interest expense on the amount owed, and a depreciation expense for the asset. The reduction of rent expense can be estimated as the average of two years of rent expense. Interest expense is estimated as the interest rate times the PV of the lease payments. Depreciation is estimated on a straight-line basis based on the number of years of future lease payments.

In summary, adjusting a company's financial statements to include amounts of lease payments gives a more complete picture of the company's financial condition and enables the comparison of companies with varying arrangements for financing assets. It may additionally be necessary to adjust for amounts associated with other off-balance-sheet financing arrangements.

7. SUMMARY

This chapter describes selected applications of financial statement analysis, including the evaluation of past financial performance, the projection of future financial performance, the assessment of credit risk, and the screening of potential equity investments. In addition, the chapter introduced analyst adjustments to reported financials. In all cases, the analyst needs to have a good understanding of the financial reporting standards under which financial statements are prepared. Because standards evolve over time, analysts must stay current in order to make good investment decisions. The main points in the chapter include the following:

- Evaluating a company's historical performance addresses not only what happened but also the causes behind the company's performance and how the performance reflects the company's strategy.
- The projection of a company's future net income and cash flow often begins with a top-down sales forecast in which the analyst forecasts industry sales and the company's market share. By projecting profit margins or expenses and the level of investment in working and fixed capital needed to support projected sales, the analyst can forecast net income and cash flow.
- Projections of future performance are needed for discounted cash flow valuation of equity and are often needed in credit analysis to assess a borrower's ability to repay interest and principal of a debt obligation.
- Credit analysis uses financial statement analysis to evaluate credit-relevant factors, including tolerance for leverage, operational stability, and margin stability.
- When ratios using financial statement data and market data are used to screen for potential equity investments, fundamental decisions include which metrics to use as screens, how many metrics to include, what values of those metrics to use as cutoff points, and what weighting to give each metric.
- Analyst adjustments to a company's reported financial statements are sometimes necessary (e.g., when comparing companies that use different accounting methods or assumptions). Adjustments include those related to investments; inventory; property, plant, and equipment; goodwill; and off-balance-sheet financing.

PRACTICE PROBLEMS

1. Projecting profit margins into the future on the basis of past results would be *most* reliable when the company
   A. is a large, diversified company operating in mature industries.
   B. is in the commodities business.
   C. operates in a single business segment.

2. Galambos Corporation had an average receivable collection period of 19 days in 2003. Galambos has stated that it wants to decrease its collection period in 2004 to match the industry average of 15 days. Credit sales in 2003 were $300 million, and analysts expect credit sales to increase to $400 million in 2004. To achieve the company's goal of decreasing the collection period, the change in the average accounts receivable balance from 2003 to 2004 that must occur is *closest* to
   A. −$420,000.
   B. $420,000.
   C. $836,000.

3. Credit analysts are likely to consider which of the following in making a rating recommendation?
   A. Business risk, but not financial risk
   B. Financial risk, but not business risk
   C. Both business risk and financial risk

4. When screening for potential equity investments based on return on equity, to control risk an analyst would be *most likely* to include a criterion that requires
   A. positive net income.
   B. negative net income.
   C. negative shareholders' equity.

5. One concern when screening for low price-to-earnings stocks is that companies with low price-to-earnings ratios may be financially weak. What criteria might an analyst include to avoid inadvertently selecting weak companies?
   A. current-year sales growth lower than prior-year sales growth
   B. net income less than zero
   C. debt-to-total assets ratio below a certain cutoff point

6. When a database eliminates companies that cease to exist because of a merger or bankruptcy, this can result in
   A. look-ahead bias.
   B. backtesting bias.
   C. survivorship bias.

7. In a comprehensive financial analysis, financial statements should be
   A. used as reported without adjustment.
   B. adjusted after completing ratio analysis.
   C. adjusted for differences in accounting standards, such as IFRS and U.S. GAAP.

8. When comparing financial statements prepared under IFRS with those prepared under U.S. GAAP, analysts may need to make adjustments related to
   A. realized losses.
   B. unrealized gains and losses for trading securities.
   C. unrealized gains and losses for available-for-sale securities.

9. When comparing a U.S. company using the LIFO method of inventory to companies preparing their financial statements under IFRS, analysts should be aware that according to IFRS, the LIFO method of inventory
   A. is never acceptable.
   B. is always acceptable.
   C. is acceptable when applied to finished goods inventory only.

10. An analyst is evaluating the balance sheet of a U.S. company that uses LIFO accounting for inventory. The analyst collects the following data:

	31 Dec 05	31 Dec 06
Inventory reported on balance sheet	$500,000	$600,000
LIFO reserve	$50,000	$70,000
Average tax rate	30%	30%

    After adjustment to convert to FIFO, inventory on 31 December 2006 would be closest to
    A. $600,000.
    B. $620,000.
    C. $670,000.

11. An analyst gathered the following data for a company ($ millions):

	31 Dec 2000	31 Dec 2001
Gross investment in fixed assets	$2.8	$2.8
Accumulated depreciation	$1.2	$1.6

    The average age and average depreciable life, respectively, of the company's fixed assets at the end of 2001 are *closest* to

	Average Age	Average Depreciable Life
A.	1.75 years	7 years
B.	1.75 years	14 years
C.	4.00 years	7 years

12. To compute tangible book value, an analyst would
    A. add goodwill to stockholders' equity.
    B. add all intangible assets to stockholders' equity.
    C. subtract all intangible assets from stockholders' equity.

13. Which of the following is an off-balance-sheet financing technique? The use of
    A. the LIFO inventory method.
    B. capital leases.
    C. operating leases.

14. To better evaluate the solvency of a company, an analyst would most likely add to total liabilities
    A. the present value of future capital lease payments.
    B. the total amount of future operating lease payments.
    C. the present value of future operating lease payments.

CHAPTER 10

INVENTORIES

Elbie Antonites, CFA

University of Pretoria
Pretoria, South Africa

Michael A. Broihahn, CFA

Barry University
Miami, Florida

LEARNING OUTCOMES

After completing this chapter, you will be able to do the following:

- Explain International Financial Reporting Standards (IFRS) and U.S. generally accepted accounting principles (U.S. GAAP) rules for determining inventory cost including which costs are capitalized and methods of allocating costs between cost of goods sold and inventory.
- Discuss how inventories are reported in the financial statements and how the lower of cost or net realizable value is used and applied.
- Compute ending inventory balances and cost of goods sold using the first in, first out (FIFO), weighted average cost, and last in, first out (LIFO) methods to account for product inventory and explain the relationship among and the usefulness of inventory and cost of goods sold data provided by the FIFO, weighted average cost, and LIFO methods when prices are (1) stable, (2) decreasing, or (3) increasing.
- Discuss ratios useful for evaluating inventory management.
- Analyze the financial statements of companies using different inventory accounting methods to compare and describe the effect of the different methods on cost of goods sold, inventory balances, and other financial statement items; and compute and describe the effects of the choice of inventory method on profitability, liquidity, activity, and solvency ratios.
- Make adjustments to reported financial statements related to inventory assumptions in order to aid in comparing and evaluating companies.

- Discuss the reasons that a LIFO reserve might rise or decline during a given period and discuss the implications for financial analysis.

1. INTRODUCTION

Merchandising and manufacturing companies generate their sales and profits through inventory transactions on a regular basis. Merchandisers (wholesalers and retailers) purchase their inventory from manufacturers and thus account for only one type of inventory—finished goods inventory. Manufacturers, however, must account for three different types of inventory: raw materials, work-in-process, and finished goods. A manufacturer purchases raw materials from supplier companies and then adds value by transforming the raw materials into work-in-process and, ultimately, finished goods through the application of direct labor and factory overhead costs. Work-in-process inventories are those inventories that have started the conversion process from raw materials but have not yet been completed or "finished." Manufacturers may report the separate carrying values of their raw materials, work-in-process, and finished goods inventories on the balance sheet or choose instead to report just the total inventory value. If the latter approach is used, the company must disclose the carrying values of its raw materials, work-in-process, and finished goods inventories in a footnote to the financial statements.

An important consideration in calculating profits for these types of companies is measuring the cost of goods sold when inventory is sold to business customers. The measurement process would be simple if inventory costs remained constant over time; however that is simply not economic reality. Also, financial analysis would be much easier if all companies used the same inventory cost flow assumption; however, that is not an accounting reality in today's complex business environment. IFRS as promulgated by the International Accounting Standards Board (IASB) allow companies complying with IFRS to opt from three sanctioned methods: specific identification, weighted average cost, and FIFO. U.S. GAAP allows the same three methods, but also includes a fourth method called LIFO.

Given the complexity introduced by having several allowable inventory accounting methods, the analyst must clearly understand the various approaches to inventory costing that companies use and be able to understand the related impact on financial statements and financial ratios. A beneficial outcome of this knowledge will be an improved evaluation of a company's performance and better comparisons of a company with industry peers.

2. INVENTORY COST AND INVENTORY ACCOUNTING METHODS

Because inventory purchase costs and manufacturing conversion costs generally change over time, the allocation of these total inventory costs (cost of goods available for sale) between cost of goods sold on the income statement and inventory on the balance sheet will vary depending on the cost flow assumption used by the company. If more cost is allocated to cost of goods sold under one inventory method than another (with a corresponding lower cost allocated to inventory), that inventory method will cause reported gross profit (and thus net income) to be lower and reported inventory carrying value to be lower than if the other inventory method had been used. Accounting for inventory, and consequently the allocation of costs, thus has a direct impact on the financial statements.

2.1. Determination of Inventory Cost

According to International Accounting Standard (IAS) 2, the IFRS rule governing inventory accounting, the cost of inventories shall comprise all costs of purchase, costs of conversion, and other costs incurred in bringing the inventories to their present location and condition. Companies must also allocate to inventory a portion of fixed production overhead based on normal capacity levels, though any unallocated portion of the overhead is expensed when incurred. IAS 2 excludes from inventory cost all abnormal costs incurred due to waste of materials and abnormal waste incurred for labor and overhead conversion costs from the production process, any storage costs (unless required as part of the production process), and all administrative overhead and selling costs. These excludable costs are expensed and treated as period costs instead of being capitalized as inventory product costs. Under U.S. GAAP, Accounting Research Bulletin (ARB) 43 and Statement of Financial Accounting Standards (SFAS) No. 151 provide similar treatment for the determination of inventory cost.

Capitalizing inventory-related costs defers their recognition as an expense in the income statement until the inventory is sold. Any capitalization of costs that should otherwise be expensed will overstate profitability on the income statement (due to the inappropriate deferral of cost recognition) and create an overstated inventory value on the balance sheet. WorldCom used a variation of this ploy (i.e., capitalization of expenses to long-term fixed assets) to construct the fictitious financial statements that resulted in very costly accounting fraud for the deceived creditors and investors.

EXAMPLE 10-1   Capitalization of Inventory Related Costs

Acme Enterprises, a hypothetical company, produces folding tables at a factory that has a normal capacity of 1 million folding tables per year. Acme prepares its financial statements in accordance with IFRS. In 2008, the factory produced 900,000 finished folding tables and incurred €2 million of fixed production overhead costs. Raw material costs for the finished folding tables were €9 million and labor conversion costs were €18 million. In addition, Acme scrapped 1,000 folding tables (attributable to abnormal waste) at a total production cost of €30,000 (€10,000 raw material cost and €20,000 labor conversion costs). During the year, Acme spent €1 million for freight-in charges and also incurred €500,000 for storage related costs prior to selling the manufactured folding tables. Acme does not have any work-in-process inventory at the end of the year.

1. What are the total capitalized inventory costs for Acme in 2008?
2. What is the finished goods inventory cost of an Acme folding table in 2008?
3. What costs did Acme treat as period costs and, therefore, expense in 2008?

Solution to 1. Capitalized inventory costs will include 90 percent (900,000 units produced ÷ 1 million units normal capacity) of the fixed production overhead costs or €1.8 million (0.90 × €2 million total fixed production overhead costs), the €9 million cost of raw materials and the €18 million labor conversion costs for the 900,000 finished good folding tables, and also €1 million for the raw material freight-in costs. The total capitalized inventory costs are thus €29.8 million.

Solution to 2. The finished good inventory cost of one folding table is €33.11 (€29.8 million capitalized inventory costs ÷ 900,000 finished good folding tables).

Solution to 3. The period costs include the remaining unallocated fixed production overhead of €200,000, the €30,000 incurred cost for abnormal waste, and the €500,000 spent for storage related costs prior to selling the manufactured folding tables. The total period costs that Acme expensed in 2008 is thus €730,000.

2.2. Declines in Inventory Value

IAS 2 states that inventories shall be measured at the lower of cost and "net realizable value." **Net realizable value** is the estimated selling price in the ordinary course of business less the estimated costs necessary to make the sale. In the event that the value of inventory declines below the cost carried on the balance sheet (historical cost), a write-down (loss) must be recorded. Reversal (limited to the amount of the original write-down) is required for a subsequent increase in value of inventory previously written down. The amount of any write-down of inventories to net realizable value and all losses of inventories are recognized as an expense in the period the write-down or loss occurs. Likewise, the amount of any reversal of any write-down of inventories, arising from an increase in net realizable value, are recognized as a reduction in the amount of inventories recognized as an expense (cost of sales) in the period in which the reversal occurs.

In certain industries, inventories may be valued and recorded at amounts greater than their historical cost. IAS 41 allows the inventories of producers and dealers of agricultural and forest products, agricultural produce at the point of harvest, and minerals and mineral products to be carried at net realizable value even if above historical cost. If an active market exists for these products, the quoted market price in that market is the appropriate basis for determining the fair value of that asset. If an active market does not exist, a company may use market-determined prices or values (such as the most recent market transaction price) when available. A gain or loss from the change in fair value is included in net profit or loss for the period in which it arises.

U.S. GAAP (ARB 43) is broadly consistent with IFRS, in that the lower of cost and market is used to value inventories. Market value (frequently referred to as fair value following the receipt of SFAS No. 157) is defined as being current replacement cost subject to an upper limit of net realizable value and a lower limit of net realizable value less a normal profit margin. Reversal of a write-down is prohibited, as a write-down creates a new cost basis. The treatment is similar to IFRS for inventories of agricultural and forest products and mineral ores. Mark-to-market inventory accounting is allowed for refined bullion of precious metals.

EXAMPLE 10-2   Accounting for Declines and Recoveries of Inventory Value

Acme Enterprises, a hypothetical company, manufactures folding tables and prepares its financial statements in accordance with IFRS. In 2007, the carrying (book) value of its inventory was €5.2 million before a €0.3 million write-down was recorded. In 2008, the fair value of Acme's inventory was €0.5 million greater than the carrying value.

1. What was the effect of the write-down on Acme's 2007 financial statements? What was the effect of the recovery on Acme's 2008 financial statements?
2. What would be the effect of the recovery on Acme's 2008 financial statements if Acme's inventory were agricultural assets instead of folding tables?

Solution to 1. For 2007, Acme would record the €0.3 million write-down as a loss, thereby decreasing inventory and increasing cost of goods sold. For 2008, Acme would record a €0.3 million recovery as a gain, thereby increasing inventory and decreasing cost of goods sold. Acme is limited to a €0.3 million recovery because its inventories are not agricultural, forest, or mineral products.

Solution to 2. If Acme's inventory were agricultural assets instead of folding tables, IAS 41 would be applicable. Acme would, therefore, record a €0.5 million gain for 2008.

2.3.   Inventory Accounting Methods

According to IAS 2, the cost of inventories is generally assigned by using either the FIFO or weighted average cost method. The specific identification method is used for inventories of items that are not ordinarily interchangeable and for goods or services produced and segregated for specific projects (i.e., for products that are not typically purchased, manufactured, or sold to customers in the ordinary course of business). Specific identification is also commonly used for costly goods that are uniquely identifiable, such as precious gemstones. The FIFO and weighted average methods (as well as the LIFO method that is permissible under U.S. GAAP) are cost flow *assumptions,* whereas the specific identification method is not. A business entity must use the same cost formula for all inventories having a similar nature and use to the entity. For inventories with a different nature or use, different cost formulas may be justified (e.g., using the weighted average method for one type of product and FIFO or specific identification methods for another). When inventories are sold, the carrying amount of the inventory is recognized as an expense according to the inventory cost flow formula. U.S. GAAP is similar in all respects to IFRS with the exception that the LIFO method is also permissible. The LIFO inventory method will be discussed and illustrated in section 4 of this chapter.

The choice of inventory method would not be much of an issue if inventory unit costs remained relatively constant from period to period. That is because the allocation of cost flow between cost of goods sold and inventory carrying value would be very similar under the specific identification, weighted average cost, and FIFO inventory methods. But because inventory unit costs typically change from period to period, the choice of inventory method does in fact matter to a company.

The specific identification method matches the physical flow of the specific inventory items sold to their actual historic cost. Under the weighted average cost method, inventory value and inventory cost recognition are determined by using a weighted average mix of the actual costs incurred for all inventory items available for sale. The FIFO method assumes that companies sell their oldest purchased inventory units first before selling the next oldest purchased inventory units, and so on. Under the FIFO method, ending inventory will always consist of those units that have been most recently purchased and are valued at their historic purchase costs (subject to subsequent potential net realizable value inventory declines and recoveries as discussed in section 2.2).

EXAMPLE 10-3   Inventory Cost Flow Illustration for the Specific Identification, Weighted Average Cost, and FIFO Methods

Global Sales, Inc. (GSI), a hypothetical company, sells electric razors at retail. GSI began operations in 2006, during which it purchased 50,000 razors and sold 46,000 razors. The razors were purchased at a cost of €20.00 per unit. In 2007, GSI purchased another 53,000 razors at a cost of €23.00 per unit. GSI sold 55,000 razors during 2007 (3,000 of the razors sold were purchased in 2006 and 52,000 sold were purchased in 2007). GSI's sales price for razors was €30.00 per unit in 2006 and €33.00 per unit in 2007.

1. What is the reported cost of goods sold on GSI's income statement for 2007 under the specific identification method? What is the carrying value of inventory on GSI's balance sheet at year-end 2007 under the specific identification method?
2. What is the reported cost of goods sold on GSI's income statement for 2007 under the weighted average cost method? What is the carrying value of inventory on GSI's balance sheet at year-end 2007 under the weighted average cost method?
3. What is the reported cost of goods sold on GSI's income statement for 2007 under the FIFO cost method? What is the carrying value of inventory on GSI's balance sheet at year-end 2007 under the FIFO method?

Solution to 1. Under the specific identification method, the physical flow of the specific inventory items sold is matched to their actual historic cost. GSI's cost of goods sold for 2007 is €1,256,000 (52,000 razors sold at €23.00 cost per razor and 3,000 razors sold at €20.00 cost per razor). The inventory carrying value at year-end 2007 is €43,000 (1,000 razors remaining from those purchased in 2006 at €20.00 cost per razor and 1,000 razors remaining from those purchased in 2007 at €23.00 cost per razor).

Solution to 2. Under the weighted average cost method, inventory value and inventory cost recognition are determined by using a weighted average mix of the actual costs incurred for all inventory items. The weighted average cost of the razor inventory available for sale in 2007 is €1,299,000 (4,000 razors in beginning inventory purchased at €20.00 cost per razor and the 53,000 razors purchased in 2007 at €23.00 cost per razor). Accordingly, the weighted average cost of a razor inventory unit that was available for sale in 2007 is €22.7895 (€1,299,000 total purchase cost of the razor inventory available for sale divided by 57,000 razors available). The cost of goods sold is thus €1,253,421 (55,000 razors sold at €22.7895 weighted average cost per razor) and the inventory carrying value at year-end 2007 is €45,579 (2,000 razors remaining in inventory at a weighted average cost of €22.7895 cost per razor).

Solution to 3. Under the FIFO method, the cost flow assumption is that the oldest inventory units acquired are the first units to be sold. Ending inventory, therefore, consists of those inventory units most recently acquired. GSI's cost of goods sold for 2007 is €1,253,000 (4,000 razors sold at €20.00 cost per razor and 51,000 razors sold at €23.00 cost per razor). The inventory carrying value at year-end 2007 is €46,000

(2,000 razors remaining in inventory from those purchased in 2007 at €23.00 cost per razor).

The following table summarizes the ending inventory and the cost of goods sold that was calculated for each of the three inventory methods. Note that, as would be expected, the sum (the total cost of goods available for sale) is the same under all three methods.

Inventory Method	Specific ID	Weighted Average Cost	FIFO
Cost of goods sold	€1,256,000	€1,253,421	€1,253,000
Ending inventory	43,000	45,579	46,000
Total cost of goods available for sale	€1,299,000	€1,299,000	€1,299,000

2.4. Comparison of Inventory Accounting Methods

As shown in Example 10-3, the allocated cost of inventories available for sale to cost of goods sold on the income statement and to ending inventory on the balance sheet are each different under the specific identification, weighted average, and FIFO methods. The allocation of cost will be different again if the LIFO method were applied under U.S. GAAP.

In an environment of rising inventory unit costs and constant or increasing inventory quantities, FIFO (in comparison with weighted average cost) will allocate a lower amount of cost flow to cost of goods sold on the income statement and a greater amount of cost flow to the carrying value of inventory on the balance sheet. Accordingly, because cost of goods sold will be lower under FIFO, a company's gross profit, operating profit, and income before taxes will be higher. The book value of inventories under FIFO will more closely reflect current replacement values because inventories consist of the most recently purchased items that are carried at their higher purchase costs.

Conversely, in an environment of declining inventory unit costs and constant or increasing inventory quantities, FIFO (in comparison with weighted average cost) will allocate a greater amount of cost flow to cost of goods sold on the income statement and a lower amount of cost flow to the carrying value of inventory on the balance sheet. Accordingly, because cost of goods sold will be greater under FIFO, a company's gross profit, operating profit, and income before taxes will be lower. Once again, the book value of inventories under FIFO will more closely reflect current replacement values because inventories consist of the most recently purchased items that are carried at their lower purchase costs.

3. FINANCIAL ANALYSIS OF INVENTORIES

The choice of inventory method impacts the financial statements and any financial ratios that are derived from them. As a consequence, the analyst must carefully consider inventory method differences when evaluating a company's performance or when comparing a company with industry data or industry competitors.

3.1. Inventory Ratios

The **inventory turnover** ratio, **number of days of inventory** ratio, and **gross profit margin ratio are directly and fully impacted by a company's choice of inventory method.**[1] Analysts should be aware, however, that many other ratios are also affected by the choice of inventory method, although less directly. Some examples include the current ratio because inventory is a component of current assets, return on assets ratio because cost of goods sold is a component in deriving net income and inventory is a component of total assets, and even the debt-to-equity ratio because the cumulative measured net income from the inception of a business is an aggregate component of retained earnings.

The inventory turnover ratio indicates the resources tied up in inventory (the carrying costs) and can be used to evaluate inventory management effectiveness. The higher the inventory turnover ratio, the shorter the period that inventory is held, and so the lower the number of days of inventory ratio. In general, inventory turnover and the number of days of inventory should be benchmarked against industry norms.

A high inventory turnover ratio to industry norms might indicate highly effective inventory management. Alternatively, a high inventory ratio (and commensurately low number of days of inventory) could possibly indicate that the company does not carry adequate inventory, so shortages could potentially result in lost sales and reduced revenue. To assess which explanation is more likely, the analyst can compare the company's revenue growth with that of the industry. Slower growth combined with higher inventory turnover could indicate inadequate inventory levels. Revenue growth at or above the industry's growth supports the interpretation that the higher turnover reflects greater inventory management efficiency.

A low inventory turnover ratio (and commensurately high number of days of inventory) relative to the rest of the industry could be an indicator of slow-moving or obsolete inventory. Again, comparing the company's sales growth with the industry can provide insight.

3.2. Financial Analysis Illustration

Selected consolidated financial statements and financial notes for Alcatel-Lucent (NYSE: ALU) are presented in Exhibits 10-1, 10-2, and 10-3. Note 1(i) from Exhibit 10-3 discloses that ALU's finished goods inventories and work-in-process are valued at the lower of cost or net realizable value and that cost is primarily determined by the weighted average cost method.[2] Note 2(a) in Exhibit 10-3 discloses that the impact of inventory and work-in-process write-down on Alcatel-Lucent income before tax was a net charge of €77 million in 2006, a net charge of €18 million in 2005, and a net gain of €20 million in 2004. These amounts are included as a component (additions/reversals) of ALU's change in valuation allowance as disclosed in Note 19(b) from Exhibit 10-3. Observe also that ALU breaks out the valuation allowance on 31 December 2006, 2005, and 2004 (€378 million for 2006) in Note 19(b) for inventories (€355 million for 2006) and for construction contracts (€23 million for 2006). Finally, observe that the €2,259 net value for inventories on 31 December 2006 (excluding construction contracts) in Note 19(a) reconciles to the balance sheet amount for inventories and work-in-process, net on 31 December 2006 as presented in Exhibit 10-2.

---

[1]The number of days of inventory ratio is also commonly referred to as the *average inventory processing period.*

[2]Alcatel-Lucent's financial statements and notes refer to *work-in-progress* rather than *work-in-process.* Both terms are commonly used and mean the same thing.

EXHIBIT 10-1   Alcatel-Lucent: Consolidated Income Statements (€millions except per-share data)

For years ended 31 December	2006	2005	2004
Revenues	€12,282	€11,219	€10,263
Cost of sales	(8,212)	(7,085)	(6,169)
Gross profit	4,070	4,134	4,094
Administrative and selling expenses	(1,910)	(1,815)	(1,771)
Research and development costs	(1,466)	(1,298)	(1,320)
Income from Operating Activities before Restructuring Costs, Impairment of Intangible Assets, and Gain on Disposal of Consolidated Assets	694	1,021	1,003
Restructuring costs	(707)	(79)	(313)
Impairment of intangible assets	(141)	—	(88)
Gain on disposal of consolidated entities	15	129	—
Income (Loss) from Operating Activities	(139)	1,071	602
Financial interest on gross financial debt	(241)	(215)	(211)
Financial interest on cash and cash equivalents	143	122	103
Finance costs	(98)	(93)	(108)
Other financial income (loss)	(112)	43	32
Share in net income (losses) of equity affiliates	22	(14)	(61)
Income (loss) before Tax, Related Reduction of Goodwill and Discontinued Operations	(327)	1,007	465
Reduction of goodwill related to realized unrecognized loss carryforwards	(5)	—	—
Income tax expense (benefit)	42	(146)	(34)
Income (loss) from continuing operations	(290)	861	431
Income from discontinued operations	159	110	214
Net Income (Loss)	€(131)	€971	€645
Attributable to:			
Equity holders of parent	(176)	930	576
Minority interests	45	41	69
Net Income (Loss) Attributable to the Equityholders of the Parent per Share			
Basic earnings per share	€(0.12)	€0.68	€0.43
Diluted earnings per share	(0.12)	0.68	0.42
Net Income (Loss) before Discontinued Operations Attributable to the Equityholders of the Parent per Share			
Basic earnings per share	(0.23)	0.60	0.27
Diluted earnings per share	(0.23)	0.60	0.26
Net Income (Loss) of Discontinued Operations per Share			
Basic earnings per share	0.11	0.08	0.16
Diluted earnings per share	0.11	0.08	0.16

EXHIBIT 10-2   Alcatel-Lucent: Consolidated Balance Sheets (€ millions)

31 December	2006	2005	2004
Goodwill, net	€10,977	€3,772	€3,774
Intangible assets, net	5,347	819	705
Goodwill and intangible assets, net	16,324	4,591	4,479
Property, plant and equipment, net	2,026	1,111	1,095
Share in net assets of equity affiliates	682	606	604
Other noncurrent financial assets, net	803	306	554
Deferred tax assets	1,692	1,768	1,638
Prepaid pension costs	2,734	294	287
Marketable securities, net	697	—	—
Other noncurrent assets	203	468	332
Total Noncurrent Assets	25,161	9,144	8,989
Inventories and work in progress, net	2,259	1,438	1,273
Amounts due from customers on construction contracts	615	917	729
Trade receivables and related accounts, net	3,877	3,420	2,693
Advances and progress payments	87	124	90
Other current assets	1,006	827	1,418
Assets held for sale	2,117	50	196
Current income taxes	256	45	78
Marketable securities, net	1,245	640	552
Cash and cash equivalents	4,749	4,510	4,611
Total Current Assets	16,211	11,971	11,640
Total Assets	**€41,372**	**€21,115**	**€20,629**
Capital stock (€2 nominal value: 2,309,679,141 shares issued on 31 December 2006; 1,428,541,640 ordinary shares issued at 31 December 2005; and 1,305,455,461 ordinary shares issued and 120,780,519 shares to be issued related to Orane on 31 December 2004)	€4,619	€2,857	€2,852
Additional paid-in capital	16,443	8,308	8,226
Less treasury stock at cost	(1,572)	(1,575)	(1,607)
Retained earnings, fair value and other reserves	(3,706)	(4,467)	(4,951)
Cumulative translation adjustments	(115)	174	(183)
Net income (loss)—attributable to the equityholders of the parent	(176)	930	576
Shareholders' Equity—Attributable to the Equityholders of the Parent	15,493	6,227	4,913
Minority interests	498	477	373
Total Shareholders' Equity	15,991	6,704	5,286

31 December	2006	2005	2004
Pensions, retirement indemnities, and other postretirement benefits	5,331	1,468	1,466
Bonds and notes issued, long term	4,901	2,393	3,089
Other long-term debt	147	359	402
Deferred tax liabilities	2,524	162	132
Other noncurrent liabilities	303	295	201
Total Noncurrent Liabilities	13,206	4,677	5,290
Provisions	2,331	1,621	2,049
Current portion of long-term debt	1,161	1,046	1,115
Customers' deposits and advances	778	1,144	973
Amounts due to customers on construction contracts	273	138	133
Trade payables and related accounts	4,022	3,755	3,350
Liabilities related to disposal groups held for sale	1,606	—	97
Current income tax liabilities	66	99	179
Other current liabilities	1,938	1,931	2,157
Total Current Liabilities	12,175	9,734	10,053
Total Liabilities and Shareholders' Equity	€41,372	€21,115	€20,629

EXHIBIT 10-3   Alcatel-Lucent: Selected Notes to Consolidated Financial Statements

Note 1—Summary of Significant Accounting Policies

(i) Inventories and Work in Progress

Inventories and work in progress are valued at the lower of cost (including indirect production costs where applicable) or net realizable value. Cost is primarily calculated on a weighted average basis. Net realizable value is the estimated sales revenue for a normal period of activity less expected completion and selling costs.

Note 2—Principal Uncertainties Regarding the Use of Estimates

(a) Valuation Allowance for Inventories and Work in Progress

Inventories and work in progress are measured at the lower of cost or net realizable value. Valuation allowances for inventories and work in progress are calculated based on an analysis of foreseeable changes in demand, technology or the market, in order to determine obsolete or excess inventories and work in progress.

The valuation allowances are accounted for in cost of sales or in restructuring costs depending on the nature of the amounts concerned.

The impact of inventory and work in progress write-down on Alcatel-Lucent income before tax was a net charge of €77 million in 2006 (a net charge of €18 million in 2005 and a net gain of €20 million in 2004), representing new write-down taken in 2006 which more than offset the reversal of existing provisions of €98 million due to asset sales that occurred in 2006.[a]

(Continued)

EXHIBIT 10-3   *(Continued)*

Note 19—Inventories and Work in Progress

(a) Analysis of Net Value

	(€ millions)		
	2006	**2005**	**2004**
Raw materials and goods	542	467	501
Work in progress excluding construction contracts	752	712	592
Finished goods	1,320	653	645
Gross Value (Excluding Construction Contracts)	2,614	1,832	1,738
Valuation allowance	(355)	(394)	(465)
Net value (Excluding Construction Contracts)	2,259	1,438	1,273
Work in progress on construction contracts, gross (*)	137	281	291
Valuation allowance	(23)	(29)	(30)
Work in Progress on Construction Contracts, Net	114	252	261
Total, net	2,373	1,690	1,534

(*) Included in the amounts due from/to construction contracts

(b) Change in Valuation Allowance

	(€ millions)		
	2006	**2005**	**2004**
On January 1	(423)	(495)	(978)
(Additions)/reversals	(77)	(18)	20
Utilization	54	131	427
Changes in consolidation group	54	11	40
Net effect of exchange rate changes and other changes	14	(52)	(4)
On December 31	(378)	(423)	(495)

[a]For 2006, €175 million was added to the allowance for inventory write-downs; however, €98 million was reversed because inventory that had been written down in earlier years was sold in 2006. Because the company uses a valuation allowance, the inventory that is sold would have the valuation allowance associated with the sold inventory removed from the total valuation.

Some companies use and disclose an inventory valuation allowance in their financial footnotes. The inventory valuation allowance represents the total amount of inventory write-down that was taken for the inventory reported on the balance sheet (which is measured at the lower of cost or net realizable value). The analyst can, therefore, determine the historical cost of the company's inventory by adding the inventory valuation allowance to the reported inventory carrying value on the balance sheet.

EXAMPLE 10-4   Financial Analysis Illustration

The consolidated income statements and consolidated balance sheets for Alcatel-Lucent (NYSE: ALU) are provided in Exhibits 10-1 and 10-2, respectively. Exhibit 10-3 includes selected financial note disclosures concerning ALU's inventory accounting policies.

1. What are ALU's inventory turnover ratios, number of days of inventory ratios, gross margin ratios, current ratios, return on total assets ratios, and debt-to-equity ratios for 2006, 2005, and 2004, respectively, under the weighted average cost method?
2. What trends are apparent for ALU's inventory turnover ratio, number of days of inventory, and gross profit margin ratios?
3. If ALU had used the FIFO inventory method instead of the weighted average cost method during 2004, 2005, and 2006, what would be the effect on ALU's reported cost of goods sold and inventory values? What would be the directional impact on the financial ratios that were calculated in part 1 above for ALU?

Solution to 1. The financial ratios are as follows:

	2006	**2005**	**2004**
Inventory turnover ratio	3.64	4.93	4.85
Number of days of inventory	100.4 days	74.1 days	75.3 days
Gross profit margin	33.14%	36.85%	39.89%
Current ratio	1.33	1.23	1.16
Return on assets	−0.32%	4.60%	3.13%
Debt-to-equity ratio	1.59	2.15	2.90

The inventory turnover ratio (cost of goods sold ÷ ending inventory) is 3.64 (€8,212 ÷ €2,259) for 2006, 4.93 (€7,085 ÷ €1,438) for 2005, and 4.85 (€6,169 ÷ €1,273) for 2004.[3]

The number of days of inventory (365 days ÷ inventory turnover ratio) is 100.4 days (365 days ÷ 3.64) for 2006, 74.1 days (365 days ÷ 4.93) for 2005, and 75.3 days (365 days ÷ 4.85) for 2004.

The gross profit margin (gross profit ÷ total revenue) is 33.14% (€4,070 ÷ €12,282) for 2006, 36.85% (€4,134 ÷ €11,219) for 2005, and 39.89% (€4,094 ÷ €10,263) for 2004.

The current ratio (current assets ÷ current liabilities) for ALU is 1.33 (€16,211 ÷ €12,175) for 2006, 1.23 (€11,971 ÷ €9,734) for 2005, and 1.16 (€11,640 ÷ €10,053) for 2004.

The return on assets (net income ÷ ending total assets) is −0.32% (− €131 ÷ €41,372) for 2006, 4.60% (€971 ÷ €21,115) for 2005, and 3.13% (€645 ÷ €20,629) for 2004.[4]

The debt-to-equity ratio (total debt ÷ total shareholders' equity) for ALU is 1.59 (€25,381 ÷ €15,991) for 2006, 2.15 (€14,411 ÷ €6,704) for 2005, and 2.90 (€15,343 ÷ €5,286) for 2004.

[3,4]For simplicity of example, the ending values of balance sheet accounts were used in calculating the financial ratios in this example (e.g., ending inventory, ending total assets). In practice, it is generally preferable to use average values (e.g., average inventory, average total assets).

Solution to 2. The inventory turnover ratio declined sharply in 2006 and the number of days of inventory increased in 2006 from the relatively constant levels that existed in 2005 and 2004. ALU's gross profit margin declined sharply in 2005 and declined sharply again in 2006 (more than a 3 percent margin erosion in each successive year from 2004). The analyst should investigate the reasons for the sharp decline in ALU's gross profit margin.

Solution to 3. If inventory replacement costs were increasing during 2004, 2005, and 2006 (and inventory quantity levels were stable or increasing), ALU's cost of goods sold would have been lower under the FIFO inventory method than what it reported under the weighted average cost method (assuming no inventory write-downs that would otherwise neutralize the differences between the inventory methods). Consequently, ALU's reported gross profit, net income, and retained earnings would also be higher for those years. Because FIFO always allocates the oldest inventory costs to cost of goods sold, the reported cost of goods sold would be lower under the FIFO method. Under the FIFO method, inventory carrying values would be higher than under weighted average cost because the more recently purchased inventory items would be included in inventory at their higher costs (again assuming no inventory write-downs that would otherwise neutralize the differences between the inventory methods).

The inventory turnover ratios would all be lower under the FIFO inventory method because the numerator (cost of goods sold) would be lower and the denominator (inventory) would be higher than what was reported by ALU under the weighted average cost method.

The number of days of inventory ratios would all be longer under the FIFO inventory method because the inventory turnover ratios would be lower under FIFO.

The gross profit margin ratios would all be higher under the FIFO inventory method because cost of goods sold would be lower under FIFO than under the weighted average method.

The current ratios would all be higher under the FIFO inventory method because inventory carrying values would be higher under FIFO (current liabilities would be the same under both methods).

The return on assets ratios would all be higher under the FIFO inventory method because the incremental profit added to the numerator (net income) has a greater impact than the incremental increase to the denominator (total assets). By way of example, assume that a company has €3 million in net income and €100 million in total assets using the weighted average cost method. If the company earns another €1 million in net income by using FIFO instead of weighted average cost, it would then also have another €1 million in total assets (after tax). Based on this example, the return on assets under the weighted average cost method is 3.00 percent (€3/€100), and 3.96 percent (€4/€101) under the FIFO method.

The debt-to-equity ratios would all be lower under the FIFO inventory method because retained earnings would be higher under FIFO (again assuming no inventory write-downs that would otherwise neutralize the differences between the inventory methods).

If inventory replacement costs were decreasing during 2004, 2005, and 2006 (and inventory quantity levels were stable or increasing), ALU's cost of goods sold would have been higher under the FIFO inventory method than what it reported under the weighted average cost method (assuming no inventory write-downs that would otherwise neutralize the differences between the inventory methods). As a consequence, the ratio assessment that was performed above would result in directly opposite conclusions.

4. LIFO ACCOUNTING METHOD UNDER U.S. GAAP

In the United States, there are four basic methods that companies may choose from to report inventory value and to allocate inventory cost. They are the specific identification, weighted average cost, first-in, first-out (FIFO), and last-in, first-out (LIFO) methods. The specific identification, weighted average cost, and FIFO methods are also permissible under IFRS; however, the LIFO method is not. In the United States, the LIFO method is widely used (approximately 30 percent of U.S. companies use the LIFO method) because of potential income tax savings.[5] Under the "LIFO conformity rule," the U.S. tax code requires that companies using LIFO for tax purposes must also use LIFO for financial reporting.

4.1. The LIFO Method

The LIFO method assumes that companies sell their most recently purchased inventory units first before selling the next most recently purchased inventory units, and so on. Under this method, ending inventory will consist of those units that have been held the longest and valued at their historic purchase costs.

EXAMPLE 10-5   LIFO Inventory Method Illustration

American Sales, Inc. (ASI), a hypothetical company, sells portable hair dryers on a retail basis. ASI began operations in 2006 during which it purchased 50,000 hair dryers and sold 46,000 hair dryers. The hair dryers were purchased at a cost of $20 per unit. In 2007, ASI purchased another 60,000 hair dryers at a cost of $23 per unit. ASI sold 55,000 hair dryers during 2007. ASI's sales price for hair dryers was $30 per unit in 2006 and $33 per unit in 2007. ASI uses the LIFO inventory method.

1. What is the reported cost of goods sold on ASI's income statement for 2007 under LIFO?
2. What is the reported gross profit on ASI's income statement for 2007 on a LIFO basis?
3. What is the carrying value of inventory on ASI's balance sheet at year-end 2007 under LIFO?
4. What would be the reported cost of goods sold, gross profit, and inventory carrying value if ASI used the weighted average cost inventory method instead of LIFO?
5. What would be the reported cost of goods sold, gross profit, and inventory carrying value if ASI used the FIFO inventory method instead of LIFO?

---

[5]The tax consequences and their effect on cash flows are a unique consequence of the U.S. tax system. Many countries specify the tax treatment independent of whether a particular treatment is adopted in the accounts.

Solution to 1. ASI's cost of goods sold for 2007 is $1,265,000 (55,000 hair dryers sold at $23 cost per hair dryer). Under the LIFO method, the cost flow assumption is that the most recently purchased inventory units are the first units to be sold. Because ASI purchased more hair dryers than it sold in 2007, the units allocated to cost of goods sold are those that were purchased in 2007 at a unit cost of $23 per hair dryer.

Solution to 2. ASI's gross profit for 2007 is $550,000. The reported sales are $1,815,000 (55,000 hair dryers sold at $33 sales price per hair dryer) and the reported cost of goods sold is $1,265,000.

Solution to 3. ASI's inventory carrying value at year-end 2007 is $195,000 (4,000 hair dryers purchased in 2006 at $20 per hair dryer plus 5,000 hair dryers purchased in 2007 at $23 per hair dryer). Under the LIFO method, the ending inventory consists of those units that have been held the longest at their historical purchase cost. Because there were 4,000 unsold hair dryers at the end of 2006 (ASI's first year of operations), ASI's beginning inventory for 2007 carries those 4,000 hair dryers at a historical cost of $80,000. Furthermore, because 5,000 more hair dryers were purchased than sold by ASI in 2007, the ending inventory at year-end 2007 will increase by an additional $115,000 over year-end 2006.

Solution to 4. Under the weighted average cost method, inventory value and inventory cost recognition are determined by using a weighted average mix of the actual costs incurred for all inventory items. The weighted average cost of the hair dryer inventory available for sale in 2007 is $1,460,000 (4,000 hair dryers in beginning inventory purchased at $20 cost per hair dryer and the 60,000 hair dryers purchased in 2007 at $23 cost per hair dryer). Accordingly, the weighted average cost of a hair dryer inventory unit that was available for sale in 2007 is $22.8125 ($1,460,000 total purchase cost of the hair dryer inventory available for sale divided by 64,000 hair dryers available). The cost of goods sold is thus $1,254,688 (55,000 hair dryers sold at $22.8125 weighted average cost per hair dryer). ASI's gross profit for 2007 is $560,312. The reported sales are $1,815,000 (55,000 hair dryers sold at $33 sales price per hair dryer). Ending inventory carrying value at year-end 2007 under the weighted average cost method is $205,313 (9,000 hair dryers remaining in inventory at a weighted average cost of $22.8125 cost per hair dryer).

Solution to 5. Under the FIFO method, the cost flow assumption is that the oldest inventory units acquired are the first units to be sold. ASI's cost of goods sold for 2007 is $1,253,000 (4,000 hair dryers sold at $20.00 cost per hair dryer and 51,000 hair dryers sold at $23.00 cost per hair dryer). ASI's gross profit for 2007 is $562,000. The reported sales are $1,815,000 (55,000 hair dryers sold at $33 sales price per hair dryer). Ending inventory thus consists of those inventory units most recently acquired. The inventory carrying value at year-end 2007 under FIFO is $207,000 (9,000 hair dryers remaining in inventory from those purchased in 2007 at $23 cost per hair dryer).

    The following table summarizes the cost of goods sold, ending inventory, and gross profit that was calculated for each of the three inventory methods. Note that any difference in gross profit among the three methods is attributable by the same amount of difference in their respective ending inventory balances. Finally, it should be noted that because inventory unit purchase costs increased in 2007 relative to the inventory unit purchase costs that were incurred in 2006 (the initial year of business), the LIFO method will report the lowest gross profit and the lowest ending inventory balance, and the FIFO method will report the highest gross profit and the highest ending inventory balance. Whether inventory unit purchase costs are increasing or decreasing over time, the weighted average cost method will always result in a gross profit and ending inventory balance that falls somewhere between the LIFO and FIFO methods.

Inventory Method	LIFO	Weighted Average Cost	FIFO
Cost of goods sold	$1,265,000	$1,254,688	$1,253,000
Ending inventory	195,000	205,312	207,000
Total cost of goods available for sale	$1,460,000	$1,460,000	$1,460,000
Gross profit	$550,000	$560,312	$562,000

In general, the weighted average cost method valuations assigned to cost of goods sold and ending inventory are typically near or approximately the valuations that would otherwise be allocated under the FIFO method. This is primarily due to the fact that the cost flow allocation using the weighted average method closely trails the cost flows that are allocated under the FIFO method. Because the differences between the two inventory methods are often immaterial, an analyst will not typically make adjustments when comparing a company using the weighted average cost method with a company using FIFO. This is not the case, however, when the analyst is comparing a company using the LIFO method with a company using FIFO. Over a period of time, a continuous cycle of increasing inventory unit purchase costs and stable or rising inventory unit levels will often lead to significant and material differences between the LIFO and FIFO inventory methods. For this reason, the analyst must carefully evaluate valuations allocated to cost of goods sold and ending inventory for LIFO reporting companies when comparing them to FIFO reporting companies.

4.2. LIFO Reserve

Under the LIFO method, inventory write-downs are less likely to occur than under other inventory methods (assuming a long-term environment of rising inventory costs). This is mostly attributable to LIFO inventories being valued at older and lower costs (and thus less likely to be carried at values that are greater than their net realizable values) than are inventories valued under the FIFO and weighted average cost methods.

Under U.S. GAAP, companies that use the LIFO inventory method must disclose in their financial notes the amount of the **LIFO reserve** or the amount that would have been reported in inventory if the FIFO method had been used. The LIFO reserve is the difference between inventory reported at FIFO and inventory reported at LIFO (FIFO inventory value less LIFO inventory value). When inventory unit costs are rising over time, the FIFO inventory value will always exceed the LIFO inventory value. Accordingly, when inventory unit costs are rising over time and new LIFO unit layers are added to inventory, the LIFO reserve will increase. Likewise, to the extent that older LIFO unit layers are depleted, the LIFO reserve will decrease. The analyst may, therefore, determine whether LIFO liquidations are occurring by closely examining the change in the LIFO reserve from year to year (or by deriving the LIFO reserve for each year by taking the difference between inventory reported at FIFO and inventory reported at LIFO) (see Exhibits 10-4, 10-5, and 10-6).

The LIFO reserve disclosure may also be used by the analyst to compare a U.S. company that uses LIFO accounting with another company in its industry that uses FIFO accounting. This comparison is especially critical when comparing a U.S. company that uses the LIFO accounting method with international companies for which this method is not allowable.

EXHIBIT 10-4   Caterpillar Inc.: Consolidated Results of Operation ($ millions except per-share data)

For the years ended 31 December	2006	2005	2004
Sales and Revenues			
Sales of machinery and engines	$38,869	$34,006	$28,336
Revenue of financial products	2,648	2,333	1,970
Total sales and revenues	41,517	36,339	30,306
Operating Costs			
Cost of goods sold	29,549	26,558	22,497
Selling, general, and administrative expenses	3,706	3,190	2,926
Research and development expenses	1,347	1,084	928
Interest expense of financial products	1,023	768	524
Other operating expenses	971	955	747
Total operating costs	36,596	32,555	27,622
Operating Profit	4,921	3,784	2,684
Interest expense excluding financial products	274	260	230
Other income (expense)	214	377	253
Consolidated Profit before Taxes	4,861	3,901	2,707
Provision for income taxes	1,405	1,120	731
Profit of consolidated companies	3,456	2,781	1,976
Equity in profit of unconsolidated affiliated companies	81	73	59
Profit	$ 3,537	$ 2,854	$ 2,035
Profit per Common Share	$ 5.37	$ 4.21	$ 2.97
Profit per Common Share—Diluted	$ 5.17	$ 4.04	$ 2.88
Weighted Average Common Shares Outstanding (millions)			
Basic	658.7	678.4	684.5
Diluted	683.8	705.8	707.4
Cash Dividends Declared per Common Share	$ 1.15	$ 0.96	$ 0.80

EXHIBIT 10-5 Caterpillar Inc.: Consolidated Financial Position ($ millions)

31 December	2006	2005	2004
Assets			
Current assets:			
Cash and short-term investments	$530	$1,108	$445
Receivables—trade and other	8,168	7,526	7,463
Receivables—finance	6,804	6,442	5,182
Deferred and refundable income taxes	733	255	330
Prepaid expenses and other current assets	507	2,146	1,369
Inventories	6,351	5,224	4,675
Total current assets	$23,093	$22,701	$19,464
Property and equipment—net	8,851	7,988	7,682
Long-term receivables—trade and other	860	1,037	764
Long-term receivables—finance	11,531	10,301	9,903
Investments in unconsolidated companies	562	565	517
Deferred income taxes	1,949	857	742
Intangible assets	387	424	315
Goodwill	1,904	1,451	1,450
Other assets	1,742	1,745	2,258
Total Assets	$50,879	$47,069	$43,095
Liabilities			
Current liabilities:			
Short-term borrowings			
Machinery and engines	$165	$871	$93
Financial products	4,990	4,698	4,064
Accounts payable	4,085	3,412	3,524
Accrued expenses	2,923	2,617	2,261
Accrued wages, salaries and employee benefits	938	1,601	1,543
Customer advances	921	454	503
Dividends payable	194	168	141
Deferred and current income taxes payable	575	528	259
Long-term debt due within one year:			
Machinery and engines	418	340	6
Financial products	4,043	4,159	3,525
Total current liabilities	19,252	18,848	15,919
Long-term debt due after one year			
Machinery and engines	3,694	2,717	3,663
Financial products	13,986	12,960	12,174

(*Continued*)

EXHIBIT 10-5 *(Continued)*

31 December	2006	2005	2004
Liability for postemployment benefits	5,879	3,161	3,126
Deferred income taxes and other liabilities	1,209	951	746
Total Liabilities	44,020	38,637	35,628
Commitments and Contingencies (Notes 22 and 23)			
Stockholders' equity			
Common stock of $1.00 par value:			
Authorized shares: 900,000,000			
Issued shares (2006, 2005, and 2004–814,894,624) at paid-in amount	2,465	1,859	1,231
Treasury stock (2006, 169,086,448 shares; 2005, 144,027,405 shares; and 2004, 129,020,726 shares) at cost	(7,352)	(4,637)	(3,277)
Profit employed in the business	14,593	11,808	9,937
Accumulated other comprehensive income	(2,847)	(598)	(424)
Total Stockholders' Equity	6,859	8,432	7,467
Total Liabilities and Stockholders' Equity	$50,879	$47,069	$43,095

EXHIBIT 10-6   Caterpillar Inc.: Selected Notes to Consolidated Financial Statements.
Note 1. Operations and Summary of Significant Accounting Policies

D. Inventories

Inventories are stated at the lower of cost or market. Cost is principally determined using the last-in, first-out (LIFO) method. The value of inventories on the LIFO basis represented about 75% of total inventories at December 31, 2006 and about 80% of total inventories at December 31, 2005 and 2004.

If the FIFO (first-in, first-out) method had been in use, inventories would have been $2,403 million, $2,345 million and $2,124 million higher than reported at December 31, 2006, 2005 and 2004, respectively.

L. New accounting standards

SFAS 151– In November 2004, the Financial Accounting Standards Board (FASB) issued Statement of Financial Accounting Standards No. 151 (SFAS 151), "Inventory Costs—An Amendment of ARB No. 43, Chapter 4." SFAS 151 discusses the general principles applicable to the pricing of inventory. Paragraph 5 of ARB 43, Chapter 4 provides guidance on allocating certain costs to inventory. This Statement amends ARB 43, Chapter 4, to clarify that abnormal amounts of idle facility expense, freight, handling costs, and wasted materials (spoilage) should be recognized as current-period charges. In addition, this Statement requires that allocation of fixed production overheads to the costs of conversion be based on the normal capacity of production facilities. As required by SFAS 151, we adopted this new accounting standard on January 1, 2006. The adoption of SFAS 151 did not have a material impact on our financial statements.

EXAMPLE 10-6   LIFO Reserve Illustration

The Consolidated Results of Operations (Income Statements) and Consolidated Financial Position (Balance Sheets) for Caterpillar Inc. (NYSE: CAT) are provided in Exhibits 10-4 and 10-5, respectively. Exhibit 10-6 includes selected financial note disclosures concerning CAT's inventory accounting policies.

1. What inventory value would CAT report on its 2006 balance sheet if it used the FIFO inventory method instead of LIFO?
2. What amount would cost of goods sold be on CAT's 2006 income statement if it used the FIFO inventory method instead of LIFO?
3. What amount would net income (profit) be on CAT's 2006 income statement if it used the FIFO inventory method instead of LIFO?
4. What is the cumulative amount of income tax savings that CAT has generated through 2006 by using the LIFO inventory method instead of FIFO?
5. What amounts would be added to CAT's deferred income tax liabilities and retained earnings (profit employed in the business) respectively, at 31 December 2006 if CAT used the FIFO inventory method instead of LIFO?
6. What is CAT's inventory turnover ratio, number of days of inventory ratio, gross margin ratio, current ratio, return on total assets ratio, and debt-to-equity ratio for 2006 under the LIFO method? What would CAT's inventory turnover ratio, number of days of inventory ratio, gross margin ratio, current ratio, return on total assets ratio, and debt-to-equity ratio be for 2006 if the company used the FIFO inventory method instead of LIFO?

Solution to 1. CAT's 2006 inventory value would be $8,754 (in millions) if the FIFO inventory method was used instead of LIFO. Exhibit 10-5 reports that CAT's inventories (valued on a LIFO basis) on 31 December 2006 were $6,351. Financial note D in Exhibit 10-6 discloses that CAT's inventories would have been $2,403 higher than reported at 31 December 2006 if the FIFO method had been used instead.

Solution to 2. CAT's cost of goods sold for 2006 would be $29,491 (in millions) if the FIFO inventory method was used instead of LIFO. Exhibit 10-4 reports that CAT's cost of goods sold (valued on a LIFO basis) for 2006 was $29,549. Financial note D in Exhibit 10-6 discloses that CAT's inventories would have been $2,403 higher and $2,345 higher than reported at 31 December 2006 and 2005, respectively, if the FIFO method had been used instead. Because the LIFO reserve increased by $58 during 2006 ($2,403 LIFO reserve at 31 December 2006 less $2,345 LIFO reserve at 31 December 2005), the reported cost of goods sold would accordingly be lower by that amount if the FIFO method had been used instead of LIFO.

Solution to 3. CAT's net income (profit) for 2006 would be $3,578 (in millions) if the FIFO inventory method was used instead of LIFO. Exhibit 10-4 reports that CAT's profit (based on the LIFO method) for 2006 was $3,537. Under the FIFO method, CAT's cost of goods sold would have been $58 lower than what CAT reported under the LIFO method (determined in the solution to 2 above). The resulting $58 increase to CAT's gross profit would, however, be reduced by income taxes of $17 because CAT's 2006 income tax rate was approximately 29% ($1,405 provision for income taxes ÷ $4,861 consolidated profit before taxes). CAT's profit for 2006 would thus be $41 ($58 incremental gross profit less $17 incremental income tax expense) higher if the FIFO inventory method had been used instead of LIFO.

Solution to 4. The cumulative amount of income tax savings that CAT has generated by using the LIFO method instead of FIFO is approximately $697 (in millions). Financial note D in Exhibit 10-6 discloses that the LIFO reserve on 31 December 2006 is $2,403. Accordingly, under the FIFO inventory method, cumulative gross profits would have been $2,403 higher. Because CAT's income tax rate is approximately 29 percent (determined in the solution to 3 above), the cumulative additional income tax expense would be approximately $697 ($2,403 LIFO reserve × 29% income tax rate). The estimated savings would be higher (lower) if income tax rates in prior years were higher (lower) than the 29% average tax rate incurred by CAT in 2006.

Solution to 5. The amount that would be added to CAT's deferred income tax liabilities at 31 December 2006 is $697 (in millions). The $2,403 LIFO reserve would be taxed at an income tax rate of approximately 29%. Likewise, the amount that would be added to CAT's retained earnings (profit employed in the business) is $1,706 because CAT would keep approximately 71% (after income taxes) of the $2,403 LIFO reserve.

Solution to 6. The LIFO and FIFO ratios are as follows:

	LIFO	FIFO
Inventory turnover ratio	4.65	3.37
Number of days of inventory	78.5 days	108.3 days
Gross profit margin	28.83%	28.97%
Current ratio	1.20	1.28
Return on assets	6.95%	6.72%
Debt-to-equity ratio	6.42	5.22

The inventory turnover ratio (cost of goods sold ÷ ending inventory) under LIFO is 4.65 ($29,549 ÷ $6,351) and under FIFO is 3.37 ($29,491 ÷ $8,754). The ratio is higher under LIFO than under FIFO because, in a long-term environment of rising inventory costs, cost of goods sold will be higher and inventory carrying value will be lower under LIFO than what it would otherwise be under FIFO.[6]

The number of days of inventory (365 days ÷ inventory turnover ratio) under LIFO is 78.5 days (365 days ÷ 4.65) and under FIFO is 108.3 days (365 days ÷ 3.37). The number of days of inventory is lower under LIFO than under FIFO because the inventory turnover ratio is higher under LIFO in a long-term environment of rising inventory costs.

---

[6]As before, the ending values of balance sheet accounts were used in calculating the financial ratios in this example. In practice, it is generally preferable to use average values.

Consolid

for the yea

The gross profit margin (gross profit ÷ total revenue) under LIFO is 28.83 percent [($41,517 − $29,549) ÷ $41,517] and under FIFO is 28.97 percent [($41,517 − $29,491) ÷ $41,517]. The gross profit margin is lower under LIFO than under FIFO because cost of goods sold is higher under LIFO in an environment of rising inventory costs.

The current ratio (current assets ÷ current liabilities) for CAT under LIFO is 1.20 ($23,093 ÷ $19,252) and under FIFO is 1.28 [($23,093 + $2,403 LIFO reserve) ÷ ($19,252 + $697 deferred income tax liability)]. The current ratio is lower under LIFO primarily because inventories are carried at a lower value (in an environment of rising inventory costs) than what it would otherwise be carried at under FIFO.

The return on assets (net income ÷ ending total assets) under LIFO is 6.95 percent ($3,537 ÷ $50,879) and under FIFO is 6.72 percent [$3,578 ÷ ($50,879 + $2,403 LIFO reserve)]. In this instance, the return on assets is higher under LIFO than under FIFO. This is due to the current year's increase in the LIFO reserve having less of an impact on FIFO net income than the impact of the total LIFO reserve on FIFO total assets.

Finally, the debt-to-equity ratio (total debt ÷ total shareholders' equity) for CAT under LIFO is 6.42 ($44,020 ÷ $6,859) and under FIFO is 5.22 [($44,020 + $697 additional deferred income tax liability from the LIFO reserve) ÷ ($6,859 + $1,706 after-tax addition to retained earnings from the LIFO reserve)]. In this instance, the ratio is higher under LIFO than under FIFO. This is due to the current year's increase in the deferred income tax liability having less of an impact on FIFO total debt than the total after-tax addition to retained earnings from the LIFO reserve on FIFO total equity.

4.3. LIFO Liquidations

LIFO liquidation occurs when the number of units in ending inventory declines from the number of units that were present at the beginning of the year. This occurs whenever the sale of units from inventory exceeds the purchase or production of new inventory units within any given year. If inventory unit costs have generally risen from year to year, the phenomenon of inventory-related "phantom" gross profits occurs. Inventory phantom gross profits occur because the lower inventory costs of the liquidated units are matched with unit sales to generate a higher gross profit than what would otherwise occur if those sold units were matched with units purchased at current replacement costs. Phantom inventory profits are one-time accounting events that are not sustainable in the future. Accordingly, the analyst must be attuned to the fact that some companies may potentially manipulate and inflate their reported gross profits at critical times by intentionally liquidating older layers of LIFO inventory.

Companies may also incur LIFO liquidations because of recession, labor strikes, or declining product demand. The ensuing liquidation may result in outsized phantom profits that boost reported gross profit during economic downturns (a somewhat paradoxical phenomenon).

LIFO liquidations are most likely to occur if a company uses a specific-goods LIFO approach. If LIFO layers of individual inventory items are temporarily depleted and not replaced by fiscal year-end, LIFO liquidation will occur resulting in phantom profits. In order to mitigate this liquidation problem, companies can opt to combine individual inventory items into inventory pools or groups of items that are similar in nature. Under the pooled approach, a decrease of some individual inventory items may be offset by an increase in other individual items within the pool.

EXAMPLE 10-7   LIFO Liquidation Illustration

Industrial Fan Sales, Inc. (IFS), a hypothetical company, sells an industrial-grade fan at retail and has been in business since 2004. Exhibit 10-7 provides relevant data and financial statement information about IFS's inventory purchases and sales of fan inventory for the years 2004 through 2007. IFS uses the LIFO inventory method. What is IFS's inventory phantom gross profit for 2007?

EXHIBIT 10-7   IFS Financial Statement information under LIFO

	2004	2005	2006	2007
Fans—units purchased	12,000	12,000	12,000	12,000
Purchase cost per fan	$100	$105	$110	$115
Fans—units sold	10,000	10,000	10,000	16,000
Sales price per fan	$200	$205	$210	$215
LIFO Method				
Beginning inventory	$0	$200,000	$410,000	$630,000
Purchases	1,200,000	1,260,000	1,320,000	1,380,000
Goods available for sale	1,200,000	1,460,000	1,730,000	2,010,000
Ending inventory	(200,000)	(410,000)	(630,000)	(200,000)
Cost of goods sold	$1,000,000	1,050,000	$1,100,000	$1,810,000
Income Statement				
Sales	$2,000,000	$2,050,000	$2,100,000	$3,440,000
Cost of goods sold	1,000,000	1,050,000	1,100,000	1,810,000
Gross profit	$1,000,000	$1,000,000	$1,000,000	$1,630,000
Balance Sheet				
Inventory	$200,000	$410,000	$630,000	$200,000

Solution. IFS's phantom gross profit for 2007 is $30,000. The reported gross profit is $1,630,000. If IFS had purchased 16,000 fans in 2007 rather than 12,000 fans, the cost of goods sold under the LIFO method would have been $1,840,000 (16,000 fans sold at $115.00 purchase cost per fan), and the reported gross profit would have been $1,600,000 ($3,440,000 reported sales less $1,840,000 cost of goods sold). The phantom gross profit is thus $30,000 ($1,630,000 reported gross profit less the $1,600,000 gross profit that would have been reported without the LIFO liquidation). The phantom gross profit may alternatively be determined by multiplying the number of units liquidated times the difference between the replacement cost of the units liquidated and their historical purchase cost. For IFS, the $30,000 phantom gross profit would be the 2,000 fans that are liquidated from its LIFO inventory from 2006 multiplied by $5.00 per fan ($215 replacement cost per fan less the $210 historical cost per fan) plus the 2,000 fans that are liquidated from its LIFO inventory from 2005 multiplied by $10 per fan ($215 replacement cost per fan less the $205 historical cost per fan).

in accounting for their inventories. Financial note L in Exhibit 10-6 describes Caterpillar changes in accounting for its inventories because of the adoption of SFAS No. 151 (which was mandatory for all manufacturing companies under U.S. GAAP) in 2006. Another required financial note disclosure for manufacturing companies is the breakout of the inventory values for raw materials, work-in-process, and finished goods inventories if these values are not already separately reported on the balance sheet. Exhibit 10-8 provides an example of this required disclosure from Note 9 of Caterpillar's 2006 annual report. See that the total inventories in the note disclosure ($6,351 for CAT at 31 December 2006) must reconcile to the inventories amount stated on the balance sheet (the $6,351 for inventories in Exhibit 10-5).

EXHIBIT 10-8   Caterpillar Inc.: Selected Notes to Consolidated Financial Statements. Note 9. Inventories

31 December ($ millions)	2006	2005	2004
Raw Materials	$2,182	$1,689	$1,592
Work-in-process	977	814	664
Finished goods	2,915	2,493	2,209
Supplies	277	228	210
Total inventories	$6,351	$5,224	$4,675

We had long-term material purchase obligations of approximately $231 million on December 31, 2006.

5. EFFECTS OF INVENTORY METHOD CHOICE

As was discussed earlier, the choice of inventory method would not be much of an issue if inventory unit costs remained relatively constant from period to period because the allocation of cost flow between cost of goods sold and inventory carrying value would be very similar under the weighted average cost, FIFO, and LIFO inventory methods. But because inventory unit costs typically change from period to period, the choice of inventory method does in fact matter to a company. In an environment of rising inventory unit costs and generally constant or increasing inventory quantities, U.S. companies have an economic incentive to use the LIFO method because of the related income tax savings.

5.1. Financial Statement Effects of Using LIFO

In an environment of rising inventory unit costs and constant or increasing inventory quantities, LIFO (in comparison with FIFO) will allocate a greater amount of cost flow to cost of goods sold on the income statement and a lesser amount of cost flow to the carrying value of inventory on the balance sheet. Accordingly, because cost of goods sold will be greater under LIFO, a company's gross profit, operating profit, and income before taxes will be lower. Income tax expense will thus be lower under LIFO, causing the company's net operating cash flow to increase. On the balance sheet, a lower inventory carrying value will also cause reported working capital and total assets to be lower.

When the financial statement impact from using LIFO is significantly different from the impact of using FIFO, the company's profitability, liquidity, activity, and solvency ratios will be materially affected as well. When confronted with these conditions, a restatement to the FIFO method (see Example 10-5) is critical for the analyst to make a valid comparison with other companies using FIFO (or other companies reporting under IFRS).

Although an environment of rising inventory unit costs is far more prevalent than an environment of falling unit prices, there are some industries (such as the computer hardware and peripheral equipment industry) where declining unit prices are the norm. Companies do not usually select the LIFO method when they conduct business in a normal environment of falling inventory unit costs. In such an environment, these companies would more likely opt for the FIFO method because using this method would generate the lowest amount of income tax expense. In fact, the effect on financial statements and ratios from using FIFO (in comparison with LIFO) in an environment of declining inventory unit costs is the same as when using LIFO (in comparison with FIFO) in an environment of rising inventory unit costs.

5.2. Inventory Method Changes

Companies sometimes decide to change inventory methods. Under IFRS, changes in accounting policy are accounted for retrospectively. According to IAS 8, a change in policy is acceptable only if the change results in the financial statements providing reliable and more relevant information about the effects of transactions, other events, or conditions on the business entity's financial position, financial performance, or cash flows. If the change is justifiable, historical information is restated for all accounting periods (typically the previous one or two years that are presented for comparability purposes with the current year in annual financial reports). Adjustment amounts relating to accounting periods that are prior to those financial statements presented and restated are adjusted against the opening balance of retained earnings of the earliest year presented for comparison purposes. An exemption to the restatement applies when it is impracticable to determine either the period-specific effects or the cumulative effect of the change.

Under U.S. GAAP, accounting for a change in inventory policy is now similar to IFRS due to the adoption of SFAS No. 154 for fiscal years beginning after 15 December 2005. Because of U.S. GAAP consistency requirements, a company must thoroughly explain why the newly adopted inventory accounting method is superior and preferable to the old method. In addition, U.S. tax regulations may also restrict changes and require permission from the Internal Revenue Service (IRS). If a company decides to change from LIFO to another inventory method, U.S. GAAP requires a retrospective restatement of inventory and retained earnings. Historical financial statements are also restated for the effects of the change. If a company decides to change to the LIFO method, it must do so on a prospective basis.

Retrospective adjustments are not made to the financial statements. Instead, the carrying value of inventory under the old method will become the initial LIFO layer in the year of LIFO adoption.

6. SUMMARY

Inventory cost flow is a major determinant in measuring income for merchandising and manufacturing companies. In addition, inventories are usually a significant asset on the balance sheets of these companies. The financial statements and financial notes of a company provide important information that the analyst needs to correctly assess and compare financial performance with other companies. Key concepts in this chapter are as follows:

- Inventories are a major factor in the analysis of merchandising and manufacturing companies. Such companies generate their sales and profits through inventory transactions on a regular basis. An important consideration in determining profits for these companies is measuring the cost of goods sold when inventories are sold to business customers.
- The cost of inventories comprises all costs of purchase, costs of conversion, and other costs incurred in bringing the inventories to their present location and condition. Also, any allocation of fixed production overhead is based on normal capacity levels, with unallocated production overhead expensed as incurred.
- Under IFRS, the cost of inventories is assigned by using either the FIFO or weighted average cost formula. The specific identification method is required for inventories of items that are not ordinarily interchangeable and for goods or services produced and segregated for specific projects. A business entity must use the same cost formula for all inventories having a similar nature and use to the entity.
- Inventories are measured at the lower of cost or "net realizable value." Net realizable value is the estimated selling price in the ordinary course of business less the estimated costs necessary to make the sale. Reversals of write-downs are permissible under IFRS but not U.S. GAAP.
- The choice of inventory method impacts the financial statements and any financial ratios that are derived from them. As a consequence, the analyst must carefully consider inventory method differences when evaluating a company's performance or when comparing a company with industry data or industry competitors.
- The inventory turnover ratio, number of days of inventory ratio, and gross profit margin ratio are directly and fully affected by a company's choice of inventory method.
- Under U.S. GAAP, the LIFO method is widely used for both tax and financial reporting purposes because of potential income tax savings.
- LIFO reserve liquidation occurs when the number of units in ending inventory declines from the number of units that were present at the beginning of the year. If inventory unit costs have generally risen from year to year, the phenomenon of inventory "phantom" gross profits occurs on liquidation.
- Under U.S. GAAP, companies that use the LIFO inventory method must disclose in their financial notes the amount of the LIFO reserve or the amount that would have been reported in inventory if the FIFO method had been used.
- Consistency of inventory costing is required under both U.S. GAAP and IFRS. If a company changes an accounting policy, the change must be justifiable and all financial statements are accounted for retrospectively.

PRACTICE PROBLEMS

1. Inventory cost is *least likely* to include
   A. production-related storage costs.
   B. costs incurred due to normal waste of materials.
   C. transportation costs of shipping inventory to customers.

2. Ajax Factories produces pencils at a factory designed to produce 10 million pencils per year. In 2007 the fixed production overhead related to the factory was $1 million and the factory produced 9 million pencils. The inventory cost for each pencil related to the fixed production overhead is *closest* to
   A. $0.00
   B. $0.10
   C. $0.11

3. Mustard Seed PLC adheres to IFRS. It recently purchased inventory for €100 million and spent €5 million for storage prior to selling the goods. The amount it charged to inventory expense (in € millions) was *closest* to
   A. €95.
   B. €100.
   C. €105.

4. Carrying inventory at a value above its historical cost would *most likely* be permitted if
   A. the inventory was held by a produce dealer.
   B. financial statements were prepared using U.S. GAAP.
   C. the change resulted from a reversal of a previous write-down.

5. Eric's Used Bookstore prepares its financial statements in accordance with U.S. GAAP. Inventory was purchased for $1 million and later marked down to $550,000. However, one of the books was later discovered to be a rare collectible item and the inventory is now worth an estimated $3 million. The inventory is *most likely* reported on the balance sheet at
   A. $550,000.
   B. $1,000,000.
   C. $3,000,000.

6. Fernando's Pasta purchased inventory and later wrote it down, though the current realizable value is higher than the value when written down. Fernando's inventory balance will *most likely* be
   A. higher if it complies with IFRS.
   B. higher if it complies with U.S. GAAP.
   C. the same under U.S. GAAP and IFRS.

7. Cinnamon Corp. started business in 2007 and uses the weighted average cost inventory method. During 2007 it purchased 45,000 units of inventory at €10 each and sold 40,000 units for €20 each. In 2008 it purchased another 50,000 units at €11 each and sold 45,000 units for €22 each. Its 2008 cost of goods sold (in € thousands) was *closest* to
   A. €490.
   B. €491.
   C. €495.

8. Zimt AG started business in 2007 and uses the FIFO inventory method. During 2007 it purchased 45,000 units of inventory at €10 each and sold 40,000 units for €20 each. In 2008 it purchased another 50,000 units at €11 each and sold 45,000 units for €22 each. Its 2008 ending inventory balance (in € thousands) was *closest* to
   A. €105.
   B. €109.
   C. €110.

9. Zimt AG uses the FIFO inventory accounting method, and Nutmeg Inc. uses the LIFO method. Compared to the cost of replacing the inventory, during periods of rising prices the cost of goods sold reported by
   A. Zimt is too low.
   B. Nutmeg is too low.
   C. Nutmeg is too high.

10. Zimt AG uses the FIFO inventory accounting method, and Nutmeg Inc. uses the LIFO method. Compared to the cost of replacing the inventory, during periods of rising prices the ending inventory balance reported by
    A. Zimt is too high.
    B. Nutmeg is too low.
    C. Nutmeg is too high.

11. Like many technology companies, TechnoTools operates in an environment of declining prices. Its reported profits will tend to be *highest* if it accounts for inventory using the
    A. FIFO method.
    B. LIFO method.
    C. weighted average cost method.

12. Compared to using the weighted average cost method to account for inventory, during a period in which prices are generally rising the current ratio of a company using the FIFO method would *most likely* be
    A. lower.
    B. higher.
    C. dependent upon the interaction with accounts payable.

13. Zimt AG wrote down the value of inventory in 2007 and reversed the write-down in 2008. Compared to ratios calculated if the write-down had never occurred, Zimt's reported 2007
    A. current ratio was too high.
    B. gross margin was too high.
    C. inventory turnover was too high.

14. Zimt AG wrote down the value of inventory in 2007 and reversed the write-down in 2008. Compared to results reported if the write-down had never occurred, Zimt's reported 2008
    A. profit was overstated.
    B. cash flow from operations was overstated.
    C. year-end inventory balance was overstated.

15. Compared to a company that uses the FIFO inventory accounting method, during periods of rising prices a company that uses the LIFO method will *most likely* appear more
    A. liquid.
    B. efficient.
    C. profitable.

16. Nutmeg, Inc. uses the LIFO method to account for inventory. During years in which inventory unit costs are generally rising and in which the company purchases more inventory than it sells to customers its reported gross profit margin will *most likely* be
    A. lower than it would have been if the company used the FIFO method.
    B. higher than it would have been if the company used the FIFO method.
    C. about the same as it would have been if the company used the FIFO method.

17. Sauerbraten Corp. reported 2007 sales ($ in millions) of $2,157 and cost of goods sold of $1,827. The company uses the LIFO method for inventory valuation and discloses that if the FIFO inventory valuation method had been used, inventories would have been $63.3 million and $56.8 million higher in 2007 and 2006, respectively. If Sauerbraten used the FIFO method exclusively, it would have reported 2007 gross profit *closest* to
    A. $324.
    B. $330.
    C. $337.

18. Sauerbraten Corp. reported 2007 sales ($ in millions) of $2,157 and cost of goods sold of $1,827. Inventories at year-end 2007 and 2006, respectively, were $553 and $562. The company uses the LIFO method for inventory valuation and discloses that if the FIFO inventory valuation method had been used, inventories would have been $63.3 million and $56.8 million higher in 2007 and 2006, respectively. Compared to the inventory turnover ratio reported, if Sauerbraten had exclusively used the FIFO method its inventory turnover ratio would have been *closest* to
    A. 2.96.
    B. 3.28.
    C. 3.49.

19. Compared to using the FIFO method to account for inventory, during periods of rising prices a company that uses the LIFO method is *most likely* to report higher
    A. net income.
    B. cost of sales.
    C. income taxes.

20. In order to compare the results of a company that uses the LIFO method to one using FIFO, the required adjustments to the financial statements of the LIFO user include adding the
    A. LIFO reserve to inventory.
    B. change in the LIFO reserve to inventory.
    C. change in the LIFO reserve to cost of goods sold.

21. Carey Company adheres to U.S. GAAP, while Jonathan Company adheres to IFRS. It is *least likely* that
    A. Carey has reversed an inventory write-down.
    B. Jonathan has reversed an inventory write-down.
    C. Jonathan and Carey both use the FIFO inventory accounting method.

CHAPTER 11

LONG-LIVED ASSETS

Elaine Henry, CFA

University of Miami
Coral Gables, Florida

Elizabeth A. Gordon

Temple University
Philadelphia, Pennsylvania

LEARNING OUTCOMES

After completing this chapter, you will be able to do the following:

- Explain the accounting standards related to the capitalization of expenditures as part of long-lived assets, including interest costs.
- Compute and describe the effects of capitalizing versus expensing on net income, shareholders' equity, cash flow from operations, and financial ratios including the effect on the interest coverage ratio of capitalizing interest costs.
- Explain the circumstances in which software development costs and research and development costs are capitalized.
- Identify the different depreciation methods for long-lived tangible assets and discuss how the choice of method, useful lives, and salvage values affect a company's financial statements, ratios, and taxes.
- Discuss the use of fixed asset disclosures to compare companies' average age of depreciable assets, and calculate, using such disclosures, the average age and average depreciable life of fixed assets.
- Describe amortization of intangible assets with finite useful lives, and the estimates that affect the amortization calculations.
- Discuss the liability for closure, removal, and environmental effects of long-lived operating assets, and discuss the financial statement impact and ratio effects of that liability.
- Discuss the impact of sales or exchanges of long-lived assets on financial statements.

- Define impairment of long-lived tangible and intangible assets and explain what effect such impairment has on a company's financial statements and ratios.
- Calculate and describe both the initial and long-lived effects of asset revaluations on financial ratios.

1. INTRODUCTION

[handwritten: Capitalized Interest [Interest coverage Ratios.]

Long-lived assets, also commonly referred to as long-term assets, are assets that are expected to provide economic benefits over a future period of time, typically greater than one year.[1] Long-lived assets may be tangible, intangible, or financial assets. Examples of **tangible assets** include land (property), plant, and equipment; examples of **intangible assets** (assets lacking physical substance) include patents and trademarks; and examples of financial assets include investments in equity or debt securities issued by other companies. In this chapter, we cover long-lived tangible and intangible assets. A subsequent chapter will discuss financial assets.

The costs of most long-lived assets are allocated as expenses over the period of time during which they are expected to provide economic benefits. The two main types of long-lived assets whose costs are *not* allocated over time are land, which is not depreciated, and those intangible assets with indefinite useful lives. Intangible assets with indefinite lives are tested periodically for any reduction in their fair value as compared to their recorded value, known as an *impairment,* which is reflected as an impairment loss on the income statement.

This chapter is organized as follows: Sections 2 and 3 describe and illustrate accounting for the acquisition of long-lived tangible assets and long-lived intangible assets. Sections 4 and 5 describe the allocation of the costs of long-lived assets over their useful lives. Section 6 discusses the treatment of obligations arising in connection with the ultimate retirement of an asset. Section 7 describes accounting for the disposal of long-lived operating assets. Sections 8 and 9 cover the concepts of impairment (reduction in the value of an asset) and revaluation (change in the value of an asset). Section 10 summarizes the chapter and is followed by practice problems in the CFA Institute multiple-choice format.

2. ACCOUNTING FOR THE ACQUISITION OF LONG-LIVED TANGIBLE ASSETS

Upon acquisition, a long-lived asset is recorded on the balance sheet at its cost, which is typically the same as its fair value.[2] In addition to the purchase price, the buyer also records, as part of the cost of an asset, all the expenditures necessary to prepare the asset for its intended use. The following paragraphs discuss accounting for the acquisition of long-lived tangible assets and selected relevant analytical issues.

---

[1]In some instances, it is industry practice (such as with tobacco and alcohol distillers) to include as current assets rather than long-lived assets those assets with lives that are longer than one year, for example, leaf tobacco, which is cured and aged over a period longer than one year, and whiskey, which is barrel-aged for a period longer than one year.
[2]*Fair value* is defined formally in the Statement of Financial Accounting Standards (SFAS) No. 157, Paragraph 5 as "the price that would be received to sell an asset or paid to transfer a liability in an orderly transaction between market participants at the measurement date."

2.1. Accounting Standards Related to Capitalization of Expenditures

Expenditures related to long-lived assets are included as part of the recorded value of assets on the balance sheet (i.e. capitalized) if they are expected to provide benefits in the future, typically beyond one year; alternatively, expenditures are treated as an expense if they are not expected to provide benefits in future periods. Before turning to specific instances, we will consider the general financial statement impact of capitalizing versus expensing and two analytical issues related to the decision—namely, the effect on an individual company's trend analysis and on comparability across companies.

In the period of the expenditure, an expenditure that is capitalized increases the amount of assets on the balance sheet and appears as an investing cash outflow on the statement of cash flows. In subsequent periods, a company allocates the capitalized amount over the asset's useful life (except land and intangible assets with indefinite lives) as depreciation or amortization expense. This expense reduces net income on the income statement and reduces the value of the asset on the balance sheet. Depreciation is a non-cash expense and therefore, apart from its effect on taxable income, has no impact on the cash flow statement. In the section of the statement of cash flows that reconciles net income to operating cash flow, depreciation expense is added back to net income.

Alternatively, an expenditure that is expensed reduces net income by the entire amount of the expenditure in the period it is made. No asset is recorded on the balance sheet and thus no depreciation or amortization can occur in subsequent periods. The lower amount of net income is reflected in lower retained earnings on the balance sheet. An expenditure that is expensed appears as operating cash outflow in the period it is made. There is no effect on the financial statements of subsequent periods.

Example 11-1 illustrates the impact on the financial statements of capitalizing versus expensing an expenditure.

EXAMPLE 11-1   Financial Statement Impact of Capitalizing versus Expensing

Assume two identical (hypothetical) companies, CAP Inc. and NOW Inc., start up with €1,000 cash and €1,000 common stock. Each year the companies receive total revenues of €1,500 cash and pay cash expenses, excluding an equipment purchase, of €500. At the beginning of operations, each company spends €900 to purchase equipment. CAP estimates the equipment will have a useful life of three years and an estimated salvage value of €0 at the end of the three years. NOW estimates a much shorter useful life and expenses the equipment immediately. The companies have no other assets and make no other asset purchases during the three year period. Assume the companies pay no dividends, earn zero interest on cash balances, have a tax rate of 30 percent, and use the same accounting method for financial and tax purposes.

The left side of the table below shows CAP's financial statements, i.e. with the expenditure capitalized and depreciated at €300 per year based on the straight-line method of depreciation (€900 cost minus €0 salvage value equals €900, divided by a three-year life equals €300 per year). The right side of the table below shows NOW's financial statements, with the entire €900 expenditure treated as an expense in the first year.

| CAP Inc. | | | | NOW Inc. | | | |
| Capitalize €900 as Asset and Depreciate | | | | Expense €900 Immediately | | | |
For Year	1	2	3	For Year	1	2	3
Revenue	€1,500	€1,500	€1,500	Revenue	€1,500	€1,500	€1,500
Cash expenses	500	500	500	Cash expenses	1,400	500	500
Depreciation	300	300	300	Depreciation	0	0	0
Income before tax	€700	€700	€700	Income before tax	€100	€1,000	€1,000
Tax at 30%	210	210	210	Tax at 30%	30	300	300
Net income	€490	€490	€490	Net income	€70	€700	€700
Cash from operations	€790	€790	€790	Cash from operations	€70	€700	€700
Cash used in investing	(900)	0	0	Cash used in investing	0	0	0
Total change in cash	(€110)	€790	€790	Total change in cash	€70	€700	€700

1. Which company reports higher net income over the three years? Total cash flow? Cash from operations?
2. Based on return on equity (ROE) and net profit margin, how do the two companies' profitability compare?
3. Why does NOW Inc. report change in cash of €70 in year 1, while CAP Inc. reports total change in cash of (€110)?

Solution to 1. Neither company reports higher net income nor total cash flow over the three years. The sum of net income over the three years is identical (€1,470 total) whether the €900 is capitalized or expensed. Also, the sum of the change in cash (€1,470 total) is identical under either scenario. CAP Inc. reports higher cash from operations by an amount of €900 because, under the capitalization scenario, the €900 purchase is treated as an investing cash flow.

> *Note: Because the companies use the same accounting method for both financial and taxable income, absent the assumption of zero interest on cash balances, expensing the €900 would have resulted in higher income and cash flow for NOW Inc. because the lower taxes paid in the first year (€30 versus €210) would have allowed NOW Inc. to earn interest income on the tax savings.*

Solution to 2. Computing ROE requires forecasting shareholders' equity. In general, ending shareholders' equity = beginning shareholders' equity + net income + other comprehensive income − dividends + net capital contributions from shareholders. Because the companies in this example do not have other comprehensive income, did not pay dividends, and reported no capital contributions from shareholders, ending retained earnings = beginning retained earnings + net income, and ending shareholders' equity = beginning shareholders' equity + net income. The forecasts are presented below.

CAP Inc.					NOW Inc.				
Capitalize €900 as Asset and Depreciate					**Expense €900 Immediately**				
Time	**0**	**1**	**2**	**3**	**Time**	**0**	**1**	**2**	**3**
Retained earnings	€0	€490	€980	€1,470	Retained earnings	€0	€70	€770	€1,470
Common stock	1,000	1,000	1,000	1,000	Common stock	1,000	1,000	1,000	1,000
Total shareholders' equity	1,000	1,490	1,980	2,470	Total shareholders' equity	1,000	1,070	1,770	2,470

ROE is calculated as net income divided by average shareholders' equity, and net profit margin is calculated as net income divided by total revenue. For example, CAP Inc. had year 1 ROE of 39 percent (€490/[(€1,000 + €1,490)/2]), and year 1 net profit margin of 33 percent (€490/€1,500).

CAP Inc.				NOW Inc.			
Capitalize €900 as Asset and Depreciate				**Expense €900 Immediately**			
For year	**1**	**2**	**3**	**For year**	**1**	**2**	**3**
ROE	39%	28%	22%	ROE	7%	49%	33%
Net profit margin	33%	33%	33%	Net profit margin	5%	47%	47%

As shown, capitalizing results in higher profitability ratios (ROE and net profit margin) in the first year, and lower profitability ratios in the subsequent years. For example, CAP Inc.'s year 1 ROE of 39 percent was higher than NOW Inc.'s year 1 ROE of 7 percent, but in years 2 and 3, NOW Inc. reports superior profitability.

Note also that NOW's superior growth in net income between year 1 and year 2 is not attributable to superior performance but rather to a different accounting decision, namely to recognize the expense sooner than CAP. In general, all else equal, accounting decisions that result in recognizing expenses sooner will give the appearance of greater subsequent growth. Comparison of the growth of the two companies' net income without an awareness of the difference in accounting methods would be misleading. As a corollary, NOW's income and profitability exhibit greater volatility across the three years, not because of more volatile performance but rather because of the different accounting decision.

Solution to 3. NOW Inc. reports change in cash of €70 in year 1, while CAP Inc. reports total change in cash of €110 because NOW's taxes were €180 lower than CAP Inc.'s (€30 versus €210).

Note that this problem assumes the two companies use identical accounting methods for financial reporting and taxes. Recall that in the United States, companies are allowed to use different depreciation methods for financial reporting and taxes, which, in practice, often gives rise to deferred taxes.

As shown, discretion regarding whether to expense or capitalize expenditures can impede comparability across companies. Example 11-1 assumes the companies purchase a single asset in one year. Because the sum of net income over the three-year period is identical whether the asset is capitalized or expensed, it illustrates that although capitalizing results in higher profitability compared to expensing in the first year, it results in lower profitability ratios in the subsequent years. Conversely, expensing results in lower profitability in the first year, but higher profitability in later years, indicating a favorable trend.

Similarly, shareholders' equity for a firm that capitalizes the expenditure will be higher in the early years because the initially higher profits result in initially higher retained earnings. Example 11-1 assumes the companies purchase a single asset in one year and report identical amounts of total net income over the three-year period, so shareholders' equity (and retained earnings) for the firm that expenses will be identical to shareholders' equity (and retained earnings) for the capitalizing firm at the end of the three-year period.

Although the example above shows companies purchasing an asset only in the first year, if a company continues to purchase similar or increasing amounts of assets each year, the profitability-enhancing effect of capitalizing continues so long as the amount of the expenditure in a period is less than the depreciation expense for a single year. Example 11-2 illustrates this point.

EXAMPLE 11-2   Impact of Capitalizing versus Expensing for Ongoing Purchases

A company buys a £300 computer in year 1 and capitalizes the expenditure. The computer has a useful life of three years and an expected salvage value of £0, so the annual depreciation expense using the straight-line method is £100 per year. Compared to expensing the entire £300 immediately, the company's pre-tax profit in year 1 is £200 greater.

1. Assume that the company continues to buy an identical computer each year at the same price. Assuming the company uses an identical accounting treatment for each of the computers, when does the profit-enhancing effect of capitalizing versus expensing end?
2. If the company buys another identical computer in year 4, using identical accounting treatment as the prior years, what is the effect on year 4 profits of capitalizing versus expensing these expenditures?

Solution to 1. The profit-enhancing effect of capitalizing versus expensing would end in year 3. In year 3, the depreciation expense on each of the three computers bought in years 1, 2, and 3 would total £300 (£100 + £100 + £100). Therefore, the total depreciation expense for year 3 will be exactly equal to the capital expenditure in year 3. The expense in year 3 would be £300, regardless of whether the company capitalized or expensed the annual computer purchases.

Solution to 2. There is no impact on year 4 profits. As in the previous year, the depreciation expense on each of the three computers bought in years 2, 3, and 4 would total £300 (£100 + £100 + £100). Therefore, the total depreciation expense for year 4 will be exactly equal to the capital expenditure in year 4. Pretax profits would be reduced by £300, regardless of whether the company capitalized or expensed the annual computer purchases.

Capitalizing an expenditure rather than expensing it also results in greater amounts reported as cash from operations. Cash from operations is an important consideration in valuation, so companies may aim to maximize reported cash from operations. WorldCom is an infamous example of a company violating U.S. GAAP to maximize reported cash from operations; in 2001, the company wrongly capitalized over $3 billion in line costs (charges paid for access to telecommunication lines) that should have been expensed. It is, of course, important to distinguish between WorldCom's fraudulent financial reporting and allowable accounting discretion. Nonetheless, the general concept is that a capitalized expenditure would typically be shown as an investment cash outflow whereas an expense would reduce operating cash.

The discussion now turns to specific instances of the capitalization of expenditures.

2.2.   Costs Incurred at Acquisition

The most obvious cost incurred to acquire a tangible asset (such as property, plant, and equipment) is its purchase price. In addition to the purchase price, the buyer also records, as part of the cost of an asset, all the expenditures necessary to get the asset ready for its intended use. For example, freight costs borne by the purchaser and special installation costs are included in the total cost of the asset.

In a monetary exchange, the purchase price is easily determined. If an asset is acquired in a nonmonetary exchange, its cost is based on the fair value of the asset given up, or the fair value of the asset acquired if it is more readily determinable.[3] Examples of nonmonetary exchanges of operating assets include exchanges of mineral leases or real estate. For an example, refer to the disclosure of a nonmonetary exchange shown in Exhibit 11-1.

An analyst would want to understand the nature of a nonmonetary exchange that gave rise to a significant gain or loss. Presumably, neither counterparty to an exchange would be willing to sacrifice an asset of higher value to obtain an asset of lower value. Therefore, one reason for an exchange giving rise to a significant gain or loss would be differences between the values placed on the assets exchanged by the different counterparties. Another explanation for an exchange is to achieve a fair value measurement of assets. As we will discuss below, International Financial Reporting Standards (IFRS), unlike U.S. GAAP, allows companies the option to value long-lived assets based on historical costs or based on fair value. The net result of the exchange described in Exhibit 11-1 was that the company now reports the exchanged coal reserves at fair value, which is $38.2 million higher than the book value of the assets exchanged.

EXHIBIT 11-1   Example of a Nonmonetary Exchange: Massey Energy Company (NYSE: MEE) Disclosed a Nonmonetary Exchange in Its 2006 Financial Statements

---

During the third quarter of 2005, we exchanged coal reserves with a third party, recognizing a gain of $38.2 million (pretax) in accordance with SFAS 153. The fair value of the assets surrendered by both parties was determined by use of a future cashflows valuation model. The difference in the fair value of the assets surrendered and their book basis resulted in the gain recognized. The gain from this transaction is recorded in Other revenue. The acquired coal reserves were recorded in Property, plant and equipment at the fair value of the reserves surrendered.

Source: Massey Energy Company's Form 10-K filed with the SEC on 1 March 2007, p. 60.

---

[3]APB 29 and SFAS No. 153 specify U.S. GAAP accounting for assets acquired in nonmonetary exchanges, and the latter standard uses language similar to that in IAS 16, *Property, Plant and Equipment,* and IAS 38, *Intangible Assets.*

2.3. Capitalization of Interest Costs

Companies generally must capitalize interest costs associated with acquiring or constructing an asset that requires a long period of time to get ready for its intended use.[4] For example, constructing a building to sell or for a company's own use typically requires a substantial amount of time; any interest cost incurred in order to finance construction is capitalized as part of the cost of the asset. The company determines the interest rate to use based on its existing borrowings or, if applicable, on a borrowing specifically incurred for constructing the asset. If a company takes out a loan specifically to construct a building, the interest cost on that loan during the time of construction would be capitalized as part of the building's cost.

As a consequence of this accounting treatment, a company's interest costs for a period can appear either on the balance sheet (to the extent they are capitalized) or on the income statement (to the extent they are expensed).

If the interest expenditure is incurred in connection with constructing an asset for the company's own use, the capitalized interest appears on the balance sheet as a part of the relevant long-lived asset (i.e., property, plant, and equipment). The capitalized interest is expensed over time as the property is depreciated and is thus part of depreciation expense rather than interest expense. If the interest expenditure is incurred in connection with constructing an asset to sell, for example, by a home builder, the capitalized interest appears on the company's balance sheet as part of inventory. The capitalized interest is expensed as part of the cost of goods sold when the asset is sold.

The treatment of capitalized interest poses certain issues that analysts may want to consider. First, capitalized interest appears as part of investing cash outflows, whereas expensed interest reduces operating cash flow. Although the treatment is consistent with accounting standards, an analyst may want to examine the impact on reported cash flows. Second, recall that interest coverage ratios are solvency indicators measuring the extent to which a company's earnings (or cash flow) in a period covered its interest costs. To provide a true picture of a company's interest coverage, the entire amount of interest expenditure, both the capitalized portion and the expensed portion, should be used in calculating interest coverage ratios. Additionally, if a company is depreciating interest that it capitalized in a previous period, income should be adjusted to eliminate the effect of that depreciation. Example 11-3 illustrates the calculation.

EXAMPLE 11-3   Effect of Capitalized Interest Costs on Coverage Ratios and Cash Flow

MTR Gaming Group, Inc. (NasdaqGS: MNTG) disclosed the following information in one of the footnotes to its financial statements: "Interest is capitalized to construction in progress based on the product resulting from applying the company's cost of borrowing rate to qualifying assets. Interest capitalized in 2005 was $1,301,000. There

---

[4]SFAS No. 34 specifies U.S. GAAP accounting for capitalization of interest costs. Under the recently revised IAS 23 (March, 2007), international standards now require capitalization of interest costs. Although the standards are not completely converged, the new international standard eliminates the previously allowed alternative of immediately expensing interest costs.

was no interest capitalized during 2004 and 2003 (Form 10-K filed 29 March 2006, F-6)" (see Exhibit 11-2).

EXHIBIT 11-2   MTR Gaming Group Selected data, as reported ($ thousands)

	2005	2004	2003
EBIT (from income statement)	$25,736	$36,321	$35,869
Interest expense (from income statement)	12,179	13,599	11,896
Interest capitalized (from footnote)	1,301	0	0
Net cash provided by operating activities	$39,484	$46,569	$37,806
Net cash used in investing activities	(45,778)	(45,922)	(46,541)

1. Calculate and interpret MTR's interest coverage ratio, with and without capitalized interest.
2. Calculate MTR's percentage change in operating cash flow from 2004 to 2005. What were the effects of capitalized interest on operating and investing cash flows?

Solution to 1. MTR did not capitalize any interest during 2003 or 2004, so the interest coverage ratio for each of those two years is not affected by capitalized interest. The interest coverage ratio, measured as earnings before interest and taxes (EBIT) divided by interest expense, was as follows:

3.02 ($35,869 ÷ $11,896) for 2003
2.67 ($36,321 ÷ $13,599) for 2004

For the year 2005, interest coverage ratios with and without capitalized interest were as follows:

2.11 ($25,736 ÷ $12,179) excluding capitalized interest
1.91 [$25,736 ÷ ($12,179 + $1,301)] including capitalized interest

Because MTR did not capitalize interest in previous years, no adjustment for depreciation of capitalized interest costs is required.

The above calculations indicate that MTR's interest coverage deteriorated over the three-year period from 2003 to 2005. In addition, the 2005 interest coverage ratio of 1.91 that includes capitalized interest is substantially lower than the ratio with capitalized interest excluded.

Solution to 2. If the interest had been expensed rather than capitalized, operating cash flows would have shown an even greater decline and investing cash outflows would have declined rather than remaining stable over the 2004 to 2005 period.

For 2005 compared with 2004, MTR's operating cash flow declined by 15.2 percent $39,484 ÷ $46,569 − 1. If the $1,301 of interest had been expensed rather than capitalized, the decline in cash flow would have been even greater, 18.0 percent ($39,484 − $1,301) ÷ $46,569 − 1.

Further, including capitalized interest in investing activities, as reported, the company's investing cash flows appear approximately flat between 2004 and 2005. However, excluding capitalized interest from investing activities, the company's investing cash flows declined over the period by 3.1 percent ($45,778 − $1,301) ÷ $45,922 − 1.

Generally, including capitalized interest in the calculation of interest coverage ratios provides a better assessment of a company's solvency. In assigning credit ratings, rating agencies include capitalized interest in coverage ratios. For example, Standard & Poor's calculates the EBIT interest coverage ratio as EBIT divided by gross interest (defined as interest prior to deductions for capitalized interest or interest income).

Maintaining a minimum interest coverage ratio is a financial covenant often included in bank loans. The definition of the coverage ratio can be found in the company's credit agreement. The definition is relevant because treatment of capitalized interest in calculating coverage ratios would affect an assessment of how close a company's actual ratios are to the levels specified by its financial covenants and thus the probability of breaching those covenants.

3. ACCOUNTING FOR THE ACQUISITION OF LONG-LIVED INTANGIBLE ASSETS

Intangible assets are assets lacking physical substance. Intangible assets include items that involve exclusive rights such as patents, copyrights, trademarks, and franchises. Intangible assets also include goodwill, which arises when one company purchases another and the acquisition price exceeds the fair value of the identifiable assets acquired. Accounting for an intangible asset depends on how it is acquired. The following sections describe accounting for intangible assets obtained in three ways: purchased in situations other than business combinations, developed internally, and acquired in business combinations.

3.1. Intangible Assets Purchased in Situations Other than Business Combinations

Intangible assets purchased in situations other than business combinations are treated the same as long-lived tangible assets; namely, they are recorded at their fair value when acquired, which is assumed to be equivalent to the purchase price.[5] If several intangible assets are acquired as part of a group, the purchase price is allocated to each asset based on its fair value.

In deciding how to treat individual intangible assets for analytical purposes, analysts are particularly aware that companies must use a substantial amount of judgment and numerous assumptions to determine the fair value of individual intangible assets. For analysis, therefore,

---

[5]SFAS No. 142 specifies U.S. GAAP accounting for intangible assets, and IAS 38 specifies requirements under international standards.

understanding the types of intangible assets acquired can often be more useful than focusing on the values assigned to the individual assets.

3.2. Intangible Assets Developed Internally

Costs to internally develop intangible assets are generally expensed when incurred, although there are some exceptions, described in the following sections. The general analytical issues related to the capitalizing-versus-expensing decision apply here, namely, comparability across companies and the effect on an individual company's trend analysis.

3.2.1.   Effect of Differences in Strategy (Developing Internally versus Acquiring)

The general requirement that costs of internally developing intangible assets be expensed should be compared with capitalizing the cost of acquiring intangible assets, described in the previous section. Because costs associated with internally developing intangible assets are usually expensed, a company that has obtained its intangible assets such as patents, copyrights, or brands internally through expenditures on research and development (R&D) or advertising will reflect a lower amount of assets than a company that has obtained its intangible assets by acquisition. In addition, on the statement of cash flows, costs of internally developing intangible assets are treated as operating cash outflows, while costs of acquiring intangible assets are investing cash outflows. Differences in strategy (developing versus acquiring intangible assets) can thus impact financial ratios.

3.2.2.   Research and Development (R&D)

IFRS (IAS 38) requires that expenditures on research (or during the research phase of an internal project) be expensed rather than capitalized as an intangible asset. Research is defined in IAS 38, paragraph 8, as "original and planned investigation undertaken with the prospect of gaining new scientific or technical knowledge and understanding." The "research phase of an internal project" refers to the period during which a company cannot demonstrate that an intangible asset is being created, for example the search for alternative materials or systems to use in a production process. IFRS allows companies to recognize an internal asset arising from development (or the development phase of an internal project) if certain criteria are met, including a demonstration of the technical feasibility of completing the intangible asset and the intent to use or sell the asset. Development is defined in IAS 38 as "the application of research findings or other knowledge to a plan or design for the production of new or substantially improved materials, devices, products, processes, systems or services before the start of commercial production or use."

Generally, U.S. accounting standards require that R&D costs be expensed. But the standards do require that certain costs related to software development be capitalized.[6] Costs incurred to develop a software product for sale are expensed until the product's feasibility is established, and capitalized after the product's feasibility has been established. In addition, companies capitalize costs related directly to developing software for internal use, such as the costs of employees who help build and test the software.

Even though standards require companies to capitalize software development costs after a product's feasibility is established, judgment in determining feasibility means that companies' capitalization practices differ. For example, as illustrated in Exhibit 11-3, Microsoft judges

---

[6]SFAS No. 86 and SOP 98-1 specify U.S. GAAP accounting for software development costs.

EXHIBIT 11-3   Disclosure on Software Development Costs: Excerpt from Management
Discussion and Analysis (MD&A) of Microsoft Corporation (NasdaqGS: MSFT)

Judgment is required in determining when technological feasibility of a product is established. We have
determined that technological feasibility for our software products is reached shortly before the products are released to manufacturing. Costs incurred after technological feasibility is established have not
been material, and accordingly, we have expensed all research and development costs when incurred.

Source: Microsoft 2005 10-K filed 26 August 2006, p. 39.

product feasibility to be established very shortly before manufacturing begins and therefore
effectively expenses—rather than capitalizing—R&D costs.

Expensing rather than capitalizing development costs results in lower net income in the
current period. The cumulative effect will also reduce net income so long as the amount of
the current period development costs is higher than the expense that would have resulted
from amortizing prior periods' capitalized development costs—the typical situation when a
company's development costs are increasing. On the statement of cash flows, expensing rather
than capitalizing development costs lowers net operating cash flows and lowers investing cash
outflows.

In comparing the financial performance of one company that expenses all software
development costs, such as Microsoft, with another company that capitalizes software development costs, adjustments can be made to make the two comparable. For the company that
capitalizes software development costs, an analyst can adjust (a) the income statement to
include software development costs as an expense and to exclude amortization of prior years'
software development costs; (b) the balance sheet to exclude capitalized software; and (c) the
statement of cash flows to decrease operating cash flows and decrease cash used in investing by the amount of the current period development costs. Any ratios that include income,
long-lived assets, or cash flow from operations—such as ROE—will also be affected.

Look Into This

EXAMPLE 11-4   Software Development Costs

You are working on a project involving the analysis of JHH Software, a (hypothetical) software development company that established technical feasibility for its first
product in 2004. Part of your analysis involves computing certain market-based ratios,
which you will use to compare JHH to another company that expenses all of its software development expenditures. Relevant data and extracts from the company's annual
report are included in Exhibit 11-4.

EXHIBIT 11-4   JHH SOFTWARE ($ thousands, except per-share amounts)

CONSOLIDATED STATEMENT OF EARNINGS (abbreviated)

For Year Ended 31 December	2006	2005	2004
Total revenue	$91,424	$91,134	$96,293
Total operating expenses	78,107	78,908	85,624
Operating income	$13,317	$12,226	$10,669

Provision for income taxes	3,825	4,232	3,172
Net income	$9,492	$7,934	$7,479
Earnings per share (EPS)	$1.40	$0.81	$0.68

STATEMENT OF CASH FLOWS (abbreviated)

For Year Ended 31 December	2006	2005	2004
Net cash provided by operating activities	$15,007	$14,874	$15,266
Net cash used in investing activities*	(11,549)	(4,423)	(5,346)
Net cash used in financing activities	(8,003)	(7,936)	(7,157)
Net change in cash and cash equivalents	($4,545)	$2,515	$2,763
*Includes software development expenses of:	($6,000)	($4,000)	($2,000)
and capital expenditures of:	($2,000)	($1,600)	($1,200)

Additional Information:

For Year Ended 31 December	2006	2005	2004
Market value of outstanding debt	0	0	0
Amortization of capitalized software development expenses	($2,000)	($667)	0
Depreciation expense	($2,200)	($1,440)	($1,320)
Market price per share of common stock	$42	$26	$17
Shares of common stock outstanding (thousands)	6,780	9,765	10,999

Footnote disclosure of accounting policy for software development:
Expenses that are related to the conceptual formulation and design of software products are expensed to research and development as incurred. The company capitalizes expenses that are incurred to produce the finished product after technological feasibility has been established.

1. Compute the following ratios for JHH based on the reported financial statements for fiscal year ended 31 December 2006, with no adjustments, and determine the approximate impact on these ratios if the company had expensed rather than capitalized its investments in software. (Assume the financial reporting does not affect reporting for income taxes, so there would be no change in the effective tax rate.)
   A. P/E: Price/Earnings per share.
   B. P/CFO: Price/Operating cash flow per share.
   C. EV/EBITDA: Enterprise value/EBITDA, where enterprise value is defined as the total market value of all sources of a company's financing, including equity and debt, and EBITDA is earnings before interest tax, depreciation, and amortization.
2. Interpret the changes in the ratios.

Solution to 1. JHH's 2006 ratios are presented in the following table ($ thousands except per-share amounts):

Ratios	Solution to 1 (As reported)	Solution (As adjusted)
A. P/E ratio	30.0	42.9
B. P/CFO	19.0	31.6
C. EV/EBITDA	16.3	24.7

A. Based on information as reported, the P/E ratio was 30.0 ($42 ÷ $1.40). Based on EPS adjusted to expense software development costs, the P/E ratio was 42.9 ($42 ÷ $0.98).
- Price: Assuming that the market value of the company's equity is based on its fundamentals, the price per share is $42, regardless of a difference in accounting.
- EPS: As reported, EPS was $1.40. Adjusted EPS was $0.98. Expensing software development costs would have reduced JHH's 2006 operating income by $6,000, but the company would have reported no amortization of prior years' software costs, which would have increased operating income by $2,000. The net change of $4,000 would have reduced operating income from the reported $13,317 to $9,317. The effective tax rate for 2006 ($3,825 ÷ $13,317) is 28.72 percent, and using this effective tax rate would give an adjusted net income of $6,641 [$9,317 × (1 − 0.2872)], compared to $9,492 before the adjustment. The EPS would therefore be reduced from the reported $1.40 to $0.98 (adjusted net income of $6,641 ÷ 6,780 shares).

B. Based on information as reported, the P/CFO was 19.0 ($42 ÷ $2.21). Based on CFO adjusted to expense software development costs, the P/CFO was 31.6 ($42 ÷ $1.33).
- Price: Assuming that the market value of the company's equity is based on its fundamentals, the price per share is $42, regardless of a difference in accounting.
- CFO per share, as reported, was $2.21 (total operating cash flows $15,007 ÷ 6,780 shares).
- CFO per share, as adjusted, was $1.33. The company's $6,000 expenditure on software development costs was reported as a cash outflow from investing activities, so expensing those costs would reduce cash from operating activities by $6,000, from the reported $15,007 to $9,007. Dividing adjusted total operating cash flow of $9,007 by 6,780 shares results in cash flow per share of $1.33.

C. Based on information as reported, the EV/EBITDA was 16.3 ($284,760 ÷ $17,517). Based on EBITDA adjusted to expense software development costs, the EV/EBITDA was 24.7 ($284,760 ÷ $11,517).
- Enterprise Value: Enterprise value is the sum of the market value of the company's equity and debt. JHH has no debt, and therefore the enterprise value is equal to the market value of its equity. The market value of its equity is $284,760 ($42 per share × 6,780 shares).
- EBITDA, as reported, was $17,517 (earnings before interest and taxes of $13,317 plus $2,200 depreciation plus $2,000 amortization).
- EBITDA, adjusted for expensing software development costs by the inclusion of $6,000 development expense and the exclusion of $2,000

amortization of prior expense, would be $11,517 (earnings before interest and taxes of $9,317 plus $2,200 depreciation plus $0 amortization).

Solution to 2. Expensing software development costs would decrease historical profits, operating cash flow, and EBITDA, and would thus increase all market multiples. So JHH's stock would appear more expensive if it expensed rather than capitalized the software development costs.

   If the unadjusted market-based ratios were used in the comparison of JHH to its competitor that expenses all software development expenditures, then JHH might appear to be under-priced when the difference is solely related to accounting factors. JHH's adjusted market-based ratios provide a better basis for comparison.

For the company in Example 11-4, current period software development expenditures exceed the amortization of prior periods' capitalized software development expenditures. As a result, expensing rather than capitalizing software development costs would have the effect of lowering income. If, however, software development expenditures slowed such that current expenditures were lower than the amortization of prior periods' capitalized software development expenditures, then expensing software development costs would have the effect of increasing income relative to capitalizing it.

3.3. Intangible Assets Acquired in a Business Combination

When one company acquires another company, the transaction is accounted for using the **purchase method** of accounting.[7] Under the purchase method, the company identified as the acquirer allocates the purchase price to each asset acquired (and each liability assumed) on the basis of its fair value. If the purchase price exceeds the sum of the amounts that can be allocated to individual assets and liabilities, the excess is recorded as goodwill. Goodwill is an intangible asset that cannot be identified separately from the business as a whole.

   U.S. accounting standards present two criteria to judge whether an intangible asset should be treated separately from goodwill; namely, it must be either an item arising from contractual or legal rights or an item that can be separated from the acquired company. Examples of intangible assets that are treated separately from goodwill include the intangible assets mentioned above that involve exclusive rights (patents, copyrights, franchises, licenses), as well as items such as Internet domain names, video and audiovisual materials, and numerous others. International accounting standards specify that an intangible asset meet the definition of an intangible asset and be capable of being measured reliably.

   Exhibit 11-5, for example, describes how one company allocated a portion of the $19 million purchase price of an acquisition to intangible assets—licenses, customer lists, and goodwill.

   One item with somewhat different accounting treatment under U.S. GAAP is in-process R&D. Amounts considered in-process R&D are amounts related to a particular project that is incomplete at the time of an acquisition. Any part of the purchase price that is allocated to in-process R&D must be expensed at the time of acquisition.

---

[7]SFAS No. 141 specifies U.S. GAAP accounting for business combinations, and IFRS 3 specifies requirements under international standards. Both sets of standards require use of the purchase method.

EXHIBIT 11-5   Acquisition of Intangible Assets through a Business Combination: Except from Annual Report of United States Cellular Corporation (AMEX: USM)

On April 21, 2006, U.S. Cellular purchased the remaining ownership interest in the Tennessee RSA No. 3 Limited Partnership, a wireless market operator in which it had previously owned a 16.7% interest, for approximately $19.0 million in cash, subject to a working capital adjustment. This acquisition increased investments in licenses, goodwill and customer lists by $5.5 million, $4.1 million and $2.0 million, respectively.

Source: Company's 10-K filed 23 April 2007, p. 61.

EXHIBIT 11-6   Disclosure of In-Process R&D: Excerpt from Earnings Announcement by Becton, Dickinson and Company (NYSE: BDX)

We present research and development expense, both alone and as a percentage of revenues, for the first six months of fiscal year 2007 after excluding the impact of the in-process research and development ("R&D") charge relating to the acquisition of TriPath Imaging, Inc. . . . We also present these measures for the second quarter and first six months of fiscal year 2006 after excluding the impact of the in-process R&D charge relating to the acquisition of GeneOhm Sciences Inc. . . . These noncash charges are not considered by management to be part of ordinary operations and served to increase reported R&D expense for the period in which they were incurred. Management believes that these adjusted measures are more indicative of BD's R&D activities for the period presented. Management also presents these adjusted measures in order to assist investors in comparing BD's R&D expense for the period to other periods.

Source: Company's Form 8-K filed 25 April 2007 announcing results for the second fiscal quarter ending 31 March 2007.

In analyzing a company reporting a write-off of in-process R&D, items to consider are the effect on a company's future earnings trend and relevance to forecasting earnings. Appearance of a favorable earnings trend would result from a company's decision to allocate a greater amount of the acquisition price to in-process R&D, which would reduce earnings in the current year but contribute to a more favorable earnings trend in future years. With respect to forecasting, if the current period earnings are used as a baseline for forecasting future earnings, they should usually be adjusted to eliminate the effect of an in-process R&D write-off because such an item would not typically be viewed as a recurring part of operations.

Exhibit 11-6 illustrates how one company provided information, adjusted for the effects of in-process R&D, and the rationale for doing so. The example disclosures in Exhibit 11-6 should facilitate an analyst's evaluation of the trend in the company's R&D expenditures, both including and excluding R&D expenditures related to acquisitions.

Unlike U.S. GAAP, IFRS does not require the immediate write off of in-process R&D acquired in a business combination. A company may either identify the amount of in-process R&D as a separate asset with a finite life, or include the asset as part of goodwill. Exhibit 11-7 provides an example of the disclosures by one Dutch company that reports under IFRS, but reconciles their results to U.S. GAAP.

To summarize accounting treatment for R&D, Exhibit 11-8 shows the types of R&D expenditures discussed in this section and their treatment under IFRS and U.S. GAAP.

EXHIBIT 11-7   Differences in Accounting for In-Process R&D between U.S. GAAP and IFRS: Excerpt from Earnings Announcement by CRUCELL NV (Euronext, NASDAQ: CRXL; Swiss Exchange: CRX)

RECONCILIATION IFRS TO U.S. GAAP

Shareholders equity under U.S. GAAP is €413.4 million, €50.9 million lower than under IFRS. This is primarily due to the different method to determine the Berna acquisition price and write-off of in-process R&D of €61.8 million required under U.S. GAAP. . . . Net loss under U.S. GAAP for the six months ended June 30, 2006, is €102.4 million versus a loss of €40.9 million under IFRS. The difference is mainly due to the write-off of in-process R&D under U.S. GAAP as well as some other minor differences.

Source: Company's Form 6-K filed 29 August 2006 announcing results for the second quarter of 2006.

EXHIBIT 11-8   Accounting Treatment for R&D

Type of expenditure	IFRS	U.S. GAAP
Research	Expense as incurred	Expense as incurred
Development	Capitalize if certain criteria are met	Expense as incurred, except for: Costs to develop a software product to sell after feasibility established Certain costs to develop software for internal use
In-process R&D (IPRD) acquired in a business combination	Either identify IPRD as a separate asset with a finite life, or include as part of goodwill	Expense immediately upon acquisition

Having described the accounting for acquisition of long-lived assets, we turn to the topic of allocating their costs to subsequent periods.

4. DEPRECIATING LONG-LIVED TANGIBLE ASSETS

As described in an earlier chapter, the capitalized cost of a long-lived tangible asset (other than land, which is not depreciated) is allocated to subsequent periods as a depreciation expense. The sum of historical depreciation expenses, i.e. accumulated depreciation, is netted against the asset's historical cost on the balance sheet. Detail on depreciation expense and the amount of accumulated depreciation typically appears in a footnote to the financial statements. Companies also describe the depreciation method used along with information on the assumptions used. The following paragraphs review depreciation methods, discuss estimates required for depreciation calculations, and present an analytical tool for using fixed asset disclosure to estimate the average age of companies' depreciable assets.

4.1. Depreciation Methods

As described in Chapter 4, "Understanding the Income Statement," depreciation methods include the **straight-line** method, in which the cost of an asset is evenly distributed over its useful life; **accelerated** methods, in which the allocation of cost is greater in earlier years; and **units-of-production** methods, in which the allocation of cost corresponds to the actual use of an asset in a particular period.

The straight-line method is calculated as depreciable cost divided by estimated useful life, where depreciable cost is the historical cost minus the estimated salvage (i.e., residual) value. A common accelerated method is the declining balance method, in which the amount of depreciation expense is calculated as some percentage of the remaining balance of cost, net of accumulated depreciation (i.e., carrying value). In the units-of-production method, the amount of depreciation expense is based on the proportion of the asset's production during a period compared to the total estimated productive capacity of the asset over its useful life. Example 11-5 provides a review of these depreciation methods.

Depreciation can differ amongst industry and companies.

EXAMPLE 11-5   Review of Depreciation Methods

You are analyzing three (hypothetical) companies: EVEN-LI Co., SOONER Inc., and AZUSED Co. Each of the companies buys an identical piece of box-manufacturing equipment, but each uses a different method of depreciation. Each company's depreciation method, as disclosed in the footnotes to their financial statements, and assumptions are as follows:

Depreciation Method
- EVEN-LI Co.: straight-line method.
- SOONER Inc.: double-declining balance method for the first year, switching to straight-line for the remaining years.
- AZUSED Co.: units-of-production method.

Assumptions
- Cost of equipment: $2,300
- Estimated salvage value: $100
- Useful life: 4 years
- Total productive capacity: 800 boxes
- Production in each of the four years: 200 boxes in the first year, 300 in the second year, 200 in the third year, and 100 in the fourth year.
- For each company, revenues in each year were $3,000, and expenses, other than depreciation, were $1,000. The tax rate is 32 percent.

1. Using the following sample template, record each company's beginning and ending net book value, end-of-year accumulated depreciation, and annual depreciation expense for the box-manufacturing equipment.
2. Explain the significant differences in the timing of the recognition of the depreciation expense.
3. Calculate each company's net profit margin (net income divided by sales) for each of the four years, and assess the impact of the depreciation methods on that ratio.

SAMPLE TEMPLATE

	Beginning Net Book Value	Depreciation Expense	Accumulated Depreciation	Ending Net Book Value
Year 1				
Year 2				
Year 3				
Year 4				

Solution to 1. For *every* company, the following apply: Accumulated year-end depreciation equals the balance from the previous year plus the current year's depreciation expense; ending net book value equals original cost minus accumulated year-end depreciation (which is the same as beginning net book value minus depreciation expense); beginning net book value in year 1 equals the purchase price; and beginning net book value in years 2 and 3 equals the ending net book value of the prior year. The following notes describe how depreciation *expense* is calculated for each company.

EVEN-LI Co. uses the straight-line method, so depreciation expense in each year equals $550, which is calculated as ($2,300 original cost − $100 salvage value) ÷ 4 years.

	Beginning Net Book Value	Depreciation Expense	Accumulated Year-End Depreciation	Ending Net Book Value
Year 1	$2,300	$550	$550	$1,750
Year 2	1,750	550	1,100	1,200
Year 3	1,200	550	1,650	650
Year 4	650	550	2,200	100

SOONER Inc. uses the double-declining balance method for the first year, switching to straight-line for the remaining years. The depreciation rate for the double-declining balance method is double the depreciation rate for the straight-line method. The straight-line method is depreciating at a rate of one-fourth per year, thus the depreciation rate for the double-declining balance method is one-half. So the depreciation expense for the first year is one-half of the beginning balance $1,150 (one-half of initial balance of $2,300). Note that under this method, the depreciation rate of one-half is applied to the total cost of the asset, without adjustment for expected salvage value. After the first year, the ending net book value is $1,150 (original cost of $2,300 minus accumulated depreciation of $1,150.) Switching to the straight-line method for the remaining years gives a depreciation expense of $350, calculated as ($1,150 remaining book value − $100 salvage value) ÷ 3 years.

	Beginning Net Book Value	Depreciation Expense	Accumulated Year-End Depreciation	Ending Net Book Value
Year 1	$2,300	$1,150	$1,150	$1,150
Year 2	1,150	350	1,500	800

	Beginning Net Book Value	Depreciation Expense	Accumulated Year-End Depreciation	Ending Net Book Value
Year 3	800	350	1,850	450
Year 4	450	350	2,200	100

AZUSED Co. uses the units-of-production method. Dividing the equipment's total depreciable cost by its total productive capacity gives a cost per unit of $2.75, calculated as ($2,300 original cost − $100 salvage value) ÷ 800. So the depreciation expense each year is the number of units produced times $2.75. For year 1, the amount of depreciation expense is $550 (200 units × $2.75). For year 2, the amount is $825 (300 units × $2.75). For year 3, the amount is $550. For year 4, the amount is $275.

	Beginning Net Book Value	Depreciation Expense	Accumulated Year-End Depreciation	Ending Net Book Value
Year 1	$2,300	$550	$550	$1,750
Year 2	1,750	825	1,375	925
Year 3	925	550	1,925	375
Year 4	375	275	2,200	100

Solution to 2. All three methods result in the same total depreciation expense over the life of the equipment. The significant differences are simply in the timing of the recognition of the expense with the straight-line method recognizing the expense evenly, the accelerated method recognizing most of the expense in the first year, and the units-of-production method recognizing the expense based on usage.

Under all three methods, the ending net book value is $100; however, because the accelerated method recognizes depreciation expense earlier, the net book value declines more quickly under the accelerated method.

Solution to 3. Because revenues and expenses other than depreciation are assumed equal in each year, EVEN-LI, which uses straight-line depreciation, reports the same income before tax, net income, and net profit margin for each of the four years. SOONER, which uses an accelerated depreciation method in the first year, reports lower income before tax, net income, and net profit margin in the initial year because its depreciation expense is higher in that year. AZUSED, which employs a usage-based depreciation method, reports income before tax, net income, and a net profit margin that varies with the variations in usage of the asset.

Calculations in the table below are as follows:

- Income before tax = Revenues of $3,000 − expenses (other than depreciation) of $1,000 − depreciation expense for each company
- Net income = Income before tax × (1 − tax rate)
- Net profit margin = Net income ÷ sales

EVEN-LI Co.	Income Before Tax	Net Income	Net Profit Margin
Year 1	$1,450	$986	32.9%
Year 2	1,450	986	32.9
Year 3	1,450	986	32.9
Year 4	1,450	986	32.9
SOONER Inc.			
Year 1	$850	$578	19.3%
Year 2	1,650	1,122	37.4
Year 3	1,650	1,122	37.4
Year 4	1,650	1,122	37.4
AZUSED Co.			
Year 1	$1,450	$986	32.9%
Year 2	1,175	799	26.6
Year 3	1,450	986	32.9
Year 4	1,725	1,173	39.1

Recall that in the United States, a company need not use the same depreciation method for financial reporting and taxes. (In many countries, a company must follow the same accounting methods for financial and tax reporting.) Typically, companies use the straight-line method for financial reporting and an accelerated depreciation method prescribed by the Internal Revenue Service, known as the Modified Accelerated Cost Recovery System (MACRS), for tax purposes. Differences in depreciation methods create differences in the amount of taxes computed based on financial reporting and the amount of taxes actually owed. Although these differences eventually reverse because the total depreciation is the same regardless of the timing of its recognition in the financial statements versus the tax return, during the period of the difference the balance sheet will show deferred taxes. Specifically, if a company uses straight-line depreciation for financial reporting and an accelerated depreciation method for tax purposes, the company's financial statements will report lower depreciation expenses and thus higher pretax income in the first year, compared with the amount of depreciation expense and taxable income included in its tax reporting. (Compare the depreciation expense in year one for EVEN-LI and SOONER, Inc. in the preceding example.) Tax expense calculated based on pretax income shown in the financial statements will be higher than taxes payable based on taxable income; the difference between the two amounts is deferred tax.

4.2.   Estimates Required for Depreciation Calculations

As mentioned in an earlier chapter, significant estimates required for depreciation calculations include the useful life of the equipment (or its total lifetime productive capacity) and its expected residual value at the end of that useful life. A longer useful life and higher expected residual value decrease the amount of annual depreciation relative to a shorter useful life and lower expected residual value.

Additional estimates are required to allocate depreciation expense between the cost of goods sold and sales, general, and administrative expenses (SG&A). Footnotes to the financial statements often disclose some information regarding which income statement line item includes depreciation, although the exact amount of detail disclosed by individual companies varies. Including a higher proportion of depreciation expense in cost of goods sold lowers the gross margin, and lowers the operating expenses, but does not affect the operating margin. When comparing two companies, apportionment of depreciation to cost of goods versus SG&A can contribute to explaining differences in gross margins and operating expenses.

4.3. Using Fixed Asset Disclosures to Compare Companies' Average Age of Depreciable Assets

Under U.S. GAAP, companies value long-lived assets at historical cost net of accumulated depreciation. International accounting standards (IAS 16) permit companies to measure property, plant, and equipment (PP&E) either under a cost model (i.e., historical cost minus accumulated depreciation) or under a revaluation model (i.e., fair value).[8] Under the revaluation model, the relationship between carrying value, accumulated depreciation, and depreciation expense will differ when the carrying value differs significantly from the historical cost. The following discussion applies primarily to PP&E reported under a historical cost model.

The balance sheet reports PP&E at historical cost net of accumulated depreciation. The statement of cash flows typically shows depreciation expense (or depreciation plus amortization) as a line item in the adjustments of net income to cash from operations. The notes to the financial statements describe the company's accounting method(s), the range of estimated useful lives, historical cost by main category of fixed asset, and annual depreciation expense.

Chapter 9, "Financial Statement Analysis: Applications," provided an example of using the amount of depreciation expense and the balance of net PP&E to estimate the average remaining useful life of a company's asset base. Specifically, the average remaining useful life of a company's assets can be estimated as net PP&E divided by depreciation expense. In this section, we review that analysis as well as the estimation of the average age of a company's depreciable assets. To estimate the average age of the asset base, divide accumulated depreciation by depreciation expense.

These estimates simply reflect the following relationships for assets accounted for on a historical cost basis: total historical cost minus accumulated depreciation equals net PP&E; and, under straight-line depreciation, total historical cost less salvage value divided by estimated useful life equals annual depreciation expense. Equivalently, total historical cost less salvage value divided by annual depreciation expense equals estimated useful life.

---

[8]Research indicates that revaluations of property, plant, and equipment permitted under IFRS but prohibited under U.S. GAAP are an important cause of the lack of comparability of financial statements prepared under the two sets of standards. For example see J.L. Haverty, "Are IFRS and U.S. GAAP converging? Some evidence from People's Republic of China companies listed on the New York Stock Exchange," *Journal of International Accounting, Auditing and Taxes* 15(1) (2006): 48–71.

Assuming, for simplicity, straight-line depreciation and no salvage value, we have the following:

Estimated total useful life	=	Time elapsed since purchase (age)	+	Estimated remaining life
Historical cost ÷ annual depreciation expense	=	Estimated total useful life		
Historical cost	=	Accumulated depreciation	+	Net PP&E

Equivalently,

| Estimated total useful life | = | Estimated age of equipment | + | Estimated remaining life |
| Historical cost ÷ annual depreciation expense | = | Accumulated depreciation ÷ annual depreciation expense | + | Net PP&E ÷ annual depreciation expense |

The application of these estimates can be illustrated by a hypothetical example of a company with a single depreciable asset. Assume the asset initially cost $100, had an estimated useful life of 10 years, and an estimated salvage value of $0. Each year, the company records a depreciation expense of $10, so accumulated depreciation will equal $10 times the number of years since the asset was acquired (when the asset is 7 years old, accumulated depreciation will be $70) and, equivalently, the age of the asset will equal accumulated depreciation divided by the annual depreciation expense.

In practice, such estimates are difficult to make with great precision. Companies use depreciation methods other than the straight-line method and have numerous assets with varying useful lives and salvage values, including some assets that are fully depreciated, so this approach produces an estimate only. Moreover, fixed-asset disclosures are often quite general. Consequently, these estimates may be primarily useful to identify areas for further investigation.

One further general metric compares annual capital expenditures to annual depreciation expense. The metric provides a very general indicator of the rate at which a company is replacing its PP&E relative to the rate at which the PP&E is being depreciated.

EXAMPLE 11-6   Using Fixed Asset Disclosure to Compare Companies' Average Age of Depreciable Assets

You are analyzing the property, plant, and equipment of three international paper and paper products companies:

- Abitibi-Consolidated Inc. (NYSE: ABY; TSX: A) is a Canadian company that manufactures newsprint, commercial printing papers, and other wood products.
- International Paper Company (NYSE: IP) is a U.S. paper and packaging company.
- UPM-Kymmene Corporation (UPM) is a Finnish company that manufactures fine and specialty papers, newsprint, magazine papers, and other related products. The company's common stock is listed on the Helsinki and New York stock exchanges.

The following table presents selected information from the companies' financial statements.

	ABY	IP	UPM
Currency (millions)	Canadian $	U.S. $	Euro €
Historical cost total PP&E	$7,768	$23,043	€16,997
Accumulated depreciation	3,784	14,050	10,497
Net PP&E	3,984	8,993	6,500
Land included in PP&E	Not separated	Not separated	632
Annual depreciation expense (annual impairment)	424	1,158	804 (239)
Capital expenditure	165	1,009	635
Accounting standards	Canadian GAAP	U.S. GAAP	IFRS
PP&E measurement	Historical cost	Historical cost	Historical cost
Depreciation method	Straight-line	Units-of-production for pulp and paper mills*; straight-line for other	Straight-line
Useful life of assets, in years, except as noted	20–25 (buildings, pulp and paper mills); 10–12 (sawmill equip.); 10–20 (roads, camps, woodlands); 40 (power plants)	Straight-line depreciation rates are 2.5% to 8.5% (buildings), and 5% to 33% (machinery and equipment)	25–40 (buildings); 15–20 (heavy equip.); 5–15 (light equip.)

*Pulp and paper mills' historical cost as disclosed in a footnote total $16,665 million. Depreciation expense and accumulated depreciation is not separately reported for mills.

Sources:
For ABY, Form 40-F for the year ended 31 December 2006, filed 15 March 2007.
For IP, Form 10-K for the year ended 31 December 2006, filed 28 February 2007.
For UPM, Form 20-F for the year ended 31 December 2006, filed 15 March 2007.

1. Based on the above data for each company, use the standard formulas to estimate the total useful life, age, and remaining useful life of PP&E.
2. Interpret the estimates. What items might affect comparisons across these companies?
3. How does each company's 2006 depreciation expense compare to its capital expenditures for the year?

Solution to 1. The following table presents the estimated total useful life, estimated age, and estimated remaining useful life of PP&E using the standard formulas.

Estimates	ABY	IP	UPM
Estimated total useful life (years)	18.3	19.9	21.1
Estimated age (years)	8.9	12.1	13.1
Estimated remaining life (years)	9.4	7.8	8.1

The computations are explained using UPM's data. The estimated total useful life of PP&E is total historical cost of PP&E of €16,997 divided by annual depreciation expense of €804, giving 21.1 years. Estimated age and estimated remaining life are obtained by dividing accumulated depreciation of €10,497 and net PP&E of €6,500 by the annual depreciation expense of €804, giving 13.1 years and 8.1 years, respectively.

Ideally, the estimates of asset lives illustrated in this example should exclude land, which is not depreciable, when the information is available; however, UPM is the only one of the three companies for which land appeared to be disclosed separately, and the above table thus presents the estimates without adjusting UPM for land costs in order to compare it with the other two companies. As an illustration of the calculations to exclude land, excluding UPM's land would give an estimated total useful life of 20.4 years [(total cost €16,997 – land cost of €632) divided by annual depreciation expense of €804].

Solution to 2. The estimated total useful life suggests that UPM depreciates its PP&E over the longest period—21.1 years versus 19.9 and 18.3 for IP and ABY, respectively— although the differences are not dramatic across the companies. This result can be compared, to an extent, to the useful life of assets noted by the companies. UPM depreciates its buildings over 25 to 40 years, while ABY depreciates its buildings over 20 to 25 years. IP depreciates its buildings (other than pulp and paper mills) over 12 years (1 ÷ a depreciation rate of 8.5 percent) to 40 years (1 ÷ a depreciation rate of 2.5 percent).

The estimated age of the equipment suggests that ABY has the newest PP&E with an estimated age of 8.9 years. Additionally, the estimates suggest that only 49 percent of ABY's assets' useful lives have passed (8.9 years ÷ 18.3 years, or equivalently, C$3,784 million divided by C$7,768 million). In comparison, over 60 percent of the useful lives of the PP&E of both IP and UPM have passed.

Items that can affect comparisons across the companies include business differences, such as differences in composition of the companies' operations and differences in acquisition and divestiture activity. In addition, the companies all use different sets of accounting standards, and IP discloses that it uses the units-of-production method for the largest component of its PP&E. Differences in disclosures, for example, in the categories of assets disclosed, also can affect comparisons.

Solution to 3. Capital expenditure as a percentage of depreciation is 39 percent for ABY, 87 percent for IP, and 79 percent for UPM. Based on this metric, IP is replacing its PP&E at a rate almost comparable to the rate its PP&E is being depreciated. Because IP uses the units-of-production method of depreciation, this implies that IP is replacing its PP&E at nearly the same rate of usage. ABY's metric suggests the company is replacing its PP&E at a slower rate than the PP&E is being depreciated, suggesting that further examination of the company's capital expenditure policies may be needed.

5. AMORTIZING INTANGIBLE ASSETS WITH FINITE USEFUL LIVES

This section discusses cost allocation for intangible assets with finite useful lives (i.e., amortization). As noted, amortization is effectively the same concept as depreciation. The term *amortization* applies to intangible assets, and the term *depreciation* applies to tangible assets.[9]

5.1. Amortizing Intangible Assets with Finite Useful Lives

Intangible assets with finite useful lives are amortized over their useful lives, following the pattern in which the benefits are used up. Assets without a finite useful life, that is, with an indefinite useful life, are not amortized. In both cases, the assets are periodically reviewed for impairment (discussed in section 8).

Examples of intangible assets with finite useful lives include: an acquired customer list expected to provide benefits to a direct-mail marketing company for two to three years; an acquired patent or copyright with a specific expiration date; an acquired license with a specific expiration date and no right to renew the license; or an acquired trademark for a product that a company plans to phase out over a specific number of years. Examples of intangible assets with indefinite useful lives include: an acquired license which, although it has a specific expiration date, can be renewed at little or no cost; or an acquired trademark which, although it has a specific expiration, can be renewed at a minimal cost and relates to a product that a company plans to continue selling for the foreseeable future.

5.2. Estimates Required for Amortization Calculations

As with tangible assets, the estimates required for amortization calculations include the original amount at which the intangible asset is valued, its residual value at the end of its useful life, and the length of its useful life. Useful lives are estimated based on the expected use of the asset, considering any factors that may limit the life of the asset such as legal, regulatory, contractual, competitive, or economic.

6. ASSET RETIREMENT OBLIGATIONS

For many types of long-lived tangible assets, ownership involves not only a right to use the asset but also an obligation that must be fulfilled at the end of the asset's service life. For example, a company that owns and operates a landfill will have legal obligations, such as covering the land with topsoil and planting vegetation when sections of the landfill become full, and legal obligations after the end of the asset's service life, such as monitoring the ground water and air quality. These obligations are referred to as **asset retirement obligations** (AROs).

As soon as a company is able to make a reasonable estimate of the costs it will incur as a result of those asset retirement obligations, the company reports the fair value of these estimated costs, with the fair value determined using a discounted cash flow approach. The fair

---

[9]*Depletion* is the term applied to a similar concept for natural resources; costs associated with those resources are allocated to a period based on the usage or extraction of those resources.

value of the asset retirement obligations is reported as a liability, with the balancing offset being an increase in the carrying value of the asset. Afterward, the amount added to the asset's carrying value is expensed systematically (a concept similar to depreciation). The amount reported as a liability increases each year with the passage of time because it is based on the discounted present value of future cash flows. The increase in the amount of the liability is recognized as an operating expense, referred to as accretion expense.

Treated as debt.

EXAMPLE 11-7   Reporting an Asset Retirement Obligation

A (hypothetical) company, Wastaway Inc., disposes of waste at a landfill site. The landfill site is recorded as an asset, which the company is depreciating on a straight-line basis over its useful life of 10 years.[10] In the future, after the company finishes using the landfill site, state and federal laws require that the company undertake procedures to cap and close the landfill. Landfill caps range from a single layer of soil to a multi-layer system of soils and synthetic materials. Regulations also require that the location be monitored after closure to prevent future damage to the air and water around the site. Wastaway Inc. estimates that the costs for capping, closing, and postclosure monitoring its landfill at the end of its 10-year useful life will total $450,000 (adjusted for inflation), equal to a present value of $200,872 when discounted at a rate of 8.4 percent, which is based on the company's credit standing. So the company will record the asset retirement costs of $200,872 as part of the cost of the long-lived asset (landfill site) and an ARO liability equal to $200,872.

The company will write off the asset at the same rate that it depreciates the landfill site asset and show this as a depreciation expense. The company will show changes in the ARO liability that occur because of the passage of time as an accretion expense. In this example, each year the company will recognize a depreciation expense equal to one-tenth (1/10) of the asset retirement costs ($20,087), and an accretion expense equal to 8.4 percent of the ARO liability balance. In year 1, the accretion expense will be $16,873 (8.4 percent × $200,872). For year 1, the total expense associated with the asset retirement obligation will be $36,960 ($20,087 + $16,873). At the end of year 1 (i.e., the beginning of year 2), the ARO liability balance will have grown to $217,745 ($200,872 + $16,873), so the accretion expense for year 2 will be $18,291 (8.4 percent × $217,745). The total expense associated with the asset retirement obligation in year 2 will be $38,378 ($20,087 + $18,291).

1. What will be the accretion expense for year 3?
2. What will be the total expense associated with the asset retirement obligation in year 3?
3. At the end of the useful life of the landfill, what will be the balance of the ARO? What will be the balance of the asset?

---

[10]While land in and of itself is not depreciated, Wastaway Inc. can depreciate the landfill site (including site improvements and capital expenditures necessary to prepare the site) over its useful life.

Solution to 1. The accretion expense for year 3 will be $19,827. At the beginning of year 3, the ARO liability balance will have grown to $236,036 (the $217,745 balance at the beginning of year 2 plus the accretion expense of $18,291 for year 2). This ARO liability balance can also be computed as the present value of $450,000 discounted at a rate of 8.4 percent for the remaining period of 8 years. The accretion expense for year 3 equals $19,827 (8.4% $\times$ $236,036).

Solution to 2. The total expense associated with the asset retirement obligation in year 3 will be $39,914, which is determined by adding the accretion expense of $19,827 for year 3 to the annual depreciation expense of $20,087.

Solution to 3. At the end of the useful life of the landfill, the balance of the ARO liability will be $450,000. The beginning balance of the ARO liability was determined as the present value of $450,000 for 10 years at 8.4 percent, and each year's accretion reflects the increase in the ARO liability for 1 year at 8.4 percent; so after 10 years, the ARO liability equals $450,000. At the end of the useful life of the landfill, the balance of the asset will be $0. Each year's depreciation expense reduces the balance of the asset by one-tenth; therefore, after 10 years, the balance of the asset will be zero.

For financial analysis, and particularly credit analysis, adjustments can reflect the debt-like nature of AROs. These adjustments, described in Standard & Poor's Corporate Ratings Criteria (2006), consider the AROs as debt and treat the related financial statement items in a manner consistent with debt. For example, to treat the AROs as debt, increase the amount of debt by the amount of the AROs, adjusted for such offsetting items as dedicated retirement fund assets and any tax savings that the company is likely to utilize. Anticipated tax savings reduce any deferred tax asset. To reclassify items consistent with treating the AROs as debt, reclassify the accretion amount, which is similar to an interest accrual, as an interest expense.

Some companies, such as utilities, have trust funds in excess of their asset retirement obligations. For example, Exhibit 11-9 shows that Constellation Energy Group Inc. (CEG) had an asset retirement obligation, primarily nuclear decommissioning costs, totaling $974.8 million at the end of 2006. However, the company's nuclear decommissioning trust fund totaled $1,240.1 million, i.e., $265.3 million more than the amount of the ARO. In addition, the company's net investments in the trust fund were $8.8 million for the year, compared to $3.1 million of new ARO liabilities, indicating that in 2006, the fund increased by more than the amount of the AROs. The U.S. Nuclear Regulatory Commission (NRC) requires nuclear power plant owners to decommission nuclear plants. Owners are required to prefund the decommissioning over the plants' 40-year life. For CEG, changes in the trust fund relative to the ARO liability reflect in part actions by utility regulators that control the rates customers can be charged and amounts allocated to decommissioning funds. Although the size of the asset retirement obligation and the trust fund are each large enough to merit separate disclosure on the face of the company's balance sheet, the significant size of the trust fund relative to the ARO indicates that the ARO would not have a negative credit impact.

EXHIBIT 11-9 Asset Retirement Obligations: Constellation Energy Group Inc. (NYSE: CEG), Selected Information for 2006

Line Item ($ millions)	As Reported	Where Reported
Nuclear decommissioning trust funds (asset)	$1,240.1	B/S
Asset retirement obligations (liability)	$974.8	B/S
Investment in nuclear decommissioning trust fund securities	$394.6	CF
Proceeds from nuclear decommissioning trust fund securities	$385.8	CF
Net investments in nuclear decommissioning trust fund securities	$8.8	Calculated
ARO liabilities incurred, net of liabilities settled	$3.1	FT 1

B/S, balance sheet; CF, statement of cash flows; FT, footnote

Explanation in the MD&A (page 37)

Our nuclear decommissioning costs represent our largest asset retirement obligation. This obligation primarily results from the requirement to decommission and decontaminate our nuclear generating facilities in connection with their future retirement. We utilize site-specific decommissioning cost estimates to determine our nuclear asset retirement obligations. However, given the magnitude of the amounts involved, complicated and ever-changing technical and regulatory requirements, and the very long time horizons involved, the actual obligation could vary from the assumptions used in our estimates, and the impact of such variations could be material.

Source: Constellation Energy Group Inc. and Subsidiaries Form 10-K for the year ending 31 December 2006, filed 27 February 2007

In contrast with the company in Exhibit 11-9, the following example illustrates a company in which the amounts of the asset retirement obligation were not significant enough to warrant separate line item disclosure on the face of the company's balance sheet; however, there is a noticeable, if not dramatic, impact on the company's solvency ratios.

EXAMPLE 11-8 Asset Retirement Obligation

Exhibit 11-10 provides selected information on Waste Management, Inc. (WMI), a company involved in the collection, treatment, disposal, and recycling of waste.

1. Adjust the company's reported financial information to reflect the ARO liability as part of long-term debt. Assume that the company will be able to use all tax deductions when the ARO liability is paid. Then calculate and compare the company's interest coverage ratio and debt-to-equity ratio based on the information as reported and as adjusted.
2. Interpret the ratios.

EXHIBIT 11-10   Waste Management, Inc., Selected Information for 2006

Line Item ($ millions)	As Reported	Where Reported
Income from continuing operations before taxes	$1,474	I/S
Interest expense (including capitalized interest)	563	FT 3
EBIT	2,037	I/S
Total long-term debt	$8,317	B/S
Common shareholders equity	6,222	B/S
Other information		
Trust funds and escrow accounts for environmental remediation obligations (asset)	$219	FT 3
Landfill and environment remediation liabilities (liability)	1,389	FT 4
Accretion on liability	79	FT 4
Effective tax rate	22.1%	FT 8

I/S, income statement; B/S, balance sheet; FT, footnote.
Form 10-K for the year ended 31 December 2006, filed 15 February 2007.
Source: Waste Management Inc.

Solution to 1. To calculate the company's interest coverage ratio and debt-to-equity ratio reflecting the ARO liability as part of long-term debt, first adjust the ARO for the following offsetting items:

$219 million trust funds and escrow accounts for environmental remediation obligations;

$307 million tax savings when the ARO is paid (22.1 percent tax rate × $1,389 million ARO). The adjustment is made on a tax-adjusted basis because it is considered likely that the company will be able to make use of the tax deduction.

The ARO, after deducting these offsetting adjustments is $863 million.

Interest expense for the period is adjusted by the amount of the accretion, which is $79 million.

The following table summarizes these adjustments and presents the ratios before and after these adjustments ($ millions):

Line Item	As Reported	Adjustment	As Adjusted
Income from continuing operations before taxes	$1,474		$1,474
Interest expense (including capitalized interest)	$563	$79	$642
EBIT	$2,037	$79	$2,116
Total long-term debt	$8,317	$863	$9,180

Common shareholders' equity	$6,222		$6,222
Ratios			
Interest coverage	3.6x		3.3x
Debt-to-equity	1.34		1.48

The interest coverage ratio is 3.6 ($2,037 million ÷ $563 million) before any adjustment and 3.3 ($2,116 million ÷ $642 million) after the adjustment. The debt-to-equity ratio before adjustment is 1.34 ($8,317 million ÷ $6,222 million) and 1.48 ($9,180 million ÷ $6,222 million) after the adjustment.

Solution to 2. The interest coverage ratio, after adjusting to treat the current period accretion as interest expense, declines from 3.6x to 3.3x. This solvency indicator shows that the company's coverage is lower, i.e. the company has a somewhat lower safety cushion against a decline in income on an adjusted basis.

The company's debt-to-equity ratio increases from 1.34 to 1.48. Prior to adjustment, the company had $1.34 in debt for every $1 of equity, but after adjusting to treat the asset retirement obligation as debt, the company has $1.48 in debt for every $1 of equity. This ratio indicates that the company's solvency position is weaker after adjusting to treat the asset retirement obligation as debt.

7. DISPOSAL OF LONG-LIVED OPERATING ASSETS

A company may dispose of a long-lived operating asset by selling it, exchanging it, or abandoning it. Assets that are to be sold are classified as assets held for sale, in contrast to assets held for use.

7.1. Sale of Long-Lived Assets

The gain or loss on the sale of long-lived assets is computed as the sales proceeds minus the carrying value of the asset at the time of sale. An asset's carrying value is typically the net book value, that is, the historical cost minus accumulated depreciation (unless the asset's carrying value has been changed to reflect impairment and/or revaluation, as discussed in sections 8 and 9).

EXAMPLE 11-9   Calculation of Gain or Loss on the Sale of Long-Lived Assets

Moussilauke Diners Inc. (hypothetical company), as a result of revamping its menus to focus on healthier food items, sells 450 used pizza ovens and reports a gain on the sale of $1.2 million. The ovens had a carrying value of $1.9 million (original cost $5.1 million less $3.2 million of accumulated depreciation). At what price did Moussilauke sell the ovens?

A. $0.7 million
B. $0.9 million
C. $3.1 million
D. $3.3 million

Solution. C is correct. Moussilauke sold the ovens at a price of $3.1 million, and recognized a gain of $1.2 million ($3.1 million – $1.9 million) on the sale.

A gain or loss on the sale of an asset is disclosed on the income statement, either as a component of other gains and losses or in a separate line item when the amount is material. A company typically discloses further detail about the sale in the MD&A and/or financial statement footnotes. In addition, a statement of cash flows prepared using the indirect method adjusts net income to remove any gain or loss on the sale from operating cash flow, and to include the amount of proceeds from the sale in cash from investing activities. Recall that the indirect method of the statement of cash flows begins with net income and makes all adjustments to arrive at cash from operations, including removal of gains or losses from nonoperating activities.

During an accounting period in which a company makes the decision to dispose of a long-lived operating asset by selling it and commences the sale process, the company classifies the asset (or group of assets) as held for sale. The asset or group of assets, referred to as a *component of an entity*, can be a subsidiary, a business segment, or an asset group (defined in SFAS No. 144 as the "lowest level for which identifiable cash flows are largely independent of the cash flows of other groups of assets and liabilities"). So a component could be a subsidiary or a division that produces some product or a manufacturing plant within that division, so long as the plant's cash flows could be clearly distinguished. In IFRS 5, a "component of an entity" is defined as "Operations and cash flows that can be clearly distinguished, operationally and for financial reporting purposes, from the rest of the entity."

The company measures the value of the held-for-sale asset at the lower of its carrying value or fair value less cost to sell.[11] Costs to sell include items such as legal fees and title transfer fees. The company no longer records depreciation on the asset. If the fair value of the asset, net of the cost to sell it, is less than its carrying value, the company records an impairment loss. Assets that comprise a component of a company (defined above) are reported in "discontinued operations" if they have been sold or classified as held for sale in an accounting period.

To illustrate the financial statement impact of an asset sale, consider the sale by Pfizer Inc. (Pfizer) of its Consumer Healthcare business in 2006. Pfizer's MD&A in its 2006 annual report (page 8) discloses that, "In the fourth quarter of 2006, we sold our Consumer Healthcare business for $16.6 billion, and recorded a gain of approximately $10.2 billion ($7.9 billion, net of tax)." Exhibit 11-11 illustrates the impact on the company's balance sheet, income statement, and statement of cash flows. At year-end 2005, Pfizer's balance sheet shows

---

[11]SFAS No. 144 specifies U.S. GAAP accounting for long-lived assets to be disposed of by sale, and IFRS 5 specifies requirements under international standards. Accounting for long-lived assets held for sale and the classification and presentation of discontinued items is considered to be substantially the same under the two standards (IFRS 5, IN5).

EXHIBIT 11-11   Disclosures on Pfizer's Financial Statements Related to the Consumer Healthcare Business

On Balance Sheet as of 31 December 2005	
Assets of discontinued operations and other assets held for sale	$6,659 million
On Income Statement for the year ended 31 December 2006	
Gains on sales of discontinued items, net of tax	$7,880 million
On Statement of Cash Flows for the year ended 31 December 2006	
Operating activities	
Adjustments to reconcile net income to net cash provided by operating activities:	
Gains on sales of discontinued operations	($10,243 million)
Supplemental cash flow information	
Noncash transactions:	
Sale of the Consumer Healthcare business (portion of proceeds received in the form of short-term investments)	$16,429 million

$6.7 billion in assets of discontinued operations and other assets held for sale, a significant portion of which related to the consumer healthcare business. Pfizer's income statement for 2006 shows the $7.9 billion gain on the sale, net of tax. The statement of cash flows shows a reconciliation item to remove the $10.2 billion gain (pre-tax) from net income. Because most of the sale proceeds were apparently received in the form of short-term investments rather than cash, Pfizer discloses a noncash transaction of $16.4 billion as supplemental information on its statement of cash flows. The $200 million difference between the total sales proceeds disclosed in the MD&A and the amount received as short-term investments ($16.6 billion minus $16.4 billion) would be included among the company's investing cash inflows.

Differences in asset sales transactions result in different presentations. Example 11-10 shows an instance where a portion of a sale was considered to be the sale of assets that were part of the company's continuing operations, and the other portion of the sale was considered to be the sale of assets that constituted discontinued operations by the company. The gain on the portion of the sale transaction considered part of the company's continuing operations is shown in operating income. The gain on the portion considered discontinued operations of the company is shown as a gain on the sale of discontinued operations. The amount of Jupitermedia's 2005 asset sale was relatively large and had a significant impact on reported financial performance. Evaluating the company, excluding the asset sales, can provide a better picture of the company's past operating performance and the outlook for its future performance.

EXAMPLE 11-10   Financial Statement Reporting of the Sale of Long-Lived Assets

Jupitermedia (NasdaqGS: JUPM) sells photos, clip art, music, and online information to customers in information technology and media design. For the year ended 2005, the company's income statement and statement of cash flow (abbreviated versions in

Exhibit 11-12A and Exhibit 11-12B) provide information about an asset sale, which is further described in the MD&A. From the company's MD&A:

- "On August 5, 2005, Jupitermedia sold its Search Engine Strategies and its ClickZ. com network of Web sites (collectively known as "SES") to Incisive Media plc, a London Stock Exchange listed media company, for $43.0 million in cash, subject to certain post-closing adjustments." (Company's 2006 10-K, p. 26)
- "As part of the sale of SES on August 5, 2005, we sold our ClickZ.com Network of Web sites to Incisive Media plc, which resulted in a gain of $13.3 million." (Company's 2006 10-K, p. 30)

EXHIBIT 11-12A   Excerpts from Jupitermedia Corporation Financial Statements: [Abbreviated] Consolidated Statements of Operations

	Year Ended 31 December		
Line Items ($ thousands)	2004	2005	2006
Revenues	$52,636	$113,754	$137,530
Cost of revenues (exclusive of items shown separately below)	15,917	36,841	50,683
Advertising, selling, general	19,929	40,170	57,112
Depreciation and amortization	2,970	6,579	13,386
Gain on sale of assets, net	0	13,259	0
Total operating expenses	$38,816	$70,331	$121,181
Operating income	$13,820	$43,423	$16,349
Interest and investment income (loss), net	353	392	138
Interest expense	(130)	(3,508)	(5,544)
Income before income taxes, minority interests, and equity income (loss) from investments, net	$14,043	$40,307	$10,943
Provision (benefit) for income taxes	288	(19,692)	3,625
Minority interests	(89)	(46)	(34)
Equity income (loss) from investments, net	(31)	270	256
Income from continuing operations	$13,635	$60,223	$7,540
Income from discontinued operations, net of taxes	2,102	2,332	11
Gain on sale of discontinued operations, net of taxes	0	15,844	5,573
Net income	$15,737	$78,399	$13,124

A footnote discloses that the benefit for income taxes of $19.7 million in 2005 was the result of reversing a valuation allowance related to a deferred tax asset.

EXHIBIT 11-12B   Jupitermedia Corporation: [Abbreviated] Consolidated Statements of
Cash Flows

Line Items ($ thousands)	Year Ended 31 December		
	2004	2005	2006
Cash flows from operating activities:			
Income from continuing operations	$13,635	$60,223	$7,540
Adjustments to reconcile income from continuing operations to net cash provided by operating activities:			
Depreciation and amortization	2,970	6,579	13,386
Gain on sale of assets, net	0	(13,259)	0
Deferred income taxes	0	(24,549)	1,665
All other nonoperating or noncash items	(204)	(228)	3,065
Changes in current assets and liabilities:			
Accounts receivable, net	(1,155)	(606)	(3,653)
Prepaid expenses and other	134	1,230	72
Accounts payable and accrued expenses	(470)	(4,451)	(11,325)
Deferred revenues	2,208	101	1,644
Discontinued operations	2,693	1,287	1,054
Net cash provided by operating activities	$19,811	$26,327	$13,448
Cash flows from investing activities:			
Purchases of property, equipment, images, businesses	(37,088)	(149,024)	(41,013)
Proceeds from sale of assets and other	211	14,911	368
Proceeds from sale of discontinued operations	0	28,135	9,600
Distribution from internet.com venture funds	148	105	0
Net cash used in investing activities	($36,729)	($105,873)	($31,045)
Net cash provided by financing activities	$37,537	$68,136	$7,692

Source: Jupitermedia Corporation 10-K filed 27 March 2007.

1. Where do Jupitermedia's income statement and statement of cash flows reflect the disposal of SES?
2. What was the company's operating profit margin in 2005? What is the operating profit margin excluding the gain on the sale of assets?
3. What was the company's net profit margin in 2005? What is the effect on this profitability measure of considering only continuing operations and excluding the gain on the sale of assets?
4. By what percentage did the company's operating income and cash from operations change from 2005 to 2006? Excluding the gain on the sale of assets, what were the changes in these metrics?

Solution to 1. Jupitermedia's disclosures indicate that they sold SES for $43 million. On the income statement, a gain of $13.3 million on a portion of the disposal (sale of assets) appears in operating income and a gain of $15.8 million on a portion classified as discontinued operations appears separately at the bottom of the statement. From the MD&A excerpt above indicating a gain of $13.3 million from the sale of CickZ.com's network of web sites, we infer that the gain of $15.8 million is from the sale of the other part of SES, namely Search Engine Strategies.

On the statement of cash flows, the $43 million cash proceeds from the sale appear in the investing section, approximately $14.9 million from asset sales and $28.1 million from the sale of discontinued operations. (The $14.9 million is an approximation because it may not be entirely from the asset sale based on the label "proceeds from sale of assets and other.") From the statement of cash flows, we infer that the $13.3 million gain on asset sales was realized from the $14.9 million proceeds from asset sales, and the gain of $15.8 million occurred on the $28.1 million proceeds from the sale of discontinued operations.

Solution to 2. The company's operating profit margin in 2005 was 38.2 percent (operating income of $43,423 ÷ revenues of $113,754), as reported. Excluding the gain on the sale of assets, the operating profit margin would be 26.5 percent [(operating income of $43,423 − $13,259) ÷ revenues of $113,754].

Solution to 3. The company's net profit margin in 2005 was 68.9 percent (net income $78,399 ÷ revenues of $113,754). Using income from continuing operations, however, rather than net income, better reflects the ongoing profitability of the company, and on this basis, the net margin is 52.9 percent (income from continuing operations $60,223 ÷ revenues of $113,754). Excluding the asset sale, the net margin would be 41.3 percent [(income from continuing operations $60,223 − $13,259) ÷ revenues of $113,754].

Solution to 4. The company's operating income declined by 62.3 percent ($16,349 ÷ $43,423 − 1). Excluding the 2005 sale of assets, the company's operating income declined by 45.8 percent ($16,349 ÷ ($43,423 − $13,259) − 1). The company's cash from operations declined by 48.9 percent ($13,448 ÷ $26,327 − 1). Because the sale of assets was excluded from operating cash and shown in investing cash, the 2005 sale of assets had no impact on reported operating cash flow.

7.2. Long-Lived Assets Disposed of Other than by a Sale

Long-lived assets to be disposed of other than by a sale, for example, abandoned, exchanged for another asset, or distributed to owners in a spin-off, are classified as held for use until disposal.[12] Thus, the long-lived assets continue to be depreciated and tested for impairment as required for other long-lived assets owned by the company.

When an asset is retired or abandoned, the accounting is similar to a sale, except that the company does not record cash proceeds. Assets are reduced by the carrying value of the asset at the time of retirement or abandonment, and a loss is recorded.

---

[12]In a spin-off, shareholders of the parent company receive a proportional number of shares in a new, separate entity.

EXHIBIT 11-13   Altria Group, Inc. and Subsidiaries: Pro Forma Condensed Consolidated Balance Sheet [Partial], as of 31 December 2006 (Unaudited)

Assets ($ millions)	Historical Altria[a]	Spin-off of Kraft[b]	Adjustments[c]	Pro Forma Altria
Cash and cash equivalents	$5,020	($239)	$369	$5,150
Receivables, net	6,070	(3,869)		2,201
Inventories	12,186	(3,506)		8,680
Other current assets	2,876	(640)		2,236
Total current assets	$26,152	($8,254)	$369	$18,267
Property, plant, and equipment, net	17,274	(9,693)		7,581
Goodwill	33,235	(25,553)	($1,485)	6,197
Other intangible assets, net	12,085	(10,177)		1,908
Other assets	8,734	(1,897)	$305	7,142
Total consumer products assets	$97,480	($55,574)	($811)	$41,095
Financial services assets	6,790	0		6,790
Total assets	$104,270	($55,574)	($811)	$47,885

[a]Historical consolidated balance sheet of Altria.
[b]Reflects the removal of Kraft's consolidated balance sheet from the Altria historical consolidated balance sheet.
[c]Represents adjustments, such as for pro forma cash payments by Kraft to Altria, arising from modifications to existing stock awards and tax contingencies, adjustments to goodwill, and other.
Source: Altria's Form 8-K filed with the SEC on 5 April 2007.

When an asset is exchanged for another asset, the asset acquired is recorded at the fair value of the asset given up or the fair value of the asset acquired, whichever is more readily available. Accounting for the exchange involves reducing assets by the carrying value of the asset given up, increasing assets by the value of the asset acquired, and reporting any difference as a gain or loss. A gain would be reported when the newly acquired asset's value exceeds the carrying value of the asset given up.

As an illustration of a spin-off, Altria Group, Inc. ("Altria") effected a spin-off of Kraft Foods ("Kraft") on 30 March 2007 by distributing about 89 percent of Kraft's shares to Altria's shareholders. The company prepared unaudited pro forma income statements and balance sheets (for illustrative purposes only) as if the spin-off had occurred at the beginning of the year. Exhibit 11-13 summarizes information from the asset portion of the company's pro forma balance sheets. The items in Column (b) reflect Kraft's assets being removed from Altria's balance sheet at the time of the spin-off. For example, Kraft's property, plant, and equipment (net of depreciation) total $9.7 billion.

8. IMPAIRMENT OF LONG-LIVED ASSETS

In contrast with depreciation and amortization charges, which serve to allocate the cost of a long-lived asset over its useful life, impairment charges reflect an unanticipated decline in the fair value of an asset. Accounting for impairment charges differs with assets held for use versus assets held for sale. Further, within the category of assets held for use, accounting for impairment may differ depending on the type of asset. The differences primarily involve when to test for impairment and what test is applied. The following paragraphs describe the accounting treatments and discuss implications for financial statement analysis.

8.1. Impairment of Long-Lived Tangible Assets Held for Use

For long-lived tangible assets held for use, impairment losses are recognized when the asset's carrying amount is not recoverable and its carrying value exceeds its fair value. Both of these concepts are based on the asset's carrying amount relative to its expected future cash flows. Recoverability, under U.S. standards, relates to undiscounted future cash flows, and fair value relates to discounted cash flows. The asset is considered not recoverable when the asset's carrying amount exceeds the undiscounted expected future cash flows. Then, if the asset is considered not recoverable, the impairment loss is measured as the difference between its fair value and carrying amount.

The impairment loss will reduce the carrying value of the asset on the balance sheet and will reduce net income on the income statement. The impairment loss is a noncash item and will not affect cash from operations. As with any accounting estimate, management's estimate of an impairment loss may be affected by motivations to manage earnings.

EXAMPLE 11-11   Implications of Impairment Charges in Financial Statement Analysis

Assume a (hypothetical) company, OmeTech, owns one asset with a carrying value of $2,000, manufacturing equipment that produces two products: the Ome-Gizmo and the Tech-Gizmo. An adverse event occurs that requires evaluation for impairment, namely one of OmeTech's competitors wins a lawsuit confirming their right to a patent on the technology underlying the Tech-Gizmo, leaving OmeTech with a single product. Because the equipment is highly specialized and can now be used only to manufacture a single product for which there is finite demand, OmeTech believes that this adverse event reduces the recoverable value of their manufacturing equipment to an amount below its carrying cost. Based on new estimates that the future cash flows from the equipment will total $300 per year for the next five years, and an assumed discount rate of 10 percent, the company estimates the fair value of the equipment is now $1,137 (calculated as the present value of a $300 per year cash flow for five years). The company thus determines it has an impairment loss of $863.

1. Where will the impairment loss appear in the company's financial statements?
2. How should the impairment loss be viewed in the context of evaluating past earnings and cash flow?

3. How should the impairment loss be viewed in the context of projecting future earnings and cash flow?

Solution to 1. On the balance sheet, the impairment loss will reduce the carrying amount of the relevant long-lived asset, with detail on the impairment loss itself in the footnotes to the financial statements and the MD&A. On the income statement (and thus ultimately in the retained earnings account on the balance sheet), the impairment loss will reduce income. In the operating section of the statement of cash flows, the reconciliation of net income to cash flows from operating activities will add back the impairment charge because it represents a noncash item.

Solution to 2. Because the historical depreciation charge was insufficient to represent the full decline in the equipment's value, historical earnings may have been overstated. In evaluating past earnings, it should be understood that recognition and measurement of impairment charges are highly judgmental and thus can offer the potential for a company to manage its earnings. The direction of earnings management, to the extent that it exists, is driven by the motivational context. For example, a new management team might be motivated to show improvements in future performance, so recognizing a substantial impairment charge in the current period will contribute to presenting a favorable trend. Alternatively, a management team that is close to missing a targeted earnings benchmark might be motivated to underestimate the impairment loss. In the context of evaluating past cash flow, an impairment charge does not affect cash flow. However, if the impairment loss relates to an asset that was relatively recently acquired, comparing the impairment loss to the amount invested to acquire the asset may offer some insight into management's ability to make successful acquisitions.

Solution to 3. In projecting future earnings, impairment losses would typically be considered nonrecurring and thus would not be included in future projections. In projecting future cash flows, the impairment loss can provide some guidance. In this hypothetical example with only a single machine, the disclosures would provide a fairly transparent picture of management's expectations about its future cash flows. If an analyst or other user of the financial statements made identical assumptions of a five-year remaining life of the equipment and a 10 percent discount rate, the user could derive the expected future annual cash flows by calculating what annuity a present value of $1,137 would yield over five years at an interest rate of 10 percent, namely $300 per annum. The information from the impairment loss could be used as input to an analyst's own future cash flow projections, based on his own expectations about the company's sales and profit margins, given information and assumptions about future demand for the product and competitive pressures.

In practice, neither companies' businesses nor their disclosures are as simplistic as the above example. Nonetheless, impairment disclosures can provide similarly useful information. Exhibit 11-14 provides a footnote from the financial statements of Abitibi-Consolidated. The footnotes provide information about three properties assessed for potential impairment. Based on the information, we can estimate that the company forecasts undiscounted future

EXHIBIT 11-14   Disclosure of Impairment of Long-Lived Assets: Excerpt from Financial
Statement Footnotes of Abitibi-Consolidated Inc. (NYSE: ABY; TSK: A)

IMPAIRMENT OF LONG-LIVED ASSETS

During the fourth quarter of 2006, the Company conducted the initial step of the impairment tests on
the Bridgewater, United Kingdom, paper mill and on the "Wood products" segment as a result of operating losses. The Company also conducted the initial step on the indefinitely idled Lufkin, Texas, paper
mill. Estimates of future cash flows used to test the recoverability of a long-lived asset are mainly derived
in the same manner as the projections of cash flows used in the initial step of the goodwill impairment
test. In addition, the impairment test for the Lufkin paper mill was performed in light of a scenario of
the mill's restart producing lightweight coated paper under a partnership structure.

The Company concluded that the recognition of an impairment charge for the business units analyzed
was not required, as the estimated undiscounted cash flows exceeded the book values by at least 32%.
Certain paper mills and sawmills are particularly sensitive to the key assumptions. Given the inherent
imprecision and corresponding importance of the key assumptions used in the impairment test, it is
reasonably possible that changes in future conditions may lead management to use different key assumptions, which could require a material change in the book value of these assets. The total book value of
these assets was $250 million, $174 million and $344 million for the "Newsprint," "Commercial print-
ing papers," and "Wood products" segments, respectively, as at December 31, 2006.

Source: Form 40-F for the year ended 31 December 2006, page 5, filed 15 March 2007.

cash flows on the three properties of around C$1,014 million (32 percent more than the
book value of the three properties: C$250 million + C$174 million + C$344 million.) An
assumption that the average remaining life of these assets is approximately the same as the
estimated remaining life of the company's overall PP&E asset base of 9.4 years (calculated in
Example 11-6), would indicate projected annual future cash flows from these three properties
of C$108 million (C$1,014 million ÷ 9.4 years). While this cash flow projection is clearly a
broad estimate, it could provide a useful basis of comparison for an analyst's own projections
based on his own assumptions about the future cash flows of the company.

Continuously testing the value of all these assets would obviously be impractical, so
accounting standards set guidelines for when the tests must be done. SFAS No. 144 provides
examples of events that give rise to the need to test for impairment, including a significant
adverse change in an asset's physical condition, a significant adverse change in legal or economic factors, or a significant decrease in the market price.

International standards differ somewhat in both the guidelines for determining that
impairment has occurred and in the measurement of an impairment loss. For example, under
IAS 36, measurement of an impairment loss is based on the recoverable amount of the asset
(defined as "the higher of its fair value less costs to sell and its value in use") rather than its
fair value (generally based on discounted cash flows) as in the United States.

8.2. Impairment of Intangible Assets with a Finite Life

Impairment accounting for intangible assets with a finite life is essentially the same as for
tangible assets.

Intangible assets with a finite life are amortized. They may become impaired, but are not
tested annually for impairment. Instead, they are tested only when significant events suggest
the need to test. Examples of such events include a significant decrease in the market price or
a significant adverse change in legal or economic factors.

8.3.   Impairment of Goodwill and Other Intangibles with Indefinite Lives

Goodwill and other intangible assets with indefinite lives are not amortized. Instead they are carried on the balance sheet at historical cost but tested at least annually for impairment. Impairment exists when the carrying value exceeds its fair value.[13] Measuring the value of goodwill differs somewhat from measurement of other assets because the nature of goodwill is that it cannot be separated from an overall business. Because of this inseparability, goodwill is valued for an overall reporting unit, defined as an operating segment or some component of an operating segment.

Testing for an impairment loss to goodwill in accordance with SFAS No. 142 involves two steps. First, if the carrying value of the reporting unit (including associated goodwill) exceeds its fair value, the second step is required; otherwise, there is no impairment and the second step is not required. The second step compares the carrying value of the goodwill to the fair value of the goodwill based on the valuation in the first step. If the carrying value exceeds the fair value, an impairment loss is reported. Example 11-12 provides an illustration.

EXAMPLE 11-12   Calculating Goodwill Impairment

Destroblow Inc., a (hypothetical) manufacturing company reporting under U.S. GAAP, acquired Subblow Company in 2006 for $1.2 billion. The fair value of the net assets of Subblow were $900 million, so Destroblow recorded $300 million in goodwill and will perform a goodwill impairment test at the end of each year. Subblow continues to operate as a separate company. At the end of 2007, the carrying value of Subblow is $1,010 million, including the $300 million in goodwill. The fair value of Subblow at that date is now only $950 million, and the fair value of the net assets is $875 million.

The goodwill impairment test involves two steps: (1) determining whether the fair value of Subblow is less than its carrying amount including goodwill, in which case an impairment loss exists; and (2) if an impairment loss exists, measuring the goodwill impairment loss as the difference between the carrying value of goodwill and the implied value of goodwill.

The first step of the test determines that an impairment loss exists because the $950 million fair value of Subblow is less than the $1,010 million carrying value. The second step of the test determines that the impairment loss equals $225 million, which is the excess of the $300 million book value of goodwill over the $75 million implied value of goodwill ($950 million fair value of Subblow − $875 million fair value of Subblow's net assets = $75 million implied value of goodwill).

---

[13]According to U.S. GAAP (SFAS No. 141, paragraphs 23-25), the fair value of an asset (or liability) is the amount at which that asset (or liability) could be bought (or incurred) or sold (or settled) in a current transaction between willing parties, that is, other than in a forced or liquidation sale. Perhaps the best source of fair values is the quoted market prices in active markets, if available. If not available, other methods such as the present value of future cash flows or multiples of earnings or revenues can be used.

1. If at the end of 2007, the fair value of Subblow was determined to be $950 million and the fair value of its net assets were $900 million, what would be the amount of the goodwill impairment loss?
2. If, at the end of 2007, the fair value of Subblow was determined to be $1.1 billion and the fair value of its net assets were $1 billion, what would be the amount of the goodwill impairment loss?

Solution to 1. The first step of the goodwill impairment test indicates that an impairment loss exists because Subblow's fair value of $950 million is less than its carrying value of $1,010 million. The second step determines that the amount of the goodwill impairment loss equals $250 million, which is the excess of the $300 million book value of goodwill over the $50 million implied value of goodwill ($950 million fair value of Subblow – $900 million fair value of Subblow's net assets).

Solution to 2. The first step of the goodwill impairment tests indicates that an impairment loss would not exist because Subblow's fair value of $1.1 billion exceeds its carrying value of $1,010 million. The amount of goodwill impairment loss would be $0.

Goodwill accounting under U.S. GAAP and IFRS are fairly similar conceptually, although there are several differences. Under IFRS, annual tests of goodwill (under IAS 36) relate to a "cash-generating unit" rather than a reporting unit, as under U.S. GAAP. Under IFRS, calculation of impairment of goodwill involves only one step rather than two steps, namely a comparison of the carrying value of the cash-generating unit with its "recoverable amount." The recoverable amount of an asset, as defined in IAS 36, paragraph 6, is "the higher of its fair value less costs to sell and its value in use." The fair value less costs to sell is based on the amount that would be obtained from selling the asset, and value in use is based on the present value of future cash flows that would be obtained from using the asset. If the carrying value is higher than the recoverable amount, an impairment loss is reported.

8.4. Impairment of Long-Lived Assets Held for Sale

Long-lived assets held for sale are tested for impairment at the time they are categorized as held for sale. If the carrying value exceeds the fair value less costs to sell, an impairment loss is recognized.

Reversal is reported as Profit

8.5. Reversals of Impairments of Long-Lived Assets

After an asset has been deemed impaired and an impairment loss reported, the asset's value could potentially increase. For instance, a lawsuit appeal may successfully challenge a patent infringement. The accounting for reversals of impairments depends on whether the asset is classified as held for use or held for sale. Under U.S. GAAP, once an impairment loss has been recognized for assets held for use it cannot be reversed. In other words, once the value of an asset held for use has been decreased by an impairment charge, it cannot be increased.[14]

---

[14]See SFAS No. 144, paragraph 14.

For assets held for sale, if the fair value of an asset increases after an impairment loss, the loss can be reversed.[15]

In contrast, international accounting standards permit impairment losses to be reversed if the value of an asset increases regardless of whether the asset was held for use or held for sale. The reversal is reported in profit.

8.6. Implications for Financial Statement Analysis

Significant judgment is involved in projecting the future cash flows that an asset will generate and in assessing fair values. Companies, therefore, have considerable discretion about the timing of loss recognition. One important consideration in financial statement analysis is how these charges should be included in analyzing past performance and in projecting future performance.

9. REVALUATION OF LONG-LIVED ASSETS

As previously discussed, under U.S. accounting standards, the value of long-lived assets is reported at depreciated historical cost and adjusted for impairments (decreases in value). In contrast, International Accounting Standards (IAS 16) allow companies to value long-lived assets either under a cost model (i.e., historical cost minus accumulated depreciation) or under a revaluation model (i.e., fair value). A key difference between the two is that where U.S. GAAP allows only decreases in the value of long-lived assets held for use (due to impairments), IFRS also permits increases in value to an amount above historical cost.

Under IFRS, whether an asset **revaluation** affects earnings depends on whether the revaluation initially increases or decreases an asset's carrying value. If an asset revaluation initially decreases the carrying value, the decrease is recognized in profit or loss (similar to an asset impairment). Later, if the asset's carrying value increases, the increase is recognized in profit or loss to the extent that it reverses a revaluation decrease of the same asset previously recognized in profit or loss. Contrast this treatment with an upward revaluation where the increase in the asset's carrying value bypasses the income statement and goes directly to equity under the heading of revaluation surplus. Any subsequent decrease in the asset's value first decreases the revaluation surplus then goes to income.

Exhibit 11-15 provides an example of a company's disclosures concerning revaluation. The exhibit shows an excerpt from the annual report of KPN, the Dutch telecommunications and multimedia company. The excerpt is from the section in which the company explains differences between its reporting under IFRS and its reporting under U.S. GAAP. One of these differences, as noted above, is that U.S. GAAP does not allow revaluation of fixed assets held for use. KPN explains that they elected to report fixed assets at fair value, so under U.S. GAAP (historical cost), the value of the assets at the end of 2006 would have been EUR 350 million lower.

Asset revaluations offer several considerations for financial statement analyses. First, an increase in the carrying value of depreciable long-lived assets increases total assets and shareholders' equity; so, asset revaluations that increase the carrying value of an asset can be used to reduce reported leverage (recall leverage is defined as average total assets divided by average

---

[15]See SFAS No. 144, paragraph 37.

EXHIBIT 11-15   Selected Excerpts from Annual Report of Koninklijke KPN N.V. (NYSE: KPN): Excerpt from the Explanation of Certain Differences between IFRS and U.S. GAAP Regarding "Deemed Cost Fixed Assets"

KPN elected the exemption to revalue certain of its fixed assets upon the transition to IFRS to fair value and to use this fair value as their deemed cost. KPN applied the depreciated replacement cost method to determine this fair value. The revalued assets pertain to certain cables, which form part of property, plant & equipment. Under U.S. GAAP, this revaluation is not allowed and therefore results in a reconciling item. As a result, the value of these assets as of December 31, 2006 under U.S. GAAP is EUR 350 million lower (2005: EUR 415 million; 2004: EUR 487 million) than under IFRS.

Source: Company's Form 20-F, p.168, filed 1 March 2007.

shareholders' equity).[16] Therefore, the leverage motivation for the revaluation should be considered in analysis. For example, a company may revalue assets up if it is seeking new capital or approaching leverage limitations set by financial covenants. Second, assets revaluations that decrease the carrying value of the assets reduce net income. In the year of the revaluation, profitability measures such as return on assets and return on equity decline. However, because total assets and shareholders' equity are also lower, the company may appear more profitable in future years. Additionally, reversals of downward revaluations also go through income, thus increasing earnings. Managers can then opportunistically time the reversals to manage earnings and increase income. Third, assets revaluations that increase the carrying value of an asset initially increase depreciation expense, total assets, and shareholders' equity. Therefore, profitability measures, such as return on assets and return on equity, would decline. Although upward asset revaluations also generally decrease income (through higher depreciation expense) the increase in the value of the long-lived asset is presumably based on increases in the operating capacity of the asset, which will be likely evidenced in increased future revenues. Finally, an analyst would also want to understand who does the appraisal, that is, an independent external appraiser or management, and how often revaluations are made. Appraisals of the fair value of long-lived assets involve considerable judgment and discretion. Presumably, appraisals of assets from independent external sources are more reliable. How often assets are revalued can provide an indicator of whether their reported value continues to be representative of their fair values.

EXAMPLE 11-13   Asset Revaluation

You are analyzing a company (hypothetical), RevUp PLC, that is planning to raise new debt in the coming year. Part of your analysis involves understanding the company's solvency to help determine its capacity to handle additional debt. You observe that in 2006 RevUp made an asset revaluation that increased the reported value of its assets by €150 million and increased depreciation expense by €25 million. Other relevant data and extracts from the company's annual report are included in Exhibit 11-16.

---

[16]Though both the numerator (assets) and denominator (equity) increase, we know that leverage decreases because mathematically, when a ratio is greater than one, as in this case, an increase in both the numerator and the denominator by the same amount leads to a decline in the ratio.

EXHIBIT 11-16   RevUp PLC: Excerpts from Financial Statements

Line Items (S millions)	2005	2006
On 31 December:		
Property, plant, and equipment, net	€700	€750
Total assets	3,000	3,650
Total liabilities	1,400	1,900
Revaluation surplus (part of shareholders' equity)	—	150
Total shareholders' equity	1,600	1,750
For the Year Ended 31 December		
Depreciation expense	€100	€125
Income before taxes	1,000	975
Tax expense	400	400
Net income	600	575

1. Compute the company's financial leverage (defined as average total assets divided by average shareholders' equity) based on reported financial statements fiscal year 2006, with no adjustments, and with adjustment for the impact of the asset revaluation on leverage. (Assume the asset revaluation is not taxable and any increases in deprecation expense related to the revaluation are not tax deductible, so there would be no change in taxes.)
2. Interpret the change in leverage.

Solution to 1. RevUp's 2006 ratios are as follows:

	With Asset Revaluation (as reported)	Without Asset Revaluation (as adjusted)
Leverage	1.99	2.03

Based on information as reported, leverage with the asset revaluation was 1.99 (average total assets divided by average shareholders' equity).

- Average total assets: €3,325. Beginning assets of €3,000 + ending total assets of €3,650 ÷ 2.
- Average shareholders' equity: €1,675. Beginning shareholders' equity of €1,600 + ending shareholders' equity of €1,750 ÷ 2.
  Based on information as reported, leverage without the asset revaluation was 2.03 (average total assets ÷ average shareholders' equity).
- Average total assets: €3,250. Beginning assets of €3,000 + ending total assets of €3,500 (€3,650 − €150 increase in the value of the asset surplus) ÷ 2.
- Average shareholders' equity: €1,600. Beginning shareholders' equity of €1,600 + ending shareholders' equity of €1,600 (€1,750 − €150 asset surplus) ÷ 2.

Solution to 2. Increasing the value of the assets through revaluation would decrease leverage. So, RevUp would appear to have more capacity for any new debt issues.

10. SUMMARY

Key points include the following:

- Expenditures related to long-lived assets are included as part of the value of assets on the balance sheet (i.e., capitalized) if they are expected to provide future benefits, typically beyond one year.
- Although capitalizing expenditures, rather than expensing, results in higher reported profitability in the initial year, it results in lower profitability in subsequent years; however, if a company continues to purchase similar or increasing amounts of assets each year, the profitability-enhancing effect of capitalizing continues.
- Capitalizing an expenditure rather than expensing it results in greater amounts reported as cash from operations.
- If an asset is acquired in a nonmonetary exchange, its cost is based on the fair value of the asset given up, or the fair value of the asset acquired if it is more reliably determinable.
- Companies must capitalize interest costs associated with acquiring or constructing an asset that requires a long period of time to prepare for its intended use.
- Including capitalized interest in the calculation of interest coverage ratios provides a better assessment of a company's solvency.
- Generally, U.S. accounting standards require that research and development costs be expensed; however, certain costs related to software development are required to be capitalized. IFRS also require research costs be expensed but allows development costs to be capitalized under certain conditions.
- If companies apply different approaches to capitalizing software development costs, adjustments can be made to make the two comparable.
- When one company acquires another company, the transaction is accounted for using the purchase method of accounting in which the company identified as the acquirer allocates the purchase price to each asset acquired (and each liability assumed) on the basis of its fair value.
- Under purchase accounting, if the purchase price of an acquisition exceeds the sum of the amounts that can be allocated to individual assets and liabilities, the excess is recorded as goodwill.
- U.S. GAAP requires the immediate write-off of in-process R&D acquired in a business combination, but IFRS does not.
- Depreciation methods include: the straight-line method, in which the cost of an asset is allocated in equal amounts over its useful life; accelerated methods, in which the allocation of cost is greater in earlier years; and units-of-production methods, in which the allocation of cost corresponds to the actual use of an asset in a particular period.
- Significant estimates required for depreciation calculations include the useful life of the equipment (or its total lifetime productive capacity) and its expected residual value at the end of that useful life. A longer useful life and higher expected residual value decrease the amount of annual depreciation relative to a shorter useful life and lower expected residual value.
- Estimates of average age and remaining useful life of a company's assets reflect the relationship between assets accounted for on a historical cost basis and depreciation amounts.
- The average remaining useful life of a company's assets can be estimated as net PP&E divided by depreciation expense.
- To estimate the average age of the asset base, divide accumulated depreciation by depreciation expense.

- Intangible assets with finite useful lives are amortized over their useful lives.
- Intangible assets without a finite useful life, that is, with an indefinite useful life, are not amortized, but are reviewed for impairment whenever changes in events or circumstances indicate that the carrying amount of an asset may not be recoverable.
- For many types of long-lived tangible assets, ownership involves obligations that must be fulfilled at the end of the asset's service life, referred to as asset retirement obligations (AROs). Financial analysts often adjust financial statements to treat AROs in a manner consistent with debt.
- The gain or loss on the sale of long-lived assets is computed as the sales proceeds minus the carrying value of the asset at the time of sale.
- Long-lived assets to be disposed of other than by a sale—for example, abandoned, exchanged for another asset, or distributed to owners in a spin-off—are classified as held for use until disposal. Thus, they continue to be depreciated and tested for impairment.
- In contrast with depreciation and amortization charges, which serve to allocate the cost of a long-lived asset over its useful life, impairment charges reflect a decline in the fair value of an asset to an amount lower than its carrying value.
- Impairment disclosures can provide useful information about a company's expected cash flows.
- Under U.S. accounting standards, the value of long-lived assets is reported at depreciated historical cost. This value may be decreased by impairment charges, but cannot be increased. International accounting standards, however, permit impairment losses to be reversed, with the reversal reported in profit.

PRACTICE PROBLEMS

1. The Schneider Candy Company has decided to capitalize the interest costs it incurs during and related to construction of its new storage and shipping facility. This practice is
   A. permitted only if the company complies with U.S. GAAP.
   B. permitted only if the company complies with IFRS.
   C. permissible under either U.S. GAAP or IFRS.

2. The Juniper Juice Company reports that it has capitalized the interest costs it incurred during and related to construction of its new bottling plant. A creditor assessing Juniper Juice's solvency ratios would *most likely*
   A. add capitalized interest to reported interest expense.
   B. subtract capitalized interest from reported interest expense.
   C. add any depreciation from previously capitalized interest to interest expense.

3. Anna Lyssette is evaluating the performance of two biotechnology companies: Biotech Holdings and Advanced Biotech. Both companies released their first new drugs early in the year, but Lyssette is worried about a possible lack of comparability due to differing strategies. Biotech Holdings acquired the research and development for its drug from another company while Advanced Biotech developed its drug internally. In the current accounting period, all else equal, Biotech Holdings would *most likely* report
   A. lower total assets.
   B. higher net income.
   C. similar cash flow from operations.

4. Amerisoft complies with U.S. GAAP, while EuroWare complies with IFRS. When comparing the two companies, it would *most likely* be necessary to adjust the financial statements of
   A. Amerisoft to remove charges related to acquired in-process R&D.
   B. EuroWare to remove charges related to acquired in-process R&D.
   C. Both companies to remove charges related to acquired in-process R&D.

5. When comparing a company that complies with IFRS to a company that complies with U.S. GAAP, it is *most* important to remember that under IFRS
   A. research-phase R&D expenditures are capitalized.
   B. acquired in-process R&D is expensed immediately.
   C. development-phase R&D expenditures may be capitalized.

The following information relates to Problems 6 through 9:
   The Asset Intensive Company (AIC) has purchased equipment for $1 million. The equipment is expected to have a three-year useful life and a salvage value of $100,000. AIC reports under U.S. GAAP.

6. Over the full life of the machine, all else equal, the volatility of AIC's net income will be
   A. the same regardless of whether AIC expenses or capitalizes the cost of the machine.
   B. highest if the company expenses the entire cost of the machine in the year of its purchase.
   C. highest if the company capitalizes the cost of the machine and depreciates it over its useful life.

7. Assuming AIC capitalizes the cost of the equipment, depreciation expense over the life of the machine will be
   A. the same regardless of the chosen depreciation method.
   B. lowest if the company uses the double-declining balance method.
   C. highest if the company uses the double-declining balance method.

8. In year 3, the return on equity will *most likely* be
   A. highest if the company expenses the cost of the equipment.
   B. highest if the company capitalizes the cost of the equipment.
   C. the same regardless of whether the cost of the equipment is expensed or capitalized.

9. Regardless of the depreciation method used for reporting purposes, the company will use MACRS for tax purposes. In year 1, the reported income tax expense will be
   A. the same regardless of depreciation method.
   B. highest if the company uses the straight-line method.
   C. highest if the company uses the double-declining balance method.

10. Bobcat Company's balance sheet shows PP&E valued at a historical cost of $22,983 million and accumulated depreciation of $7,879 million. Depreciation expense in the most recent year was $2,459 million. What is the average remaining useful life of Bobcat's assets?
    A. 3.2 years.
    B. 6.1 years.
    C. 9.3 years.

11. Francis Acana is comparing the property and equipment disclosures for three airline companies, as summarized in the following table:

	Airline A	Airline B	Airline C
Historical cost, aircraft	$17,239	£23,584	€45,266
Accumulated depreciation, aircraft	6,584	13,654	21,745
Net cost, aircraft	10,655	9,930	23,521
Annual depreciation expense	575	786	1,509

Acana finds that the average fleet age is
A. lowest for Airline A.
B. lowest for Airline B.
C. lowest for Airline C.

12. Relative to assets with finite lives, an intangible asset determined to have an indefinite life will result in lower reported
A. assets.
B. net income.
C. amortization expense.

13. With regard to intangible assets, a company's reported profit margin the year the asset is acquired will be highest if it estimates a
A. six-year useful life and no salvage value.
B. six-year useful life and a positive salvage value.
C. five-year useful life and a positive salvage value.

14. With regard to intangible assets, the company's cash flow from operating activities the year the asset is acquired will *most likely* be highest if it estimates a
A. five-year useful life and no salvage value.
B. six-year useful life and a positive salvage value.
C. five-year useful life and a positive salvage value.

15. When a company is able to estimate the future costs it will incur when an asset is retired, it is *least likely* to
A. increase the carrying value of the asset.
B. decrease the carrying value of the liability through an accretion charge.
C. decrease the carrying value of the asset over time through an accretion charge.

16. Compared to an asset that will not require a retirement obligation, an asset that will require a retirement obligation is *most likely* to result in a
A. one-time charge at the time of retirement.
B. rising debt/equity ratio as the retirement date approaches.
C. declining debt/equity ratio as the retirement date approaches.

17. A credit analyst reviewing a company with asset retirement obligations (ARO) would *least likely* adjust
    A. interest expense by the amount of accretion.
    B. shareholders' equity by the amount of the ARO.
    C. the reported ARO by the amount of any related trust funds or escrow.

18. Fisherman Enterprises purchased $1 million of equipment with an estimated 10-year useful life and a $100,000 expected salvage value. The company uses the straight-line method of depreciation. At the end of five years it sells the equipment for $500,000. Fisherman's income statement will include a $50,000
    A. loss recorded as a separate line item.
    B. gain recorded as a separate line item.
    C. offset to depreciation and amortization.

19. A company that has decided to sell an asset is *least likely* to record a
    A. gain at the time the asset is sold.
    B. loss at the time the decision is made.
    C. gain at the time the decision is made.

20. An asset is considered impaired when
    A. its fair value exceeds its carrying value.
    B. its carrying value exceeds its fair value.
    C. it ceases to provide an economic benefit.

21. An asset impairment is *most likely* to impact reported
    A. depreciation expense in future periods.
    B. depreciation expense in the year impaired.
    C. cash flow from operating activities in the year impaired.

22. When comparing the reported results of a company that complies with U.S. GAAP to a company that complies with IFRS, return on assets is *least likely* to require an adjustment for
    A. goodwill amortization.
    B. upwardly revalued assets.
    C. acquired in-process R&D charges.

23. In the year of the revaluation, an asset revaluation that increases the carrying value of an asset is *most likely* to
    A. increase return on equity.
    B. decrease reported leverage.
    C. decrease shareholders' equity.

CHAPTER 12

INCOME TAXES

Elbie Antonites, CFA

University of Pretoria
Pretoria, South Africa

Michael A. Broihahn, CFA

Barry University
Miami, Florida

LEARNING OUTCOMES

After completing this chapter, you will be able to do the following:

- Explain the differences between accounting profit and taxable income, and define key terms including deferred tax assets, deferred tax liabilities, valuation allowance, taxes payable, and income tax expense.
- Explain how deferred tax liabilities and assets are created and the factors that determine how a company's deferred tax liabilities and assets should be treated for the purposes of financial analysis.
- Determine the tax base of a company's assets and liabilities.
- Calculate income tax expense, income taxes payable, deferred tax assets and deferred tax liabilities, and calculate and interpret the adjustment to the financial statements related to a change in the income tax rate.
- Evaluate the impact of tax rate changes on a company's financial statements and ratios.
- Distinguish between temporary and permanent items in pretax financial income and taxable income.
- Discuss the implications of a valuation allowance for deferred tax assets (i.e., when it is required, what impact it has on financial statements, and how it might affect an analyst's view of a company).
- Compare and contrast a company's deferred tax items and effective tax rate reconciliation between reporting periods.

- Analyze disclosures relating to deferred tax items and the effective tax rate reconciliation, and discuss how information included in these disclosures affects a company's financial statements and financial ratios.
- Identify the key provisions of and differences between income tax accounting under International Financial Reporting Standards (IFRS) and U.S. generally accepted accounting principles (U.S. GAAP).

1. INTRODUCTION

For those companies reporting under IFRS, International Accounting Standard (IAS) 12 covers accounting for a company's income taxes and the reporting of deferred taxes. For those companies reporting under U.S. GAAP, Statement of Financial Accounting Standards (SFAS) No. 109 is the primary source for information on accounting for income taxes. Although IFRS and U.S. GAAP follow similar conventions on many income tax issues, there are some key differences that will be discussed in the chapter.

Differences between how and when transactions are recognized for financial reporting purposes relative to tax reporting can give rise to differences in tax expense and related tax assets and liabilities. To reconcile these differences, companies that report under either IFRS or U.S. GAAP create a provision on the balance sheet called *deferred tax assets* or *deferred tax liabilities* depending on the nature of the situation.

Deferred tax assets or liabilities usually arise when accounting standards and tax authorities recognize the timing of revenues and expenses at different times. Because timing differences such as these will eventually reverse over time, they are called *temporary differences.* Deferred tax assets represent taxes that have been recognized for tax reporting purposes (or often the carrying forward of losses from previous periods) but have not yet been recognized on the income statement prepared for financial reporting purposes. Deferred tax liabilities represent tax expense that has appeared on the income statement for financial reporting purposes, but has not yet become payable under tax regulations.

This chapter provides a primer on the basics of income tax accounting and reporting. The chapter is organized as follows: Section 2 describes the differences between taxable income and accounting profit. Section 3 explains the determination of tax base, which relates to the valuation of assets and liabilities for tax purposes. Section 4 discusses several types of timing differences between the recognition of taxable and accounting profit. Section 5 examines unused tax losses and tax credits. Section 6 describes the recognition and measurement of current and deferred tax. Section 7 discusses the disclosure and presentation of income tax information on companies' financial statements and illustrates its practical implications for financial analysis. Section 8 provides an overview of the similarities and differences for income tax reporting between IFRS and U.S. GAAP. Section 9 summarizes the chapter, and practice problems in the CFA Institute multiple-choice format conclude the chapter.

2. DIFFERENCES BETWEEN ACCOUNTING PROFIT AND TAXABLE INCOME

A company's **accounting profit** is reported on its income statement in accordance with prevailing accounting standards. Accounting profit (also referred to as *income before taxes* or *pretax income*) does not include a provision for income tax expense.[1] A company's **taxable**

---

[1] As defined under IAS 12, paragraph 5.

income is the portion of its income that is subject to income taxes under the tax laws of its jurisdiction. Because of different guidelines for how income is reported on a company's financial statements and how it is measured for income tax purposes, accounting profit and taxable income may differ.

A company's taxable income is the basis for its **income tax payable** (a liability) or **recoverable** (an asset), which is calculated on the basis of the company's tax rate and appears on its balance sheet. A company's **tax expense,** or tax benefit in the case of a recovery, appears on its income statement and is an aggregate of its income tax payable (or recoverable in the case of a tax benefit) and any changes in deferred tax assets and liabilities.

When a company's taxable income is greater than its accounting profit, then its income taxes payable will be higher than what would have otherwise been the case had the income taxes been determined based on accounting profit. **Deferred tax assets**, which appear on the balance sheet, arise when an excess amount is paid for income taxes (taxable income higher than accounting profit) and the company expects to recover the difference during the course of future operations. Actual income taxes payable will thus exceed the financial accounting income tax expense (which is reported on the income statement and is determined based on accounting profit). Related to deferred tax assets is a **valuation allowance**, which is a reserve created against deferred tax assets. The valuation allowance is based on the likelihood of realizing the deferred tax assets in future accounting periods. **Deferred tax liabilities**, which also appear on the balance sheet, arise when a deficit amount is paid for income taxes and the company expects to eliminate the deficit over the course of future operations. In this case, financial accounting income tax expense exceeds income taxes payable. → *LIFO or Accelerated Depreciation.*

Income tax paid in a period is the actual amount paid for income taxes (not a provision, but the actual cash outflow). The income tax paid may be less than the income tax expense because of payments in prior periods or refunds received in the current period. Income tax paid reduces the income tax payable, which is carried on the balance sheet as a liability.

The **tax base** of an asset or liability is the amount at which the asset or liability is valued for tax purposes whereas the **carrying amount** is the amount at which the asset or liability is valued according to accounting principles.[2] Differences between the tax base and the carrying amount also result in differences between accounting profit and taxable income. These differences can carry through to future periods. For example, a **tax loss carryforward** occurs when a company experiences a loss in the current period that may be used to reduce future taxable income. The company's tax expense on its income statement must not only reflect the taxes payable based on taxable income, but also the effect of these differences.

2.1. Current Tax Assets and Liabilities   *book vs. Tax*

A company's current tax liability is the amount payable in taxes and is based on current taxable income. If the company expects to receive a refund for some portion previously paid in taxes, the amount recoverable is referred to as a current tax asset. The current tax liability or asset may, however, differ from what the liability would have been if it was based on accounting profit rather than taxable income for the period. Differences in accounting profit and taxable income are the result of the application of different rules. Such differences between accounting profit and taxable income can occur in several ways, including:

- Revenues and expenses may be recognized in one period for accounting purposes and a different period for tax purposes.

---

[2]The terms *tax base* and *tax basis* are interchangeable. *Tax basis* is more commonly used in the United States. Similarly, *carrying amount* and *book value* refer to the same concept.

- Specific revenues and expenses may be either recognized for accounting purposes and not for tax purposes, or not recognized for accounting purposes but recognized for tax purposes.
- The carrying amount and tax base of assets and/or liabilities may differ.
- The deductibility of gains and losses of assets and liabilities may vary for accounting and income tax purposes.
- Subject to tax rules, tax losses of prior years might be used to reduce taxable income in later years, resulting in differences in accounting and taxable income (tax loss carryforward).
- Adjustments of reported financial data from prior years might not be recognized equally for accounting and tax purposes or might be recognized in different periods.

2.2. Deferred Tax Assets and Liabilities

Deferred tax assets represent taxes that have been paid (or often the carrying forward of losses from previous periods) but have not yet been recognized on the income statement. Deferred tax assets and liabilities occur when financial accounting income tax expense is greater than regulatory income tax expense. Deferred tax assets and liabilities usually arise when accounting standards and tax authorities recognize the timing of taxes due at different times; for example, when a company uses accelerated depreciation when reporting to the tax authority (to increase expense and lower tax payments in the early years) but uses the straight-line method on the financial statements. Although not similar in treatment on a year-to-year basis (e.g., depreciation of 5 percent on a straight-line basis may be permitted for accounting purposes, whereas 10 percent is allowed for tax purposes) over the life of the asset, both approaches allow for the total cost of the asset to be depreciated (or amortized). Because these timing differences will eventually reverse or self-correct over the course of the asset's depreciable life, they are called *temporary differences*.

Under IFRS, deferred tax assets and liabilities are always classified as noncurrent. Under U.S. GAAP, however, deferred tax assets and liabilities are classified on the balance sheet as current and noncurrent based on the classification of the underlying asset or liability.

Any deferred tax asset or liability is based on temporary differences that result in an excess or a deficit amount paid for taxes, which the company expects to recover from future operations. Because taxes will be recoverable or payable at a future date, it is only a temporary difference and a deferred tax asset or liability is created. Changes in the deferred tax asset or liability on the balance sheet reflect the difference between the amounts recognized in the previous period and the current period. The changes in deferred tax assets and liabilities are added to income tax payable to determine the company's income tax expense (or credit) as it is reported on the income statement.

At the end of each fiscal year, deferred tax assets and liabilities are recalculated by comparing the tax bases and carrying amounts of the balance sheet items. Identified temporary differences should be assessed on whether the difference will result in future economic benefits. For example, Pinto Construction (a hypothetical company) depreciates equipment on a straight-line basis of 10 percent per year. The tax authorities allow depreciation of 15 percent per year. At the end of the fiscal year, the carrying amount of the equipment for accounting purposes would be greater than the tax base of the equipment, thus resulting in a temporary difference. A deferred tax item may be created only if it is not doubtful that the company will realize economic benefits in future. In our example, the equipment is used in the core business of Pinto Construction. If the company is a going concern and stable, there should be no doubt that future economic benefits will result from the equipment and it would be appropriate to create the deferred tax item.

Should it be doubtful that future economic benefits will be realized from a temporary difference (such as Pinto Construction being under liquidation), the temporary difference will not lead to the creation of a deferred tax asset or liability. If a deferred tax asset or liability resulted in the past, but the criteria of economic benefits are not met on the current balance sheet date, then an existing deferred tax asset or liability related to the item will be reversed (or for U.S. GAAP a full valuation allowance will be established). In assessing future economic benefits, much is left to the discretion of the auditor in assessing the temporary differences and the issue of future economic benefits.

IFRS → Always Current, US GAAP → A portion to long-term and a portion to short term.

EXAMPLE 12-1   Deferred Tax Liability

The following information pertains to a fictitious company, Reston Partners.

Reston Partners Consolidated Income Statement Period Ending 31 March (£ millions)	2006	2005	2004
Revenue	£40,000	£30,000	£25,000
Other net gains	2,000	0	0
Changes in inventories of finished goods and work in progress	400	180	200
Raw materials and consumables used	(5,700)	(4,000)	(8,000)
Depreciation expense	(2,000)	(2,000)	(2,000)
Other expenses	(6,000)	(5,900)	(4,500)
Interest expense	(2,000)	(3,000)	(6,000)
Profit before Tax	£26,700	£15,280	£4,700

The financial performance and accounting profit of Reston Partners on this income statement is based on accounting principles appropriate for the jurisdiction in which Reston Partners operates. The principals used to calculate accounting profit (profit before tax in the example above) may differ from the principles applied for tax purposes (the calculation of taxable income). For illustrative purposes, however, assume that all income and expenses on the income statement are treated identically for tax and accounting purposes *except* depreciation.

The depreciation is related to equipment owned by Reston Partners. For simplicity, assume that the equipment was purchased at the beginning of the 2004 fiscal year. Depreciation should thus be calculated and expensed for the full year. Assume that accounting standards permit equipment to be depreciated on a straight-line basis over a 10-year period, whereas the tax standards in the jurisdiction specify that equipment should be depreciated on a straight-line basis over a 7-year period. For simplicity, assume a salvage value of £0 at the end of the equipment's useful life. Both methods will result in the full depreciation of the asset over the respective tax or accounting life.

The equipment was originally purchased for £20,000. In accordance with accounting standards, over the next 10 years the company will recognize annual depreciation of £2,000 (£20,000 ÷ 10) as an expense on its income statement and for the determination of accounting profit. For tax purposes, however, the company will recognize £2,857 (£20,000 ÷ 7) in depreciation each year. Each fiscal year the depreciation expense related to the use of the equipment will, therefore, differ for tax and accounting purposes (tax base vs. carrying amount), resulting in a difference between accounting profit and taxable income.

The income statement above reflects accounting profit (depreciation at £2,000 per year). The following table shows the taxable income for each fiscal year:

Taxable Income (£ millions)	2006	2005	2004
Revenue	£40,000	£30,000	£25,000
Other net gains	2,000	0	0
Changes in inventories of finished goods and work in progress	400	180	200
Raw materials and consumables used	(5,700)	(4,000)	(8,000)
Depreciation expense	(2,857)	(2,857)	(2,857)
Other expenses	(6,000)	(5,900)	(4,500)
Interest expense	(2,000)	(3,000)	(6,000)
Taxable income	£25,843	£14,423	£3,843

The carrying amount and tax base for the equipment is as follows:

(£ millions)	2006	2005	2004
Equipment value for accounting purposes (carrying amount) (depreciation of £2,000/year)	£14,000	£16,000	£18,000
Equipment value for tax purposes (tax base)(depreciation of £2,857/year)	£11,429	£14,286	£17,143
Difference	£2,571	£1,714	£857

At each balance sheet date, the tax base and carrying amount of all assets and liabilities must be determined. The income tax payable by Reston Partners will be based on the taxable income of each fiscal year. If a tax rate of 30 percent is assumed, then the income taxes payable for 2004, 2005, and 2006 are £1,153 (30% × 3,843), £4,327 (30% × 14,423) and £7,753 (30% × 25,843).

Remember, though, that if the tax obligation is calculated based on accounting profits, it will differ because of the differences between the tax base and the carrying amount of equipment. The difference in each fiscal year is reflected in the table above. In each fiscal year the carrying amount of the equipment exceeds its tax base. For tax purposes, therefore, the asset tax base is less than its carrying value under financial accounting principles. The difference results in a deferred tax liability.

(£ millions)	2006	2005	2004
Deferred tax liability	£771	£514	£257
(Difference between tax base and carrying amount)			
2004: £(18,000 − 17,143) × 30% = 257			
2005: £(16,000 − 14,286) × 30% = 514			
2006: £(14,000 − 11,429) × 30% = 771			

The comparison of the tax base and carrying amount of equipment shows what the deferred tax liability should be on a particular balance sheet date. In each fiscal year, only the change in the deferred tax liability should be included in the calculation of the income tax expense reported on the income statement prepared for accounting purposes.

On the income statement, the company's income tax expense will be the sum of the deferred tax liability and income tax payable.

(£ millions)	2006	2005	2004
Income Tax Payable (Based on Tax Accounting)	£7,753	£4,327	£1,153
Deferred Tax Liability	257	257	257
Income Tax (Based on Financial Accounting)	£8,010	£4,584	£1,410
(Difference between tax base and carrying amount)			
2004: £(18,000 − 17,143) × 30% = 257			
2005: £(16,000 − 14,286) × 30% − 257 = 257			
2006: £(14,000 − 11,429) × 30% − 514 = 257			

Note that because the different treatment of depreciation is a temporary difference, the income tax on the income statement is 30 percent of the accounting profit, although only a part is income tax payable and the rest is a deferred tax liability.

The consolidated income statement of Reston Partners including income tax is presented as follows:

Reston Partners (Consolidated Income Statement)			
Period Ending 31 March (£ millions)	**2006**	**2005**	**2004**
Revenue	£40,000	£30,000	£25,000
Other net gains	2,000	0	0
Changes in inventories of finished goods and work in progress	400	180	200
Raw materials and consumables used	(5,700)	(4,000)	(8,000)
Depreciation expense	(2,000)	(2,000)	(2,000)
Other expenses	(6,000)	(5,900)	(4,500)

Interest expense	(2,000)	(3,000)	(6,000)
Profit before Tax	£26,700	£15,280	£4,700
Income Tax	(8,010)	(4,584)	(1,410)
Profit after Tax	£18,690	£10,696	£3,290

Any amount paid to the tax authorities will reduce the liability for income tax payable and be reflected on the cash flow statement of the company.

3. DETERMINING THE TAX BASE OF ASSETS AND LIABILITIES

As mentioned in section 2, temporary differences arise from a difference in the tax base and carrying amount of assets and liabilities. The tax base of an asset or liability is the amount attributed to the asset or liability for tax purposes whereas the carrying amount is based on accounting principles. Such a difference is considered temporary if it is expected that the taxes will be recovered or payable at a future date.

3.1. Determining the Tax Base of an Asset

The tax base of an asset is the amount that will be deductible for tax purposes in future periods as the economic benefits become realized and the company recovers the carrying amount of the asset.

For example, our previously mentioned Reston Partners (from Example 12-1) depreciates equipment on a straight-line basis at a rate of 10 percent per year. The tax authorities allow depreciation of approximately 15 percent per year. At the end of the fiscal year, the carrying amount of equipment for accounting purposes is greater than the asset tax base, thus resulting in a temporary difference.

EXAMPLE 12-2   Determining the Tax Base of an Asset

The following information pertains to Entiguan Sports, a hypothetical developer of products used to treat sports-related injuries. (The treatment of items for accounting and tax purposes is based on fictitious accounting and tax standards and is not specific to a particular jurisdiction.) Calculate the tax base and carrying amount for each item.

1. *Dividends receivable.* On its balance sheet, Entiguan Sports reports dividends of €1 million receivable from a subsidiary. Assume that dividends are not taxable.
2. *Development costs.* Entiguan Sports capitalized development costs of €3 million during the year. Entiguan amortized €500,000 of this amount during the year. For tax purposes amortization of 25 percent per year is allowed.
3. *Research costs.* Entiguan incurred €500,000 in research costs, which were all expensed in the current fiscal year for financial reporting purposes. Assume that applicable tax legislation requires research costs to be expensed over a four-year period rather than all in one year.

4. *Accounts receivable.* Included on the income statement of Entiguan Sports is a provision for doubtful debt of €125,000. The accounts receivable amount reflected on the balance sheet, after taking the provision into account, amounts to €1,500,000. The tax authorities allow a deduction of 25 percent of the gross amount for doubtful debt.

Solutions:

	Carrying Amount (€)	Tax Base (€)	Temporary Difference (€)
1. Dividends receivable	1,000,000	= 1,000,000 *No tax*	0
2. Development costs	2,500,000	2,250,000	250,000
3. Research costs	(*expensed*) 0	375,000	(375,000)
4. Accounts receivable	1,500,000	1,218,750	281,250

Comments:

1. *Dividends receivable.* Although the dividends received are economic benefits from the subsidiary, we are assuming that dividends are not taxable. Therefore, the carrying amount equals the tax base for dividends receivable.

2. *Development costs.* First, we assume that development costs will generate economic benefits for Entiguan Sports. Therefore, it may be included as an asset on the balance sheet for the purposes of this example. Second, the amortization allowed by the tax authorities exceeds the amortization accounted for based on accounting rules. Therefore, the carrying amount of the asset exceeds its tax base. The carrying amount is (€3,000,000 − €500,000) = €2,500,000 whereas the tax base is [€3,000,000 − (25% × €3,000,000)] = €2,250,000.

3. *Research costs.* We assume that research costs will result in future economic benefits for the company. If this were not the case, creation of a deferred tax asset or liability would not be allowed. The tax base of research costs exceeds their carrying amount. The carrying amount is €0 because the full amount has been expensed for financial reporting purposes in the year in which it was incurred. Therefore, there would not have been a balance sheet item "Research costs" for tax purposes, and only a proportion may be deducted in the current fiscal year. The tax base of the asset is (€500,000 − €500,000/4) = €375,000.

4. *Accounts receivable.* The economic benefits that should have been received from accounts receivable have already been included in revenues included in the calculation of the taxable income when the sales occurred. Because the receipt of a portion of the accounts receivable is doubtful, the provision is allowed. The provision, based on tax legislation, results in a greater amount allowed in the current fiscal year than would be the case under accounting principles. This results in the tax base of accounts receivable being lower than its carrying amount. Note that the example specifically states that the balance sheet amount for accounts receivable after the provision for accounting purposes amounts to €1,500,000. Therefore, accounts receivable before any provision was €1,500,000 + €125,000 = €1,625,000. The tax base is calculated as (€1,500,000 + €125,000) − [25% × (€1,500,000 + €125,000)] = €1,218,750.

3.2. Determining the Tax Base of a Liability

The tax base of a liability is the carrying amount of the liability less any amounts that will be deductible for tax purposes in the future. With respect to payments from customers received in advance of providing the goods and services, the tax base of such a liability is the carrying amount less any amount of the revenue that will not be taxable in future. Keep in mind the following fundamental principle: In general, a company will recognize a deferred tax asset or liability when recovery/settlement of the carrying amount will affect future tax payments by either increasing or reducing the taxable profit. Remember, an analyst is not only evaluating the difference between the carrying amount and the tax base, but the relevance of that difference on future profits and losses and thus by implication future taxes.

IFRS offers specific guidelines with regard to revenue received in advance: IAS 12 states that the tax base is the carrying amount less any amount of the revenue that will not be taxed at a future date. Under U.S. GAAP, an analysis of the tax base would result in a similar outcome. The tax legislation within the jurisdiction will determine the amount recognized on the income statement and whether the liability (revenue received in advance) will have a tax base greater than zero. This will depend on how tax legislation recognizes revenue received in advance.

EXAMPLE 12-3   Determining the Tax Base of a Liability

The following information pertains to Entiguan Sports for the 2006 year-end. The treatment of items for accounting and tax purposes is based on fictitious accounting and tax standards and is not specific to a particular jurisdiction. Calculate the tax base and carrying amount for each item.

1. *Donations.* Entiguan Sports made donations of €100,000 in the current fiscal year. The donations were expensed for financial reporting purposes, but are not tax deductible based on applicable tax legislation.
2. *Interest received in advance.* Entiguan Sports received in advance interest of €300,000. The interest is taxed because tax authorities recognize the interest to accrue to the company (part of taxable income) on the date of receipt.
3. *Rent received in advance.* Entiguan recognized €10 million for rent received in advance from a lessee for an unused warehouse building. Rent received in advance is deferred for accounting purposes but taxed on a cash basis.
4. *Loan.* Entiguan Sports secured a long-term loan for €550,000 in the current fiscal year. Interest is charged at 13.5 percent per annum and is payable at the end of each fiscal year.

Solutions:

	Carrying Amount (€)	Tax Base (€)	Temporary Difference (€)
1. Donations	0	0	0
2. Interest received in advance	300,000	0	(300,000)
3. Rent received in advance	10,000,000	0	(10,000,000)
4. Loan (capital)	550,000	550,000	0
Interest paid	0	0	0

Comments:

1. *Donations.* The amount of €100,000 was immediately expensed on Entiguan's income statement; therefore, the carrying amount is €0. Tax legislation does not allow donations to be deducted for tax purposes, so the tax base of the donations equals the carrying amount. Note that while the carrying amount and tax base are the same, the difference in the treatment of donations for accounting and tax purposes (expensed for accounting purposes, but not deductible for tax purposes) represents a permanent difference (a difference that will not be reversed in future). Permanent and temporary differences are elaborated on in section 4 and it will refer to this particular case with an expanded explanation.

2. *Interest received in advance.* Based on the information provided, for tax purposes, interest is deemed to accrue to the company on the date of receipt. For tax purposes it is thus irrelevant whether it is for the current or a future accounting period, it must be included in taxable income in the financial year received. Interest received in advance is, for accounting purposes though, included in the financial period in which it is deemed to have been earned. For this reason, the interest income received in advance is a balance sheet liability. It was not included on the income statement because the income relates to a future financial year. Because the full €300,000 is included in taxable income in the current fiscal year, the tax base is €300,000 − 300,000 = €0. Note that although interest received in advance and rent received in advance are both taxed, the timing depends on how the particular item is treated in tax legislation.

3. *Rent received in advance.* The result is similar to interest received in advance. The carrying amount of rent received in advance would be €10 million while the tax base is €0.

4. *Loan.* Repayment of the loan has no tax implications. The repayment of the capital amount does not constitute an income or expense. The interest paid is included as an expense in the calculation of taxable income as well as accounting income. Therefore, the tax base and carrying amount is €0. For clarity, the interest paid that would be included on the income statement for the year amounts to 13.5% × €550,000 = €74,250 if the loan was acquired at the beginning of the current fiscal year.

3.3   Changes in Income Tax Rates

The measurement of deferred tax assets and liabilities is based on current tax law. But if there are subsequent changes in tax laws or new income tax rates, existing deferred tax assets and liabilities must be adjusted for the effects of these changes. The resulting effects of the changes are also included in determining accounting profit in the period of change.

When income tax rates change, the deferred tax assets and liabilities are adjusted to the new tax rate. If income tax rates increase, deferred taxes (i.e., the deferred tax assets and liabilities) will also increase. Likewise, if income tax rates decrease, deferred taxes will decrease. A decrease in tax rates decreases deferred tax liabilities, which reduces future tax payments to the taxing authorities. A decrease in tax rates will also decrease deferred tax assets, which reduces their value toward the offset of future tax payments to the taxing authorities.

To illustrate the effect of a change in tax rate, consider Example 12-1 again. In that illustration, the timing difference that led to the recognition of a deferred tax liability for Reston Partners was attributable to differences in the method of depreciation and the related effects on the accounting carrying value and the asset tax base. The relevant information is restated below.

The carrying amount and tax base for the equipment is:

(£ millions)	2006	2005	2004
Equipment value for accounting purposes (*carrying amount*) (depreciation of £2,000/year)	£14,000	£16,000	£18,000
Equipment value for tax purposes (*tax base*) (depreciation of £2,857/year)	£11,429	£14,286	£17,143
Difference	£2,571	£1,714	£857

At a 30 percent income tax rate, the deferred tax liability was then determined as follows:

(£ millions)	2006	2005	2004
Deferred Tax Liability	£771	£514	£257
(Difference between tax base and carrying amount)			
2004: £(18,000 − 17,143) × 30% = £257			
2005: £(16,000 − 14,286) × 30% = £514			
2006: £(14,000 − 11,429) × 30% = £771			

For this illustration, assume that the taxing authority has changed the income tax rate to 25 percent for 2006. Although the difference between the carrying amount and the tax base of the depreciable asset are the same, the deferred tax liability for 2006 will be £643 (instead of £771 or a reduction of £128 in the liability). 2006: £(14,000 − 11,429) × 25% = £643.

Reston Partners' provision for income tax expense is also affected by the change in tax rates. Taxable income for 2006 will now be taxed at a rate of 25 percent. The benefit of the 2006 accelerated depreciation tax shield is now only £214 (£857 × 25%) instead of the previous £257 (a reduction of £43). In addition, the reduction in the beginning carrying value of the deferred tax liability for 2006 (the year of change) further reduces the income tax expense for 2006. The reduction in income tax expense attributable to the change in tax rate is £85: (30% − 25%) × £1714 = £85. Note that these two components together account for the reduction in the deferred tax liability (£43 + £85 = £128).

As may be seen from this discussion, changes in the income tax rate have an effect on a company's deferred tax asset and liability carrying values as well as an effect on the measurement of income tax expense in the year of change. The analyst must thus note that proposed changes in tax law can have a quantifiable effect on these accounts (and any related financial ratios that are derived from them) if the proposed changes are subsequently enacted into law.

4. TEMPORARY AND PERMANENT DIFFERENCES BETWEEN TAXABLE AND ACCOUNTING PROFIT

Temporary differences arise from a difference between the tax base and the carrying amount of assets and liabilities. The creation of a deferred tax asset or liability from a temporary difference is only possible if the difference reverses itself at some future date and to such an extent that the balance sheet item is expected to create future economic benefits for the company. IFRS and U.S. GAAP both prescribe the balance sheet liability method for recognition of deferred tax. This balance sheet method focuses on the recognition of a deferred tax asset or liability should there be a temporary difference between the carrying amount and tax base of balance sheet items.[3]

Permanent differences are differences between tax and financial reporting of revenue (expenses) that *will not* be reversed at some future date. Because they will not be reversed at a future date, these differences do not give rise to deferred tax. These items typically include:

- Income or expense items not allowed by tax legislation.
- Tax credits for some expenditures that directly reduce taxes.

Because no deferred tax item is created for permanent differences, all permanent differences result in a difference between the company's effective tax rate and statutory tax rate. The effective tax rate is also influenced by different statutory taxes should an entity conduct business in more than one tax jurisdiction. The formula for the reported effective tax rate is thus equal to:

Reported effective tax rate = Income tax expense ÷ Pretax income (accounting profit)

The net change in deferred tax during a reporting period is the difference between the balance of the deferred tax asset or liability for the current period and the balance of the previous period.

4.1. Taxable Temporary Differences

Temporary differences are further divided into two categories, namely taxable temporary differences and deductible temporary differences. **Taxable temporary differences** are temporary differences that result in a taxable amount in a future period when determining the taxable profit as the balance sheet item is recovered or settled. Taxable temporary differences result in a deferred tax liability when the carrying amount of an asset exceeds its tax base and, in the case of a liability, when the tax base of the liability exceeds its carrying amount.

Under U.S. GAAP, a deferred tax asset or liability is not recognized for unamortizable goodwill. Discounting deferred tax assets or liabilities is generally not allowed for temporary differences related to business combinations as it is for other temporary differences.

IFRS provides an exemption (i.e., deferred tax is not provided on the temporary difference) for the initial recognition of an asset or liability in a transaction that: (a) is not

---

[3]Previously, IAS 12 required recognition of deferred tax based on the deferred method (also known as the income statement method), which focused on timing differences. Timing differences are differences in the recognition of income and expenses for accounting and tax purposes that originate in one period and will reverse in a future period. Given the definition of timing differences, all timing differences are temporary differences, such as the different treatment of depreciation for tax and accounting purposes (although the timing is different with regard to the allowed depreciation for tax and accounting purposes, the asset will eventually be fully depreciated).

a business combination (e.g., joint ventures, branches and unconsolidated investments); and (b) affects neither accounting profit nor taxable profit at the time of the transaction. U.S. GAAP does not provide an exemption for these circumstances.

As a simple example, assume that a fictitious company, Corporate International, a holding company of various leisure-related businesses and holiday resorts, buys an interest in a hotel in the current financial year. The goodwill related to the transaction will be recognized on the financial statements, but the related tax liability will not, as it relates to the initial recognition of goodwill.

4.2. Deductible Temporary Differences

Deductible temporary differences are temporary differences that result in a reduction of or deduction from taxable income in a future period when the balance sheet item is recovered or settled. Deductible temporary differences result in a deferred tax asset when the tax base of an asset exceeds its carrying amount and, in the case of a liability, when the carrying amount of the liability exceeds its tax base. The recognition of a deferred tax asset is only allowed to the extent there is a reasonable expectation of future profits against which the asset or liability (that gave rise to the deferred tax asset) can be recovered or settled.

To determine the probability of sufficient future profits for utilization, one must consider the following: (1) Sufficient taxable temporary differences must exist that are related to the same tax authority and the same taxable entity; and (2) The taxable temporary differences are expected to reverse in the same periods as expected for the reversal of the deductible temporary differences.

As with deferred tax liabilities, IFRS and U.S. GAAP state that deferred tax assets should not be recognized in cases that would arise from the initial recognition of an asset or liability in transactions that are not a business combination and when, at the time of the transaction, there is no impact on either accounting or taxable profit. Any deferred tax assets that arise from investments in subsidiaries, branches, associates, and interests in joint ventures are recognized as a deferred tax asset.

IFRS and U.S. GAAP allow the creation of a deferred tax asset in the case of tax losses and tax credits. These two unique situations will be further elaborated on in section 6. IAS 12 *does not* allow the creation of a deferred tax asset arising from negative goodwill. Negative goodwill arises when the amount that an entity pays for an interest in a business is less than the net fair market value of the portion of assets and liabilities of the acquired company, based on the interest of the entity.

4.3. Examples of Taxable and Deductible Temporary Differences

Exhibit 12-1 summarizes how differences between the tax bases and carrying amounts of assets and liabilities give rise to deferred tax assets or deferred tax liabilities.

EXHIBIT 12-1   Treatment of Temporary Differences

Balance Sheet Item	Carrying Amount vs. Tax Base	Results in Deferred Tax Asset/Liability
Asset	Carrying amount > tax base	Deferred tax liability
Asset	Carrying amount < tax base	Deferred tax asset
Liability	Carrying amount > tax base	Deferred tax asset
Liability	Carrying amount < tax base	Deferred tax liability

EXAMPLE 12-4   Taxable and Deductible Temporary Differences

Examples 12-2 and 12-3 illustrated how to calculate the tax base of assets and liabilities, respectively. Based on the information provided in Examples 12-2 and 12-3, indicate whether the difference in the tax base and carrying amount of the assets and liabilities are temporary or permanent differences and whether a deferred tax asset or liability will be recognized based on the difference identified.

Solution to Example 12-2:

	Carrying Amount (€)	Tax Base (€)	Temporary Difference (€)	Will Result in Deferred Tax Asset/Liability
1. Dividends receivable	1,000,000	1,000,000	0	NA
2. Development costs	2,500,000	2,250,000	250,000	Deferred tax liability
3. Research costs	0	375,000	(375,000)	Deferred tax asset
4. Accounts receivable	1,500,000	1,218,750	281,250	Deferred tax liability

Example 12-2 included comments on the calculation of the carrying amount and tax base of the assets.

1. *Dividends receivable.* As a result of nontaxability, the carrying amount equals the tax base of dividends receivable. This constitutes a permanent difference and will not result in the recognition of any deferred tax asset or liability. A temporary difference constitutes a difference that will, at some future date, be reversed. Although the timing of recognition is different for tax and accounting purposes, in the end the full carrying amount will be expensed/recognized as income. A permanent difference will never be reversed. Based on tax legislation, dividends from a subsidiary are not recognized as income. Therefore, no amount will be reflected as dividend income when calculating the taxable income and the tax base of dividends receivable must be the total amount received, namely, €1 million. The taxable income and accounting profit will permanently differ with the amount of dividends receivable, even on future financial statements as an effect on the retained earnings reflected on the balance sheet.

2. *Development costs.* The difference between the carrying amount and tax base is a temporary difference that, in the future, will reverse. In this fiscal year, it will result in a deferred tax liability.

3. *Research costs.* The difference between the carrying amount and tax base is a temporary difference that results in a deferred tax asset. Remember the explanation in section 2 for deferred tax assets—a deferred tax asset arises because of an excess amount paid for taxes (when taxable income is greater than accounting profit), which is expected to be recovered from future operations. Based on accounting principles, the full amount was deducted resulting in a lower accounting profit,

while the taxable income by implication, should be greater because of the lower amount expensed.

4. *Accounts receivable*: The difference between the carrying amount and tax base of the asset is a temporary difference that will result in a deferred tax asset.

Solution to Example 12-3:

	Carrying Amount (€)	Tax Base (€)	Temporary Difference (€)	Will Result in Deferred Tax Asset/Liability
1. Donations	0	0	0	NA
2. Interest received in advance	300,000	0	(300,000)	Deferred tax asset
3. Rent received in advance	10,000,000	0	(10,000,000)	Deferred tax asset
4. Loan (capital)	550,000	550,000	0	NA
Interest paid	0	0	0	NA

Example 12-3 included extensive comments on the calculation of the carrying amount and tax base of the liabilities.

1. *Donations*. It was assumed that tax legislation does not allow donations to be deducted for tax purposes. No temporary difference results from donations, and thus a deferred tax asset or liability will not be recognized. This constitutes a permanent difference.
2. *Interest received in advance*. Interest received in advance results in a temporary difference that gives rise to a deferred tax asset. A deferred tax asset arises because of an excess amount paid for taxes (when taxable income is greater than accounting profit), which is expected to be recovered from future operations.
3. *Rent received in advance*. The difference between the carrying amount and tax base is a temporary difference that leads to the recognition of a deferred tax asset.
4. *Loan*. There are no temporary differences as a result of the loan or interest paid, and thus no deferred tax item is recognized.

4.4. Temporary Differences at Initial Recognition of Assets and Liabilities

In some situations the carrying amount and tax base of a balance sheet item may vary at initial recognition. For example, a company may deduct a government grant from the initial carrying amount of an asset or liability that appears on the balance sheet. For tax purposes, such grants may not be deducted when determining the tax base of the balance sheet item. In such circumstances, the carrying amount of the asset or liability will be lower than its tax base. Differences in the tax base of an asset or liability as a result of the circumstances described above may not be recognized as deferred tax assets or liabilities.

For example, a government may offer grants to small, medium, and micro enterprises (SMME) in an attempt to assist these entrepreneurs in their endeavors that contribute to the country's gross domestic product (GDP) and job creation. Assume that a particular grant is offered for infrastructure needs (office furniture, property, plant, and equipment, etc). In these circumstances, although the carrying amount will be lower than the tax base of the asset, the related deferred tax may not be recognized. As mentioned earlier, deferred tax assets and liabilities should not be recognized in cases that would arise from the initial recognition of an asset or liability in transactions that are not a business combination and when, at the time of the transaction, there is no impact on either accounting or taxable profit.

A deferred tax liability will also not be recognized at the initial recognition of goodwill. Although goodwill may be treated differently across tax jurisdictions, which may lead to differences in the carrying amount and tax base of goodwill, IAS 12 does not allow the recognition of such a deferred tax liability. Any impairment that an entity should, for accounting purposes, impose on goodwill will again result in a temporary difference between its carrying amount and tax base. Any impairment that an entity should, for accounting purposes, impose on goodwill and if part of the goodwill is related to the initial recognition, that part of the difference in tax base and carrying amount should not result in any deferred taxation because the initial deferred tax liability was not recognized. Any future differences between the carrying amount and tax base as a result of amortization and the deductibility of a portion of goodwill constitutes a temporary difference for which provision should be made.

4.5. Business Combinations and Deferred Taxes

The fair value of assets and liabilities acquired in a business combination is determined on the acquisition date and may differ from the previous carrying amount. It is highly probable that the values of acquired intangible assets, including goodwill, would differ from their carrying amounts. This temporary difference will affect deferred taxes as well as the amount of goodwill recognized as a result of the acquisition.

4.6. Investments in Subsidiaries, Branches, and Associates and Interests in Joint Ventures

Investments in subsidiaries, branches, associates, and interests in joint ventures may lead to temporary differences on the consolidated versus the parent's financial statements. The related deferred tax liabilities as a result of temporary differences will be recognized unless both of the following criteria are satisfied:

- The parent is in a position to control the timing of the future reversal of the temporary difference.
- It is probable that the temporary difference will not reverse in the future.

With respect to deferred tax assets related to subsidiaries, branches, and associates and interests, deferred tax assets will be recognized only if the following criteria are satisfied:

- The temporary difference will reverse in the future.
- Sufficient taxable profits exist against which the temporary difference can be used.

5. UNUSED TAX LOSSES AND TAX CREDITS

IAS 12 allows the recognition of unused tax losses and tax credits only to the extent that it is probable that in the future there will be taxable income against which the unused tax losses and credits can be applied. Under U.S. GAAP, a deferred tax asset is recognized in full but is then reduced by a valuation allowance if it is more likely than not that some or all of the deferred tax asset will not be realized. The same requirements for creation of a deferred tax asset as a result of deductible temporary differences also apply to unused tax losses and tax credits. The existence of tax losses may indicate that the entity cannot reasonably be expected to generate sufficient future taxable income. All other things held constant, the greater the history of tax losses, the greater the concern regarding the company's ability to generate future taxable profits.

Should there be concerns about the company's future profitability, then the deferred tax asset may not be recognized until it is realized. When assessing the probability that sufficient taxable profit will be generated in the future, the following criteria can serve as a guide:

- If there is uncertainty as to the probability of future taxable profits, a deferred tax asset as a result of unused tax losses or tax credits is recognized only to the extent of the available taxable temporary differences.
- Assess the probability that the entity will in fact generate future taxable profits before the unused tax losses and/or credits expire pursuant to tax rules regarding the carryforward of the unused tax losses.
- Verify that the above is with the same tax authority and based on the same taxable entity.
- Determine whether the past tax losses were a result of specific circumstances that are unlikely to be repeated.
- Discover if tax planning opportunities are available to the entity that will result in future profits. These may include changes in tax legislation that is phased in over more than one financial period to the benefit of the entity.

It is imperative that the timing of taxable and deductible temporary differences also be considered before creating a deferred tax asset based on unused tax credits.

6. RECOGNITION AND MEASUREMENT OF CURRENT AND DEFERRED TAX

Current taxes payable or recoverable from tax authorities are based on the applicable tax rates at the balance sheet date. Deferred taxes should be measured at the tax rate that is expected to apply when the asset is realized or the liability settled. With respect to the income tax for a current or prior period not yet paid, it is recognized as a tax liability until paid. Any amount paid in excess of any tax obligation is recognized as an asset. The income tax paid in excess or owed to tax authorities is separate from deferred taxes on the company's balance sheet.

When measuring deferred taxes in a jurisdiction, there are different forms of taxation such as income tax, capital gains tax (any capital gains made), or secondary tax on companies (tax payable on the dividends that a company declares) and possibly different tax bases for a balance sheet item (as in the case of government grants influencing the tax base of an asset such as property). In assessing which tax laws should apply, it is dependent on how the related asset or liability will be settled. It would be prudent to use the tax rate and tax base that is consistent with how it is expected the tax base will be recovered or settled.

Although deferred tax assets and liabilities are related to temporary differences expected to be recovered or settled at some future date, neither are discounted to present value in determining the amounts to be booked. Both must be adjusted for changes in tax rates.

Deferred taxes as well as income taxes should always be recognized on the income statement of an entity unless it pertains to:

- Taxes or deferred taxes charged directly to equity.
- A possible provision for deferred taxes relates to a business combination.

The carrying amount of the deferred tax assets and liabilities should also be assessed. The carrying amounts may change even though there may have been no change in temporary differences during the period evaluated. This can result from: *Deferring Taxes*

- Changes in tax rates.
- Reassessments of the recoverability of deferred tax assets.
- Changes in the expectations for how an asset will be recovered and what influences the deferred tax asset or liability.

All unrecognized deferred tax assets and liabilities must be reassessed at the balance sheet date and measured against the criteria of probable future economic benefits. If such a deferred asset is likely to be recovered, it may be appropriate to recognize the related deferred tax asset. *Subject to estimation errors.*

Different jurisdictions have different requirements for determining tax obligations that can range from different forms of taxation to different tax rates based on taxable income. When comparing financial statements of entities that conduct business in different jurisdictions subject to different tax legislation, the analyst should be cautious in reaching conclusions because of the potentially complex tax rules that may apply.

6.1. Recognition of a Valuation Allowance

Deferred tax assets must be assessed at each balance sheet date. If there is any doubt whether the deferral will be recovered, then the carrying amount should be reduced to the expected recoverable amount. Should circumstances subsequently change and suggest the future will lead to recovery of the deferral, the reduction may be reversed.

Deferred tax assets are reduced by creating a valuation allowance. Establishing a valuation allowance reduces the deferred tax asset and income in the period in which the allowance is established. Should circumstances change to such an extent that a deferred tax asset valuation allowance may be reduced, the reversal will increase the deferred tax asset and operating income. Because of the subjective judgment involved, an analyst should carefully scrutinize any such changes.

6.2. Recognition of Current and Deferred Tax Charged Directly to Equity

In general, IFRS and U.S. GAAP require that the recognition of deferred tax liabilities and current income tax should be treated similarly to the asset or liability that gave rise to the deferred tax liability or income tax based on accounting treatment. Should an item that gives rise to a deferred tax liability be taken directly to equity, the same should hold true for the resulting deferred tax.

The following are examples of such items:

- Revaluation of property, plant, and equipment (revaluations are not permissible under U.S. GAAP).
- Long-term investments at fair value.
- Changes in accounting policies.
- Errors corrected against the opening balance of retained earnings.
- Initial recognition of an equity component related to complex financial instruments.
- Exchange rate differences arising from the currency translation procedures for foreign operations.

Whenever it is determined that a deferred tax liability will not be reversed, an adjustment should be made to the liability. The deferred tax liability will be reduced and the amount by which it is reduced should be taken directly to equity. Any deferred taxes related to a business combination must also be recognized in equity.

Depending on the items that gave rise to the deferred tax liabilities, an analyst should exercise judgment regarding whether the taxes should be included with deferred tax liabilities or whether it should be taken directly to equity. It may be more appropriate simply to ignore deferred taxes.

EXAMPLE 12-5   Taxes Charged Directly to Equity

The following information pertains to Anderson Company (a hypothetical company). A building owned by Anderson Company was originally purchased for €1 million on 1 January 2004. For accounting purposes, buildings are depreciated at 5 percent a year on a straight-line basis and depreciation for tax purposes is 10 percent a year on a straight-line basis. On the first day of 2006 the building is revalued at €1,200,000. It is estimated that the remaining useful life of the building from the date of revaluation is 20 years. *Important:* For tax purposes the revaluation of the building is not recognized.

Based on the information provided, the following illustrates the difference in treatment of the building for accounting and tax purposes.

	Carrying Amount of Building	Tax Base of Building
Balance on 1 January 2004	€1,000,000	€1,000,000
Depreciation 2004	50,000	100,000
Balance on 31 December 2004	€950,000	€900,000
Depreciation 2005	50,000	100,000
Balance on 31 December 2005	€900,000	€800,000
Revaluation on 1 January 2006	300,000	NA
Balance on 1 January 2006	€1,200,000	€800,000
Depreciation 2006	60,000	100,000
Balance on 31 December 2006	€1,140,000	€700,000

Accumulated depreciation

Balance on 1 January 2004	€0	€0
Depreciation 2004	50,000	100,000
Balance on 31 December 2004	€50,000	€100,000
Depreciation 2005	50,000	100,000
Balance on 31 December 2005	€100,000	€200,000
Revaluation at 1 January 2006	(100,000)	NA
Balance on 1 January 2006	€0	€200,000
Depreciation 2006	60,000	100,000
Balance on 30 November 2006	€60,000	€300,000

	Carrying Amount	Tax Base
On 31 December 2004	€950,000	€900,000
On 31 December 2005	€900,000	€800,000
On 31 December 2006	€1,140,000	€700,000

31 December 2004: On 31 December 2004, different treatments for depreciation expense result in a temporary difference that gives rise to a deferred tax liability. The difference in the tax base and carrying amount of the building was a result of different depreciation amounts for tax and accounting purposes. Depreciation appears on the income statement. For this reason the deferred tax liability will also be reflected on the income statement. If we assume that the applicable tax rate in 2004 was 40 percent, then the resulting deferred tax liability will be 40% × (€950,000 − €900,000) = €20,000.

31 December 2005: As of 31 December 2005, the carrying amount of the building remains greater than the tax base. The temporary difference again gives rise to a deferred tax liability. Again, assuming the applicable tax rate to be 40 percent, the deferred tax liability from the building is 40% × (€900,000 − €800,000) = €40,000.

31 December 2006: On 31 December 2006, the carrying amount of the building again exceeds the tax base. This is not the result of disposals or additions, but is a result of the revaluation at the beginning of the 2006 fiscal year and the different rates of depreciation. The deferred tax liability would seem to be 40% × (€1,140,000 − €700,000) = €176,000, *but* the treatment is different than it was for the 2004 and 2005. In 2006, revaluation of the building gave rise to a balance sheet liability, namely "Revaluation surplus" in the amount of €300,000, which is not recognized for tax purposes.

The deferred tax liability would usually have been calculated as follows:

	2006	2005	2004
Deferred Tax Liability (Closing Balance at End of Fiscal Year)	€176,000	€40,000	€20,000
(Difference between tax base and carrying amount)			
2004: €(950,000 − 900,000) × 40% = 20,000			
2005: €(900,000 − 800,000) × 40% = 40,000			
2006: €(1,140,000 − 700,000) × 40% = 176,000			

The change in the deferred tax liability in 2004 is €20,000, in 2005: €20,000 (€40,000 − €20,000) and, it would seem, in 2006: €136,000 (€176,000 − €40,000). In 2006, although it would seem that the balance for deferred tax liability should be €176,000, the revaluation is not recognized for tax purposes. Only the portion of the difference between the tax base and carrying amount that is not a result of the revaluation is recognized as giving rise to a deferred tax liability.

The effect of the revaluation surplus and the associated tax effects are accounted for in a direct adjustment to equity. The revaluation surplus is reduced by the tax provision associated with the excess of the fair value over the carry value and it affects retained earnings (€300,000 × 40% = €120,000).

The deferred tax liability that should be reflected on the balance sheet is thus not €176,000 but only €56,000 (€176,000 − €120,000). Given the balance of deferred tax liability at the beginning of the 2006 fiscal year in the amount of €40,000, the change in the deferred tax liability is only €56,000 − €40,000 = €16,000.

In the future, at the end of each year, an amount equal to the depreciation as a result of the revaluation minus the deferred tax effect will be transferred from the revaluation reserve to retained earnings. In 2006 this will amount to a portion of depreciation resulting from the revaluation, €15,000 (€300,000 ÷ 20), minus the deferred tax effect of €6,000 (€15,000 × 40%), thus €9,000.

7. PRESENTATION AND DISCLOSURE

We will discuss the presentation and disclosure of income tax related information by way of example. The Consolidated Statements of Operations (Income Statements) and Consolidated Balance Sheets for Micron Technology (MU) are provided in Exhibits 12-2 and 12-3, respectively. Exhibit 12-4 provides the income tax note disclosures for MU for the 2004, 2005, and 2006 fiscal years.

MU's income tax provision (i.e., income tax expense) for fiscal year 2006 is $18 million (see Exhibit 12-2). The income tax note disclosure in Exhibit 12-4 reconciles how the income tax provision was determined beginning with MU's reported income before taxes (shown in Exhibit 12-2 as $433 million for fiscal year 2006). The note disclosure then denotes the income tax provision for 2006 that is current ($42 million), which is then offset by the deferred tax benefit for foreign taxes ($24 million), for a net income tax provision of $18 million. Exhibit 12-4 further shows a reconciliation of how the income tax provision was derived from the U.S. federal statutory rate. Many public companies comply with this required disclosure by displaying the information in percentage terms, but MU has elected to provide the disclosure in absolute dollar amounts. From this knowledge, we can see that the dollar amount shown for U.S. federal income tax provision at the statutory rate ($152 million) was determined by multiplying MU's income before taxes by the 35 percent U.S. federal statutory rate ($433 × 0.35 = $152). Furthermore, after considering tax credits and changes in the valuation allowance for deferred tax assets, MU's $18 million tax provision for 2006 is only 4.16 percent of its income before taxes ($18 ÷ $433 = 4.16%).

In addition, the note disclosure in Exhibit 12-4 provides detailed information about the derivation of the deferred tax assets ($26 million current and $49 million noncurrent) and deferred tax liabilities ($28 million noncurrent) that are shown on MU's consolidated balance sheet for fiscal year 2006 in Exhibit 12-3.

EXHIBIT 12-2   Micron Technology, Inc.: Consolidated Statements of Operations
($ millions except per share)

For the Year Ended	31 Aug. 2006	1 Sept. 2005	2 Sept. 2004
Net sales	$5,272	$4,880	$4,404
Cost of goods sold	4,072	3,734	3,090
Gross margin	1,200	1,146	1,314
Selling, general, and administrative	460	348	332
Research and development	656	604	755
Restructure	—	(1)	(23)
Other operating (income) expense, net	(266)	(22)	—
Operating income	350	217	250
Interest income	101	32	15
Interest expense	(25)	(47)	(36)
Other nonoperating income (expense), net	7	(3)	3
Income before taxes	433	199	232
Income tax (provision)	(18)	(11)	(75)
Noncontrolling interests in net income	(7)	—	—
Net income	$408	$188	$157
Earnings per share:			
Basic	$0.59	$0.29	$0.24
Diluted	$0.56	$0.27	$0.24
Number of shares used in per share calculations:			
Basic	692	648	641
Diluted	725	702	646

EXHIBIT 12-3   Micron Technology, Inc.: Consolidated Balance Sheets ($ millions)

As of	31 Aug. 2006	1 Sept. 2005
Assets		
Cash and equivalents	$1,431	$524
Short-term investments	1,648	766
Receivables	956	794
Inventories	963	771
Prepaid expenses	77	39
Deferred income taxes	26	32
Total current assets	5,101	2,926

(*Continued*)

EXHIBIT 12-3 *Continued*

As of	31 Aug. 2006	1 Sept. 2005
Intangible assets, net	388	260
Property, plant, and equipment, net	5,888	4,684
Deferred income taxes	49	30
Goodwill	502	16
Other assets	293	90
Total assets	$12,221	$8,006
Liabilities and Shareholders' Equity		
Accounts payable and accrued expenses	1,319	753
Deferred income	53	30
Equipment purchase contracts	123	49
Current portion of long-term debt	166	147
Total current liabilities	1,661	979
Long-term debt	405	1,020
Deferred income taxes	28	35
Other liabilities	445	125
Total liabilities	2,539	2,159
Commitments and contingencies	—	—
Noncontrolling interests in subsidiaries	1,568	—
Common stock of $0.10 par value, authorized 3 billion shares, issued and outstanding 749.4 million and 616.2 million shares	75	62
Additional capital	6,555	4,707
Retained earnings	1,486	1,078
Accumulated other comprehensive loss	(2)	—
Total shareholders' equity	8,114	5,847
Total liabilities and shareholders' equity	$12,221	$8,006

EXHIBIT 12-4 Micron Technology, Inc.: Income Taxes Note to the Consolidated Financial Statements

Income (loss) before taxes and the income tax (provision) benefit consisted of the following:

($ millions)	2006	2005	2004
Income (loss) before taxes:			
U.S.	$351	$108	($19)
Foreign	82	91	251
	$433	$199	$232

Income tax (provision) benefit:

Current:

U.S. federal	($12)	$—	$—
State	(1)	(3)	—
Foreign	(29)	(18)	(12)
	(42)	(21)	(12)

Deferred:

U.S. federal	—	—	—
State	—	—	—
Foreign	24	10	(63)
	24	10	(63)
Income tax (provision)	($18)	($11)	($75)

The company's income tax (provision) computed using the U.S. federal statutory rate and the company's income tax (provision) benefit is reconciled as follows:

($ millions)	2006	2005	2004
U.S. federal income tax (provision) benefit at statutory rate	$(152)	$(70)	$(81)
State taxes, net of federal benefit	5	6	(9)
Foreign operations	3	9	(44)
Change in valuation allowance	103	(7)	(11)
Tax credits	7	28	7
Export sales benefit	13	16	16
Resolution of tax matters	—	—	37
Other	3	7	10
	$(18)	$(11)	$(75)

State taxes reflect investment tax credits of $23 million, $14 million, and $9 million for 2006, 2005, and 2004, respectively. Deferred income taxes reflect the net tax effects of temporary differences between the bases of assets and liabilities for financial reporting and income tax purposes. The company's deferred tax assets and liabilities consist of the following as of the end of the periods shown below:

($ millions)	2006	2005
Deferred tax assets:		
Net operating loss and credit carryforwards	$929	$1,202
Basis differences in investments in joint ventures	301	—
Deferred revenue	160	76
Accrued compensation	51	40

Accounts payable	43	25
Inventories	16	33
Accrued product and process technology	11	12
Other	36	87
Gross deferred assets	1,547	1,475
Less valuation allowance	(915)	(1,029)
Deferred tax assets, net of valuation allowance	632	446
Deferred tax liabilities:		
Excess tax over book depreciation	(308)	(315)
Receivables	(91)	—
Intangibles	(68)	—
Unremitted earnings on certain subsidiaries	(58)	(49)
Product and process technology	(45)	(39)
Other	(15)	(16)
Deferred tax liabilities	(585)	(419)
Net deferred tax assets	$47	$27
Reported as:		
Current deferred tax assets	$26	$32
Noncurrent deferred tax assets	49	30
Noncurrent deferred tax liabilities	(28)	(35)
Net deferred tax assets _Overall_	$47	$27

Position

   The company has a valuation allowance against substantially all of its U.S. net deferred tax assets. As of 31 August 2006, the company had aggregate U.S. tax net operating loss carryforwards of $1.7 billion and unused U.S. tax credit carryforwards of $164 million. The company also has unused state tax net operating loss carryforwards of $1.4 billion and unused state tax credits of $163 million. During 2006, the company utilized approximately $1.1 billion of its U.S. tax net operating loss carryforwards as a result of IMFT, MP Mask, and related transactions.[4] Substantially all of the net operating loss carryforwards expire in 2022 to 2025 and substantially all of the tax credit carryforwards expire in 2013 to 2026.
   The changes in valuation allowance of ($114) million and $25 million in 2006 and 2005, respectively, are primarily a result of uncertainties of realizing certain U.S. net operating losses and certain tax credit carryforwards. The change in the valuation allowance in 2006 and 2005 includes $12 million and $2 million, respectively, for stock plan deductions, which will be credited to additional capital if realized.

---

[4]Micron Technology entered into profitable joint ventures and acquired profitable companies in 2006. The company was able to apply its net operating tax loss carryforwards (NOLs) toward these profits thereby reducing the income tax payments that would otherwise have been made without the NOLs.

Provision has been made for deferred taxes on undistributed earnings of non-U.S. subsidiaries to the extent that dividend payments from such companies are expected to result in additional tax liability. Remaining undistributed earnings of $686 million as of 31 August 2006 have been indefinitely reinvested; therefore, no provision has been made for taxes due upon remittance of these earnings. Determination of the amount of unrecognized deferred tax liability on these unremitted earnings is not practicable.

EXAMPLE 12-6   Financial Analysis Example

Use the financial statement information and disclosures provided by MU in Exhibits 12-2, 12-3, and 12-4 to answer the following questions:

1. MU discloses a valuation allowance of $915 million (see Exhibit 12-4) against total deferred assets of $1,547 million in 2006. Does the existence of this valuation allowance have any implications concerning MU's future earning prospects?
2. How would MU's deferred tax assets and deferred tax liabilities be affected if the federal statutory tax rate was changed to 32 percent? Would a change in the rate to 32 percent be beneficial to MU?
3. How would reported earnings have been affected if MU were not using a valuation allowance?
4. How would MU's $929 million in net operating loss carryforwards in 2006 (see Exhibit 12-4) affect the valuation that an acquiring company would be willing to offer?
5. Under what circumstances should the analyst consider MU's deferred tax liability as debt or as equity? Under what circumstances should the analyst exclude MU's deferred tax liability from both debt and equity when calculating the debt-to-equity ratio?

Solution to 1. According to Exhibit 12-4, MU's deferred tax assets expire gradually until 2026 (2022 to 2025 for the net operating loss carryforwards and 2013 to 2026 for the tax credit carryforwards). Because the company is relatively young, it is likely that most of these expirations occur toward the end of that period. Because cumulative federal net operating loss carryforwards total $1.7 billion, the valuation allowance could imply that MU is not reasonably expected to earn $1.7 billion over the next 20 years. However, as we can see in Exhibit 12-2, MU has earned profits for 2006, 2005, and 2004, thereby showing that the allowance could be adjusted downward if the company continues to generate profits in the future, making it more likely than not that the deferred tax asset would be recognized.

Solution to 2. MU's total deferred tax assets exceed total deferred tax liabilities by $47 million. A change in the federal statutory tax rate to 32 percent from the current rate of 35 percent would make these net deferred assets less valuable. Also, because it is possible that the deferred tax asset valuation allowance could be adjusted downward in the future (see discussion to solution 1 above), the impact could be far greater in magnitude.

Solution to 3. The disclosure in Exhibit 12-4 shows that the reduction in the valuation allowance reduced the income tax provision as reported on the income statement by $103 million in 2006. Additional potential reductions in the valuation allowance could similarly reduce reported income taxes (actual tax income taxes would not be affected by a valuation allowance established for financial reporting) in future years (see discussion to solution 1 above).

Solution to 4. If an acquiring company is profitable, it may be able to use MU's tax loss carryforwards to offset its own tax liabilities. The value to an acquirer would be the present value of the carryforwards, based on the acquirer's tax rate and expected timing of realization. The higher the acquiring company's tax rate, and the more profitable the acquirer, the sooner it would be able to benefit. Therefore, an acquirer with a high current tax rate would theoretically be willing to pay more than an acquirer with a lower tax rate.

Solution to 5. The analyst should classify the deferred tax liability as debt if the liability is expected to reverse with subsequent tax payment. If the liability is not expected to reverse, there is no expectation of a cash outflow and the liability should be treated as equity. By way of example, future company losses may preclude the payment of any income taxes or changes in tax laws could result in taxes that are never paid. The deferred tax liability should be excluded from both debt and equity when both the amounts and timing of tax payments resulting from the reversals of temporary differences are uncertain.

8. COMPARISION OF IFRS AND U.S. GAAP

As mentioned earlier, though IFRS and U.S. GAAP follow similar conventions on many tax issues, there are some notable differences (such as revaluation). Exhibit 12-5 summarizes many of the key similarities and differences between IFRS and U.S. GAAP. Though both frameworks require a provision for deferred taxes, there are differences in the methodologies.

EXHIBIT 12-5: Deferred Income Tax Issues: IFRS and U.S. GAAP Methodology
Similarities and Differences *Goodwill Writeoff*

Issue	IFRS	U.S. GAAP
General Considerations		
General approach	Full provision	Similar to IFRS.
Basis for deferred tax assets and liabilities	Temporary differences—i.e., the difference between carrying amount and tax base of assets and liabilities (see exceptions below).	Similar to IFRS.
Exceptions (i.e., deferred tax is not provided on the temporary difference)	Nondeductible goodwill (that which is not deductible for tax purposes) does not give rise to taxable temporary differences.	Similar to IFRS, except no initial recognition exemption and special requirements apply in computing deferred tax on leveraged leases.
	Initial recognition of an asset or liability in a transaction that: (a) is not a business combination; and	

Issue	IFRS	U.S. GAAP
	(b) affects neither accounting profit nor taxable profit at the time of the transaction. Other amounts that do not have a tax consequence (commonly referred to as permanent differences) exist and depend on the tax rules and jurisdiction of the entity.	
Specific Applications		
Revaluation of plant, property, and equipment and intangible assets	Deferred tax recognized in equity.	Not applicable, as revaluation is prohibited.
Foreign nonmonetary assets/liabilities when the tax reporting currency is not the functional currency	Deferred tax is recognized on the difference between the carrying amount, determined using the historical rate of exchange, and the tax base, determined using the balance sheet date exchange rate.	No deferred tax is recognized for differences related to assets and liabilities that are remeasured from local currency into the functional currency resulting from changes in exchange rates or indexing for tax purposes.
Investments in subsidiaries—treatment of undistributed profit	Deferred tax is recognized except when the parent is able to control the distribution of profit and it is probable that the temporary difference will not reverse in the foreseeable future.	Deferred tax is required on temporary differences arising after 1992 that relate to investments in domestic subsidiaries, unless such amounts can be recovered tax-free and the entity expects to use that method. No deferred taxes are recognized on undistributed profits of foreign subsidiaries that meet the indefinite reversal criterion.
Investments in joint ventures—treatment of undistributed profit	Deferred tax is recognized except when the venturer can control the sharing of profits and if it is probable that the temporary difference will not reverse in the foreseeable future.	Deferred tax is required on temporary differences arising after 1992 that relate to investment in domestic corporate joint ventures. No deferred taxes are recognized on undistributed profits of foreign corporate joint ventures that meet the indefinite reversal criterion.
Investment in associates—treatment of undistributed profit	Deferred tax is recognized except when the investor can control the sharing of profits and it is probable that the temporary difference will not reverse in the foreseeable future.	Deferred tax is recognized on temporary differences relating to investments in investees.
Uncertain tax positions	Reflects the tax consequences that follow from the manner in which the entity expects, at the balance sheet date, to be paid to (recovered from) the taxation authorities.	A tax benefit from an uncertain tax position may be recognized only if it is "more likely than not" that the tax position is sustainable based on its technical merits. The tax position is measured as the largest amount of tax benefit that is greater than 50 percent likely of being realized upon ultimate settlement.

(Continued)

EXHIBIT 12-5   *Continued*

Issue	IFRS	U.S. GAAP
Measurement of Deferred Tax		
Tax rates	Tax rates and tax laws that have been enacted or substantively enacted.	Use of substantively enacted rates is not permitted. Tax rate and tax laws used must have been enacted.
Recognition of deferred tax assets	A deferred tax asset is recognized if it is probable (more likely than not) that sufficient taxable profit will be available against which the temporary difference can be utilized.	A deferred tax asset is recognized in full but is then reduced by a valuation allowance if it is more likely than not that some or all of the deferred tax asset will not be realized.
Business Combinations—Acquisitions		
Step-up of acquired assets/liabilities to fair value	Deferred tax is recorded unless the tax base of the asset is also stepped up.	Similar to IFRS.
Previously unrecognized tax losses of the acquirer	A deferred tax asset is recognized if the recognition criteria for the deferred tax asset are met as a result of the acquisition. Offsetting credit is recorded in income.	Similar to IFRS, except the offsetting credit is recorded against goodwill.
Tax losses of the acquiree (initial recognition)	Similar requirements as for the acquirer except the offsetting credit is recorded against goodwill.	Similar to IFRS.
Subsequent resolution of income tax uncertainties in a business combination	If the resolution is more than one year after the year in which the business combination occurred, the result is recognized on the income statement.	The subsequent resolution of any tax uncertainty relating to a business combination is recorded against goodwill.
Subsequent recognition of deferred tax assets that were not "probable" at the time of the business combination	A deferred tax asset that was not considered probable at the time of the business combination but later becomes probable is recognized. The adjustment is to income tax expense with a corresponding adjustment to goodwill. The income statement shows a debit to goodwill expense and a credit to income tax expense. There is no time limit for recognition of this deferred tax asset.	The subsequent resolution of any tax uncertainty relating to a business combination is recorded first against goodwill, then noncurrent intangibles, and then income tax expense. There is no time limit for recognition of this deferred tax asset.
Presentation of Deferred Tax		
Offset of deferred tax assets and liabilities	Permitted only when the entity has a legally enforceable right to offset and the balance relates to tax levied by the same authority.	Similar to IFRS.

Issue	IFRS	U.S. GAAP
Current/noncurrent	Deferred tax assets and liabilities are classified net as noncurrent on the balance sheet, with supplemental note disclosure for (1) the components of the temporary differences, and (2) amounts expected to be recovered within 12 months and more than 12 months from the balance sheet date.	Deferred tax assets and liabilities are either classified as current or noncurrent, based on the classification of the related non-tax asset or liability for financial reporting. Tax assets not associated with an underlying asset or liability are classified based on the expected reversal period.
Reconciliation of actual and expected tax expense	Required. Computed by applying the applicable tax rates to accounting profit, disclosing also the basis on which the applicable tax rates are calculated.	Required for public companies only. Calculated by applying the domestic federal statutory tax rates to pre-tax income from continuing operations.

Sources: IFRS: IAS 1, IAS 12, and IFRS 3.
U.S. GAAP: FAS 109 and FIN 48.
"Similarities and Differences–A Comparison of IFRS and U.S. GAAP,"
PricewaterhouseCoopers, October 2006

9. SUMMARY   *Current Assets, Current For Both*

Income taxes are a significant category of expense for profitable companies. Analyzing income tax expenses is often difficult for the analyst because there are many permanent and temporary timing differences between the accounting that is used for income tax reporting and the accounting that is used for financial reporting on company financial statements. The financial statements and notes to the financial statements of a company provide important information that the analyst needs to assess financial performance and to compare a company's financial performance with other companies. Key concepts in this chapter are as follows:

- Differences between the recognition of revenue and expenses for tax and accounting purposes may result in taxable income differing from accounting profit. The discrepancy is a result of different treatments of certain income and expenditure items.
- The tax base of an asset is the amount that will be deductible for tax purposes as an expense in the calculation of taxable income as the company expenses the tax basis of the asset. If the economic benefit will not be taxable, the tax base of the asset will be equal to the carrying amount of the asset.
- The tax base of a liability is the carrying amount of the liability less any amounts that will be deductible for tax purposes in the future. With respect to revenue received in advance, the tax base of such a liability is the carrying amount less any amount of the revenue that will not be taxable in future.
- Temporary differences arise from recognition of differences in the tax base and carrying amount of assets and liabilities. The creation of a deferred tax asset or liability as a result of a temporary difference will only be allowed if the difference reverses itself at some future date and to the extent that it is expected that the balance sheet item will create future economic benefits for the company.

- Permanent differences result in a difference in tax and financial reporting of revenue (expenses) that will not be reversed at some future date. Because it will not be reversed at a future date, these differences do not constitute temporary differences and do not give rise to a deferred tax asset or liability.
- Current taxes payable or recoverable are based on the applicable tax rates on the balance sheet date of an entity; in contrast, deferred taxes should be measured at the tax rate that is expected to apply when the asset is realized or the liability settled.
- All unrecognized deferred tax assets and liabilities must be reassessed on the appropriate balance sheet date and measured against their probable future economic benefit.
- Deferred tax assets must be assessed for their prospective recoverability. If it is probable that they will not be recovered at all or partly, the carrying amount should be reduced through the use of a deferred asset valuation allowance.

PRACTICE PROBLEMS

1. Using the straight-line method of depreciation for reporting purposes and accelerated depreciation for tax purposes would *most likely* result in a
   A. valuation allowance.
   B. deferred tax liability.
   C. temporary difference.

2. In early 2009 Sanborn Company must pay the tax authority €37,000 on the income it earned in 2008. This amount was recorded on the company's 31 December 2008 financial statements as
   A. taxes payable.
   B. income tax expense.
   C. a deferred tax liability.

3. Income tax expense reported on a company's income statement equals taxes payable, plus the net increase in
   A. deferred tax assets and deferred tax liabilities.
   B. deferred tax assets, less the net increase in deferred tax liabilities.
   C. deferred tax liabilities, less the net increase in deferred tax assets.

4. Analysts should treat deferred tax liabilities that are expected to reverse as
   A. equity.
   B. liabilities.
   C. neither liabilities nor equity.

5. Deferred tax liabilities should be treated as equity when
   A. they are not expected to reverse.
   B. the timing of tax payments is uncertain.
   C. the amount of tax payments is uncertain.

6. When both the timing and amount of tax payments is uncertain, analysts should treat deferred tax liabilities as

    A. equity.
    B. liabilities.
    C. neither liabilities nor equity.

7. When accounting standards require recognition of an expense that is not permitted under tax laws, the result is a
    A. deferred tax liability.
    B. temporary difference.
    C. permanent difference.

8. When certain expenditures result in tax credits that directly reduce taxes, the company will *most likely* record
    A. a deferred tax asset.
    B. a deferred tax liability.
    C. no deferred tax asset or liability.

9. When accounting standards require an asset to be expensed immediately but tax rules require the item to be capitalized and amortized, the company will *most likely* record
    A. a deferred tax asset.
    B. a deferred tax liability.
    C. no deferred tax asset or liability.

10. A company incurs a capital expenditure that may be amortized over five years for accounting purposes, but over four years for tax purposes. The company will *most likely* record
    A. a deferred tax asset.
    B. a deferred tax liability.
    C. no deferred tax asset or liability.

11. A company receives advance payments from customers that are immediately taxable but will not be recognized for accounting purposes until the company fulfills its obligation. The company will *most likely* record
    A. a deferred tax asset.
    B. a deferred tax liability.
    C. no deferred tax asset or liability.

Use the following disclosure related to income taxes to answer Problems 12–14.
NOTE I
Income Taxes
The components of earnings before income taxes are as follows ($ thousands):

	2007	**2006**	**2005**
Earnings before income taxes:			
United States	$88,157	$75,658	$59,973
Foreign	116,704	113,509	94,760
Total	$204,861	$189,167	$154,733

The components of the provision for income taxes are as follows ($ thousands):

	2007	2006	2005
Income taxes			
Current:			
Federal	$30,632	$22,031	$18,959
Foreign	28,140	27,961	22,263
	$58,772	$49,992	$41,222
Deferred:			
Federal	($4,752)	$5,138	$2,336
Foreign	124	1,730	621
	(4,628)	6,868	2,957
Total	$54,144	$56,860	$44,179

12. In 2007, the company's U.S. GAAP income statement recorded a provision for income taxes *closest* to
   A. $30,632.
   B. $54,144.
   C. $58,772.

13. The company's effective tax rate was *highest* in
   A. 2005.
   B. 2006.
   C. 2007.

14. Compared to the company's effective tax rate on U.S. income, its effective tax rate on foreign income was
   A. lower in each year presented.
   B. higher in each year presented.
   C. higher in some periods and lower in others.

15. Zimt AG presents its financial statements in accordance with International Financial Reporting Standards. In 2007, Zimt discloses a valuation allowance of €1,101 against total deferred tax assets of €19,201. In 2006, Zimt disclosed a valuation allowance of €1,325 against total deferred tax assets of €17,325. The change in the valuation allowance *most likely* indicates that Zimt's
   A. deferred tax liabilities were reduced in 2007.
   B. expectations of future earning power has increased.
   C. expectations of future earning power has decreased.

16. Cinnamon, Inc. recorded a total deferred tax asset in 2007 of $12,301, offset by a $12,301 valuation allowance. Cinnamon *most likely*
   A. fully utilized the deferred tax asset in 2007.
   B. has an equal amount of deferred tax assets and deferred tax liabilities.
   C. expects not to earn any taxable income before the deferred tax asset expires.

Use the following income tax disclosure to answer Problems 17–19.

The tax effects of temporary differences that give rise to deferred tax assets and liabilities are as follows ($ thousands):

	2007	**2006**
Deferred tax assets:		
Accrued expenses	$8,613	$7,927
Tax credit and net operating loss carryforwards	2,288	2,554
LIFO and inventory reserves	5,286	4,327
Other	2,664	2,109
Deferred tax assets	18,851	16,917
Valuation allowance	(1,245)	(1,360)
Net deferred tax assets	$17,606	$15,557
Deferred tax liabilities:		
Depreciation and amortization	(27,338)	(29,313)
Compensation and retirement plans	(3,831)	(8,963)
Other	(1,470)	(764)
Deferred tax liabilities	(32,639)	(39,040)
Net deferred tax liability	($15,033)	($23,483)

17. A reduction in the statutory tax rate would *most likely* benefit the company's
    A. income statement and balance sheet.
    B. income statement but not the balance sheet.
    C. balance sheet but not the income statement.

18. If the valuation allowance had been the same in 2007 as it was in 2006, the company would have reported $115 *higher*
    A. net income.
    B. deferred tax asset.
    C. income tax expense.

19. Compared to the provision for income taxes in 2007, the company's cash tax payments were
    A. lower.
    B. higher.
    C. the same.

Use the following income tax disclosure to answer Problems 20–22.

A company's provision for income taxes resulted in effective tax rates attributable to loss from continuing operations before cumulative effect of change in accounting principles that varied from the statutory federal income tax rate of 34 percent, as summarized in the table below.

Year ended 30 June	2007	2006	2005
Expected federal income tax expense (benefit) from continuing operations at 34 percent	($112,000)	$768,000	$685,000
Expenses not deductible for income tax purposes	357,000	32,000	51,000
State income taxes, net of federal benefit	132,000	22,000	100,000
Change in valuation allowance for deferred tax assets	(150,000)	(766,000)	(754,000)
Income tax expense	$227,000	$56,000	$82,000

20. In 2007, the company's net income (loss) was *closest* to
   A. ($217,000).
   B. ($329,000).
   C. ($556,000).

21. The $357,000 adjustment in 2007 *most likely* resulted in
   A. an increase in deferred tax assets.
   B. an increase in deferred tax liabilities.
   C. no change to deferred tax assets and liabilities.

22. Over the three years presented, changes in the valuation allowance for deferred tax assets were *most likely* indicative of
   A. decreased prospect for future profitability.
   B. increased prospects for future profitability.
   C. assets being carried at a higher value than their tax base.

CHAPTER 13

LONG-TERM LIABILITIES AND LEASES

Elizabeth A. Gordon

Temple University
Philadelphia, Pennsylvania

Elaine Henry, CFA

University of Miami
Coral Gables, Florida

LEARNING OUTCOMES

After completing this chapter, you will be able to do the following:

- Compute the effects of debt issuance and amortization of bond discounts and premiums on financial statements and ratios.
- Explain the role of debt covenants in protecting creditors by restricting a company's ability to invest, pay dividends, or make other operating and strategic decisions.
- Describe the presentation of, and disclosures relating to, financing liabilities.
- Determine the effects of changing interest rates on the market value of debt and on financial statements and ratios.
- Describe two types of debt with equity features (convertible debt and debt with warrants) and calculate the effect of issuance of such instruments on a company's debt ratios.
- Discuss the motivations for leasing assets instead of purchasing them and the incentives for reporting the leases as operating leases rather than finance leases.
- Determine the effects of finance and operating leases on the financial statements and ratios of the lessees and lessors.
- Distinguish between a sales-type lease and a direct financing lease, and determine the effects on the financial statements and ratios of the lessors.

- Describe the types and economic consequences of off-balance-sheet financing, and determine how take-or-pay contracts, throughput arrangements, and the sale of receivables affect financial statements and selected financial ratios.

1. INTRODUCTION

A **long-term liability** broadly represents a probable sacrifice of economic benefits over a future period generally greater than one year. Common types of long-term liabilities reported in a company's financial statements include long-term debt (i.e., bonds payable, long-term notes payable), finance leases, and pension liabilities. Other contractual obligations, referred to as "off-balance-sheet financing," are not reported as debt in the financial statements, yet represent probable future cash outflows that are similar in nature to debt and must be disclosed. This chapter focuses on bonds payable, leases, and off-balance-sheet financing. A subsequent chapter will cover pension liabilities.

   This chapter is organized as follows: Section 2 describes and illustrates the accounting for long-term bonds including issuing bonds, recording interest expense and interest payments, amortizing any discount or premium, extinguishing debt, and disclosing information about debt financings. Section 3 describes the treatment of debt with equity features. Section 4 describes accounting for leases including benefits of leasing, finance versus operating leases, and direct financing versus sales-type leases. Section 5 discusses other types of off-balance-sheet financing, their economic consequences, and their effect on selected financial ratios. Section 6 summarizes the chapter, and practice problems in the CFA Institute multiple-choice format conclude the chapter.

2. BONDS PAYABLE

This section discusses accounting for bonds payable, the most common form of long-term debt. In some contexts (e.g., some government debt obligations), the word *bond* is used only for a debt security with a maturity of 10 years or longer, with *note* referring to a debt security with a maturity between 2 and 10 years, and *bill* referring to a debt security with a maturity of less than 2 years. In this chapter, we will use the terms *bond* and *note* interchangeably. In the following sections, we discuss bond issuance, bond interest expense and payment, repayment of bonds including retirements and redemptions, and other issues concerning disclosures related to debt. We will also present debt covenants and an issue related to market rates and fair values.

2.1. Accounting for Bond Issuance

Bonds are contractual promises of cash payments in the future in exchange for cash received today, issued by a company (or other borrowing entity) to its lenders (i.e., bondholders). The cash a company receives when it issues bonds (sales proceeds) is based on the value of the bonds when issued, determined as the present value of future cash payments the company promises in the bond agreement.

   Ordinarily, bonds consist of two types of future cash payments that are discounted to present value: (1) the face value of the bonds, and (2) periodic interest payments. The **face value** of the bonds is the amount of cash payable by the company to the bondholders when the bonds mature. The face value is also referred to as the principal, par value, stated value, or maturity value. The maturity of the bonds (the date on which the face value is paid to bond-holders) is also stated in the bond contract and is generally a number of years in the future. Periodic interest payments are made based on the interest rate promised in the bond contract applied to the bonds' face value. The rate at which the periodic interest payments are calculated is also referred to as the **stated rate**, nominal rate, or coupon rate. For fixed-rate bonds (the primary focus of our discussion here), the stated rate remains unchanged throughout the life of the bonds. How often interest payments are made (i.e., frequency) is also stated in the bond agreement. For instance, bonds paying interest semiannually will make two interest payments a year.

The **market rate** of interest is the rate demanded by purchasers of the bonds, given the risks associated with future cash payment obligations of the particular bond issue. The market rate of interest often differs from the stated rate because of interest rate fluctuations that occur between the time the issuer establishes the stated rate and the day the bonds are actually available to investors. If the market rate of interest when the bonds are issued equals the stated rate, the market value of the bonds, and thus the amount of cash the company receives (the selling price produces the sales proceeds), will equal the face value of the bonds. When a bond is issued at a price equal to its face value, the bond is said to have been issued at par. Alternatively, if the stated rate of interest when the bonds are issued is higher than the market rate, the market value of the bonds, and thus the amount of cash the company receives, will be higher than the face value of the bonds. In other words, the bonds will sell at a premium to face value. If the stated rate of interest is lower than the market rate, the market value and thus the sale proceeds from the bonds will be less than the face value of the bonds (i.e., will sell at a discount to face value). The market rate at the time of issuance is the effective interest rate or borrowing rate that the company incurs on the debt. For the issuing company, interest expense reported for the bonds in the financial statements is based on the effective interest rate.

On the issuing company's statement of cash flows, the cash received (sales proceeds) from issuing bonds is reported as a financing cash inflow. On the issuing company's balance sheet, bonds payable are normally reported at **net book value,** that is, the face value of the bonds minus any unamortized discount or plus any unamortized premium. In a later section, we will briefly discuss instances where bonds payable are not reported at net book value.

The following two examples illustrate accounting for bonds issued at face value and then accounting for bonds issued at a discount to face value. Accounting for bonds issued at a premium involves steps similar to the steps followed in the examples below. For simplicity, these examples assume a flat interest rate yield curve, that is, that the market rate of interest is the same for each period. More precise bond valuations use the interest rate applicable to each time period in which a payment of interest or principal occurs.

EXAMPLE 13-1   Bonds Issued at Face Value

Debond Corp. (a hypothetical company) issues £1 million worth of five-year bonds, dated 1 January 2008, when the market interest rate is 5 percent per annum. The bonds pay 5 percent interest annually on 31 December. What are the sales proceeds of the bonds when issued, and how is the issuance reflected in the financial statements?

Solution. The sales proceeds of the bonds when issued are £1 million. The issuance is reflected on the balance sheet as a long-term liability, bonds payable, of £1 million. The issuance is reflected in the statement of cash flows as a financing cash inflow of £1 million.

Calculating the value of the bonds at issuance and thus the sales proceeds involves three steps: identifying key features of the bonds, determining future cash flows, and discounting the future cash flows to the present.

First, identify key features of the bonds to determine sales proceeds:

Face value (principal)	£1,000,000	
Time to maturity	5 years	
Stated interest rate	5%	
Market rate at issuance	5%	
Frequency of interest payments	1 per year	
Interest payment	£50,000	Each annual interest payment is the face value times the stated interest rate. Here, £1,000,000 × 5 percent. If interest is paid other than annually, adjust the interest rate to match the interest payment period (e.g., divide the annual stated rate by two for semiannual interest payments).

Second, determine future cash outflows. Debond will pay bondholders £1 million when the bonds mature in five years. On 31 December of each year until the bonds mature, Debond will make an interest payment of £50,000 (£1 million face value times 5 percent stated interest rate).

Date	Interest Payment	Present Value at Market Rate (5%)	Face Value Payment	Present Value at Market Rate (5%)	Total
31 December 2008	£ 50,000	£47,619			
31 December 2009	50,000	45,351			
31 December 2010	50,000	43,192			
31 December 2011	50,000	41,135			
31 December 2012	50,000	39,176	£1,000,000	£783,526	
Total		£216,474		£783,526	£1,000,000
					Sales proceeds: Cash inflow when bonds are issued

Third, sum the present value of the future payments of interest and principal to obtain the value of the bonds and thus the sales proceeds from issuing the bonds. In this example, the sum is £1 million (£216,474 + £783,526).

The present value of each cash outflow shown in the table above is calculated as:

$$PV = \frac{\text{Cash Outflow}}{(1 + r)^t}$$

where:

r = market rate
t = number of periods

For example, the present value of the £50,000 interest payment to be made at the end of 2011 is calculated as £50,000 ÷ $(1.05)^4$ = £41,135.

Because it is assumed that the market rate is the same for each year, an alternative way to calculate the present value of interest payments is to treat the five annual interest payments as an annuity and use the formula for finding the present value of an annuity:

$$PV = PMT\left[\frac{1 - \dfrac{1}{(1 + r)^t}}{r}\right]$$

where:

PMT = annual payment
r = market rate
t = number of periods

In this example, the present value of the five annual interest payments is:

£50,000 × [(1 − (1 ÷ $(1.05)^5$) ÷ 0.05]
= £50,000 × [(1 − 0.7835) ÷ 0.05]
= £50,000 × 4.3295
= £216,474

The amount of sales proceeds is reported as a financing cash inflow in the issuing company's statement of cash flows. Because these bonds are issued at par, there is no discount or premium to face value. Therefore, the amount of debt reported as a long-term liability on the issuing company's balance sheet (i.e., the net book value) is equal to the face value of the bonds.

The price of bonds is also expressed in terms of face value. For instance, the price of bonds issued at par, as in the above example, is 100 (i.e., 100 percent of face value). In the following example, in which bonds are issued at a discount, the price is 95.79 (i.e., 95.79 percent of face value).

EXAMPLE 13-2   Bonds Issued at a Discount

Debond Corp. (a hypothetical company) issues £1 million worth of five-year bonds, dated 1 January 2008, when the market interest rate is 6 percent. The bonds pay 5 percent interest annually on 31 December. What are the sales proceeds of the bonds when issued, and how is the issuance reflected in the financial statements?

Solution: The sales proceeds from the bond issuance is £957,876. The issuance is reflected on the balance sheet as a long-term liability, bonds payable, of £957,876, which is composed of the face value of £1 million minus a discount of £42,124. The issuance is reflected in the statement of cash flows as a financing cash inflow of £957,876.

     Calculating the value of the bonds at issuance and thus the sales proceeds involves three steps: identifying key features of the bonds, determining future cash flows, and discounting the future cash flows to the present.

     First, identify key features of the bonds to determine sales proceeds:

Face value (principal)	£1,000,000	
Time to maturity	5 years	
Stated interest rate	5%	
Market rate at issuance	6%	
Frequency of interest payments	1 per year	
Interest payment	£50,000	Each annual interest payment is the face value times the stated interest rate. Here, £1 million × 5%. If interest is paid other than annually, adjust the interest rate to match the interest payment period (e.g., divide the annual stated rate by two for semiannual interest payments).

     Second, determine future cash outflows. Debond will pay bondholders £1 million when the bonds mature in five years. On 31 December each year until the bonds mature, Debond makes an interest payment of £50,000 (£1 million face value times 5 percent stated interest rate).

Date	Interest Payment	Present Value at Market Rate (6%)	Face Value Payment	Present Value at Market Rate (6%)	Total
31 December 2008	£50,000	£47,170			
31 December 2009	50,000	44,500			
31 December 2010	50,000	41,981			
31 December 2011	50,000	39,605			
31 December 2012	50,000	37,363	£1,000,000	£747,258	
Total		£210,618		£747,258	£957,876
					Sales proceeds: Cash inflow when bonds are issued

Third, sum the present value of the principal payment and the present value of the interest payments to obtain the value of the bonds at issuance of £957,876 (£210,618 + £747,258). This is the amount of sales proceeds at issuance. Because the market rate when the bonds are issued (6 percent) is greater than the bonds' stated rate (5 percent), the bonds sell at a discount of £42,124 (£1 million − £957,876). Present values are calculated as in the previous example.

Cash of £957,876 from the bonds issuance is reported as a financing cash inflow in the issuing company's statement of cash flows. The amount of debt reported as a long-term liability on the issuing company's balance sheet is also £957,876 which is composed of the face value of the bonds of £1 million minus a discount of £42,124.

In Example 13-2, the bonds were issued at a discount to face value because the bonds' stated rate of 5 percent was less than the market rate. Bonds may also be issued with a stated rate of zero, i.e. zero-coupon bonds. The value of zero-coupon bonds is based on the present value of the principal payment only (because there are no periodic interest payments), so zero-coupon bonds are always issued at a discount to face value.

Most corporate bonds, other than zero-coupon bonds, are currently issued at face value. Exhibit 13-1 lists four new issues of corporate bonds, including two that were priced at other than par. The list provides information about each issue's credit rating, coupon rate, coupon frequency, maturity date, issue price, yield to maturity (YTM) or market rate, and call provisions (provisions allowing the issuer to redeem the bonds prior to maturity). The final column in the list shows the estimated total cost to buy 25 bonds with a face value of $1,000 each, simply because these examples were obtained in response to a requested price quote for purchasing $25,000 face value of bonds. (Note that a bond purchaser pays the quoted price plus any interest accrued since the last interest payment. Because these bonds are all new issues, there is no accrued interest in the estimated total cost of the bonds.)

The first issue in the exhibit is an offering of 11-year, noncallable notes by General Electric Capital, with a credit rating of AAA/Aaa. The coupon rate of 5.45 percent is equal to the market rate of 5.45 percent, so the price per bond is 100.[1] The total price of 25 bonds with a face value of $1,000 each would be $25,000. The second issue in the exhibit is an offering of 5-year, callable notes by Genworth Financial with a rating of A/A2. Because the coupon rate of 5.65 percent is higher than the market rate of 5.627 percent, the price per note is 100.098. Similarly, the 97.2 price of the 20-year bonds issued by Lehman Brothers reflects the fact that the coupon rate of 6.2 percent is less than the market rate of 6.451 percent. One reason for the difference in rates is that the coupon may be set several days prior to the bonds' issuance date, and market rates may change in the interim.

Costs such as printing, legal fees, commissions, and other types of charges are incurred when bonds are issued. Under International Financial Reporting Standards (IFRS), all debt issue costs are included in the measurement of the liability. Under U.S. generally accepted accounting principles (U.S. GAAP), companies generally show these debt issue costs as an asset (a prepaid expense), which is amortized over the life of the bonds.

---

[1] We are using market rate in this discussion to refer to the specific rate investors demand for the particular bonds in question based on risks unique to the particular bond issue as well as on risks relating to all bonds.

EXHIBIT 13-1   List of Corporate Bond New Issues (Prices as of 7 June 2007, Total Cost for 25 Bonds)

Credit Ratings			Coupon						Est. Total Cost
S&P	Moody's	Description	Rate	Frequency	Maturity	Price	YTM	Callable	
AAA	Aaa	GENL ELEC CAP CP INTERNOTES 36966RS80 New Issue	5.45	Semiannual	6/15/2018	100	5.45	No	$25,000.00
A	A2	GENWORTH FINL SR NOTES 37247DAJ5 New Issue	5.65	Semiannual	6/15/2012	100.098	5.627	Yes	$25,024.50
A+	A1	LEHMAN BROS HLDG 6.2%2752517P2S9 New Issue	6.2	Semiannual	6/15/2027	97.2	6.451	Yes	$24,300.00
AAA	Aaa	TOYOTA MTR CRDT CORENOTE 89240AGP9New Issue	5.25	Semiannual	6/20/2012	100	5.25	Yes	$25,000.00

2.2. Accounting for Bond Amortization, Interest Expense, and Interest Payments

As discussed above, companies initially report bonds as a liability on their balance sheet at the amount of the sales proceeds. The amount at which bonds are reported on the company's balance sheet is referred to as the *book value, net book value,* or *carrying value.* If the bonds are issued at par, the book value will be identical to the face value, and usually the book value will not change over the life of the bonds. For bonds issued at face value, the amount of periodic interest *expense* will be the same as the amount of the periodic interest *payment* to bondholders.

If, however, the market rate differs from the bonds' stated rate at issuance such that the bonds are issued at a premium or discount, the premium or discount is amortized systematically over the life of the bonds as a component of interest expense. For bonds issued at a premium to face value, the book value of the bonds is initially greater than the face value. As the premium is amortized, the book value of the bonds will decrease to the face value, reducing reported debt. For bonds issued at a discount to face value, the book value of the bonds is initially less than the face value. As the discount is amortized, the book value of the bonds will increase, increasing reported debt.

This accounting treatment for bonds issued at a discount, for example, reflects the fact that the company essentially paid some of its borrowing costs at issuance by selling its bonds at a discount. Rather than a cash transfer, this "payment" was made in the form of accepting less than face value for the bonds. The remaining borrowing cost occurs as a cash interest payment to investors each period. The total interest expense reflects both components of the borrowing cost. When the bonds mature, the book value will be equal to the face value.

Two methods for amortizing the book value of bonds that were issued at a price other than par are the effective interest rate method and the straight-line method. The effective interest rate method applies the market rate in effect when the bonds were issued (historical market rate) to the current amortized cost (book value) of the bonds to obtain interest expense for the period. The difference between the interest expense and the interest payment made is the **amortization** of the discount or premium. The straight-line method of amortization evenly amortizes the premium or discount over the life of the bond, similar to straight-line depreciation on long-lived assets. The effective interest rate method is required under IFRS and preferred under U.S. GAAP because it better reflects the economic substance of the transaction.

Interest payments on bonds are based on the bonds' stated rate applied to its face value. Example 13-3 illustrates both methods of amortization for bonds issued at a discount.

EXAMPLE 13-3   Amortizing a Bond Discount

Debond Corp. (a hypothetical company) issues £1 million worth of five-year bonds, dated 1 January 2008, when the market interest rate is 6 percent. The bonds pay 5 percent interest annually on 31 December.

1. What is the interest *payment* on the bonds each year?
2. What amount of interest *expense* on the bonds would be reported in 2008 and 2009, using the effective interest rate method?
3. Determine the reported value of the bonds (i.e., the book value) at 31 December 2008 and 2009, assuming the effective interest rate method is used to amortize the discount.
4. What amount of interest expense on the bonds would be reported under the straight-line method of amortizing the discount?

Solution to 1. The interest payment, as shown in the previous example, equals £50,000 annually (£1,000,000 × 5 percent).

Solution to 2. As shown in the previous example, the bonds are issued at £957,876. The sales proceeds are less than the face value, i.e., the bonds were issued at a discount of £42,124 (£1,000,000 − £957,876). Over time, the discount is amortized.

Under the effective interest rate method, interest expense on the bonds is determined based on the bonds' book value times the market rate in effect when the bonds are issued (historical market rate). For 2008, interest expense is £57,473 (£957,876 × 6 percent). The amount of the discount that will be amortized in 2008 is the difference between the interest expense of £57,473 and the interest payment of £50,000 (i.e., £7,473). The bonds' book value increases by the discount amortization, so at 31 December 2008 the bonds' book value is £965,349 (beginning balance of £957,876 plus £7,473 discount amortization). At this point, the book value reflects the remaining unamortized discount of £34,651 (£42,124 discount at issuance minus £7,473 amortized).

For 2009, interest expense is £57,921 (£965,349 × 6 percent). The amount of the discount that will be amortized in 2009 is the difference between the interest expense of £57,921 and the interest payment of £50,000, i.e. £7,921. The bonds' book value increases by the discount amortization, so at 31 December 2009 the bonds' book value is £973,270 (beginning balance of £965,349 plus £7,921 discount amortization).

The following table illustrates interest expense, discount amortization, and book value over the life of the bonds.

Year	Book Value (Beginning of Year)	Interest Expense (at Market Interest Rate of 6%)	Interest Payment (at Stated Interest Rate of 5%)	Amortization of Discount	Book Value (End of Year)
	(a)	(b)	(c)	(d)	(e)
2008	£957,876	£57,473	£50,000	£7,473	£965,349
2009	965,349	57,921	50,000	7,921	973,270
2010	973,270	58,396	50,000	8,396	981,666
2011	981,666	58,900	50,000	8,900	990,566
2012	990,566	59,434	50,000	9,434	1,000,000
Total				£42,124	

Column (a) shows the book value at the beginning of the year. The beginning amount in 2008 reflects the proceeds from the bonds' issuance of £957,876. The amounts in each subsequent year equal the ending book value from the prior year.

Column (b) shows interest expense for the year calculated as the book value at the beginning of the year multiplied by the historical market rate of interest when the bonds were issued.

Column (c) shows the annual interest payment on the bonds calculated as the bonds' face value multiplied by the bonds' stated interest rate.

Column (d) shows the amortization of the discount, calculated as the difference between the interest expense and interest payment. It is the amount of the original issuance discount allocated to this period and the amount by which the book value increases during the year.

Column (e) shows the book value at the end of the year, calculated as the book value at the beginning of the year (Column a) plus the amortization of the discount (Column d).

Solution to 3. From Column (e) in the table above, the book values of the bonds at 31 December 2008 and 2009 are £965,349 and £973,270, respectively. Observe that the book value of the bonds issued at a discount is increasing over the life of the bonds. At maturity, 31 December 2012, the book value of the bonds will equal face value.

Solution to 4. Under the straight-line method, the discount (or premium) is evenly reduced over the life of the bonds. In this example, the £42,124 discount would be amortized by £8,424.80 (£42,124 divided by 5 years) each year under the straight-line method. So, the annual interest expense under the straight-line method would be £58,424.80 (£50,000 plus £8,424.80).

The section in which interest payments are reported on the statement of cash flows can differ under IFRS and U.S. GAAP. U.S. GAAP requires interest payments on bonds to be shown as a reduction of operating cash flows. (Some financial statement users consider the placement of interest payments in the operating section to be inconsistent with the placement of bond issue proceeds in the financing section of the statement of cash flows.) Typically, cash interest paid is not shown directly on the statement of cash flows, but companies are required to disclose interest paid separately. Under IFRS interest payments on bonds can be shown as an outflow in the operating section, consistent with U.S. GAAP, or may be shown as an outflow in the financing section.

Amortization of a discount (premium) is a noncash expense (reduction in expense) and thus, apart from its effect on taxable income, has no effect on cash flow. In the section of the statement of cash flows that reconciles net income to operating cash flow, amortization of a discount (premium) is added back to (subtracted from) net income.

The bonds in the examples above pay a periodic interest payment. The accounting and reporting for zero-coupon bonds is similar to the examples above except that no interest payments are made, so the amount of interest expense each year is the same as the amount of the discount amortization for the year.

2.3. Debt Extinguishment

Once bonds are issued, a company can leave the bonds outstanding until they mature, or can redeem bonds before maturity either by calling the bonds (if the bond issue includes a call provision) or by purchasing the bonds in the open market. If the bonds remain outstanding until the maturity date, the company pays bondholders the face value of the bonds at maturity. Repayment appears in the statement of cash flows as a financing cash outflow. On the balance sheet, repayment reduces bonds payable by the net book value. Recall that any discount or premium on the bonds would be fully amortized by the time the bonds mature such that net book value equals face value. So, at maturity, the repayment reduces the balance in bonds payable by the face value of the bonds.

If a company decides to redeem bonds before maturity and thus extinguish the liability, a gain or loss on the extinguishment is computed by subtracting the cash required to pay off the bonds from the book value of the bonds at the time of redemption. For example, assume a $10 million bond issuance with a current book value equal to its face value is called at a call price of 103; the company's loss on redemption would be $300 thousand ($10 million book value minus $10.3 million cash paid to call the bonds). Recall that under U.S. GAAP debt issue costs are accounted for separately, so any remaining debt issue costs must be written off and are also included in the gain or loss on debt extinguishment. Under IFRS, debt issue costs are included in the measurement of the liability and are thus part of its book value.

A gain or loss on the extinguishment of debt is disclosed on the income statement, in a separate line item, when the amount is material. A company typically discloses further detail about the extinguishment in the management discussion and analysis (MD&A) and/or financial statement footnotes.[2] In addition, a statement of cash flows prepared using the indirect

---

[2]We use the term *MD&A* generally to refer to any management commentary that may be provided on a company's financial condition, changes in financial condition, and results of operations. In the United States, the SEC requires a management discussion and analysis for companies listed on U.S. public markets. For IFRS reporters, reporting requirements for a commentary such as the SEC-required MD&A vary across exchanges, but some are similar to the SEC requirements. Currently, the IASB is developing a standard for a management commentary, which would be consistent for all IFRS reporters.

method adjusts net income to remove any gain or loss on the extinguishment of debt from operating cash flow, and to include the amount of payment in cash used for financing activities. (Recall that the indirect method of the statement of cash flows begins with net income and makes necessary adjustments to arrive at cash from operations, including removal of gains or losses from nonoperating activities.)

As illustration of the financial statement impact of the extinguishment of debt, consider the notes payable repurchase by Ciena Corporation below.

EXAMPLE 13-4   Debt Extinguishment Disclosure

Ciena Corporation (NASDAQ: CIEN) reported a gain on the extinguishment of debt of $6.7 million in the "Management's Discussion and Analysis of Financial Condition and Results of Operations" section of its first quarter 2006, 10-Q filing as follows:

> **Gain on extinguishment of debt** *for the first quarter of fiscal 2006 resulted from our repurchase of $106.5 million in aggregate principal on our outstanding 3.75 percent convertible notes in open market transactions for $98.8 million. We recorded a gain on the extinguishment of debt in the amount of $6.7 million, which consists of the $7.7 million gain from the repurchase of the notes, less $1.0 million of associated debt issuance costs.*

The company's income statement includes a line entitled "Gain on extinguishment of debt" showing the $6.7 million. On the statement of cash flows, the gain is subtracted from net income as a noncash adjustment to arrive at operating cash flows. Under financing cash flows, the $98.8 million repurchase costs appear as a cash outflow.

Using the information provided in the financial statements and 10-Q filing, the gain can be summarized as follows ($ millions):

Aggregate principal on notes	$106.5
Less: Cash required to repurchase notes	98.8
Gain before deducting unamortized debt issue costs	7.7
Less: Debt issue costs	1.0
Gain on repurchase of notes	$6.7

2.4. Debt Covenants

Borrowing agreements often include restrictions called covenants that protect creditors by restricting a company's ability to invest, pay dividends, or make other operating and strategic decisions that might adversely affect the company's ability to pay interest and principal. Debt covenants also benefit borrowers to the extent that they lower default risk and thus reduce the cost of borrowing.

Common covenants include limitations on how borrowed monies can be used, maintenance of collateral pledged as security (if any), restrictions on future borrowings, requirements that limit dividends, and requirements to meet specific working capital requirements. Covenants may also include minimum acceptable liquidity and solvency, expressed by particular levels of financial ratios such as debt-to-equity, current ratio, or interest coverage. The example below illustrates common disclosures on debt covenants included in financial statement footnotes.

EXAMPLE 13-5   Illustration of Debt Covenant Disclosures

The following excerpt from American Greeting Corporation's (NYSE: AM) 2006 financial statements illustrates common debt covenants and their disclosure:

NOTE 11—LONG AND SHORT-TERM DEBT (Excerpt)

The credit agreement contains certain restrictive covenants that are customary for similar credit arrangements, including covenants relating to limitations on liens, dispositions, issuance of debt, investments, payment of dividends, repurchases of capital stock, acquisitions and transactions with affiliates. There are also financial performance covenants that require the corporation to maintain a maximum leverage ratio and a minimum interest coverage ratio. The credit agreement also requires the corporation to make certain mandatory prepayments of outstanding indebtedness using the net cash proceeds received from certain dispositions, events of loss and additional indebtedness that the corporation may incur from time to time.

When a company violates a debt covenant, it is said to be in default. Lenders can choose to waive the covenant, renegotiate, or call for payment of the debt. Bond issues typically require that the decision about whether to call for immediate repayment be made on behalf of all the bondholders by holders of some minimum percentage of the principal amount of the bond issue.

2.5.   Presentation and Disclosure of Long-Term Debt

The long-term liabilities section of the balance sheet usually includes a single line item of the total amount of a company's long-term debt due after one year, with the portion of long-term debt due in the next 12 months shown as a short-term liability. Financial statement footnotes provide more information on the types and nature of a company's debt. These footnote disclosures can be used to determine the amount and timing for future cash outflows. The footnotes generally include stated and effective interest rates, maturity dates, restrictions imposed by creditors, and collateral pledged (if any). The amount of scheduled debt repayments for the next five years is also shown in the footnotes. Below is an excerpt from Johnson & Johnson's 2006 10-K filing that illustrates common disclosures.

EXAMPLE 13-6   Illustration of Long-Term Debt Disclosures

The excerpt from footnote 6 of Johnson & Johnson's (NYSE: JNJ) 2006 financial statements illustrates financial statement disclosure for long-term debt including type and nature of long-term debt, effective interest rates, and required payments over the next five years.

6. Borrowings (Excerpt)

The components of long-term debt are as follows:

	2006	Effective Rate%	2005	Effective Rate%
		($ millions)		
3% zero-coupon convertible subordinated debentures due 2020	$182	3.00	$202	3.00
4.95% debentures due 2033	500	4.95	500	4.95
3.80% debentures due 2013	500	3.82	500	3.82
6.95% notes due 2029	293	7.14	293	7.14
6.73% debentures due 2023	250	6.73	250	6.73
6.625% notes due 2009	199	6.80	199	6.80
Industrial revenue bonds	29	5.21	31	3.90
Other	70	—	55	—
	2,023	5.23 (1)	2,030	5.18 (1)
Less current portion	9		13	
	$2,014		$2,017	

(1) Weighted average effective rate.

The Company has access to substantial sources of funds at numerous banks worldwide. Total unused credit available to the Company approximates $10.8 billion, including $9 billion of credit commitments, of which $3.75 billion expire September 27, 2007, $4 billion expire October 30, 2007, and $1.25 billion expire September 28, 2011. Also included are $0.75 billion of uncommitted lines with various banks worldwide that expire during 2007. Interest charged on borrowings under the credit line agreements is based on either bids provided by banks, the prime rate or London Interbank Offered Rate (LIBOR), plus applicable margins. Commitment fees under the agreement are not material.

Aggregate Maturities of Long-Term Obligations Commencing in 2007 Are ($ millions):

2007	2008	2009	2010	2011	After 2011
$ 9	9	240	9	6	1,750

In addition to disclosures in the financial statement footnotes, an MD&A commonly provides other information on a company's capital resources, including debt financing and off-balance sheet financing. In the MD&A, management often provides a qualitative discussion on any material trends, favorable or unfavorable, in capital resources and indicates any expected material changes in their mix and relative cost. Additional quantitative information is typically provided, including schedules summarizing a company's contractual obligations (such as bond payables) and other commitments (such as lines of credit and guarantees) in total and over the next five years.

2.6.   Current Market Rates and Fair Values

Recall in the discussion of reporting bonds on the balance sheet, the reported value (net book value) of bonds is based on the market rate at the time the bonds were issued (i.e. historical rate). Over time, as market rates change, the bonds' book value diverges from the bonds' fair market value. For instance, when interest rates decline, the market value of debt increases, so a company's reported debt—based on historical market rates—will be lower than the value of its economic liabilities. Using financial statement amounts will then underestimate a company's debt-to-total capital employed and similar leverage ratios.

The availability of fair value information of financial liabilities has been limited. For example, under U. S. financial accounting standards for derivatives (SFAS No. 133), if a company hedged its obligations under fixed-rate bonds by entering into an interest rate swap (i.e., a swap to receive fixed and pay floating that converts the fixed rate obligation into a floating rate), the company would be allowed to mark the hedged bonds to market value. Any loss in the bonds' value would be offset by a gain on the swap, and any gain in the bonds' value would be offset by a loss on the swap. A hedge qualifying for such treatment is known as a *fair value hedge.* Implementing SFAS No. 133 created difficulties for a number of companies resulting in a significant number of restatements. A recently issued U.S. accounting standard (SFAS No. 159) is expected to reduce some of the difficulty in accounting for financial liabilities (and thus reduce the number of restatements associated with hedge accounting) because it provides companies with more flexibility in reporting both financial assets and liabilities at fair value. Overall, recently issued U.S. accounting standards (SFAS No. 159 and SFAS No. 157) and international standards (IAS 32, IAS 39, and IFRS 7) expand disclosures of fair value of financial assets and liabilities and allow companies to report fair values on the balance sheet.[3]

3.   DEBT WITH EQUITY FEATURES

This section discusses two types of debt with equity features, **convertible debt** and **debt with warrants**, and briefly describes reporting for certain financial instruments with characteristics of both liabilities and equity.

Common with manufacturing firms.

3.1.   Convertible Debt

Some bonds include provisions allowing the bondholders to convert the bonds to equity in the future. The economic effect of issuing such instruments is substantially the same as

---

[3]Statement of Financial Accounting Standard No. 159, "The Fair Value Option for Financial Assets and Financial Liabilities—Including an amendment of SFAS No. 115," and SFAS No. 157, "Fair Value Measurements."

issuing a debt instrument with an early settlement provision and options to purchase shares. The convertibility feature of the debt usually provides financing at a lower interest rate than straight debt (debt without a conversion feature) because the option to convert is valuable to the bond purchaser. The conversion feature typically gives bondholders the right to convert the bonds into a prespecified number of common equity shares, equivalently expressed as the right to convert at a specific price.

Accounting for convertible debt differs under U.S. GAAP and IFRS. Under U.S. GAAP, accounting for convertible bond issues is essentially the same as accounting for regular bond issues. The issue proceeds (composed of face value adjusted for any discount or premium) are classified as a liability on the balance sheet and as a cash inflow from financing activities. If the bonds are converted, liabilities decrease by the book value of the bonds and equity increases by the same amount. This method for recording the amount of equity at conversion is referred to as the book value method and does not reflect the market value of the equity issued at conversion. When bonds are converted, there is no effect on cash flows. However, the conversion is a significant noncash financing activity and is reported as supplemental information on the statement of cash flows.

Accounting under IFRS recognizes the economic effect of issuing convertible debt. Accordingly, a company presents the liability and equity (option) components separately on its balance sheet. The debt is initially valued at fair value. Any difference between the debt's fair value and issue proceeds is allocated to the conversion feature and reported as equity.

When evaluating a company's capital structure, convertible debt may merit special consideration. As debt, convertible bonds are classified as a liability on the balance sheet, yet at conversion the amount of the bonds would appear as equity. If the conversion features are such that a conversion is imminent, for example if the current market price is well above the conversion price and the company may force conversion by calling the bonds, an analyst can estimate the effect of treating the convertibles as equity rather than debt. In calculating ratios, for example debt-to-total capital, convertible bonds would change both the numerator and denominator. Because accounting at the conversion is based on the bonds' carrying value (or book value), the numerator decreases and the denominator increase by the carrying value of the convertible bonds. It is, however, difficult to predict when and if the company's stock price will rise above the conversion price, and thus when the debt is more likely to be converted. Even when market prices are well above conversion prices, the timing of conversions is not necessarily easy to predict. Finally, convertible bonds are potentially dilutive securities that decrease the claims of current shareholders. As discussed in another chapter, the dilutive effect of these securities is considered when reporting diluted earnings per share. The example below illustrates how common disclosures provided on convertible bonds may be used to assess the effect on equity and debt-to-total-capital ratio if the debt were to be converted.

EXAMPLE 13-7   Convertible Debt

Below is an excerpt from Sirius Satellite Radio, Inc.'s (NasdaqGS: SIRI) long-term debt footnote. The company's shareholders' equity at 31 December 2006 was ($389,071) and the number of shares outstanding was 1,434,635,501. All dollar amounts are in thousands. For 2006, use the disclosures and additional information provided to estimate the following:

1. The number of additional shares that would be issued and the percentage increase in shares that would result if all convertible bonds were converted to common stock.
2. The effect on the debt-to-capital ratio if all convertible bonds were converted.

Long-Term Debt and Accrued Interest *(excerpt from footnote)*

Our Long-Term Debt Consists of the Following:

	Conversion Price (per share)	Book Value as of 31 December	
		2006	**2005**
9⅝% senior notes due 2013	N/A	$500,000	$500,000
3¼% convertible notes due 2011	$5.3	230,000	230,000
2½% convertible notes due 2009	4.41	300,000	300,000
3½% convertible notes due 2008	1.38	36,505	52,693
8¾% convertible subordinated notes due 2009	28.4625	1,744	1,744
Total long-term debt		$1,068,249	$1,084,437

3½% Convertible Notes Due 2008

In May 2003, we issued $201,250 in aggregate principal amount of our 3½% convertible notes due 2008 resulting in net proceeds of $194,224. These notes are convertible, at the option of the holder, into shares of our common stock at any time at a conversion rate of 724.6377 shares of common stock for each $1,000.00 principal amount, or $1.38 per share of common stock, subject to certain adjustments. Our 3½% convertible notes due 2008 mature on June 1, 2008 and interest is payable semiannually on June 1 and December 1 of each year. The obligations under our 3½% convertible notes due 2008 are not secured by any of our assets.

During the year ended December 31, 2006, holders of $16,188 in aggregate principal amount of our 3½% convertible notes due 2008 presented such notes for conversion in accordance with the terms of the indenture. We issued 11,730,431 shares of our common stock upon conversion of these notes. During the year ended December 31, 2005, we issued 10,548,545 shares of our common stock in exchange for $14,557 in aggregate principal amount of our 3½% Convertible Notes due 2008, including accrued interest.

Solution to 1. The disclosures indicate the conversion price of the convertible bonds. Dividing the amount of bonds by the conversion price gives the additional shares if the bonds are converted. As shown in the table below, the number of additional shares that would be issued if all convertible debt were converted to common stock is 137,938,000, representing a 9.6 percent increase in the number of shares outstanding (137,938,000 ÷ 1,434,635,501).

	Conversion Price (per share)	Convertible Debt 31 Dec. 2006	Additional Shares (in thousands), if Converted
3¼% convertible notes due 2011	$5.3	$230,000	43,396
2½% convertible notes due 2009	4.41	300,000	68,027
3½% convertible notes due 2008	1.38	36,505	26,453
8¾% convertible subordinated notes due 2009	28.4625	1,744	61
Total long-term convertible debt		$568,249	137,938

Solution to 2. The company's debt-to-capital ratio at 31 December 2006 is 1.57. If all convertible debt were converted the ratio would decrease to 0.74, reflecting a strengthening in the company's capital structure.

	Current	Adjustment to Convert Debt to Equity at Book Value	If Converted
Shareholder's equity	(389,071)	568,249	179,178
Long-term debt	1,068,249	(568,249)	500,000
Debt-to-capital ratio	1.57		0.74

In the Sirius example above, conversion prices range from $1.38 to over $28 per common share. Given the company's recent share price range from $2.66 to $4.84, only the 3.5 percent notes due 2008 are "in the money" (i.e., the conversion price is below the share price). As indicated in the footnote excerpt, some holders of those bonds exercised the conversion option in 2005 and 2006.

3.2. Debt with Warrants

Some bonds are issued with warrants giving holders the right to purchase additional shares of the issuer's common stock at a specific price, similar to stock options. Warrants, issued directly by a company, share many characteristics of stock options, such as requiring a specific payment to acquire the stock (strike price), a certain time when they can be exercised (like an American or European option), and an expiration date. A company will also specify a conversion ratio defining the number of warrants required to acquire a share of stock. Like the conversion feature of convertible bonds, warrants provide a purchaser of debt with additional value and thus lower the required interest rate on the bonds. Warrants are also included in debt offerings to attract buyers, who may value the opportunity to participate in any future appreciation of the company's equity.

One difference between warrants and the conversion feature of convertible bonds is that the conversion feature is an integral part of convertible bonds, but warrants are usually detachable from bonds. Under both IFRS and U.S. GAAP, accounting for bonds issued with warrants essentially accounts for the bonds and the warrants as two separate securities. The issuer records the issuance by allocating the issue price between the bonds and the warrants, based on their respective fair values that are determined as follows. Initially, debt is valued at fair value, as if there is no warrant. Any difference between the debt's fair value and issue proceeds is allocated to the warrants, which are reported in equity. Warrants, too, are potentially dilutive securities that are considered when reporting diluted earnings per share.

Issuance of bonds with warrants is more common by non-U.S. companies. Example 13-8 provides an illustrative announcement of an issuance of bonds with warrants by a small German company, and Example 13-9 provides an example of a financial statement disclosure of bonds with warrants by a major Japanese company.

[handwritten margin note: Structured Notes → a way to execute a certain market play.]

EXAMPLE 13-8   Press Release Announcing an Issuance of Bonds with Warrants

The following excerpts are from a press release issued by a German company with market capitalization of around €500 million, listed on the Frankfurt Stock Exchange:

ORCO Germany S.A.: Bond with warrants issued by Orco Germany for €100 million

Orco Germany issues €100 million of bonds with warrants attached. This marks the first significant fund raising realized by Orco Germany.

The characteristics of the offer are the following: the maturity of the bond is 5 years (2012) and the bond coupon is 4 percent. 9,328,851 warrants were issued with a maturity of seven years (2014) and an exercise price of €16.90. Each warrant gives the holder the right to subscribe to one share.

"The deal was placed to institutional investors and the bond will be used to finance our further growth and to further develop our property portfolio," says Rainer Bormann, CEO of Orco Germany.

Source: Release of a Corporate News (1 June 2007), transmitted by DGAP; a company of EquityStory AG; retrieved from Lexis-Nexis.

EXAMPLE 13-9   Financial Statement Disclosure of Bonds with Warrants

The following excerpt is from the Form 20-F of Sony Corporation, filed 1 September 2006. (Form 20-F is the form filed annually with the Securities and Exchange Commission [SEC] by non-U.S. companies that list their shares on a major U.S. stock exchange. It is the equivalent of Form 10-K for U.S. companies.)

11.   Short-Term Borrowings and Long-Term Debt (Excerpt): Sony Corporation and Consolidated Subsidiaries—Notes To Consolidated Financial Statements (Continued)

A summary of the exercise rights of the detachable warrants as of March 31, 2006, is as follows:

Issued on	Exercisable During	Exercise Price		Number of Shares per Warrant	Status of Exercise
		Yen	Dollars		
October 19, 2000	November 1, 2001, through October 18, 2006	12,457	106	100 shares of common stock of Sony Corporation	9,224 warrants outstanding
December 21, 2001	January 6, 2003 through December 20, 2007	6,039	52	100 shares of common stock of Sony Corporation	11,459 warrants outstanding

3.3.   Financial Instruments with Characteristics of Both Debt and Equity

This section provides a brief description of accounting standards regarding how an issuer characterizes and measures financial instruments with characteristics of both debt and equity (SFAS No. 150). Broadly, the standards now require that issuers report as liabilities any financial instruments that will require repayment of principal in the future. A few representative examples of financial instruments that must be reported as debt are the following: (1) a financial instrument that includes an unconditional obligation for the issuing company to redeem it in the future (mandatorily redeemable financial securities); (2) a financial instrument that includes an obligation for the issuing company to repurchase its own equity in the future (forward purchase contract); and (3) an obligation that the company must settle by issuing a variable number of its own shares, when the amount of the obligation is a fixed monetary amount, known at inception.

These accounting standards are particularly applicable to structured finance transactions that aim to achieve favorable accounting (i.e., treatment as equity rather than debt). When a company issues a financial instrument that is reported as equity rather than debt, solvency ratios based on the financial statements appear stronger. Accounting standards now limit this favorable treatment for many financial instruments with characteristics of both debt and equity. For instance, mandatorily redeemable preferred stock has many of the same characteristics as bonds with required payments (dividends in the case of preferred stock) at a stated rate. Importantly, the feature that the preferred stock must be redeemed, rather than have an unlimited life, is similar to the final payment of principal on bonds. Previously, mandatorily redeemable preferred stock appeared as equity, or in the mezzanine section of the balance sheet, between debt and equity; but it must now be reported as debt. Dividends on mandatorily preferred stock are reported as interest expense, consistent with the view that mandatorily redeemable preferred stock is debt. The example below illustrates the implications of and financial statement effects of the change in classification of mandatorily preferred stock from equity to a liability.

EXAMPLE 13-10 The Effect of SFAS No. 150

The following excerpts illustrate how SFAS No. 150 affected several companies with mandatorily redeemable securities outstanding.

- CMS Energy Corp.:

  At July 1, 2003, mandatorily redeemable preferred securities totaling $883 million, were reclassified from the mezzanine equity section to the liability section of CMS Energy's consolidated balance sheet.

  Consumers is subject to covenants in its financing agreements . . . [including] agreements to maintain specified levels of cash coverage of its interest requirements and to not allow its indebtedness to exceed specified levels of its consolidated capitalization . . . Consumers is in compliance with these requirements as of the most recent measurement date, June 30, 2003. . . . After giving effect to the adoption of SFAS No. 150 regarding the balance sheet classification of its Trust Preferred Securities and to expected future use of its revolving credit facilities, Consumers currently estimates that its ratio of indebtedness to total capitalization at the end of the third and fourth quarters of 2003 will still comply with the Debt Percentage Tests but will approach the limits specified in some of the Debt Percentage Tests. Consumers plans to seek amendments to the relevant financing agreements to modify the terms of the Debt Percentage Tests in order to, among other things, remove the effect of the adoption of SFAS No. 150 regarding Trust Preferred Securities on the calculations. Consumers believes that it will receive the necessary consents of its lenders to these amendments.

  Source: CMS Energy Corp. 10-Q for the period ended 30 June 2003, filed 14 August 2003.

- AOL Time Warner Inc.:

Abbreviated Balance Sheet as of 30 June 2003	($millions)
Long-term debt	$25,898
All other liabilities	36,759
Shareholders' equity	
Convertible preferred stock	1,500
Common Stock	45
Paid-in capital	155,388
Accumulated other comprehensive loss	(460)
Retained earnings (loss)	(100,474)
Total shareholders' equity	55,999
Total liabilities and shareholders' equity	118,656

  Source: AOL Time Warner Inc. 10-Q for the period ended 30 June 2003, filed 13 August 2003.

1. What were the concerns faced by CMS Energy Inc. when the accounting standards began requiring mandatorily redeemable preferred stock to be shown as debt rather than equity?
2. How did the reclassification required by SFAS No. 150 affect AOL's reported leverage (as measured by its debt-to-equity and debt-to-total-capital ratios)?

Solution to 1. CMS expressed concern that reclassifying its mandatorily redeemable preferred securities from mezzanine equity to debt would approach the limits specified in one of the financial covenants contained in its financing arrangements, namely the ratio of indebtedness to total capitalization. Accordingly, the company planned to seek consent from its lenders to amend the calculation of the ratio.

Solution to 2. The reclassification of its mandatorily redeemable preferred stock from equity to debt would significantly increase AOL's reported leverage. AOL's long-term debt-to-equity ratio would increase from 46.2 percent ($25,898/$55,999) to 50.3 percent ($27,398/$54,499), and the company's debt-to-capital ratio would increase from 31.6 percent [$25,898/($25,898 + $55,999)] to 33.5 percent [$27,398/($27,398 + $54,499)].

	As Reported	Adjusted
Long-term debt	$25,898	$27,398
All other liabilities	36,759	36,759
Shareholders' Equity		
Convertible preferred stock	1,500	0
Common stock	45	45
Paid-in capital	155,388	155,388
Accumulated other comprehensive loss	–460	–460
Retained earnings (loss)	–100,474	–100,474
Total shareholders' equity	55,999	54,499
Total liabilities and shareholders' equity	$118,656	$118,656
Long-term debt-to-equity	46.2%	50.3%
Debt-to-capital	31.6%	33.5%

While the recent standards solved many of the accounting problems created by financial instruments with characteristics of both debt and equity, structured finance is an active field and new products and financial instruments are continuously created, some of which may serve to enhance an issuer's reported financial position. Therefore, where new transactions similar to those covered by these accounting standards are treated as equity, an analyst should evaluate whether the classification as equity significantly enhances the appearance of strong solvency ratios; if so, further analysis of the specifics of the transactions may be warranted.

4. LEASES

A company wishing to obtain the use of an asset can borrow money and purchase the asset. Alternatively, a company can lease the asset for some finite period of time or lease the asset as a means of buying the asset over time. The following paragraphs first describe some advantages to leasing from the viewpoint of the **lessee** (the party obtaining the use of an asset through a lease) and then describe the accounting treatment of different types of leases. The final portion of this section evaluates leases from the perspective of the owner of the asset.

4.1. Advantages of Leasing

A lease is a contract between the owner of an asset—the **lessor**—and another party seeking use of the assets—the lessee. Through the lease, the lessor grants the right to use the asset to the lessee. The right to use the asset could be a long period, such as 20 years, or a much shorter period such as a month. In exchange for the right to use the asset, the lessee makes periodic lease payments to the lessor. A lease, then, is a form of financing to the lessee provided directly from the lessor in order to enable the lessee to purchase the *use* of the leased asset.

There are several advantages to leasing an asset compared to purchasing it. Leases can provide less costly financing, usually require little, if any, down payment, and are often at fixed interest rates. Because the lease contract is negotiated between the lessor and lessee, the lease may contain less restrictive provisions than other forms of borrowing. A lease can also reduce the risk of obsolescence to the lessee because the lessee does not own the asset.

Importantly, leases also have potential financial and tax reporting advantages. While providing a form of financing, certain types of leases are not shown as debt on the balance sheet. The items leased under these types of leases also do not appear as assets on the balance sheet. Therefore, no interest expense or depreciation expense is included in the income statement. In addition, in the United States, because financial reporting rules differ from tax regulations, in some cases a company may own an asset for tax purposes (and thus obtain deductions for depreciation expense for tax purposes) while not reflecting the ownership in its financial statements. A lease that is structured to provide a company with the tax benefits of ownership while not requiring the asset to be reflected on the company's financial statements is known as a synthetic lease. Next, we will discuss the two main types of leases—finance and operating—and the lessee's and lessor's accounting for them.

4.2. Finance (or Capital) Leases versus Operating Leases

The economic substance of a finance (or capital) lease is very different from an operating lease, as are the implications of each for the financial statements for the lessee and lessor.[4] In substance, a **finance lease** is the purchase of some asset (lease to own) by the buyer (lessee) that is directly financed by the seller (lessor). An **operating lease** is an agreement allowing the lessee to use some asset for a period of time, essentially a rental.

---

[4]Finance leases are also commonly referred to as capital leases, particularly in the United States.

U.S. accounting standards have four specific requirements that define when a lease is a finance lease:

1. Ownership of the leased asset transfers to lessee at end of lease.
2. The lease contains an option for the lessee to purchase the leased asset cheaply (bargain purchase option).
3. The lease term is 75 percent or more of the useful life of the leased asset.
4. The present value of lease payments is 90 percent or more of the fair value of the leased asset.

Only one of these requirements has to be met for the lease to be considered a finance lease by the lessee. On the lessor side, satisfying only one of these four specific requirements determines a finance lease plus the lessor must also meet revenue recognition requirements (i.e., be reasonably assured of cash collection and have performed substantially under the lease). If none of the four specific requirements are met or if at least one is met but the revenue recognition requirement is not, the lessor reports the lease as an operating lease. International standards are less prescriptive in their criteria for categorizing finance and operating leases, relying on broad definitions of economic substance and managerial judgment to determine whether a lease is a finance or operating lease.

4.2.1. Accounting and Reporting by the Lessee

Because a finance lease is economically similar to borrowing money and buying an asset, a company that enters into a finance lease as the lessee reports an asset (leased asset) and related debt (lease payable) on the balance sheet. The initial value of both the leased asset and lease payable is the present value of future lease payments. On the income statement, the company reports interest expense on the debt, and if the asset acquired is depreciable, the company reports depreciation expense. (The lessor, as we will illustrate in the next section, reports the sale of an asset and a lease as receivable.)

Because an operating lease is economically similar to renting an asset, a company that enters into an operating lease as the lessee records a lease expense on its income statement during the period it uses the asset. No asset or liability is recorded on its balance sheet. The main accounting differences between a finance lease and an operating lease, then, are that reported debt is higher and expenses are generally higher in the early years under a finance lease. Because of the higher debt and expenses, lessees often prefer operating leases to finance leases. As we will illustrate in the next section, lessors' preferences generally differ. Lessors would prefer a finance lease because under an operating lease, lessors continue to show the asset and its associated financing on their balance sheets.

On the lessee's statement of cash flows, for an operating lease, the full lease payment is shown as an operating cash outflow. For a finance lease, only the portion of the lease payment relating to interest expense reduces operating cash flow; the portion of the lease payment that reduces the lease liability appears as a cash outflow in the financing section.

The following example illustrates the effect on a lessee's income, debt, and cash flows when reporting a lease as a finance versus operating lease.

Finance Lease - Higher Debt
Higher Costs
(Depreciation)

EXAMPLE 13-11 Financial Statement Impact of a Finance versus Operating Lease for the Lessee

Assume two similar (hypothetical) companies CAPBS Inc. and OPIS Inc. enter into similar lease agreements for a piece of machinery on 1 January 2008. The leases require four annual payments of €28,679 starting on 1 January 2008. The useful life of the machine is four years and its salvage value is zero. CAPBS accounts for the lease as a finance lease while OPIS has determined the lease is an operating lease. For simplicity, this example assumes that the accounting rules governing these hypothetical companies do not mandate either type of lease. The present value of lease payments and fair value of the equipment is €100,000. (A reminder relevant for present value calculations: Lease payments are made at the beginning of each period.)

At the beginning of 2008, before entering into the lease agreements, both companies reported liabilities of €100,000 and equity of €200,000. Each year the companies receive total revenues of €50,000 cash. Assume the companies have a tax rate of 30 percent, and use the same accounting for financial and tax purposes. Both companies' discount rate is 10 percent. In order to focus only on the differences in the type of lease, assume neither company incurs expenses other than those associated with the lease and neither invests excess cash.

1. Which company reports higher expenses/net income in 2008? Over the four years?
2. Which company reports higher total cash flow from operations?
3. Based on return on equity (ROE), how do the two companies' profitability measures compare?
4. Based on the ratio of debt-to-equity, how do the two companies' solvency positions compare?

Solution to 1. In 2008 and 2009, CAPBS reports higher expenses because the depreciation expense and interest expense of its finance lease exceeds the lease expense of OPIS's operating lease. Therefore, OPIS reports higher net income in 2008 and 2009. The companies' total expense over the entire four-year period, however, is equal as is the companies' total net income.

Each year, OPIS reports lease expense of €28,679 associated with its operating lease. For CAPBS, its finance lease is treated as being economically similar to borrowing money and purchasing an asset. So, on its income statement, CAPBS reports depreciation expense on the leased asset acquired and interest expense on the lease liability.

The table below shows by year CAPBS's depreciation expense and book values on the leased asset.

Year	Acquisition Cost	Depreciation Expense	Accumulated Depreciation	Book Value (year end)
	(a)	(b)	(c)	(d)
2008	€100,000	€25,000	€25,000	€75,000
2009	100,000	25,000	50,000	50,000
2010	100,000	25,000	75,000	25,000
2011	100,000	25,000	100,000	0
		€100,000		

- Column (a) is acquisition cost of €100,000 of the leased equipment.
- Column (b) is depreciation expense of €25,000 per year, calculated using the straight line convention, as the acquisition costs less salvage value divided by useful life [(€100,000 − €0)/4 years].
- Column (c) is the accumulated depreciation on the leased asset calculated as the prior year's accumulated depreciation plus the current year's depreciation expense.
- Column (d) is the book value of the leased equipment, which is the difference between the acquisition cost and accumulated depreciation.

The table below shows CAPBS's lease payment, interest expense, and carrying values for its lease liability by year.[5]

Year	Lease Liability 1 January	Annual Lease Payment, 1 January	Interest (at 10%; accrued in previous year)	Reduction of Lease Liability, 1 January	Lease Liability on 31 December after Lease Payment on 1 January Same Year
	(a)	(b)	(c)	(d)	(e)
2008	€100,000	€28,679	€0	€28,679	€71,321
2009	71,321	28,679	7,132	21,547	49,774
2010	49,774	28,679	4,977	23,702	26,072
2011	26,072	28,679	2,607	26,072	0
		€114,717	€14,717	€100,000	

[5]The computations included throughout the example were made using an Excel worksheet; small apparent discrepancies in the calculations are due to the rounding.

- Column (a) is the lease liability at the beginning of the year.
  2008: €100,000
  Years thereafter: lease liability at end of previous year

- Column (b) is the annual lease payment made at the beginning of the year. A portion of the lease payment reduces any interest accrued in the previous year, and the remainder of the lease payment reduces the lease liability.

  For example, in 2009, the €28,679 paid on 1 January reduces the interest payable of €7,132 that accrued in 2008 (0.10 × 71,321) and then reduces the lease liability by €21,547.

- Column (c) is the interest portion of the 1 January lease payment made on that date. This amount of interest was accrued as interest payable during the *prior* year and is reported as the interest expense of the *prior* year.

- Column (d) is the reduction of the lease liability, which is the difference between the annual lease payment and the interest portion.

- Column (e) is the lease liability on 31 December of a given year just before the lease payment is made on the first day of the next year. It is equal to the lease liability on 1 January of the same year (column a) less the reduction of the lease liability (column d).

The table below summarizes and compares the income statement effects of the lease for CAPBS and OPIS. Notice that over the four year lease, both companies report the same total amount of expense but CAPBS shows higher expenses earlier in the life of the lease.

| Year | CAPBS | | | OPIS | |
	Depreciation Expense	Interest Expense	Total	Lease Expense	Difference
2008	€25,000	€7,132	€32,132	€28,679	€3,453
2009	25,000	4,977	29,977	28,679	1,298
2010	25,000	2,607	27,607	28,679	(1,072)
2011	25,000	—	25,000	28,679	(3,679)
Total	€100,000	€14,717	€114,717	€114,717	€(0)

The complete income statements for CAPBS and OPIS are presented below. Notice under the assumptions that the same accounting is used for financial and tax purposes, CAPBS's taxes are lower in 2008 and 2009. The lower taxes in the earlier years reflect the higher expenses in those years.

Income Statements	CAPBS					OPIS				
	2008	2009	2010	2011	Total	2008	2009	2010	2011	Total
Sales	€50,000	€50,000	€50,000	€50,000	€200,000	€50,000	€50,000	€50,000	€50,000	€200,000
Depreciation expense	25,000	25,000	25,000	25,000	€100,000					
Interest expense	7,132	4,977	2,607		14,717					
Lease expense						28,679	28,679	28,679	28,679	114,717
Income before taxes	17,868	20,023	22,393	25,000	85,283	21,321	21,321	21,321	21,321	85,283
Tax expense	5,360	6,007	6,718	7,500	25,585	6,396	6,396	6,396	6,396	25,585
Net income	€12,508	€14,016	€15,675	€17,500	€59,698	€14,925	€14,925	€14,925	€14,925	€59,698

Solution to 2. On the statement of cash flows, observe that over the four years, both CAPBS and OPIS report the same total change in cash of €59,698. Operating cash flows reported by CAPBS are higher because a portion of the lease payment each year is categorized as a financing cash flow rather than an operating cash flow. In the first two years, CAPBS change in cash is higher due to its lower taxes in those years.

Statements of Cash Flows	CAPBS					OPIS				
	2008	2009	2010	2011	Total	2008	2009	2010	2011	Total
Sales	€50,000	€50,000	€50,000	€50,000	€200,000	€50,000	€50,000	€50,000	€50,000	€200,000
Interest paid	—	7,132	4,977	2,607	€14,717					
Taxes paid	5,360	6,007	6,718	7,500	25,585	6,396	6,396	6,396	6,396	€25,585
Lease expense	—	—	—	—	—	28,679	28,679	28,679	28,679	114,717
Operating cash flows	44,640	36,861	38,305	39,893	159,698	14,925	14,925	14,925	14,925	59,698
Payment to reduce lease liability	(28,679)	(21,547)	(23,702)	(26,072)	(100,000)					
Financing cash flows	(28,679)	(21,547)	(23,702)	(26,072)	(100,000)	—	—	—	—	—
Total change in cash	€15,960	€15,314	€14,603	€13,821	€59,698	€14,925	€14,925	€14,925	€14,925	€59,698

Solution to 3. Based on ROE, CAPBS looks less profitable than OPIS in the earlier years. Computing ROE requires forecasting shareholders' equity. In general, ending Shareholders' Equity = Beginning Shareholders' Equity + Net Income + Other Comprehensive Income − Dividends + Net Capital Contributions by Shareholders. Because the companies in this example do not have other comprehensive income, did not pay dividends, and experienced no capital contributions from shareholders, Ending shareholders' equity = Beginning shareholders' equity + Net income. The forecasts are presented below.

CAPBS	2007	2008	2009	2010	2011
Retained earnings	€0	€12,508	€26,523	€42,198	€59,698
Common stock	200,000	200,000	200,000	200,000	200,000
Total shareholders' equity	€200,000	€212,508	€226,523	€242,198	€259,698
OPIS					
Retained earnings	€0	€14,925	€29,849	€44,774	€59,698
Common stock	200,000	200,000	200,000	200,000	200,000
Total shareholders' equity	€200,000	€214,925	€229,849	€244,774	€259,698

ROE is calculated as net income divided by average shareholders' equity. For example, CAPBS Inc. had 2008 ROE of 6.1 percent: €12,508 ÷ [(€200,000 + €212,508) ÷ 2].

CAPBS	2008	2009	2010	2011
ROE	6.1%	6.4%	6.7%	7.0%

OPIS	2008	2009	2010	2011
ROE	7.2%	6.7%	6.3%	5.9%

Solution to 4. Based on the ratio of debt-to-equity, the solvency position of CAPBS is weaker than that of OPIS.

For the debt-to-equity ratio, take the total shareholders' equity from part 3 above. Initially, both companies had reported liabilities of €100,000. For OPIS, the amount of total liabilities remains constant at €100,000. For CAPBS, add the lease liability at the end of the year and the amount of accrued interest payable at the end of each year from part 1 above. So for year end 2008, CAPBS's total liabilities are €178,453 (€100,000 + €71,321 lease liability + €7,132 accrued interest payable at the end of the year), and its debt-to-equity ratio is 0.84 (€178,453 ÷ €212,508). For year-end 2009, CAPBS total liabilities equal €154,751 (€100,000 + €49,774 lease liability + €4,977 accrued interest payable at the end of the year). The table below presents the ratios for each year.

CAPBS	2008	2009	2010	2011
Total debt	178,453	154,751	128,679	100,000
Shareholders' equity	212,508	226,523	242,198	259,698
Debt-to-equity ratio	0.84	0.68	0.53	0.39

OPIS	2008	2009	2010	2011
Total debt	100,000	100,000	100,000	100,000
Shareholders' equity	214,925	229,849	244,774	259,698
Debt-to-equity ratio	0.47	0.44	0.41	0.39

In summary, a company reporting a lease as an operating lease will typically show higher profits in early years, higher return measures in early years, and a stronger solvency position than an identical company reporting an identical lease as a finance lease.[6] However, the company reporting the lease as a finance lease will show higher operating cash flows because a portion of the lease payment will be reflected as a financing cash outflow rather than an operating cash outflow.

Because of the well-defined accounting standards in the United States that determine when a company should report an operating versus finance lease, a company can structure a lease to avoid the four finance lease criteria and so record an operating lease. Similar to debt disclosures, lease disclosures show payments under both capital and operating leases for the next five years and afterwards. These disclosures can help to estimate the extent of a company's off-balance-sheet lease financing through operating leases. The example below illustrates the disclosures and how these disclosures can be used to determine the effect on the financial statements if all operating leases were capitalized.

EXAMPLE 13-12   Financial Statement Impact of Treating Operating Leases as Finance Leases for the Lessee

CEC Entertainment, Inc. (NYSE: CEC) has significant commitments under finance (capital) and operating leases. Presented below is selected financial statement information and footnote disclosure to the financial statements for the company.

Commitments and Contingencies Footnote from CEC's Financial Statements

6. Commitments and contingencies:

The company leases certain restaurants and related property and equipment under operating and capital leases. All leases require the company to pay property taxes, insurance, and maintenance of the leased assets. The leases generally have initial terms of 10 to 20 years with various renewal options.

Scheduled annual maturities of the obligations for capital and operating leases as of December 31, 2006, are as follows:

| Years | ($ thousands) | |
	Capital	Operating
2007	$1,679	$62,521
2008	1,679	61,199
2009	1,679	59,892

---

[6]Example 13-11 assumes the company uses the straight-line depreciation method, which is common under IFRS and U.S. GAAP. But if the company estimated depreciation expense based on the "economic" depreciation of the leased asset, there would be no difference in reported income under a finance lease and operating lease.

2010	1,679	61,858
2011	1,679	59,777
2012–2028 (aggregate payments)	13,080	486,831
Minimum future lease payments	21,475	$792,078
Less amounts representing interest	(7,894)	
Present value of future minimum lease payments	13,581	
Less current portion	(693)	
Long-term finance lease obligation	$12,888	

Selected Financial Statement Information for CEC

	31 December 2006	1 January 2006
Total liabilities	$344,979	$308,737
Shareholders' equity	$359,206	$343,183

1. A. Calculate the implicit interest rate used to discount the "scheduled annual maturities" under finance leases to obtain the "present value of future minimum lease payments" of $13,851 disclosed in the Commitments and Contingencies footnote. To simplify the calculation, assume that future minimum lease payments on the company's finance leases are $1,679 on 31 December of each year from 2012 to 2018 and $1,327 in 2019. This is approximately the average annual minimum lease payment for the period 2007 to 2011.

   B. Why is the implicit interest rate estimate in Part A important in assessing a company's leases?

2. If the operating agreements had been treated as finance leases, what additional amount would be reported as a lease obligation on the balance sheet at 31 December 2006? To simplify the calculation, assume that future minimum lease payments on the company's operating leases are $59,777 on 31 December each year from 2012 to 2019 and $8,615 in 2020 ($59,777 is the latest annual minimum lease payment disclosed). Use the implicit interest rate obtained in Part 1A to discount future cash flows on the operating leases.

3. What would be the effect on the debt-to-equity ratio of treating all operating leases as finance leases (i.e., the ratio of total liabilities to equity) at 31 December 2006?

Solutions to 1:

   A. The implicit interest rate on finance leases is 7.4 percent. The implicit interest rate used to discount the finance lease payments is the internal rate of return on the stream of cash flows, i.e. the interest rate that will make the present value of the lease payments equal to $13,581. You can use an Excel spreadsheet or a financial calculator for the computations. Set the cash flow at time zero equal to $13,581 (note on Excel and on most financial calculators, you will input this amount as a negative number), input each of the annual payments on the finance leases, and solve for the internal rate of return.

To demonstrate how the internal rate of return corresponds to the individual present values, refer to the following schedule of the undiscounted minimum lease payments based on information from footnote 6 and the assumptions given. The table below presents the present value computations.

Implicit Interest Rate (the internal rate of return)				7.4%
Fiscal Year	Years to Discount	Minimum Lease Payment	× Present Value Factor	= Present Value
2007	1	$1,679	$1 \div (1 + \text{interest rate})^1$	$1,563
2008	2	1,679	$1 \div (1 + \text{interest rate})^2$	1,456
2009	3	1,679	$1 \div (1 + \text{interest rate})^3$	1,355
2010	4	1,679	$1 \div (1 + \text{interest rate})^4$	1,262
2011	5	1,679	$1 \div (1 + \text{interest rate})^5$	1,175
2012	6	1,679	$1 \div (1 + \text{interest rate})^6$	1,094
2013	7	1,679	$1 \div (1 + \text{interest rate})^7$	1,019
2014	8	1,679	$1 \div (1 + \text{interest rate})^8$	948
2015	9	1,679	$1 \div (1 + \text{interest rate})^9$	883
2016	10	1,679	$1 \div (1 + \text{interest rate})^{10}$	822
2017	11	1,679	$1 \div (1 + \text{interest rate})^{11}$	766
2018	12	1,679	$1 \div (1 + \text{interest rate})^{12}$	713
2019	13	1,327	$1 \div (1 + \text{interest rate})^{13}$	525
Undiscounted sum of minimum future lease payments		$21,475		
Present value of future minimum lease payments			$13,581	$13,581

The interest rate of 7.4 percent equates the future minimum lease payments with the present value of future minimum lease payments of $13,581 that CEC reports.

B. The implicit interest rate is important because it will be used to estimate the present value of the lease obligations reported as a liability, the value of the leased assets on the balance sheet, the interest expense, and the lease amortization on the income statement. For instance, by selecting a higher rate a company can opportunistically reduce reported debt, if desired. The reasonableness of the implicit interest rate can be gauged by comparing it to the interest rates of the company's other debt outstanding, which are disclosed in financial statement footnotes, and considering recent market conditions.

Solution to 2. If the operating leases had been treated as finance leases, the additional amount that would be reported as a lease obligation on the balance sheet at 31 December 2006 using a discount rate of 7.4 percent determined in part 1 above is $497,078. The table below presents the present value computations. An alternative short cut approach is to divide the discounted finance lease cash flows of $13,581 by the undiscounted finance lease cash flows of $21,475, and then apply the resulting percentage of 63.24 percent to the undiscounted operating lease cash flows of $792,078. The shortcut approach estimates the present value of the operating lease payments as $500,918, which is close to the estimate obtained using the longer method. It is likely to be most accurate when the temporal pattern of the two sets of cash flows is similar.

Implicit Interest Rate				7.4%
Fiscal Year	**Years to Discount**	**Operating Lease Payments**	**× Present Value Factor**	**= Present Value**
2007	1	$62,521	$1 \div (1 + 0.074)^1$	$58,213
2008	2	61,199	$1 \div (1 + 0.074)^2$	53,056
2009	3	59,892	$1 \div (1 + 0.074)^3$	48,345
2010	4	61,858	$1 \div (1 + 0.074)^4$	46,492
2011	5	59,777	$1 \div (1 + 0.074)^5$	41,832
2012	6	59,777	$1 \div (1 + 0.074)^6$	38,950
2013	7	59,777	$1 \div (1 + 0.074)^7$	36,266
2014	8	59,777	$1 \div (1 + 0.074)^8$	33,768
2015	9	59,777	$1 \div (1 + 0.074)^9$	31,441
2016	10	59,777	$1 \div (1 + 0.074)^{10}$	29,275
2017	11	59,777	$1 \div (1 + 0.074)^{11}$	27,258
2018	12	59,777	$1 \div (1 + 0.074)^{12}$	25,379
2019	13	59,777	$1 \div (1 + 0.074)^{13}$	23,631
2020	14	8,615	$1 \div (1 + 0.074)^{14}$	3,171
Undiscounted sum of future operating lease payment		$792,078		
Present value of future operating lease payments				$497,078

Solution to 3. The debt-to-equity ratio increases to 234.4 percent from 96.0 percent when capitalizing the operating leases. The adjusted debt-to-equity ratio is computed as follows:

	Unadjusted for Operating Leases	**Adjustment to Capitalize Operating Leases**	**Adjusted to Capitalize Operating Leases**
Total liabilities	$344,979	$497,078	$842,057
Common shareholders' equity	359,206		359,206
Debt-to-equity ratio	96.0%		234.4%

4.2.2. Accounting and Reporting by the Lessor

As previously mentioned, lessors that report under U.S. GAAP determine whether a lease is a finance (also called *capital lease*) or operating lease using the same four criteria as a lessee, plus additional revenue recognition criteria. If a lessor enters into an operating lease, the lessor records any lease revenue when earned. The lessor also continues to report the leased asset on the balance sheet and the asset's associated depreciation expense on the income statement.

From the lessor's perspective, there are two types of finance leases: (1) **direct financing leases**, and (2) **sales-type leases**.[7] A direct financing lease results when the present value of lease payments (and thus the amount recorded as a lease receivable) equals the carrying value of the leased asset. Because there is no "profit" on the asset itself, the lessor is essentially providing financing to the lessee, and the revenues earned by the lessor are financing in nature (i.e., interest revenue). If, however, the present value of lease payments (and thus the amount recorded as a lease receivable) exceeds the carrying value of the leased asset, the lease is treated as a sale.

Both types of finance lease have two similar effects on the balance sheet: the lessor reports a lease receivable based on the present value of future lease payments, and the lessor also reduces its assets by the carrying value of the asset leased. The carrying value of the asset leased relative to the present value of lease payments distinguishes a direct financing lease from a sales-type lease. The income statement effect will thus differ based on the type of lease. See Example 13-13.

In a sales-type lease, the lessor "sells" the asset to the lessee and also provides financing on the sale. Therefore, in a sales-type lease, a lessor reports revenue from the sale, cost of goods sold (i.e., the carrying value of the asset leased), profit on the sale, and interest revenue earned from financing the sale.

---

[7]IFRS do not make the distinction between a sales-type lease and a direct financing lease. However, a similar treatment to "sales-type" is allowed for finance leases originated by "manufacturer or dealer lessors," within the general provisions for finance leases.

EXAMPLE 13-13 Financial Statement Impact of a Direct Financing Lease versus Operating Lease for the Lessor

Assume two similar (hypothetical) companies, DIRFIN Inc. and LOPER Inc., own a similar piece of machinery and make similar agreements to lease the machinery on 1 January 2008. In the lease contract, each company requires four annual payments of €28,679 starting on 1 January 2008. The useful life of the machine is four years and its salvage value is zero. DIRFIN Inc. accounts for the lease as a direct financing lease while LOPER has determined the lease is an operating lease. (For simplicity, this example assumes that the accounting rules governing these hypothetical companies do not mandate either type of lease.) The present value of lease payments and fair value of the equipment is €100,000.

At the beginning of 2008, before entering into the lease agreement, both companies reported liabilities of €100,000 and equity of €200,000. Assets on hand include the asset about to be leased. Each year the companies receive total revenues of €50,000 cash, apart from any revenue earned on the lease. Assume the companies have a tax rate of 30 percent, and use the same accounting for financial and tax purposes. Both companies' discount rate is 10 percent. In order to focus only on the differences in the type of lease, assume neither company incurs expenses other than those associated with the lease and neither invests excess cash.

1. Which company reports higher expenses/net income in 2008? Over the four years?
2. Which company reports higher total cash flow over the four years? Cash flow from operations?
3. Based on ROE, how do the two companies' profitability measures compare?

Solution to 1. LOPER reports higher expenses in 2008 because under an operating lease, the lessor retains ownership of the asset and continues to report associated depreciation expense. DIRFIN, treating the lease as a finance lease, does not reflect ownership of the asset or associated depreciation expense. DIRFIN has higher net income in 2008 because the interest revenue component of the lease payment in that year exceeds the lease revenue net of depreciation reported by LOPER.

On its income statement, LOPER reports depreciation expense for the asset it has leased and lease revenue based on the lease payment received. The following table shows LOPER's depreciation and book values on leased equipment by year.[8]

---

[8]The computations included throughout the example were made using an Excel worksheet; small apparent discrepancies in the calculations are due to the rounding.

Year	Cost	Depreciation Expense	Accumulated Depreciation	Book Value (Year End)
	(a)	(b)	(c)	(d)
2008	€100,000	€25,000	€25,000	€75,000
2009	100,000	25,000	50,000	50,000
2010	100,000	25,000	75,000	25,000
2011	100,000	25,000	100,000	0
		€100,000		

- Column (a) is the cost of €100,000 of the leased equipment.
- Column (b) is depreciation expense of €25,000 per year, calculated using the straight-line method as the cost less the salvage value divided by the useful life [(€100,000 − €0) ÷ 4 years].
- Column (c) is the accumulated depreciation on the leased asset calculated as the prior year's accumulated depreciation plus the current year's depreciation expense.
- Column (d) is the ending book value of the leased equipment, which is the difference between the cost and accumulated depreciation.

However, DIRFIN records the lease as a direct financing lease. It removes the leased asset from its records and records a lease receivable. On its income statement, DIRFIN reports interest revenues earned from financing the lease. The table below shows DIRFIN's interest revenue and carrying values on the lease receivable.

Year	Lease Receivable, 1 January	Annual Lease Payment Received, 1 January	Interest (at 10%; accrued in previous year)	Reduction of Lease Receivable, 1 January	Lease Receivable on 31 December after Lease Payment on 1 January of Same Year
	(a)	(b)	(c)	(d)	(e)
2008	€100,000	€28,679	€0	€28,679	€71,321
2009	71,321	28,679	7,132	21,547	49,774
2010	49,774	28,679	4,977	23,702	26,072
2011	26,072	28,679	2,607	26,072	0
		€114,717	€14,717	€100,000	

- Column (a) is the lease receivable at the beginning of the year.
- Column (b) is annual lease payment received at the beginning of the year, which is allocated to interest and reduction of the lease receivable.
- Column (c) is interest for the year calculated as the lease receivable outstanding for the year multiplied by the interest rate.
- Column (d) is the reduction of the lease receivable which is the difference between the annual lease payments received and interest. Because the lease payment is due on 1 January, this amount of interest is a receivable at the end of the *prior* year and the interest revenue of the *prior* year.
- Column (e) is the lease receivable after the lease payment is received and at the end of the year. It is the lease receivable at 1 January (Column a) less the reduction of the lease receivable (Column d).

The table below summarizes and compares the income statement effects of the lease for DIRFIN and LOPER. Notice that over the four-year lease, both companies report the same total amount of revenue, but DIRFIN's revenues in the earlier years of the lease are higher than the net of lease revenues less depreciation reported by LOPER in those years.

Year	DIRFIN Lease Revenue	LOPER Lease Revenue	Depreciation Expense	Total	Difference
2008	€7,132	€28,679	€25,000	€3,679	€3,453
2009	4,977	28,679	25,000	3,679	1,298
2010	2,607	28,679	25,000	3,679	(1,072)
2011	—	28,679	25,000	3,679	(−3,679)
Total	€14,717	€114,717	€100,000	€14,717	€0

The complete income statements for DIRFIN and LOPER are presented in the following table. Notice that, under the assumption that the same accounting is used for financial and tax purposes, DIRFIN's taxes are higher than those of LOPER in 2008 and 2009.

Income Statements	DIRFIN					LOPER				
	2008	2009	2010	2011	Total	2008	2009	2010	2011	Total
Sales	€50,000	€50,000	€50,000	€50,000	€200,000	€50,000	€50,000	€50,000	€50,000	€200,000
Depreciation expense						(25,000)	(25,000)	(25,000)	(25,000)	(100,000)
Interest revenue	7,132	4,977	2,607		14,717					
Lease revenue						28,679	28,679	28,679	28,679	114,717
Income before taxes	€57,132	€54,977	€52,607	€50,000	€214,717	€53,679	€53,679	€53,679	€53,679	€214,717
Tax expense	17,140	16,493	15,782	15,000	64,415	16,104	16,104	16,104	16,104	64,415
Net income	€39,992	€38,484	€36,825	€35,000	€150,302	€37,575	€37,575	€37,575	€37,575	€150,302

Solution to 2. Looking at the statement of cash flows, observe that operating cash flows reported by DIRFIN are lower, but investing cash flows are higher than LOPER. Over the four years, both DIRFIN and LOPER report the same total change in cash.

Statements of Cash Flows	DIRFIN					LOPER				
	2008	2009	2010	2011	Total	2008	2009	2010	2011	Total
Net income	€39,992	€38,484	€36,825	€35,000	€150,302	€37,575	€37,575	€37,575	€37,575	€150,302
Increase(decrease) in interest receivable	7,132	(2,155)	(2,370)	(2,607)	0					
Add back depreciation expense						25,000	25,000	25,000	25,000	100,000
Operating cash flows	€32,860	€40,639	€39,195	€37,607	€150,302	€62,575	€62,575	€62,575	€62,575	€250,302
Payments received on finance leases	28,679	21,547	23,702	26,072	100,000					
Investing cash flows	28,679	21,547	23,702	26,072	100,000					
Change in cash	€61,540	€62,186	€62,897	€63,679	€250,302	€62,575	€62,575	€62,575	€62,575	€250,302

Solution to 3. Based on ROE, DIRFIN appears more profitable than LOPER in the early years of the lease. Computing ROE requires forecasting shareholders' equity. In general, ending Shareholders' equity = Beginning shareholders' equity + Net income + Other comprehensive income − Dividends + Net capital contributions by shareholders. Because the companies in this example do not have other comprehensive income, do not pay dividends, and have no capital contributions, Ending shareholders' equity = Beginning shareholders' equity + Net income. The forecasts are presented below.

DIRFIN	2007	2008	2009	2010	2011
Retained earnings	€0	€39,992	€78,477	€115,302	€150,302
Common stock	200,000	200,000	200,000	200,000	200,000
Total shareholders' equity	€200,000	€239,992	€278,477	€315,302	€350,302

LOPER					
Retained earnings	€0	€37,575	€75,151	€112,726	€150,302
Common stock	200,000	200,000	200,000	200,000	200,000
Total shareholders' equity	€200,000	€237,575	€275,151	€312,726	€350,302

ROE is calculated as net income divided by average shareholders' equity. For example, DIRFIN Inc. had 2008 ROE of 18.2 percent: €39,992 ÷ [(€200,000 + €239,992) ÷ 2].

DIRFIN	2008	2009	2010	2011
ROE	18.2%	14.8%	12.4%	10.5%

LOPER	2008	2009	2010	2011
ROE	17.2%	14.7%	12.8%	11.3%

From the comparisons above, DIRFIN looks more profitable in the early years of the lease, but less profitable in the later years.

543

When a company enters into a sales-type lease, a lease agreement where the present value of lease payment is greater than the value of the leased asset to the lessor, it will show a profit on the transaction in the year of inception and interest revenue over the life of the lease.

EXAMPLE 13-14   Financial Statement Impact of a Sales-Type Lease for the Lessor

Assume a (hypothetical) company, Selnow Inc., owns a piece of machinery and enters into an agreement to lease the machinery on 1 January 2008. In the lease contract, the company requires four annual payments of €28,679 starting on 1 January 2008. The present value of the lease payments (using a 10 percent discount rate) is €100,000, and the fair value of the equipment is €90,000. The useful life of the machinery is four years and its salvage value is zero.

1. Is the lease above a direct financing or sales-type lease?
2. What is Selnow's income related to the lease in 2008? In 2009? Ignore taxes.

Solution to 1. The above lease is a sales-type lease. The present value of lease payments is more than the lessor's carrying value of the leased asset, the difference being the lessors' profit from selling the machinery. The lessor will record a profit of €10,000 on the sale of the leased equipment in 2008 (€100,000 present value of lease payments receivable less €90,000 value of leased equipment).

Solution to 2. In 2008, Selnow shows income of €17,132 related to the lease. One part of this is the €10,000 gain on the sale of the lease equipment (sales revenues of €100,000 less costs of goods sold of €90,000). Selnow also shows interest revenue of €7,132 on its financing of the lease (lease receivable of €71,321 after the initial lease payment is received times the 10 percent discount rate). In 2009, Selnow reports only the interest revenue of €4,977 (lease receivable of €49,774 after the 1 January lease payment is received times the 10 percent discount rate). The table below shows lease payments received, interest revenue, and reduction of the lease receivable for Selnow's sales-type lease. Note that this table is the same as DIRFIN's table in the previous example with the direct financing lease. They are the same because the present value of the lease payments in both cases is the same. It is the fair value of the equipment that differs between the two examples.

	Lease Receivable, 1 January	Annual Lease Payment Received, 1 January	Interest (at 10%; accrued in previous year)	Reduction of Lease Receivable, 1 January	Lease Receivable on 31 December after Lease Payment on 1 January Same Year
	(a)	(b)	(c)	(d)	(e)
2008	€100,000	€28,679	€0	€28,679	€71,321
2009	71,321	28,679	7,132	21,547	49,774
2010	49,774	28,679	4,977	23,702	26,072
2011	26,072	28,679	2,607	26,072	0
		€114,717	€14,717	€100,000	

5. OTHER TYPES OF OFF-BALANCE-SHEET FINANCING

An operating lease is only one type of contractual obligation that is not recognized as a liability on the balance sheet. Companies can engage in other types of off-balance-sheet arrangements that do not result in additional liabilities reported on the balance sheet but nonetheless create economic obligations. Examples include (but are not limited to) take-or-pay contracts, throughput arrangements, and the sale of receivables. Each of these is described below. An analyst should consider the effect on financial statements and financial ratios of adjustments to reflect the economic reality of **off-balance-sheet financing** activities.

5.1. Take-or-Pay and Throughput

With a take-or-pay contract, a company commits to buying a minimum quantity of an item (such as raw materials and other inputs) over a certain time period. Even if the company does not take delivery, it must still pay for the item. Similarly, with a throughput arrangement, a company commits to pay a minimum amount for transporting its production through a delivery channel. For example, a gas company or group of gas companies may commit to pay a minimum amount periodically to use a pipeline for delivering gas. Prices in the arrangements can be fixed or related to market prices. One reason for making such arrangements is to secure access to raw materials or to transport capacity. Another reason for making such arrangements is to facilitate the financing of a large project, such as a pipeline, on a standalone basis by providing a committed stream of cash inflows to the project.

Even though the company has committed to make minimum payments under take-or-pay and throughput arrangements, accounting standards do not require the liability to be recognized on the balance sheet. As a corollary, the standards also do not require the item being purchased to be recognized as an asset on the balance sheet. However, the purchaser commonly discloses the nature and minimum required payments in the footnotes to the financial statements and in the MD&A. The U.S. SEC (in a 2003 rule adopted at the direction of the Sarbanes-Oxley Act of 2002) specifically requires companies to explain off-balance-sheet arrangements in a separately captioned disclosure in the MD&A and also to provide a tabular summary of known contractual obligations, including both on- and off-balance-sheet obligations. Footnote disclosures about obligations not reflected on a company's balance sheet generally appear under the caption "Commitments and Contingencies."

For analytical purposes, disclosures about financial commitments are useful in assessing how a company's solvency position, as reflected in leverage ratios, is affected by off-balance-sheet items. Example 13-15 illustrates the effect of adjusting a company's debt-to-capital ratio by adding the commitments under a take-or-pay arrangement to the company's total debt. For ratios involving assets, the adjustment would include adding both the assets to be purchased and the associated debt commitments to the relevant balance sheet amounts. Disclosures about financial commitments in forthcoming years are also useful when assessing a company's liquidity position.

EXAMPLE 13-15   Financial Statement Impact of Off-Balance-Sheet Take-or-Pay Arrangements

Wheeling-Pittsburgh Corporation (NasdaqGM: WPSC) provides information about contractual obligations in its "Management's Discussion and Analysis [MD&A] of Financial Condition and Results of Operations" section of its 2006 10-K filing and in the footnotes to its 2006 financial statements.

The first excerpt is from the contractual obligations disclosures in the company's MD&A, and the second excerpt is from the "Commitments and Contingencies" footnote to the company's financial statements.

Excerpt from the Contractual Obligations table included in the company's MD&A showing the company's purchase commitments

CONTRACTUAL OBLIGATIONS (as of December 31, 2006)

...	Contractual Payments Due ($ millions)				
	Total	Less than 1 Year	1–3 Years	3–5 Years	More than 5 Years
Purchase commitments:					
Oxygen supply	93.3	10.0	20.0	23.2	40.1
Electricity	83.7	7.5	15.0	14.0	47.2
Coal	8.4	8.4	—	—	—
Coal	11.3	11.3	—	—	—

We entered into a 15-year take-or-pay contract in 1999 that was amended in 2003. The contract requires us to purchase oxygen, nitrogen and argon each month with a minimum monthly charge of approximately $0.7 million, subject to escalation clauses.

We entered into a 20-year take-or-pay contract in 1999, which was amended in 2003. The contract requires us to purchase steam and electricity each month or pay a minimum monthly charge of approximately $0.5 million, subject to increases for inflation, and a variable charge calculated at a minimum of $3.75 times the number of tons of iron produced each month with an agreed-to minimum of 3,250 tons per day, regardless of whether any tons are produced. At December 31, 2006, a maximum termination payment of $27.7 million would have been required to terminate the contract.

In 2004, we amended our contract to purchase coal each month to a minimum monthly charge of approximately $0.7 million. The term of the contract expires on December 31, 2007.

In 2005, we entered into contracts to purchase 20,000 tons of coal each month from August 2006 through May 2007 at a price approximating $94.50 per ton.

Excerpt from the Commitments and Contingencies footnote to 2006 financial statements:

Commitments

The Company entered into a 15-year take-or-pay contract in 1999, which was amended in 2003 and requires the Company to purchase oxygen, nitrogen and argon each month with a minimum monthly charge of approximately $600, *subject to escalation clauses. Payments for deliveries under this contract totaled $12,150, $10,621 and $14,200 during 2006, 2005 and 2004, respectively.*

The Company entered into a 20-year contract in 1999, which was amended in 2003 and requires the Company to purchase steam and electricity each month or pay a minimum monthly charge of approximately $500, subject to increases for inflation, and a variable charge calculated at a minimum of $3.75 times the number of tons of iron produced each month, with an agreed-to minimum of 3,250 tons per day, regardless of whether any tons are produced. Payments for delivery of steam and electricity under this contract totaled $12,867, $9,652 and $9,150 during 2006, 2005 and 2004, respectively. At December 31, 2006, a maximum termination payment of approximately $27,750 would have been required to terminate the contract.

Additional information:

The company's shareholders' equity at 31 December 2006 was $286.2 million, and total debt was $287.1 million. All dollar amounts are in millions.

Required: Use the disclosures and additional information provided to estimate the effect on WPSC's debt-to-capital ratio for 2006 if the purchase commitments were included as debt.

Solution: The company's debt-to-capital ratio increases to 0.63 from 0.50 when its purchase commitments are included on the balance sheet. The company has two take-or-pay contracts disclosed in its MD&A and the footnotes to its financial statements totaling commitments of $196.7 million (93.3 + 83.7 + 8.4 + 11.3) at 31 December 2006. Including these off-balance-sheet arrangements in the financial statement would reflect a deterioration in the company's ratio.

	As Reported	Adjustment for Purchase Commitments	Adjusted
Total debt	$287.1	$196.7	$483.8
Total capital (debt plus equity)	573.3	196.7	770.0
Debt-to-capital ratio	0.50		0.63

In this example, the purchase commitments do not dramatically increase the debt-to-total capital ratio. If the debt-to-capital ratio increased enough to be of concern, the analyst might discount the purchase commitments to their present value, which would provide a better estimate. Such an estimate would produce a debt-to-capital ratio between 0.50 and 0.63.

5.2. Sale of Receivables

To accelerate cash flows, a company can sell its accounts receivable to a third party. A securitization of receivables typically involves the company first selling the receivables to a trust (set up as a special purpose entity, or SPE), and then the SPE selling debt securities backed by the receivables. The receivables may be trade receivables, mortgages, or various other types of financial assets.

The company selling the receivables, however, often retains some of the risk that the receivable is not collected. Roughly, this means if the borrower owing under the receivable sold to the SPE defaults, the company that sold the receivables would be obligated to reimburse the SPE for some of the amount of the default. Depending on the amount of default risk that the company retains, the sale of receivables can be viewed as the economic equivalent of collateralized borrowing. Accounting standards (SFAS No. 140 and IAS 39) discuss the circumstances in which a company recognizes the transaction as a collateralized borrowing (in which the company's financial statements would reflect a liability) versus a sale (in which the company would not reflect a liability). Additionally, companies disclose information about securitized assets in the footnotes to their financial statements, including the principal amounts and losses arising from defaults (SFAS No. 140 and IFRS 7).

Disclosures about accounts receivable facilitate assessment of a company's financial position. When receivables are transferred, and the transfer is accounted for as a sale, accounts receivable decrease and operating cash flows increase. To the extent that an analyst considers the transfer of receivables as borrowings, the cash received should be reclassified to financing cash flows from operating cash flows. Additionally, accounts receivable and current liabilities should be increased by the amount of receivables that were sold before computing ratios.

EXAMPLE 13-16   Financial Statement Impact of Sale of Receivables

Stanley Works (NYSE: SWK) discloses the following information on the sale of accounts receivable in its 2006 financial statement footnotes:

Excerpt from footnotes to 2006 financial statements:

B. ACCOUNTS AND NOTES RECEIVABLE

The Company has agreements to sell, on a revolving basis, undivided interests in defined pools of notes receivable to a Qualified Special Purpose Entity ("QSPE"). The entity is designed to facilitate the securitization of certain trade accounts receivable and is used as an additional source of liquidity. . . . The proceeds from sales of such eligible receivables to the QSPE in revolving-period securitizations were $43.9 million in 2006 and $4.7 million in 2005. There were no gains or losses on these sales. The amounts deducted from receivables in the December 30, 2006 and December 31, 2005 Consolidated Balance Sheets under this arrangement were $60.3 million and $16.4 million, respectively. The Company is responsible for servicing and collecting the receivables sold and held in the QSPE. . . .

The company's statement of cash flows shows that operating cash flows for fiscal 2006 were $439.1 million. Its balance sheet on 30 December 2006 shows total current assets and total current liabilities of $1,638.5 million and $1,251.1 million, respectively. All dollar amounts are in millions.

Use the disclosures and additional information provided to estimate the following for 2006:

- The effect on the operating cash flows if the proceeds from the sale of accounts receivable had been classified as financing cash flows.
- The effect on the current ratio of treating the asset transfer as a collateralized borrowing (i.e., continuing to include the receivables in both current assets and current liabilities).

Solution: The company's operating cash flows decrease by approximately 10 percent to $395.2 million from $439.1 million when proceeds from the sale of accounts receivable are reclassified to financing cash flows. Its current ratio decreases only slightly from 1.31 to 1.30.

	As Reported	Adjustment for Sale of Trade A/R	Adjusted
Operating cash flows	$439.1	$43.9	$395.2
Total current assets	1,638.5	60.3	1,698.8
Total current liabilities	1,251.1	60.3	1,311.4
Current ratio	1.31		1.30

6. SUMMARY

Key points include the following:

- The sales proceeds of a bond issue are determined by discounting future cash payments using the market rate of interest. The reported interest expense on bonds is based on the market interest rate.
- Future cash payments on bonds usually include periodic interest payments (made at the stated rate) and the principal amount at maturity.
- When the market rate of interest is the stated rate for the bonds, the bonds will sell at par (i.e., at a price equal to the face value). When the market rate of interest is higher than the bonds' stated rate, the bonds will sell at a discount. When the market rate of interest is lower than the bonds' stated rate, the bonds will sell at a premium.
- An issuer amortizes any issuance discount or premium on bonds over the life of the bonds.
- If a company redeems bonds before maturity, it may show a gain or loss on debt extinguishment computed as the net book value of the bonds (including bond issuance costs under IFRS) less the amount required to redeem the bonds.
- Debt covenants impose restrictions on borrowers such as limitations on future borrowing or requirements to maintain a minimum debt-to-equity ratio.
- The book value of bonds is based on the face value adjusted for any unamortized discount or premium, which can differ from its fair value. Such a difference will be due to

the implicit discount rate, established at the time of issue, being different from the current market rate.

- Under U.S. GAAP, convertible bonds, which allow bondholders to convert the bonds to equity, are reported at issuance with no separate value attributed to the conversion feature. IFRS separates the debt from the conversion feature, which is reported as equity.
- Bonds with warrants giving the holder the right to purchase additional shares of the issuer's common stock are reported at issuance with the issue proceeds allocated between the bonds and the warrants.
- Some financial instruments have characteristics of both debt and equity. If the financial instruments are treated as equity, solvency ratios based on the financial statements appear stronger.
- Accounting standards generally define two types of leases: operating leases and finance (or capital) leases. U.S. accounting standards have four specific requirements that define when a lease is a finance lease. International standards are less prescriptive.
- When a lessee reports a lease as an operating lease rather than a finance lease, it usually appears more profitable in early years of the lease and less so later, and it appears more solvent over the whole period.
- When a company has a substantial amount of operating leases, adjusting reported financials to include the impact of capitalizing these leases better reflects the company's solvency position.
- When a lessor reports a lease as a finance lease rather than an operating lease, it usually appears more profitable in early years of the lease.
- In direct financing leases, a lessor earns only interest revenue. In a sales-types lease, a lessor earns both interest revenue and a profit (or loss) on the sale of the leased asset.
- Companies can engage in other types of off-balance-sheet arrangements to avoid reporting additional liabilities on the balance sheet such as take-or-pay contracts, throughput arrangements, and the sale of receivables. Analysis should assess the impact on financial statements and financial ratios of adjustments reflecting the economic reality of off-balance-sheet financing activities.

PRACTICE PROBLEMS

1. A company issues $1 million of bonds at face value. When the bonds are issued, the company will record a
   A. cash inflow from investing activities.
   B. cash inflow from financing activities.
   C. cash inflow from operating activities.

2. Alpha Aircraft receives $1 million for bonds issued at face value, and Beta Bizjets receives $1 million for bonds issued at a discount. As a result of the bond issue, compared to Alpha Aircraft, Beta Bizjets will *most likely* record higher
   A. periodic interest expense on the income statement.
   B. liabilities on the balance sheet at the time of issue.
   C. periodic interest payments on the cash flow statement.

3. Oil Exploration LLC paid $45,000 related to printing, legal fees, commissions, and other costs associated with its recent bond issue. Under U.S. GAAP it is most likely to record these costs on its financial statements as

   A. an asset.

   B. a liability.

   C. a cash outflow from investing activities.

4. On 1 January 2008, Elegant Fragrances Company issues $1 million worth of five-year bonds with annual interest payments of $55,000 paid each 31 December. The market interest rate is 6.0 percent. Using the effective interest rate method of amortizing, Elegant Fragrances is *most likely* to record

   A. interest expense of $55,000 on its 2008 income statement.

   B. a liability of $982,674 on the 31 December 2008 balance sheet.

   C. a $58,736 cash outflow from operating activity on the 2008 statement of cash flows.

5. Consolidated Enterprises issues $10 million worth of five-year bonds with a stated rate of 6.5 percent at a time when the market interest rate is 6.0 percent. Using the effective interest rate method of amortizing, the carrying value after one year will be *closest to*

   A. $10.17 million.

   B. $10.21 million.

   C. $10.28 million.

6. Innovative Inventions, Inc. needs to raise $10 million and typically would issue coupon-bearing bonds at par value. If the company chooses to issue zero-coupon bonds instead, its debt-to-equity ratio will

   A. rise as the maturity date approaches.

   B. decline as the maturity date approaches.

   C. remain constant throughout the life of the bond.

7. Fairmont Golf issued fixed rate debt when interest rates were 6 percent. Rates have since risen to 7 percent. Using the values reported on the financial statements would *most likely* cause an analyst to

   A. overestimate Fairmont's economic liabilities.

   B. underestimate Fairmont's economic liabilities.

   C. underestimate Fairmont's interest coverage ratio.

8. Debt covenants are *least likely* to place restrictions on the issuer's ability to

   A. pay dividends.

   B. issue additional debt.

   C. issue additional equity.

9. Sheila Cummins is analyzing the financial statements of a company that has issued convertible bonds that are currently reported as debt. Cummins is considering potential adjustments to the debt-to-equity ratio as part of her analysis. The *least appropriate* action would be to

   A. make no adjustment.

   B. adjust debt but not equity.

   C. adjust equity but not debt.

10. Why-Fi Incorporated reports total equity of $10 million. It has also issued convertible bonds with a book value of $10 million that are convertible into equity with a current

market value of $15 million. Under U.S. GAAP, if the bonds are converted, Why-Fi will report total equity *closest to*

A. $10 million.
B. $20 million.
C. $25 million.

11. When analyzing the financial statements of Energy Resources, Inc., Frederico Montalban, CFA, is treating its convertible bonds issue as equity rather than debt. Montalban's analysis is *most likely* appropriate

A. if the conversion price is near the current market price of the stock.
B. if the conversion price is significantly above the current market price of the stock.
C. if the conversion price is significantly below the current market price of the stock.

12. Capitol Services Corp. has $300 million in shareholders' equity and $400 million in long-term debt, of which $200 million are convertible bonds. What would Capitol's long-term debt-to-equity ratio be if the bonds were converted?

A. 0.40
B. 0.80
C. 0.67

13. Assets that are being used under a synthetic lease are reported as though the lessee owns them

A. for tax purposes and on the financial statements.
B. on the financial statements but not for tax purposes.
C. for tax purposes but not on the financial statements.

14. Compared to using a finance lease, a lessee that makes use of an operating lease will report higher

A. debt.
B. rent expense.
C. cash flow from operating activity.

15. The notes to the financial statements of Bargain Apparel Corp. disclose that the company has finance lease commitments with minimum future payments of $20 million, of which $6 million represents interest payments. It also has operating leases with minimum future payments of $25 million. If Robert Xu, CFA, wishes to adjust the financial statements to treat all leases as debt, he should increase reported total liabilities by an amount *closest to*

A. $17.5 million.
B. $25.0 million.
C. $45.0 million.

16. Compared to an identical company that uses an operating lease, a company that uses a finance lease will *most likely* produce a reported return on equity (ROE) that

A. starts lower but rises during the life of the lease.
B. starts higher but decline during the life of the lease.
C. starts lower and remains so during the life of the lease.

17. For a lessor, the leased asset appears on the balance sheet and continues to be depreciated when the lease is classified as
    A. a sales-type lease.
    B. an operating lease.
    C. a direct financing lease.

18. A lessor's reported revenues at lease inception will be *highest* if the lease is classified as
    A. a sales-type lease.
    B. an operating lease.
    C. a direct financing lease.

19. The lessor will record interest income if the lease is classified as
    A. sales-type only.
    B. direct financing only.
    C. either sales-type or direct financing.

20. Cavalier Copper Mines has $840 million in total liabilities and $520 million in shareholders' equity. It has disclosed $100 million in purchase commitments over the next five years. An analyst wishing to treat the purchase commitments as debt would calculate a debt to total capital ratio *closest to*
    A. 0.58.
    B. 0.59.
    C. 0.64.

21. Charles McKimmon, CFA, is analyzing the financial statements of Computers On Credit, Inc. (COC). COC has sold $60 million of accounts receivable for proceeds of $50 million, and McKimmon wishes to treat the transaction as collateralized borrowing. McKimmon's financial statement adjustments will *most likely* include adding
    A. $50 million to accounts receivable.
    B. $50 million to cash flows from financing activity.
    C. $50 million to cash flows from operating activity.

CHAPTER 14

EMPLOYEE COMPENSATION: POSTRETIREMENT AND SHARE-BASED

Elaine Henry, CFA

University of Miami
Coral Gables, Florida

Elizabeth A. Gordon

Temple University
Philadelphia, Pennsylvania

LEARNING OUTCOMES

After completing this chapter, you will be able to do the following:

- Explain the types of postretirement benefit plans and the implications for financial reports.
- Explain the measures of a defined-benefit pension plan's liabilities, including the projected benefit obligation, accumulated benefit obligation, and vested benefit obligation.
- Describe the components of a company's defined-benefit pension expense and explain the impact of plan assumptions on that pension expense.
- Explain the impact on financial statements of International Financial Reporting Standards (IFRS) and U.S. generally accepted accounting principles (U.S. GAAP) for pension and other postretirement benefits that permit some items to be reported in the footnotes rather than being reflected in the financial statements themselves.
- Evaluate pension plan footnote disclosures, including cash flow–related information.

- Evaluate the underlying economic liability (or asset) of a company based upon pension and other postretirement benefit disclosures.
- Calculate the underlying economic pension and other postretirement expense (income) based on disclosures.
- Discuss the main issues involved in accounting for share-based compensation.
- Explain the impact on financial statements of accounting for stock grants and stock options, and the importance of companies' assumptions in valuing these grants and options.

1. INTRODUCTION

This chapter covers two aspects of employee compensation that involve some complexity: postretirement benefits and share-based compensation. Postretirement benefits include pensions and other postretirement benefits such as health insurance. Examples of share-based compensation are stock options and stock grants.

A common theme across both aspects of employee compensation discussed here is the difficulty in measuring the value of these types of compensation. This chapter will provide an overview of these measurement issues and review the implications for financial statement analysis.

The chapter is organized as follows: Section 2 addresses pensions and other postretirement benefits, and section 3 covers share-based compensation, with a focus primarily on the accounting for and analysis of stock options. Section 4 summarizes the chapter, and practice problems in the CFA Institute item set format conclude the chapter.

2. PENSIONS AND OTHER POSTRETIREMENT BENEFITS

This section discusses the accounting and reporting of pensions and other post retirement benefits by the companies that provide these benefits (accounting and reporting by pension and other retirement funds are not covered in this chapter). The discussion begins with an overview of the types of benefits and measurement issues involved. It then continues with financial statement reporting of pension and other postretirement benefits including an overview of critical assumptions used to value these benefits. The section concludes with a discussion of evaluating pension and other postretirement benefit disclosures.

2.1. Types of Postretirement Benefit Plans and the Implications for Financial Reports

Companies may offer various types of benefits to their employees following retirement, including pension plans, medical insurance, and life insurance. Some of these benefits involve payments in the current period but many are promises of future benefits, and implications for financial reports differ accordingly.

Pension plans may be either defined-contribution plans or defined-benefit plans. **Defined-contribution (DC) pension plans** establish individual accounts for participating employees, which the employee can make contributions to, typically on a tax-advantaged basis (e.g., 401(k) plans in the United States), and typically with the employer also contributing to the plan. These plans are known as *defined contribution* because the amounts of contributions to the pension plan are defined at the outset, but the future value of the benefit is unknown. The future value of the benefits to be received by the employee after retirement depends on the performance of the investments within the plan. Any gains or losses related to the investments accrue to the employee. In other words, in DC pension plans, the employee bears the investment risk of the plan assets. The employer makes its contributions, if any, to the plan in each period and reflects these contributions as expenses on the income statement; it bears no future responsibility, and thus no pension-related liabilities accrue.

In contrast to defined-contribution plans, in **defined-benefit (DB) pension plans** the company promises to pay a certain annual amount to its employees after retirement; in other words, the benefit is defined. The future benefit is typically based on a formula relating the amount of promised annual pension payment to an individual employee's length of service and final year's salary level. For example, a DB plan may provide for the retiree to be paid 1 percent times number of years of service times final year's salary. The pension payments to be paid in the future represent a liability or obligation of the company. Most DB pension plans are funded; that is, the company contributes funds to a pension trust, a separate legal entity whose assets will be used to make the payments to the company's retirees. Most countries have regulatory requirements specifying minimal funding levels for DB plans, but those requirements vary by country.

If the amount of assets in the DB pension trust exceeds the present value of the estimated liability, the DB plan is said to be overfunded; conversely, if the amount of assets in the pension trust is less than the estimated liability, the plan is said to be underfunded. Because the company has promised a defined amount of benefit to the employees, it is obligated to make those pension payments regardless of whether the pension plan assets generate sufficient returns to provide that benefit when it is due. In other words, the company bears the investment risk.

Similar to DB pension plans, **other postretirement benefits** (OPBs) are promises by the company to pay benefits in the future, such as life insurance premiums and all or part of health care insurance for its retirees. Unlike DB pension plans, however, companies typically do not fund OPBs in advance to the same degree as DB plans, partly because they represent a much smaller financial liability and partly because OPBs are often easier to eliminate should the costs become onerous.

Exhibit 14-1 summarizes these three types of postretirement benefits.

Information about a company's pension plans often appears throughout the company's disclosures. Exhibit 14-2 provides excerpts of disclosures describing the pension plans of the Dutch company CNH Global N.V., which manufacturers agricultural and construction equipment and is listed on the New York Stock Exchange (NYSE). The company was formed by the merger of Case and New Holland and is a majority-owned subsidiary of Fiat S.p.A. The first excerpt in the exhibit, from the financial statement footnote number 2, succinctly summarizes the company's accounting for pensions and other postretirement plans. The note explains that the "cost of providing defined-benefit pension and other postretirement benefits is based on actuarial valuations" while contributions to its defined-contribution plans are expensed during the period of the employee's service. The second excerpt in the exhibit, from the operating and financial review section, discloses the separate funding of the U.S. and U.K. pension plans and that plans in Germany and other countries are not funded. This disclosure illustrates differences in countries' regulatory requirements for companies to fund pensions. The third excerpt, from the description of risk factors, clearly describes the underfunded status of the company's pension and postretirement plans.

EXHIBIT 14-1   Types of Postretirement Benefits

Type of benefit	Amount of postretirement benefit to employee	Obligation of sponsoring company	Sponsoring company's prefunding of its future obligation
Defined-contribution pension plan	Amount of benefit is *not* defined. Actual benefit will depend on the future value of plan assets. Investment risk is borne by the employee.	The amount of the company's contribution is defined. The contribution, if any, is made on a periodic basis with no future obligation.	Not applicable.
Defined-benefit pension plan	Amount of employee's benefit is defined. Pension is based on plan formula (often a function of length of service and final year's salary). Investment risk is borne by company.	The amount of the future obligation, based on the plan formula, must be estimated in the current period.	Companies typically prefund the plans by contributing funds to a pension trust. Regulatory requirements to prefund vary by country.
Other postretirement benefits (OPB), e.g., retirees' health care	Amount of benefit depends on plan specifications and type of benefit.	The eventual benefits are specified. The amount of the future obligation must be estimated in the current period.	Companies typically do not prefund other postretirement benefit obligations.

EXHIBIT 14-2   Excerpts from the Pension Plan Disclosures of CNH Global N.V. (NYSE: CNH)

Excerpt 1

Retirement Programs [excerpt from Note 2 to financial statements on Page F-11]

CNH operates numerous defined benefit and defined contribution pension plans, the assets of which are held in separate trustee-administered funds. The pension plans are generally funded by payments from employees and CNH. The cost of providing defined benefit pension and other postretirement benefits is based upon actuarial valuations. The liability for termination indemnities is accrued in accordance with labor legislation in each country where such benefits are required. CNH contributions to defined contribution plans are charged to income during the period of the employee's service.

Excerpt 2

Defined Benefit Pension and Other Postretirement Benefits [excerpt from Operating Review and Financial Prospects on Page 61]

As more fully described in "Note 12: Employee Benefit Plans and Postretirement Benefits" of our consolidated financial statements, we sponsor pension and other retirement plans in various countries. In the U.S. and the U.K., we have major defined benefit pension plans that are separately funded. Our pension plans in Germany and certain other countries, however, are not funded. . . .

Excerpt 3

An Increase in Health Care or Pension Costs Could Adversely Affect Our Results of Operations and Financial Position [excerpt from management's discussion of risk factors on Page 8].

The funded status of our pension and postretirement benefit plans is subject to developments and changes in actuarial and other related assumptions. At both December 31, 2006, and 2005, pension plans which we fund had an underfunded status of approximately $947 million and $1.0 billion, respectively. Pension plan obligations for plans that we do not currently fund were $553 million and $521 million at December 31, 2006, and 2005, respectively.

Our U.S. pension plans are subject to the Employee Retirement Income Security Act of 1974 (ERISA). Under ERISA the Pension Benefit Guaranty Corporation ("PBGC"), has the authority to terminate underfunded pension plans under limited circumstances. In the event our U.S. pension plans are terminated for any reason while the plans are underfunded, we will incur a liability to the PBGC that may be equal to the entire amount of the U.S. plans underfunding.

Actual developments, such as a significant change in the performance of the investments in the plan assets or a change in the portfolio mix of plan assets, may result in corresponding increases or decreases in the valuation of plan assets, particularly with respect to equity securities. Lower or higher plan assets and a change in the rate of expected return on plan assets can result in significant changes to the expected return on plan assets in the following year and, as a consequence, could result in higher or lower net periodic pension cost in the following year.

"Unlike certain of our defined benefit pension plans, our other postretirement benefit obligations are currently unfunded. At December 31, 2006 and 2005, our other postretirement benefit obligations had an underfunded status of $1.5 billion and $1.7 billion, respectively.

In addition, pension and postretirement benefit plan valuation assumptions could have an effect on the funded status of our plans. Changes in assumptions, such as discount rates, rates for compensation increase, mortality rates, retirement rates, health care cost trend rates and other factors, may lead to significant increases or decreases in the value of the respective obligations, which would affect the reported funded status of our plans and, as a consequence, could affect the net periodic pension cost in the following year.

Source: CNH GLOBAL N.V. Form 20-F filed 30 March 2007.

The following sections provide additional detail on how DB pension plan liabilities and periodic costs are measured, the financial statement impact of reporting pension and other postretirement benefits, and how other footnote disclosures can be used to gain insights about the underlying economics of a company's defined-benefit pension plan.

2.2.   Measuring a Defined-Benefit Pension Plan's Liabilities

Under U.S. GAAP, three measures are used in estimating a defined-benefit pension plan's liabilities, each increasingly more inclusive. First, the **vested benefit obligation** is defined as the "actuarial present value of vested benefits" (SFAS No. 87, 106). The term *vested* refers to a typical provision in pension plans that an employee gains rights to future benefits only after reaching a prespecified number of years of service, or sometimes service in combination with age. Second, the **accumulated benefit obligation** is defined as "the actuarial present value of benefits (whether vested or nonvested) attributed by the pension benefit formula to employee service rendered before a specified date and based on employee service and compensation (if applicable) prior to that date" (SFAS No. 87, 96). Both the vested benefit obligation and the accumulated benefit obligation are based on the amounts promised as a result of an employee's service up to a specific date.

The third measure of a defined-benefit pension plan's liabilities is the **projected benefit obligation** that includes not only the benefit obligation attributable to an employee's service up to a specific date, but additionally an estimate of benefit obligations based on future compensation levels where applicable. Thus, the projected benefit obligation is defined as "the actuarial present value as of a date of all benefits attributed by the pension benefit formula to employee service rendered prior to that date. The projected benefit obligation is measured using assumptions as to future compensation levels if the pension benefit formula is based on those future compensation levels (pay-related, final-pay, final-average-pay, or career-average-pay plans)" (SFAS No. 87, 104). If the pension benefit formula is not linked to future compensation levels, the accumulated benefit obligation and projected benefit obligation will be equal (see Exhibit 14-3).

EXHIBIT 14-3   Summary of Measures of Defined-Benefit Pension Obligation under U.S. GAAP

| Measure | PV of Benefits Based on Service Up to Measurement Date | | PV of Estimated Benefits Based on Future Compensation Levels, Where Applicable |
	Vested Service	Nonvested Service	
Vested benefit obligation	✓		
Accumulated benefit obligation	✓	✓	
Projected benefit obligation	✓	✓	✓

For analysis, the projected benefit obligation is typically the most appropriate measure because it assumes that the company will continue to operate in the future (the so-called *going-concern assumption*) and recognizes that benefits will increase with future compensation increases.

IFRS (IAS 19, *Employee Benefits*) employs only one measure of the DB pension obligation. Although the terminology differs somewhat from U.S. GAAP, international standards also require companies to estimate pension liabilities by discounting the estimated amount of future benefits, similar to the projected benefit obligation. Instead of a separate measure of the amount of pension obligation relating to vested service, IFRS provides that companies estimate the probability of employees satisfying the vesting requirements. The IFRS approach to measuring the DB obligation is called the Projected Unit Credit Method because it treats "each period of service as giving rise to an additional unit of benefit entitlement and measures each unit separately to build up the final obligation" (IAS 19, 65).

In the remainder of this chapter, unless otherwise specified, the term *defined-benefit (DB) pension obligation* will refer to the obligation inclusive of any effects of estimated future compensation levels, that is, the *defined benefit obligation* under IFRS and *projected benefit obligation* under U.S. GAAP.

2.3. Measuring a Defined-Benefit Pension Plan's Periodic Costs

Broadly, the periodic cost of a company's DB pension plan can be thought of as the increases in its pension obligations, offset by earnings on pension plan assets. As will be discussed below, current accounting rules do not require companies to reflect this entire amount as an expense of the period; however, it is a useful starting point for understanding periodic pension expense.

Items that can increase a company's DB pension obligation in a particular period include the following:

- Employees' service during the period, which increases the amount of pension benefit the employee will be paid in retirement.
- Interest expense accrued on the beginning pension obligation.
- Changes to the terms of a pension plan that increase the benefit obligation applicable to employees' service during previous period.
- Actuarial gains and losses, which can occur when changes are made to the assumptions on which a company's estimated pension obligation has been based (e.g., employee turnover, mortality rates, retirement ages, compensation increases, etc.).

IFRS and U.S. GAAP use somewhat different terminology for items that are substantively the same. For example, the increase in the present value of a company's estimated pension obligation that results from employees' service during a period is known as the *current service cost* in IFRS and as the *service cost component of net periodic pension cost* in U.S. GAAP. An increase in the present value of a company's estimated pension obligation that results from changes to the terms of a pension plan applicable to employees' service during previous periods is known as *past service cost* in IFRS and *prior service cost* in U.S. GAAP. In the remainder of this chapter, we will use the IFRS terms *current service cost* and *past service cost*.

2.4. Financial Statement Reporting of Pension and Other Postretirement Benefits

The next few sections describe how pensions and other postretirement benefits are reflected on the financial statements of the sponsoring company.

2.4.1. Balance Sheet

Because companies make contributions to defined-contribution plans as the expense arises, no liabilities accrue for that type of plan. The discussion in this section of balance sheet reporting relates to DB plans and other postretirement benefits where a liability does accrue and thus must be measured and reported. As noted, companies typically contribute to a trust fund that holds assets specifically dedicated to satisfying their liabilities for DB plans.

IFRS (IAS 19, paragraph 54) requires companies' balance sheets to reflect as a defined benefit liability the net of the present value of the pension obligation minus the fair value of plan assets, with certain adjustments for actuarial gains or losses or for any prior service costs not yet recognized. As noted above, actuarial gains and losses can occur when changes are made to the assumptions on which a company's estimated pension obligation has been based. In addition, the term encompasses differences between actual experience and previous actuarial assumptions, for example when asset returns vary. The reason that actuarial gains or losses or any past service costs might not yet be recognized is that the standard allows companies to smooth the effects of these two items over time rather than immediately reflecting the effect as income or expense. The next section on expenses explains the smoothing mechanism. If the net of the plan obligation minus the plan assets, with adjustments, is negative (an asset), IFRS places several restrictions on the amount that can be shown as an asset.

Under U.S. GAAP's new accounting standard (SFAS No. 158 adopted in September 2006), companies' balance sheets fully recognize the over-funded or underfunded status of the companies' pension plans and other postretirement benefit plans as assets (if over-funded) or liabilities (if underfunded). The standard requires companies' balance sheets to reflect "the funded status of a benefit plan—measured as the difference between the fair value of plan assets and the benefit obligation" (SFAS No. 158, 2). Prior to SFAS No. 158, accounting standards allowed a company to recognize the funded position of its benefit plans, net of adjustments for various unamortized costs (similar to the adjustments still allowed under IFRS). In addition to requiring more complete recognition of benefits-related liabilities, the new U.S. accounting standard requires companies to disclose the effect of implementing the new requirements. For companies with under-funded plans, the new standard typically will: increase liabilities such that the total underfunded position appears on the balance sheet; decrease shareholders' equity by the amount of unamortized costs, net of tax; and increase deferred tax assets, reflecting the future tax deductions. To illustrate the significant effect of this accounting standard, Example 14-1 presents excerpts from disclosures by CNH and a U.S. competitor, Caterpillar Inc., regarding the incremental effects of the new accounting standard. As shown, CNH's reported pension-related liabilities increased by around 17 percent, and Caterpillar's reported pension-related liabilities increased by around 35 percent. Because the standard requires full recognition of the funded status of companies' pension plans, some companies with underfunded plans faced concerns about potential breaches of financial covenants. Note, for example, Caterpillar's disclosure that the $2.7 billion reduction in shareholders' equity did not result in the violation of any debt covenants. The example demonstrates the importance of this change in accounting to a ratio-based trend analysis.

The new U.S. accounting standard, which affects the balance sheet, is only the first phase in a comprehensive review of accounting for pensions and postretirement benefits. A subsequent anticipated change in accounting standards will address those aspects of current accounting standards that smooth the income effects of fluctuations in the values of pension assets and liabilities (discussed in the following section). Although SFAS No. 158 is a U.S. GAAP standard, because the IASB and the FASB have identified this area of accounting as a major project for collaborative efforts, the changes under SFAS No. 158 are also relevant for anticipating future changes for companies using IFRS. Therefore, the following example focuses on the new U.S. standard.

Note that in the example, one disclosure refers to an additional minimum liability (AML), a concept that will no longer be relevant for U.S. GAAP after the adoption of SFAS No. 158. Smoothing adjustments under old U.S. accounting standards resulted in the funded position reflected on a company's balance sheet differing from the actual funded position of the plan; when the difference between the reported and actual funded positions became too great, the old standards required an adjustment to make the reported position closer to the actual funded position. The adjustments were reflected as an AML. Because the following example is taken from the year in which SFAS No. 158 was first implemented, companies separately disclosed the AML effect at that time.

EXAMPLE 14-1   Impact of New Pension Accounting and Analysis of Trends in Key Financial Ratios

Companies are required to disclose the impact of the new accounting standard for pensions, SFAS No. 158. These disclosures can be particularly important in trend analysis. Exhibit 14-4 presents disclosures by CNH and selected supplemental information. Exhibit 14-5 presents the pension disclosures and supplemental information for Caterpillar (CAT).

EXHIBIT 14-4   CNH Global N.V. Pension Disclosures and Selected Supplemental Information

Excerpt from footnote on Employee Benefit Plans and Post-retirement Benefits (from Note 12 to the financial statements in the company's Form 20-F filed 30 March 2007, p. F-33)

The incremental effects of adopting the provisions of SFAS No. 158 on the Company's consolidated balance sheet at December 31, 2006 are presented in the following table. The adoption of SFAS No. 158 had no effect on the Company's consolidated statement of income for the year ended December 31, 2006, or for any prior period presented, and it will not affect the Company's operating results in future periods. . . .

($ millions)	Prior to Adopting SFAS No. 158	Effect of Adopting SFAS No. 158	As Reported on 31 December 2006
Intangible assets, net	$728	$(20)	$708
Other assets	1,671	(215)	1,456
Other accrued liabilities	2,072	72	2,144
Pension, postretirement, and postemployment benefits	1,731	557	2,288
Accumulated other comprehensive loss, net of tax	422	396	818

Selected Supplemental Information for CNH Global N.V. (from financial statements in the company's Form 20-F filed 30 March 2007, 29 April 2005, and 7 April 2004)

($ millions)	2006	2005	2004	2003	2002
Net income	$292	$163	$125	$(157)	$(426)
Ending shareholders' equity	5,120	5,052	5,029	4,874	2,761
Long term debt, including current maturities	5,132	4,765	4,906	4,886	5,115
Pension, postretirement, and postemployment benefits	2,288	2,132	2,224	2,040	1,759

EXHIBIT 14-5   Caterpillar Inc. Pension Disclosures and Selected Supplemental Information

Pension disclosure: Excerpt from Note L to the financial statements in the company's Form 10-K filed 23 February 2007, p. A-12.

SFAS 158—In September 2006, the FASB issued Statement of Financial Accounting Standards No. 158 (SFAS 158), "Employers' Accounting for Defined Benefit Pension and Other Postretirement Plans—an amendment of FASB Statements No. 87, 88, 106 and 132R." SFAS 158 requires recognition of the overfunded or underfunded status of pension and other postretirement benefit plans on the balance sheet. . . . The following summarizes the effect of the required changes in the AML, as well as the impact of the initial adoption of SFAS 158, as of December 31, 2006.

Initial adoption of SFAS 158 ($ millions)	31 Dec. 2006 Prior to AML and SFAS 158 Adjustments	AML Adjustment per SFAS 87	SFAS 158 Adjustment	31 Dec. 2006 Post AML and SFAS 158 Adjustments
Prepaid expenses and other current assets	$2,336	$—	$(1,829)	$507
Investments in unconsolidated affiliated companies	568	—	(6)	562
Deferred income taxes	552	(97)	1,494	1,949
Intangible assets	639	(60)	(192)	387
Accrued wages, salaries and employee benefits	1,440	—	(502)	938
Liability for postemployment benefits	3,625	(386)	2,640	5,879
Accumulated other comprehensive income	(405)	229	(2,671)	(2,847)

Pension disclosure: Further excerpt from Note L to the financial statements in the company's Form 10-K filed 23 February 2007, p. A-59.

The adoption of SFAS 158 reduced December 31, 2006 assets by approximately $500 million, increased liabilities by approximately $2.20 billion and reduced stockholders' equity by approximately $2.70 billion. Also, we reclassified approximately $500 million from current liabilities to long-term liabilities based on the classification guidelines provided in SFAS 158. We did not incur any violation of debt covenant agreements as a result of the reduction in stockholders' equity. The adoption of this Statement did not affect our results of operations.

Selected Supplemental Information for Caterpillar Inc. (from financial statements in the company's Form 10-K filed 23 February 2007 and 24 February 2005)

($ millions)	2006	2005	2004	2003	2002
Net income	$3,537	$2,854	$2,035	$1,099	$798
Ending shareholders' equity	6,859	8,432	7,467	6,078	5,472
Long-term debt, including current maturities	22,141	20,176	19,368	17,527	15,686
Pension- and postretirement-related liabilities	5,879	3,161	3,126	3,172	3,333

Using the information from Exhibit 14-4 and Exhibit 14-5:

1. Calculate each company's return on equity (ROE) and debt-to-capital ratio using the financial information reported, and the financial information adjusted for the effect of SFAS 158.
2. Describe the effect of the new accounting standard on each company's 2006 ROE.
3. Describe the effect of the new accounting standard on each company's 2006 debt-to-capital ratio.
4. Explain the implications for an analysis of the trends for these companies, based on each company's return on equity (ROE) and debt-to-capital ratio from 2003 to 2006.

Solution to 1. For CNH, the calculation of return on equity (ROE) and debt-to-capital ratio using the financial information reported, and the financial information adjusted for the impact of SFAS 158 is as follows:

($ millions)	2006 as Reported	2006 w/out SFAS 158	
Net income	$292	$292	a
Ending shareholders' equity (E)	5,120	5,516	b
Long-term debt, including current maturities	5,132	5,132	c
Pension, postretirement, and postemployment benefits	2,288	1,731	d
ROE	5.74%	5.53%	e
LTD/(LTD including pension-related liabilities + E)	59.17	55.44	f
LTD/(LTD excluding pension-related liabilities + E)	50.06	48.20	g

a. Accounting change did not affect reported net income.

b. Accounting change increased the company's accumulated other comprehensive loss, thus reducing shareholders' equity, by $396. In other words, absent the change, the company's shareholders' equity would have been $396 higher.

c. Accounting change did not affect reported long term debt.

d. Accounting change increased the company's pension liabilities by $557; that is, absent the change, the company's pension liabilities would have been $557 lower.

e. ROE = net income divided by average shareholders equity.

As reported, ROE = $292 ÷ [($5,052 + $5,120) ÷ 2] = 5.74%

Absent the accounting change, ROE = $292 ÷ [($5,052 + $5,516)/2] = 5.53%

f. Debt-to-capital ratio = Long-term debt ÷ (Long-term debt + Shareholders' equity).

Including the pension-related liabilities in long-term debt:

As reported, the ratio = ($5,132 + $2,288) ÷ ($5,132 + $2,288 + $5,120) = 59.17%

Absent the accounting change, the ratio = ($5,132 + $1,731) ÷ ($5,132 + $1,731 + $5,516) = 55.44%

g. Debt-to-capital ratio = Long-term debt ÷ (Long-term debt + Shareholders' equity)

Excluding the pension-related liabilities in long-term debt:

As reported, the ratio = $5,132 ÷ ($5,132 + $5,120) = 50.06%

Absent the accounting change, the ratio = $5,132 ÷ ($5,132 + $5,516) = 48.20%

For CAT, the calculation of return on equity (ROE) and debt-to-capital ratio using the financial information reported, and the financial information adjusted for the impact of SFAS 158 is as follows:

($ millions)	2006 as reported	2006 w/out SFAS 158
Net income	$3,537	$3,537
Ending shareholders' equity (E)	6,859	9,301
Long-term debt, including current maturities	22,141	19,887
Pension- and postretirement-related liabilities	5,879	3,625
ROE	46.26%	39.89%
LTD/(LTD including pension-related liabilities + E)	80.33%	71.65%
LTD/(LTD excluding pension-related liabilities + E)	76.35%	68.13%

Solution to 2. The new accounting standard does not affect reported income but does reduce reported shareholders' equity for both companies, thus increasing each company's return on equity. The new standard increases CNH's 2006 ROE slightly, from

5.53 percent to 5.74 percent. The new standard increases CAT's 2006 ROE more significantly, from 39.89 percent to 46.26 percent.

Solution to 3. The new accounting standard reduces reported shareholders' equity and increases reported liabilities for both companies, thus increasing each company's debt-to-capital ratio. The new standard increases CNH's 2006 debt-to-capital ratio from 48.20 percent to 50.06 percent; and if pension liabilities are treated as debt, the new standard increases the company's ratio from 55.44 percent to 59.17 percent. The new standard increases CAT's 2006 Debt-to-Total Capital ratio from 68.13 percent to 76.35 percent; and if pension liabilities are treated as debt, the new standard increases the company's ratio from 71.65 percent to 80.33 percent.

Solution to 4. In examining the trends in these companies' profitability (for example, as measured by ROE) and leverage (e.g., as measured by debt-to-capital), an analyst should recognize that the accounting change—rather than an actual economic change—creates the appearance of a greater improvement in the companies' profitability ratios and shows a deterioration rather than improvement in the companies' leverage ratios. While both companies show a positive trend in profitability as measured by ROE, the 2006 ratios based on the reported numbers overstate the improvement from prior years. Similarly, both companies show increasing leverage in 2006 based on the reported financials; however, the apparent trend toward higher leverage is actually the result of the change in accounting for pensions.

For CNH, the ratios for 2003 to 2006 are:

	2006 as reported	2006 w/out SFAS 158	2005	2004	2003
ROE	5.74%	5.53%	3.23%	2.52%	−4.11%
LTD/(LTD including pension-related liabilities + E)	59.17	55.44	57.72	58.64	58.69
LTD/(LTD excluding pension-related liabilities + E)	50.06	48.20	48.54	49.38	50.06

For CAT, the ratios for 2003 to 2006 are:

	2006 as reported	2006 w/out SFAS 158	2005	2004	2003
ROE	46.26%	39.89%	35.90%	30.05%	19.03%
LTD/(LTD including pension-related liabilities + E)	80.33	71.65	73.46	75.08	77.30
LTD/(LTD excluding pension-related liabilities + E)	76.35	68.13	70.53	72.17	74.25

In Example 14-1 above, the solution shows the debt-to-capital ratio both with and without pension-related liabilities included as debt. The argument for including pension-related liabilities in the calculation is that these liabilities reflecting underfunded defined pension and other postretirement plans are indeed debt-like in nature. One difference in pension-related liabilities and debt is that pension-related liabilities are often tax deductible; therefore, a further refinement in analyses similar to the one shown above is to reflect the pension-related liabilities after taxes. Note, however, that companies do include tax considerations in reporting under SFAS No. 158. Exhibit 14-5 shows that Caterpillar reflects a $1,494 increase in deferred income tax asset.

2.4.2. Pension Expense

Pension expense for defined-contribution pension plans is simply an amount equal to the companies' annual contribution to the plans, so the discussion in this section relates to pension expense for DB plans, which has several components.

As noted above, the periodic cost of a company's DB pension plan can be thought of as the increases in its pension obligations, offset by earnings on pension plan assets. As will be discussed below, current accounting rules do not require companies to reflect this entire amount as an expense. Items that can increase a company's pension liability in a particular period include the following: (1) current service costs; (2) interest expense accrued on the pension obligation; (3) past service costs; and (4) actuarial gains and losses. (An additional item that can affect pension obligations and periodic expenses is the curtailment [i.e., elimination] of a pension plan for some or all employees, details of which are beyond the scope of this chapter.) Increases in a company's pension obligation are offset by earnings on the pension plan's assets, including: interest income, dividend income, gains or losses on sales of securities, and unrealized gains and losses, that is, changes in the value of the assets held by the plan.

Note that the amount of assets in the fund increases when the company makes contributions and decreases when the fund pays out benefits to current retirees; however, such changes are essentially deposits into and withdrawals from the fund, not earnings on plan assets.

Under both IFRS and U.S. GAAP current accounting rules, two items that increase a company's pension liability in a particular period are fully and immediately reflected as components of a company's DB pension expense: current service costs and interest expense on the pension obligation. In contrast, both sets of accounting standards include various provisions (sometimes referred to as smoothing mechanisms because they result in a smoother pattern of income) providing for some of the effects of past service costs and of actuarial gains and losses to be reflected in a company's DB pension expense over time.

Under U.S. GAAP, past service costs are shown as part of other comprehensive income for the period in which the change giving rise to the costs occurred. Subsequently, other comprehensive income is adjusted in each period as these costs are amortized over the service lives of the affected employees and become a component of DB pension expense. Similarly, actuarial gains and losses arising from changes in the pension obligation attributable to changes in actuarial assumptions are shown as part of other comprehensive income for the period in which the change in actuarial assumptions occurred. In addition, current accounting rules (both U.S. GAAP and IFRS) do not require companies to use the *actual* amount of earnings on pension plan assets as a component of defined-benefit pension expense; instead, companies report the "expected return" on plan assets. Any difference between the actual and expected return on plan assets (which is included in actuarial gains and losses) bypasses the income statement and is included as part of other comprehensive income. If the cumulative amount of gains and losses in accumulated other comprehensive income becomes too great over time (more than 10 percent of the greater of the value of plan assets, or of the projected benefit obligation for an underfunded plan), the difference must be amortized over the remaining service period of active employees and becomes a component of periodic DB pension expense. The difference may be amortized more quickly, so long as the method is systematic, consistently applied to both gains and losses, and disclosed. One rationale for this accounting treatment is that the actual return on pension plan assets is typically volatile. Showing the full amount of these volatile returns might distort the company's overall performance; therefore, the pension accounting rules provide for a volatility-smoothing mechanism.

Under IFRS, past service costs are recognized immediately to the extent that the benefits are vested, and, otherwise, on a straight-line basis over the relevant vesting period. Similar to U.S. GAAP, IFRS requires companies to recognize only a portion of actuarial gains and losses. As with U.S. GAAP, actuarial gains and losses encompass both changes in the value of the DB obligation arising from changes in actuarial assumptions and differences between actual return on plan assets and the expected return on plan assets. If the cumulative unrecognized actuarial gains and losses becomes too large (i.e., exceeds 10 percent of the greater of the value of the plan assets, or of the present value of the DB obligation), similar to U.S. GAAP, IFRS require the difference to be amortized over the remaining service period of active employees, and permits faster amortization. IFRS also allow companies to recognize actuarial gains and losses in a statement of changes in equity (i.e., outside profit and loss).

In summary, the components of a company's defined-benefit pension expense are listed in Exhibit 14-6 on page 570.

2.4.3. Impact of Assumptions and of Actuarial Gains and Losses on Pension and Postretirement Benefit Expense

As noted, periodic pension expense for a DC pension plan is simply an amount equal to the company's contribution to the plan in the period, so the discussion in this section relates to the effect of assumptions on expenses for DB pension plans and for other post retirement benefits.

For DB pension plans, the company's pension obligation is an estimate based on many assumptions. The amount of future pension payments requires assumptions about employee turnover, length of service, and rate of increase in compensation levels. The length of time the pension payments will be made requires assumptions about employees' life expectancy postretirement. Finally, the present value of these future payments requires assumptions about the appropriate discount rate and the rate at which interest will subsequently accrue on the pension liability. Changes in any of these actuarial assumptions will increase or decrease the pension obligation. An increase in pension obligation resulting from changes in actuarial assumptions would be considered an actuarial loss, and a decrease would be considered an actuarial gain.

The estimate of the company's pension liability affects several components of annual pension expense, apart from actuarial gains and losses. First, the service cost component of annual pension expense is essentially the amount by which the pension liability increases as a result of the employees' service during the year. Second, the interest cost component of annual pension expense is based on the amount of the liability. Third, the prior service cost component of annual pension expense is the amount by which the pension liability increases because of changes to the plan.

Look at other comprehensive Income. (handwritten)

Pension Template (handwritten, left margin)

EXHIBIT 14-6 Components of a Company's Defined-Benefit Pension Expense

Component	Effect on Defined-Benefit Pension Expense	Direction of Effect on Defined-Benefit Pension Expense
Service costs: estimated increase in the pension obligation resulting from employees' service during the period	Immediately and fully recognized.	Increases the expense.
Interest expense on the pension obligation	Immediately and fully recognized.	Increases the expense.
Past service costs: Increase in the pension obligation resulting from changes to the terms of a pension plan applicable to employees' service during previous periods	IFRS: Vested employees' portion expensed immediately; unvested employees' portion expensed over average period until vesting. U.S. GAAP: Portion not immediately recognized as an expense is shown in other comprehensive income and subsequently amortized over service life of employees.	Typically increases the expense.
Actuarial gains and losses, including changes in a company's pension obligation arising from changes in actuarial assumptions as well as differences between the actual return on plan assets and the expected return on plan assets	IFRS: If the cumulative unrecognized amount of actuarial gains and losses exceeds specified levels,[a] a portion of the excess is recognized as an expense. U.S. GAAP: Portion not immediately recognized as an expense is shown in other comprehensive income and subsequently amortized if the cumulative amount in other comprehensive income exceeds specified levels.[a]	May increase or decrease the expense.
Return on plan assets	_Expected return_ on plan assets is immediately and fully recognized as a reduction of pension expense. Any differences between expected and actual return is considered part of actuarial gains and losses and treated as described above.	Decreases the expense.[b]

[a] If the cumulative amount of unrecognized actuarial gains and losses exceeds 10 percent of the greater of the value of the plan assets or of the present value of the DB obligation (under U.S. GAAP, the projected benefit obligation), the difference must be amortized over the service lives of the employees.
[b] If the actual return on plan assets is lower than the expected return on plan assets such that the cumulative difference becomes large enough to require amortization, the amortization of the difference increases pension expense.

Estimates related to plan assets also affect annual pension expense. Because a company's pension expense includes the expected return on pension assets rather than the actual return, another important assumption affecting pension expense is the assumption about the "expected return" on plan assets. In turn, the expected return on plan assets requires estimating which period in the future benefits will be paid. As noted above, a divergence of actual returns on pension assets from expected returns would also be considered an actuarial gain or loss.

Understanding the effect of actuarial assumptions on the estimated pension obligation and on periodic expenses is important both for interpreting a company's financial statements and for evaluating whether a company's actuarial assumptions appear relatively conservative or aggressive. The following simplified example, using a single employee, illustrates the effect on a company's pension obligation of changes in certain key assumptions.

EXAMPLE 14-2   Calculation of Defined-Benefit Pension Obligation for an Individual Employee

Assume that a (hypothetical) company offers a defined benefit pension plan that will pay a pension equal to 1.5 percent of the employee's final salary times the number of years of employment. The following table illustrates the computation of the pension liability for a single employee who: has a current salary of $100 thousand; is expected to work for the company for a total of 40 years; and is expected to live, and receive a pension payment, for 20 years following retirement. The assumed discount rate is 6 percent and the assumed annual compensation increase is 4.75 percent. Assume, for simplicity, that all compensation increases are awarded on the last day of the service year.

The change in the pension obligation between year 1 and year 2 has two components: (a) an increase in the payment based on the employee having worked an additional year; and (b) an increase in the obligation based on the passage of time.

Given	Year 1	Year 2	
Current salary	$ 100,000	$ 104,750	
Service years to date	10	11	
Years until retirement	30	29	
Years of receiving pension	20	20	
Assumptions			
Annual compensation increases	4.75%	4.75%	
Discount rate	6.00%	6.00%	
Computations: Base case			
Final year's estimated salary	$402,365.70	$402,365.70	a
Amount of annual pension using plan formula based on service years to date	$60,354.85	$66,390.34	b
Present value of pension annuity during retirement discounted to retirement date	$692,265.43	$761,491.97	c
Pension obligation: present value from retirement date to today	$120,530.42	$140,538.47	d

Notes: This "base case" follows Spiceland et al. (2007). The computations above were made using an Excel worksheet; answers derived from using a calculator may differ slightly due to rounding in interim calculations.

a. Final year's estimated salary =
   current year's salary $\times$ [(1 + annual compensation increase)$^{\text{Years until retirement}}$]
   At year 1, final year's estimated salary = $100,000 \times$ [(1 + 0.0475)^{30}] = $402,365.70.
   At year 2, assuming the employee's salary increased by 4.75% to $104,750, the final year's estimated salary = ($104,750 $\times$ [(1 + 0.0475)^{29}] = $402,365.70.

b. Amount of annual pension using plan formula based on service years to date = years to date $\times$ final year's estimated salary $\times$ 1.5%
   At year 1, amount of annual pension = 10 $\times$ $402,365.70 $\times$ 1.5% = $60,354.85

c. Present value of pension annuity during retirement discounted to the beginning of retirement, based on year 1 information = $692,265.43, calculated with the following input:
   Annuity Payment = $60,354.85; Number of years = 20; Discount rate = 6%.[1]

d. Present value from retirement date to today based on year 1 information = $120,530.41, calculated with the following input:
   Future Value = $692,265.43; Number of years = 30; Discount rate = 6%.

Based on the information given above:

1. Estimate the effect on the year 1 pension obligation of a 1 percent increase in the assumed discount rate—from 6 percent to 7 percent.
2. Estimate the effect on the year 1 pension obligation of a 1 percent increase in the assumed annual compensation increase—from 4.75 percent to 5.75 percent.

Solution to 1. A one percent increase in the assumed discount rate (from 6 percent to 7 percent) would *decrease* the pension obligation by $36,534.25 ($120,530.42 base case estimated obligation minus new estimate of obligation $83,996.16 from step *d* below).

a. No change in estimated final year's salary. A change in the discount rate assumption does not affect the estimated final year's salary. At year 1, final year's estimated salary = $100,000 $\times$ [(1 + 0.0475)^{30}] = $402,365.70.

b. No change in estimated amount of annual pension. A change in the discount rate assumption does not affect the estimated amount of annual pension using plan formula based on service years to date = years to date $\times$ final year's estimated salary $\times$ 1.5%. At year 1, amount of annual pension = 10 $\times$ $402,365.70 $\times$ 1.5% = $60,354.85.

c. Present value of pension annuity during retirement discounted to the beginning of retirement, based on year 1 information = $639,400.19, calculated with the following input:
   Annuity Payment = $60,354.85; Number of years = 20; Discount rate = 7%.

---

[1]This is a simplification of the valuation process for illustrative purposes. For instance, the actuarial valuation would use mortality rates, not just assumed life expectancy. Additionally, taking the present value of an ordinary annuity annually likely understates the liability because the actual benefit payments are usually made monthly or biweekly rather than annually.

d. Present value from retirement date to today based on year 1 information = $83,996.16, calculated with the following input:
Future Value = $639,400.19; Number of years = 30; Discount rate = 7%.

Solution to 2. A one percent increase in the assumed annual compensation increase (from 4.75 percent to 5.75 percent) would *increase* the pension obligation by $39,752.43 ($120,530.42 base case estimated obligation minus $160,284.84 new estimate of obligation from step *d* below.)

a. A change in the assumed annual compensation increase assumption *increases* the estimated final year's salary. At year 1, final year's estimated salary = $100,000 × [(1 + 0.0575)^{30}] = $535,070.84.

b. A change in the assumed annual compensation increase assumption *increases* the estimated amount of annual pension. Using the plan formula based on service years to date = years to date × final year's estimated salary × 1.5%:
At year 1, estimated amount of annual pension = 10 × $535,070.84 × 1.5% = $80,260.63.

c. Present value of pension annuity during retirement discounted to the beginning of retirement, based on year 1 information = $920,583.10, calculated with the following input:
Annuity Payment = $80,260.63; Number of years = 20; Discount rate = 6%.

d. Present value from retirement date to today based on year 1 information = $160,282.84, calculated with the following input:
Future Value = $920,583.10; Number of years = 30; Discount rate = 6%.

The simplified case in Example 14-2, using a single employee, illustrates that increases in the assumed discount rate will *decrease* a company's pension obligation. The discount rate used in calculating the obligation is also used to calculate the following year's interest component of the periodic benefit-related expense (calculated as the discount rate times the obligation at the beginning of the year). Typically, an increase in the assumed discount rate will decrease the interest component of a company's periodic benefit-related expenses because, expressed in percentage the decrease in the obligation will more than offset the increase in the discount rate; an exception occurs when the pension obligation is of a short duration.

Example 14-2 also illustrates that increases in the assumed rate of annual compensation increase will *increase* a company's projected benefit obligation—when the pension formula is based on final year's salary. In addition, a higher assumed rate of annual compensation increase will increase the service component of a company's periodic pension expense.

For postretirement health plans, an increase in the assumed trends in health care costs will increase the obligation and associated periodic expense of these plans.

Finally, because the expected return on plan assets is an offset to interest expense, a higher expected return will reduce the expense. Exhibit 14-7 summarizes the impact of these key assumptions on the balance sheet and the periodic benefit-related expense.

Accounting for other postretirement benefits also requires assumptions. For example, assumed trends in health care costs are an important component of estimating costs of postretirement health care plans. A higher assumed medical expense inflation rate will result in a higher postretirement medical obligation. Companies also estimate various patterns of health

EXHIBIT 14-7   Impact of Key DB Pension Assumptions on Balance Sheet and Periodic Expense

Assumption	Impact of assumption on Balance Sheet	Impact of assumption on periodic expense
Higher discount rate	Lower obligation.	The interest expense will typically be lower.
Higher rate of compensation increase	Higher obligation.	Higher service expense.
Higher expected return on plan assets		Lower expense.

Sensitivity Analysis

care cost trend rates, for example, higher in the near term, but becoming lower after some point in time.

The next section evaluates disclosures of pension and other postretirement benefits, including disclosures about key assumptions.

2.5. Evaluating Disclosures of Pension and Other Postretirement Benefits

Several aspects of the accounting for pensions and other post retirement benefits described above can affect comparative financial analysis using ratios based on financial statements. First, differences in key assumptions can affect comparisons across companies. Second, the balance sheet reports a company's net funded position, with the separate components (i.e. plan assets and plan liabilities) disclosed in the footnotes. Third, the smoothing mechanisms within the accounting standards can obscure the underlying economic expense. In addition, the entire pension expense is treated as an operating expense on the income statement, but actually includes items of a financial nature, such as accruals on pension liabilities and returns on pension assets. Finally, cash flow information related to pensions can be obtained from various portions of the footnoted disclosure and appropriate analytical adjustments can be made. In the following sections, we examine pension plan footnote disclosures to address these analytical issues.

2.5.1. Assumptions

Companies disclose their assumptions about discount rates, expected compensation increases, medical expense inflation, and expected return on plan assets. Comparing these assumptions over time and across companies provides a basis to assess any conservative or aggressive biases. Some companies also disclose the effect of a change in their assumptions.

First we consider disclosures about assumed discount rates. Exhibit 14-8 on page 576 presents the assumed discount rates to estimate pension obligations for four companies operating in the industrial goods sector: CNH Global N.V., a Dutch manufacturer of agricultural and construction equipment; Caterpillar Inc., a U.S. manufacturer of construction and mining equipment, engines, and turbines; ABB Ltd., a Swiss-based provider of power and automation products; and Deere & Co., a U.S. manufacturer of agricultural and commercial equipment. All four companies have used U.S. GAAP in their financial statements filed with the Securities and Exchange Commission (SEC), which facilitates comparison.

The assumed discount rates to estimate pension obligations are based on the market interest rates of high quality fixed income investments with a maturity profile similar to the timing of a company's future pension payments. The trend in discount rates across the companies is similar: a decrease from 2004 to 2005, followed by an increase from 2005 to 2006. CNH has the highest assumed discount rate across these companies. Recall that a higher discount rate assumption results in a lower estimated pension obligation. Therefore, a higher discount rate compared to peers may indicate a less conservative bias.

Explanations for differences in the level of the assumed discount rates, apart from a reporting bias, are differences in the regions involved and differences in the timing of obligations. In this example, difference in regions would not appear to explain the difference in the rates shown for CNH and Caterpillar, because the assumptions shown for those two companies relate only to their U.S. plans. The timing of companies' obligations under their DB pension plans vary and, therefore, the relevant market interest rates selected as the discount rate will vary. Because the timing of each company's pension obligations is not readily observable from the disclosed information, differences in the timing of pension obligations cannot be ruled out as an explanation for differences in the company's discount rates.

Another important consideration is whether the assumptions are internally consistent. For example, do a company's assumed discount rates and assumed compensation increases reflect a consistent view of inflation? For ABB, both the assumed discount rates and the assumed annual compensation increases are lower than those assumed by the other companies; so both of the assumptions appear internally consistent with plans related to lower inflation regions. For Caterpillar, unlike the trend in assumed discount rates, the assumed annual compensation increase is unchanged over the period, possibly reflecting the terms of the company's agreement with its labor union. For CNH, no assumed annual compensation increase for the U.S. plans is disclosed. An explanation for the omission can be found in the company's descriptive disclosure that "benefits for salaried employees in the U.S. were frozen for pay and service as of December 31, 2000."

Comparing Deere and Caterpillar, Deere's assumed discount rate is higher and assumed annual compensation increase is lower in each year. Both a higher discount rate assumption and a lower compensation increase assumption result in a lower estimated pension obligation. Absent additional information, Deere's assumptions to estimate pension obligations appear less conservative than Caterpillar's (see Exhibit 14-8).

Exhibit 14-9 presents a comparison of the four companies' assumptions about the expected return on U.S. pension assets. As noted, a higher expected return on plan assets lowers the periodic benefit expense. (Of course, a higher expected return on plan assets presumably reflects more risky investments, so one would not conclude that a company would simply invest in riskier investments to reduce periodic benefit expense.) At this point, we will compare the company's assumptions in the context of its chosen asset allocation. In a later section, we will assess the effect of using actual returns on plan assets rather than expected returns.

Caterpillar shows the highest expected return. This higher expected return appears consistent with the company's higher percentage allocation of plan assets to equity securities. Similarly, ABB shows the lowest expected return and this expectation appears consistent with the company's significantly lower allocation of plan assets to equity securities. Further, ABB's lower expected returns are consistent with the company's assumptions discussed above. Overall, none of the companies' assumptions appear significantly higher or lower than what would be reasonably expected given the companies' asset allocations.

EXHIBIT 14-8 Assumed Discount Rates to Estimate Pension Obligations

	2006	2005	2004
CNH Global N.V. (U.S. plans)	5.80%	5.50%	5.75%
Caterpillar Inc. (U.S. plans)	5.50	4.70	5.50
ABB Ltd.	4.39	4.29	4.60
Deere & Co.	5.70	5.50	6.00
Assumed Annual Compensation Increase to Estimate Pension Obligations			
CNH Global N.V. (U.S. plans)	NA	NA	NA
Caterpillar Inc. (U.S. plans)	4.00%	4.00%	4.00%
ABB Ltd.	2.39	2.41	2.23
Deere & Co.	3.80	3.90	3.90

EXHIBIT 14-9 Expected Return on U.S. Pension Plan Assets and Asset Allocation

	2006	2005	2004
CNH Global N.V. (U.S. plans)	8.25%	8.25%	8.75%
	E: 53%; F: 47%	E: 53%; F: 47%	—
Caterpillar Inc. (U.S. plans)	9.00	9.00	9.00
	E: 74; F: 26	E: 72; F: 28	E: 74; F: 26
ABB Ltd.	4.92	5.45	5.57
	E: 33; F: 56;	E: 34; F: 54;	
	RES 7; O: 4	RES 7; O: 5	
Deere & Co.	8.50	8.50	8.50
	E: 57; F: 20;	E: 62; F: 18;	—
	RES 4; O: 19	RES 3; O: 17	

Note: Equity securities (E); Fixed-income securities (F); Real Estate (RES); and Other (O).

Companies with postretirement health plans also disclose assumptions about increases in health care costs. The assumptions are typically that the inflation rate in health care costs will taper off to some lower, constant rate at some year in the future. That future inflation rate is known as the ultimate health care trend rate. Holding all else equal, the following assumptions would each result in a higher benefit obligation and a higher periodic expense: a higher assumed near-term increase in health care costs; a higher assumed ultimate health care trend rate; and a later year in which the ultimate health care trend rate is assumed to be reached. Conversely, holding all else equal, the following assumptions would each result in a lower benefit obligation and a lower periodic expense: a lower assumed near-term increase in health care costs; a lower assumed ultimate health care trend rate; and an earlier year in which the ultimate health care trend rate is assumed to be reached.

Example 14-3 examines two companies' assumptions about trends in U.S. health care costs.

EXAMPLE 14-3   Comparison of Assumptions about Trends in U.S. Health Care Costs

In addition to disclosing assumptions about health care costs, companies also disclose information on the sensitivity of the measurements of both the obligation and periodic expense to a change in those assumptions. Exhibit 14-10 presents information obtained from the footnotes to the financial statements for CNH Global N.V. and Caterpillar Inc. Panel A in the exhibit shows the companies' assumptions about health care costs and the amounts each reported for post-retirement health care benefit plans. For example, CNH assumes that the initial year's increase in health care costs will be 10 percent, and this rate of increase will decline to 5 percent over the next 5 years, that is, 9 percent increase in the second year, 8 percent increase in the third year, and so on.

Panel B in the exhibit shows the effect of a 1 percent increase or decrease in the assumed increase in the near-term health care trend. For example, a 1 percent increase in CNH's assumed initial trend rate would increase the estimated benefit obligation by $159 million.

EXHIBIT 14-10   Postretirement Health Care Plan Disclosures

Panel A. Assumptions and Reported Amounts for U.S. Postretirement Health Care Benefit Plans

	Assumptions about Health Care Costs			Amounts Reported for Other Postretirement Benefits ($ millions)	
	Initial Trend Rate	Ultimate Health Care Trend Rate	Year in Which Ultimate Rate Attained	Accumulated Benefit Obligation Year-End 2006	Periodic Expense for Benefits for 2006
CNH Global N.V.	10% (I)	5%	2012	$1,481	$131
Caterpillar Inc.	8.5 (I)	5	2013	5,661	363

Panel B. Effect of 1 Percent Increase (Decrease) in Assumed Health Care Cost Trend Rate on 2006 Total Accumulated Postretirement Benefit Obligations and Periodic Expense

	1% Increase	1% Decrease
CNH Global N.V.	+$159 million (Obligation)	−$133 million (Obligation)
	+$12 million (Expense)	−$10 million (Expense)
Caterpillar Inc.	+$444 million (Obligation)	−$389 million (Obligation)
	+$35 million (Expense)	−$31 million (Expense)

Based on the information in Exhibit 14-10, answer the following questions:

1. Which company's assumptions about health care costs appear less conservative?
2. What would be the effect of adjusting the postretirement benefit obligation of the less conservative company to reflect an equivalent assumption about health care cost trends?
3. What would be the effect of adjusting the periodic post retirement benefit expense of the less conservative company to reflect an equivalent assumption about health care cost trends?

Solution to 1. Caterpillar's assumptions about health care costs appear less conservative than CNH's. Caterpillar's near term assumed health care cost increase of 8.5 percent is significantly lower than CNH's assumed 10 percent. Even though CNH's assumption is that the ultimate health care cost trend rate will be reached one year earlier, a year-by-year extrapolation of the companies assumed costs (below) shows that Caterpillar's assumed growth rate is equal to or lower than CNH's in every year except for small amounts in 2010 and 2011.

	2006	2007	2008	2009	2010	2011	2012	2013
CNH	10.00%	9.00%	8.00%	7.00%	6.00%	5.00%	5.00%	5.00%
Caterpillar	8.50	7.92	7.33	6.75	6.17	5.58	5.00	5.00
Difference	1.50%	1.08%	0.67%	0.25%	−0.17%	−0.58%	0.00%	0.00%

Year-to-year change in assumed growth in health care costs are estimated by extrapolating from the assumptions as follows: (near-term health care cost trend rate minus ultimate health care trend rate) divided by years until the ultimate trend rate is reached. For Caterpillar, 8.50 percent minus 5.00 percent divided by 6 years equals 0.005833 per year, so the health care cost trend rate extrapolated to 2007 equals 7.92 percent (8.50 percent minus 0.005833), and the trend rate extrapolated to 2008 equals 7.33 percent (7.92 percent minus 0.005833).

Solution to 2. To reflect an equivalent assumption about health care cost trends, Caterpillar's assumed rate for 2006 would need to be increased by 1.5 percent, from 8.50 percent to 10 percent. The sensitivity disclosures indicate that a 1 percent increase in the assumed rate would increase the postretirement benefit obligation by $444 million. Although the sensitivity to an increase more or less than 1 percent cannot be assumed to be exactly linear, the sensitivity information can be used to estimate the impact. So Caterpillar's postretirement benefit obligation would increase by approximately $666 million (1.5 × $444 million) using an assumption equivalent to CNH's about health care cost trends. Caterpillar's postretirement benefit obligation would increase to approximately $6,327 million ($5,661 million + $666 million), using the more conservative assumption.

Solution to 3. To reflect an equivalent assumption about health care cost trends, Caterpillar's assumed rate for 2006 would need to be increased by 1.5 percent, from 8.50 percent to 10.0 percent. The sensitivity disclosures indicate that a 1 percent increase in the assumed rate would increase the periodic post retirement benefit expense by $35 million. Although the sensitivity to an increase more or less than 1 percent cannot be assumed to be exactly linear, the sensitivity information can be used to estimate the impact. So, Caterpillar's periodic postretirement benefit expense for 2006 would increase by approximately $52.5 million (1.5 times $35 million) using an assumption equivalent to CNH's about health care cost trends. Caterpillar's periodic postretirement benefit expense for 2006 would increase from $363 million to approximately $415.5 million using the more conservative assumption.

This section has explored the use of pension and post retirement benefit disclosures to assess a company's assumptions and explore how the assumptions can affect comparisons across companies. The following sections turn to the use of disclosures in understanding the underlying economics of a company's pension and post retirement plans.

2.5.2. Underlying Economic Liability (or Asset)

A company's balance sheet reports the net funded position (or simply funded position or funded status) of a company's pension and post retirement benefits. Footnotes to the financial statements disclose the components of the net funded position, i.e., the total obligation and the total assets allocated to pay this obligation. Prior to SFAS No. 158, the amount of pension obligation appearing on a company's balance sheet reflected a number of deferred items; however, companies now reflect the entire net pension obligation on the balance sheet. An overfunded plan results in an asset, and an underfunded plan results in a liability.

Even following SFAS No. 158, the amount appearing in the balance sheet is a net amount: the pension obligation minus the plan assets. Some analysts use information from the footnotes to adjust a company's assets and liabilities for the gross amount of the benefit plan assets and the gross amount of the benefit plan liability. A related adjustment is to include the actual return on plan assets as income and the interest on the plan liability as an expense. Such adjustments effectively consolidate the benefit plans with the sponsoring company. An argument for making such adjustments is that they reflect the underlying economic liability (or asset); however, it should be recognized that an actual consolidation is precluded by laws protecting a pension or other benefit plan as a separate legal entity.

At a minimum, an analyst will compare the gross benefit obligation (i.e., the benefit obligation without deducting related plan assets) to the sponsoring company's total assets, shareholders' equity, and earnings. If the gross benefit obligation is large relative to these items, a small change in the pension liability can have a significant financial result on the sponsoring company.

2.5.3. Underlying Economic Expense (or Income)

As illustrated in Exhibit 14-11, the two main reasons for changes in the net funded status of a DB pension plan are the periodic cost of the pension plan and contributions into the plan by the sponsoring company. Benefits paid to retirees decrease the pension obligation and the plan assets by an identical amount and thus have no impact on the net funded status. As noted above, the periodic cost of a company's DB pension plan comprise net increases in pension obligations, offset by earnings on pension plan assets. So the periodic cost of a company's DB pension plan can be calculated in either of the following ways: by summing each item that increases or decreases the pension obligation and deducting earnings on pension plan assets; or, equivalently, by calculating the change in the plan's net funded status over the period, excluding any contributions made by the company.

explanation of template *(handwritten)*

Comment on Assumptions *(handwritten)*

EXHIBIT 14-11 Summary of Underlying Economic Liability (or Asset) and Economic Expense of the Period

Beginning of Period Economic Liability or Asset ⇨	Economic Expense of the Period	Benefits Paid Out of and Contributions to the Pension Plan ⇨	End of Period Economic Liability or Asset
Beginning pension obligation	Service costs increase the obligation and the economic expense of the period.	Benefits paid to retirees decrease the pension obligation.	Ending pension obligation
	Interest costs increase the obligation and the economic expense of the period.		
	Actuarial gains/losses affecting pension obligation may increase or decrease the obligation and the economic expense of the period.		
Beginning plan assets	Actual returns on plan assets (typically) increase the plan assets and thus decrease the economic expense of the period.	Benefits paid to retirees decrease the plan assets.	Ending plan assets
		Contributions by the sponsoring company increase the plan assets.	
Pension obligation minus plan assets equals beginning net funded position.	Increases in the economic cost of the period minus decreases in the economic costs of the period equals net economic expense of the period.		Pension obligation minus ending net funded position.
If negative, economic liability.			If negative, economic liability.
If positive, economic asset.			If positive, economic asset.

(handwritten annotations: "Is this reflected accurately in the B/S", "Discount Rate?")

EXAMPLE 14-4   Summary of Underlying Economic Liability (or Asset)

Summary of underlying economic liability (or asset) and economic expense of the period, with *assumed* numbers based on the following information:

- A company's beginning pension obligation is $5,798 and plan assets are $3,852, giving a beginning net funded position of −$1,946.

- Two items increase the company's pension obligation: service costs of $1,112 and interest costs of $333.
- The following items decrease the company's pension obligation: actuarial gains of $59, foreign exchange impact, and benefits paid to retired employees of $436;
- Actual returns on the plan assets are $241.
- The sponsoring company contributed $1,223 to the plan.

#'s

Beginning-of-Period Economic Liability or Asset	Economic Expense of the Period	Benefits Paid Out of and Contributions to the Pension Plan	End-of-Period Economic Liability or Asset
Beginning pension obligation: $5,798	Service costs: $1,112 Interest costs: $333 Actuarial gain decreases the obligation: −$59 Foreign exchange impact: −$25	Benefits paid to retirees: −$436	Ending pension obligation: $6,723
Beginning plan assets: $3,852	Actual returns on plan assets: $241	Benefits paid to retirees decrease the plan assets: −$436 Contributions by the sponsoring company increase the plan assets: $1,223	Ending plan assets: $4,880
Pension obligation minus plan assets equals beginning net funded position: −$1,946	Total net economic expense of the period is calculated by summing the above: $1,112 + $333 − $59 − $25 − $241 = $1,120 Or equivalently Calculated as the change in net funded position of $103 excluding sponsoring company contributions of $1,223 (i.e., $103 − $1,223)		Pension obligation minus ending net funded position: −$1,843

For Raytheon 0|00

Change in net funded position equals ending underfunded position of −$1,843 minus beginning underfunded position of −$1,946.

What number goes on the Balance Sheet? Net pension obligation.

Based on this assumed information, the economic expense of the period equals $1,120. One way to compute the economic expense is to sum the items that increase the pension obligation, subtract the items that decrease the obligation other than retiree payments, and deduct the return on the plan assets. Alternatively, the economic pension expense can be computed by calculating the change in the net funded position of the plan, excluding the sponsoring company's contributions. Because the computations (and variations presented in these examples) yield equivalent results, analysts can use the approach they consider most intuitive to determine the economic pension expense.

As discussed in an earlier section of the chapter, the pension expense shown on a company's income statement does not reflect the economic expense of the period, primarily because, under certain conditions, accounting standards permit several components of pension expense to be smoothed into income over time. (Recall that the components of the cost that are smoothed into income over time include past service costs and actuarial gains and losses. Also, actuarial gains and losses include both changes in the pension obligation resulting from changes in actuarial assumptions as well as any differences between expected and actual returns on plan assets.) To better reflect the company's operating performance, analysts can adjust for these items to obtain the underlying economic expense (or income) and financial ratios based on it. Using either of the calculations to estimate the economic pension expense of the period effectively includes actual returns on plan assets, all actuarial gains and losses arising in the period, and all service costs arising in the period (whether they relate to current service or past service), and effectively excludes any amortization of prior service cost and amortization of net actuarial gains and losses. Below is an example illustrating the estimation of economic pension expense for Coach, Inc. (NYSE: COH). Note that the actual numbers in the Coach example are identical to those in the assumed exhibit above, except that the Coach numbers are in thousands.

EXAMPLE 14-5   Adjusting Pension and Postretirement Benefits Expense to Underlying Economic Expense

Use the following pension-related information reported by Coach, Inc. in fiscal 2006 to answer the following. All amounts are in thousands.

1. Estimate the economic pension expense of the period.
2. Compute the difference between estimated economic pension expense of the period and reported pension expense, which was $748, the components of which are shown below.
3. Adjust reported net income to reflect the underlying economic pension expense. Coach's net income in fiscal 2006 was $494,277, and their effective tax rate was 38 percent.

Excerpt from footnote on retirement plans:	
Change in Benefit Obligation	
Benefit obligation at beginning of year	$5,798
Service cost	357

Interest cost	333
Actuarial (gain) loss	−59
Prior service cost	755
Foreign exchange impact	−25
Benefits paid	−436
Benefit obligation at end of year	$6,723
Change in Plan Assets	
Fair value of plan assets at beginning of year	$3,852
Actual return on plan assets	241
Employer contributions	1,223
Benefits paid	−436
Fair value of plan assets at end of year	$4,880
Components of Net Periodic Benefit Costs:	
Service costs	$357
Interest cost	333
Expected return on plan assets	−255
Amortization of net actuarial loss	313
Net periodic benefit cost	$748

Solution to 1. Economic pension expense is $1,120, calculated as the change in the pension obligation less change in pension plan assets adjusted for cash contributions and benefit payments.

Change in Benefit Obligation	$ 925
Adjust for non-expense items	
Benefits paid	436
Adjusted change in benefit obligation	$1,361
Change in Plan Assets	$1,028
Adjust for non-income items	
Employer contributions	−1,223
Benefits paid	436
Adjusted change in plan assets	$241
Net Increase in Net Pension Obligation = Economic Pension Expense	**$1,120**
Alternative, equivalent calculations	
Net funded position at beginning of period (underfunded) $5,798 benefit obligation minus $3,852 plan assets	−$1,946
Net funded position at end of period (underfunded) $6,723 benefit obligation minus $4,880 plan assets	−1,843

Change in net funded position, before employer's contribution	103
Employer's contribution	1,223
Change in net funded position, excluding employer's contribution = Economic pension expense	**$1,120**

Solution to 2. Adjusting to economic pension expense increases pension expense from the reported amount of $748 to $1,120 (i.e., by $372 or about 50 percent).

Solution to 3. Net income for Coach would decrease to $494,046, a relatively minor change, if adjusted for economic pension expense. In companies where the pension expense is a greater percentage of income, the effects are expected to be greater.

Economic pension expense from Part 1	$1,120
Reported pension expense	748
Increase in pension expense	$372
Net income (as reported)	494,277
Adjusted for after tax increase in pension expense [$372 × (1−0.38 tax rate)]	$231
Net income (adjusted)	$494,046

Source: Coach, Inc. Form 10-K, filed with the SEC 25 August 2006.

The components of pension expense conceptually can be classified as operating, investing, or financing costs; however, the expense is generally treated as a single item and deducted as an operating expense. It can be argued that only the service cost component of the pension expense is an operating expense, whereas the interest component and asset returns are both nonoperating. The interest cost component of pension expense is conceptually similar to the interest cost on any of the company's other liabilities. The pension liability is essentially equivalent to a borrowing from employees, and the interest costs of that borrowing can be considered financing costs. Similarly, the return on pension plan assets is conceptually similar to returns on any of the company's other financial assets.

To better reflect a company's operating performance, an adjustment can be made to operating income by adding in the full pension expense and then subtracting out the service cost. Note that this approach also excludes from operating income the amortization of prior service cost and the amortization of net actuarial gains and losses. This adjustment also eliminates the interest cost component and the return on plan assets component from the company's operating income. The interest cost component would be added to the company's interest expense, and the return on plan assets would be treated as nonoperating income. Recall that the *expected* return on plan assets is included as a component of pension expense. The difference between the actual and expected return is shown as a component of other comprehensive income. This difference can be taken to current year so that current year earnings reflect the *actual return* on plan assets. This adjustment changes net income, and potentially introduces earnings volatility. The reclassification of interest expense would not change net income. Below is an example illustrating adjustments to operating and nonoperating income.

EXAMPLE 14-6   Adjusting Pension and Postretirement Benefits Expense to Underlying Economic Expense and Reclassifying Components between Operating and Nonoperating Income

Use the fiscal 2006 pension-related information below reported by SABMiller plc., a U.K. based company that brews and distributes beer and other beverages, to estimate operating income and income before taxes for the period adjusted to include the economic pension and post-retirement expense. All amounts are in millions of U.S. dollars.

Excerpt from Consolidated Income Statement
For the year ended 31 March, 2007
SABMiller plc.
(US$ millions)

Revenue	$18,620
Net operating expenses	−15,593
Operating income	3,027
Interest payable and similar charges	−668
Interest receivable	240
Share of post-tax results of associates	205
Income before taxation	$2,804

Excerpt from footnote on retirement plans:
Components of pension and other postretirement benefits expense

Current service costs	$54
Interest costs	114
Expected return on plan assets	72
Total	96
Actual return on plan assets	$100

Solution. Operating income adjusted to include the economic pension expense is $3,069. The $96 pension and other postretirement benefits expense from the footnote is subtracted from operating income. Only the service cost component of $54 is added back as an operating expense.

Profit before taxation is $2,832 based on additional adjustments. Below operating income, interest costs of $114 are reclassified to "Interest payable and similar charges." The *actual* return on plan assets is added as investment income. All adjustments are summarized below.

Take to
Time to
make adjustments so
you will be reworded.

	Reported	Adjustments		Adjusted
Revenue	$18,620			$18,620
Net operating expenses	−15,593	Subtract 96	Add 54	−15,551
Operating income	3,027			3,069
Interest payable and similar charges	−668	Add 114		−782
Interest receivable	240			240
Share of post-tax results of associates	205			205
Actual return on plan assets		Add 100		100
Income before taxation	$2,804			$2,832

Note that SFAS No. 158 did not change the measurement of pension expense or its components. Issues with the measurements of the pension liability and expense are on the current FASB agenda.

2.5.4. Cash Flow Information

For a sponsoring company, the cash flow impact of pension and postretirement benefits is the amount of contributions that the company makes to fund the plan, or for unfunded plans, the amount of benefits paid. The amount of contributions a company makes to fund a pension or postretirement benefit plan is determined by regulations of the countries in which the company operates. In the United States, for example, the amount of contributions to DB pension plans are governed by the Employee Retirement and Income Security Act (ERISA) and depend on the funded status of the plan.

The previous section described the economic pension expense of a period. If a sponsoring company's periodic contributions to a plan exceed the economic pension expense of the period, the excess can be viewed from an economic perspective as a reduction of the overall pension obligation. In other words, the contribution would cover not only the pension obligation arising in the current period but also the pension obligations of another period. Such a contribution would be similar in concept to making a principal payment on a loan in excess of the scheduled principal payment. Conversely, a periodic contribution that is less than the economic pension expense of the period can be viewed as a source of financing.

In Example 14-5, Coach's economic pension expense for the period was $1,120 million, and the company's contribution to the plan was $1,223 million. The excess of $103 million can be viewed as a reduction of the overall pension obligation. The company covered not only the $1,120 million net pension obligation arising in this period but also part of the pension obligation from another period. Where the amounts of benefit obligations are material, an analyst may choose to adjust the cash flows that a company presents in its statement of cash flows. In this instance, the adjustment would reclassify the $103 million excess contribution as an outflow related to financing activities rather than to operating activities. Example 14-7 describes such an adjustment.

EXAMPLE 14-7   Adjusting Cash Flow

Vassiliki Doukas is analyzing the cash flow statement of Caterpillar Inc. as one component of a valuation. Doukas suggests to her colleague, Dimitri Krontiras, that the difference between the company's 2005 contributions to the pension plan and the economic pension costs incurred during that period is similar to a form of borrowing that enhances the company's reported cash from operations.

Using the information from the notes below and Exhibit 14-12, determine the following:

1. What is the company's economic pension expense for 2005?
2. How did the company's 2005 contribution to the pension plan compare to the economic expense for the year?
3. How would cash from operating activities and financing activities be adjusted to illustrate Doukas's interpretation of the difference between the company's contribution and the economic pension cost?

Notes:

a. Caterpillar's effective tax rate for 2005 was 29.5 percent.
b. Caterpillar reported 2005 cash from operating activities of $3,113 million and cash from financing activities of $1,153 million.

EXHIBIT 14-12   Excerpt from Caterpillar Inc. 10-K Postretirement Benefit Plans

($ millions)	U.S. Pension Benefits
Note 14 A	**2005**
Change in benefit obligation:	
Benefit obligation, beginning of year	$9,593
Service cost	150
Interest cost	555
Plan amendments	204
Actuarial losses (gains)	863
Benefits paid	−686
Acquisitions/Special termination benefits	—
Benefit obligation end of year	$10,679
Note 14 B	
Change in plan assets:	
Fair value of plan assets, beginning of year	$8,725
Actual return on plan assets	860
Company contributions	542

Benefits paid	−686
Acquisitions	—
Fair value of plan assets end of year	$9,441

Note 14 E

Components of net periodic benefit costs:

Service cost	150
Interest cost	555
Expected return on plan assets	−712
Amortization of:	
Prior service cost	59
Net actuarial loss	197
Total cost included in operating profit	$249

Solution to 1. The economic pension expense for 2005 is $912 million.

Calculation of Economic Pension Expense	
Net funded position at beginning of period (underfunded) $9,593 benefit obligation minus $8,725 plan assets	−$868
Net funded position at end of period (underfunded) $10,679 benefit obligation minus $9,441 plan assets	−$1,238
Change in net funded position, before company's contribution	−370
Company's contribution	−542
Change in net funded position, excluding employer's contribution = **Economic pension expense**	**−$912**

This economic pension expense calculation is equivalent to the $1,086 million increase in the benefit obligation ($10,679 million minus $9,593 million), minus the $174 million increase in the plan assets excluding the company's contributions ($9,441 million minus $8,725 million minus $542 million). Thus, the change in the company's net pension obligation, excluding the company's contribution (i.e., the economic pension expense), was $912 ($1,086 million minus $174 million.)

The following table shows the components of economic pension expense and where the items are disclosed in the company's footnotes.

Reported Information	2005	Source
Service cost	−$150	Notes 14 A, E
Interest cost	−$555	Notes 14 A, E
Actuarial losses and plan amendments	−$1,067	Note 14 A, sum
Actual return on plan assets	$860	Note 14 B
Economic pension expense	−$912	Items 1 + 2 + 3 minus item 4

Solution to 2. The company's contribution to the pension plan in 2005 was $542 million. Thus, the contribution was $370 million less than the economic pension expense of $912 million. The $370 difference equals $261 on a tax-effected basis, using the effective tax rate of 29.5 percent.

Economic pension expense (above)	−$912	Above
Amount of contribution	$542	Note 14 B
Amount by which economic pension expense exceeds the sponsoring company's contribution (pretax)	−$370	
Tax rate	29.50%	Given
Tax-effected amount by which economic pension expense exceeds the sponsoring company's contribution	−$261	$370 × (1−0.2950)

Solution to 3. The company's contribution to the pension plan in 2005 was $370 million ($261 million tax-effected) less than the 2005 economic pension expense. Interpreting this difference as similar to a source of borrowing rather than as an operating cash flow would increase the company's cash flow from financing from $1,153 to $1,414 million and decrease cash flow from operations.

Adjustment		
Cash from financing as reported	$1,153	Given
Financing inflow	261	From above
Adjusted cash from financing	$1,414	

3. SHARE-BASED COMPENSATION [*Not Coupied*]

In this section, we provide an overview of executive compensation focusing on share-based compensation. We first briefly discuss common components of executive compensation packages, their objectives, and advantages and disadvantages of share-based compensation. The discussion of share-based compensation then moves to accounting and reporting of stock grants before concentrating on stock options. The explanation of accounting and reporting stock options includes discussion of fair value accounting, the choice of valuation models, assumptions used, common disclosures, and important dates in measuring and reporting compensation expense.

Employee compensation packages are structured to fulfill varied objectives including satisfying employees' needs for liquidity, retaining employees, and motivating employees. Common components of employee compensation packages are salary, bonuses, and share-based compensation.[2] The salary component provides for the liquidity needs of an employee. Bonuses, generally in the form of cash, motivate and reward employees for short or long

---

[2]An extensive overview of different employee compensation mechanisms can be found in Lynch and Perry (2003).

term performance or goal achievement linking pay to performance. Share-based compensation is intended to align employees' interest with those of the shareholders. In the United States, disclosure of the key elements of management compensation is made in a company's proxy statement filed with the SEC. IFRS 2 requires similar disclosures. Exhibit 14-13 gives a description of the components and objectives of American Eagle Outfitters, Inc.'s (NYSE: AEO) executive compensation program.

Share-based compensation has the added advantage of requiring no cash outlays.[3] But a compensation expense is recorded and it reduces earnings as further discussed below. Although share-based compensation is generally viewed as motivating employees and aligning managers' interests with those of the shareholders, there are several disadvantages of share-based compensation. One disadvantage is that the managers may have limited influence over the company's market value (consider the scenario of overall market decline), so share-based compensation does not necessarily provide the desired incentives. A second disadvantage is that the increased ownership may lead managers to be risk averse. That is, fearing a large

EXHIBIT 14-13   Excerpts from Executive Compensation Disclosures of American Eagle Outfitters, Inc. (NYSE: AEO)

Compensation Program Elements

Our executive compensation program is designed to place a large amount of pay at risk based on company performance for all executives. Our philosophy serves to cultivate a pay-for-performance environment. Our executive compensation plan design has five key elements:

- Base Salary

- Annual Incentive Bonus

- Long-Term Incentive Cash Plan ("LTICP")

- Restricted Stock ("RS")

- Non-Qualified Stock Options ("NSO")

Three of the elements (Annual Incentive Bonus, Long-Term Incentive Cash Plan, and Restricted Stock) are entirely "at risk" based on company performance and are subject to forfeiture if the Company does not achieve threshold performance goals. Company performance below threshold levels results in forfeiture of all elements of direct compensation other than base salary and Non-Qualified Stock Options. At threshold performance, the CEO's total annual compensation declines by an average 45% relative to target performance.

We strategically allocate compensation between short-term and long-term components and between cash and equity in order to maximize executive performance and retention. While we endeavor to design compensation packages consistently for our executives, long-term compensation and equity awards comprise an increasingly larger proportion of total compensation as position level increases. The portion of total pay attributable to long-term incentive cash/equity compensation increases at successively higher levels of management, which ensures that executive compensation closely aligns with changes in shareholder value and achievement of performance objectives and that executives are held accountable for results relative to position level.

Source: American Eagle Outfitters, Inc. Form Def 14A filed 1 May 2007.

---

[3]While issuing employee stock options requires no initial cash outlay, the company implicitly forgoes issuing new shares of stock (and receiving cash) when the options are exercised.

market value decline (and loss in individual wealth), managers may seek less risky (and less profitable) projects. An opposite effect, excessive risk-taking, can also occur with options awards. Because options have skewed pay-out that rewards excessive risk-taking, managers may seek more risky projects. Finally, when share-based compensation is granted to employees, existing shareholders ownership is diluted.

For financial reporting, a company reports compensation expense during the period in which employees earn their salary. Accounting for cash payments and cash bonuses is relatively straightforward. When the employee has earned the salary or bonus an expense is recorded. Commonly, compensation expense for managers is reported in sales, general, and administrative expenses on the income statement.

Share-based compensation is more varied and can include stock, stock options, or stock appreciation rights and phantom shares. Compensation expense reported for share-based compensation is reported at fair value under U.S. GAAP (SFAS No. 123 (R)) and IFRS (IFRS 2), but the specifics of the accounting depend on the type of share-based compensation given to the employee. Under both U.S. GAAP and IFRS, the usual disclosures required for share-based compensation include: (1) the nature and extent of share-based compensation arrangements during the period, (2) how the fair value of a share-based grant was determined, and (3) the effect of share-based compensation on income for the period and on its financial position.

Two common forms of share-based compensation are discussed below: **stock grants** and **stock options**.

3.1. Stock Grants

A company can grant stock to employees outright, with restrictions, or contingent upon performance. For an outright stock grant, compensation expense is reported based on the fair value of the stock on the grant date, generally the market value at grant date. Compensation expense is allocated over the period benefited by the employee's service, referred to as the service period.

Another type of stock award is a restricted stock grant that is given subject to the shares being returned to the company if certain conditions are not met. Common restrictions include the requirement that employees remain with the company for a specified period or that certain performance goals are met. Compensation expense for restricted stock grants is equal to the fair value (usually market value) of the shares issued at the grant date. This compensation expense is allocated over the employee service period.

Shares granted contingent on meeting performance goals are called performance shares. The amount of the grant is usually determined by performance measures other than the change in stock price, such as accounting earnings or return on assets. Basing the grant on accounting performance addresses employees' concerns that stock price is beyond their control. However, it can provide incentives to manipulate accounting numbers. Compensation expense is equal to the fair value (usually market value) of the shares issued at the grant date. This compensation expense is allocated over the employee service period.

3.2. Stock Options

Like stock grants, compensation expense related to option grants is reported at fair value under SFAS No. 123(R) and IFRS 2. Until recently, companies reporting under U.S. GAAP were allowed to use the intrinsic value of stock option grants as a measure of the value of options granted. The **intrinsic value** is the difference between the market price on the day the options is granted and the exercise price of the option. Usually, the exercise price of stock options granted to employees is the market value of the stock at the grant date. So, the intrinsic value would be zero (and compensation expense would also be zero).

Accounting rules now require fair value to be estimated using a valuation model such as the Black–Scholes model or a binomial model. Using the fair value of stock options granted rather than the intrinsic value generally results in increased compensation expense.

Where the fair value of stock grants is usually based on the market value at the date of the grant, the fair value of option grants must be estimated. Because features of employee stock options generally differ from traded options, companies must choose a valuation technique rather than rely on a market value. One key choice in estimating fair value is the valuation technique, or option pricing model, that the company uses. Several methods are commonly seen such as the Black–Scholes model or a binomial model. Accounting standards do not prescribe a certain model. Generally, though, the valuation method should be: (1) consistent with the fair value measurement, (2) based on established principles of financial economic theory, and (3) reflect all substantive characteristics of the award.

Once a valuation technique is selected, a company must determine the input to the option pricing model often including items such as exercise price, stock price volatility, estimated life of each award, estimated number of options that will be forfeited, and the risk-free rate of interest.[4] Certain input is known at the time of the grant, such as the exercise price. Other critical input is highly subjective, such as stock price volatility or the estimated life of stock options, and can greatly change the estimated fair value and thus compensation expense. Higher volatility, a longer estimated life, and higher risk-free interest rate would generally increase the estimated fair value while a higher assumed dividend yield would decrease the estimated fair value. Using different assumptions coupled with different valuation models can significantly impact the fair value of employee stock options. Exhibit 14-14 is an excerpt for Coca Cola, Inc (NYSE: KO) explaining the assumptions used in valuing stock options.

In accounting for stock options, there are several important dates including the grant date, vesting date, exercise date, and expiration date. The **grant date** is the day that options are granted to employees. The **vesting date** is the date that employees can first exercise stock options. The vesting can be immediate or over a future period. The **exercise date** is the day that employees actually exercise the options and convert them to stock. If the options go unexercised, they may expire at some pre-determined future date, commonly 5 or 10 years from the grant date.

The grant date is also usually the date that compensation expense is measured if both the number of shares and option price are known. If facts affecting the value of options granted depend on events after the grant date, then compensation expense is measured at the exercise date. Compensation expense is allocated over the period benefited by the employee's service, referred to as the service period. The **service period** is usually the period between the grant date and the vesting date.

In Example 14-8, Coca Cola, Inc. (NYSE: KO) reported $324 million of compensation expense in fiscal 2006 from option grants. It also disclosed that $376 million, related to stock options already granted, will be recorded as compensation expense in the future as options vest over the next 1.7 years.

---

[4] The estimated life of an option award incorporates such assumptions as employee turnover and is usually shorter than the expiration period.

EXHIBIT 14-14   Assumptions Used in Stock Options Pricing Models: Excerpts from Financial Statements of Coca Cola, Inc. (NYSE: KO)

Note 15—Stock Compensation Plans

The fair value of each option award is estimated on the date of the grant using a Black–Scholes–Merton option pricing model that uses the assumptions noted in the following table. The expected term of the options granted represents the period of time that options granted are expected to be outstanding and is derived by analyzing historic exercise behavior. Expected volatilities are based on implied volatilities from traded options on the Company's stock, historical volatility of the Company's stock, and other factors. The risk-free interest rate for the period matching the expected term of the option is based on the U.S. Treasury yield curve in effect at the time of the grant. The dividend yield is the calculated yield on the Company's stock at the time of the grant.

The following table sets forth information about the weighted-average fair value of options granted during the past three years and the weighted-average assumptions used for such grants:

Fiscal Year	2006	2005	2004
Fair value of options at grant date	$8.16	$8.23	$8.84
Dividend yields	2.7%	2.6%	2.5%
Expected volatility	19.3%	19.9%	23.0%
Risk-free interest rates	4.5%	4.3%	3.8%
Expected term of the option	6 years	6 years	6 years

Source: Coca Cola, Inc. Form 10-K, filed 21 February 2007.

EXAMPLE 14-8   Disclosure of Stock Options Current Compensation Expense, Vesting, and Future Compensation Expense

Coca Cola, Inc. (NYSE: KO) reports $324 million of compensation expense in fiscal 2006 from option grants. It also provides disclosures related to stock options already granted. Using the information from the following note, determine:

1. What total compensation expense will be in future years as options vest.
2. What compensation expense will be in 2007 and 2008 for options already granted.

Excerpts from Financial Statements of Coca Cola, Inc. (NYSE: KO):

Note 15—Stock Compensation Plans

Our total stock-based compensation expense was approximately $324 million, $324 million and $345 million in 2006, 2005 and 2004, respectively. These amounts were recorded in selling, general and administrative expenses in 2006,

2005 and 2004, respectively. As of December 31, 2006, we had approximately $376 million of total unrecognized compensation cost related to non-vested share-based compensation arrangements granted under our plans. This cost is expected to be recognized as stock-based compensation expense over a weighted-average period of 1.7 years. . . .

Stock options granted in December 2003 and thereafter generally become exercisable over a four-year annual vesting period and expire 10 years from the date of grant. Stock options granted from 1999 through July 2003 generally become exercisable over a four-year annual vesting period and expire 15 years from the date of grant. Prior to 1999, stock options generally became exercisable over a three-year vesting period and expired 10 years from the date of grant.

Source: Coca Cola, Inc. Form 10-K filed 21 February 2007.

Solution to 1. Coca Cola, Inc. discloses that unrecognized compensation expense relating to stock options already granted totals $376 million.

Solution to 2. The options already granted will vest over the next 1.7 years. So, compensation expense related to stock options already granted will be $221 million ($376/1.7 years) in 2007 and $155 in 2008 ($376 total less $221 expensed in 2007). New options may also be granted in the future, raising the reported compensation expense.

3.3. Other Issues Related to Share-Based Compensation

In addition to decreasing income through compensation expense, stock options have the potential to dilute earnings per share. Both stock grants and stock options allow the employee to obtain direct ownership in the company. Other types of share-based compensation, such as stock appreciation rights (SARs) or phantom stock, compensate an employee based on changes in the value of shares without requiring the employee to hold the shares. With SARs, an employee's compensation is based on increases in a company's share price. Like other forms of stock-based compensation, SARs serve to motivate employees and align their interest with shareholders. Two additional advantages of SARs are (1) the potential for risk aversion is limited because employees have limited downside risk and unlimited upside potential similar to employee stock options and (2) shareholder ownership is not diluted. A disadvantage is that SARs require a current-period cash outflow. Similar to other share-based compensation, SARs are valued at fair value and compensation expense is allocated over the service period of the employee. While phantom share plans are similar to other types of share-based compensation, they differ somewhat because compensation is based on the performance of hypothetical stock rather than the company's actual stock. Unlike SARs, phantom shares can be used by private companies or business units within a company that are not publicly traded, or by highly illiquid companies.

4. SUMMARY

This chapter discusses two different forms of employee compensation: postretirement benefits and share-based compensation. While different, the two share similarities in that they are forms of compensation outside of the standard salary arrangements. They also involve complex valuation, accounting, and reporting issues. While U.S. GAAP and IFRS are converging on accounting and reporting, it is important to note that differences in a country's social system, laws, and regulations can result in differences in a company's pension and share-based compensation plans that may be reflected in the company's earnings and financial reports.

Key points include the following:

- Defined-contribution pension plans specify only the amount of contribution to the plan; the eventual amount of the pension benefit to the employee will depend on the value of an employee's plan assets at the time of retirement.
- Defined-benefit pension plans specify the amount of the pension benefit, often determined by a plan formula, under which the eventual amount of the benefit to the employee is a function of length of service and final salary.
- Differences exist in countries' regulatory requirements for companies to fund DB pension plan obligations.
- DB pension plan obligations are funded by the sponsoring company contributing assets to a pension trust, a separate legal entity.
- Three measures are used in estimating a DB pension plan's liabilities, each increasingly more inclusive: the vested benefit obligation, the accumulated benefit obligation, and the projected benefit obligation.
- For analysis, the projected benefit obligation is typically the most appropriate measure because it recognizes future salary increases.
- Balance sheet reporting is less relevant for DC plans because companies make contributions to DC plans as the expense arises and thus no liabilities accrue for that type of plan.
- IFRS requires companies' balance sheets to reflect as a DB liability the pension obligation minus the fair value of plan assets, with certain adjustments for actuarial gains or losses, and any past service costs not yet recognized.
- New U.S. accounting standards require that companies' balance sheets reflect as a DB liability the pension obligation minus the fair value of plan sets, with no further adjustments.
- Because the IASB and the FASB have identified pensions and postretirement benefit accounting as a major area for collaborative efforts, the new U.S. accounting standards are also relevant for anticipating future changes for companies using IFRS.
- Pension expense includes the following components: service cost, interest expense, prior service cost, actuarial gains and losses, and return on plan assets (which reduces pension expense).
- Estimates of the future obligation under DB pension plans and other postretirement benefits are sensitive to numerous assumptions, including discount rates, assumed annual compensation increases, expected return on plan assets, and assumed health care cost inflation.
- Employee compensation packages are structured to fulfill varied objectives including satisfying employees' needs for liquidity, retaining employees, and providing incentives to employees.
- Common components of employee compensation packages are salary, bonuses, and share-based compensation.

- Share-based compensation serves to align employees' interest with those of the shareholders. It includes stocks and stock options.
- Share-based compensation has the advantage of requiring no current-period cash outlays.
- Share-based compensation is reported at fair value under U.S. GAAP and IFRS.
- The valuation technique, or option pricing model, that the company uses is an important choice in determining fair value and is disclosed.
- Key assumptions and input into option pricing models include items such as exercise price, stock price volatility, estimated life of each award, estimated number of options that will be forfeited, and the risk-free rate of interest. Certain assumptions are highly subjective, such as stock price volatility or the expected life of stock options, and can greatly change the estimated fair value and thus compensation expense.

PRACTICE PROBLEMS

The following information relates to Problems 1 through 6.

Magenta Corp. is based in the United States and offers its employees a defined-benefit pension plan. The company's effective tax rate for 2008 is 40 percent. Excerpts from a financial statement footnote on Magenta's retirement plans are presented in Exhibit 14-15.

EXHIBIT 14-15   Magenta Corp. Defined-Benefit Pension Plan

($ millions)	2008
Change in benefit obligation	
Benefit obligations at beginning of year	$28,416
Service cost	96
Interest cost	1,557
Actuarial (gains) losses	−306
Prior service costs	132
Foreign exchange impact	−42
Benefits paid	−1,332
Benefit obligations at end of year	$28,531
Change in plan assets	
Fair value of plan assets at beginning of year	$23,432
Actual return on plan assets	1,302
Employer contributions	693
Benefits paid	−1,332
Fair value of plan assets at end of year	$24,105
Components of net periodic benefit cost	
Service cost	$96
Interest cost	1,557
Expected return plan assets	−1,874
Amortization of net actuarial loss	264
Net periodic benefit cost	$43

1. At year-end 2008, $28,531 represents the defined benefit pension plan's
   A. vested benefit obligation.
   B. projected benefit obligation.
   C. accumulated benefit obligation.

2. The economic pension expense for Magenta's DB plan is *closest to*
   A. $135 million
   B. $1,251 million
   C. $2,509 million

3. The difference between Magenta's estimated economic pension expense for the period
   and the reported pension expense is *closest to*
   A. $92 million
   B. $1,208 million
   C. $1,302 million

4. To adjust Magenta's reported net income to reflect the company's underlying economic
   pension expense, an analyst would decrease net income by an amount *closest to*
   A. $43 million.
   B. $55 million.
   C. $135 million.

5. In order to reflect the underlying economic liability of Magenta's defined-benefit pension
   plan, an analyst would adjust Magenta's 2008 balance sheet to include a $24,105
   A. increase in assets and equity.
   B. increase in assets and liabilities.
   C. increase in liabilities and reduction to equity.

6. An adjustment to the Magenta's statement of cash flows to reclassify the company's excess
   contribution for 2008 would *most likely* entail reclassifying $558 million as an outflow
   related to
   A. investing activities rather than operating activities
   B. financing activities rather than operating activities
   C. operating activities rather than financing activities

The following information relates to Problems 7 through 12.

EXHIBIT 14-16   Components of Expense (Income)

	Year Ended 31 December		
	2008	**2007**	**2006**
Components of expense/(income)			
Service cost	$908	$910	$831
Interest cost	2,497	2,457	2,378
			(Continued)

EXHIBIT 14-16   *Continued*

	Year Ended 31 December		
	2008	**2007**	**2006**
Expected return on plan assets	(3,455)	(3,515)	(3,378)
Amortization of prior service costs	188	185	180
Recognized net actuarial loss/(gain)	912	1,266	440
Net periodic benefit cost	$1,050	$1,303	$451

EXHIBIT 14-17   Funded Status of Plan

At 31 December ($ millions)	**2008**	**2007**
Change in benefit obligation		
Beginning balance	$45,183	$42,781
Service cost	908	910
Interest cost	2,497	2,457
Plan participants' contributions	9	12
Amendments	156	270
Actuarial (gain)/loss	(925)	2,778
Settlement/curtailment/acquisitions/dispositions, net	85	(1,774)
Benefits paid	(2,331)	(2,251)
Ending balance	$45,582	$45,183
Change in plan assets		
Beginning balance at fair value	$43,484	$38,977
Actual return on plan assets	4,239	5,460
Company contribution	526	2,604
Plan participants' contributions	9	12
Settlement/curtailment/acquisitions/dispositions, net	216	(1,393)
Benefits paid	(2,286)	(2,208)
Exchange rate adjustment	15	32
Ending balance at fair value	$46,203	$43,484

EXHIBIT 14-18   Volatility Assumptions Used to Value Stock Option Grants

Grant Year	**Weighted Average Expected Volatility**
2008 valuation assumptions	
2004–2008	21.50%
2007 valuation assumptions	
2003–2007	23.00%

Passaic Industries is based in the United States and offers its employees both a defined-benefit pension plan and stock options. Several of the disclosures related to these plans are presented in Exhibits 14-16, 14-17, and 14-18.

7. With regard to its defined-benefit pension plan, Passaic's year-end 2008 balance sheet *most likely* presents a
   A. $621 million asset.
   B. $621 million liability.
   C. $1,699 million liability.

8. The pension expense reported on the Passaic Industries income statement for the year ending 31 December 2008 is *closest* to
   A. $908 million.
   B. $1,050 million.
   C. $2,331 million.

9. The Passaic Industries statement of cash flows for the year ended 31 December 2008 shows the reconciliation of net income to cash flows from operating activities for the period. The associated adjustment to net income related to the DB plan is *closest* to
   A. $526 million.
   B. $2,331 million.
   C. $4,239 million.

10. The estimated increase in the pension obligation due to benefits earned by current employees in 2008 is *closest* to
    A. $908 million.
    B. $1,050 million.
    C. $2,331 million.

11. Because of the changes in pension plan assets and benefit obligations reported in the Funded Status of Plan reported at 31 December 2007 and 31 December 2008, the 2008 Passaic Industries balance sheet compared to the 2007 balance sheet will show a $2,320 increase in
    A. assets.
    B. liabilities.
    C. shareholders' equity.

12. Compared to 2008 net income as reported, if Passaic Industries had used the same expected volatility assumption for its 2008 option grants that it had used in 2007, its 2008 net income would have been
    A. lower.
    B. higher.
    C. the same.

The following information relates to Problems 13 through 18.
Stereo Warehouse is a U.S. retailer that offers employees a defined-benefit pension plan and stock options as part of its compensation package. Peter Friedland, CFA, is an equity analyst concerned with earnings quality. He is particularly interested in whether the discretionary assumptions the company is making regarding compensation plans are contributing

EXHIBIT 14-19   Assumptions Used for Stereo Warehouse Defined-Benefit Plan

	2008	2007	2006
Expected long-term rate of return on plan assets	6.06%	6.14%	6.79%
Discount rate	4.85	4.94	5.38
Salary increases	4.00	4.44	4.25
Inflation	3.00	2.72	2.45

EXHIBIT 14-20   Allocation of Stereo Warehouse Defined-Benefit Plan Assets

	2008	2007
Equity securities	90%	80%
Debt securities	10	20

EXHIBIT 14-21   Option Valuation Assumptions

	2008	2007	2006
Risk free rate	4.6%	3.8%	2.4%
Expected life	5.0 yrs	4.5 yrs	5.0 yrs
Dividend yield	1.0%	0.0%	0.0%
Expected volatility	29%	31%	35%

to the recent earnings growth at Stereo Warehouse. He gathers information from the company's regulatory filings regarding the pension plan assumptions in Exhibit 14-19, the actual asset allocation for the pension plan in Exhibit 14-20, and the assumptions related to option valuation in Exhibit 14-21.

13. Compared to the 2008 reported financial statements, if Stereo Warehouse had used the same expected long-term rate of return on plan assets assumption in 2008 as it used in 2006, its year-end 2008 pension obligation would *most likely* have been
    A. lower.
    B. higher.
    C. the same.

14. Compared to the reported 2008 financial statements, if Stereo Warehouse had used the same discount rate as it used in 2006, it would have *most likely* reported lower
    A. net income.
    B. total liabilities.
    C. cash flow from operating activities.

15. Compared to the assumptions Stereo Warehouse used to compute its pension expense in 2007, earnings in 2008 were *most favorably* impacted by the change in the
    A. discount rate.
    B. expected salary increases.
    C. expected long-term rate of return on plan assets.

16. The pension assumptions being used by Stereo Warehouse may be *internally inconsistent* with respect to
    A. asset returns only.
    B. inflation expectations only.
    C. both inflation expectations and asset returns.

17. Compared to the reported 2008 financial statements, if Stereo Warehouse had used the 2006 expected volatility assumption to value its employee stock options it would have *most likely* reported higher
    A. net income.
    B. compensation expense.
    C. deferred compensation liability.

18. Compared to the assumptions Stereo Warehouse used to value stock options in 2007, earnings in 2008 were most favorably impacted by the change in the
    A. expected life.
    B. risk-free rate.
    C. dividend yield.

The following information relates to Problems 19 through 24.

EXHIBIT 14-22   Pension Plan Assumptions for Aero Euro

	2008	**2007**	**2006**
Discount rate	4.51%	4.49%	4.55%
Salary inflation rate	2.62%	2.70%	2.91%
Expected long-term rate of return on plan assets	5.70%	5.70%	5.13%

EXHIBIT 14-23   Information Related to Aero Euro's Defined-Benefit Plans

	Pension Benefits (€ millions)		
	2008	**2007**	**2006**
Benefit obligation at beginning of year	10,921	10,313	9,208
Service cost	368	359	275
Interest cost	489	461	447
Employees' contribution	40	36	32

(Continued)

EXHIBIT 14-23   *Continued*

	Pension Benefits(€ millions)		
	2008	**2007**	**2006**
Plan amendments	150	49	16
Settlements/curtailments	(28)	(11)	(1)
Benefits paid	(423)	(398)	(352)
Actuarial loss / (gain)	68	106	707
Currency translation adjustment	(3)	6	(19)
Benefit obligation at end of year	11,582	10,921	10,313
Fair value of plan assets at beginning of year	12,538	10,782	9,936
Actual return on plan assets	936	1,763	920
Employers' contributions	323	358	261
Employees' contributions	40	36	32
Settlements/curtailments	(6)	(6)	—
Benefits paid	(423)	(398)	(352)
Currency translation adjustment	(4)	3	(15)
Fair value of plan assets at end of year	13,404	12,538	10,782
Funded status	1,822	1,617	469
Unrecognized prior service cost	190	59	25
Unrecognized actuarial (gains) / losses	(857)	(710)	322
Prepaid (accrued) pension cost	1,155	966	816
Amounts recorded in the balance sheet:			
Pension asset	2,097	1,903	1,767
Provision for retirement benefits	(942)	(937)	(951)
Net amount recognized	1,155	966	816
Net periodic cost :			
Service cost	368	359	275
Interest cost	489	461	447
Expected return on plan assets	(714)	(616)	(532)
Settlement/curtailment	(18)	(8)	—
Amortization of prior service cost	19	12	15
Amortization of unrecognized actuarial (gain) loss	(1)	16	(4)
Other	—	(1)	—
Net periodic cost	143	223	201
Accumulated benefit obligation	10,018	9,656	9,081

Andreas Kordt is an equity analyst examining the financial statements of Aero Euro. Aero Euro is based in Belgium and complies with IFRS. Kordt believes that the accounting guidelines for defined-benefit plans do not reflect the underlying economic financial conditions and he intends to adjust Aero Euro's financial statements accordingly. He also wants to compare the reported financial statements to those of a company that follows U.S. GAAP. As an initial step, he pulled certain information relating to the plans, which is presented in Exhibits 14-22 and 14-23.

19. At year-end 2008, €10,018 million represents the total present value of benefits Aero Euro's employees
    A. have earned to date.
    B. would receive if they left the company.
    C. are expected to earn during their career.

20. The adjustments Kordt needs to make in order to reflect the underlying economic pension expense for 2008 include subtracting
    A. €423 million from the change in benefit obligation.
    B. €423 million from the change in the value of plan assets.
    C. €323 million from the change in the value of plan assets.

21. The 2008 pension expense recognized on Aero Euro's income statement is *closest* to
    A. €143 million.
    B. €423 million.
    C. €1,155 million.

22. Adjusting Aero Euro's 2008 balance sheet to reflect the underlying economic position of the company's defined benefit plan would result in a €667 increase in
    A. assets.
    B. liabilities.
    C. shareholders' equity.

23. Compared to the reported 2008 financial statements, if Aero Euro used the 2006 salary inflation rate in 2008 it would have *most likely* reported higher
    A. net income.
    B. benefit obligation.
    C. amortization of prior service cost.

24. Compared to the reported 2008 financial statements, if Aero Euro used the 2006 expected long-term rate of return on plan assets in 2008 it would have *most likely* reported higher
    A. net assets.
    B. net income.
    C. pension expense.

CHAPTER 15

INTERCORPORATE INVESTMENTS

Susan Perry Williams

McIntire School of Commerce
University of Virginia
Charlottesville, Virginia

LEARNING OUTCOMES

After completing this chapter, you will be able to do the following:

- Explain the categorization of intercorporate investments into minority passive, minority active, joint ventures, and controlling interest.
- Describe the reporting under International Financial Reporting Standards (IFRS) and U.S. generally accepted accounting principles (U.S. GAAP) of the four categories of intercorporate investments including the use of different accounting methods: equity, proportionate consolidation, and consolidation; and including the treatment of goodwill.
- Contrast the purchase method, the pooling of interest method, and the acquisition method, used in business combinations and evaluate the impact of each method on reported financial results.
- Explain the implications on performance ratios of the different accounting methods used for intercorporate investments.
- Identify the accounting issues associated with special purpose entities (SPEs) or variable interest entities.

1. INTRODUCTION

Intercompany investments play a significant role in business activities. Diversification, entry into global markets, growth, and competitive opportunities lead many companies to make investments in other companies. Companies often invest in the marketable debt and equity securities of other companies. Debt securities include corporate and government bonds, notes, redeemable preferred stock, and municipal securities. Equity securities include common and nonredeemable preferred stock. The percentage of ownership a company decides to acquire of an investee depends on resources available, the desired level of involvement, and the ability to acquire the investment.

There are several accounting methods available to account for these investments, but the choice of accounting method is not discretionary. The characteristics of each investment dictate the appropriate accounting treatment. Differences in reporting standards for intercompany investments can reduce the comparability of financial statements and make it difficult for the analyst to correctly assess the performance and financial position of the company.

The growth of global markets and recent accounting scandals make it even more important for the analyst to understand differences in accounting standards. The European Union (EU) recently adopted IFRS as their required financial reporting standard for member countries. Global convergence of reporting standards facilitates financial analysis but significant differences still exist. The analyst should be aware of these differences when comparing the financial statements of companies using IFRS, U.S. GAAP, or other standards. The International Accounting Standards Board (IASB) and the Financial Accounting Standards Board (FASB) are currently working on a joint business combination project that addresses accounting for controlling interest investments. This project is expected to reduce the number and significance of differences between IFRS and U.S. GAAP related to business combinations. The joint business combination project is beginning to produce results and in late 2007, FASB issued SFAS No. 141R and SFAS No. 160. These two standards will have a significant impact on financial reporting for business combinations. In the near future, the IASB is also expected to issue standards that will result in a substantial convergence on business combination issues.

Understanding the appropriate accounting treatment for different types of intercorporate investment and understanding the differences between IFRS and U.S. GAAP related to these investments will enable analysts to make better comparisons and improve investment decisions.

This chapter is organized as follows: Section 2 explains the basic categorization of corporate investments. Section 3 describes reporting for minority passive investments a company may make in other corporations. Section 4 describes the financial reporting for minority active investments, and section 5 explores joint ventures, a common, important type of minority active investment. Section 6 describes controlling interests in other companies, the parent/subsidiary relationship, and consolidated financial statements. Section 7 describes the financial reporting for special purpose entities. Section 8 summarizes the chapter, and practice problems in the CFA Institute item set format complete the chapter.

2. BASIC CORPORATE INVESTMENT CATEGORIES

In general, investments in marketable debt and equity securities can be categorized as (1) **minority passive investments** in which the investor has no significant influence or control over the operations of the investee, (2) **minority active investments** in which investors exert significant influence (but not control) over the investee, and (3) **controlling interest** (a greater than 50 percent ownership) in an investee. Although the determination is based on influence rather than percent holding, lack of influence is generally presumed when the investor holds less than 20 percent interest, significant influence is generally presumed between

20 percent and 50 percent, and investments in excess of 50 percent are usually presumed to be controlling interests. A fourth category, **joint ventures**, relates to shared control by two or more entities.

Volvo Group, a Swedish manufacturer of commercial vehicles, states in its 2006 Annual Report that:

> *Consolidated financial statements comprise the Parent Company, subsidiaries, joint ventures, and associated companies. Subsidiaries are defined as companies in which Volvo holds more than 50% of the voting rights or in which Volvo otherwise has a controlling interest. Joint ventures are companies over which Volvo has joint control together with one or more external parties. Associated companies are companies in which Volvo has a significant influence, which is normally when Volvo's holding equals at least 20% but less than 50% of the voting rights.*
>
> Source: Volvo Group Annual Report 2006

A summary of the accounting treatments for various types of corporate investment is presented in Exhibit 15-1. The reader should be alert to the fact that value measurement can be different depending on the portfolio classification and whether the standards are IFRS or U.S. GAAP. These alternative treatments are discussed later in this chapter.

EXHIBIT 15-1   Summary of Accounting Treatments for Investments

	Minority Passive	**Minority Active**	**Controlling Interest**	**Joint Ventures**
Influence	Not significant	Significant	Controlling	Shared control
Typical percentage interest	Usually < 20%	Usually 20%–50%	Usually > 50%	Varies
Methodology	Investments are classified as held-to-maturity, held-for-trading, or available-for-sale. Investors may also designate the portfolio as fair value. Debt: Held-to-maturity (amortized cost) Held-for-trading securities (fair value) Available-for-sale (fair value) Equity: Held-for-trading securities (fair value) Available-for-sale (fair value)	Equity method	Consolidation	IFRS: Equity method or proportionate consolidation U.S. GAAP: Equity method (except for unincorporated ventures in specialized industries)
Applicable IFRS	IAS 39	IAS 28	IAS 27 IFRS 3	IAS 31
Applicable U.S. GAAP	SFAS 115 SFAS 159	SFAS 142 APB 18	SFAS 141 SFAS 142 SFAS 141R SFAS 160	SFAS No. 94

3. MINORITY PASSIVE INVESTMENTS

Investments are considered **passive** when the investor can exert no significant influence or control over the operations of the investee. When, and if, the investee pays dividends, the investor records dividend income. Recognition of additional income depends on the classification of the passive investment.

IFRS and U.S. GAAP are similar regarding the accounting for passive investments. Both define three basic categories of financial instruments: (1) held-to-maturity investments, (2) held-for-trading (or simply "trading securities"), and (3) available-for-sale. Additionally, both standards permit companies to designate passive investments at fair value with unrealized gains and losses in earnings.

3.1. Held-to-Maturity Investments

Held-to-maturity investments are debt securities the entity currently intends to hold until the maturity date. The most common examples are bonds, notes, or convertible debt. In order to support this designation, both IFRS and U.S. GAAP require a positive intent and ability to hold a financial asset to maturity. IFRS require that securities be reported at their initial fair value whereas U.S. GAAP requires held-to-maturity assets to be carried at cost. In most cases, cost is the initial fair market value, so the treatment is identical. Companies report short-term held-to-maturity securities at their original cost. But long-term held-to-maturities are carried at amortized cost because long-term investments are adjusted for amortization and impairment. A discount or premium arises if the investor's cost differs from the par value of the debt security because of disparities between the stated interest rate and the effective interest rate. This discount or premium is amortized over the life of the investment and has an impact on the carrying value of the debt security. Any interest payments, adjusted for amortization, are reported as income.

3.2. Held-for-Trading Securities

Held-for-trading securities are debt or equity financial assets bought with the intention to sell them in the near term, usually less than three months. Held-for-trading securities are reported at fair value, with unrealized gains and losses included in income. The income statement also includes interest from debt securities and dividends from equity securities.

3.3. Available-for-Sale Investments

Available-for-sale investments include debt and equity securities not classified as either held-to-maturity or held-for-trading securities. In general, available-for-sale securities are reported at fair value on the balance sheet. Interest income from debt securities and dividends from equity securities are included in income when earned. Under U.S. GAAP, unrealized gains or losses are reported in the equity section of the balance sheet as part of other comprehensive income until the securities are sold. Upon sale, the realized gain or loss is reported as income (and reversed out of other comprehensive income). U.S. GAAP comprehensive income includes net income as reported on the income statement plus other comprehensive income.

IFRS treatment is similar to U.S. GAAP except for foreign exchange gains and losses. IFRS (IAS 1 revised 2007) established disclosure requirements for the statement of recognized income and expense. Disclosures include net income recognized directly in equity, transfers from equity, and profit or loss for the year. IFRS treats gains or losses on available-for-sale securities as net income recognized directly in equity, except for foreign exchange gains or losses on available-for-sale securities that are included as profit or loss.

3.4. Designated Fair Value

Designated fair value instruments can be financial assets or financial liabilities. Using this designation can reduce measurement or recognition inconsistency and can mitigate earnings volatility caused by measuring related assets and liabilities on different bases. IFRS (IAS 39) criteria are more restrictive than U.S. GAAP (SFAS No. 159). Gains or losses are recognized as income.

The differences between standards for investments are illustrated in Exhibit 15-2. This excerpt from the 2006 annual report of Novartis, a health care product company in Switzerland, shows a reconciliation of net income from continuing operations between IFRS and U.S. GAAP.

EXHIBIT 15-2   Novartis: Significant Differences between IFRS and U.S. GAAP

	Notes	**2006 (US$ millions)**	**2005 (US$ millions)**
Net Income from continuing operations under IFRS		7,019	6,072
U.S. GAAP adjustments:			
Available-for-sale securities	**33.2**	−114	**278**
Inventory	33.3	103	20
Associated companies	**33.4**		**−6**
Intangible assets	33.5	−1,743	−1,238
Property, plant, and equipment	33.6	58	53
Pensions and other postemployment benefits	33.7	−198	−181
Deferred taxes	33.8	125	178
Share-based compensation	33.9	−5	−44
Minority interests	33.10	−27	−11
Others	33.11	−68	
Net income from continuing operations under U.S. GAAP		5,150	5,121

Note 33.2—Available-for-sale marketable securities and derivative financial instruments:

Under IFRS, fair value changes that relate to underlying movement in exchange rates on available-for-sale debt securities have to be recognized on the income statement. U.S. GAAP requires the entire movement in the fair value of these securities to be recognized in equity, including any part that relates to foreign exchange movements. This resulted in an additional U.S. GAAP expense of US$114 million in 2006 (2005: income of US$278 million)

Note 33.4—Investments in associated companies include purchase price adjustments and amortization differences due to diverging implementation rules for U.S. GAAP SFAS No. 141 and IFRS 3 on accounting for business combinations and investments in associated companies.

The different treatment of unrealized gains and losses on available-for-sale investments is described in note 33.2 above. In the case of Novartis, an unrealized foreign exchange loss (as a result of movements in exchange rates) of $278 million is recognized for available-for-sale securities under IFRS for 2005, whereas the same losses would have been recognized in other comprehensive income under U.S. GAAP. Thus, the loss is added back to IFRS income to reconcile to U.S. GAAP income. For 2006, the company reports an unrealized gain of $114 million on foreign exchange, whereas the gain would have again been reported as part of other comprehensive income under U.S. GAAP. The adjustment because of the accounting for associated companies is discussed in section 6.

EXAMPLE 15-1   Accounting for Minority Passive Investments

On 1 January 2007, fictitious company Baxter Inc. invested $300,000 in fictitious company Cartel Co. debt securities (with a 6 percent coupon rate on par value, payable each 31 December). The par value of the securities was $275,000. On 31 December 2007, the fair value of Baxter's investment in Cartel is $350,000.

Assume that the market interest rate in effect when the bonds were issued was 4.5 percent.[1] If the investment is designated as held-to-maturity, the investment is reported at amortized cost using the effective interest method. A portion of the amortization table is as follows:

End of Year	Interest Payment	Interest Income	Amortization	Carrying Value
0				$300,000
1	$16,500	$13,500	$3,000	$297,000
2	$16,500	$13,365	$3,135	$293,865
3	$16,500	$13,224	$3,276	$290,589

How would this investment be reported on the balance sheet, income statement, and statement of shareholder's equity at 31 December 2007, under both U.S. GAAP and IFRS, if Baxter designated the investment as (1) held-to-maturity, (2) held-for-trading security, (3) available-for-sale, or (4) designated as fair value?

Solution:

	Income Statement	Balance Sheet	Statement of Shareholder's Equity
Held-to-maturity	Interest income[a] $13,500 ($16,500 − $3,000)	Reported at amortized cost of $297,000	No effect

---

[1]The effective interest rate method applies the market rate in effect when the bonds were issued to the current amortized cost (book value) of the bonds to obtain interest expense for the period.

Held-for-trading security	Interest income $16,500 and $50,000 unrealized gain is recognized	Reported at fair value $350,000	No effect
Available-for-sale U.S. GAAP	Interest income of $16,500	Reported at fair value $350,000	$50,000 unrealized gain is reported as other comprehensive income
Available-for-sale IFRS	Interest income of $16,500	Reported at fair value $350,000	$50,000 unrealized gain is reported in net income reported directly as equity on the statement of recognized income and expenses
Designated fair value	Interest income $16,500 and $50,000 unrealized gain is recognized	Reported at fair value $350,000	No effect

[a]6% × par value of $275,000 = $16,500; 4.5% × carrying value of $300,000 = $13,500.

If the investment is held-to-maturity, the reported amount at amortized cost at the end of year 2 on the balance sheet would be $293,865. Held-for-trading securities and available-for-sale would be measured at the fair value at the end of year 2.

If the debt securities were sold on 1 January 2008 for $352,000, gain recognition would be as follows:

- Held-to-maturity: gain on income statement of $55,000 [$352,000 − ($300,000 − $3,000)]
- Held-for-trading security: gain on income statement of $2,000 ($352,000 − $350,000)
- Available-for-sale: gain on income statement of $52,000 ($352,000 − $300,000); $50,000 removed from other comprehensive income (U.S. GAAP) or income reported directly in equity (IFRS).

If the investment had been in Cartel Co. equity securities rather than debt securities, the analysis would change in the following ways:

1. There would not be a held-to-maturity option.
2. Dividend income (if any) would replace interest income.

The differences in classifying passive investments and the differences in reporting standards between IFRS and U.S. GAAP can make it particularly difficult for analysts to evaluate investment returns. Analysts typically evaluate performance separately for operating and investing activities. Operating performance analysis should exclude items related to investing activities such as interest income, dividends, and realized and unrealized gains and losses.

For comparative purposes, analysts should exclude nonoperating assets in the determination of return on net operating assets. IFRS (IAS 7) and U.S. GAAP (SFAS No. 115) require disclosure of fair value of each class of minority passive investment. Using market values and pro forma financial statements for consistency improves assessments of performance ratios across companies.

4. MINORITY ACTIVE INVESTMENTS

When an entity holds 20 to 50 percent of the voting rights of an investee it is presumed (unless circumstances demonstrate otherwise) that the entity has significant influence, but not control, over the investee's business activities. IAS No. 28 applies to most investments in which an investor has significant influence but not control or shared control. In the United States, SFAS No. 142 and APB No. 18 provide guidance on accounting for equity method investments. Both U.S. GAAP (APB 18) and IFRS (IAS 28) note that significant influence may be evidenced by:

- Representation on the board of directors.
- Participation in the policy-making process.
- Material transactions between the parties.
- Interchange of managerial personnel.
- Technological dependency.

Because the entity can exert significant influence over financial and operating policy decisions including the amount and timing of dividends, the **equity method** provides a more objective basis for reporting investment income. Under the equity method, the investing entity recognizes a share of income as earned rather than as dividends when received. IFRS often refers to these transactions as Investment in Associates whereas they are typically referred to as Equity Method Investments under U.S. GAAP. On the balance sheet, the investing entity's investment account balance increases (decreases) as the investee (associate) earns and reports income (losses). The investor's account balance also decreases whenever a dividend is received.

4.1. Equity Method of Accounting: Basic Principles

The basic accounting principle under the equity method of accounting is that an equity investment is initially recorded at cost. In subsequent periods, the equity investment is adjusted to reflect the investor's share of income or loss. Dividends or other distributions constitute a return of capital, and thus reduce the carrying amount of the investment. The investment account is reflected as a single line item on the balance sheet, and the investor's share of the investee's reported net income, adjusted for certain cost amortizations, as a single line on the income statement (contrast this disclosure with the disclosure on consolidated statements in section 6). Equity method investments (investments in associates) are classified as noncurrent assets, and the investor's share of the profit or loss of equity method investments, and the carrying amount of those investments, must be separately disclosed on the income statement and balance sheet.

EXAMPLE 15-2   Equity Method: Balance in Investment Account

Branch, a fictitious company, purchases a 20 percent interest in Williams (a fictitious company) for $200,000 on 1 January 2007. Williams reports income and dividends as follows:

	Income	Dividends
2007	$200,000	$50,000
2008	300,000	100,000
2009	400,000	200,000
	$900,000	$350,000

Calculate the balance in the investment in Williams's account that appears on Branch's balance sheet.

Solution:

Investment in Williams on 31 December 2009:

Initial cost	$200,000
Equity income 2007	$40,000 (20% of $200,000 Income)
Dividends received 2007	($10,000) (20% of $50,000 Dividends)
Equity income 2008	$60,000 (20% of $300,000 Income)
Dividend received 2008	($20,000) (20% of $100,000 Dividends)
Equity income 2009	$80,000 (20% of $400,000 Income)
Dividends received 2009	($40,000) (20% of $200,000 Dividends)
Balance	$310,000 [$200,000 + 20% × ($900,000 − $350,000)]

This simplified example implicitly assumes that the 1 January 2007 purchase price equals the purchased equity in the book value of Williams's net assets, recorded and unrecorded. Later, sections 4.2 and 4.3 will cover the more common cases in which price does not equal book value.

Notice that, in contrast to passive investments, the fair value is not used for valuing investments under the equity method. But for fiscal years beginning after 15 November 2007, SFAS No. 159 creates a fair value option for investments currently accounted for under the equity method. Changes in the fair value under this irrevocable election are included in earnings.

Using the equity method, the investor includes its share of the investee's profit and losses on the income statement. The equity investment is carried at cost, plus its share of post-acquisition income less dividends received. The recorded investment value can decline as a result of investee losses or a permanent decline in the investee's market value (see section 4.4 for treatment of impairments). If the investment value is reduced to zero the investor usually discontinues the equity method and does not record further losses. If the investee subsequently recovers, the equity method is resumed after equity income equals the share of losses not recognized during the suspension of the equity method.

COCA-COLA'S 2006 ANNUAL REPORT

In its 2006 annual report, the Coca-Cola Company disclosed its equity method investments in several affiliates:

> Coca-Cola Enterprises Inc. (CCE) is a marketer, producer, and distributor of bottle and can nonalcoholic beverages, operating in eight countries. As of December 31, 2006, our Company owned approximately 35 percent of the outstanding common stock of CCE. We account for our investment by the equity method of accounting and, therefore, our net income includes our proportionate share of income resulting from our investment in CCE.
>
> Our other equity method investments include our ownership interests in Coca-Cola HBC, Coca-Cola FEMSA, and Coca-Cola Amatil. As of December 31, 2006, we owned approximately 23 percent, 32 percent, and 32 percent, respectively, of these companies' common shares.

Although Coca-Cola has subsidiaries, the investments in this note are not controlling interests and, therefore, these equity investments of the company are not reported on a consolidated basis. Rather, the financial results of these equity method investments are reported as a one-line, nonoperating item entitled Equity income—net on the Coca-Cola Company and Subsidiaries Consolidated Statement of Income. The amounts ($102 million in 2006) reflect the proportionate share of income accruing to the investor (Coca-Cola), after any necessary adjustments (as discussed in sections 4.2 and 4.3).

THE COCA-COLA COMPANY AND SUBSIDIARIES: CONSOLIDATED STATEMENTS OF INCOME ($ millions except per-share data)

Year Ended December 31	2006	2005	2004
NET OPERATING REVENUES	$24,088	$23,104	$21,742
Cost of goods sold	8,164	8,195	7,674
GROSS PROFIT	15,924	14,909	14,068
Selling, general, and administrative expenses	9,431	8,739	7,890
Other operating charges	185	85	480
OPERATING INCOME	6,308	6,085	5,698
Interest income	193	235	157
Interest expense	220	240	196
Equity income—net	102	680	621
Other income (loss)—net	195	(93)	(82)
Gains on issuances of stock by equity method investees[2]	—	23	24

---

[2]If an investee issues additional stock and the Coca-Cola Company does not purchase some of this stock, its percentage holding in the investee declines—its ownership interest drops. U.S. GAAP allows firms to view this as an equivalent to the sale of some of its ownership. Therefore, even though Coca-Cola may own the same number of shares, the company in this case booked a gain on its change in ownership in the investee as if Coca-Cola had sold some percentage of its ownership.

INCOME BEFORE INCOME TAXES	6,578	6,690	6,222
Income taxes	1,498	1,818	1,375
NET INCOME	$5,080	$4,872	$4,847
BASIC NET INCOME PER SHARE	$2.16	$2.04	$2.00
DILUTED NET INCOME PER SHARE	$2.16	$2.04	$2.00
AVERAGE SHARES OUTSTANDING	2,348	2,392	2,426
Effect of dilutive securities	2	1	3
AVERAGE SHARES OUTSTANDING ASSUMING DILUTION	2,350	2,393	2,429

Refer to Notes to Consolidated Financial Statements.

Source: 2006 Coca-Cola Company annual report.

The equity method reflects the close relationship between the investor and investees. The Coca-Cola Company does not control Coca-Cola Enterprises, Coca-Cola HBC, Coca-Cola FEMSA, or Coca-Cola Amati, but its ownership (23 to 35 percent) implies that it has significant influence over the associates' operating and financial policies. Because the investor can potentially influence the timing of dividend distributions, the equity method provides a more objective basis for reporting investment income than the passive investment variations.

4.2.   Investment Costs that Exceed the Book Value of the Investee

The cost to acquire shares of an investee often differs from the book value of those shares. Book values of assets and liabilities generally reflect historical costs rather than fair values. For example, U.S. GAAP requires historical costs (less accumulated depreciation) for property, plant, and equipment (PP&E). IFRS allow either historical measures or revalued amounts.

More importantly, however, successful companies should be able to generate more economic good through the productive use of assets than the resale value of the assets themselves. Therefore, investors may be willing to pay a premium in anticipation of future benefits. These benefits could be a result of general market conditions, the investors' ability to exert significant influence on the investee, or other synergies.

IFRS and U.S GAAP both treat the difference between the cost of the acquisition and investor's share of the fair value of the net identifiable assets as **goodwill**. Because the investment is reported as a single line item on the balance sheet, the goodwill is included in the carrying amount of the investment.

EXAMPLE 15-3   Equity Method Investment in Excess of Book Value

Assume that the hypothetical Blake Co. acquires 30 percent of the outstanding shares of the hypothetical Brown Co. At the acquisition date, book values and fair values of Brown's recorded assets and liabilities are as follows:

	Book Value	Fair Value
Current assets	$10,000	$10,000
Plant and equipment	$190,000	$220,000
Land	$120,000	$140,000
	$320,000	$370,000
Liabilities	$100,000	$100,000
Net assets	$220,000	$270,000

Blake Co. believes the value of Brown Co. is higher than the fair value of the identifiable net assets. They offer $100,000 for a 30 percent interest in Brown Co. Part of the excess purchase price is attributable to the $50,000 difference between book value and fair value of the identifiable assets and part of the excess is attributable to goodwill. Calculate goodwill.

Solution:

Purchase price	$100,000
30 percent of book value of Brown	66,000
(30% × $220,000)	
Excess purchase price	$34,000
Attributable to net assets	
Plant and equipment	
(30% × $30,000)	$9,000
Land	
(30% × $20,000)	$6,000
Goodwill (residual)	$19,000
	$34,000

As illustrated above, goodwill is the residual excess not allocated to identifiable assets or liabilities.

4.3. Amortization of Excess Purchase Price

The excess purchase price allocated to the assets and liabilities are accounted for consistent with the accounting treatment for the specific asset or liability to which they are assigned. Amounts allocated to assets and liabilities that are expensed or periodically amortized (PP&E and inventory) must be treated in a consistent manner. Because these allocated amounts are not on the books of affiliates, their income statements cannot reflect the necessary periodic adjustments. Therefore, the investor company must directly record the effects by debiting (or crediting) the equity income and crediting (or debiting) the investment account. Amounts allocated to assets or liabilities that are not systematically amortized (e.g., land) will continue to be reported at their values on the date the investment was acquired. Goodwill is considered to have an indefinite life and is not amortized.

Using the example above and assuming a 10-year useful life for PP&E and using straight-line depreciation, the annual amortization is as follows:

Account	Excess Price	Useful Life	Amortization/Year
Plant and equipment	$9,000	10 years	$900
Land	$6,000	Indefinite	$0
Goodwill	$19,000	Indefinite	$0

Annual amortization would reduce the investor's share of investee's reported income (equity income) and the balance in the investment account by $900 for each year over the 10-year period.

EXAMPLE 15-4   Equity Method Investments with Goodwill

On 1 January 2009 Parker Company acquired 30 percent of Prince Inc. common shares for the cash price of €500,000 (both companies are fictitious). It is determined that Parker has the ability to exert significant influence on Prince's financial and operating decisions. The following information concerning Prince's assets and liabilities on 1 January 2009 is provided:

Prince, Inc	Book Value	Fair Value	Difference
Current assets	€100,000	€100,000	0
Plant and equipment	1,900,000	2,200,000	300,000
	€2,000,000	€2,300,000	€300,000
Liabilities	800,000	800,000	0
Net assets	€1,200,000	€1,500,000	€300,000

The plant and equipment are depreciated on a straight-line basis and have 10 years of remaining life. Prince reports net income for 2009 of €100,000 and pays dividends of €50,000. Calculate the following:

1. Goodwill.
2. Balance in the investment in associate (Prince) at the end of 2009.

Solution to 1: Goodwill

Purchase price	€500,000
Acquired equity in book value of Prince's net assets	
(30% × €1,200,000)	360,000
Excess purchase price	€140,000

Attributable to plant and equipment
(30% × €300,000)   90,000
Goodwill (residual)   50,000
                                                           €140,000

Solution to 2. Investment in Associate
Purchase price   €500,000
Parker's share of Prince's net income   30,000
(30% × €100,000)
Dividends received (30% of €50,000)   (15,000)
Amortization on excess purchase price attributable
to plant and equipment (€90,000 ÷ 10 years)   (9,000)
31 December 09 balance in
investment in Prince   €506,000

An alternate way to look at the balance in the investment account reflects the basic valuation principle of the equity method. At any point in time, the investment account balance equals the investor's (Parker) monetary equity in the recorded net assets of the investee (Prince) plus the unamortized balance of the original excess purchase price. Applying this principle to this example:

Parker's Monetary Equity in Prince's Recorded Net Assets
[30% × (€1,200,000 + 100,000 − 50,000)]   €375,000
Unamortized excess purchase price
(€140,000 − 9,000)   131,000
Investment in Prince   €506,000

Note that the unamortized excess purchase price is a cost incurred by Parker, not Prince. Therefore, the total amount (not 30 percent) is included in the investment account balance.

4.4. Impairment

Equity method investments are subject to review for impairment. If the fair value of the investment declines below the carrying value *and* the decline is determined to be permanent, U.S. GAAP (APB Opinion 18) requires an impairment loss be recognized on the income statement and the asset is reduced to fair value on the balance sheet. This impairment cannot be reversed even if the fair value later increases. IFRS (IAS 28) provide similar guidance, but IAS 36 allows reversal of impairment losses in certain circumstances.

Section 6.8 discusses impairment tests for the goodwill attributed to the consolidated subsidiary. Note the distinction between the disaggregated goodwill impairment test for consolidated statements and the total fair value of impairment test for equity method investments.

4.5. Transactions with Associates

Because an investor company can influence the terms and timing of transactions with associates, profits from such transactions cannot be realized until confirmed through use or sale to third parties. Accordingly, the investor company's share of any unrealized profit must be deferred by reducing the amount recorded under the equity method. In the subsequent period(s) when this deferred profit is considered confirmed, it is added back to the equity income. At that time, the equity income is again based on the recorded values in the associates' accounts.

Transactions between the two affiliates may be **upstream** (associate to investor) or **downstream** (investor to associate). In an upstream sale, the profit on the intercompany transaction is recorded on the associate's profit and loss (income) statement. The investor's share of the unrealized profit is thus included in equity income on the investor's profit and loss (income) statement. In a downstream sale, the profit is recorded on the investor's profit and loss (income) statement. Both U.S. GAAP (Interpretation 1 of APB 18) and IFRS (IAS 28) require that the unearned profits be eliminated to the extent of the investor's interest in the associate. The result is an adjustment to equity income on the investor's profit and loss (income) statement.

EXAMPLE 15-5   Equity Method with Sale of Inventory: Upstream Sale

On 1 January 2009, Wicker Company acquired a 25 percent interest in Foxworth Company (both companies are fictitious) for $1 million and used the equity method to account for its investment. The book value of Foxworth's net assets on that date was $3,800,000. An analysis of fair values revealed that all assets and liabilities were equal to book values except for a building. The building was undervalued by $40,000 and has a 20-year remaining life. The company used straight-line depreciation for the building. Foxworth paid $3,200 in dividends in 2009. During 2009, Foxworth reported net income of $20,000. During the year, Foxworth sold Inventory to Wicker. At the end of the year, goods remained in Wicker's inventory that Foxworth had recognized $8,000 of profit on.

1. Calculate the equity income to be reported as a line item on Wicker's 2009 income statement.
2. Calculate the balance in the investment in Foxworth to be reported on the 31 December 2009 balance sheet.

Purchase price	$1,000,000
Acquired equity in book value	
of Foxworth's net assets (25% × $3,800,000)	950,000
Excess purchase price	$50,000
Attributable to:	
Building (25% × $40,000)	$10,000
Goodwill (residual)	$40,000
	$50,000

Solution to 1: Equity Income

Wicker's share of Foxworth's reported Income (25% × $20,000)	$5,000

Amortization of excess purchase price attributable to building ($10,000/20)	(500)
Unrealized profit (25% × $8,000)	(2,000)
Equity income 2009	$2,500

Solution to 2: Investment in Foxworth

Purchase price	$1,000,000
Equity income 2009	2,500
Dividends received (25% × $3,200)	(800)
Investment in Foxworth, 31 Dec 2009	$1,001,700

Composition of investment account:

Wicker's monetary equity in Foxworth's recorded net assets [25% × ($3,800,000 + (20,000 − 8,000) − 3,200)]	$952,200
Unamortized excess purchase price ($50,000 − 500)	49,500
	$1,001,700

EXAMPLE 15-6   Equity Method with Sale of Inventory: Downstream Sale

Jones Company owns 25 percent of Jason Company (both fictitious companies) and appropriately applies the equity method of accounting. Excess amortization related to undervalued assets at the time of the investment is $8,000 per year. During 2009 Jones sold $96,000 of inventory to Jason for $160,000. Jason resold $120,000 of this inventory during 2009. The remainder was sold in 2010. Jason reports income from its operations of $800,000 in 2009 and $820,000 in 2010.

1. Calculate the equity income to be reported as a line item on Jones's 2009 income statement.
2. Calculate the equity income to be reported as a line item on Jones's 2010 income statement.

Solution to 1: Equity Income 2009

Jones's share of Jason's reported Income (25% × $800,000)	$200,000
Amortization of excess purchase price	(8,000)
Unrealized profit (25% × $16,000)	(4,000)
Equity income 2009	$188,000

Profit margin: 40 percent ($64,000/$160,000)
Inventory on 31 Dec 2009: $40,000 (profit of 40 percent or $16,000)

Solution to 2: Equity Income 2010

Jones's share of Jason's reported Income (25% × $820,000)	$205,000
Amortization of excess purchase price	(8,000)
Realized profit (25% × $16,000)	4,000
Equity income 2010	$201,000

4.6. Disclosure

The notes to the financial statements are an integral part of the information necessary for investors. Both IFRS and U.S. GAAP require disclosure about the assets, liabilities, and results of equity method investments. For example, Volvo Group reports that:

> . . . *holdings in associated companies are reported in accordance with the equity method. The Group's share of reported income in such companies is included in the consolidated income statement in Income from investments in associated companies, reduced in appropriate cases by depreciation of surplus values and the effect of applying different accounting principles. Income from associated companies is included in operating income due to that the investments are of operating nature.*

For practical reasons, associated companies' results are sometimes included in the investor's accounts with a certain time lag, normally not more than one quarter. Dividends from associated companies are not included in investor income because it would be a double counting. Applying the equity method recognizes the investor's full share of the associate's income. Dividends received involves exchanging a portion of equity interest for cash. In the consolidated balance sheet, the book value of shareholdings in associated companies is increased by the investor's share of the company's net income, and reduced by depreciation of surplus values and the amount of dividends received.

4.7. Issues for Analysts

Equity method accounting presents several challenges for analysis. First, analysts should question whether the equity method is appropriate. For example, an investor holding 19 percent of an associate may, in fact, exert significant influence but may attempt to avoid using the equity method to avoid reporting associate losses. On the other hand, an investor holding 25 percent of an associate may be unable to exert significant influence and may be unable to access cash flows, and yet prefers the equity method to capture associate income.

Second, because the investment account represents the investor's percentage ownership in the net assets of the investee company, the investment account is often referred to as one-line consolidation. There can be significant assets and liabilities of the investee that are not reflected on the investor's balance sheet, which will significantly affect debt ratios. Net margin ratios could be overstated because income for the associate is included in investor net income but is not specifically included in sales. An investor may actually control the investee with less than 50 percent ownership but prefer the financial results using the equity method. Careful analysis can reveal financial performance driven by accounting structure.

Finally, the analyst must consider the quality of the equity method earnings. The equity method assumes that a dollar earned by the investee company is a dollar earned by the investor (i.e., a fraction of the dollar equal to the fraction of the company owned), even if cash is not received. Analysts should, therefore, consider potential restrictions on dividend cash flows (cash flow statement).

5. JOINT VENTURES

A **joint venture** is an entity (partnership, corporations, and other legal forms) that is owned and operated by a small group of investors (often two) called **venturers**. Some are primarily contractual relationships whereas others share common ownership of assets. Each venturer usually plays an active role in the management of the joint venture, but no one venturer can be said to be in control. Control is joint because operating and financing decisions require the approval of all venturers. Joint ventures can be a convenient way to enter foreign markets, specialized activities, or risky undertakings. For example, in 2007, General Electric Company and Fanuc Ltd of Japan celebrated the 20th anniversary of their joint venture to produce automation hardware and software.

IFRS and U.S. GAAP currently apply different standards to joint ventures, although this subject is now under review as part of the convergence program. IAS No. 31 recommends **proportionate consolidation** but permits equity method accounting as a non-recommended alternative, whereas SFAS No. 94 requires equity method accounting for joint ventures.[3] In the United States, proportionate consolidation is generally not permitted except for unincorporated entities operating in certain industries.

IFRS distinguish between three types of joint ventures:

- *Jointly controlled entities.* The arrangement is carried on through a separate entity, incorporated or unincorporated.
- *Jointly controlled operations.* Each venturer uses its own assets for a specific project.
- *Jointly controlled assets.* A project carried on with assets that are jointly owned.

Proportionate consolidation requires the venturer's share of the assets, liabilities, income, and expenses of the joint venture to be *combined on a line-by-line* basis with similar items on the venturer's financial statements. In contrast, as explained in section 4, the equity method results in a single line item (equity in income of the joint venture) on the income statement and a single line item (investment in joint venture) on the balance sheet.

Because the single line item equity in joint venture reflects the net effect of the sales and expenses, the total income recognized is identical under the two methods. And because the single line item investment in joint venture reflects the venturer's share of assets and liabilities, the total net assets are identical. There can be significant differences, however, in ratio analysis between the two methods because of the differential effects on values for total assets, liabilities, sales, expenses, etc.

---

[3]In September 2007, the IASB issued an Exposure Draft proposing the removal of proportionate consolidation in favor of the equity method.

EXAMPLE 15-7   Joint Venture

Assume that hypothetical Companies A and B enter into a joint venture, each with a 50 percent interest. The first column presents the assumed financial statement for the joint venture in its first year. Columns 2 and 3 reflect the financial result for Company A under the two methods of accounting for its interest in the joint venture.

	Joint Venture	Company A Venturer	
		Equity Method[a]	Proportionate Consolidation
Income Statement			
Sales	$400,000	$1,000,000	$1,200,000
Equity in joint venture income		60,000	
Cost of sales	200,000	500,000	600,000
Other expenses	80,000	240,000	280,000
Net income	$120,000	$320,000	$320,000
Balance Sheet			
Cash	$40,000	$400,000	$420,000
Inventory		$500,000	$500,000
Investment in joint venture		$450,000	
Other assets	1,160,000	1,500,000	2,080,000
	$1,200,000	$2,850,000	$3,000,000
Accounts payable		$200,000	$200,000
Long-term debt	300,000	1,650,000	1,800,000
Capital stock		600,000	600,000
Retained earnings		400,000	400,000
Venturers' (Companies A and B) equity	900,000		
	$1,200,000	$2,850,000	$3,000,000

[a]The data (other than the subtotals) shown under the equity method are the same as if there had been no joint venture except for "Equity in joint venture income," "Investment in joint venture," and "Retained earnings."

First, examine the income statement. Notice that net income is $320,000 using either the equity method or proportionate consolidation. But sales, cost of sales, and expenses are different because under the equity method the net effect of sales, cost of sales, and expenses is reflected in the $60,000 equity in joint venture income.

On the balance sheet, the line item investment in joint venture observed under the equity method is replaced by the proportionate share of each balance sheet account in the proportionate consolidation method. The single line item is replaced with a line-by-line consolidation. Because the venturer has a 50 percent interest in the joint venture, 50 percent of joint venture assets and liabilities are included in the proportionate balance sheet.

The analyst will observe differences in performance ratios based on the accounting method used for joint ventures.

	Equity Method	Proportionate Consolidation
Net profit margin	32.0%	26.7%
Return on assets	11.2%	10.7%
Debt/Equity	1.65	1.80

The proportional consolidation method is currently the preferred method for joint ventures under IFRS but has limited approval (it is used in the construction industry) under U.S GAAP. The IFRS Exposure Draft now under consideration proposes a change from proportional consolidation to the equity method.

6. CONTROLLING INTEREST INVESTMENTS

Controlling interest investments involve the combination of two or more organizations into a larger economic entity. Business combinations are typically motivated by expectations of added value through synergies, including elimination of duplicate costs, tax advantages, coordination of the production process, and efficiency gains from asset management.

Business combinations can take several forms: the statutory merger, acquisition, statutory consolidation, or variable interest (special purpose) entity. Each of these types of business combinations has distinctive characteristics that are described in Exhibit 15-3.

In the past, statutory mergers, acquisitions, or statutory consolidations as legal forms of combination could be accounted for either as a purchase transaction or as a uniting (or pooling) of interests. In June 2001, FASB issued SFAS No. 141 that prohibits the use of the pooling of interests method for business combinations and the IASB followed this with a similar standard prohibiting the uniting of interests (IFRS 3) in 2004. Both the IASB (IFRS 3) and FASB (SFAS 141) currently require that all business combinations be accounted for using the purchase method. Though the broad principles are the same, the current application of the purchase method differs between the two standard setters. As part of the joint project with the IASB, U.S. GAAP has adopted SFAS No. 141R for fiscal years beginning after 15 December 2008. This standard calls for the acquisition method (described in section 6.11) to account for all business combinations. This standard substantially reduces any differences between IFRS and U.S. GAAP for business combinations.

6.1. Pooling of Interests

Prior to June 2001, under U.S. GAAP, combining companies that met twelve strict criteria used the **pooling of interests accounting method** for the business combination. Companies not meeting these criteria used the purchase method. In a pooling of interests, the combined companies were portrayed as if they had always operated as a single economic entity.

EXHIBIT 15-3   Types of Business Combinations

Statutory Merger

The distinctive feature of a merger is that only one of the affiliates remains in existence. One hundred percent of the target is absorbed into the acquiring company. Company A may issue common stock, preferred stock, bonds, or pay cash to acquire the net assets. The net assets of Company B are transferred to Company A. Company B ceases to exist and Company A is the only entity that remains.

$$\text{Company A} + \text{Company B} = \text{Company A}$$

Acquisition

The distinctive feature of an acquisition is the legal continuity of the affiliated companies. Both companies continue operations, but are now affiliated through a parent–subsidiary relationship. Both companies are individual entities and keep financial records, but the parent provides consolidated financial statements in each reporting period. Unlike a statutory merger or consolidation, the acquiring company does not need to acquire 100 percent of the target. In fact, in some cases, it may acquire less than 50 percent and still exert control (see section 6.5.2). If the acquiring company acquires less than 100 percent, minority (noncontrolling) shareholders' interests are reported on the consolidated financial statements.

$$\text{Company A} + \text{Company B} = (\text{Company A} + \text{Company B})$$

Statutory Consolidation

The distinctive feature of a consolidation is that a new legal entity is formed and none of the predecessor affiliates remain in existence. A new company is created to take over the net assets of Company A and Company B. Company A and Company B cease to exist and Company C is the only entity that remains.

$$\text{Company A} + \text{Company B} = \text{Company C}$$

Variable Interests

The distinctive feature of a variable interest (also referred to as special purpose) entity is that control is not usually based on voting control, as equity investors do not have a sufficient amount at risk for the entity to finance its activities without additional subordinated financial support. Furthermore, the equity investors may lack a controlling financial interest. The sponsoring company usually creates a special purpose entity (SPE) for a narrowly defined purpose. FASB Interpretation (FIN No. 46R) requires consolidation when the sponsor is the primary beneficiary in a variable interest that bears the risks and rewards or absorbs the majority of expected returns or losses.[4] IFRS require consolidation if the substance of the relationship indicates control by the sponsor. Variable interests will be discussed more thoroughly in section 7.

Consequently, assets and liabilities were recorded at book values and the pre-combination retained earnings were included in the balance sheet of the combined companies. This treatment was consistent with the view that there was a continuity of ownership and no new basis of accounting existed. Similar rules applied under IFRS, which used the term **uniting of interests** in reference to the same concept. IFRS permitted use of the uniting of interests method until March 2004. Currently, neither IFRS nor U.S. GAAP allows use of the pooling/uniting of interests method.

In contrast, a combination accounted for as a purchase is viewed as a purchase of net assets and those net assets are recorded at fair values. This usually results in additional amortization for depreciable assets. As a result, for the same level of revenue, the purchase method resulted in lower reported income than the pooling of interests method. For this reason, managers had a tendency to favor the pooling of interests method.

---

[4]Qualified special purpose entities (QSPEs) do not require consolidation.

Although the pooling of interests method is no longer allowed, companies may continue to use pooling of interests accounting for business combinations prior to June 2001. We illustrate the method here because pooling of interests accounting was commonly used and will have an impact on financial statements for the foreseeable future. Because of the ongoing effect, an understanding of pooling of interests will facilitate the analyst's assessment of the performance and financial position of the company.

6.2. Purchase Method

IFRS and U.S. GAAP currently require the purchase method of accounting for statutory mergers, acquisitions, and statutory consolidations, although both have a few specific exemptions.

The cost of the acquisition is the sum of the cash or cash equivalents paid plus the fair value of other purchase consideration given, plus some direct costs of the business combination such as professional and legal fees, valuation experts, and consultants.

IFRS 3 requires that assets, liabilities, and contingent liabilities be recorded at fair value. Even if the business combination is an acquisition of less than 100 percent, IFRS require the full fair value to be reported such that the fair value of the minority (noncontrolling) interest (excluding goodwill arising from the purchase transaction) is included on the consolidated balance sheet. U.S. GAAP is similar except that minority interest is recorded at the pre-acquisition carrying value (book value) rather than fair value when the parent adopts parent company theory for applying the purchase method. Parent company theory looks at valuation from the perspective of the parent company shareholders. Therefore, cost is allocated to the minority shareholders based on book value.

Example 15-8 illustrates the pooling of interests and purchase method of consolidation.

EXAMPLE 15-8   Pooling of Interests and Purchase Method Post-Combination Balance Sheet

Franklin Company, headquartered in the United States, acquired 100 percent of the outstanding shares of Jefferson, Inc. by issuing 1 million shares of its $1 par common stock ($15 market value). Immediately before the transaction, the two companies compiled the following information:

	Franklin Book Value	Jefferson Book Value	Jefferson Fair Value
	(000)	**(000)**	**(000)**
Cash and receivables	$10,000	$300	$300
Inventory	12,000	1,700	3,000
PP&E (net)	27,000	2,500	4,500
	$49,000	$4,500	$7,800

Current payables	8,000	600	600
Long-term debt	16,000	2,000	1,800
	24,000	2,600	2,400
Net assets	$25,000	$1,900	$5,400
Shareholders' equity:			
Capital stock ($1 par)	$5,000	$400	
Additional paid-in capital	6,000	700	
Retained earnings	$14,000	$800	

Show the balances in the post-combination balance sheet using

1. The pooling of interests method.
2. The purchase method.

Solution to 1: Pooling-of-Interest Method
If the Franklin and Jefferson combination were accounted for as a statutory merger using the pooling of interests method, the post-combination balance sheet of the combined entity would appear as follows:

Franklin Post-Combination Balance Sheet	
(Pooling of Interests)	**(000)**
Cash and receivables	$10,300
Inventory	13,700
PP&E (net)	29,500
	$53,500
Current payables	$8,600
Long-term debt	18,000
	$26,600
Capital stock ($1 par)	$6,000
Additional paid-in capital	6,100
Retained earnings	14,800
Total stockholders' equity	$26,900
Total liabilities and stockholders' equity	$53,500

Under the pooling of interests method, assets and liabilities are combined using book values. For example, Franklin's $10,000 cash and receivables are added to Jefferson's $300 cash and receivables for a combined balance of $10,300. One of the criteria to qualify for pooling of interests is that the transaction must be a stock for stock exchange.

Prior to the transaction, Franklin had 5 million shares of $1 par stock outstanding ($5 million). The combined entity reflects the Franklin capital stock issuance of $6 million ($5 million plus the additional 1 million shares of $1 par stock issued to effect the transaction). Jefferson's paid in capital is eliminated on consolidation, being replaced by the stock issued by Franklin, and Jefferson's retained earnings are carried forward to the post-combination balance sheet. Jefferson's $1,100,000 of paid in capital is shown on the post-combination balance sheet as capital stock of $1 million (par value of Franklin stock issued) and $100,000 of additional paid in capital (residual amount of the total of capital stock (400,000) and of additional paid in capital (700,000) i.e., $1,100,000). Franklin's additional paid in capital of $6 million is combined with the $100,000 for a total of $6,100,000.

Retained earnings of the target company are generally carried to combined financial statements. Franklin's retained earnings of $14 million are combined with Jefferson's retained earnings of $800,000 for reported retained earnings of $14,800,000.

Solution to 2: Purchase Method

If the Franklin and Jefferson combination were accounted for as a statutory merger using the purchase method, the purchase price allocation would be as follows:

Cost (stock issued is 1,000,000 shares at market value of $15)	$15,000,000
Book value of Jefferson's net assets	1,900,000
Excess purchase price	$13,100,000
Cost	$15,000,000
Fair value of net assets	5,400,000
Goodwill	$9,600,000
Allocation of excess purchase price (based on the differences between fair values and book values):	
Inventory	$ 1,300,000
PP&E (net)	2,000,000
Long-term debt	200,000
Goodwill	9,600,000
	$13,100,000

Both IFRS and U.S. GAAP record the purchase price of the acquisition at the market value of stock issued, or $15 million. In this case, the purchase price exceeds the book value of Jefferson by $13,100,000. Inventory, PP&E (net), and long-term debt are adjusted to fair values. The excess of purchase price over fair values of the net assets results in goodwill recognition of $9,600,000.

The post-combination balance sheet of the combined entity would appear as follows:

Franklin Consolidated Balance Sheet (Purchase Method) ($ thousands)

Cash and receivables	$10,300
Inventory	15,000
PP&E (net)	31,500
Goodwill	9,600
Total assets	$66,400
Current payables	$8,600
Long-term debt	17,800
Total liabilities	$26,400
Capital stock ($1 par)	$6,000
Additional paid-in capital	20,000
Retained earnings	14,000
Total stockholders' equity	$40,000
Total liabilities and stockholders' equity	$66,400

Assets and liabilities are combined using book values of Franklin plus fair values for the assets and liabilities acquired from Jefferson. For example, the book value of Franklin's inventory ($12 million) is added to the fair value of inventory acquired from Jefferson ($3 million) for a combined inventory of $15 million. Long-term debt has a book value of $16 million on Franklin's pre-acquisition statements and Jefferson's fair value of debt is $1,800,000. The combined long-term debt is recorded as $17,800,000.

Franklin's post-merger financial statement reflects in stockholders' equity the stock issued by the Franklin, the acquiring company. Franklin issues stock with a par value of $1 million in exchange for Jefferson's paid in capital (capital stock plus additional paid in capital) of $1,100,000.

Shares issued are measured at fair value under both U.S. GAAP and IFRS. Therefore, the purchase price is 1 million shares at market value of $15, or $15 million. Prior to the transaction, Franklin had 5,000,000 shares of $1 par stock outstanding ($5 million). The combined entity reflects the Franklin capital stock outstanding of $6 million ($5 million plus the additional 1 million shares of $1 par stock issued to effect the transaction). Franklin's additional paid in capital of $6 million is increased by the $14 million additional paid in capital from the issuance of the 1 million shares ($15 million less par value of $1 million) for a total of $20 million. At the merger date, only the acquirer's retained earnings are carried to the combined entity. Earnings of the target are included on the consolidated income statement and retained earnings only in post-acquisition periods.

6.3. Impact of Pooling of Interests versus Purchase Method on Financial Statements: Date of Acquisition

Comparison of Pooling of Interests and Purchase Method

	Pooling of Interests ($ thousands)	Purchase ($ thousands)
Cash and receivables	$10,300	$10,300
Inventory	13,700	15,000
PP&E (net)	29,500	31,500
Goodwill		9,600
Total assets	$53,500	$66,400
Current payables	$8,600	$8,600
Long-term debt	18,000	17,800
Total liabilities	$26,600	$26,400
Capital stock ($1 par)	$6,000	$6,000
Additional paid-in capital	6,100	20,000
Retained earnings	14,800	14,000
Total stockholders' equity	$26,900	$40,000
Total liabilities and stockholders' equity	$53,500	$66,400

These differences can be significant for the analyst. The assets and liabilities of Franklin and Jefferson are combined at book value under pooling of interests. The purchase method combines the book value of Franklin's assets and liabilities with the fair value of assets and liabilities of Jefferson, the acquired company. In this example, under the purchase method inventory and PP&E are reported at higher values and long-term debt is at a lower value. Because the companies are combined at book value, no goodwill is recognized under the pooling of interests method. Goodwill is recognized as the excess of purchase price over the fair value of net assets acquired under the purchase method. Common stock at par is Franklin's common stock issued at par in both cases. But, under the purchase method, the cost of acquisition is based on the market value of the stock issued. The excess over par value is included in additional paid-in capital. The result is significantly higher paid-in capital (common stock plus additional paid-in capital) under the purchase method. Under the pooling of interest method the retained earnings of Jefferson are carried forward to the merged entity. Under the purchase method only post-acquisition earnings are combined in the new entity.

6.4. Impact of Pooling of Interests versus Purchase Method on Financial Statements: Post-Acquisition

In the periods subsequent to the business combination, the financial reports continue to be affected by the choice of accounting method. Net income reflects the performance of the new entity. Under the pooling of interests method, depreciation is computed based on the historical book values for both Franklin and Jefferson. Under the purchase method, however, amortization/depreciation is based on historical cost for Franklin and fair value for Jefferson. For example, using Example 15-8, in the year the inventory is sold, the cost of goods sold is $13,700,000 under pooling of interests but $15 million under purchase method. Depreciation on PP&E under the purchase method would be $2 million higher over the life of the asset ($31.5 million versus $29.5 million).

The result is that the analyst must be aware of companies that used pooling of interests prior to the method being disallowed in 2004 for companies reporting under IFRS and 2001 for companies reporting under U.S. GAAP. In future periods, including periods after pooling was disallowed, the assets may be understated and income overstated relative to the purchase method companies as a result of pooling of interests accounting. These differences will affect the comparability of return on investment ratios. Example 15-9 illustrates the potential impact on performance evaluation.

EXAMPLE 15-9   Post-Acquisition Results Using Pooling-of-Interests and Purchase Method

For this example, make the following assumptions related to the Franklin and Jefferson merger introduced in Example 15-8: the merger was effective on 1 January 2001; the 1 January inventory was sold during 2001; the PP&E had a four-year remaining life and no purchase or sale was made during the year; and long-term debt had two years remaining.[5] The following assumed income data for 2007, and balance sheet values at 31 December 2001, reflect the differences that would exist under the pooling-of-interest and purchase methods:

	Pooling-of-Interest Method ($ thousands)	Purchase Method ($ thousands)
Income Statement		
Sales	$34,000	$34,000
Cost of goods sold	(19,000)	(20,300)
Interest expense	(900)	(1,000)
Depreciation expense	(7,375)	(7,875)
Net income	$6,725	$4,825
Balance Sheet		
Cash and receivables	$38,400	$38,400
Inventory	12,700	12,700
PP&E (net)	22,125	23,625
Goodwill		9,600
Total assets	$73,225	$84,325

---

[5]This example assumes straight-line amortization, which is consistent with U.S. GAAP, but other patterns would be possible under IFRS.

Current payables:		
Long-term debt	21,600	21,600
Total liabilities	18,000	17,900
Shareholders' equity	$39,600	$39,500
Capital stock ($1 par)	6,000	6,000
Additional paid in capital	6,100	20,000
Retained earnings	21,525	18,825
Total stockholders' equity	$33,625	$44,825
Total liabilities and shareholders' equity	$73,225	$84,325
Impact on Ratios		
Return on assets	9.18%	5.72%
Return on equity	20.00%	10.76%

Income is $1,900,000 greater under the pooling of interests method than the purchase method ($6,725,000 versus 4,825,000). This difference is because of differences in the cost of goods sold, interest expense, and depreciation. The cost of goods sold differs by $1,300,000 because the 1 January 2001 inventory was sold in 2001 and the inventory values on 1 January 2001 differed between the two methods. Interest expense is $100,000 higher using the purchase method, which reflects the amortization of the undervalued debt ($200,000) with a life of two years. Finally, depreciation expense is greater under the purchase method by $500,000 ($2 million/4), which is the excess over book value with a life of four years. As a rule, managers preferred pooling of interests because income was greater, which had a significant impact on return on assets and return on equity, as illustrated above.

6.5. Consolidated Financial Statements

Consolidated financial statements combine the results of operations for distinct legal entities, the parent and its subsidiaries, as if they were one economic unit. IFRS and U.S. GAAP both require **consolidation**, but each is based on a different control model. The definition of control differs in certain respects between the two models. For example, the IFRS consolidation model is based on voting control or when the parent has legal or contractual control rights. U.S. GAAP adopts a consolidation model that includes both a variable interest model and a voting interest model. FIN 46(R) defines when a sponsor of a variable interest entity should base consolidation on factors other than voting rights and instead use a "risks and rewards" model.

6.5.1. The Consolidation Process

Consolidation combines the assets, liabilities, revenues, and expenses of subsidiaries with the parent company. Transactions between the parent and subsidiary (intercompany transactions) are eliminated to avoid double counting or premature income recognition.

Although the consolidated statements are presumed to be more meaningful for fair presentation, the analyst will need to consider that differences in IFRS and U.S. GAAP accounting standards, valuation bases, and other factors can impair the validity of comparative analyses.

6.5.2.   Business Combination with Less than 100 Percent Acquisition

When an acquiring company decides to make an investment in another company, 100 percent ownership is not required in order to achieve control. Although many companies acquire 100 percent ownership, control is generally achieved when the acquiring company possesses more than 50 percent of the target company's stock. The acquiring company may be constrained by resources or they may be unable to acquire all the outstanding shares. Both the acquirer and target companies remain separate legal entities. The acquiring company is the parent and the target company is the subsidiary. Both the parent and the subsidiary prepare their own financial records, but consolidated financial statements are prepared at each reporting period. It is the consolidated financial statements that are the primary source of information for investors.

6.5.3.   Minority (Noncontrolling) Interests: Balance Sheet

If the parent acquires a controlling interest but less than 100 percent of the subsidiary, the remaining shares are not controlled by the parent and are referred to as **minority** or **noncontrolling** interests.

IFRS and U.S. GAAP both require using the purchase method to account for business combinations. But the purchase method differs between the two standards. Two of the more significant differences apply to situations in which minority shareholders exist. First, U.S. GAAP currently deems that only the acquired portion of the subsidiary has been purchased and therefore, only that portion should be carried at fair value. Minority or noncontrolling interests are at book value. IFRS consider the company as one, indivisible entity, and thus require that all assets and liabilities be recorded at fair value, including the minority (noncontrolling) interest (except that no goodwill is attributed to minority interest as a result of the acquisition).

Note that this is the current position under IFRS 3 and SFAS No. 141, but FASB issued SFAS No. 141R in November 2007. After 15 December 2008, minority or noncontrolling interest will be carried at fair value including full goodwill. IASB is expected to issue a new standard that also allows, but does not require, the full goodwill method. The joint project is discussed further in section 6.11.

Second, U.S. GAAP and IFRS differ on the placement of the minority (noncontrolling) interest on the balance sheet. IFRS present the minority interest on the balance sheet as a separate line item in the equity section that is presented separately from the parent's shareholders' equity. U.S. GAAP presents minority interests as either long-term liabilities or as a separate line item between total liabilities and shareholder's equity (SFAS No. 160 also moves this placement to equity after November 2007).

Example 15-10 illustrates the current differences in reporting requirements.

EXAMPLE 15-10   Acquisition with Noncontrolling Interest

On 1 January 2008, the hypothetical Parent Co. acquired 80 percent of the outstanding shares of the hypothetical Subsidiary Co. in exchange for shares of Parent Co.'s no par common stock with a fair value of $128,000. The subsidiary stock had a fair market value on the date of the exchange of $160,000. Immediately prior to the exchange of shares (before the parent recorded the acquisition), the two companies had the following information compiled.

Parent	Book Value	Subsidiary Book Value	Fair Value
Cash and receivables	$40,000	$15,000	$15,000
Inventory	125,000	80,000	80,000
PP&E (net)	235,000	95,000	155,000
	$400,000	$190,000	$250,000
Payables	55,000	20,000	20,000
Long-term debt	120,000	70,000	70,000
	175,000	90,000	90,000
Net assets	$225,000	$100,000	$160,000
Shareholders' equity:			
Capital stock (no par)	$87,000	$34,000	
Retained earnings	$138,000	$66,000	

Calculate the value of PP&E on the consolidated balance sheet under both U.S. GAAP and IFRS.

Solution. Relative to fair values, the PP&E is understated by $60,000. If the parent had purchased 100 percent of the subsidiary's stock, these assets would be valued at $155,000 (fair value) on the consolidated balance sheet. But when the controlling interest is less than 100 percent, IFRS would still include the fair value of the PP&E of $155,000 on the consolidated balance sheet, whereas U.S. GAAP would include 80 percent of the fair value (the portion that was purchased) and 20 percent of the book value (the minority portion) for a total of $143,000. An equivalent way of viewing this is to observe that the full book value is carried forward plus 80 percent of the excess of fair value over book value [$95,000 + (80% × $60,000) = $143,000]. Because the purchase price is equal to 80 percent of the fair value of the identifiable assets, there is no goodwill in this transaction.

Therefore, PP&E on the consolidated balance sheet would be valued at $390,000 under IFRS and $378,000 under U.S. GAAP.

Minority interest at the acquisition date using IFRS is 20 percent of fair value of acquired identifiable assets, liabilities, and contingent liabilities, or $32,000 (20% × $160,000). Minority interest at the acquisition date using U.S. GAAP is 20 percent of the pre-acquisition carrying value of net assets, or $20,000 (20% × $100,000). Notice that the difference in the minority interest values ($12,000) is equal to the difference in the minority interest's share in the values assigned to PP&E.

For comparative purposes, below is the balance sheet at the acquisition date under IFRS and U.S. GAAP.

Comparative Consolidated Balance Sheet at Acquisition Date: Purchase Method

	IFRS	U.S. GAAP
Cash and receivables	$55,000	$55,000
Inventory	205,000	205,000
PP&E (net)	390,000	378,000
Total assets	$650,000	$638,000
Payables	$75,000	$75,000
Long-term debt	190,000	190,000
Total liabilities	$265,000	$265,000
Minority interests		$20,000
Shareholders' equity:		
Capital stock (no par)	$215,000	$215,000
Retained earnings	138,000	138,000
Minority interests	32,000	—
Total equity	$385,000	$373,000
Total liabilities and shareholders' equity	$650,000	$638,000

6.5.4. Minority (Noncontrolling) Interests: Income Statement

On the income statement, minority (noncontrolling) Interests are presented as a line item showing the allocation of profit or loss for the period. Intercompany transactions, if any, are eliminated in full.

Using some assumed data consistent with the facts in Example 15-10, the consolidated income statements under IFRS and U.S. GAAP are presented below:

	IFRS	U.S. GAAP
Sales	$200,000	$200,000
Cost of goods sold	110,000	110,000
Interest expense	8,000	8,000
Depreciation expense	39,000	37,800
Income from continuing operations	$43,000	$44,200
Minority interest	8,600	9,800
Consolidated net income to shareholders	$34,400	$34,400

Income to shareholders is $34,400 whether the company uses IFRS or U.S. GAAP. Recall that IFRS allocated the fair value of the PP&E to the minority shareholders as well as to the controlling shareholders. Therefore, the minority shareholders will share in the adjustment for excess depreciation because of the $60,000 increase in PP&E. Under U.S. GAAP, only the parent's share of the excess value was written up and, therefore, minority shareholders do not share in the increased depreciation. Depreciation expense is higher and minority interest income is lower under IFRS, resulting in identical net income to shareholders of the parent company.

6.6. Financial Statement Presentation Subsequent to the Business Combination

The presentation of consolidated financial statements differs slightly between IFRS and U.S. GAAP, but the quality of the presentation is similar. For example, selected financial statements for GlaxoSmithKline are shown in Exhibits 15-4 and 15-5. GlaxoSmithKline is a leading pharmaceutical company headquartered in the United Kingdom.

The consolidated balance sheet in Exhibit 15-4 combines the operations of GlaxoSmithKline and its subsidiaries. The analyst can observe that in 2006 GlaxoSmithKline

EXHIBIT 15-4   GlaxoSmithKline: Consolidated Balance Sheet (on 31 December 2006)

	Notes	2006 (£ million)	2005 (£ million)
Noncurrent assets			
Property, plant, and equipment	15	6,930	6,652
Goodwill	16	758	696
Other intangible assets	17	3,293	3,383
Investments in associates and joint ventures	18	295	276
Other investments	19	441	362
Deferred tax assets	12	2,123	2,214
Other noncurrent assets	20	721	438
Total noncurrent assets		14,561	14,021
Current assets			
Inventories	21	2,437	2,177
Current tax recoverable	12	186	416
Trade and other receivables	22	5,317	5,348
Liquid investments	30	1,035	1,025
Cash and cash equivalents	23	2,005	4,209
Assets held for sale	24	12	2
Total current assets		10,992	13,177
Total assets		25,553	27,198
Current liabilities			
Short-term borrowings	30	(718)	(1,200)
Trade and other payables	25	(4,871)	(5,147)
Current tax payable	12	(621)	(2,269)
Short-term provisions	27	(1,055)	(895)
Total current liabilities		(7,265)	(9,511)

Noncurrent liabilities

Long-term borrowings	30	(4,772)	(5,271)
Deferred tax provision	12	(595)	(569)
Pensions and other postemployed benefits	26	(2,339)	(3,069)
Other provisions	27	(528)	(741)
Other noncurrent liabilities	28	(406)	(467)
Total noncurrent liabilities		(8,640)	(10,117)
Total liabilities		(15,905)	(19,628)
Net assets		9,648	7,570
Equity			
Share capital	31	1,498	1,491
Share premium account	31	858	549
Retained earnings	32	6,965	5,579
Other reserves	32	65	(308)
Shareholders' equity		9,386	7,311
Minority interests		262	259
Total equity		9,648	7,570

had passive investments (other investments of £441 million and liquid investments of £1,035 million), minority active investments (investments in associates and joint ventures of £295 million), and controlling investments (consolidated subsidiaries). The goodwill on the balance sheet implies that GlaxoSmithKline acquired another company and paid an amount in excess of the fair value of the identifiable net assets. The analyst can also note that GlaxoSmithKline is the parent company in a less than 100 percent acquisition. The minority interest of £262 million in the equity section is the portion of the combined entity that accrues to minority shareholders. Because the statement is prepared using IFRS, the minority interest was reflected at the acquisition date based on the minority's share of the fair value of the net assets acquired. As the value of the subsidiaries change as a result of net income and changes in equity, the minority interests will also change.

The consolidated income statement for GlaxoSmithKline is presented in Exhibit 15-5. U.S. GAAP and IFRS have similar treatment for consolidated income statements. Each line item (e.g., turnover [sales], cost of sales, etc.) includes 100 percent of the parent and the subsidiary transactions after eliminating any upstream (subsidiary sells to parent) or downstream (parent sells to subsidiary) intercompany transactions. The portion of income accruing to minority shareholders is presented as a separate line item on the consolidated income statement. Note that net income is the same under IFRS and U.S. GAAP.[6] Because IFRS record the fair value of the minority interest in net assets and recognize expense on this amount, the minority's share of income is also adjusted so that income to parent company shareholders is unaffected. The analyst will need to make adjustments for any analysis that compares specific line items that might differ between IFRS and U.S. GAAP.

---

[6]It is possible, however, for differences to arise through the application of different accounting rules (e.g., valuation of fixed assets).

EXHIBIT 15-5   GlaxoSmithKline: Consolidated Income Statement (for the year ended 31 December 2006)

	Notes	2006 (£ million)	2005 (£ million)	2004 (£ million)
Turnover		23,225	21,660	19,986
Cost of sales	5	(5,010)	(4,764)	(4,360)
Gross profit		18,215	16,896	15,626
Selling, general, and administration		(7,257)	(7,250)	(7,201)
Research and development		(3,457)	(3,136)	(2,904)
Other operating income	6	307	364	235
Operating profit	7,8	7,808	6,874	5,756
Finance income	9	287	257	176
Finance costs	10	(352)	(451)	(362)
Share of after tax profits of associates and joint ventures	11	56	52	60
Profit on disposal of interest in associates	36	—	—	149
Profit before taxation		7,799	6,732	5,779
Taxation	12	(2,301)	(1,916)	(1,757)
Profit after taxation for the year		5,498	4,816	4,022
Profit attributable to minority interests		109	127	114
Profit attributable to shareholders		5,389	4,689	3,908
		5,498	4,816	4,022
Basic earnings per share (pence)	13	95.5p	82.6p	68.1p
Diluted earnings per share (pence)	13	94.5p	82.0p	68.0p

6.7. Goodwill

Goodwill is recognized as the excess purchase price over the fair value of the identifiable net assets. Using data from Example 15-10 above, assume that Parent Co. issued stock with a market value of $180,000 to acquire the 80 percent interest in Subsidiary Co.

Purchase price	$180,000
80% fair value	$128,000
Goodwill	$52,000

The goodwill is not amortized under either IFRS or U.S. GAAP, but it is tested for impairment at least annually.

6.8. Goodwill Impairment

Under current IFRS (IAS No. 36) and U.S. GAAP (SFAS No. 142), goodwill is recognized as the cost of the acquisition less the acquirer's share of the fair value of all tangible and intangible assets, liabilities, and contingent liabilities acquired. There is a small difference between

IFRS and U.S. GAAP in their inclusion of contingent liabilities. IFRS include contingent liabilities if their fair values can be reliably measured. U.S. GAAP includes only those contingent liabilities that are probable and can be reasonably estimated. Goodwill is considered to have an indefinite life and is, therefore, not amortized. Goodwill, however, is tested for **impairment** annually or more frequently if events or circumstances indicate that goodwill might be impaired.

U.S. GAAP uses a two-step approach to test for impairment at the reporting unit level. The carrying amount of the unit is compared to its fair value. If the fair value of the unit exceeds the carrying value, goodwill is not considered to be impaired. If the carrying value exceeds the fair value, the implied fair value of the unit's goodwill is compared to its carrying amount to determine the amount of impairment loss. The implied fair value of goodwill is determined in the same manner as in a business combination. The fair value of the unit is allocated to all assets and liabilities of the unit. The excess is the implied fair value of goodwill. If the goodwill is deemed to be impaired, an impairment loss will be recorded as a separate line item in the operating section of the consolidated income statement. IFRS 36 retains a one-step approach and requires the comparison of the carrying amount of the cash-generating unit to which goodwill has been allocated to the recoverable amount. If the carrying amount of the unit exceeds the recoverable amount of the unit, the entity recognizes an impairment loss on the profit and loss statement.

EXAMPLE 15-11   Impairment of Goodwill

The reporting unit of a U.S. corporation (e.g., a division) has a fair value of $1,300,000 and a carrying book value of $1,400,000 that includes recorded goodwill of $300,000. The estimated fair value of the identifiable assets minus liabilities is $1,200,000. Calculate the impairment loss.

Solution.

Fair market value of unit	$1,300,000
Current assets	400,000
PP&E	1,100,000
Liabilities	300,000
Net assets	$1,200,000
Implied goodwill	$100,000
Current carrying value of goodwill	300,000
Impairment loss	$200,000

The impairment loss of $200,000 is reported on the income statement and a portion of the goodwill on the consolidated balance sheet is reduced accordingly.

6.9. Purchase Price Less than Fair Value (Bargain Purchase)

Occasionally, a company faces negative circumstances such that the market value drops below the fair value of the net assets. If the company is acquired and the purchase price is less than the fair value of the net assets, the acquisition is considered to be a **bargain purchase**. IFRS requires that the identifiable assets, liabilities, and contingent liabilities be reassessed. Any excess after reassessments is recognized as a profit or loss. U.S. GAAP also requires reassessment but any excess is allocated proportionately to reduce noncurrent assets. If noncurrent assets are reduced to zero, any remaining negative goodwill will be recognized as an extraordinary gain on the income statement.

6.10. Additional Issues in Business Combinations that Impair Comparability

Accounting for business combinations is a complex topic. In addition to the basics covered so far in this chapter, we briefly mention some of the more common issues that impair comparability between IFRS and U.S. GAAP.

6.10.1. Contingent Liabilities

Under IFRS, the cost of an acquisition is allocated to the fair value of assets, liabilities, and contingent liabilities. Contingent liabilities are recorded at fair value provided their fair values can be measured reliably. U.S. GAAP calls for recognition only if the contingency is probable and can be reasonably estimated. U.S. GAAP does not recognize contingent liabilities of the target company at the date of the acquisition but instead recognizes them when the contingency is resolved or the amount is determinable.

6.10.2. Contingent Consideration

Contingent consideration may be negotiated as part of the purchase price. For example, the parent may agree to pay additional money to the subsidiary shareholders if certain sales levels are attained by the combined entity. If the cost of an acquisition is dependent on future events, IFRS requires the estimated amount be included as part of the cost at the acquisition date. Under U.S. GAAP, the additional cost is recognized when the contingent consideration is resolved or the amount can be determined.

6.10.3. In-Process Research and Development

IFRS and U.S. GAAP recognize in-process research and development (R&D) acquired in a business combination at fair value. If the in-process R&D meets the definition of an intangible asset and can be measured reliably, IFRS allow recognition as a separate intangible asset. U.S. GAAP generally requires that in-process R&D be expensed immediately.

6.11. Proposed Joint Project of the IASB and FASB

A joint IASB–FASB project, "Business Combinations: Applying the Acquisition Method: Joint Project of the IASB and FASB" was completed in 2007. In November 2007, FASB issued SFAS No. 141R that provides significant changes for accounting for business combinations. This standard is effective for companies with fiscal years ending after 15 December 2008. The IASB will issue its standards soon, with an expected application date of January 2009. The result will be a substantial convergence between IFRS and U.S. GAAP for the accounting of business combinations.

The goal of the project is to create a standard that ensures high quality financial information that can be used across borders. Although there is significant improvement in comparability, there are still some differences between the IFRS and U.S. GAAP on various issues. To achieve consistency, analysts will need to adjust consolidated financial statements when assessing performance.

We summarize some of the more significant changes to the current standards:

- Business combinations will be accounted for using the **acquisition method**. The acquisition method requires the acquirer to measure each identifiable asset and liability at fair value. This is similar to the purchase method under IFRS but represents a change for U.S. GAAP. Recall that currently U.S. GAAP (SFAS No. 141) calls for fair value only for the purchased portion of assets and liabilities but book value for minority interest. The acquisition method (SFAS No. 141R) will improve comparability between U.S. GAAP and IFRS.
- Direct costs under U.S. GAAP (SFAS No. 141R) are not included in the acquisition cost but are expensed unless the costs are associated with the issue of debt and equity securities.
- Contingent assets and liabilities that meet the definition of an asset or liability will be recognized at fair value at the acquisition date of the business combination; any subsequent changes will be reflected as a profit or loss.
- All identifiable R&D acquired in a business combination will be measured at fair value. The in-process R&D will have an indefinite life until completion or abandonment. Like goodwill, recorded in-process R&D will not be amortized but will be tested annually for impairment.
- The IASB and FASB did not reach convergence on the measurement of noncontrolling interests in a business combination. FASB (SFAS No. 141R) requires that fair value at the acquisition date be used for the measurement of the noncontrolling interest. Thus, "full goodwill" will be recognized. IASB (IFRS 3) will allow an acquisition-by-acquisition option to use either total fair value at the acquisition date (full goodwill) or the noncontrolling proportionate interest in the fair value of the acquiree's identifiable assets and liabilities (partial goodwill).
- Disclosure of noncontrolling interests is in the equity section of the balance sheet.
- Bargain purchases (purchase price less than fair value) may result in a gain to income.

EXAMPLE 15-12   Acquisition Method Illustrated

Assume that Carter Company acquired an 80 percent interest in Novel Company on 1 January 2008 for $320,000 in cash (both companies are fictitious). Novel's assets and liabilities were as follows:

	Novel Company	
	Book Value	Fair Value
Cash and receivables	$40,000	$40,000
Inventory	80,000	90,000
PP&E (net)	200,000	260,000
	320,000	390,000

Payables	10,000	10,000
Long-term debt	50,000	50,000
	60,000	60,000
Net assets	$260,000	$330,000
Shareholders' equity:		
Capital stock (no par)	$80,000	
Retained earnings	$180,000	

Because the consideration paid, $320,000 cash, is presumed to be a sufficient measure of the fair value, the fair value of 100 percent of Novel is $400,000 ($320,000/0.80).

The fair value of the identifiable assets and liabilities is $330,000. This implies that the total goodwill associated with Novel is $70,000. Based on the new standard, FASB would require recognition of noncontrolling interests on the balance sheet of $80,000. IASB would allow recognition of the minority's percentage interest (20 percent) of either the fair value of the identifiable assets and liabilities ($66,000) or the fair value of all assets and liabilities ($80,000).

7. VARIABLE INTEREST AND SPECIAL PURPOSE ENTITIES

For many years, sponsors avoided consolidation of **special purpose entities** (SPEs). As a result, assets and liabilities were not reported on the balance sheet and financial performance as measured by unadjusted financial statements was obscured. The benefit to the sponsor company was improved asset turnover and improved financial leverage metrics. Enron used SPEs to achieve off-balance-sheet financing and disguise the company's financial problems. Enron's subsequent collapse made SPEs notorious. Both the IASB and FASB addressed the accounting issues related to SPEs to improve consistency and transparency. FASB currently uses the term **variable interest entity** (VIE), but IFRS use the term *special purpose entity.*

SPEs can be a legitimate financing mechanism for a company to segregate certain activities and thereby reduce risk. The special purpose entity can be a corporation, partnership, trust, limited liability, or partnership formed to facilitate a specific type of business activity. SFAS No. 140 and Interpretation FIN 46R provide guidance for U.S. GAAP, which classifies special purpose entities as variable interest entities if:

- Total equity at risk is insufficient to finance activities without financial support from other parties, and
- Equity investors lack any one of the following:

  1. The ability to make decisions.
  2. The obligation to absorb losses.
  3. The right to receive return.

An entity classified as a variable interest entity under FIN 46R must be consolidated by its primary beneficiary. The sponsoring entity is the primary beneficiary if it absorbs the majority of risks and residual returns of a variable interest entity. Common examples of variable interests are entities created to lease real estate or other property, entities created for the securitization of financial assets, or entities created for R&D activity.

IAS No. 27 and Interpretation SIC 12 provide guidance for IFRS for consolidation of special purpose entities. Under IFRS a sponsoring entity must consolidate a special purpose entity when the sponsoring entity controls "in substance" the SPE. Indicators of control under SIC No. 12 include the following:

- The SPE activities are conducted for the benefit of the sponsoring entity.
- The sponsoring entity has decision making powers to obtain benefits.
- The sponsoring entity is able to absorb the risks and rewards of the SPE.
- The sponsoring entity has a residual interest in the SPE.

7.1. Illustration of an SPE for a Leased Asset

Consider the situation in which a sponsoring company creates a special purpose entity with minimal and independent third party equity. The SPE borrows from the debt market and acquires or constructs an asset. The asset may be purchased from the sponsoring company or from an outside source. The sponsoring company then leases the asset and the cash flow from lease payments is used to repay the debt and provide a return to equity holders. Because the asset is pledged as collateral, risk is reduced and a lower interest rate may be offered by the financing organization. In addition, because equity investors are not exposed to all the business risks of the sponsoring company but only those of the restricted SPE, they may be more willing to invest in this relatively safe investment. The sponsor retains the risk of default and receives the benefits of ownership of the leased asset through a residual value guarantee. Under these conditions, the sponsor is the primary beneficiary and consolidates the SPE (see Exhibit 15-6).

In 1996, Dreamworks Animation SKG entered into an agreement with financial institutions to construct their Glendale Animation Campus in Glendale, California. The 326,000 square foot facility houses a majority of Dreamworks employees. In 2002, Dreamworks created an SPE that acquired the property from the financial institution for $73.0 million. The SPE leases the facility back to Dreamworks. It has been determined that Dreamworks Animation SKG is the primary beneficiary of the SPE. Dreamworks Animation SKG discloses the following information about their use of SPEs in their 2006 annual report:

> *We operate an animation campus in Glendale, California. The **lease** on the property, which was originally acquired for $76.5 million, qualified as an operating **lease**. In March 2002, we renegotiated the **lease** through the creation of a **special purpose entity** that acquired the property for $73.0 million and leased the facility to us for an initial term of five years, which was subsequently extended through October 2009. In accordance with the provisions of FIN 46, we have included the asset, debt and non-controlling interest on our combined balance sheet as of December 31, 2006 and 2005. In addition to the principal amount of $73 million that is due in October 2009, we are obligated to pay interest based primarily on 30-day commercial paper rates (5.32% at December 31, 2006). For further discussion, please see Note 6 to our audited consolidated financial statements.*

> *Source:* Dreamworks Animation SKG, Inc. Form 10-K, 2006

EXHIBIT 15-6   SPE for a Leased Asset

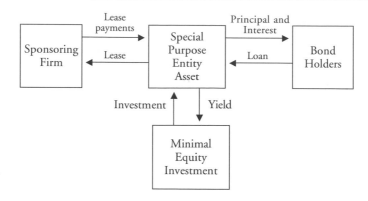

7.2. Securitization of Assets

SPEs are often established for the securitization of receivables. The SPE issues debt to purchase all or a portion of the sponsoring company receivables. Repayment of the debt and interest are made with the cash flow generated by the receivables. For example, Fiat S.p.A. sells its trade receivables to an SPE to improve its cash flows in a cost-effective manner. Fiat, one of the largest industrial companies in Italy, is engaged principally in the manufacture and sale of automobiles, agricultural and construction equipment, trucks, and commercial vehicles. Regarding the sale of receivables in their 2006 Form 20-F, Fiat reports:

> *The Fiat Group sells a significant part of its financial, trade and tax receivables through either securitization programs or factoring transactions. A securitization transaction entails the sale of a portfolio of receivables to a securitization vehicle. This special purpose entity finances the purchase of the receivables by issuing asset-backed securities (i.e., securities whose repayment and interest flow depend upon the cash flow generated by the portfolio). Asset-backed securities are divided into classes according to their degree of seniority and rating: the most senior classes are placed with investors on the market; the junior class, whose repayment is subordinated to the senior classes, is normally subscribed for by the seller. The residual interest in the receivables retained by the seller is therefore limited to the junior securities it has subscribed for. In accordance with SIC-12-Consolidation-Special Purpose Entities (SPE), all securitization vehicles are included in the scope of consolidation, because the subscription of the junior asset-backed securities by the seller entails its control in substance over the SPE. Furthermore, factoring transactions may be with or without recourse to the seller; certain factoring agreements without recourse include deferred purchase price clauses (i.e., the payment of a minority portion of the purchase price is conditional upon the full collection of the receivables), require a first loss guarantee of the seller up to a limited amount or imply a continuing significant exposure to the receivables cash flow.*

Securitizations raise several issues for the analyst. First, the analyst should assess the relationship to ensure that SPEs are consolidated when appropriate. Second, securitization can have a significant impact on operating cash flows and financial leverage and may need to be adjusted for analysis. Finally, securitization may affect the volatility of operating cash flows.

7.3. Qualifying Special Purpose Entities

Under U.S. GAAP, it is possible to structure an SPE that does not meet the variable interest criteria in FIN 46R. **Qualifying special purpose entities** (QSPEs) are structured to avoid consolidation and must meet qualification criteria. The use of QSPEs has increased in recent years, probably as a consequence of FIN 46R requiring consolidation. Under U.S. GAAP, the QSPE is independent and legally separate from the sponsor and has total control over the purchased asset. The QSPE can hold only financial assets. The sponsoring company does not have effective control over the assets and is not the primary beneficiary. The financial risk of the sponsor is limited, for example, to its investment or explicit recourse obligation in the SPE. In other words, the sponsor is *bankruptcy remote*. SFAS No. 140 provides guidance for situations in which the transfer of an asset to the QSPE is considered to be a sale to an independent entity. The sponsor company removes the asset from the balance sheet and recognizes a gain or loss on the sale. IFRS do not permit QSPEs.

Toyota Motor Corp., which elects to use U.S. GAAP for its annual consolidated statements, describes its securitization program in its 2006 SEC Form 20-F:

> *Toyota's securitization program involves a two-step transaction. Toyota sells discrete pools of retail finance receivables to a wholly-owned bankruptcy remote special purpose entity ("SPE"), which in turn transfers the receivables to a qualified special purpose entity ("QSPE" or "securitization trust") in exchange for the proceeds from securities issued by the securitization trust. Once the receivables are transferred to the QSPE, the receivables are no longer assets of Toyota and, therefore, no longer appear on Toyota's consolidated balance sheet. These securities are secured by collections on the sold receivables and structured into senior and subordinated classes.*

There is significant judgment required in determining whether an entity is a QSPE. Analysts should consider the impact of nonconsolidation on performance metrics. Substantial QSPE transactions can result in material distortion of liquidity, leverage, and profitability measures.

For example, Caterpillar Financial Services Corp. noted in their 2006 10-K that during one period the trust they created to securitize receivables did not qualify as a QSPE. The transferor is not allowed to hold more than 90 percent of the fair market value of the beneficial interest. Because Caterpillar exceeded the 90 percent limit on the beneficial interest, the trust did not qualify as a QSPE. During this period, the company was required to consolidate the trust in accordance with FIN 46R. In another case, the Federal National Mortgage Association (Fannie Mae) admitted that they transferred assets to a trust that did not meet QSPE criteria and acknowledged errors in applying SFAS No. 140 to their SPEs.

Federal National Mortgage Association (Fannie Mae)

> *We incorrectly recorded asset sales that did not meet the sale accounting criteria set forth in SFAS No. 125 and SFAS No. 140, primarily because the assets were transferred to an MBS trust that did not meet the QSPE criteria. We failed to consolidate MBS trusts that were not considered QSPEs and for which we were deemed to be the primary beneficiary or sponsor of the trust. These entities included those to which we transferred assets in a transaction that initially qualified as a sale and for QSPE status, but where the trust*

subsequently failed to meet the criteria to be a QSPE, primarily because our ownership interests in the trust exceeded the threshold permitted for a QSPE.

There is significant judgment used to determine whether a trust is a QSPE. To maintain QSPE status, the trust must continue to meet the QSPE criteria both initially and in subsequent periods. We have analyzed the governing pooling and servicing agreements for each of our securitizations and believe that the terms are industry standard and are consistent with the QSPE criteria. If at any time we determine a trust no longer qualifies as a QSPE, each trust will need to be reviewed to determine if there is a need to recognize the commercial mortgage loan asset in the statement of financial position along with the offsetting liability. In addition, certain industry practices related to the qualifying status of QSPEs are being discussed by the FASB and could impact the accounting for existing and/or future transactions.

7.4. Consolidated versus Nonconsolidated Securitization Transactions

A common type of QSPE is a securitization transaction. To illustrate the differences between a consolidated and nonconsolidated securitization transaction, consider the following:

Securitized Transaction: Qualified Special Purpose Entity	Securitized Transaction: Special Purpose Entity
Originator of receivables sell financial assets to an SPE.	Originator of receivables sell financial assets to an SPE.
The originator does not own or hold or expect to receive beneficial interest.	Seller is primary beneficiary; absorbs risks and rewards.
SFAS No. 140 allows seller to derecognize the sold assets if transferred assets have been isolated from the transferor and are beyond the reach of bankruptcy, and are financial assets.	Seller maintains some level of control.
	Seller is required to consolidate.
	Seller's balance sheet would still show receivables as an asset.
	Debt of SPE would appear on seller's balance sheet.

IFRS do not recognize a QSPE. As Deutsche Telekom AG notes in its 2006 20-F filing with the SEC:

We have entered into agreements to sell, on a continual basis, certain eligible trade receivables to Special Purpose Entities (SPEs). Under IFRS, these SPEs are consolidated and included in our consolidated financial statements, whereas under U.S. GAAP, these SPEs are considered Qualifying Special Purpose Entities (QSPEs) and are therefore not consolidated. As a result, the transferred receivables are removed from the balance sheet, with a gain or loss recognized on the sale for U.S. GAAP. The measurement of the gain or loss depends on the carrying bases of the transferred receivables, allocated between the receivables sold and the interests and obligations retained, based on their relative fair values as of the date of transfer. Under these agreements, we retain without remuneration the servicing obligation relating to the sold receivables, which are recognized for U.S. GAAP, but not for IFRS.

Capital One, in its 2006 10-K filing, provides a reconciliation that illustrates the effect on some common performance inputs. The first column reflects the information as reported and does not include consolidation of QSPEs. The third column reflects the "as if" consolidated. This provides the analyst with an example of how off-balance-sheet accounting can affect financial analysis ratios.

Capital One

Reconciliation to GAAP Financial Measure

The Company's consolidated financial statements prepared in accordance with accounting principles generally accepted in the United States (GAAP) are referred to as its "reported" financial statements. Loans included in securitization transactions that qualify as sales under GAAP have been removed from the Company's "reported" balance sheet. However, servicing fees, finance charges, and other fees, net of charge-offs, and interest paid to investors of securitizations are recognized as servicing and securitization income on the "reported" income statement.

The Company's "managed" consolidated financial statements reflect adjustments made related to effects of securitization transactions qualifying as sales under GAAP. The Company generates earnings from its "managed" loan portfolio that includes both the on-balance-sheet loans and off-balance-sheet loans. The Company's "managed" income statement takes the components of the servicing and securitizations income generated from the securitized portfolio and distributes the revenue and expense to appropriate income statement line items from which it originated. For this reason, the company believes the "managed" consolidated financial statements and related managed metrics to be useful to stakeholders.

As of and for the year ended 31 December 2006.

(Dollars in millions)	Total Reported	Securitization Adjustments	Total Managed
Income Statement Measures			
Net interest income	$5,100	$3,841	$8,941
Noninterest income	$6,997	($2,094)	$4,903
Total revenue	$12,097	$1,747	$13,844
Provision for loan losses	$1,476	$1,748	$3,224
Net charge-offs	$1,407	$1,751	$3,158
Balance Sheet Measures			
Loans held for investment	$96,512	$49,639	$146,151
Total assets	$149,739	$48,906	$198,645
Average loans held for investment	$63,577	$47,752	$111,329
Average earnings assets	$84,522	$45,726	$130,248
Average total assets	$95,810	$47,172	$142,982
Delinquencies	$2,648	$1,766	$4,414

The impact is apparent in this example. Noninterest income is higher and total assets are lower when the qualified special purpose entity is not consolidated. Therefore, noninterest return on assets is significantly higher without consolidation (4.67 percent versus 2.47 percent).

There is also significant debt that is not reported on the balance sheet when the special purpose entity is not required to be consolidated. This disclosure by Capital One illustrates the effect of off-balance-sheet SPEs and the usefulness of this type of financial information for performance analysis.

8. SUMMARY

Intercompany investments play a significant role in business activities and create significant challenges for the analyst in assessing company performance. Investments in other corporations can take four basic forms: minority passive investments, minority active investments, joint ventures, and controlling interest investments. Key concepts are as follows:

- Minority passive investments are those in which the investor has no significant influence. They can be designated as: held-to-maturity investments, held-for-trading securities, or available-for-sale securities. Additionally, both IFRS and U.S GAAP allow investments to be designated at fair value. IFRS and U.S. GAAP treat minority passive investments in a similar manner.
  ○ Held-to-maturity investments are carried at cost.
  ○ Held-for-trading securities are carried at fair value; unrealized gains and losses are reported on the profit and loss (income) statement.
  ○ Available-for-sale securities are carried at fair value; unrealized gains and losses are reported in the statement of recognized income and expenses (IFRS) or other comprehensive income (U.S. GAAP) in the equity section of the balance sheet.
  ○ Gains or losses on investments designated as fair value are reported on the profit and loss (income) statement.
- Minority active investments are those in which the investor has significant influence, but not control, over the investee's business activities. Because the investor can exert significant influence over financial and operating policy decisions, the equity method of accounting provides a more objective basis for reporting investment income.
  ○ The equity method requires the investor to recognize income as earned rather than when dividends are received.
  ○ The equity investment is carried at cost, plus its share of post-acquisition income (after adjustments) less dividends received.
  ○ The equity investment is reported as a single line item on the balance sheet and on the income statement.
- Joint ventures are entities owned and operated by a small group of investors with shared common control. IFRS and U.S. GAAP apply different standards to joint ventures. IFRS favor proportionate consolidation that requires the venturer's share of the assets, liabilities, income, and expenses of the joint venture to be combined on a line-by-line basis with similar items in the venturer's financial statements. U.S. GAAP requires the equity method accounting for joint ventures. The IASB is expected to issue a statement that changes accounting for joint ventures from proportionate consolidation to the equity method.
- Controlling interests investments can be structured as mergers, acquisitions, or statutory consolidation.

- In a statutory merger, two or more companies combine such that only one of the companies remains in existence. In a statutory consolidation, two or more companies are folded into a new entity with the new entity becoming the surviving company.
- An acquisition allows for the legal continuity for each of the combining companies. Both companies continue as separate entities but are now affiliated through a parent–subsidiary relationship.
  - Unlike a statutory merger or consolidation, the acquiring company does not need to acquire 100 percent of the target. If the acquiring company acquires less than 100 percent, minority (noncontrolling) shareholders' interests are reported on the consolidated financial statements.
  - Consolidated financial statements are prepared in each reporting period.
- Current accounting standards (IFRS and U.S. GAAP) require the purchase method for business combinations. Fair value is the appropriate measurement for identifiable assets and liabilities acquired in the business combination. If the acquisition is less than 100 percent, U.S. GAAP revalues only the portion of the company acquired, whereas IFRS revalue the total assets or liabilities. FASB (SFAS No. 141R), effective after 15 December 2008 and the soon to be released IASB revision of IFRS 3 (effective after 1 January 2009) will require the acquisition method for business combinations. Identifiable assets and liabilities will be measured at fair value.
- The pooling of interests method for business combinations was not allowed after June 2001 in U.S. GAAP (March 2004 in IFRS).
- Goodwill is the excess purchase price after recognizing the fair market value of all tangible and intangible assets acquired. U.S. GAAP (SFAS No. 141R) will also recognize goodwill for the noncontrolling interest (full goodwill), whereas the new IASB standard will provide the option for full or proportionate goodwill.
- Goodwill has an indefinite life and is not amortized but is evaluated at least annually for impairment. Impairment losses are reported on the income statement.
- Variable interests (SPEs) require consolidation with the sponsoring company if the sponsoring company bears the majority of risks and rewards from the transaction.
  - U.S. GAAP allows for qualified special purpose entities to avoid consolidation if the sponsoring company is not the primary beneficiary.

PRACTICE PROBLEMS

The following information relates to Problems 1 through 6.

Cinnamon, Inc. is a diversified manufacturing company headquartered in the United States, and it complies with U.S. GAAP. In 2008, Cinnamon held a 19 percent passive stake in Cambridge Processing that was classified as available for sale. During the year, the value of this stake rose by $2 million. In December 2008, Cinnamon announced that it would be increasing its ownership to 50 percent effective 1 January 2009.

Peter Lubbock, an analyst following both Cinnamon and Cambridge, is curious how the increased stake will affect Cinnamon's consolidated financial statements. He asks Cinnamon's chief financial officer how the company will account for the stake, and is told that the decision has not yet been made. Lubbock decides to use his existing forecasts for both companies' financial statements to compare various alternative outcomes.

Lubbock gathers abbreviated financial statement data for Cinnamon (Exhibit 15-7) and Cambridge (Exhibit 15-8) for this purpose.

EXHIBIT 15-7   Selected Financial Statement Estimates for Cinnamon, Inc. ($ millions)

Year ending 31 December	2008	2009[a]
Revenue	$1,400	$1,575
Operating income	126	142
Net income	62	69
Total assets	1,170	1,317
Shareholders' equity	616	685

[a]Estimates made prior to announcement of increased stake in Cambridge.

EXHIBIT 15-8   Selected Financial Statement Estimates for Cambridge Processing ($ millions)

Year ending 31 December	2008	2009
Revenue	$1,000	$1,100
Operating income	80	88
Net income	40	44
Dividends paid	20	22
Total assets	800	836
Shareholders' equity	440	462

1. In 2008, Cinnamon's earnings before taxes includes a contribution (in $ millions) from its investment in Cambridge Processing *closest* to
   A. $2.5 million.
   B. $3.8 million.
   C. $5.0 million.

2. In 2009, Cinnamon is *least likely* to account for its investment in Cambridge under which of the following methods?
   A. Equity
   B. Purchase method
   C. Proportionate consolidation

3. On 31 December 2009, Cinnamon's shareholders' equity amount on the balance sheet would *most likely* be
   A. highest if Cinnamon is deemed to have control of Cambridge.
   B. independent of the accounting method used for the investment in Cambridge.
   C. highest if Cinnamon is deemed to have significant influence over Cambridge.

4. In 2009, Cinnamon's net profit margin would be *highest* if
   A. it is deemed to have control of Cambridge.
   B. it had not increased its stake in Cambridge.
   C. it is deemed to have significant influence over Cambridge.

5. On 31 December 2009, Cinnamon's reported debt-to-equity ratio will most likely be *highest* if it is deemed to have
   A. control of Cambridge.
   B. joint control of Cambridge.
   C. significant influence over Cambridge.

6. Compared to Cinnamon's operating margin in 2008, if it is deemed to have control of Cambridge, its operating margin in 2009 will *most likely* be
   A. lower.
   B. higher.
   C. the same.

The following information relates to Problems 7 through 12.

Zimt AG is a consumer products manufacturer headquartered in Austria. It complies with IFRS.

In 2008, Zimt held a 10 percent passive stake in Oxbow Limited that was classified as held-for-trading securities. During the year, the value of this stake declined by €3 million.

In December 2008, Zimt announced that it would be increasing its ownership to 50 percent effective 1 January 2009.

Franz Gelblum, an analyst following both Zimt and Oxbow, is curious how the increased stake will affect Zimt's consolidated financial statements. Because Gelblum is uncertain how the company will account for the increased stake, he uses his existing forecasts for both companies' financial statements to compare various alternative outcomes.

Gelblum gathers abbreviated financial statement data for Zimt (Exhibit 15-9) and Oxbow (Exhibit 15-10) for this purpose.

EXHIBIT 15-9   Selected Financial Statement Estimates for Zimt AG (€ millions)

Year ending 31 December	2008	2009
Revenue	€1,500	€1,700
Operating income	135	153
Net income	66	75
Total assets	1,254	1,421
Shareholders' equity	660	735

EXHIBIT 15-10   Selected Financial Statement Estimates for Oxbow
Limited (€ millions)

Year ending 31 December	2008	2009
Revenue	€1,200	€1,350
Operating income	120	135
Net income	60	68
Dividends paid	20	22
Total assets	1,200	1,283
Shareholders' equity	660	706

7. In 2008, Zimt's earnings before taxes includes a contribution (in € millions) from its investment in Oxbow Limited *closest* to
   A. (€0.6) million.
   B. €1.0 million.
   C. €1.9 million.

8. On 31 December 2009, Zimt's total assets balance would *most likely* be
   A. highest if Zimt is deemed to have control of Oxbow.
   B. highest if Zimt is deemed to have significant influence over Oxbow.
   C. unaffected by the accounting method used for the investment in Oxbow.

9. Based on Gelblum's estimates, if Zimt is deemed to have significant influence over Oxbow, its 2009 operating income would be *closest* to
   A. €153.
   B. €221.
   C. €288.

10. Based on Gelblum's estimates, if Zimt is deemed to have joint control of Oxbow, and Zimt uses the proportionate consolidation method, its 31 December 2009 total liabilities will *most likely* be *closest* to
   A. €686.
   B. €975.
   C. €1,263.

11. Based on Gelblum's estimates, if Zimt is deemed to have control over Oxbow, its 2009 consolidated sales will be *closest* to
   A. €1,700.
   B. €2,375.
   C. €3,050.

12. Based on Gelblum's estimates, Zimt's net income in 2009 will *most likely* be
   A. highest if Zimt is deemed to have control of Oxbow.
   B. highest if Zimt is deemed to have significant influence over Oxbow.
   C. independent of the accounting method used for the investment in Oxbow.

The following information relates to Problems 13 through 18.

Burton Howard, CFA, is an equity analyst with Maplewood Securities. Howard is preparing a research report on Confabulated Materials, SA, a publicly traded company based in France that complies with IFRS. As part of his analysis, Howard has assembled data gathered from the financial statement footnotes of Confabulated's 2008 annual report and from discussions with company management. Howard is concerned about the effect of this information on Confabulated's future earnings.

Information about Confabulated's investment portfolio for the years ended 31 December 2007 and 2008 is presented in Exhibit 15-11. As part of his research, Howard is considering the possible effect on reported income of Confabulated's accounting classification for fixed income investments.

EXHIBIT 15-11   Confabulated's Investment Portfolio (€ thousands)

Characteristic	Bugle AG	Cathay Corp.	Dumas SA
Classification	Available-for-sale	Held-to-maturity	Held-to-maturity
Cost[a]	€25,000	€40,000	€50,000
Market value, 31 December 2007	29,000	38,000	54,000
Market value, 31 December 2008	28,000	37,000	55,000

[a]All securities were purchased at par value.

In addition, Confabulated's financial reports discuss a transaction under which receivables were factored through an SPE for Confabulated's benefit.

13. The balance sheet carrying value of Confabulated's investment portfolio (in € thousands) at 31 December 2008 is *closest* to
    A. 112,000.
    B. 115,000.
    C. 118,000.

14. The balance sheet carrying value of Confabulated's investment portfolio (in € thousands) at 31 December 2008 would have been higher if which of the securities had been reclassified as a held-for-trading security?
    A. Bugle.
    B. Cathay.
    C. Dumas.

15. Compared to Confabulated's reported interest income in 2009, if Dumas had been classified as available-for-sale, the interest income would have been
    A. lower.
    B. the same.
    C. higher.

16. Compared to Confabulated's reported earnings before taxes in 2009, if Bugle had been classified as a held-for-trading security, the earnings before taxes would have been
    A. the same.
    B. €1,000 lower.
    C. €3,000 higher.

17. Confabulated's reported interest income would be higher if the cost were the same but the par value of
    A. Bugle was €28,000.
    B. Cathay was €37,000.
    C. Dumas was €55,000.

18. Confabulated's special purpose entity is *most likely* to be
    A. held off balance sheet.
    B. consolidated on Confabulated's financial statements.
    C. consolidated on Confabulated's financial statements only if it is a QSPE.

The following information relates to Problems 19 through 24.

BetterCare Hospitals, Inc. operates a chain of hospitals throughout the United States. The company has been expanding by acquiring local hospitals. Its largest acquisition, that of Statewide Medical, was made under the pooling of interests method. BetterCare complies with U.S. GAAP.

BetterCare is currently forming a 50/50 joint venture with Supreme Healthcare, under which the companies will share control of several hospitals. Supreme Healthcare complies with IFRS and will comply with the preferred accounting methods for joint ventures.

Erik Ohalin is an equity analyst who covers both companies. He has estimated the joint venture's financial information for 2009 in order to prepare his estimates of each company's earnings and financial performance. This information is presented in Exhibit 15-12.

EXHIBIT 15-12   Selected Financial Statement Forecasts
for Joint Venture ($ millions)

Year ending 31 December	2009
Revenue	$1,430
Operating income	128
Net income	62
Total assets	1,500
Shareholders' equity	740

BetterCare recently announced it had formed a qualifying special purpose entity through which it can sell up to $100 million of its accounts receivable at any given time. Ohalin wants to estimate the impact this will have on BetterCare's consolidated financial statements.

19. Compared to accounting principles currently in use, the pooling method BetterCare used for its Statewide Medical acquisition has *most likely* caused its reported
    A. revenue to be higher.
    B. total equity to be lower.
    C. total assets to be higher.

20. Based on Ohalin's estimates, the amount of joint venture revenue included on BetterCare's consolidated 2009 financial statements should be *closest* to
    A. $0.
    B. $715.
    C. $1,430.

21. Based on Ohalin's estimates, the amount of joint venture operating income included on the consolidated financial statements of each venturer will *most likely* be
    A. higher for BetterCare.
    B. higher for Supreme Healthcare.
    C. the same for both BetterCare and Supreme Healthcare.

22. Based on Ohalin's estimates, the amount of the joint venture's 31 December 2009 total assets that will be included on Supreme Healthcare's consolidated financial statements will be *closest* to
    A. $0.
    B. $750.
    C. $1,500.

23. Based on Ohalin's estimates, the amount of joint venture shareholders' equity at 31 December 2009 included on the consolidated financial statements of each venturer will *most likely* be
    A. higher for BetterCare.
    B. higher for Supreme Healthcare.
    C. the same for both BetterCare and Supreme Healthcare.

24. If BetterCare uses its special purpose entity, its consolidated financial results will most likely show a *higher*
    A. revenue figure for 2009.
    B. cash balance at 31 December 2009.
    C. accounts receivable balance at 31 December 2009.

CHAPTER 16

MULTINATIONAL OPERATIONS

Timothy S. Doupnik

Moore School of Business
University of South Carolina
Columbia, South Carolina

LEARNING OUTCOMES

After completing this chapter, you will be able to do the following:

- Distinguish local currency, functional currency, and the presentation currency.
- Analyze the impact of changes in exchange rates on the translated sales of the subsidiary and parent company.
- Compare and contrast the current rate method and the temporal method, analyze and evaluate the effects of each on the parent company's balance sheet and income statement, and distinguish which method is appropriate in various scenarios.
- Calculate the translation effects, evaluate the translation of a subsidiary's balance sheet and income statement into the parent company's currency, use the current rate method and the temporal method to analyze how the translation of a subsidiary's financial statements will affect the subsidiary's financial ratios, and analyze how using the temporal method versus the current rate method will affect the parent company's financial ratios.
- Illustrate and analyze alternative accounting methods for subsidiaries operating in hyperinflationary economies.

1. INTRODUCTION

According to the World Trade Organization, merchandise exports worldwide exceeded US$10 trillion in 2005.[1] The top five exporting countries, in order, were Germany, the United States, China, Japan, and France. From 2000 to 2005, international trade grew by 62 percent.

---

[1] World Trade Organization, *International Trade Statistics 2006*, Table A6.

The U.S. Department of Commerce identified 239,100 U.S. companies as exporters in 2005. Only 3 percent of those companies were large (more than 500 employees). The vast majority of U.S. companies with export activity were small or medium-sized entities.

The point made by these statistics is that many companies engage in transactions that cross national borders. The parties to these transactions must agree on the currency in which to settle the transaction. Generally, this will be the currency of either the buyer or the seller. Exporters that receive payment in foreign currency and allow the purchaser time to pay must carry a foreign currency receivable on their books. Conversely, importers that agree to pay in foreign currency will have a foreign currency account payable. To be able to include them in the total amount of accounts receivable (payable) reported on the balance sheet, these foreign currency–denominated accounts receivable (payable) must be translated into the currency in which the exporter (importer) keeps its books and presents financial statements.

The prices at which foreign currencies can be purchased or sold are called foreign exchange rates. Because foreign exchange rates fluctuate over time, the value of foreign currency payables and receivables also fluctuate. The major accounting issue related to foreign currency transactions is how to reflect the changes in value for foreign currency payables and receivables in the financial statements.

Many companies have operations located in foreign countries. As examples, the Swiss food products company Nestlé SA reports that it has subsidiaries in more than 90 different countries, and U.S.-based Coca-Cola Company discloses that it has 144 foreign wholly owned subsidiaries located in 40 countries around the world. Foreign subsidiaries are generally required to keep accounting records in the currency of the country in which they are located. To prepare consolidated financial statements, the parent company must translate the foreign currency financial statements of its foreign subsidiaries into its own currency. Nestlé, for example, must translate the assets and liabilities its various foreign subsidiaries carry in foreign currency into Swiss francs to be able to consolidate those amounts with the Swiss franc assets and liabilities located in Switzerland.

A multinational company like Nestlé is likely to have two types of foreign currency activities that require special accounting treatment. Most multinationals (1) engage in transactions that are denominated in a foreign currency, and (2) invest in foreign subsidiaries that keep their books in a foreign currency. To prepare consolidated financial statements, a multinational company must translate the foreign currency amounts related to both types of international activities into the currency in which the company presents its financial statements.

This chapter presents the accounting for foreign currency transactions and the translation of foreign currency financial statements. The conceptual issues related to these accounting topics are discussed and the specific rules embodied in International Financial Reporting Standards (IFRS) and U.S. generally accepted accounting principles (U.S. GAAP) are demonstrated through examples. Fortunately, differences between IFRS and U.S. GAAP with respect to foreign currency translation issues are minimal.

Analysts need to understand the impact that fluctuations in foreign exchange rates have on the financial statements of a multinational company and how foreign currency gains and losses, whether realized or not, are reflected in the company's financial statements.

2. FOREIGN CURRENCY TRANSACTIONS

When companies from different countries agree to conduct business with one another, they must decide which currency will be used. For example, if a Mexican electronic components manufacturer agrees to sell goods to a customer in Finland, the two parties must agree whether the Finnish company will pay for the goods in Mexican pesos, euros, or perhaps even a third currency such as the U.S. dollar. If the transaction is denominated in Mexican pesos, the Finnish company has a foreign currency transaction but the Mexican company does not. To account for the inventory being purchased and the account payable in Mexican pesos, the Finnish company must translate the Mexican peso amounts into euros using appropriate exchange rates. Although the Mexican company also has entered into an international transaction (an export sale), it does not have a foreign currency transaction and no translation is necessary. It simply records the sales revenue and account receivable in Mexican pesos, which is the currency in which it keeps its books and prepares financial statements.

The currency in which financial statement amounts are presented is known as the **presentation currency.** In most cases, the presentation currency of a company will be the currency of the country where the company is located. Finnish companies are required to keep accounting records and present financial results in euros, U.S. companies in U.S. dollars, Chinese companies in Chinese yuan, and so on.

Another important concept in accounting for foreign currency activities is the **functional currency**, which is the currency of the primary economic environment in which an entity operates. Normally, the functional currency is the currency in which an entity primarily generates and expends cash. In most cases, the functional currency of an entity will be the same as its presentation currency. And, because most companies primarily generate and expend cash in the currency of the country where they are located, the functional and presentation currencies are most often the same as the **local currency** where the company operates.

Because the local currency generally is an entity's functional currency, a multinational corporation with subsidiaries in a variety of different countries is likely to have a variety of different functional currencies. The Thai subsidiary of a Japanese parent company, for example, is likely to have the Thai baht as its functional currency whereas the Japanese parent's functional currency is the Japanese yen. But in some cases, the foreign subsidiary could have the parent's functional currency as its own. Intel Corporation, for example, has determined that all of its significant foreign subsidiaries have the U.S. dollar as their functional currency.

By definition, a foreign currency is any currency other than the functional currency of a company and **foreign currency transactions** are transactions that are denominated in a currency other than the company's functional currency. Foreign currency transactions occur when a company (1) makes an import purchase or an export sale that is denominated in a foreign currency, or (2) borrows or lends funds where the amount to be repaid or received is denominated in a foreign currency. In each of theses cases, the company has an asset or a liability that is denominated in a foreign currency.

2.1. Foreign Currency Transaction Exposure to Foreign Exchange Risk

Assume that FinnCo, a Finnish-based company, imports goods from Mexico in January under 90-day credit terms and the purchase is denominated in Mexican pesos. By deferring payment until April, FinnCo runs the risk that from the date the purchase is made until the date of payment, the value of the Mexican peso might increase relative to the euro. FinnCo would then need to spend more euros to settle its Mexican peso account payable. In this case, FinnCo is said to have an **exposure to foreign exchange risk**. Specifically, FinnCo has a foreign currency **transaction exposure**. Transaction exposure related to imports and exports can be summarized as follows:

Import purchase. A transaction exposure arises when the importer is obligated to pay in foreign currency and is allowed to defer payment until sometime after the purchase date. The importer is exposed to the risk that from the purchase date until the payment date the foreign currency might increase in value thereby increasing the amount of functional currency that must be spent to acquire enough foreign currency to settle the account payable.

Export sale. A transaction exposure arises when the exporter agrees to be paid in foreign currency and allows payment to be made sometime after the purchase date. The exporter is exposed to the risk that from the purchase date until the payment date the foreign currency might decrease in value thereby decreasing the amount of functional currency into which the foreign currency can be converted when it is received.

The major issue in accounting for foreign currency transactions is how to account for the foreign currency risk, that is, how to reflect in the financial statements the change in value of the foreign currency asset or liability. Both International Accounting Standard (IAS) 21, "The Effects of Changes in Foreign Exchange Rates," and FASB Statement (SFAS) No. 52, "Foreign Currency Translation," require the change in the value of the foreign currency asset or liability resulting from a foreign currency transaction to be treated as a gain or loss reported on the income statement.

2.1.1. Accounting for Foreign Currency Transactions with Settlement before Balance Sheet Date

Example 16-1 demonstrates the accounting that would be done by FinnCo assuming that it purchased goods on account from a Mexican supplier who required payment in Mexican pesos, and that it made payment before the balance sheet date. The basic principle is that all transactions are recorded at the spot rate on the date of the transaction. The foreign currency risk on *transactions*, therefore, arises only when the transaction date and the payment date are different.

EXAMPLE 16-1   Accounting for Foreign Currency Transactions with Settlement before Balance Sheet Date

---

FinnCo purchases goods from its Mexican supplier on 1 November 2008; the purchase price is 100,000 Mexican pesos. Credit terms allow payment in 45 days, and FinnCo makes payment of 100,000 pesos on 15 December 2008. FinnCo's functional and presentation currency is the euro. Spot exchange rates between the euro (€) and Mexican peso (Ps.) are as follows:

1 November 2008	Ps. 1 = €0.0684
15 December 2008	Ps. 1 = €0.0703

FinnCo's fiscal year end is 31 December. How will FinnCo account for this foreign currency transaction and what effect will it have on the 2008 financial statements?

Solution. The euro value of the Mexican peso account payable on 1 November 2008 was €6,840 (Ps. 100,000 × €0.0684). FinnCo could have paid for its inventory on 1 November by converting 6,840 euros into 100,000 Mexican pesos. Instead, the company purchases 100,000 Mexican pesos on 15 December 2008, when the value of the peso has increased to €0.0703. Thus, FinnCo pays 7,030 euros to purchase 100,000 Mexican pesos. This results in a loss of 190 euros (€7,030 − €6,840).

Although the cash outflow to acquire the inventory is €7,030, the cost capitalized in the inventory account is only €6,840. This represents the amount that FinnCo could have paid if it had not waited 45 days to settle its account. By deferring payment, and because the Mexican peso increased in value between the transaction date and settlement date, FinnCo has to pay an additional 190 euros. A foreign exchange loss of €190 will be reported in FinnCo's net income in 2008. This is a realized loss in that the company actually spent an additional 190 euros to purchase its inventory. The net effect on the financial statements can be seen as follows:

Balance Sheet				Income Statement		
Assets = Liabilities + Stockholders' Equity				**Revenues and Gains**	**Expenses and Losses**	
Cash	−7,030	Retained			Foreign	
Inventory	6,840	Earnings	−190	←	Exchange Loss	−190

2.1.2. Accounting for Foreign Currency Transactions with Intervening Balance Sheet Dates

Another important issue related to the accounting for foreign currency transactions is what should be done, if anything, if a balance sheet date falls between the initial transaction date and the settlement date. For foreign currency transactions that occur with settlement dates that fall in subsequent accounting periods, both IFRS and U.S. GAAP require adjustments to reflect intervening changes in currency exchanges rates. Foreign currency transaction gains and losses are reported on the income statement creating one of the very few situations in which accounting rules allow, indeed require, companies to include an unrealized gain or loss in income before it has been realized.

Subsequent foreign currency transaction gains and losses are recognized from the balance sheet date through the date the transaction is settled. Adding together foreign currency transaction gains and losses for both accounting periods (transaction initiation to balance sheet date and balance sheet date to transaction settlement) produces an amount equal to the actual realized gain or loss on the foreign currency transaction.

EXAMPLE 16-2   Accounting for Foreign Currency Transaction with Intervening Balance Sheet Date

FinnCo sells goods to a customer in the United Kingdom for £10,000 on 15 November 2008, with payment to be received in British pounds on 15 January 2009. FinnCo's functional and presentation currency is the euro. Spot exchange rates between the euro (€) and British pound (£) are as follows:

15 November 2008	£1 = €1.460
31 December 2008	£1 = €1.480
15 January 2009	£1 = €1.475

FinnCo's fiscal year end is 31 December. How will FinnCo account for this foreign currency transaction, and what effect will it have on the 2008 and 2009 financial statements?

Solution. The euro value of the British pound account receivable at each of the three relevant dates is determined as follows:

Date	€ per £ Exchange Rate	Account Receivable (£10,000)	
		Euro Value	Change in Euro Value
15 Nov 2008	€1.460	€14,600	NA
31 Dec 2008	€1.480	€14,800	+200
15 Jan 2009	€1.475	€14,750	−50

A change in the euro value of the British pound receivable from 15 November to 31 December would be recognized as a foreign currency transaction gain or loss on FinnCo's 2008 income statement. In this case, the increase in the value of the British pound results in a transaction gain of €200 [£10,000 × (€1.48 − €1.46)]. Note that the gain recognized in 2008 income is unrealized and remember that this is one of few situations where companies include an unrealized gain in income.

Any change in the exchange rate between the euro and British pound that occurs from the balance sheet date (31 December 2008) to the transaction settlement date (15 January 2009) likewise will result in a foreign currency transaction gain or loss. In our example, the British pound weakened slightly against the euro during this period, resulting in an exchange rate of €1.475 per British pound on 15 January 2009. The £10,000 account receivable now has a value of €14,750, which is a decrease in value of €50 from 31 December 2008. FinnCo will recognize a foreign currency transaction loss on 15 January 2009 of €50 that will be included in the company's calculation of net income for the first quarter of 2009.

From the transaction date to the settlement date, the British pound has increased in value by €0.015 (€1.475 − €1.46), which generates a realized foreign currency transaction gain of €150. A gain of €200 was recognized in 2008 and a loss of €50 is recognized in 2009. Over the two month period, the net gain recognized in the financial statements is equal to the actual realized gain on the foreign currency transaction.

In Example 16-2, FinnCo's British pound account receivable resulted in a net foreign currency transaction gain because the British pound strengthened (increased) in value between the transaction date and the settlement date. In this case FinnCo has an asset exposure to foreign exchange risk. This asset exposure benefited the company because the foreign currency strengthened. If FinnCo instead had a British pound account payable, a liability exposure would have existed. The euro value of the British pound account payable would have increased as the British pound strengthened and FinnCo would have recognized a foreign currency transaction loss as a result.

Whether a change in exchange rate results in a foreign currency transaction gain or loss depends on (1) the nature of the exposure to foreign exchange risk (asset or liability) and (2) the direction of change in the value of the foreign currency (strengthens or weakens).

		Foreign Currency	
Transaction	**Type of Exposure**	**Strengthens**	**Weakens**
Export sale	Asset (account receivable)	Gain	Loss
Import purchase	Liability (account payable)	Loss	Gain

A foreign currency receivable arising from an export sale creates an asset exposure to foreign exchange risk. If the foreign currency strengthens, the receivable increases in value in terms of the company's functional currency and a foreign currency transaction gain arises. The company will be able to convert the foreign currency when received into more units of functional currency because the foreign currency has strengthened. Conversely, if the foreign currency weakens, the foreign currency receivable loses value in terms of the functional currency and a loss results.

A foreign currency payable resulting from an import purchase creates a liability exposure to foreign exchange risk. If the foreign currency strengthens, the payable increases in value in terms of the company's functional currency and a foreign currency transaction loss arises. The company will have to spend more units of functional currency to be able to settle the foreign currency liability because the foreign currency has strengthened. Conversely, if the foreign currency weakens, the foreign currency payable loses value in terms of the functional currency and a gain exists.

2.2. Analytical Issues

Both IFRS (IAS 21) and U.S. GAAP (FASB 52) require foreign currency transaction gains and losses to be reported in net income (even if they have not yet been realized), but neither standard indicates where on the income statement these gains and losses should be placed. The two most common treatments are (1) as a component of other operating income/expense or (2) as a component of nonoperating income/expense, in some cases as a part of net financing cost. The calculation of operating profit margin is affected by where foreign currency transaction gains or losses are placed on the income statement.

EXAMPLE 16-3 Placement of Foreign Currency Transaction Gains/Losses on the Income Statement—Effect on Operating Profit

Assume that FinnCo had the following income statement information in both 2008 and 2009, excluding a foreign currency transaction gain of €200 in 2008 and a transaction loss of €50 in 2009.

	2008	2009
Revenues	€20,000	€20,000
Cost of goods sold	12,000	12,000
Other operating expenses, net	5,000	5,000
Nonoperating expenses, net	1,200	1,200

FinnCo is deciding between two alternatives for the treatment of foreign currency transaction gains and losses. Alternative 1 calls for the reporting of foreign currency transaction gains/losses as part of "other operating expenses, net." Under Alternative 2, the company would report this information as part of "nonoperating expenses, net."

FinnCo's fiscal year end is 31 December. What impact will the decision of Alternatives 1 and 2 have on the company's gross profit margin, operating profit margin, and net profit margin for 2008? For 2009?

Solution. Remember that a gain would serve to reduce expenses whereas a loss would have the effect of increasing expenses.

2008—Transaction gain of €200

	Alternative 1	Alternative 2
Revenues	€20,000	€20,000
Cost of goods sold	12,000	12,000
Gross profit	8,000	8,000
Other operating expenses, net	4,800 incl. gain	5,000
Operating profit	3,200	3,000
Nonoperating expenses, net	1,200	1,000 incl. gain
Net profit	€2,000	€2,000

Profit margins in 2008 under the two alternatives would be calculated as follows:

	Alternative 1	Alternative 2
Gross profit margin	€8,000/€20,000 = 40.0%	€8,000/€20,000 = 40.0%
Operating profit margin	3,200/20,000 = 16.0%	3,000/20,000 = 15.0%
Net profit margin	2,000/20,000 = 10.0%	2,000/20,000 = 10.0%

2009—Transaction loss of €50

	Alternative 1	Alternative 2
Revenues	€20,000	€20,000
Cost of goods sold	12,000	12,000
Gross profit	8,000	8,000
Other operating expenses, net	5,050 incl. loss	5,000
Operating profit	2,950	3,000
Nonoperating expenses, net	1,200	1,250 incl. loss
Net profit	€1,750	€1,750

Profit margins in 2009 under the two alternatives would be calculated as follows:

	Alternative 1	Alternative 2
Gross profit margin	€8,000 ÷ €20,000 = 40.0%	€8,000 ÷ €20,000 = 40.0%
Operating profit margin	2,950 ÷ 20,000 = 14.75%	3,000 ÷ 20,000 = 15.0%
Net profit margin	1,750 ÷ 20,000 = 8.75%	1,750 ÷ 20,000 = 8.75%

Gross profit and net profit are unaffected, but operating profit differs under the two alternatives. In 2008, the operating profit margin is larger under Alternative 1, which includes the transaction gain as part of "other operating expenses, net." In 2009, Alternative 1 results in a smaller operating profit margin than Alternative 2. Alternative 2 has the same operating profit margin in both periods. Because exchange rates do not fluctuate by the same amount or in the same direction from one accounting period to the next, Alternative 1 will cause greater volatility in operating profit and operating profit margin over time.

Because accounting standards do not provide guidance on the placement of foreign currency transaction gains and losses on the income statement, companies are free to choose among the alternatives. Two companies in the same industry could choose different alternatives, which would distort the direct comparison of operating profit and operating profit margins between those companies.

A second issue that should be of interest to analysts relates to the fact that unrealized foreign currency transaction gains and losses are included in net income when the balance sheet date falls between the transaction and settlement dates. The implicit assumption underlying this accounting requirement is that the unrealized gain or loss as of the balance sheet date is reflective of the ultimate net gain or loss to the company. In reality, though, the ultimate net gain or loss may vary dramatically because of the possibility for changes in trend and volatility of currency prices.

This effect was seen in the previous hypothetical Example 16-2 with FinnCo. Using actual currency exchange rate data shows that the real-world effect can also be quite dramatic. Assume that a French company purchased goods from a Canadian supplier on 1 December 2006, with payment of 100,000 Canadian dollars (C$) to be made on 15 May 2007. Actual exchange rates between the Canadian dollar and euro during the period 1 December 2006 and 15 May 2007, the euro value of the Canadian dollar account payable, and foreign currency transaction gain or loss are shown below:

	€ per C$	€ Value	Account Payable (C$100,000)	Change in € Value (Gain/Loss)
01 Dec 06	0.6656	66,560	N/A	
31 Dec 06	0.6504	65,040	1,520	gain
31 Mar 07	0.6490	64,900	140	gain
15 May 07	0.6658	66,580	1,680	loss

As the Canadian dollar weakened against the euro in late 2006 and early 2007, the French company would have recorded a foreign currency transaction gain of €1,520 in the fourth quarter of 2006 and an additional transaction gain of €140 in the first quarter of 2007. The Canadian dollar reversed course and strengthened against the euro in the second quarter of 2007, resulting in a transaction loss of €1,680. At the time payment is made on 15 May 2007, the French company realizes a net foreign currency transaction loss of €20 (€66,580 – €66,560). In this case, the transaction gains reported in net income in 2006 and the first quarter of 2007 did not accurately reflect the loss that ultimately was realized.

2.3. Disclosures Related to Foreign Currency Transaction Gains and Losses

Because accounting rules allow companies to choose where they present foreign currency transaction gains and losses on the income statement it is useful for companies to disclose both the amount of transaction gain or loss that is included in income and the presentation alternative they have selected. IAS 21 requires disclosure of "the amount of exchange differences recognized in profit or loss" and SFAS No. 52 requires disclosure of "the aggregate transaction gain or loss included in determining net income for the period," but neither standard specifically requires disclosure of the line item in which these gains and losses are located.

Exhibit 16-1 provides disclosures from BASF AG's 2006 annual report that the German company made related to foreign currency transaction gains and losses. Exhibit 16-2 presents similar disclosures found in the Netherlands-based Heineken NV's 2006 annual report. Both companies use IFRS to prepare their consolidated financial statements.

EXHIBIT 16-1   Excerpts from BASF AG's 2006 Annual Report Related to Foreign Currency Transactions: Consolidated Statements of Income

Million €	Explanation in Notes	2006	2005
Sales	4	52,609.7	42,744.9
Cost of sales		37,697.5	29,566.8
Gross profit on sales		**14,912.2**	**13,178.1**
Selling expenses		4,995.5	4,329.9
General and administrative expenses		893.2	780.1
Research and development expenses		1,276.6	1,063.7
Other operating income	5	934.1	600.2
Other operating expenses	6	1,931.1	1,775.1
Income from operations		**6,749.9**	**5,829.5**
Income from companies accounted for using the equity method		35.0	5.6
Other income from participations		36.7	342.4
Interest result		(371.9)	(170.0)
Other financial result		77.0	(81.9)
Financial result	7	**(223.2)**	**96.1**

Income before taxes and minority interests		**6,526.7**	**5,925.6**
Income taxes	8	3,060.6	2,758.1
Income before minority interests		**3,466.1**	**3,167.5**
Minority interests	9	250.9	160.8
Net income		**3,215.2**	**3,006.7**

Notes

1. Summary of Accounting Policies

Foreign currency transactions: The cost of assets acquired in foreign currencies and revenues from sales in foreign currencies are recorded at the exchange rate at the date of the transaction. Foreign currency receivables and liabilities are valued at the exchange rates on the balance sheet date.

5. Other Operating Income

Million €	2006	2005
Reversal and adjustment of provisions	275.2	118.4
Revenue from miscellaneous revenue-generating activities	62.3	85.3
Gains from foreign currency transactions	119.7	43.3
Gains from the translation of financial statements in foreign currencies	10.8	57.3
Gains from disposal of property, plant and equipment and divestitures	127.8	107.4
Gains on the reversal of allowance for doubtful receivables	89.0	92.1
Other	249.3	96.4
	934.1	600.2

Gains from foreign currency transactions represent gains arising from foreign currency positions and foreign currency derivatives as well as from the valuation of receivables and liabilities denominated in foreign currencies at the spot rate at the balance sheet date.

6. Other Operating Expenses

Million €	2006	2005
Integration and restructuring measures	399.4	446.5
Environmental protection and safety measures, costs of demolition and planning costs related to the preparation of capital expenditure projects not subject to mandatory capitalization	180.5	158.3
Amortization of intangible assets and depreciation of property, plant and equipment	430.3	204.6
Costs from miscellaneous revenue-generating activities	85.1	84.7
Losses from foreign currency transactions	48.4	189.5
Losses from the translation of financial statements in foreign currencies	51.6	23
Losses from the disposal of property, plant, and equipment	21.8	15.5
Oil and gas exploration expenses	167.3	172.9

(Continued)

EXHIBIT 16-1   *(Continued)*

Million €	2006	2005
Expenses from additions to allowances for doubtful receivables	90.4	102.9
Other	456.3	377.2
	1,931.1	1,775.1

Losses from foreign currency transactions include losses from foreign currency positions and derivatives and the valuation of receivables and liabilities in foreign currencies at the closing rate on the balance sheet date.

BASF's income statement in Exhibit 16-1 does not include a separate line item for foreign currency gains and losses. From Note 5 in Exhibit 16-1, an analyst can determine that BASF has chosen to include "Gains from foreign currency transactions" in other operating income. Of the total amount of €934.1 million reported as other operating income in 2006, €119.7 million is attributable to foreign currency transaction gains. It is not possible to determine from BASF's financial statements whether these gains were realized in 2006 or not. And any unrealized gain reported in 2006 income might or might not be realized in 2007.

Note 6 in Exhibit 16-1 indicates that "Losses from foreign currency transactions" in 2006 were €48.4 million, making up 2.5 percent of other operating expenses. Combining foreign currency transaction gains and losses results in a net gain of €71.3 million, which comprised 1.06 percent of BASF's income from operations.

In Exhibit 16-2, Heineken's Note 2, Basis of Preparation, part (c) explicitly states that the euro is the company's functional currency. Note 3(b)(*i*) indicates that monetary assets and liabilities denominated in foreign currencies at the balance sheet are translated to the functional currency and foreign currency differences arising on the translation (i.e., translation gains and losses) are recognized on the income statement. Note 3(o) discloses that foreign currency gains are included in other finance income and foreign currency losses are included in other finance expense. These two amounts are combined into a part of the line item reported on the income statement as other net finance income. Note 11, Other Net Finance Income, shows that a net translation loss of €16 million existed in 2006 and a net gain of €19 million arose in 2005. The net foreign currency transaction gain in 2005 amounted to 1.63 percent of Heineken's profit before income tax that year, while the net translation loss in 2006 represented 0.94 percent of the company's profit before income tax in that year.

In applying U.S. GAAP's SFAS No. 52 to account for its foreign currency transactions, Yahoo! Inc. reported the following in its quantitative and qualitative disclosures about market risk in its 2006 annual report:

In the year ended December 31, 2006, we recorded net foreign currency transaction gains, realized and unrealized, of approximately $5 million, net losses of $8 million and net gains of $6 million in 2005 and 2004, respectively, which were recorded in other income, net on the consolidated statements of income.

Yahoo! explicitly acknowledges that both realized and unrealized foreign currency transaction gains and losses are reflected in income, specifically as a part of nonoperating activities. The net foreign currency transaction gain in 2006 of $5 million represented only 0.6 percent of the company's net income for the year.

EXHIBIT 16-2   Excerpts from Heineken NV's 2006 Annual Report Related to Foreign Currency Transactions: Consolidated Income Statement (for the year ended 31 December 2006)

(€ millions)	Note	2006	2005
Revenue	5	**11,829**	**10,796**
Other income	7	**379**	**63**
Raw materials, consumables and services	8	7,376	6,657
Personnel expenses	9	2,241	2,180
Amortisation, depreciation and impairments	10	786	768
Total expenses		**10,403**	**9,605**
Results from operating activities		**1,805**	**1,254**
Interest income		52	60
Interest expenses		(185)	(199)
Other net finance income	11	11	25
Net finance expenses		**(122)**	**(114)**
Share of profit of associates		27	29
Profit before income tax		**1,710**	**1,169**
Income tax expense	12	(365)	(300)
Profit		**1,345**	**869**
Attributable to:			
Equity holders of the Company (net profit)		1,211	761
Minority interest		134	108
Profit		**1,345**	**869**

Notes

2. Basis of Preparation

   (c) Functional and Presentation Currency

These consolidated financial statements are presented in euros, which is the company's functional currency. All financial information presented in euros has been rounded to the nearest million.

3. Significant Accounting Policies

   (b) Foreign Currency
   (i) Foreign Currency Transactions

Transactions in foreign currencies are translated to the respective functional currencies of Heineken entities at the exchange rates at the dates of the transactions. Monetary assets and liabilities denominated in foreign currencies at the balance sheet date are retranslated to the functional currency at the exchange rate at that date. . . . Foreign currency differences arising on retranslation are recognized in the income statement, except for differences arising on the retranslation of available-for-sale (equity) investments.[2]

(Continued)

---

[2] Note that this excerpt uses *retranslation* in the same way that *translation* is used throughout the rest of this chapter.

EXHIBIT 16-2   (*Continued*)

(o) Interest Income, Interest Expenses, and Other Net Finance Expenses

Other finance income comprises dividend income, gains on the disposal of available-for-sale financial assets, changes in the fair value of financial assets at fair value through profit or loss, foreign currency gains, and gains on hedging instruments that are recognized in the income statement. Dividend income is recognised on the date that Heineken's right to receive payment is established, which in the case of quoted securities is the ex-dividend date.

Other finance expenses comprise unwinding of the discount on provisions, changes in the fair value of financial assets at fair value through profit or loss, foreign currency losses, impairment losses recognized on financial assets, and losses on hedging instruments that are recognised in the income statement.

11. Other Net Finance Income

(€ millions)	2006	2005
Impairment investments	—	(6)
Dividend income	13	13
Exchange rate differences	(16)	19
Other	14	(1)
	11	**25**

Companies often neglect to disclose either the location or the amount of foreign currency transaction gains and losses, presumably because the amounts involved are immaterial. The disclosure made by Altria Group, Inc., in its 2006 annual report is indicative of this approach. Note 2, Summary of Significant Accounting Policies, contains a subheading, Foreign Currency Translation, in which the company states:

Transaction gains and losses are recorded in the consolidated statements of earnings and were not significant for any of the periods presented.

There are several reasons why the amount of transaction gains and losses can be immaterial for a company:

- The company engages in a limited number of foreign currency transactions that involve relatively small amounts of foreign currency.
- The exchange rates between the company's functional currency and the foreign currencies in which it has transactions tend to be relatively stable.
- Gains on some foreign currency transactions are naturally offset by losses on other transactions, such that the net gain or loss is immaterial.

  For example, if a U.S. company sells goods to a customer in Canada with payment in Canadian dollars to be received in 90 days and at the same time purchases goods from a supplier in Canada with payment to be made in Canadian dollars in 90 days, any loss that arises on the Canadian dollar receivable due to a weakening in the value of the Canadian dollar will be exactly offset by a gain of equal amount on the Canadian dollar payable.

- The company engages in foreign currency hedging activities to offset the foreign exchange gains and losses that arise from foreign currency transactions. Hedging foreign exchange risk is a common practice for many companies engaged in foreign currency transactions.

The two most common types of hedging instruments used to minimize foreign exchange risk are foreign currency forward contracts and foreign currency options. Corning, Inc., describes its foreign exchange risk management approach in its 2006 annual report in Note 15, Hedging Activities. An excerpt from that note follows:

> We operate and conduct business in many foreign countries and as a result are exposed to movements in foreign currency exchange rates. Our exposure to exchange rate effects includes:
>
> - Exchange rate movements on financial instruments and transactions denominated in foreign currencies that impact earnings, and
>
> - Exchange rate movements upon translation of net assets in foreign subsidiaries for which the functional currency is not the U.S. dollar that impact our net equity.[3]
>
> Our most significant foreign currency exposures related to Japan, Korea, Taiwan, and western European countries. We selectively enter into foreign exchange forward and option contracts with durations generally 15 months or less to hedge our exposure to exchange rate risk on foreign source income and purchases. The hedges are scheduled to mature coincident with the timing of the underlying foreign currency commitments and transactions. The objective of these contracts is to neutralize the impact of exchange rate movements on our operating results.
>
> We engage in foreign currency hedging activities to reduce the risk that changes in exchange rates will adversely affect the eventual net cash flows resulting from the sale of products to foreign customers and purchases from foreign suppliers. The hedge contracts reduce the exposure to fluctuations in exchange rate movements because the gains and loses associated with foreign currency balances and transactions are generally offset with gains and losses of the hedge contracts. Because the impact of movements in foreign exchange rates on the value of hedge contracts offsets the related impact on the underlying items being hedged, these financial instruments help alleviate the risk that might otherwise result from currency exchange rate fluctuations.

Corning goes on to indicate that "changes in the fair value of undesignated hedges are recorded in current period earnings in the other income, net component, *along with the foreign currency gains and losses arising from the underlying monetary assets or liabilities in the consolidated statement of operations*" (p. 171, emphasis added). Amounts, however, are not disclosed, presumably because they are immaterial.

3. TRANSLATION OF FOREIGN CURRENCY FINANCIAL STATEMENTS

Many companies have operations in foreign countries. Most operations located in foreign countries keep their accounting records and prepare financial statements in the local currency. For example, the U.S. subsidiary of German automaker BMW AG keeps its books in U.S. dollars.

---

[3]The translation of currency for foreign subsidiaries will be covered in the next section.

IFRS and U.S. GAAP require parent companies to prepare consolidated financial statements in which the assets, liabilities, revenues, and expenses of both domestic and foreign subsidiaries are added to those of the parent company. To prepare worldwide consolidated statements, parent companies must translate the foreign currency financial statements of their foreign subsidiaries into the parent company's presentation currency. BMW AG, for example, must translate the U.S. dollar financial statements of its U.S. subsidiary and the South African rand financial statements of its South African subsidiary into euros to consolidate these foreign operations.

The IASB (in IAS 21) and FASB (in SFAS No. 52) have established very similar rules for the translation of foreign currency financial statements. To fully understand the results from applying these rules, however, several conceptual issues must first be examined.

3.1. Translation Conceptual Issues

In translating foreign currency financial statements into the parent company's presentation currency, two questions must be addressed:

1. What is the appropriate exchange rate to be used in translating each financial statement item?
2. How should the translation adjustment that inherently arises from the translation process be reflected in the consolidated financial statements? In other words, how is the balance sheet brought back into balance?

These issues and the basic concepts underlying the translation of financial statements are demonstrated through the following example.

Spanco is a hypothetical Spanish-based company that uses the euro as its presentation currency. Spanco establishes a wholly owned subsidiary, Amerco, in the United States on 31 December 2008 by investing €10,000 when the exchange rate between the euro and the U.S. dollar is €1 = US$1. The equity investment of €10,000 is physically converted into US$10,000 to begin operations. In addition, Amerco borrows US$5,000 from local banks on 31 December 2008. Amerco purchases inventory that costs US$12,000 on 31 December 2008, and retains US$3,000 in cash. Amerco's balance sheet at 31 December 2008 appears as follows:

Amerco Balance Sheet, 31 December 2008 (US$)

Cash	$3,000	Notes payable	$5,000
Inventory	12,000	Common stock	10,000
Total	$15,000	Total	$15,000

To prepare a consolidated balance sheet in euros at 31 December 2008, Spanco must translate all of the U.S. dollar balances on Amerco's balance sheet at the €1 = US$1 exchange rate. The translation worksheet at 31 December 2008 is as follows:

Translation Worksheet for Amerco, 31 December 2008

	USD	Exchange Rate	EUR
Cash	$3,000	€1.00	€3,000
Inventory	12,000	€1.00	12,000
Total	$15,000		€15,000
Notes payable	5,000	€1.00	5,000
Common stock	10,000	€1.00	10,000
Total	$15,000		€15,000

By translating each U.S. dollar balance at the same exchange rate (€1.00), Amerco's translated balance sheet in euros reflects an equal amount of total assets and total liabilities plus equity and remains in balance.

During the first quarter of 2009, Amerco engages in no transactions. However, during that period the U.S. dollar weakens against the euro such that the exchange rate at 31 March 2009 is €0.80 = US$1.

To prepare a consolidated balance sheet at the end of the first quarter 2009, Spanco now must choose between the current exchange rate of €0.80 and the historical exchange rate of €1.00 to translate Amerco's balance sheet amounts into euros. The original investment made by Spanco of €10,000 is a historical fact, so the company wants to translate Amerco's common stock in such a way that it continues to reflect this amount. This is achieved by translating common stock of US$10,000 into euros using the historical exchange rate of €1 = US$1.

Two different approaches for translating the foreign subsidiary's assets and liabilities are:

1. All assets and liabilities are translated at the **current exchange rate** (the spot exchange rate on the balance sheet date), or
2. Only **monetary assets and liabilities** are translated at the current exchange rate; **nonmonetary assets and liabilities** are translated at **historical exchange rates** (the exchange rates that existed when the assets and liabilities were acquired). Monetary items are cash and receivables (payables) that are to be received (paid) in a fixed number of currency units. Nonmonetary assets include inventory, fixed assets, and intangibles, and nonmonetary liabilities include deferred revenue.

These two different approaches are demonstrated and the results analyzed in turn.

3.1.1. All Assets and Liabilities Are Translated at the Current Exchange Rate
The translation worksheet at 31 March 2009 in which all assets and liabilities are translated at the current exchange rate (€0.80) is as follows:

Translation Worksheet for Amerco, 31 March 2009

	US$	Exchange Rate	Euro	Change in Euro Value since 31 Dec. 2008
Cash	$3,000	€0.80 C	€2,400	−€600
Inventory	12,000	€0.80 C	9,600	−2,400
Total	$15,000		€12,000	−€3,000
Notes payable	5,000	€0.80 C	4,000	−1,000
Common stock	10,000	€1.00 H	10,000	0
Subtotal	$15,000		14,000	−1,000
Translation adjustment			(2,000)	−2,000
Total			€12,000	−€3,000

C, current exchange rate; H, historical exchange rate.

By translating all assets at the lower current exchange rate, total assets are written down from 31 December 2008 to 31 March 2009 in terms of their euro value by €3,000. Liabilities are written down by €1,000. To keep the euro translated balance sheet in balance, a *negative* translation adjustment of €2,000 is created and included in stockholders' equity on the consolidated balance sheet.

Those foreign currency balance sheet accounts that are translated using the current exchange rate are revalued in terms of the parent's functional currency. This process is very similar to the revaluation of foreign currency receivables and payables related to foreign currency transactions. The net translation adjustment that results from translating individual assets and liabilities at the current exchange rate can be viewed as the *net* foreign currency translation gain or loss caused by a change in the exchange rate:

(€600)	Loss on cash
(€2,400)	Loss on inventory
€1,000	Gain on notes payable
(€2,000)	Net translation loss

The negative translation adjustment (net translation loss) does not result in a cash outflow of €2,000 for Spanco and thus is unrealized. The loss could be realized, however, if Spanco were to sell Amerco at its book value of US$10,000. The proceeds from the sale would be converted into euros at €0.80 per US$1, resulting in a cash inflow of €8,000. Because Spanco originally invested €10,000 in its U.S. operation, a *realized* loss of €2,000 would result.

The second conceptual issue related to the translation of foreign currency financial statements is whether the unrealized net translation loss should be included in the determination of consolidated net income currently or should be deferred in the stockholders' equity section of the consolidated balance sheet until the loss is realized through sale of the foreign subsidiary. There is some debate as to which of these two treatments is most appropriate. This issue is discussed in more detail after considering the second approach for translating assets and liabilities.

3.1.2. Only Monetary Assets and Monetary Liabilities Are Translated at the Current Exchange Rate

Now assume only monetary assets and monetary liabilities are translated at the current exchange rate. The translation worksheet at 31 March 2009 in which only monetary assets and liabilities are translated at the current exchange rate (€0.80) is as follows:

Translation Worksheet for Amerco, 31 March 2009

	US$	Exchange Rate	Euro	Change in Euro Value since 31 Dec. 2008
Cash	$3,000	€0.80 C	€2,400	−€600
Inventory	12,000	€1.00 H	12,000	0
Total	$15,000		€14,400	−€600
Notes payable	5,000	€0.80 C	4,000	−1,000
Common stock	10,000	€1.00 H	10,000	0
Subtotal	$15,000		14,000	−1,000
Translation adjustment			400	400
Total			€14,400	−€600

C, current exchange rate; H, historical exchange rate.

Using this approach, cash is written down by €600 but inventory continues to be carried at its euro historical cost of €12,000. Notes payable is written down by €1,000. To keep the balance sheet in balance, a positive translation adjustment of €400 must be included in stockholders' equity. The translation adjustment reflects the *net* translation gain or loss related to monetary items only:

(€600)	Loss on cash
€1,000	Gain on notes payable
€400	Net translation gain

The positive translation adjustment (net translation gain) also is *unrealized*. However, the gain could be *realized* if:

1. The subsidiary uses its cash (US$3,000) to pay as much of its liabilities as possible, and
2. The parent sends enough euros to the subsidiary to pay its remaining liabilities (US$5,000 − US$3,000 = US$2,000). At 31 December 2008, at the €1.00 per US$1 exchange rate, Spanco would have sent €2,000 to Amerco to pay liabilities of US$2,000. At 31 March 2009, given the €0.80 per US$1 exchange rate, the parent needs to send only €1,600 to pay US$2,000 of liabilities. As a result, Spanco would enjoy a foreign exchange gain of €400.

The second conceptual issue again arises under this approach. Should the unrealized foreign exchange gain be recognized in current period net income or deferred on the balance sheet as a separate component of stockholders' equity? The answer to this question, as provided by IFRS and U.S. GAAP, is described in section 3.2, Translation Rules.

3.1.3. Balance Sheet Exposure

Those assets and liabilities translated at the *current* exchange rate are revalued from balance sheet to balance sheet in terms of the parent company's presentation currency. These items are said to be *exposed* to translation adjustment. Balance sheet items translated at *historical* exchange rates do not change in parent currency value and therefore are not exposed to translation adjustment. Exposure to translation adjustment is referred to as balance sheet translation, or accounting exposure.

A foreign operation will have a **net asset balance sheet exposure** when assets translated at the current exchange rate are greater in amount than liabilities translated at the current exchange rate. A **net liability balance sheet exposure** exists when liabilities translated at the current exchange rate are greater than assets translated at the current exchange rate. Another way to think about the issue is to realize that there is a net asset balance sheet exposure when exposed assets are greater in amount than exposed liabilities and a net liability balance sheet exposure when exposed liabilities are greater in amount than exposed assets. The sign (positive or negative) of the current period's translation adjustment is a function of two factors: (1) the nature of the balance sheet exposure (asset or liability) and (2) the direction of change in the exchange rate (strengthens or weakens). The relationship between exchange rate fluctuations, balance sheet exposure, and the current period's translation adjustment can be summarized as follows:

	Foreign Currency (FC)	
Balance Sheet Exposure	**Strengthens**	**Weakens**
Net asset	Positive	Negative
	Translation adjustment	Translation adjustment
Net liability	Negative	Positive
	Translation adjustment	Translation adjustment

These relationships are the same as those summarized in section 2.2 with respect to foreign currency transaction gains and losses. In reference to the example in section 3.1.2, for instance, exposed assets ($3,000) were less than exposed liabilities ($5,000) implying that there was a net liability exposure. Further the foreign currency (US$) weakened, resulting in a positive translation adjustment.

The combination of balance sheet exposure and direction of exchange rate change determine whether the current period's translation adjustment will be positive or negative. After the initial period of operations, a cumulative translation adjustment is required to keep the translated balance sheet in balance. The cumulative translation adjustment will be the sum of the translation adjustments that arise over successive accounting periods. For example, assume that Spanco translates all of Amerco's assets and liabilities using the current exchange rate (a net asset balance sheet exposure exists), which due to a weakening U.S. dollar in the first quarter of 2009 resulted in a negative translation adjustment at 31 March 2009 of €2,000 (as shown in section 3.1.1). Assume further that in the second quarter of 2009, the U.S. dollar strengthens against the euro and there still is a net asset balance sheet exposure, which results in a *positive* translation adjustment of €500 for that quarter. Although the current period translation adjustment for the second quarter of 2009 is positive, the cumulative translation adjustment at 30 June 2009 still will be negative, but the amount now will be only €1,500.

3.2. Translation Methods

The two approaches to translating foreign currency financial statements described in the previous section are known as (1) the **current rate method** (all assets and liabilities are translated at the current exchange rate), and (2) the **monetary/nonmonetary method** (only monetary assets and liabilities are translated at the current exchange rate). A variation of the monetary/nonmonetary method requires not only monetary assets and liabilities but also nonmonetary assets and liabilities that are measured at their current value on the balance sheet date to be translated at the current exchange rate. This variation of the monetary/nonmonetary method sometimes is referred to as the **temporal method**. The basic idea underlying the temporal method is that assets and liabilities should be translated in such a way that the measurement basis (either current value or historical cost) in the foreign currency is preserved after translating to the parent's presentation currency. To achieve this objective, assets and liabilities carried on the foreign currency balance sheet at a current value should be translated at the current exchange rate and assets and liabilities carried on the foreign currency balance sheet at historical costs should be translated at historical exchange rates. Although neither the IASB nor the FASB specifically refer to translation methods by name, the procedures required by IFRS and U.S. GAAP in translating foreign currency financial statements essentially require the use of either the current rate or the temporal method.

Which method is appropriate for an individual foreign entity depends on that entity's functional currency. As noted earlier, the functional currency is the currency of the primary economic environment in which an entity operates. A foreign entity's functional currency can be either the parent's presentation currency or another currency, typically the currency of the country in which the foreign entity is located. Exhibit 16-3 lists the factors that IAS 21 indicates should be considered in determining a foreign entity's functional currency. Although not identical, SFAS No. 52 provides similar indicators for determining a foreign entity's functional currency.

When the functional currency indicators listed in Exhibit 16-3 are mixed and the functional currency is not obvious, IAS 21 indicates that management should use its best

EXHIBIT 16-3   Factors Considered in Determining the Functional Currency

In accordance with IAS 21, The Effects of Changes in Foreign Exchange Rates, the following factors should be considered in determining an entity's functional currency:

1. The currency that influences sales prices for goods and services.

2. The currency of the country whose competitive forces and regulations mainly determine the sales price of its goods and services.

3. The currency that mainly influences labor, material, and other costs of providing goods and services.

4. The currency in which funds from financing activities are generated.

5. The currency in which receipts from operating activities are usually retained.

Additional factors to consider in determining whether the foreign entity's functional currency is the same as the parent's are:

6. Whether the activities of the foreign operation are an extension of the parent's or are carried out with a significant amount of autonomy.

7. Whether transactions with the parent are a large or a small proportion of the foreign entity's activities.

8. Whether cash flows generated by the foreign operation directly affect the cash flow of the parent and are available to be remitted to the parent.

9. Whether operating cash flows generated by the foreign operation are sufficient to service existing and normally expected debt or whether the foreign entity will need funds from the parent to service its debt.

---

judgment in determining the functional currency. However, in this case, indicators 1 and 2 should be given priority over indicators 3 through 9.

The following three steps outline the functional currency approach required by both IFRS and U.S. GAAP in translating foreign currency financial statements into the parent's presentation currency:

1. Identify the functional currency of the foreign entity.
2. Translate foreign currency balances into the foreign entity's functional currency.
3. Use the current exchange rate to translate the foreign entity's functional currency balances into the parent's presentation currency, if they are different.

To illustrate how this approach is applied, consider a U.S. parent company with a Mexican subsidiary that keeps its accounting records in Mexican pesos. Assume that the vast majority of the subsidiary's transactions are carried out in Mexican pesos but it also has an account payable in Guatemalan quetzals. In applying the three steps, the U.S. parent company first determines that the Mexican peso is the functional currency of the Mexican subsidiary. Second, the Mexican subsidiary translates its foreign currency balances, that is, the Guatemalan quetzal account payable, into Mexican pesos using the current exchange rate. In step 3, the Mexican peso financial statements (including the translated account payable) are translated into U.S. dollars using the current rate method.

Now assume that the primary operating currency of the Mexican subsidiary is the U.S. dollar, which thus is identified as the Mexican subsidiary's functional currency. In that case, in addition to the Guatemalan quetzal account payable, all of the subsidiary's accounts that are denominated in Mexican pesos also are considered to be foreign currency balances (because they are not denominated in the subsidiary's functional currency, which is the U.S. dollar). Along with the Guatemalan quetzal balance, each of the Mexican peso balances must be translated into U.S. dollars as if the subsidiary kept its books in U.S. dollars. Assets and liabilities carried at current value in Mexican pesos are translated into U.S. dollars using the current exchange rate, and assets and liabilities carried at historical cost in Mexican pesos are translated into U.S. dollars using historical exchange rates. After completing this step, the Mexican subsidiary's financial statements are stated in terms of U.S. dollars, which is both the subsidiary's functional currency and the parent's presentation currency. As a result, there is no need to apply step 3.

The procedures to be followed in applying the functional currency approach embodied in IFRS and U.S. GAAP are described in more detail in the following two sections.

3.2.1. Foreign Currency Is the Functional Currency

In most cases, a foreign entity will primarily operate in the currency of the country where it is located, which will be different from the currency in which the parent company presents its financial statements. For example, the Japanese subsidiary of a French parent company is likely to have the Japanese yen as its functional currency, whereas the French parent company must prepare consolidated financial statements in euros. When a foreign entity has a functional currency that is different from the parent's presentation currency, the foreign entity's foreign currency financial statements are translated into the parent's presentation currency using the following procedures:

1. All assets and liabilities are translated at the current exchange rate at the balance sheet date.
2. Stockholders' equity accounts are translated at historical exchange rates.
3. Revenues and expenses are translated at the exchange rate that existed when the transactions took place. For practical reasons, a rate that approximates the exchange rates at the dates of the transactions, such as an average exchange rate, may be used.

These procedures essentially describe the current rate method.

Under both IAS 21 and SFAS No. 52, when the current rate method is used, the cumulative translation adjustment needed to keep the translated balance sheet in balance is reported as a separate component of stockholders' equity.

The basic concept underlying the current rate method is that the entire investment in a foreign entity is exposed to translation gain or loss. Therefore, all assets and all liabilities must be revalued at each successive balance sheet date. But the net translation gain or loss that results from this procedure is unrealized and will be realized only when the entity is sold. In the meantime, the unrealized translation gain or loss that accumulates over time is deferred on the balance sheet as a separate component of stockholders' equity. When a specific foreign entity is sold, the cumulative translation adjustment related to that entity is reported as a realized gain or loss in net income.

The current rate method results in a net asset balance sheet exposure (except in the rare case in which an entity has negative stockholders' equity):

Items Translated at Current Exchange Rate

Total Assets > Total Liabilities   ➔   Net Asset Balance Sheet Exposure

When the foreign currency increases in value (strengthens), application of the current rate method results in an increase in the positive cumulative translation adjustment (or a decrease in the negative cumulative translation adjustment) reflected in stockholders' equity. When the foreign currency decreases in value (weakens), the current rate method results in a decrease in the positive cumulative translation adjustment (or increase in the negative cumulative translation adjustment) in stockholders' equity.

3.2.2. Parent's Presentation Currency Is the Functional Currency

In some cases, a foreign entity might have the parent's presentation currency as its functional currency. For example, a German-based manufacturer might have a 100 percent–owned distribution subsidiary in Switzerland that primarily uses the euro in its day-to-day operations. But as a Swiss company, the subsidiary is required to record its transactions and keep its books in Swiss francs. In that situation, the subsidiary's Swiss franc financial statements must be translated into euros as if the subsidiary's transactions had originally been recorded in euros. SFAS No. 52 refers to this process as *remeasurement*. IAS 21 does not refer to this process as remeasurement, but instead describes this situation as "reporting foreign currency transactions in the functional currency." To achieve the objective of translating to the parent's presentation currency as if the subsidiary's transactions had been recorded in that currency, the following procedures are used:

1. a. Monetary assets and liabilities are translated at the current exchange rate.
    b. Nonmonetary assets and liabilities measured at historical cost are translated at historical exchange rates.
    c. Nonmonetary assets and liabilities measured at current value are translated at the exchange rate at the date when the current value was determined.
2. Stockholders' equity accounts are translated at historical exchange rates.
3. a. Revenues and expenses, other than those expenses related to nonmonetary assets (as explained in 3.b. below), are translated at the exchange rate that existed when the transactions took place (for practical reasons, average rates may be used).
    b. Expenses related to nonmonetary assets, such as cost of goods sold (inventory), depreciation (fixed assets), and amortization (intangible assets), are translated at the exchange rates used to translate the related assets.

These procedures essentially describe the temporal method.

Under the temporal method, companies must keep record of the exchange rates that exist when nonmonetary assets (inventory, prepaid expenses, fixed assets, and intangible assets) are acquired, because these assets (normally measured at historical cost) are translated at historical exchange rates. Keeping track of the historical exchange rates for these assets is not necessary under the current rate method. Translating these assets (and their related expenses) at historical exchange rates complicates application of the temporal method.

The historical exchange rates used to translate inventory (and cost of goods sold) under the temporal method will differ depending on the cost flow assumption—first in, first out (FIFO); last in, first out (LIFO); or average cost—used to account for inventory. Ending inventory reported on the balance sheet is translated at the exchange rate that existed when the inventory assumed to still be on hand at the balance sheet date (using FIFO or LIFO) was acquired. If FIFO is used, ending inventory is assumed to be composed of the most recently acquired items and thus inventory will be translated at relatively recent exchange rates. If LIFO is used, ending inventory is assumed to consist of older items and thus inventory will be translated at older exchange rates. The weighted average exchange rate for the year is used when inventory is carried at weighted average cost. Similarly, cost of goods sold is translated using the exchange rates that existed when the inventory items assumed to have been sold during the year (using FIFO or LIFO) were acquired. If weighted average cost is used to account for inventory, cost of goods sold will be translated at the weighted average exchange rate for the year.

Under both IAS 21 and SFAS No. 52, when the temporal method is used, the translation adjustment needed to keep the translated balance sheet in balance is reported as a gain or loss in net income. SFAS No. 52 refers to these as *remeasurement* gains and losses.

The basic assumption supporting the recognition of a translation gain or loss in income when the temporal method is used is that if the foreign entity primarily uses the parent's currency in its day-to-day operations, then the foreign entity's monetary items that are denominated in a foreign currency generate translation gains and losses that will be realized in the near future and thus should be reflected in current net income.

The temporal method generates either a net asset or a net liability balance sheet exposure depending on whether assets translated at the current exchange rate, that is, monetary assets and nonmonetary assets measured on the balance sheet date at current value (exposed assets), are greater than or less than liabilities translated at the current exchange rate, that is, monetary liabilities and nonmonetary liabilities measured on the balance sheet date at current value (exposed liabilities):

Items Translated at Current Exchange Rate

Exposed Assets > Exposed Liabilities   ➡   Net Asset Balance Sheet Exposure

Exposed Assets < Exposed Liabilities   ➡   Net Liability Balance Sheet Exposure

Most liabilities are monetary liabilities. Only cash and receivables are monetary assets, and nonmonetary assets generally are measured at their historical cost. As a result, liabilities translated at the current exchange rate (exposed liabilities) often exceed assets translated at the current exchange rate (exposed assets), which results in a net liability balance sheet exposure when the temporal method is applied.

3.2.3. Translation of Retained Earnings

Stockholders' equity accounts are translated at historical exchange rates under both the current rate and the temporal methods. This creates somewhat of a problem in translating retained earnings (R/E), which is the accumulation of previous years' income less dividends over the life of the company. At the end of the first year of operations, foreign currency (FC) retained earnings are translated into the parent's currency (PC) as follows:

Net income in FC	[Translated according to the method used to translate the income statement]	=	Net income in PC
− Dividends in FC	× Exchange rate when dividends declared	=	− Dividends in PC
R/E in FC			R/E in PC

Retained earnings in parent currency at the end of the first year becomes the beginning retained earnings in parent currency for the second year and the translated retained earnings in the second year (and subsequent years) is then calculated in the following manner:

Beginning R/E in FC	[From last year's translation]	→	Beginning R/E in PC
+ Net income in FC	[Translated according to the method used to translate the income statement]	=	+ Net income in PC
− Dividends in FC	× Exchange rate when dividends declared	=	− Dividends in PC
Ending R/E in FC			Ending R/E in PC

Exhibit 16-4 summarizes the translation rules as discussed in sections 3.2.1 and 3.2.2.

3.2.4. Highly Inflationary Economies

When a foreign entity is located in a highly inflationary economy, the entity's functional currency is irrelevant in determining how to translate its foreign currency financial statements into the parent's presentation currency. IAS 21 requires that the financial statements of the foreign entity first be restated for local inflation using the procedures outlined in IAS 29, "Financial Reporting in Hyperinflationary Economies." Then, the inflation-restated foreign currency financial statements are translated into the parent's presentation currency using the current exchange rate (i.e., using the current rate method).

EXHIBIT 16-4   Rules for the Translation of a Foreign Subsidiary's Foreign Currency Financial Statements into the Parent's Presentation Currency under IFRS and U.S. GAAP

	Foreign Subsidiary's Functional Currency	
	Foreign Currency	**Parent's Presentation Currency**
Translation method:	**Current Rate Method**	**Temporal Method**
Exchange rate at which financial statement items are translated from the foreign subsidiary's bookkeeping currency to the parent's presentation currency:		
Assets		
Monetary, e.g., cash; receivables	Current rate	Current rate
Nonmonetary		
Measured at current value (e.g., marketable securities); inventory measured at market under the lower of cost or market rule	Current rate	Current rate
Measured at historical costs (e.g., inventory measured at cost under the lower of cost or market rule); property, plant, and equipment; intangible assets	Current rate	Historical rates
Liabilities		
Monetary (e.g., accounts payable); accrued expenses; long-term debt; deferred income taxes	Current rate	Current rate
Nonmonetary		
Measured at current value	Current rate	Current rate
Not measured at current value (e.g., deferred revenue)	Current rate	Historical rates

(*Continued*)

EXHIBIT 16-4   *(Continued)*

| | Foreign Subsidiary's Functional Currency | |
	Foreign Currency	Parent's Presentation Currency
Equity		
Other than retained earnings	Historical rates	Historical rates
Retained earnings	Beginning balance plus translated net income less dividends translated at historical rate	Beginning balance plus translated net income less dividends translated at historical rate
Revenues	Average rate	Average rate
Expenses		
Most expenses	Average rate	Average rate
Expenses related to assets translated at historical exchange rate (e.g., cost of goods sold); depreciation; amortization	Average rate	Historical rates
Treatment of the translation adjustment in the parent's consolidated financial statements	Accumulated as a separate component of equity	Included as gain or loss in net income

U.S. GAAP requires a very different approach for translating the foreign currency financial statements of foreign entities located in highly inflationary economies. SFAS No. 52 does not allow restatement for inflation, but instead requires the temporal method to translate financial statements kept in a highly inflationary currency. However, despite the use of the temporal method, the resulting translation adjustment is included as a gain or loss in determining net income.

SFAS No. 52 defines a highly inflationary economy as one in which the cumulative three-year inflation rate exceeds 100 percent. This equates to an average of approximately 26 percent per year. IAS 21 does not provide a specific definition of high inflation, but IAS 29 does indicate that a cumulative inflation rate approaching or exceeding 100 percent over three years would be one indicator of hyperinflation. If a country in which a foreign entity is located ceases to be classified as highly inflationary, the functional currency of that foreign entity must be identified to determine the appropriate method for translating the entity's foreign currency financial statements.

The FASB initially proposed that companies restate for inflation and then translate the financial statements, but this approach met with stiff resistance from U.S. multinational corporations. By requiring the temporal method, SFAS No. 52 ensures that companies avoid a "disappearing plant problem" that exists when the current rate method is used in a country with high inflation. In a highly inflationary economy, as the local currency loses purchasing power within the country, it also tends to weaken in value in relation to other currencies. Translating the historical cost of assets such as land and buildings at progressively lower exchange rates causes these assets to slowly disappear from the parent company's consolidated financial statements. Example 16-4 demonstrates the effect of three different translation approaches when books are kept in the currency of a highly inflationary economy.

EXAMPLE 16-4   Foreign Currency Translation in a Highly Inflationary Economy

Turkey was one of the few remaining highly inflationary countries at the beginning of the twenty-first century. Annual inflation rates and selected exchange rates between the Turkish lira (TL) and U.S. dollar during the period 2000–2002 were as follows:

Date	Exchange Rates	Year	Inflation Rate
01 Jan 2000	TL 542,700 = US$1		
31 Dec 2000	TL 670,800 = US$1	2000	38%
31 Dec 2001	TL 1,474,525 = US$1	2001	69%
31 Dec 2002	TL 1,669,000 = US$1	2002	45%

Assume that a U.S.-based company established a subsidiary in Turkey on 1 January 2000. The U.S. parent sent the subsidiary US$1,000 on 1 January 2000 to purchase a piece of land at a cost of TL 542,700,000 (TL 542,700/US$ × US$1,000 = TL 542,700,000). Assuming no other assets or liabilities, what are the annual and cumulative translation gains or losses that would be reported under each of three possible translation approaches?

Solution:

Approach 1: Translate Using the Current Rate Method

The historical cost of the land is translated at the current exchange rate, which results in a new translated amount at each balance sheet date.

Date	Carrying Value in TL	Current Exchange Rate	Translated Amount in US$	Annual Translation Gain (Loss)	Cumulative Translation Gain (Loss)
01 Jan 2000	542,700,000	542,700	$1,000	NA	NA
31 Dec 2000	542,700,000	670,800	809	($191)	($191)
31 Dec 2001	542,700,000	1,474,525	368	(441)	(632)
31 Dec 2002	542,700,000	1,669,000	325	(43)	(675)

At the end of three years, land that was originally purchased with US$1,000 would be reflected on the parent's consolidated balance sheet at US$325 (and remember that land is not a depreciable asset). A cumulative translation loss of US$675 would be reported as a separate component of stockholders' equity on 31 December 2002. Because this method accounts for adjustments in exchange rates but does not account for likely changes in the local currency values of assets, it does a poor job accurately reflecting the economic reality of situations such as the one in our example. That is the major reason this approach is not acceptable under either IFRS or U.S. GAAP.

Approach 2: Translate Using the Temporal Method (SFAS No. 52)

The historical cost of land is translated using the historical exchange rate, which results in the same translated amount at each balance sheet date.

Date	Carrying Value in TL	Historical Exchange Rate	Translated Amount in US$	Annual Translation Gain (Loss)	Cumulative Translation Gain (Loss)
01 Jan 2000	542,700,000	542,700	$1,000	NA	NA
31 Dec 2000	542,700,000	542,700	1,000	NA	NA
31 Dec 2001	542,700,000	542,700	1,000	NA	NA
31 Dec 2002	542,700,000	542,700	1,000	NA	NA

Under this approach, land continues to be reported on the parent's consolidated balance sheet at its original cost of US$1,000 each year. There is no translation gain or loss related to balance sheet items translated at historical exchange rates. This approach is required by SFAS No. 52 and ensures that nonmonetary assets do not disappear from the translated balance sheet.

Approach 3: Restate for Inflation/Translate Using Current Exchange Rate (IAS 21)

The historical cost of the land is restated for inflation and then the inflation-adjusted historical cost is translated using the current exchange rate.

Date	Inflation Rate	Restated Carrying Value in TL	Current Exchange Rate	Translated Amount in US$	Annual Translation Gain (Loss)	Cumulative Translation Gain (Loss)
01 Jan 00		542,700,000	542,700	$1,000	NA	NA
31 Dec 00	38%	748,926,000	670,800	1,116	$116	$116
31 Dec 01	69%	1,265,684,940	1,474,525	858	(258)	(142)
31 Dec 02	45%	1,835,243,163	1,669,000	1,100	242	100

Under this approach, land is reported on the parent's 31 December 2002 consolidated balance sheet at US$1,100 with a cumulative, unrealized gain of US$100. Although the cumulative translation gain on 31 December 2002 is unrealized, it could have been realized if (1) the land had appreciated in TL value by the rate of local inflation, (2) the Turkish subsidiary sold the land for TL 1,835,243,163, and (3) the sale proceeds were converted into US$1,100 at the current exchange rate on 31 December 2002.

This approach is required by IAS 21. It is the approach that perhaps best represents economic reality in the sense that it reflects both the likely change in the local currency value of the land as well as the actual change in the exchange rate.

3.3. Illustration of Translation Methods (Excluding Hyperinflationary Economies)

To demonstrate the procedures required by IAS 21 and SFAS No. 52 in translating foreign currency financial statements, assume that Interco is a European-based company that has the euro as its presentation currency. On 1 January 2008, Interco establishes a wholly owned subsidiary in Canada, Canadaco. In addition to Interco making an equity investment in

Canadaco, a long-term note payable to a Canadian bank was negotiated to purchase property and equipment. The subsidiary begins operations with the following balance sheet in Canadian dollars (C$):

Canadaco Balance Sheet, 1 January 2008 (C$)

Assets

Cash	$1,500,000
Property and equipment	3,000,000
	$4,500,000

Liabilities and Equity

Long-term note payable	$3,000,000
Capital stock	1,500,000
	$4,500,000

Canadaco purchases and sells inventory in 2008, generating net income of C$1,180,000, out of which C$350,000 in dividends are paid. The company's income statement and statement of retained earnings for 2008 and balance sheet at 31 December 2008 follow:

Canadaco Income Statement and Statement of Retained Earnings, 2008 (C$)

Sales	$12,000,000
Cost of sales	(9,000,000)
Selling expenses	(750,000)
Depreciation expense	(300,000)
Interest expense	(270,000)
Income tax	(500,000)
Net income	1,180,000
less: Dividends, 1 Dec. 08	(350,000)
Retained earnings, 31 Dec. 2008	$830,000

Canadaco Balance Sheet, 31 December 2008 (C$)

Assets		Liabilities and Equity	
Cash	$980,000	Accounts payable	$450,000
Accounts receivable	900,000	Total current liabilities	450,000
Inventory	1,200,000	Long-term notes payable	3,000,000
Total current assets	3,080,000	Total liabilities	3,450,000
Property and equipment	3,000,000	Capital stock	1,500,000
Less: accumulated depreciation	(300,000)	Retained earnings	830,000
Total	$5,780,000	Total	$5,780,000

Inventory is measured at historical cost on a FIFO basis.

To translate Canadaco's Canadian dollar financial statements into euros for consolidation purposes, the following exchange rate information was gathered:

Date	€ per C$
1 January 2008	0.70
Average, 2008	0.75
Weighted average rate when inventory was acquired	0.74
1 December 2008, when dividends were declared	0.78
31 December 2008	0.80

During 2008, the Canadian dollar strengthened steadily against the euro from an exchange rate of €0.70 at the beginning of the year to €0.80 at year end.

The translation worksheet below shows Canadaco's translated financial statements under each of the two translation methods. Assume first that Canadaco's functional currency is the Canadian dollar and therefore the current rate method must be used. The Canadian dollar income statement and statement of retained earnings are translated first. Income statement items for 2008 are translated at the average exchange rate for 2008 (€0.75), and dividends are translated at the exchange rate that existed when they were declared (€0.78). The ending balance in retained earnings at 31 December 2008 of €612,000 is transferred to the C$ balance sheet. The remaining balance sheet accounts are then translated. Assets and liabilities are translated at the current exchange rate on the balance sheet date of 31 December 2008 (€0.80), and the capital stock account is translated at the historical exchange rate (€0.70) that existed on the date that Interco made the capital contribution. A positive translation adjustment of €202,000 is needed as a balancing amount, which is reported in the stockholders' equity section of the balance sheet.

If instead Interco determines that Canadaco's functional currency is the euro, the parent's presentation currency, the temporal method must be applied as shown in the far right columns of the table. The differences in procedure from the current rate method are that inventory, property, and equipment (and accumulated depreciation), as well as their related expenses (cost of goods sold and depreciation), are translated at the historical exchange rates that existed when the assets were acquired: €0.70 in the case of property and equipment, and €0.74 for inventory. The balance sheet is translated first, with €472,000 determined as the amount of retained earnings needed to keep the balance sheet in balance. This amount is transferred to the income statement and statement of retained earnings as the ending balance in retained earnings on 31 December 2008. Income statement items then are translated, with cost of goods sold and depreciation expense being translated at historical exchange rates. A negative translation adjustment of €245,000 is determined as the amount that is needed to arrive at the ending balance in retained earnings of €472,000, and is reported as a translation loss on the income statement.

The positive translation adjustment under the current rate method can be explained by the fact that Canadaco has a net asset balance sheet exposure (total assets exceed total liabilities) during 2008 and the Canadian dollar strengthened against the euro. The negative translation adjustment (translation loss) under the temporal method is due to the fact that Canadaco has exposed liabilities (accounts payable plus notes payable) that exceed exposed assets (cash plus receivables) during 2008 when the Canadian dollar strengthened against the euro.

Canadaco Income Statement and Statement of Retained Earnings 2008

	C$	Current Rate			Temporal		
		Exch. Rate		€	Exch. Rate		€
Sales	12,000,000	0.75	A	9,000,000	0.75	A	9,000,000
Cost of goods sold	(9,000,000)	0.75	A	(6,750,000)	0.74	H	(6,660,000)
Selling expenses	(750,000)	0.75	A	(562,500)	0.75	A	(562,500)
Depreciation expense	(300,000)	0.75	A	(225,000)	0.70	H	(210,000)
Interest expense	(270,000)	0.75	A	(202,500)	0.75	A	(202,500)
Income tax	(500,000)	0.75	A	(375,000)	0.75	A	(375,000)
Income before trans. gain (loss)	1,180,000			885,000			990,000
Translation gain (loss)	N/A			N/A	to balance		(245,000)
Net income	1,180,000			885,000			745,000
Less: Dividends, 12/1/2008	(350,000)	0.78	H	(273,000)	0.78	H	(273,000)
Retained earnings, 12/31/2008	830,000			612,000	from	B/S	472,000

C, current exchange rate; A, average-for-the-year exchange rate; H, historical exchange rate.

Canadaco Balance Sheet, 31 December 2008

	C$	Current Rate			Temporal		
		Exch. Rate		€	Exch. Rate		S
Assets							
Cash	980,000	0.80	C	784,000	0.80	C	784,000
Accounts receivable	900,000	0.80	C	720,000	0.80	C	720,000
Inventory	1,200,000	0.80	C	960,000	0.74	H	888,000
Total current assets	3,080,000			2,464,000			2,392,000
Property and equipment	3,000,000	0.80	C	2,400,000	0.70	H	2,100,000
Less: accumulated depreciation	(300,000)	0.80	C	(240,000)	0.70	H	(210,000)
Total assets	5,780,000			4,624,000			4,282,000
Liabilities and Equity							
Accounts payable	450,000	0.80	C	360,000	0.80	C	360,000
Total current liabilities	450,000			360,000			360,000
Long-term notes payable	3,000,000	0.80	C	2,400,000	0.80	C	2,400,000
Total liabilities	3,450,000			2,760,000			2,760,000
Capital stock	1,500,000	0.70	H	1,050,000	0.70	H	1,050,000
Retained earnings	830,000	from	I/S	612,000	to balance		472,000
Translation adjustment	N/A	to balance		202,000			N/A
Total	5,780,000			4,624,000			4,282,000

C, current exchange rate; A, average-for-the-year exchange rate; H, historical exchange rate.

3.4. Translation Analytical Issues

The two different translation methods used to translate Canadaco's C$ financial statements into euros result in very different amounts that will be included in Interco's consolidated financial statements. The chart below summarizes some of these differences:

| Item | Translation Method | | |
	Current Rate	Temporal	Difference
Net income	€885,000	€745,000	+18.8%
Income before translation gain (loss)	885,000	990,000	−10.6
Total assets	€4,624,000	€4,282,000	+8.0
Total equity	€1,864,000	€1,522,000	+22.5

In this particular case, the current rate method results in a significantly larger net income than the temporal method. This occurs because under the current rate method the translation adjustment is not included in the calculation of income. If the translation loss were excluded from net income, the temporal method would result in a significantly larger amount of net income. The combination of smaller net income under the temporal method and a positive translation adjustment reported on the balance sheet under the current rate method results in a much larger amount of total equity under the current rate method. Total assets also are larger under the current rate method because all assets are translated at the current exchange rate, which is higher than the historical exchange rates at which inventory and fixed assets are translated under the temporal method.

To examine the impact that translation has on the underlying relationships that exist in Canadaco's C$ financial statements, several significant ratios are calculated from the original C$ financial statements and the translated (€) financial statements and presented in the table below.

	C$	Current Rate (€)	Temporal (€)
Current Ratio			
Current assets	3,080,000	2,464,000	2,392,000
Current liabilities	450,000	360,000	360,000
	6.84	6.84	6.64
Debt-to-Assets Ratio			
Total debt	3,000,000	2,400,000	2,400,000
Total assets	5,780,000	4,624,000	4,282,000
	0.52	0.52	0.56
Debt-to-Equity Ratio			
Total debt	3,000,000	2,400,000	2,400,000
Total equity	2,330,000	1,864,000	1,522,000
	1.29	1.29	1.58
Interest Coverage			
EBIT	1,950,000	1,462,500	1,567,500

	C$	Current Rate (€)	Temporal (€)
Interest payments	270,000	202,500	202,500
	7.22	7.22	7.74
Gross Profit Margin			
Gross profit	3,000,000	2,250,000	2,340,000
Sales	12,000,000	9,000,000	9,000,000
	0.25	0.25	0.26
Operating Profit Margin			
Operating profit	1,950,000	1,462,500	1,567,500
Sales	12,000,000	9,000,000	9,000,000
	0.16	0.16	0.17
Net Profit Margin			
Net income	1,180,000	885,000	745,000
Sales	12,000,000	9,000,000	9,000,000
	0.10	0.10	0.08
Receivables Turnover			
Sales	12,000,000	9,000,000	9,000,000
Accounts receivable	900,000	720,000	720,000
	13.33	12.50	12.50
Inventory Turnover			
Cost of goods sold	9,000,000	6,750,000	6,660,000
Inventory	1,200,000	960,000	888,000
	7.50	7.03	7.50
Fixed Asset Turnover			
Sales	12,000,000	9,000,000	9,000,000
Property and equipment, net	2,700,000	2,160,000	1,890,000
	4.44	4.17	4.76
Return on Assets			
Net income	1,180,000	885,000	745,000
Total assets	5,780,000	4,624,000	4,282,000
	0.20	0.19	0.17
Return on Equity			
Net income	1,180,000	885,000	745,000
Total equity	2,330,000	1,864,000	1,522,000
	0.51	0.47	0.49

Comparing the current rate method (€) and temporal method (€) columns in the above table shows that financial ratios calculated from Canadaco's translated financial statements (in €) differ significantly depending on which method of translation is used. Of the ratios presented, only receivables turnover is the same under both translation methods. This is the only ratio presented in which there is no difference in the type of exchange rate used to translate the items that comprise the numerator and the denominator. Sales are translated at the average exchange rate and receivables are translated at the current exchange rate under both methods. For each of the other ratios, at least one of the items included in either the numerator or the denominator is translated at a different type of rate (current, average, or historical rate) under the temporal method than under the current rate method. For example, the current ratio has a different value under the two translation methods because inventory is translated at the current exchange rate under the current rate method and at the historical exchange rate under the temporal method. In this case, because the €/C$ exchange rate on 31 December 2008 (€0.80) is higher than the historical exchange rate when the inventory was acquired (€0.74), the current ratio is larger under the current rate method of translation.

Comparing the ratios in the C$ and current rate method (€) columns of the above table shows that many of the underlying relationships that exist in Canadaco's C$ financial statements are preserved when the current rate method of translation is used (i.e., the ratio calculated from the C$ and € translated amounts is the same). The current ratio, the leverage ratios (debt-to-assets and debt-to-equity ratios), the interest coverage ratio, and the profit margins (gross profit margin, operating profit margin, and net profit margin) are the same in the C$ and current rate method (€) columns of the above table. This occurs because each of the ratios is calculated using information from either the balance sheet or the income statement, but not both. Those ratios that compare amounts from the balance sheet with amounts from the income statement (e.g., turnover and return ratios) are different. In this particular case, each of the turnover and return ratios is larger when calculated from the C$ amounts than when calculated using the current rate (€) amounts. The underlying C$ relationships are distorted when translated using the current rate method because the balance sheet amounts are translated using the current exchange rate while revenues and expenses are translated using the average exchange rate. (These distortions would not exist if revenues and expenses also were translated at the current exchange rate.)

Comparing the ratios in the C$ and temporal method (€) columns of the table shows that translation using the temporal method distorts all of the underlying relationships that exist in the C$ financial statements, except inventory turnover. Moreover, it is not possible to generalize the direction of the distortion across ratios. In Canadaco's case, using the temporal method results in a larger gross profit margin and operating profit margin but a smaller net profit margin as compared with the values of these ratios calculated from the original C$ amounts. Similarly, receivables turnover is smaller, inventory turnover is the same, and fixed asset turnover is larger when calculated from the translated amounts.

In translating Canadaco's C$ financial statements into euros, the temporal method results in a smaller amount of net income than the current rate method only because IFRS and U.S. GAAP require the resulting translation loss to be included in net income when the temporal method is used. The translation loss arises because the C$ strengthened against the euro and Canadaco has a larger amount of liabilities translated at the current exchange rate (monetary liabilities) than it has assets translated at the current exchange rate (monetary assets). If Canadaco had a net monetary asset exposure (i.e., if monetary assets exceeded monetary liabilities), a translation gain would arise and net income under the temporal method (including the translation gain) would be greater than under the current rate method. Example 16-5 demonstrates how different types of balance sheet exposure under the temporal method can affect translated net income.

EXAMPLE 16-5   Impacts of Different Balance Sheet Exposures under the Temporal Method

Canadaco begins operations on 1 January 2008 with cash of C$1,500,000 and property and equipment of C$3,000,000. In Case A, Canadaco finances the acquisition of property and equipment with a long-term note payable, and begins operations with net monetary liabilities of C$1,500,000 (C$3,000,000 long-term note payable less C$1,500,000 cash). In Case B, Canadaco finances the acquisition of property and equipment with capital stock, and begins operations with net monetary assets of C$1,500,000. To isolate the effect that balance sheet exposure has on net income under the temporal method, assume that Canadaco continues to have C$270,000 in interest expense in Case B, even though there is no debt financing. This assumption is inconsistent with reality, but it allows us to more clearly see the effect that balance sheet exposure has on net income. The only difference between Case A and Case B is the net monetary asset/liability position of the company, as shown below:

Canadaco Balance Sheet, 1 January 2008 ($C)

	Case A	Case B
Assets		
Cash	$1,500,000	$1,500,000
Property and equipment	3,000,000	3,000,000
	4,500,000	4,500,000
Liabilities and Equity		
Long-term note payable	3,000,000	0
Capital stock	1,500,000	4,500,000
	$4,500,000	$4,500,000

Canadaco purchases and sells inventory in 2008, generating net income of C$1,180,000, out of which dividends of C$350,000 are paid. The company has total assets of C$5,780,000 at 31 December 2008. Canadaco's functional currency is determined to be the euro, the parent's presentation currency, and the company's Canadian dollar financial statements are translated into euros using the temporal method. Relevant exchange rates are:

Date	€ per C$
1 January 2008	0.70
Average, 2008	0.75
Weighted average rate when inventory was acquired	0.74
1 December 2008 when dividends were declared	0.78
31 December 2008	0.80

What impact does the nature of Canadaco's net monetary asset or liability position have on the euro translated amounts?

Solution. Translation of Canadaco's 31 December 2008 balance sheet under the temporal method in Case A and Case B is shown below:

Canadaco Balance Sheet, 31 December 2008: Temporal Method

	Case A: Net Monetary Liabilities				Case B: Net Monetary Assets			
	C$	Exch. Rate		€	C$	Exch. Rate		€
Assets								
Cash	980,000	0.80	C	784,000	980,000	0.80	C	784,000
Accounts receivable	900,000	0.80	C	720,000	900,000	0.80	C	720,000
Inventory	1,200,000	0.74	H	888,000	1,200,000	0.74	H	888,000
Total current assets	3,080,000			2,392,000	3,080,000			2,392,000
Property and equipment	3,000,000	0.70	H	2,100,000	3,000,000	0.70	H	2,100,000
Less: accum. deprec.	(300,000)	0.70	H	(210,000)	(300,000)	0.70	H	(210,000)
Total assets	5,780,000			4,282,000	5,780,000			4,282,000
Liabilities and Equity								
Accounts payable	450,000	0.80	C	360,000	450,000	0.80	C	360,000
Total current liabilities	450,000			360,000	450,000			360,000
Long-term notes pay.	3,000,000	0.80	C	2,400,000	0			0
Total liabilities	3,450,000			2,760,000	450,000			360,000
Capital stock	1,500,000	0.70	H	1,050,000	4,500,000	0.70	H	3,150,000
Retained earnings	830,000			472,000	830,000			772,000
Total	5,780,000			4,282,000	5,780,000			4,282,000

C, current exchange rate; A, average-for-the-year exchange rate; H, historical exchange rate.

To keep the balance sheet in balance, retained earnings must be €472,000 in Case A (net monetary liability exposure) and €772,000 in Case B (net monetary asset exposure). The difference in retained earnings of €300,000 is equal to the translation loss that results from holding a C$ note payable during a period in which the C$ strengthens against the euro. This difference is determined by multiplying the amount of long-term note payable in Case A by the change in exchange rate during the year (C$3,000,000 × [€0.80 − €0.70] = C$300,000). Notes payable are exposed to foreign exchange risk under the temporal method, whereas capital stock is not. Canadaco could avoid the €300,000 translation loss related to long-term debt by financing the acquisition of property and equipment with equity rather than debt.

Translation of Canadaco's 2008 income statement and statement of retained earnings under the temporal method for Case A and Case B is shown below:

Canadaco Income Statement and Statement of Retained Earnings 2008: Temporal Method

	Case A: Net Monetary Liabilities			Case B: Net Monetary Assets			
	C$	Exch. Rate	€	C$	Exch. Rate		€
Sales	12,000,000	0.75 A	9,000,000	12,000,000	0.75	A	9,000,000
Cost of goods sold	(9,000,000)	0.74 H	(6,660,000)	(9,000,000)	0.74	H	(6,660,000)
Selling expenses	(750,000)	0.75 A	(562,500)	(750,000)	0.75	A	(562,500)
Depreciation expense	(300,000)	0.70 H	(210,000)	(300,000)	0.70	H	(210,000)
Interest expense	(270,000)	0.75 A	(202,500)	(270,000)	0.75	A	(202,500)
Income tax	(500,000)	0.75 A	(375,000)	(500,000)	0.75	A	(375,000)
Income before translation gain (loss)	1,180,000		990,000	1,180,000			990,000
Translation gain (loss)	N/A		(245,000)	N/A			55,000
Net income	1,180,000		745,000	1,180,000			1,045,000
Less: Dividends on 1 Dec. 2008	(350,000)	0.78 H	(273,000)	(350,000)	0.78	H	(273,000)
Retained earnings on 31 Dec. 2008	830,000		472,000	830,000			772,000

C, current exchange rate; A, average-for-the-year exchange rate; H, historical exchange rate.

Income before translation gain (loss) is the same in both cases. To obtain the amount of retained earnings needed to keep the balance sheet in balance, a translation loss of €245,000 must be subtracted from net income in Case A (net monetary liabilities), whereas a translation gain of €55,000 must be added to net income in Case B (net monetary assets). The difference in net income between the two cases is €300,000, which is equal to the translation loss related to the long-term note payable.

When the temporal method is used, companies have more ability to manage their exposure to translation gain (loss) than when the current rate method is used. If a company can manage the balance sheet of a foreign subsidiary such that monetary assets equal monetary liabilities, no balance sheet exposure exists. Elimination of balance sheet exposure under the current rate method occurs only when total assets equal total liabilities. This is difficult to achieve because it would require the foreign subsidiary to have no stockholders' equity.

For Canadaco, in 2008, applying the current rate method results in larger euro amounts of total assets and total equity being reported in the consolidated financial statements than would result from applying the temporal method. The direction of these differences between the two translation methods is determined by the direction of change in the exchange rate between the Canadian dollar and the euro. For example, total exposed assets are greater under the current rate method because all assets are translated at the current exchange rate. The current exchange rate on 31 December 2008 is greater than the exchange rates that existed when the nonmonetary assets were acquired, which is the translation rate for these assets under the temporal method. Therefore, the current rate method results in a larger amount of total assets because the Canadian dollar strengthened against the euro. The current rate method would result in a smaller amount of total assets than the temporal method if the Canadian dollar had weakened against the euro.

Applying the current rate method also results in a much larger amount of stockholders' equity than the temporal method. A positive translation adjustment arises under the current rate method, which is included in equity, whereas a translation loss reduces total equity (through retained earnings) under the temporal method.

Example 16-6 shows the effect that the direction of change in the exchange rate has on the translated amounts. Canadaco's Canadian dollar financial statements are translated into euros first assuming no change in the exchange rate during 2008, and then assuming the Canadian dollar strengthens and weakens against the euro. Using the current rate method to translate the foreign currency financial statements into the parent's presentation currency, the foreign currency strengthening increases the revenues, income, assets, liabilities, and total equity reported on the parent company's consolidated financial statements. Likewise, smaller amounts of revenues, income, assets, liabilities, and total equity would be reported if the foreign currency weakens against the parent's presentation currency.

When the temporal method is used to translate the foreign currency financial statements, foreign currency strengthening still increases revenues, assets, and liabilities reported in the parent's consolidated financial statements. Net income and stockholders' equity, however, translate into smaller amounts (assuming that the foreign subsidiary has a net monetary liability position) because of the translation loss. The opposite results are obtained when the foreign currency weakens against the parent's presentation currency.

EXAMPLE 16-6 Effect of Direction of Change in the Exchange Rate on Translated Amounts

Canadaco's Canadian dollar (C$) financial statements are translated into euros (€) under three assumptions: (1) the Canadian dollar remains stable against the euro, (2) the Canadian dollar strengthens against the euro, and (3) the Canadian dollar weakens against the euro. Relevant exchange rates are as follows:

Date	€ per C$		
	Stable	Strengthens	Weakens
1 January 2008	0.70	0.70	0.70
Average, 2008	0.70	0.75	0.65
Weighted average rate when inventory was acquired	0.70	0.74	0.66
Rate when dividends were declared	0.70	0.78	0.62
31 December 2008	0.70	0.80	0.60

What amounts will be reported on the parent's consolidated financial statements under the three different exchange rate assumptions if Canadaco's Canadian dollar financial statements are translated using the:

1. Current rate method?
2. Temporal method?

Solution to 1: Current rate method. Using the current rate method, Canadaco's Canadian dollar financial statements would be translated into euros as follows under the three different exchange rate assumptions:

Canadaco Income Statement and Statement of Retained Earnings 2008: Current Rate Method

	C$	C$ Stable			C$ Strengthens			C$ Weakens		
		Exch. Rate	€		Exch. Rate	€		Exch. Rate	€	
Sales	12,000,000	0.70	8,400,000	0.75	A	9,000,000	0.65	A	7,800,000	
Cost of goods sold	(9,000,000)	0.70	(6,300,000)	0.75	A	(6,750,000)	0.65	A	(5,850,000)	
Selling expenses	(750,000)	0.70	(525,000)	0.75	A	(562,500)	0.65	A	(487,500)	
Deprec. expense	(300,000)	0.70	(210,000)	0.75	A	(225,000)	0.65	A	(195,000)	
Interest expense	(270,000)	0.70	(189,000)	0.75	A	(202,500)	0.65	A	(175,500)	
Income tax	(500,000)	0.70	(350,000)	0.75	A	(375,000)	0.65	A	(325,000)	
Net income	1,180,000		826,000			885,000			767,000	
Less: Dividends	(350,000)	0.70	(245,000)	0.78	H	(273,000)	0.62	H	(217,000)	
Retained earnings	830,000		581,000			612,000			550,000	

C, current exchange rate; A, average-for-the-year exchange rate; H, historical exchange rate.

Compared to the translated amount of sales and net income under a stable Canadian dollar assumption, a stronger Canadian dollar results in a larger amount of Sales and Net income being reported in the consolidated income statement, and a weaker Canadian dollar results in a smaller amount of Sales and Net income being reported in consolidated net income.

Canadaco Balance Sheet, 31 December 2008: Current Rate Method

	C$	C$ Stable			C$ Strengthens			C$ Weakens		
		Exch. Rate	€	Exch. Rate		€	Exch. Rate		€	
Assets										
Cash	980,000	0.70	686,000	0.80	C	784,000	0.60	C	588,000	
Accounts receivable	900,000	0.70	630,000	0.80	C	720,000	0.60	C	540,000	

	C$	C$ Stable		C$ Strengthens			C$ Weakens		
	C$	Exch. Rate	€	Exch. Rate		€	Exch. Rate		€
Inventory	1,200,000	0.70	840,000	0.80	C	960,000	0.60	C	720,000
Total current assets	3,080,000		2,156,000			2,464,000			1,848,000
Property and equipment	3,000,000	0.70	2,100,000	0.80	C	2,400,000	0.60	C	1,800,000
Less: accum. deprec.	(300,000)	0.70	(210,000)	0.80	C	(240,000)	0.60	C	(180,000)
Total assets	5,780,000		4,046,000			4,624,000			3,468,000
Liabilities and equity									
Accounts payable	450,000	0.70	315,000	0.80	C	360,000	0.60	C	270,000
Total current liabilities	450,000		315,000			360,000			270,000
Long-term notes pay.	3,000,000	0.70	2,100,000	0.80	C	2,400,000	0.60	C	1,800,000
Total liabilities	3,450,000		2,415,000			2,760,000			2,070,000
Capital stock	1,500,000	0.70	1,050,000	0.70	H	1,050,000	0.70	H	1,050,000
Retained earnings	830,000		581,000			612,000			550,000
Translation adjustment	NA		0			202,000			(202,000)
Total equity	2,330,000		1,631,000			1,864,000			1,398,000
Total	5,780,000		4,046,000			4,624,000			3,468,000

C, current exchange rate; A, average-for-the-year exchange rate; H, historical exchange rate.

The translation adjustment is zero when the Canadian dollar remains stable for the year; it is positive when the Canadian dollar strengthens and negative when the Canadian dollar weakens. Compared to the amounts that would appear in the euro consolidated balance sheet under a stable Canadian dollar assumption, a stronger Canadian dollar results in a larger amount of assets, liabilities, and equity being reported on the consolidated balance sheet, and a weaker Canadian dollar results in a smaller amount of assets, liabilities, and equity being reported on the consolidated balance sheet.

Solution to 2: Temporal Method. Using the temporal method, Canadaco's financial statements would be translated into euros as follows under the three different exchange rate assumptions:

Canadaco Balance Sheet, 31 December 2008

| | | Temporal Method | | | | | | |
| | | C$ Stable | | C$ Strengthens | | | C$ Weakens | | |
	C$	Exch. Rate	€	Exch. Rate		€	Exch. Rate		€
Assets									
Cash	980,000	0.70	686,000	0.80	C	784,000	0.60	C	588,000
Accounts receivable	900,000	0.70	630,000	0.80	C	720,000	0.60	C	540,000
Inventory	1,200,000	0.70	840,000	0.74	H	888,000	0.66	H	792,000
Total current assets	3,080,000		2,156,000			2,392,000			1,920,000
Property and equipment	3,000,000	0.70	2,100,000	0.70	H	2,100,000	0.70	H	2,100,000
Less: accum. deprec.	(300,000)	0.70	(210,000)	0.70	H	(210,000)	0.70	H	(210,000)
Total assets	5,780,000		4,046,000			4,282,000			3,810,000
Liabilities and Equity									
Accounts payable	450,000	0.70	315,000	0.80	C	360,000	0.60	C	270,000
Total current liabilities	450,000		315,000			360,000			270,000
Long-term notes pay.	3,000,000	0.70	2,100,000	0.80	C	2,400,000	0.60	C	1,800,000
Total liabilities	3,450,000		2,415,000			2,760,000			2,070,000
Capital stock	1,500,000	0.70	1,050,000	0.70	H	1,050,000	0.70	H	1,050,000
Retained earnings	830,000		581,000			472,000			690,000
Total equity	2,330,000		1,631,000			1,522,000			1,740,000
Total	5,780,000		4,046,000			4,282,000			3,810,000

C, current exchange rate; A, average-for-the-year exchange rate; H, historical exchange rate.

Compared to the stable Canadian dollar scenario, a stronger Canadian dollar results in a larger amount of assets and liabilities, but a smaller amount of equity reported on the consolidated balance sheet. A weaker Canadian dollar results in a smaller amount of assets and liabilities, but a larger amount of equity reported on the consolidated balance sheet.

Canadaco Income Statement and Statement of Retained Earnings 2008: Temporal Method

	C$	**C$ Stable**		**C$ Strengthens**			**C$ Weakens**		
		Exch. Rate	**€**	**Exch. Rate**		**€**	**Exch. Rate**		**€**
Sales	12,000,000	0.70	8,400,000	0.75	A	9,000,000	0.65	A	7,800,000
Cost of sales	(9,000,000)	0.70	(6,300,000)	0.74	H	(6,660,000)	0.66	H	(5,940,000)
Selling expenses	(750,000)	0.70	(525,000)	0.75	A	(562,500)	0.65	A	(487,500)
Depreciation expense	(300,000)	0.70	(210,000)	0.70	H	(210,000)	0.70	H	(210,000)
Interest expense	(270,000)	0.70	(189,000)	0.75	A	(202,500)	0.65	A	(175,500)
Income tax	(500,000)	0.70	(350,000)	0.75	A	(375,000)	0.65	A	(325,000)
Income before translation gain (loss)	1,180,000		826,000			990,000			662,000
Translation gain (loss)	N/A		0			(245,000)			245,000
Net income	1,180,000		826,000			745,000			907,000
less: Dividends	(350,000)	0.70	(245,000)	0.78	H	(273,000)	0.62	H	(217,000)
Retained earnings	830,000		581,000			472,000			690,000

C, current exchange rate; A, average-for-the-year exchange rate; H, historical exchange rate.

No translation gain or loss exists when the Canadian dollar remains stable during the year. Because the subsidiary has a net monetary liability exposure to changes in the exchange rate, a stronger Canadian dollar results in a translation loss and a weaker Canadian dollar results in a translation gain. Compared to a stable Canadian dollar, a stronger Canadian dollar results in a larger amount of sales and a smaller amount of net income reported on the consolidated income statement. This difference in direction is due to the translation loss that is included in net income. (As was demonstrated in Example 16-5, a translation gain would have resulted if the subsidiary had a net monetary asset exposure). A weaker Canadian dollar results in a smaller amount of sales, but a larger amount of net income than if the Canadian dollar had remained stable.

Exhibit 16-5 summarizes the relationships illustrated in Examples 16-5 and 16-6, focusing on the effect that a strengthening or weakening of the foreign currency has on financial statement amounts compared to what these amounts would be if the foreign currency were to remain stable.

EXHIBIT 16-5   Effect of Currency Exchange Rate Movement on Financial Statements

	Temporal Method, Net Monetary Liability Exposure	Temporal Method, Net Monetary Asset Exposure	Current Rate Method
Foreign currency strengthens relative to parent's presentation currency	↑ Revenues ↑ Assets ↑ Liabilities ↓ Net income ↓ Shareholders' equity Translation loss	↑ Revenues ↑ Assets ↑ Liabilities ↑ Net income ↑ Shareholders' equity Translation gain	↑ Revenues ↑ Assets ↑ Liabilities ↑ Net income ↑ Shareholders' equity Positive translation adjustment
Foreign currency weakens relative to parent's presentation currency	↓ Revenues ↓ Assets ↓ Liabilities ↑ Net income ↑ Shareholders' equity Translation gain	↓ Revenues ↓ Assets ↓ Liabilities ↓ Net income ↓ Shareholders' equity Translation loss	↓ Revenues ↓ Assets ↓ Liabilities ↓ Net income ↓ Shareholders' equity Negative translation adjustment

3.5. Translation When a Foreign Subsidiary Operates in a Hyperinflationary Economy

As noted earlier, IAS 21 and SFAS No. 52 differ substantially in their approach to translating the foreign currency financial statements of foreign entities operating in the currency of a hyperinflationary economy. SFAS No. 52 simply requires the foreign currency financial statements of such an entity to be translated as if the parent's currency is the functional currency, i.e., the temporal method must be used with the resulting translation gain or loss reported in net income. IAS 21 requires the foreign currency financial statements first to be restated for inflation using the procedures of IAS 29, and then the inflation-adjusted financial statements are translated using the current exchange rate.

IAS 29 requires the following procedures in adjusting financial statements for inflation:

Balance Sheet

- Monetary assets and monetary liabilities are not restated because they are already expressed in terms of the monetary unit current at the balance sheet date. Monetary items consist of cash, receivables, and payables.
- Nonmonetary assets and nonmonetary liabilities are restated for changes in the general purchasing power of the monetary unit. Most nonmonetary items are carried at historical cost. In these cases, the restated cost is determined by applying to the historical cost the change in the general price index from the date of acquisition to the balance sheet date. Some nonmonetary items are carried at revalued amounts, for example, property, plant, and equipment revalued according to the allowed alternative treatment in IAS 16, "Property, Plant and Equipment." These items are restated from the date of revaluation.

- All components of stockholders' equity are restated by applying the change in the general price level from the beginning of the period or, if later, from the date of contribution to the balance sheet date.

Income Statement

- All income statement items are restated by applying the change in the general price index from the dates when the items were originally recorded to the balance sheet date.
- The net gain or loss in purchasing power that arises from holding monetary assets and monetary liabilities during a period of inflation is included in net income.

The procedures for adjusting financial statements for inflation are similar in concept to the procedures followed when using the temporal method for translation. By restating non-monetary assets and liabilities along with stockholders' equity in terms of the general price level at the balance sheet date, these items are carried at their historical amount of purchasing power. Only the monetary items, which are not restated for inflation, are exposed to inflation risk. The effect of that exposure is reflected through the purchasing power gain or loss on the net monetary asset or liability position.

Holding cash and receivables during a period of inflation results in a **purchasing power loss**, whereas holding payables during inflation results in a **purchasing power gain**. This can be demonstrated through the following examples.

Assume that the general price index (GPI) at 1 January 2008 is 100; that is, a representative basket of goods and services can be purchased on that date for $100. At the end of 2008, the same basket of goods and services costs $120; thus, the country has experienced an inflation rate of 20 percent ([$120 − $100]/$100). Cash of $100 can be used to acquire one basket of goods at 1 January 2008. One year later, however, when the GPI stands at 120, the same $100 in cash can now purchase only 83.3 percent of a basket of goods and services. At the end of 2008 it now takes $120 to purchase the same amount as $100 could purchase at the beginning of the year. The difference between the amount of cash needed to purchase one market basket at year-end ($120) and the amount actually held ($100) results in a purchasing power loss of $20 from holding cash of $100 during the year.

Borrowing money during a period of inflation increases purchasing power. Assume that a company expects to receive $120 in cash at the end of 2008. If it waits until the cash is received, the company will be able to purchase exactly 1.0 baskets of goods and services when the GPI stands at 120. If instead, the company borrows $120 at 1 January 2008 when the GPI is 100, it can acquire 1.2 baskets of goods and services. This results in a purchasing power gain of $20. Of course, there is an interest cost associated with the borrowing that offsets a portion of this gain.

A net purchasing power gain will arise when a company holds a greater amount of monetary liabilities than monetary assets, and a net purchasing power loss will result when the opposite situation exists. As such, purchasing power gains and losses are analogous to the translation gains and losses that arise when the currency is weakening in value and the temporal method of translation is applied.

Although the procedures required by SFAS No. 52 and IAS 21 for translating the foreign currency financial statements in high inflation countries are fundamentally different, the results, in a rare occurrence, can be very similar. Indeed, if the exchange rate between two currencies changes by exactly the same percentage amount as the change in the general price index in the highly inflationary country, then the two methodologies produce the same results. This is demonstrated in Example 16-7.

EXAMPLE 16-7   Translation of Foreign Currency Financial Statements of a Foreign Entity Operating in a High Inflation Country

ABC Company formed a subsidiary in a foreign country on 1 January 2008, through a combination of debt and equity financing. The foreign subsidiary acquired land on 1 January 2008, which it rents to a local farmer. The foreign subsidiary's financial statements for its first year of operations, in foreign currency units (FC), are as follows:

Foreign Subsidiary Income Statement

(in FC)	2008
Rent revenue	1,000
Interest expense	(250)
Net income	750

Foreign Subsidiary

Balance Sheets

(in FC)	1 Jan 08	31 Dec 08
Cash	1,000	1,750
Land	9,000	9,000
Total	10,000	10,750
Note payable (5%)	5,000	5,000
Capital stock	5,000	5,000
Retained earnings	0	750
Total	10,000	10,750

The foreign country experienced significant inflation in 2008, especially in the second half of the year. The general price index during 2008 was:

1 January 2008	100
Average, 2008	125
31 December 2008	200

The rate of inflation in 2008 was 100 percent, and the foreign country clearly meets the definition of a highly inflationary economy under both IFRS and U.S. GAAP.

As a result of the high rate of inflation in the foreign country, the FC weakened substantially during the year relative to other currencies. Relevant exchange rates between ABC's presentation currency (U.S. dollars) and the FC during 2008 were:

	$ per FC
1 January 2008	1.00
Average, 2008	0.80
31 December 2008	0.50

What amounts will ABC Company include in its consolidated financial statements for the year ended 31 December 2008 related to this foreign subsidiary?

Solution. Assuming that ABC Company wishes to prepare its consolidated financial statements in accordance with IFRS, the foreign subsidiary's 2008 financial statements would be restated for local inflation and then translated into ABC's presentation currency using the current rate method as follows:

	FC	Restatement Factor	Inflation-Adjusted FC	Exch. Rate	$
Cash	1,750	200/200	1,750	0.50	875
Land	9,000	200/100	18,000	0.50	9,000
Total	10,750		19,750		9,875
Note payable	5,000	200/200	5,000	0.50	2,500
Capital stock	5,000	200/100	10,000	0.50	5,000
Retained earnings	750		4,750	0.50	2,375
Total	10,750		19,750		9,875
Revenues	1,000	200/125	1,600	0.50	800
Interest expense	(250)	200/125	(400)	0.50	(200)
Subtotal	750		1,200		600
Purchasing power gain/loss			3,550	0.50	1,775
Net income			4,750		2,375

All financial statement items are restated to the GPI at 31 December 2008. The net purchasing power gain of FC 3,550 can be explained as follows:

Gain from holding note payable	FC 5,000 × (200 − 100)/100 = FC 5,000
Loss from holding beginning balance in cash	−1,000 × (200 − 100)/100 = (1,000)
Loss from increase in cash during the year	−750 × (200 − 125)/125 = (450)
Net purchasing power gain (loss)	FC 3,550

Note that all inflation-adjusted FC amounts are translated at the current exchange rate, and thus no translation adjustment is needed.

Now assume that ABC Company wishes to comply with U.S. GAAP in preparing its consolidated financial statements. In that case, the foreign subsidiary's FC financial statements are translated into U.S. dollars using the temporal method, with the resulting translation gain/loss reported in net income, as follows:

	FC	Exch. Rate	$
Cash	1,750	0.50 C	875
Land	9,000	1.00 H	9,000
Total	10,750		9,875

Note payable	5,000	0.50 C	2,500
Capital stock	5,000	1.00 H	5,000
Retained earnings	750		2,375
Total	10,750		9,875
Revenues	1,000	0.80 A	800
Interest expense	(250)	0.80 A	(200)
Subtotal	750		600
Translation gain[a]			1,775
Net income			2,375

C, current exchange rate; A, average-for-the-year exchange rate; H, historical exchange rate.

[a]The dividend is zero and the increase in retained earnings is 2,375 (from the balance sheet), so net income is $2,375, and thus the translation gain is $1,775.

Application of the temporal method as required by U.S. GAAP in this situation results in exactly the same U.S. dollar amounts as were obtained under the restate/translate approach required by IFRS. The equivalence of results under the two approaches exists because of the exact one-to-one inverse relationship between the change in the GPI in the foreign country and the change in the dollar value of the FC, as predicted by the theory of purchasing power parity. The GPI doubled and the FC lost half its purchasing power, which caused the FC to lose half its value in dollar terms. To the extent that this relationship does not hold, and it rarely if ever does, the two different methodologies will generate different translated amounts. For example, if the 31 December 2008 exchange rate had adjusted to only $0.60 per FC (rather than $0.50 per FC), then translated net income would have been $2,050 under U.S. GAAP and $2,850 under IFRS.

3.6. Companies Use Both Translation Methods at the Same Time

Under both IFRS and U.S. GAAP it is possible that a multinational corporation will need to use both the current rate and the temporal methods of translation at a single point in time. This will be true when some foreign subsidiaries have a foreign currency as their functional currency (and therefore are translated using the current rate method) and other foreign subsidiaries have the parent's currency as their functional currency (and therefore are translated using the temporal method). As a result, the consolidated financial statements of a multinational corporation can reflect at the same time both a net translation gain or loss that is included in the determination of net income (from foreign subsidiaries translated using the temporal method) and a separate cumulative translation adjustment that is reported on the balance sheet in stockholders' equity (from foreign subsidiaries translated using the current rate method).

Exxon Mobil Corporation is an example of a company that has a mixture of foreign currency and parent currency functional currency subsidiaries, as evidenced by the following excerpt from its 2006 annual report:

Exxon Mobil Corporation, Note 1.
Summary of Significant Accounting Policies

Foreign Currency Translation. *The Corporation selects the functional reporting currency for its international subsidiaries based on the currency of the primary economic environment in which each subsidiary operates. Downstream and Chemical operations primarily use the local currency. However, the U.S. dollar is used in highly inflationary countries (primarily in Latin America) and Singapore, which predominantly sells into the U.S. dollar export market. Upstream operations which are relatively self-contained and integrated within a particular country, such as Canada, the United Kingdom, Norway and continental Europe, use the local currency. Some Upstream operations, primarily in Asia, West Africa, Russia and the Middle East, use the U.S. dollar because they predominantly sell crude and natural gas production into U.S. dollar-denominated markets. For all operations, gains or losses from remeasuring foreign currency transactions into the functional currency are included in income.*

Because of the judgment involved in determining the functional currency of foreign operations, two companies operating in the same industry might apply this judgment differently. For example, while Exxon Mobil has identified the local currency as the functional currency for many of its international subsidiaries, Chevron Corporation has designated the U.S. dollar as the functional currency for substantially all of its overseas operations as indicated in the company's 2006 Annual Report:

Chevron Corporation, Note 1.
Summary of Significant Accounting Policies

Currency Translation *The U.S. dollar is the functional currency for substantially all of the company's consolidated operations and those of its equity affiliates. For those operations, all gains and losses from currency translations are currently included in income. The cumulative translation effects for those few entities, both consolidated and affiliated, using functional currencies other than the U.S. dollar are included in the currency translation adjustment in "Stockholders' Equity."*

Evaluating net income reported by Exxon Mobil against net income reported by Chevron presents a comparability problem. This problem can be partially resolved by adding the translation adjustments reported in stockholders' equity to net income for both companies. The feasibility of this solution is dependent on the level of detail disclosed by multinational corporations with respect to the translation of foreign currency financial statements.

3.7. Disclosures Related to Translation Methods

Both IAS 21 and SFAS No. 52 require two types of disclosures related to foreign currency translation:

1. The amount of exchange differences recognized in net income.
2. The amount of cumulative translation adjustment classified in a separate component of equity, along with a reconciliation of the amount of cumulative translation adjustment at the beginning and end of the period.

SFAS No. 52 also specifically requires disclosure of the amount of translation adjustment transferred from stockholders' equity and included in current net income as a result of the disposal of a foreign entity.

The amount of exchange differences recognized in net income consists of:

- Foreign currency *transaction* gains and losses, and
- *Translation* gains and losses resulting from application of the temporal method.

Neither IAS 21 nor SFAS No. 52 requires disclosure of the two separate amounts that comprise the total exchange difference recognized in net income, and most companies do not provide disclosure at that level of detail. However, BASF AG (shown in Exhibit 16-1) is an exception. Note 5 in BASF's annual report separately discloses gains from foreign currency transactions and gains from translation of financial statements, both of which are included in the line item "Other Operating Income" on the income statement, as shown below:

5. Other Operating Income

(€ millions)	2006	2005
Reversal and adjustment of provisions	275.2	118.4
Revenue from miscellaneous revenue-generating activities	62.3	85.3
Gains from foreign currency transactions	119.7	43.3
Gains from the translation of financial statements in foreign currencies	10.8	57.3
Gains from disposal of property, plant and equipment and divestitures	127.8	107.4
Gains on the reversal of allowance for doubtful receivables	89.0	92.1
Other	249.3	96.4
	934.1	600.2

The company provides a similar level of detail in Note 6 related to other operating expenses.

Disclosures related to foreign currency translation commonly are found in both the Management Discussion & Analysis (MD&A) and the Notes to Financial Statements sections of an annual report. Exhibit 16-6 provides foreign currency–related disclosures made by Swedish appliance manufacturer Electolux AB in its 2006 annual report along with an analysis of those disclosures. As a company based in the European Union, Electrolux uses IFRS in preparing its consolidated financial statements.

Exhibit 16-7 (page 708) provides an analysis of the foreign currency-related disclosures made in 2006 by Yahoo! Inc., a U.S.-based company that prepares financial statements in accordance with U.S. GAAP.

EXHIBIT 16-6   Disclosures Related to Foreign Currency Translation: Electrolux AB 2006 Annual Report

Electrolux provides the following information related to exchange rate exposure in its discussion of Financial Risks and Commitment in the MD&A:

Exchange-rate exposure

Operations in a number of different countries throughout the world expose Electrolux to the effects of changes in exchange rates. These affect Group income through translation of income statements in foreign subsidiaries to SEK, i.e., translation exposure, as well as through exports of products and sales outside the country of manufacture, i.e., transaction exposure.

(Continued)

(Continued)

> *Translation exposure is related mainly to EUR and USD. Transaction exposure is greatest in EUR, USD, GBP and HUF. The Group's global presence and widespread production and sales enable exchange-rate effects to be balanced.*

The last sentence suggests that natural hedges exist among Electrolux's different exchange rate exposures that results in a relatively small *net* gain or loss arising from fluctuations in exchange rates.

Note 1, Accounting and Valuation Principles, discloses the principles used by the company to account for foreign currency translation:

Foreign currency translations

> *Foreign currency transactions are translated into the functional currency using the exchange rates prevailing at the dates of the transactions.*

> *The consolidated financial statements are presented in SEK, which is the Parent Company's functional and presentation currency.*

> *The balance sheets of foreign subsidiaries have been translated into SEK at year-end rates. The income statements have been translated at the average rates for the year. Translation differences thus arising have been taken directly to equity.*

> *Prior to consolidation, the financial statements of subsidiaries in countries with highly inflationary economies and whose functional currency is other than the local currency have been remeasured into their functional currency and the exchange-rate differences arising from that remeasurement have been charged to income. When the functional currency is the local currency, the financial statements have been restated in accordance with IAS 29. When a foreign operation is partially disposed of or sold, exchange differences that were recorded in equity are recognized in the income statement as part of the gain or loss on sales.*

Monetary assets and liabilities in foreign currency

> *Monetary assets and liabilities denominated in foreign currency are valued at year-end exchange rates and the exchange-rate differences are included in the income statement, except when deferred in equity for the effective part of a qualifying net investment hedge. Exposure from net investments (balance sheet exposure)*

> *The net of assets and liabilities in foreign subsidiaries constitute a net investment in foreign currency, which generates a translation difference in connection with consolidation. This exposure can have an impact on the Group's equity, and on the capital structure, and is hedged according to the Financial Policy. The Financial Policy stipulates the extent to which the net investments can be hedged and also sets the benchmark for risk measurement. The benchmark was changed at the end of 2006 and only investments with an equity capitalization exceeding 60% are hedged unless the exposure is considered too high by the Group. The result of this change is that only a limited number of currencies are hedged on a continuous basis. Group Treasury is allowed to deviate from the benchmark under a given risk mandate. Hedging of the Group's net investments is implemented within the Parent Company in Sweden.*

Notes 4 and 9 indicate that the company includes exchange rate differences as components of both operating income and financial income and expense. Note 9, Financial Income and Financial Expenses, discloses that: *Exchange-rate differences on foreign currency loans and borrowings, net* amounted to SEK 46 million in 2006 (approximately 1.2 percent of pretax income). These are one type of transaction gain or loss.

Note 4, Net Sales and Operating Income, indicates that in 2006: *The Group's operating income includes net-exchange-rate differences in the amount of SEK 76 million.* This represented approximately 2 percent of pretax income. Although not explicitly stated, the amount of exchange rate difference included in operating income presumably includes both transaction gains and losses related to foreign currency accounts payable and accounts receivable as well as translation gains and losses related to those foreign subsidiaries whose financial statements are translated using the temporal method.

Note 1 shown above indicates that translation differences arising from the translation of the foreign currency financial statements of local currency functional currency subsidiaries are taken directly to equity. The equity section of the consolidated balance sheet is as follows:

Equity attributable to equity holders of the Parent Company (SEK in millions)	Note	31 December 2006	31 December 2005
Share capital	20	1,545	1,545
Other paid-in capital		2,905	2,905
Other reserves	18	−11	1,653
Retained earnings		8,754	19,784
		13,193	**25,887**
Minority interests		1	1
Total equity		13,194	25,888

Note 18 reveals that translation differences are included in other reserves as a currency translation reserve, as shown below:

Note 18, Other Reserves in Equity

(SEK millions)	Available-for-sale instruments	Hedging reserve	Currency translation reserve	Total other reserves
Opening balance, 1 January 2005			(489)	(489)
Effects of changes in accounting principles		7		7
Opening balance, 1 January 2005, after adoption of IAS 32 and IAS 39		7	(489)	(482)
Available-for-sale instruments				
Gain/loss taken to equity	24			24
Cash flow hedges				
Gain/loss taken to equity		16		16
Transferred to profit and loss on sale		(7)		(7)
Exchange differences on translation of foreign operations				—
Equity hedge			(615)	(615)
Translation difference			2,717	2,717
Net income recognized directly in equity	24	9	2,102	2,135
Closing balance, 31 December 2005	24	16	1,613	1,653

(Continued)

EXHIBIT 16-6   (*Continued*)

(SEK millions)	Other reserves			
	Available-for-sale instruments	Hedging reserve	Currency translation reserve	Total other reserves
Available-for-sale instruments				
Gain/loss taken to equity	30			30
Cash flow hedges				
Gain/loss taken to equity		(34)		(34)
Transferred to profit and loss on sale				
Exchange differences on translation of foreign operations				
Equity hedge			421	421
Translation difference	—	—	(2,081)	(2,081)
Net income recognized directly in equity	30	(34)	(1,660)	(1,664)
Closing balance, 31 December 2006	54	(18)	(47)	(11)

The opening balance in the currency translation reserve on 1 January 2005 was a negative SEK 489 million. The translation adjustment in 2005 was a positive SEK 2,717 million. Assuming that most if not all of Electrolux's foreign subsidiaries have more assets than liabilities, the positive sign of the adjustment suggests that, on average, the functional currencies in which the company's foreign subsidiaries operate strengthened against the Swedish krona (SEK) in 2005. The opposite is true in 2006 as evidenced by the negative translation difference of SEK 2,081 million. The currency translation reserve also includes amounts related to equity hedges. Although there is no further description of these items, it is reasonable to assume that these reflect the gains and losses on financial instruments used to hedge the translation differences related to balance sheet exposure. The effect of the equity hedges is of the opposite sign from the translation difference in each year indicating that the hedges were effective in partially offsetting the translation difference. Nonetheless, the balance in the currency translation reserve fluctuates greatly from year-to-year; from SEK −489 million at 31 December 04 to SEK +1,613 million at 31 December 05 and SEK –47 million at 31 December 06.

EXHIBIT 16-7   Disclosures Related to Foreign Currency Translation: Yahoo! Inc. 2006 Annual Report

Yahoo! Inc. is a U.S.-based provider of internet services. In the Management Discussion & Analysis section of the 2006 Annual Report, the company reports that 32 percent of revenues are generated from international operations, up from 30 percent in 2005 and 28 percent in 2004 (p. 44). As part of its Quantitative and Qualitative Disclosures about Market Risk, the company states that:

The growth in our international operations has increased our exposure to foreign currency fluctuations. Revenues and related expenses generated from our international subsidiaries are generally denominated in the functional currencies of the local countries. Primary currencies include Euros, British Pounds, Japanese Yen, Korean Won and Australian Dollars. The statements of income of our international operations are translated into United States dollars at the average exchange rate in each applicable period. To the extent the United States dollar strengthens against foreign currencies, the translation of these foreign currency denominated transactions results in reduced revenues, operating expense and net income for our International segment.

Similarly, our revenues, operating expenses and net income will increase for our International segment, if the United States dollar weakens against foreign currencies.

Note that Yahoo! describes its foreign currency risk from the perspective of how the U.S. dollar fluctuates against foreign currencies. If the U.S. dollar strengthens, then foreign currencies must weaken, which will result in reduced revenues, expenses, and income from foreign operations.

The stockholders' equity section of Yahoo!'s Consolidated Balance Sheet includes the following line item, in which several types of unrealized gains and losses have been accumulated:

	31 December	
	2005	2006
Accumulated other comprehensive income (loss)	(35,965)	150,505

The Consolidated Statement of Stockholders' Equity provides detail on the components comprising Accumulated other comprehensive income (loss). The relevant portion of that statement appears below:

	Years Ended 31 December		
	2004	2005	2006
Accumulated other comprehensive income (loss)			
Balance, beginning of year	3,598	535,736	(35,965)
Net change in unrealized gains/losses on available-for-sale securities, net of tax	471,425	(491,532)	38,018
Foreign currency translation adjustments, net of tax	60,713	(80,169)	148,452
Balance, end of year	535,736	(35,965)	150,505

The foreign currency translation adjustments arise from applying the current rate method to translate the foreign currency functional currency financial statements of foreign subsidiaries. Assuming that Yahoo!'s foreign subsidiaries have positive net assets, the negative translation adjustment in 2005 is the result of a weakening in the foreign functional currencies in which Yahoo!'s foreign subsidiaries operate. Conversely, this can be viewed as a strengthening in the U.S. dollar. The positive translation adjustment in 2006 results from a strengthening in foreign currencies (weakening in the U.S. dollar). If these translation adjustments had been included in the calculation of income, net income would have been as follows:

	2005	2006	% Change
Net income	$1,896,230	$751,391	–60.4%
Foreign currency translation adjustment	(80,169)	148,452	
	$1,816,061	$899,843	–50.5%

The percentage decrease in reported net income from 2005 to 2006 of 60.4 percent would have been somewhat smaller if the translation adjustments had been treated as gains and losses in net income.

As noted in the previous section, because of the judgment involved in determining the functional currency of foreign operations, two companies operating in the same industry might use different predominant translation methods. As a result, income reported by these companies is not directly comparable. Exxon Mobil Corporation and Chevron Corporation, both operating in the petroleum industry, are an example of two companies for which this is the case. Whereas Chevron has identified the U.S. dollar as the functional currency for substantially all of its foreign subsidiaries, Exxon Mobil indicates that its downstream and chemical operations, as well as some of its upstream operations, primarily use the local currency as the functional currency. As a result Chevron primarily uses the temporal method with translation gains and losses included in income, while Exxon Mobil uses the current rate method to a much greater extent with the resulting translation adjustments excluded from income. To make the income of these two companies more comparable, an analyst can use the disclosures related to translation adjustments to include these as gains and losses in determining an adjusted amount of income. Example 16-8 demonstrates this process for Exxon Mobil and Chevron.

EXAMPLE 16-8   Comparing Net Income for Exxon Mobil Corporation and Chevron Corporation

Exxon Mobil Corporation uses the current rate method to translate the foreign currency financial statements of a substantial number of its foreign subsidiaries and includes the resulting translation adjustments in the "Accumulated other nonowner changes in equity" line item in the stockholders' equity section of the Consolidated Balance Sheet. Detail on the items composing "Accumulated other nonowner changes in equity," including "Foreign exchange translation adjustment," is provided in the Consolidated Statement of Shareholders' Equity.

Chevron Corporation uses the temporal method to translate the foreign currency financial statements of substantially all of its foreign subsidiaries. However, for those few entities using functional currencies other than the U.S. dollar, the current rate method is used and the resulting translation adjustments are included in the "Accumulated other comprehensive loss" component of stockholders' equity. The Consolidated Statement of Stockholders' Equity provides detail on the changes in the component of stockholders' equity, including a "Currency translation adjustment."

Combining net income from the income statement and the change in the cumulative translation adjustment account from the statement of stockholders' equity, an adjusted net income in which translation adjustments are treated as gains and losses can be calculated for each company as shown in the table below (amounts in millions of U.S. dollars):

Exxon Mobil	2006	2005	2004
Reported net income	39,500	36,130	25,330
Translation adjustment	2,754	(2,619)	2,177
Adjusted net income	42,254	33,511	27,507

Chevron

Reported net income	17,138	14,099	13,328
Translation adjustment	55	(5)	36
Adjusted net income	17,193	14,094	13,364

The sign (positive or negative) of the translation adjustment is the same for both companies in each of the years 2004 through 2006. But Exxon Mobil has significantly larger translation adjustments than Chevron because Exxon Mobil designates the local currency as functional currency for a substantially larger portion of it foreign operations.

A comparison of the relative amounts of net income generated by the two companies is different depending on whether reported net income or adjusted net income is used. Exxon Mobil's reported net income in 2004 is 1.90 times larger than Chevron's, whereas its adjusted net income is 2.06 times larger. This is shown in the table below, which also shows that the year-to-year percentage change in the ratio of net income between the two companies differs significantly depending on the income measure used. For example, based on reported net income, the ratio of net income decreased from 2005 to 2006 by 10 percent (from 2.56 down to 2.30); based on adjusted net income, the ratio increased from 2005 to 2006 by 3 percent (from 2.38 to 2.46).

	2006	**2005**	**2004**
Exxon Mobil reported net income/ Chevron reported net income	2.30	2.56	1.90
Year-to-year % change	−10%	+35%	
Exxon Mobil adjusted net income/ Chevron adjusted net income	2.46	2.38	2.06
Year-to-year % change	+3%	+16%	

Including translation adjustments as gains and losses in the measurement of an adjusted net income provides a more comparable basis for evaluating the profitability of two companies that are using different predominant translation methods. However, bringing the translation adjustments into the calculation of adjusted net income still might not provide truly comparable measures because of the different impact that the different translation methods have on reported net income. For example, both Exxon Mobil and Chevron reported a positive translation adjustment in 2006 because foreign currencies generally strengthened against the U.S. dollar that year. Assuming Chevron's U.S. dollar functional currency foreign subsidiaries mostly had net monetary liability positions, application of the temporal method in a year in which foreign currencies strengthened against the U.S. dollar resulted in a net translation loss that was included in net income. However, because Exxon Mobil has designated many of its foreign subsidiaries as foreign currency functional currency operations, a similar loss would not be recognized; instead, a positive translation adjustment would result (knowing that Exxon has positive net assets). All else equal, Chevron's 2006 adjusted net income is likely to be less than Exxon Mobil's adjusted net income simply because Chevron has designated a larger portion of its foreign operations as having the U.S. dollar as the functional currency.

Some analysts believe that all nonowner changes in stockholders' equity, such as translation adjustments, should be included in the determination of net income. This is referred to as **clean-surplus accounting,** as opposed to **dirty-surplus accounting**, in which some income items are reported as part of stockholders' equity rather than as gains and losses on the income statement. One of the **dirty-surplus items** found in both IFRS and U.S. GAAP financial statements is the translation adjustment that arises when a foreign currency is determined to be the functional currency of a foreign subsidiary. Disclosures made in accordance with IFRS and U.S. GAAP provide analysts with the detail needed to be able to calculate net income on a clean-surplus basis. In fact, both sets of standards allow (but do not specifically require) companies to prepare a statement of comprehensive income in which unrealized gains and losses that have been deferred in stockholders' equity are included in a measure of comprehensive income. Chevron Corporation is one U.S. company that has elected to prepare a statement of comprehensive income. Exhibit 16-8 presents Chevron's Consolidated Statement of Comprehensive Income as shown in the company's 2006 annual report.

EXHIBIT 16-8	Excerpt from Chevron Corporation 2006 Annual Report: Consolidated Statement of Comprehensive Income

	Year ended 31 December		
($ millions)	**2006**	**2005**	**2004**
Net income	$17,138	$14,099	$13,328
Currency translation adjustment			
Unrealized net change arising during period	55	(5)	36
Unrealized holding (loss) gain on securities			
Net (loss) gain arising during period	(88)	(32)	35
Reclassification to net income of net realized (gain)	—	—	(44)
Total	(88)	(32)	(9)
Net derivatives gain (loss) on hedge transactions			
Net gain (loss) arising during period			
Before income taxes	2	(242)	(8)
Income taxes	6	89	(1)
Reclassification to net income of net realized gain (loss)			
Before income taxes	95	34	—
Income taxes	(36)	(12)	—
Total	67	(131)	(9)
Minimum pension liability adjustment			
Before income taxes	(88)	89	719
Income taxes	50	(31)	(247)
Total	(38)	58	472
Other comprehensive (loss) gain, net of tax	(4)	(110)	490
Comprehensive income	$17,134	$13,989	$13,818

Chevron has four "dirty-surplus items" that are required under U.S. GAAP to be reported as "other comprehensive income" in stockholders' equity rather than as gains and losses in net income. In the Statement of Comprehensive Income, these items are added to net income to determine comprehensive income. The first of these four items is the currency translation adjustment that arises when the current rate method is used to translate the foreign currency financial statements of those foreign operations that have been determined to have a foreign currency as their functional currency.

4. SUMMARY

The translation of foreign currency amounts is an important accounting issue for companies with multinational operations. Fluctuations in foreign exchange rates cause the functional currency values of foreign currency assets and liabilities resulting from foreign currency transactions as well as from foreign subsidiaries to change over time, giving rise to foreign exchange differences that must be reflected in the financial statements. Determining how to measure these foreign exchange differences and whether to include them in the calculation of net income are the major issues in accounting for multinational operations.

- The local currency is the national currency of the country where an entity is located. The functional currency is the currency of the primary economic environment in which an entity operates. Normally, the local currency is an entity's functional currency. For accounting purposes, any currency other than an entity's functional currency is a foreign currency for that entity. The currency in which financial statement amounts are presented is known as the presentation currency. In most cases, the presentation currency will be the same as the local currency.

- When an export sale (import purchase) on account is denominated in a foreign currency, the sales revenue (inventory) and foreign currency account receivable (account payable) are translated into the seller's (buyer's) functional currency using the exchange rate on the transaction date. Any change in the functional currency value of the foreign currency account receivable (account payable) that occurs from the transaction date to the settlement date is recognized as a foreign currency transaction gain or loss in net income.

- If a balance sheet date falls between the transaction date and the settlement date, the foreign currency account receivable (account payable) is translated at the exchange rate at the balance sheet date. The change in the functional currency value of the foreign currency account receivable (account payable) is recognized as a foreign currency transaction gain or loss in income. Analysts should understand that these gains and losses are unrealized at the time they are recognized, and might or might not be realized when the transactions are settled.

- A foreign currency transaction gain arises when an entity has a foreign currency receivable and the foreign currency strengthens or it has a foreign currency payable and the foreign currency weakens. A foreign currency transaction loss arises when an entity has a foreign currency receivable and the foreign currency weakens or it has a foreign currency payable and the foreign currency strengthens.

- Companies must disclose the net foreign currency gain or loss included in income. They may choose to report foreign currency transaction gains and losses as a component of operating income or as a component of non-operating income. If two companies choose to report foreign currency transaction gains and losses differently, making a direct comparison of operating profit and operating profit margin between the two companies is questionable.

- To prepare consolidated financial statements, foreign currency financial statements of foreign operations must be translated into the parent company's presentation currency. The major conceptual issues related to this translation process are what is the appropriate exchange rate for translating each financial statement item and how should the resulting translation adjustment be reflected in the consolidated financial statements. Two different translation methods are used worldwide.

- Under the current rate method, assets and liabilities are translated at the current exchange rate, equity items are translated at historical exchange rates, and revenues and expenses are translated at the exchange rate that existed when the underlying transaction occurred. For practical reasons, an average exchange rate is often used to translate income items.

- Under the temporal method, monetary assets (and nonmonetary assets measured at current value) and monetary liabilities (and nonmonetary liabilities measured at current value) are translated at the current exchange rate. Nonmonetary assets and liabilities not measured at current value and equity items are translated at historical exchange rates. Revenues and expenses, other than those expenses related to nonmonetary assets, are translated at the exchange rate that existed when the underlying transaction occurred. Expenses related to nonmonetary assets are translated at the exchange rates used for the related assets.

- Under both IFRS and U.S. GAAP, the functional currency of a foreign operation determines the method to be used in translating its foreign currency financial statements into the parent's presentation currency and whether the resulting translation adjustment is recognized in income or as a separate component of equity.

- The foreign currency financial statements of a foreign operation that has a foreign currency as its functional currency are translated using the current rate method and the translation adjustment is accumulated as a separate component of equity. The cumulative translation adjustment related to a specific foreign entity is transferred to net income when that entity is sold or otherwise disposed of. The balance sheet risk exposure associated with the current rate method is equal to the foreign subsidiary's net asset position.

- The foreign currency financial statements of a foreign operation that has the parent's presentation currency as its functional currency are translated using the temporal method and the translation adjustment is included as a gain or loss in income. U.S. GAAP refers to this process as *remeasurement*. The balance sheet exposure associated with the temporal method is equal to the foreign subsidiary's net monetary asset/liability position (adjusted for nonmonetary items measured at current value).

- IFRS and U.S. GAAP differ with respect to the translation of foreign currency financial statements of foreign operations located in a highly inflationary country. Under IFRS, the foreign currency statements are first restated for local inflation and then translated using the current exchange rate. Under U.S. GAAP, the foreign currency financial statements are translated using the temporal method, without any restatement for inflation.

- Application of the different translation methods for a given foreign operation can result in very different amounts reported in the parent's consolidated financial statements.

- Companies must disclose the total amount of translation gain or loss reported in income and the amount of translation adjustment included in a separate component of stockholders' equity. Companies are not required to separately disclose the component of translation gain or loss arising from foreign currency transactions and the component arising from application of the temporal method.

- Disclosures related to translation adjustments reported in equity can be used to include these as gains and losses in determining an adjusted amount of income following a clean-surplus approach to income measurement.

Foreign currency translation rules are well-established in both IFRS and U.S. GAAP. Fortunately, except for the treatment of foreign operations located in highly inflationary countries, there are no major differences between the two sets of standards in this area. The ability to understand the impact of foreign currency translation on the financial results of a company using IFRS should apply equally as well in the analysis of financial statements prepared in accordance with U.S. GAAP.

PRACTICE PROBLEMS

The following information relates to Problems 1 through 6.

Pedro Ruiza is an analyst for a credit rating agency. One of the companies he follows, Eurexim SA, is based in France and complies with International Financial Reporting Standards (IFRS). Ruiz has learned that Eurexim used €220 million of its own cash and borrowed an equal amount to open a subsidiary in Ukraine. The funds were converted into hryvnia (UAH) on 31 December 2007 at an exchange rate of €1.00 = UAH6.70 and used to purchase UAH1,500 million in fixed assets and UAH300 of inventories.

Ruiz is concerned about the effect that the subsidiary's results might have on Eurexim's consolidated financial statements. He calls Eurexim's Chief Financial Officer, but learns little. Eurexim is not willing to share sales forecasts and has not even made a determination as to the subsidiary's functional currency.

Absent more useful information, Ruiz decides to explore various scenarios to determine the potential impact on Eurexim's consolidated financial statements. Ukraine is not currently in a hyperinflationary environment, but Ruiz is concerned that this situation could change. Ruiz also believes the euro will appreciate against the hryvnia for the foreseeable future.

1. If Ukraine's economy becomes highly inflationary, Eurexim will *most likely* translate inventory by
   A. restating for inflation and using the temporal method.
   B. restating for inflation and using the current rate method.
   C. using the temporal method with no restatement for inflation.

2. Given Ruiza's belief about the direction of exchange rates, Eurexim's gross profit margin would be *highest* if it accounts for the Ukraine subsidiary's inventory using
   A. FIFO and the temporal method.
   B. weighted average cost and the temporal method.
   C. weighted average cost and the current rate method.

3. If the euro is chosen as the Ukraine subsidiary's functional currency, Eurexim will translate its fixed assets using the
   A. average rate for the reporting period.
   B. rate in effect when the assets were purchased.
   C. rate in effect at the end of the reporting period.

4. If the euro is chosen as the Ukraine subsidiary's functional currency, Eurexim will translate its accounts receivable using the
   A. rate in effect at the transaction date.
   B. average rate for the reporting period.
   C. rate in effect at the end of the reporting period.

5. If the hryvnia is chosen as the Ukraine subsidiary's functional currency, Eurexim will translate its inventory using the
   A. average rate for the reporting period.
   B. rate in effect at the end of the reporting period.
   C. rate in effect at the time the inventory was purchased.

6. Based on the information available and Ruiza's expectations regarding exchange rates, if the hryvnia is chosen as the Ukraine subsidiary's functional currency Eurexim will *most likely* report
   A. an addition to the cumulative translation adjustment.
   B. a subtraction from the cumulative translation adjustment.
   C. a translation gain or loss as a component of net income.

The following information relates to Problems 7 through 12.

Consolidated Motors is a U.S.-based corporation that sells mechanical engines and components used by electric utilities. Its Canadian subsidiary, Consol-Can, operates solely in Canada. It was created on 31 December 2006 and Consolidated Motors determined at that time that it should use the U.S. dollar as its functional currency.

Chief Financial Officer Monica Templeton was asked to explain to the Board of Directors how exchange rates affect the financial statements of both Consol-Can and the consolidated financial statements of Consolidated Motors. For the presentation, Templeton collects Consol-Can's balance sheets for the years ended 2006 and 2007 (Exhibit 16-9), as well as relevant exchange rate information (Exhibit 16-10).

Templeton explains that Consol-Can uses the FIFO inventory accounting method, and that purchases of C$300 million and the sell-through of that inventory occurred evenly throughout 2007. Her presentation includes reporting the translated amounts in U.S. currency for each item, as well as associated translation related gains and losses. The Board responds with several questions.

- Would there be a reason to change the functional currency to the Canadian dollar?
- Would there be any translation effects for Consolidated Motors if the functional currency for Consol-Can were changed to the Canadian dollar?
- Would a change in the functional currency have any impact on financial statement ratios for the parent company?
- What would be the balance sheet exposure to translation effects if the functional currency were changed?

7. After translating Consol-Can's inventory and long-term debt into the parent currency (US$), the amounts reported on Consolidated Motor's financial statements at 31 December 2007 would be *closest* to (in millions)
   A. $71 for inventory and $161 for long-term debt.
   B. $71 for inventory and $166 for long-term debt.
   C. $73 for inventory and $166 for long-term debt.

8. After translating Consol-Can's 31 December 2007 balance sheet into the parent currency, the translated value of retained earnings will be *closest to*
   A. $41 million.
   B. $44 million.
   C. $46 million.

EXHIBIT 16-9   Consol-Can Condensed Balance Sheet, Fiscal
Years Ending 31 December (C$ millions)

Account	2007	2006
Cash	135	167
Accounts receivable	98	—
Inventory	77	30
Fixed assets	100	100
Accumulated depreciation	(10)	—
Total assets	400	297
Accounts payable	77	—
Long-term debt	175	175
Common stock	100	100
Retained earnings	48	—
Total liabilities and shareholders' equity	400	275

EXHIBIT 16-10   Exchange Rate Information

	C$/US$
Rate on 31 December 2006	0.86
Average rate in 2007	0.92
Weighted average rate for inventory purchases	0.92
Rate on 31 December 2007	0.95

9. In response to the Board's first question, Templeton should reply that such a change
   would be *most* justified if
   A. the inflation rate in the United States became hyperinflationary.
   B. management wanted to flow more of the gains through net income.
   C. Consol-Can were making autonomous decisions about operations, investing, and
      financing.

10. In response to the Board's second question, Templeton should note that if the change
    is made, the consolidated financial statements for Consolidated Motors would begin to
    recognize
    A. realized gains and losses on monetary assets and liabilities.
    B. realized gains and losses on non-monetary assets and liabilities.
    C. unrealized gains and losses on non-monetary assets and liabilities.

11. In response to the Board's third question, Templeton should note that the change will
    most likely affect
    A. the cash ratio.
    B. fixed asset turnover.
    C. receivables turnover.

12. In response to the Board's fourth question, the balance sheet exposure (in millions) would be *closest* to
    A. −19.
    B. 148.
    C. 400.

The following information relates to Problems 13 through 18.

Romulus Corp. is a U.S.-based company that prepares its financial statements in accordance with U.S. GAAP. Romulus Corp. has two European subsidiaries: Julius and Augustus. Anthony Marks, CFA, is an analyst trying to forecast Romulus's 2008 results. Marks has prepared separate forecasts for both Julius and Augustus, as well as for Romulus's other operations (prior to consolidating the results.) He is now considering the impact of currency translation on the results of both the subsidiaries and the parent company's consolidated financials. His research has provided the following insights:

- The results for Julius will be translated into U.S. dollars using the current rate method.
- The results for Augustus will be translated into U.S. dollars using the temporal method.
- Both Julius and Augustus use the FIFO method to account for inventory.
- Julius had year-end 2007 inventory of €340 million. Marks believes Julius will report €2300 in sales and €1400 in cost of sales in 2008.

Marks also forecasts the 2008 year-end balance sheet for Julius (Exhibit 16-11). Data and forecasts related to euro/dollar exchange rates are presented in Exhibit 16-12.

EXHIBIT 16-11   Forecasted Balance Sheet Data
for Julius, 31 December 2008 (€ millions)

Cash	50
Accounts receivable	100
Inventory	700
Fixed assets	1,450
Total assets	2,300
Liabilities	700
Common stock	1,500
Retained earnings	100
Total liabilities and shareholder equity	2,300

EXHIBIT 16-12   Exchange Rates ($/€)

31 December 2007	1.47
31 December 2008	1.61
2008 average	1.54
Rate when fixed assets were acquired	1.25
Rate when 2007 inventory was acquired	1.39
Rate when 2008 inventory was acquired	1.49

13. Based on the translation method being used for Julius, the subsidiary is *most likely*
    A. a sales outlet for Romulus's products.
    B. a self-contained, independent operating entity.
    C. using the U.S. dollar as its functional currency.

14. To account for its foreign operations, Romulus has *most likely* designated the euro as the functional currency for
    A. Julius only.
    B. Augustus only.
    C. both Julius and Augustus.

15. When Romulus consolidates the results of Julius, any unrealized exchange rate holding gains on monetary assets should be
    A. reported as part of operating income.
    B. reported as a nonoperating item on the income statement.
    C. reported directly to equity as part of the cumulative translation adjustment.

16. When Marks translates his forecasted balance sheet for Julius into U.S. dollars, total assets on 31 December 2008 (dollars in millions) will be *closest* to
    A. $1,429.
    B. $2,392.
    C. $3,703.

17. When Marks converts his forecasted income statement data into U.S. dollars, the 2008 gross profit margin for Julius will be *closest* to
    A. 39.1 percent.
    B. 40.9 percent.
    C. 44.6 percent.

18. Relative to the gross margins the subsidiaries' report in local currency, Romulus's consolidated gross margin *most likely*
    A. will not be distorted by currency translations.
    B. would be distorted if Augustus were using the same translation method as Julius.
    C. will be distorted due to the translation and inventory accounting methods Augustus is using.

The following information relates to Problems 19 through 24.
    Redline Products, Inc. is a U.S.-based multinational with subsidiaries around the world. One such subsidiary, Acceletron, operates in Singapore, which has seen mild but not excessive rates of inflation. Acceletron was acquired in 2000 and has never paid a dividend. It records inventory using the FIFO method.
    Chief Financial Officer Margot Villiers was asked by Redline's Board of Directors to explain how the functional currency selection and other accounting choices affect Redline's consolidated financial statements. She gathers Acceletron's financial statements denominated in Singapore dollars (SGD) in Exhibit 16-13 and the U.S. dollar/Singapore dollar exchange rates in Exhibit 16-14. She does not intend to identify the functional currency actually in use, but rather to use Acceletron as an example of how the choice of functional currency affects the consolidated statements.

EXHIBIT 16-13   Selected Financial Data for Acceletron,
31 December 2007 (SGD millions)

Cash	SGD	125
Accounts receivable		230
Inventory		500
Fixed assets		1,640
Accumulated depreciation		(205)
Total assets	SGD	2,290
Accounts payable		185
Long-term debt		200
Common stock		620
Retained earnings		1,285
Total liabilities and equity		2,290
Total revenues	SGD	4,800
Net income	SGD	450

EXHIBIT 16-14   Exchange Rates Applicable to Acceletron

Exchange Rate in Effect at Specific Times	USD per SGD
Rate when first 1,000 of fixed assets were acquired	0.568
Rate when remaining 640 of fixed assets were acquired	0.606
Rate when long-term debt was issued	0.588
31 December 2006	0.649
Weighted average rate when inventory was acquired	0.654
Average rate in 2007	0.662
31 December 2007	0.671

19. Compared to using the Singapore dollar as Acceletron's functional currency for 2007, if
    the U.S. dollar were the functional currency it is *most likely* that Redline's consolidated
    A. inventories will be higher.
    B. receivable turnover will be lower.
    C. fixed-asset turnover will be higher.

20. If the U.S. dollar were chosen as the functional currency for Acceletron in 2007, Redline
    could reduce its balance sheet exposure to exchange rates by
    A. selling SGD 30 of fixed-assets for cash.
    B. issuing SGD 30 of long-term debt to buy fixed assets.
    C. issuing SGD 30 in short-term debt to purchase marketable securities.

21. Redline's consolidated gross profit margin for 2007 would be *highest* if Acceletron
    accounted for inventory using
    A. FIFO and its functional currency were the U.S. dollar.
    B. LIFO and its functional currency were the U.S. dollar.
    C. FIFO and its functional currency were the Singapore dollar.

22. If the current rate method is used to translate Acceletron's financial statements into U.S. dollars, Redline's consolidated financial statements will *most likely* include Acceletron's
    A. $3,178 in revenues.
    B. $118 in long-term debt.
    C. negative translation adjustment to shareholder equity.

23. If Acceletron's financial statements are translated into U.S. dollars using the temporal method, Redline's consolidated financial statements will *most likely* include Acceletron's
    A. $336 in inventory.
    B. $956 in fixed assets.
    C. $152 in accounts receivable.

24. When translating Acceletron's financial statements into U.S. dollars, Redline is *least likely* to use an exchange rate of USD per SGD
    A. 0.671.
    B. 0.588.
    C. 0.654.

CHAPTER 17

EVALUATING FINANCIAL REPORTING QUALITY

Scott Richardson

Barclays Global Investors
San Francisco, California

İrem Tuna

The Wharton School
University of Pennsylvania
Philadelphia, Pennsylvania

LEARNING OUTCOMES

After completing this chapter, you will be able to do the following:

- Contrast accrual accounting and cash accounting and explain why accounting discretion exists in an accrual accounting system.
- Describe the relationship between the level of accruals and the persistence of earnings, and the relative multiples which the cash and accrual components of earnings should rationally receive in valuation.
- List and explain the opportunities and motivations for management to intervene in the external financial reporting process, and the mechanisms that discipline such intervention.
- Discuss earnings quality, explain simple measures of earnings quality, and compare and contrast the earnings quality of peer companies.
- Explain mean reversion in earnings and the expected relations between the speed of mean reversion and the accruals component of earnings.
- Identify and explain problems in financial reporting related to revenue recognition, expense recognition, the reporting of assets and liabilities, and the cash flow statement.

- Explain and interpret warning signs of potential problems in each of the major areas of financial reporting (i.e., revenue, expenses, assets, liabilities, and cash flow) and warning signs of overall vulnerability to financial reporting problems.

1. INTRODUCTION

Financial statement analysis involves taking a systematic approach to using information contained in the financial statements to assist in decision making. The set of decision makers using financial statements is varied. However, one thing they have in common is an interest in assessing a company's future cash flow generating capability. Equity investors and analysts, credit investors and analysts, rating agencies, customers, employees, tax authorities, and others all have a need to estimate a company's future cash flows. Although there are many sources of information relevant to such forecasting, one of the principal sources, and our focus in this chapter, is the company's financial statements (inclusive of supplemental information to the main financial statements).

Financial reporting quality relates to the accuracy with which a company's reported financials reflect its operating performance and to their usefulness for forecasting future cash flows. Our focus in introducing this topic is on the income statement and the discretion (exercise of choice) embedded in the recording of various revenues and expenses—this affects net income, which is simply net revenue less total expense. Simple measures that capture the aggregate discretion reflected in reported net income are a very effective way to measure financial reporting quality. Companies exercising more (less) discretion can usually be classified as having weaker (stronger) financial reporting quality. This separation is especially useful in identifying companies who will have weaker (stronger) future cash flow generating capability.

The discussion in this chapter extends the material introduced in the chapter on financial statement analysis techniques. We begin with some fundamentals to highlight the extent of discretion that is embedded in financial statements. This discretion is a necessary part of financial reporting, but it brings with it unintended consequences. Discretion necessitates preparers of financial statements to make numerous "estimates," which suffer from neutral errors as well as strategic manipulation. We will walk through many examples of how discretion in the financial reporting system manifests itself in the form of systematic biases which analysts would be foolhardy to ignore, given the ever increasing role that accounting numbers play in contracts and asset pricing. Our discussion will be broad, and will be generally from the perspective of an equity or credit analyst. However, much of the material covered is also relevant to the corporate financial analyst for evaluating acquisitions, restructurings, and other investments, and for calculating the value generated by strategic scenarios.

The remainder of this chapter is organized as follows: Section 2 introduces discretion in accounting systems, comparing accrual and cash bases of accounting. Understanding this basic, yet often subtle, difference is crucial to all of the material in the chapter, as it defines the scope for discretion that resides in the financial statements. Section 3 lays out the general context for financial reporting quality and introduces simple measures of financial reporting quality. Section 4 provides a structure for computing, analyzing, and interpreting various indicators and measures of financial reporting and earnings quality. Section 5 briefly discusses the implications for financial reporting quality of the trend towards fair value accounting. Section 6 summarizes the key points from the chapter, and practice problems in the CFA Institute format conclude the chapter.

2. DISCRETION IN ACCOUNTING SYSTEMS

To understand the issues in evaluating the quality of financial reporting, the analyst should be familiar with the context in which managerial discretion in accounting is exercised and with the principles and objectives of accrual accounting. The following sections provide that background.

2.1. Distinguishing Cash Basis from Accrual Basis Accounting

Our focus on external financial statements centers on the three primary financial statements: the balance sheet, income statement, and statement of cash flows. The balance sheet is a snapshot of the various asset, liability, and equity accounts. It reflects the financial status of the entity at a point in time. The income statement reports revenues less expenses, and the statement of cash flows which, when reported using the indirect method (which starts with net income), articulates how the change in cash observed on the balance sheet can reconcile to reported income.

To help put these statements in context and clarify the importance of accrual accounting, consider a bicycle repair shop, Cadence Cycling. At the start of the current year the owner contributes $100 cash into the business. The opening balance sheet would look as follows:

Cadence Cycling Balance Sheet (Cash-Basis Accounting) as of 1 January 2007

Assets		Liabilities	
Cash	100		0
		Equity	
		Common stock	100

During 2007, Cadence Cycling attracted two customers who brought their bikes to the store for service. The first customer pays $20 up front for the bike service and repairs. The second customer does not pay for the service up front; the estimated price for the service is $25. By the end of 2007, Cadence has completed work for the second customer but has not started the work for the first customer (we are ignoring the associated inventory parts to keep the example simple). Under pure **cash basis** accounting, the only relevant transactions for the financial statements are those that involve cash. Thus, the balance sheet needed for this example includes only cash and cash equivalents, and the income statement (and statement of cash flows) is simply the change in cash and cash equivalents not attributable to external capital providers. The income statement and balance sheet under the cash basis would be as follows:

Cadence Cycling Income Statement (Cash-Basis Accounting) for the Year Ended 31 December 2007

Revenues	
Cash collected from Customer #1	20
Expenses	**0**
Net Income	**20**

Cadence Cycling Balance Sheet (Cash-Basis Accounting) as of 31 December 2007

Assets		Liabilities	
Cash	120		0
		Equity	
		Common stock	100
		Retained earnings	20

Note: We ignored the associated inventory costs to focus the discussion on revenue.

Obviously, we do not see such financial statements in practice for publicly traded companies (although we will see how financial statements can be recast to compute a pure cash basis of earnings, which can be used to benchmark accrued earnings). Instead, we see an accrual accounting system. In contrast to cash basis accounting, under **accrual basis** of accounting it is *not* the cash flow that defines when revenues and expenses are recorded in the financial statements; rather, there is an earnings process that triggers the recognition of revenues and expenses. **Revenues** are increases in net assets that result from the principal income generating activity of the company, and **expenses** are reductions in net assets associated with the creation of those revenues. Thus, for example, accrual accounting records revenue not when cash is collected, but when a good or service has been provided to the customer. The income statement and balance sheet under the accrual basis for Cadence Cycling would be as follows:

Cadence Cycling Income Statement (Accrual-Basis Accounting) for the Year Ended 31 December 2007

Revenues	
Bike services for Customer #2	25
Expenses	**0**
Net Income	**25**

Cadence Cycling Balance Sheet (Accrual-Basis Accounting) as of 31 December 2007

Assets		Liabilities	
Cash	120	Unearned revenue	20
Receivable	25		
		Equity	
		Common stock	100
		Retained earnings	25

Note: We ignored the associated inventory costs to focus the discussion on revenue.

There is a striking difference in the summary performance measure across the two sets of financial statements. Under the cash basis, Cadence Cycling reports return on average total assets (ROA) of $20/[($100 + $120)/2] = 18.2\%$, whereas under the accrual basis the ROA is

$25/[($100 + $145)/2] = 20.4\%$. There is good reason to focus on the accrual-based earnings measure of performance, as it gives a better indication of the "true" value-creating activities during the year. The differences between ROA on a cash basis and on an accrual basis of accounting are even greater if we consider investment activities in noncurrent assets (assets that have long useful lives). Under cash basis accounting, if these noncurrent investments, such as the purchase of property, plant, and equipment (PP&E), are paid for with cash, the cash outflow would constitute a reduction to income in the year of the investment, whereas under the accrual basis of accounting that amount initially gets capitalized as an asset and is then periodically depreciated over the useful life of the asset. In the year of the investment, an ROA measure from the cash basis will be substantially lower than under the accrual basis. Conversely, in later periods, if the company makes fewer such investments in PP&E, then ROA will be higher under the cash basis in those future periods as the depreciation charge will continue to flow through the income statement under the accrual basis of accounting. This example naturally leads to the question: What are the relative merits of cash basis and accrual earnings?

One of the main objectives of external financial statements is to provide information that is useful to investors. Accrual accounting has emerged as the accepted method of achieving this objective. Accrual accounting centers on the identification and measurement of assets and liabilities, with accruals representing changes in noncash assets and liabilities. The financial analyst should be able to analyze whether a company's use of discretion in implementing accruals facilitates or hampers investor decision making. The potential usefulness of the accrual system can be seen with the accruals and deferrals related to revenue recognition. For a company that sells a lot of its goods and services on credit terms, waiting until cash is received will not result in timely indication of the future cash flow generating ability of that enterprise. Instead, the company accrues revenues as the good is delivered or the service is provided. This is a desirable property of the accrual accounting system: it provides more timely and relevant information for decision-making purposes. For example, if Cadence Cycling sold a bike during 2007 to a customer on credit, then under the cash basis of accounting that sale will not appear in the calculation of income for 2007. Instead, it will be recorded as revenue when the cash is collected in a future period. Under the accrual basis that sale will be recorded as revenue during 2007, with an adjustment for doubtful accounts (i.e., the full amount of the credit sale will be reduced based on an expectation of amounts that are not likely to be collected). The accrual basis of accounting therefore produces a net income figure that is more timely in communicating profit generating activity to users of financial statements.

It is important to note that these same accruals bring with them discretion in estimating the amount of revenues that get allocated between fiscal periods. A number of questions must be answered before a number for revenue can be assigned to a given time period. For example, were the goods actually delivered? Were the services provided? Do the customers have recourse to return the merchandise? Do the customers have the ability, or creditworthiness, to pay the receivable when it falls due? The answers to these questions are often subjective and create opportunities for strategic use of accrual accounting. By "strategic use" we mean that accounting numbers such as net income are important in a variety of contractual settings such as executive compensation. The economic incentives created by such contracts create an opportunity for management to be "strategic" or "opportunistic" when making determinations such as when a good has been provided, or how large a provision for doubtful accounts should be. We describe some of these incentives in more detail in section 2.3.

Considerable research has examined whether cash basis or accrual basis performance measures are superior indicators of future cash flows and stock returns. The broad takeaway from the relevant literature is that accrual accounting earnings are superior to cash accounting earnings at summarizing company performance.[1] However, accrual accounting aggregates numerous estimations with respect to the deferral and accrual of various revenue and expenses. For example, choices on useful life and residual value for the purposes of estimating periodic depreciation, choices on provisioning for doubtful accounts, choices on assumptions for computing postretirement obligations, etc., are all relevant in determining periodic net income. A simple way to isolate these aggregate accruals is to decompose accrued earnings into a cash flow and accrual component (we cover measurement of the components in section 3.2). Extensive research has examined the benefits from this decomposition.[2] There is clear evidence that the accrual component of earnings is less persistent (i.e., more transitory) than the cash component of earnings. (To explain *persistence* further, a completely persistent earnings stream is one for which a euro of earnings today implies a euro of earnings for all future periods.) The implication is that while accrual accounting is superior to cash accounting, the accrual component of earnings should receive a lower weighting than the cash component of earnings in evaluating company performance. This lower persistence is at least partly attributable to the greater subjectivity involved in the estimation of accruals.

The lower persistence of earnings resulting from high levels of accruals does not have to be a direct result of **earnings management activity** (i.e., deliberate activity aimed at influencing reporting earnings numbers, often with a goal of placing management in a favorable light). The nature of accrual accounting is to accrue and defer past, current, and anticipated future cash receipts and disbursements. The accrual process involves a significant amount of estimation of future cash receipts and payments, and a subjective allocation of past cash receipts and payments. In doing so, the accrual process creates accounts of varying reliability. For example, recording the net realizable value of receivables involves estimation of default risk across a portfolio of debtors. Other examples include estimating recoverable amounts of inventories, depreciating and amortizing long lived assets, and estimating post-retirement benefit obligations. Estimation errors (either intentional or unintentional) for the various asset, liability, and associated revenue and expense accounts will all lead to lower persistence in earnings. Collectively, these estimations manifest themselves in the magnitude of reported accruals. We will examine detailed examples related to these accounting distortions later in the chapter. Specifically, we will introduce some broad measures of accruals that are useful from an investment perspective. To the extent that investors do not assign a lower weighting to accruals (because they are unable to fully comprehend the greater subjectivity involved in the estimation of accruals), securities become mispriced with respect to that information. A good analyst should not make this error. The accrual component of earnings should rationally receive a lower multiple in valuation than the cash component.

2.2. Placing Accounting Discretion in Context

In this section we outline some of the key areas of discretion embedded in the financial statements and identify why this discretion could be used strategically by management. Financial statements prepared under generally accepted accounting principles are riddled with estimates. These estimates lower the reliability of reported earnings as a result of both neutral estimation errors and the opportunistic use of discretion. For example, when estimating the allowance for doubtful accounts on credit sales and the related provision for bad debts, an estimate of 3 percent of sales may be made; but the actual rate of default could turn out to be 5 percent. The 2 percent understatement

---

[1]See, for example, Dechow (1994).
[2]See, for example, Sloan (1996).

of expense in the year the provision was created may simply be an error in estimation or it could be the result of management intervention to report a lower expense. Disentangling whether the estimation error is neutral or strategic can be difficult, but the net result is the same for the financial analyst. If you see choices made that tend to over-(under) state current income, then on average *future* cash flows will be lower (higher) respectively.

Examples of sources of accounting discretion include the following:

- *Revenue recognition.* Provisions for doubtful accounts, warranty provisions, returns and allowances, channel stuffing (forcing more products through a sales distribution channel than the channel can sell), timing of service or provision of goods, and so on.
- *Depreciation choices.* Estimation of useful lives, residual value, method choice.
- *Inventory choices.* Cost flow assumptions, obsolescence estimation, and so on.
- *Choices related to goodwill and other noncurrent assets.* Periodic impairment tests.
- *Choices related to taxes.* Valuation allowances.
- *Pension choices.* Estimated return on plan assets, discount rates, wage growth, employee turnover.
- *Financial asset/liability valuation.* Recent accounting pronouncements (e.g., SFAS 157 on fair value measurement in the United States) focus on fair value as the basis for recording financial assets and liabilities. For certain types of financial assets and liabilities that rarely trade, there is considerable discretion in specifying the model inputs that would be used to assign a fair value.
- *Stock option expense estimates.* Volatility estimates, discount rates, etc.

The above is only a partial list. Everything other than cash (excluding fraudulently reported cash) is the result of choice. We want to understand this choice and learn how to utilize disclosures in financial statements to quantify the extent that these choices are driving reported earnings.

It is important to keep in mind that the accounting discretion we discuss in this chapter is part of a broader set of management decisions and interactions with financial markets that affect investor expectations. For example, the strategic use of accounting discretion can be combined with real business decisions such as the cutting of research and development activity or timing inventory purchases under last in, first out (LIFO) accounting (permitted under U.S. GAAP but not IFRS), which also have a direct impact on financial statements. Management also can communicate directly with capital markets via their investor relations departments, conference calls, and conference presentations. There is a large industry set up to facilitate these communications which are used by companies to explain company performance and help set expectations for future performance.

2.3. Manipulation Incentives

Financial statement information is used in a variety of settings that can create the incentive for the preparers of those statements to be opportunistic when reporting results. In particular, preparers may hope to influence capital markets and/or measured performance under various contracts. We examine these incentives in more detail in the following sections.

2.3.1. Capital Markets
When financial information is reported to capital markets, security prices move. This creates a clear incentive for management to report financial performance that meets or exceeds current expectations and to manage expectations going forward.

Research has focused on the propensity for companies to report earnings that meet various thresholds (e.g., beat historical earnings and beat consensus analyst forecasts). The exhibits below neatly summarize this phenomenon. Exhibit 17-1 reports the relative frequency of return on the market value equity (defined as net income divided by the market value of equity). The sample included is all U.S. Securities and Exchange Commission (SEC) registrants from 1988 to 2003 (effectively, all companies with securities that were publicly traded in the United States in that period). The horizontal axis groups companies into "NI (net income) class" buckets. These buckets are formed by cross-sectional ranking all companies into groups based on the magnitude of net income scaled by market capitalization. Each bar corresponds to a 50-basis-point interval. For example, the bolded vertical bars correspond to firm-years where net income scaled by market capitalization is between 0 and 0.005 for the first bar, and between 0.005 and 0.01 for the second bolded bar. There is a clear "kink" in this distribution where more companies than expected report small profits (the bolded bars) compared to small losses. Some have claimed this kink is at least partly attributable to financial reporting manipulation.

Exhibit 17-2 reports the distribution of forecast errors for the same sample of companies. A forecast error is defined as the difference between reported earnings and the most recent consensus analyst earnings forecast prior to the earnings announcement. There is a clear incidence of an asymmetry around the "zero" forecast error (i.e., where more companies report earnings that slightly exceed sell-side analyst forecasts than companies who report earnings that just miss these forecasts). (*Sell-side analysts* work at firms that sell trading and related services.) This pattern appears to illustrate a combination of earnings management (i.e., opportunistic use of accruals) and **earnings expectations management** (i.e., encouraging analysts to forecast a slightly lower number than they would otherwise).

The target that the company is trying to achieve is a moving benchmark: the consensus sell-side forecast. Using strategic communications with the investment community, management is able to move this benchmark. Likewise, the reported earnings number is a moving

EXHIBIT 17-1   Distribution of Net Income Deflated by Market Value of Equity

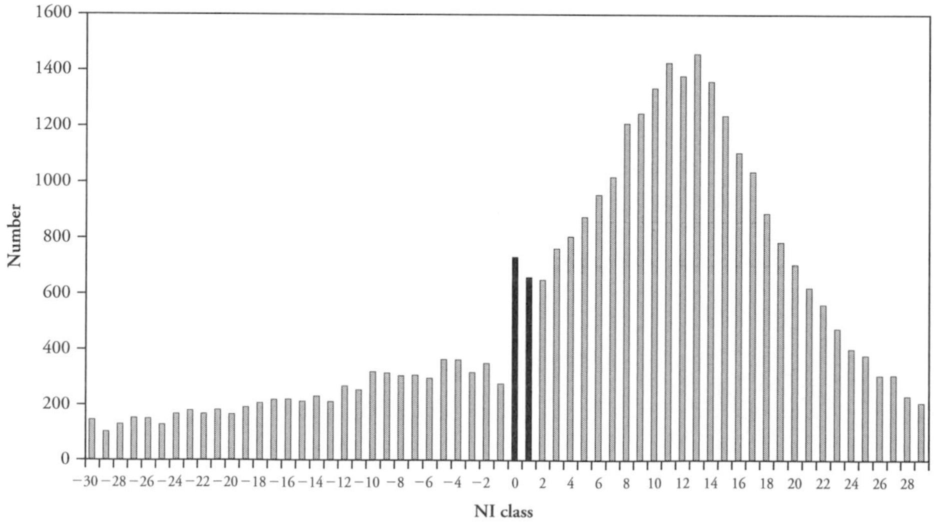

Source: Dechow, Richardson, and Tuna (2003).

EXHIBIT 17-2   Distribution of Analyst Forecast Errors

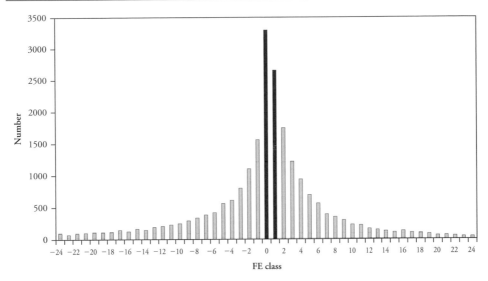

Source: Dechow, Richardson, and Tuna (2003).

target attributable to the discretion afforded to management. The focus on reporting earnings that meet consensus estimates has often been referred to as **the earnings game**. Indeed, there is evidence that this "game" is related to capital market pressures facing a company. If one looks at the pattern of forecast errors throughout the fiscal year, initial forecasts tend to be optimistic relative to reported earnings (i.e., analysts are forecasting a number early in the year that is greater than what the company ends up reporting), and the later forecasts tend to be pessimistic (i.e., analysts are forecasting a number later in the year that is less than what the company ends up reporting). This switch from early optimism to late pessimism leads to a positive earnings surprise when earnings are finally announced. Exhibit 17-3 on page 732 summarizes this pattern for the same sample of companies, and it is clear that this pattern has become increasingly common in more recent years. Furthermore, this pattern is stronger for companies that are subsequently issuing equity, or where insiders are, on average, selling their equity stake.

Besides capital markets, a variety of contracts can provide manipulation incentives, as discussed in the next section.

2.3.2. Contracts
Accounting information is used in a variety of contracts, including managerial contracts and contracts related to financial securities. Both types of contracts can provide the incentive for management to use accounting discretion opportunistically.

For example, managerial compensation is typically set as a function of reported earnings numbers (either in absolute terms or relative to a benchmark) as well as linked to stock price information, which in turn is a function of reported earnings. As an example, Textron Inc. reports in its 2006 proxy statement that the performance criteria used for its short-term and long-term incentive plans includes various financial statement based measures including return on assets, and various profit margin and turnover measures. Financial statement information is regularly used as a basis for the determination of executive compensation. These contracts

EXHIBIT 17-3   Forecast Errors Across the Fiscal Year

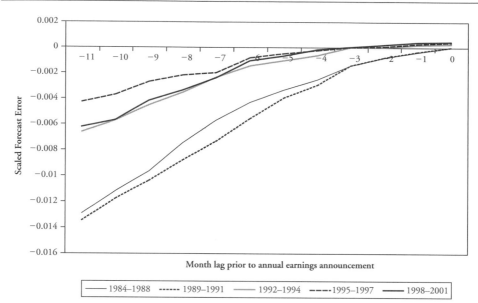

Source: Richardson, Teoh and Wysocki (2004).

provide a very direct incentive for management to be opportunistic in their use of accounting discretion.

There are other contracts where accounting information also is used, such as debt contracts. Companies with outstanding debt are parties to one or more **debt covenants** (agreements between the company as borrower and its creditors) that typically have a variety of restrictions (e.g., the company must maintain a minimum interest coverage ratio to avoid technical default and potentially costly debt renegotiation) and possibly performance pricing grids where interest costs are explicitly tied to financial performance. Collectively, these contracts provide very clear incentives for management to strategically use the accounting discretion afforded to them.

2.4. Mechanisms Disciplining Management

The discussion thus far points to many opportunities for management to manipulate reported financial results. Should we therefore place very little value on the output of this system? No. Financial statements provide very useful information in part due to the standard set of rules according to which they are prepared despite the discretion allowed by the standards. There any many mechanisms curtailing abuse of that discretion. Some examples of the mechanisms ensuring truthful reporting include:

• *External auditors.* Every public company is required to have their financial statements audited by a registered auditor. This process provides independent verification of the statements. Specifically, the external auditor's responsibility is to express an opinion on the truthfulness of consolidated financial statements, an opinion on management's assessment of internal controls, and an opinion on the effectiveness of internal financial reporting controls. Auditors' opinions that are other than "unqualified" reflect a disagreement about the treatment or disclosure of information in the financial statements.

- *Internal auditors, audit committee, and the board.* The board of directors, through its committees and oversight of internal auditors, has the capacity to act as a check on management.
- *Management certification.* For companies subject to the U.S. Sarbanes–Oxley Act of 2002, the CEO and CFO must now certify the financial statements increasing their litigation risk, so they have more personal risk than formerly in manipulating reported financial results.
- *Lawyers.* Class action lawsuits are a potentially effective way to mitigate incentives to game the financial reporting system.
- *Regulators.* Regulatory actions, up to criminal prosecution for certain misdeeds, can make managers think twice about their actions.
- *General market scrutiny.* Financial journalists, short sellers, activist institutions, employee unions, analysts, and the like are constantly poring over financial statements in an effort to identify financial shenanigans.

3. FINANCIAL REPORTING QUALITY: DEFINITIONS, ISSUES, AND AGGREGATE MEASURES

In this section we lay out a broad framework for financial reporting quality, focusing on earnings quality. Earnings quality is typically defined in terms of persistence and sustainability. For example, analysts often claim that earnings are considered to be of high quality when they are sustainable or when they "expect the reported level of earnings to be sustained or continued." These approaches have at their core a view on forecasting future cash flows or earnings which is central to valuation. A summary performance measure that better forecasts future cash flows or earnings is arguably of higher quality than one which is a less effective forecaster, as it better serves that valuation purpose. Other discussions of earnings quality look at the extent of aggressive or conservative choices that have been made in the financial statements of the companies under examination. For example, companies that have used an accelerated depreciation method, have high allowances for inventory obsolescence and doubtful accounts, or have large unearned revenue balances could be considered to have employed conservative accounting choices. This is because earnings have been depressed in the current period. However, given the range of potential earnings outcomes, simply equating choices that lower reported earnings with high earnings quality provides at best a marginal indictor of financial reporting quality as defined in the introduction of this chapter. Reporting earnings that are too high or too low results in an inferior earnings measure for the purpose of forecasting future company performance. Accruals are not independent over time. Rather, accruals have a natural self-correcting property. For example, an aggressive accounting choice in the past that capitalized an excess amount of cost into a noncurrent asset will lead to larger writedowns of that asset in future periods. Thus, the earlier aggressive choice (avoiding expensing at the time of capitalization) is associated with a later conservative action (expensing). Focusing on changes in balance sheet accounts, or equivalently the multitude of accruals and deferrals embedded in net income, is an efficient and effective way to capture cross-sectional variation in earnings quality. These accrual-based measures capture both aggressive and conservative accounting choices that impair the ability of accrued earnings to forecast future company performance.

3.1. Mean Reversion in Earnings

Our focus on accruals and deferrals for earnings quality has valuation at its core. Our aim is to identify companies that have earnings which are more persistent or sustainable than their peers. In that context, the analyst should be aware of the empirically observed tendency of earnings at extreme levels to revert back to normal levels (mean reversion in earnings). The phenomenon has an economic explanation. Competitive markets (including the market for corporate control) tend to lead to correction of strategic or managerial problems causing poor performance; poorly performing businesses and segments tend to be abandoned. Subject to barriers to entry, capital migrates toward more profitable businesses and segments, increasing competition and reducing returns. The net effect of these competitive forces is to move earnings back to a "normal" level. Data analyzed by Nissim and Penman (2001) show that this pattern of mean reversion in earnings is very pervasive. Exhibit 17-4 below summarizes the mean-reverting behavior in return on net operating assets (RNOA) for a large sample of SEC registrants. Every year companies are sorted into ten equal groups and the average RNOA for these 10 portfolios are tracked over the next six years. There is a clear reversion back to a range between 8 percent and 20 percent by the end of six years.

Understanding this reverting property of earnings is of fundamental importance for financial statement analysis. To build a meaningful forecast of future cash flows one should recognize that very low and very high earnings are not expected to continue into the future. Using information in accruals we can improve these forecasts of future cash flow further. As mentioned earlier, earnings have a cash flow and an accrual component. Algebraically, earnings are equal to cash flows plus accruals. When earnings are largely comprised of accruals, the evidence referenced in section 2.1 suggest that future accounting rates of return and future cash flows would be lower. This is equivalent to saying that earnings will revert back to a normal level even quicker when earnings are largely

EXHIBIT 17-4   Mean Reversion in Accounting Rates of Return (Return on Net Operating Assets)

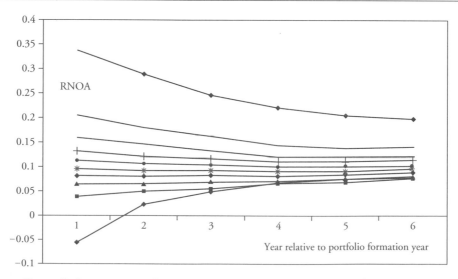

Source: Figure 4b from Nissim and Penman (2001). With kind permission of Springer Science and Business Media.

comprised of accruals as opposed to cash flows. This is not surprising: The accrual component of earnings is where the accounting distortions are greatest and for which we expect there to be lower persistence.

In summary, earnings that are more persistent are viewed as higher quality. This decomposition of earnings into its accrual and cash flow components creates a superior forecast for future earnings and cash flows; furthermore, as already mentioned, earnings components that are less persistent should rationally receive a lower multiple in valuation. In a later section, we will walk through many examples of transactions that give rise to low quality earnings streams. One thing that is common to all of the examples of low earnings quality is the fact that current earnings are temporarily distorted relative to "true" earnings, due to various accounting choices, but cash flows are unaffected.

3.2. Measures of the Accrual Component of Earnings and Earnings Quality

In this section, we lay out the framework for measuring the cash and accrual components of earnings using standardized financial statements. We explain various measures of the accrual component of earnings (the cash component being the remainder after subtracting the accrual component from reported earnings). Finally, we present scaled measures of accrual components as simple measures of earnings quality that working analysts can readily compute and use.

Exhibit 17-5 presents the three primary financial statements in standardized formats. The format selected is based on the one used by Compustat in processing the reported financials of companies trading in the Unites States, with simplifications.[3] Using a standardized format has advantages in facilitating cross-sectional comparisons across companies.[4] Note that "income before extraordinary items" is possible under U.S. generally accepted accounting principles (U.S. GAAP) but not under International Financial Reporting Standards (IFRS), and "minority interest" must appear in the equity section under IFRS but can be placed in liabilities, in the equity section, or in between according to U.S. GAAP (Compustat places it in liabilities). Making adjustments for such differences where required is part and parcel of analysts' work.

The financial statements presented here are based on an accrual accounting system. Other than cash, every line item in the balance sheet is the result of subjective choices surrounding recognition and valuation rules. For example: (1) Receivables are reported on a net basis after making a determination that a sale was made and those credit sales are to customers with sufficient capacity to make good on the amounts they owe; (2) inventories are also reported on a net basis assuming that there is sufficient future sales demand to be able to sell

---

[3]The simplifications include using one line for items that are usually broken down into multiple lines. As examples, "cash and short-term investments" in actual financial statements is often presented in two lines as "cash and cash equivalents" and "short-term investments," and "Common equity—Total" is analyzed into multiple components (Compustat gives seven lines) including "common stock," "capital surplus," "retained earnings," "accumulated other comprehensive income," etc.

[4]A good example of the usefulness of a standardized format relates to the disclosure of depreciation and amortization. Most companies include this charge as part of selling, general, and administrative (SG&A) expenses or cost of goods sold in their regulatory filings. But analysts are able to identify these data from supplemental footnote disclosures, which the data providers capture and then treat systematically.

EXHIBIT 17-5   Financial Statements (in a Standardized Format)

Panel A: Balance Sheet

Cash and short-term investments	a	Debt in current liabilities	i
Receivables (net)	b	Accounts payable	j
Inventories (net)	c	Income taxes payable	k
Other current assets	d	Other current liabilities	l
Total current assets (TCA):	**a+b+c+d**	**Total current liabilities (TCL):**	**i+j+k+l**
Property, plant, and equipment (net)	e	Long-term debt	m
Investments and advances	f	Deferred taxes	n
Intangibles (net)	g	Other noncurrent liabilities	o
Other noncurrent assets	h	**Total noncurrent liabilities (TNL):**	**m+n+o**
Total noncurrent assets (TNA):	**e+f+g+h**	**Minority interest**	**MI**
Total assets	**TCA+TNA**	**Total liabilities (TL):**	**TCL+TNL+MI**
		Preferred stock (book value)	p
		Common equity—Total	q
		Total shareholders' equity (OE)	**p+q**
		Total liabilities and shareholders' equity	**TL + OE**

Panel B: Income Statement

Net revenue	a
less: Cost of goods sold	b
less: Selling, general & admin.	c
Operating income before depreciation (OIBD)	**a−b−c**
less: Depreciation and amortization expense	d
Operating income after depreciation (OIAD)	**OIBD-d**
less: Interest expense (net)	e
less: Special items and other nonoperating items	f
less: Tax expense	g
Income before extraordinary items (IBXI)	**OIAD-e-f-g**
less: Extraordinary items	h
Net Income (NI)	**IBXI-h**

Panel C: Cash Flow Statement

Income before extraordinary items	**IBXI**
+ Depreciation and amortization expense	a
+ Deferred taxes	b
+ Equity in net loss (earnings)	c
+ (−) Gain (loss) on sale of noncurrent assets	d
+ Other funds from operations	e
+ (−) Decrease (increase) in net working capital	f
Operating cash flows	**CFO = IBXI + a + b + c + d + e + f**
− Increase in investments	g
+ Sale of investments	h
− Capital expenditures	i
+ Sale of property, plant, and equipment	j
− Acquisitions	k
Investing cash flows	**CFI = − g+h−i+j −k**
+ Sale of common and preferred stock	l
− Stock repurchases and dividends	m
+ Issuance of debt	n
− Reduction of debt	o
Financing cash flows	**CFF + l − m + n − o**
Change in cash and cash equivalents	**CFO + CFI + CFF**

Notes:

1. Debt in current liabilities includes the current portion of long-term debt and notes payable.

2. Equity in net loss (earnings) is sometimes called "equity income or loss, net of dividends."

3. Other funds from operations can include items such as stock-based compensation expense and foreign currency adjustments.

4. In the cash flow statement, net working capital is (Accounts receivable + Inventory) − (Accounts payable + Accrued liabilities); the term is not used by Compustat, but is introduced here to summarize four Compustat line items.

these items at an amount greater than their historical cost. Similar explanations can be made for every other line item in the balance sheet. Considerable discretion resides throughout the accrual based financial statements.

In contrast, financial statements based on a pure cash basis are devoid of this discretion: "cash is cash." Absent fraud, there is no disputing ownership and the valuation of cash. Contrasting financial statements prepared on a cash basis with those prepared on an accrual basis is therefore a natural way to identify the extent of discretion embedded in the reported financial statements. Effectively, this amounts to comparing a pure change in cash measure of earnings with the reported earnings under the relevant set of accrual accounting principles (e.g., U.S. GAAP or IFRS). The difference is aggregate accruals or the accrual component of earnings:

$$\text{Aggregate accruals} = \text{Accrual-basis earnings} - \text{Cash earnings} \qquad (17\text{-}1)$$

There are several ways that we can decompose reported accrual earnings into a cash flow and accrual component. We can focus on information in the balance sheet, or we can focus on information in the statement of cash flows. We prefer the latter approach because it generates a cleaner measure that is free from the effects of noncash acquisitions and foreign currency translation adjustment effects. We now outline the two approaches to this decomposition of accruals and the definition of a quantity ("accrual ratio") for comparing accruals across companies or for one company over time.

First, using balance sheet data, we can measure the net change across all noncash accounts to compute the aggregate accruals for that fiscal period. With the sample balance sheet reported above, aggregate accruals are simply the change in net assets (net of the cash and debt related accounts) from the start to the end of the period. We first define **net operating assets** (NOA) as the difference between operating assets (total assets less cash) and operating liabilities (total liabilities less total debt):

$$NOA_t = [(\text{Total assets}_t - \text{Cash}_t) - (\text{Total liabilities}_t - \text{Total debt}_t)] \qquad (17\text{-}2)$$

We exclude cash (shorthand here for "cash and short-term investments") and debt from our measure as these accounts are essentially discretion free. (This is not entirely true as there are some accounting accruals/deferrals embedded in debt, e.g., amortization of discounts/premium, but these can be ignored for our purposes here.)

From a balance sheet perspective, we measure aggregate accruals for period t as the change in NOA over the period:

$$\text{Aggregate accruals}_t^{B/S} = NOA_t - NOA_{t-1} \qquad (17\text{-}3)$$

We can call the measure presented in Equation 17-3 **balance-sheet-based aggregate accruals**. To adapt the measure as an indicator of earnings quality, it must be made comparable across companies by adjusting for differences in company size. An easy way to do the adjustment is to deflate (i.e., scale) the aggregate accrual measure by the *average* value of NOA. If one just used the opening or ending value of NOA as the scaling quantity, the ratio would be distorted by companies that have experienced significant growth or contractions during the fiscal period. The scaled measure (which we can call the **balance-sheet-based accruals ratio**) is our first measure of financial reporting quality and given by

$$\text{Accruals ratio}_t^{B/S} = \frac{(\text{NOA}_t - \text{NOA}_{t-1})}{(\text{NOA}_t + \text{NOA}_{t-1})/2} \tag{17-4}$$

The accruals measures defined in Equations 17-3 and 17-4 involve the summation of all of the line items of the balance sheet. If you are interested in subcomponents of accrual activity, then simply focus on the relevant line item from the balance sheet. For example, looking at the change in net receivables over a fiscal period deflated by average NOA will give you a sense of the magnitude of accrued revenue attributable to net credit sales.

We can also look at the statement of cash flows. For this approach we are looking at the difference between reported accrual earnings and the cash flows attributable to operating and investing activities. From a cash flow statement perspective, a measure of aggregate accruals can be defined as follows:[5]

$$\text{Aggregate accruals}_t^{CF} = \text{NI}_t - (\text{CFO}_t + \text{CFI}_t) \tag{17-5}$$

We can call this **cash-flow-statement-based aggregate accruals**. The corresponding scaled measure (**cash-flow-statement-based accruals ratio**) is our second simple measure of financial reporting quality:

$$\text{Accruals ratio}_t^{CF} = \frac{[\text{NI}_t - (\text{CFO}_t + \text{CFI}_t)]}{(\text{NOA}_t + \text{NOA}_{t-1})/2} \tag{17-6}$$

The measures in Equations 17-5 and 17-6 aggregate all of the operating and investing activities and their impact on cash flows relative to accrued earnings. The result is a cash flow statement-based measure of aggregate accruals. The inclusion of the cash flow from investing activities (CFI_t) in Equations 17-5 and 17-6 may require explanation. From a valuation perspective, there are essentially only two sides to the company: the operating side (broadly conceived) and the financing side. However, the cash flow statement splits the operating side into "operating" and "investing" pieces (roughly, current and noncurrent operating pieces). When calculating a broad accruals ratio, the appropriate treatment is to include both cash flow pieces (CFO and CFI). In applying Equations 17-5 and 17-6, the analyst should make any needed adjustments for differences in the cash flow statement treatment of interest and dividends across companies being examined.[6] These adjustments ensure consistency in the treatment of operating and financing activities. For example, if Company A treats interest paid as an operating cash outflow (under U.S. GAAP) and Company B treats interest paid as a financing cash flow (under IFRS), the systematic differences in leverage across the two companies could create significant differences in a computed aggregate accrual measure. Treating interest paid consistently across the companies (e.g., as a financing cash outflow) will mitigate this problem.

Example 17-1 illustrates the calculation of the ratios for an actual company.

---

[5]In applying Equations 17-5 and 17-6 for companies reporting under U.S. GAAP, where comparison with non-U.S GAAP reporting companies is not an issue, analysts may prefer to use IBXI_t rather than NI_t.

[6]In particular, IFRS allows operating or financing cash flow treatment of interest paid and dividends paid whereas U.S. GAAP currently specifies operating cash flow treatment of interest paid and financing cash flow treatment of dividends paid.

EXAMPLE 17-1   The Coca-Cola Company: An Illustration of Accrual Analysis

Below, recent financial statements for the Coca-Cola Company (NYSE: KO) have been put in the format of Exhibit 17-5.[7]

Panel A: Balance Sheet	2006	2005
Cash and short-term investments	2,590	4,767
Receivables (net)	2,587	2,281
Inventories (net)	1,641	1,424
Other current assets	1,623	1,778
Total current assets	8,441	10,250
Property, plant, and equipment (net)	6,903	5,786
Investments and advances	6,783	6,922
Intangibles (net)	5,135	3,821
Other noncurrent assets	2,701	2,648
Total noncurrent assets	21,522	19,177
Total assets	29,963	29,427
Debt in current liabilities	3,268	4,546
Accounts payable	929	2,315
Income taxes payable	567	797
Other current liabilities	4,126	2,178
Total current liabilities	8,890	9,836
Long-term debt	1,314	1,154
Deferred taxes	608	352
Other noncurrent liabilities	2,231	1,730
Total noncurrent liabilities	4,153	3,236
Minority interest	0	0
Total liabilities	13,043	13,072
Preferred stock (book value)	0	0
Common equity—total	16,920	16,355
Total shareholders' equity	16,920	16,355
Total Liabilities and Shareholders' Equity	29,963	29,427

---

[7]In Panel A, the balance sheet, *deferred taxes* refers to *accumulated* deferred taxes. In Panel B, the statement of cash flows, "deferred taxes" refers to deferred tax expense related to the single period being reported, 2006. Note also that the concise balance sheet pools cash and cash equivalents and short-term investments into one line so the change in cash and cash equivalents of –2,261 shown in the statement of cash flows cannot be confirmed directly. However, the more detailed balance sheet in the Form 10-K disclosure for Coca-Cola shows that cash and cash equivalents in 2005 to 2006 were $4,701 and $2,440 respectively; as $2,440 − 4,701 = −$2,261, this confirms the value shown in the statement of cash flows.

Panel B: Income Statement	2006
Net revenue	24,088
Less: Cost of goods sold	7,358
Less: Selling, general & admin. expenses	9,195
Operating income before depreciation	**7,535**
Less: Depreciation and amortization expense	938
Operating income after depreciation	**6,597**
Less: Interest expense (net)	220
Plus: Special items and other nonoperating items	201
Less: Tax expense	1,498
Income before extraordinary items	**5080**
Less: Extraordinary items	0
Net income	**5,080**

Panel C: Statement of Cash Flows	
Income before extraordinary items	**5,080**
+ Depreciation and amortization expense	938
+ Deferred taxes	−35
+ Equity in net loss (earnings)	124
+ (−) Gain (loss) on sale of noncurrent assets	−303
+ Other funds from operations	768
+ (−) Decrease (increase) in net working capital	−615
Operating cash flows	**5,957**
− Increase In Investments	1,045
+ Sale of investments	640
− Capital expenditures	1,407
+ Sale of property, plant, and equipment	112
− Acquisitions	0
Investing cash flows	**−1700**
+ Sale of common stock	148
− Stock repurchases and dividends	5,327
+ Issuance of debt	617
− Reduction of debt	2,021
Financing cash flows	**−6,583**
Less: exchange rate effects	65
Change in cash and cash equivalents	**−2261**

Based on the information given, address the following problems:

1. Calculate net operating assets for Coke for 2006 and 2005.
2. Calculate balance-sheet-based aggregate accruals for Coke for 2006.
3. Calculate the balance-sheet-based accruals ratio for Coke for 2006.
4. Calculate cash-flow-statement-based aggregate accruals for Coke for 2006.
5. Calculate the cash-flow-statement-based accruals ratio for Coke for 2006.
6. State and explain which of the measures calculated in Problems 1 through 5 would be appropriate to use in evaluating relative financial reporting quality of a group of companies.

Solutions to 1, 2, and 3. These are given in the worksheet below.

Balance Sheet Computation of Aggregate Accruals

	2006	2005	
Operating Assets			
Total Assets	29,963	29,427	
Less: Cash and Short-term Investments	2,590	4,767	
Operating Assets (**A**)	27,373	24,660	
Operating Liabilities			
Total Liabilities	13,043	13,072	
Less: Long-term Debt	1,314	1,154	
Less: Debt in Current Liabilities	3,268	4,546	
Operating liabilities (**B**)	8,461	7,372	
Net Operating Assets = (A) − (B)	**18,912**	**17,288**	Solution to 1
Balance-Sheet-Based Aggregate Accruals **BSA = NOA$_{2006}$ − NOA$_{2005}$**	**1,624**		Solution to 2
Average Net Operating Assets (AvgNOA)	18,100		
Balance-Sheet-Based Accruals **Ratio = BSA/AvgNOA**	**8.97%**		Solution to 3

Problem 1. The amount of net operating assets is found as the difference between operating assets (total assets minus cash and short-term investments) and operating liabilities (total liabilities minus total debt). For 2005 and 2006, net operating assets amount to $17,288 million and $18,912 million, respectively.

Problem 2. The amount of balance-sheet-based aggregate accruals for 2006 is found as the change in net operating assets from 2005 to 2006. This amount is $1,624 million.

Problem 3. The balance-sheet-based accruals ratio for 2006 is found by dividing balance-sheet-based aggregate accruals for 2006, $1,624 million, by average net operating assets, (18,912 + 17,288) ÷ 2 = $18,100 million. This ratio is equal to 1,624 ÷ 18,100 = 8.97 percent.

Solutions to 4 and 5. These are given in the worksheet below:

Cash Flow Statement Computation of Aggregate Accruals		
	2006	
Income Before Extraordinary Items	5,080	
Less: Operating Cash Flows	5,957	
Less: Investing Cash Flows	−1700	
Cash-Flow-Statement Based Aggregate Accruals (A)	**823**	Solution to 4
Cash-Flow-Statement Based Accruals = (A)/AvgNOA	**4.55%**	Solution to 5

Note: AvgNOA is 18,100 (see previous worksheet).

Solution to 6. Among the measures presented in Problems 2 through 5, only the size-scaled measures calculated in Problems 3 and 5 are appropriate for cross-company comparisons. The unscaled measures in Problems 2 and 4 would be affected by differences in company size.

Consistent with the discussion above on the balance sheet approach to measuring accruals, we also could focus on current versus noncurrent accruals by looking only at the difference between reported income and operating cash flows for current accruals. It is important to note that while the two approaches (balance sheet and statement of cash flows) are conceptually equivalent, they will not generate the exact same numbers due to a combination of noncash acquisitions, currency translation, and inconsistent classification across the balance sheet and statement of cash flows. These differences, however, are typically small and can be ignored for our purpose. The typical correlation between a broad accrual measure based on balance sheet data with one based on statement of cash flow data is in excess of 0.80. The important thing to remember is to compare companies using the same method. If you prefer to use a balance sheet approach or a statement of cash flow approach, be sure to keep that method constant across companies. If you use different methods across companies, this will distort your comparison. But using one approach systematically will give a very similar rank ordering of companies as using the other approach systematically.

3.3. Applying the Simple Measures of Earnings Quality

The simple measures of earnings quality defined by Equations 17-4 and 17-6 are an effective way to partition companies into low and high earnings quality groups. Given the broad discretion afforded to management, it can be difficult to identify specifically which accrual or deferral was manipulated in a given fiscal period. Rather than attempt to measure discretion embedded within each accrual, an effective alternative is to focus on the aggregate. This aggregate measure will reflect the portfolio of discretion and its impact on income for a given fiscal period. In this section we give further examples to illustrate the measures. Example 17-2 compares two companies. In contrast to Example 17-1, the original account labels have been retained in the example.

EXAMPLE 17-2   A Quality-of-Earnings Comparison of Two Companies

Siemens AG is a global electronics and electrical engineering company headquartered in Munich, Germany. Selected data (in € millions) from Siemens' financial statements for the years ended 30 September 2006, 2005, and 2004 are presented below.

Siemens AG: Fiscal Years Ended 30 September (€ millions)

Selected Income Statement Data	2006	2005	2004
Net sales	87,325	75,445	70,237
Income from continuing operations, before tax	4,371	4,185	4,369
Income (loss) from discontinued operations	(54)	(810)	(45)
Net income	3,033	2,248	3,405
Selected Balance Sheet Data as of 31 December			
Cash and equivalents	10,214	8,121	12,190
Marketable securities	596	1,789	1,386
Total current assets	51,611	46,803	45,946
Total assets	90,973	86,117	79,518
Short-term debt	2,175	3,999	1,434
Total current liabilities	38,957	39,631	33,372
Long-term debt	13,399	8,436	9,785
Total liabilities	61,667	59,095	52,663
Selected Statement of Cash Flows Data			
Net cash provided by (used in) operating activities	4,981	3,121	5,080
Net cash provided by (used in) operating activities—continuing operations	5,174	4,217	4,704
Net cash provided by (used in) investing activities	(4,614)	(5,824)	(1,818)
Net cash provided by (used in) investing activities—continuing operations	(4,435)	(5,706)	(1,689)
Net cash provided by (used in) financing activities	1,802	(1,403)	(3,108)

General Electric is a diversified global industrial corporation headquartered in Fairfield, Connecticut, USA. Selected data (in $ millions) from GE's financial statements for the years ended 31 December 2006, 2005, and 2004 are presented below.

General Electric Company and Consolidated Affiliates, Years Ended 31 December ($ millions)

Selected Income Statement Data	2006	2005	2004
Net sales	163,391	147,956	134,291
Income from continuing operations, before tax	24,620	22,696	20,297
Income (loss) from discontinued operations	163	(1,950)	559
Net income	20,829	16,711	17,160
Selected Balance Sheet Data as of 31 December			
Cash and equivalents	14,275	8,825	12,152
Marketable securities	47,826	42,148	56,923
Total current assets	87,456	76,298	93,086
Total assets	697,239	673,321	750,507
Short-term debt	172,153	158,156	157,195
Total current liabilities	220,514	204,970	200,047
Long-term debt	260,804	212,281	207,871
Total liabilities	577,347	555,916	627,083
Selected Statement of Cash Flows Data			
Net cash provided by (used in) operating activities	30,646	37,691	36,493
Net cash provided by (used in) operating activities—continuing operations	33,019	32,664	30,872
Net cash provided by (used in) investing activities	(51,402)	(35,099)	(38,423)
Net cash provided by (used in) investing activities—continuing operations	(51,019)	(29,366)	(30,772)
Net cash provided by (used in) financing activities	23,230	(6,119)	4,594

Based on the information given, address the following:

1. Calculate net operating assets for Siemens and GE for each year presented.
2. Calculate aggregate accruals using both the balance sheet and cash flow statement methods for Siemens and GE for each year presented.
3. Calculate the balance-sheet-based and cash-flow-statement-based accruals ratios for Siemens and GE for each year presented.
4. A.   State and explain which company had higher earnings quality in 2005 and 2006.
   B.   Identify any trends in earnings quality for each company.

5. Would the results of question 4 be different if the accruals ratios were calculated based only on continuing operations?
6. General Electric recorded net financing receivables of $334,232 in 2006 and $292,639 in 2005. It describes these receivables in the notes to its financial statements as largely relating to direct financing leases. Evaluate this disclosure with respect to GE's earnings quality.

Solution to 1. Net operating assets is defined as (Total assets − Cash and marketable securities) − (Total liabilities − Total debt). For example, in 2006 Siemens reported total assets of 90,973 and cash and marketable securities of 10,214 + 596 = 10,810. Total liabilities were 61,667 and total debt was 2,175 + 13,399 = 15,574. (90,973 − 10,810) − (61,667 − 15,574) = 80,163 − 46,093 = 34,070. The values for each firm are summarized below.

Net Operating Assets	2006	2005	2004
Siemens	34,070	29,547	24,498
General Electric	490,748	436,869	419,415

Solution to 2. Balance sheet aggregate accruals are defined as the change in net operating assets. As such, only two years worth of accruals can be calculated from the data given. For example, for Siemens, using the answers to Problem 1, balance sheet aggregate accruals for 2006 equals €34,070 − €29,547 = €4,523.

Balance Sheet Aggregate Accruals	2006	2005
Siemens	4,523	5,049
General Electric	53,879	17,454

Cash flow statement aggregate accruals are defined as Net income − (Cash flows from operating activity + Cash flows from investing activity). For example, for Siemens in 2006, cash flow statement aggregate accruals is found as NI of €3,033 − [CFO of €4,981 + (CFI of − €4,614)] = €3,033 − €367 = €2,666.

Cash Flow Statement Aggregate Accruals	2006	2005	2004
Siemens	2,666	4,951	143
General Electric	41,585	14,119	19,090

Solution to 3. The accrual ratio is defined as aggregate accruals divided by average net operating assets. Because the denominator requires an average of two years' data, only two years of accrual ratios can be calculated. For example, for Siemens, average net operating assets for 2006 were (€34,070 + €29,547) ÷ 2 = €31,808.5. With aggregate accruals for 2006 of €4,523 and €2,666 by the balance sheet and cash flow statement methods respectively, the corresponding accrual ratios were €4,523 ÷ €31,808.5 = 14.2 percent and €2,666 ÷ €31,808.5 = 8.4 percent.

Balance Sheet-Based Accrual Ratio	2006	2005
Siemens	14.2%	18.7%
General Electric	11.6%	4.1%
Cash Flow Statement-Based Accrual Ratio		
Siemens	8.4%	18.3%
General Electric	9.0%	3.3%

Solutions to 4.

A. Using the balance-sheet-based accrual ratio, General Electric has higher earnings quality (i.e., lower accruals ratio) in both years. Using the cash-flow-statement-based measure, GE actually shows lower earnings quality than Siemens only in 2006.

B. Using either earnings quality measure, Siemens shows improving earnings quality from 2005 to 2006, while GE shows deteriorating earnings quality.

Solution to 5. Subtracting the results of discontinued operations from net income and using the cash flow data from continuing operations, the results of the calculations are:

Cash Flow Statement Accruals—Continuing operations	2006	2005	2004
Siemens	2,348	4,547	435
General Electric	38,666	15,363	16,501
Accrual Ratio—Continuing Operations			
Siemens	7.4%	16.8%	
General Electric	8.3%	3.6%	

Using continuing operations does not significantly alter either the level or trends in accruals for these companies.

Solution to 6. The $41,593 million change in financing receivables accounts for a large portion of GE's $53,879 million change in net operating assets. Compared to treating the leases as operating leases (see the chapter on long-term liabilities), accounting for leases as direct financing leases increases net income in the early years of a lease but the same total net income is recognized over the lease life. Under operating lease accounting, operating cash flow is lower, but investing cash flows are higher. When considering the cash versus accrual portions of earnings, this disclosure allows us to conclude that GE's 2006 earnings are likely less persistent (of lower quality) than its 2005 earnings.

EXHIBIT 17-6   Relative Frequency of Earnings Restatements as a Function of Aggregate Accruals

Source: Richardson, Tuna, and Wu (2002).

Broad measures of aggregate accruals are quite effective in identifying companies with financial reporting quality issues. Using a broad sample of earnings restatements from 1979 through 2002, Richardson, Tuna, and Wu (2002) found strong evidence that these restatements are concentrated in companies reporting the highest level of total accruals. Exhibit 17-6 summarizes these findings. Every year, SEC registrants are sorted into ten equal sized groups based on the magnitude of total accruals, using the statement of cash flow definition above (Equation 17-6). Exhibit 17-6 reports the relative frequency of earnings restatements across these 10 equal sized groups. The upward sloping line is quite telling: Of the 440 earnings restatements examined, there is a concentration in the highest accrual group (low earnings quality). Specifically, for the lowest accrual group (high earnings quality) only 7.5 percent of the 440 restatements are to be found, but in the highest accrual group we see 18 percent of the 440 restatement companies.

This ability to discriminate restatement companies from non-restatement companies is beneficial to analysts looking to avoid significant "torpedoes" in their portfolios. This clearly can be seen in Exhibit 17-7. In this exhibit, we plot the cumulative equity returns for the 440 earnings restatement companies examined above. We cumulate stock returns for 120 trading days either side of the first press release describing the earnings announcement (i.e., the "0" point on the horizontal axis corresponds to the announcement date). There is a marked decrease in market value around this announcement. For the average company in that group, the loss of market value in the few days surrounding the announcement of the restatement is around 10 percent. Having information ahead of time as to the likelihood of a restatement is clearly of value to the equity investor. The analysis above demonstrates just that: Broad accrual measures are effective in identifying egregious accounting irregularities of the type that precipitate earnings restatements. Importantly, these measures identify such companies well ahead of the restatement announcement. For the 440 restatement companies examined, the announcement date is (on average) more than one year after the fiscal year during which the alleged manipulation occurred.

EXHIBIT 17-7   Cumulative Abnormal Returns around Earnings Restatements

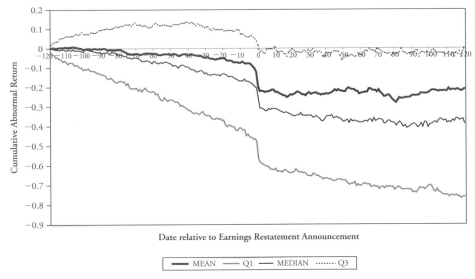

Date relative to Earnings Restatement Announcement

——— MEAN   ——— Q1   ——— MEDIAN   ········· Q3

Source: Richardson, Tuna and Wu (2002).

To make this point even more clear, research also has shown that broad measures of accruals are also leading indicators of SEC enforcement actions. Exhibit 17-8 reports aggregate accruals for companies subject to SEC enforcement actions. (The measure used [ACC] is the same as what we have called the balance-sheet-based accruals ratio in this chapter.) Aggregate accruals are tracked for five years on either side of the period of alleged manipulation giving rise to the

EXHIBIT 17-8   Aggregate Accruals (ACC) around SEC Enforcement Actions

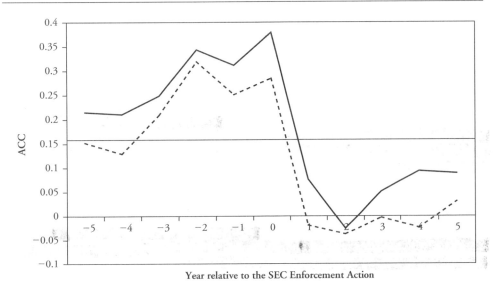

Year relative to the SEC Enforcement Action

Source: Richardson, Sloan, Soliman, and Tuna (2006).

enforcement action. The bold (hatched) line reports the average (median) aggregate accruals for the SEC enforcement action sample. For comparison purposes the horizontal line shows the aggregate accruals for the average listed company (a little over 15 percent). Note the clear pattern for companies subject to enforcement actions from the SEC: The accrual measure peaks at between 30 percent and 35 percent in the two years prior to the SEC enforcement action.

It is important to note that while this broad approach does not tell us which accruals were used as part of that manipulation, it is effective at summarizing all sources of accruals that were used to achieve an earnings target. More detailed analysis focusing on components of total accruals that are particularly germane to a given sector is likely to generate even more effective discriminatory power to identify earnings restatements. Some examples include focusing on the unearned revenue accounts in the software industry, claim loss development reserves in the insurance industry, loan loss provisions for financial institutions, fair value adjustments for complicated derivative instruments held by financial institutions, inventory adjustments for manufacturing companies, and so on.

In the next section, we focus on the various component accruals (e.g., provision for doubtful accounts, depreciation choices, unearned revenue, inventory obsolescence, etc.) that drive the aggregate accrual measures we have discussed so far.

4. A FRAMEWORK FOR IDENTIFYING LOW-QUALITY FINANCIAL REPORTING

This section focuses on specific approaches and measures used to quantify financial reporting quality. This framework builds on a sound understanding of the key risk and success factors facing the company. As with any quantitative analysis, the quality of the output depends on the quality of inputs and on a structured analysis of those inputs. Furthermore, the relevance of the reporting quality measures we will discuss (1) varies across companies and (2) can vary through time for a given company. As examples of point 1, measures related to inventory are particularly relevant for retail and manufacturing companies, measures relating to depreciation choices are particularly relevant for capital intensive companies, and measures relating to off balance sheet financing vehicles are especially relevant for financial institutions or entities with linked financial subsidiaries. As an example of point 2, it is often easier for management of a company to "hide" their use of discretion in periods of growth. Consequently, the most effective way to utilize the quantitative measures discussed below is through a combination of peer group comparison and year over year changes. Sector-neutralizing measures of financial reporting quality—by subtracting the mean or median ratio for a given sector group from a given company's ratio—is particularly useful in identifying companies with extreme good or poor quality. However, the degree of homogeneity within a sector or industry group may vary, so supplementing this kind of analysis with information on how the company itself has changed through time can help mitigate any heterogeneity. The company may change through time via divestitures, acquisitions, and changes in strategy. Such changes need to be kept in mind so you have a comparison that is as close to "apples to apples" as possible. Finally, as with any ratio analysis, the analyst should work with standardized financial statements so companies of different sizes are comparable. This is easily achieved by dividing a flow measure from the income statement or statement of cash flows by a measure from the balance sheet such as average total assets.

As we work through the various line items of the financial statements below, it is important to keep in mind the link between the primary financial statements. If there is an issue to be measured in the context of revenues or expenses, there will be an associated implication on the net assets reported in the balance sheet. To keep the sections manageable, we have focused on revenue and expense quality issues. We could easily have included a complete asset and liability section as well, but this would be the flip side of a combination of the revenue and expense items. For example, discussion on the *unearned revenue* account which typically appears as part of *other current liabilities* on the balance sheet is subsumed by the discussion of revenue recognition below. Therefore, instead of repeating our discussion, we highlight the relevant asset and liability accounts associated with the respective revenue and expense accounts.

4.1. Revenue Recognition Issues

Misstating current revenue, recognizing revenue early, or classifying nonoperating income or gains as resulting from operating activities can make current operating performance appear better than it actually is—generally impairing the persistence or sustainability of reported earnings. The following sections highlight the major types of revenue recognition issues.

4.1.1. Revenue Misstatement

This section focuses on the discretion available when reporting revenue. Revenue can be over or understated for a given period. Examples of overstatement include recording smaller provisions for doubtful accounts and warranty provisions. Examples of understatement include recording opportunistic use of unearned revenue. We will discuss these in turn.

4.1.1.1. The Range of Problems   Revenue accounting is one of the simplest, yet most challenging aspects of interpreting financial statements. As described in section 2, accrual accounting records revenue not when cash is collected, but when a good or service has been provided to the customer. Total revenue reported in a given fiscal period is equal to the cash collected from customers plus the increase in net accounts receivable less the increase in unearned revenue (unearned revenue or deferred revenue is payment received in advance of providing a good or service). Receivables capture credit sales made in the past that as yet have not been collected. While companies have to report these receivables on a net basis by making a best guess as to what will become uncollectible, there is considerable discretion in determining the amount that is expected to be uncollectible. Likewise, unearned revenue contains discretion. The existence of this account typically lowers the reported revenue relative to cash received in the current period. But note that unearned revenues from prior fiscal periods can be used to create revenue in the current fiscal period. For example, if a company collected cash in 2006 for services to be provided over several periods the appropriate treatment is to record that cash collection as a liability in 2006. During future periods, a determination has to be made as to whether the services have in fact been provided. Often, there is discretion in deciding when a service has been provided, especially for software companies where the service and licensing agreements are typically bundled together. Related to estimates about credit sales and unearned revenue, companies also must estimate warranty provisions, and sales returns and allowances. The net effect of all of these estimates is the single line item, total revenue, reported at the top of the income statement. Collectively, the discretion embedded in the revenue line item is the culprit for the majority of earnings restatements, fraud cases, and related SEC enforcement actions

(Huron Consulting report that the main driver of earnings restatements in recent years is revenue recognition issues).

4.1.1.2. Warning Signs   To detect quality issues with reported revenues, it is best to focus on the balance sheet accounts associated with revenue (accounts receivable and unearned revenue). Large changes in these accounts should be viewed as "red flag" indicators of revenue quality issues. Specifically, large increases in accounts receivable or large decreases in unearned revenue are indicators of low quality revenue. Companies reporting earnings where a large portion of the revenue is attributable to growth in receivables or a contraction in unearned revenue, on average report lower accounting rates of return and cash flows in the future, and these earnings reversals are not anticipated in a timely fashion by the stock market.[8]

We can use the example of Microsoft to illustrate various revenue recognition issues. In Exhibit 17-9, we see the balance sheet for the 30 June 2007 fiscal year for Microsoft.

There is a roughly $1.6 billion increase in the short-term unearned revenue account (the opening balance is $9.138 billion and the closing balance is $10.779 billion, creating a positive change of $1.641 billion), and a roughly $0.1 billion increase in the long-term unearned

EXHIBIT 17-9   Microsoft Corporation Balance Sheets: Fiscal Year Ended 30 June 2007 and 30 June 2006 ($ millions)

30 June	2007	2006
Assets		
Current assets:		
Cash and equivalents	**$6,111**	$6,714
Short-term investments (including securities pledged as collateral of $2,356 and $3,065)	**17,300**	27,447
Total cash and short-term investments	**23,411**	34,161
Accounts receivable, net of allowance for doubtful accounts of $117 and $142	*11,338*	*9,316*
Inventories	**1,127**	1,478
Deferred income taxes	**1,899**	1,940
Other	**2,393**	2,115
Total current assets	**40,168**	49,010
Property and equipment, net	**4,350**	3,044
Equity and other investments	**10,117**	9,232
Goodwill	**4,760**	3,866
Intangible assets, net	**878**	539
Deferred income taxes	**1,389**	2,611
Other long-term assets	**1,509**	1,295
Total assets	**$63,171**	$69,597

[8]See, for example, Sloan (1996).

Liabilities and stockholders' equity

Current liabilities:

Accounts payable	**$3,247**	$2,909
Accrued compensation	**2,325**	1,938
Income taxes	**1,040**	1,557
Short-term unearned revenue	**10,779**	*9,138*
Securities lending payable	**2,741**	3,117
Other	**3,622**	3,783
Total current liabilities	**23,754**	22,442
Long-term unearned revenue	**1,867**	*1,764*
Other long-term liabilities	**6,453**	5,287
Commitments and contingencies Stockholders' equity:		
Common stock and paid-in capital—shares authorized 24,000; outstanding 9,380 and 10,062	**60,557**	59,005
Retained deficit, including accumulated other comprehensive income of $1,654 and $1,229	**(29,460)**	(18,901)
Total stockholders' equity	**31,097**	40,104
Total liabilities and stockholders' equity	**$63,171**	$69,597

Note: Italics added by authors.

revenue account (the opening balance is $1.764 billion and the closing balance is $1.867 billion, creating a positive change of $0.103 billion). There is also a roughly $2 billion increase in net accounts receivable (the opening balance is $9.316 billion and the closing balance is $11.338 billion, creating a positive change of $2.022 billion). To place these magnitudes in context, Microsoft reported revenue of $51.122 billion and net income of $14.065 billion for the fiscal period. The difference between revenue and cash collected from customers can be computed by aggregating the changes in accounts receivable and unearned revenue accounts as follows:

$$\text{Revenue} - \text{Cash collected from customers} = \text{Increase in net A/R} - \text{Increase in unearned revenue}$$
$$= \$2.022 \text{ billion} - (1.641 \text{ billion} + 0.103 \text{ billion})$$
$$= \$0.278 \text{ billion}.$$

The net effect of the increase in receivables and increase in unearned revenue is to report revenue greater by $0.278 billion relative to cash collected from customers. The magnitude of the absolute changes in these two accounts is over $3.5 billion, suggesting that Microsoft has considerable flexibility in reporting revenue in a given fiscal period. For example, the unearned revenue account could be built up in periods of strong growth as customers prepay for services, and tapped into when times are tough. In effect, with the unearned revenue account, Microsoft has flexibility to be strategic as to when it chooses to recognize revenue. Note that few companies disclose unearned revenue separately in the financial statements; however, this information can often be found in supplemental footnote disclosures to the financial statements.

To place the accrual items described above (change in accounts receivable and change in unearned revenue) in context, we can express these changes as a fraction of average net operating assets. For the year ended 30 June 2007, Microsoft reports in millions of dollars: opening (closing) total assets of $69,597 ($63,171), opening (closing) cash and short-term investments of $34,161 ($23,411), opening (closing) total liabilities of $29,493 ($32,074), and opening (closing) total debt of $0 ($0). Using the balance-sheet-based accruals ratio described in Equation 17-4, we can compute aggregate accruals as follows:

	2007	2006
Operating Assets		
Total assets	63,171	69,597
Less: Cash and short-term investments	23,411	34,161
Operating assets (OA)	39,760	35,436
Operating Liabilities		
Total liabilities	32,074	29,493
Less: Long-term debt	0	0
Less: Debt in current liabilities	0	0
Operating liabilities (OL)	32,074	29,493
Net Operating Assets NOA = OA − OL	7,686	5,943
Balance-sheet-based aggregate accruals [= **NOA(2007)** − **NOA(2006)**]	1,743	
Average Net Operating Assets	6,814.5	
Balance-Sheet-Based Accruals Ratio (= **1,743/6,814.5**)	25.58%	

The revenue-related accruals in accounts receivable and unearned revenue, calculated above as the increase in net accounts receivable minus the increase in unearned revenue, total $278 million, which accounts for about 16 percent of the total accruals ($278 million ÷ $1743 million) for the 2007 fiscal year. There are other ways to use this information to make statements about earnings quality. For example, measures of days sales outstanding (DSO) are useful to inform about revenue quality. DSO is simply the ratio of net accounts receivable divided by total revenue multiplied by 365. This ratio gives a sense for how quickly the company is able to convert its credit sales into cash. Increases in this ratio are a red flag for questionable credit sales that take longer to convert into cash. Of course, in assessing this ratio, one should be careful to see if the company's credit policy or product mix has changed substantially, or whether the company has securitized or factored its receivables (this leads to a dramatic lowering of DSO, which is not sustainable). If you notice that a company has securitized a large portion of its receivables, then do not treat the accompanying improvement in DSO as a signal of improving earnings quality because it is a one-off occurrence. For example, Federated Stores sold its credit card business in 2005 effectively lowering its DSO ratio to zero.

4.1.2. Accelerating Revenue

In addition to the issues described above relating to credit sales and unearned revenue, there is also considerable discretion as to when a sale has been made. The issue here is deciding in which fiscal period revenue should be recognized.

4.1.2.1. The Range of Problems   Related to the discussion in section 4.1.1, revenue is recognized when a good is "delivered" to the customer or a service has been performed. There is considerable discretion as to when the transaction is deemed to have taken place. It is easy to understand the incentives of sales people who are struggling to meet internal targets toward the end of the fiscal period: to sell as much as possible as the period ends, for example, by lowering credit standards or by moving sales from the next period to the current fiscal period. This latter option is acceptable as long as the sale has been made, that is, the good has been delivered and/or the service has been provided. For companies that provide goods or services where it is sometimes difficult to assess the completion of the revenue generating process (i.e., the delivery of the good or the provision of service), there is the potential for these companies to accelerate the recognition of revenue by reporting revenue in the current period that should be reported in a future period. Companies that provide goods and services as bundled products are a classic example where there may be opportunity for the acceleration of revenues. Consider a company selling computer software licenses with a multiperiod service agreement. The revenue associated with the provision of that service component of the software license should not be recognized at point of sale but at the time the service is provided to the customer. For example, consider a software provider that sells desktop applications in bulk to large corporations on 1 November 2007. This contract comes with built-in options to upgrade and extensive product support for the next two years. A determination needs to be made to allocate the revenue associated with this software sale over the 2007, 2008, and 2009 fiscal periods.

4.1.2.2. Warning Signs   The analyst needs to be particularly skeptical about revenue reporting practices when:

- Top management has a significant portion of vested options in the money,
- The company is trying to maintain its track record of successively meeting analyst forecasts, or
- The company is looking to raise additional financing.

The preceding are risk factors in the sense of describing circumstances that can provide incentives for accelerating the recognition of revenue.

The warning signs for accelerated revenue are similar to what was described for overstated revenue: Look for large positive changes in net accounts receivable and large decreases in unearned revenue accounts (to the extent these are separately disclosed). A large increase in accounts receivable could indicate credit sales made late in the fiscal period with associated deteriorations in credit quality. Large decreases in unearned revenue could be indicative of management's aggressive determination that prior goods and services have been delivered/ provided in the current fiscal period. Combining an analysis of the accrual activity in revenue related accounts with the current market environment (e.g., pressing need to meet analyst forecasts or extensive outstanding vested options for top executives) can be an effective way to identify companies who have the incentive to be aggressive in the timing of revenue recognition and who have utilized accrual accounting choices to deliver revenue growth.

A good example is Microstrategy. Exhibit 17-10 below outlines the evolution of Microstrategy's stock price for the 1999–2000 period. Microstrategy announced that it would be restating its earnings in March 2000. They had accelerated the recognition of revenue by booking legitimate future sales orders in the current fiscal period. At first glance this does not seem particularly egregious: after all, these would have been legitimate sales. But placed in the context of significant capital market pressures, where analysts and investors generally were looking for exponential sales growth to support very lofty stock prices, the front-loading of revenues allowed Microstrategy to report very large revenue increases over the 1998–1999 period, fueling the stock price appreciation during 1999. When investors learned that this revenue growth was the result of front-loading future sales, there was a very quick correction in the market. There are numerous other cases of companies accelerating revenue recognition. A skeptical view on receivable growth and changes in unearned revenue, combined with an assessment of incentives to manipulate earnings, can help identify these companies before the stock price collapses.

One way to detect acceleration of revenue recognition is to analyze the ratio of revenue to cash collected from customers. Cash collected from customers can be computed as Revenue + Decrease (minus increase) in accounts receivable + Increase (minus decrease) in

EXHIBIT 17-10   Daily Stock Prices for Microstrategy, 1 September 1999–29 September 2000

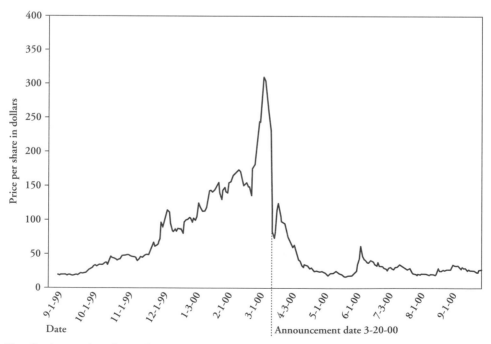

Note: Stock prices have been adjusted to account for the 26 January 2000 2:1 stock split.
Source: GAO (2002), Figure 18, based on the GAO's analysis of NYSE TAQ data.

deferred income (or "deferred revenue"). In normal circumstances, the relation between revenue and cash collected from customers should be relatively stable. Large swings in revenue as a percent of cash collected from customers could occur for several reasons including the acceleration of revenue. Reported revenue as a percent of cash collected from customers would be expected to initially increase as the aggressive revenue recognition is adopted. Example 17-3 below illustrates one technique of revenue acceleration: bill-and-hold sales.

EXAMPLE 17-3   Revenue Recognition Practices

Diebold, Inc. (NYSE: DBD) is a leading manufacturer of automated teller machines (ATMs) used in banks, as well as electronic voting machines. Certain of Diebold's financial results for the years ended 31 December 2006, 2005, and 2004 are summarized as follows:

	2006	**2005**	**2004**
Revenues	$2,906,232	$2,587,049	$2,357,108
Net income	86,547	96,746	183,797
Cash flow from operating activities	250,424	102,741	221,610
Accounts receivable, net	610,893	676,361	583,658
Deferred income	170,921	136,135	92,862
Other current liabilities	258,103	228,699	202,713

In its 2006 annual report, Diebold described its revenue recognition practice as follows:

1. The company considers revenue to be realized or realizable and earned when the following revenue recognition requirements are met: persuasive evidence of an arrangement exists, which is a customer contract; the products or services have been provided to the customer; the sales price is fixed or determinable within the contract; and collectibility is probable. (From the Notes to the Financial Statements)

2. Revenue is recognized only after the earnings process is complete. For product sales, the company determines that the earnings process is complete when the customer has assumed risk of loss of the goods sold and all performance requirements are substantially complete. (From the Management Discussion and Analysis)

On 25 July 2007, Diebold announced it would be delaying the release of its earnings for the second quarter due to regulatory questions about the way it reports revenue. The stock had closed on 24 July at $53.71 per share.

On 2 October 2007, Diebold Inc. issued a press release titled "Diebold Provides Update on Revenue Recognition Practice."

Diebold, Incorporated has been engaged in an ongoing discussion with the Office of the Chief Accountant (OCA) of the Securities and Exchange Commission

(SEC) regarding the company's practice of recognizing certain revenue on a "bill and hold" basis within its North America business segment. As a result of these discussions, Diebold will discontinue the use of bill and hold as a method of revenue recognition in both its North America and international businesses. . . .

The change in the company's revenue recognition practice, and the potential amendment of prior financial statements, would only affect the timing of recognition of certain revenue. While the percentage of the company's global bill and hold revenue varied from period to period, it represented 11 percent of Diebold's total consolidated revenue in 2006. The company does not anticipate that the change in the timing of revenue recognition would impact previously reported cash provided by operating activities or the company's net cash position. . . .

While the company cannot predict with certainty the length of time it will take to complete this analysis and review, it anticipates the process will take at least 30 days. Upon completing this process, Diebold will be in a position to provide updated revenue and earnings guidance for the full-year 2007.

That day, shares continued a slide that had begun with the announced delay, reaching $44.50. As of late 2007, the stock had fallen more than 20 percent since the initial announcement.

In a document titled "Report Pursuant to Section 704 of the Sarbanes–Oxley Act of 2002," the U.S. Securities and Exchange Commission noted that:

Improper accounting for bill-and-hold transactions usually involves the recording of revenue from a sale, even though the customer has not taken title of the product and assumed the risks and rewards of ownership of the products specified in the customer's purchase order or sales agreement. In a typical bill-and-hold transaction, the seller does not ship the product or ships it to a delivery site other than the customer's site. These transactions may be recognized legitimately under GAAP when special criteria are met, including being done pursuant to the buyer's request.

Based on the information given, address the following problems:

1. State whether bill-and-hold sales are consistent with the revenue recognition practices described in Diebold's annual report. Explain your response.
2. Describe the incentives for recording revenue on a bill and hold basis.
3. The SEC report notes that bill and hold sales may be appropriate when done at the customer's request. Explain a circumstance in which a customer may choose to be billed for a product that has not been delivered.
4. Critique the argument in the press release of 2 October 2007 that "the change in the company's revenue recognition practice, and the potential amendment of prior financial statements, would only affect the timing of recognition of certain revenue."
5. Describe a warning sign that might alert investors to the presence of improper bill and hold accounting. Illustrate the warning sign for the case of Diebold.

Solution to 1. No, they are not consistent. Diebold says it recognizes revenue only after "the products or services have been provided to a customer." In a bill and hold transaction, "the seller does not ship the product or ships it to a delivery site other than the customer's site."

Solution to 2. Incentives include meeting revenue growth expectations or prior company guidance on revenue growth. Investors may reward positive "surprises" in revenues (revenue in excess of expected revenue) with a higher stock price. Conversely, disappointing news with respect to revenue targets may result in stock price declines. Thus, meeting or exceeding revenue growth expectations can help support the stock price. Furthermore, individual employees may have bonuses that depend in part upon their ability to meet certain sales targets in a given period, creating another incentive to recognize revenue on a bill and hold basis.

In Diebold's case, it is possible that nearly all of the 12.3 percent growth in revenues was provided by the 11 percent of revenue recorded on a bill-and-hold basis. The accounting for the bill-and-hold transaction was not adequately disclosed in the financial statements, and thus it is no surprise that the practice drew negative attention from regulators.

Solution to 3. Customers may also have incentives to "time" their expenditures. For example, they might have provided their own investors with an indication of how much they planned to invest in new capital and may request that some equipment be provided on a bill-and-hold basis in order to meet that guidance. Alternatively, department heads may want to spend any remaining money in their budget at fiscal year-end to avoid budget cuts the following year, and not be particularly concerned about taking possession at the time of purchase. Another reason could be that the seller offers discounts if the buyer "requests" bill and hold.

Solution to 4. The statement is correct in that the bill and hold revenue recognition involves the timing of revenue recognition. However, the statement is incomplete in not pointing out that the effect of bill and hold sales is to speed up of the recognition of revenue and often to distort the revenue growth rate in a manner that is temporarily favorable to the company.

Solution to 5. The first sign could come from comparing revenue into cash collections from customers. For Diebold, the calculations for 2005 and 2006 are as follows:

	2006	2005
Revenue	$2,906,232	$2,587,049
Plus decrease (increase) in accounts receivable	65,468	(92,703)
Plus increase in deferred income	34,786	43,273
Equals cash collected from customers	$3,006,486	$2,537,619
Revenue/Cash collected from customers	96.7%	101.9%

In normal circumstances, the relationship between revenue and cash collected from customers would be expected to remain relatively stable. In Diebold's case, there was a 6.1 percent decrease from 2005 to 2006. In particular, the large increase in accounts receivable in 2005 provided a warning sign more than one year in advance of the restatement. As noted earlier, increases in accounts receivable capture aggressive accruals related to revenue recognition.

The net profit margin declined from 7.8 percent in 2004 to 3.7 percent in 2005 and 3.0 percent in 2006. The declining profitability could have been a signal that the company was pricing aggressively for customers willing to accept early billing. At the same time, the deferred income rose by 84 percent between 2004 and 2006 while sales grew just 23 percent.

Taking a more holistic approach to analysis, investors should also have been skeptical of the company's accounting practices on the basis of past infractions. The SEC lawsuit that led to the change was disclosed in the 10-Q filed in August 2006.

4.1.3. Classification of Nonrecurring or Nonoperating Revenue as Operating Revenue

Investors view operating income numbers as being most informative about the on-going earnings power of a business. For example, many investors base forward price-to-earnings ratio estimates on forecasts of operating earnings, which exclude nonrecurring items. Broadly, management may have an incentive to include nonrecurring revenues in operating income that might not belong there.

4.1.3.1. The Range of Problems Capital markets tend to focus on operating income numbers. This is important, because items that are outside the core operating activity of the company are not as relevant for assessing the long-term cash flow generating capability of the company. For example, a company operating in the retail sector may have a portfolio of financial assets which is required to be periodically revalued. These revaluations, to the extent the securities are held for trading purposes, will be included in net income. But these earnings are not reflective of the core operating activity of the company. Likewise, gains or losses associated with the divestiture of noncurrent assets typically fall outside the core operating activities of most companies, yet these transac tions will affect net income. The challenge for the analyst is in separating operating from nonoperating activities. Companies do this as evidenced by the operating, investing, and financing sections of the statement of cash flows and the pro forma earnings numbers that are the focal point of earnings announcements and conference calls. However, there is discretion in making this distinction. Consequently, there is room in defining what is core or operating earnings. One of the advantages of this earnings game for management is the absence of an *ex post* settling up mechanism: For this type of earnings management, there is no accrual or deferral reversal in future periods.

Note that the opportunistic classification of items into operating income as opposed to a nonrecurring item is not about *net income* reported under generally accepted accounting principles. Rather, the issue relates to the earnings number generally provided to the capital markets. This has been described cynically by some as "earnings before bad stuff." Pro forma earnings numbers fall outside of the domain of U.S. GAAP and as such no uniform methodology exists for calculating them.[9]

---

[9] Note that the SEC cracked down on abuses of reporting pro forma results back in 2001 with Release Nos. 33-8039, 34-45124, FR-59.

Pro Forma statements

4.1.3.2. Warning Signs One red flag for the opportunistic classification of nonrecurring items into operating income is to look at the temporal inconsistency with respect to the included revenues and expenses in a company's definition of operating income. For example, if a company excludes different items from its computation of pro forma earnings across quarters, this is a good indication that the company is opportunistically using its discretion to classify items as recurring or nonrecurring. This information can be gleaned from the press releases associated with earnings announcements, and the greater disclosure required currently makes this easier to do.

4.2. Expense Recognition Issues

Having discussed revenue recognition as it relates to financial reporting quality issues, we will now focus on expense recognition, the other chief area of earnings discretion. Expense issues include:

- Understating expenses.
- Deferring expenses.
- Classifying ordinary expenses as nonrecurring or nonoperating.

We address these in order.

4.2.1. Understating Expenses

Income can be increased by both overstating revenue and understating expenses. In this section, we focus on the improper capitalization of costs.

4.2.1.1. The Range of Problems Our focus in discussing expense recognition will be selling, general, and administrative (SG&A) expenses and the cost of goods sold (COGS).

The classic expense account with considerable discretion is depreciation and amortization, which is typically reported as part of SG&A or COGS on the income statement. Companies are required to determine the capital costs associated with noncurrent assets and then depreciate the depreciable amount (the difference between the capitalized costs and an estimate of the salvage value) over an estimated useful life. Reported depreciation expense is the result of many choices—which costs to capitalize, residual value assumptions, useful life assumptions—as well as an allocation method (e.g., straight line, accelerated or some other method).

Another primary expense account that contains considerable discretion is COGS. Accrual accounting only expenses costs associated with inventory when that inventory is sold. For companies with large inventory balances, there is considerable discretion as to the costs that are capitalized into inventory as well as how to value that inventory at the end of the fiscal period. Obsolescence must be accounted for and inventory, as with other assets, cannot be reported on the balance sheet at greater than fair value. Identification of obsolete inventory and valuation at the end of the fiscal period is subjective. As with receivables, care should be taken to monitor significant changes in inventory balances.

4.2.1.2. Warning Signs Financial statements contain ample disclosures related to depreciation and amortization. Companies must disclose their method (straight line or otherwise) along with broad summaries of useful lives. Ratios of depreciation rates relative to the gross value of property, plant and equipment or ratios of changes in depreciation rates relative to contemporaneous sales, can easily be computed and compared to other companies to assess conservative or aggressive depreciation rates.

Financial statement information also can be combined with additional disclosure that companies make at earnings announcements or via conference calls. Companies typically give more detailed information than what you see in the 10-Q or 10-K filing, especially for segment information. A good example of the information contained in conference calls is Ford Motor Company. For the quarter ended 30 September 2004, Ford reported net income of $266 million compared to a net loss of $25 million for the quarter ended 30 September 2003. A key driver of this improved profitability is the financial services arm of Ford. That unit reported an increase of net income from $1.031 billion for Q3, 2003 to $1.425 billion for Q3, 2004. Revenues fell marginally from $6.499 billion for the financial services arm to $6.198 million, but this was coupled with a significant reduction in depreciation from $2.072 billion to $1.570 billion. Conference call participants were quick to pick this up, and noticed that the bulk of the improvement in the financial services profitability was attributable to growth in Ford Motor Credit, with over half of the improvement coming from lease residual value improvements (i.e., the company reassessed the residual value of its fleet based on recent auctions, increasing residual values and consequently lowering periodic depreciation charges). This choice as to residual value affected the depreciation accrual. The net effect allowed Ford to report a profit for Q3, 2004 as opposed to a loss. This example also illustrates that the information used to identify financial reporting quality issues need not be limited to the financial statements themselves. Conference calls and other company communications provide additional information for the interpretation of reported financial statements. In the case of Ford, it was detailed segment disclosure in the conference call that alerted conference call participants to the reasons Ford moved to a profit in Q3, 2004.

NetFlix is a good example of low quality financial reporting attributable to depreciation related choices. NetFlix has a simple business model: It maintains an extensive DVD warehouse with an online distribution channel. This business model was very effective, primarily due to a first mover advantage in implementing the strategy. Part of the financial performance of NetFlix is attributable to the amortization method for its rental library. NetFlix uses an accelerated amortization method known as "sum of the months."[10] Prior to 2004, NetFlix used this accelerated method with a one year useful life assumption. Post 2004, NetFlix switched to a three year useful life assumption for back catalogue DVDs. This had the effect of slowing the expensing of back-catalog DVDs. Going into 2005, the back catalogue DVDs that would have been expensed from the acquisitions during 2004 would be spread out over the next three years. The change in amortization method at NetFlix had the consequence of increasing reported earnings in the year following the change by slowing the expense rate of back catalogue DVDs. Blockbuster is an interesting counter-example. They employ a similar accelerated depreciation method over one year for all DVDs, and have kept this method constant.

Reporting quality issues with inventory can be tracked by monitoring large changes in the inventory balance. Inventory build up will be explained by companies as necessary to support future product demand. On average, however, an inventory build up is a good indication that the company has problems with managing its inventory levels and/or has not been sufficiently aggressive in writing down the value of that inventory as the turnover slows. As with the days sales outstanding ratio discussed for revenue issues, a similar days

---

[10]Using one year as the useful life and a "sum of the months" digit method, the sum of the months over one year totals 78 $(1 + 2 + 3 + \ldots + 12 = 78)$. 12/78 of the amortizable amount would be charged to the first month, 11/78 to the second month, 10/78 to the third month, and so forth.

inventory outstanding ratio can be looked at to identify inventory quality issues. This ratio is equal to net inventory divided by cost of goods sold multiplied by 365. This ratio gives a sense for how quickly the company is able to convert inventory into revenue. Increases in this ratio may indicate potential problems related to earnings quality. But be careful in treating all increases and decreases equally. Companies can shift their inventory management systems leading to significant periodic changes in this ratio. For example, companies expecting some instability in inventory supply chains from overseas locations may rationally build up additional inventory to act as a buffer from potential disruptions. But companies will always try to explain away unfavorable movements in key ratios. The right question to ask of management in this scenario is "Why were supply chains set up with such political risk in the first place?" Finally, for companies utilizing the LIFO cost flow assumption to value their inventories, check the footnotes carefully to see the extent to which LIFO liquidations have contributed to profit in a given fiscal period. If you see a LIFO liquidation has contributed to an improvement in profitability as COGS are lower by "dipping" into the older inventory cost layers, this one time advantage should be removed from current earnings to give a better indication of long-term profitability.

4.2.2. Deferring Expenses

In addition to simply understating expenses, companies are able to shift the recording of expenses across fiscal periods under the accrual accounting system. In this section we look at some of these deferral choices in detail.

4.2.2.1. The Range of Problems One of the largest areas of accounting abuse is the practice of capitalizing costs that should have been expensed. Given the significant discretion in capitalizing costs for various noncurrent assets such as PP&E and intangibles, some companies abuse this discretion and include costs in the noncurrent portion of the balance sheet that should have been expensed.

4.2.2.2. Warning Signs The simplest way to get a sense for inappropriate capitalization is to track growth in net noncurrent assets: capitalization activity is what we are interested in. The broad measures of accruals described in section 2 will flag companies that have experienced significant growth in their net operating assets. On average, this growth in net operating assets is associated with lower future company performance. This is due to a combination of over-investment tendencies from these companies and diminishing marginal returns to investment activity. However, not all companies that grow will perform poorly. Identifying, ex ante, which companies are growing at a rate that is not likely to lead to lower future performance is a challenging task. The approach is to place the asset growth in context relative to sales growth, expected future sales growth both for the company itself and sector group which it belongs to. If a company is growing its asset base in an environment where capacity utilization is very tight and margins are quite attractive, this asset growth is less likely to be indicative of poor future performance as compared to a company which is growing its asset base and has excess capacity and deteriorating margins. But note that this is a challenging task: It is very difficult to separate good asset growth from bad asset growth. Your presumption should be to treat all asset growth as bad and impose a tough standard to reject that hypothesis.

The example below touches on the issue of capitalization of software development costs. It also illustrates the care that must be taken in selecting valuation metrics when costs that might be included in operating expenses are capitalized.

EXAMPLE 17-4   Expense Recognition for an Information Service Provider

Thomson Corporation, based in Canada, is one of the world's leading information services providers. The software industry is an interesting sector to examine because it allows considerable discretion with respect to capitalization decisions. Software providers are allowed to capitalize costs associated with software development and then amortize these costs over a period in which the product is expected to be sold. Thomson's income statement for the year ended 31 December 2006, along with selected notes related to its treatment of software development costs, is presented below.

Thomson Corporation: Consolidated Statement of Earnings (US$ millions except per-common-share amounts)

	Year ended 31 December	
	2006	**2005**
Revenues	6,641	6,173
Cost of sales, selling, marketing, general and administrative expenses	(4,702)	(4,351)
Depreciation (Notes 11 and 12)	(439)	(414)
Amortization (Note 13)	(242)	(236)
Operating profit	1,258	1,172
Net other income (expense) (Note 4)	1	(28)
Net interest expense and other financing costs (Note 5)	(221)	(221)
Income taxes (Note 6)	(119)	(261)
Earnings from continuing operations	919	662
Earnings from discontinued operations, net of tax (Note 7)	201	272
Net earnings	1,120	934
Dividends declared on preference shares (Note 16)	(5)	(4)
Earnings attributable to common shares	1,115	930
Earnings per Common Share (Note 8)		
Basic and diluted earnings per common share:		
From continuing operations	$1.41	$1.00
From discontinued operations	0.32	0.42
Basic and diluted earnings per common share	$1.73	$1.42

Note 1: Summary of Significant Accounting Policies: Computer Software

Capitalized Software for Internal Use

Certain costs incurred in connection with the development of software to be used internally are capitalized once a project has progressed beyond a conceptual, preliminary stage to that of application development. Costs which qualify for capitalization include both internal and external costs, but are limited to those that are directly related to the specific project. The capitalized amounts, net of accumulated amortization, are included in "Computer software, net" in the consolidated balance sheet. These costs are amortized over their expected useful lives, which range from three to ten years. The amortization expense is included in "Depreciation" in the consolidated statement of earnings.

Capitalized Software to Be Marketed

In connection with the development of software that is intended to be marketed to customers, certain costs are capitalized once technological feasibility of the product is established and a market for the product has been identified. The capitalized amounts, net of accumulated amortization, are also included in "Computer software, net" in the consolidated balance sheet. The capitalized amounts are amortized over the expected period of benefit, not to exceed three years, and this amortization expense is included in "Cost of sales, selling, marketing, general and administrative expenses" in the consolidated statement of earnings.

Note 12: Computer Software

Computer software consists of the following:

As of 31 December 2006	Cost	Accumulated Amortization	Net Computer Software
Capitalized software for internal use	1,791	(1,228)	563
Capitalized software to be marketed	212	(128)	84
	2,003	(1,356)	647
Capitalized software for internal use	1,608	(1,085)	523
Capitalized software to be marketed	143	(98)	45
	1,751	(1,183)	568

The amortization charge for internal use computer software in 2006 was $241 million (2005, $224 million) and is included in "Depreciation" in the consolidated statement of earnings. The amortization charge for software intended to be marketed was $25 million (2005, $21 million) and is included in "Cost of sales, selling, marketing, general and administrative expenses" in the consolidated statement of earnings.

Based on the information given, address the following problems:

1. Contrast Thomson's recognition of software related costs in 2006 with the actual cash spent acquiring and developing the software.
2. Estimate Thomson's 2006 operating profit and earnings from continuing operations assuming Thomson expensed all software related costs when the related cash flows occurred.

3. Contrast the implications for the cash flow statement from expensing software development costs rather than capitalizing and amortizing them.

4. Many analysts use EV/EBITDA (enterprise value divided by earnings before interest, taxes, depreciation and amortization) as a valuation measure for software companies. Enterprise value is simply the sum of the market capitalization and the book value of outstanding debt. Critique the use of this measure when software related costs are being capitalized.

Solution to 1. The total balance for capitalized computer software increased from $568 in 2005 to $647 in 2006, a total of $79. This is the amount by which computer software costs exceeded the amount recognized as an expense on the income statement.

Solution to 2. Operating profit would have been $1,258 − 79 = $1,179. The effective tax rate for 2006 is 11.5% [= 119 ÷ (1,258 + 1 − 221)]. Net income would be reduced by $79 adjusted for tax, or $79(1 − 0.115) = $70, so the adjusted earnings from continuing operations is $919 − 70 = 849. Earnings from continuing operations were effectively overstated by 8.2 percent (= 70 ÷ 849) relative to cash costs.

Solution to 3. Software development costs would typically be expensed as part of research and development, or in Thomson's case as part of cost of sales. With such treatment, software development costs affect (reduce) cash flow from operating activities. By contrast, capitalized software costs are amortized to expense over time. The initial expenditure is recorded as a cash flow from investing activities. Amortization of the capitalized amount is added back to net income when calculating cash flow from operating activities. In effect, capitalizing software costs reclassifies them from an operating cash flow to an investing cash flow, and then allocates that amount to amortization expense over time.

Solution to 4. EBITDA ignores the costs related to software development by adding amortization back to operating income. Unless either the initial capitalized amount or the subsequent amortization is deducted, investors are effectively ignoring a software company's software development costs altogether in evaluating the company. Because software companies must develop software in order to stay in business, valuing the companies on the basis of EBITDA potentially ignores a critical component of expense, akin to ignoring a retailer's inventory costs. In the case of Thomson, the amortization of software to be marketed is included in SG&A expenses, so it is captured in the computation of EBITDA. However, most of Thomson's software costs related to software to be marketed and was not included in SG&A. Thus, using EBITDA in this case would result in ignoring most software costs.

4.2.3. Classification of Ordinary Expenses as Nonrecurring or Nonoperating
The final set of expense issues that we will touch on relate to a possible way to mask a decline in operating performance by reclassifying operating expenses.

4.2.3.1. The Range of Problems   There is an incentive for management at companies with deteriorating core income to reclassify some recurring or operating expenses as nonoperating. The issue here is the inappropriate classification of a recurring item that would normally be recorded as part of SG&A or COGS. These costs are then classified as a nonrecurring or special charge and are reported as a separate line item on the income statement. This is easiest for companies that have experienced a genuine special item such as a restructuring. Recurring costs can then be "piggy-backed" onto these nonrecurring items.

4.2.3.2. Warning Signs   McVay (2006) examines this issue in detail and identifies one way to track this behavior based on the core operating margin, defined as (Sales − COGS − SGA) ÷ Sales. This ratio represents the pretax return on a money unit (e.g., euro) of sales resulting from the company's operating activities. To use it, analysts should compute year-over-year changes in the core operating margin and look for spikes in the incidence of negative special items for companies that have experienced a decrease in this margin. Observing an increase in core operating margins coincident with a negative special item is consistent with opportunistic classification of a recurring expense as a nonrecurring expense. More sophisticated approaches would include building models of expected core operating margin in year *t* rather than focusing on a simple change in core operating margin. Examples of these sophisticated approaches include building regression-based models that forecast next period's core operating margin using the prior period's core operating margin in addition to other variables such as expected growth rates, macroeconomic conditions, sector affiliation, etc. The goal is the same: To build an expected core operating margin to compare against the realized core operating margin. If you see a large positive unexpected increase in core operating margin and the company contemporaneously reports a negative special item or nonrecurring charge, this may indicate a reclassification of a recurring item as a nonrecurring item. Absent this opportunistic reclassification, the company would not have reported an increase in its core operating margin. Furthermore, this reclassification tendency is stronger for companies that do not regularly report special items, and the expense classification shifting is more pervasive when incentives are greatest (e.g., the desire to meet/beat analyst forecasts). McVay (2006) notes Borden, Inc. as a good example of this type of behavior. The SEC determined that Borden had inappropriately classified $192 million of marketing expenses, which should have been included in standard selling, general, and administrative expenses, as part of a 1992 restructuring charge.

EXAMPLE 17-5   Core Operating Margin Warning Sign

Based in Canada, NOVA Chemicals Corporation, together with its subsidiaries, engages in the production and marketing of plastics and chemicals. The company operates in three business units: Olefins/Polyolefins, Performance Styrenics, and STYRENIX. NOVA's income statements and an associated note are presented below.

Consolidated Statements of Income (Loss) and Reinvested Earnings (Deficit), (US$ millions except number of shares and per-share amounts)

	Year ended 31 December		
	2006	**2005**	**2004**
Revenue	$6,519	$5,616	$5,270
Feedstock and operating costs	5,663	4,906	4,378

	Year ended 31 December		
	2006	2005	2004
Depreciation and amortization	299	290	297
Selling, general and administrative	201	199	274
Research and development	51	50	48
Restructuring charges (Note 14)	985	168	8
	7,199	5,613	5,005
Operating income (loss)	(680)	3	265

14. Restructuring Charges

During the past three years, NOVA Chemicals has undertaken several restructuring steps to reduce costs. As a result of these actions, the Company estimates it will reduce costs by about $100 million per year beginning in 2007. In addition to this, depreciation will be reduced by about $80 million per year in the three reportable segments within the STYRENIX business unit. In 2006, NOVA Chemicals recorded a restructuring charge of $985 million before tax ($861 million after tax) related to the following:

The Company recorded an impairment charge of $860 million related to the STYRENIX business unit assets. The STYRENIX business unit includes the Styrene Monomer, North American Solid Polystyrene and NOVA Innovene European joint venture segments. The STYRENIX business unit has not been profitable due to poor market conditions, and in recent years both NOVA Chemicals and the NOVA Innovene joint venture have reduced production capacity through plant closures. In July 2006, NOVA Chemicals announced it would investigate various alternatives for the STYRENIX business unit, including sale, formation of a joint venture with other producers, or spin out. NOVA Chemicals has assessed the recoverability of the STYRENIX assets and determined that the carrying value exceeded the estimated future cash flows from these assets. Based on this analysis, the fair market value of these STYRENIX facilities was determined to be $242 million.

NOVA Innovene permanently closed its Carrington, U.K., solid polystyrene facility in October 2006. The Company recorded a restructuring charge of $57 million related primarily to noncash asset write-downs of the plant including $8 million related to total expected severance and other departure costs. As of December 31, 2006, $5 million of the severance costs was paid to employees.

During 2006, NOVA Chemicals restructured its North American operations to better align resources and reduce costs. As a result, the Company recorded a $53 million restructuring charge related to severance, pension and other employee-related costs. Of this amount, $10 million related to one-time pension curtailment and special termination benefits. Of the remaining $43 million, $22 million has been paid to employees by the end of 2006 with the majority of the remainder to be paid in 2007.

A $15 million charge was recorded related to the accrual of total expected severance costs for the Chesapeake, Virginia, polystyrene plant, which was closed in 2006. To date, $3 million has been paid to employees.

NOVA's PP & E balance declined from $3,626 in 2005 to $2,719 in 2006. Net operating assets were $3,088 in 2005 and $2,349 in 2006. Based on the information given, address the following problems:

1. What was NOVA's core operating margin in each of the three years ended 31 December 2006, 2005 and 2004?
2. What was NOVA's balance-sheet-based accruals ratio in 2006?
3. Are there any warning signs related to NOVA's earnings quality based on the information presented?

Solution to 1. Core operating margins, when calculated as (Sales − Cost of sales − SGA) ÷ Sales, for NOVA were 10.0 percent, 9.1 percent, and 11.7 percent in 2006, 2005, and 2004, respectively (feedstock and operating costs being used as the most representative of cost of sales). When calculated using all operating items other than the restructuring charge, core operating margins were 4.7 percent, 3.0 percent, and 5.2 percent, which is directionally similar.

	2006	2005	2004
Revenue	$ 6,519	$ 5,616	$ 5,270
Feedstock and operating costs	5,663	4,906	4,378
Depreciation and amortization	299	290	297
Selling, general and administrative	201	199	274
Research and development	51	50	48
Core operating income	305	171	273
Core operating margin	4.7%	3.0%	5.2%

Solution to 2. The balance-sheet-based accruals ratio is equal to the Change in NOA/ Average NOA. In NOVA's case, $(2{,}349 - 3{,}088) \div [0.5 \times (2{,}349 + 3{,}088)] = -739 \div 2{,}718.5 = -27.2\%$.

Solution to 3. Yes. The large accrual ratio suggests that a significant portion of NOVA's net income was due to discretionary items. The increase in core operating margin from 2005 to 2006, combined with a large special item in 2006, fits McVay's warning sign that the company may be classifying ordinary operating expenses as nonoperating or nonrecurring. This is an indication of opportunistic use of expense classification. The reported numbers for NOVA should be viewed skeptically.

EXAMPLE 17-6   The Classification of Expenses

Matsushita Electric Industrial Co., Ltd., best known for its Panasonic brand name, is one of the world's leading manufacturers of electronic and electric products for a wide range of consumer, business, and industrial uses, as well as a wide variety of components. Excerpted below are Matsushita's income statements for the years ended 31 March.

Years ended 31 March	Yen (millions)		
	2007	2006	2005
Revenues, costs and expenses:			
Net sales:			
Related companies (Note 4)	250,863	204,740	192,489
Other	8,857,307	8,689,589	8,521,147
Total net sales	9,108,170	8,894,329	8,713,636
Cost of sales (Notes 4 and 16)	(6,394,418)	(6,155,297)	(6,176,046)
Selling, general, and administrative expenses (Note 16)	(2,254,211)	(2,324,759)	(2,229,096)
Interest income	30,553	28,216	19,490
Dividends received	7,597	6,567	5,383
Gain from the transfer of the substitutional portion of Japanese Welfare Pension Insurance (Note 10)	—	—	31,509
Other income (Notes 5, 6, 16 and 17)	114,545	147,399	82,819
Interest expense	(20,906)	(21,686)	(22,827)
Goodwill impairment (Note 8)	(30,496)	(50,050)	(3,559)
Other deductions (Notes 4, 5, 7, 8, 15, 16 and 17)	(121,690)	(153,407)	(174,396)
Income before income taxes	439,144	371,312	246,913
Provision for income taxes (Note 11):			
Current	119,465	96,341	96,529
Deferred	72,398	70,748	56,805
	191,863	167,089	153,334
Income before minority interests and equity in earnings (losses) of associated companies	247,281	204,223	93,579
Minority interests	31,131	(987)	27,719
Equity in earnings (losses) of associated companies (Note 4)	1,035	(50,800)	(7,379)
Net income	217,185	154,410	58,481

As shown, Matsushita includes a line "other deductions," which would be understood to be nonoperating items because it appears below such items as "other income" and "interest expense." Without further examination, analysts may be inclined to treat this item as nonoperating or nonrecurring. However, the deductions amount to a high percentage of pretax income (as high as 70 percent in 2005) and revenue (2 percent in 2005.) Clearly the distinction is worth further analysis. Consider the associated notes, which are excerpted below:

4. Investments in and Advances to, and Transactions with Associated Companies

During the years ended March 31, 2006 and 2005, the Company incurred a writedown of 30,681 million yen and 2,833 million yen, respectively, for other-than-temporary impairment of investments and advances in associated companies.

5. Investments in Securities

During the years ended March 31, 2007, 2006 and 2005, the Company incurred a write down of 939 million yen, 458 million yen and 2,661 million yen, respectively, for other-than-temporary impairment of available-for-sale securities, mainly reflecting the aggravated market condition of certain industries in Japan.

7. Long-Lived Assets

The Company periodically reviews the recorded value of its long-lived assets to determine if the future cash flows to be derived from these assets will be sufficient to recover the remaining recorded asset values. . . .

8. Goodwill and Other Intangible Assets

The Company recognized an impairment loss of 27,299 million yen during fiscal 2007 related to goodwill of a mobile communication subsidiary. This impairment is due to a decrease in the estimated fair value of the reporting unit caused by decreased profit expectation and the intensification of competition in a domestic market which was unforeseeable in the prior year.

The Company recognized an impairment loss of 3,197 million yen during fiscal 2007 related to goodwill of JVC due primarily to profit performance in JVC's consumer electronics business being lower than the Company's expectation.

The Company recognized an impairment loss of 50,050 million yen during fiscal 2006 related to goodwill of a mobile communication subsidiary. This impairment is due to a decrease in the estimated fair value of the reporting unit caused by decreased profit expectation and the closure of certain businesses in Europe and Asia.

15. Restructuring Charges

The Company has provided early retirement programs to those employees voluntarily leaving the Company. The accrued early retirement programs are recognized when the employees accept the offer and the amount can be reasonably estimated. Expenses associated with the closure and integration of locations include amounts such as moving expense of facilities and costs to terminate leasing contracts incurred at domestic and overseas manufacturing plants and sales offices. An analysis of the accrued restructuring charges for the years ended March 31, 2007, 2006 and 2005 is as follows:

	Yen (millions)		
	2007	**2006**	**2005**
Balance at beginning of the year	1,335	3,407	—
New charges	19,574	48,975	110,568
Cash payments	(10,889)	(51,047)	(107,161)
Balance at end of the year	10,020	1,335	3,407

16. Supplementary Information to the Statements of Income and Cash Flows

Foreign exchange gains and losses included in other deductions for the years ended March 31, 2007, 2006 and 2005 are losses of 18,950 million yen, 13,475 million yen and 7,542 million yen, respectively.Included in other deductions for the year ended March 31, 2006 are claim expenses of 34,340 million yen.

Based on the information given, address the following problems:

1. Based on the description in the notes for each item, comment on whether it is appropriate to treat the following charges as nonoperating or nonrecurring:
    A. Investments in and advances to and transactions with associated companies.
    B. Investments in securities.
    C. Long-lived assets.
    D. Goodwill and other intangible assets.
    E. Restructuring charges.
    F. Supplementary information to the statements of income and cash flows.
2. How would analyzing balance-sheet-based or cash-flow-statement-based accruals ratios help in assessing the impact of movements in the accounts above? (No calculations are needed.)

Solutions to 1. Discretion is required in analyzing many items. When in doubt, analysts may wish to prepare separate sets of financial statements to understand the effect of treating individual items in different manners.

A. Classifying changes in the value of the investments as nonoperating is appropriate for a nonfinancial company such as Matsushita.

B. Securities held available for sale are typically used as alternatives to investing in low-yielding cash. Treating losses on such securities as nonoperating is appropriate. Again, however, persistent losses raise the question of whether management is capable of selecting worthwhile alternative investments.

C. The value of long-lived assets is typically charged to expense over time as depreciation, which is considered to be an operating item. The impairment charges shift future depreciation expense into the current year, which reduces the future depreciation and also suggests that past depreciation charges were too low. Analysts should reclassify the impairment expense to treat it on par with normal depreciation.

D. Accounting principles call for periodic testing of goodwill for impairment. No amortization expense is otherwise charged. Because the impairment does not offset a normal operating expense, it can be appropriate to classify it as nonoperating, as Matsushita does. However, analysts should pay attention to goodwill impairment. Large impairments can appear conservative at the time they are announced, but the need for them can result from previous aggressive accounting (aggressive at least from an after-the-fact perspective). In the case of Matsushita, it appears that management overpaid for its past investments.

E. Early retirement programs and expenses associated with the closure and integration of locations include amounts such as moving expense of facilities and costs to terminate leasing contracts. Given that these expenses would be incurred from time to time as part of normal business operations, they should be reclassified as operating expenses.

F. Matsushita is an international operation and should thus be expected to incur foreign currency gains and losses as part of normal operations, although they are typically considered outside management's control. Foreign exchange gains are typically treated as adjustments to net financing costs and are treated as nonoperating.

Solution to 2. Marketable securities (if treated as short-term investments) and equity investments would not be included in either net operating assets or cash flow from operating activities, so the accruals ratios would provide the correct interpretation of these items. Foreign currency and goodwill may appear in a balance sheet driven accruals ratio, but not in the ratio based on the cash flow statement. These were also items of questionable operating significance, so the mixed treatment in an accruals ratio reflects the ambiguity. The charges to long-lived assets and for restructuring would deservedly be reflected in the accruals ratios.

4.3. Balance Sheet Issues

The focus of our discussion has been quality of earnings issues as contained in various revenue and expense accounts. There are additional sources of information related to the balance sheet that pertain to our discussion of earnings quality. We will introduce this topic with brief discussion of two balance sheet issues, off-balance-sheet debt and goodwill.

4.3.1. Off-Balance-Sheet Liabilities

Off-balance-sheet debt includes items not reported in the body of the balance sheet but that might be associated with an obligation for future payments. Information contained here is related to our discussion of earnings quality, as the net assets that are acquired from this off-balance-sheet financing is a form of growth that an on-balance sheet measure of accruals would fail to capture.

4.3.1.1. The Range of Problems Current accounting standards allow for a significant portion of assets and liabilities to avoid recognition in the primary financial statements. A consequence of this is that companies will appear to have less leverage than they actually do when leverage is measured using only on-balance-sheet information. The classic example is leases. U.S. GAAP recognizes two types of leases (operating and capital) and provides different accounting rules for each. The distinction between the two types of leases rests primarily on a consideration of the present value of minimum lease payments relative to the fair value of the asset leased (greater than 90 percent constitutes a capital lease under U.S. GAAP), and a consideration of whether the life of the lease is greater than 75 percent of the useful life of the leased asset (greater than 75 percent constitutes a capital lease under U.S. GAAP). There are other issues to consider such as the existence of a bargain purchase option, but they typically are less relevant for the determination of whether a lease is operating or not. The treatment of operating leases relative to capital leases is dramatically different. An operating lease treats the cash outflow associated with the lease as a rental expense which will flow through the income statement over the life of the lease. With a capital lease, the fair value of the asset is recognized as both an asset and liability at inception of the lease, and subsequently amortized over the life of the lease. Companies have a strong preference for operating lease classification, as this keeps the lease obligation off the balance sheet. With the current rules under U.S. GAAP, there is significant discretion in structuring the terms of the lease contract so as not to trigger one of the thresholds described above.

Currently there are few companies reporting capital leases: operating leases have become the norm, largely attributable to their preferred accounting treatment. Estimates range to over $1 trillion dollars for the amount of undiscounted future cash flow obligations associated with operating leases for SEC registrants. This is clearly a nontrivial issue. The use of operating leases is pervasive in the retail sector with companies such as Walgreens, Wal-Mart, CVS, and others having very large off-balance-sheet operating lease obligations. The consequence of bringing these leases onto the balance sheet will be to increase leverage ratios; and depending on how these companies amortize the value of the leased asset, there could also be significant impacts on reported income directly.

4.3.1.2. Warning Signs While the Financial Accounting Standards Board (FASB) has governed the determination of operating and capital leases and the appropriate accounting treatment, SEC disclosures have improved in recent years with the addition of tabular presentation of future cash flow obligations associated with debt, operating leases, and other commitments in the 10-K. From these disclosures it is now possible to identify future cash flow obligations from many contractual obligations including current operating leases. These numbers can be discounted to their present value to get a rough estimate of the off-balance-sheet obligations, which in turn can be brought on to the balance sheet and amortized using the companies' reported depreciation schedule for other noncurrent assets. Furthermore, tracking year over year changes in these off-balance-sheet leases can highlight less transparent financing activities for these companies, which are arguably as important as on-balance sheet financing activities for forecasting future company performance.

The following example explores the use of off-balance-sheet debt of a major U.S. retailer.

EXAMPLE 17-7   Off-Balance-Sheet Debt

In its 10-K for the year ended 31 January 2007, Wal-Mart's (NYSE: WMT) balance sheet included total obligations under capital leases of $3,798 million, of which $285 million was due within one year and the remainder was long term. The notes to the financial statements also broke out the following information regarding long-term contractual obligations:

Contractual Obligations and Other Commercial Commitments

The following table sets forth certain information concerning our obligations and commitments to make contractual future payments, such as debt and lease agreements, and contingent commitments:

($ millions)	Payments due during fiscal years ending 31 January				
	Total	2008	2009–2010	2011–2012	Thereafter
Recorded Contractual Obligations:					
Long-term debt	$32,650	$5,428	$9,120	$5,398	$12,704
Commercial paper	2,570	2,570	—	—	—
Capital lease obligations	5,715	538	1,060	985	3,132
Unrecorded Contractual Obligations:					
Noncancelable operating leases	*10,446*	*842*	*1,594*	*1,332*	*6,678*
Interest on long-term debt	17,626	1,479	2,482	1,705	11,960
Undrawn lines of credit	6,890	3,390	—	3,500	—
Trade letters of credit	2,986	2,986	—	—	—
Standby letters of credit	2,247	2,247	—	—	—
Purchase obligations	15,168	11,252	3,567	126	223
Total commercial commitments	$96,298	$30,732	$17,823	$13,046	$34,697

Based on the information given, address the following problems:

1. Contrast the relative importance of on- and off-balance-sheet treatment of contractual obligations for Wal-Mart.
2. Determine the relative importance of Wal-Mart's off-balance-sheet obligations, given that Wal-Mart's 2007 cost of sales was $264 billion.
3. Estimate the impact on Wal-Mart's financial statements if operating leases were treated as though they were capital leases.

Solution to 1. Wal-Mart lists $40.9 billion of recorded contractual obligations ($32.650 + $2.570 + 5.715), and $55.4 ($10.446 + $17.626 + $6.890 + $2.986 + $2.247 + $15.168) billion of future obligations that are not recorded on the balance sheet.

Solution to 2. Noncancelable operating leases are similar in nature to capital leases, or assets financed with debt. They should be treated as though they were capital leases. The interest on long-term debt is the total future sum, and represents a financing cost rather than an actual liability. Analysis of interest coverage ratios should be adequate, with no adjustments to financial statements required. Undrawn lines of credit represent credit available, not currently in use. It is a potential obligation rather than an actual one. Letters of credit and purchase obligations are normal parts of business, and the related amounts ($20.4 billion) are small relative to Wal-Mart's operations. Wal-Mart's 2007 cost of sales was $264 billion—so the $15 billion in purchase obligations (which will eventually flow through cost of sales) amounts to less than three weeks worth of the actual purchases by Wal-Mart.

Solution to 3. The present value of Wal-Mart's operating leases can be estimated by comparing them to its capital leases. Ideally, an analyst would discount the future capital lease payments, $5,715, to their carrying value of $3,798 to determine the implicit interest rate (an internal rate of return), then discount the operating lease obligations at the same rate. However, the disclosures give only broad ranges of when the payments are due, so analysts must estimate the timing. A shortcut approach is to simply apply the same overall discount to each type of lease. So, if the present value of capital leases is $3,798 ÷ $5,715 = 66.5% of the future payments, the present value of operating leases would be estimated at $10,446 × 0.665 = $6,942. To capitalize the operating leases, the analyst would add $6,942 to property, plant, and equipment and also to long-term liabilities. Leverage ratios, asset turnover, and other ratios involving assets and liabilities would be affected. In addition, the existing lease payments would ideally be allocated to depreciation and interest components rather than the current classification as rent. This would also impact interest coverage ratios and operating margins. The precise impact would depend on the amortization assumptions made. Note: Operating lease obligations of $10.4 billion are 1.83 times larger than the $5.7 billion in capital leases. The operating leases are slightly longer duration, as evidenced by the fact that 64 percent ($6,678 ÷ $10,446) of the payments are due in more than five years, compared with 55 percent ($3,132 ÷ $5,715) of the capital lease payments. Because the payments are due over a longer time horizon, their discounted value is lower, and the $6.9 billion estimated value is somewhat high (though considerably more accurate than the current balance sheet valuation of zero).

4.3.2. Goodwill

Goodwill is an intangible asset, subject to an annual impairment test, that is typically paid for in a business combination when the consideration paid to acquire the target exceeds the fair value of the target's net assets. For a company with many past acquisitions, the impairment of goodwill can have a major effect on reported financials.

4.3.2.1. The Range of Problems When a company acquires another company and records part of the acquisition price as goodwill, the goodwill is capitalized as an asset and no periodic amortization charges are taken against it. Instead, companies evaluate goodwill and other acquired intangible assets for impairment annually or whenever events or changes in circumstances indicate that the value of such an asset is impaired. This assessment requires estimates of the future cash flows associated with continued use of the asset, growth rates, and general market conditions. There is considerable discretion in conducting this impairment test, and this is one of the key risks associated with the external audit function: Auditors typically hire external appraisers to help with their assessment of fair value of goodwill and other intangibles.

4.3.2.2. Warning Signs Disclosures for goodwill can be found in the supplemental information to the primary financial statements. Typically, a company will provide tabular disclosure for year-over-year changes in reported goodwill. Given the inherent subjectivity in how this account is valued, analysts should look carefully at changes (or the absence of an impairment given overall economic conditions) in reported goodwill. Companies that continue to report goodwill on their balance sheets, but that have market capitalization less than the book value of equity, are certainly worthy of detailed examination to understand why an impairment was not taken. Karthik and Watts (2007) provide an interesting illustration of this situation for Orthodontic Centers of America (OCA). For the fiscal year ended 31 December 2003, OCA had reported book value of equity in excess of the market value of equity, yet continued to report a sizeable goodwill on its balance sheet ($87 million out of its $660 million total assets were attributable to goodwill). OCA was subsequently delisted from the stock exchange and in 2006 filed for bankruptcy.

4.4.   Cash Flow Statement Issues

The material discussed in the preceding sections has highlighted many problems with earnings measures as predictors of a company's ability to generate future free cash flows. In this section, we outline a few caveats related to blindly following cash flow based measures. We will discuss three key items: (1) classification issues in the cash flow statement, (2) omitted investing and financing activities, and (3) real earnings management activity.

4.4.1.   Classification Issues
Accounting standards define cash and cash equivalents to include only very short-term highly liquid investments. This narrow definition leads to the possibility that companies' investment of cash in liquid assets may appear in the investing as well as the operating section of statement of cash flows.[11]

Many firms carry large cash balances which are invested in a portfolio of reasonable liquid investments. These cash balances are kept for various reasons. For example, Microsoft Corporation holds very large cash balances in part to help finance new investment opportunities when they arise, eliminating the need to obtain costly external financing. The cash that companies like Microsoft hold is not always invested in highly liquid short-term investments such as Treasury bills because companies can often obtain higher expected rates of return by investing elsewhere. To the extent that cash is invested in marketable securities such as equity and other fixed income products, these investments are not strictly a "cash equivalents" under most accounting standards. This allows companies to classify them as longer term investments. The result is that some liquid investments end up appearing in the investing section of the statement of cash flows. If the analyst focuses solely on an operating cash flow number, these "investing" cash flows will be missed. An easy solution to this problem is to take a holistic view to cash flows, and include operating and investing cash flows when assessing financial reporting quality. The aggregate accrual measures described in this chapter do this for you by capturing the net cash flow generated from both operating and investing activities.

---

[11]Note that the IASB in its 2007 revision to IAS 1 "Presentation of Financial Statements" has decided to make "cash" rather than "cash and cash equivalents" the basis for presenting the statement of cash flows. See the document FSP-0710b08a-obs at www.iasb.org for more information.

4.4.2. Omitted Investing and Financing Activities

The aggregate accrual measures outlined in this chapter are based solely on investing and financing activity that is reported in the primary financial statements. There are certain types of investing and financing activity that are (1) not reported in *either* the balance sheet or statement of cash flows, or (2) not reported in the financial statements at all. An example of the first category is common-stock-based acquisition activity. Such activity will be picked up via the balance sheet measure of aggregate accruals and the net assets acquired through the acquisition will be reported in the balance sheet post acquisition for the new entity. It is important for the analyst to utilize both a balance-sheet-based and cash-flow-statement-based measure of aggregate accruals so as not to miss capturing the effects of such activity. An example of the second category is operating leases. This was described in detail in section 4.3.1. The recommended approach is to capitalize the operating lease and adjust the balance sheet to reflect this off-balance-sheet source of asset growth. What the analyst should pay attention to is not the existence of operating leases per se, but growth in operating lease activity. A good example is JetBlue Airways Corporation (NASDAQ: JBLU). Like most airline operators JetBlue makes extensive use of operating leases in its business model. From the perspective of 2007, over the last three years JetBlue has expanded extensively in part by increasing the use of operating leases related to terminal usage and flight equipment. Exhibit 17-11 shows three panels extracted from the annual reports filed by JetBlue for the fiscal years ended 31 December 2004 through 31 December 2006.

EXHIBIT 17-11　JetBlue Annual Reports

Panel A. Contractual Obligations for Year ended December 31, 2004 (in millions)

		Payments due in					
	Total	**2005**	**2006**	**2007**	**2008**	**2009**	**Thereafter**
Long-term debt (1)	$2,011	$173	$166	$163	$179	$129	$1,201
Operating leases	*1,035*	*110*	*114*	*98*	*92*	*88*	*533*
Flight equipment obligations	7,280	820	1,120	1,170	1,210	1,240	1,720
Short-term borrowings	44	44	—	—	—	—	—
Facilities and other (2)	271	143	28	28	30	27	15
Total	$10,641	$1,290	$1,428	$1,459	$1,511	$1,484	$3,469

Panel B. Contractual Obligations for Year ended December 31, 2005 (in millions)

	Total	**2006**	**2007**	**2008**	**2009**	**2010**	**Thereafter**
Long-term debt	$3,400	$3,400	$282	$282	$207	$200	$2,123
Lease commitments	*1,707*	*1,707*	*155*	*155*	*129*	*119*	*1,002*
Flight equipment obligations	6,440	6,440	1,170	1,170	1,230	1,180	545
Short-term borrowings	65	65	—	—	—	—	—
Financing obligations and other	2,439	2,439	83	83	147	158	1,748
Total	$14,051	$14,051	$1,690	$1,690	$1,713	$1,657	$5,418

Panel C. Contractual Obligations for Year ended December 31, 2006 (in millions)

	Payments due in						
	Total	**2007**	**2008**	**2009**	**2010**	**2011**	**Thereafter**
Long-term debt and capital lease obligations (1)	$4,312	$350	$387	$282	$275	$271	$2,747
Lease commitments	*2,177*	*217*	*216*	*190*	*170*	*159*	*1,225*
Flight equipment obligations	5,705	775	835	965	1,030	1,000	1,100
Short-term borrowings	39	39	—	—	—	—	—
Financing obligations and other (2)	2,333	147	119	138	147	168	1,614
Total	$14,566	$1,528	$1,557	$1,575	$1,622	$1,598	$6,686

Note: Italics within added by the authors.

There is a clear increase in the extent of operating lease activity for JetBlue over the three years from 2004 through 2006. To the extent that the growth in operating lease activity is not associated with asset growth that is recorded on the balance sheet, this lease activity represents an investing activity that is missing from the primary financial statements—limiting the potential usefulness of statement-of-cash-flow- or balance-sheet-based measures of aggregate accruals. A recommended approach is to capitalize the future cash flow obligations reported in the contractual obligation tables that companies are required to disclose (at least in the United States). As described in section 4.3.1, simple assumptions with respect to discount rates and treatment of the cash flows that extend beyond five years are sufficient for our purposes. This capitalized amount then gets added to the asset and liability side of the balance sheet. Given that our measures focus on net operating asset growth, this growth in operating lease activity will lead to a direct change in our aggregate accrual measures as the liability side of this transaction is a financing activity.

4.4.3. Real Earnings Management Activity

Our focus on financial reporting quality has concentrated on the embedded discretion in the accrual-based accounting system. We have ignored real operating decisions that management may take to meet the same capital market and contracting pressures described in section 2.3. For example, management may cut the budget for research and development activity toward the end of the fiscal period when it becomes clear they are struggling to meet earnings-based targets. Note that under U.S. GAAP research and development expenditures are expensed in the year that they are incurred and not capitalized for expensing over future periods. Such myopic behavior is not uncommon for management. The longer term implications from these real operating decisions are to sacrifice future free cash flows at the expense of meeting short term earnings targets.

4.5. A Summary of Financial Reporting Quality Warning Signs

In the course of this chapter, we have presented some key indicators of possibly low quality financial reporting. In Exhibit 17-12, we indicate some key red flags to look for across the various revenue, expense, and balance sheet issues. We include the main warning signs discussed in the text as well as a selection of other warning signs that the reader may find helpful for further study. The expanded list is only a selection, of course.

EXHIBIT 17-12   Accounting Warning Signs (Selection)

Category	Observation	Potential Interpretation
Revenues and gains	Large increases in accounts receivable or large decreases in unearned revenue.	Financial statement indicator of potential for revenue quality issues.
	Large swings in the ratio of revenue to cash collected from customers.	Financial statement indicator of potential revenue acceleration issues.
	Recognizing revenue early; for example:	Acceleration in the recognition of revenue boosts reported income masking a decline in operating performance.
	Bill-and-hold sales	
	Lessor use of capital lease classification	
	Recording sales of equipment or software prior to installation and acceptance by customer	
	Classification of nonoperating income or gains as part of operations.	Income or gains may be nonrecurring and may not relate to true operating performance. May mask a decline in operating performance.
	Recognizing revenue from barter transactions.	Value of transaction may be overstated. Both parties may be striving to report revenues where no cash flow occurs. Revenues and expenses may be overstated.
	Growth in revenues out of line with industry, peers, inventory growth, receivables growth, or cash flow from operations.	May indicate aggressive reporting of sales. If receivables are growing more rapidly than sales, may indicate that credit standards have been lowered or that shipments have been accelerated. If inventories are growing more rapidly than sales, may indicate a slowdown in demand for the company's products.
	Large proportion of revenue occurs in the last quarter of the year for a non-seasonal business.	May indicate aggressive reporting of sales or acceleration of shipments at year-end.
Expenses and losses	Inconsistency over time in the items included in operating revenues and operating expenses.	May indicate opportunistic use of discretion to boost reported operating income.
	Classification of ordinary expenses as nonrecurring or nonoperating.	May reflect an attempt to mask a decline in operating performance.
	Declines in the core operating margin (Sales − COGS − SGA) ÷ Sales accompanied by spikes in negative special items.	May indicate opportunistic classification of recurring expenses as nonrecurring.
	Use of nonconservative deprecation and amortization estimates, assumptions, or methods; for example, long depreciable lives.	May indicate actions taken to boost current reported income. Changes in assumptions may indicate an attempt to mask problems with underlying performance in the current period.
	Buildup of high inventory levels relative to sales or decrease in inventory turnover ratios.	May indicate obsolete inventory or failure to take needed inventory write-downs.

	Deferral of expenses by capitalizing expenditures as an asset; for example: Customer acquisition costs Product development costs	May boost current income at the expense of future income. May mask problems with underlying business performance.
	Lessee use of operating leases.	May result in higher net income in early years under an operating lease, not reflecting depreciation expense and interest expense. Leased asset and associated liability not reflected on balance sheet.
	Use of reserves, such as Restructuring or impairment charges reversed in a subsequent period. Use of high or low level of bad debt reserves relative to peers.	May allow company to "save" profits in one period to be used when needed in a later period. May be used to smooth earnings and mask underlying earnings variability.
Balance sheet issues (may also impact earnings)	Lessee preference for capital lease classification.	Tends to reduce leverage ratios based only on on-balance-sheet-items.
	Market value less than book value for companies with substantial reported goodwill	May indicate that appropriate goodwill impairments have not been taken.
	Use of aggressive acquisition accounting, such as write-off of purchased in-process research and development costs[12]	May indicate that assets and liabilities are not recorded at economic cost to the entity and that earnings may be overstated in future years relative to peers
	Use of special purpose vehicles (SPVs)[13]	Assets and/or liabilities may not be properly reflected on the balance sheet. Income may also be overstated by sales to the special purpose entity or a decline in the value of assets transferred to the SPE.
	Large changes in deferred tax assets and liabilities.	May have near-term cash flow consequences. Particularly investigate the reason for the existence of deferred tax asset valuation allowances.
	Sales of receivables with recourse.	The use of debt may not be fully reflected on the balance sheet and the risks of non-collection may not be reflected for receivables.
	Use of unconsolidated joint ventures or equity method investees when substantial ownership (near 50 percent) exists.	May reflect off balance sheet liabilities. Profitability ratios may be overstated due to share on income reported in income statement but related sales or assets are not reflected in parent financial statements.

Source: Adapted from Stowe, Robinson, Pinto, McLeavey (2002), Chapter 1, Table 1-1, with additions and deletions.

---

[12]**Purchased in-process research and development** costs are the costs of research and development in progress at an acquired company; often part of an acquired company's purchase price is allocated to such costs.
[13]A **special purpose vehicle** is a non-operating entity created to carry out a specified purpose, such as leasing assets or securitizing receivables. The use of SPVs is frequently related to off-balance-sheet financing (financing that does not currently appear on the balance sheet).

5. THE IMPLICATIONS OF FAIR VALUE REPORTING FOR FINANCIAL REPORTING QUALITY: A BRIEF DISCUSSION

As a final point of discussion before concluding, it is worth noting how the recent push from the FASB and the IASB to bring greater relevance to the financial statements has the ironic side effect of increasing accounting discretion. The IASB and FASB recently have made serious efforts to embrace fair value accounting as a basis for financial reporting. The general theme is that the balance sheet should reflect fair values of assets and liabilities. While for some assets, such as equity investments in companies listed on the New York Stock Exchange, the fair value is readily determinable and easily audited (just pick up a copy of the *Wall Street Journal* on the last day of the fiscal period and multiply the number of shares held by the quoted market price), it is not as clear for some other assets. For example, how should one value a large block of equity or bonds in another public entity? Should a discount from the current market value be recorded from the market impact cost associated with selling such a large position? What about investments in private entities where there is no observable market (even for over-the-counter corporate bond trading in the United States, it is difficult to get an accurate price). This is not to mention the more common problem of valuing assets whose economic lives are quite long and may be quite specific to the entity— for example, specialized manufacturing equipment. The turmoil in credit markets over the summer of 2007, stemming from concerns about the collateral quality for many securitized asset-backed securities, illustrates the difficulty in identifying reliable estimates of fair value for many assets (even financial assets) that reside on company balance sheets. Of course, the FASB and International Accounting Standards Board (IASB) have very detailed guidelines defining approaches one can take to place a fair value on such items. But ultimately, fair value accounting opens the door for considerable discretion to be placed on balance sheet valuations.

What is an analyst to do when faced with this increasing uncertainty about balance sheet valuations? First, remember that financial statements should be used as an anchor for your valuation. Keep in mind that there is considerable discretion in the financial statements; appreciate where it is and be skeptical of the numbers presented to you. Second, search for disclosures relating to how the values of assets and liabilities reported in the balance sheet are determined. Financial statements should not be read in isolation from the detailed footnotes accompanying them. There is often useful detail in those footnotes that greatly assists in understanding the choices made by a company in a given fiscal period. With sufficient disclosure about the choices a company has made, it is possible to reverse engineer and place companies back on an equal footing with respect to that choice set.

6. SUMMARY

We have touched on major themes in financial reporting quality. This is a broad area with considerable academic and practitioner research. Indeed, many of the techniques described here are used by analysts to make security recommendations and by asset managers in making portfolio allocation decisions. The interested reader would be well served by exploring this topic in greater detail. Among the points the chapter has made are the following:

• Financial reporting quality relates to the accuracy with which a company's reported financial statements reflect its operating performance and to their usefulness for forecasting future cash flows. Understanding the properties of accruals is critical for understanding and evaluating financial reporting quality.

- The application of accrual accounting makes necessary use of judgment and discretion. On average, accrual accounting provides a superior picture to a cash basis accounting for forecasting future cash flows.

- Earnings can be decomposed into cash and accrual components. The accrual component has been found to have less persistence than the cash component, and therefore (1) earnings with higher accrual components are less persistent than earnings with smaller accrual components, all else equal; and (2) the cash component of earnings should receive a higher weighting in evaluating company performance.

- Aggregate accruals = Accrual earnings – Cash earnings.

- Defining net operating assets as $NOA_t = [(\text{Total assets}_t - \text{Cash}_t) - (\text{Total liabilities}_t - \text{Total debt}_t)]$ one can derive the following balance-sheet-based and cash-flow-statement-based measures of aggregate accruals/the accruals component of earnings:

  ○ Aggregate accruals$_t^{B/S}$ = $NOA_t - NOA_{t-1}$

  ○ Aggregate accruals$_t^{CF}$ = $NI_t - (CFO_t + CFI_t)$

With corresponding scaled measures that can be used as simple measures of financial reporting quality:

  ○ Accruals Ratio$_t^{B/S}$ = $\dfrac{(NOA_t - NOA_{t-1})}{(NOA_t + NOA_{t-1})/2}$

  ○ Accruals ratio$_t^{CF}$ = $\dfrac{[NI_t - (CFO_t + CFI_t)]}{(NOA_t + NOA_{t-1})/2}$

- Aggregate accruals ratios are useful to rank companies for the purpose of evaluating earnings quality. Companies with high (low) accruals ratios are companies with low (high) earnings quality. Companies with low (high) earnings quality tend to experience lower (higher) accounting rates of return and relatively lower excess stock returns in future periods.

- Sources of accounting discretion include choices related to revenue recognition, depreciation choices, inventory choices, choices related to goodwill and other noncurrent assets, choices related to taxes, pension choices, financial asset/liability valuation, and stock option expense estimates.

- A framework for detecting financial reporting problems includes examining reported financials for revenue recognition issues and expense recognition issues.

- Revenue recognition issues include overstatement of revenue, acceleration of revenue, and classification of nonrecurring or nonoperating items as operating revenue.

- Expense recognition issues include understating expenses, deferring expenses, and the classification of ordinary expenses as nonrecurring or nonoperating expenses.

- Discretion related to off-balance sheet liabilities (e.g., in the accounting for leases) and the impairment of goodwill also can affect financial reporting quality.

PRACTICE PROBLEMS

1. Which of the following mechanisms is *least likely* to discourage management manipulation of earnings?
   A. Debt covenants.
   B. Securities regulators.
   C. Class action lawsuits.

2. High earnings quality is *most likely* to
   A. Result in steady earnings growth.
   B. Improve the ability to predict future earnings.
   C. Be based on conservative accounting choices.

3. The *best* justification for using accrual-based accounting is that it
   A. Reflects the company's underlying cash flows.
   B. Reflects the economic nature of a company's transactions.
   C. Limits management's discretion in reporting financial results.

4. The *best* justification for using cash-based accounting is that it
   A. Is more conservative.
   B. Limits management's discretion in reporting financial results.
   C. Matches the timing of revenue recognition with that of associated expenses.

5. Which of the following is *not* a measure of aggregate accruals?
   A. The change in net operating assets.
   B. The difference between operating income and net operating assets.
   C. The difference between net income and operating and investing cash flows.

6. Consider the following balance sheet information for Profile, Inc.:

Year ended 31 December	2007	2006
Cash and short-term investments	14,000	13,200
Total current assets	21,000	20,500
Total assets	97,250	88,000
Current liabilities	31,000	29,000
Total debt	50,000	45,000
Total liabilities	87,000	79,000

Profile's balance-sheet-based accruals ratio in 2007 was *closest* to
   A. 12.5%.
   B. 13.0%.
   C. 16.2%.

7. Rodrigue SA reported the following financial statement data for the year ended 2007:

Average net operating assets	39,000
Net income	14,000
Cash flow from operating activity	17,300
Cash flow from investing activity	(12,400)

Rodrigue's cash-flow-based accruals ratio in 2007 was *closest* to
   A. −8.5%.
   B. −19.1%.
   C. 23.3%.

8. Cash collected from customers is *least likely* to differ from sales due to changes in
   A. Inventory.
   B. Deferred revenue.
   C. Accounts receivable.

9. Reported revenue is *most likely* to have been reduced by management's discretionary estimate of
   A. Warranty provisions.
   B. Inventory damage and theft.
   C. Interest to be earned on credit sales.

10. Zimt AG reports 2007 revenue of €14.3 billion. During 2007, its accounts receivable rose by €0.7 billion, accounts payable increased by €1.1 billion, and unearned revenue increased by €0.5 billion. Its cash collections from customers in 2007 were *closest* to
    A. €14.1 billion.
    B. €14.5 billion.
    C. €15.2 billion.

11. Cinnamon Corp. began the year with $12 million in accounts receivable and $31 million in deferred revenue. It ended the year with $15 million in accounts receivable and $27 million in deferred revenue. Based on this information, the accrual-basis earnings included in total revenue were *closest* to
    A. $1 million.
    B. $7 million.
    C. $12 million.

12. Which of the following is *least likely* to be a warning sign of low-quality revenue?
    A. A large decrease in deferred revenue.
    B. A large increase in accounts receivable.
    C. A large increase in the allowance for doubtful accounts.

13. An unexpectedly large reduction in the unearned revenue account is *most likely* a sign that the company
    A. Accelerated revenue recognition.
    B. Overstated revenue in prior periods.
    C. Adopted more conservative revenue recognition practices.

14. Canelle SA reported 2007 revenue of €137 million. Its accounts receivable balance began the year at €11 million and ended the year at €16 million. At year-end, €2 million of receivables had been securitized. Canelle's cash collections from customers (in € millions) in 2007 were *closest* to
    A. €130.
    B. €132.
    C. €134.

15. In order to identify possible understatement of expenses with regard to noncurrent assets, an analyst would *most likely* beware management's discretion to
    A. Accelerate depreciation.
    B. Increase the residual value.
    C. Reduce the expected useful life.

16. A sudden rise in inventory balances is *least likely* to be a warning sign of
    A. Understated expenses.
    B. Accelerated revenue recognition.
    C. Inefficient working capital management.

17. A warning sign that a company may be deferring expenses is sales revenue growing at a slower rate than
    A. Unearned revenue.
    B. Noncurrent liabilities.
    C. Property, plant, and equipment.

18. An asset write-down is *least likely* to indicate understatement of expenses in
    A. Prior years.
    B. Future years.
    C. The current year.

19. Ranieri Corp. reported the following 2007 income statement:

Sales	93,000
Cost of sales	24,500
SG & A	32,400
Interest expense	800
Other income	1,400
Income taxes	14,680
Net income	22,020

Ranieri's core operating margin in 2007 was *closest* to
A. 23.7%.
B. 38.8%.
C. 73.7%.

20. Sebastiani AG reported the following financial results for the years ended 31 December:

	2007	2006
Sales	46,574	42,340
Cost of sales	14,000	13,000
SGA	13,720	12,200
Operating income	18,854	17,140
Income taxes	6,410	5,656
Net income	12,444	11,484

Compared to core operating margin in 2006, Sebastiani's core operating margin in 2007 was
A. Lower.
B. Higher.
C. Unchanged.

21. A warning sign that ordinary expenses are being classified as nonrecurring or nonoperating expenses is
    A. Falling core operating margin followed by a spike in positive special items.
    B. A spike in negative special items followed by falling core operating margin.
    C. Falling core operating margin followed by a spike in negative special items.

22. Which of the following obligations must be reported on a company's balance sheet?
    A. Capital leases.
    B. Operating leases.
    C. Purchase commitments.

23. The *most accurate* estimate for off-balance-sheet financing related to operating leases consists of the sum of
    A. future payments.
    B. future payments less a discount to reflect the related interest component.
    C. future payments plus a premium to reflect the related interest component.

24. The intangible asset goodwill represents the value of an acquired company that cannot be attached to other tangible assets. This noncurrent asset account is charged to an expense
    A. As amortization.
    B. When it becomes impaired.
    C. At the time of the acquisition.

25. Total accruals measured using the balance sheet is *most likely* to differ from total accruals measured using the statement of cash flows when the company has made acquisitions
    A. Financed by debt.
    B. In exchange for cash.
    C. In exchange for stock.

GLOSSARY

Accelerated methods of depreciation   Depreciation methods that allocate a relatively large proportion of the cost of an asset to the early years of the asset's useful life.

Account   With the accounting systems, a formal record of increases and decreases in a specific asset, liability, component of owners' equity, revenue, or expense.

Account format   A method of presentation of accounting transactions in which effects on assets appear at the left and effects on liabilities and equity appear at the right of a central dividing line; also known as T-account format.

Accounting profit (income before taxes or pretax income)   Income as reported on the income statement, in accordance with prevailing accounting standards, before the provisions for income tax expense.

Accounts payable   Amounts that a business owes to its vendors for goods and services that were purchased from them but which have not yet been paid.

Accrual basis   Method of accounting in which the effect of transactions on financial condition and income are recorded when they occur, not when they are settled in cash.

Accrued expenses (accrued liabilities)   Liabilities related to expenses that have been incurred but not yet paid as of the end of an accounting period—an example of an accrued expense is rent that has been incurred but not yet paid, resulting in a liability "rent payable."

Accumulated benefit obligation   Under U.S. GAAP, a measure used in estimating a defined-benefit pension plan's liabilities, defined as "the actuarial present value of benefits (whether vested or nonvested) attributed by the pension benefit formula to employee service rendered before a specified date and based on employee service and compensation (if applicable) prior to that date."

Accumulated depreciation   An offset to property, plant, and equipment (PP&E) reflecting the amount of the cost of PP&E that has been allocated to current and previous accounting periods.

Acquisition method   A method of accounting for a business combination where the acquirer is required to measure each identifiable asset and liability at fair value. This method was the result of a joint project of the IASB and FASB aiming at convergence in standards for the accounting of business combinations.

Activity ratios (asset utilization or operating efficiency ratios)   Ratios that measure how efficiently a company performs day-to-day tasks, such as the collection of receivables and management of inventory.

Allowance for bad debts   An offset to accounts receivable for the amount of accounts receivable that are estimated to be uncollectible.

Amortization   The process of allocating the cost of intangible long-term assets having a finite useful life to accounting periods; the allocation of the amount of a bond premium or discount to the periods remaining until bond maturity.

Antidilutive   With reference to a transaction or a security, one that would increase earnings per share (EPS) or result in EPS higher than the company's basic EPS—antidilutive securities are not included in the calculation of diluted EPS.

Asset retirement obligations (AROs)   The fair value of the estimated costs to be incurred at the end of a tangible asset's service life. The fair value of the liability is determined on the basis of discounted cash flows.

Assets   Resources controlled by an enterprise as a result of past events and from which future economic benefits to the enterprise are expected to flow.

Available-for-sale investments   Debt and equity securities not classified as either held-to-maturity or held-for-trading securities. The investor is willing to sell but not actively planning to sell. In general, available-for-sale securities are reported at fair value on the balance sheet.

Available-for-sale securities   Securities that a company does not intend to actively trade or (in the case of debt securities) hold to maturity.

Backtesting   With reference to portfolio strategies, the application of a strategy's portfolio selection rules to historical data to assess what would have been the strategy's historical performance.

Balance sheet (statement of financial position or **statement of financial condition)**   The financial statement that presents an entity's current financial position by disclosing resources the entity controls (its assets) and the claims on those resources (its liabilities and equity claims), as of a particular point in time (the date of the balance sheet).

Balance sheet ratios   Financial ratios involving balance sheet items only.

Balance-sheet-based accruals ratio   The difference between net operating assets at the end and the beginning of the period compared to the average net operating assets over the period.

Balance-sheet-based aggregate accruals   The difference between net operating assets at the end and the beginning of the period.

Bargain purchase   When a company is acquired and the purchase price is less than the fair value of the net assets. The current treatment of the excess of fair value over the purchase price is different under IFRS and U.S. GAAP. The excess is never accounted for as negative goodwill.

Basic EPS   Net earnings available to common shareholders (i.e., net income minus preferred dividends) divided by the weighted average number of common shares outstanding.

Bottom-up analysis   With reference to investment selection processes, an approach that involves selection from all securities within a specified investment universe; that is, without prior narrowing of the universe on the basis of macroeconomic or overall market considerations.

Capitalized inventory costs   Costs of inventories including costs of purchase, costs of conversion, other costs to bring the inventories to their present location and condition, and the allocated portion of fixed production overhead costs.

Carrying amount (book value)   The amount at which an asset or liability is valued according to accounting principles.

Cash   In accounting contexts, cash on hand (e.g., petty cash and cash not yet deposited to the bank) and demand deposits held in banks and similar accounts that can be used in payment of obligations.

Cash basis   Accounting method in which the only relevant transactions for the financial statements are those that involve cash.

Cash conversion cycle (net operating cycle)   A financial metric that measures the length of time required for a company to convert cash invested in its operations to cash received as a result of its operations; equal to days of inventory on hand plus days of sales outstanding minus number of days of payables.

Cash equivalents   Very liquid short-term investments, usually maturing in 90 days or less.

Cash flow from operations (cash flow from operating activities or **operating cash flow)**   The net amount of cash provided from operating activities.

Cash flow statement (statement of cash flows)   A financial statement that reconciles beginning-of-period and end-of-period balance sheet values of cash; consists of three parts: cash flows from operating activities, cash flows from investing activities, and cash flows from financing activities.

Cash ratio   A liquidity ratio calculated as (cash plus short-term marketable investments) divided by current liabilities.

Cash-flow-statement-based accruals ratio   The difference between reported net income on an accrual basis and the cash flows from operating and investing activities compared to the average net operating assets over the period.

Cash-flow-statement-based aggregate accruals   The difference between reported net income on an accrual basis and the cash flows from operating and investing activities.

Chart of accounts   A list of accounts used in an entity's accounting system.

Classified balance sheet   A balance sheet organized so as to group together the various assets and liabilities into subcategories (e.g., current and noncurrent).

Clean-surplus accounting   The bottom-line income reflects all changes in shareholders' equity arising from other than owner transactions. In the absence of owner transactions, the change in shareholders' equity should equal net income. No adjustments such as translation adjustments bypass the income statement and go directly to shareholders equity.

Common-size analysis   A tool used in financial statement analysis that involves expressing financial data in relation to a single financial statement item or base; an example is an income statement in which all items are expressed as a percent of revenue.

Completed contract   A method of revenue recognition in which the company does not recognize any revenue until the contract is completed; used particularly in long-term construction contracts.

Comprehensive income   The change in equity of a business enterprise during a period from non-owner sources; includes all changes in equity during a period except those resulting from investments by owners and distributions to owners; comprehensive income equals net income plus other comprehensive income.

Consolidation   The combining of the results of operations of subsidiaries with the parent company to present financial statements as if they were a single economic unit. The asset, liabilities, revenues and expenses of the subsidiaries are combined with those of the parent company, eliminating intercompany transactions.

Contra account   An account that offsets another account.

Controlling interest   An investment where the investor exerts control over the investee, typically by having a greater than 50 percent ownership in the investee.

Convertible debt   Debt with the added feature that the bondholder has the option to exchange the debt for equity at prespecified terms.

Cost of goods sold   For a given period, equal to beginning inventory minus ending inventory plus the cost of goods acquired or produced during the period.

Cost recovery method   A method of revenue recognition in which is the seller does not report any profit until the cash amounts paid by the buyer—including principal and interest on any financing from the seller—are greater than all the seller's costs for the merchandise sold.

Credit   With respect to double-entry accounting, a credit records increases in liability, owners' equity, and revenue accounts or decreases in asset accounts; with respect to borrowing, the willingness and ability of the borrower to make promised payments on the borrowing.

Credit analysis   The evaluation of credit risk; the evaluation of the creditworthiness of an borrower or counterparty.

Credit risk   The risk of loss caused by a counterparty's or debtor's failure to make a promised payment.

Cross-sectional analysis   Analysis that involves comparisons across individuals in a group over a given time period or at a given point in time.

Current assets   Assets that are expected to be consumed or converted into cash in the near future, typically one year or less.

Current cost   With reference to assets, the amount of cash or cash equivalents that would have to be paid to buy the same or an equivalent asset today; with reference to liabilities, the undiscounted amount of cash or cash equivalents that would be required to settle the obligation today.

Current exchange rate   For accounting purposes, the spot exchange rate on the balance sheet date.

Current liabilities   Those liabilities that are expected to be settled in the near future, typically one year or less.

Current rate method   Approach to translating foreign currency financial statements for consolidation in which all assets and liabilities are translated at the current exchange rate. The current rate method is the prevalent method of translation.

Current ratio   A liquidity ratio calculated as current assets divided by current liabilities.

Current taxes payable   Tax expenses that have been recognized and recorded on a company's income statement but which have not yet been paid.

Days of inventory on hand (DOH) An activity ratio equal to the number of days in the period divided by inventory turnover over the period.

Days of sales outstanding (DSO) An activity ratio equal to the number of days in period divided by receivables turnover.

Dealing securities Securities held by banks or other financial intermediaries for trading purposes.

Debit With respect to double-entry accounting, a debit records increases of asset and expense accounts or decreases in liability and owners' equity accounts.

Debt covenants Agreements between the company as borrower and its creditors.

Debt with warrants Debt issued with warrants that give the bondholder the right to purchase equity at prespecified terms.

Debt-to-assets ratio A solvency ratio calculated as total debt divided by total assets.

Debt-to-capital ratio A solvency ratio calculated as total debt divided by total debt plus total shareholders' equity.

Debt-to-equity ratio A solvency ratio calculated as total debt divided by total shareholders' equity.

Deductible temporary differences Temporary differences that result in a reduction of or deduction from taxable income in a future period when the balance sheet item is recovered or settled.

Defensive interval ratio A liquidity ratio that estimates the number of days that an entity could meet cash needs from liquid assets; calculated as (cash plus short-term marketable investments plus receivables) divided by daily cash expenditures.

Deferred tax assets A balance sheet asset that arises when an excess amount is paid for income taxes relative to accounting profit. The taxable income is higher than accounting profit and income tax payable exceeds tax expense. The company expects to recover the difference during the course of future operations when tax expense exceeds income tax payable.

Deferred tax liabilities A balance sheet liability that arises when a deficit amount is paid for income taxes relative to accounting profit. The taxable income is less than the accounting profit and income tax payable is less than tax expense. The company expects to eliminate the liability over the course of future operations when income tax payable exceeds tax expense.

Defined-benefit pension plans Plan in which the company promises to pay a certain annual amount (defined benefit) to the employee after retirement. The company bears the investment risk of the plan assets.

Defined-contribution pension plans Individual accounts to which an employee and typically the employer makes contributions, generally on a tax-advantaged basis. The amounts of contributions are defined at the outset, but the future value of the benefit is unknown. The employee bears the investment risk of the plan assets.

Depreciation The process of systematically allocating the cost of long-lived (tangible) assets to the periods during which the assets are expected to provide economic benefits.

Derivative A financial instrument whose value depends on the value of some underlying asset or factor (e.g., a stock price, an interest rate, or exchange rate).

Designated fair value instruments Financial instruments that an entity chooses to measure at fair value per IAS 39 or SFAS 159. Generally, the election to use the fair value option is irrevocable.

Diluted EPS The EPS that would result if all dilutive securities were converted into common shares.

Diluted shares The number of shares that would be outstanding if all potentially dilutive claims on common shares (e.g., convertible debt, convertible preferred stock, and employee stock options) were exercised.

Diminishing balance method An accelerated depreciation method; that is, one that allocates a relatively large proportion of the cost of an asset to the early years of the asset's useful life.

Direct financing lease A type of finance lease, from a lessor perspective, where the present value of the lease payments (lease receivable) equals the carrying value of the leased asset. The revenues earned by the lessor are financing in nature.

Direct format (direct method) With reference to the cash flow statement, a format for the presentation of the statement in which cash flow from operating activities is shown as operating cash receipts less operating cash disbursements.

Direct write-off method   An approach to recognizing credit losses on customer receivables in which the company waits until such time as a customer has defaulted and only then recognizes the loss.

Dirty-surplus accounting   Accounting in which some income items are reported as part of stockholders' equity rather than as gains and losses on the income statement; certain items of comprehensive income bypass the income statement and appear as direct adjustments to shareholders' equity.

Dirty-surplus items   Direct adjustments to shareholders' equity that bypass the income statement.

Double-declining balance depreciation   An accelerated depreciation method that involves depreciating the asset at double the straight-line rate. This rate is multiplied by the book value of the asset at the beginning of the period (a declining balance) to calculate depreciation expense.

Double-entry accounting   The accounting system of recording transactions in which every recorded transaction affects at least two accounts so as to keep the basic accounting equation (assets equal liabilities plus owners' equity) in balance.

Downstream   A transaction between two affiliates, an investor company and an associate company, such that the investor company records a profit on its income statement. An example is a sale of inventory by the investor company to the associate.

DuPont analysis   An approach to decomposing return on investment (e.g., return on equity) as the product of other financial ratios.

Earnings expectation management   Attempts by management to encourage analysts to forecast a slightly lower number for expected earnings than the analysts would otherwise forecast.

Earnings game   Management's focus on reporting earnings that meet consensus estimates.

Earnings management activity   Deliberate activity aimed at influencing reporting earnings numbers, often with the goal of placing management in a favorable light; the opportunistic use of accruals to manage earnings.

Earnings per share   Earnings per common share of the corporation; (net income minus preferred dividends) divided by the weighted average number of common shares outstanding.

Equity   Assets minus liabilities; the residual interest in the assets after subtracting the liabilities.

Equity method   A basis for reporting investment income in which the investing entity recognizes a share of income as earned rather than as dividends when received. These transactions are typically reflected in investments in associates or equity method investments.

Exercise date   The day that employees actually exercise the options and convert them to stock.

Expensed   Taken as a deduction in arriving at net income.

Expenses   Outflows of economic resources or increases in liabilities that result in decreases in equity (other than decreases because of distributions to owners); reductions in net assets associated with the creation of revenues.

Exposure to foreign exchange risk   The risk of a change in value of an asset or liability denominated in a foreign currency due to a change in exchange rates.

Face value (also principal, par value, stated value, or maturity value)   The amount of cash payable by a company to the bondholders when the bonds mature.

Fair market value   The market price of an asset or liability that trades regularly.

Fair value   The amount at which an asset could be exchanged, or a liability settled, between knowledgeable, willing parties in an arm's-length transaction; the price that would be received to sell an asset or paid to transfer a liability in an orderly transaction between market participants.

FIFO method   The first in, first out, method of accounting for inventory, which matches sales against the costs of items of inventory in the order in which they were placed in inventory.

Finance lease (capital lease)   Essentially, the purchase of some asset by the buyer (lessee) that is directly financed by the seller (lessor).

Financial flexibility   The ability to react and adapt to financial adversities and opportunities.

Financial leverage   The extent to which a company can effect, through the use of debt, a proportional change in the return on common equity that is greater than a given proportional change in operating income; also, short for the financial leverage ratio.

Financial leverage ratio   A measure of financial leverage calculated as average total assets divided by average total equity.

Financial reporting quality   The accuracy with which a company's reported financials reflect its operating performance and their usefulness for forecasting future cash flows.

Financing activities   Activities related to obtaining or repaying capital to be used in the business (e.g., equity and long-term debt).

Fixed asset turnover   An activity ratio calculated as total revenue divided by average net fixed assets.

Fixed charge coverage   A solvency ratio measuring the number of times interest and lease payments are covered by operating income, calculated as (EBIT plus lease payments) divided by (interest payments plus lease payments).

Fixed costs   Costs that stay the same within some range of activity.

Foreign currency transactions   Transactions that are denominated in a currency other than a company's functional currency.

Free cash flow   The excess of operating cash flow over capital expenditures.

Functional currency   The currency of the primary economic environment in which an entity operates.

Gains   Asset inflows not directly related to the ordinary activities of the business.

Goodwill   An intangible asset that represents the excess of the purchase price of an acquired company over the value of the net assets acquired.

Grant date   The day that options are granted to employees; usually the date that compensation expense is measured if both the number of shares and option price are known.

Gross profit (gross margin)   Sales minus the cost of sales (i.e., the cost of goods sold for a manufacturing company).

Gross profit margin   A profitability ratio calculated as gross profit divided by revenue.

Grouping by function   With reference to the presentation of expenses in an income statement, the grouping together of expenses serving the same function (e.g., all items that are costs of good sold).

Grouping by nature   With reference to the presentation of expenses in an income statement, the grouping together of expenses by similar nature (e.g., all depreciation expenses).

Growth investors   With reference to equity investors, investors who seek to invest in high-earnings-growth companies.

Held-for-trading securities (trading securities)   Debt or equity financial assets bought with the intention to sell them in the near term, usually less than three months; securities that a company intends to trade.

Held-to-maturity investments   Debt (fixed-income) securities that a company intends to hold to maturity; these are presented at their original cost, updated for any amortization of discounts or premiums.

Historical cost   In reference to assets, the amount paid to purchase an asset, including any costs of acquisition and/or preparation; with reference to liabilities, the amount of proceeds received in exchange in issuing the liability.

Historical exchange rates   For accounting purposes, the exchange rates that existed when the assets and liabilities were initially recorded.

Horizontal analysis   Common-size analysis that involves comparing a specific financial statement with that statement in prior or future time periods; also, cross-sectional analysis of one company with another.

Identifiable intangible   An intangible that can be acquired singly and is typically linked to specific rights or privileges having finite benefit periods (e.g., a patent or trademark).

If-converted method   A method for accounting for the effect of convertible securities on earnings per share (EPS) that specifies what EPS would have been if the convertible securities had been converted at the beginning of the period, taking account of the effects of conversion on net income and the weighted average number of shares outstanding.

Impairment   Diminishment in value as a result of carrying (book) value exceeding fair value and/or recoverable value.

Income   Increases in economic benefits in the form of inflows or enhancements of assets, or decreases of liabilities that result in an increase in equity (other than increases resulting from contributions by owners).

Income statement (statement of operations or **profit and loss statement)** A financial statement that provides information about a company's profitability over a stated period of time.

Income tax paid The actual amount paid for income taxes in the period; not a provision, but the actual cash outflow.

Income tax payable The income tax owed by the company on the basis of taxable income.

Income tax recoverable The income tax expected to be recovered, from the taxing authority, on the basis of taxable income. It is a recovery of previously remitted taxes or future taxes owed by the company.

Indirect format (indirect method) With reference to cash flow statements, a format for the presentation of the statement which, in the operating cash flow section, begins with net income, then shows additions and subtractions to arrive at operating cash flow.

Installment Said of a sale in which proceeds are to be paid in installments over an extended period of time.

Installment method (installment-sales method) With respect to revenue recognition, a method that specifies that the portion of the total profit of the sale that is recognized in each period is determined by the percentage of the total sales price for which the seller has received cash.

Intangible assets Assets lacking physical substance, such as patents and trademarks.

Interest coverage A solvency ratio calculated as EBIT divided by interest payments.

Intrinsic value The greater of zero and the difference between the market price of the stock and the exercise price of the stock option.

Inventory The unsold units of product on hand.

Inventory turnover An activity ratio calculated as cost of goods sold divided by average inventory.

Investing activities Activities which are associated with the acquisition and disposal of property, plant, and equipment; intangible assets; other long-term assets; and both long-term and short-term investments in the equity and debt (bonds and loans) issued by other companies.

Joint venture An entity (partnership, corporation, or other legal form) where control is shared by two or more entities called venturers.

Lessee The party obtaining the use of an asset through a lease.

Lessor The owner of an asset that grants the right to use the asset to another party.

Liabilities Present obligations of an enterprise arising from past events, the settlement of which is expected to result in an outflow of resources embodying economic benefits; creditors' claims on the resources of a company.

LIFO layer liquidation (LIFO liquidation) With respect to the application of the LIFO inventory method, the liquidation of old, relatively low-priced inventory; happens when the volume of sales rises above the volume of recent purchases so that some sales are made from relatively old, low-priced inventory.

LIFO method The last in, first out, method of accounting for inventory, which matches sales against the costs of items of inventory in the reverse order the items were placed in inventory (i.e., inventory produced or acquired last are assumed to be sold first).

LIFO reserve The difference between inventory reported at FIFO and inventory reported as LIFO (FIFO inventory value minus LIFO inventory value).

Liquidity With reference to a firm's financial condition, the ability to meet short-term obligations.

Liquidity ratios Financial ratios measuring the company's ability to meet its short-term obligations.

Local currency The currency of the country where a company is located.

Long-lived assets (long-term assets) Assets that are expected to provide economic benefits over a future period of time, typically greater than one year.

Long-term contract A contract that spans a number of accounting periods.

Long-term liability An obligation that is expected to be settled, with the outflow of resources embodying economic benefits, over a future period generally greater than one year.

Losses Asset outflows not directly related to the ordinary activities of the business.

Market rate The rate demanded by purchasers of bonds, given the risks associated with future cash payment obligations of the particular bond issue.

Market-oriented investors   With reference to equity investors, investors whose investment disciplines cannot be clearly categorized as value or growth.

Mark-to-market   The revaluation of a financial asset or liability to its current market value or fair value.

Matching principle   The accounting principle that expenses should be recognized when the associated revenue is recognized.

Materiality   The condition of being of sufficient importance so that omission or misstatement of the item in a financial report could make a difference to users' decisions.

Minority active investments   Investments in which investors exert significant influence, but not control, over the investee. Typically, the investor has 20 percent to 50 percent ownership in the investee.

Minority interest   The portion of consolidated subsidiaries' net assets not owned by the parent.

Minority interests (noncontrolling interests)   The proportion of the ownership of a subsidiary not held by the parent (controlling) company.

Minority passive investments (passive investments)   Investments in which the investor has no significant influence or control over the operations of the investee.

Monetary assets and liabilities   Assets and liabilities with value equal to the amount of currency contracted for, a fixed amount of currency. Examples are cash, accounts receivable, mortgages receivable, accounts payable, bonds payable, and mortgages payable. Inventory is not a monetary asset. Most liabilities are monetary.

Monetary/nonmonetary method   Approach to translating foreign currency financial statements for consolidation in which monetary assets and liabilities are translated at the current exchange rate. Nonmonetary assets and liabilities are translated at historical exchange rates (the exchange rates that existed when the assets and liabilities were acquired).

Multi-step format   With respect to the format of the income statement, a format that presents a subtotal for gross profit (revenue minus cost of goods sold).

Net asset balance sheet exposure   When assets translated at the current exchange rate are greater in amount than liabilities translated at the current exchange rate. Assets exposed to translation gains or losses exceed the exposed liabilities.

Net book value   The remaining (undepreciated) balance of an asset's purchase cost. For liabilities, the face value of a bond minus any unamortized discount, or plus any unamortized premium.

Net income (loss)   The difference between revenue and expenses; what remains after subtracting all expenses (including depreciation, interest, and taxes) from revenue.

Net liability balance sheet exposure   When liabilities translated at the current exchange rate are greater than assets translated at the current exchange rate. Liabilities exposed to translation gains or losses exceed the exposed assets.

Net operating assets   The difference between operating assets (total assets less cash) and operating liabilities (total liabilities less total debt).

Net profit margin (profit margin or return on sales)   An indicator of profitability, calculated as net income divided by revenue.

Net realizable value   Estimated selling price in the ordinary course of business less the estimated costs necessary to make the sale.

Net revenue   Revenue after adjustments (e.g., for estimated returns or for amounts unlikely to be collected).

Noncurrent   Not due to be consumed, converted into cash, or settled within one year after the balance sheet date.

Noncurrent assets   Assets that are expected to benefit the company over an extended period of time (usually more than one year).

Nonmonetary assets and liabilities   Assets and liabilities that are not monetary assets and liabilities. Nonmonetary assets include inventory, fixed assets, and intangibles, and nonmonetary liabilities include deferred revenue.

Notes payable   Amounts owed by a business to creditors as a result of borrowings that are evidenced by (short-term) loan agreements.

Number of days of inventory   An activity ratio equal to the number of days in a period divided by the inventory ratio for the period; an indication of the number of days a company ties up funds in inventory.

Number of days of payables   An activity ratio equal to the number of days in a period divided by the payables turnover ratio for the period; an estimate of the average number of days it takes a company to pay its suppliers.

Off-balance-sheet financing   Arrangements that do not result in additional liabilities on the balance sheet but nonetheless create economic obligations.

Operating activities   Activities that are part of the day-to-day business functioning of an entity, such as selling inventory and providing services.

Operating lease   An agreement allowing the lessee to use some asset for a period of time; essentially a rental.

Operating leverage   The use of fixed costs in operations.

Operating profit (operating income)   A company's profits on its usual business activities before deducting taxes.

Operating profit margin (operating margin)   A profitability ratio calculated as operating income divided by revenue.

Operating return on assets (operating ROA)   A profitability ratio calculated as operating income divided by average total assets.

Ordinary shares (common stock or common shares)   Equity shares that are subordinate to all other types of equity (e.g., preferred equity).

Other comprehensive income   Items of comprehensive income that are not reported on the income statement; comprehensive income minus net income.

Other postretirement benefits   Promises by the company to pay benefits in the future, other than pension benefits, such as life insurance premiums and all or part of health care insurance for its retirees.

Other receivables   Amounts owed to the company from parties other than customers.

Owners' equity   The excess of assets over liabilities; the residual interest of shareholders in the assets of an entity after deducting the entity's liabilities.

Payables turnover   An activity ratio calculated as purchases divided by average trade payables.

Percentage-of-completion   A method of revenue recognition in which, in each accounting period, the company estimates what percentage of the contract is complete and then reports that percentage of the total contract revenue in its income statement.

Period costs   Costs (e.g., executives' salaries) that cannot be directly matched with the timing of revenues and which are thus expensed immediately.

Permanent differences   Differences between tax and financial reporting of revenue (expenses) that will not be reversed at some future date. These result in a difference between the company's effective tax rate and statutory tax rate and do not result in a deferred tax item.

Pooling-of-interests accounting method   A method of accounting in which combined companies were portrayed as if they had always operated as a single economic entity. Called pooling of interests under U.S. GAAP and uniting of interests under IFRS. (No longer allowed under U.S. GAAP or IFRS.)

Prepaid expense   A normal operating expense that has been paid in advance of when it is due.

Present value   The present discounted value of future cash flows: for assets, the present discounted value of the future net cash inflows that the asset is expected to generate in the normal course of business; for liabilities, the present discounted value of the future net cash outflows that are expected to be required to settle the liabilities in the normal course of business.

Presentation currency   The currency in which financial statement amounts are presented.

Pretax margin   A profitability ratio calculated as earnings before taxes divided by revenue.

Price to book value   A valuation ratio calculated as price per share divided by book value per share.

Price to cash flow   A valuation ratio calculated as price per share divided by cash flow per share.

Price to sales   A valuation ratio calculated as price per share divided by sales per share.

Profitability ratios   Ratios that measure a company's ability to generate profitable sales from its resources (assets).

Projected benefit obligation   Under U.S. GAAP, a measure used in estimating a defined-benefit pension plan's liabilities, defined as "the actuarial present value as of a date of all benefits attributed by the pension benefit formula to employee service rendered prior to that date. The projected benefit obligation is measured using assumptions as to future compensation if the pension benefit formula is based on those future compensation levels."

Proportionate consolidation   A method of accounting for joint ventures where the venturer's share of the assets, liabilities, income and expenses of the joint venture are combined on a line-by-line basis with similar items on the venturer's financial statements.

Provision   In accounting, a liability of uncertain timing or amount.

Purchase method   A method of accounting for a business combination where the acquiring company allocates the purchase price to each asset acquired and liability assumed at fair value. If the purchase price exceeds the allocation, the excess is recorded as goodwill.

Purchased in-process research and development costs   The costs of research and development in progress at an acquired company.

Purchasing power gain   A gain in value caused by changes in price levels. Monetary liabilities experience purchasing power gains during periods of inflation.

Purchasing power loss   A loss in value caused by changes in price levels. Monetary assets experience purchasing power losses during periods of inflation.

Qualifying special purpose entities   Under U.S. GAAP, a special purpose entity structured to avoid consolidation that must meet qualification criteria.

Quick ratio   A liquidity ratio calculated as (cash plus short-term marketable investments plus receivables) divided by current liabilities.

Realizable value (settlement value)   With reference to assets, the amount of cash or cash equivalents that could currently be obtained by selling the asset in an orderly disposal; with reference to liabilities, the undiscounted amount of cash or cash equivalents expected to be paid to satisfy the liabilities in the normal course of business.

Receivables turnover   An activity ratio equal to revenue divided by average receivables.

Report format   With respect to the format of a balance sheet, a format in which assets, liabilities, and equity are listed in a single column.

Residual claim   The owners' remaining claim on the company's assets after the liabilities are deducted.

Retail method   An inventory accounting method in which the sales value of an item is reduced by the gross margin to calculate the item's cost.

Return on assets (ROA)   A profitability ratio calculated as net income divided by average total assets.

Return on common equity (ROCE)   A profitability ratio calculated as (net income minus preferred dividends) divided by average common equity; equal to the return on equity ratio when no preferred equity is outstanding.

Return on equity (ROE)   A profitability ratio calculated as net income divided by average shareholders' equity.

Return on total capital   A profitability ratio calculated as EBIT divided by the sum of short- and long-term debt and equity.

Revaluation   The process of valuing long-lived assets at fair value, rather than at cost less accumulated depreciation. Any resulting profit or loss is either reported on the income statement and/or through equity under revaluation surplus.

Revenue   The amount charged for the delivery of goods or services in the ordinary activities of a business over a stated period; the inflows of economic resources to a company over a stated period.

Sales   Generally, a synonym for revenue; "sales" is generally understood to refer to the sale of goods, whereas "revenue" is understood to include the sale of goods or services.

Sales returns and allowances   An offset to revenue reflecting any cash refunds, credits on account, and discounts from sales prices given to customers who purchased defective or unsatisfactory items.

Sales-type lease A type of finance lease, from a lessor perspective, where the present value of the lease payments (lease receivable) exceeds the carrying value of the leased asset. The revenues earned by the lessor are operating (the profit on the sale) and financing (interest) in nature.

Salvage value The amount the company estimates that it can sell the asset for at the end of its useful life.

Sarbanes–Oxley Act An act passed by the U.S. Congress in 2002 that created the Public Company Accounting Oversight Board (PCAOB) to oversee auditors.

Scenario analysis Analysis that shows the changes in key financial quantities that result from given (economic) events, such as the loss of customers, the loss of a supply source, or a catastrophic event.

Screening The application of a set of criteria to reduce a set of potential investments to a smaller set having certain desired characteristics.

Sector neutralizing Measure of financial reporting quality by subtracting the mean or median ratio for a given sector group from a given company's ratio.

Securities Act of 1933 An act passed by the U.S. Congress in 1933 that specifies the financial and other significant information that investors must receive when securities are sold, prohibits misrepresentations, and requires initial registration of all public issuances of securities.

Securities Exchange Act of 1934 An act passed by the U.S. Congress in 1934 that created the Securities and Exchange Commission (SEC), gave the SEC authority over all aspects of the securities industry, and empowered the SEC to require periodic reporting by companies with publicly traded securities.

Segment debt ratio Segment liabilities divided by segment assets.

Segment margin Segment profit (loss) divided by segment revenue.

Segment ROA Segment profit (loss) divided by segment assets.

Segment turnover Segment revenue divided by segment assets.

Sensitivity analysis Analysis that shows the range of possible outcomes as specific assumptions are changed.

Service period The period benefited by the employee's service, usually the period between the grant date and the vesting date.

Simulation Computer-generated sensitivity or scenario analysis that is based on probability models for the factors that drive outcomes.

Single-step format With respect to the format of the income statement, a format that does not subtotal for gross profit (revenue minus cost of goods sold).

Solvency With respect to financial statement analysis, the ability of a company to fulfill its long-term obligations.

Solvency ratios Ratios that measure a company's ability to meet its long-term obligations.

Special purpose entity (special purpose vehicle or variable interest entity) A nonoperating entity created to carry out a specified purpose, such as leasing assets or securitizing receivables; can be a corporation, partnership, trust, limited liability, or partnership formed to facilitate a specific type of business activity.

Specific identification method An inventory accounting method that identifies which specific inventory items were sold and which remained in inventory to be carried over to later periods.

Standard cost With respect to inventory accounting, the planned or target unit cost of inventory items or services.

Stated rate (nominal rate or coupon rate) The rate at which periodic interest payments are calculated.

Statement of cash flows (cash flow statement) A financial statement that reconciles beginning-of-period and end-of-period balance sheet values of cash; provides information about an entity's cash inflows and cash outflows as they pertain to operating, investing, and financing activities.

Statement of changes in shareholders' equity (statement of owners' equity) A financial statement that reconciles the beginning-of-period and end-of-period balance sheet values of shareholders' equity; provides information about all factors affecting shareholders' equity.

Statement of retained earnings   A financial statement that reconciles beginning-of-period and end-of-period balance sheet values of retained income; shows the linkage between the balance sheet and income statement.

Stock grants   The granting of stock to employees as a form of compensation.

Stock options (stock option grants)   The granting of stock options to employees as a form of compensation.

Straight-line method   A depreciation method that allocates evenly the cost of a long-lived asset less its estimated residual value over the estimated useful life of the asset.

Tangible assets   Long-term assets with physical substance that are used in company operations, such as land (property), plant, and equipment.

Tax base (tax basis)   The amount at which an asset or liability is valued for tax purposes.

Tax expense   An aggregate of an entity's income tax payable (or recoverable in the case of a tax benefit) and any changes in deferred tax assets and liabilities. It is essentially the income tax payable or recoverable if these had been determined based on accounting profit rather than taxable income.

Tax loss carry-forward   A taxable loss in the current period that may be used to reduce future taxable income.

Taxable income   The portion of an entity's income that is subject to income taxes under the tax laws of its jurisdiction.

Taxable temporary differences   Temporary differences that result in a taxable amount in a future period when determining the taxable profit as the balance sheet item is recovered or settled.

Temporal method   A variation of the monetary/nonmonetary translation method that requires not only monetary assets and liabilities, but also nonmonetary assets and liabilities that are measured at their current value on the balance sheet date to be translated at the current exchange rate. Assets and liabilities are translated at rates consistent with the timing of their measurement value. This method is typically used when the functional currency is other than the local currency.

Top-down analysis   With reference to investment selection processes, an approach that starts with macro selection (i.e., identifying attractive geographic segments and/or industry segments) and then addresses selection of the most attractive investments within those segments.

Total asset turnover   An activity ratio calculated as revenue divided by average total assets.

Total invested capital   The sum of market value of common equity, book value of preferred equity, and face value of debt.

Trade receivables (commercial receivables or accounts receivable)   Amounts customers owe the company for products that have been sold as well as amounts that may be due from suppliers (such as for returns of merchandise).

Trading securities (held-for-trading securities)   Securities held by a company with the intent to trade them.

Transaction exposure   The risk of a change in value between the transaction date and the settlement date of an asset or liability denominated in a foreign currency.

Treasury stock method   A method for accounted for the effect of options (and warrants) on earnings per share (EPS) that specifies what EPS would have been if the options and warrants had been exercised and the company had used the proceeds to repurchase common stock.

Unbilled revenue (accrued revenue)   Revenue that has been earned but not yet billed to customers as of the end of an accounting period.

Unclassified balance sheet   A balance sheet that does not show subtotals for current assets and current liabilities.

Unearned fees   Fees that are recognized when a company receives cash payment for fees prior to earning them.

Unearned revenue (deferred revenue)   A liability account for money that has been collected for goods or services that have not yet been delivered; payment received in advance of providing a good or service.

Unidentifiable intangible   An intangible that cannot be acquired singly and that typically possesses an indefinite benefit period; an example is accounting goodwill.

Uniting-of-interests method   A method of accounting in which combined companies were portrayed as if they had always operated as a single economic entity. Called uniting of interests under IFRS and pooling of interests under U.S. GAAP. (No longer allowed under IFRS or U.S. GAAP.)

Units-of-production method   A depreciation method that allocates the cost of a long-lived asset based on actual usage during the period.

Upstream   A transaction between two affiliates, an investor company and an associate company such that the associate company records a profit on its income statement. An example is a sale of inventory by the associate to the investor company.

Valuation allowance   A reserve created against deferred tax assets, based on the likelihood of realizing the deferred tax assets in future accounting periods.

Valuation ratios   Ratios that measure the quantity of an asset or flow (e.g., earnings) in relation to the price associated with a specified claim (e.g., a share or ownership of the enterprise).

Value investors   With reference to equity investors, investors who are focused on paying a relatively low share price in relation to earnings or assets per share.

Variable costs   Costs that rise proportionally with revenue.

Venturers   The owners of a joint venture. Each is active in the management and shares control of the joint venture.

Vertical analysis   Common-size analysis using only one reporting period or one base financial statement; for example, an income statement in which all items are stated as percentages of sales.

Vested benefit obligation   Under U.S. GAAP, a measure used in estimating a defined-benefit pension plan's liabilities, defined as the "actuarial present value of vested benefits."

Vested benefits   Future benefits promised to the employee regardless of continuing service. Benefits typically vest after a specified period of service or a specified period of service combined with age.

Vesting date   The date that employees can first exercise stock options; vesting can be immediate or over a future period.

Weighted average cost method   An inventory accounting method that averages the total cost of available inventory items over the total units available for sale.

Working capital   The excess of current assets over current liabilities.

Working capital turnover   An activity ratio calculated as revenue divided by average working capital.

REFERENCES

"A Comprehensive Business Reporting Model: Financial Reporting for Investors." 2005. CFA Institute Centre for Financial Market Integrity, October.

Abarbanell, J. S., and B. J. Bushee. 1997. "Fundamental Analysis, Future Earnings, and Stock Prices." *Journal of Accounting Research* 35(1):1–24.

Abarbanell, J. S., and B. J. Bushee. 1998. "Abnormal Returns to a Fundamental Analysis Strategy." *Accounting Review* 73(1):19–46.

Altman, E. 1968. "Financial Ratios, Discriminant Analysis and the Prediction of Corporate Bankruptcy." *Journal of Finance* 23(4):589–609.

Altman, E. 2000. "Predicting Financial Distress of Companies: Revisiting the Z-Score and Zeta Models." Working paper at www.stern.nyu.edu/~ealtman/Zscores.pdf.

Altman, E., R. Haldeman, and P. Narayanan. 1977. "Zeta Analysis: A New Model to Identify Bankruptcy Risk of Corporations." *Journal of Banking and Finance* 1(1).

Beaver, W. 1967. "Financial Ratios as Predictors of Failures." Empirical Research in Accounting, selected studies supplement to *Journal of Accounting Research* 4 (1).

Benninga, S. Z., and O. H. Sarig. 1997. *Corporate Finance: A Valuation Approach.* New York: McGraw-Hill Publishing.

Chan, L. K. C., and J. Lakonishok. 2004. "Value and Growth Investing: Review and Update." *Financial Analysts Journal* 60(1):71–86.

Chan, L. K. C., Y. Hamao, and J. Lakonishok. 1991. "Fundamentals and Stock Returns in Japan." *Journal of Finance* 46(5):1739–1764.

Conrad, J., M. Cooper, and G. Kaul. 2003. "Value versus Glamour." *Journal of Finance* 58(5):1969–96.

Davis, J. L. 1994. "The Cross-Section of Realized Stock Returns: The Pre-COMPUSTAT Evidence." *Journal of Finance* 49(5):1579–93.

Dechow, P. M. 1994. "Accounting Earnings and Cash Flows as Measures of Firm Performance: the Role of Accounting Accruals." *Journal of Accounting and Economics* 18(1):3–42.

Dechow, P. M., S. A. Richardson, and I. Tuna. 2003. "Why are Earnings Kinky? An Examination of the Earnings Management Explanation." *Review of Accounting Studies* 8(2–3):355–84.

Ederington, L. H. 1986. "Why Split Ratings Occur." *Financial Management* 15(1):37–47.

Ederington, L. H., J. B. Yawitz, and B. E. Roberts. 1987. "The Information Content of Bond Ratings." *Journal of Financial Research* 10(3):211–26.

Fama, E. F., and K. R. French. 1992. "The Cross-Section of Expected Stock Returns." *Journal of Finance* 47(2):427–65.

General Accounting Office. 2002. "Financial Statement Restatements: Trends, Market Impacts, Regulatory Responses, and Remaining Challenges." GAO-03-138.

Haugen, R. A., and N. L. Baker. 1996. "Commonality in the Determinants of Expected Stock Returns." *Journal of Financial Economics* 41(3):401–39.

Haverty, J. L. 2006. "Are IFRS and U.S. GAAP Converging? Some Evidence from People's Republic of China Companies Listed on the New York Stock Exchange." *Journal of International Accounting, Auditing and Taxation* 15(1):48–71.

Henry, E., and Y. Yang. 2006. "Making the Right Comparisons: Novartis AG Case Study." Working paper. University of Miami.

Herrmann, D., and I. P. N. Hague. 2006. "Convergence: In Search of the Best." *Journal of Accountancy* online edition, January.

Hopwood, W. S., J. C. McKeown, and J. F. Mutchler. 1994. "A Reexamination of Auditor versus Model Accuracy within the Context of the Going Concern Opinion Decision." *Contemporary Accounting Research* 10:409–31.

Jegadeesh, N., and S. Titman. 2001. "Profitability of Momentum Strategies: An Evaluation of Alternative Explanations." *Journal of Finance* 56(2):699–720.

Karthik, R., and R. L. Watts. 2007. "Evidence on the Effects of Unverifiable Fair Value Accounting." Working paper, Harvard Business School and MIT.

Lakonishok, J., A. Shleifer, and R.W. Vishny. 1994. "Contrarian Investment, Extrapolation and Risk." *Journal of Finance* 49(5):1541–78.

Lev, B., and S. R. Thiagarajan. 1993. "Fundamental Information Analysis." *Journal of Accounting Research* 31(2):190–215.

Lynch, L. J., and S. E. Perry. 2003. "An Overview of Management Compensation." *Journal of Accounting Education* 21(1):43–60.

McVay, S. E. 2006. "Earnings Management using Classification Shifting." *Accounting Review* 81:501–31.

Modigliani, F., and Miller, M. 1958. "The Cost of Capital, Corporation Finance and the Theory of Investment." *American Economic Review* 48:261–98.

Modigliani, F., and Miller, M. 1963. "Corporate Income Taxes and the Cost of Capital: A Correction." *American Economic Review* 53:433–44.

Moody's Investors Service. 2006. "Rating Methodology: Global Paper & Forest Products Industry." June.

"Moving the Market—Tracking the Numbers/Outside Audit: Sarbanes-Oxley Changes Take Root; Jump in Profit Restatements Shows Impact of Controls." *Wall Street Journal,* March 3, 2006: C3.

Nissim, D., and S. H. Penman. 2001. "Ratio Analysis and Equity Valuation: From Research to Practice." *Review of Accounting Studies* 6(1):109–54.

Ohlson, J. A. 1980. "Financial Ratios and the Probabilistic Prediction of Bankruptcy." *Journal of Accounting Research* 18(1):109–31.

Oppenheimer, H. R., and G. Schlarbaum. 1981. "Investing with Ben Graham: An Ex Ante Test of the Efficient Markets Hypothesis." *Journal of Financial and Quantitative Analysis* 16(3):341–60.

Ou, J. A., and S. H. Penman, 1989a. "Financial Statement Analysis and the Prediction of Stock Returns." *Journal of Accounting and Economics* 11(4):295–329.

Ou, J. A., and S. H. Penman. 1989b. "Accounting Measurement, Price-Earnings Ratio, and the Information Content of Security Prices." *Journal of Accounting Research* 27 (Supplement):111–44.

Piotroski, J. D. 2000. "Value Investing: The Use of Historical Financial Statement Information to Separate Winners from Losers." *Journal of Accounting Research* 38 (Supplement):1–41.

Pownall, G. and K. Schipper. 1999. "Implications of Accounting Research for the SEC's Consideration of International Accounting Standards for U.S. Securities Offerings." *Accounting Horizons* 13(3):259–80.

Richardson, S. A., İ. Tuna, and M. Wu. 2002. "Predicting Earnings Management: The Case of Earnings Restatements." Working paper, University of Pennsylvania.

Richardson, S. A., R. G. Sloan, M. T. Soliman, and İ. Tuna. 2006. "The Implications of Accounting Distortions and Growth for Accruals and Profitability." *Accounting Review,* 81(3):713–43.

Richardson, S. A., S. H. Teoh, and P. D. Wysocki. 2004. "The Walk-Down to Beatable Analyst Forecasts: The Role of Equity Issuance and Insider Trading Incentives." *Contemporary Accounting Research* 21(4):885–924.

Robinson, T., and P. Munter. 2004. "Financial Reporting Quality: Red Flags and Accounting Warning Signs." *Commercial Lending Review* 19(1):2–15.

Securities and Exchange Commission (SEC). 2005. "Report and Recommendations Pursuant to Section 401(c) of the Sarbanes-Oxley Act of 2002 On Arrangements with Off-Balance Sheet Implications, Special Purpose Entities, and Transparency of Filings by Issuers." June 15. Available at: www.sec.gov.

Sloan, R. G. 1996. "Do Stock Prices Fully Reflect Information in Accruals and Cash Flows About Future Earnings?" *Accounting Review* 71(3):289–315.

Spiceland, D., J. Sepe, and L. Tomassini. 2007. *Intermediate Accounting,* 4th ed. New York: McGraw-Hill Irwin.

Standard & Poor's Corporate Ratings Criteria. 2006. Available at www.standardandpoors.com.

Standards of Practice Handbook, 9th ed. 2006. Charlottesville, VA: CFA Institute.

Stowe, J. D., T. R. Robinson, J. E. Pinto, and D. W. McLeavey. 2002. *Analysis of Equity Investments: Valuation.* Charlottesville, VA: CFA Institute.

van Greuning, H. 2006. *International Financial Reporting Standards—A Practical Guide.* Washington, DC: World Bank.

van Greuning, H., and S. Brajovic Bratanovic. 2003. *Analyzing and Managing Banking Risk: A Framework for Assessing Corporate Governance and Financial Risk.* Washington, DC: World Bank.

ABOUT THE AUTHORS

Elbie Antonites, CFA, is a senior lecturer in Investment Management and Financial Risk Management in the Department of Financial Management at the University of Pretoria located in Pretoria, South Africa. She also acts as program coordinator of undergraduate CFA Institute Educational Partner Program, BCom (Investment Management) at the University of Pretoria. Ms. Antonites joined the University of Pretoria in 2002 after gaining experience in private practice with a portfolio management and export company, respectively. She received her BCom and BCom (Hons) degrees in Financial Management from the University of Pretoria in 1999 and 2001, respectively, and was awarded the CFA charter in 2004. In 2007, she became a board member of CFA South Africa, the local society of CFA Institute.

Michael A. Broihahn, CFA, is Associate Professor of Accounting and Director of Graduate Programs at Barry University in Miami Shores, Florida. Mr. Broihahn received his BS, MBA, and MS degrees from the University of Wisconsin, majoring in accounting and finance. He is licensed as a Certified Public Accountant in Florida and Wisconsin, and also holds the professional credentials of Certified Internal Auditor, Certified Management Accountant, Certified in Financial Management, Certified Financial Planner®, and Certified Fund Specialist.

Mr. Broihahn began his business career in 1976 with Price Waterhouse in Milwaukee, Wisconsin, where he worked on the audits of Fortune 500 manufacturing companies. He has worked with Fox & Carskadon Financial Corporation in San Mateo, California, as a portfolio controller, and with ComputerLand Corporation as Corporate Controller and Director of Financial Reporting. In 1985, he returned to Milwaukee as the CFO for ComputerBay, also a franchisor of computer retail stores. In 1988, he joined the faculty of the Andreas School of Business at Barry University, where he presently teaches courses in financial accounting, auditing, and financial statement analysis. He has been a CFA charterholder since 1990 and currently serves CFA Institute in a number of capacities.

Timothy S. Doupnik, PhD, is Professor of Accounting in the Moore School of Business at the University of South Carolina. He received his PhD from the University of Illinois and joined the University of South Carolina faculty in 1982. He teaches courses in financial accounting, international accounting, and financial statement analysis. Dr. Doupnik is coauthor of two textbooks: *Advanced Accounting* and *International Accounting*. He is a past president of the International Accounting Section of the American Accounting Association, and has served as editor of *Advances in International Accounting* and associate editor of *Journal of International Accounting Research*. His research has been published in a variety of academic journals including *Abacus*, *Accounting Organizations and Society*, *International Journal of Accounting*, *Journal of Accounting Literature*, and *Journal of International Business Studies*.

Elizabeth A. Gordon is an Associate Professor of Accounting with tenure at Temple University and is a Merves Scholar. She specializes in the areas of international accounting and corporate governance, investigating topics such as accounting restatements, corporate communications, executive compensation, related-party transactions, market development and corporate disclosure, and International Financial Reporting Standards. Her research is published in top journals in her field including the *Journal of Accounting Research, Journal of Accounting, Auditing and Finance,* and *Accounting Review.* She serves on the editorial review boards of the *Journal of International Accounting Research* and *International Journal of Accounting.* Dr. Gordon has taught courses in financial accounting and international accounting at the graduate and undergraduate levels, receiving a number of teaching awards. Dr. Gordon was an auditor with Price Waterhouse and interned at the Office of Management and Budget before entering academe. Prior to joining Temple, she was on the faculty of the Graduate School of Business at the University of Chicago, and the Rutgers Business School. Dr. Gordon received her PhD from Columbia University, MBA from Yale University, and BS in accounting with highest distinction from Indiana University.

Elaine Henry, PhD, CFA, is an Assistant Professor of Accounting at the University of Miami, where she teaches courses in accounting, financial statement analysis, and valuation. Dr. Henry received her BA and BBA from Millsaps College and her MBA with high distinction from the Harvard Business School. After working in corporate finance at Lehman Brothers, strategy consulting at McKinsey & Company, and corporate banking at Citibank (Athens, London, and New York), she obtained a PhD from Rutgers University, where she majored in accounting and minored in finance. She has published articles in a number of journals, including *Advances in Financial Economics, Journal of Emerging Technologies in Accounting, Accounting Horizons*, and *Issues in Accounting Education.*

Dr. Henry served as project team leader for the Public Company Accounting Oversight Board (PCAOB) research synthesis project on related-party transactions in 2006 and 2007. She served as the treasurer of the Harvard Business School of London from 1996 to 1998, as a trustee of British Friends of HBS from 1996 to 2000, and as a member of the board of trustees and finance committee of the United Way of Greater Mercer County from 2002 to 2005. Dr. Henry is a member of the American Accounting Association and CFA Miami, and has served as a CFA standard setting participant.

Scott Richardson, PhD, is Global Head of Credit Research at BGI within the Fixed Income group. Mr. Richardson joined BGI in 2006 from the Wharton School at the University of Pennsylvania. His academic research includes security market implications of accounting information, earnings management activity, and corporate governance. He has published widely in leading accounting and finance journals, including the *Journal of Accounting and Economics, Journal of Finance* and *Journal of Accounting Research.* He serves on the editorial advisory boards of the *Accounting Review*, the *Review of Accounting Studies*, and *Journal of Business, Finance and Accounting.* Mr. Richardson graduated with a BEc (first-class honors) from the University of Sydney, and has a PhD in business administration from the University of Michigan. Before joining BGI, Mr. Richardson was the exclusive consultant to Criterion Research, which provides quantitative financial statement analysis. Criterion was acquired by CFRA and is now a part of RiskMetrics.

Thomas R. Robinson, PhD, CFA, is Head, Educational Content, in the Education Division of CFA Institute, where he leads and develops the teams responsible for producing and delivering educational content to candidates, members, and others encompassing CFA Program Content, Professional Development Content, Private Wealth, Publications, University Relations, and Conferences.

Previously, he was Associate Professor of Accounting and Director of the Master of Professional Accounting program at the University of Miami. He also was Managing Director of TR Robinson & Associates, LLC, a state-registered investment advisory firm. Dr. Robinson primarily taught financial statement analysis, personal financial planning, and valuation. He has a BA in economics from the University of Pennsylvania and a master's and PhD from Case Western Reserve University. He is a Certified Public Accountant (Ohio) and Certified Financial Planner® certificant. Prior to joining the University of Miami, Dr. Robinson practiced public accounting and financial planning for 10 years, primarily with Deloitte & Touche and Pritchett Dlusky & Saxe in Columbus, Ohio. He has also served as a consultant to law firms, accounting firms, professional associations and governmental agencies in the areas of financial statement analysis and valuation.

Dr. Robinson was active locally and nationally with the CFA Institute prior to joining the staff, and has served in various capacities including president and board member of CFA Miami (formerly the Miami Society of Financial Analysts). In addition, he has been coauthor, lead author, and consultant for curriculum readings for the CFA program.

Karen O'Connor Rubsam, CPA, CFA, has over twenty years experience in the public accounting/finance and insurance industries. She holds a BBA in accounting, with honors, from the University of Notre Dame and a master's in banking and financial management from Boston University. Since 1999, she has been a private investor and independent business/financial consultant. Her clients include legal and hedge fund firms. She has also served as an adjunct accounting instructor for Chandler Gilbert Community College. Prior to moving to Arizona, Ms. O'Connor Rubsam was the chief financial officer for PartnerRe Ltd., a reinsurer traded on the NYSE. From 1993 to 1997, she was part of the financial management team at another public reinsurer, Zurich Reinsurance Centre Holdings, serving first as the corporate controller and later as the CFO. Her other experience includes roles as a senior manager at Coopers & Lybrand (now part of PriceWaterhouseCoopers), an internal auditor (NAC Re Corporation) and a research analyst for Paulsen, Dowling Securities, Inc.

İrem Tuna, PhD, is Assistant Professor of Accounting at the Wharton School in Philadelphia. She joined the Wharton School of the University of Pennsylvania in 2002. Her academic research focuses on the use of accounting information in valuation, corporate governance, and earnings management. Professor Tuna has published in top-tier accounting journals, including *Accounting Review*, *Journal of Accounting Research*, and *Journal of Accounting and Economics*. She recently joined the editorial and advisory board of *Accounting Review*. Professor Tuna holds a BSc from the Middle East Technical University, an MAS from the University of Illinois at Urbana-Champaign, and a PhD from the University of Michigan.

Hennie van Greuning, CFA, is a senior advisor in the World Bank's Treasury, Washington DC. He joined the World Bank as a Senior Financial Sector Specialist in the Financial Sector Development Department and moved to the Europe and Central Asia region as Financial Sector Manager in 1997. As Financial Sector Manager, he was responsible for inputs into financial sector strategy, as well as technical guidance for financial sector operations in the 27 member countries in the Europe and Central Asia region. In July 2000, he joined the World Bank Treasury, where he is currently a senior adviser concentrating on risk-based management and securities accounting information, operational risk, and central bank portfolio management capacity building. He previously worked with the South African Reserve Bank, where he served as Head of South African Bank Supervision and Controller/Financial Manager. He was actively involved in financial market regulation issues. Prior to that, he was a partner with Deloitte & Touche, where he had spent 10 years.

Mr. van Greuning majored in accounting at Stellenbosch University and has since completed a Doctorate in economics as well as a Doctorate in accounting science. He qualified as a chartered accountant in both South Africa and Canada and is a CFA charterholder. His World Bank publication on *International Financial Reporting Standards* has appeared in four editions. He also coauthored *Analyzing and Managing Banking Risk*. The books have been translated into more than 15 languages.

Susan Perry Williams, PhD, is the KPMG Professor of Accounting at the McIntire School of Commerce, University of Virginia. Professor Williams earned her PhD from the University of Wisconsin–Madison in 1990. She currently teaches advanced financial accounting and special topics in financial reporting at the McIntire School. She has published in a number of academic accounting journals. Professor Williams serves on the audit committee of the McIntire School of Commerce Foundation. She has also served on various committees of the American Accounting Association, and holds both CPA and CMA certificates.

ABOUT THE CFA PROGRAM

The Chartered Financial Analyst® designation (CFA®) is a globally recognized standard of excellence for measuring the competence and integrity of investment professionals. To earn the CFA charter, candidates must successfully pass through the CFA Program, a global graduate-level self-study program that combines a broad curriculum with professional conduct requirements as preparation for a wide range of investment specialties.

Anchored by a practice-based curriculum, the CFA Program is focused on the knowledge identified by professionals as essential to the investment decision-making process. This body of knowledge maintains current relevance through a regular, extensive survey of practicing CFA charterholders across the globe. The curriculum covers 10 general topic areas, ranging from equity and fixed-income analysis to portfolio management to corporate finance, all with a heavy emphasis on the application of ethics in professional practice. Known for its rigor and breadth, the CFA Program curriculum highlights principles common to every market so that professionals who earn the CFA designation have a thoroughly global investment perspective and a profound understanding of the global marketplace.

www.cfainstitute.org

INDEX

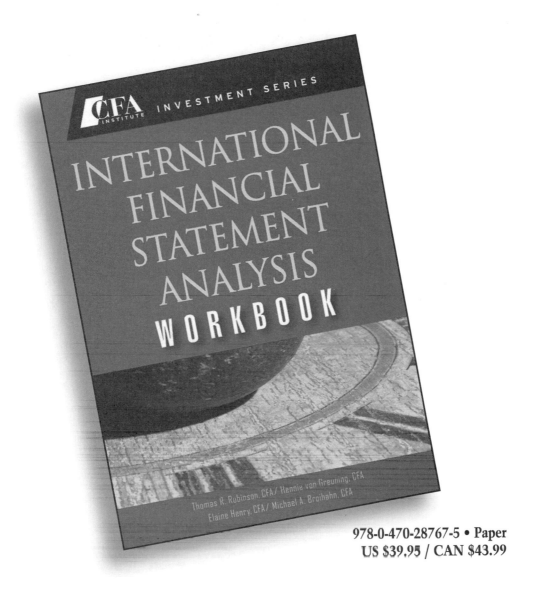

978-0-470-28767-5 • Paper
US $39.95 / CAN $43.99

Master International Financial Statement Analysis with the companion Workbook

The CFA Institute
Investment Series:
Setting the Industry Standard

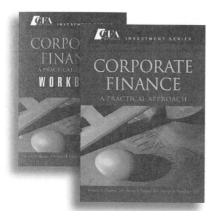
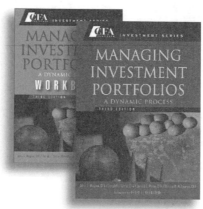

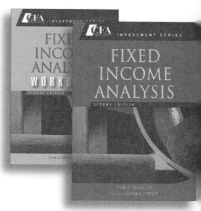